Hoover Bibliographical Series: 50

LEON TROTSKY

A Bibliography

by

Louis Sinclair

1972

Hoover Institution Press

Stanford University, Stanford, California

The Hoover Institution on War, Revolution and Peace, founded
at Stanford University in 1919 by the late President Herbert
Hoover, is a center for advanced study and research on public
and international affairs in the twentieth century. The views
expressed in its publications are entirely those of the authors
and do not necessarily reflect the views of the Hoover Institution.

Hoover Institution Bibliographical Series 50
Standard Book Number 8179-2501-5
Library of Congress Number 78-185240
Printed in the United States of America
Copyright 1972 by the Board of Trustees of
    the Leland Stanford Junior University

CONTENTS

E R R A T A

P. 486   <u>insert</u>   321013(4)   The lesson of Mil's treason.
                         <u>Trans.</u>: Am. <u>CLA</u>, (6), 15.I.33
                         [On ILOpp.]

P.1026   <u>insert</u>   at <u>CLA</u>, (12), 19.IV.33 index number 330228

The problems in compiling a list of the published works of Leon Trotsky are as to be expected, and they can be stated briefly: locating the material and finding complete files of the relevant periodicals and bulletins of organizations which directly or otherwise supported his political struggles. In addition, there are the problems of pseudonymous and anonymous matter. Some help is available, from works like Kamenev's Catalogue and from the notes to the earlier editions of Lenin's Collected Works. But the passage of time has made these areas of enquiry extremely complex. Work remains to be done in the post-exilic period, too.

A complete bibliography cannot be considered for many more years. There are uncounted unpublished items in the spheres of Trotsky's activities in the Russian Communist Party, in the Soviet Government, in the Red Army and in the Comintern. It is reported that there are some 20,000 items in the closed section of his Archives at Harvard; some of these may fall within the limits of this work. The private papers of his correspondents which are untraced or unpublished is a further area to be researched.

The present draft marks the position reached at the end of August, 1970. Besides the books, pamphlets and other material published or advertized, notes are inserted of Trotsky's attendance at meetings where he may have spoken although no texts have as yet been traced.

With the original sources there is a listing of reprints and translations, and where possible, variations are noted. Because Trotsky himself vigorously objected to the Spanish versions of two of his books (reported in a private communication), they are omitted from this draft. Nor are pirate editions included.

Assessments of Trotsky vary between extremes. For his own part, in his diary for March 25, 1935, he wrote:

"... the work in which I am engaged now, ... is the most important work of my life.... I cannot speak of the 'indispensability' of my work, even about the period from 1917 to 1921. But now my work is 'indispensable' in the full sense of the word.... There is now no one except me to carry out the mission of arming a new generation over the heads of the Second and Third International.... I need at least about five more years of uninterrupted work to ensure the succession."

Stalin allowed him just that measure of time -- for interrupted work.

Little more should be necessary by way of preface. The Notes which follow these lines explain the construction of the book and offer some suggestions which may be useful to the reader.

To conclude: it is a pleasure and a privilege to pay tribute to very many people.- They have made possible this catalogue at its present level of completeness and accuracy by making available their private collections and sound advice. The overwhelming majority have preferred to guard their anonymity, and this cover is, regretably, and with apologies, extended to all -- with two necessary exceptions. Dr Chimon Abramsky and Professor Pierre Naville have allowed themselves to be cited as the authorities, in the first case for information on certain Hebrew and Yiddish items, and in the second for the identification of and notes on certain unsigned material in French. Librarians and their staffs have, almost without exception, been sympathetic and helpful, often beyond the limits of their office. Members of political organizations have co-operated to the fullest. All this generous aid has been indispensable. The errors of omission and commission remain, of course, the responsibility of the compiler.

May, 1971.   L.Sinclair

PART I

The material of the text is arranged in chronological order. The date, reversed, is taken as the index number of the item. When 2 or more items are assigned to the same number they are distinguished by the addition of (1), (2), etc. There are no priorities in such cases. The example illustrates the pattern followed.

220501(1)   Rech. (A speech.) (Iz, (96), 3.V.22; Trud, (94), 3.V.22)
            Repr.: 230000(7).III.ii: 60-1.
            Trans.: Eng. p.q. Russian Information Review, 8.VI.22.
            |To parade in Red Square.|

This condenses the information that Trotsky made a speech on 1 May, 1922. It was (first) printed in Izvestiya, No. 96 of 3 May, 1922 and also in Trud, No. 94, of the same date. A reprint will be found in the item indexed at 230000(7). This is the book KAK VOORUZHALAS REVOLYUTSIYA, and on pages 60-1 of Vol. III, part ii is the item. The speech was partially translated in the English-language periodical Russian Information Review of 8 June, 1922. [   ] enclose an editorial note.

There are a few refinements to the above example.

(a) / after an index number signifies that the old Russian calendar is being used. |e.g. 171230(2)/.| For the modern calendar add 13 days.

(b) | | enclose a number when the date is tentative. |e.g. |700000(13)|.|

(c) Sometimes the reprint is fuller than the first |newspaper| report. This requires to be checked but is often obvious from the number of pages involved.

(d) When earlier drafts were revised some numbers were dropped but subsequent numbers were not stepped up.

(e) Books |entered in CAPITALS| are indexed at date of publication or of printing, whichever is fuller.

(f) Only titles and headings in cyrillic script are translated.

In reverse: to trace the original of an item found e.g. in Russian Information Review of 8 June 1922, consult the concordance to periodicals in Part II where the index number 220501(1) is given. Part I shows the details as above. Similarly, if faced with a blank reference to, say, Vol. IX of the SOCHINENIYA, pages 38-40, Part III shows Vol. IX to be EVROPA V VOINE whose index number is 270000(1), and in the concordance to books (cyrillic script), pages 38-40 show up as part of an article running from page 36 to 43 whose index number is 150115(1). The rest follows.

For cross-reference, the procedure is the same. First establish an index number. E.g. to find the Chinese translation of the French HISTOIRE DE LA RÉVOLUTION RUSSE. Begin at 330100(3) -- or at the number of any of the reprints --go back to 310000(1) and there the information sought is recorded.

Sometimes the best procedure to follow is to work through PUBLICATIONS BY LANGUAGES, in Part III, although this can be tedious. Except for Russian, American, English, French and German, all languages are covered. The exceptions were too long. Items which appear in books are not listed separately.

There is no list of separate items in any language, nor of untranslated nor of uncollected pieces.

Translations of titles from cyrillic are literal and do not necessarily concide with published forms. THE DEFENCE OF TERRORISM and DICTATORSHIP VS DEMOCRACY are published titles for TERRORIZM I KOMMUNIZM (TERRORISM AND COMMUNISM).

In a few instances Trotsky's work is shown as the source although in fact the item was reprinted from another author. |e.g. 171230(2)/.|

PART II

The BOOK LISTS give the information more properly called bibliographical, together with some locations, cyrillic and non-cyrillic separately. Similarly with PERIODICALS. The CONCORDANCES follow immediately after each section. No information is given as to the sponsors of the periodicals.

The arrangement is alphabetical, as the English eye sees it.

PART III

Some sections are self-explanatory: PSEUDONYMS, PROSPECTUS OF SOCHINENIYA, and MATERIAL printed FROM Trotsky's personal ARCHIVES.

The SUBJECT INDEX IS NEITHER COMPREHENSIVE NOR DETAILED. As with TRANSLATIONS BY LANGUAGES, the reader is referred to volumes rather than to individual entries.

Not all the material in the SECONDARY SOURCES will be found cited in the text (e.g. Sukhanov). Some of the books in this section may also have appeared in other languages but this is not always indicated.

ABBREVIATIONS

| Abbreviations for Periodicals and Bulletins will be found in their respective sections. |

Abr   Abridged

B   Berlin
Br   Britain

c.   cited/summarized in ...
Cat   Catalogue. See: Catalogues cited
CC   Central Committee
CCC   Central Control Commission
Ch.   Chapter
Ch.A.   Chimon Abramsky
CLA   Communist League of America
CP   Communist Party

D   Harvard Archives, catalog no....
Doc   Document: unidentified origin
DVPS   DOKUMENTY VNESHNEI POLITIKI SSSR

et a.   and others
et al. and others

FI   Fourth International

i dr.   and others
ILOpp   International Left Opposition (Bolshevik-Leninists)
IS   International Secretariat of the ILOpp/FI
ISFI   International Secretariat of the Fourth International

L   Leningrad
Ln   London
Loc   Located at .... See Location Guide
LOpp   Left Opposition

M   Moscow
M-L   Moscow-Leningrad

NY   New York

P   Paris
Pet   Petrograd
P.N.   Pierre Naville

p.q.	partially quoted/summarized in ...
Pref.	Preface
RCP	Revolutionary Communist Party, Britain
Red.	Editor/Editorial Board
Repr.	Reprinted in ...
RS–DLP	Russian Social-Democratic Labour Party
RSDRP	Russian Social-Democratic Labour Party
SI	Secrétariat International
SOCH.	SOCHINENIYA (COLLECTED WORKS)
SRs	Social Revolutionaries
StP	St Petersburg
SWP	Socialist Workers Party, USA
T	Harvard Archives catalog number ...
Trans.	Translated/published in the language of .../ published in ...
Trans. Afr.	Afrikaans
Am.	America/Canada/Mexico/USA
Arab.	Arabic
Ben.	Bengal
Bul.	Bulgaria
Ch.	China
Cz.	Czecho-Slovakia
Den.	Denmark
Eng.	England/Britain/Australia/Ceylon/India/So. Africa
Esp.	Esperanto
Esth.	Esthonia
Fin.	Finland
Fr.	France
Ger.	Germany/Austria
Gr.	Greece
Heb.	Hebrew/Israel
Hol.	Holland/Flemish
Hung.	Hungary
Ice.	Iceland
It.	Italy
Jap.	Japan
Kar.	Karantaisch Sprache [a Georgian dialect]
Lat.	Latvia

Trans. Lith.   Lithuania

Mal.   Malayalam [Kerala, India]

Nor.   Norway

Pol.   Poland

Port.   Portugal/Brazil

Rum.   Rumania

Scand.   Scandinavia

Serb.   Serbia/Serbo-Croatian

Sin.   Sinhalese/Ceylon

Sp.   Spain/Latin America/Mexico [including Castellan]

Swed.   Sweden

Tat.   Tatar [/Tartar]

Tur.   Turkey

Turc.   Turcoman

Ukr.   Ukraine

Viet.   Vietnam/French Indo-China

Yid.   Yiddish

TsIK   Central Executive Committee

TsK   Central Committee

u.   and

u.a.   and others

V   Harvard Archives catalog number ...

VS"ezdsov All-Russian Congress of Soviets

VTsIK   All-Russian CEC

WP   Workers Party, USA

SIGLIA

*   unchecked

†   See Part II for details of contents

§   Contains more than 2 items; not necessarily detailed in notes

¢   File incomplete/partially checked

--:   unsigned

++++   continued

LOCATIONS

AAO	Arbeiderbevegelsens Arkiv, Oslo
AAS	Arbetarrörelsens Arkiv, Stockholm
ABC	Arbejderbevaegelsens Bibliotek og Arkiv, Copenhagen
AN	Archives Nationales, Paris
BDIC	Bibliothèque de Documentation Internationale Contemporaine, Paris
BM	British Museum, London
BN	Bibliothèque Nationale, Paris
BRB	Bibliothèque Royale, Brussels
BU	Birmingham University Library
CDI	Centre de Documentation Internationale de L'URSS et Pays Slaves, Paris
CU	Cambridge University Library
GDS	Institute of Soviet and East European Studies, Glasgow
HIS	Hoover Institution, Stanford, California
IISG	International Instituut voor Sociale Geschiedenis, Amsterdam
J	Hebrew University, Jerusalem
KBC	Det Kongelige Bibliotek, Copenhagen
KBS	Kungl Biblioteket, Stockholm
LC	Library of Congress, Washington, USA. ⌊See also NUC⌉
LnL	London Library
LOV	Ecole Nationale de Langue Vivantes Orientales, Paris
LSE	London School of Economics
MLG	Mitchell Library, Glasgow
MS	Musée Sociale, Paris
MU	Manchester University Library
NDL	National Diet Library, Tokyo
NLS	National Library of Scotland, Edinburgh
NUC	National Union Catalog. ⌊Continuation of LC⌋
NYPL	New York Public Library
O	Bodleian Library, Oxford
O(T)	Taylorian Institute, Oxford

Per	Personal collection
PPA	Pioneer Publishers, New York. |Later Merit; later Pathfinder|
PSB	Parti Socialiste Belge |Library|, Brussels
SEES	School of Slavonic and East European Studies, London University
SHL	Seely Historical Library, Cambridge
TPL	Public Library, Toronto
UCB	University of California, Berkeley
ULH	University Library, Helsinki
ULO	University Library, Oslo

Per	Personal collection
PPA	Pioneer Publishers, New York. |Later Merit; later Pathfinder|
PSB	Parti Socialiste Belge |Library|, Brussels

CATALOGUES CITED

BABH   Bulletin analytique de Bibliographie Hellénique
BB   Bibliografia Brasileira
BBA   Boletin Bibliográfico Argentino
BE   Bibliografia Española
BibEzh Bibliograficheskii Ezhegodnik
BNS   Bibliothèque Nationale de Sofia
BT   Berliner Titeldrucke

CUBI   Catalogo Cumulativo. 1886-1957. Bolletino della Pubblicazioni Italiani

DB   Deutsches Bücherverzeichnis

GB   Bakalov (Georgi), BIO-BIBLIOGRAFIYA
GV   Vértes (György), A MAGYAR TANÁCSKÖZTÁRSASÁG KIADVÁHYAI ES ELSÖ
                KOMMUNISTA KIADVÁNYOK

IK   Knizhnik (Iv.), SISTEMATICHESKII UKAZATEL LITERATURY PO OBSHCHESTVENNYM
                NAUKAM

ILO   International Labour Office, Geneva
IT   Index Translationium

KAB   Kommunisticheskaya Akademiya Biblioteka. Pervaya Russkaya Revolyutsiya.
        Ukazatel literatury
Kam   Kamenev (L.), SOTSIALDEMOKRATICHESKAYA IZDANIYA, 1883-1905 g.g.
KL   KNIZHNAYA LETOPIS

LEHA   Libreria española e hispano-americano
LI   Catalogo della libreria italiana

PLVK   Pyat Let Voennoi Knigi
Postnikov RUSSKII ISTORICHESKII ARKHIV

SČL   Soupis Československé Literatury (1901-1925)

Z   Zaleski (E.), MOUVEMENTS OUVRIERS ET SOCIALISTES: LA RUSSIE
ZK   Kormanowa (Zanna), MATERIALY DO BIBLIOGRAFII POLSKIEGO RUCHU ROBOTNICZEGO
                (1918-1939)

PART I

970000   Editor, <u>Nashe Delo</u>.
         [c. 180000(55). 3 issues.]

980000(1)   Revolutionary verse.
               <u>Trans</u>.: Am. p.q. Eastman, LEON TROTSKY: Ch. VI.

*980000(2)   *Essay on his arrest.
               [c. Deutscher, PA: 37.]

*980000(3)   *Essay on freemasonry.
               [c. 300000(1): Ch. VIII.]

000700   i Y.M.Steklov: IZ RABOCHAGO DVIZHENIYA V ODESSE I NIKOLAEVE. (THE
           WORKERS MOVEMENT IN ODESSA AND NIKOLAEV.)
           Repr.: ProlRev, (9), 1922.

[001015]   Antid Oto: "Malo zametnyi, no vsema vazhnyi vintik v gosudarstvennoi
           mashine." ("A little noticed but highly important cog in the state
           machine.") (VOb, (230), 15.X.00)
           Repr.: 260000(16): 3-7.

[001222]   Antid Oto: Koe-chto o filosofii "sverkhcheloveka". (Something about
           the "Superman" philosophy.) (VOb, (284,286,287,289), 22,24,25,30.XII.00)
           Repr.: 260000(12): 147-62.

[001223]   Antid Oto: Koe-chto o zemstve. (Something about zemstvos.) (VOb, (285),
           23.XII.00)
           Repr.: 260000(16): 7-12.

010000   Istoriya literatury, g. Boborykin i russkaya kritika. (A history of
                literature; Mr. Boborykin and Russian criticism.) (260000(12): 125-32)

[010114]   Antid Oto: "Staryi dom." ("The old home.") (VOb, (10), 14.I.01)
                Repr.: 260000(12): 162-6.

[010125]   Antid Oto: "Otryvnoi" kalendar kak kul´turtreger. (The "tear-off"
                calendar as a carrier of culture. (VOb, (19), 25.I.01)
                Repr.: 260000(12): 71-4.

[010214]   Antid Oto: Ob odnom starom voprose. (On a certain old question.)
                (VOb, (33,34), 14,15.II.01)
                Repr.: 260000(16): 12-6.
                [The woman question.]

[010217]   Antid Oto: O pessimizme, optimizme, XX stoletii, i mnogom drugom.
                (Pessimism, optimism, the 20th century, and many more things.)
                (VOb, (36), 17.II.01)
                Repr.: 260000(12): 74-9.
                Trans.: Am. p.q. 640800: 40-1;
                        Eng. p.q. Deutscher, PA: 53;
                        Jap. p.q. 681125: 46-7;
                        Sp. p.q. 670000(5): 43-4;
                        Swed. p.q. 691100(2): 33-4.

[010313]   Antid Oto: "Deklaratsiya prav" i "Barkhatnaya kniga". (The "Declaration
                of Rights" and the "Velvet Book".) (VOb, (56,57), 13,14.III.01)
                Repr.: 260000(12): 79-86.
                Trans.: Eng. p.q. Deutscher, PA: 68.

[010318]   Antid Oto: O Bal´monte. (Balmont.) (VOb, (61), 18.III.01)
                Repr.: 260000(12): 167-70.

[010329]   Antid Oto: Obyknovennoe derevenskoe. (Ordinary rural matters.)
                (VOb, (70), 29.III.01)
                Repr.: 260000(16): 17-20.

[010422]   Antid Oto: Hertsen i Molodoe Pokolenie. (Herzen and Molodoe Pokoleie.)
                (VOb, (88,91), 22,26.IV.01)
                Repr.: 260000(12): 20-7.

[010505]   Antid Oto: Poslednyaya drama Gauptmana i kommentarii k nei Struve.
(Hauptmann's latest play and Struve's commentary on it.) (VOb,
(99,102), 5,9.V.01)
Repr. 260000(12): 170-81.

[010530]   Antid Oto: Obyknovennoe derevenskoe. (Ordinary rural matters.)
(VOb, (117), 30.V.01)
Repr.: 260000(16): 20-6.

[010603]   Antid Oto: Ob Ibsene. (Ibsen.) (VOb, (121,122,126), 3,4,9.VI.01)
Repr.: 260000(12): 181-95.

[010620]   Antid Oto: Penitentsiarnye idealy i gumannoe tyur'movozzrenie.
(Penitentiary ideals and a humane prison system.) (VOb, (135,136),
20,21.VI.01)
Repr.: 260000(12): 86-93.

[010713]   Antid Oto: My sozreli. (We have matured.) (VOb, (154), 13.VII.01)
Repr.: 260000(12): 93-7.

[010722]   Antid Oto: Novye vremena -- novye pesni. (New times -- new songs.)
(VOb, (162,164,165), 22,25,26.VII.01)
Repr.: 260000(12): 97-113.

[010804]   Antid Oto: Obyknovennoe derevenskoe. (Ordinary rural matters.)
(VOb, (173), 4.VIII.01)
Repr.: 260000(16): 26-31.

[010809]   Antid Oto: Obyknovennoe derevenskoe. (Ordinary rural matters.)
(VOb, (176), 9.VIII.01)
Repr.: 260000(16): 32-5.

[010820]   Antid Oto: Dve pisatel'skie dushi vo vlasti metafizicheskogo besa.
(The souls of two writers in the grip of a metaphysical demon.)
(VOb, (189), 20.VIII.01)
Repr.: 260000(12): 195-9.
[On Berdyaev and Mikhailovsky.]

[010902]   Antid Oto: "Neliberal'nyi" moment "liberal'nykh" otnoshenii. (An
"illiberal" feature of "liberal" relations.) (VOb, (194), 2.IX.01)
Repr.: 260000(16): 42-3.

[010908]   **Antid Oto: Poeziya, mashina i poeziya mashiny.** (Poetry, the machine, and the poetry of the machine. (<u>VOb</u>, (197), 8.IX.01)
<u>Repr</u>.: 260000(12): 199-204.
⌊On Ruskin.⌋

[010926]   **Antid Oto: Obyknovennoe derevenskoe.** (Ordinary rural matters.) (<u>VOb</u>, (212), 26.IX.01)
<u>Repr</u>.: 260000(16): 35-42.

[011013]   **Antid Oto: S.F.Sharapov i nemetskie agrarii.** (S.F.Sharapov and the German landowners.) (<u>VOb</u>, (225), 13.X.01)
<u>Repr</u>.: 260000(12): 113-6.

[011114]   **Antid Oto: "Russkii Darvin."** ("The Russian Darwin.") (<u>VOb</u>, (251), 14.XI.01)
<u>Repr</u>.: 260000(12): 116-8.
<u>Trans</u>.: Eng. p.q. Deutscher, PA: 52.
⌊On Sharapov on Solovyev.⌋

[011117]   **Antid Oto: N.A.Dobrolyubov i <u>Svistok</u>.** (N.A.Dobrolyubov and <u>Svistok</u>.) (<u>VOb</u>, (253), 17.XI.01)
<u>Repr</u>.: 260000(12): 27-32.

[020110]   Antid Oto: Koe-chto o "svobode tvorcheskogo spazma". (Something about "the freedom of the creative soasm".) (VOb, (8), 10.I.02)
Repr.: 260000(12): 204-10.

[020124]   Antid Oto: Obshchestvennaya tavtologiya. (Social tautology.) (VOb, (20), 24.I.02)
Repr.: 260000(12): 119-25.

[020202(1)]   Antid Oto: O nastroenii. (A mood.) (VOb, (28), 2.II.02)
Repr.: 260000(12): 132-42.

[020202(2)]   Nechto o somnambulizme. (Something about sleepwalking.) (260000(12): 142-4)

[020221]   Antid Oto: N.V.Gogol (1852-1902 g.g.) (VOb, (43), 21.II.02)
Repr.: 260000(12): 9-20.
Trans.: Am. 650900: 317-24;
        Eng. 640000(5): 317-24; 640000(10): 317-24;
        Sp. 690000(8).I: 191-200.

[020309]   Antid Oto: O romane voobshche, o romane "Troe" v chastnosti. (The novel in general, the novel "Three" in particular.) (VOb, (56), 9.III.02)
Repr.: 260000(12): 210-5.
["Three", by Gorky.]

[020400]   O Glebe Ivanoviche Uspenskom. (Gleb Ivanovich Uspensky.) (Nauchnoe Obozrenie, IV.02)
Repr.: 260000(12): 41-67.

[020418]   Antid Oto: Gleb Ivanovich Uspenskii. (VOb, (88), 18.IV.02)
Repr.: 260000(12): 33-40.
Trans.: Eng. p.q. Deutscher, PA: 52.

[020419]   Antid Oto: V.A.Zhukovskii (1783-1852 g.g.) (VOb, (89), 19.IV.02)
Repr.: 260000(12): 3-9.

[020518]   Antid Oto: Ob Arture Shnitslere. (Arthur Schnitzler) (VOb, (114,115), 18,19.V.02)
Repr.: 260000(12): 215-26.

[020605]   Antid Oto: O Leonide Andreeve. (Leonid Andreev.) (VOb, (129), 5.VI.02)
Repr.: 260000(12): 226-40.

[020817]   Antid Oto: "Da zdravstvuet zhizn!" ("Hail life!") (<u>VOb</u>, (192), 17.VIII.02)

Repr.: 260000(12): 240-6.

Trans.: Eng. p.q. Deutscher, PA: 69.

[021101(1)]   —: K 200-letiyu prisoedineniya Shlissel´burga. (The 200th anniversary of the annexation of the Schlusselburg Fortress.) (<u>Iskra</u>, (27), 1.XI.02)

Repr.: 260000(16): 44-5.

[021101(2)]   —: Bobchinskie v oppozitsii. (Bobchinskys in the opposition.) (<u>Iskra</u>, (27), 1.XI.02)

Repr.: 260000(16): 48-50.

[021115]   —: Shulera slavyanofil´stva. (Cheats of slavophilism.) (<u>Iskra</u>, (28), 15.XI.02)

Repr.: 260000(16): 45-8.

Trans.: Eng. p.q. Deutscher, PA: 68.

[021201]   —: Zakonnaya oppozitsiya bezzakonnomu pravitel´stvu. (Lawful opposition to a lawless government.) (<u>Iskra</u>, (29), 1.XII.02)

Repr.: 260000(16): 51-6.

Trans.: Eng. p.q. Deutscher, PA: 68.

[021215]   —: Zubatovshchina v Peterburge. (Zubatovism in Petersburg.) (<u>Iskra</u>, (30), 15.XII.02)

Repr.: 260000(16): 56-9.

[Zubatov, chief of Moscow okhrana.]

[030101] —: Opekaemoe studenchestvo. (The students under guardianship.)
(Iskra, (31), 1.I.03)
Repr.: 260000(16): 129-32.

*030127 *Pis'mo. (A letter.)
[c. Lenin, SOCH. XXVIII: 170.]

[030201(1)] —: Idealisticheskaya gamma. (The range of idealism.) (Iskra, (33),
1.II.03)
Repr.: 260000(16): 61-3.

[030201(2)] —: Yubileinoe kholopstvo. (Jubilee servility.) (Iskra, (33), 1.II.03)
Repr.: 260000(16): 63.

[030201(3)] —: Pechat patrioticheskogo donosa o Finlyandii. (The patriotic press
denounces Finland.) (Iskra, (33), 1.II.03)
Repr.: 260000(16): 64-5.

[030201(4)] —: Blagorodstvo, vmesto programmy, i nervnost, vmesto taktiki.
(Nobility instead of a programme, and neurosis instead of tactics.)
(Iskra, (33), 1.II.03)
Repr.: 260000(16): 138-41.

[030215(1)] —: Novyi pokhod g. fon-Pleve. (A new campaign by Mr. von Plehve.)
(Iskra, (34), 15.II.03)
Repr.: 260000(16): 59-61.

[030215(2)] —: V mire merzosti i zapusteniya. (In a world of abomination and
desolation.) (Iskra, (34), 15.II.03)
Repr.: 260000(16): 65-7.

[030301] —: Kak oni "primiryayut". (How they "make it up.") (Iskra, (35),
1.III.03)
Repr.: 260000(16): 133-7.

[030315] —:"Sotsializatsiya", "kooperatsiya" i populyarnaya literatura
"sotsialistov-revolyutsionerov". ("Socialization," "co-operation"
and the popular literature of the "social-revolutionaries".)
(Iskra, (36), 15.III.03)
Repr.: 260000(16): 141-6.

[030415] —: "Reformistskii" sotsializm g. Mil´erana. (The "reformist" socialism of M.Millerand.) (<u>Iskra</u>, (38), 15.IV.03)
[Identified in CatKam.]

[030601] —: Eshche o tartyufakh. (More on the Tartuffes.) (<u>Iskra</u>, (41), 1.IV.03)
<u>Repr.</u>: 260000(16): 146-50.

030700 N.Trotskii: VTOROI S"EZD ROS. SOTS. DEM. R.P. OTCHET SIBIRSKOI DELEGATSII. (THE 2nd RSDLP CONGRESS. REPORT OF THE SIBERIAN DELEGATION.)
<u>Trans.</u>: Fr. p.q. 680000(4): 184-8; 700000(5).

[030701(1)] —: Zubatovtsy v podpol´noi pechati. (Zubatovites in the underground press.) (<u>Iskra</u>, (43), 1.VII.03)
<u>Repr.</u>: 260000(16): 67-70.

[030701(2)] —: Fabrichnaya inspektsiya i detsentralizovannaya pompaduriya. (Factory inspection and decentralized pompadourism.) (<u>Iskra</u>, (43), 1.VII.03)
<u>Repr.</u>: 260000(16): 70-7.
[Pompadourism, the practice of searching workers leaving a factory.]

030900 Speech at 2nd (Geneva) Congress RSDLP. (PROTOKOLY: 448-500)
<u>Trans.</u>: Am. p.q. Haimson: 177.

030920 & Martov: Resolution at 2nd (Geneva) Congress RSDLP; to boycott <u>Iskra</u>.
<u>Trans.</u>: Am. p.q. Haimson: 183;
   Eng. p.q. Deutscher, PA: 85.

[031125] —: Politicheskie pis´ma. (Political letters.) (<u>Iskra</u>, (53), 25.XI.03)
<u>Repr.</u>: 260000(16): 77-84; ISKRA ZA I.: 17-23.

031126 i dr.: Pis´mo. (A Letter.) (KOMMENTARII: 28-34)
[From Opposition in the <u>Iskra</u> dispute.]

[031215] —: Politicheskie pis´ma. (Political letters.) (<u>Iskra</u>, (55), 15.XII.03)
<u>Repr.</u>: 260000(16): 84-7; ISKRA ZA.I: 34-7.

040000 N.Trotskii: † NASHI POLITICHESKIYA ZADACHI. (OUR POLITICAL TASKS.)
Repr.: *280000(1).
Trans.: Fr. p.q. 680000(4): passim; 700228;
   Serb. p.q. BIROKRATIJA.I: 207.
[Pref. 040823.]

[040101] —: Razlozhenie sionizma i ego vozmozhnye preemniki. (The decay of zionism and its possible successors.) (Iskra, (56), 1.I.04)
Repr.: 260000(16): 124-8.

[040210] T.: Politicheskie pis´ma. (Political letters.) (Iskra, (59), 10.II.04)
Repr.: 260000(16): 87-94; ISKRA ZA.I: 50-7.

[040225] T.: Politicheskie pis´ma. (Political letters.) (Iskra, (60), 25.II.04)
Repr.: 260000(16): 94-102; ISKRA ZA.I: 57-65.

040300 Pis´mo. (A letter.) (040000: 82-4)
Trans.: Fr. 700228: 167-9.

[040305] T.: Politicheskie pis´ma. (Dve tolpy.) (Political letters: Two mobs.) (Iskra, (61), 5.III.04)
Repr.: 260000(16): 102-6; ISKRA ZA.I: 65-9.

[040315] T.: Nasha "voennaya" kampaniya. (Our "military" campaign.) (Iskra, (62), 15.III.04)

[040625] T.: Otvet na "Pis´mo v redaktsiyu". (Reply to a"letter to the Editorial Board".) (Iskra, (68), 25.VI.04)

040700 Pis´mo. (A letter.) (040000: 85-9)
Trans.: Fr. 700228: 174.

040823 Pref. NASHI POLITICHESKIYA ZADACHI, 040000.
Trans.: Fr. 700228: 39-44.

040900 Open letter to comrades.
[c. 300000(1): Ch. XIII.]

[041005] —: Politicheskie pis´ma. ("Pered katastrofoi.") (Political letters: "Before the catastrophe.") (Iskra, (75), 5.X.04)
Repr.: 260000(16): 107-12; ISKRA ZA I.: 163-9.

[041020(1)]   T.: Politicheskie pis'ma. (Political letters.) (<u>Iskra</u>, (76), 20.X.04)
                <u>Repr.</u>: 260000(16): 112-9.

[041020(2)]   N.Trotskii: Yavlenie liberalov narodu. (The appearance of the liberals
                to the people.) (<u>Iskra</u>, (76), 20.X.04)
                <u>Repr.</u>: 260000(16): 119-23; ISKRA ZA.I: 507-10.

[041100]   —: Sredi gazet. (In the newspapers.) (<u>Sotsdem</u>, (3), 04)
                [Identified in CatKam.]

041220   Do devyatago yanvarya. (Before the 9th of January.) (050000(1))
                <u>Repr.</u>: 060000(6): 17-63; 250000(6).I: 3-53; 250000(7): 5-59.
                <u>Trans.</u>: Am. p.q. 180000(40): 29-44; p.q. [180000(53)]: 6; p.q. 640800: 41-50;
                        Eng. p.q. 531200: 2-8;
                        Jap. p.q. 681125: 47-56;
                        Sp. p.q. 670000(5): 44-52;
                        Swed. p.q. 691100(2): 34-41;
                        Yid. p.q. 190000(68): 29-43; p.q. 210000(51): 29-43.
                [See further, 050120.]

050000(1)   N.Trotskii: DO DEVYATAGO YANVARYA. (BEFORE JANUARY 9th.)
Repr.: 250000(7).
[See 041220, 050120 for other repr., trans., notes. 250000(7) includes
additional material.]

050000(2)   N.Trotskii: CHEMU UCHAT SOTSIALISTY-REVOLYUTSIONERY? (WHAT DO THE
SOCIAL-REVOLUTIONARIES TEACH?)
[See [051116(5)] for all repr., notes.]

[050000(3)]   Bulyginskaya duma i nashi zadachi. (The Bulygin duma and our tasks.)
(250000(6).I: 185-93)
[Letter to Petersburg comrades.]

050120   Chto zhe dal'she? (What next?) (050000(1))
Repr.: 060000(6): 63-73; 250000(6).I: 54-67; 250000(7): 59-71.
Trans.: Am. p.q. 180000(40): 51-61; p.q. 650900: 62-6;
         Eng. p.q. 531200: 10-5; p.q. 640000(5): 62-6; p.q. 640000(10):
              62-6.
[See also 041220.]

050303(1)   TsK RS-DRP: Krest'yane, k vam nashe slovo! (Peasants, we address
ourselves to you!) (DELO, No. 146)
Repr.: 250000(6).I: 210-7; 250000(7): 72-80.
Trans.: Eng. p.q. Deutscher, PA: 123.

[050303(2)]   T.: Politicheskie pis'ma. (Political letters.) (Iskra, (90), 3.III.05)
Repr.: 250000(6).I: 230-4; ISKRA ZA.II: 167-77.

[050310]   Neofit: Nechto o kvalifitsirovannykh demokratakh. (Something about
qualified democrats.) (Iskra, (92), 10.III.05)
Repr.: 250000(6).I: 153-8; ISKRA ZA.II: 541-6.
[Letter from Russia.]

[050317]   T.: Politicheskie pis'ma. (Political letters.) (Iskra, (93), 17.III.05)
Repr.: 250000(6).I: 234-40.

050415   Novye tsarskie milosti. (New tsarist favours.) (DELO, No. 193)
Repr.: 250000(6).I: 217-24.

050500(1) Doloi pozornuyu boimyu! (Down with the shameful massacre!)
(250000(6).I: 251-4)

050500(2) Amendment to resolution on armed insurrection and provisional government.
[c. 270600(1). Sent to 3rd Congress RSDLP; read by Krassin.]

050501 TsK RSDRP: Pervoe maya. (May Day.) (DELO, No. 127)
Repr.: 250000(6).I: 240-5.

[050502] Peterburgskaya gruppa RSDRP: Tovarishchi-rabochie Peterburga!
(Comrade-workers of Petersburg!) (250000(6).I: 245-7)

[050503] Peterburgskaya gruppa RSDRP: Grazhdane, otbros'te vashi somneniya!
(Citizens, shed your doubts!) (250000(6).I: 247-8)

[050600(1)] Peterburgskaya gruppa RSDRP: Tovarishchi-rabochie! (Comrade-workers!)
(250000(6).I: 249-50)

[050600(2)] Peterburgskaya gruppa RSDRP: Zapasnye, oboronyaites! (Reservists,
defend yourselves!) (250000(6).I: 250-1)

[050600(3)] Peterburgskaya gruppa RSDRP: Rabochie, trebuite prekrashcheniya boiny!
(Workers, demand the end of the massacre!) (250000(6).I: 254-6)

[050600(4)] Peterburgskaya gruppa RSDRP: Ne tsar, ne zemtsy, a narod! (No tsar,
no zemstvos, but the people!) (250000(6).I: 256-8)

050614 Peterburgskaya gruppa RSDRP: Soldaty russkoi armii i russkogo flota!
(Soldiers of the Russian army and Russian fleet!) (250000(6).I: 248-9)

050700(1) Kapital v oppozitsii. (Capital in opposition.) (060000(6): 74-94)
Repr.: 250000(6).I: 71-93.

050700(2) N.Trotskii: F.Lassal, RECH PERED SUDOM PRISYANNYKH. (F.Lassalle,
SPEECH TO THE JURY.)
Repr.: p.q. 060600.
[The role of the proletariat and of the bourgeoisie in Germany, in 1848.
Trans. from Ger. Ed. with pref. by T. LocNYPL.]

[050707] Zayavlenie peterburgskikh rabochikh predstavitelyam zemstv i dum.
(Declaration of the Petersburg workers to the representatives of the
zemstvos and duma.) (Sotsdem, (9), 7.VII.05)
Repr.: 250000(6).I: 193-6.

050800   Otkrytoe pis'mo professoru P.N.Milyukovu. (Open letter to Professor P.N.Milyukov.) (060000(6): 136-44)
Repr.: 250000(6).I: 196-205.
Trans.: Eng. p.q. Deutscher, PA: 120.
[PS 060800.]

050900   Kak delali gosudarstvennuyu dumu. (How they made the State Duma.) (060000(6): 110-35)
Repr.: 250000(6).I: 159-85.

[051018(1)] Ot federativnogo soveta. (From the federative soviet.) (Iz(SRD), (2), 18.X.05)
Repr.: 250000(6).I: 278.

[051018(2)] Rezolyutsiya. (A resolution.) (Iz(SRD), (2), 18.X.05)
Repr.: 250000(6).I: 278-9.

[051018(3)] Stachka prodolzhaetsya. (The strike is ended.) (Iz(SRD), (2), 18.X.05)
Repr.: 250000(6).I: 279-80.

051018(4) Rezolyutsiya. (A resolution.) (Iz(SRD), (3), 20.X.05)
Repr.: 250000(6).I: 495-6.
[Resolution No. 18 of the soviet; in reply to Manifesto of October 17.]

051018(5) Speech at Technological Institute.
[c. 100000(2): Ch. IX.]

051019   Rezolyutsiya. (A resolution.) (Iz(SRD), (3), 20.X.05)
Repr.: 250000(6).I: 280.
[On ending of general political strike.]

[051020(1)] Tsarskii manifest. (The Tsar's Manifesto.) (Iz(SRD), (3), 20.X.05)
Repr.: 250000(6).I: 281-3.

[051020(2)] [Item.] (Iz(SRD), (3), 20.X.05)
[Date-line: Petersburg, 20 oktyabrya.]

051022(1)   Rezolyutsiya. (A resolution.) (<u>Iz</u>(SRD), (4), 30.X.05)

                 <u>Repr</u>.: 250000(6).I: 283-4.

                 [On solemn funeral for first victims of the constitution.]

051022(2)   Rezolyutsiya. (A resolution.) (<u>Iz</u>(SRD), (4), 30.X.05)

                 <u>Repr</u>.: 250000(6).I: 285.

                 [On measures to prevent pogroms.]

051028   Rezolyutsiya. (A resolution.) (<u>Iz</u>(SRD), (5), 3.XI.05)

                 <u>Repr</u>.: 250000(6).I: 285

                 [On introduction of 8-hour working day.]

[051030]   L.Yanovskii: Pis'mo v redaktsiyu. (Letter to Editorial Board.) (<u>Iz</u>(SRD),

                 (4), 30.X.05)

                 <u>Repr</u>.: 250000(6).I: 284.

                 [Known as Yanovsky when chairman of the soviet. See PROTSESS SOVETA

                 RABOCHIKH DEPUTATOV: 5.]

051100   Address to bourgeois meeting.

                 [c. 100000(2): Ch. XV.]

051101(1)   Rech. (A speech.) (<u>Iz</u>(SRD), (5), 3.XI.05)

                 <u>Repr</u>.: 250000(6).I: 285-6.

                 [At extraordinary meeting of soviet.]

051101(2)   Rezolyutsiya. (A resolution.) (<u>Iz</u>(SRD), (5), 3.XI.05)

                 <u>Repr</u>.: 250000(6).I: 286-7.

                 [Of EC of soviet; on general strike.]

051103   Otvet sovet rabochikh deputatov na telegrammu grafa Vitte "K bratsam-

                 rabochim". (Reply of soviet of workers deputies to Count Witte's

                 telegram, "To brother-workers".) (<u>Iz</u>(SRD), (6), 5.XI.05;<u>NZh</u>(05), (7),

                 7.XI.05)

                 <u>Repr</u>.: 250000(6).I: 287.

051104   K oproverzheniyu gr. Vitte. (In refutation of Count Witte.) (<u>Tovarishch</u>,

                 (106), 5.XI.05)

                   <u>Repr</u>.: 250000(6).I: 463-9.

                 [Letter to Editorial Board.]

[051105(1)]   N.T--kii: Otvet grafu Vitte. (Reply to Count Witte.) (<u>Iz</u>(SRD), (6),5.XI.05)

                 <u>Repr</u>.: 250000(6).I: 288.

051105(2)   Rech. (A speech.) (Iz(SRD), (7), 7.XI.05)
             Repr.: 250000(6).I: 290-3.
             [Report of soviet EC.]

051105(3)   Rezolyutsiya. (A resolution.) (Iz(SRD), (7), 7.XI.05)
             Repr.: 250000(6).I: 293-4.

051105(4)   Manifest k soldatam. (Manifesto to the soldiers.) (Iz(SRD), (8),
             [8.XII.05])
             Repr.: 250000(6).I: 299-300.
             [Not traced in Iz(SRD), (8).]

051106   Rezolyutsiya. (A resolution.) (NZh(05), (8), 8.XI.05)
             Repr.: 250000(6).I: 295.
             [On 8-hour working day.]

[051109]   N.Trotskii: Zemsty protiv naroda! (The zemstvos against the people!)
             (RussG, (383), 9.XI.05)

051112(1)   Rezolyutsiya. (A resolution.) (NZh(05), (13), 15.XI.05)
             Repr.: 250000(6).I: 297.
             [On suspension of 8-hour working day.]

[051112(2)] N.T.: Athinskim sovam na Mokhovoi. (To the owls of Athene on the
             Mokhovaya.) (NZh(05), (11), 12.XI.05)
             [The Mokhovaya, the street in Moscow where the University stood.]

[051113(1)] —: Birzha vyrazhaet sochuvstvie gr. Vitte; Grazhdanii dovolen liberalami;
             Liberaly b'yut otboi. (The Stock Exchange expresses sympathy for Count
             Witte; Grazhdanii pleases the liberals; The liberals sound the retreat.)
             (N(05), (1), 13.XI.05)
             Repr.: 250000(6).I: 305-7.

[051113(2)] N.Trotskii: Stachka v oktyabre. (The October strike.) (N(05), (1,2),
             13,15.XI.05)
             Repr.: 060000(6): 149-64; 220000(12): 83-100; 250000(6).I: 261-77.
             [See 220000(12) for other repr., trans., notes.]

051114   Rezolyutsiya. (A resolution.) (NZh(05), (13), 15.XI.05)
             Repr.: 250000(6).I: 298-9.
             [On struggle against lock-outs.]

[051115(1)] Dobrogo utra, peterburgskii dvornik! (Good morning, Petersburg caretakers!) (RussG, (388), 15.XI.05)
Repr.: 250000(6).I: 300-1.

[051115(2)] Kadetskie professora v roli krest'yanskikh tribunov; Politicheskaya ekonomiya eserov; Professora v roli politicheskikh dvornikov; Burzhuazny zhurnalist o chernoi sotne i revolyutsii. (Cadet professors in the role of peasant tribunes; The political economy of the SRs; Professors in the role of political caretakers; A bourgeois journalist on the Black Hundreds and the revolution.) (N(05), (2), 15.XI.05)
Repr.: 250000(6).I: 307-10.

[051116(1)] Vitte - agent birzhi, Struve - agent Vitte. (Witte, agent of the Stock Exchange; Struve, agent of Witte.) (N(05), (3), 16.XI.05)
Repr.: 250000(6).I: 289.

[051116(2)] Telegramma Sevastopol'tsam. (Telegram to [comrades in] Sevastopol.) (NZh(05), (14), 16.XI.05)
Repr.: 250000(6).I: 299.
[From the soviet.]

[051116(3)] Suvorin razoblachaet liberalov; Professorskaya gazeta kleveshchet; Syn Otechestva i polemicheskoe mirolyubie; Bol'sheviki i deyatel'nost soveta. (Suvorin unmasks the liberals; A professorial newspaper slanders; Syn Otechestva and controversial peacefulness; The bolsheviks and the soviet's activities.) (N(05), (3), 16.XI.05)
Repr.: 250000(6).I: 310-3.

[051116(4)] N.Trotskii: "Nezavisimitsy" i svoboda. (The "Independents" and freedom.) (RussG, (389), 16.XI.05)

[051116(5)] —: Chemu uchat sotsialisty-revolyutsionery? (What do the social-revolutionaries teach?) (RussG, (389), 16.XI.05)
Repr.: 050000(2); 250000(6).I: 225-9.
[Brochure subject to confiscation.]

[051117(1)] Esery nedovol'ny sotsial-demokratami; "Utonchennye metody" monarkhicheskoi gazety. (The SRs are displeased with the social-democrats; "Subtle methods" of a monarchist newspaper.) (N(05), (4), 17.XI.05)
Repr.: 250000(6).I: 313-5.

[051117(2)]   Kontr-revolyutsiya rabotaet. (The counter-revolution is at work.)
(N(05), (4), 17.XI.05)
Repr.: 250000(6).I: 326-7.

[051118(1)]   N.Trotskii: Ne privetstvuite nas! (Don't greet us!) (N(05), (5),
18.XI.05)
Repr.: 250000(6).I: 327-9.

[051118(2)]   Novoe Vremya za liberal´nuyu zhandarmeriyu; "Intendanty" revolyutsii;
Russkie Vedemosti za parlamentskii obraz deistvii. (Novoe Vremya is for
a liberal gendarmerie; "Supervisors" of the revolution; Russkie Vedemosti
is for the parliamentary form of action.) (N(05), (5), 18.XI.05)
Repr.: 250000(6).I: 315-7.

[051119(1)]   —: Ili-ili. (Either-or.) (N(05), (6), 19.XI.05)
Repr.: 060000(6): 165-8; 250000(6).I: 329-32.

[051119(2)]   Voennoe polozhenie v Pol´she sbrosheno! (The military posture in Poland
has been abandoned!) (N(05), (6), 19.XI.05)

[051120]   Nuzhno dodumat do kontsa; Legitimist ob uchasti zhirondistov; Reaktsiya v
sudorogakh trakha. (It is necessary to think things out to the end; A
legitimist on the fate of the girondists; Reaction in convulsions of fear.)
(N(05), (7), 20.XI.05)
Repr.: 250000(6).I: 317-9.

[051123(1)]   Nakanune. (On the eve.) (N(05), (8), 23.XI.05)
Repr.: 250000(6).I: 295-7.

[051123(2)]   Liberaly b'yut otboi; Syn Otechestva o svoikh grekhakh molodosti. (The
liberals sound the retreat; Syn Otechestva on the sins of its youth.)
(N(05), (8), 23.XI.05)
Repr.: 250000(6).I: 319-22.

[051124]   Toskuyut po Bonapartu; Meshchanii poka eshche ne trebuet "poryadka";
Zheltaya gazeta spekuliruet. (They long for a Bonaparte; The philistine
meantime still does not call for "order"; A yellow newspaper gambles.)
(N(05), (9), 24.XI.05)
Repr.: 250000(6).I: 322-4.

[051125]   N.Trotskii: Sotsialdemokratiya i revolyutsiya. (The social democracy and
the revolution.) (N(05), (10), 25.XI.05)
Repr.: 060000(6): 168-73.

[051126]   Nasha Zhizn i Plekhanov. (Nasha Zhizn and Plekhanov.) (N(05), (11),
              26.XI.05)
              Repr.: 250000(6).I: 324-5.

[051127(1)]   Zashchishchaite svobodnoe slovo! (Defend free speech!) (RussG, (399),
              27.XI.05)
              Repr.: 250000(6).I: 301-3.

051127(2)   Rezolyutsiya. (A resolution.) (NZh(05), (26), 30.XI.05)
              Repr.: 250000(6).I: 303.
              [Of soviet; on arrest of Khrustalev-Nosar.]

[051127(3)]   N.Trotskii: Nuzhno stroit partiyu! (It is necessary to build the party!)
              (N(05), (12), 27.XI.05)
              Repr.: 060000(6): 173-6.

051200   Cherez tritsat pyat let, 1871-1906. (Thirty-five years later, 1871-1906.)
              [Pref., Karl Marx, PARIZHSKAYA KOMMUNA. LocBDIC.]

[051202]   Derzaite! (Risk it!) (RussG, (404), 2.XII.05)
              Repr.: 250000(6).I: 303-4.

060000(1)   L.Takhotskii: GOSPODIN PETR STRUVE V POLITIKE. (THE POLITICS OF MR. PETER
STRUVE.)
Repr.: 060000(2); 060000(6): 177-223; 250000(6).I: 333-88.
[Pref. to 1st ed. 060208; pref. to 2nd ed. 060711. Author's name in 2nd
ed. is given as N.Trotskii.]

060000(2)   N.Trotskii: GOSPODIN PETR STRUVE V POLITIKE. (THE POLITICS OF MR. PETER
STRUVE.)
[2nd ed. See 060000(1) for all repr., notes.]

060000(3)   [Red.]: † ISTORIYA SOVETA RABOCHIKH DEPUTATOV G. S-PETERBURGA. (HISTORY
OF THE ST. PETERSBURG SOVIET OF WORKERS DEPUTIES.]
[Pref. [061200(2).]

060000(4)   ITOGI SUDA NAD SOVETOM RABOCHIKH DEPUTATOV. (REVIEW OF THE TRIAL OF THE
DEPUTIES OF THE WORKERS SOVIET.)
Repr.: 250000(6).I: 469-77.

060000(5)   L.T—ii: NASHA TAKTIKA V BOR´BE ZA UCHREDITEL´NOE SOBRANIE. (OUR TACTIC
IN THE STRUGGLE FOR A CONSTITUENT ASSEMBLY.)
Repr.: 250000(6).I: 423-37; p.q. 300000(3).

060000(6)   N.Trotskii: † NASHA REVOLYUTSIYA. (OUR REVOLUTION.)
Trans.: Am. p.q. 180000(40).
[Pref. [061200(3)]. See 180000(40) for other p.q. trans.]

[060000(7)] REVOLYUTSIYA I EYA SILY. (THE REVOLUTION AND ITS FORCES.)
Repr.: 250000(6).I: 438-52.
[Repr. reads REVOLYUTSIYA I EE SILY.]

[060000(8)] IZ ISTORII ODNOGO GODA...I: INTELLIGENTSIYA. (THE HISTORY OF ONE
YEAR...II: THE INTELLIGENTSIA.)
Repr.: 250000(6).I: 94-153.

[060000(9)] N.Trotskii: KONSTITUTSIYA "OSVOBOZHDENTSEV". (THE CONSTITUTION OF THE
"LIBERTY" UNION.)
Repr.: 060000(6): 95-109; 250000(6).I: 407-22.
[The "Liberty" Union was founded by Struve.]

[060000(11)] Voznikovenie soveta rabochikh deputatov. (How the soviet of workers
deputies arose.) (220000(12): 101-9)
Repr.: 250000(6).II: 178-85.
[See 220000(12) for other repr., trans., notes.]

[060000(12)]   Itogi. (Results.) (220000(12): 225-45)

Repr.: 250000(6).II: 185-205.

[See 220000(12) for other repr.., trans. Repr. as Istoricheskoe znachenie soviet rabochikh deputatov (The historical significance of the soviet of workers deputies).]

060000(13)   [Notes on Novoe Vremya, Osvobozhdenie, Russkie Vedemosti.] (250000(6).I: 524-5, 530-1, 538-9)

Repr.: 260000(16): 543-4, 545-6.

060208   Pref. GOSPODIN PETR STRUVE V POLITIKE, 060000(1).

[See 060000(1) for repr., notes.]

060212   Kataya gorodskaya duma nuzhna Peterburgu. (The sort of city duma Petersburg needs.) (260000(16): 153-69)

[Archives.]

060216   L.Takhotskii, ODNA ILI DVE PALATY? (ONE CHAMBER OR TWO?)

Repr.: 250000(6).I: 389-407; p.q. 300000(3).

060600   Itogi i perspektivy. (Results and pros ects.) (060000(6): 224-86)

Repr.: 171200(3); 190000(6); p.q. 310000(1).II: App. III.

Trans.: Am. p.q. 180000(40): 69-144; 650000(3): 161-254; 690000(20): 36-122; 700000(8): 36-122; [700000(12)]: 36-122;

Ar. 650000(4): 27-139;

Eng. 210000(39); p.q. 540300; 620700(1): 161-254;

Fr. p.q. 680000(4): 220-5; 690415: 397-463;

Ger. 670000(6);

Jap. *610805; 661130: 6-54; 670131: 117-44;

Yid. p.q. 190000(68): 49-82; p.q. 210000(51): 49-82.

[See 190312, Pref. to Eng. trans. 210000(39); 310000(1) other p.q. trans. Re-titled PERSPEKTIVY RUSSKOI REVOLYUTSII (PROSPECTS OF THE RUSSIAN REVOLUTION).]

060614   V tsentral'nyi komitet RSDRP. (In the Central Committee of the RSDLP.) (250000(6).I: 459-62)

[Archives.]

060700   Sovet i prokuratura. (The soviet and the Procurator's Office.) (060000(3): 311-23)

Repr.: 220000(12): 331-45; 250000(6).II: 149-63.

[See 220000(12) for other repr., trans., notes.]

060711   Pref. GOSPODIN PETR STRUVE V POLITIKE, 060000(2).
          [2nd ed. See 060000(1) note.]

060800   PS 050800. (060000(6): 144-8)
          Repr.: 250000(6).I: 205-9.

060912   Pis´mo P.B.Aksel´rodu. (Letter to P.B.Axelrod. (070000(1): 38-49)

061004/   Moya rech pered sudom. (My speech in court.) (220000(12): 346-60)
          Repr.: 220000(13): 346-60; 250000(6).II: 163-77.
          Trans.: Am. p.q. 640800: 56-61; FI, III.42;
                  Eng. 541000; p.q. Workers' Fight(M/r), (7), VI.68;
                  Fr. p.q. 680000(4): 261-3;
                  Jap. p.q. 681125: 62-7;
                  Sp. p.q. 670000(5): 59-62;
                  Swed. p.q. 691100(2): 47-51.
          [See 100000(2), 220000(12) for other repr., trans. Tovarishch, (I.84,85),
          11,12.X.06 (LocULH) carries report of trial, with brief extracts.]

[061100] Pamyati Arama Ter-Mkrtchyants. (In memory of Aram Ter-Mkrtchyants.)
          (060000(3): 5)
          Repr.: 250000(6).I: 462-3.
          [Archives.]

061104/   Protsess soveta rabochikh deputatov. (The trial of the soviet of
          workers deputies.) (220000(12): 317-30)
          Repr.: 220000(13): 317-30; 250000(6).II: 137-49.
          [See 100000(2), 220000(12) for trans.]

[061200(1)] Sovet i revolyutsiya: Pyat´desyat dnei. (The soviet and the revolution:
          Fifty days.) (060000(3): 9-21)
          Repr.: 220000(12): [Last Ch. of Part I]; p.q. 250000(6).II: 205-6.
          Trans.: Am. p.q. 180000(40): 151-61; p.q. 640800: 51-6;
                  Eng. p.q. 531200: 16-20;
                  Ger. NZeit, (25), VI.07;
                  Sp. p.q. 670000(5): 53-8;
                  Swed. p.q. 691100(2): 42-7;
                  Yid. p.q. 190000(68): 113-23; p.q. 210000(51): 113-23.
          [See 100000(2), 220000(12) for other repr., trans.]

[061200(2)] Pref. ISTORIYA SOVETA RABOCHIKH DEPUTATOV G. S-PETERBURGA, 060000(3).
          Repr.: p.q. 250000(6).I: 507-8.

[061200(3)]   Pref. NASHA REVOLYUTSIYA, 060000(6).

061201(1)   Pis'mo k tov. Larinu. (Letter to cde. Larin.) (070000(1): 49-74)

061201(2)   V zashchitu partii. (In defence of the party.) (070000(1): 75-121)

061223   Kautskii o russkoi revolyutsii. (Kautsky on the Russian revolution.)
          (070000(1): 122-48)

070000(1)   N.Trotskii: † V ZASHCHITU PARTII. (IN DEFENCE OF THE PARTY.)
       [Pref. 070101.]

070000(3)   N.Trotskii: § TUDA I OBRATNO. (THERE AND BACK.)
       Repr.: 190000(28); 220000(12): 361-422; 260000(13); p.q. 300000(1):Ch.IV.
       Trans.: Am. 230000(30); 250000(25);
           Eng. 690100;
           Ger. 100000(2): 297-359; 220000(25); p.q. Jug-Int,(III.11-IV.4-5),
             VII.22-I.23;
           It. *300000(16);
           Swed. 240000(46).
       [Pref. 070408; pref. to 2nd ed. 260000(13), 250929. See 070212,
       220000(12), 300000(1) for other/p.q. trans. 2nd ed. has new title.]

[070000(4)]   Na poroge vtoroi dumy/ Na puti vo vtoroyu dumu. (On the road to the
       second duma.) (070000(1): 1-37)
       Repr.: 260000(16): 175-207.
       [Title in Contents page differs from heading of article.]

[070000(5)]   Politicheskie pis'ma. (Political letters.) (260000(16): 169-74)
       [Archives.]

[070000(6)]   Perspektivy dal'neishego razvitiya revolyutsii. (Prospects of further
       revolutionary upsurge.) (250000(6).I: 452-5)
       Repr.: 260000(16): 179-81.
       [Reply to criticisms by Iordansky and others of NASHA REVOLYUTSIYA,
       060000(6).]

[070100]   Über den Marxismus in Russland. (NZeit, (XXVI.i: 7-10), 1907-8)
       [Trans. Ger. For 25th anniversary of the paper.]

070101   Pref. V ZASHCHITU PARTII, 070000(1).

070103   See 070212.

070105   i dr.: Proshchal'noe pis'mo sov. rab. dep. k peterburgskomu proletariatu.
       (Farewell letter of soviet of workers deputies to the Petersburg
       proletariat.) (250000(6).I: 477-8)

070110   See 070212.

070111   See 070212.

070112   See 070212.

070116   See 070212.

070118   See 070212.

070123   See 070212.

070126   See 070212.

070129   See 070212.

070201   See 070212.

070202   See 070212.

070204   See 070212.

070206   See 070212.

070208   See 070212.

070209   See 070212.

070212   § Tuda. (There.) (070000(3): 11-43)

                Repr. 220000(12).

                Trans. Fr. p.q. Contre leC, (II.7), 22.I.28; Ger.
                        Ger. p.q. ArbStim, (19), 3.XII.27.

                [See 070000(3) for other repr., trans., notes.]

[070221]   Neofit: Kadetskiya zhivyya kartiny. (Life portraits of Cadets.)
                (NLuch, 21.II.07)

[070225]   Neofit: Na kozlakh u Milyukova. (On the coachbox at Milyukov's.)
                (NLuch, (6), 25.II.07)

[070227]   Neofit: Dzholamanov sekret. (Dzholaman's secret.) (NLuch, (7),
                27.II.07)

070408/   Pref. TUDA I OBRATNO, 070000(3).

                Trans.: Am. 180000(40): 163-8;
                        Eng. 531200: iii-iv; 690100: 11-2;
                        Fr. p.q. 680000(4): 348-9.

                [Not all trans. of 070000(3) contain the pref. See 070000(3), 220000(12)
                for repr., trans., notes.]

070501   Rech. (A speech.) (V(Ln) S"EZD [1963])
                [To 5th(London) Congress RSDLP.)

070502   Rech. (A speech.) (V(Ln) S"EZD [1963])

070508 Rech. (A speech.) (V(Ln)S"EZD [1963])
     Repr.: Lenin, p.q. SOCH.XI: 573-4.

070512 Partiya proletariata i burzhuaznye partii v revolyutsii. (The party of
     the proletariat and the bourgeois parties in the revolution.) (V KON.
     PART.I: 180-5)
     Repr.: 220000(12): 249-56; p.q. 300000(3); V(Ln) S"EZD [1963])
     [See 220000(12) for trans.]

070516(1) Popravka k prinyatoi s"ezdom rezolyutsii bol´shevikov ot otnoshenii k
     burzhuaznym partiyam. (Correction to resolution of majority on
     relations with bourgeois parties.) (V(Ln) S"EZD)
     Repr.: Lenin, POLNOE SOBRANIE SOCH.:XV: 505; Lenin, SOCH.:XI: 577.

070516(2) Rech. (A speech.)
     [c. V(Ln) S"EZD [1963].]

070524 Speech at meeting in London.
     [In French. c. Kendall.]

[070600] Die Duma und die Revolution. (NZeit, (25), VI.07: 377-85)
     Russian: 260000(16): 207-18.
     [Trans. Ger.]

[070700] Moral londonskogo s"ezda. (The ethics of the London Congress.)
     (Vestnik Zhizni, (6,7), 1907: 65-84)

071202 Lecture: Capitalisme et socialisme.
     [c. Kriegel, Dossier. In Paris. See 071206.]

071206 [Lecture resumed.]
     [See 071202. cf. PIS´MA: 177.]

*080000(1)   *O GERMANSKOI SOTSIALDEMOKRATII. (ON THE GERMAN SOCIAL DEMOCRACY.)

080000(2)   Das Proletariat und die russische Revolution. (NZeit, (XXVI.II), 1907-8: 782-91)

Russian: 220000(12): 257-69.

[Trans. Ger. Review of A.Tscherewanin, DAS PROLETARIAT UND DIE RUSSISCHE REVOLUTION. See 220000(12) for all repr., trans.]

*080000(3)   *KAPITALIZM I SOTSIALIZM. (CAPITALISM AND SOCIALISM.)

[c. 300000(1): Ch. XVII. Lecture delivered in different European countries. cf. 071202.]

080214   Frank Wedekind. (NZeit, (XXVI.ii), 1907-8: 63-70)

Russian: 230000(9): 324-43; 260000(12): 401-19; LITERATURNYI
         RASPAD.I: 203-20.

Trans.:   Ger. 680800(2): 366-86;
         Jap. 641225.II: 175-202.

[Trans. Ger. PS [080400(1)].]

[080300]   Losy rewolucji rosyjskiej. Artykul pierwszy. (PS-D, (IV.1), III.08)

[Trans. Pol. See further in series [080400(2)], [080500], [080600(2)], [080700], [090600].]

[080400(1)]   PS 080214.

[See 080214 for all repr., trans. Lacking in LITERATURNYI RASPAD.]

[080400(2)]   Trzecia Duma. (PS-D, (IV.2), IV.08)

Russian: 260000(16): 219-29.

[Trans. Pol. See [080300] for series.]

[080400(3)]   Tretya duma. (The third duma.) (NZeit, (XXVI.ii), 1907-8: 388-95)

Russian: 260000(16): 230-8.

[Trans. Ger.]

080412   Nashe otechestvo v vremeni. (Our native land in the present time.)
(230000(9): 193-201)

Repr.:   260000(12): 267-75.

Trans. Ger. 680800(2): 218-27;
         Jap. 641225.II: 1-12.

[f.n. 220600(4).]

[080500]   Duma i budẑet. (PS-D, (IV.3), V.08)

[Trans. Pol. See [080300] for series.]

[080506] O smerti i ob erose. (On death and Eros.) (<u>Odesskie Novosti</u>, (7510), 6.V.08)

Repr.: 230000(9): 201-12; 260000(12): 275-85.

Trans.: Ger. 680800(2): 227-38;
   Jap. 641225.II: 12-27.

[080600(1)] Druzyna carska przy pracy. (<u>PS-D</u>, (IV.4), VI.08)

Russian: 220000(12): 118-23; 250000(6).II: 42-8; 260000(16): 238-44.

[Trans. P$_o$l. See 220000(12) for other repr., trans. Review of MATERIALY K ISTORII RUSSKOI KONTR-REVOLYUTSII, Tom. I.]

[080600(2)] Kryzys w partji. (<u>PS-D</u>, (IV.4), VI.08)

[Trans. Pol. See [080300] for series.]

[080629] "Simplitsissimus." ("Simplicissimus.") (<u>KM</u>, (178), 29.VI.08)

Repr.: 230000(9): 306-18; 260000(12): 420-32.

Trans.: Ger. 680800(2): 346-59;
   Jap. 641225.II: 153-68.

[PS 220600(3). PIS´MA: 322 says the pseudonym Antid Oto is found for all <u>KM</u> articles.]

[080700] W czym sie róznimy. (<u>PS-D</u>, (IV.5), VII.08)

Russian: 220000(12): 270-86.

Trans.: Eng. p.q. Deutscher, PA: 178.

[Trans. Pol. See 220000(12) for all repr., trans.; author's note on text in 220000(12).]

080705 N.Trotskii: Pis´mo. (A letter.) (<u>Prol</u>, (32), 2(15).VII.08)

[Correcting Cherevanin's interpetration of "permanent revolution."]

[080800] Polityka miedzynarodowa i rewolucja. (<u>PS-D</u>, (IV.6), VIII.08)

[Trans. Pol.]

[080806] Graf Vitte. (Stranichka is istorii byurokraticheskoi kul´tury.) (Count Witte: A little page from the history of bureaucratic culture.) (<u>KM</u>, (216,218), 6,8.VIII.08)

Repr.: 260000(17): 97-105.

[080818] Eklektichesky Sankho-Pansa i ego mistichesky oruzhenosets Don Kikhot. (An eclectic Sancho Panza and his mystic armour-bearer, Don Quixote.) (<u>KM</u>, (228), 18.VIII.08)

Repr.: 230000(9): 219-21; 260000(12): 285-7.

Trans.: Ger. 680800(2): 248-9; ++++

[080818] ++++ Jap.: 641225.II: 38-40;
                Sp.: 690000(8).I: 201-2.

[080915]   Leo Tolstoi. (NZeit, (XXV.II: 900-9), 15.IX.09)
                Russian: 260000(12): 249-60.
                Trans.: Am. 640800: 326-31; FI, V-VI.51;
                        Fr. 640911: 233-45; Monde, 1.IX.28;
                        Gr. 660000(6): 218-31; Logotekhnes, (I.4,5), XI,XII.56;
                        It. 581000: 119-31; 680000(6): 19-34;
                        Jap. 681125: 340-6;
                        Nor. p.q. Monde(Verden), (I.3), XII.28;
                        Sp. 640900(1): 275-89; 670000(5): 330-4; 690000(8).II: 19-30;
                        Swed. 690600(1): 209-20.
                [Trans. Ger.]

[081001]   Die russische Sozialdemokratie. (Kampf, (II.1), 1.X.08)
                [Trans. Ger.]

[081003]   --: Samoubiitsy i ekspropriatory. (Suicides and expropriators.)
                (Pr(V), (1), 3.X.08)
                Repr.: 260000(16): 245.

081014   Balkany, kapitalisticheskaya Evropa i tsarizm. (The Balkans, capitalist
                Europe, and tsarism.) (Prol, (38), 1.XI.08)
                Repr.: 260000(1): 13-26.
                Trans.: Pol. PS-D, (IV.8-9), X-XI.08.

[081024]   Zatmenie solntsa. (The eclipse of the sun.) (KM, (295), 24.X.08)
                Repr.: 230000(9): 318-24; 260000(12): 432-8.
                Trans.: Ger. 680800(2): 360-6;
                        Jap. 641225,II: 168-75.

[081106]   Aristotel i chasoslov. (Aristotle and the Prayer-book.) (KM, (308),
                6.XI.08)
                Repr.: 230000(9): 221-7; 260000(12): 287-93.
                Trans.: Ger. 680800(2): 250-6;
                        Jap. 641225.II: 41-9.

[081123]   Vzalkali "kul´tury" ... (Thirst for "culture" ...) (KM, (325),
                23.XI.08)
                Repr.: 230000(9): 227-35; 260000(12): 293-300.
                Trans.: Ger. 680800(2): 256-65;
                        Jap. 641225.II: 49-55.

[081125]   Dlya krasoty sloga. (On beautiful style.) (KM, (327), 25.XI.08)
               Repr.: 230000(9): 235-7; 260000(12): 311-4.
               Trans.: Ger. 680800(2): 265-8;
                       Jap. 641225.II: 59-63.

[081200]   Nationalpsychologie oder Klassenstandpunkt. (NZeit, (XXVII.i: 76-84)
               1908-9)
               [Trans. Ger.]

081216   Duma a "ustawa 22 listopade". (PS-D, (IV.10), XII.08)
               Russian: 260000(16): 322-32.
               [Trans. Pol.]

[081217(1)]   —: Chernaya Duma za rabotoi. (The Black Duma at work.) (Pr(V), (2),
               17.XII.08)
               Repr.: 260000(16): 246-50.

[081217(2)]   —: Na bor'bu s bezrabotitsei i golodom. (For a struggle against
               unemployment and famine.) (Pr(V), (2), 17.XII.08)
               Repr.: 260000(16): 250-5.

[081217(3)]   —: Turetskaya revolyutsiya i zadachi proletariata. (The Turkish
               revolution and the tasks of the proletariat.) (Pr(V), (2), 17.XII.08)
               Repr.: 260000(1): 3-6.

[081230]   Novogodny razgovor ob isskustva. (A New Year talk on art.) (KM, (358),
               30.XII.08)
               Repr.: 230000(9): 212-9; 260000(12): 301-8.
               Trans.: Ger. 680800(2): 239-47;
                       Jap. 641225.II: 27-38.

[090103]   Novaya Turtsiya. (The new Turkey.) (<u>KM</u>, (3), 3.I.09)
Repr.: 260000(1): 6-13.

[090109]   Zhores. (Jaurès.) (<u>KM</u>, (9), 9.I.09)
<u>Repr.</u>: 260000(17): 16-20.
<u>Trans.</u>: Eng. p.q. Deutscher, PA: 187.

[090127]   Slabost kak istochnik sily. (Puriskevich.) (Weakness as a source of
strength: Puriskevich.) (<u>KM</u>, (27), 27.I.09)
<u>Repr.</u>: p.q. 260000(16): 578-9; 260000(17): 168-71.

[090129]   Belyi Bychok i kul'tura. ("A little White Bull" and culture.)
(<u>KM</u>, (29), 29.I.09)
<u>Repr.</u>: 230000(9): 238-41; 260000(12): 308-11.
<u>Trans.</u>: Ger. 680800(2): 268-72;
        Jap. 641225.II: 63-8.
[Reference is to Dostoevsky, THE FRIEND OF THE FAMILY: Ch. VI.]

[090130]   Na zapade. (In the West.) (<u>KM</u>, (30,37,63), 30.I, 6.II, 3.III.09)
<u>Repr.</u>: 230000(9): 357-73; 260000(12): 438-52.
<u>Trans.</u>: Ger. 680800(2): 401-16;
        Jap. 641225.II: 217-35.
[Unsystematic notes.]

[090208]   Khodatai ili deputaty? (K evolyutsii narodovtsev.) (Intercessors or
deputies? On the evolution of the Populists.) (<u>KM</u>, (39), 8.II.09)
<u>Repr.</u>: 260000(16): 373-7.

[090210]   --: Nasha dumskaya fraktsiya. (Our duma fraction.) (<u>Sotsdem</u>, (2),
10.II.09)
[Identified in CatKam.]

*[090300]   *Pis'mo t. Katslerovichu. (Letter to cde. Katslerovich.) (<u>Radnik</u>, (15),
1909)
[Trans. Serb.]

[090322]   N.Trotsky: Die verdorbene Suppe. (<u>NZeit</u>, (XXVII.i: 892-9), III.09)
Russian: 260000(16): 338-45; <u>Sotsdem</u>, (3), 22.III.09.
[Trans. Ger.]

[090327(1)]   Pered pervym maya. (Before May Day.) (<u>Pr</u>(V), (3), 27.III.09)
<u>Repr.</u>: 260000(16): 256-60.

[090327(2)] —: Nuzhna zheleznaya metla. (An iron broom is needed.) (Pr(V), (3), 27.III.09)

Repr.: 260000(16): 263-5.

[On the occasion of the Nobles' Congress.]

[090327(3)] —: Iz russkoi zhizni. (From Russian life.) (Pr(V), (3), 27.III.09)

Repr.: 260000(16): 261-3.

090327(4) —: Krakh terrora i ego partii. (The failure of terror and its party.) (Pr(V), (3), 27.III.09)

Repr.: 260000(16): 345-58.

Trans.: Am./Eng. p.q. THE CASE: 258,490; p.q. NOT GUILTY: 251;

Fr. p.q. 371116(2);

Ger. p.q. 370000(17);

Gr. p.q. 620000(18);

It. p.q. 670000(11);

Pol. p.q. *370000(28); PS-D, (V.11), V.09;

Por. p.q. *440000(1);

Sp. p.q. *380000(15); p.q. *470000(9); p.q. 620000(10).

[The Azef affair.]

[090421] Gospodin Petr Struve. (Popytka ob"yasneniya.) (Mr. Peter Struve: An attempt at an explanation.) (KM, (109), 21.IV.09)

Repr.: p.q. 260000(16): 546-7; 260000(17): 238-46.

[090430] Venskaya "Secession" 1909 g. (The Vienna "Secession" in 1909.) (KM, (118), 30.IV.09)

Repr.: 230000(9): 372-6; 260000(12): 463-9.

Trans.: Ger. 680800(2): 417-21;

Jap. 641225.II: 235-40.

["Secession", an annual Art exhibition by Impressionists and others, held in Vienna. See further [130623].]

[090500] Die revol. Romantik und Asew. (NZeit, (XXVII.ii: 184-7), V.09)

Russian: 260000(16): 358-61.

Trans.: Am./Eng. p.q. THE CASE: 258,491.

Fr. p.q. 371116(2);

Ger. p.q. 370000(17);

Gr. p.q. 620000(18);

It. p.q. 670000(11);

Pol. p.q. *370000(28);

Por. p.q. *440000(1); ++++

[090500]   ++++   Sp. p.q. *380000(15); p.q. *470000(9); p.q. 620000(10).
[Trans. Ger. Reply to M.L.]

[090518]   Speech to meeting of Russian revolutionaries.
[c. Kriegel: 277.]

[090600]   Włościaństwo a socjaldemokracja. (PS-D, (V.12), VI.09)
Russian: 260000(16): 311-22.
[Trans. Pol. See [080300] for series.]

[090602]   —: K chemu prishli. (What they have come to.) (Pr(V), (4), 2.VI.09)
Repr.: 260000(16): 266-71.

[090821]   Zatrudneniya vneshnie i vnutrennie. (Difficulties abroad and at home.)
(Sotsdem, (7-8), 21.VIII.09)
Trans.: Pol. PS-D, (V.14-15), VIII-IX.09.

[090920(1)]   —: Vneshnyaya politika kontr-revolyutsii. (The foreign policy of the
counter-revolution.) (Pr(V), (5), 20.IX.09)
Repr.: 260000(16): 278-84.

[090920(2)]   —: Iz russkoi zhizni. (From Russian life.) (Pr(V), (5), 20.IX.09)
Repr.: 260000(16): 272-8.

[090920(3)]   —: My ne znaem eshche ikh imen.... (We don't even know their names....)
(Pr(V), (5), 20.IX.09)
Repr.: 260000(16): 271-2.

091000   Pref. RUSSLAND IN DER REVOLUTION, 100000(2).
[Trans. Ger. See 220000(12) for Russian and other trans.]

[091105(1)]   —: Imperskie zagovorshchiki i Finlyandiya. (Imperial conspirators
and Finland.) (Pr(V), (6), 5.XI.09)
Repr.: 260000(16): 377-9.

[091105(2)]   Vivos Voco: Pis'mo k russkim rabochim. (Letter to the Russian workers.)
(Pr(V), (6), 5.XI.09)

[091105(3)]   —: Iz russkoi zhizni. (From Russian life.) (Pr(V), (6), 5.XI.09)

[091121(1)]   —: Zhelezo i krov. (Iron and blood.) (Pr(V), (7), 21.XI.09)
Repr.: 260000(16): 379-82.
[The national question in Russia.]

[091121(2)] —: Karl Marks i Rossiya v 1909 g. (Karl Marx and Russia in 1909.)
(Pr(V), (7), 21.XI.09)
Repr.: 260000(16): 287-90.

[091121(3)] —: V ozhidanii promyshlennogo podema. (In expectation of industrial
revival.) (Pr(V), (7), 21.XI.09)
Repr.: 260000(16): 397-404; p.q. 300000(1): Ch. XVII.

[091208(1)] —: Natsional´naya bor´ba i edinstvo proletariata. (The national
struggle and the unity of the proletariat.) (Pr(V), (8), 8.XII.09)
Repr.: 260000(16): 370-3.

[091208(2)] —: M.Gor´kii i sotsial-demokratiya. (M.Gorky and the social democracy.)
(Pr(V), (8), 8.XII.09)
Repr.: 260000(16): 286-7.

[091208(3)] —: Cherespolositsa i sotsializm. (Overlapping and socialism.) (Pr(V),
(8), 8.XII.09)
Repr.: 260000(16): 337.
[Overlapping, a scattered-strip system, one of the complicated forms
of land-tenure in tsarist Russia.]

[091208(4)] —: Mezhdunarodnyi sotsialisticheskii kongress v Kopengagene. (The
international socialist congress in Copenhagen.) (Pr(V), (8),
8.XII.09)
[T. was the Pravda(V) correspondent at this congress and further,
unsigned, articles on it, in this periodical, are credited to him.]

[091208(5)] —: Kurlovskii nabeg. (Kurlov's raid.) (Pr(V), (8), 8.XII.09)
Repr.: 260000(16): 284-6.

100000(1)   RUSKATA REVOLYUTSIYA. (THE RUSSIAN REVOLUTION.)
              [Trans. Bul. See 100712 for Russian, note.]

100000(2)   § RUSSLAND IN DER REVOLUTION.
              Russian: 220000(12).
              Trans.: Am. p.q. 650900: 43-61;
                      Eng. p.q. 640000(5): 43-61; 640000(10): 43-61;
                      Ger. p.q. Arbeiterpolitik, (II.41),13.X.17.
              [Trans. Ger. Russian 220000(12) is expanded ed. See 220000(12) for
              repr., trans., notes. Pref. 091000.]

[100000(3)]   Rezension. (NZeit, XXVIII.ii: 687, 1909-10)
              [Trans. Ger. Review of P.Chasles, LE PARLEMENT RUSSE.]

[100000(4)]   Conversation with Boris Eliacheff. (Démocratie, (190), 13.VI.63)
              [Trans. Fr.]

*[100000(5)] *Bebelovi memoari. (In memory of Bebel.) (Radnichke Novine, (21),
              1910)
              [Trans. Serb.]

[100101(1)]   —: Nel'zya molchat! (It is impossible to be silent!) (Pr(V), (9),
              1.I.10)
              Repr.: 260000(16): 382-4.
              [On national question in Russia.]

[100101(2)]   —: Gde nashi, gde vashi? (Where are ours, where yours?), (Pr(V), (9),
              1.I.10)
              Repr.: 260000(16): 362-4.
              Trans.: Am/Eng.: p.q. THE CASE: 258, 491;
                      Fr. p.q. 371116(2);
                      Ger. p.q. 370000(17);
                      Gr. p.q. 620000(18);
                      It. p.q. 670000(11);
                      Pol. p.q. *370000(28);
                      Por. p.q. *440000(1);
                      Serb. Radnichke Novine, (27), 1911;
                      Sp. p.q. *380000(15); p.q. *470000(9); p.q. 620000(10).

[100101(3)]   —: Vokrug muzhitskoi zemli. (About the muzhik's land.) (Pr(V), (9),
              1.I.10)
              Repr.: 260000(16): 332-7.

[100101(4)]   —: 9 yanvarya. (January 9th.) (<u>Pr</u>(V), (9), 1.I.10)
Repr.: 250000(7): 93-4.

100115   [At Plenum CC RSDLP, in Paris.]
[c. Lenin, SOCH. XVI: 744.]

[100212(1)]   —: Finlyandskie vybory. (The Finnish elections.) (<u>Pr</u>(V), (10), 12.II.10)
Repr.: 260000(16): 384-6.

[100212(2)]   —: Iz russkoi zhizni. (From Russian life.) (<u>Pr</u>(V), (10), 12.II.10)

[100318(1)]   —: Udar v serdtse. (A blow to the heart.) (<u>Pr</u>(V), (11), 18.III.10)
Repr.: 260000(16): 386-8.

[100318(2)]   —: S dumoi ili bez dumy? (With or without a duma?) (<u>Pr</u>(V), (11),
18.III.10)
Repr.: 260000(16): 290-5.

[100403(1)]   —: Chto zhe dal´she? (What next?) (<u>Pr</u>(V), (12), 3.IV.10)
Repr.: 260000(16): 388-90.

[100403(2)]   —: K mezhdunarodnomu sotsialisticheskomu kongressu v Kopengagene.
(To the international socialist congress in Copenhagen.) (<u>Pr</u>(V),
(12,13,14), 3.IV, 15.V, 24.VI.10)

[100403(3)]   Pervomaiskoi listok. (May Day supplement.) (<u>Pr</u>(V), (12), 3.IV.10)
Repr.: 260000(16): 404-7.

[100403(4)]   —: Iz russkoi zhizni. (From Russian life.) (<u>Pr</u>(V), (12), 3.IV.10)

[100403(5)]   —: K edinstvu cherez vse prepyatsviya. (Unity despite all obstacles.)
[<u>Pr</u>(V), (12), 3.IV.10)
[c. Lenin, SOCH. XIV: 439.]

[100501]   K pervomu maya. (For May Day.) (260000(16): 407-10)
[May Day supplement to <u>Pravda</u>(V).]

[100515]   —: Pravo gosudarstvennogo perevorota. (The right to state revolution.)
(<u>Pr</u>(V), (13), 15.V.10)
Repr.: 260000(16): 296-9.

[100624(1)]   —: Konets Finlyandii? (The end of Finland?) (<u>Pr</u>(V), (14), 24.VI.10)
Repr.: 260000(16): 390-3.

[100624(2)] Neunyvayushchii: Zametki nablyudatelya. (Notes of an observer.)
(<u>Pr</u>(V), (14), 24.VI.10)
<u>Repr</u>.: 260000(16): 299-302.

100712 Ruskata revolyutsiya. (The Russian revolution.)
Russian: 250000(6).II: 207-23.
[Trans. Bul. Speech to XVII Congress Bulgarian Workers Social-
democratic Party, in Sofia. See 100000(1).]

100721 Letter to Kautsky. (p.q. Nettl: 433)
[Trans. Eng. On Kautsky's relations with Luxemburg.]

[100801(1)] —: Balkanskii vopros i sotsial-demokratiya. (The Balkan question
and the social democracy.) (<u>Pr</u>(V), (15), 1.VIII.10)
<u>Repr</u>.: 260000(1): 36-41.

[100801(2)] N.Trotskii: S bolgarskogo s"ezda. (At the Bulgarian Congress.)
(<u>Pr</u>(V), (15), 1.VIII.10)
<u>Repr</u>.: 260000(1): 41-5.

[100801(3)] —: Kooperativy i sotsializm. (Co-operatives and socialism.)
(<u>Pr</u>(V), (15), 1.VIII.10)
[Address to International Socialist Congress, Copenhagen.]

[100828] —: Die russische Sozialdemokratie. (<u>Vorwärts</u>, (201), 28.VIII.10)
[c. Lenin, SOCH. XIV: 56.]

[100909] Die Entwicklungtendenzen der russischen Sozialdemokratie.
(<u>NZeit</u>, (XXVIII.ii: 860-71), 9.IX.10)
[Trans. Ger. c. 300000(1): Ch. XVI.]

[100924(1)] —: Navstrechu pod"emu. (To meet the revival.) (<u>Pr</u>(V), (16), 24.IX.10)
<u>Repr</u>.: 260000(16): 411-5.

[100924(2)] —: Krasnyi parlament v Kopengagene. (A red parliament in Copenhagen.)
(<u>Pr</u>(V), (16), 24.IX.10)

[101100] Intelligentsiya i sotsializm. (The intelligentsia and socialism.)
(<u>SovMir</u>, XI.10)
<u>Repr</u>.: 230000(9): 344-57; 260000(12): 452-65.
<u>Trans</u>.: Arab. *<u>Arab Studies</u>, (11), IX.69;
    Eng. 660100; <u>FI</u>(Ln), Aut-Winter, 1964-5;
    Ger. 680800(2): 387-401; ++++

[101100]   ++++ Trans.: Jap. 641225.II: 202-17;

                         Sp. 690000(8).I: 179-90.

                   [Review of Max Adler, SOTSIALIZM I INTELLIGENTSIYA (SOCIALISM AND
                   THE INTELLIGENTSIA).]

[101101]   Na Balkanu.

                   Trans.: Serb. Borba, (II.17), 1911.

[101120(1)]   —: Tolstoi. (Pr(V), (17), 20.XI.10)

                   Repr.: 260000(12): 260-4.

[101120(2)]   Neunyvayushchii: Zametki nablyudatelya. (Notes of an observer.)
                   (Pr(V), (17), 20.XI.10)

                   Repr.: 260000(16): 302-5.

[101120(3)]   —: Chto zhe dal'she? (What next?) (Pr(V), (17), 20.XI.10)

*101126   *O sovremennoi rabochei presse. (On the contemporary workers press.)
                   [c. Lenin, SOCH. XIV: 554. See f.n. p. 37.]

[110129(1)] —: Pavel Zinger. (Pr(V), (18–19), 29.I.11)
Repr.: 260000(17): 3–5.
Trans.: Eng. Keep Left, (XIX.3), III.70.

[110129(2)] —: Polozhenie v strane i nashi zadachi. (The situation in the country and our tasks.) (Pr(V), (18–19), 29.I.11)
Repr.: 260000(16): 416–26.

[110129(3)] T—skii: "Ty trudishsya nedarom!" ("You toil in vain!") (Pr(V), (18–19), 29.I.11)

[110200(1)] [Rezension.] (NZeit, (XXIX.ii: 643–5), 1910–1)
[Trans. Ger. Review of Gart, WARUM HAT RUSSLAND ZU WANKEN BEGONNEN?]

[110200(2)] [Lectures to marxist school, in Bologna.]
[c. 300000(1): Ch. XXXVI. The school opened 21.XI.10 and closed III.11.]

[110416] —: Razvyazka nadvigaetsya. (The denouement is coming.) (Pr(V), (20), 16.IV.11)
Repr.: 260000(16): 426–35.

[110508] Evno Azef. (KM, (126), 8.V.11)
Repr.: 260000(17): 105–14.

[110519] Merezhkovskii. (KM, (137,140), 19,22.IV.11)
Repr.: 230000(9): 241–54; 260000(12): 314–27.
Trans.: Ger. 680800(2): 272–87;
          Jap. 641225.II: 68–86.

[110527] Dve venskie vystavki, 1911 g. (Two Viennese exhibitions in 1911.) (KM, (145), 27.V.11)
Repr.: 230000(9): 378–85; 260000(12): 469–78.
Trans.: Ger. 680800(2): 422–31;
          Jap. 641225.II: 240–50.

[110601] N.Trotskii: Der russischen Paragraph 14. (Kampf, (IV.9), 1.VI.11)
[Trans. Ger.]

[110625] —: Evropeiskaya rabochaya gazeta na russkom yazyke. (A European workers paper in the Russian language.) (Pr(V), (21), 25.VI.11)
[c. Lenin, SOCH. XV: 578.]

[111100]   Nestlozhnye voprosy. (Urgent problems.) (Nasha Zarya, (II.11: 116-28), 1911)

[111101]   N.Trotskii: Terrorismus. (Kampf, (V.2), 1.XI.11)
            Russian: 260000(16): 364-9.
            Trans.: Am/Eng. p.q. THE CASE: 259, 492; p.q. NOT GUILTY: 251-2;
                    Fr. p.q. 371116(2);
                    Ger. p.q. 370000(17);
                    Gr. p.q. 620000(18);
                    It. p.q. 670000(11);
                    Pol. p.q. *370000(28);
                    Por. p.q. *440000(1);
                    Serb. Borba, (IV.21), 1911;
                    Sp. p.q. *380000(15); p.q. *470000(9); p.q. 620000(10).
            [Trans. Ger.]

[111116(1)] —: Krovozhadnyi i beschestnyi. (Bloodthirsty and dishonorable.)
            (Pr(V), (22), 16.XI.11)
            Repr.: 260000(16): 440-1.
            [On Stolypin.]

[111116(2)] —: "Politika ne zavisit ot lichnosti." ("Politics do not depend on
            personality.") (Pr(V), (22), 16.XI.11)
            Repr.: 260000(16): 441-4.

[111116(3)] —: Vpered. (Forward.) (Pr(V), (22), 16.XI.11)
            [c. Lenin, SOCH. XV: 302.]

[111210]   —: Nichto im ne pomozhet. (No one will help them.) (Pr(V), (23),
            10.XII.11)
            Repr.: 260000(16): 435-40.

[120000(1)]   Balkanskie strany i sotsializm. (The Balkan countries and socialism.)
(230000(19): 9-18)
Repr.: 260000(1): 27-35.

120000(2)   Domov i N.Trotskii: YUBILEI POZORA NASHEGO (1613-1913). (THE JUBILEE
OF OUR SHAME (1613-1913).)
Repr.: 260000(17): 140-51.
Trans.: Swed. 130000.
[Title of T's contribution BLAGOCHESTIVEISHII, SAMODERZHAVNEISHII
(MOST PIOUS, MOST AUTOCRATIC).]

120222   N.Trotskii: Politicheskie pis'ma. Est li u nas konstitutsiya?
(Political letters: Do we have a constitution?) (ZhiDel, (7), 2.III.12)
Repr.: 260000(16): 305-10.

120225   Rezolyutsiya redaktsii Pravda. (Resolution of the Pravda Editorial
Board.) (Listok Golosa Sotsialdemokrata, (5), III.12)
[Arrangements for forthcoming ["August bloc"] conference.]

[120304]   Ob intelligentsii. (The intelligentsia.) (KM, (64,72), 4,12.III.12)
Repr.: 230000(9): 255-68; 260000(12): 327-42.
Trans.: Am. Partisan Review, Fall, 1968;
      Ger. 680800(2): 288-305;
      Jap. 641225.II: 87-106.
[f.n. 220600(1).]

[120314(1)]   —: Tovarishchi! (Comrades!) (Pr(V), (24), 14.III.12)
[c. Lenin, POLNOE. XXI: 601.]

[120314(2)]   —: Voprosy izbiratel'noi kampanii. (Problems of the electoral
campaign.) (Pr(V), (24), 14.III.12)
[c. Lenin, POLNOE. XXI: 601.]

[120326]   Aus dem russischan Parteileben. (Vorwärts, (72), 26.III.12)
[Trans. Ger. c. Lenin, SOCH. XV: 423.]

[120329]   Gertsen i zapad. (Herzen and the West.) (KM, (87), 29.III.12)
Repr.: 260000(17): 231-8.

[120423(1)]   —: Lenskaya boinya i otvet proletariata. (The Lena massacre and the
proletariat's response.) (Pr(V), (25), 23.IV.12)
Repr.: 260000(16): 444-52.

[120423(2)]   —: K pervomu maya. (For May Day.) (Pr(V), (25), 23.IV.12)
Repr.: 260000(16): 452-62.
[Supplement.]

[120423(3)]   Red.: My zhdem otveta. (We await a reply.) (Pr(V), (25), 23.IV.12)

[120423(3)]   Red.: Otkrytoe pis´mo kievskim tovarishcham. (Open letter to Kiev
comrades.) (Pr(V), (25), 23.IV.12)

[120428]   Pod kontrol. (Under control.) (ZhiDel, (16), 28.IV.12)
[c. Lenin, SOCH. XVI: 42,43. cf. [121016].]

[120500]   N.Trotskii: Printsipy i predrassudki. (Principles and prejudices.)
(Nasha Zarya, (III.5), 1912)
[c. Lenin, SOCH. XVI: 675.]

[120510]   Literatura razocharovannykh stipendiatov. (Writings of disappointed
grant-aided students.) (KM, (129,130), 10,11.V.12)
Repr.: 260000(17): 114-22.
[On Men´shchikov and Bakai.]

[120518]   Chukovskii. (KM, (136), 18.V.12)
Repr.: 260000(12): 351.
[See further, 140209.]

[120525]   Nechto ob anketakh. (A few words about questionnaires.) (KM, (143),
25.V.12)
Repr.: 260000(12): 342-50.

120810   Pis´mo. (A letter.)
[c. PIS´MA: 255. To Martov.]

[120918]   Rossiya o sotsial-demokraticheskoi platforme. (Rossiya on the
social-democratic platform.) (Luch, (2,3,8), 18,19,25.IX.12)
Repr.: 260000(17): 131-8.

[120922]   Milyukov. (Luch, (6,7), 22,23.IX.12)
Repr.: 260000(17): 171-6.

[120926]   N.Trotskii: S zapada na vostok. (From west to east.) (Luch, (9),
26.IX.12)
[Part I, only; remainder not traced.]

[121003(1)]   Pervye vpechatleniya. (First impressions.) (<u>KM</u>, (274), 3.X.12)
Repr.: 260000(1): 64-8.
[Balkan war.]

[121003(2)]   N.Trotskii: Otvet putilovtsam. (Reply to Putilov workers.) (<u>Luch</u>, (15), 3.X.12)

[121004(1)]   V doroge. (En route.) (<u>Den</u>, (3), 4.X.12)
Repr.: 260000(1): 57-61.

[121004(2)]   Belgrade. (<u>Den</u>, (3), 4.X.12)
Repr.: 260000(1): 61-4.

[121004(3)]   T.: O germanskoi sotsial-demokratii. (On the German social-democrats.) (<u>Luch</u>, (16), 4.X.12)

[121005(1)]   Serbiya v siluetakh. (Serbia in silhouettes.) (<u>Den</u>, (4), 5.X.12)
Repr.: 260000(1): 73-8.
[Pashich, Pachu, and Prodanovich.]

[121005(2)]   Laza Pachu. (<u>KM</u>, (276), 5.X.12)
Repr.: 260000(1): 79-82.

[121013]   Pered sobytiyami. (Before the events.) (<u>Den</u>, (12), 13.X.12)
Repr.: 230000(19): 47-57; 260000(1): 134-9.

[121014]   Voina ob"yavlena.... (War declared....) (<u>KM</u>, (285), 14.X.12)
Repr.: 260000(1): 140-4.

[121015]   Politicheskie partii i voina. (Dva monologa.) (The political parties and the war: Two monologues.) (<u>KM</u>, (286), 15.X.12)
Repr.: 260000(1): 153-60.

[121016]   N.Trotskii: Rabochuyu pressu — pod kontrol! (To the workers press — Under control!) (<u>Luch</u>, (26), 16.X.12)
[cf.[120428].]

[121019(1)]   Nablyudeniya i obobshcheniya. (Observations and generalizations.) (<u>Odesskie Novosti</u>, (8852), 19.X.12)
Repr.: 260000(1): 144-53.

[121019(2)]   Iznanka pobedy: Dva potoka. (The seamy side of victory: Two streams.) (<u>KM</u>, (290), 19.X.12)
Repr.: 230000(19): 68-77; 260000(1): 174-9.

[121019(3)] Bolgarskaya voennaya tsenzura. (Bulgarian military censorship.)
(Den, (18), 19.X.12)
Repr.: 230000(19): 95-100; 260000(1): 244-8.

[121019(4)] Bolgarskaya pressa. (The Bulgarian press.) (230000(19): 92-5)

[121022] Chetnichestvo i voina. (Chetnikism and the war.) (KM, (293), 22.X.12)
Repr.: 230000(19): 107-15; 260000(1): 218-25.

[121024] Vokrug voiny. (About the war.) (KM, (295), 24.X.12)
Repr.: 260000(1): 127-9.

[121031] Ranenye. (The wounded.) (KM, (302), 31.X.12)
Repr.: 260000(1): 180-5.

[121100(1)] Okolo Kirkilisse. (Around Kirkilisse.) (230000(19): 58-67)
Repr.: 260000(1): 165-74.

[121100(2)] Dlinnyi mesyats. (A long month.) (230000(19): 78-80)
Repr.: 260000(1): 205-7.

[121104] So slov uchastnikov. (From the words of participants.) (KM, (306),
4.XI.12)
Repr.: 260000(1): 185-91.

[121109] Bolgariya i russkaya diplomatiya. (Bulgaria and Russian diplomacy.)
(Den, (38), 9.XI.12)
Repr.: 260000(1): 211-7.
[Interview with Bulgarian officials.]

[121110(1)] U plennykh ofitserov. (With captured officers.) (KM, (312), 10.XI.12)
Repr.: 230000(19): 73-7; 260000(1): 191-4.

[121110(2)] K dialektike sobytyi. (The dialectics of events.) (230000(19): 77)

121112 Razlozhenie Turtsii i armyanskii vopros. (The disintegration of
Turkey and the Armenian question.) (260000(1): 225-35)
[Archives.]

[121118] V zapozdaloi strane. (In a backward country.) (KM, (320), 18.XI.12)
Repr.: 230000(19): 19-24; 260000(1): 46-50.

[121119(1)]   Bolgarskii parlamentarizm. (Bulgarian parliamentarism.) (KM, (322), 19.XI.12)
          Repr.: 230000(19): 24-5; 260000(1): 50-2.

[121119(2)]   Demokratiya i absolyutizm. (Democracy and absolutism.) (KM, (322), 19.XI.12)
          Repr.: 230000(19): 25-7; 260000(1): 52-4.

[121120(1)]   Doma. (At home.) (230000(19): 80-3)
          Repr.: 260000(1): 259-61.

[121120(2)]   V novykh provintsiyakh. (In new provinces.) (230000(19): 83-5)
          Repr.: 260000(1): 262-3.

[121120(3)]   Serbskaya pressa. (The Serbian press.) (Den, (49,51), 20,22.XI.12)
          Repr.: 260000(1): 97-104.

121120(4)   Pis'mo P.Todorova. (A letter from P.Todorov.) (KM, (332), 30.XI.12)
          Repr.: 260000(1): 263-7.
          Trans.: Eng. p.q. Deutscher, PA: 204.

121127   Otvet P.Todorovu. (Reply to P.Todorov.) (KM, (334), 2.XII.12)
          Repr.: 230000(19): 100-6; 260000(1): 267-73.

[121129]   Pressa i tsenzura. (The press and censorship.) (KM, (331), 29.XI.12)
          Repr.: 260000(1): 160-5.

[121200]   Rasskaz ofitsera. (An officer's account.) (260000(1): 199-204)
          [Archives.]

[121206]   Armiya pobeditelei. (An army of victors.) (KM, (338), 6.XII.12)
          Repr.: 230000(19): 86-91; 260000(1): 248-53.

[121213]   Klubok protivorechii. (A tangle of contradiction.) (KM, (345), 13.XII.12)
          Repr.: 260000(1): 68-73.

[121214]   Nikola Pashich. (KM, (346,349), 14,17.XII.12)
          Repr.: 260000(1): 89-97.

[121219]   Stoyan Novakovich. (Odesskie Novosti, (8902), 19.XII.12)
          Repr.: 260000(1): 82-9.

[121221]   Serbiya i Chernogoriya. (Serbia and Montenegro.) (<u>KM</u>, (353), 21.XII.12)

Repr.: 260000(1): 112-5.

[121223]   Za kraem zavesy. (Beyond the curtain edge.) (<u>KM</u>, (355), 23.XII.12)

Repr.: 260000(1): 253-9.

[121225]   Iz istorii odnoi brigady. (From the history of one brigade.) (<u>Den</u>, (84,86), 25,29.XII.12)

Repr.: 260000(1): 115-27.

[121229]   Zhest g-na Bryanchaninova. (A gesture from Mr. Bryanchaninov.) (<u>KM</u>, (360), 29.XII.12)

Repr.: 260000(1): 129-33.

[Russia and Serbia; slavophils.]

[121230]   Politicheskie partii. (The political parties.) (<u>Den</u>, (87), 30.XII.12)

Repr.: 260000(1): 105-12.

[The Balkan parties.]

130000   Domov och Trotskij, VÅR VANHEDERS JUBILEUM (1613-1913).
                [Trans. Swed. See 120000(2) for all trans., note.]

[130129]   N.Trotskii: Rasskaz ranenago. (A wounded man's story.) (Luch, (23),
                29.I.13)
                Repr.: 260000(1): 194-9.

[130130]   N.Trotskii: Vnedumskii vopros g-mu P.Milyukovu. (A pre-duma question
                to Mr. P.Milyukov.) (Luch, (24:110), 30.I.13)
                Repr.: 260000(1): 273-5.

[130202(1)]   N.Trotskii: Pis'mo ob edinstve: Odna ili dve partii? (A letter on unity:
                One or two parties?) (Luch, (27), 2.II.13)
                [c. Lenin, SOCH. XVI: 675.]

[130202(2)]   N.Trotskii: Pis'mo ob edinstve: Rabochie i polemika. (A letter on unity:
                The workers and the polemic.) (Luch, (27), 2.II.13)
                [c. Lenin, SOCH. XVI: 675.]

[130205]   N.Trotskii: Pis'mo ob edinstve. III: Vozstanovlenie fraktsii? (A letter
                on unity. III: Re-making fractions?) (Luch, (29:115), 5.II.13)
                [See also [130202(1)], [130202(2)].]

130207   Pis'mo. (A letter.) (PIS'MA: 274)
                [To Nasha Zarya.]

[130208(1)]   U groba Frantsa Shumaiera. (At the grave of Franz Schumayer.) (Luch,
                (32), 8.II.13)
                Repr.: 260000(17): 5-7.
                Trans.: Eng. Keep Left, (XIX.3), III.70.

[130208(2)]   Filosofiya i moral ukryvatel'stva. (The philosophy and morality of
                receiving stolen goods.) (KM, (39), 8.II.13)
                Repr.: 260000(1): 283-94.

[130219]   N.Trotskii: Itogi "Balkanskogo zaprosa". (Results of a "Balkan Inquiry."
                (Luch, (41,43,44), 19,21,22.II.13)
                Repr.: 260000(1): 275-83.

[130224]   N.Trotskii: Kazennaya nedotykomka. (Official hypersensitivity.)
                (Luch, (46), 24.II.13)
                Repr.: 260000(17): 138-40.

[130305]   N.Trotskii: V poryadke veshchei! (In the order of things!) (Luch, (53:139), 5.III.13)
Repr.: 260000(1): 294-5.

[130306]   N.Trotskii: Karl Kautskii i nashi raznoglasiya. (Karl Kautsky and our differences.) (Luch, (54,56,66:140,142,152), 6,8,20.III.13)

[130307]   Na zashchite dobrosovestnogo molchaniya. (In defence of conscientious silence.) (KM, (66), 7.III.13)
Repr.: 260000(1): 295-300.

[130313(1)]   —: Byudzhet i rabochii klass. (The budget and the working class.) (Luch, (60,69,71-3,78,82), 13,23,26-8.III, 3,7.IV.13)
Repr.: 260000(16): 516-25.

[130313(2)]   N.T.: "Surovyi klimat." ("A severe climate.") (Luch, (60), 13.III.13)

[130314]   Ikh rabota. (Their work.) (Luch, (61:147), 14.III.13)
Repr.: 260000(1): 301-3.
Trans.: Serb. Radnichke Novine, (44), 1914.
[On the Balkan social democracy.]

[130315]   Rabota proletariata. (The proletariat's work.) (Luch, (62:148), 15.III.13)
Repr.: 260000(1): 303-5.
Trans.: Serb. Radnichke Novine, (43), 1913.

[130320]   Sotsial-demokraticheskoi fraktsii avstriiskogo reikhsrata: Pravleniyu vengerskoi sotsial-demokratii. (The social-democratic fraction in the Austrian parliament: To the leadership of the Hungarian social democrats.) (260000(1): 306-9)
[Archives.]

[130321]   Khrustalev. (Luch, (67), 21.III.13)
Repr.: 250000(6).I: 508-10; 260000(17): 190-2.

[130331]   N.Trotskii: Otvet na vopros. (Answer to a question.) (Luch, (76), 31.III.13)

130401   [Pis'mo.] [A letter.] (LENIN O T.: 171-3)
Trans.: Eng. p.q. Deutscher, PA: 232;
    Fr. p.q. TROTSKI ET: 61-2;
    It. p.q. TROTSKI ED: 60-1.
[To Chkeidze.]

[130402]　　　Yuch-Bunar.　(Luch, (77), 2.IV.13)
　　　　　　　Repr.:　260000(1): 207-11.

[130516]　　　K likvidatsii legendy.　(Pis'mo v redaktsiyu.)　(For the liquidation of
　　　　　　　a legend: Letter to the Editorial Board.)　(KM, (137), 16.V.13; Luch,
　　　　　　　(111): 16.V.13)
　　　　　　　Repr.:　250000(6).I: 510-4; 260000(17): 192-7.
　　　　　　　[On Khrustalev-Nosar.]

[130623]　　　"Secession" 1913 g.　("Secession" in 1913.)　(KM, (171,172), 23,24.VI.13)
　　　　　　　Repr.:　230000(9): 385-92; 260000(12): 478-85.
　　　　　　　Trans.: Ger. 680800(2): 432-9;
　　　　　　　　　　　　Jap. 641225.II: 251-9.
　　　　　　　[See [090430].]

[130703]　　　Balkanskii razgovor.　(A Balkan conversation.)　(KM, (181), 3.VII.13)
　　　　　　　Repr.:　260000(1): 310-9.

130707　　　　Pervye vpechatleniya.　(First impressions.)　(230000(20): 11-8)
　　　　　　　Repr.:　260000(1): 343-9.
　　　　　　　[Post-war Rumania.]

[130710]　　　Organizatory katastrofy.　(Organizers of catastrophe.)　(KM, (188),
　　　　　　　10.VII.13)
　　　　　　　Repr.:　230000(19): 28-34; 260000(1): 320-5.

[130713]　　　Viktor Adler.　(KM, (191), 13.VII.13)
　　　　　　　Repr.:　260000(17): 7-16.
　　　　　　　Trans.: Eng. Keep Left, (XIX.3), III.70.
　　　　　　　[PS 190400(1).]

130717　　　　See 130707.

[130719]　　　Andranik i ego otryad.　(Andranik and his detachment.)　(KM, (197),
　　　　　　　19.VII.13)
　　　　　　　Repr.:　260000(1): 235-43.

[130728]　　　Bukharestskii mir.　(The Peace of Bucharest.)　(KM, (206), 28.VII.13)
　　　　　　　Repr.:　230000(20): 19-25; 260000(1): 350-5.

[130731]　　　Rumyno-bolgarskie otnosheniya.　(Rumano-Bulgarian relations.)　(KM,
　　　　　　　(209,211), 31.VII, 2.VIII.13)
　　　　　　　Repr.:　230000(20): 26-32; 260000(1): 356-61.

[130809]   Sredi zatrudnenii. (In the midst of difficulties.) (<u>KM</u>, (218), 9.VIII.13)
Repr.: 230000(20): 33-44; 260000(1): 361-71.

[130827]   Poezdka v Dobrudzhu. (A trip to Dobrudzha.) (<u>KM</u>, (243,245,246,253), 3,5,6,13.IX.13)
Repr.: 230000(20): 93-116; 260000(1): 411-32.
[PS 220712.]

[130912]   Rabochaya partiya. (The workers party.) (<u>KM</u>, (252), 12.IX.13)
Repr.: 230000(20): 63-71; 260000(1): 386-94.
[In Rumania.]

[130917]   Vokrug reform. (About reform.) (<u>KM</u>, (257), 17.IX.13)
Repr.: 230000(20): 45-52; 260000(1): 371-8.

[130921]   Na putyakh vnutrennei katastrofy. (On the road to internal catastrophe.) (<u>KM</u>, (261), 21.IX.13)
Repr.: 230000(20): 53-62; 260000(1): 378-86.

[131006]   Guchkov i guchkovshchina. (Guchkov and guchkovism.) (<u>KM</u>, (276), 6.X.13)
Repr.: 260000(17): 176-80.

[131015]   Ne pomozhet li natsional-liberalizm? (Won't national-liberalism help?) (<u>KM</u>, (285), 15.X.13)
Repr.: 260000(16): 477-82.

[131017]   "Golyama pouka." ("A big lesson.") (<u>KM</u>, (287), 17.X.13)
Repr.: 230000(20): 117-22; 260000(1): 334-9.
[Title in Bulgarian.]

[131019]   Soblaznitel'nye paralleli. (Tempting parallels.) (<u>KM</u>, (289), 19.X.13)
Repr.: 260000(12): 368-72.

[131025]   Georgy Zamyslovskii. (<u>KM</u>, (295), 25.X.13)
Repr.: 260000(17): 180-9.

[131100]   Die Beilis-Affäre. (<u>NZeit</u>, (XXXII.i: 310-20), XI.13)
Russian: 260000(16): 462-76.
Trans.: It. *[180000(51)].
[Trans. Ger. Jewry.]

[131102]   Krizis Bolgarii. (The Bulgarian crisis.) (<u>KM</u>, (313), 2.XI.13)
Repr.: 230000(19): 35-43; 260000(1): 326-33.

[131206]   N.I.Pirigov. (<u>KM</u>, (337,343), 6,12.XII.13)
Repr.: 260000(17): 215-31.

140000(1)   DER KRIEG UND DIE INTERNATIONALE.
            [Trans. Ger. See [140000(3)] for all repr., trans., notes.]

140000(2)   DER KRIEG UND DIE INTERNATIONALE.
            [Trans. Ger. See [140000(3)] for all repr., trans., notes.]

[140000(3)]   Leo N.Trotsky: DER KRIEG UND DIE INTERNATIONALE.
              Russian: 220000(3).I: 75-154; p.q. Golos, (59,60,79), 20,21.XI, 13.XII.14)
              Repr.: 140000(1); 140000(2); 170000(7); 180000(37): 3-84; [180000(52)];
                      190000(49); [190000(63)]; p.q. Jug-Int, (11), V.18.
              Trans.: Am. 180000(32); p.q. 640800: 71-9; p.q. FI, X.44;
                      Bul. *180000(1);
                      Cz. p.q. Rude Pravo, (65), 7.XII.20;
                      Eng. p.q. 180000(45);
                      Gr. p.q. Diethnistes, (1), I.[65];
                      Hol. 150000(1);
                      It. 200000(54); *210000(29); p.q. 680200(2): 59-69; 700000(16);
                      Jap. p.q. 681125: 77-85;
                      Sp. 190000(41); *190000(42); *210000(55); 220000(38); p.q.
                          670000(5): 71-9;
                      Swed. p.q. 691100(2): 60-8;
                      Yid. p.q. 190000(68): 153-90; p.q. 210000(51): 153-90.
              [Trans. Ger. Pref. 141031; f.n. 220400(2).]

[140000(4)]   Povechan´e ruske vojski. (Borba, (VII.208), 1914)
              [Trans. Serb.]

[140110]   Stranichka iz proshlogo. (A little page from the past.) (KM, (10),
              10.I.14)
              Repr.: 260000(17): 198-205.
              [P.A.Zlydnev obituary.]

[140209]   Chukovskii. (KM, (40), 9.II.14)
              Repr.: 230000(9): 270-80; 260000(12): 351-68.
              Trans.: Ger. 680800(2): 305-16;
                      Jap. 641225.II: 107-21.
              [See [120518].]

[140215]   Kak ozdorovit vlast? (How restore the state power to health?) (KM, (46),
              15.II.14)
              Repr.: 260000(16): 482-8.

[140219] Popranie sillogizma. (Scorn for the syllogism.) (<u>KM</u>, (50), 19.II.14)
     <u>Repr</u>.: 230000(9): 280-5; 260000(12): 372-7.
     <u>Trans</u>.: Ger. 680800(2): 316-22;
        Jap. 641225.II: 121-7.

[140220] Osvobozhdenie slova. (Liberation of the word.) (<u>KM</u>, (51), 20.II.14)
     <u>Repr</u>.: 230000(9).: 285-91; 260000(12): 377-83.
     <u>Trans</u>.: Ger. 680800(2): 322-9;
        Jap. 641225.II: 127-34.

*[140221] N.Trotskii: #Rabochaya gazeta. (A workers paper) (<u>Severnaya</u>
     <u>Rabochaya Gazeta</u>, (11), 21.II.14)
     [c. Lenin, SOCH. XVII: 669.]

[140222(1)] T.: Pamyati N.L.Grossera-Zel´tsera. (In memory of N.L.Grosser-Zeltser.)
     (<u>Bor´ba</u>, (1), 22.II.14)
     <u>Repr</u>.: 260000(17): 208-11.

[140222(2)] Ot redaktsii. (From the Editorial Board.) (<u>Bor´ba</u>, (1), 22.II.14)
     [c. Lenin, SOCH. XVII: 669.]

[140222(3)] --: Parlamentarizm i rabochii klass. (Parliamentarism and the working
     class.) (<u>Bor´ba</u>, (1), 22.II.14)
     [c. Lenin, SOCH. XVII: 392.]

[140222(4)] --: Istoricheskoe desyatiletie. (1904-1914 g.g.) (An historical
     decade:, 1904-1914.) (<u>Bor´ba</u>, (1), 22.II.14)
     <u>Repr</u>.: 260000(16): 497-506.

[140301] Svetskie bogoslovy i Van´kina lichnost. (Worldly theologians and
     Vanka's personality.) (<u>KM</u>, (60), 1.III.14)
     <u>Repr</u>.: 230000(9): 291-7; 260000(12): 383-9.
     <u>Trans</u>.: Ger. 680800(2): 329-36;
        Jap. 641225.II: 134-42.

140315 Pamyati P.A.Zlydneva. (In memory of P.A.Zlydnev.) (<u>Bor´ba</u>, (3), 9.IV.14)
     <u>Repr</u>.: 260000(17): 205-8.

[140316] Sud´ba tolstogo zhurnala. (The fate of a thick journal.) (<u>KM</u>,
     (75,78), 16,19.III.14)
     <u>Repr</u>.: 230000(9): 297-305; 260000(12): 389-97.
     <u>Trans</u>.: Ger. 680800(2): 336-46;
        Jap. 641225.II: 142-51.
     [f.n. 220600(2).]

[140318]   —: Gosudarstvo i narodnoe khozyaistvo. (The state and the national economy.) (Bor´ba, (2), 18.III.14)
Repr.: 260000(16): 525-33.

[140409]   N.Trotskii: Rabochiya koalitsii. (A workers coalition.) (Bor´ba, (3), 9.IV.14)

140414   T.: S.L.Klyachko. Nekrolog. (S.L.Klyachko: An obituary.) (Bor´ba, (4), 28.IV.14)
Repr.: 260000(17): 211-4.

[140428]   Martovskie itogi. (A review of March.) (Bor'ba, (4), 28.IV.14)
Repr.: 260000(16): 506-14.

[140516(1)]   Dumskii lokaut. (A duma lock-out.) (Bor´ba, (5), 16.V.14)
Repr.: 260000(16): 488-97.

[140516(2)]   Lozung momenta. (The slogan of the moment.) (Bor´ba, (5), 15.V.14)
Repr.: 260000(16): 514-5.

[140516(3)]   Redaktor: K druz´yam edinstva! (To friends of unity!) (Bor´ba, (5), 16.V.14)

[140516(4)]   Redaktsiya: Po povodu pis´ma t.t. vperedovtsev. (On a letter from comrade-adherents of Vpered.) (Bor´ba, (5), 16.V.14)

[140602]   Rossiya i Evropa. (Russia and Europe.) (KM, (158), 2.VI.14)
Repr.: 260000(12): 485-93.

[140619]   Masarik o russkom marksizme. (Masaryk on Russian marxism.) (KM, (166), 19.VI.14)
Repr.: 260000(12): 493-7.
Trans.: Ger. Kampf, (VII): 519-27, 1913-1914.

[140621]   Garting i Menshchikov. (Harting and Menshchikov.) (KM, (168), 21.VI.14)
Repr.: 260000(17): 122-31.

140807   Iz shveitsarskogo dnevnika. (From a Swiss diary.) (220000(3).I: 49-50)

140809(1)   Iz shveitsarskogo dnevnika. (From a Swiss diary.) (220000(3).I: 50-1)
Repr.: p.q. 300000(1): Ch. XVIII.

[140809(2)]   "Den nemetskogo naroda." ("The Day of the German people.) (220000(3).I: 52-3)

140810   Iz shveitsarskogo dnevnika. (From a Swiss diary.) (220000(3).I: 53-4)

140811   Iz shveitsarskogo dnevnika. (From a Swiss diary.) (220000(3).I: 54-5)
Repr.: p.q. 300000(1): Ch. XVIII.

140812   Iz shveitsarskogo dnevnika. (From a Swiss diary.) (220000(3).I: 55-60)
[f.n. 220400(1).]

140813   Iz shveitsarskogo dnevnika. (From a Swiss diary.) (220000(3).I: 60-3)

140814   Iz shveitsarskogo dnevnika. (From a Swiss diary.) (220000(3).I: 63-4)

140815   Iz shveitsarskogo dnevnika. (From a Swiss diary.) (220000(3).I: 64-5)

140817   Iz shveitsarskogo dnevnika. (From a Swiss diary.) (220000(3).I: 65-6)

140818   Iz shveitsarskogo dnevnika. (From a Swiss diary.) (220000(3).I: 66)

140826   Iz shveitsarskogo dnevnika. (From a Swiss diary.) (220000(3).I: 66-9)

140901   Iz shveitsarskogo dnevnika. (From a Swiss diary.) (220000(3).I: 69-71)

140910   Manifesto against the war; for "Eintracht".
[c. 300000(1): Ch. XVIII.]

141031   Pref. DER KRIEG UND DIE INTERNATIONALE, [140000(3)].
Russian: 220000(3).I: 75-6.
Trans.: Fr. p.q. 680000(4): 108-15.
[Trans. Ger. See [140000(3)] for other trans., repr.]

141120   Politicheskii moratorium. (A political moratorium.) (KM, (328),
28.XI.14)
Repr.: 190000(10): 7-12; 270000(1): 3-6.

[141124/]   N.Trotskii: Verno li? (Is it true?) (Golos, (62), 24.XI.14)
Repr.: 220000(3).II: 67/66.

[141125]   N.Trotskii: Neobkhodimaya popravka. (A necessary correction.) (Golos,
(63), 25.XI.14)

[141127]   N.Trotskii: Proletariat v voine. (The proletariat in the war.) (Golos),
(65,66), 27,28.XI.14)

[141204]   Dve armii. (Two armies.) (KM, (334), 4.XII.14)
Repr.: 190000(2): 7-19; 270000(1): 7-15.

[141210]   N.Trotskii: Gregus po demokraticheskomu spiska. (Gregus on the
Democratic list.) (<u>Golos</u>, (76), 10.XII.14)
<u>Repr</u>.: 220000(3).I: 223–7; 270000(1): 129–33.

[141214]   Bosnyak volonter. (A Bosnian volunteer.) (<u>KM</u>, (344), 14.XII.14)
<u>Repr</u>.: 270000(1): 15–7.

141226   Tre mesyatsa vo frantsuzskom flote. (Three months in the French fleet.)
(190000(1): 20–32)
[Conversation with a Serbian volunteer.]

[141230]   Pechal'nyi dokument. (A wretched document.) (<u>Golos</u>, (93), 30.XII.14)
<u>Repr</u>.: 220000(3).I: 295–9.
[Plekhanov on the war.]

150000(1) DE OORLOG EN DE INTERNATIONALE.
    [Trans. Hol. See [140000(3)] for all trans., notes.]

150000(2) M.S.Uritskomu. (To M.S.Uritsky.) (p.q. LENIN O T.: 173)

[150106] "Yaponskii" vopros. (The "Japanese" question.) (<u>KM</u>, (6), 6.I.15)
    <u>Repr</u>.: 270000(1): 31-6.

[150108] N.Trotskii: K 100-mu nom. <u>Golosa</u>. (The 100th issue of <u>Golos</u>.) (<u>Golos</u>,
    (100), 8.I.15)
    <u>Repr</u>.: 220000(3).II: 68-9/66-7.

[150113] French. (The military uniform.) (<u>KM</u>, (13), 15.I.15)
    <u>Repr</u>.: 270000(1): 26-31.

150115(1) "Guerre d'usure." (<u>NS</u>, (60), 9.IV.15)
    <u>Repr</u>.: 190000(2): 20-30; 270000(1): 36-43.

[150115(2)] N.Trotskii: Nash politicheskii lozung. (Our political slogans.)
    (<u>Golos</u>, (106,108), 15,17.I.15)

150116 Ot Pontiya k Pilatu. (From Pontius to Pilate.) (270000(1): 43-9)
    [Archives.]

[150120] Vse dorogi vedut v Rim. (All roads lead to Rome.) (<u>KM</u>, (20), 20.I.15)
    <u>Repr</u>.: 270000(1): 17-21.

150200 Mal´chiki kotorye "vyzvali" voinu. (Young lads "conscripted" for war.)
    (190000(1): 7-19)

[150213] N.Trotskii: Zayavlenie. (A statement.) (<u>NS</u>, (14), 13.II.15)
    [Reply to Y.Larin.]

[150214] N.Trotskii: Parvus. (<u>NS</u>, (15), 14.II.15)
    <u>Repr</u>.: 190000(10): 44-7.
    <u>Trans</u>.: Fr. <u>V</u>(M), (II.67), 15.II.18.

150216 "Sed´moi pekhotnyi" v bel´giiskoi epopee. (The "7th Infantry" in the
    Belgian epic.) (<u>KM</u>, (63,65), 4,6.III.15)
    <u>Repr</u>.: 190000(1): 69-92; 270000(1): 58-74.

[150223] N.Trotskii: Nash politicheskii lozung. (Our political slogans.)
    (<u>NS</u>, (22,23), 23,24.II.15)
    <u>Trans</u>.: Eng. p.q. Deutscher, PA: 237.

[150300]   Iz tetradi o Bel'gii. (From a notebook on Belgium.) (190000(1): 33-68)

[150301]   N.Trotskii: Nekriticheskaya otsenka kriticheskoi epokhi. (An uncritical
           estimate of a critical epoch.) (NS, (28,35,41), 1,10,17.III.15)
           Repr.: 220000(3).I: 306-12.
           [Part III, in NS, completely censored.]

[150317]   See note, [150301].

[150322]   Otkuda poshlo. (Where it came from.) (KM, (81), 22.III.15)
           Repr.: 270000(1): 49-58.

[150325]   —: Petrogradskie royalisty i frantsuzskaya respublika. (Petrograd
           royalists and the French republic.) (NS, (48), 25.III.15)
           Repr.: 220000(3).I: 227-8.
           [Censored in NS.]

[150331]   —: Eshche est na svete sotsialdemokraty. (There are still social
           democrats in the world.) (NS, (53), 31.III.15)
           Repr.: 220000(3).II: 251-2/243-4.

[150401]   N.T.: Vremya nynche takovskoe. (The time is good enough.) (NS, (54)
           1.IV.15)
           Repr.: 220000(3).II: 321-4/313-6.

[150409]   N.T.: Nekhorosho-s! (It's bad!) (NS, (60), 9.IV.15)

[150411]   —: Do kontsa! (To the end!) (NS, (62), 11.IV.15)
           Repr.: 220000(3).II: 69-71/67-9.

[160416]   Al'fa: Porazhenchestvo i iskazhenchestvo. (Defeatism and distortion.)
           (NS, (66), 16.IV.15)

[150417]   N.Trotskii: Sytinskii "malyi" o Rakovskom. (A Sytinite "little man"
           on Rakovsky.) (NS, (67), 17.IV.15)
           Repr.: 190000(10): 65-7; 220000(3).II: 305-6/297-8.

[150425]   —: Klevetnikam! (A slander!) (NS, (74), 25.IV.15)
           Repr.: 220000(3).II: 307-10/299-302.
           [On Rakovsky.]

[150429]   —: Va banque! (NS, (77), 29.IV.15)
           Repr.: 220000(3).I: 228-30; 270000(1): 133-4.

[150501]   N.Trotskii: Pervoe maya (1890-1915 g.g.) (May Day: 1890-1915.)
(NS, (79), 1.V.15)
Repr.: 220000(3).II: 71-7/69-74.

[150505]   N.Trotskii: Kommentarii k telegramme t. Kh. Rakovskogo. (Commentary on
a telegram from cde. Ch. Rakovsky.) (NS, (81), 5.V.15)
Repr.: 220000(3).II: 310-1/302-3.

[150506]   —: Imperializm i natsional'naya ideya. (Imperialism and the national
idea.) (NS, (82), 6.V.15)

[150515]   —: Nasha pozitsiya. (Our position.) (NS, (89,100,106,107),
15,29.V, 5,6.VI.15)
Repr.: 220000(3).II: 78-93/76-90.
[See note [150723]; PIS'MA: 344. Proletarian struggle against the war.]

[150516]   Red.: P.B.Akselrod i sotsial-patriotizm. (P.B.Axelrod and social-
patriotism.) (NS, (90), 16.V.15)
Repr.: 220000(3).II: 127-9/123-5.

[150529]   N.T.: Privet tov. Dobrodzhanu-Gerea. (Greetings to cde. Dobrodjanu-
Gherea.) (NS, (100), 29.V.15)
Repr.: 220000(3).II: 77-8/75-6; 260000(17): 80-1.

[150601]   T.: [Article completely censored.] (NS, (102), 1.VI.15)

[150604]   N.Trotskii: Otkrytoe pis'mo v redaktsiyu zhurnala Kommunist. (Open
letter to Editorial Board of the journal Kommunist.) (NS, (105), 4.VI.15)
Trans.: Am. Gankin & Fisher: 170-3.

[150613]   —: "Oni — drugogo dukha." ("They are of a different spirit.")
(NS, (113), 13.VI.15)
Repr.: 220000(3).II: 253-6/245-8.
[On the German social democracy.]

[150617]   —: Kautskii o Plekhanove. (Kautsky on Plekhanov.) (NS, (116-8),
17-19.VI.15)
Repr.: 220000(3).I: 299-306.

[150623]   —: Nemetskaya oppozitsiya i nemetskaya diplomatiya. (The German
Opposition and German diplomacy.) (NS, (121), 23.VI.15)
Repr.: 270000(1): 115-8.

[150624]   Al´fa: Pervyi shag sdelan. (The first step has been taken.)
(NS, (122), 24.VI.15)
Repr.: 220000(3).I: 230-2; 260000(17): 156-8.
[Political portraits of Shcherbatov and Kaknin.]

[150703]   N.Trotskii: Natsiya i khozyaistvo. (The nation and the economy.)
(NS, (130,135), 3,9.VII.15)
Repr.: 270000(1): 209-16.

[150711(1)]   —: "Levaya" i "tsentr" v nemetskoi sots.-dem. ("Left" and "Centre" in
the German social-democracy.) (NS, (137), 11.VII.15)
Repr.: 220000(3).II: 256-8/248-50.

[150711(2)]   N.Trotskii: Diversii. (Acts of sabotage.) (NS, (137), 11.VII.15)

[150712]   Na severo-zapad. (In the North-West.) (KM, (191), 12.VII.15)
Repr.: 270000(1): 21-6.

[150717(1)]   —: Bez masshtaba. (Without measure.) (NS, (141), 17.VII.15)
Repr.: 220000(3).II: 258-62/250-3.
[The German social-democracy.]

[150717(2)]   Zhan Zhores. (Jean Jaurès.) (KM, (196), 17.VII.15)
Repr.: 190000(10): 127-43; 260000(17): 20-32.
Trans.: Eng. Keep Left, (XIX.5,6), V,VI.70;
         Hol. NTijd, (XXI.2), II.16.
[cf. *170000(1).]

[150718(1)]   N.Trotskii: Otkrytoe pis´mo t. Plekhanovu. (Open letter to cde. Plekhanov.)
(NS, (142), 18.VII.15)

[150718(2)]   —: Na Balkanakh. (In the Balkans.) (NS, (142,143), 18,20.VII.15)
Repr.: 220000(3).I: 163-7; 270000(1): 77-81.

[150722]   —: Politika "tyla". (Politics "in the rear.") (NS, (145), 22.VII.15)
Repr.: 220000(3).I: 232-4; 270000(1): 134-7.

[150723]   —: Nasha pozitsiya. (Our position.) (NS, (146,147), 23,24.VII.15)
[Given in NS as Part IV of [150515]. Polemic with Sotsial-Demokrat.]

[150804]   —: God voiny. (One year of war.) (NS, (156), 4.VIII.15)
Repr.: 190000(2): 54-61; 220000(3).II: 93-8/90-5; 270000(1): 216-21.

[150815]   Al´fa: Ne v ochered. (Out of order.) (NS, (166), 15.VIII.15)
Repr.: 270000(1): 137-9.

[150818]   —: Konvent rasteryannosti i bezsiliya. (A convention of confusion and
             weakness.) (NS, (167), 18.VIII.15)
             Repr.: 220000(3).I: 234-7; 270000(1): 139-42.

[150826]   —: Voennyi krizis i politicheskaya perspektivyi. (The war crisis and
             political perspectives.) (NS, (174,179-182), 26.VIII, 1-4.IX.15)
             Repr.: 220000(3).I: 238-53; p.q. 270000(1): 142-51.

[150827]   —: Haaze — Ebert — David. (NS, (175), 27.VIII.15)
             Repr.: 190000(10): 70-2; 260000(17): 36-8.

[150900(1)] Imperialisticheskaya programma. (An imperialist programme.)
             (190000(2): 62-74)
             [A peace programme.]

[150900(2)] "Frantsuzskaya" programma mira. (The "French" peace programme.)
             (190000(2): 75-96)

[150900(3)] Psikhologiya voennoi zony. (Psychology of the war zone.)
             (190000(2): 104-12)

[150900(4)] Vykinye iz voennoi zony. (Thrown out of the war zone.)
             (190000(2): 123-41)

150907(1)   [Speech at Zimmerwald conference.) (Lademacher.I: 132-4)
             [Trans. Ger.]

[150907(2)] u. Roland Holst: Entwurf. (Lademacher.I: 134-7)
             [Trans. Ger.]

[150911]   Psikhologicheskaya zagadki voiny. (A psychological riddle of the war.)
             (KM, (252), 11.IX.15)
             Repr.: 190000(2): 97-103; 270000(1): 244-8.
             Trans.: Eng. p.q. Deutscher, PA: 231-2.

150915   Manifest internatsional'noi sotsialisticheskoi konferentsii v
             Tsimmervalde. (Manifesto of the international socialist Zimmerwald
             conference.) (220000(3).II: 52-5/51-4)
             Repr.: LETUCHII.
             Trans.: Am. Gankin & Fisher: 329-33; 640800: 80-3;
                     Eng. 510900; Lenin, CW. XVIII: 379-82;
                     Fr. Humbert-Droz: L'ORIGINE: 139-42;Levy: 105-9; Maitron &
                         Chambelland: 184-7; Rosmer.I: 379-82;   ++++

150915   ++++   Jap. 681125: 86-9;
                      Sp. 670000(5): 79-83; *Pereyra: 57-63;
                      Swed. 691100(2): 68-71.

[150920]   Transheya. (Trenches.) (KM, (261,262), 20,21.IX.15)
            Repr.: 190000(2): 113-22; 270000(1): 196-203.

[150930]   —: Rakovskii o russkikh sotsial-patriotakh. (Rakovsky on the Russian
            social-patriots.) (NS, (204), 30.IX.15)
            Repr.: 220000(3).II: 311-5/303-7.

151001   Krepost ili transheya? (Fortress or trenches?) (KM, (306), 4.XI.15)
            Repr.: 190000(2): 47-53; 270000(1): 191-6.

[151003]   Vyvody. (Editorials.) (NS, (207,209), 3,6.X.15)
            Repr.: 220000(3).II: 56-60/55-9.

[151005]   N.Trotskii: Pis´mo v redaktsiyu l'Humanité. (Letter to Editorial Board
            Humanité.) (NS, (208), 5.X.15)

[151006]   See [151003].

[151007(1)] Al´fa: "Les Russes d'abord!" (NS, (210), 7.X.15)
            Repr.: 270000(1): 151-2.

[151007(2)] N.T.: Nemetskaya s.-d. oppozitsiya. (The German s-d opposition.)
            (NS, (210), 7.X.15)
            [From a notebook.]

[151009]   N.T.: Rossiiskaya sektsiya internatsionala. (The Russian section of
            the International.) (NS, (212), 9.X.15)
            [From a notebook.]

[151012]   —: Bolgarskaya sots.-dem. i voina. (The Bulgarian soc-dem. and the
            war.) (NS, (214), 12.X.15)
            Repr.: 220000(3).II: 99-102/95-8.

[151013]   N.T.: Osnovnye tezisy. (Fundamental theses.) (NS, (215,216),
            13,14.X.15)
            Repr.: 220000(3).II: 44-51/43-51.
            [On Zimmerwald. From a notebook.]

[151014]   —: Ostavte nas v pokoe! (Leave us in peace!) (NS, (216), 14.X.15)
            Repr.: 190000(10): 103-7; 260000(17): 62-4.

[151017(1)]   N.Trotskii: Osnovnye voprosy. (Fundamental problems.) (NS, (217),
              17.X.15)
              Repr.: 190000(6); 220000(12): 287-93.
              Trans.: Eng. 210000(39): 83-90;
                      Fr. 690415: 465-70;
                      Ger. 670000(6): 129-36;
                      Jap. 670131: 145-56.
              [See 220000(12) for other trans.]

[151017(2)]   —: Voennye tainy i politicheskie misterii. (War secrets and political
              mysteries.) (NS, (217), 17.X.15)
              Repr.: 220000(3).I: 167-71.

[151019]   —: Ona byla, konferentsiya v Tsimmerval'de! (The Zimmerwald conference
              is over!) (NS, (218), 19.X.15)
              [Censored in NS.]

[151022(1)]   N.T.: Konferentsiya v Tsimmerval'de. (The Zimmerwald conference.)
              (NS, (221), 22.X.15)
              Repr.: 220000(3).II: 24-8.
              [f.n. 220400(3).]

[151022(2)]   R.Grimm i O.Morgari. (R.Grimm and O.Morgari.) (190000(10): 47-53)
              Repr.: 220000(3).II: 28-32.
              [f.n. 220400(4).]

[151022(3)]   Morgari ob Italii. (Morgari on Italy.) (190000(10): 53-60)

[151023]   Kh.Rakovskii i V.Kolarov. (Ch.Rakovsky and V.Kolarov.) (KM, (294),
              23.X.15)
              Repr.: 190000(10): 60-5; 220000(3).II: 32-5; 260000(17): 77-80.

[151024]   A.: Zametki chitatelya. (A reader's notes.) (NS, (223,224),
              24,26.X.15)
              Repr.: 220000(3).I: 208-10; p.q. 270000(1): 151, 152-3.

[151025]   Ledebur -- Goffman. (Ledebour -- Hoffman.) (KM, (296), 25.X.15)
              Repr.: 190000(10): 78-83; 220000(3).II: 36-9/35-8; 260000(17): 74-7.

[151026]   See [151024].

[151027]   N.T.: Otvet P.B.Aksel´rodu. (Reply to P.B.Axelrod.) (<u>NS</u>, (225), 27.X.15)

Repr.: 190000(10): 73-8; 220000(3).II: 60-4.

[See further [151031].]

[151028(1)]   Kautskii, Bernshtein, Haaze. (190000(10): 83-90)

Repr.: 220000(3).II: 39-42.

[Repr. with slight modifications.]

[151028(2)]   Deyatel´nost levykh v Germanii. (Left activity in Germany.) (220000(3).II: 42-4/42-3)

[151029]   Lyud: Khvostov! (<u>NS</u>, (227), 29.X.15)

Repr.: 190000(10): 107-10; 260000(17): 151-3.

[151030(1)]   —: Gallienne. (<u>NS</u>, (228), 30.X.15)

Repr.: 220000(3).I: 171-3.

[151030(2)]   —: Sushchnost krizisa. (Substance of the crisis.) (<u>NS</u>, (228), 30.X.15)

Repr.: 220000(3).I: 173-5.

[151031]   N.T.: K Tsimmerval´dskoi konferentsii. (The Zimmerwald conference.) (<u>NS</u>, (229,232,240,244), 31.X, 5,14,19.XI.15)

Repr.: 190000(10): 73-8; 220000(3).II: 60-4/59-62.

[See also [151027].]

151100(1)   La famille Declerc. (<u>Huma</u>, 22.I.22)

Repr.: <u>Humbles</u>, (XIX.5-6), V-VI.34.

Trans.: Cz. <u>Rude Pravo</u>, (49), 26.II.22;
        It. <u>Ordine Nuovo</u>, (II.44), 13.II.22.

[Wartime France. Trans. Fr.]

151100(2)   [Loriot et T.]: LES SOCIALISTES DE ZIMMERWALD ET LA GUERRE.

Trans.: Ger. p.q. <u>Arbeiterpolitik</u>, (II.4), 27.I.17.

[Trans. Fr. Identified in Rosmer.I: 464.]

[151105]   —: Svoim poryadkom. (In their own order.) (<u>NS</u>, (232), 5.XI.15)

Repr.: 220000(3).I: 254-5; 270000(1): 153-4.

[151106]   —: Bez programmy, bez perspektiv, bez kontrolya. (Without programme, without perspektiv, without control.) (<u>NS</u>, (233), 6.XI.15)

Repr.: 220000(3).I: 175-7.

[151110]   —: O sovmestnykh vystuplennykh s sotsial-patriotami. (On joint
action with the social patriots.) (NS, (236), 10.XI.15)
Repr.: 220000(3).II: 129-34/126-30.
[On a letter of Martov's.]

[151111]   —: Nuzhno sdelat vse vyvody. (All the conclusions must be drawn.)
(NS, (237), 11.XI.15)
Repr.: 220000(3).II: 139-44/135-9.
[On the election of workers to War-Production Committees.]

[151113]   Postoronnii: Neveroyatno! (It's unbelievable!) (NS, (239), 13.XI.15)

[151117]   —: Gruppirovki v nemetskoi sotsial-demokratiya. (Groupings in the
German social democracy.) (NS, (242), 17.XI.15)
Repr.: 220000(3).II: 262-4/254-6.

[151119]   Postoronnii: Akh, vot ono chto! (Alas, but there it is!) (NS, (244),
19.XI.15)
Repr.: 220000(3).I: 210-1.

[151124]   N.Trotskii: Pod bremenem ob"ektivizma. (Under the burden of objectivity.)
(NS, (248,249), 24,25.XI.15)

[151127]   Al'fa: Zametki chitatelya. (A reader's notes.) (NS, (251), 27.XI.15)

[151128]   N.T.: Vpered. (Forward.) (NS, (252), 28.XI.17)

[151130]   N.T.: Chto eto za informator? (How's that for an informer?) (NS, (253),
30.XI.15)

[151203]   —: Byli i ostemsya krasnymi. (We were and we remain Reds.) (NS, (256),
3.XII.15)
Repr.: 220000(3).II: 324-7/316-9.

[151205]   Postoronnii: 79 rue de Grenelle. (NS, (258), 5.XII.15)
Repr.: 220000(3).I: 211-2.

[151212]   —: Sotrudnichestvo s sotsial-patriotami. (Collaboration with the
social-patriots.) (NS, (264), 12.XII.15)
Repr.: 220000(3).II: 134-9/130-4.
[Reply to Martov.]

[151218]   —: Chudesa, kotorye ne snilis mudretsam. (Wonders which don't deceive the wise.) (<u>NS</u>, (269), 18.XII.15)

Repr.: 220000(3).II: 327-30/319-22.

[151219]   —: Fakty i vyvody. (Facts and conclusions.) (<u>NS</u>, (270), 19.XII.15)

Repr.: 220000(3).II: 144-8/139-44.

[Again on the Petrograd elections.]

[151221]   Voina i tekhnika. (War and technique.) (<u>KM</u>, (353), 21.XII.15)

Repr.: 190000(2): 31-46; 270000(1): 187-91.

151222   Otkhodit epokha. (An epoch has passed.) (<u>KM</u>, (1), 1.I.16; <u>NS</u>, (273), 22.XII.15)

Repr.: 190000(10): 143-51; 220000(3).II: 215-20/207-12; 260000(17): 49-55.

Trans.: Fr. 670306; <u>BulCom</u>, (IV.52), 27.XII.23.

[On the occasion of the death of E.Vaillant.]

[151225]   N.Trotskii: Ni sub"ektivizma, ni fatalizma! (No subjectivism, no fatalism!) (<u>NS</u>, (275), 25.XII.15)

Repr.: 220000(3).I: 312-6.

[151228(1)]   —: Deklaratsiya dvadtsati. (The Declaration of the Twenty.) (<u>NS</u>, (276), 28.XII.15)

Repr.: 220000(3).II: 264-7/256-8.

[The German social democrats opposed to the war.]

[151228(2)]   Al´fa: Na nachalakh vzaimnosti. (The beginning of reciprocity.) (<u>NS</u>, (276), 28.XII.15)

Repr.: 270000(1): 118.

[151229(1)]   —: Politicheskie shtreikbrekhery: Novye "vybory" v voenno-promyshlennyi komitet. (Political strike-breakers: The new "elections" to the War-Production Committees.) (<u>NS</u>, (277), 29.XI.15)

Repr.: 220000(3).II: 149-52/144-7.

[151229(2)]   Postoronnii: Itak? (So?) (<u>NS</u>, (277), 29.XII.15)

[160000(1)] L'EXPULSION DE LÉON TROTZKY. Lettre à Jules Guesde.
      [Trans.Fr. See 161011 for all repr., trans., notes.]

160000(2) O russkom imperializme. (On Russian imperialism.) (270000(1): 181-3)
      [Archives, 1916.]

[160100] Vavilony otechestvennoi mysli. (A babel of patriotic thoughts.)
      (220000(3).I: 317-29)
      [Maslow on Plekhanov, Plekhanov on Kant, Alexinsky on Tikhomirov.]

[160101(1)] —: K novomu godu. (For the new year.) (NS, (1:388), 1.I.16)
      Repr.: 220000(3).II: 102-4/99-101.

[160101(2)] Al´fa: Ikh literatura. (Their literature.) (NS, (1:388), 1.I.16)
      Repr.: 220000(3).I: 329-32; 270000(1): 224-7.
      [Instead of a New Year review.]

[160106] N.Trotskii: Sotsializm i sotsial-natsionalism. (Socialism and social-
      nationalism.) (NM(NY), (564,565,568,569), 6,7,11,12.I.16)

[160113(1)] —: Sobytiya idut svoim cheredom. (Events take their own course.)
      (NS, (10:397), 13.I.16)
      Repr.: 270000(1): 154-7.

[160113(2)] N.T.: Vokrug Tsimmerval´da. (About Zimmerwald.) (NS, (10:397), 13.I.16)
      [On an article by Martov.]

[160114] —: Tsimmerval´d ili gvozdevshchina? (Zimmerwald or gvozdevism?)
      (NS, (11:398), 14.I.16)
      Repr.: 220000(3).II: 152-6/147-51.

[160116] N.T.: Sbornik "Samozashchita". (The collection "Samozashchita.")
      (NS, (13:400), 16.I.16)
      [Review of social-patriotic collection "Samozashchita".]

[160117] Letter to Grimm. (Lademacher.II: 386-7)
      [Trans. Ger.]

[160125] —: Ikh perspektivy. (Their prospects.) (NS, (20:407), 25.I.16)
      Repr.: 270000(1): 221-4.

[160129] N.Trotskii: Programma mira. (A peace programme.) (NS, (24,25,28,29,86-8:
      411,412,415,416,473-5), 29,30.I, 3,4.II, 11-13.IV.16)
      [Revised version 170512/.]

[160200]   Letter to Roland Holst. (van Rossum)
Trans.: Eng. Spokesman, (4), VI.70.
[Trans. Ger. Text in Russian and Ger. On relations with Lenin.]

[160201]   Postoronnii: Eto nedorazumenie! (There is a misunderstanding!)
(NS, (26:413), 1.II.16)

[160204]   Letter to Grimm. (Lademacher.II: 438-9)
[Trans. Ger.]

[160208(1)]   Al´fa: Narodnaya Mysl. (NS, (32:419), 8.II.16)
Repr.: 220000(3).I: 212-3; 270000(1): 157-8.
[Correcting NS issue number.]

[160208(2)]   Al´fa: "Zakon mekhaniki." ("A law of mechanics.") (NS, (32:419), 8.II.16)
[Correcting NS issue number.]

[160210]   —: Sotsial-patriotizm v Rossii. (Social patriotism in Russia.) (NS,
(34,35,53,54,62,63: 421,422,440,441,449,450), 10,11.II, 3,4,14,15.III.16)
Repr.: 220000(3).II: 156-77/151-71.

[160211]   Al´fa: Plekhanov o Khvostove. (Plekhanov on Khvostov.) (NS, (35:422),
11.II.16)
Repr.: 220000(3).I: 213-4; 270000(1): 158.

[160216]   N.Trotskii: Informator nashelsya. (An informer among us.) (NS,
39:426), 16.II.16)

[160217]   Al´fa: Jusqu'au bout. (NS, (40:427), 17.II.16)
Repr.: 220000(3).I: 255-7; 270000(1): 158-60.

[160220]   Al´fa: "Est eshche tsenzura v Parizhe." ("There's censorship again in
Paris.") (NS, (43:430), 20.II.16)
Repr.: 220000(3).I: 178.

[160224]   Al´fa: [Article completely censored.] (NS, (46:433), 24.II.16)

[160229]   [For a 3rd International.] (NS:437), 29.II.16)
Trans.: Fr. p.q. Kriegel: 273.

[160303]   Red.: Privet F.Meringu i R.Lyuksemburg. (Greetings to F.Mehring and
R.Luxemburg.) (NS, (53:440), 3.III.16)
Repr.: 190000(10): 116-8; 260000(17): 70-1.

[160305]   --: Ot "istoshcheniya" -- k "dvizheniyu". (From "spring" to "motion".)
           (NS, (55:442), 5.III.16)
           Repr.: 220000(3).I: 179-81.

[160307]   --: Amnistiya -- da ne a toi storony. (Amnesty, yes, not from that
           side.) (NS, (56:443), 7.III.16)
           Repr.: 270000(1): 160-3.

[160309]   N.Trotskii: "Samozashchita." (NS, (58,69:445,456), 9,22.III.16)
           Repr.: 190000(10): 95-102; 220000(3).I: 332-42.
           [On Potresov, a social-patriot.]

160316   Na novye rel'sy. (On new rails.) (190000(2): 142-8)

[160324]   --: Ne polnaya, no simmetriya. (Not fulness but symmetry.)
           (NS, (71:458), 24.III.16)
           Repr.: 190000(10): 122-7; 220000(3).I: 182-5.
           [Akkambrei not Liebknecht.]

[160325]   --: Po tu storonu Vogez. (On this side of the Vosges.) (NS, (72:459),
           25.III.16)
           Repr.: 220000(3).I: 185-7; 270000(1): 119-21.

[160326(1)]   --: Ironicheskii shchelchok istorii. (An ironical fillip of history.)
           (NS, (73:460), 26.III.16)
           Repr.: 220000(3).I: 357-61; 270000(1): 163-7.

160326(2) Leon Dode, Sharl Morras, Miguel Almereida. (Stranitsa literaturnykh
           nravov.) (Léon Daudet, Charles Maurras, Miguel Almereida: A page of
           literary morals.) (190000(10): 31-43)

[160331]   --: Nasha dumskaya fraktsiya. (Our duma fraction.) (NS, (77;78:
           404,405), 31.III, 1.IV.16)
           [See [160420].]

[160409]   --: Logika plokhogo polozheniya. (The logic of a bad situation.)
           (NS, (85:472), 9.IV.16)
           Repr.: 220000(3).II: 177-81/172-5.
           [Reply to Martov.]

[160414]   --: Otechestvennoe. (Patriots.) (NS, (89:476), 14.IV.16)
           Repr.: 220000(3).I: 266-8; 260000(17): 163-5.
           [Khvostov, Sukhomlinov.]

160415   Lecture, "Histoire du mouvement professionel ouvrier".
                [c. Kriegel: 296.]

[160419]   —: Po povodu "zayavleniya" tov. Martova. (On cde. Martov's "statement.")
                (NS, (93:480), 19.IV.16)

[160420]   —: Nasha dumskaya fraktsiya. (Our duma fraction.) (NS, (94,95: 481,482),
                20,21.IV.16)
                Repr.: 220000(3).II: 181-4/175-8.
                [See also [160331].]

[160423]   —: Dva printsipa. (Two principles.) (NS, (97:484), 23.IV.16)
                Trans.: Eng. p.q. Deutscher, PA: 235.
                [Reply to article by Lozovsky.]

[160426]   —: K.Kautskii ob Internatsionale. (K.Kautsky on the International.)
                (NS, (98:485), 26.IV.16)
                Repr.: 220000(3).I: 342-6.

160500   Po zapisnoi knizhke odnogo serba. (According to the notebook of a Serb.)
                (190000(1): 92-127)
                Repr.: 270000(1): 87-112.

[160501(1)]   Al'fa: Fantastika: Pervomaiskiya razmyshleniya. (A fantasy: May Day
                reflections.) (NS, (102:488), 1.V.16)
                Repr.: 190000(10): 110-6; 220000(3).I: 261-3; 260000(17): 158-63.
                [Khvostov, Kaprov and others.]

[160501(2)]   —: Pervoe maya (1916 g.) (May Day: 1916) (NS, (102:488), 1.V.16)
                Repr.: 220000(3).II: 104-8/101-4.

[160501(3)]   [Speech at Comité pour la reprise des relations internationales.]
                [c. Kriegel: 290.]

[160504]   —: Bez sterzhenya. (Without substance.) (NS, (104:490), 4.V.16)
                Repr.: 220000(3).II: 184-8/178-82.

[160506(1)]   —: Kheglund i Libknekht. (Hoeglund and Liebknecht.) (NS, (106:492),
                6.V.16)
                Repr.: 190000(10): 118-21.

[160506(2)]   N.Trotskii: Nuzhdat'sya v proverke. (Need for a check-up.) (NS,
                (106:492), 6.V.16)

160508   [Speech at meeting of Comité pour la reprise des relations internationales]
[c. Kriegel: 290.]

[160510]   —: V bor'be za tretii internatsional. (The struggle for a 3rd
International.) (NS, (109:495), 10.V.16)
Repr.: 220000(3).II: 108-11/105-7.

[160511(1)]   —: Clémence! (NS, (110:496), 11.V.16)
Repr.: 220000(3).I: 187-9.

[160511(2)]   —: Vtoraya tsimmerval'dskaya konferentsiya. (The second Zimmerwald
Conference.) (NS, (110-3:496-9), 11-14.V.16)
[c. Deutscher, PA: 235.]

[160516(1)]   —: Servantes i Svift. (Cervantes and Swift.) (*NS, (114:500), 16.V.16)
Repr.: 220000(3).I: 214-5; 270000(1): 121-2.

[160516(2)]   —: Dve velichiny, poroza ravnye tret'e.... (Two magnitudes separately
equal to a third....) (*NS, (114:500), 16.V.16)
Repr.: 220000(3).I: 216-8.

[160516(3)]   Al'fa: Zametki chitatelya. (A reader's notes.) (NS, (114:500), 16.V.16)
Repr.: 220000(3).II:111-5/107-11.
[On 500th issue of NS.]

160519   Lecture, Révolte d'Irlande.
[c. Kriegel: 290.]

[160521(1)]   —: Pochemu ne nazvali Plekhanova? (Why didn't they invite Plekhanov?)
(NS, (119:505), 21.V.16)
Repr.: 220000(3).I: 218-9.

[160521(2)]   —: V Avstrii. (In Austria.) (NS, (119:505), 21.V.16)
Repr.: 220000(3).II: 287-90/279-82.

[160524]   —: So slavyanskim aktsentom i ulybkoi na slavyanskikh gubakh. (G—n
Milyukov v Parizhe.) (With a slavonic accent and a smile on his
slavonic lips: Mr. Milyukov in Paris.) (NS, (121:507), 24.V.16)
Repr.: 190000(10): 90-5; 270000(1): 167-70.

[160527]   —: Nedomoganie. (Lethargy.) (NS, (124:510), 27.V.16)
Repr.: 220000(3).I: 192-4.

[160604]   —: Voennye zametki: "Voina v voine". (War notes: "War against war.)
              (NS, (130:516), 4.VI.16)
              Repr.: 220000(3).II: 290-4/282-6.

[160615]   —: Klyuch k pozitsii. (The key to the position.) (NS, (138:524),
              15.VI.16)
              Repr.: 220000(3).I: 194-6; 270000(1): 327-8.

[160621]   —: Razocharovaniya i bespokoistva. (Disappointment and worry.)
              (NS, (143:529), 21.VI.16)
              Repr.: 220000(3).I: 268-71; 270000(1): 171-3.

[160624]   —: Kto iz nikh luchshe? (Which of them is the better?) (NS, (146:532),
              24.VI.16)
              Repr.: 220000(3).II: 294-6/286-8.

[160629]   —: Argument ot kopyta. (An argument from the hoof.) (NS, (150:536),
              29.VI.16)
              Repr.: 220000(3).II: 188-90/182-4.

[160701]   —: Karl Libknekht. (NS, (152:538), 1.VII.16)
              Repr.: 190000(10): 121-2.

[160704(1)]   —: K Dublinskim itogam. (Results of the Dublin events.) (NS, (154:540),
              4.VII.16)
              Repr.: 220000(3).I: 189-92.
              Trans.: Eng. Lace Curtain, [1970];
                      Workers Press, (188), 16.VI.70.

[160704(2)]   —: Khristyu Rakovskii. (NS, (154:540), 4.VII.16)
              Repr.: 190000(10): 68-70; 220000(3).II: 316-7/307-9.

160704(3)   [At la Comité pour la reprise des relations internationales.]
              Trans.: Fr. p.q. Kriegel: 291.

[160706]   Etapy. (Stages.) (NS, (156:542), 6.VII.16)
              Repr.: 220000(3).II: 115-9/111-5.

[160712]   —: Uroki poslednei dumskoi sessii. (Lessons of the last duma session.)
              (NS, (161:547), 12.VII.16)

[160713]   —: Vokrug natsional'nago printsipa. (Concerning the national principle.)
              (NS,(162:548), 13.VII.16)
              Repr.: 220000(3).I: 196-9; 270000(1): 228-31.

160717   [At la Comité pour la reprise des relations internationales.]
                Trans.: Fr. p.q. Kriegel: 291.

[160718]   [On Levenburg (Dmitriev) as a German agent.]
                [c. Kriegel: 299-300 from *NS. See further [160813(2)], [160815],
                [160824].]

[160712]   —: Korennoe raskhozhdenie. (A radical difference.) (NS, (165,166):
                551,552), 19,20.VII.16)
                Repr.: 220000(3).II: 190-7/184-91.

[160727(1)]   N.T.: Pamyati D.M.Gertsensteina. (In memory of D.M.Herzenstein.)
                (NS, (172:558), 27.VII.16)
                Repr.: 260000(17): 214.

[160727(2)]   —: Ravnenie po Makarovu. (Lining up with Makarov.) (NS, (172:558),
                27.VII.16)
                Repr.: 220000(3).I: 274-7; 270000(1): 177-9.

[160728]   —: Dve telegrammy. (Two telegrams.) (NS, (173:559), 28.VII.16)
                Repr.: 220000(3).I: 277-8; 270000(1): 179-81.

[160729]   —: Dva litsa. (Two sides.) (NS, (174:560), 29.VII.16)
                Repr.: 220000(3).II: 197/191-3.

160731   [At la Comité pour la reprise des relations internationales.]
                Trans.: Fr. p.q. Kriegel: 292-3.

160800(1)   Gruppirovki v rossiiskoi sotsial-demokratii. (Groupings in the Russian
                social democracy.) (220000(3).II: 200-4/194-7)
                [Theses.]

[160800(2)]   Parizh letom 1916 g. (Paris in 1916.) (Krasnaya Niva, (1), I.23)
                Trans.: Fr. 640911: 246-57;
                        Sp. 690000(8).II: 31-42;
                        Swed. 690600(1): 221-31.
                [From an old notebook.]

[160802]   —: Sredi germanskoi oppozitsii. (Inside the German opposition.)
                (NS, (177-9;563-5), 2-4.VIII.16)
                Repr.: 220000(3).II: 267-71/259-63.

[160803(1)]   Al´fa: Nash konkurs. (Our assembly.) (NS, (178:564), 3.VIII.16)
                Repr.: 220000(3).II: 220-1/212-3.

[160803(2)] N.T.: Gustav Ekshtein. (<u>NS</u>, (178:564), 3.VIII.16)
 <u>Repr</u>.: 260000(17): 38-9.

[160804] —: Dva goda. (Two years.) (<u>NS</u>, (179:565), 4.VIII.16)
 <u>Repr</u>.: 220000(3).II: 119-20/115-7; 270000(1): 231-3.
 [Censored in <u>NS</u>.]

[160806] —: "Sud´ba idei." ("The fate of an idea.") (<u>NS</u>, (181:567), 6.VIII.16)
 <u>Repr</u>.: 220000(3).I: 199-202; 270000(1): 233-5.

[160808(1)] —: Proekt deklaratsiya. (A draft declaration.) (<u>NS</u>, (182:568),
 8.VIII.16)
 <u>Repr</u>.: 220000(3).II: 223-6/215-8.
 [To la Comité pour la reprise des relations internationales. Censored
 in <u>NS</u>.]

[160808(2)] —: V komitete dlya vosstanovleniya internatsional´nykh svyazei. (At
 la Comité por la reprise des relations internationales.) (<u>NS</u>, (182,188:
 568,574), 8,17.VIII.16)
 <u>Repr</u>.: 220000(3).II: 227-8/218-9.

160810 [At la Comité pour la reprise des relations internationales.]
 [c. Kriegel: 293.]

[160813(1)] —: Po adresu longetistov. (For the attention of the Longuetists.)
 (<u>NS</u>, (187:573), 13.VIII.16)
 <u>Repr</u>.: 220000(3).II: 221-2/213-5.

[160813(2)] N.T.: Istoriya s moral´yu. (A story with a moral.) (<u>NS</u>, (187:573),
 13.VIII.16)
 <u>Repr</u>.: 220000(3).II: 330-3/322-5.
 [See [160718].]

[160815] See [160718].

[160818(1)] Red.: O chem molchit frantsuzskaya pressa. (What the French press is
 silent about.) (<u>NS</u>, (189:575), 18.VIII.16)
 <u>Repr</u>.: 220000(3).II: 228-31/219-22.
 [On longuetism.]

160818(2) [At la Comité pour la reprise des relations internationales.]
 [c. Kriegel: 294.]

[160820]   —: Konferentsiya neitral´nykh tenei. (A conference of neutral shadows.) (NS, (191:577), 20.VIII.16)

Repr.: 220000(3).II: 121-4/117-20.

[160822(1)]   —: Vandervel´de, Nashe Slovo i Vorwärts. (Vandervelde, Nashe Slovo and Vorwärts.) (NS, (192:578), 22.VIII.16)

Repr.: 220000(3).I: 202-4.

[160822(2)]   N.Trotskii: Strategiya i sotsialisticheskaya politika. (Strategy and socialist policy.) (NS, (192:578), 22.VIII.16)

Repr.: 220000(3).I: 347-50.

[Censored in NS.]

[160823]   N.T.: Vpechatleniya i obobshcheniya g.Milyukova. (Impressions and generalisations of Mr. Milyukov.) (NS, (193,194:579,580), 23,24.VIII.16)

Repr.: 220000(3).I: 280-7.

[160824]   See [160718].

[160826]   Lettre. (Ce qu'il faut dire, 26.VIII.16)

[Trans. Fr.]

[160827]   —: "Bor´ba za vlast": Progressivno-kadetskaya Moskva i ministerstvo Shtyurmera. ("The struggle for power": Progressive-kadet Moscow and the Shturmer ministry.) (NS, (197:583), 27.VIII.16)

Repr.: 220000(3).I: 278-80.

[160900(1)]   Krizis frantsuzskogo sotsializma. (The crisis of French socialism.) (220000(3).II: 241-8/232-9)

[160900(2)]   [Letter to Grimm.] (p.q. Lademacher.II: 611)

[Trans. Ger.]

[160901]   —: "Garantii mira". (K kharakteristike patsifizma.) ("Peace guarantees." For a characterization of pacifism.) (NS, (201,202: 587,588), 1,2.IX.16)

Repr.: 220000(3).I: 350-5; 270000(1): 235-40.

[160903]   —: Poezdka deputata Chkheidze. (Deputy Chkheidze's tour.) (NS, (203:589), 3.IX.16)

Repr.: 220000(3).II: 204-7/197-201.

[160905]   —: Stavka na sil'nykh. (Betting on the strong.) (<u>NS</u>, (204:590), 5.IX.16)

Repr.: 270000(1): 240-3.

[Censored in <u>NS</u>.]

160907(1)   N.Trotskii: Vo frantsuzskom vagone. (In a French railway carriage.) (<u>NM</u>(NY), (900,901), 1,2.II.17)

Repr.: 190000(2): 149-64.

[160907(2)]   —:"Solidnye argumenty". ("Solid arguments.") (<u>NS</u>, (206:592), 7.IX.16)

Repr.: 220000(3).I: 204-6; 270000(1): 81-3.

[160908]   —: V atmosfere neustoichivosti i rastleniya. (In an atmosphere of instability and depravity.) (<u>NS</u>, (207:593), 8.IX.16)

[160910]   —: <u>Prizyv</u> i ego Aleksinskii. (<u>Prizyv</u> and its Alexinsky.) (<u>NS</u>, (209:595), 10.IX.16)

Repr.: 220000(3).II: 334-5/325-6.

160911   [At la Comité pour la reprise des relations internationales.]

[c. Kriegel:294.]

[160912]   —: Aleksinskii i ego <u>Prizyv</u>. (Alexinsky and his <u>Prizyv</u>.) (<u>NS</u>, (210:596), 12.IX.16)

Repr.: 220000(3).II: 335-6/327-8.

[160914(1)]   —: Novyi tsenzurnyi rezhim. (The new censor regime.) (<u>NS</u>, (212:598), 14.IX.16)

Repr.: 220000(3).I: 219-20.

[160914(2)]   —: Frantsuzskii i nemetskii sotsialpatriotizm. (French and German social patriotism.) (<u>NS</u>, (212,213:598:599), 14,15.IX.16)

Repr.: 220000(3).II: 231-41/222-32.

[Censored in <u>NS</u>.]

160925   [At la Comité pour la reprise des relations internationales.]

[c. Kriegel: 298.]

160927   [At la Comité pour la reprise des relations internationales.]

[c. Kriegel: 294.]

[160930]   Én: Rodnye teni. (Their own shadows.) (<u>Nach</u>, (1), 30.IX.16)

Repr.: 220000(3).I: 287-9; 260000(17): 153-6.

[Dumbadze and others.]

[161001] Én: Prestuplenie i nakazanie. (Crime and punishment.) (<u>Nach</u>, (2), 1.I.16)

[161006] —: Imperializm i sotsializm. (Imperialism and socialism.) (<u>Nach</u>, (6,16,21), 6,18,24.X.16)
<u>Repr</u>.: 220000(3).II: 271-83/263-74.

161009 [At la Comité pour la reprise des relations internationales.] [c. Kriegel:294.]

161011 Lettre ouverte à Jules Guesde. (<u>VieOuv</u>, (3), 1916)
Russian: 220000(3).II: 348-55/340-7.
<u>Repr</u>.: [160000(1)]; [580000(8)]; 670306: 42-8; <u>BulCom</u>, (V.29), 18.VII.24; <u>Demain</u>, (I.16), VIII.17; <u>Humbles</u>, (XIX.5-6), V-VI.34; <u>V</u>(M),(II.27), 6.I.18; Rosmer.II: 228-32.
<u>Trans</u>.: Am. 180000(33): 25-32;
Eng. 520300; Schuster;
Yid. Zukunft, II.17.
[Trans. Fr. PS. 170121. Supplement to <u>VieOuv</u>, (3), 1916.]

[161012] —: Iz'yan v tverdom kurse. (A flaw in the hard way.) (<u>Nach</u>, (9), 12.X.16)
<u>Repr</u>.: 220000(3).I: 289-92.

[161022] Én: Negodyai. (A scoundrel.) (<u>Nach</u>, (20), 22.X.16)
<u>Repr</u>.: 220000(3).II: 336-7/328-9; 260000(17): 68-9.
[Purishkevich.]

[161025] —: Fritz Adler. (<u>Nach</u>, (22), 25.X.16)
<u>Repr</u>.: 220000(3).II: 297-302/288-93; 260000(17): 39-44.
[PS. 220501(2).]

[161103] K poezdke deputata Chkheidze. (On deputy Chkheidze's tour.) (<u>Nach</u>, (29), 3.XI.16)
<u>Repr</u>.: 220000(3).II: 207-11/201-4.

[161105] N.Trotskii: Privet druzyam iz Ispanii. (Greetings to friends,from Spain.) (<u>Nach</u>, (31), 5.XI.16)

161110 Tyurma. (Prison.) (260000(5): 26-40)
<u>Repr</u>.: 270000(1): 267-74.
<u>Trans</u>.: Sp. 290000(5): 49-69; 680000(9).

161111   [Mas sobre la Carcel.] (260000(5): 41-9)

Repr.: 270000(1): 274-9.

Trans.: Sp. 290000(5): 71-82; 680000(9).

[Sp. titles are given as above where none is in Russian.]

161112   [En Libertad vigilada.] (260000(5): 50-3)

Repr.: 270000(1): 280-1

Trans.: Sp. 290000(5): 83-8; 680000(9).

161113(1)   Na yug. (Southwards.) (260000(5): 54-62)

Repr.: 270000(1): 281-6.

Trans.: Sp. 290000(5): 89-102; 680000(9).

161113(2)   [Lettre.] (190600: 10)

Repr.: 390000(10): 10.

Trans.: Eng. Soc(G), 24.VII.19.

[Trans. Fr.]

161114(1)   [Lettre.] (190600:9)

Repr.: 390000(10):9.

Trans.: Eng. Soc(G), 24.VII.19.

161114(2)   [Lettre.] (190600: 10-1)

Repr.: 390000(10): 10-1.

Trans.: Eng. Soc(G), 24.VII.19

[Trans. Fr.]

161114(3)   V Kadikse. (In Cadiz.) (Nach, (42), 18.XI.16)

Repr.: 260000(5): 63-77; 270000(1): 286-93; p.q. NM(NY), (851), 6.XII.16.

Trans.: Eng. Soc(G), 24.VII.19;

        Fr. 190600: 11-4; 390000(10): 11-4;

        Sp. 290000(5): 103-29; 680000(9).

[Completely censored in Nach.]

161115(1)   [Lettre.] (190600: 11)

Repr.: 390000(10): 11; Rosmer.II: 125.

Trans.: Eng. Soc(G), 24.VII.19.

[Trans. Fr.]

161115(2)   [V Kadikse.] [(In Cadiz.)] (260000(5): 77-80)

Repr.: 270000(1): 293-6.

[Sp. see 290000(5): 103-29; 680000(9).]

161119   [Lettre.] (190600: 14)
                Repr.: 390000(10): 14; Rosmer.II: 125.
                Trans.: Eng. Soc(G), 24.VII.19.

161121   En: Ispanskiya "vpechatleniya" (Pochti arabskaya skazka.) (Spanish
                "impressions"; A quasi-Arabian Night's tale.) (Nach, (54), 2.XII.16)
                Repr.: 220000(3).II: 359-64; 270000(1): 251-6.

161122(1)   [Lettre.] (190600: 14-5)
                Repr.: 390000(10): 14-5.
                Trans.: Eng. Soc(G), 24.VII.19.
                [Trans. Fr.]

161122(2)   [Lettre.] (190600: 15-6)
                Repr.: 390000(10): 15-6.
                Trans.: Eng. Soc(G), 24.VII.19.
                [Trans. Fr.]

161126   [Siguen la Lecturas.] (260000(5): 91-7)
                Repr.: 270000(1): 303-8.
                Trans.: Sp. 290000(5): 145-54; 680000(9).

161129   [Lettre.] (190600: 16-7)
                Repr.: 390000(10): 16-7; Rosmer.II: 125-7.
                Trans.: Eng. Soc(G), 31.VII.19.
                [Trans. Fr.]

[161130]   [Lettre.] (190600: 17-20)
                Repr.: 390000(10): 17-20.
                Trans.: Eng. Soc(G), 31.VII.19.
                [Trans. Fr.]

[161201]   [Lettre.] (190600: 20-2)
                Repr.: 390000(10): 20-2.
                Trans.: Eng. Soc(G), 31.VII.19.
                [Trans. Fr.]

161202   [Lettre.] (190600: 22-3)
                Repr.: 390000(10): 22-3.
                Trans.: Eng. Soc(G), 31.VII.19.

161208   [Fiestas y Espectacules.] (260000(5): 105-7)
                Repr.: 270000(1): 308-10.
                Trans.: Sp. 290000(5): 165-9; 680000(9).

161209   [Lettre.] (190600: 23-4)

Repr.: 390000(10): 23-4.

Trans.: Eng. Soc(G), 7.VIII.19.

[Trans. Fr.]

161211   [Lettre.] (190600: 24-7)

Russian: 220000(3).II: 359-64/351-6.

Repr.: 390000(10): 24-7; 670306: 51-4.

Trans.: Eng. Call(Ln), 31.VII.19; Soc(G), 7.VIII.19.

[Trans. Fr.]

161213   [Lettre.] (190600: 27-8)

Repr.: 390000(10): 27-8.

Trans.: Eng. Soc(G), 7.VIII.19.

[Trans. Fr.]

[161214(1)]   [Lettre.] (190600: 28-30)

Repr.: 390000(10): 28-30.

Trans.: Eng. Soc(G), 7.VIII.19.

[Trans. Fr.]

[161214(2)]   [Lettre.] (190600: 30-1)

Repr.: 390000(10): 30-1.

Trans.: Eng. Soc(G), 7.VIII.19.

[Trans. Fr.]

161215   [Lettre.] (190600: 31-2)

Repr.: 390000(10): 31-2.

Trans.: Eng. Soc(G), 21.VIII.19.

[Trans. Fr.]

161216   [Ensenanzas historicas.] (260000(5): 108-14)

Repr.: 270000(1): 310-4.

Trans.: Sp. 290000(5): 171-9; 680000(9).

161217   [Lettre.] (190600: 32-3)

Repr.: 390000(10): 32-3.

Trans.: Eng. Soc(G), 21.VIII.19.

[Trans. Fr.]

161221   V Barselonu i v Barselone. (To Barcelona and in Barcelona.)

(260000(5): 115-20)

Repr.: 270000(1): 314-7.

Trans. Sp. 290000(5): 181-9; 680000(9).

[161227]   N.Trotskii: Vnusheniya "chefov" i otkroveniya "agentov". (The hints
           of the "chiefs" and the revelations of the "agents.") (Nach, (74),
           27.XII.16)
           Repr.: 220000(3).II: 364-6/356-8; 260000(5); 270000(1): 256-9; Krasnaya
                   Nov, (7), 1922.
           Trans.: Am. Living Age, 25.XI, 9.XII.22;
                   Fr. Revue Mondiale, (150,151), 15.X, 1.XI.22;
                   Sp. 200000(85): 29-40; 290000(5); 680000(9).

161231(1) V Ameriku. (In America.) (260000(5): 121-6)
           Repr.: 270000(1): 317-20.
           Trans.: Sp. 290000(5): 191-9; 680000(9).

161231(2) ⌊Lettre.⌋ (190600: 33)
           Re r.: 390000(10): 33.
           Trans.: Eng. Soc(G), 21.VIII.19.
           ⌊Trans. Fr.⌋

*170000(1)   *ZHAN ZHORES. (JEAN JAURÈS.)
                Repr.: 180000(4).
                Trans.: Fr. 180000(36); 240000(43); 600000(4); 670306: 25-35; BulCom,
                        (IV.47), 22.XI.23; CahiersCom, (3), 1924;
                        Yid. *190000(46).
                [cf. 150717(2). 3rd anniversary of Jaurès assassination.]

170000(2)   KOGDA ZHE KONETS PROKLYATOI BOINE? (WHEN WILL THE CURSED SLAUGHTER END?)
                [See [170901(2)/] for all repr., trans.]

170000(3)   KOGDA ZHE KONETS PROKLYATOI BOINI? (WHEN WILL THE CURSED SLAUGHTER END?)
                [See [170901(2)/] for all repr., trans.]

170000(4)   PROGRAMMA MIRA. (A PEACE PROGRAMME.)
                [See 170512/ for all repr., trans., notes.]

170000(5)   § CHTO ZHE DAL'SHE? (ITOGI I PERSPEKTIVY.) (WHAT NEXT? RESULTS AND
                PROSPECTS.)
                Repr.: 240000(32).I: 219-52.
                Trans.: Am. [180000(53)]: 239-79;
                        Eng. 671100(2);
                        Ger. 210000(25).
                [Pref. 170907/.]

170000(6)   V PLENU U ANGLICHAN. (PRISONER OF THE ENGLISH.)
                [See 170423/ for all repr., trans.]

*170000(7)   *DER KRIEG UND DIE INTERNATIONALE.
                [Trans. Ger. See [140000(3)] for all repr., trans., notes.]

170000(8)   DER PAZIFISMUS IM DIENST DES IMPERIALISMUS.
                [Trans. Ger. See [170617/] for all repr., trans., notes.]

170000(9)   u. Lenin: AN DIE DEUTSCHEN SOLDATEN.
                [Trans. Ger. See 171205/. Flugblatt.]

[170000(11)]   Doblavenie. (An addendum.) (240000(32).II: 370-4)
                [Pref. A.A.Joffe, KRAKH MEN'SHEVIZMA (THE COLLAPSE OF MENSHEVISM) in 1917.
                On the unification of the internationalists.]

*170000(12)   *DER CHARAKTER UNSERER REVOLUTION.
                [Trans. Ger. See [170822/] for all trans.]

170101   See 170113(2).

170102(1)   [Lettre.] (190600: 34)
            Repr.: 390000(10): 34.
            Trans.: Eng. Soc(G), 21.VIII.19
            [Trans. Fr.]

170102(2)   See 170113(2).

170103   Lettre de Cadiz. (190600: Frontispiece)
            Repr.: 390000(10): Frontispiece.
            [Trans. Fr.]

170113(1)   See[161227].

170113(2)   [Aqui Termina España.] (260000(5): 127-32)
            Repr.: 270000(1): 321-3.
            Trans.: Sp. 290000(5): 201-7; 680000(9).

170115   Interview, on arrival in New York. (Call, 1917)
            Repr.: p.q. Draper.I: 77.
            [Trans. Am.]

170116(1)   Interview. (Call, 1917)
            Repr.: p.q. Draper.I: 77.
            [Trans. Am.]

[170116(2)]   N.Trotskii: Da zdravstvuet bor´ba! (Long live the struggle!)
            (NM(NY), (886), 16.I.17)
            Repr.: 220000(3).II: 369-70/361-2; p.q. 300000(1): Ch. XXII.

[170120]   N.Trotskii: Uroki velikogo god. 9 yanvarya 1905 — 9 yanvarya 1917 g.)
            (Lessons of a great year. 9 January, 1905 — 9 January, 1917.)
            (NM(NY), (890), 20.I.17)
            Repr.: 220000(3).II: 424-8/414-8.
            Trans.: Am. 180000(40): 171-7;
                   Eng. 531200: 21-3.

170121   PS to LETTRE A JULES GUESDE, [160000(1)].
            Trans.: Yid. Zukunft, II.17.

170125   Pod znamenem sotsial´noi revolyutsii. (Under the banner of socialist
            revolution.) (220000(3).II: 370-7/362-8)
            [Speech to Welcome Meeting, in New York.]

[170126]   N.Trotskii: Za dva s polovinoi goda voiny v Evrope. (Iz dnevnika.)
(Two-and-a-half years of war in Europe: From a diary.) (<u>NM</u>(NY), (895),
26.I.17)

Repr.: 190000(10): 12-7; 220000(3).I: 35-8; 270000(1): 84-7.

Trans.: Am. 180000(33): 3-10;
        Cz. *[190000(62)].

[See further [170205], [170217], [170322(3)] for series.]

170200   Revolyutsionnyi tsenz Khilkvita. (Hillquit's revolutionary qualification.)
(220000(3).II: 390-2/381-3)

[Letter to NY<u>Volkszeitung</u>.]

[170203]   Al'fa: Dokumenty voiny. (War documents.) (<u>NM</u>(NY), (902), 3.II.17)

[170205]   N.Trotskii: Za dva s polovinoi goda voiny v Evrope. (Iz dnevnika.)
(Two-and-a-half years of war in Europe: From a diary.) (<u>NM</u>(NY), (903),
5.II.17)

Repr.: 190000(10): 17-21; 220000(3).I: 38-41; 260000(17): 33-6.

[f.n. 220400(7). See [170126] for series.]

[170206]   N.Trotskii: V shkole voiny. (In the school of war.) (<u>NM</u>(NY), (904),
6.II.17)

Repr.: 220000(3).II: 411-4/401-4.

[170207]   N.Trotskii: Povtorenie proidennogo. (A repetition of past happenings.)
(<u>NM</u>(NY), (905), 7.II.17)

Repr.: 220000(3).II: 377-9/369-70; 270000(1): 328-30.

[170208]   --: Bol'she obyazatel'stvo. (A great obligation.) (<u>NM</u>(NY), (906),
8.II.17)

Repr.: 220000(3).II: 379-82/371-3.

[170210]   Lev N.Trotskii: Tsarizm na respublikanskoi pochve. (Tsarism on
republican soil.) (<u>NM</u>(NY), (908,909), 10,12.II.17)

Repr.: 220000(3).II: 341-8/333-40.

[170213]   Klaru Tsetkin luchshe im ostavit v pokoe. (Clara Zetkin would do better
to keep still.) (<u>NM</u>(NY), (910), 13.II.17)

Repr.: 220000(3).II: 392-3/384.

[Letter to Ed.]

[170216]   A vse-taki Klaru Tsetkin naprasno trevozhite! (But, even so, Clara
Zetkin is getting alarmed for nothing!) (<u>NM</u>(NY), (913), 16.II.17)

Repr.: 220000(3).II: 393-4/384-5.

[170217]   Lev N.Trotskii: Za dva s polovinoi goda voiny v Evrope. (Iz dnevnika.)
(Two-and-a-half years of war in Europe: From a diary.) (<u>NM</u>(NY),
(914,928), 17.II, 16.III.17)
<u>Repr.</u>: 190000(10): 21-6; 220000(3).I: 42-5.
<u>Trans.</u>: Am. 180000(33): 11-20;
        Cz. *[190000(62)].
[See [170126] for series.]

[170223]   Lev N.Trotskii: Nuzhno vybirat put. (It is necessary to go the whole
road.) (<u>NM</u>(NY), (919), 23.II.17)
<u>Repr.</u>: 220000(3).II: 382-5/373-6.

[170227]   Lev N.Trotskii: Chto govoril Internatsional o zashchite otechestva?
(What did the International say about defence of the fatherland?)
(<u>NM</u>(NY), (922), 27.II.17)
<u>Repr.</u>: 220000(3).II: 414-8/404-8.

*[170300]   *Zeier pazifism un unser pazifism. Wi azoy der burgeoiser pazifism
fihrt zu militarizm. (<u>Zukunft</u>, III.17)
[Trans. Yid. cf. 170617/.]

[170303(1)]   Lev N.Trotskii: Na zaprosy chitatelei. (On readers' questions.)
(<u>NM</u>(NY), (926), 3.III.17)
<u>Repr.</u>: 220000(3).II: 394-7/386-8.

[170303(2)]   Al´fa: U okna. (Through the window.) (<u>NM</u>(NY), (926), 3.III.17)
<u>Repr.</u>: 220000(3).II: 453; 270000(1): 330-1.

[170306(1)]   Obshchei pochvy s <u>Vorwärts</u> u nas net. (We have no common ground with
Vorwärts.) (<u>NM</u>(NY), (928), 6.III.17)
<u>Repr.</u>: 220000(3).II: 398-9/389-90.
[Letter to Ed.]

[170306(2)]   Al´fa: Trezvye mysli. (Sober thoughts.) (<u>NM</u>(NY), (928), 6.III.17)
<u>Repr.</u>: 220000(3).II: 454-5.

[170307]   Al´fa: Kto otgadaet? (Who can guess?) (<u>NM</u>(NY), (929), 7.III.17)
<u>Repr.</u>: 220000(3).II: 455-7; 270000(1): 331-3.

[170308(1)]   —: Gotovte soldat revolyutsii. (Prepare the soldiers of the revolution.)
(<u>NM</u>(NY), (930), 8.III.17)
<u>Repr.</u>: 220000(3).II: 397-8/388-9.

[170308(2)]   Lev N.Trotskii: Dva voyuyushchikh lagerya. (The two warring camps.)
(<u>NM</u>(NY), (930), 8.III.17)
<u>Repr</u>.: 220000(3).II: 418-9/408-9.

[170308(3)]   Al´fa: Opyat otkryli Dumu. (The Duma has been re-opened.) (<u>NM</u>(NY),
(930), 8.III.17)
<u>Repr</u>.: 220000(3).II: 428-9/418-9; 260000(17): 166-7.

[170309(1)]   Lev N.Trotskii: Dlya chego Amerike voina? (What does the war mean to
America?) (<u>NM</u>(NY), (931), 9.III.17)
<u>Repr</u>.: 220000(3).II: 385-7/376-8; 270000(1): 333-5.

[170309(2)]   Al´fa: Zatrudneniya chitatelya. (A reader's difficulties.) (<u>NM</u>(NY),
(931), 9.III.17)
<u>Repr</u>.: 220000(3).II: 457-8; 270000(1): 335-6.

[170309(3)]   L.N.T.: Nepravda! (Untrue!) (<u>NM</u>(NY), (931), 9.III.17)
<u>Repr</u>.: 220000(3).II: 399/390.

[170310]   Al´fa: Zhvachka. (Chewing the cud.) (<u>NM</u>(NY), (932), 10.III.17)
<u>Repr</u>.: 220000(3).II: 459-60.

[170313(1)]   Lev N.Trotskii: U poroga revolyutsii. (On the threshold of revolution.)
(<u>NM</u>(NY), (934), 13.III.17)
<u>Repr</u>.: 220000(3).II: 430-2/419-21; 240000(32).I: 3-5.
<u>Trans</u>.: Am. 180000(40): 181-5;
      Eng. 531200: 24-5;
      Fr. <u>Huma</u>, 14.III.23;
      Yid. 190000(68): 129-32; 210000(51): 129-32.

[170313(2)]   Al´fa: Pravosudie na kryshe. (Justice on the roof.) (<u>NM</u>(NY), (934),
13.III.17)
<u>Repr</u>.: 220000(3).II: 460-1.

[170314]   —: Neobkhodimo ochishchenie ryadov; rol <u>Forvertsa</u> v evreiskom rabochem
dvizhenii. (It is necessary to cleanse the ranks; the role of <u>Vorwärts</u>
in the Jewish workers movement.) (<u>NM</u>(NY), (935), 14.III.17)
<u>Repr</u>.: 220000(3).II: 399-401/390-2; p.q. 320513.

[170315(1)]   —: Baranya konstitutsiya. (A sheep's constitution.) (<u>NM</u>(NY), (936),
15.III.17)
<u>Repr</u>.: 220000(3).II: 387-9/379-81.
[On a conference of Gompers and Co.]

[170315(2)]   Lev N.Trotskii: Nespokoino v Evrope. (Unrest in Europe.) (NM(NY), (936), 15.III.17)

        Repr.: 220000(3).II: 419-21/410-2.

[170316(1)]   —: Revolyutsiya v Rossii. (Revolution in Russia.) (NM(NY), (937), 16.III.17)

        Repr.: 220000(3).II: 432-4/422-4; 240000(32).I: 5-7.

        Trans.: Eng. p.q. Deutscher, PA: 244.

[170316(2)]   Al´fa: Obrabotka i pozolota. (Processing and gilding.) (NM(NY), (937), 16.III.17)

        Repr.: 220000(3).II: 461-3; 270000(1): 337-8.

[170317(1)]   —: Pod znamenem Kommuny. (Under the banner of the Commune.) (NM(NY), (938), 17.III.17)

        Repr.: 220000(3).II: 422-4/412-4.

        Trans.: Am. NMil, 21.III.36;

                Eng. 550900: 1-3; WIN, II-III.46;

                Sin. 510000(1): 6-9.

[170317(2)]   Lev N.Trotskii: Dva litsa. (Two faces.) (NM(NY), (938), 17.III.17)

        Repr.: 220000(3).II: 435-8 /424-8 ; 240000(32).I: 7-11.

        Trans.: Am. 180000(40): 189-97;

                Eng. 531200: 26-9.

[170319]   Lev N.Trotskii: Narastayushchii konflikt. (Growing conflict.) (NM(NY), (940), 19.III.17)

        Repr.: 220000(3).II: 438-40/428-30; 240000(32).I: 11-3.

        Trans.: Am. 180000(40): 201-4;

                Eng. 531200: 30-1.

[170320(1)]   Lev N.Trotskii: Voina ili mir? (War or peace?) (NM(NY), (941), 20.III.17)

        Repr.: 220000(3).II: 440-3/430-3; 240000(32).I: 13-4.

        Trans.: Am. 180000(40): 207-12;

                Eng. 531200: 32-4;

                Yid. 190000(68): 193-8; 210000(51): 193-8.

[170320(2)]   —: G┬-n Kagan, kak istolkovatel russkoi revolyutsii pered rabochimi Nyu Yorka. (Mr. Kagan as interpreter of the Russian revolution to the workers of New York.) (NM(NY), (941), 20.III.17)

        Repr.: 220000(3).II: 401/392.

[170321]   Lev N.Trotskii: Ot kogo i kak zashchishchat revolyutsiyu. (From whom
             and how defend the revolution.) (<u>NM</u>(NY), (942), 21.III.17)
             <u>Repr.</u>: 220000(3).II: 444-7/433-7; 240000(32).I: 17-20.
             <u>Trans.</u>: Eng. p.q. Deutscher, PA: 245.

[170322(1)] —: Voina i revolyutsiya. (War and revolution.) (<u>NM</u>(NY), (943), 22.III.17)
             <u>Repr.</u>: 220000(3).II: 402-3/393-4; 270000(1): 339-40.

[170322(2)] —: Kto izmenniki? (Who are the traitors?) (<u>NM</u>(NY), (943), 22.III.17)
             <u>Repr.</u>: 220000(3).II: 463; 240000(32).I: 20-1.

[170322(3)] Lev N.Trotskii: Za dva s polovinoi goda voiny v Evrope. (Tw-and-a-half
             years of war in Europe.) (<u>NM</u>(NY), (943), 22.III.17)
             <u>Repr.</u>: 190000(10): 26-31; 220000(3).I: 157-60.
             <u>Trans.</u>: Am. 180000(33): 20-4;
                    Cz. *[190000(62)].
             [See [170126] for series.]

[170327]   Al´fa: Pokladistyi bozhestvennyi promysel. (A pleasant, good-natured
             business.) (<u>NM</u>(NY), (948), 27.III.17)
             <u>Repr.</u>: 220000(3).II: 464-5; 240000(32).I: 21-3.

[170400(1)] 1905-1917 g.g. (220000(3).II: 447-53/437-42)
             <u>Repr.</u>: 240000(32).I: 23-8.
             <u>Trans.</u>: Eng. p.q. Deutscher, PA: 245;
                    Yid. <u>Zukunft</u>, IV.17.

[170400(2)] Russkomu General´nomu Konsulu. (To the Russian Consul-General.)
             (240000(32).I: 331-2)

[170400(3)] Dokument. (A document.) (240000(32).I: 332-4)

170423/   V PLENU U ANGLICHAN. (PRISONER OF THE ENGLISH.)
             <u>Repr.</u>: 180000(2); 220000(3).II: 469-81/445-56; 240000(32).I: 31-42.
             <u>Trans.</u>: Eng. p.q. Deutscher, PA: 247.

170505/   Rech.   (A speech.)   (<u>Iz</u>, (60), 7.V.17)

                <u>Repr</u>.:   240000(32).I: 45-6.

                <u>Trans</u>.:   Am. p.q. 640800: 96-7; p.q. Golder: 357; p.q. Sack: 349;

                       Eng. p.q. Deutscher, PA: 253;

                       It. p.q. 680200(2): 86-8;

                       Jap. p.q. 681125: 103-5;

                       Sp. 670000(5): 96-7(p.q.);

                       Swed. p.q. 691100(2): 83-4.

                [At 1st Petrograd soviet.]

170507(1)/   Rech.   (A speech.)   (<u>NZh</u>, (18), 9.V.17)

                <u>Repr</u>.:   240000(32).I: 46-8.

                [At municipal conference on unity; on Uritsky's report on relations with the government.]

170507(2)/   Rezolyutsiya.   (A resolution.)   (<u>NZh</u>, (18), 9.V.17)

                <u>Repr</u>.:   240000(32).I: 48-9.

                [See 170507(1)/.]

170507(3)/   Rezolyutsiya.   (A resolution.)   (<u>NZh</u>, (18), 9.V.17)

                <u>Repr</u>.:   240000(32).I: 49-50.

                [See 170507(1)/.; on relations with Tseretelli and Skobelev.]

170510/   [On the fusion of the inter-regionalists with the bolsheviks.]

                <u>Trans</u>.: Eng. p.q. Carr, BR.I: 89.

                [From Lenin, *SBORNIK.IV, 1925: 301-3.]

170512/   Programma mira.   (A peace programme.), 170000(4).

                <u>Repr</u>.:   220000(3).II: 485-509/459-82; 240000(32).I: 70-93.

                <u>Trans</u>.: Am. 180000(48); [180000(53)]: 328-47; p.q. <u>FI</u>, V.42; p.q. IX.44;

                       Eng. 180000(58); 180200; 560600; [620000(12)]; <u>Free Expression</u>,

                           III,IV,VI.44;

                       Fr. p.q. [620000(5)]; p.q. <u>QI</u>, IX-X, XI-XII.47;

                       Ger. 180000(46).

                [Revision of [160129]. Pref. 171212/to Eng. 180000(48); PS 220000(33). Written originally for Stockholm conference.]

170513/   Rech.   (A speech.)   (<u>NZh</u>, (23), 14.V.17)

                <u>Repr</u>.:   240000(32).I: 50-1.

                <u>Trans</u>.: Eng. p.q. Deutscher, PA: 261.

                [On report of socialist ministers.]

170526/   Rech. (A speech.) (<u>Iz</u>, (76), 27.V.17; <u>NZh</u>, (33), 27.V.17)
<u>Repr</u>.:   p.q. 180000(5); 240000(32).I: 51-2.
[At extraordinary session of Petrograd soviet; on Kronstadt.]

170527/   Ot kronshtadtskikh matrosov, soldat i rabochikh — k revolyutsionnomu
narodu Petrograda i vsei Rossii. (From the Kronstadt sailors, soldiers
and workers — To the revolutionary people of Petrograd and of all
Russia.) (<u>Pr</u>, (69), 31.V.17)
<u>Repr</u>.: 240000(32).I: 53-6.

[170600(1)]   Tsentral´naya zadacha. (The central tasks.) (<u>Vpered</u>, (1), 2.VI.17)
<u>Repr</u>.: 240000(32).I: 56-9.
<u>Trans</u>.: Am. [180000(53)]: 179-84;
       Eng. 660500: 21-6.
[Peace and the reactionary forces. Archives.]

170600(2)   [Letter from CC Bolsheviks to CEC of soviets.]
[c. 271021, Par. 9. cf. 170604/.]

170601/   Rech. (A speech.) (<u>NZh</u>, (38), 2.VI.17)
<u>Repr</u>.: 240000(32).I: 107-8.
[At joint meeting of S.D. and all-russian soviets. On the war.]

[170602(1)/]   Red.: Vpered! (Forward!) (<u>Vpered</u>, (1), 2.VI.17)
<u>Repr</u>.: 240000(32).I: 59-61.

[170602(2)/]   Dvoebezvlastie. (Dual power.) (<u>Iz</u>, (82), 3.VI.17; <u>Vpered</u>, (1), 2.VI.17)
<u>Repr</u>.: 240000(32).I: 61-9.
<u>Trans</u>.: Am. [180000(53)]: 185-92; <u>Class Struggle</u>, (II.2), III-IV.18;
       Browder & Kerensky: 1118-9 (p.q.);
       Eng. 660500: 27-34;
       Yid. 190000(68): 135-48; 210000(51): 135-48.
[Characterization of current situation.]

170604/   Zayavlenie fraktsii bol´shevikov. (Statement of Bolshevik fraction.)
(<u>Pr</u>, (75), 7.VI.17)
<u>Repr</u>.: 240000(32).I: 136-7; p.q. 300000(1): Ch. XXVI.
[To 1st all-russian congress of soviets. On proposed advance on the
front. See 300000(1) for all p.q. trans.]

170605(1)/   Rech. (A speech.) (<u>Iz</u>, (85), 7.VI.17; <u>Vpered</u>, (3), 15.VI.17)
                <u>Repr</u>.: 240000(32).I: 113-22; p.q. 300000(1): Ch. XXV.
                <u>Trans</u>.: Am. p.q. [180000(53)]: 163-4; p.q. Sack: 350-1;
                       Eng. p.q. Deutscher, PA: 263.
                [To 1st all-russian congress of soviets. On relations with Provisional Government. See 300000(1) for other p.q. trans.]

170605(2)/   Vystuplenie. (A statement.) (<u>Iz</u>, (86), 8.VI.17; <u>NZh</u>, (41), 6.VI.17)
                <u>Repr</u>.: 240000(32).I: 122.
                <u>Trans</u>.: Eng. p.q. Deutscher, PA: 264.
                [To evening session of all-russian congress of soviets. On personal questions.]

[170607/]   Na puti k razvyazke. (On the road to an outcome.) (<u>Vpered</u>, (2), 7.VI.17)
                <u>Repr</u>.: 240000(32).I: 109-12.

170608/   Rech. (A speech.) (I VSEROS. S"EZD SOVETOV: 353)
                <u>Trans</u>.: Eng. p.q. Deutscher, PA: 265-6.
                [On the army.]

170609(1)/   Rech. (A speech.) (<u>Iz</u>, (88), 10.VI.17)
                <u>Repr</u>.: 240000(32).I: 122-4; STEN. OTCHET I VSEROS. S"EZD SOVETOV.
                [To 1st all-russian congress of soviets. On the State Duma.]

170609(2)/   Rech. (A speech.) (<u>Vpered</u>, (4), 17.VI.17)
                <u>Repr</u>.: 240000(32).I: 124-32; STEN. OTCHET I VSEROS. S"EZD SOVETOV.
                [At evening session of 1st all-russian congress of soviets. On the war.]

170612/   Zayavlenie fraktsii bol´shevikov. (Declaration of Bolshevik fraction.) (<u>Pr</u>, (80), 13.VI.17)
                <u>Repr</u>.: 240000(32).I: 133-5.
                [To 1st all-russian congress of soviets.]

[170615/]   Na etom puti vykhoda net. (This way there is no way out.) (<u>Vpered</u>, (3), 15.VI.17)
                <u>Repr</u>.: 240000(32).I: 94-9.
                <u>Trans</u>.: Eng. p.q. Deutscher, PA: 273.
                [On peace programme.]

[170617/] Patsifizm na sluzhbe imperializma. (Pacifism in the service of
imperialism.) (Vpered, (4), 17.VI.17)
Repr.: 220000(3).II: 403-10/394-401, 240000(32).I: 99-106.
Trans.: Am. ⌊180000(53)⌋: 193-200; Class Struggle, XI-XII.17; p.q.
SocAp, 2.IV.38;
Eng. 660500: 35-41; CI, (5), IX.24; CI(Ln), (5), 21.VII.24;
Inprecor, (IV.45), 21.VII.24;
Fr. Ce qu'il faut dire, 22.XII.17; CorInt, (IV.44), 15.VII.24;
Demain, (II.1), 18.X.17;
Ger. Arbeiterpolitik, (II.33,34), 18,25.VIII.17; Inprekor,
(IV.83), 8.VII.24; Jug-Int, (10), X.17.
⌊cf. [170300].⌋

[170623/] Pis´mo v redaktsiyu. (Letter to Editorial Board.) (NZh, (56), 23.VI.17)
Repr.: 240000(32).I: 253-4.

[170627/] 10,000 dollarov, Ferein i klevetniki. (10,000 dollars, Verein and
slanders.) (NZh, (59), 27.VI.17)
Repr.: 240000(32).I: 154-8; p.q. 300000(1): Ch. XIV.
Trans.: p.q. 300000(1): Ch. XIV.
⌊Letter to Editor.⌋

⌊170628(1)/⌋ Nastuplenie i nastuplentsy. (An attack and the attackers.) (Vpered,
(5), 28.VI.17)
Repr.: 240000(32).I: 138-40.
Trans.: Am. [180000(53)]: 201-3;
Eng. 660500: 42-5.

⌊170628(2)/⌋ L.T.: Tezisy o voine. (Theses on the war.) (Vpered, (5), 28.VI.17)
Repr.: 240000(32).I: 141-4.

[170628(3)/] Ot slov -- k delu. (From words to action.) (Vpered, (5), 28.VI.17)
Repr.: 240000(32).I: 144-9.
⌊On the unification of the internationalists.⌋

⌊170700(1)⌋ Rezolyutsiya. (A resolution.) (240000(32).I: 335)

⌊170700(2)⌋ ⌊Item: no title.⌋ (240000(32).I: 338)

⌊170702/⌋ Nuzhno nemedlenno ob"edinit sya na dele. (Unity in action is
necessary immediately.) (Pr, (97), 2.VII.17; Pr(Ist), (97), 5.VII.17)
Repr.: 240000(32).I: 149
⌊Reply to a question.⌋

170706/   Vystuplenie. (A statement.) (<u>Iz</u>, (112), 8.VII.17)

           <u>Repr</u>.: 240000(32).I: 162.

           [To Central Bureau of Trade Unions. On the events of July 2-3.]

[170708/]   Parvus i ego "agenty". (Parvus and his "agents.") (<u>Iz</u>, (112), 8.VII.17;

           <u>NZh</u>, (69), 8.VII.17)

           <u>Repr</u>.: 240000(32).I: 158-9.

[170709/]   Dni ispytaniya. (Days of test.) (<u>Vpered</u>, (6), 9.VII.17)

           <u>Repr</u>.: 240000(32).I: 163-5.

           <u>Trans</u>.: Am. [180000(53)]: 201-3;

                Eng. 660500: 43-5.

170710/   Pis'mo vremennomu pravitel'stvu. (Letter to Provisional Government.)

           (<u>NZh</u>, (73), 13.VII.17)

           <u>Repr</u>.: 240000(32).I: 165-6.

           <u>Trans</u>.: Am. 640800: 98-9; Golder: 460-2;

                Jap. 681125: 105-7;

                Sp. 670000(5): 98-9;

                Swed. 691100(2): 85-6.

170717/   Rech. (A speech.) (<u>Iz</u>, (121), 19.VII.17)

           <u>Repr</u>.: 240000(32).I: 167-70.

           <u>Trans</u>.: Am. p.q. Ross: 169-70.

170720(1)/   Vystuplenie. (A statement.) (<u>Iz</u>, (124), 22.VII.17)

           <u>Repr</u>.: 240000(32).I: 171.

           [On the counter-revolution.]

170720(2)/   i dr.: Zayavlenie. (A declaration.) (240000(32).I: 345)

           [On the counter-revolution.]

170721/   Rech. (A speech.) (<u>Iz</u>, (125), 23.VII.17)

           <u>Repr</u>.: 240000(32).I: 172-4.

           [To CEC of soviets and EC of peasants deputies. On conference in

           Winter Palace.]

170722/   Alternative for 170721/.

170723/   Alternative for 170725(3)/.

170725(1)/   Sdacha pozitsii. (Surrender of position.) (<u>RabiSol</u>, (2), 18.X.17)

           <u>Repr</u>.: 240000(32).I: 174-6.

           [Arrest of Chernov.]

[170725(2)/]   "Revolyutsiya v opasnosti!"   ("The revolution is in danger!")
(<u>Vpered</u>, (7), 25.VII.17)
<u>Repr</u>.:   240000(32).I: 177-92.

170725(3)/   Pis´mo Vremennomu Pravitel´stvu.   (Letter to the Provisional
Government.)   (<u>NZh</u>, (88), 30.VII.17)
<u>Repr</u>.:   240000(32).I: 201-2.
<u>Trans</u>.: Ger. <u>Prawda</u>, (15), 5.VIII.17.

[170802/]   Pis´mo ministru yustitsii.   (Letter to the Minister of Justice.)
(<u>NZh</u>, (90), 2.VIII.17)
<u>Repr</u>.:   240000(32).I: 203.
<u>Trans</u>.: Am. [180000(53)]: 168.
[To Zarudny.   Reply to Burtsev's slanders.]

170808/   Zayavlenie.   (A declaration.)   (240000(32).I: 204-5; 339-40)
[2 items.   To Commission of Inquiry into the July Days.]

[170813/]   T.: Chto sluchilos?   (What happened?)   (<u>Prol</u>, (1), 13.VIII.17)
<u>Repr</u>.:   170000(5); 240000(32).I: 220-4.
<u>Trans</u>.: Am. [180000(53)]: 241-6;
        Eng. 671100(2): 11-5;
        Ger. 210000(25): 9-15;
        Yid. 190000(68): 205-14; 210000(51): 205-14.

[170815(1)/]   T.: Elementy bonapartizma.   (Elements of bonapartism.)   (<u>Prol</u>, (2),
15.VIII.17)
<u>Repr</u>.:   170000(5); 240000(32).I: 224-32.
<u>Trans</u>.: Am. [180000(53)]: 247-54;
        Eng. 671100(2): 16-22;
        Ger. 210000(25): 16-25.

[170815(2)/]   —: Pozor!   (Shame!)   (<u>Prol</u>, (2), 15.VIII.17)
<u>Repr</u>.:   240000(32).I: 206-11.
[On Ministry of Justice.]

[170817/]   T.: Chto dal´she?   (What next?)   (<u>Prol</u>, (4), 17.VIII.17)
<u>Repr</u>.:   170000(5); 240000(32).I: 238-42.
<u>Trans</u>.: Am. [180000(53)]: 263-7;
        Eng. 671100(2): 30-3;
        Ger. 210000(25): 35-9.

[170818/]   T.: Krov´yu i zhelezom.... (Blood and iron....) (<u>Prol</u>, (5), 18.VIII.17)
       <u>Repr</u>.: 240000(32).I: 253-6.

[170820(1)/]   P.Tanas: Aleksinskii-Milyukov. (<u>Prol</u>, (7), 20.VIII.17)
       <u>Repr</u>.: 240000(32).I: 159-61.

[170820(2)/]   —: Ministr yustitsii A.S.Zarudnyi zanyat vospitaniem t. Trotskogo.
       (The Minister of Justice, A.S.Zarudny, undertakes the education of
       cde. Trotsky.) (<u>Prol</u>, (7), 20.VIII.17)
       <u>Repr</u>.: 240000(32).I: 211-2.

[170820(3)/]   T.: Armiya i revolyutsiya. (The army and the revolution.)
       (<u>Prol</u>, (7), 20.VIII.17)
       <u>Repr</u>.: 170000(5); 240000(32).I: 232-8.
       <u>Trans</u>.: Am. [180000(53)]: 255-62;
             Eng. 671100(2): 23-9;
             Ger. 210000(25): 26-34; ALMANACH: 244-51.

[170822/]   T.: Kharakter russkoi revolyutsii. (The character of the Russian
       revolution.) (<u>Prol</u>, (8), 22.VIII.17)
       <u>Repr</u>.: 170000(5); 240000(32).I: 242-8.
       <u>Trans</u>.: Am. [180000(53)]: 268-74; p.q. <u>FI</u>, VIII.48;
             Eng. 671100(2): 34-9;
             Ger. 210000(25): 48-53;
             Yid. 190000(68): 217-27; 210000(51): 217-27.

[170823/]   T.: Internatsional´naya taktika. (International tactics.)
       (<u>Prol</u>, (10), 24.VIII.17; <u>RabPut</u>, (1), 23.VIII.17)
       <u>Repr</u>.: 170000(5); 240000(32).I: 248-52.
       <u>Trans</u>.: Am. [180000(53)]: 275-9;
             Eng. 671100(2): 40-3;
             Ger. 210000(25): 48-53;
             Yid. 190000(68): 231-8; 210000(51): 231-8.

[170825/]   T.: Itogi i perspektivy. (Results and prospects.) (<u>Rab</u>, (1), 25.VIII.17)
       [Sub-titled as Section 4; earlier parts not identified.]

[170827/]   [Item.] (240000(32).I: 347-9)

170831/   Rezolyutsiya. (A resolution.) (240000(32).I: 346)
       <u>Trans</u>.: Am. p.q. 410000(1): Ch. VII.
       [At Petrograd soviet; on the Bolsheviks. See 410000(1) for other
       p.q. trans.]

170901(1)/   Pis'mo v TsIK. (Letter to CEC.) (RabPut, (2), 5.IX.17)

Repr.: 240000(32).I: 213-5.

⌊To soviets; on the Bolsheviks.⌋

[170901(2)/]   Kogda zhe konets proklyatoi boini? (When will the cursed slaughter end?)
(Rab, (10,12), 1,2.IX.17)

Repr.: 170000(2); 170000(3); 240000(32).I: 256-69.

Trans.: Fr. 180000(28);
         Swed. 180000(38).

[170901(3)/]   Protokol predvaritel'nogo sledstviya po delu 3-5 iyulya. (Protocols of
the preliminary inquiry into the events of 3-5 July.) (240000(32).I:
193-200; 212-3)

Repr.: p.q. 300000(1): Ch. XXV.

⌊See 300000(1) for p.q. trans.⌋

170903/   P.Tanas: Bonapartizm. (Bonapartism.) (RabPut, (4), 7.IX.17)

[170904/]   Tov. M.Gor'komu. (To cde. M.Gorky.) (p.q. 240000(32).I: 346-7)

170907/   Pref. CHTO ZHE DAL'SHE? 170000(5).

Repr.: 240000(32).I: 219-20.

Trans.: Am. ⌊180000(53)⌋: 239-40;
       Eng. 671100(2): 9
       Ger. 210000(25): 7.

⌊170908/⌋   L.T.: Na chistuyu vodu! (At the clean water!) (RabPut, (5), 8.IX.17)

Repr.: 240000(32).I: 270-4.

⌊On Kornilov.⌋

170909(1)/   Rech. (A speech.) (Iz, (168), 12.IX.17)

Repr.: 240000(32).I: 276-7.

⌊At Petrograd soviet; on July Days.⌋

170909(2)/   Rezolyutsiya. (A resolution.) (RabPut, (8), 12.IX.17)

Repr.: 240000(32).I: 277-9.

[See 170909(1)/.]

170909(3)/   Rech. (A speech.) (RabPut, (8), 12.IX.17)

Repr.: 240000(32).I: 279-80.

⌊At Petrograd soviet; on Presidium.⌋

[170910(1)/]   i Y.Kamenev: Zapros v byuro TsIK. (An inquiry in CEC Bureau.)
(RabPut), (7), 10.IX.17)   ++++

[170910(1)/]++++ Repr.: 240000(32).I: 274-5.

170910(2)/   Rech. (A speech.) (RabPut, (8), 12.IX.17)
                  Repr.: 240000(32).I: 280-2.
                  [At Petrograd soviet; on sending a delegation to Finland.]

170911/   Rech. (A speech.) (Iz, (169), 13.IX.17)
                  Repr.: 240000(32).I: 283-4.
                  [At Petrograd soviet; on Democratic Conference.]

170915/   Doklad. (A report.) (NZh, (122), 16.IX.17)
                  Repr.: 240000(32).I: 285.
                  [To Bolshevik fraction; on Democratic Conference.]

170918(1)/   Rech. (A speech.) (AiFSvobRos, (215), 20.IX.17; Iz, (176), 20.IX.17;
                  RabPut, (15), 20.IX.17)
                  Repr.: 240000(32).I: 285-93.
                  Trans.: Eng. p.q. Inprecor, (VII.55), 29.IX.27.

170918(2)/   Deklaratsiya fraktsii bol'shevikov. (Declaration of Bolshevik fraction.)
                  (RabPut, (15), 20.IX.17)
                  Repr.: 240000(32).I: 293-8/351-7.
                  [At Democratic Conference.]

170919/   Vystuplenie. (A statement.) (Iz, (176), 20.IX.17)
                  Repr.: 240000(32).I: 298-9.
                  Trans.: Eng. 671100(2): 44-5.
                  [At Democratic Conference; voting against Coalition amendments.]

170920(1)/   Vystuplenie. (A statement.) (Iz, (177), 21.IX.17)
                  Repr.: 240000(32).I: 299-300; PROTOKOLY RSDRP VIII.17-II.18 (1958),49-54.
                  [At Democratic Conference; on Tseretelli's amending resolution.]

170920(2)/   Doklad. (A report.) (Iz, (177), 21.IX.17)
                  Repr.: 240000(32).I: 300-1.
                  [To Workers Section, Petrograd soviet; on Democratic Conference.]

170921(1)/   Zasedanie fraktsii bol'shevikov Demokraticheskogo Soveshchaniya.
                  (Session of Bolshevik fraction of Democratic Conference.) (NZh, (134),
                  22.IX.17)
                  Repr.: 240000(32).I: 301-2.

170921(2)/   Rech. (A speech.) (RabPut, (19), 24.IX.17)

Repr.: 240000(32).I: 302-5.

Trans.: Eng. Inprecor, (VII.56), 6.X.27;
        Fr. CorInt, (VII.104), 15.X.27.

⌊At Petrograd Soviet; on report on Democratic Conference.⌋

170922(1)/   Deklaratsiya fraktsii bol'shevikov. (Declaration of the Bolshevik
fraction.) (RabPut, (18), 23.IX.17)

Trans.: Am. Golder: 549-53.

⌊At Democratic Conference.⌋

170922(2)/   Rezolyutsiya. (A resolution.) (RabPut, (19), 24.IX.17)

Repr.: 240000(32).I: 305-7.

⌊See 170921(2)/.⌋

170923(1)/   Zasedanie TsIK s uchastiem predstavitelei provintsial'nykh sovetov
(uchastnikov Demokraticheskogo Soveshchaniya). (Session of CEC with
representatives of the Provincial Soviets, participants in the
Democratic Conference.) (Iz, (180), 24.IX.17)

Repr.: 240000(32).I: 309-10.

170923(2)/   Rech. (A speech.) (Iz, (181), 26.IX.17)

Repr.: 240000(32).I: 310-3; PROTOKOLY RSDRP, VIII.17-II.18: 68.

⌊On Tseretelli's report on joint-session of Provisional Government and
Democratic Conference delegation.⌋

170923(3)/   & Kamenev: ⌊On Kornilov.⌋

Trans.: Eng. Inprecor, (VII.54), 22.IX.17.

⌊Russian original not traced.⌋

170925(1)/   Rech. (A speech.) (RabPut, (21), 27.IX.17)

Repr.: 240000(32).I: 314.

⌊At Petrograd Soviet after election of new President.⌋

170925(2)/   Rech. (A speech.) (RabPut, (23), 29.IX.17)

Repr.: 240000(32).I: 314-7.

⌊At Petrograd Soviet; on report on current situation.⌋

170925(3)/   Rezolyutsiya. (A resolution.) (RabPut, (21), 27.IX.17)

Repr.: 240000(32).I: 318-8.

170926(1)/   O "Dne". (On "Dnya".) (NZh, (138), 27.IX.17)

Repr.: 240000(32).I: 318-9.

⌊"Dnya", a column in NZh.⌋

170926(2)/   Rech. (A speech.) (NZh, (138), 27.IX.17)

               Repr.: 240000(32).I: 319-20.

               [At Bureau of CEC; on calling a session of soviets.]

[171000]   [Draft resolution.] (240000(32).I: 336-8)

171005/   Proekt platforma. (A draft platform.)

               [c. PROTOKOLY TsK: 76 (1958).]

171006(1)/   Rech. (A speech.) (Iz, (191), 7.X.17)

               Repr.: 240000(32).I: 320.

               [At soldiers section Petrograd soviet; on current situation.]

171006(2)/   Rezolyutsiya. (A resolution.) (Iz, (191), 7.X.17)

               Repr.: 240000(32).I: 321.

               [See 171006(1)/.]

171007(1)/   Deklaratsiya fraktsii bol'shevikov. (Declaration of Bolshevik fraction.)

               (RabPut, (31), 8.X.17)

               Repr.: 240000(32).I: 321-3; PROTOKOLY TsK: 77 (1958).

               Trans.: Am. Browder & Kerensky: 1728-30; p.q. Ross: 257-9;

                     Eng. Lenin, CW.XXI.ii: 323-4; Reed, Appendix 4 Chap. II.

               [At Democratic Conference.]

171007(2)/   V sovet rossiiskoi respubliki. (In the soviet of the Russian Republic.)

               (Iz, (192), 8.X.17)

               [1st session.]

171009(1)/   Rech. (A speech.) (Iz, (193), 10.X.17; RabPut, (33), 11.X.17)

               Repr.: 240000(32).I: 324-5.

               Trans.: Am. p.q. Golder: 594-5;

                     Pol. p.q. Front, (74), 13.X.17.

               [At Petrograd soviet; on Pre-Parliament.]

171009(2)/   Zaklyuchitel'noe slovo. (Summary speech.) (RabPut, (33), 11.X.17)

               Repr.: 240000(32).I: 325-6.

               [See 171009(1)/.]

171009(3)/   Rezolyutsiya. (A resolution.) (RabPut, (32), 10.X.17)

               Repr.: 240000(32).I: 326-7.

               [See 171009(1)/.]

171009(4)/   Rezolyutsiya. (A resolution.) (RabPut, (32), 10.X.17)
Repr.: 240000(32).I: 327.
[Of Petrograd soviet; on withdrawal of troops from Petrograd.]

171010(1)/   Doklad. (A report.) (RabPut, (34), 12.X.17)
Repr.: 240000(32).II: 3-4.
Trans.: Ger. Bote, (7), 27.X.17.
[To 4th conference of Petrograd factory committees; on the Constituent
Assembly.]

171010(2)/   [Report to CC that EC has decided to organize a military staff.]
[c. 410000(1): Ch. VII.]

171011(1)/   Doklad. (A report.) (Iz, (195), 12.X.17; RabPut, (35), 13.X.17)
Repr.: 240000(32).II: 5-6,6-7.
Trans.: Am. p.q. Golder: 599;
         Fr. Oldenbourg: 41-2.
[To congress of soviets of Northern Regions; on activities of the
Petrograd soviet.]

171011(2)/   Privetstvie Baltiiskomu flotu ot s"ezda Sovetov Severnoi oblasti.
(Greetings to the Baltic Fleet from the Soviets of the Northern
Regions.) (RabPut, (35), 13.X.17)
Repr.: 240000(32).II: 7-8.

171012(1)/   Doklad. (A report.) (RabPut, (38), 17.X.17)
Repr.: 240000(32).II: 8-10.
[To Soviets of Northern Regions; on current situation.]

171012(2)/   Zaklyuchitel'noe slovo. (Summary speech.) (RabPut, (36), 14.X.17)
Repr.: 240000(32).II: 11.
[See 171012(1)/.]

171012(3)/   Rezolyutsiya. (A resolution.) (RabPut, (35), 13.X.17)
Repr.: 240000(32).II: 11-3.
Trans.: Fr. p.q. Oldenbourg: 43.
[See 171012(1)/.]

171013(1)/   Radiotelegramma. (A radiogram.) (RabPut, (41), 20.X.17)
Repr.: 240000(32).II: 13-4.
[From Soviets of Norther Regions; calling for an All-Russian congress
of soviets. See further 171013(2)/.

171013(2)/   Sovetam, armeiskim organizatsiyam, vsem rabochim i soldatam.
(To soviets, army organizations, all workers and soldiers.)
(240000(32).II: 345)
⌊See 171013(1)/.⌋

171016(1)/   Rech. (A speech.) (RabPut, (39), 18.X.17)
Repr.: 240000(32).II: 14-6.
Trans.: Am. p.q. Golder: 590;
         Eng. p.q. Reed: Ch. III;
         Fr. Oldenbourg: 65-7.
[At Petrograd soviet; on Military Revolutionary Committee.]

171016(2)/   ⌊At CC.⌋
Trans.: Eng. Lenin, CW.XXI.ii: 338.
⌊On date of insurrection.⌋

171017(1)/   Beseda s Dzhonom Ridom. (Interview with John Reed.)
(240000(32).II: 21-3)
Trans.: Am. Liberator, III.18;
         Eng. Reed: Ch. III.

[171017(2)/]   Rabochii i Soldat. (RabiSol, (1), 17.X.17)
Repr.: 240000(32).II: 16-7.

[171017(3)/]   Ugroza Petrogradu i bor´ba za mir. (The threat to Petrograd and the
struggle for peace.) (RabiSol, (1), 17.X.17)
Repr.: 240000(32).II: 18-21.

[171017(4)/]   [Order to Sestroretski Factory to issue arms to Red Guards.]
[c. 180000(5): § Narastenie priliva (The swelling tide).]

⌊171018(1)/⌋   Pogromnaya agitatsiya. (Pogrom agitation.) (RabiSol, (2), 18.X.17)
Repr.: 240000(32).II: 23-4.

171018(2)/   Doklad. (A report.) (RabPut, (42), 21.X.17)
Repr.: 240000(32).II: 25-9.
⌊To All-Russian conference of factory committees; on current situation.⌋

171018(3)/   Rezolyutsiya. (A resolution.) (RabPut, (43), 22.X.17)
Repr.: 240000(32).II: 30.
⌊See 171018(2)/.⌋

171018(4)/   Soobshchenie na zasedaniiPetrogradskogo Soveta o vzimanii tramvainoi
platy s soldat. (Communication to session of Petrograd Soviet on the
lifting of the tramway lines by the soldiers.) (<u>Iz</u>, (201), 19.X.17;
<u>RabPut</u>, (41), 20.X.17)
<u>Repr</u>.: 240000(32).II: 30-1.
<u>Trans</u>.: Am. Browder & Kerensky: 1767.

171018(5)/   Zayavlenie o "vystuplenii" na zasedanii Petrogradskogo Soveta.
(Declaration on the "revelation" at the session of the Petrograd Soviet.)
(<u>RabPut</u>, (41), 20.X.17)
<u>Repr</u>.: 240000(32).II: 31-3.
<u>Trans</u>.: Am. p.q. Golder: 613;
       Eng. p.q. Deutscher, PA: 302;
       Fr. Oldenbourg: 86-8.

[171019/]   Nam nuzhen mir. (We need peace.) (<u>RabiSol</u>, (3), 19.X.17)
<u>Repr</u>.: 240000(32).II: 33-5.

171020/   Rech. (A speech.) (PROTOKOLY RSDRP VIII.17-II.18 (1958): 106-8)

171021(1)/   Doklad. (A report.) (<u>Iz</u>, (204), 22.X.17)
<u>Repr</u>.: 240000(32).II: 35-6.
<u>Trans</u>.: Fr. Oldenbourg: 113-5.
[To Extraordinary Meeting of Regimental Committees of Petrograd Garrison.]

171021(2)/   Rezolyutsii. (Resolutions.) (<u>RabPut</u>, (43), 22.X.17)
<u>Repr</u>.: 240000(32).II: 35-6.
<u>Trans</u>.: Am. Bunyan & Fisher: 79;
       Fr. Oldenbourg: 116-7.
[3 items: on Military Revolutionary Committee; on October 22; on All-
Russian congress of soviets. See 171021(1)/.]

[171021(3)/]   Brat'ya Kazaki! (Brother-Cossacks!) (240000(32).II: 38-40)
<u>Trans</u>.: Am. Bunyan & Fisher: 80.
[Appeal of Petrograd Soviet.]

171022(1)/   Rech. (A speech.) (Popov: 159)
<u>Repr</u>.: 240000(32).II: 40.
<u>Trans</u>.: Eng. p.q. Chamberlin.I: 303; p.q. Deutscher, PA: 305.
[On "Soviet Day" in Petrograd.]

171022(2)/   Resolution at meeting in People's House.
<u>Trans</u>.: Eng. Reed: Ch. III.

171022(3)/   Garnizonu goroda Petrograda i ego okrestnostei. (To the Garrison of
Petrograd and District.) (RabPut, (44), 24.X.17)
Repr.: 240000(32).II: 37-8.
Trans.: Am. Bunyan & Fisher: 79;
        Fr. Oldenbourg: 118-9.

171023(1)/   Rech. (A speech.) (Iz, (205), 24.X.17; Russkaya Volya, (252),
24.X.17)
Repr.: 240000(32).II: 44.
Trans.: Eng. Reed: Ch. III.
⌊At Petrograd Soviet; on report of Military Revolutionary Committee.⌋

171023(2)/   Rezolyutsiya. (A resolution.) (RabPut, (45), 25.X.17)
Repr.: 240000(32).II: 44-5.
Trans.: Fr. Oldenbourg: 122.
⌊See 171023(1)/.⌋

171023(3)/   Interview. (p.q. Dosch-Fleurot: 178)
Trans.: Eng.
⌊On Bolshevik aims.⌋

171023(4)/   Speech in Peter and Paul Fortress.
⌊c. 180812.⌋

171024(1)/   Petrogradskii Sovet frontu. (Petrograd Soviet, to the front.)
(RabPut, (44), 24.X.17)
Repr.: 240000(32).II: 40-4.

171024(2)/   K naseleniyu Petrograda. (To the people of Petrograd.) (Iz, (205),
24.X.17)
Repr.: 240000(32).II: 45.
Trans.: Fr. Oldenbourg: 121.

171024(3)/   Rech. (A speech.) (Iz, (207), 26.X.17)
Repr.: 240000(32).II: 46,46-7; PROTOKOLY (1958): ⌊Session 29⌋.
Trans.: Eng. p.q. Reed: Ch. III;
        Fr. p.q. Lévy: 112-3.
⌊At Extraordinary Session of CC together with delegates of the Soviet
Congress; on report on current events.⌋

171024(4)/   Doklad. (A report.) (<u>Iz</u>, (206), 25.X.17; <u>RabPut</u>, (46), 26.X.17)

           <u>Repr</u>.: 240000(32).II: 51-4,54-5.

           <u>Trans</u>.: Am. p.q. Golder: 616-7;

               Eng. p.q. Chamberlin.I: 311-2; p.q. <u>Inprecor</u>, (VII.63), 10.XI.27;

               Fr. Oldenbourg: 148-51.

           [To Extraordinary Session of Petrograd Soviet; on report of activities of Military Revolutionary Committee.]

171024(5)/   K naseleniyu Petrograda. (To the people of Petrograd.) (<u>Iz</u>, (208), 27.X.17; <u>NZh</u>, (158:164), 27.X.17)

           <u>Repr</u>.: 240000(32).II: 60.

           <u>Trans</u>.: Fr. Oldenbourg: 153.

[171025(1)/]   Ot Voenno-Revolyutsionnogo Komiteta. (From the Military Revolutionary Committee.) (<u>Iz</u>, (207), 26.X.17; <u>RabPut</u>, (45), 25.X.17)

           <u>Repr</u>.: 240000(32).II: 51.

           <u>Trans</u>.: Eng. Chamberlin.I: 315;

               Fr. Oldenbourg: 214-5; <u>V</u>, (130), 3.XI.32.

171025(2)/   Doklad. (A report.) (<u>Iz</u>, (207), 26.X.17; <u>RabPut</u>, (46), 26.X.17)

           <u>Repr</u>.: 240000(32).II: 55-8; LENINGRADSKIE: 165-7.

           <u>Trans</u>.: Am. p.q. Bunyan & Fisher: 103; Golder: 617-8;

               Eng. Reed: Ch. III;

               Fr. Oldenbourg: 167-9, 170-1.

           [To Extraordinary Session of Petrograd Soviet; on the overthrow of the Provisional Government. Including second speech, of later hour.]

171025(3)/   Rezolyutsiya. (A resolution.) (<u>RabPut</u>, (46), 26.X.17)

           <u>Repr</u>.: 240000(32).II: 58-9.

           <u>Trans</u>.: Fr. Oldenbourg: 172-3.

           [See 171025(2)/.]

171025(4)/   Vsem armeiskim komitetam deist deistvuyushchei armii, vsem Sovetam Soldatskikh Deputatov. (To all Army Committees of Forces in the field, to all Soviets of Soldiers Deputies.) (<u>RabPut</u>, (46), 26.X.17)

           <u>Repr</u>.: 240000(32).II: 59-60.

171025(5)/   Rech. (A speech.) (<u>Iz</u>, (208,209), 27,28.X.17; <u>Pr</u>, (170), 27.X.17)

           <u>Repr</u>.: 240000(32).II: 61-2.

           <u>Trans</u>.: Am. p.q. Bunyan & Fisher: 113-4;

               Fr. Oldenbourg: 204,205-6.

           [At 2nd All-Russian Congress of Soviets; on walk-out by Mensheviks and SR.]

171025(6)/   K grazhdanam Rossii. (To the citizens of Russia.) (240000(32).II: 350-1)

171026(1)/   Rech. (A speech.) (<u>DerBed</u>, (16), 31.X.17; <u>Iz</u>, (208,209), 27,28.X.17; <u>Pr</u>, (172), 29.X.17)
<u>Repr</u>.: 240000(32).II: 62-3.
<u>Trans</u>.: Fr. Oldenbourg: 245-6.
[At 2nd All-Russian Congress of Soviets; on arrest of socialist ministers.]

171026(2)/   Rech. (A speech.) (II VSEROS. S"EZD SOV.: 84-7)
<u>Repr</u>.: 240000(32).II: 63-7; p.q. 310000(1). Bk. III. Ch. X.
<u>Trans</u>.: Am. p.q. Bunyan & Fisher: 135-7;
     Eng. p.q. Reed: Ch. IV;
     Fr. Oldenbourg: 251-5.
[At 2nd All-Russian Congress of Soviets; on organization of State power.]

171026(3)/   [Proposal to 2nd All-Russian Congress of Soviets.]
[c. Oldenbourg: 236.]

[171027(1)/]   Brat´ya-Kazaki! (Brother-Cossacks!) (<u>Iz</u>, (208), 27.X.17)
<u>Repr</u>.: 240000(32).II: 67-8.

171027(2)/   Vsem raionnym Sovetam Rabochikh Deputatov i fabrichno-zavodskim komitetam. (To all District Soviets of Workers Deputies and to factory committees.) (<u>Iz</u>, (210), 29.X.17)
<u>Repr</u>.: 240000(32).II: 68-9.
<u>Trans</u>.: Eng. Antonelli: 78; Reed: Ch. VII;
     Fr. Oldenbourg: 281-2.
[An order.]

[171027(3)/]   i Lenin: Dekret o pechati. (Decree on the Press.)
[c. PROTOKOLY TsK (1958): n.232, p. 242.]

171028(1)/   Ot Voenno-Revolyutsionnogo Komiteta k naseleniyu Petrograda.) (From the Military Revolutionary Committee to the people of Petrograd.) (<u>Iz</u>, (210/211), 29/30.X.17; <u>Pr</u>, (173), 30.X.17)
<u>Repr</u>.: 240000(32):II: 74-5.
<u>Trans</u>.: Am. Bunyan & Fisher: 148-9;
     Ger. RÜSTZEUG (8).

171028(2)/   i dr.: Ko vsemu naseleniyu. (To all the people.) (<u>Iz</u>, (210), 29.X.17)
<u>Repr</u>.: 240000(32).II: 353-4.

171029(1)/   Rech. (A speech.) (<u>Iz</u>, (211), 30.X.17)

Repr.: 240000(32).II: 69-72.

Trans.: Am. p.q. Bunyan & Fisher: 153;

       Eng. p.q. Reed: Ch. V;

       Ger. RÜSTZEUG, (8).

[At Petrograd Soviet; on current situation.]

171029(2)/   Zaklyuchitel'noe slovo. (Summary speech.)

Repr.: 240000(32).II: 72-3.

[See 171029(1)/.]

171029(3)/   Doklad. (A report.) (<u>Iz</u>, (212), 31.X.17; <u>Pr</u>, (174), 31.X.17)

Repr.: 240000(32).II: 73-4.

Trans.: Fr. Oldenbourg: 313-5.

[To meeting of Petrograd Garrison; on communications with the Front.]

171029(4)/   Interview. (Dosch-Fleurot: 182)

[Trans. Eng. On Kerensky.]

171030(1)/   Prikaz po garnisonu. (Order to the Garrison.) (<u>Iz</u>, (212), 31.X.17)

Repr.: 240000(32).II: 75-6.

171030(2)/   Rech. (A speech.) (<u>Iz</u>, (212), 31.X.17)

Repr.: 240000(32).II: 76-8.

Trans.: Eng. p.q. Reed: Ch. III,VIII.

[At Petrograd Soviet; on the situation at the Front.]

171031/   Telegramma. (A telegram.) (<u>Iz</u>, (213), 1.XI.17; <u>Pr</u>, (175), 1.XI.17)

Repr.: 180000(5); 240000(32).II: 78/312.

Trans.: Eng. Reed: Ch. VIII;

       Fr. Oldenbourg: 333-4; <u>LOuv</u>(B), (II.45), 6.XI.37;

       Ger. <u>PermRev</u>, (I.5), XII.31.

[On check to Kerensky at Pulkovo. See 180000(5) for other trans.]

171101(1)/   Rech. (A speech.)

Repr.: PROTOKOLY TsK (1958): No. 31.

Trans.: Fr. Oldenbourg: 367-8.

[At CC; on Vikzhel, the Railwaymen's Union.]

171101(2)/   [Resolution to CC.]

[c. 171101(3)/.]

171101(3)/   Rech. (A speech.)
Repr.: PROTOKOLY TsK (1958): 133-4; Lenin, SOCH.XXVI: 247-9.
Trans.: Am. Bunyan & Fisher: 200-2.
[At CC; declaration to minority.]

171102(1)/   Razgovor s predstavitelam Vikzhel. (Talk with representatives of the
Railwaymen's Union.) (NZh, (171), 3.XI.17; VechPochta, (3), 3.XI.17)

171102(2)/   Telegramma iz Tsarskoe Selo. (Telegram from Tsarskoe Selo.)
(Iz, (214), 2.XI.17)
Trans.: Fr. Oldenbourg: 150.

[171103(1)/]   Vozzvanie. (An appeal.) (Iz, (215), 3.XI.17)
Repr.: 240000(32).II: 103.

171103(2)/   Rech. (A speech.) (Iz, (216), 4.XI.17)
Trans.: Eng. Lloyd George.V: 2598-600.

[171104(1)/]   Otvet t.t. samokatchikam. (Reply to cdes. of Bicycle Units.)
(Iz, (216), 4.XI.17)
Repr.: 240000(32).II: 103-4.

171104(2)/   Rech. (A speech.) (Iz, (217,218), 5,7.XI.17)
Repr.: 240000(32).II: 104-5; PROTOKOLY TsIK: 24.
Trans.: Am. p.q. Bunyan & Fisher: 221-2;
       Eng. p.q. Reed: Ch. XI;
       Fr. Oldenbourg: 400-2.
[At CEC; on the Press.]

171104(3)/   Rezolyutsiya. (A resolution.) (PROTOKOLY TsIK: 24)
Repr.: 240000(32).II: 105-6.
Trans.: Am. p.q. Bunyan & Fisher: 221-2.
[See 171104(2)/.]

171104(4)/   Rech. (A speech.) (Iz, (217), 5.XI.17; Pr, (181,182), 5,7.XI.17)
Repr.: 240000(32).II: 106-8; PROTOKOLY TsIK: 28.
[At CEC; on inquiry into Left SRs.]

171104(5)/   Rezolyutsiya. (A resolution.) (PROTOKOLY TsIK: 31-2)
Repr.: 240000(32).II: 108-9.
Trans.: Am. Bunyan & Fisher: 189.
[See 171104(4)/.]

171105/   [To Shliapnikov.] (640000(1): 2)
Trans.: Eng. 640000(1): 3.

171106(1)/   Prikaz po ministerstvu inostrannykh del. (Order of the Ministry of
Foreign Affairs.) (Pr, (185), 10.XI.17)
Repr.: 240000(32).II: 110; PROTOKOLY RSDRP VIII.17-II.18 (1958): 147.
Trans.: Eng. Antonelli: 89.
[To Foreign Office employees.]

171106(2)/   Zayavlenie. (A statement.) (NM(NY), (1143), 9.XI.17)
[By Chairman of CEC to its members.]

171106(3)/   Interv´yu s New York Globe. (Interview with New York Globe.)
(NM(NY), (1143), 9.XI.17)
Trans.: Am. New York Globe, 1917.

[171107(1)/]   Vnimaniyu vsekh grazhdan. (For the attention of all citizens.)
(Iz, (218), 7.XI.17)
Repr.: 240000(32).II: 109-10.
Trans.: Am. p.q. Bunyan & Fisher: 202-3.

171107(2)/   [Radio appeal to Allied countries and Central Powers for a general peace.]
[c. 300000(1): Ch. XXXI. Magnes dates this 171108.]

171107(3)/   i Lenin: Pravitel´stvennoe predpisanie Verkhovnomu Glavnokomanduyushchemu
Dukhonimu.) (Government instruction to Supreme Commander-in-Chief
Dukhonim.) (DVPS.I: 15-6)
[cf. 171108(3)/.]

171108(1)/   Pravitel´stvennaya nota poslam soyuznykh stran. (Government Note to
Ambassadors of the Allied countries.) (Iz, (220/221), 9/10.XI.17;
Pr, (184), 9.XI.17)
Repr.: 240000(32).II: 157; GazVKP, (19), 26.XI.17; DVPS.I: 16-7.
Trans.: Am. Bunyan & Fisher: 243; Cumming & Pettit: 44;
     Eng. Antonelli: 173; Barbusse: 25-6; Degras, SOVDOC.I: 4;
       ManGuard, 24.XI.17;
    Fr. Lévy: 110-1; Oldenbourg: 428-9;
    Nor. Ny Tid, 24.XI.17; S.(M.): 71-2.
[On formation of new government; proposing armistice on all fronts.]

171108(2)/   Doklad. (A report.) (<u>Iz</u>, (220), 9.XI.17; <u>Pr</u>, (184), 9.XI.17)

           <u>Repr</u>.: 240000(32).II: 158-63; PROTOKOLY TsIK: 40-4.

           <u>Trans</u>.: Am. p.q. Magnes: 12;

                Eng. p.q. Degras, SOVDOC.I: 4.

           [To CEC; on activities of Foreign Office.]

171108(3)/   i dr.: Telegramma. (A telegram.) (<u>Iz</u>, (221), 10.XI.17; <u>NZh</u>, 9.XI.17;

           <u>Pr</u>, (184), 9.XI.17)

           <u>Repr</u>.: Piontkovskii: 265.

           <u>Trans</u>.: Am. Bunyan & Fisher: 233;

                Eng. Degras, SOVDOC.I: 3-4;

                Fr. Oldenbourg: 425-6;

                Nor. S.(M.): 70-1.

           [To General Dukhonin; to cease hostilities. cf. 171107(3)/.]

171109/   Tainye dogovory i tainaya diplomatiya. (Secret treaties and secret

           diplomacy.) (<u>Iz</u>, (221), 10.XI.17; <u>Pr</u>, (187), 12.XI.17)

           <u>Repr</u>.: 240000(32).II: 164-5; DVPS.I: 21-2.

           <u>Trans</u>.: Am. Pref, RUSSIAN REVOLUTIONARY PAMPHLETS, No. 1;

                Eng. Pref, RUSSIAN REVOLUTIONARY PAMPHLETS, No. 1 (3 eds.);

                   Degras, SOVDOC.I: 8-9; <u>New Europe</u> (Special Supplement),

                   20.XII.17.

           [Am. pamphlet Loc BN; Eng. pamphlets loc HIS.]

171110(1)/   Pravitel'stvennaya nota poslam neitral'nykh stran. (Government Note

           to Ambassadors of Neutral Countries.) (<u>Iz</u>, (222), 11.XI.17)

           <u>Repr</u>.: 240000(32).II: 165-6; <u>GazVKP</u>, (19), 26.XI.17; DVPS.I: 22-3.

           <u>Trans</u>.: Am. Cumming & Pettit: 45-6;

                Eng. Degras, SOVDOC.I: 9-10.

171110(2)/   [Conversation with Peskovsky.] (Farbman: 125)

           [Trans. Eng.]

[171111(1)/]   i Lenin: Vsem armeiskim organizatsiyam, voenno-revolyutsionnym komitetam,

           vsem soldatam na fronte. (To all Army organizations, Military

           Revolutionary Committees, to all soldiers at the front.) (<u>GazVKP</u>, (8),

           11.XI.17; <u>Pr</u>, (186), 11.XI.17)

           <u>Repr</u>.: 240000(32).II: 111-2; <u>GazVKP</u>, (19), 26.XI.19.

           <u>Trans</u>.: Fr. Oldenbourg: 439-40.

171111(2)/   Polkovym, divizionnym, korpusnym i armeiskim komitetam, Sovetam
Rabochikh, Soldatskikh i Krest'yanskikh Deputatov. (To regiments,
divisions, corps and army committees, Soviets of Workers, Soldiers and
Peasants Deputies.) (<u>Iz</u>, (223), 12.XI.17)

Repr.: 240000(32).II: 166–8; DVPS.I: 23–4.

Trans.: Am. p.q. Bunyan & Fisher: 246–7;

        Fr. Oldenbourg: 453–5;

        Nor. S.(M.): 72–5.

[On Allied note protesting against separate peace.]

171111(3)/   Interview with Associated Press.

Trans.: Am. <u>NYHerald</u>, 24.XI.17;

        Ger. <u>Vorwärts</u>, 18.XI.17.

[Possibly trans. Yid. not Ger.]

171111(4)/   & Lenin: The Soviet Government and the food crisis.

Trans.: Am. p.q. Bunyan & Fisher: 329–30.

[171112/]   Chto glasyat tainye dogovory? (What will the secret treaties reveal?)
(<u>Pr</u>, (187), 12.XI.17)

Repr.: 240000(32).II: 171–5.

[171113(1)/]   Pis'mo velikobritanskomu poslu. (Letter to British Ambassador.)
(<u>Pr</u>, (188), 13.XI.17)

Repr.: 240000(32).II: 110–1.

171113(2)/   Prikaz po ministerstvu inostrannykh del. (Order of the Ministry of
Foreign Affairs.) (<u>Iz</u>, (225), 14.XI.17)

Repr.: 240000(32).II: 113.

[171114(1)/]   —: Dva dokumenta. (Two documents.) (<u>Iz</u>, (225), 14.XI.17)

Repr.: 240000(32).II: 168–71.

[Peace proposals.]

171114(2)/   i Lenin: Obrashchenie Soveta Narodnykh Komissarov k pravitel'stvam
i narodam soyuznykh s Rossiei stran. (Address of the Soviet of
Peoples Commissars to the governments and peoples allied with Russia.)
(<u>AiF</u>, (1), 21.XI.17)

Repr.: 240000(32).II: 173–5; Popov: 254.

Trans.: Eng. Coates: 34.

171114(3)/   K svedeniyu diplomaticheskikh predstavitelei soyuznykh s Rossiei stran. (For the information of diplomatic representatives allied with Russia.) (Iz, (228), 17.XI.17)

         Repr.: 240000(32).II: 175-6; DerBed, (38), 25.XI.17; Sots-Dem, (215), 21.XI.17.

         Trans.: Am. Cumming & Pettit: 51;
                Eng. Degras, SOVDOC.I: 10;
                Fr, Oldenbourg: 485-6.

171115(1)/   Privetsvennoe slovo. (Speech of welcome.) (Iz, (227), 16.XI.17)
         Repr.: 240000(32).II: 176-8; PROTOKOLY TsIK: 56-7.
         [At joint meeting of CEC, All-Russian Peasant Congress and Petrograd Soviet.]

171115(2)/   i Lenin: Narodam voyushchikh stran. (To the peoples of the belligerent countries.) (DerBed, (31), 17.XI.17; Pr, (190), 15.XI.17; Sots-Dem, (210), 16.XI.17)
         Repr.: DVPS.I: 28-30.
         Trans.: Eng. Barbusse: 26-8; Degras, SOVDOC.I: 11-2;
                Fr. Oldenbourg: 471-3;
                Ger. *[170000(10)];
                Nor. Ny Tid, 30.XI.17; S.(M.): 83-5.

[171116(1)/]   Prikaz po ministerstvu inostrannykh del. (Order of the Ministry of Foreign Affairs.) (Iz, (227), 16.XI.17)

171116(2)/   i dr.: Prikaz No. 80 po ministerstvu pocht i telegrafov. (Order, No. 80, of the Ministry of Post and Telegraph.) (Iz, (234), 24.XI.17)

171116(3)/   Otvet velikobritanskomu posol'stvu. (Reply to British Ambassador.) (Iz, (228), 17.XI.17; Pr, (191), 18.XI.17)
         Repr.: 240000(32).II: 183; DVPS.I: 30-1.
         Trans.: Eng. Degras, SOVDOC.I: 14.

171117(1)/   Rech. (A speech.) (Iz, (229), 18.XI.17; Pr, (194), 19.XI.17)
         Repr.: 240000(32).II: 178-82.
         Trans.: Eng. Carr, p.q. BR.III: 26-7; p.q. Degras, SOVDOC.I: 12-3;
                Fr. p.q. Lévy: 112-3.
         [At Petrograd Soviet; on international and home situation.]

[171117(3)/]   Prikaz po ministerstvu inostrannykh del. (Order of the Ministry of Foreign Affairs.) (Iz, (228), 17.XI.17)
         Repr.: 240000(32).II: 113.

171118(1)/   Pravitel´stvu Avstro-Vengrii. (To the Austro-Hungarian Government.)
(AiF, (1), 21.XI.17; Iz, (229), 18.XI.17)
Repr.: 240000(32).II: 182; DVPS.I: 32.
Trans.: Fr. Oldenbourg: 484-5.

171118(2)/   Neobkhodimoe preduprezhdenie. (Necessary measures.) (Iz, (229), 18.XI.17)
Repr.: 240000(32).II: 184.
[For peace.]

171118(3)/   Beseda nachal´nika amerikanskoi voennoi missii. (Interview with head
of the American Military Mission.) (Iz, (230), 19.XI.17)
Repr.: 240000(32).II: 185.
Trans.: Am. Cumming & Pettit: 54-5;
        Eng. Degras, SOVDOC.I: 14.

171118(4)/   Statement on the Note of Lt.-Col. Kerth. (*Iz, (229/230), 18/19.XI.17)
Trans.: Am. Cumming & Pettit: 54.

[171118(5)/]   i dr.: Prikaz po ministerstvu vnutrennykh del. (Order of the Ministry
of Home Affairs.) (Iz, (229), 18.XI.17)

171119/   Interview on armistice negotiations.
Trans.: Eng. p.q. Times, 7.XII.17.

171120/   Doklad. (A report.) (AiF, (3), 23.XI.17; Pr, (195), 21.XI.17)
Repr.: 240000(32).II: 185-9.
Trans.: Am. ⌊180000(53)⌋: 315-8;
       Eng. 560600; [620000(12)].
[In "Modern" Circus; on government activities.]

171121/   Rech. (A speech.) (AiF, (3), 23.XI.17; Iz, (233), 23.XI.17)
Repr.: 240000(32).II: 114-5; PROTOKOLY TsIK: No. 14.
⌊At CEC; on calling the Constituent Assembly.⌋

[171122(1)/]   Vsem Sovetam Rabochikh, Soldatskikh i Krest´yanskikh Deputatov, vsem
armeiskim organizatsiyam. (To all Sŏviets of Workers, Soldiers and
Peasants Deputies, to all army organizations.) (Iz, (232), 22.XI.17)
Repr.: 240000(32).II: 115-6.

171122(2)/   Khod mirnykh peregovorov. (The progress in the peace negotiations.)
(Iz, (233), 23.XI.17)
Repr.: 240000(32).II: 190-2.
[Government communique.]

171123/   Obrashchenie Narodnogo Komissara po inostrannym delam. (Note of the Peoples Commissar for Foreign Affairs.) (AiF, (4), 24.XI.17; Iz, (234), 24.XI.17)

Repr.: 240000(32).II: 192-4; DVPS.I: 41-2.

Trans.: Am. Cumming & Pettit: 56-7;

         Eng. p.q. Degras, SOVDOC.I: 17-8.

[For information of ambassadors.]

171124(1)/   Razgovor Narodnogo Komissara po inostrannym delam s Verkhovnym Glavnokomanduyushchim. (Conversation between the People's Commissar for Foreign Affairs and the Commander-in-Chief.) (AiF, (7), 20.XI.17; DerBed, (39), 26.XI.17; Iz, (235), 25.XI.17; Pr, (200), 25.XI.17)

Repr.: 240000(32).II: 116-20.

171124(2)/   [& others: Appeal to the Moslem workers in Russia and in the East.] (*Iz, (235), 25.XI.17)

Trans.: Eng. Degras, SOVDOC.I: 15-7.

[171124(3)/]   Vnimaniyu vsekh chlenov Petrogradskogo Soveta. (For the attention of all members of the Petrograd Soviet.) (Iz, (234), 24.XI.17)

Trans.: Fr. Lévy: 114.

171124(4)/   Prikaz. (Order of the Day.) (Iz, (235), 25.XI.17)

Trans.: Am. p.q. Bunyan & Fisher.

[Order to advance against the Cossacks.]

171124(5)/   Prikaz komissara po inostrannym delam. (Order of the Commissar for Foreign Affairs.) (AiF, (5), 25.XI.17)

[Abolishing titles and honours.]

[171124(6)/]   i dr.: Dekret o sude. (Decree on Law Courts.) (DerBed, (37), 24.XI.17)

[171124(7)/]   Otchet o deyatel´nosti Rabochago i Krest´yanskago pravitel´stva. (Report on activities of the Workers and Peasants Government.) (DerBed, (37), 24.XI.17)

[171125(1)/]   Prikaz komissara po inostrannym delam. (Order of the Commissar for Foreign Affairs.) (Pr, (199), 25.XI.17)

Repr.: 240000(32).II:121.

[171125(2)/]   Vopros ob osvobozhdenii t. Chicherina i dr. (The question of the release of cde. Chicherin and others.) (Pr, (199), 25.XI.17)

Repr.: 240000(32).II: 121.

171125(3)/   Ko vsemu naseleniyu. (To all the people.) (<u>Iz</u>, (230), 26.XI.17)
Repr.: 240000(32).II: 121-3.

171125(4)/   [Conversation with Lenin.] (240000(24): Ch. II)

[171125(5)/]   i dr.: Dekret. (A decree.) (<u>AiF</u>, (5), 25.XI.17; <u>Iz</u>, (237), 27.XI.17)

171125(6)/   i dr.: Postanovlenie. (A decree.) (<u>AiF</u>, (7), 28.XI.17; <u>Iz</u>, (237),
27.XI.17)

[171126(1)/]   O sabotazhe chinovnikov. (On sabotage by officials.) (<u>GazVKP</u>, (19),
26.XI.17; <u>Iz</u>, (237), 27.XI.17)
Repr.: 240000(32).II: 120.
Trans.: Am. Bunyan & Fisher: 230.

171126(2)/   Prikaz Narodnogo Komissara po inostrannym delam. (Order of the People's
Commissar for Foreign Affairs.) (<u>AiF</u>, (8), 30.XI.17; <u>Pr</u>, (201), 27.XI.17)
Repr.: 240000(32).II: 123-4; DVPS.I: 43-4.
Trans.: Eng. <u>Times</u>, 12.XII.17.
[Appointment of ambassadors.]

171126(3)/   Rech. (A speech.) (<u>AiF</u>, (9), 1.XII.17; <u>Iz</u>, (237/240), 27/30.XI.17;
<u>Pr</u>, (202), 30.XI.17)
Repr.: 240000(32).II: 125-7.
Trans.: Eng. p.q. Deutscher, PA: 337; p.q. <u>Times</u>, 13.XII.17.
[At Riding School of Grenadier Guards; on freedom of the Press.]

[171128(1)/]   Ot Soveta Narodnykh Komissarov trudovym kazakam. (From Sovnarkom to
toiling Cossacks.) (<u>Iz</u>, (238), 28.XI.17)
Repr.: 240000(32).II: 128-31.
[cf. 171124(2)/.]

[171128(2)/]   K rabochim i soldatam Petrograda. (To the workers and soldiers of
Petrograda.) (<u>Iz</u>, (238), 28.XI.17)
Repr.: 240000(32).II: 131/355.

171128(3)/   i dr.: Dekret. (A decree.) (<u>AiF</u>, (8), 30.XI.17; <u>Iz</u>, (239), 29.XI.17;
<u>Iz</u>(H), (215), 1.XII.17)
Repr.: 240000(32).II: 353.
Trans.: Am. Bunyan & Fisher: 359;
       Eng. DECREES.I: 28;
       Swed. PÅBUD.
[No. 239. For arrest of leaders of civil war against the Government.]

[171128(4)/]   i dr.: Dekret. (A decree.) (<u>AiF</u>, (7), 28.XI.17; <u>Iz</u>, (238), 28.XI.17)
[Of Special Defence conference.]

[171128(5)/]   i dr.: Dekret po ministerstvu finansov. (Decree of Ministry of Finance.)
(<u>AiF</u>, (7), 28.XI.17)

[171128(6)/]   i dr.: Prikaz. (An order.) (<u>AiF</u>, (7), 28.XI.17)

[171129(1)/]   K vsem trudyashchimsya i eksploatiruemya. (To all toilers and exploited.)
(<u>Iz</u>, (239), 29.XI.17; <u>Iz</u>(H), (215), 1.XII.17)
<u>Repr</u>.: 240000(32).II: 131-3; PROTOKOLY TsK (1958): 157-9.
[Government communique.]

171129(2)/   [At CC meeting which elected an inner group.]
<u>Repr</u>.: PROTOKOLY TsK (1958): 148.
<u>Trans</u>.: Am. p.q. 410000(1): Ch. VIII.

[171130/]   Bor'ba za mir. (The struggle for peace.) (<u>DerBed</u>, (42), 1.XII.17;
<u>Iz</u>, (240), 30.XI.17; <u>Iz</u>(H), (215), 1.XII.17; <u>ZT</u>, (84), 30.XI.17)
<u>Repr</u>.: 240000(32).II: 194-5.
<u>Trans</u>.: Am. p.q. Bunyan & Fisher: 273; p.q. Magnes: 25;
      Eng. p.q. <u>Times</u>, 30.XII.17.

171200(2)   Interview.
<u>Trans</u>.: Am. <u>Independent</u>, 9.III.18; Ross, *RUSSIA: 207-14.
[On Russian industry.]

171200(3)   PERSPEKTIVY RUSSKOI REVOLYUTSII. (PERSPECTIVES OF THE RUSSIAN
REVOLUTION.)
[See 060600 for all repr., trans., notes.]

[171201(1)/]   Po povodu t.t. Chicherina i Petrova. (On cdes. Chicherin and Petrov.)
(<u>Pr</u>, (203), 1.XII.17)
<u>Repr</u>.: 240000(32).II: 114.
<u>Trans</u>.: Eng. <u>Morning Post</u>, 17.XII.17.
[Government note to Britain.]

171201(2)/   i Petrovskii: Ob"yavlenie. (A statement.) (<u>Pr</u>, (213), 13.XII.17)
<u>Repr</u>.: 240000(32).II: 141.

171201(3)/   K svedeniyu inostrannykh grazhdan. (For the attention of foreign citizens.) (GazVKP, (23), 2.XII.17; Iz, (241), 1.XII.17)
Repr.: 240000(32).II: 133.

171201(4)/   & Others: Decree of CEC, establishing Supreme Council of National Economy.
Trans.: Am. p.q. Bunyan & Fisher: 291-2.

171202(1)/   Rech. (A speech.) (Iz, (244), 6.XII.17)
Repr.: 240000(32).II: 134-8.
[At Petrograd Soviet; on attitude to Constituent Assembly and Cadet Party.]

171202(2)/   Rezolyutsiya. (A resolution.) (Iz, (244), 6.XII.17)
Repr.: 240000(32).II: 138-9..
[See 171202(2)/.]

171202(3)/   Zaklyuchitel´naya rech. (Summary speech.) (Iz, (244), 6.XII.17)
Repr.: 240000(32).II: 139-40.
[See 171202(1)/.]

171202(4)/   Rezolyutsiya. (A resolution.) (Iz, (244), 6.XII.17)
Repr.: 240000(32).II: 140-1.
[See 171202(3)/.]

171202(5)/   [Annotation to note found in documents of Foreign Ministry.]
Trans.: Fr. Bol(S), (III.1), 2.I.18.

171203(1)/   Ot Narodnogo Komissariata po inostrannym delam. (From the People's Commissar of Foreign Affairs.) (AiF, (12), 5.XII.17; Iz, (243), 3.XII.17)
Repr.: 240000(32).II: 141-2.

[171203(2)/]   Prikaz po Narodnomu Komissariatu po inostrannym delam. (Iz, (243), 3.XII.17)
Repr.: 240000(32).II: 195.
[Order of the People's Commissariat for Foreign Affairs.]

171203(3)/   Doklad. (A report.) (Iz, (245), 7.XII.17; NZh, (193:187), 5.XII.17)
Repr.: 240000(32).II: 196-203.
Trans.: Eng. p.q. Deutscher, PA: 354; p.q. Times, 20.XII.17;
      Nor. p.q. Ny Tid, 14.XII.17.
[To 2nd All-Russian Congress of Peasant Deputies; on progress of peace negotiations.]

171203(4)/   Rezolyutsiya. (A resolution.) (Iz, (245), 7.XII.17)

Repr.: 240000(32).II: 203-4.

[See 171203(3)/.]

171203(5)/   Predatel´stvu Kharbinskikh vlastei. (To the Government of Harbin
territory.) (AiF, (18), 12.XII.17; Iz, (249), 12.XII.17)

Repr.: 240000(32).II: 151.

171203(6)/   i dr.: Po petrogradskomu voennomu okrugu polkevogo shtaba
glavnokomanduyushchago za No. 13. (For the Petrograd Military District
Commanding Staff, No. 13.) (AiF, (12), 5.XII.17)

171204(1)/   Sovet Narodnykh Komissarov — Rade. (The Sovnarkom to the Rada.)
(Iz, (244), 6.XII.17)

Repr.: 240000(32).II: 142-4.

[No. 262.]

171204(2)/   Note to Allied Embassies on progress of peace negotiations.

Trans.: Am. p.q. Magnes: 28.

171205/   Lenin & T.: An Appeal to the German Soldiers.

Trans.: Am. Lutz.I: 112; ONE YEAR: 21-3;
       Ger. 170000(9); Drahn: 14-5.

[171206(1)/]   i Gromokhov: Ot Narodnogo Komissariata po inostrannym delam delegatsii
v Brest-Litovske. (From the People's Commissariat for Foreign Affairs
to the delegation at Brest-Litovsk.) (Pr, (207), 6.XII.17)

Repr.: 240000(32).II: 204-5.

[171206(2)/]   Rezolyutsiya. (A resolution.) (Pr, (207), 6.XII.17)

Repr.: 240000(32).II: 205-6.

[See ⌊171206(1)/⌋.]

[171206(3)/]   Svidanie Narodnogo Komissara po inostrannym delam s frantsuzskim
poslom. (Communique of People's Commissar for Foreign Affairs and
French Ambassador.) (Pr, (207), 6.XII.17)

Repr.: 240000(32).II: 209-10.

⌊171206(4)/⌋   K trudyashchimsya, ugnetennym i obeskrovlennym narodam Evropy. (To
the toiling, oppressed,and exhausted peoples of Europe.) (Iz, (244),
6.XII.17)

Repr.: 240000(32).II: 206-9.

Trans.: Eng. Barbusse: 30-3; Degras, SOVDOC.I: 18-21;
       Ger. ALMANACH: 218-22.

171206(5)/   Otchet. (A report.) (AiF, (16), 9.XII.17; Bed, (505), 9.XII.17;
DerBed, (90), 9.XII.17; Iz, (247), 9.XII.17)
Repr.: 240000(32).II: 217-21.
Trans.: Am. p.q. Bunyan & Fisher: 260.
[To Petrograd Soviet; on foreign policy.]

[171207(1)/]   K konfliktu s Radoi. (On the conflict with the Rada.) (Iz, (245),
7.XII.17)
Repr.: 240000(32).II: 144-7.
[The Kaledin-Cadet counter-revolution.]

[171207(2)/]   Golos pechati. (The voice of the Press.) (Pr, (208), 7.XII.17)
Repr.: 240000(32).II: 210-1.
Trans.: Eng. p.q. Deutscher, PA: 356.

171207(3)/   Otvet na zapros o konflikte mezhdu Sovnarkomom i ukrainskoi Radoi.
(Reply to an inquiry about the conflict between the Sovnarkom and the
Ukrainian Rada.) (Iz, (247), 9.XII.17)
Repr.: 240000(32).II: 147-8.
[To delegation from 2nd All-Russian Congress of Peasant Deputies.]

[171208(1)/]   Pol-pravdy. (A half-truth.) (Iz, (246), 8.XII.17)
Repr.: 240000(32).II: 148-9.

171208(2)/   Rech. (A speech.) (Iz, (247), 9.XII.17)
Repr.: 240000(32).II: 211-7; PROTOKOLY TsIK.
Trans.: Eng. p.q. Deutscher, PA: 357-8; p.q. Times, 24.XII.17.
[To joint-session of Government, CEC of Soviets, Petrograd Soviet,
City Duma, Trade Union and Worker Organizations; on peace negotiations.]

[171208(3)/]   i dr.: Dekret. (A decree.) (AiF, (16), 9.XII.17; Iz, (246), 8.XII.17;
ZT, (90), 8.XII.17)

171208(4)/   Torzhestvennoe zasedanie v Aleksandrinskom Teatre. (At a celebration
meeting in Alexandry Theatre.) (Iz, (248,249), 10,12.XII.17)

[171209(1)/]   Zagovor imperialistov s kaledintsami. (The imperialist conspiracy with
the Kaledinists.) (Iz, (247), 9.XII.17; Pr, (221), 22.XII.17)
Repr.: 240000(32).II: 149-50.
Trans.: Eng. p.q. Times, 26.XII.17.
[A last warning.]

[171209(2)/]   "Vooruzhdenie" plennykh avstriitsev. (The "arming" of Austrian
                prisoners.) (Pr, (210), 9.XII.17)
                Repr.: 240000(32).II: 150-1.

171209(3)/   Otvet sotsialisticheskoi fraktsii frantsuzskogo parlamenta. (Reply
                to the socialist fraction in the French parliament.) (Iz, (248),
                10.XII.17)
                Repr.: 240000(32).II: 221-4.
                Trans.: Am. ⌊180000(53)⌋: 323-4;
                        Eng. ManGuard, 8.I.18;
                        Fr. ⌊180000(57)⌋; V(M), (II.26), 5.I.18.

171212/   Pref. WHAT IS A PEACE PROGRAMME? 180000(48).
                ⌊Trans. Eng. See 170512 for all repr., trans., notes.⌋

[171213/]   i Lenin: Postanovlenie Soveta Narodnykh Komissarov. (A decree of the
                Sovnarkom.) (Iz, (250), 13.XII.17; Pr, (213), 13.XII.17)
                Repr.: 240000(32).II: 151-2; PROTOKOLY TsIK.
                Trans.: Am. p.q. Bunyan & Fisher: 484-5.
                ⌊An appropriation of 2 million roubles for the international movement.⌋

171214(1)/   Doklad. (A report.) (Iz, (253), 16.XII.17; Pr, (217,218), 17,18.XII.17)
                Repr.: 240000(32).II: 225-9; PROTOKOLY TsIK: 137-40.
                Trans.: Fr. p.q. Lévy: 116-7;
                        Swed. Pol(S), (III.3), 4.I.18.
                ⌊To CEC; on course of peace negotiations.⌋

171214(2)/   Otvet belorussam i serbskim soldatam. (Reply to Byelo-Russian and
                Serbian soldiers.) (Pr, (215), 15.XII.17)
                Repr.: 240000(32).II: 229-30.

[171216/]   i dr.: Deistviya pravitel'stva. (Activities of the Government.)
                (Iz, (253), 16.XII.17)

[171217(1)/]   Ot Narodnogo Komissariata po inostrannym delam. (From the People's
                Commissariat of Foreign Affairs.) (Pr, (217), 17.XII.17)
                Repr.: 240000(32).II: 231.
                Trans.: Eng. ManGuard, 4.I.18.
                ⌊To Allies; on suspension of peace negotiations for 10 days.⌋

[171217(2)/] Narodam i pravitel´stvam soyuznykh stran. (To the peoples and governments of the Allied countries.) (AiF, (23), 17.XII.17; Iz, (254), 17.XII.17)
Repr.: 240000(32).II: 231-5; DVPS.I: 67-70.
Trans.: Am. Cumming & Pettit: 61-4;
Eng. Barbusse: 35-9; Call (Ln), 10.I.18.

[171218(1)/] Nota rumynskomu posol´stvu. (Note to Rumanian Ambassador.)
(Iz, (255), 18.XII.17; Pr, (218), 18.XII.17)
Repr.: 240000(32).II: 235-6.
Trans.: Eng. Degras, SOVDOC.I: 23.

[171218(2)/] i dr.: Nezavisimost Finlyandii. (The independence of Finland.)
(AiF, (25), 20.XII.17; Iz, (255), 18.XII.17; Iz(TsIK), 19.XII.17;
Pr, (218), 18.XII.17)
Repr.: 260000(18).I: 622; DVPS.I: 71.
Trans.: Nor. Ny Tid, 5.I.18.

[171218(3)/] Oproverzhenie. (A refutal.) (Iz, (255), 18.XII.17.
Repr.: 240000(32).II: 242.
[Of report of an interview by Keyserling.]

171219(1)/ Rech. (A speech.) (AiF, (27), 21.XII.17; Iz, (257), 21.XII.17; NZh,
(207:201), 21.XII.17; Pr, (220), 21.XII.17)
Repr.: 240000(32).II: 236-9; PROTOKOLY TsIK.
Trans.: Eng. p.q. ManGuard, 4.I.18.
[At joint meeting of CEC, Petrograd Soviet and All-Army Congress; on
demobilization of army during peace negotiations.]

171219(2)/ Rezolyutsiya. (A resolution.) (PROTOKOLY TsIK: 169)
Repr.: 240000(32).II: 240-2.
Trans.: Eng. Degras, SOVDOC.I: 24-6.
[See 171219(1)/.]

171219(3)/ Appointment of Litvinov.
Trans.: Eng. Times, 3.I.18.

[171220/] Interv´yu. (An interview.) (Iz, (256), 20.XII.17)
Repr.: 240000(32).II: 242-7.
Trans.: Eng. p.q. Degras, SOVDOC.I: 26-8.
[With Press Bureau.]

[171221/]   Vo frantsuzskuyu voennuyu missiyu. (To the French military mission.)
(Iz, (257), 21.XII.17; PetGol, (21), 23.XII.17)
Repr.: 240000(32).II: 247-8; 300000(1): Ch. XXIX.
[See 300000(1) for all trans.]

171222(1)/   Frantsuzskaya voennaya missiya — istochnik lzhi i otravlennykh slukhov.
(The French military mission is a source of lies and poisonous rumours.)
(AiF, (29), 24.XII.17; Iz, (259), 23.XII.17; Pr, (222), 23.XII.17)
Repr.: 240000(32).II: 248-50.

171222(2)/   Russko-persidskie otnosheniya. (Russo-Persian relations.) (AiF, (29),
24.XII.17; Iz, (259), 23.XII.17; Pr, (222), 23.XII.17)
Repr.: 240000(32).II: 251; DVPS.I: 72-3.
Trans.: Eng. Degras, SOVDOC.I: 28.

[171222(3)/]   Po vedomostvu inostrannykh del. (For the Department of Foreign Affairs.)
(Iz, (258), 22.XII.17)

[171222(4)/]   Naznachenie poslov. (Appointment of Ambassadors.) (GazVKP, (40),
23.XII.17; Pr, (221), 22.XII.17)
Repr.: 240000(32).II: 152-3.
Trans.: Am. Magnes: 94;
        Eng. p.q. Deutscher, PA: 371.

[171222(5)/]   Imenem Sovetov Rabochikh, Soldatskikh i Krest´yanskikh Deputatov.
(In the name of the Soviets of Workers, Soldiers and Peasants Deputies.)
(Pr, (221), 22.XII.17)

[171224/]   i dr.: Komissar po prodovol´stvo. (The Commissar for Food.)
(Iz, (260), 24.XII.17)

171227/   Bor´ba za glasnost i svobodu propagandy. (The struggle for publicity
and freedom for propaganda.) (260000(18).I: 3)
Repr.: Joffe: 48.

171228(1)/   Rech. (A speech.) (260000(18).I: 3-11)
Repr.: Joffe: 52.
Trans.: Am. p.q. Bunyan & Fisher: 492; p.q. Magnes: 58-61;
       Eng. p.q. Wheeler-Bennet: 156; p.q. Times, 14.I.18.
[To Plenary Session, Brest-Litovsk.]

171228(2)/   Obrashchenie k Kyul´manu o dopushchenii v Brest predstavitelei pechati.
(Appeal to Kuhlmann for admission of Press to Brest ⌊negotiations⌋.)
(260000(18).I: 11)
Repr.: Joffe: 246-7.

171228(3)/   Zasedaniya. (A session.) (260000(18).I: 15-6)
Repr.: Joffe: 61.
⌊Political Commission at Brest-Litovsk; on occupied territories,
self-determination.⌋

171228(4)/   Zasedanie. (A session.) (260000(18).I: 69-71)
Repr.: Joffe: 52.
Trans.: Am. p.q. Magnes: 63.
⌊At Brest-Litovsk; on Russo-Ukrainian relations.⌋

171228(5)/   Bor´ba za glasnost. (The struggle for publicity.) (Joffe: 246-7)
⌊Letter to Kuhlmann.⌋

171229(1)/   Utrenee zasedanie. (Morning session.) (Iz, (4), 6.I.18)
Repr.: 260000(18).I: 16-24; Joffe: 65.
Trans.: Nor. p.q. Ny Tid, 16.I.18.
⌊At Brest-Litovsk; on occupied territories, self-determination.⌋

171229(2)/   Vechernee zasedanie. (Evening session.) (260000(18).I: 24-8)
Repr.: Joffe: 81.
⌊At Brest-Litovsk; on occupied territories; self-determination.⌋

171230(1)/   Eshche raz obyasneniya s Goffmanom. (Once again, an explanation to
Hoffman.) (260000(18).I: 12-4)
Repr.: Joffe: 88.
Trans.: Am. p.q. Magnes: 67-73, 78;
       Eng. p.q. Wheeler-Bennet: 103,174.
⌊At Plenary Session, Brest-Litovsk.⌋

171230(2)/   Zasedanie. (A session.) (260000(18).I: 28-32)
Repr.: Joffe: 91.
⌊Declaration at Political Commission, Brest-Litovsk; on occupied
Russian territories.⌋

171230(3)/   Zasedanie. (A session.) (260000(18).I: 71-2)
⌊At Brest-Litovsk; on Russo-Ukrainian relations.⌋

171231(1)/   Protiv tendentsioznykh iskazhenii. (Against tendentious distortions.)
(__Pr__, (1), 3.I.18)

__Repr__.: 260000(18).I: 11-2; Joffe: 83.

__Trans__.: Am. p.q. Magnes: 83-5.

⌊At Brest-Litovsk.⌋

171231(2)/   Rech. (A speech.) (__Pr__, (2), 4.I.18)

⌊At Brest-Litovsk.⌋

*180000(1)   *BOLSHEVIKITIE I SVIETSKIYA MIR. (THE BOLSHEVIKS AND WORLD PEACE.)
             ⌊See ⌊140000(3)⌋ for all trans., notes.⌋

180000(2)   V PLENU U ANGLICHAN. (PRISONER OF THE ENGLISH.)
             ⌊See 170423/ for all repr., trans., notes.⌋

180000(3)   DOKLAD. (A REPORT.)
             ⌊See 180422(1) for all repr., trans.⌋

180000(4)   ZHAN ZHORES. (JEAN JAURÈS.)
             ⌊See *170000(1) for all repr., trans., notes.⌋

180000(5)   ISTORIYA OKTYABR´SKOI REVOLYUTSII. (HISTORY OF THE OCTOBER REVOLUTION.)
             Repr.: 180000(15); *190000(31); *230000(42); *240000(26);
                     240000(32).II: 255-329; *250000(34); ⌊310000(3)⌋.
             Trans.: Am. 190000(44); 630000(8): 23-111; p.q. Current History, XII.19;
                     Bul. *190000(5);
                     Ch. *⌊200000(96)⌋;
                     Cz. *200000(65); 210000(62); Rude Pravo, (II.167-240),
                         19.VII-13.X.21;
                     Den. 190000(61);
                     Eng. 190000(81); 190400(2); 190700; 520600; 630000(9): 23-111;
                     Esth. *190000(52);
                     Fin. ⌊190000(72)⌋;
                     Fr. 180000(34); 190000(40); 200000(53);
                     Ger. 180000(43); ⌊180000(54)⌋; 190000(58); 190000(59);
                         ⌊190000(65)⌋; 190000(70); p.q. Kom(B), (II.27), 1.II.19;
                         p.q. Leipziger Volksztg, 18.X.18; p.q. RusKor, (I.ii.14-16),
                         X.20; p.q. Vossische Ztg, 18.X.18;
                     It. 190000(43); 200000(55); *450000(1);
                     Nor. 190000(56);
                     Pol. *200000(97);
                     Port. 200000(106);
                     Sp. 190000(45); 190000(66); 190000(69); 200000(80);
                         ⌊200000(85)⌋; *300000(7);
                     Swed. 180000(41);
                     Yid. *210000(37).
             ⌊Pref. 180212; PS to 180212, 180529(2); Pref. 2nd ed. 180716(5).⌋

180000(6)   KRASNAYA ARMIYA. (THE RED ARMY.)
             ⌊See 180422(1) for all repr., trans., notes.⌋

180000(7) KRASNAYA ARMIYA. (THE RED ARMY.)
[See 180422(1) for all repr., trans., notes.]

180000(8) MEZHDUNARODNOE POLOZHENIE I KRASNAYA ARMIYA. (THE INTERNATIONAL
SITUATION AND THE RED ARMY.)
[See 180616(1) for all repr., trans.]

180000(9) MEZHDUNARODNOE POLOZHENIE I KRASNAYA ARMIYA. (THE INTERNATIONAL
SITUATION AND THE RED ARMY.)
[See 180616(1) for all repr., trans., notes.]

180000(10) MEZHDUNARODNOE POLOZHENIE I KRASNAYA ARMIYA. (THE INTERNATIONAL
SITUATION AND THE RED ARMY.)
[Trans. Tatar. See 180616(1) for all trans., repr., notes. Text in
Tatar, title in Russian.]

180000(12) NA BOR´BU S GOLODOM! (A STRUGGLE AGAINST FAMINE!)
[See 180609 for all repr., trans.]

*180000(13) *NASHA POLITIKA V DELE SOZDANIYA ARMII. (OUR POLICY IN THE MATTER OF
CREATING AN ARMY.)
[Theses.]

180000(14) O MYATEZHE LEVYKH S.-R. (THE INSURRECTION OF THE LEFT SRs.)
[See 180709(1) for all repr., notes.]

180000(15) OKTYABR´SKAYA REVOLYUTSIYA. (THE OCTOBER REVOLUTION.)
[See 180000(5) for all repr., trans., notes.]

180000(16) ORGANIZATSIYA KRASNOI ARMII. (THE ORGANIZATION OF THE RED ARMY.)
[See 180710(1).]

180000(17) SLOVO RUSSKIM RABOCHIM I KREST´YANAM O NASHAKH DRUZ´YAKH I VRAGAKH I
O TOM, KAK UBERECH I UPROCHIT SOVETSKUYU RESPUBLIKU. (A WORD TO THE
RUSSIAN WORKERS AND PEASANTS ON OUR FRIENDS AND ENEMIES AND ON HOW TO
PRESERVE AND STRENGTHEN THE SOVIET REPUBLIC.)
[See 180414 for all repr., trans., notes.]

180000(18) SLOVO RUSSKIM RABOCHIM I KREST´YANAM O NASHAKH DRUZ´YAKH I VRAGAKH I
O TOM, KAK UBERECH I UPROCHIT SOVETSKUYU RESPUBLIKU. (A WORD TO THE
RUSSIAN WORKERS AND PEASANTS ON OUR FRIENDS AND ENEMIES AND ON HOW TO
PRESERVE AND STRENGTHEN THE SOVIET REPUBLIC.)
[See 180414 for all repr., trans., notes.]

*180000(19)   *SLOVO RUSSKIM RABOCHIM I KREST´YANAM O NASHAKH DRUZ´YAKH I VRAGAKH I O TOM, KAK UBERECH I UPROCHIT SOVETSKUYU RESPUBLIKU. (A WORD TO THE RUSSIAN WORKERS AND PEASANTS ON OUR FRIENDS AND ENEMIES AND ON HOW TO PRESERVE AND STRENGTHEN THE SOVIET REPUBLIC.)
[See 180414 for all repr., trans., notes.]

180000(20)   SOVETSKAYA VLAST I MEZHDUNARODNYI IMPERIALIZM. (SOVIET POWER AND INTERNATIONAL IMPERIALISM.)
[See 180421 for all repr., trans., notes.]

180000(21)   SOVETSKAYA VLAST I MEZHDUNARODNYI IMPERIALIZM. (SOVIET POWER AND INTERNATIONAL IMPERIALISM.)
[See 180421 for all repr., trans., notes.]

180000(22)   SOVETSKAYA VLAST I MEZHDUNARODNYI IMPERIALIZM. (SOVIET POWER AND INTERNATIONAL IMPERIALISM.)
[See 180421 for all repr., trans., notes.]

180000(23)   SLOVO RUSSKIM RABOCHIM I KREST´YANAM O NASHAKH DRUZ´YAKH I VRAGAKH I O TOM, KAK UBERECH I UPROCHIT SOVETSKUYU RESPUBLIKU. (A WORD TO THE RUSSIAN WORKERS AND PEASANTS ON OUR FRIENDS AND ENEMIES AND ON HOW TO PRESERVE AND STRENGTHEN THE SOVIET REPUBLIC.)
[See 180414 for all repr., trans., notes.]

180000(24)   TRUD, DISTSIPLINA, PORYADOK SPASUT SOTSIALISTICHESKU SOVETSKUYU RESPUBLIKU. (WORK, DISCIPLINE AND ORDER WILL SAVE THE SOCIALIST SOVIET REPUBLIC.)
[See 180328(1) for all repr., trans.]

180000(25)   TRUD, DISTSIPLINA, PORYADOK SPASUT SOTSIALISTICHESKU SOVETSKUYU RESPUBLIKU. (WORK, DISCIPLINE AND ORDER WILL SAVE THE SOCIALIST SOVIET REPUBLIC.)
[See 180328(1) for all repr., trans.]

*[180000(26)]   *VNUTRENNIE I VNESHNIE ZADACHI SOVETSKOI VLAST. (INTERNAL AND EXTERNAL TASKS OF THE SOVIET POWER.)
[See 180421 for all repr., trans., notes.]

180000(27)   SOZDANIE RABOCHIE I KREST´YANSKOI KRASNOI ARMII. (CREATING THE WORKERS AND PEASANTS RED ARMY.)
[See 180710(1) for all repr., trans., notes.]

180000(28) A QUAND LA FIN DE CE MAUDIT CARNAGE?
⌊Trans. Fr. See ⌊170901(2)/⌋ for all trans.⌋

180000(29) ARBEIT, DISZIPLIN UND ORDNUNG WERDEN DIE SOZIALISTISCHE SOWJET-REPUBLIK
RETTEN!
⌊Trans. Ger. See 180328(1) for all repr., trans., notes.⌋

*180000(30) *ARBET, DISZIPLIN UN ORDNUNG WELN RATEVEN DI RATEN REGIRUNG.
⌊Trans. Yid. See 180328(1) for all trans., notes.⌋

180000(31) et a.: AUX MASSES LABORIEUSES DU FRANCE, D'ANGLETERRE, D'AMÉRIQUE
ET DU JAPON.
⌊Trans. Fr. See 180801(1) for all trans.⌋

180000(32) THE BOLSHEVIKI AND WORLD PEACE.
⌊Trans. Am. See ⌊140000(3)⌋ for all trans., notes.⌋

180000(33) § CHAPTERS FROM MY DIARY.
⌊Trans. Am. 4 articles.⌋

180000(34) DE LA RÉVOLUTION D'OCTOBRE A LA PAIX DE BREST-LITOVSK.
⌊Trans. Fr. See 180000(5) for all repr., trans., notes.⌋

180000(35) DISCURSUL.
⌊Trans. Rum. Printed with Lenin, PUTEREA SOVITELOR SI CRIZA SOCIALA
DIN GERMANIA. ? 180421.⌋

180000(36) JEAN JAURÈS.
⌊Trans. Fr. See *170000(1) for all repr., trans.⌋

180000(37) Lenin u. T.: § KRIEG UND REVOLUTION.
⌊Trans. Ger. Ed. E.Lewin-Dorsch.⌋

180000(38) NÄR SKALL DET FÖRBANNADE KRIGET SLUTA?
⌊Trans. Swed. See ⌊170901(2)/⌋ for all trans.⌋

180000(39) § NEUVOSTOVALTA JA YLEISMAAILLINEN VALLANKUMOUS.
⌊Trans. Fin. See 180421, 180616(1), 181003 for all trans., notes.⌋

180000(40) § OUR REVOLUTION.
Trans.: Eng. 531200 + 540300;
          Yid. p.q. 190000(68); p.q. 210000(51).
⌊Trans. Am. Selected essays, some p.q. 1905-17.⌋

180000(41) DEN RYSKA ARBETARREVOLUTION. FRAN NOVEMBERREVOLUTION TILL
BRESTFREDEN.
[Trans. Swed. See 180000(5) for all trans., notes.]

180000(42) DIE SOWJET-MACHT UND DER INTERNATIONALE IMPERIALISMUS.
[Trans. Ger. See 180421 for all trans.]

180000(43) VON DER OKTOBER REVOLUTION BIS ZUM BRESTER FRIEDENSVERTRAG.
[Trans. Ger. See 180000(5) for all repr., trans., notes.]

180000(44) VON DER OKTOBER REVOLUTION BIS ZUM BRESTER FRIEDENSVERTRAG.
[Trans. Ger. See 180000(5) for all repr., trans., notes.]

180000(45) WAR OR REVOLUTION.
[Trans. Eng. p.q. [140000(3)].]

180000(46) WAS IST EIN FRIEDENSPROGRAMM?
[Trans. Ger. See 170512/ for all trans., notes.]

180000(48) WHAT IS A PEACE PROGRAMME?
[Trans. Am. See 170512/ for all repr., trans., notes.]

180000(49) ARBEJDE, DISCIPLIN OG ORDEN KAN REDDE SOVJETREPUBLIKEN.
[Trans. Den. See 180328(1) for all trans., notes.]

*[180000(50)] Lenin u T.: *DEUTSCHE DESERTEURE BERICHTEN.
[Trans. Ger. See *180106/.]

*[180000(51)] *UN DRAMMA GIUDIZARIO. IL PROCESSO BEILIS.
[Trans. It. See [131100].]

[180000(52)] DER KRIEG UND DIE INTERNATIONALE.
[Trans. Ger. See [140000(3)] for all repr., trans., notes.]

[180000(53)] Lenin & T.: † THE PROLETARIAN REVOLUTION.
Trans.: Am;
  Eng. p.q. 660500;
  Yid. p.q. 190000(68); p.q. 210000(51).
[Ed. L.Fraina.]

[180000(54)] VON DER OKTOBER REVOLUTION BIS ZUM BRESTER FRIEDENSVERTRAG.
[Trans. Ger. See 180000(5) for all repr., trans., notes.]

[180000(55)] Avtobiograficheskaya zametka. (Autobiographical sketch.)
              (ProlRev, 1921: 244-9.)
              Trans.: Am. Living Age, 28.IV.23;
                      Fr. CorInt, (III.6), 16.II.23;
                      It. Avanti, 3.III.23;
                      Nor. Ny Tid, 14,28.IV.23;
                      Sp. Batalla, (I.10), 1.III.23.
              [Written late Dec. 1917 or early Jan. 1918, after joining CPR.]

*180000(56)   *CUVANT CATRE TARANII SI MUNICITORII RUSI.
              [Trans. Rum. See 180414 for all trans.]

[180000(57)] RÉPONSE AU GROUPE SOCIALISTE PARLEMENTAIRE.
              [Trans. Fr. No. 3 of brochure POUR L'ACTION. See 171209(3)/ for
              all trans.]

180000(58)   WHAT IS A PEACE PROGRAMME?
              [Trans. Eng. See 170512/ for all repr., trans.]

180000(59)   TRUD, DISTSIPLINA, PORYADOK SPASUT SOTSIALISTICHESKUYU SOVETSKUYU
              RESPUBLIKU. (WORK, DISCIPLINE AND ORDER WILL SAVE THE SOCIALIST
              SOVIET REPUBLIC.)
              [See 180328(1) for all repr., trans.]

*180000(60)   *[Interview with Mahandra Pratep.]
              [c. Bailey: 223.]

180000(61)   TYD, KURI JA JÄRJESTYS PELASTAVAT SOSIALISTISEN NEUVOSTOTASAVALLAN.
              [Trans. Fin. See 180328(1) for all trans.]

180000(62)   TRUD, DISTSIPLINA, PORYADOK SPASUT SOTSIALISTICHESKUYU SOVETSKUYU
              RESPUBLIKU. (WORK, DISCIPLINE AND ORDER WILL SAVE THE SOCIALIST
              SOVIET REPUBLIC.)
              [See 180328(1) for all repr., trans.]

180100(1)   Conversation with Robins. (Wheeler-Bennet: 142)
              [Trans. Eng. On Russia and USA.]

[180100(2)]   LETTER TO LENIN.
              Trans.: Am. Magnes: 122-3;
                      Eng. Bernstein: 192-4; Wheeler-Bennet: 155-6.
              [From Brest-Litovsk. Advancing formula "Neither war nor peace."]

180101/   Zayavlenie. (A declaration.) (260000(18).I: 14)

Repr.: Joffe: 100.

[At Political Commission, Brest-Litovsk.]

180102(1)/   Utrenee zasedanie. (Morning session.) (Iz, (5,6), 8,9.I.18)

Repr.: 260000(18).I: 38-44; Joffe: 107; OmV, (7), 11.I.18.

[Political Commission, Brest-Litovsk.]

180102(2)/   Vechernee zasedanie. (Evening session.) (OmV, (8), 12.I.18)

Repr.: 260000(18).I: 44-9; Joffe: 110.

[Political Commission, Brest-Litovsk.]

180102(3)/   Protest protiv zakulisnykh soglashenii Ukrainskoi delegatsii s imperialistami. (Protest against behind-the-scenes agreements between the Ukrainian delegation and the imperialists.) (260000(18).I: 72-3)

Repr.: Joffe: 248.

180102(4)/   [Telephone conversation with Lenin, from Brest-Litovsk.] (410000(1): Ch. VIII.)

180105(1)/   Utrenee zasedanie. (Morning session.) (Iz, (5), 7.I.18; Pr, (5), 7.I.18)

Repr.: 260000(18).I: 49-50; Joffe: 123.

Trans.: Am. p.q. Bunyan & Fisher: 498; p.q. Magnes: 91.

[Political Commission, Brest-Litovsk.]

180105(2)/   Vechernee zasedanie. (Evening session.) (260000(18).I: 51-3)

Repr.: Joffe: 130.

[Political Commission, Brest-Litovsk.]

*180106/   u. Lenin: *DEUTSCHE DESERTEURE BERICHTEN.

[Trans. Ger. Flugblatt.]

180110/   Rech. (A speech.) (Iz, (8), 12.I.18; Pr, (8), 12.I.18)

[At 3rd Congress of Soviets.]

180111/   [At CC.] (PROTOKOLY TsK (1958): 169,170,171)

[re Brest-Litovsk negotiations.]

180112/   Rech. (A speech.) (Iz, (11), 16.I.18)

[At 3rd Congress of Soviets.]

180113(1)/   Rech. (A speech.) (<u>Iz</u>, (10,11), 14,16.I.18; <u>Pr</u>, (11,12), 16,17.I.18)
            <u>Repr</u>.: 260000(18).I: 53-62.
            <u>Trans</u>.: Am. p.q. Bunyan & Fisher: 506; Magnes: 103-4;
                   Eng. p.q. Wheeler-Bennet: 194;
                   Ger. p.q. Drahn: 48-51.
            [At 3rd Congress of Soviets; on peace negotiations.]

180113(2)/   Zaklyuchitel'noe slovo. (Summary speech.) (260000(18).I: 62-5)
            [See 180113(1)/.]

180113(3)/   Predatel'stvo rumynskoi burzhuazii i izmena generala Shcherbacheva.
            (The treachery of the Rumanian bourgeoisie and the treason of General
            Shcherbachev.) (<u>Iz</u>, (10), 14.I.18)
            <u>Repr</u>.: 260000(18).I: 628-9.

180114(1)/   Rezolyutsiya. (A resolution.) (<u>Iz</u>, (11), 16.I.18)
            <u>Repr</u>.: 260000(18).I: 66.
            <u>Trans</u>.: Eng. Degras, SOVDOC.I: 40-1.
            [See 180113(1)/.]

180114(2)/   Persidsku poslanniku v Petrograde. (To the Persian Ambassador in
            Petrograd.) (<u>Iz</u>, (11), 16.I.18)
            <u>Repr</u>.: DVPS.I: 91-2.

180115/   Interview.
            <u>Trans</u>.: Eng. p.q. <u>Times</u>, 1.II.18.
            [On Rumania.]

180116/   RSFSR i Finlyandiya. (The RFSSR and Finland.) (<u>Iz</u>, (11), 16.I.18;
            <u>Pr</u>, (11), 16.I.18)
            <u>Repr</u>.: 260000(18).I: 91-2; DVPS.I: 94.
            <u>Trans</u>.: Eng. p.q. Antonelli: 150; <u>Daily News</u> (Ln), 30.I.18.
            [To the government of bourgeois Finland.]

180117(1)/   Proekt deklaratsiya posle pereryva. (Draft of declaration after the
            break [at Brest-Litovsk].) (260000(18).I: 67-9)
            [Archives.]

180117(2)/   Plenarnoe zasedanie mirnoi konferentsii. (Plenary session of the Peace
            Conference.) (<u>Iz</u>, (20), 26.I.18; <u>Pr</u>, (20), 26.I.18)
            <u>Repr</u>.: 260000(18).I: 73-6; Joffe: 135.

180118(1)/   Zasedanie. (A session.) (<u>Iz</u>, (21), 27.I.18; <u>Pr</u>, (21), 27.I.18)
                   <u>Repr</u>.: 260000(18).I: 76-8; Joffe: 135.
                   [Political Commission, Brest-Litovsk.]

180118(2)/   Vopros o Pol'she. (The question of Poland.) (260000(18).I: 84-5)
                   <u>Trans</u>.: Fr. LIVRE ROUGE: 13-6.
                   [At Political Commission, Brest-Litovsk.]

*180123(1)/   *AN ALLER VOLKER.
                   [Trans. Ger. Flugblatt.]

*180123(2)/   *OFFIZIELLES TELEGRAM DER RUSSISCHEN VOLKSKOMMISSARE.
                   [Trans. Ger. Flugblatt.]

180126/   Gospodin Ministru Inostrannykh Del Grafu Cherninu. (To the Minister
                   of Foreign Affairs, Count Czernin.) (300000(1): Ch. XXXII)
                   <u>Repr</u>.: 640000(1): 8-10.
                   <u>Trans</u>.: 300000(1): Ch. XXXII;
                         Eng. 640000(1): 9-11.
                   [T3.]

180131(1)   Zapiska t. Leninu. (Note to cde. Lenin) (260000(18).I: 96-7)
                   <u>Repr</u>.: 640000(1): 10; 300000(1): Ch. XXXII.
                   <u>Trans</u>.: 300000(1): Ch. XXXII; 640000(1): 11.
                   [From Brest-Litovsk. T7.]

180131(2)/   [Telegram.] (640000(1): 14)
                   <u>Trans</u>.: Eng. 640000(1): 15.
                   [To Chicherin.]

180200   WHAT IS A PEACE PROGRAMME?
                   [Trans. Eng. See 170512/ for all repr., trans., notes.]

[180201]   Plenarnoe zasedanie. (Plenary session.) (<u>Pr</u>, (25), 1.II.18)
                   <u>Repr</u>.: Joffe: 149.
                   [At Brest-Litovsk.]

180202(1)   i Karakhan: Pravitel'stvu raboche-krest'yanskoi Finlyandii. (To the
                   workers and peasants government of Finland.) (<u>Iz</u>, (15), 20.I.18)
                   <u>Repr</u>.: 260000(18).I: 92.
                   <u>Trans</u>.: Eng. <u>Times</u>, 6.II.18;
                         Swed. <u>Pol</u>(S), (III.30), 6.II.18.

180202(2)   Gospodinu generalu Goffmanu. (To General Hoffman) (640000(1): 24)

Trans.: Eng. 640000(1): 25.

⌊T9.⌋

180203(1)   Vopros o Pol'she. (The question of Poland.) (260000(18).I: 85-9)

Repr.: Joffe: 157.

Trans.: Am. p.q. Magnes: 113-4;

          Eng. Degras, SOVDOC.I: 41-3;

          Lith. p.q. Ka sukas: 488.

⌊At Political Commission, Brest-Litovsk.⌋

⌊180203(2)⌋   Vopros o Finlyandii na mirnoi konferentsii. (The question of Finland at the Peace Conference.) (260000(18).I: 92-3)

⌊180206(1)⌋   Telegramma. (A telegram.) (Joffe: 263)

180206(2)   ⌊Conversation with Schuller.⌋

Trans.: Eng. Wheeler-Bennet: 216.

180207(1)   Vopros o Pol'she. (The question of Poland.) (260000(18).I: 89-91)

Repr.: Joffe: 166.

180207(2)   Zasedanie. (A session.) (260000(18).I: 94-6)

⌊Political Commission, Brest-Litovsk; Soviet delegation accused of dragging-out the negotiations.⌋

180209   Zasedanie. (A session.) (260000(18).I: 97-102)

Repr.: Joffe: 206.

Trans.: Am. Magnes: 124-7, 129-31;

          Eng. Coates: 56.

⌊Political Commission, Brest-Litovsk.⌋

180210(1)   Zasedanie. (A session.) (260000(18).I: 102-5)

Repr.: Joffe: 206.

⌊Political Commission, Brest-Litovsk.⌋

180210(2)   i dr.: Zayavlenie delegatsii RSFSR o prekrashchenii voiny. (Statement of RFSSR delegation on discontinuation of the war.) (Iz, (25), 14.II.18; NZh, (22:236), 30.I(12.II).18; Pr, (23), 30.I.18)

Repr.: 260000(18).I: 106; Joffe: 210.

Trans.: Am. Current History, IV.18;

          Eng. Barbusse: 39-41; Times, 13.II.18.

180210(3)   ⌊Conversation with Schuller.⌋

Trans.: Eng. Wheeler-Bennet: 225.

180212   Pref. ISTORIYA OKTYABR´SKOI REVOLYUTSII, 180000(5).
[PS 180529(2). See 180000(5) for all repr., trans., notes.]

180214   Itogi peregovorov. (Results of the negotiations.) (Iz, (26), 15.II.18;
Pr, (26,27), 15,16.II.18)
Repr.: p.q. 180000(5); 260000(18).I: 107-11; PROTOKLY VTsIK.
Trans.: Am. [180000(53)]: 348-54; p.q. Magnes: 134-41;
      Eng. 560600; 620000(12);
      Ger. Drahn: 61-6.
[Report to CEC.]

180216(1)   Doklad. (A report.) (Iz, (27,28), 17,19.II.18)
Repr.: 260000(18).I: 111-6.
[To Petrograd Soviet; on peace negotiations.]

180216(2)   i Vladimirov: Ot Chrezvychainoi komissii po prodovol´stviyu transportu.
(From the Extraordinary Commission for food transport.) (Iz, (41),
6.III.18; Pr, (39), 2.III.18)
Trans.: Am. p.q. Bunyan & Fisher: 661.

180217(1)   [Votes against Lenin, re German advance.]
[c. 410000(1): Ch. VIII.]

180217(2)   Germanskoe nastuplenie i podpisanie Brestskogo mira. (The German
advance and the signing of the Brest Peace [Treaty].) (Iz, (28),
19.II.18)
Repr.: 260000(18).I: 116; Joffe: 263.
Trans.: Eng. Times, 18.II.18;
      Fr. V(M), (II.71), 19.II.18.

180217(3)   Alternative for 180219(2).

180218   Zapros Avstro-Vengrii. (Inquiry re Austria-Hungary.) (Iz, (29), 20.II.18)
Repr.: 260000(18).I: 116-7; DVPS.I: 107; Joffe: 151.
Trans.: Am. Magnes: 151;
      Swed. Pol(S), (III.44), 21.II.18.
[Telegram to Czernin on possibility of Austro-Hungary renewing
hostilities.]

180219(1)   i Lenin: Zayavlenie o soglasii podpisat mir. (Statement on agreement to sign peace [treaty].) (Iz, (29), 20.II.18; Pr, (30), 20.II.18)

Repr.: 260000(18).I: 117.

Trans.: Am. Magnes: 150;
        Eng. Coates: 51.

180219(2)   Alternative for 180218.

180219(3)   i Lenin: Radiotelegramma. (Radiotelegram.) (Iz, (29), 20.II.18)

Repr.: DVPS.I: 106.

Trans.: Eng. Times, 27.II.18;
        Swed. Pol(S), (III.45), 22.II.18.

⌊To Berlin. cf. 180219(1).⌋

180220   i dr.: K trudyashchemusya naseleniyu vsei Rossii. (To the toiling people of all Russia.) (Iz, (30), 21.II.18)

Repr.: 260000(18).I: 117-20; DVPS.I: 107-9.

⌊An appeal from the Sovnarkom.⌋

180221   i dr.: Sotsialisticheskoe otechestvo v opasnosti. (The socialist fatherland is in danger.) (Iz, (31), 22.II.18)

Repr.: 260000(18).I: 120-1.

Trans.: Am. p.q. Magnes: 153.

⌊An appeal from the Sovnarkom.⌋

[180222(1)]   i Lenin: Soobshchenie o prinyatii TsIK"om germanskikh uslovii mira. (Communique on acceptance by CEC of German peace terms.) (Pr, (32), 22.II.18)

Repr.: 260000(18).I: 124; Joffe: 265.

Trans.: Am. Bunyan & Fisher: 520; Magnes: 156;
        Eng. Degras, SOVDOC.I: 46; Times, 25.II.18;
        Nor. Ny Tid, 4.III.18.

180222(2)   Pochemu my soglasilis na germanskie usloviya mira? (Why did we agree to the German peace terms?) (Iz, (33), 24.II.18; Pr, (33), 23.II.18)

Repr.: 260000(18).I: 121-4.

Trans.: Eng. Bernstein: 187-92;
        Nor. Ny Tid, 23.II.18.

⌊Interview with Bernstein, NYHerald correspondent. ? printed in NYHerald.

180223   i Lenin: Postanovlenie. (A regulation.) (Iz, (34), 26.II.18)

Repr.: DVPS.I: 112.

180224   [Interview.] (Bruce Lockhart: Ch. III)
[Trans. Eng.]

180226   Obyazatel'noe postanovleniya Chrezvychainoi komissii po prodovol'stviyu
i transportu. (Compulsory regulation of Extraordinary Commission for
food and transport.) (Iz, (36), 28.II.18)

[180228(1)]   Ot Chrezvychainoi komissii po prodovol'stviyu i transportu. (From the
Extraordinary Commission for food and transport.) (Iz, (36), 28.II.18)

[180228(2)]   Obyazatel'noe postanovlenie. (Compulsory regulation.) (Iz, (36),
28.II.18)

180301(1)   i dr.: Dogovor mezhdu Finlyandskoi i Rossiiskoi sotsialisticheskimi
respublikami. (Treaty between the Finnish and Russian Socialist
Republics.) (Pr, (46), 10.III.18)
Trans.: Eng. Degras, SOVDOC.I: 47-8.

180301(2)   [To Murmansk Soviet.] (Kedrov: 28)
Trans.: Am. Kennan: 46; Strakhovsky: 29;
         Eng. Lloyd George.VI: 3165-6.
[Telegram. To co-operate with Allies. See [180329].]

180304   i Lenin: Mir podpisan. (Peace signed.) (Iz, (40), 5.III.18)
Repr.: 260000(18).I: 125.
[Public notice.]

180305(1)   [Conversation with Robins.] (Wheeler-Bennet: 290)
[Trans. Eng.]

180305(2)   [Note to Robins.] (Wheeler-Bennet: 56-7)
[Trans. Eng.]

[180305(3)]   Postanovlenie. (A regulation.) (Iz, (40), 5.III.18)
Repr.: 260000(18).I: 704-5.

180306(1)   [Interview with Bruce Lockhart.] (Bruce Lockhart: Ch. IV)
[Trans. Eng.]

[180306(2)]   i Vladimirov: Ot Chrezvychainoi komissii po prodovol'stviyu i transportu.
(From the Extraordinary Commission for food and transport.) (Iz, (41),
6.III.18)

180307   Rech. (A speech.) (PROTOKOLY VII S"EZD: 77-86)
                Repr.: 260000(18).I: 134-43; p.q. 300000(1): Ch. XXXII.
                Trans.: p.q. 300000(1): Ch. XXXII.

180308(1)   Zayavlenie. (A statement.) (PROTOKOLY VII S"EZD: 147)
                Repr.: 260000(18): 143-4.
                ⌊To 7th Congress CPR; on peace negotiations.⌋

180308(2)   ⌊Interview with Ruggles and Riggs.⌋
                ⌊c. Strakhovsky: 9.⌋

[180310]   Vtoraya voina i podpisanie mira. (A second war and the signing of
                peace.) (260000(18).I: 125-8)

[180314]   Ot Voenno-Revolyutsionnogo Komissariata ri petrogradsk. sov. (From
                the Military Revolutionary Commissariat for the Petrograd Soviet.)
                (Pr, (48/49), 14/15.III.18)

180315   ⌊Interview.⌋ (Bruce Lockhart: Ch. IV)
                ⌊Trans. Eng.⌋

180316   ⌊Interview.⌋ (Bruce Lockhart: Ch. IV)
                ⌊Trans. Eng.⌋

180318   Perenesenie stolitsy v Moskvu. (The transfer of the capital to
                Moscow.) (Iz, (51), 19.III.18)
                Repr.: 260000(18).I: 130-1.

180319(1)   Nam nuzhna armiya. (We need an army.) (Iz, (52,53), 20,21.III.18;
                Pr, (51), 21.III.18)
                Repr.: 230000(7).I: 25-8; 260000(18).I: 227-31.
                Trans.: Am. p.q. FI, X.41;
                        Fr. 680000(1): 43-8;
                        Ger. 240000(40): 19-23; p.q. PermRev, (III.8), II.33.
                ⌊Speech to Moscow Soviet.⌋

⌊180319(2)⌋   ⌊Conversation with Sadoul.⌋ (Sadoul: 273)
                ⌊Trans. Fr.⌋

[180319(3)]   Ni pyadi zemli bez boya! (Not an inch of ground without a fight!)
                (Iz, (51), 19.III.18)
                Repr.: 260000(18).I: 128-30.
                ⌊Appeal to working people. Archives.⌋

180320(1) [Letter to Robins.]
           Trans.: Am. Kennan: 217.

180320(2) [Interview with Arthur Ransome.]
           Trans.: Eng. Daily News(Ln), 25.III.18 p.q. Dennis: 278.
           [On Japanese intervention.]

180320(3) i Sklyanskii: Prikaz, No. 223. (Iz(NKVD), (21), 23.V.18)
           [Prikaz, Order of the Day; trans. discontinued.]

180321(1) Nasha zadacha. (Our tasks.) (Iz, (56), 24.III.18)
           Repr.: 230000(7).I: 29-30; 260000(18).I: 232-4.
           Trans.: Fr. 680000(1): 48-50; Niessel: 327-9;
                   Ger. 240000(40): 24-6.
           [Appeal of Commissar of War.]

180321(2) [Letter to Ruggles.]
           Trans.: Am. p.q. Kennan: 114-5.

180321(3) [Message to Colonel Lavergne.]
           Trans.: Fr. p.q. Niessel: 329-30.
           [Asking for technical assistance for the army.]

180322   Novaya armiya. (A new army.) (Iz, (55), 23.III.18)
           Repr.: 230000(7).I: 99-100; 260000(18).I: 234-6.
           Trans.: Fr. 680000(1): 127-9;
                   Ger. 240000(40): 27-8.
           [Speech in Alexeev People's House.]

[180324(1)] i Podvoiskii: Ot narodnogo komissariata po voennym delam. (From the
           People's Commissariat for War.) (Iz, (56), 24.III.18; Pr, (58),
           26.III.18)

180324(2) Sovetskaya vlast i mezhdunarodnaya burzhuaziya. (Soviet power and
           the international bourgeoisie.) (Iz, (57), 26.III.18)

180328(1) TRUD, DISTSIPLINA, PORYADOK SPASUT SOTSIALISTICHESKU SOVETSKUYU
           RESPUBLIKU. (WORK, DISCIPLINE AND ORDER WILL SAVE THE SOCIALIST
           SOVIET REPUBLIC), 180000(24).
           Repr.: 180000(25); 180000(59); *180000(62); 190000(26); *190000(27);
                   *200000(92); 230000(7).I: 31-45; p.q. 240000(28): 125-6;
                   260000(18).I: 155-72.

++++

180328(1) ┼┼┼┼ <u>Trans</u>.: Am. <u>Class Struggle</u>, (III.4), XI.19;

Cz. p.q. <u>SocDem</u>, (II.41), 10.XII.20;

Den. ⌊180000(49)⌋;

Eng. <u>Soc</u>(G), (XVIII.238-40), 6-20.XI.19; p.q. Deutscher, PA:407;
p.q. LABOUR CONDITIONS: 150;

Fin. 180000(61);

Fr. 680000(1): 50-66; <u>RevueCom</u>, (I.2,3), IV,V.20;

Ger. 180000(29); 190000(36); 190000(37); ⌊190000(60)⌋; p.q.
<u>KomArb</u>, (I.40), 18.VI.19;

Hol. ⌊200000(8)⌋;

Hun. *190000(75); *190000(76);*⌊190000(77)⌋;

It. 190000(50); 700000(18);

Sp. *⌊200000(86)⌋;

Yid. *180000(30).

180328(2)   Zashchitinku kapitana Sadulya. (To the counsel for the defence of
Captain Sadoul.) (260000(18).I: 132-4)
⌊Sadoul's trial.⌋

⌊180329⌋   ⌊To Petrozavodsk Soviet.⌋
<u>Trans</u>.: Am. Strakhovsky: 32.
⌊See 180301(2).⌋

⌊180330(1)⌋   O zapreshchenii uvolnyayushchimsya. (Ban on resignations from the
armed forces.) (<u>Iz</u>, (61), 30.III.18)

180330(2)   i dr.: Prikaz, No. 230. (Order of the Day, No. 230.) (<u>Iz</u>, (63),
2.IV.18)
<u>Repr</u>.: Iz(NKVD), (11/12/13), 10/11/12.V.18.
⌊The full head: Prikaz narodnogo komissar⌊iat⌋a po voennym ⌊and/ i
morskim⌋ delam (Order of the Day of the People's Commissar⌊iat⌋ for
War ⌊and/ Maritime Affairs⌋, variant and abbreviated forms, with
translations is not given in later cases. Places of origin of the
Orders are also omitted.⌋

180401(1)   i Sklyanskii: Prikaz, No. 244. (<u>Iz</u>, (65), 4.IV.18)
<u>Repr</u>.: VKVD, (10), 15.IV.18.

180401(2)   i Sklyanskii: Prikaz, No. 246. (<u>Iz</u>, (71), 11.IV.18)

180401(3)   i Sklyanskii: Prikaz, No. 248. (<u>Iz</u>, (65), 4.IV.18)

180403(1)   i Sklyanskii: Prikaz, No. 250. (<u>Iz</u>, (71), 11.IV.18)

                <u>Repr</u>.: DEKRETY: 4-5.

                <u>Trans</u>.: Fr. Lévy: 122.

180403(2)   i Sklyanskii: Prikaz, No. 252. (<u>Iz</u>, (70), 10.IV.18)

180404   i Sklyanskii: Prikaz, No. 256. (<u>Iz</u>, (70), 10.IV.18)

180405(1)   i Sklyanskii: Prikaz, No. 258. (<u>Iz</u>, (70), 10.IV.18)

180405(2)   i Sklyanskii: Prikaz, No. 266. (<u>Iz</u>, (71), 11.IV.18)

180405(3)   Prikaz, No. 264. (<u>VKVD</u>, (10), 15.IV.18)

180406   Prikaz. (260000(18).I: 695-6)

180407   [Interview with Sadoul.]

                [c. Strakhovsky: 20.]

180408(1)   i Sklyanskii: Prikaz, No. 270. (<u>Iz</u>, (70), 10.IV.18)

180408(2)   Dekret Soveta Narodnykh Komissarov. (Decree of the Sovnarkom.)

                (<u>Iz</u>, (73), 13.IV.18)

                <u>Repr</u>.: DEKRETY: 5-13; <u>Iz</u>(Pet), (26), 20.IV.18; <u>VKVD</u>, (10), 15.IV.18.

180408(3)   i Sklyanskii: Prikaz, No. 254. (<u>Iz</u>, (74), 14.IV.18)

180409   Prikaz, No. 1. (<u>Iz</u>, (78), 20.IV.18)

180410   i dr.: Prikaz, No. 253. (<u>Iz</u>, (75), 16.IV.18)

180411(1)   i Sklyanskii: Prikaz, No. 257. (<u>Iz</u>, (75), 16.IV.18)

180411(2)   i Sklyanskii: Prikaz, No. 259. (<u>Iz</u>, (78), 20.IV.18)

                <u>Repr</u>.: <u>VKVD</u>, (11), 24.IV.18.

180411(3)   i Podvoiskii: Prikaz, No. 261. (<u>Iz</u>, (78), 20.IV.18)

180413   i Sklyanskii: Prikaz, No. 265. (<u>Iz</u>, (78), 20.IV.18)

180414   SLOVO RUSSKIM RABOCHIM I KREST´YANAM O NASHAKH DRUZ´YAKH I VRAGAKH I
O TOM, KAK UBERECH I UPROCHIT SOVETSKUYU RESPUBLIKU (A WORD TO THE
RUSSIAN WORKERS AND PEASANTS ON OUR FRIENDS AND ENEMIES AND ON HOW TO
PRESERVE AND STRENGTHEN THE SOVIET REPUBLIC), 180000(17).

                <u>Repr</u>.: 180000(11); 180000(18); *180000(19); 180000(23); 260000(18).I:
173-98. ++++

180414 ++++   <u>Trans</u>.: Eng. 200000(62); 570900(3);
                          Rum. *[180000(56)]
                 [Address at workers meeting; includes answers to questions.]

180415(1)   i dr.: Prikaz, No. 271. (<u>Iz</u>, (78), 20.IV.18)

180415(2)   i dr.: Prikaz, No. 273. (<u>Iz</u>, (78), 20.IV.18)

180416(1)   i dr.: Ot Soveta Narodnykh Komissarov. (From the Sovnarkom.)
                 (<u>Iz</u>, (76), 17.IV.18)

180416(2)   i Sklyanskii: Prikaz, No. 272. (<u>Iz</u>, (85), 28.IV.18)

180416(3)   i dr.: Prikaz, No. 276. (<u>Iz</u>, (80), 23.IV.18)

180417(1)   i dr.: Prikaz, No. 274. (<u>Iz</u>, (78), 20.IV.18)

180417(2)   i Sklyanskii: Prikaz, No. 277. (<u>Iz</u>, (80), 23.IV.18)

180417(3)   i Sklyanskii: Prikaz, No. 278. (<u>Iz</u>, (79), 21.IV.18)

180418   i Sklyanskii: Prikaz, No. 279. (<u>Iz</u>, (85), 28.IV.18)

180420(1)   Prikaz. (<u>Iz</u>, (79), 21.IV.18)
                 <u>Trans</u>.: Eng. Degras, SOVDOC.I: 70-1.
                 [To local authorities; on prisoners of war.]

[180420(2)]   Tezisy o tekushchem momente. (Theses on the current situation.)
                 (<u>Kom</u>, (1), 20.IV.18)
                 <u>Repr</u>.: 260000(18).I: 593-610.

180420(3)   i Sklyanskii: Prikaz, No. 283. (<u>Iz</u>, (85), 28.IV.18)

180420(4)   i Sklyanskii: Prikaz, No. 284. (<u>Iz</u>, (85), 28.IV.18)

180420(5)   i dr.: Prikaz, No. 285. (<u>Iz</u>, (86), 30.IV.18)

180420(6)   i dr.: Prikaz, No. 286. (<u>Iz</u>, (82), 25.IV.18)

180420(7)   i Sklyanskii: Prikaz, No. 287. (<u>Iz</u>, (86), 30.IV.18)

180420(8)   i dr.: Prikaz, No. 288. (<u>Iz</u>, (86), 30.IV.18)

180420(9)   i Sklyanskii: Prikaz, No. 289. (<u>Iz</u>, (86), 30.IV.18)

180420(10)   i Yurenev: Prikaz, No. 291. (<u>Iz</u>, (83), 26.IV.18)

180421   KRASNAYA ARMIYA (THE RED ARMY), 180000(20).

           Repr.: 180000(21); 180000(22); *[180000(26)]; 230000(7).I: 46-67;

                  260000(18).I: 198-224; p.q. 260000(18).II: 527-8.

           Trans.: Am. p.q. Bunyan & Fisher: 572;

                  Fin. 180000(39): 3-29;

                  Fr. 200000(68); 200000(69); 680000(1): 66-92;

                  Ger. 180000(42);

                  Hol. 200000(70);

                  It. 210000(28);

                  Rum. 190000(39);

                  Serb. *190000(80).

           [Lecture in Moscow. Reprinted under various titles.]

180422(1)   Krasnaya armiya. (The Red Army.) (Iz, (80,81), 23,24.IV.18; Pr,

           (80,81), 25,26.IV.18)

           Repr.: 180000(3); 180000(6); 180000(7); *190000(67); 230000(7).I:

                  101-13; 260000(18).I: 236-51; DEKRETY: 22-37.

           Trans.: Eng. p.q. Deutscher, PA: 412;

                  Fr. 680000(1): 129-43;

                  Ger. 190000(53); 190000(55); 190000(57); 200000(67);

                     240000(40): 29-41;

                  Yid. *190000(54).

           [Speech to All-Russian CEC.]

180422(2)   Zaklyuchitel'noe slovo. (Summary speech.) (Iz, (80,81), 23,24.IV.18;

           Pr, (80,81), 25,26.IV.18)

           Repr.: 180000(6); 180000(7); 230000(7).I: 113-22; 260000(18).I: 251-62;

                  DEKRETY: 37-48.

           Trans.: Fr. 680000(1): 144-54;

                  Ger. 240000(40): 42-9.

           [See 180422(1).]

180422(3)   Dekret ob obyazatel'nom obuchenii voennomu iskusstvu. (Decree on

           compulsory military training.) (230000(7).I: 123-4; VPS, (2), 1918)

           Trans.: Fr. 680000(1): 155-7;

                  Ger. 240000(40): 50-2.

180422(4)   Sotsialisticheskaya klyatva. (The socialist oath.) (230000(7).I: 125)

           Trans.: Eng. Call(Ln), 15.I.20; Red Dawn, (II.6), VIII.20;

                  Fr. 680000(1): 157-8;

                  Ger. 240000(40): 53.

           [Red Army induction oath.]

180422(5)   i Sklyanskii: Prikaz, No. 292. (Iz, (87), 1.V.18)

180422(6)   i Sklyanskii: Prikaz, No. 293. (Iz, (91), 10.V.18)

180422(7)   i Sklyanskii: Prikaz, No. 296. (Iz, (86), 30.IV.18)

180423(1)   Neobkhodimoe raz"yasnenie. (O voenspetsakh.) (A necessary explanation:
                   On military specialists.) ((DEKRETY: 13-5)
                   Repr.: 230000(7).I: 135; 260000(18).I: 316-7.
                   Trans.: Am. 650900: 121-2;
                           Eng. 640000(5): 121-2; 640000(10): 121-2;
                           Fr. 680000(1): 165-6.

180423(2)   i dr.: Prikaz, No. 297. (Iz, (83), 26.IV.18)

180423(3)   i dr.: Prikaz, No. 298. (Iz, (85), 28.IV.18)

180423(4)   i dr.: Prikaz, No. 299. (Iz, (87), 1.V.18)

180423(5)   i dr.: Prikaz, No. 300. (Iz, (86), 30.IV.18)

180423(6)   i Yurenev: Prikaz, No. 301. (Iz, (86), 30.IV.18)

180424(1)   i Yurenev: Prikaz, No. 302. (Iz, (86), 30.IV.18)

180424(2)   i dr.: Prikaz, No. 303. (Iz, (85), 28.IV.18)

⌊180425(1)⌋   i Sklyanskii: Radiotelegramma. (A radiotelegram.) (Iz, (82), 25.IV.18)
                   Repr.: Iz(NKVD), (9), 3.V.18; VKVD, (12-3), 16.V.18.
                   ⌊Repr. on many days continuously after 3.V.18 in Iz(NKVD); not recorded
                   further.⌋

180425(2)   i dr.: Prikaz, No. 304. (Iz, (91), 10.V.18)

180425(3)   i Mekhonoshin: Prikaz, No. 305. (Iz, (85), 28.IV.18)

180425(4)   i Podvoiskii: Prikaz, No. 306. (Iz, (85), 28.IV.18)

180426   i Yurenev: Prikaz, No. 309. (Iz, (87), 1.V.18)

180427(1)   i dr.: Dekret o snabzhenii sel´skogo khozyaistva orudiyami proizvodstva
                   i metallami. (Decree on supplying agriculture with instruments of
                   production and metal.) (Iz, (84), 27.IV.18; NZh, (112:327), 9.VI.18)

180427(2)   i Yurenev: Prikaz, No. 307. (Iz, (89), 4.V.18)

180429(1)   i Mekhonoshin: Prikaz, No. 312. (<u>Iz</u>(NKVD), (8), 1.V.18)

180429(2)   i dr.: Prikaz, No. 313. (<u>Iz</u>, (NKVD), (8), 1.V.18)

180429(3)   i Sklyanskii: Prikaz, No. 314. (<u>Iz</u>(NKVD), (8), 1.V.18)

180430   i Sklyanskii: Prikaz, No. 317. (<u>Iz</u>(NKVD), (10), 9.V.18)

[180501(1)]   1-e maya i Internatsional. (May Day and the International.) (<u>Iz</u>, (87), 1.V.18)
                <u>Repr.</u>: 260000(10): 3-6.

[180501(2)]   Telegramma. (A telegram.) (<u>Iz</u>, (87), 1.V.18)

180503(1)   Prikaz. (<u>Iz</u>, (89), 4.V.18)

180503(2)   i dr.: Prikaz, No. 316. (<u>Iz</u>, (90), 9.V.18; <u>Iz</u>(NKVD), (10/11), 9/10.V.18)

180503(3)   i dr.: Prikaz, No. 318. (<u>Iz</u>(NKVD), (10), 9.V.18)

180503(4)   i dr.: Prikaz, No. 319. (<u>Iz</u>(NKVD), (10), 9.V.18)

180503(5)   i Sklyanskii: Prikaz, No. 320. (<u>Iz</u>, (91), 10.V.18; <u>Iz</u>(NKVD), (10), 9.V.18)

180504   i dr.: Dekret Soveta Narodnykh Komissarov. (Decree of the Sovnarkom.) (<u>Iz</u>(NKVD), (17), 18.V.18)
                <u>Repr.</u>: Iz, (102), 23.V.18.

180507(1)   i dr.: Prikaz, No. 321. (<u>Iz</u>, (90), 9.V.18; <u>Iz</u>(NKVD), (10), 9.V.18)

180507(2)   i dr.: Prikaz, No. 322. (<u>Iz</u>, (90), 9.V.18; <u>Iz</u>(NKVD), (10), 9.V.18)

180507(3)   i dr.: Prikaz, No. 323. (<u>Iz</u>(NKVD), (10), 9.V.18)
                <u>Repr.</u>: Iz, (92), 11.V.18.

180507(4)   i dr.: Prikaz, No. 324. (<u>Iz</u>(NKVD), (10), 9.V.18)
                <u>Repr.</u>: Iz, (92), 11.V.18.

180507(5)   i dr.: Prikaz, No. 325. (<u>Iz</u>(NKVD), (11), 10.V.18)
                <u>Repr.</u>: Iz, (93), 12.V.18.

180507(6)   i Sklyanskii: Prikaz, No. 326. (<u>Iz</u>(NKVD), (11), 10.V.18)
                <u>Repr.</u>: Iz, (94), 14.V.18; <u>Iz</u>(NKVD), (12-14), 11-14.V.18.

180508(1)   i Yurenev: Prikaz, No. 327. (Iz(NKVD), (11), 10.V.18)
                Repr.: Iz, (93/106), 12/28.V.18.

[180508(2)]   i Lenin: Prikaz rossiiskogo pravitel´stva ob okhrane russo-ukrainskoi
                granitsy. (Order of the Day of the Russian government on the defence of
                the Russo-Ukraine frontier.) (Iz, 8.V.18)
                [Special issue of Iz. LocBM.]

180508(3)   i Yurenev: Prikaz, No. 328. (Iz(NKVD), (11), 10.V.18)
                Repr.: Iz, (106), 28.V.18.

180508(4)   i dr.: Prikaz, No. 329. (Iz, (92), 11.V.18; Iz(NKVD), (11), 10.V.18)

180508(5)   i Yurenev: Prikaz, No. 330. (Iz, (92), 11.V.18; Iz(NKVD), (11), 10.V.18)

180508(6)   i Yurenev: Prikaz, No. 331. (Iz, (92), 11.V.18; Iz(NKVD), (11), 10.V.18)

180508(7)   i Yurenev: Prikaz, No. 332. (Iz, (92), 11.V.18; Iz(NKVD), (11), 10.V.18)

180508(8)   i Yurenev: Prikaz, No. 333. (Iz, (92), 11.V.18; Iz(NKVD), (11), 10.V.18)

180508(9)   i Yurenev: Prikaz, No. 334. (Iz, (92), 11.V.18; Iz(NKVD), (11), 10.V.18)
                Repr.: Iz, (101), 22.V.18.

180508(10)   i Yurenev: Prikaz, No. 335. (Iz, (92), 11.V.18; Iz(NKVD), (11), 10.V.18)

180508(11)   i Sklyanskii: Prikaz, No. 336. (Iz(NKVD), (11), 10.V.18)

180508(12)   i dr.: Prikaz, No. 337. (Iz(NKVD), (11), 10.V.18)

180508(13)   i Yurenev: Prikaz, No. 338. (Iz(NKVD), (11), 10.V.18)
                Repr.: Iz, (101), 22.V.18.

180508(14)   i dr.: Prikaz, No. 339. (Iz, (91), 10.V.18; Iz(NKVD), (11), 10.V.18)

180508(15)   i dr.: Prikaz, No. 340. (Iz(NKVD), (11), 10.V.18)
                Repr.: Iz, (101), 22.V.18.

180508(16)   i dr.: Prikaz, No. 341. (Iz, (91), 10.V.18; Iz(NKVD), (11), 10.V.18)

180508(17)   i dr.: Prikaz, No. 342. (Iz, (91), 10.V.18; Iz(NKVD), (11), 10.V.18)

180508(18)   i Mekhonoshin: Prikaz, No. 343. (Iz, (92), 11.V.18; Iz(NKVD), (11),
                10.V.18)

[180509(1)]   T.: U chem govorit perevorot na Ukraine? (What does the uprising in
                the Ukraine signify?) (Iz, (90), 9.V.18)

[180509(2)]   i dr.: Ot Vyshogo Voennogo Soveta. (From the Supreme Military Council.) (<u>Iz</u>, (90), 9.V.18; <u>Iz</u>(NKVD), (11), 10.V.18)

180509(4)   i Yurenev: Prikaz, No. 344. (<u>Iz</u>(NKVD), (12), 11.V.18)

180509(5)   i Yurenev: Prikaz, No. 345. (<u>Iz</u>(NKVD), (12), 11.V.18)
<u>Repr</u>.: <u>Iz</u>, (101), 22.V.18.

180509(6)   i Yurenev: Prikaz, No. 346. (<u>Iz</u>(NKVD), (12), 11.V.18)
<u>Repr</u>.: <u>Iz</u>, (101), 22.V.18.

180509(7)   i Yurenev: Prikaz, No. 347. (<u>Iz</u>(NKVD), (12), 11.V.18)
<u>Repr</u>.: <u>Iz</u>, (101), 22.V.18.

180509(8)   i Yurenev: Prikaz, No. 348. (<u>Iz</u>(NKVD), (12), 11.V.18)
<u>Repr</u>.: <u>Iz</u>, (101), 22.V.18.

180509(9)   i Yurenev: Prikaz, No. 349. (<u>Iz</u>(NKVD), (12), 11.V.18)
<u>Repr</u>.: <u>Iz</u>, (101), 22.V.18.

180509(10)   i dr.: Prikaz, No. 351. (<u>Iz</u>(NKVD), 12), 11.V.18)
<u>Repr</u>.: <u>Iz</u>, (101), 22.V.18.

180509(11)   i dr.: Prikaz, No. 352. (<u>Iz</u>(NKVD), (12), 11.V.18)

180509(12)   i dr.: Prikaz, No. 353. (<u>Iz</u>(NKVD), (12), 11.V.18)

180509(13)   i dr.: Prikaz, No. 354. (<u>Iz</u>(NKVD), (12), 11.V.18)

180509(14)   i dr.: Prikaz, No. 355. (<u>Iz</u>(NKVD), (12), 11.V.18)

[180510(1)]   i dr.: Dekret. (A decree.) (<u>Iz</u>(NKVD), (11), 10.V.18)

180510(2)   i dr.: Prikaz, No. 356. (<u>Iz</u>(NKVD), (13/14), 12/14.V.18)

[180511]   i dr.: Prikaz, No. 347. (<u>Iz</u>, (92), 11.V.18)

180512(1)   i dr.: Prikaz, No. 357. (<u>Iz</u>(NKVD), (14), 14.V.18)

180512(2)   i Sklyanskii: Prikaz, No. 367. (<u>Iz</u>(NKVD), (15), 16.V.18)
<u>Repr</u>.: <u>Iz</u>, (103), 24.V.18.

180512(3)   i dr.: Prikaz, No. 358. (<u>Iz</u>(NKVD), (14), 14.V.18)

180512(4)   i dr.: Prikaz, No. 359. (<u>Iz</u>(NKVD),(14), 14.V.18)
<u>Repr</u>.: <u>Iz</u>, (101), 22.V.18.

180512(5)   i dr.: Prikaz, No. 360. (Iz(NKVD), (14), 14.V.18)

180513(1)   i Yurenev: Prikaz, No. 361. (Iz(NKVD), (14), 14.V.18)
                 Repr.: Iz, (103), 24.V.18.

180513(2)   i Yurenev: Prikaz, No. 362. (Iz(NKVD), (14), 14.V.18)

180513(3)   i Yurenev: Prikaz, No. 363. (Iz(NKVD), (14), 14.V.18)

180513(4)   i Yurenev: Prikaz, No. 364. (Iz(NKVD), (14), 14.V.18)

180514(1)   i Mekhonoshin: Prikaz, No. 366. (Iz(NKVD), (15), 16.V.18)
                 Repr.: Iz, (103), 24.V.18.

180514(2)   i Sklyanskii: Prikaz, No. 391. (Iz(NKVD), (24), 28.V.18)

[180515(1)]   i dr.: Vremennoe polozhenie o kollegii narodnogo komissariata po
                 morskim delam. (Provisional proposal on College of People's Commissariat
                 for Maritime Affairs.) (Iz, (95), 15.V.18; VPS, (2), 1918)

180512(2)   i dr.: Prikaz, No. 368. (Iz(NKVD), (15), 16.V.18)
                 Repr.: Iz, (103), 24.V.18.

180515(3)   i Yurenev: Prikaz, No. 366. (Iz(NKVD), (17), 17.V.18)

180515(4)   i Yurenev: Prikaz, No. 370. (Iz(NKVD), (16), 17.V.18)
                 Repr.: Iz, (103), 24.V.18.

180516(1)   i dr.: Prikaz, No. 368. (Iz(NKVD), (16), 17.V.18)

180516(2)   i dr.: Prikaz, No. 372. (Iz(NKVD), (17), 18.V.18; VPS, (3), 1918)

[180516(3)]   Prikaz. (VKVD, (12-3), 16.V.18)

180516(4)   i Sklyanskii: Prikaz, No. 392. (Iz(NKVD), (24), 28.V.18)

180516(5)   i Sklyanskii: Prikaz, No. 393. (Iz(NKVD), (24), 28.V.18)

180516(6)   i Sklyanskii: Prikaz, No. 394. (Iz(NKVD), (24), 28.V.18)

180517   i Yurenev: Prikaz, No. 373. (Iz(NKVD), (17), 18.V.18)
                 Repr.: Iz, (103), 24.V.18.

180518(1)   i dr.: Vsem gubernskim, uezdnym i volostnym Sovetam. (To all Provincial,
                 Country and Rural Soviets.) (Iz, (100), 21.V.18; Iz(NKVD), (19),
                 21.V.18)   ++++

180518(1)   ++++   <u>Repr.</u>:   230000(7).I: 126; 260000(18).I: 263; <u>Iz</u>(NKVD), (20-2), 22-4.V.18.

              <u>Trans.</u>: Fr. 680000(1): 158-9.

180518(2)   i dr.: Postanovlenie. (A regulation.) (<u>Iz</u>, (102), 23.V.18; <u>Iz</u>(NKVD),
              (22), 24.V.18)

              ⌊On the inspection of the national institutions of the RFSSR.⌋

180520(1)   i Yurenev: Prikaz, No. 374. (<u>Iz</u>(NKVD), (19), 21.V.18)

180520(2)   i Yurenev: Prikaz, No. 375. (<u>Iz</u>(NKVD), (20), 22.V.18)
              <u>Repr.</u>: <u>Iz</u>, (106), 28.V.18.

180520(3)   i Sklyanskii: Prikaz, No. 376. (<u>Iz</u>(NKVD), (20), 22.V.18)
              <u>Repr.</u>: <u>Iz</u>, (106), 28.V.18.

180520(4)   i dr.: Prikaz, No. 377. (<u>Iz</u>, (103), 24.V.18; <u>Iz</u>(NKVD), (20), 22.V.18)

180520(5)   Letter to Robins.
              <u>Trans.</u>: Am. p.q. Kennan: 217.

180521(1)   i Sklyanskii: Prikaz, No. 378. (<u>Iz</u>, (103), 24.V.18; <u>Iz</u>(NKVD), (21),
              23.V.18)

180521(2)   i Sklyanskii: Prikaz, No. 379. (<u>Iz</u>, (103), 24.V.18; <u>Iz</u>(NKVD), (21),
              23.V.18)

180521(3)   i Sklyanskii: Prikaz, No. 380. (<u>Iz</u>(NKVD), (22), 24.V.18)
              <u>Repr.</u>: <u>Iz</u>, (106), 28.V.18.

180521(4)   i Sklyanskii: Prikaz, No. 396. (<u>Iz</u>, (108), 30.V.18; <u>Iz</u>(NKVD), (24),
              28.V.18)

180522(1)   i dr.: Ot Vserossiiskogo TsIK. Telegramma. Vsem Sovdepam. (From the
              All-Russian CEC. A Telegram. To all Sov. deps.) (‡z, (111), 2.VI.18)

180522(2)   i Lenin: Dekret. (A decree.) (<u>Iz</u>(NKVD), (24), 28.V.18)

180523(1)   Prikaz o razoruzhenii Chekho-slovakov. (Order to disarm Czecho-Slovaks.)
              (Maksakov i Turunov: 168)

180523(2)   i dr.: Prikaz, No. 381. (<u>Iz</u>(NKVD), (23), 26.V.18)
              <u>Repr.</u>: <u>Iz</u>, (107), 29.V.18.

180523(3)   i dr.: Prikaz, No. 382. (<u>Iz</u>(NKVD), (23), 26.V.18)
               <u>Repr.</u>: <u>Iz</u>, (107), 29.V.18.

180523(4)   i Sklyanskii: Prikaz, No. 383. (<u>Iz</u>(NKVD), (23), 26.V.18)
               <u>Repr.</u>: <u>Iz</u>, (107), 29.V.18.

180523(5)   i Sklyanskii: Prikaz, No. 384. (<u>Iz</u>(NKVD), (23), 26.V.18)
               <u>Repr.</u>: <u>Iz</u>, (107), 29.V.18.

180524(1)   i Sklyanskii: Prikaz, No. 385. (<u>Iz</u>(NKVD), (23), 26.V.18)
               <u>Repr.</u>: <u>Iz</u>, (107), 29.V.18.

180524(2)   i Yurenev: Prikaz, No. 386. (<u>Iz</u>(NKVD), (23), 26.V.18)
               <u>Repr.</u>: <u>Iz</u>, (107), 29.V.18.

180524(3)   i Yurenev: Prikaz, No. 387. (<u>Iz</u>(NKVD), (23), 26.V.18)
               <u>Repr.</u>: <u>Iz</u>, (107), 29.V.18.

180524(4)   i Yurenev: Prikaz, No. 388. (<u>Iz</u>(NKVD), (23), 26.V.18)
               <u>Repr.</u>: <u>Iz</u>, (107), 29.V.18.

180524(5)   i Sklyanskii: Prikaz, No. 389. (<u>Iz</u>(NKVD), (23), 26.V.18)
               <u>Repr.</u>: <u>Iz</u>, (107), 29.V.18.

180524(6)   i Yurenev: Prikaz, No. 390. (<u>Iz</u>(NKVD), (24), 28.V.18)
               <u>Repr.</u>: <u>Iz</u>, (115), 7.VI.18.

180524(7)   i Sklyanskii: Prikaz, No. 395. (<u>Iz</u>(NKVD), (24), 28.V.18)

180524(8)   i Mekhonoshin: Prikaz, No. 397. (<u>Iz</u>(NKVD), (36), 12.VI.18)
               <u>Repr.</u>: <u>Iz</u>, (124), 19.VI.18.

180525(1)   i Mekhonoshin: Prikaz, No. 398. (<u>Iz</u>(NKVD), (36), 12.VI.18)
               <u>Repr.</u>: <u>Iz</u>, (124), 19.VI.18.

180525(2)   i Mekhonoshin: Prikaz, No. 399. (<u>Iz</u>(NKVD), (36), 12.VI.18)
               <u>Repr.</u>: <u>Iz</u>, (124), 19.VI.18.

180525(3)   i Mekhonoshin: Prikaz, No. 400. (<u>Iz</u>(NKVD), (36), 12.VI.18)
               <u>Repr.</u>: <u>Iz</u>, (124), 19.VI.18.

180525(4)   i Mekhonoshin: Prikaz, No. 401. (<u>Iz</u>(NKVD), (36), 12.VI.18)
               <u>Repr.</u>: <u>Iz</u>, (124), 19.VI.18.

[180525(5)] i dr.: Dekret Soveta Narodnykh Komissarov. (Decree of the Sovnarkom.)
(Iz, (104), 25.V.18)

180525(6) [Telegram.] (Maksakov i Turunov: 168)
Trans.: Am. Bunyan & Fisher: 91;
        Eng. p.q. Footman: 92.
[To disarm Czechs.]

[180526] i dr.: Vsem gubernskim, uezdnym i volostnym sovetam. (To all Provincial,
Country and Rural Soviets.) (Iz, (105), 26.V.18)
Repr.: Iz, (106/107), 28/29.V.18.

180527(1) Postanovlenie. (A regulation.) (260000(18).I: 703)
[Arrest of Admiral Shchastny. See further 180620(1).]

180527(2) i Yurenev: Prikaz, No. 402. (Iz(NKVD), (24), 28.V.18)

180527(3) i Mekhonoshin: Prikaz, No. 403. (Iz(NKVD), (24), 28.V.18)

180528(1) i Yurenev: Prikaz, No. 404. (Iz(NKVD), (25), 30.V.18)

180528(2) i Mekhonoshin: Prikaz, No. 405. (Iz(NKVD), (25), 30.V.18)

180529(1) O chekho-slovatskikh eshelonakh. (On the Czecho-Slovak echelons.)
(Iz, (108), 30.V.18; Iz(NKVD), (25), 30.V.18)
Repr.: 230000(7).I: 210-1; 260000(18).I: 477-8; Maksakov i Turunov:
        176-7.
Trans.: Fr. 680000(1): 247-8.
[Communique on insurrection.]

180529(2) PS to 180212. (240000(32).II: 258)

180529(3) i Mekhonoshin: Prikaz, No. 406. (Iz, (109), 31.V.18; Iz(NKVD), (25),
30.V.18)

180529(4) i Mekhonoshin: Prikaz, No. 407. (Iz, (109), 31.V.18; Iz(NKVD), (25),
30.V.18)

180529(5) i dr.: Prikaz, No. 408. (Iz, (109), 31.V.18; Iz(NKVD), (25), 30.V.18)

180529(6) i Sklyanskii: Prikaz, No. 409. (Iz(NKVD), (25), 30.V.18)

180529(7) i Lenin: Postanovlenie. (A regulation.) (Iz(NKVD), (26), 31.V.18;
VPS, (3), 1918)

180530(1) i dr.: Ot Soveta Narodnykh Komissarov. (From the Sovnarkom.)
(Iz, (109), 31.V.18; Pr, (108), 1.VI.18)
Repr.: 260000(18).I: 393-9.
[An appeal; struggle for food.]

180530(2) i dr.: Trudovye Kazaki Dona i Kubani! (Cossack workers of the Don and
Kuban!) (Iz, (109), 31.V.18; Pr, (107), 31.V.18)
Repr.: 260000(18).I: 495-6; Vestnik KVD, (15-6), 1918: 11-2.

180530(3) i dr.: Rabochie i krest'yane! Chestnye trudyashchimsya grazhdane vsei
Rossii! (Workers and peasants! Honourable toiler-citizens of all
Russia!) (Iz, (109), 31.V.18)
Trans.: Fr, RevCom, (I.6), VIII.20.
[From the Sovnarkom.]

180530(4) i dr.: Postanovlenie. (A regulation.) (Iz, (109), 31.V.18; VPS, (3),
1918)

180530(5) i dr.: Polozhenie o pravakh i obyazannostyakh upravlyayushchogo delami
Narodnago Komissariata po voennym delam. (Regulation on rights and
duties of those in charge of the affairs of the People's Commissariat
for War.) (Iz, (109), 31.V.18; Iz(NKVD), (25), 30.V.18; VPS, (3), 1918)

[180530(6)] Polozhenie o voennykh komissarakh, chlenakh voennykh sovetov. (The
position of military commissars who are members of military soviets.)
(Iz(NKVD), (25), 30.V.18)

180530(7) i Yurenev: Prikaz, No. 410. (Iz(NKVD), (26), 31.V.18)

180531(1) Otvety na voprosy predstavitelya chekho-slovatskogo korpusa V.Neiberta.
(Answers to questions from V[yacheslav] Neibert, representative of the
Czecho-Slovak Corps.) (230000(7).I: 212-5)
Repr.: 260000(18).I: 478-82.
Trans.: Fr. 680000(1): 249-52.

180531(3) i Sklyanskii: Prikaz, No. 411. (Iz(NKVD), (27), 1.VI.18)
Repr.: Iz, (117), 9.VI.18.

180531(4) i Sklyanskii: Prikaz, No. 412. (Iz(NKVD), (27), 1.VI.18)
Repr.: Iz, (117), 9.VI.18.

180531(5) i Sklyanskii: Prikaz, No. 413. (Iz, (117/118), 9/11.VI.18; VPS, (3),
1918)

[180531(6)]   i dr.: Ot Soveta Narodnykh Komissarov RSFRS. (From the Sovnarkom of the RFSSR.) (<u>Iz</u>, (109), 31.V.18; <u>Pr</u>, (107), 31.V.18)

180531(7)   i Sklyanskii: Prikaz, No. 413. (<u>Iz</u>(NKVD), (28), 2.VI.18)

180531(8)   i Burdakov: Prikaz, No. 236. (<u>Iz</u>(NKVD), (27), 1.VI.18)

180601(1)   i dr.: Postanovlenie. (A regulation.) (<u>Iz</u>, (110), 1.VI.18)
<u>Repr</u>.: 180615(15).

180601(2)   i dr.: Prikaz, No. 414. (<u>Iz</u>(NKVD), (30), 5.VI.18)
<u>Repr</u>.: Iz, (117), 9.VI.18; <u>VPS</u>, (3), 1918.

180601(3)   i dr.: Prikaz, No. 415. (<u>Iz</u>(NKVD), (30), 5.VI.18)
<u>Repr</u>.: Iz, (117), 9.VI.18; <u>VPS</u>, (3), 1918.

180601(4)   i Sklyanskii: Prikaz, No. 416. (<u>Iz</u>(NKVD), (29), 4.VI.18)
<u>Repr</u>.: Iz, (118), 11.VI.18.

180601(5)   i dr.: Telegramma. (A telegram.) (<u>Iz</u>(NKVD), (29), 4.VI.18)
[To all Soviet departments.]

180601(6)   i Sklyanskii: Utverzhdaetsya. (A confirmation.) (<u>Iz</u>(NKVD), (82), 6.VIII.18)

180602   i Sklyanskii: Prikaz, No. 421. (<u>Iz</u>(NKVD), (30), 5.VI.18)
<u>Repr</u>.: Iz, (124), 19.VI.18.

180603(1)   i Sklyanskii: Prikaz, No. 417. (<u>Iz</u>(NKVD), (30), 5.VI.18)
<u>Repr</u>.: Iz, (123), 18.VI.18.

180603(2)   i Sklyanskii: Prikaz, No. 418. (<u>Iz</u>(NKVD), (30), 5.VI.18)
<u>Repr</u>.: Iz, (123), 18.VI.18.

180603(3)   i Sklyanskii: Prikaz, No. 419. (<u>Iz</u>(NKVD), (30), 5.VI.18)
<u>Repr</u>.: Iz, (123), 18.VI.18.

180604(1)   Dva puti. (Two roads.) (<u>Iz</u>, (113), 5.VI.18)
<u>Repr</u>.: 230000(7).I: 68-72; 260000(18).I: 400-5.
<u>Trans</u>.: Fr. 680000(1): 92-7.
[Speech to joint session of members of All-Russian CEC (4th Convention), Moscow Soviet, All-Russian Central Council, Trade Unions, Representatives of all trade unions in Moscow, factory committees and other workers organizations.]

180604(2)   Rezolyutsiya. (A resolution.) (230000(7).I: 72-3)
             Repr.: 260000(18).I: 405-6.
             Trans.: Fr. 680000(1): 97-8.
             [See 180604(1).]

180604(3)   Prikaz. (Iz, (113), 5.VI.18)
             Repr.: 230000(7).I: 216; Maksakov i Turunov: 177.
             Trans.: Fr. 680000(1): 252-3.
             [To all units fighting against the Czecho-Slovak counter-revolutionary
             mutineers.]

180604(4)   Pokazaniya, dannye chlenu TsIK v Kingissepu. (Evidence given to CEC
             members in Kingissep.) (260000(18).I: 317-22)
             [Shchasty's treachery.]

180604(5)   i Sklyanskii: Prikaz, No. 420. (Iz(NKVD), (30), 5.VI.18)
             Repr.: Iz, (123), 18.VI.18.

[180604(6)] i dr.: Postanovlenie Soveta Narodnykh Komissarov po voprosu o
             samostoyatelnykh zagotovkakh.) (Regulation of the Sovnarkom on the
             question of individual procurement.) (Iz, (112), 4.VI.18)
             Repr.: VPS, (3), 1918.

180604(7)   i Sklyanskii: Prikaz, No. 422. (Iz(NKVD), (30), 5.VI.18)
             Repr.: Iz, (124), 19.VI.18.

180605(1)   Prikaz, No. 423. (Iz(NKVD), (33), 8.VI.18)
             Repr.: Iz, (124), 19.VI.18.

180605(2)   i Sklyanskii: Prikaz, No. 427. (Iz(NKVD), (32), 7.VI.18)
             Repr.: Iz, (118), 11.VI.18.

180606(1)   i Mekhonoshin: Prikaz, No. 424. (Iz(NKVD), (32), 7.VI.18)
             Repr.: Iz, (118), 11.VI.18.

180606(2)   i Yurenev: Prikaz, No. 425. (Iz(NKVD), (33), 8.VI.18)

180606(3)   i Sklyanskii: Prikaz, No. 426. (Iz(NKVD), (32), 7.VI.18)
             Repr.: Iz, (118), 11.VI.18; Iz(NKVD), (40), 18.VI.18.

180606(4)   i Sklyanskii: Prikaz, No. 428. (Iz(NKVD), (33), 8.VI.18)
             Repr.: Iz, (130), 26.VI.18; Iz(NKVD), (35), 11.VI.18.
             [Iz(NKVD), (35) reads i Yurenev.]

180606(5)   i Sklyanskii: Prikaz, No. 429. (Iz(NKVD), (33), 8.VI.18)
              Repr.: Iz, (118), 11.VI.18.

180606(6)   i Sklyanskii: Prikaz, No. 524. (Iz, (143), 10.VII.18)

180606(7)   i Sklyanskii: Prikaz, No. 525. (Iz, (143), 10.VII.18)

180606(9)   i Sklyanskii: Prikaz, No. 527. (Iz, (143), 10.VII.18)

180607(1)   Organizatsiya Krasnoi Armii. (The organization of the Red Army.)
              (Iz, (116), 8.VI.18; p.q. Bednota, (86), 11.VI.18; NZh, (112:327),
              9.VI.18)
              Repr.: 230000(7).I: 127-31; 260000(18).I: 264-9.
              Trans.: Eng. p.q. Footman: 141;
                       Fr. 680000(1): 159-64;
                       Ger. 240000(40): 57-61.
              [Speech to 1st All-Russian Congress of Military Commissars.]

180607(2)   [Message to Regional Soviet, Archangel.]
              Trans.: Am. p.q. Kennan: 371; p.q. Strakhovsky: 51.

180607(3)   i Sklyanskii: Prikaz, No. 430. (Iz(NKVD), (34), 9.VI.18)
              Repr.: Iz, (124), 19.VI.18.

180607(4)   i Sklyanskii: Prikaz, No. 431. (Iz(NKVD), (34), 9.VI.18)
              Repr.: Iz, (124), 19.VI.18.

180607(5)   i Sklyanskii: Prikaz, No. 432. (Iz(NKVD), (35), 11.VI.18)
              Repr.: Iz, (124), 19.VI.18.

180607(6)   i Sklyanskii: Utverzhdaetsya. (A confirmation.) (Iz(NKVD), (82),
              8.VIII.18)

180609   NA BOR'BU S GOLODOM! (THE STRUGGLE AGAINST FAMINE!), 180000(12).
              Repr.: 190000(12); 230000(7).I: 74-95; 260000(18).I: 406-33.
              Trans.: Fr. 680000(1): 99-125.

180610(1)   i Sklyanskii: Prikaz, No. 433. (Iz(NKVD), (35), 11.VI.18)
              Repr.: Iz, (124), 19.VI.18.

180610(2)   Lenin & T.: [War declared against Siberian Provisional Government.]
              (NZh, (114:329), 12.VI.18; SvobRos, (44), 11.VI.18)
              Trans.: Am. p.q. Bunyan: 325-8.

180610(3)   i Raskol´nikov: [Prikaz.] (<u>Iz</u>(151), 19.VII.18)

                <u>Repr</u>.: p.q. 640000(1): 50.

                <u>Trans</u>.: Eng. p.q. 640000(1): 51.

                [See 640000(1): 56, n.3.]

180610(4)   i dr.: Ot Soveta Narodnykh Komissarov. (From the Sovnarkom.)
                (<u>Iz</u>, (118), 11.VI.18)

                <u>Repr</u>.: <u>VPS</u>, (4), 1918.

180611(1)   Dekret. (A decree.) (<u>Iz</u>, (119), 12.VI.18)

                <u>Repr</u>.: 260000(18).I: 482.

                <u>Trans</u>.: Am. Bunyan: 100.

180611(2)   i dr.: Prikaz, No. 327. (<u>Iz</u>(NKVD), (36), 12.VI.18)

180611(3)   i dr.: Prikaz, No. 434. (<u>Iz</u>(NKVD), (37), 13.VI.18)

180613(1)   i Lenin: Prikaz. (<u>Iz</u>, (121), 15.VI.18)

                <u>Repr</u>.: 230000(7).I: 217; Maksakov i Turunov: 188.

                <u>Trans</u>.: Fr. 680000(1): 253-4.

180613(2)   <u>Prikaz</u>. (Iz, (121), 15.VI.18)

                <u>Repr</u>.: 230000(7).I: 218; Maksakov i Turunov: 177-8.

                <u>Trans</u>.: Fr. 680000(1): 254-5.

180613(3)   Vsem chasnyam rabochei i krest´yanskoi Krasnoi Armii, srzhayushchimsya
                protiv kontr-revolyutsionnykh myatezhnikov i ikh soyuznikov Chekho-
                slovakov. (To all worker and peasant units of the Red Army on guard
                against the counter-revolutionary mutineers and their Czecho-Slovak
                allies.) (<u>Iz</u>, (121), 15.VI.18; <u>PetPr</u>, (125), 16.VI.18)

                <u>Repr</u>.: Iz(NKVD), 40), 18.VI.18; Maksakov i Turunov: 178-9.

180613(4)   i Sklyanskii: Prikaz, No. 435. (<u>Iz</u>, (122), 16.VI.18; <u>Iz</u>(NKVD), (39),
                16.VI.18)

180613(5)   i dr.: Dekret Soveta Narodnykh Komissarov. (<u>PetPr</u>, (122), 13.VI.18)

                <u>Repr</u>.: Maksakov i Turunov: 187.

                [Call-up of workers and peasants of the Rada country areas, of the
                Urals and of the Siberian military areas, for military service.]

180614(1)   Pamyati Plekhanova. (In memory of Plekhanov.) (260000(17): 65-6)

                [Archives.]

180614(2)   i dr.: Prikaz, No. 436. (<u>Iz</u>, (121), 15.VI.18; <u>Iz</u>(NKVD), (38), 14.VI.18)
<u>Repr</u>.: <u>PetPr</u>, (127), 19.VI.18.
[See 180614(15).]

180614(3)   i Sklyanskii: Prikaz, No. 437. (<u>Iz</u>(NKVD), (40), 18.VI.18)

180614(4)   i Sklyanskii: Prikaz, No. 438. (<u>Iz</u>, (124), 19.VI.18; <u>Iz</u>(NKVD), (40), 18.VI.18)

180614(5)   i Sklyanskii: Prikaz, No. 439. (<u>Iz</u>, (124), 19.VI.18; <u>Iz</u>(NKVD), (40), 18.VI.18)

180614(6)   i Sklyanskii: Prikaz, No. 440. (<u>Iz</u>, (124), 19.VI.18; <u>Iz</u>(NKVD), (40), 18.VI.18)

180614(7)   i Sklyanskii: Prikaz, No. 441. (<u>Iz</u>, (124), 19.VI.18; <u>Iz</u>(NKVD), (40), 18.VI.18)

180614(8)   Prikaz. (<u>Iz</u>, (121), 15.VI.18)
<u>Repr</u>.: <u>VPS</u>, (5), 1918.
[For all units of the peasants and workers Army resisting the Germano-Haidamak [i.e. Ukrainian nationalist] units.]

[180614(9)]   i dr.: O Voennykh Komissariatakh pri mestnykh Sovetakh. (On Military Commissariats attached to Soviets.) (<u>VKVD</u>, (15-6), 14.VI.18)

[180614(10)]   i dr.: Vozzvanie. (An appeal.) (<u>VKVD</u>, (15-6), 14.VI.18)
[Productivity crisis.]

[180614(11)]   Dekret. (<u>VKVD</u>, (15-6), 14.VI.18)
[Of Sovnarkom; on establishment of military areas.]

[180614(12)]   i dr.: Rabochie i krest'yane! Chestnye trudyashchimsya grazhdane vsei Rossii. (Workers and Peasants! Honourable toiling-citizens of all Russia.) (<u>VKVD</u>, (15-6), 14.VI.18)

[180614(13)]   i dr.: Obrashchenie. (An appeal.) (<u>VKVD</u>, (15-6), 14.VI.18)
[Of Sovnarkom; to Cossacks of Don and Kuban, on Krasnov's insurrection.]

[180614(14)]   i dr.: Postanovlenie. (A Regulation.) (<u>VKVD</u>, (15-6), 14.VI.18)
[Of Sovnarkom; on setting up unified productivity centre.]

180614(15)   [Addendum to Prikaz, No. 436.] (<u>Iz</u>(NKVD), (38), 14.VI.18)
[See 180614(2).]

180615(1)   i dr.: Dekret Soveta Narodnykh Komissarov. (Decree of the Sovnarkom.) (Iz, (123), 18.VI.18)

180615(2)   i Sklyanskii: Prikaz, No. 442. (Iz, (124), 19.VI.18; Iz(NKVD), (41), 19.VI.18)

180615(3)   i Mekhonoshin: Prikaz, No. 443. (Iz, (124), 19.VI.18; Iz(NKVD), (41), 19.VI.18)

180615(4)   i dr.: Prikaz, No. 444. (Iz(NKVD), (41), 19.VI.18)
Repr.: Iz, (126), 21.VI.18.

180615(5)   i dr.: Prikaz, No. 445. (Iz(NKVD), (41), 19.VI.18)
Repr.: Iz, (126), 21.VI.18.

180615(6)   i dr.: Prikaz, No. 446. (Iz, (124), 19.VI.18; Iz(NKVD), (41), 19.VI.18)

180615(7)   i Sklyanskii: Prikaz, No. 447. (Iz, (125), 20.VI.18; Iz(NKVD), (42), 20.VI.18)

180615(8)   i Sklyanskii: Prikaz, No. 448. (Iz(NKVD), (40), 18.VI.18)
Repr.: Iz, (127), 22.VI.18.

180615(9)   i Yurenev: Prikaz, No. 449. (Iz(NKVD), (40), 18.VI.18)
Repr.: Iz, (127), 22.VI.18.

180615(10)   i Yurenev: Prikaz, No. 450. (Iz(NKVD), (40), 18.VI.18)
Repr.: Iz, (127), 22.VI.18.

180615(11)   i Yurenev: Prikaz, No. 451. (Iz(NKVD), (40), 18.VI.18)
Repr.: Iz, (127), 22.VI.18.

180615(12)   i Yurenev: Prikaz, No. 452. (Iz(NKVD), (40), 18.VI.18)
Repr.: Iz, (127), 22.VI.18.

180615(13)   i dr.: Prikaz, No. 453. (Iz(NKVD), (40), 18.VI.18)

180615(14)   i Sklyanskii: Prikaz, No. 454. (Iz, (125), 20.VI.18; Iz(NKVD), (42), 20.VI.18)

180615(15)   i Mekhonoshin: Prikaz, No. 467. (Iz(NKVD), (42), 20.VI.18)
[Includes 180601(1).]

180616(1)   MEZHDUNARODNOE POLOZHENIE I KRASNAYA ARMIYA (THE INTERNATIONAL SITUATION
            AND THE RED ARMY), 180000(8).
            Repr.: 180000(9); 180000(11); 190000(11); 260000(18).I: 269-89.
            Trans.: Eng. p.q. Dennis: 286;
                    Fin. 180000(39): 30-41;
                    Tat. 180000(10).
            [Address in Sergei People's House, Voronezh.]

[180616(2)]   i dr.: Ko vsem trudyashchimusya musulmanam. (To all Muslim toilers.)
              (Iz, (122), 16.VI.18)

180617(1)   i Lenin: Dekret. (A decree.) (Iz, (123), 18.VI.18; Iz(NKVD), (41),
            19.VI.18)

180617(2)   i Sklyanskii: Prikaz, No. 456. (Iz, (126), 21.VI.18; Iz(NKVD), (42),
            20.VI.18)

180617(3)   i Sklyanskii: Prikaz, No. 457. (Iz, (126), 21.VI.18; Iz(NKVD), (42),
            20.VI.18)

[180618(1)]   i Lenin: Dekret. (A decree.) (Iz, (123), 18.VI.18)

180618(2)   i Sklyanskii: Prikaz, No. 455. (Iz, (126), 21.VI.18; Iz(NKVD), (42),
            20.VI.18)

180618(3)   i Sklyanskii: Prikaz, No. 458. (Iz, (126), 21.VI.18; Iz(NKVD), (42),
            20.VI.18)

180618(4)   i Sklyanskii: Prikaz, No. 459. (Iz, (126), 21.VI.18; Iz(NKVD), (42),
            20.VI.18)

180618(5)   i Sklyanskii: Prikaz, No. 460. (Iz(NKVD), (42), 20.VI.18)
            Repr.: Iz, (130), 26.VI.18.

180618(6)   i Mekhonoshin: Prikaz, No. 461. (Iz(NKVD), (42), 20.VI.18)
            Repr.: Iz, (127), 22.VI.18.

180618(7)   i Yurenev: Prikaz, No. 462. (Iz(NKVD), (42), 20.VI.18)
            Repr.: Iz, (130), 26.VI.18.

180618(8)   i Mekhonoshin: Prikaz, No. 463. (Iz(NKVD), (42), 20.VI.18)
            Repr.: Iz, (127), 22.VI.18.

180618(9)   i Mekhonoshin: Prikaz, No. 464. (Iz, (127), 22.VI.18)

180618(10)   i Mekhonoshin: Prikaz, No. 465. ($\underline{Iz}$(NKVD), (42), 20.VI.18)
               $\underline{Repr.}$: $\underline{Iz}$, (131), 27.VI.18.

180618(11)   i Mekhonoshin: Prikaz, No. 466. ($\underline{Iz}$(NKVD), (42), 20.VI.18)
               $\underline{Repr.}$: $\underline{Iz}$, (131), 27.VI.18.

180618(12)   i Mekhonoshin: Prikaz, No. 468. ($\underline{Iz}$(NKVD), (42), 20.VI.18)
               $\underline{Repr.}$: $\underline{Iz}$(NKVD), (50), 29.VI.18.
               ⌊See ⌊180629(7)⌋.⌋

180620(1)   Pokazaniya pered Verkhovnym Revolyutsionnym Tribunalom. (Evidence to
               Supreme Revolutionary Tribunal.) (230000(7).I: 136-41)
               $\underline{Repr.}$: 260000(18).I: 322-9.
               $\underline{Trans.}$: Fr. 680000(1): 166-73;
                       Ger. 240000(40): 76-82.
               ⌊Trial of Shchastny. See also 180527.⌋

180620(2)   i Sklyanskii: Prikaz, No. 535. ($\underline{Iz}$(NKVD), (63), 14.VII.18)
               $\underline{Repr.}$: $\underline{Iz}$, (148), 16.VII.18.

180621   i Sklyanskii: Prikaz, No. 469. ($\underline{Iz}$(NKVD), (44), 22.VI.18)
               $\underline{Repr.}$: $\underline{Iz}$, (146), 13.VII.18.

⌊180622(1)⌋   K interventsii. O pripisannom emu. Zayavlenie. (On the intervention.
               On a note sent to him. A statement.) ($\underline{Iz}$, (127), 22.VI.18)
               $\underline{Repr.}$: 230000(7).I: 199-200; 260000(18).I: 499-500; Maksakov i
                       Turunov: 179-80.
               $\underline{Trans.}$: Am. p.q. Bunyan: 103;
                       Fr. 680000(1): 235-6.

180622(2)   i Mekhonoshin: Prikaz, No. 470. ($\underline{Iz}$(NKVD), (46), 25.VI.18)
               $\underline{Repr.}$: $\underline{Iz}$, (146), 13.VII.18.

180622(3)   i Mekhonoshin: Prikaz, No. 471. ($\underline{Iz}$(NKVD), (46), 25.VI.18)
               $\underline{Repr.}$: $\underline{Iz}$, (146), 13.VII.18.

180622(4)   i Mekhonoshin: Prikaz, No. 472. ($\underline{Iz}$(NKVD), (46), 25.VI.18)

180623(1)   i Sklyanskii: Prikaz, No. 518. ($\underline{Iz}$, (153), 21.VII.18)

180623(2)   i Sklyanskii: Prikaz, No. 520. ($\underline{Iz}$, (136), 3.VII.18)
               $\underline{Repr.}$: $\underline{Iz}$, (148), 16.VII.18.

180624(1) i dr.: Prikaz, No. 473. (Iz(NKVD), (48), 27.VI.18)
Repr.: Iz, (146), 13.VII.18.

180624(2) i dr.: Prikaz, No. 474. (Iz, (131), 27.VI.18; Iz(NKVD), (48), 27.VI.18)

180624(3) i Mekhonoshin: Prikaz, No. 475. (Iz(NKVD), (48), 27.VI.18)

180624(4) i Mekhonoshin: Prikaz, No. 476. (Iz, (132), 28.VI.18; Iz(NKVD), (48), 27.VI.18)

180624(5) i Mekhonoshin: Prikaz, No. 477. (Iz(NKVD), (49), 28.VI.18)

180624(6) i Sklyanskii: Prikaz, No. 521. (Iz, (136), 3.VII.18)
Repr.: Iz, (148), 16.VII.18.

180625(1) i Sklyanskii: Prikaz, No. 478. (Iz(NKVD), (49), 28.VI.18)
Repr.: Iz, (135), 2.VII.18.

180625(2) i dr.: Prikaz, No. 479. (Iz(NKVD), (49), 28.VI.18)
Repr.: Iz, (135), 2.VII.18.

180625(3) Prikaz, No. 481. (Iz, (132), 28.VI.18; Iz(NKVD), (49), 28.VI.18)
Repr.: Iz, (140), 7.VII.18.

180625(4) i Podvoiskii: Prikaz, No. 508. (Iz(NKVD), (51), 30.VI.18)
Repr.: Iz, (136/141), 3/8.VII.18.

180625(5) i Yurenev: Prikaz, No. 511. (Iz(NKVD), (51), 30.VI.18)

180625(6) i Mekhonoshin: Prikaz, No. 512. (Iz, (148), 16.VII.18)

180625(7) i Mekhonoshin: Prikaz, No. 480. (Iz(NKVD), (66), 18.VII.18)

180625(8) Lenin & T.: [Telegram to Yuriev.]
Trans.: Am. Strakhovsky: 58.

180626(1) Prikaz, No. 482. (Iz(NKVD), (49), 28.VI.18)
Repr.: Iz, (145), 12.VII.18.

180626(2) Doklad. (A report.) (Iz, (131), 27.VI.18; Pr, (129), 27.VI.18)
Repr.: 260000(18).I: 289-91; VPS, (5), 1918.
Trans.: Am. p.q. Bunyan: 270-1.
[To Sovnarkom; on use of bourgeoisie in Red Army.]

[180626(3)]   [Addendum to 180422(3).] (Iz(NKVD), (47), 26.VI.18)

180627(1)   i Yurenev: Prikaz, No. 483. (Iz(NKVD), (50), 29.VI.18)

180627(2)   i Yurenev: Prikaz, No. 484. (Iz(NKVD), (50), 29.VI.18)

180627(3)   i Yurenev: Prikaz, No. 485. (Iz(NKVD), (50), 29.VI.18)

180627(4)   i Yurenev: Prikaz, No. 486. (Iz(NKVD), (50), 29.VI.18)

180627(5)   i Yurenev: Prikaz, No. 487. (Iz(NKVD), (50), 29.VI.18)

180627(6)   i Yurenev: Prikaz, No. 488. (Iz(NKVD), (50), 29.VI.18)

180627(7)   i Yurenev: Prikaz, No. 489. (Iz(NKVD), (50), 29.VI.18)

180627(8)   i Yurenev: Prikaz, No. 490. (Iz(NKVD), (50), 29.VI.18)

180627(9)   i Yurenev: Prikaz, No. 491. (Iz(NKVD), (50), 29.VI.18)

180627(10)   i Yurenev: Prikaz, No. 492. (Iz(NKVD), (50), 29.VI.18)

180627(11)   i Yurenev: Prikaz, No. 493. (Iz(NKVD), (50), 29.VI.18)

180627(12)   i Yurenev: Prikaz, No. 494. (Iz(NKVD), (50), 29.VI.18)

180627(13)   i Yurenev: Prikaz, No. 495. (Iz(NKVD), (50), 29.VI.18)

180627(14)   i Yurenev: Prikaz, No. 496. (Iz(NKVD), (50), 29.VI.18)

180627(15)   i Yurenev: Prikaz, No. 497. (Iz(NKVD), (50), 29.VI.18)

180627(16)   i Yurenev: Prikaz, No. 498. (Iz(NKVD), (50), 29.VI.18)

180627(17)   i Yurenev: Prikaz, No. 499. (Iz(NKVD), (50), 29.VI.18)

180627(18)   i Yurenev: Prikaz, No. 500. (Iz(NKVD), (50), 29.VI.18)

180627(19)   i Yurenev: Prikaz, No. 501. (Iz(NKVD), (50), 29.VI.18)

180627(20)   i Yurenev: Prikaz, No. 502. (Iz(NKVD), (50), 29.VI.18)

180627(21)   i Yurenev: Prikaz, No. 503. (Iz(NKVD), (50), 29.VI.18)

180627(22)   i Yurenev: Prikaz, No. 504. (Iz(NKVD), (50), 29.VI.18)

180627(23)   i Yurenev: Prikaz, No. 505. (Iz(NKVD), (50), 29.VI.18)

180627(24)   i Yurenev: Prikaz, No. 506. (Iz(NKVD), (50), 29.VI.18)

180627(25)   i Yurenev: Prikaz, No. 507. (Iz(NKVD), (50), 29.VI.18)

180627(26)   i Yurenev: Prikaz, No. 508. (Iz(NKVD), (50), 29.VI.18)

180628   i dr.: Postanovlenie. (A regulation.) (Iz, (132), 28.VI.18)

180629(1)   Trudyashchiesya — v armiyu, parazity — na chernuyu rabotu. (Toilers, into the army; parasites, to hard labour.) (Iz, (134), 30.VI.18)
Repr.: 260000(18).I: 291-3.
Trans.: Am. p.q. Bunyan: 268-70.
[Speech to 4th All-Country Conference of factory committees; in Moscow.]

180629(2)   i dr.: Dekret, No. 1893. (Decree, No. 1893.) (Iz, (135), 2.VII.18; Iz(NKVD), (52), 2.VII.18)
[Call-up for necessarywar service.]

180629(3)   i dr.: Dekret, No. 1894. (Decree, No. 1894. (Iz, (135), 2.VII.18; Iz(NKVD), (53), 3.VII.18)
[Call-up for necessary war service.]

180629(4)   i dr.: Dekret, No. 1895. (Decree, No. 1895.) (Iz, (135), 2.VII.18)

180629(5)   i dr.: Dekret Soveta Narodnykh Komissarov. (Decree of the Sovnarkom.) (Iz, (135), 2.VII.18)

180629(6)   i Yurenev: Prikaz, No. 511. (Iz, (146), 13.VII.18)

[180629(7)]   i Mekhonoshin:[Addendum to 180618(12).] (Iz(NKVD), (150), 29.VI.18)

180630(1)   i Yurenev: Prikaz, No. 513. (Iz, (147), 14.VII.18)

180630(2)   i Yurenev: Prikaz, No. 514. (Iz, (147), 14.VII.18)

180630(3)   i Yurenev: Prikaz, No. 515. (Iz, (147), 14.VII.18)

180630(4)   i Yurenev: Prikaz, No. 516. (Iz(147), 14.VII.18)

180630(5)   i Yurenev: Prikaz, No. 517. (Iz, (147), 14.VII.18)

180630(6)   i Sklyanskii: Prikaz, No. 519. (Iz, (146), 13.VII.18)
Repr.: Iz, (148), 16.VII.18.

180701(1)   Prikaz, (<u>Iz</u>, (135), 2.VII.18; <u>Rannee Utro</u>, (121), 2.VII.18)

               <u>Repr</u>.: 230000(7).I: 201; 260000(18).I: 490; <u>Iz</u>, (148), 16.VII.18.
               <u>Trans</u>.: Am. Bunyan: 134-5;
                     Fr. 680000(1): 237.
               [On intervention.]

180701(2)   i Sklyanskii: Prikaz, No. 522. (<u>Iz</u>, (148), 16.VII.18)
               <u>Repr</u>.: <u>Iz</u>, (153), 21.VII.18.

180701(3)   O desante v Murmanske. (The landing in Murmansk.) (<u>Iz</u>, (137), 4.VII.18;
               <u>Rannee Utro</u>, (121), 2.VII.18)
               <u>Repr</u>.: 230000(7).I: 202-4; 260000(18).I: 490-4.
               <u>Trans</u>.: Am. p.q. Bunyan: 135; p.q. Strakhovsky: 33;
                     Fr. 680000(1): 237-41.

[180701(4)]   i Lenin: Dekret. (A decree.) (<u>Iz</u>, (135), 2.VII.18)
               <u>Trans</u>.: Am. Strakhovsky: 67.

180702   [Conversation with Yurenev.]
               <u>Trans</u>.: Am. p.q. Strakhovsky: 68.

180703(1)   i Sklyanskii: Prikaz, No. 523. (<u>Iz</u>, (148), 16.VII.18)

180703(2)   i Sklyanskii: Prikaz, No. 541. (<u>Iz</u>(NKVD), (66), 18.VII.18)

180704(1)   Pered myatezhom. (Faced with insurrection.) (<u>Iz</u>, (138), 5.VII.18)
               <u>Repr</u>.: 230000(7).I: 266-9; 260000(18).I: 437-41; V VS"EZDSOV: 20-3.
               <u>Trans</u>.: Eng. p.q. Deutscher, PA: 401;
                     Fr. 680000(1): 303-6.
               [Emergency statement to 5th Congress of Soviets.]

180704(2)   Zaklyuchitel´noe slovo. (Summary speech.) (<u>Iz</u>, (138), 5.VII.18)
               <u>Repr</u>.: 230000(7).I: 269-74; 260000(18).I: 441-7.
               <u>Trans</u>.: Fr. 680000(1): 306-13.
               [See 180704(1).]

180704(3)   Rezolyutsiya. (A resolution.) (230000(7).I: 274)
               <u>Repr</u>.: 260000(18).I: 447-8.
               <u>Trans</u>.: Fr. 680000(1): 313-4.
               [See 180704(1).]

180704(4)   i Sklyanskii: Prikaz, No. 613. (<u>Iz</u>, (165), 4.VIII.18)

180706(1)   i Sklyanskii: Prikaz, No. 524. (<u>Iz</u>(NKVD), (59), 10.VII.18)

180706(2)   i Sklyanskii: Prikaz, No. 525. (<u>Iz</u>(NKVD), (59), 10.VII.18)

180706(3)   i Sklyanskii: Prikaz, No. 526. (<u>Iz</u>(NKVD), (59), 10.VII.18)

180706(4)   i Sklyanskii: Prikaz, No. 527. (<u>Iz</u>(NKVD), (59), 10.VII.18)

[180707]   Ubiistvo grafa Mirbakha. (The assassination of Count Mirbach.)
(<u>Iz</u>, (140), 7.VII.18)
<u>Repr</u>.: 230000(7).I: 275; 260000(18).I: 448-9.
<u>Trans</u>.: Fr. 680000(1): 314-5.
[By Blyumkin.]

180708(1)   Prikaz. (<u>Iz</u>(NKVD), (61), 12.VII.18)
<u>Repr</u>.: 230000(7).I: 297.
<u>Trans</u>.: Fr. 680000(1): 341.

[180708(2)]   Likvidatsiya myatezha. (The liquidation of the insurrection.)
(<u>Iz</u>, (141), 8.VII.18; <u>Iz</u>(NKVD), (58), 9.VII.18)
<u>Repr</u>.: 230000(7).I: 298-9; 260000(18).I: 449-51.
<u>Trans</u>.: Fr. 680000(1): 342-4;
Ger. 240000(40): 83-5.
[Official communique.]

180708(3)   i Sklyanskii: Prikaz, No. 533. (<u>Iz</u>(NKVD), (63), 14.VII.18)

180709(1)   Myatezh. (The insurrection.) (<u>Iz</u>, (143), 10.VII.18; <u>NZh</u>, (135;350),
11.VII.18)
<u>Repr</u>.: 180000(14); 230000(7).I: 276-87; 260000(18).I: 451-65.
<u>Trans</u>.: Fr. 680000(1): 315-28.
[Report to 5th All-Russian Congress of Soviets after the quelling of
the insurrection of the Left SRs. See also [180708(2)].]

180709(2)   Zaklyuchitel'noe slovo. (Summary speech.) (<u>Iz</u>, (143), 10.VII.18)
<u>Repr</u>.: 180000(14); 230000(7).I: 287-95; 260000(18).I: 465-75.
<u>Trans</u>.: Fr. 680000(1): 328-38.
[See 180709(1).]

180709(3)   Primechanie. (Notes.) (230000(7).I: 295-6)
<u>Repr</u>.: 260000(18).I: 475-6.
<u>Trans</u>.: Fr. 680000(1): 338-41.

180710(1)   Sozdanie Rabochei i Krest´yanskoi Krasnoi Armii. (The creation of
the Workers and Peasants Red Army.) (Iz, (144), 11.VII.18)
Repr.: 180000(16); [180000(27)]; 230000(7).I: 303-17; 260000(18).I:
294-312; Iz(NKVD), (63), 14.VII.18.
Trans.: Fr. 680000(1): 347-64;
Ger. 200000(60); p.q. 240000(40): 86-101.
[Report to 5th Congress of Soviets.]

180710(2)   Rezolyutsiya. (A resolution.) (Pr, (142), 11.VII.18)
Repr.: 230000(7).I: 317-9; 260000(18).I: 312-5; Maksakov i Turunov:
209-12.
Trans.: Fr. 680000(1): 364-7.
[See 180710(1).]

180710(3)   i Podvoiskii: Prikaz, No. 530. (Iz, (145), 12.VII.18)
Repr.: Iz, (148), 16.VII.18.

180710(4)   i Sklyanskii: Prikaz, No. 531. (Iz, (148), 16.VII.18; Iz(NKVD), (63),
14.VII.18)
[Appointments.]

180711(1)   i Yurenev: Prikaz, No. 532. (Iz, (148), 16.VII.18; Iz(NKVD), (63),
14.VII.18)

180711(2)   i Sklyanskii: Prikaz, No. 536. (Iz(NKVD), (63), 14.VII.18)

180711(3)   i Sklyanskii: Prikaz, No. 558. (Iz(NKVD), (68), 20.VII.18)
Repr.: 180723(14); Iz, (154), 23.VII.18.

[180712(1)]   i Lenin: Obrashchenie Sovnarkom. (An appeal of the Sovnarkom.)
(Iz, (145), 12.VII.18)
Repr.: 260000(18).I: 483-6.
[On Czechoslovaks.]

[180712(2)]   i Lenin:Ob izmene Murav´eva. (Muraviev's treachery.) (Iz, (145),
12.VII.18; Krasnaya Gazeta, (115), 12.VII.18)
Repr.: 260000(18).I: 487; Iz(Pet), (50), 17.VII.18.
Trans.: Am. Bunyan: 224-5.

180712(3)   i Sklyanskii: Prikaz, No. 537. (Iz, (148), 16.VII.18; Iz(NKVD), (63),
14.VII.18)
Repr.: Iz, (153), 21.VII.18.

180712(4)	i Sklyanskii: Prikaz, No. 538. (Iz, (148), 16.VII.18; Iz(NKVD), (63), 14.VII.18)
180712(5)	i Sklyanskii: Prikaz, No. 539. (Iz(NKVD), (63), 14.VII.18) Repr.: Iz, (153), 21.VII.18.
180712(6)	i Sklyanskii: Prikaz, No. 540. (Iz(NKVD), (63), 14.VII.18) Repr.: Iz, (153), 21.VII.18.
180715(1)	i Sklyanskii: Prikaz, No. 541. (Iz, (150), 18.VII.18; Iz(NKVD), (66), 18.VII.18)
180715(2)	Prikaz, No. 561. (230000(7).I: 300) Trans.: Fr. 680000(1): 344-5.
180716(1)	Krupnaya pobeda na Tsaritsinskom napravlenii. (A great victory in the Tsaritsyn area.) (Iz, (148), 16.VII.18) [Telegram to Kikvidze Division.]
180716(2)	Prikaz, No. 543. (Iz, (151), 19.VII.18; Iz(NKVD), (67), 19.VII.18)
180716(3)	i Sklyanskii: Prikaz, No. 544. (Iz, (153), 21.VII.18; Iz(NKVD), (67), 19.VII.18)
180716(4)	i Sklyanskii: Prikaz, No. 545. (Iz, (153), 21.VII.18; Iz(NKVD), (67), 19.VII.18)
180716(5)	K russkom izdaniyu. (For the Russian edition.) (240000(32).II: 255-6) [2nd Preface , ISTORIYA OKTYABR´SKOI REVOLYUTSII (HISTORY OF THE OCTOBER REVOLUTION), 180000(5).]
180716(6)	Prikaz, No. 547. (Iz(NKVD), (67), 19.VII.18)
[180717(1)]	Prikaz. (Iz, (149), 17.VII.18; Iz(NKVD), (66), 18.VII.18) Repr.: 230000(7).I: 205. Trans.: Fr. 680000(1): 241. [On intervention.]
180717(2)	Prikaz, No. 546. (Iz, (149), 17.VII.18; Iz(NKVD), (67), 19.VII.18)
[180717(3)]	Prikaz. (Iz, (149), 17.VII.18) Repr.: 230000(7).I: 142; 260000(18).I: 329-30. Trans.: Fr. 680000(1): 174-5.

180717(4)   i Yurenev: Prikaz, No. 548. (<u>Iz</u>, (153), 21.VII.18; <u>Iz</u>(NKVD), (67), 19.VII.18)

180717(5)   i Yurenev: Prikaz, No. 549. (<u>Iz</u>(NKVD), (68), 20.VII.18)
<u>Repr</u>.: <u>Iz</u>, (154), 23.VII.18.

180717(6)   i Yurenev: Prikaz, No. 550. (<u>Iz</u>(NKVD), (68), 20.VII.18)
<u>Repr</u>.: <u>Iz</u>, (154), 23.VII.18.

180717(7)   i Yurenev: Prikaz, No. 551. (<u>Iz</u>(NKVD), (68), 20.VII.18)
<u>Repr</u>.: <u>Iz</u>, (154), 23.VII.18.

180717(8)   i Yurenev: Prikaz, No. 552. (<u>Iz</u>(NKVD), (68), 20.VII.18)
<u>Repr</u>.: <u>Iz</u>, (154), 23.VII.18.

180717(9)   i Yurenev: Prikaz, No. 553. (<u>Iz</u>(NKVD), (68), 20.VII.18)
<u>Repr</u>.: <u>Iz</u>, (154), 23.VII.18.

180717(10)   i Yurenev: Prikaz, No. 554. (<u>Iz</u>(NKVD), (68), 20.VII.18)
<u>Repr</u>.: <u>Iz</u>, (154), 23.VII.18.

180717(11)   i Yurenev: Prikaz, No. 555. (<u>Iz</u>(NKVD), (68), 20.VII.18)
<u>Repr</u>.: <u>Iz</u>, (154), 23.VII.18.

180717(12)   Prikaz, No. 556. (<u>Iz</u>(NKVD), (68), 20.VII.18)
<u>Repr</u>.: <u>Iz</u>, (154), 23.VII.18.

180717(13)   i Sklyanskii: Prikaz, No. 557. (<u>Iz</u>(NKVD), (68), 20.VII.18)
<u>Repr</u>.: 180723(14); <u>Iz</u>, (154), 23.VII.18.

180717(14)   i Sklyanskii: Prikaz, No. 576. (<u>Iz</u>(NKVD), (72), 25.VII.18)
<u>Repr</u>.: <u>Iz</u>, (160), 30.VII.18.

180717(15)   i Sklyanskii: Prikaz, No. 595. (<u>Iz</u>(NKVD), (78), 1.VIII.18)

180718(1)   i Sklyanskii: Prikaz, No. 559. (<u>Iz</u>(NKVD), (68), 20.VII.18)
<u>Repr</u>.: 180723(14); <u>Iz</u>, (154), 23.VII.18.

180718(2)   i Sklyanskii: Prikaz, No. 560. (<u>Iz</u>(NKVD), (68), 20.VII.18)
<u>Repr</u>.: <u>Iz</u>, (154), 23.VII.18.

180718(3)   i Antonov: Prikaz, No. 565. (<u>Iz</u>, (157), 26.VII.18; <u>Iz</u>(NKVD), (71), 24.VII.18)

[180718(4)]   Prikaz. (<u>Iz</u>(NKVD), (66), 18.VII.18)

[180718(5)]   Prikaz, (<u>Iz</u>(NKVD), (66), 18.VII.18)

180718(6)   i Antonov: Prikaz, No. 566. (<u>Iz</u>(NKVD), (71), 24.VII.18)

180718(7)   i Antonov: Prikaz, No. 567. (<u>Iz</u>(NKVD), (71), 24.VII.18)

180719(1)   Prikaz, No. 562. (<u>Iz</u>, (154), 23.VII.18; <u>Iz</u>(NKVD), (70), 23.VII.18)

180719(2)   Prikaz, No. 563. (<u>Iz</u>, (154), 23.VII.18 ; <u>Iz</u>(NKVD), (70), 23.VII.18)

180719(3)   Prikaz, No. 564. (<u>Iz</u>, (153), 21.VII.18; <u>Iz</u>(NKVD), (70), 23.VII.18)

180719(4)   i Sklyanskii: Prikaz, No. 583. (<u>Iz</u>(NKVD), (74), 27.VII.18)
                        <u>Repr</u>.: Iz, (164), 3.VIII.18.

180720(1)   Prikaz, No. 568. (<u>Iz</u>, (157), 26.VII.18; <u>Iz</u>(NKVD), (71), 24.VII.18)

180720(2)   i Sklyanskii: Prikaz, No. 569. (<u>Iz</u>, (157), 26.VII.18; <u>Iz</u>(NKVD), (71), 24.VII.18)

[180721]   i Yurenev: Prikaz, No. 517. (<u>Iz</u>, (153), 21.VII.18)

180722(1)   i Sklyanskii: Po lichnomu sostavu. (For Staff personnel.) (<u>Iz</u>, (157), 26.VII.18; <u>Iz</u>(NKVD), (71), 24.VII.18)

180722(2)   i Sklyanskii: Prikaz, No. 571. (<u>Iz</u>(NKVD), (72), 25.VII.18)
                        <u>Repr</u>.: Iz, (164), 3.VIII.18.

180722(3)   Prikaz. (<u>Iz</u>, (154), 23.VII.18; <u>Iz</u>(NKVD), (71), 24.VII.18; <u>Iz</u>(VTsIK), (154), 23.VII.18)
                        <u>Repr</u>.: 230000(7).I: 206.
                        <u>Trans</u>.: Fr. 680000(1): 242.

180722(4)   i Sklyanskii: Prikaz, No. 572. (<u>Iz</u>(NKVD), (71), 24.VII.18)

180722(5)   No. 1. Po lichnomu sostavu. (No. 1. For Staff personnel.) (<u>Iz</u>(NKVD), (76), 30.VII.18)

[180723(1)]   Ofitserskii vopros. (The officer question.) (<u>Iz</u>, (154), 23.VII.18; <u>Iz</u>(NKVD), (70), 23.VII.18)
                        <u>Repr</u>.: 230000(7).I: 143-5; 260000(18).I: 330-4.
                        <u>Trans</u>.: Fr. 680000(1): 175-8;
                                    Ger. 240000(40): 64-7.

180723(2) Predosterezhenie. (A warning.) (Iz, (155), 24.VII.18; Iz(NKVD), (72), 25.VII.18)
Repr.: 230000(7).I: 207; Iz, (156), 25.VII.18.
Trans.: Fr. 680000(1): 242-3; Lévy: 142-3.
[On intervention.]

180723(4) Prikaz, No. 573. (Iz, (156), 25.VII.18; Iz(NKVD), (72), 25.VII.18)

180723(5) Prikaz, No. 574. (Iz, (156), 25.VII.18; Iz(NKVD), (72), 25.VII.18)

180723(6) Prikaz, No. 575. (Iz(NKVD), (72), 25.VII.18)
Repr.: Iz, (164), 3.VIII.18.

180723(7) i Sklyanskii: Prikaz, No. 577. (Iz(NKVD), (72), 25.VII.18)
Repr.: Iz, (163), 2.VIII.18.

180723(8) i Sklyanskii: Prikaz, No. 578. (Iz(NKVD), (72), 25.VII.18)
Repr.: Iz, (164), 3.VIII.18.

180723(9) i Sklyanskii: Prikaz, No. 579. (Iz, (157), 26.VII.18; Iz(NKVD), (72), 25.VII.18)
Repr.: Iz, (164), 3.VIII.18.

180723(10) i Sklyanskii: Prikaz, No. 580. (Iz(NKVD), (72), 25.VII.18)
Repr.: Iz, (164), 3.VIII.18.

180723(11) i Sklyanskii: Prikaz, No. 584. (Iz, (160), 30.VII.18; Iz(NKVD), (75), 28.VII.18)

180723(12) i Potapov: Naznachayutsya, No. 2. (Appointments; No. 2) (Iz(NKVD), (76), 30.VII.18)
Repr.: Iz, (164), 3.VIII.18.

180723(13) K revolyutsionnym moryakam. (To the revolutionary sailors.) (Pr, (152), 23.VII.18)
Trans.: Am. Bunyan: 194.
[Suppression of Yaroslavl revolt.]

180723(14) i dr.: Prikaz, No. 338. (Iz(NKVD), (73), 26.VII.18)
[Includes 180711(3), 180717(13), 180718(1).]

180723(15) i Sklyanskii: Prikaz, No. 585. (Iz(NKVD), (76), 30.VII.18)

180724(1)   T.: Posledniya sudorogi soglashatel´stva. (The last convulsions of conciliationism.) (Iz, (155), 24.VII.18)

180724(2)   Prikaz, No. 581. (Iz(NKVD), (72), 25.VII.18)
Repr.: Iz, (164), 3.VIII.18.

180724(3)   i Sklyanskii: Prikaz, No. 582. (Iz, (164), 3.VIII.18)

180724(4)   i Sklyanskii: Prikaz, No. 592. (Iz, (160), 30.VII.18; Iz(NKVD), (76), 30.VII.18)

180725   Prikaz. (Iz, (158), 27.VII.18)

180726(1)   Prikaz, No. 546. (Iz, (157), 26.VII.18)

[180726(2)]   i Antonov: Prikaz, No. 566. (Iz, (157), 26.VII.18)

[180726(3)]   i Antonov: Prikaz, No. 567. (Iz, (157), 26.VII.18)

180726(4)   i Sklyanskii: Prikaz, No. 570. (Iz, (157), 26.VII.18)

[180726(5)]   i Sklyanskii: Prikaz, No. 571. (Iz, (157), 26.VII.18)

180727(1)   i dr.: Dekret Soveta Narodnykh Komissarov. (Decree of the Sovnarkom.) (Iz, (160), 30.VII.18; Iz(NKVD), (77), 31.VII.18)

180727(2)   i Yurenev: Prikaz, No. 586. (Iz, (160), 30.VII.18; Iz(NKVD), (76), 30.VII.18)

180727(3)   i Yurenev: Prikaz, No. 587. (Iz(NKVD), (76), 30.VII.18)

180727(4)   i Yurenev: Prikaz, No. 588. (Iz(NKVD), (76), 30.VII.18)

180727(5)   i Yurenev: Prikaz, No. 589. (Iz(NKVD), (76), 30.VII.18)

180727(6)   i Yurenev: Prikaz, No. 590. (Iz(NKVD), (76), 30.VII.18)

180727(7)   i Yurenev: Prikaz, No. 591. (Iz(NKVD), (76), 30.VII.18)

180727(8)   i Sklyanskii: Prikaz, No. 593. (Iz(NKVD), (77), 31.VII.18)
Repr.: Iz, (164), 3.VIII.18.

180727(9)   i Sklyanskii: Po lichnomu sostavu. (For Staff personnel.) (Iz(NKVD), (77), 31.VII.18)
Repr.: Iz, (164), 3.VIII.18.
[No. 3.]

172

180727(10) i Potapov: Po lichnomu sostavu, No. 4. (For Staff personnel; No. 4)
(Iz, (165), 4.VIII.18; Iz(NKVD), (80), 3.VIII.18)

180729(1) Sotsialisticheskoe otechestvo v opasnosti. (The socialist fatherland
is in danger.) (230000(7).I: 219-29)
Repr.: 260000(18).I: 502-14; SOEDINENNOE: 15-23.
Trans.: Eng. p.q. Footman: 147;
        Fr. 680000(1): 255-67;
        Ger. 240000(40): 107-18.
[Report to Extraordinary Joint-session of All-Russian CEC of Soviets
(5th Convention) together with Moscow Soviet, trade union and works
committees representatives.]

180729(2) Rezolyutsiya. (A resolution.) (Pr, (158), 30.VII.18)
Repr.: 230000(7).I: 229; 260000(18).I: 514-5; Maksakov i Turunov:
       212-3.
Trans.: Fr. 680000(1): 267-8;
        Ger. 240000(40): 118-9.
[See 180729(1).]

180729(3) i Sklyanskii: Prikaz, No. 615. (Iz, (168), 8.VIII.18; Iz(NKVD), (82),
6.VIII.18)

180729(4) i Sklyanskii: Prikaz, No. 596. (Iz(NKVD), (78), 1.VIII.18)

180729(5) i Sklyanskii: Prikaz, No. 597. (Iz(NKVD), (78), 1.VIII.18)

180729(6) i Sklyanskii: Prikaz, No. 598. (Iz(NKVD), (78), 1.VIII.18)

180729(7) i Sklyanskii: Prikaz, No. 599. (Iz(NKVD), (78), 1.VIII.18)

[180730(1)] Prikaz. (Iz, (160), 30.VII.18)

[180730(2)] i Sklyanskii: Prikaz, No. 585. (Iz, (160), 30.VII.18)

[180730(3)] i Antonov: Ob uchrezhdenii prifrontovykh mestnykh sudov. (Setting up
front-line local courts.) (Iz, (160), 30.VII.18)

[180730(4)] i Antonov: Rotnye tovarishcheskie sudy. (Comrade-courts at Company
level.) (Iz, (160), 30.VII.18; Iz(NKVD), (76), 30.VII.18)

[180730(5)] i Yurenev: Prikaz, No. 587. (Iz, (160), 30.VII.18)

[180730(6)]   i Yurenev: Prikaz, No. 588. (<u>Iz</u>, (160), 30.VII.18)

[180730(7)]   i Yurenev: Prikaz, No. 589. (<u>Iz</u>, (160), 30.VII.18)

[180730(8)]   i Yurenev: Prikaz, No. 590. (<u>Iz</u>, (160), 30.VII.18)

[180730(9)]   i Yurenev: Prikaz, No. 591. (<u>Iz</u>, (160), 30.VII.18)

180730(10)   i Sklyanskii: Prikaz, No. 603. (<u>Iz</u>, (165), 4.VIII.18)

180730(11)   Manifestatsiya b. gen. Novitskogo. (Ex-general Novitsky's demonstration.) (230000(7).I: 146)
     <u>Repr.</u>: 260000(18).I: 334-5.
     <u>Trans</u>.: Fr. 680000(1): 179.
     [Letter to Commandant, General Staff Academy.]

[180731]   Prikaz. (<u>Iz</u>(NKVD), (77), 31.VII.18)

180800   [Telegram.] (640000(1): 70)
     <u>Trans</u>.: Eng. 640000(1): 71.
     [On mobilization.]

180801(1)   i dr.: K trudyashchimsya massam Frantsii, Anglii, Ameriki, Italii i Yaponii. (To the toiling masses of France, Britain, America, Italy and Japan.) (MIROVAYA BOINYA)
     <u>Trans</u>.: Am. p.q. [180000(53)]: 428-9;
           Eng. Barbusse: 41-6; Degras, SOVDOC.I: 88-92;
           Fr. 180000(31);
           Ger. ALMANACH: 223-8;
           Hun. *[190000(78)];
           Swed. <u>Pol</u>(S), (III.186), 13.VIII.18.
     [Against intervention.]

[180801(2)]   Postanovlenie. (A regulation.) (<u>Iz</u>(NKVD), (78), 1.VIII.18)

180802(1)   i dr.: Dekret Soveta Narodnykh Komissarov. (Decree of the Sovnarkom.) (<u>Iz</u>, (164), 3.VIII.18)
     <u>Repr.</u>: 230000(7).I: 175; 260000(18).I: 706-7.
     <u>Trans</u>.: Fr. 680000(1): 208-9.
     [Call-up of persons who had served as NCOs in the war.]

180802(2)   i Sklyanskii: Prikaz, No. 604. (<u>Iz</u>(NKVD), (82), 6.VIII.18)

180802(3)   i Antonov: Prikaz, No. 605. (Iz, (165), 4.VIII.18; Iz(NKVD), (82),
                 6.VIII.18)
                 Repr.: Iz(166/168), 6/8.VIII.18.

180802(4)   i Sklyanskii: Prikaz, No. 609. (Iz, (165), 4.VIII.18; Iz(NKVD), (82),
                 6.VIII.18)

180802(5)   Alternative for 180803(2).

180803(1)   Prikaz. (Iz, (165), 4.VIII.18; Iz(NKVD), (82), 6.VIII.18)
                 Repr.: 230000(7).I: 174; 260000(18).I: 339-40; Iz, (166), 6.VIII.18.
                 Trans.: Am. p.q. Bunyan: 273;
                          Fr. 680000(1): 207-8.
                 [NCOs! The country calls you!]

180803(2)   i Sklyanskii: Polozhenie ob uchebo-instruktorskikh batalonakh.
                 (Regulation on training battalions.) (Iz, (165), 4.VIII.18; Iz(NKVD),
                 (82), 6.VIII.18)

180803(3)   i Sklyanskii: Prikaz, No. 604. (Iz, (165), 4.VIII.18)

180803(4)   i Sklyanskii: Prikaz, No. 606. (Iz, (195), 10.IX.18)

180803(5)   i Sklyanskii: Prikaz, No. 608. (Iz, (165), 4.VIII.18; Iz(NKVD), (82),
                 6.VIII.18)

180803(6)   i Sklyanskii: Prikaz, No. 610. (Iz, (165), 4.VIII.18; Iz(NKVD), (82),
                 6.VIII.18)

180803(7)   i Sklyanskii: Prikaz, No. 611. (Iz, (165), 4.VIII.18; Iz(NKVD), (82),
                 6.VIII.18)

180803(8)   i Sklyanskii: Prikaz, No. 612. (Iz(NKVD), (83), 7.VIII.18)

180804(1)   Prikaz, No. 607. (Iz, (165), 4.VIII.18; Iz(NKVD), (82), 6.VIII.18)

[180804(2)]   i dr.: Postanovlenie Soveta Narodnykh Komissarov. (A regulation of
                 the Sovnarkom.) (Iz, (165), 4.VIII.18)

[180804(3)]   Prikaz. (Iz, (165), 4.VIII.18)
                 [On railway saboteurs.]

[180804(4)]   Prikaz. (Iz, (165), 4.VIII.18)

[180804(6)]   Prikaz. (Iz, (165), 4.VIII.18)

180804(7)   i Sklyanskii: Prikaz, No. 613. (Iz(NKVD), (82), 6.VIII.18)

180804(8)   Prikaz, No. 614. (Iz, (165), 4.VIII.18; Iz(NKVD), (82), 6.VIII.18)
                   Repr.: Iz, (168), 8.VIII.18.

180805(1)   Prikaz, No. 616. (Iz, (165), 4.VIII.18; Iz(NKVD), (82), 6.VIII.18)

180805(2)   Prikaz, No. 617. (Iz, (168), 8.VIII.18; Iz(NKVD), (82), 6.VIII.18)

180805(3)   i Sklyanskii: Prikaz, No. 618. (Iz(NKVD), (82), 6.VIII.18)

180805(4)   i Sklyanskii: Prikaz, No. 619. (Iz, (167), 7.VIII.18; Iz(NKVD), (83),
                   7.VIII.18)

180805(5)   i Sklyanskii: Prikaz, No. 620. (Iz, (168), 8.VIII.18; Iz(NKVD), (83),
                   7.VIII.18)

180805(6)   i Antonov: Prikaz, No. 621. (Iz, (168), 8.VIII.18; Iz(NKVD), (83),
                   7.VIII.18)

180805(7)   i Sklyanskii: Prikaz, No. 622. (Iz, (168), 8.VIII.18; Iz(NKVD), (83),
                   7.VIII.18)

180805(8)   Prikaz, No. 623. (Iz(NKVD), (83), 7.VIII.18)

180805(9)   i Sklyanskii: Prikaz, No. 624. (Iz, (167), 7.VIII.18; Iz(NKVD), (83),
                   7.VIII.18)

180805(10)   Prikaz, No. 625. (Iz(NKVD), (83), 7.VIII.18)

180805(11)   i Sklyanskii: Prikaz, No. 639. (Iz(NKVD), (85), 9.VIII.18)
                   Repr.: Iz, (172), 13.VIII.18.

180806(1)   Prikaz, No. 626. (Iz(NKVD), (83), 7.VIII.18)

180806(2)   i Yurenev: Prikaz, No. 627. (Iz(NKVD), (85), 9.VIII.18)

180806(3)   Prikaz, No. 628. (Iz(NKVD), (85), 9.VIII.18)
                   Repr.: Iz, (176), 17.VIII.18.

180806(4)   [Telegram.] (640000(1): 64)
                   Trans.: Eng. 640000(1): 65.
                   [To Lenin; on Natsaremus.]

180806(5)   Prikaz. (Iz(NKVD), (82), 6.VIII.18; Iz(TsIK), (166), 6.VIII.18)

Repr.: 230000(7).I: 208.

Trans.: Eng. p.q. Deutscher, PA: 414, 419;

Fr. 680000(1): 243-4.

[To Kedrov, People's Commissar for War. Issued at Vologda.]

180806(6)   i Yurenev: Prikaz, No. 629. (Iz(NKVD), (85), 9.VIII.18)

180806(7)   i Yurenev: Prikaz, No. 630. (Iz, (170), 10.VIII.18; Iz(NKVD), (85), 9.VIII.18)

180806(8)   i Yurenev: Prikaz, No. 631. (Iz, (170), 10.VIII.18; Iz(NKVD), (85), 9.VIII.18)

180806(9)   i Yurenev: Prikaz, No. 632. (Iz(NKVD), (85), 9.VIII.18)

180806(10)   i Yurenev: Prikaz, No. 633. (Iz(NKVD), (85), 9.VIII.18)

180806(11)   i Yurenev: Prikaz, No. 634. (Iz(NKVD), (85), 9.VIII.18)

180806(12)   i Yurenev: Prikaz, No. 635. (Iz(NKVD), (85), 9.VIII.18)

180806(13)   i Yurenev: Prikaz, No. 636. (Iz(NKVD), (85), 9.VIII.18)

180806(14)   i Yurenev: Prikaz, No. 637. (Iz(NKVD), (85), 9.VIII.18)

180806(15)   i Yurenev: Prikaz, No. 638. (Iz(NKVD), (85), 9.VIII.18)

[180807(1)]   Kleveta na tov. Okulova, Pashina i drugikh. (A slander against cdes. Okulov, Pashin and others.) (Iz, (167), 7.VIII.18; Iz(NKVD), (83), 7.VIII.18)

180807(2)   i Sklyanskii: Prikaz, No. 640. (Iz(NKVD), (85), 9.VIII.18)

180807(3)   i Sklyanskii: Prikaz, No. 641. (Iz, (170), 10.VIII.18; Iz(NKVD), (85), 9.VIII.18)

180807(4)   Prikaz, No. 1. (Iz, (172), 13.VIII.18)

180807(5)   Prikaz, No. 2. (Iz, (172), 13.VIII.18)

180807(6)   Prikaz, No. 3. (Iz, (172), 13.VIII.18)

180807(7)   Prikaz, No. 8. (Iz, (172), 13.VIII.18)

180807(8)   Prikaz, No. 642. (Iz(NKVD), (85), 9.VIII.18)
             Repr.: Iz, (172), 13.VIII.18.

180807(9)   i Sklyanskii: Prikaz, No. 643. (Iz(NKVD), (85), 9.VIII.18)
             Repr.: Iz, (172), 13.VIII.18.

180807(10)   i Sklyanskii: Prikaz, No. 647. (Iz, (172), 13.VIII.18)

180807(11)   i Sklyanskii: Prikaz, No. 653. (Iz(NKVD), (86), 10.VIII.18)
             Repr.: Iz, (175), 16.VIII.18.

180807(12)   No. 5. Po lichnomu sostavu. (No. 5. For Staff personnel.)
             (Iz(NKVD), (84), 8.VIII.18)

[180808(1)] i Sklyanskii: Prikaz. (Iz, (168), 8.VIII.18)

[180808(2)] i Sklyanskii: Prikaz. (Iz, (168), 8.VIII.18)

180808(3)   i Enukidze: Prikaz, No. 645. (Iz(NKVD), (85), 9.VIII.18)
             Repr.: Iz, (172), 13.VIII.18.

180808(4)   i Enukidze: Prikaz, No. 646. (Iz(NKVD), (85), 9.VIII.18)
             Repr.: Iz, (172), 13.VIII.18.

180808(5)   i Enukidze: Prikaz, No. 647. (Iz(NKVD), (85), 9.VIII.18)
             Repr.: Iz, (176), 17.VIII.18.

180808(6)   i Enukidze: Prikaz, No. 648. (Iz(NKVD), (85), 9.VIII.18)
             Repr.: Iz, (176), 17.VIII.18.

180808(7)   i Enukidze: Prikaz, No. 649. (Iz(NKVD), (85), 9.VIII.18)
             Repr.: Iz, (176), 17.VIII.18.

180808(8)   i Enukidze: Prikaz, No. 650. (Iz(NKVD), (85), 9.VIII.18)
             Repr.: Iz, (176), 17.VIII.18.

180808(9)   i Enukidze: Prikaz, No. 663. (Iz(NKVD), (90), 15.VIII.18)
             Repr.: Iz, (178), 20.VIII.18.

180808(10)   Prikaz. (Iz, (171), 11.VIII.18; Krasnaya Gazeta, (166), 13.VIII.18)
             Repr.: 230000(7).I: 232-3; Iz(Pet), (59), 17.VIII.18.
             Trans.: Eng. p.q. Deutscher, PA: 419;
                     Fr. 680000(1): 271-2.
             [To all, to all, to all. The struggle against the Czech White Guards
             has gone on too long.]

180809(1)   Prikaz, No. 686/11. (Iz, (176), 17.VIII.18; Iz(NKVD), (90), 15.VIII.18)
                 Repr.: 640000(1): 72.
                 Trans.: Eng. 640000(1): 73.

180809(2)   Prikaz, No. 688/11. (Iz, (174), 15.VIII.18)

180809(3)   [Telegram.] (640000(1): 68)
                 Trans.: Eng. 640000(1): 69.
                 [On transport of reinforcements.]

180810(1)   Prikaz po Armii i Flotu. (Order of the Day for the Army and Fleet.)
                 (Iz, (172), 13.VIII.18)

180810(2)   Prikaz po Krasnomu Armii i Voennomu Flotu. (Order of the Day for the
                 Red Army and Navy.) (Iz, (172), 13.VIII.18)

180810(3)   No. 7. Po lichnomu sostavu. (No. 7. For Staff personnel.)
                 (Iz(NKVD), (87), 11.VIII.18)
                 Repr.: Iz(NKVD), (95/96), 22/23.VIII.18.

180811(1)   Prikaz, No. 21. (230000(7).I: 150)
                 Trans.: Fr. 680000(1): 182.

180811(2)   Prikaz. (Iz, (172), 13.VIII.18)

180812(1)   Prikaz. (Iz, (178), 20.VIII.18)

180812(2)   [Telegram.] (640000(1): 74)
                 Trans.: Eng. 640000(1): 75.
                 [To Lenin; on Yudin's death.]

180813(1)   Latyshskii Zemgal'skii polk. (The Lettish Zemgale Regiment.)
                 (230000(7).I: 234)
                 Trans.: Fr. 680000(1): 273-4.

180813(2)   Leninu. (To Lenin.) (260000(18).I: 728-9)
                 Repr.: p.q. 300000(1): Ch. XXXVI; 640000(1): 78.
                 Trans.: p.q. 300000(1): Ch. XXXVI;
                           Eng. 640000(1): 79.
                 [From Sviyansk; on civil war.]

[180813(3)]   Vsem okruzhnym, gubernskim, uezdnym, volostnym komissariatam, shtabam,
                 otryadam. (To all military area, provincial, country and rural
                 commissariats, staffs and detachments.) (Iz(NKVD), (88), 13.VIII.18)

[180814(1)]   Prikaz, No. 18. (<u>Iz</u>, (173), 14.VIII.18)
        Repr.: 230000(7).I: 235; 260000(18).II: 569-70; p.q. 300000(1):
              Ch. XXXIII.
        Trans.: p.q. 300000(1): Ch. XXXIII;
              Fr. 680000(1): 274-5;
              Ger. 240000(40): 122.
        [On unauthorized retreats. Texts in repr. differ slightly among
        themselves.]

180814(2)   Gospoda chekho-slovatskoi Rossii. (The gentry of Czecho-Slovak
        Russia.) (<u>Iz</u>, (178), 20.VIII.18)
        Repr.: 230000(7).I: 230-1; 260000(18).I: 487-9.
        Trans.: Fr. 680000(1): 268-70;
              Ger. 240000(40): 120-1.

180814(3)   Iz shtaba vostochnogo fronta. (From HQ Western Front.) (<u>Iz</u>, (176),
        17.VIII.18)

180814(4)   [To Lenin.] (640000(1): 78)
        Trans.: Eng. 640000(1): 79.
        [Telegram; on reinforcements.]

180815(1)   O sodeistvuyushchikh chekho-belogvardeitsam. (On those who help the
        Czech White Guards.) (230000(7).I: 236)
        Trans.: Fr. 680000(1): 275.

180815(2)   Leninu. (To Lenin.) (260000(18).I: 729)
        Repr.: 640000(1): 80.
        Trans.: Eng. 640000(1): 81.
        [On civil war. T34.]

[180817(1)]   i Yurenev: Prikaz, No. 629. (<u>Iz</u>, (176), 17.VIII.18)

[180817(2)]   i Yurenev: Prikaz, No. 630. (<u>Iz</u>, (176), 17.VIII.18)

[180817(3)]   i Yurenev: Prikaz, No. 631. (<u>Iz</u>, (176), 17.VIII.18)

[180817(4)]   i Yurenev: Prikaz, No. 632. (<u>Iz</u>, (176), 17.VIII.18)

[180817(5)]   i Yurenev: Prikaz, No. 633. (<u>Iz</u>, (176), 17.VIII.18)

[180817(6)]   i Yurenev: Prikaz, No. 634. (<u>Iz</u>, (176), 17.VIII.18)

[180817(7)]   i Yurenev: Prikaz, No. 635. (<u>Iz</u>, (176), 17.VIII.18)

[180817(8)]   i Yurenev: Prikaz, N$_0$. 636. (<u>Iz</u>, (176), 17.VIII.18)

[180817(9)]   i Yurenev: Prikaz, No. 637. (<u>Iz</u>, (176), 17.VIII.18)

[180817(10)]   i Yurenev: Prikaz, No. 638. (<u>Iz</u>, (176), 17.VIII.18)

[180817(11)]   [To Lenin.] (640000(1): 86)
               <u>Trans</u>.: Eng. 640000(1): 87.

180817(12)   [Telegram.] (640000(1): 86)
               <u>Trans</u>.: Eng. 640000(1): 87.
               [On military organization.]

180819   Tovarishchi moryaki Volzhskoi flotilli! (Comrade-sailors of the
               Volga flotilla!) (230000(7).I: 237-8)
               <u>Trans</u>.: Fr. 680000(1): 275-7;
                        Ger. 240000(40): 129-30.

180821(1)   [To Lenin.] (640000(1): 98)
               <u>Trans</u>.: Eng. 640000(1): 99.

180821(2)   [To Bonch-Bruevich.] (640000(1): 100)
               <u>Trans</u>.: Eng. 640000(1): 101.

180821(3)   [To Lenin.] (640000(1): 100)
               <u>Trans</u>.: Eng. 640000(1): 101.
               [On Kazan.]

180822   Amerikanskaya lozh. (An American lie.) (<u>Iz</u>, (181), 23.VIII.18;
               Iz(NKVD), (97), 24.VIII.18)
               <u>Repr</u>.: 230000(7).I: 209; 260000(18).I: 500-1; Maksakov i Turunov:
                        167-8.
               <u>Trans</u>.: Am. Cumming & Pettit: 249-50;
                        Eng. Degras, SOVDOC.I: 95;
                        Fr. 680000(1): 244-5.

180823(1)   [To Lenin.]
               <u>Trans</u>.: p.q. 410000(1): Ch. IX.
               [On officers.]

180823(2)   [Telegram.] (640000(1): 104)
               <u>Trans</u>.: Eng. 640000(1): 105.
               [On Bonch-Bruevich.]

180823(3)   [To Lenin.] (640000(1): 106)

Trans.: Eng. 640000(1): 107.

[On Yegorov's proposals.]

180823(4)   See 180831(2).

180824(1)   Prikaz. (230000(7).I: 239)

Repr.: 260000(18).I: 516-7.

Trans.: Am. p.q. Bunyan: 301-2;

Fr. 680000(1): 277-8.

[Kazan must be taken!]

180824(2)   [To Lenin.] (640000(1): 108)

Trans.: Eng. 640000(1): 109.

[On Bonch-Bruevich.]

180825(1)   Prikaz. (Iz, (184), 27.VIII.18)

180825(2)   [To Lenin.] (640000(1): 112)

Trans.: Eng. 640000(1): 113.

[On MRC.]

180826   Myatezhnym Kazanskim voiskam, srazhayushchimsya protiv Rabochei i
Krest'yanskoi Krasnoi Armii, obmanutym chekho-slovakam, obmanutym
krest'yanam, obmanutym rabochim. (To the mutinous troops of Kazan
fighting against the Workers and Peasants Red Army, to the deceived
Czecho-Slovaks, to the deceived peasants, to the deceived workers.)
(230000(7).I: 240)

Trans.: Am. 650900: 120-1; Bunyan: 302;

Eng. 640000(5): 120-1; 640000(10): 120-1;

Fr. 680000(1): 278-9;

Ger. 240000(40): 123.

180827(1)   O mobilizatsii. (On mobilization.) (230000(7).I: 241)

Trans.: Am. p.q. Bunyan: 302-3;

Fr. 680000(1): 279-80.

[To peasants and workers of Kazan province.]

180827(2)   Prikaz. (640000(1): 112)

Trans.: Eng. 640000(1): 113.

[On appointments.]

180827(3)   [To Sverdlov.] (640000(1): 114)
              Trans.: Eng. 640000(1): 115.
              [On awards.]

[180828(1)]   Iz-za chego idet bor´ba? (Why this struggle?) (GrazhVoina, (2),
              28.VIII.18)
              Repr.: 230000(7).I: 242; 260000(18).I: 517-8.
              Trans.: Fr. 680000(1): 280-1;
                      Ger. 240000(40): 125-6.

180828(2)   [To Lenin.] (640000(1): 114)
              Trans.: Eng. 640000(1): 115.
              [On refugees.]

180829(1)   Prikaz, No. 30. (Iz, (190), 4.IX.18)

180829(2)   i Sklyanskii: Prikaz na pogranichnoi okhrane, No. 7. (Order of the
              Day, No. 7; for frontier-guards.) (Iz, (195), 10.IX.18)

180829(3)   [To Lenin.] (640000(1): 116)
              Trans.: Eng. 640000(1): 117.
              [On mobilization in Kazan province.]

180830(1)   Prikaz, No. 31. (230000(7).I: 243)
              Trans.: Fr. 680000(1): 281-2.

[180830(2)]   U vorot Kazani. (At the gates of Kazan.) (230000(7).I: 244)
              Repr.: 260000(18).I: 518.
              Trans.: Fr. 680000(1): 282.

[180830(3)]   Pomnite ob Yaroslavle! (Remember Yaroslavl!) (230000(7).I: 245)
              Trans.: Am. p.q. Bunyan;
                      Fr. 680000(1): 283.

[180830(4)]   Ot Narodnogo Komissariata po voennym delam. (From the Commissariat
              for Military Affairs.) (Iz(NKVD), (101), 30.VIII.18)

[180831(1)]   Preduprezhdenie trudovomu naseleniyu Kazani. (Warning to the toiling
              people of Kazan.) (230000(7).I: 246)
              Trans.: Fr. 680000(1): 283-4.

180831(2)   [To Lenin.] (640000(1): 118)
              Trans.: Eng. 640000(1): 119.
              [Draft of communication on military commissars.]

[180900(1)]   O voennykh komissarakh. (On military commissars.) (230000(7).I: 183-4)

            Repr.: 260000(18).I: 338-9.

            Trans.: Fr. 680000(1): 217-9;

                   Ger. 240000(40): 62-3.

            [See also 180406.]

180900(2)   Unter-ofitsery. (NCOs.) (230000(7).I: 176-80)

            Repr.: 260000(18).I: 340-6.

            Trans.: Fr. 680000(1): 209-18;

                   Ger. 240000(40): 70-5.

            [Speech at Petrograd manoeuvres of NCOs in Kozlov.]

180900(3)   Kazanskii muzhik zadnim umom krepok. (The Kazan muzhiks are wise after the event.) (230000(7).I: 247)

            Trans.: Fr. 680000(1): 284-5;

                   Ger. 240000(40): 127.

180900(4)   Chto takoe panika? (What is this panic?) (230000(7).I: 248)

            Trans.: Fr. 680000(1): 285-6;

                   Ger. 240000(40): 128.

180900(5)   Krasnye ofitsery. (Red officers.) (230000(7).I: 325-9)

            Repr.: 260000(18).I: 346-52.

            Trans.: Fr. 680000(1): 373-9.

            [Speech to students at courses in military administration.]

180902(1)   Pered vzyatiem Kazani. (Before the liberation of Kazan.) (Iz, (189), 3.IX.18; Pr, (188), 4.IX.18)

            Repr.: 230000(7).I: 320-4; 260000(18).I: 518-24.

            Trans.: Fr. 680000(1): 368-73.

            [Speech to All-Russian CEC.]

180902(2)   O ranenom. (The wounded man.) (240000(24: 151-8)

            Trans.: 240000(24);

                   Am. FI, I.43.

            [On Lenin. Speech to All-Russian CEC.]

180903(1)   Rech. (A speech.) (Iz, (190), 4.IX.18)

            [At plenary session Moscow Soviet.]

180903(2)   Voisko Donskoe. (The Don army.) (Pr, (192), 8.IX.18)

            Repr.: 230000(7).I: 330-1; 260000(18).I: 496-8.

            Trans.: Fr. 680000(1): 379-80.

180910   Prikaz, No. 33. (<u>Iz</u>, (199), 14.IX.18; <u>Pr</u>, (197), 14.IX.18)
                <u>Repr</u>.: 230000(7).I: 249.
                <u>Trans</u>.: Am. Bunyan: 303;
                        Fr. 680000(1): 286-7;
                        Ger. 240000(40): 140.
                [On liberation of Kazan.]

180911(1)   Telegramma t.t. Zinov'evu i Kamenevu. (Telegram to cdes. Zinoviev and
                Kamenev.) (<u>Iz</u>, (197), 12.IX.18)
                <u>Repr</u>.: 230000(7).I: 250.
                <u>Trans</u>.: Fr. 680000(1): 287.
                [On liberation of Kazan.]

180911(2)   [To Lenin.] (640000(1): 126)
                <u>Trans</u>.: Eng. 640000(1): 127.
                [On liberation of Kazan.]

180912(1)   Znachenie vzyatiya Kazani v khode grazhdanskoi voiny. (The significance
                of the liberation of Kazan for the course of the civil war.)
                (230000(7).I: 251-6)
                <u>Repr</u>.: 260000(18).I: 524-31; p.q. 640000(1): 128.
                <u>Trans</u>.: Am. p.q. Bunyan: 303-4;
                        Eng. p.q. 640000(1): 129;
                        Fr. 680000(1): 288-94;
                        Ger. p.q. 240000(40): 141-2.
                [Speech in Kazan. Archives.]

180912(2)   Po povodu pobedy. (A few words about the victory.) (<u>Iz</u>, (195), 14.IX.18)
                <u>Repr</u>.: 230000(7).I: 262-3; 260000(18).I: 531-2.
                <u>Trans</u>.: Fr. 680000(1): 298-300.
                [Archives. ? T2952.]

180912(3)   Prikaz. (<u>Iz</u>, (199), 14.IX.18)
                <u>Repr</u>.: 230000(7).I: 257.
                <u>Trans</u>.: Fr. 680000(1): 295.

180913(1)   Prikaz, No. 37. (<u>Iz</u>, (201), 17.IX.18)
                <u>Repr</u>.: 230000(7).I: 258.
                <u>Trans</u>.: Fr. 680000(1): 295-6.

180913(2)   Prikaz, No. 38. (<u>Iz</u>, (206), 22.IX.18; <u>Krasnaya Gazeta</u>, (195), 19.IX.18)
                <u>Repr</u>.: 230000(7).I: 259.
                <u>Trans</u>.: Fr. 680000(1): 296.

180913(3) Obrashchenie k chekho-slovakam. (An appeal to the Czecho-Slovaks.)
(<u>Iz</u>, (201), 17.IX.18)
<u>Repr.</u>: 230000(7).I: 260; Maksakov i Turunov: 246-7; <u>KrG</u>, (195), 19.IX.18.
<u>Trans.</u>: Fr. 680000(1): 296-7.

[180914(1)] O gromilakh, zakhvativshikh v Kazani chast zolotogo zapasa Rossiikoi
Sovetskoi Respubliki. (On the thieves who stole in Kazan part of the
gold reserve of the Russian Soviet Republic.) (<u>Znamya TrudKom</u>, (22),
15.IX.18; <u>Iz</u>, (199), 14.IX.18)
<u>Repr.</u>: 230000(7).I: 261.
<u>Trans.</u>: Fr. 680000(1): 297-8.

180914(2) [To Lenin.] (640000(1): 130)
<u>Trans.</u>: Eng. 640000(1): 131.
[On supplies.]

[180917(1)] Prikaz. (<u>Iz</u>, (201), 17.IX.18)
[To the fleet.]

[180917(2)] Prikaz. (<u>Iz</u>, (201), 17.IX.18)
[To all armies.]

[180926(1)] Telegramma. (A telegram.) (<u>Iz</u>, (209), 26.IX.18)
<u>Repr.</u>: <u>Iz</u>, (210), 27.IX.18.
[To Moscow organizations; on 2nd anniversary of October Revolution.]

*[180926(2)] *Stroitel'stvo proletarskoi armii. (Building a proletarian army.)
(<u>God Proletarskoi Diktatury</u>)
[Advertized in <u>Iz</u>, (209), 26.IX.18.]

180926(3) [To Lenin.] (640000(1): 132)
<u>Trans.</u>: Eng. 640000(1): 133.
[On supplies.]

180926(4) [To Lenin.] (640000(1): 134)
<u>Trans.</u>: Eng. 640000(1): 135.
[On MRC.]

180930(1) Polozhenie na frontakh. (The situation at the front.) (<u>Iz</u>, (213),
2.X.18)
<u>Repr.</u>: 230000(7).I: 363-5; 260000(18).II: 3-6.
<u>Trans.</u>: Eng. p.q. <u>Workers Dreadnought</u>, (V.43), 18.I.19;
Fr. 680000(1): 409-12.

180930(2)   Prikaz. (230000(7).I: 151)

Repr.: Maksakov i Turunov: 248.

Trans.: Am. Bunyan: 274;

        Eng. Chamberlin.II: 31;

        Fr. 680000(1): 183;

        Ger. 240000(40): 124.

[On punishing families of traitors and renegades.]

181003   Mezhdunarodnaya obstanovka. (The international setting.) (Iz, (215), 4.X.18; Pr, (214), 5.X.18)

Repr.: 230000(7).I: 366-74; p.q. 260000(7): 83-5; 260000(18).II: 6-16; p.q. 300000(1): Ch. XXXII.

Trans.: p.q. 300000(1): Ch. XXXII;

        Fin. p.q. 180000(39): 42-4;

        Fr. 680000(1): 412-22.

[Speech to Extraordinary Joint-Session of All-Russian CEC, Moscow and district Soviets, and representatives of factory-committees and trade unions.]

[181004(1)]   Rech. (A speech.) (Iz, (216), 5.X.18)

[At opening of "Supplementary Courses inArmy Administration and Political Leadership".]

181004(2)   [Telegramma, No. 552. (Telegram, No. 552.)] (300000(1): Ch. XXXVI)

Repr.: 320000(2): 205-6; 640000(1): 134.

Trans.: 300000(1): Ch. XXXVI; p.q. 410000(1): Ch. IX;

        Am. 370000(14): 209-10; 620000(3): 209-10;

        Eng. 640000(1): 135.

[To Lenin; on Tsaritsyn; for recall of Stalin.]

181004(3)   Prikaz, No. 42. (Iz, (221), 11.X.18)

181005(1)   Prikaz, No. 43. (Iz, (230), 22.X.18)

Repr.: 230000(7).I: 347-8.

Trans.: Fr. 680000(1): 395-6.

[Unification of armies of Southern Front.]

181005(2)   [To Lenin.] (320000(2): 206)

Repr.: 640000(1): 140.

Trans.: 410000(1): Ch. IX;

        Am. 370000(14): 210; 620000(3): 210;

        Eng. 640000(1): 141.

[On insubordination at Tsaritsyn.]

[181005(3)]   i dr.: Dekret Soveta Narodnykh Komissarov. (Decree of the Sovnarkom.)
(<u>Iz</u>, (216), 5.X.18)
[Call-up for military service.]

181005(4)   [To Sverdlov.] (640000(1): 140)
<u>Trans</u>.: Eng. 640000(1): 141.
[On a Stalin Order of the Day.]

[181006]   Pamyati tov. M.I.Markina. (In memory of M.I.Markin.) (<u>Iz</u>, (217),
6.X.18)
<u>Repr</u>.: 260000(17): 255-7.

181007(1)   Prikaz, No. 44. (<u>Iz</u>(NKVD), (135), 11.X.18)
<u>Repr</u>.: 230000(7).I: 349; <u>Iz</u>, (230), 22.X.18.
<u>Trans</u>.: Fr. 680000(1): 397.
[On deserters.]

181007(2)   Prikaz, No. 45. (<u>Iz</u>(NKVD), (135), 11.X.18)
<u>Repr</u>.: <u>Iz</u>, (230), 22.X.18.

181007(3)   Prikaz, No. 764. (<u>Iz</u>(NKVD), (135), 11.X.18)

181009(1)   i Yurenev: Prikaz, No. 47. (<u>Iz</u>(NKVD), (137), 13.X.18)

181009(2)   i Yurenev: Prikaz, No. 48. (<u>Iz</u>(NKVD), (140), 17.X.18)

181009(3)   i dr.: Prikaz, No. 49. (<u>Iz</u>(NKVD), (137), 13.X.18)

181009(4)   i dr.: Prikaz, No. 54. (<u>Iz</u>(NKVD), (139), 16.X.18)

181009(5)   i dr.: Prikaz, No. 55. (<u>Iz</u>(NKVD), (139), 16.X.18)

181009(6)   i dr.: Prikaz, No. 56. (<u>Iz</u>(NKVD), (139), 16.X.18)

181011(1)   [To CEC.] (640000(1): 146)
<u>Trans</u>.: Eng. 640000(1): 147.
[On mobilization of railway troops.]

181011(2)   i dr.: Prikaz, No. 57. (<u>Iz</u>(NKVD), (139), 16.X.18)

181011(3)   i dr.: Prikaz, No. 58. (<u>Iz</u>(NKVD), (139), 16.X.18)

181011(4)   i dr.: Prikaz, No. 59. (<u>Iz</u>(NKVD), (139), 16.X.18)

181011(5)   i dr.: Prikaz, No. 60. (Iz(NKVD), (139), 16.X.18)

181011(6)   i dr.: Prikaz, No. 61. (Iz(NKVD), (139), 16.X.18)

181011(7)   i dr.: Prikaz, No. 62. (Iz(NKVD), (139), 16.X.18)

181011(8)   i dr.: Prikaz, No. 63. (Iz(NKVD), (139), 16.X.18)

181012   i dr.: Prikaz, No. 68. (Iz(NKVD), (139), 16.X.18)

181013(1)   [To Lenin.] (640000(1): 146)
Trans.: Eng. 640000(1): 147.
[On appointments.]

181013(2)   [To Dzerzhinsky.] (640000(1): 148)
Trans.: Eng. 640000(1): 149.
[On arrested officers.]

181014   i dr.: Prikaz, No. 94. (Iz(NKVD), (140), 17.X.18)

181015   [To Lenin.] (640000(1): 150)
Trans.: Eng. 640000(1): 151.
[On MRC.]

181018   Doklad. (A report.) (Iz, (229), 20.X.18)
[To EC of Moscow Soviet.]

181019   Rech. (A speech.) (Krasnaya Gazeta, (223), 20.X.18)
[To new recruits.]

181020   [To Sverdlov.] (640000(1): 150)
Trans.: Eng. 640000(1): 151.

181021(1)   i dr.: Prikaz, No. 120. (Iz(NKVD), (149), 27.X.18)

181021(2)   i dr.: Prikaz, No. 122. (Iz(NKVD), (149), 27.X.18)

181021(3)   i dr.: Prikaz, No. 127. (Iz(NKVD), (149), 27.X.18)

181022(1)   i dr.: Prikaz, No. 130. (Iz(NKVD), (149), 27.X.18)

181022(2)   i dr.: Prikaz, No. 131. (Iz(NKVD), (149), 27.X.18)

181022(3)   i Rattel: Prikaz, No. 133. (Iz(NKVD), (149), 27.X.18)

181022(4)   Prikaz, No. 134. (Iz(NKVD), (149), 27.X.18)

181023(1)   [To Lenin.] (640000(1): 152)
              Trans.: Eng. 640000(1): 153.

181023(2)   [To Lenin.] (640000(1): 156)
              Trans.: Eng. 640000(1): 157.

181023(3)   [To Lenin.] (640000(1): 158)
              Trans.: Eng. 640000(1): 159.
              [On grain stocks.]

181023(4)   [On transport.]
              [c. 640000(1): 182.]

181025   [To Lenin.] (640000(1): 162)
              Trans.: Eng. 640000(1): 163.
              [On X Army.]

181027   [To MRC.] (640000(1): 164)
              Trans.: Eng. 640000(1): 165.
              [On X Army.]

181028   Rech. (A speech.) (Iz, (236), 29.X.18)
              [At Tsaritsyn.]

181030   Peredyshka. (A respite.) (230000(7).I: 375-6)
              Repr.: 260000(18).II: 16-8.
              Trans.: Eng. Chamberlin.II: 122, p.q.;
                       Fr. 680000(1): 422-4.
              [Speech to 5th Convocation of All-Russian CEC. Archives.]

181101   [To Lenin and Sverdlov.] (640000(1): 166)
              Trans.: p.q. 410000(1): Ch. IX;
                      Eng. 640000(1): 167.
              [On X Army. T67.]

181103   Prikaz, No. 56. (230000(7).I: 264)
              Repr.: Maksakov i Turunov: 247-8.
              Trans.: Fr. 680000(1): 300-1;
                      Ger. 240000(40): 144.

181104(2)   [To Lenin and Sverdlov.] (640000(1): 168)
              Trans.: Eng. 640000(1): 169.

181104(3)   [To Anisimov.] (640000(1): 170)

Trans.: Eng. 640000(1): 171.

181105   Prikaz, No. 55. (KrArmiya, (116), 6.XI.18)

Repr.: 230000(7).I: 350-1.

Trans.: p.q. 410000(1): Ch. IX;

      Fr. 680000(1): 397-9.

181107   Prikaz, No. 58. (230000(7).I: 352)

Trans.: Fr. 680000(1): 399-400.

[On anniversary of October Revolution.]

181108(1)   Voennaya Akademiya. (The Military Academy.) (230000(7).I: 162-8)

Repr.: 260000(18).I: 352-60.

Trans.: Eng. p.q. Deutscher, PA: 413;

      Fr. 680000(1): 194-201;

      Ger. 240000(40): 182-8.

[Speech at opening of Military Academy.]

181108(2)   [To Lenin.] (640000(1): 174)

Trans.: Eng. 640000(1): 175.

[On case of Tsikolini.]

181109   Voennoe polozhenie. (The military situation.) (Iz, (245), 10.XI.18;

KrArmiya, (119), 12.XI.18; Pr, (244), 12.XI.18)

Repr.: 230000(7).I: 332-41; 260000(18).II: 19-31.

Trans.: p.q. 410000(1): Ch. IX;

      Eng. p.q. Chamberlin.II: 122;

      Fr. 680000(1): 381-92;

      Ger. 240000(40): 145-56.

[Report to 6th Congress of Soviets.]

181113   Prikaz, No. 202. (Iz, (250), 16.XI.18; KrArmiya, (123), 16.XI.18;

Pr, (247), 15.XI.18)

[On the return of Czecho-Slovaks to their own country.]

181115   Prikaz, No. 60. (230000(7).I: 265)

Trans.: Fr. 680000(1): 301-2.

181116   Prikaz, No. 61. (KrArmiya, (124), 17.XI.18)

Repr.: 230000(7).I: 353.

Trans.: Fr. 680000(1): 400.

181118 NA STRAZHE MIROVOI REVOLYUTSII (ON GUARD FOR WORLD REVOLUTION),
190000(14).
Repr.: 230000(7).I: 377-98; p.q. 260000(7): 86-9; 260000(18).II: 31-58.
Trans.: Fr. 680000(1): 425-50;
    Ger. 240000(40): 191-214.

181120 Prikaz, No. 62. (230000(7).I: 354-6)
Trans.: Fr. 680000(1): 401-4;
    Ger. 240000(40): 157-60.
[To 8th Army. Secret.]

181123 i Sklyanskii: Prikaz, No. 275. (Iz, (258), 26.XI.18)
[Call-up of officers.]

181124(1) Prikaz, No. 64. (230000(7).I: 357)
Trans.: Fr. 680000(1): 404-5.
[For troops of Southern Front.]

181124(2) Prikaz, No. 65. (230000(7).I: 358)
Trans.: Fr. 680000(1): 405-6.
[For troops guarding southern front.]

181124(3) [To Lenin.] (640000(1): 178)
Trans.: Eng. 640000(1): 179.
[On 9th Army.]

181125(1) [To Lenin.] (640000(1): 182)
Trans.: Am. Wolfe: 170;
    Eng. 640000(1): 183.

181125(2) [To Lenin.] (640000(1): 182)
Trans.: Eng. 640000(1): 183.

181129(1) [To Lenin.] (640000(1): 184)
Trans.: Eng. 640000(1): 185.
[On railway transport.]

181129(2) [To Lenin.] (640000(1): 186)
Trans.: Eng. 640000(1): 187.
[On ammunition.]

181130 i dr.: Postanovlenie VTsIK. (Decree of the All-Russian CEC.)
(230000(7).I: 342-3)
Repr.: 260000(18).II: 58-60. ++++

181130 ++++   <u>Trans</u>.: Fr. 680000(1): 392-4.
    [All forces into the struggle against the enemy!]

181200   [Confidential Letter to CEC.]
    <u>Trans</u>.: Eng. p.q. Deutscher, PA: 426.
    [Against slanders. Harvard Archives.]

181201(1)   [Proposal to CEC to organize a Council for Defence.]
    [c. 410000(1): Ch. IX. T2953.]

181201(2)   [To Lenin.] (640000(1): 192)
    <u>Trans</u>.: Eng. 640000(1): 193.
    [On fodder suplies.]

181201(3)   [To Lenin.] (640000(1): 192)
    <u>Trans</u>.: Eng. 640000(1): 193.
    [On personnel.]

181203   Prikaz, No. 334. (<u>Iz</u>, (33), 13.II.19)

181204   Pref. BELGIYA I SERBIYA V VOINE (BELGIUM AND SERBIA IN THE WAR),
    190000(1).

181210   Slovo o Kazakakh i k Kazakam. (A word about the Cossacks and to the
    Cossacks.) (230000(7).I: 359-60)
    <u>Trans</u>.: Fr. 680000(1): 406-8;
        Ger. 240000(40): 161-2.

181211   Prikaz, No. 69. (230000(7).I: 185)
    <u>Trans</u>.: Eng. p.q. Footman: 150;
        Fr. 680000(1): 219-20;
        Ger. 240000(40): 181.
    [Role of communists in the war.]

181214(1)   [To Lenin.] (640000(1): 196)
    <u>Trans</u>.: Eng. 640000(1): 197.
    [On personnel.]

181214(2)   [To Lenin.] (640000(1): 198)
    <u>Trans</u>.: Eng. 640000(1): 199.
    [On personnel.]

181221   Pref. LYUDI STAROI I NOVOI EPOKH (PEOPLE OF THE OLD AND NEW EPOCH), 190000(10).

181222   Pref. VOINA I TEKHNIKA (WAR AND TECHNIQUE), 190000(2).

[181225(1)]   Beseda. (An interview.) (Iz, (283), 25.XII.18)
           [On the Red Army and the military situation.]

181225(2)   [To CC CPR.] (640000(1): 204)
           Trans.: Eng. 640000(1): 205.
           [On military opposition.]

[181226(1)]   Grazhdane, sdavaite oruzhie. (Citizens, give up your weapons.)
           (Iz, (284), 26.XII.18; Pr, (283), 27.XII.18)
           Repr.: Iz, (286), 28.XII.18.

181226(2)   [To Lenin.) (640000(1): 210)
           Trans.: Eng. 640000(1): 211.

181226(3)   [To Lenin.] (640000(1): 212)
           Trans.: Eng. 640000(1): 213.
           [On TsIK Detachment.]

181226(4)   [To Lenin.] (640000(1): 214)
           Trans.: Eng. 640000(1): 215.
           [On 6th Army.]

181227(1)   [To Lenin.] (640000(1): 218)
           Trans.: Eng. 640000(1): 219.
           [On transport difficulties.]

181227(2)   [To Lenin.] (640000(1): 218)
           Trans.: Eng. 640000(1): 219.
           [On Extraordinary Levy.]

181228   [To Lenin.] (640000(1): 220)
           Trans.: Eng. 640000(1): 221.
           [On SRs.]

181229   [To Lenin.] (640000(1): 224)
           Trans.: Eng. 640000(1): 225.
           [On SRs.]

181230(1) O byvshikh ofitserakh. Neobkhodimoe zayavlenie. (On ex-officers. A necessary statement.) (230000(7).I: 360-1)

Repr.: 260000(18).I: 360-1; Maksakov i Turunov: 248-9.

Trans.: Am. 650900: 121-2;
   Eng. 640000(5): 121-2; 640000(10): 121-2;
   Fr. 680000(1): 183-4;
   Ger. 240000(40): 68-9.

181230(2) [To Lenin.] (640000(1): 224)

Trans.: Eng. 640000(1): 225.

[On fuel.]

181231(1) Voennye spetsialisty i Krasnaya Armiya. (Military specialists and the Red Army.) (Iz, (5), 10.I.19)

Repr.: 230000(7).I: 154-61; 260000(18).I: 361-70.

Trans.: Eng. p.q. Deutscher, PA: 426-7;
   Fr. 680000(1): 185-94; Lévy: 132-42.

181231(2) Ob ofitserakh, obmanutykh Krasnovym. (On officers deceived by Krasnov.) (Iz, (7), 12.I.19)

Repr.: 230000(7).I: 147-9; 260000(18).I: 335-7.

Trans.: Fr. 680000(1): 180-1.

181231(3) [To Lenin.] (640000(1): 226)

Trans.: Eng. 640000(1): 227.

[On transport.]

181231(4) [To Lenin.] (640000(1): 226)

Trans.: Eng. 640000(1): 227.

[On Krasnov.]

190000(1)   † BELGIYA I SERBIYA V VOINE. (BELGIUM AND SERBIA IN THE WAR.)
Repr.: *190000(3).
[Pref. 181204.]

190000(2)   † VOINA I TEKHNIKA. (WAR AND TECHNIQUE.)
Repr.: *190000(3).
[Pref. 181222.]

*190000(3)   § *GODY VELIKOGO PERELOMA. (THE YEARS OF THE GREAT UPHEAVAL.)
[Comprising 190000(1), 190000(2), 190000(10).]

*190000(4)   *DEZERTIRY — POMOSHCHNIKI KOLCHAKA. (DESERTERS ARE AID TO KOLCHAK.)
[See 190503(2) for all repr., trans.]

*190000(5)   *ISTORIYA NA RUSKATA REVOLYUTSIYA. (THE HISTORY OF THE RUSSIAN
REVOLUTION.)
[Trans. Bul. See 180000(5) for all repr., trans., notes.]

190000(6)   ITOGI I PERSPEKTIVY. DVIZHUSHCHIE SILY REVOLYUTSII. (RESULTS AND
PROSPECTS. THE MOTIVE FORCES OF THE REVOLUTION.)
[See 060600 for all repr., trans., notes.]

*190000(7)   *KAVALERISTAM KORPUSA MAMONTOVA. (TO THE CAVALRYMEN OF MAMONTOV'S
CORPS.)
[See 190824 for all repr., trans.]

190000(8)   KARL LIBKNEKHT I ROZA LYUKSEMBURG. (KARL LIEBKNECHT AND ROSA
LUXEMBURG.)
[See 190118 for all repr., trans.]

*190000(9)   *KOMMUNISTAM NA VOSTOCHNOM FRONTA. (TO THE COMMUNISTS ON THE
EASTERN FRONT.)
[See 190324(1) for all repr., trans.]

190000(10)   † LYUDI STAROI I NOVOI EPOKH. (PEOPLE OF THE OLD AND NEW EPOCH.)
Repr.: *190000(3).
[Pref. 181221.]

190000(11)   MEZHDUNARODNOE POLOZHENIE I KRASNAYA ARMIYA. (THE INTERNATIONAL
SITUATION AND THE RED ARMY.)
[See 180616(1) for all repr., trans.]

190000(12)   NA BOR´BU S GOLODOM! (THE STRUGGLE AGAINST FAMINE!)
[See 180609 for all repr., trans.]

*190000(13)   *NA OBLAVU! (CHASE THEM!)

[See 190818(2) for all repr., trans.]

190000(14)   NA STRAZHE MIROVOI REVOLYUTSII. (ON GUARD FOR WORLD REVOLUTION.)

[See 181118 for all repr., trans.]

*190000(15)   *NA URAL! (TO THE URALS!)

[See 190407(1) for all repr., trans.]

190000(16)   NA FRONTAKH. (TO THE FRONT.)

[See 190224 for all repr., trans.]

190000(17)   NASHE VOENNOE STROITEL'STVO I NASHI FRONTY. (OUR MILITARY
CONSTRUCTION AND OUR FRONTS.)

[See 191207 for all repr., trans.]

*190000(18)   *OBRASHCHENIE K KAVALERISTAM KORPUSA MAMONTOVA. (AN APPEAL TO THE
CAVALRYMEN OF MAMONTOV'S CORPS.)

[See 190824 for all repr., trans.]

*190000(19)   *PIS'MO K KREST'YANAM SEREDNYAKAM. (LETTER TO THE MIDDLE PEASANTS.)

[See [190206] for all repr.]

190000(20)   PORYADOK IZ KHAOSA. (ORDER OUT OF CHAOS.)

[See 190113 for all repr., trans.]

*190000(21)   *RECH. (A SPEECH.)

[See 190224 for all repr., trans.]

*190000(22)   *RECH V ZASEDANII MOSKOVSKOGO SOVETA. (SPEECH AT MOSCOW SOVIET.)

[See 190224 for all repr., trans.]

190000(23)   RECH NA ZASEDANII VSEUKRAINSKOGO TsIK. (SPEECH TO ALL-UKRAINIAN CEC.)

[See 190519 for all repr.]

*190000(24)   *RECH NA SOEDINENNOM ZASEDANII SAMARSKOGO SOVETA RABOCHIKH I
KRASNOARMEISKIKH DEPUTATOV. (SPEECH TO JOINT-SESSION OF SAMARA
SOVIET OF WORKERS AND ARMY DEPUTIES.)

[See 190406(2) for all repr., trans., notes.]

*190000(25)   *RECH, PROIZNESENNAYA NA GORODSKIM MITINGE. (SPEECH TO CITY MEETING.)

[See 190424(2) for all repr., trans.]

190000(26) TRUD, DISTSIPLINA, PORYADOK SPASUT SOTSIALISTICHESKU SOVETSKUYU
RESPUBLIKU. (WORK, DISCIPLINE AND ORDER WILL SAVE THE SOCIALIST
SOVIET REPUBLIC.)
[See 180328(1) for all repr., trans.]

*190000(27) *TRUD, DISTSIPLINA, PORYADOK SPASUT SOTSIALISTICHESKU SOVETSKUYU
RESPUBLIKU. (WORK, DISCIPLINE AND ORDER WILL SAVE THE SOCIALIST
SOVIET REPUBLIC.)
[See 180328(1) for all repr., trans.]

190000(28) TUDA I OBRATNO. (THERE AND BACK.)
[See 070000(3) for all repr., trans., notes.]

*190000(29) *CHEREZ POBEDU K MIRU. (THROUGH VICTORY TO PEACE.)
[Order of the Day.]

*[190000(30)] *VESNA KOTORAYA RESHAET. (A SPRING WHICH WILL BE DECISIVE.)
[See 190409 for all repr., trans.]

*[190000(31)] *OT OKTYABR´SKOI REVOLYUTSII DO BRESTSKOGO MIRA. (FROM THE OCTOBER
REVOLUTION TO THE BREST PEACE.)
[See 180000(5) for all repr., trans.]

*[190000(32)] *PIS´MO K KREST´YANAM-SEREDNYAKAM. (LETTER TO THE MIDDLE-PEASANTS.)
[See [190206] for all repr.]

*[190000(33)] *PIS´MO K KREST´YANAM-SEREDNYAKAM. (LETTER TO THE MIDDLE-PEASANTS.)
[See [190206] for all repr.]

*[190000(34)] *RECH NA ZASEDANII MOSKOVSKOGO SOVETA. (SPEECH AT MOSCOW SOVIET.)
[See 190224 for all repr., trans.]

*[190000(35)] *RECH, PROIZNESENNAYA V MOSKOVSKOGO SOVETA. (SPEECH AT MOSCOW SOVIET.)
[See 190224 for all repr., trans.]

*[190000(36)] *RECH PROIZNESENNAYA NA MITINGE V g. VYATKE. (SPEECH AT MEETING IN
VYATKA.)
[See 190424(2) for all repr., trans.]

190000(37) ARBEIT, DISZIPLIN UND ORDNUNG WERDEN DIE SOZIALISTISCHE SOWJET-RESPUBLIK
RETTEN!
[Trans. Ger. See 180328(1) for all trans., repr.]

190000(38) ARBEIT, DISZIPLIN UND ORDNUNG WERDEN DIE SOZIALISTISCHE SOWJET-RESPUBLIK RETTEN!

[Trans. Ger. See 180328(1) for all trans., repr.]

190000(39) ARMATA ROSIE.

[Trans. Rum. See 180421 for all trans.]

190000(40) L'AVÈNEMENT DU BOLCHEVISME.

[Trans. Fr. See 180000(5) for all trans., repr., notes.]

190000(41) EL BOLCHEVIQUISMO ANTE LA GUERRA Y LA PAZ DEL MUNDO.

[Trans. Sp. See [140000(3)] for all trans., repr., notes.]

*190000(42) *EL BOLCHEVIQUISMO ANTE LA GUERRA Y LA PAZ DEL MUNDO.

[Trans. Sp. See [140000(3)] for all trans., repr., notes.]

190000(43) DALLA RIVOLUZIONE D'OTTOBRE AL TRATTATO DI PACE DI BREST-LITOVSK.

[Trans. It. See 180000(5) for all trans., repr., notes.]

190000(44) FROM OCTOBER TO BREST-LITOVSK.

[Trans. Am. See 180000(5) for all trans., repr., notes.]

190000(45) HISTORIA DE LA REVOLUCIÓN RUSA.

[Trans. Sp. See 180000(5) for all trans., repr., notes.]

*190000(46) *JEAN JAURÈS.

[Trans. Fr. See *170000(1) for all trans., repr., notes.]

190000(47) KARL LIBKNECHT ET ROSA LUXEMBOURG.

[Trans. Fr. See 190118 for all trans., repr., notes.]

190000(48) KARL LIEBKNECHT UND ROZA LUXEMBURG.

[Trans. Ger. See 190118 for all trans., repr., notes.]

*190000(49) *PORYADOK IZ KHAOSA. (ORDER OUT OF CHAOS.)

[See 190113 for all repr., trans.]

190000(50) LAVORO, DISCIPLINA E ORDINE SALVERANNO LA REPUBLICA SOCIALISTA DEI SOWJET.

[Trans. It. See 180328(1) for all trans., notes. Printed with Lenin, LA LOTTA PER IL PANE.]

190000(51) ---: MANIFESTO OF THE FIRST CONGRESS OF THE COMMUNIST INTERNATIONAL.

[Trans. Eng. See 190306(1) for all trans., repr., notes.]

*190000(52)   *OKTOOBRIREVOLUTSION.
                 [Trans. Esth. See 180000(5) for all trans., notes.]

190000(53)   DIE ROTE ARMEE.
                 [Trans. Ger. See 180422(1) for all trans., repr., notes.]

*190000(54)   *DI ROYTE ARMEY.
                 [Trans. Yid. See 180422(1) for all trans., notes.]

190000(55)   DIE RUSSISCHE SOZIALISTISCHE ROTE ARMEE.
                 [Trans. Ger. See 180422(1) for all trans., repr., notes.]

190000(56)   DEN RUSSISKE ARBEIDERREVOLUTION. FRA NOVEMBERREVOLUTION TIL
                 BRESTFREDEN.
                 [Trans. Nor. See 180000(5) for all trans., notes.]

190000(57)   ÜBER DIE ROTE ARMEE.
                 [Trans. Ger. See 180422(1) for all trans., repr., notes.]

190000(58)   VON DER OKTOBER REVOLUTION BIS ZUM BRESTER FRIEDENSVERTRAG.]
                 [Trans. Ger. See 180000(5) for all trans., repr., notes.]

*190000(59)   *VON OKTOBER BIS NACH BREST-LITOVSK.
                 [Trans. Ger. See 180000(5) for all trans., repr., notes.]

[190000(60)]   ARBEIT, DISZIPLIN UND ORDNUNG WERDEN DIE SOZIALISTISCHE SOWJET-RESPUBLIK.
                 RETTEN!
                 [See 180328(1) for all trans., repr., notes.]

[190000(61)]   FRA NOVEMBERREVOLUTION TIL BREST-LITOWSK-FREDEN.
                 [Trans. Den. See 180000(5) for all trans., notes.]

*[190000(62)]   *KAPITOLY Z MEHO DENNIKU.
                 [Trans. Cz. See 180000(33) for all trans., notes.]

[190000(63)]   DER KRIEG UND DIE INTERNATIONALE.
                 [Trans. Ger. See [140000(3)] for all trans., repr., notes.]

[190000(64)]   —: DAS NEUE KOMMUNISTISCHE MANIFEST.
                 [Trans. Ger. See 190306(1) for all trans., repr., notes.]

[190000(65)]   VON DER OKTOBER REVOLUTION BIS ZUM FRIEDEN VON BREST-LITOWSK.
                 [Trans. Ger. See 180000(5) for all trans., repr., notes.]

*190000(66)   *EL TRIUNFO DEL BOLCHEVISMO.
                 [Trans. Sp. See 180000(5) for all trans., repr., notes.]

*190000(67)   *KRASNAYA ARMIYA. (THE RED ARMY.)
                 [See 180422(1) for all repr., trans.]

190000(68)   § UNZER REVOLUTSION.
                 Repr.: 210000(51).
                 [Trans. Yid. p.q. 180000(40), p.q. [180000(53)].]

190000(69)   HISTORIA DE LA REVOLUCIÓN RUSA.
                 [Trans. Sp. See 180000(5) for all trans., repr., notes.]

190000(70)   VON DER OKTOBER REVOLUTION BIS ZUM BRESTER FRIEDENSVERTRAG.
                 [Trans. Ger. See 180000(5) for all trans., repr., notes.]

*190000(71)   *MANIFEST KOMMUNISTICHESKOGO INTERNATSIONALA K PROLETARIATAM VSEGO
                 MIRA. (MANIFESTO OF THE COMMUNIST INTERNATIONAL TO THE PROLETARIAT
                 OF THE WHOLE WORLD.)
                 [See 190306(1) for all repr., trans.]

[190000(72)]   VENÄJAN TYÖVÄEN VALLANKUMOUKSEN HISTORIAA.
                 [Trans. Fin. See 180000(5) for all trans. Lacks Pref. 180212.]

*190000(73)   *A KOMMUNISTA INTERNACIONALE KIÁLTVÁNYA A VILÁG PROLETÁRJAIHOZ.
                 [Trans. Hun. See 190306(1) for all trans.]

*190000(74)   *MANIFEST DER KOMMUNISTISCHE INTERNATIONALE. (A KOMMUNISTA
                 INTERNACIONALE KIÁLTVÁNYA A VILÁG PROLETÁRJAIHOZ.)
                 [Trans. Ger. See 190306(1) for all trans., repr., notes.]

*190000(75)   *MUNKA, FEGYELEM ÉS REND MENTIK MEG A PROLETÁRSÁGOT.
                 [Trans. Hun. See 180328(1) for all trans., repr., notes.]

*190000(76)   *MUNKA, FEGYELEM ÉS REND MENTIK MEG A PROLETÁRSÁGOT.
                 [Trans. Hun. See 180328(1) for all trans., repr., notes.]

*190000(77)   *MUNKA, FEGYELEM ÉES REND MENTIK MEG A PROLETRSÁGOT.
                 [Trans. Hun. See 180328(1) for all trans., repr., notes.]

*[190000(78)]   et al: *VILÁGHÁBORU ÉS VILÁGFORDALOM.
                 [Trans. Hun. See 180801(1) for all trans.]

*190000(79) *PIS´MO KREST´YANAM SEREDNYAKAM OT NARODNOGO KOMISSARA PO VOEVVYM
I MORSKIM DELAM. (LETTER TO THE MIDDLE PEASANTS FROM THE PEOPLE'S
COMMISSAR FOR WAR AND NAVAL AFFAIRS.)
[See [190206] for all repr.]

*190000(80) *VLAST SOVJETA I INTERNACIONALNI IMPERIJALIZAM.
[Trans. Serb. See 180421 for all trans.]

190000(81) THE HISTORY OF THE RUSSIAN REVOLUTION TO BREST-LITOVSK.
[Trans. Eng. See 180000(5) for all repr., trans., notes.]

190100(1) [To Lenin.] (640000(1): 266)
Trans.: Eng. 640000(1): 267.
[On General Zagiu. Misprinted in Deutscher, PA: 438 as Zagin.]

190100(2) [To Berzin.]
Trans.: 410000(1): Ch. IX.
[On counter-revolutionary orders.]

190100(3) [To comrade-deserters.] (p.q. 300000(1): Ch. XXXIV)
Trans.: p.q. 300000(1): Ch. XXXIV.

190101 To Lenin. (410000(1): Ch. IX)
Russian: p.q. 320000(2); 640000(1): 228.
Trans.: 410000(1): Ch. IX;
        Am. p.q. 370000(14): 215; p.q. 620000(3): 215;
        Eng. 640000(1): 229.
[On 3rd Army. T108.]

190102(1) Prikaz, No. 73. (Iz, (6), 11.I.19)

190102(2) [To Lenin.] (640000(1): 230)
Trans.: Eng. 640000(1): 231.
[On Ukraine.]

190102(3) [To Lenin.] (640000(1): 230)
Trans.: Eng. 640000(1): 231.
[On Podvoisky.]

190102(4) [To Lenin.] (640000(1): 236)
Trans.: Eng. 640000(1): 237.
[On food situation in Petrograd.]

190103(1) [To Lenin.] (640000(1): 238)
Trans.: Eng. 640000(1): 239.
[On operations on the Southern Front.]

190103(2) [To Saks.] (640000(1): 240)
Trans.: Eng. 640000(1): 241.
[On operations in Caspian.]

190103(3) Pamyatka dlya koe-kakikh novoispechennykh anglofilov. (A memorandum
on certain newly-fledged anglophiles.) (Iz, (4), 5.I.19)
Repr.: 230000(7).II.ii: 225-6.

190104(1) [To Lenin; on Ukraine.]
[c. Deutscher, PA: 428. T116.]

190104(2) [To Defence Council.] (640000(1): 240)
Trans.: Eng. 640000(1): 241.
[On Ukraine.]

[190105(1)] i dr.: Gruppe "Spartak" v Germanii i kommunisticheskoi partii
nemetskoi Avstrii. (The "Spartacus" group in Germany and the
communist party of Germano-Austria.) (Pr, (4), 5.I.19)
Repr.: 260000(10): 91-3; NashaPr, (4), 12.I.19)

190107(1) Pora konchat! (It is time to finish!) (V Puti, (20), 1919)
Repr.: 230000(7).II.i: 166-8; 260000(18).II: 60-4.
Trans.: Fr. 680000(1): 642-6.

190107(2) [To Lenin.] (640000(1): 246)
Trans.: Eng. 640000(1): 247.
[On appointment of Commissar for Railways.]

190109(1) "Pervaya kniga dlya chteniya." Stoit li ee chitat? ("A First Reading
Book." Is it worth reading?) (Iz, (8), 14.I.19; Pr, (8), 14.I.19;
Voennoe Delo, (2), 1919)
Repr.: 230000(7).II.i: 158-60; 270000(2): 235-7.
Trans.: Fr. 680000(1): 633-5.

190109(2) Neobkhodima surovaya chistka. (A necessary rough purge.) (V Puti,
(21), 11.I.19)
Repr.: 230000(7).II.i: 163-5; 260000(18).II: 64-7; Pr, (17), 25.I.19.
Trans.: Fr. 680000(1): 639-42.
[Southern front.]

190109(3) Prikaz, No. 74. (Iz, (10), 16.I.19)
Repr.: 230000(7).II.ii: 227.

190110(1)   [To Sverdlov.] (300000(1): Ch. XXXVI)

Repr.: p.q. 320000(2); 640000(1): 246.

Trans.: 300000(1): Ch. XXXVI; p.q. 410000(1): Ch. IX.

        Am. p.q. 370000(14): 210-1; p.q. 410000(1): Ch. IX;

           p.q. 620000(3): 210-1;

        Eng. 640000(1): 247.

[T118.]

190110(2)   Po nauke ili koe-kak? Pis'mo drugu. (Scientifically or anyhow?

Letter to a friend.) (Pr, (30), 9.II.19)

Repr.: 230000(7).I: 169-73; p.q. 240000(8): 67-70; 260000(18).I:

        371-6; p.q. 270000(2): 97-100; NashaPr, (30,31), 14,15.II.19;p.q.

        SevernayaKom, (33), 12.II.19; Voennoe Delo, (5-6:34-35),

Trans.: Am. 690000(11): 148-53;

        Eng. Labour Review, VII-VIII.59;

        Fr. 680000(1): 202-7;

        Ger. 240000(40): 176-80.

190110(3)   Telegramma. (A telegram.) (Iz, (11), 17.I.19)

Repr.: 230000(7).II.i: 171.

Trans.: Fr. 680000(1): 649.

[To HQ XVI Division; on death of cde. Kikvidze.]

190110(4)   Prikaz, No. 75. (230000(7).II.i: 88)

Trans.: Fr. 680000(1): 551-2.

190111(1)   Prikaz, No. 76. (230000(7).II.i: 169-70)

Trans.: Fr. 680000(1): 649; Lévy: 129-31.

190111(2)   [To Lenin.] (p.q. 300000(1): Ch. XXXVI)

Repr.: 320000(2); 640000(1): 248.

Trans.: p.q. 300000(1): Ch. XXXVI; p.q. 410000(1): Ch. IX;

        Am. p.q. 370000(14): 211-2; p.q. 620000(3): 211-2;

        Eng. 640000(1): 249.

[On compromise with Stalin. T119.]

190111(3)   [To Sverdlov.] (640000(1): 252)

Trans.: Eng. 640000(1): 253.

[On Panteleev affair.]

190112   [To Lenin.] (640000(1): 254)

Trans.: Eng. 640000(1): 255.

[On death of Kikvidze.]

190113   Poryadok iz khaosa. (Order out of chaos.) (Pr, (26), 5.II.19)

         Repr.: 190000(20); *190000(49); 230000(7).II.i: 7-13; 260000(10): 6-14.

         Trans.: Am. SocAp, 27.IV.40;

                 Eng. Keep Left, (XIX.2), II.70; WIN, VI.40;

                 Fr. 680000(1): 453-61.

         [Supplement to Pr.]

190118   KARL LIBKNEKHT I ROZA LYUKSEMBURG (KARL LIEBKNECHT AND ROSA LUXEMBURG),

         190000(8).

         Repr.: *190000(81); 260000(17): 82-94.

         Trans.: Bul. *220000(37);

                 Fr. p.q. 190000(47); p.q. BulCom, (I.10), 20.V.20; p.q. RevCom,

                     (I.1), III.20;

                 Ger. p.q. 190000(48); p.q. Kom(B), (III.2), 15.I.20; p.q.

                     KomArb, (II.15), 15.I.20;

                 It. Ordine Nuovo, (II.15), 15.I.22;

                 Yid. p.q. UnserK, (II.1), 15.I.33.

         [Archives.]

190119   [To Lenin.] (640000(1): 254)

         Trans.: Eng. 640000(1): 255.

         [On communications.]

190122   [To Lenin.] (640000(1): 256)

         Trans.: Eng. 640000(1): 257.

         [On communications.]

190123   [To Lenin.] (640000(1): 258)

         Trans.: Eng. 640000(1): 259.

         [On 8th Army.]

190124   i dr.: K pervomu s"ezdu Kommunisticheskogo Internatsionala. (The first

         congress of the Communist International.) (Iz, (16), 24.I.19; Pr, (16),

         24.I.19)

         Repr.: 260000(10): 33-7; Bor'ba Bol'shevikov: 113; KI, (I:30), 1924.

         Trans.: Eng. CI, (V.1), 1924;

                 Fin. KAPITALISTINEN: 14-9;

                 Ger. KomInt, (1), VIII.19.

         [Invitation to Spartakusbund to join the Comintern.]

190125   [To Lenin.] (640000(1): 260)

         Trans.: Eng. 640000(1): 261.

190126   [To MRC, Astrakhan.] (640000(1): 262)

Trans.: Eng. 640000(1): 263.

[On XIth Army.]

190127   Prikaz, No. 78. (230000(7).II.ii: 228)

[To Nikolaev Division.]

190128   i Yurenev: Prikaz, No. 153. (Iz, (20), 29.I.19)

[190200]   Kazakam! (To the Cossacks!) (230000(7).II.ii: 229)

190204   i dr.: Polozhenie o revolyutsionnykh voennykh tribunalakh. (Regulation on revolutionary military tribunals.) (Iz, (32), 12.II.19)

[190206]   Pis'mo k krest'yanam-serednyakam. (Letter to middle-peasants.) (Iz, (28), 6.II.19)

Repr.: *190000(19); *[190000(32)]; *[190000(33)]; *190000(79); 230000(7).II.ii: 230-5; 260000(18).II; 528-32; Severnaya Kommuna, (31), 9.II.19.

190211(1)   Prikaz, No. 79. (V Puti, (22), 11.II.19; Severnaya Kommuna, (34), 13.II.19)

Repr.: 230000(7).II.i: 377-8; 260000(18).II: 231-5.

Trans.: Fr. 680000(1): 867-9.

[To the army defending the approaches to Petrograd.]

190211(2)   Na Petrogradskii front! (To the Petrograd front!) (Severnaya Kommuna, (34), 13.II.19)

190214(1)   Rech. (A speech.) (Severnaya Kommuna, (36), 15.II.19)

[To Petrograd Soviet.]

190214(2)   Rezolyutsiya. (A resolution.) (Severnaya Kommuna, (36), 15.II.19)

[See 190214(1).]

190215   [To Lenin.] (640000(1): 270)

Trans.: Eng. 640000(1): 271.

[On re-enlistment of ex-officers.]

190219   Petrograd pod ugrozoi. (Petrograd under threat.) (Severnaya Kommuna, 1919)

Repr.: 260000(18).II: 235-9.

Trans.: Am. Call, 18.V.19; Living Age, 5.IV.19.

[Speech to Petrograd Soviet.]

190220   Nasha politika v dele sozdaniya armii. (Our policy in the matter of creating an army.) (<u>Iz</u>, (43), 25.II.19; <u>Pr</u>, (43), 25.II.19) [Theses of report. cf. 190323(1).]

[190323(1)]   Kakoi voennyi zhurnal nam nuzhen? (What sort of military journal do we need?) (<u>Voennoe Delo</u>, (5-6), 23.II.19)
<u>Repr</u>.: 230000(7).II.i: 152-7.
<u>Trans</u>.: p.q. 370000(12): Ch. VIII;
         Fr. 680000(1): 625-33.
[Speech at conference of editors and staffs of military publications.]

[190223(2)]   i dr.: Dekret ob nekotorykh kategorii krasnoarmeitsev k godovshchine Krasnoi Armii. (Decree on certain categories of Red Army men for the anniversary of the Red Army.) (<u>Pr</u>, (42), 23.II.19)

190224   Na frontakh. (At the front.) (<u>Iz</u>, (46), 28.II.19)
<u>Repr</u>.: 190000(16); *190000(21); *190000(22); *190000(34); *[190000(35)];
         230000(7).II.i: 14-37; 260000(18).II: 67-96.
<u>Trans</u>.: Fr. 680000(1): 461-91.

[190225]   Otsenka sostoyaniya Krasnoi Armii. (An estimate of the state of the Red Army.) (230000(7).II,i: 41-5)
<u>Trans</u>.: Fr. 680000(1): 495-500.
[Answers to questions of soviet press.]

[190226]   Lektsiya. (A lecture.) (<u>Iz</u>, (45), 27.II.19)

190300(1)   O nashe politike po otnosheniyu k krest´yanstvu. (On our policy on relations with the peasantry.) (260000(18).II: 539-41)
[Archives.]

190300(2)   [To CC.] (640000(1): 324)
<u>Trans</u>.: p.q. 300000(1): Ch. XXXVI; p.q. 410000(1): Ch. IX;
         Eng. 640000(1): 325.
[T2954.]

190300(3)   [Conversation with Lenin.] (300000(1): Ch. XXXVI)
<u>Trans</u>.: 300000(1): Ch. XXXVI; 410000(1): Ch. IX.

190300(4)   DER KRIEG UND DIE INTERNATIONALE.
[Trans. Ger. See [140000(3)] for all repr., trans., notes.]

190302(1)   Doklad ob RKP i Krasnoi Armii. (Report on CPR and the Red Army.)

(KI, (3), 1.VII.19)

Repr.: 240000(29): 14-7.

Trans.: Am. 451000: 31-4;

        Fr. IC, (3), VII.19;

        Ger. KomInt, (3), 1919.

[To 1st session of Comintern Congress.]

190302(2)   Prikaz, No. 80. (230000(7).II.i: 172)

Trans.: Fr. 680000(1): 649-50.

190302(3)   Prikaz, No. 81. (230000(7).II.ii: 234)

[Establishment of Order of the Red Banner.]

190302(4)   Prikaz, No. 82. (230000(7).II.i: 89-90)

Trans.: Fr. 680000(1): 552-3.

[A necessary explanation of the Statute, "Internal service of the
Workers and Peasants Red Army.]

190304   i dr.: Zayavlenie uchastnikov Tsimmerval dskaya konferentsym.
(Statement of participants in Zimmerwald Conferences.) (Iz, (53),
9.III.19)

Repr.: KI, (1), 1.V.19.

Trans.: Eng. Degras, CI.I; Call(Ln), 17.IV.19; CI, (1), 1.V.19;

        Fr. THÈSES: 17;

        Ger. KomInt, (1), VIII.19.

[Transmitting its functions, etc. to Comintern.]

190306(1)   —: Manifest Kommunisticheskogo Internatsionala. (Manifesto of the
Communist International.) (Iz, (52), 7.III.19; Pr, (52), 7.III.19)

Repr.: *190000(71); *[200000(100)]; *[200000(101)]; 240000(29): 3-13;

        260000(10): 38-49; KI, (1), 1.V.19; KRASNYI PETROGRAD: 3-12.

Trans.: Am. NI(WP), VI.43;

        Den. 3die: 35-46;

        Eng. 190000(51); Degras, CI.I: 38-47; CI, (1), 1.V.19;

           Soc(G), (XVIII.222), 17.VII.19; p.q. Workers Dreadnought,

           (VI.33), 11.VIII.19;

        Fin. KAPITALISTINEN: 20-34;

        Fr. THÈSES: 30-4; IC, (1), 1919;

        Ger. [190000(64)]; *190000(74); KomInt, (1), VIII.19; p.q.

           ALMANACH; PROTOKOLL: 171-95;   ++++

190306(1)   ++++ Trans.: Hun. *190000(73);

                   Lat. <u>Jelgawas Komunists</u>, (34-6), 14-16.III.19;

                   Nor. TREDJE INTERNASJONALE: 40-54; <u>Ny Tid</u>, 1,2.IV.19;

                   Swed. TREDJE INTERNATIONALEN: 65-82.

[190306(2)]   Velikoe vremya. (Great times.) (<u>Iz</u>, (51), 6.III.19; <u>Pr</u>, (51), 6.III.19)
               <u>Repr</u>.: 240000(29): 28-30; 260000(10): 28-30; <u>KI</u>, (1), 1.V.19.
               <u>Trans</u>.: Am. 451000: 48-9;

                   Eng. <u>Call</u>(Ln), 11.IX.19; <u>CI</u>, (1), 1.V.19;

                   Fin. KAPITALISTINEN: 80-2;

                   Fr. <u>IC</u>, (1), 1919;

                   Ger. <u>KomInt</u>, (1), 1919.

190306(3)   Torzhestvennoe zasedanie v chest III Internationala. (Celebration
               meeting in honour of the 3rd International.) (<u>Iz</u>, (52), 7.III.19;
               <u>Pr</u>, (52), 7.III.19)
               [Speech.]

190309(1)   Tovarishcham spartakovstam. (To comrades of the Spartacus League.)
               (240000(29): 21-5)
               <u>Repr</u>.: 260000(10): 93-7.
               <u>Trans</u>.: Am. 451000: 39-43.

190309(2)   Prikaz, No. 83. (<u>Iz</u>, (54), 11.III.19; <u>Pr</u>, (54), 11.III.19)
               <u>Repr</u>.: 230000(7).II.ii: 235; 240000(29): 17-8.
               <u>Trans</u>.: Am. 451000: 35; <u>FI</u>, VIII.45; <u>Soviet Russia</u>, 25.XII.20.

190312   Pref. A REVIEW AND SOME PERSPECTIVES, 210000(39).
               <u>Repr</u>.: 620700(1): 161-7.
               <u>Trans</u>.: Am. 650000(3): 161-7; 690000(13): 29-35;

                   Fr. 690415;

                   Ger. 670000(6): 121-8;

                   Iran. 650000(4);

                   Jap. 670131: 3-14.
               [Trans. Eng.]

190316   [At CC.]
               [c. 640000(1): 296; on Okulov as co-rapporteur on military policy.]

[190317(1)]   K VIII s"ezdu RKP. (To 8th Congress CPR.) (V Puti, 17.III.19;
                Iz, (59), 18.III.19)
                Repr.: 230000(7).II.i: 46-9.
                Trans.: Fr. 680000(1): 500-5.
                [Press interview.]

190317(2)   Ya.M.Sverdlov. (230000(7).II.ii: 236-8)
                [Obituary.]

190317(3)   [To CC.] (640000(1): 302)
                Trans.: Eng. 640000(1): 303.
                [On Sverdlov's death.]

190317(4)   [To Lenin.] (640000(1): 302)
                Trans.: Eng. 640000(1): 303.
                [On unified command of anti-soviet troops.]

190318(1)   Prikaz, No. 84. (Iz, (64), 25.III.19; Pr, (64), 25.III.19)
                Repr.: 230000(7).II.ii: 239.
                [To railwaymen.]

190318(2)   Prikaz, No. 85. (Iz, (64), 25.III.19)
                Repr.: 230000(7).II.ii: 240-1.

190318(3)   Obrashchenie k krest´yanam. (Appeal to the peasants.) (Iz, (65),
                26.III.19; Pr, (64), 25.III.19)
                Repr.: 260000(18).II: 532-4.

190318(4)   Prikaz, No. 86. (Iz, (64), 25.III.19; Pr, (64), 25.III.19)
                Repr.: 230000(7).II.ii: 242-5; 260000(18).II: 534-5.
                [Long live the unity of the Red Army and the peasantry!]

[190318(5)]   V Parizhe. (In Paris.) (220000(3).I: 13)
                Repr.: 260000(17): 48-9.
                [PS. 220424(5).]

[190318(6)]   Martov. (220000(3).I: 15-7)
                Repr.: 260000(17): 66-8.
                [PS. 220424(6).]

[190318(7)]   Karl Kautskii. (220000(3).I: 22-6)
                Repr.: 260000(17): 44-8.
                [PS. 220424(4).]

190318(8)   [Item.] (220000(3).I: 22-6)

190318(9)   [To Lenin.] (640000(1): 304)
             Trans.: Eng. 640000(1): 305.
             [On destruction of railway lines.]

190320   [To Lenin.] (640000(1): 306)
             Trans: Eng. 640000(1): 307.
             [On evacuation.]

190321(1)   [To Lenin.] (640000(1): 306)
             Trans.: Eng. 640000(1): 307.
             [On uprisings behind Eastern Front.]

190321(2)   [To Lenin.] (640000(1): 308)
             Trans.: Eng. 640000(1): 309.

190322(1)   [To Stalin.] (640000(1): 310)
             Trans.: Eng. 640000(1): 311.
             [On Volga peasantry.]

190322(2)   [To CC.] (p.q. 300000(1): Ch. XXXVI)
             Trans.: 300000(1): Ch. XXXVI.
             [On Volga peasantry.]

190323(1)   NASHA POLITIKA V DELE SOZDANIYA ARMII (OUR POLICY IN THE MATTER OF
             CREATING AN ARMY), 190000(23).
             Repr.: 230000(7).I: 186-95; 260000(18).I: 377-89.
             Trans.: Eng. p.q. Deutscher, PA: 478;
                     Am. p.q. Current History, XI.19;
                     Fr. 680000(1): 220-32;
                     Ger. 240000(40): 165-75.
             [Theses confirmed by 8th Congress CPR. cf. 190220.]

190323(2)   [To Stalin.] (640000(1): 312)
             Trans.: Eng. 640000(1): 313.
             [On Verkhovsky.]

190324(1)   Kommunistam na vostochnom fronte. (To the communists on the Eastern
             Front.) (Pr, (70), 1.IV.19)
             Repr.: *190000(9); 230000(7).II.i: 313-5; V Puti, (27), 6.IV.19.
             Trans.: Fr. 680000(1): 801-4.

190324(2)   [To Lenin.] (640000(1): 314)
                Trans.: Eng. 640000(1): 315.
                [On Verkhovsky.]

190324(3)   [To Stalin.) (640000(1): 316)
                Trans.: Eng. 640000(1): 317.
                [On Verkhovsky.]

190324(4)   [To Stalin.] (640000(1): 318)
                Trans.: Eng. 640000(1): 319.
                [On Volga inspection.]

190325   [To MRC, Serpukhov.] (640000(1): 322)
                Trans.: Eng. 640000(1): 323.
                [On 5th Army.]

190326   Prikaz, No. 87 po 2-i armii. (Order of the Day, No. 87, to 2nd Army.)
                (230000(7).II.i: 316)
                Trans.: Fr. 680000(1): 804-5.

190327   Izdykhayushchaya kontr-revolyutsiya. (The expiring counter-revolution.)
                (V Puti, (27), 6.IV.19)
                Repr.: 230000(7).II.ii: 244-6; 260000(18).II: 535-8; Pr, (86), 24.IV.19.

190329   Nashi zadachi. (Our tasks.) (230000(7).II.i: 50-2)
                Trans.: Fr. 680000(1): 505-8.
                [Interview with Rosta [predecessor of TASS]. Archives.]

190330   Ob izbranii tov. Kalinina predsedatelem VTsIK. (The election of cde.
                Kalinin as Chairman of All-Russian CEC.) (Iz, (70), 1.IV.19)
                Repr.: 260000(18).II: 541-2.
                [Speech to All-Russian CEC.]

190400(1)   PS. [130713]. (260000(17): 16)

190400(2)   THE HISTORY OF THE RUSSIAN REVOLUTION TO BREST-LITOVSK.
                [Trans. Eng. See 180000(5) for all trans., repr., notes.]

190401   Opasnost na vostoke. (Danger in the East.) (Severnaya Kommuna, (74),
                3.IV.19)
                Repr.: 260000(18).II: 99-112.
                [Report to Plenum Moscow Soviet. Archives.]

190403   Prikaz, No. 88. (<u>Iz</u>, (73), 4.IV.19)
                <u>Repr.</u>: 230000(7).II.ii: 247.

190405(1)   Kakoe pravitel'stvo prochnee? (Which government is the better based?)
                (230000(7).II.ii: 248-9)

190405(2)   [To CC CPR.] (640000(1): 338)
                <u>Trans.</u>: Eng. 640000(1): 339.
                [On appointment of Smilga.]

190406(1)   K inostrannym soldatam russkogo severa. (To the foreign soldiers of
                northern Russia.) (230000(7).II.ii: 250)

190406(2)   VOSTOCHNYI FRONT (THE EASTERN FRONT), *190000(24).
                <u>Repr.</u>: 230000(7).II.i: 317-33; 260000(18).II: 112-32.
                <u>Trans.</u>: Fr. 680000(1): 805-25.
                [Speech to Joint-session of Samara Provincial Committee CPR, and trade
                union representatives.]

190407(1)   Na Ural! (To the Urals!) (<u>Pr</u>, (83), 17.IV.19)
                <u>Repr.</u>: *190000(15); 230000(7).II.i: 334-6; 260000(18).II: 132-5.
                <u>Trans.</u>: Fr. 680000(1): 825-8.
                        Am. Copeland.

190407(2)   [To CC CPR.] (640000(1): 340)
                <u>Trans.</u>: Eng. 640000(1): 341.
                [On 5th Army.]

190407(3)   [To Central Supply Administration.] (640000(1): 340)
                <u>Trans.</u>: Eng. 640000(1): 341.
                [On 5th Army's ~~medical~~ supplies.]

190407(4)   [To Health Commissariat.] (640000(1): 342)
                <u>Trans.</u>: Eng. 640000(1): 343.
                [On 5th Army's medical supplies.]

190409   Vesna, kotoraya reshaet. (A spring which will be decisive.) (<u>V Puti</u>,
                (29), 11.IV.19)
                <u>Repr.</u>: *[190000(30)]; 230000(7).II.i: 337-9; 260000(18).II: 140-3;
                      <u>Pr</u>, (84), 18.IV.19.
                <u>Trans.</u>: Eng. Dennis: 91;
                      Fr. 680000(1): 828-31.

190410(1)   Chego khochet Kolchak? (Why does Kolchak laugh?) (V Puti, (30), 1919)
            Repr.: 230000(7).II.i: 340-2; DerKom, (84), 15.IV.19.
            Trans.: Fr. 680000(1): 831-4.

190410(2)   [To Lenin.] (640000(1): 344)
            Trans.: Eng. 640000(1): 345.
            [On Eastern Front. T152.]

190412(1)   Tezisy TsK RKP(b) v sviazi s polozheniem na vostochnom fronte. (Theses
            of CC CPR(b) on the situation on the Eastern Front.) (Iz, (79),
            12.IV.19)
            Repr.: 260000(18).II: 135-8.
            [All resources to the Eastern Front!]

190412(2)   Bor'ba za Volgu. (The struggle for the Volga.) (V Puti, (31), 15.IV.19)
            Repr.: 230000(7).II.i: 343-5; 260000(18).II: 138-40.
            Trans.: Fr. 680000(1): 834-6.

190412(3)   Krasnye moryaki — na Ural! (Red Sailors, to the Urals!)
            (Nizhnegorodskaya Kommuna, 13,15.IV.19)
            Repr.: 260000(18).II: 143-8.
            [Speech to Red Sailors in Nizhne Novgorod.]

190413   Na chto nadeetsya Kolchak? (What does Kolchak rely on?) (V Puti, (31),
            18.IV.19)
            Repr.: 230000(7).II.i: 346-7; Pr, (87), 25.IV.19.
            Trans.: Fr. 680000(1): 837-9.

190414   Chto nuzhno Rossii. (What Russia needs.) (V Puti, (32), 18.IV.19)
            Repr.: 230000(7).II.i: 348-50; 260000(18).II: 148-50; Pr, (88),
                    26.IV.19; Zvezda, (106), 1.V.19.
            Trans.: Fr. 680000(1): 839-42.

190415   [To Sklyansky.] (640000(1): 356)
            Trans.: Eng. 640000(1): 357.
            [On attack on Kolchak.]

190416   [To Tsyurupa.] (640000(1): 358)
            Trans.: Eng. 640000(1): 359.
            [On 7th Army's supplies.]

190417   Polzuchaya revolyutsiya. (A creeping revolution.) (<u>Pr</u>, (85), 23.IV.19)

         <u>Repr</u>.: 230000(7).II.ii: 251-4; 240000(29): 25-8; 260000(10): 97-101.

         <u>Trans</u>.: Am. 451000: 44-7;

                Fr. LA RÉVOLUTION ALLEMANDE: 11-4.

[190418(1)]   Za dymovoi zavesoi. (Behind the smoke screen.) (<u>V Puti</u>, (32), 18.IV.19)

         <u>Repr</u>.: 230000(7).II.i: 351-2.

         <u>Trans</u>.: Fr. 680000(1): 842-4.

190418(2)   [At Politbureau CPR(b).] (p.q. 410000(1): Ch. IX,X)

         Russian: 640000(1): 360.

         <u>Trans</u>.: p.q. 410000(1): Ch. IX,X;

                Eng. 640000(1): 361.

190418(3)   Lenin i T.: [Telegram to Rakovsky.] (p.q.260000(1a).II: 586)

         Russian: 640000(1): 364.

         <u>Trans</u>.: Am. Wolfe: 170;

                Eng. 640000(1): 365.

190419   Tovarishcham pechatnikam s fronta. (To comrade-pressmen at the front.)

         (<u>Krasnyi Sever</u>, 7.V.19)

         <u>Repr</u>.: 230000(7).II.ii: 255; 270000(2): 243-4.

190420(1)   Prikaz, No. 89. (230000(7).II.ii: 256)

[190420(2)]   Rossiya ili Kolchak? (Russia or Kolchak?) (<u>V Puti</u>, (34), 20.IV.19)

         <u>Repr</u>.: 230000(7).II.i: 364-6; 260000(18).II: 160-3.

         <u>Trans</u>.: Fr. 680000(1): 855-8.

190420(3)   Da zdravstvuet pervoe maya! Da zdravstvuet kommunizm! K

         trudyashchimsya vsego mira. (Long live May Day! Long live Communism!

         To the toilers of the whole world.) (<u>KI</u>, (1), 1.V.19)

         <u>Trans</u>.: Eng. <u>CI</u>, (1), 1.V.19;

                Fr. <u>IC</u>, (1), 1919.

190423(1)   Po povodu voennykh tribunalov. (Concerning military tribunals.)

         (<u>V Puti</u>, (35), 24.IV.19)

         <u>Repr</u>.: 230000(7).II.i: 140-2.

         <u>Trans</u>.: Fr. 680000(1): 611-4.

190423(2)   Prikaz, No. 90. (230000(7).II.i: 353-5)

         <u>Trans</u>.: Fr. 680000(1): 844-8.

         [To commissars of 3rd Army.]

190424(1) Zadacha Vostochnogo fronta. (Tasks of the Eastern front.)

(<u>V Puti</u>, (36), 1919)

<u>Repr</u>.: 230000(7).II.i: 356.

<u>Trans</u>.: Fr. 680000(1): 848-9.

190424(2) Vsem grazhdanam Vyatskoi gubernii. (To all citizens of Vyatka

Province.) (<u>V Puti</u>, (35), 24.IV.19)

<u>Repr</u>.: *190000(25); *[190000(36)]; 230000(7).II.i: 357-8.

<u>Trans</u>.: Fr. 680000(1): 849-50.

190424(3) Na zashchitu revolyutsii! (In defence of the revolution!) (<u>Krasnyi</u>

<u>Nabat</u>, 27.IV.19)

<u>Repr</u>.: 260000(18).II: 150-60.

[Speech at meeting in Vyatka.]

190426 Prikaz, No. 91. (230000(7).II.i: 359)

<u>Trans</u>.: Fr. 680000(1): 851-2.

190427 Chto delaesh, delai skoree! (What you can do, do quickly!)

(<u>V Puti</u>, (37), 27.IV.19)

<u>Repr</u>.: 230000(7).II.i: 360-1; 260000(18).II: 538-9.

<u>Trans</u>.: Fr. 680000(1): 852-3.

[Letter to cde. Yakovlev. Archives.]

[190428] Ne teryaite vremeni! (Don't lose any time!) (<u>V Puti</u>, (38), 28.IV.19)

<u>Repr</u>.: 230000(7).II.i: 362-3.

<u>Trans</u>.: Fr, 680000(1): 853-5.

[190429] Mysli o khode proletarskoi revolyutsii. (V Puti.) (Thoughts on the

progress of the proletarian revolution: En route.) (<u>Iz</u>, (90,92),

29.IV, 1.V.19; <u>KI</u>, (1), 1.V.19)

<u>Repr</u>.: 240000(29): 30-43; 260000(10): 14-28.

<u>Trans</u>.: Am. 451000: 50-63; 640800: 117-31;

   Ger. p.q. <u>KomArb</u>, (I.132), 3.X.19;

   Jap. 681125: 125-39;

   Sp. 670000(5): 117-31;

   Swed. 691100(2): 102-15.

190430 Eshche raz: Ne teryaite vremeni! (Once more, don't lose any time!)

(<u>V Puti</u>, (39), 1919)

<u>Repr</u>.: 230000(7).II.i: 367-8.

<u>Trans</u>.: Fr. 680000(1): 859-60.

190501(1)   Prikaz, No. 92. (230000(7).II.i: 369)
              Trans.: Fr. 680000(1): 861-2.
              [To those fighting on the Eastern Front.]

[190501(2)]   1-e maya. (May Day.) (230000(7).II.ii: 257)

190501(3)   [To CC CPR.] (640000(1): 386)
              Trans.: Eng. 640000(1): 387.
              [On military policy in Ukraine.]

190502(1)   [To Sklyansky.] (640000(1): 394)
              Trans.: Eng. 640000(1): 395.
              [On Panyushkin.]

190502(2)   [To Sklyansky.] (640000(1): 396)
              Trans.: Eng. 640000(1): 397.
              [On personnel.]

190503(1)   Gore dezertiram! (Woe to deserters!) (V Puti, (40), 1919)
              Repr.: 230000(7).II.i: 135-6.
              Trans.: Fr. 680000(1): 607-8.

190503(2)   Dezertiry — pomoshchniki Kolchaka. (Deserters are aid to Kolchak.)
              (V Puti, (40), 1919)
              Repr.: *190000(4); 230000(7).II.i: 135-6.
              Trans.: Fr. 680000(1): 608-10.

190503(3)   [To CC CPR] (640000(1): 398)
              Trans.: Eng. 640000(1): 399.

190504   Nachalo pereloma. (Beginning of a change.) (V Puti, (41), 1919)
              Repr.: 230000(7).II.i: 370.
              Trans.: Fr. 680000(1): 862-3.

190505   Prikaz, No. 94. (230000(7).II.i: 371)
              Trans.: Fr, 680000(1): 863-4.

190506   Prikaz, No. 95. (230000(7).II.1: 372)
              Trans.: Fr. 680000(1): 864-5.

190507(1)   Velikii ekzamen. (A great test.) (V Puti, (43), 1919)
              Repr.: 230000(7).II.i: 373-4; Iz, (99), 10.V.19.
              Trans.: Fr. 680000(1): 865-6.

190507(2)   [To Sklyansky.] (640000(1): 402)
               Trans.: Eng. 640000(1): 403.
               [On Trifonov.]

190507(3)   [To Lenin.] (640000(1): 404)
               Trans.: Eng. 640000(1): 405.
               [On Eastern Front.]

190508   [and others: Telegram to L.B.Kamenev.] (ProlRev, (6), 1925: 148)
               [c. McNeal: 86.]

190510   [Telegram to MRC, Kiev.] (p.q. Tcherikower: 286)
               [Trans. Yid. For formation of Jewish battalions.]

190511   Nash Yuzhnyi front. (Our Southern Front.) (V Puti, (45), 1919)
               Repr.: 230000(7).II.i: 173; Pr, (111), 24.V.19.
               Trans.: Fr. 680000(1): 650-1.

190512(1)   Vosstanie v tylu. (Revolt in the rear.) (V Puti, (44), 1919)
               Repr.: 230000(7).II.i: 174.
               Trans.: Fr. 680000(1): 652-3.

190512(2)   Prikaz, No. 97. (230000(7).II.i: 91)
               Trans.: Fr. 680000(1): 553-4.

190512(3)   [Telegram to Lenin; on Saratov.]
               [c. 410000(1): Ch. X. T194.]

190512(4)   [To Sklyansky.] (640000(1): 412)
               Trans.: Eng. 640000(1): 413.
               [On Saratov.]

190513   [To Sklyansky.] (640000(1): 416)
               Trans.: Eng. 640000(1): 417.
               [On Cossack uprising.]

190514   [To Lenin.] (640000(1): 420)
               Trans.: Eng. 640000(1): 421.
               [On Southern Front.]

190515   Prikaz, No. 98. (230000(7).II.i: 175)
               Trans.: Fr. 680000(1): 653.

190516(1)   Za sovetskoi ugol! (For soviet coal!) (<u>V Puti</u>, (46), 1919)

Repr.: 230000(7).II.i: 176-7.

Trans.: Fr. 680000(1): 654-5.

190516(2)   Ukrainskie uroki. (Lessons of the Ukraine.) (<u>V Puti</u>, (47), 1919)

Repr.: 230000(7).II.i: 177-82.

Trans.: Fr. 680000(1): 655-60.

190516(3)   [To Sklyansky.] (640000(1): 428)

Trans.: Eng. 640000(1): 429.

[On CC meeting.]

190516(4)   [To Sklyansky.] (640000(1): 430)

Trans.: Eng. 640000(1): 431.

[On Panyushkin.]

190517(1)   [To CC CPR.] (640000(1): 430)

Trans.: Eng. 640000(1): 431.

[On Ukrainian Front.]

190517(2)   [To Sklyansky.] (640000(1): 432)

Trans.: Eng. 640000(1): 433.

[On Ukrainian Front.]

190519   Rech. (A speech.) (<u>Iz</u>(Vseukrainskogo TsIK), 20.V.19)

Repr.: 190000(23); 260000(18).II: 167-74.

[To All-Ukrainian CEC.]

190520   Rech. (A speech.) (<u>Iz</u>(Vseukrainskogo TsIK), 22.V.19)

Repr.: 260000(18).II: 174-9.

[To workers meeting in Kiev.]

190521(1)   Rech. (A speech.) (<u>Iz</u>(Vseukrainskogo TsIK), 25.V.19)

Repr.: 260000(18).II: 179-82.

[To Kharkov Soviet.]

190521(2)   [To Sklyansky.] (640000(1): 444)

Trans.: Eng. 640000(1): 445; 410000(1): Ch. X.

[On change of personnel.]

190521(3)   [To Sklyansky.] (640000(1): 446)

Trans.: Eng. 640000(1): 447.

[On paper currency in Ukraine.]

190521(4)   [To Sklyansky.] (640000(1): 448)
              Trans.: Eng. 640000(1): 449.
              [On operations against Cossack uprising.]

190521(5)   [To Sklyansky.] (640000(1): 448)
              Trans.: Eng. 640000(1): 449.
              [On deferment of CC meeting.]

190521(6)   [To Sklyansky.] (640000(1): 451)
              Trans.: Eng. 640000(1): 453.
              [On mandate for Bonch-Bruevich.]

190522(1)   [To Sklyansky.] (320000(2): 224)
              Trans.: Am. 370000(14): 229; 620000(3): 229; NI, VIII.35.
              [For Lenin; on the Eastern Front.]

190522(2)   Prikaz, No. 99. (230000(7).II.i: 183)
              Trans.: Fr. 680000(1): 661-2.
              [For N Army.]

190522(3)   [To Lenin.] (640000(1): 454)
              Trans.: Eng. 640000(1): 455.

190522(4)   [To Lenin.] (640000(1): 456)
              Trans.: Eng. 640000(1): 457.
              [On removal of Podvoisky.]

190522(5)   [To Sklyansky.] (640000(1): 458)
              Trans.: Eng. 640000(1): 459.
              [On supplies for Mariupol area.]

190523   [To MRC, Southern Front.] (640000(1): 460)
              Trans.: Eng. 640000(1): 461.
              [On 2nd Ukrainian Army.]

190524   [To Sklyansky.] (640000(1): 464)
              Trans.: Eng. 640000(1): 465.

190525   Prikaz, No. 100. (230000(7).II.i: 186)
              Trans.: Fr. 680000(1): 664-5.
              [To N Army.]

190526(1)   Yuzhnyi front podtyanis! Pobol′she predusmotritel′nosti, tochnosti,
vyderzhki. (Souther Front, brace yourselves! A little more foresight,
accuracy and tenacity.) (<u>V Puti</u>, (49), 1919)
<u>Repr</u>.: 230000(7).II.i: 184-5; <u>Iz</u>, (115), 29.V.19.
<u>Trans</u>.: Fr. 680000(1): 662-4.

190526(2)   [To Sklyansky.] (640000(1): 466)
<u>Trans</u>.: Eng. 640000(1): 467.
[On Kalegaev.]

190527(1)   [To Sklyansky.] (640000(1): 470)
<u>Trans</u>.: Eng. 640000(1): 471.
[On operations on the Southern Front.]

190527(2)   [To Sklyansky.] (640000(1): 472)
<u>Trans</u>.: Eng. 640000(1): 473.
[On Kalegaev.]

190600   † VINGT LETTRES.
<u>Repr</u>.: 390000(10).
<u>Trans</u>.: Eng. <u>Soc</u>(G), (XVIII.223-5,7), 24.VII-7,21.VIII.19.
[Trans. Fr. Supplement to <u>La Vie Ouvrière</u>, (11), VI.19.]

190601(1)   Devyatyi val. (The ninth wave.) (<u>V Puti</u>, (50), 2.VI.19)
<u>Repr</u>.: 230000(7).II.i: 187-8; 260000(18).II: 182-4.
<u>Trans</u>.: Fr. 680000(1): 665-7.

190601(2)   [Telegram No. 79/c to Sklyansky and Lenin.] (320000(2): 208-9)
<u>Trans</u>.: Am. 370000(14): 212-3; 620000(3): 212-3.
[On food supplies of Southern Army. T254.]

190601(3)   [To Sklyansky.] (640000(1): 498)
<u>Trans</u>.: Eng. 640000(1): 499.
[On operations on Southern Front.]

190601(4)   [To Sklyansky.] (640000(1): 500)
<u>Trans</u>.: Eng. 640000(1): 501.
[On Ukrainian Army.]

190601(5)   [To Sklyansky.] (640000(1): 502)
<u>Trans</u>.: Eng. 640000(1): 503.
[On road improvement.]

190601(6)   [To Sklyansky.] (640000(1): 504)
Trans.: Eng. 640000(1): 505.

190601(7)   [To Sklyansky.] (640000(1): 506)
Trans.: Eng. 640000(1): 507.
[On Eastern Front.]

190602   Makhnovshchina. (Makhno-ism.) (V Puti, (51), 1919)
Repr.: 230000(7).II.i: 189-91; Pr, (128), 15.VI.19.
Trans.: Fr. 680000(1): 668-71.

190603   [To Sklyansky.] (640000(1): 516)
Trans.: Eng. 640000(1): 517.

190604(1)   Beseda. (An interview.) (V Puti, (52), 5.VI.19)
Repr.: 230000(7).II.i: 192-5; 260000(18).II: 184-8; Iz, (126), 13.VI.18.
Trans.: Fr. 680000(1): 672-5.
[With Kharkov press.]

190604(2)   [Prikaz, No.1824.]
[c. Footman: 272.]

190605(1)   Prikaz, No. 105. (230000(7).II.i: 196-8)
Trans.: Fr. 680000(1): 675-9.

190605(2)   [To Sklyansky.] (640000(1): 528)
Trans.: Eng. 640000(1): 529.
[On situation on Southern Front.]

190605(3)   [To Sklyansky.] (640000(1): 530)
Trans.: Eng. 640000(1): 531.
[On situation on Southern Front.]

190605(4)   [To Sklyansky.] (640000(1): 534)
Trans.: Eng. 640000(1): 535.
[On Caspian flotilla.]

190605(5)   [To Sklyansky.] (640000(1): 536)
Trans.: Eng. 640000(1): 537.
[On abandoned stores.]

190605(6)   [To Sklyansky.] (640000(1): 536)
Trans.: Eng. 640000(1): 537.
[On XI Army.]

190606(1)   Prikaz, No. 106. (230000(7).II.i: 199)
                 <u>Trans.</u>: Fr. 680000(1): 679–80.

190606(2)   Prikaz, No. 107. (230000(7).II.i: 200)
                 <u>Trans.</u>: Fr. 680000(1): 680–1.

190607   [To Sklyansky.] (640000(1): 542)
                 <u>Trans.</u>: Eng. 640000(1): 543.

190608   Prikaz, No. 108. (230000(7).II.i: 201–2)
                 <u>Trans.</u>: Fr. 680000(1): 681–3.
                 [An end to Makhno-ism!]

190609   Prikaz, No. 111. (230000(7).II.i: 203)
                 <u>Trans.</u>: Fr. 680000(1): 683–4.

190610   Styd i sram. (Shame and disgrace.) (<u>V Puti</u>, (53), 1919)
                 <u>Repr.</u>: 230000(7).II.i: 204–5; <u>Pr</u>, (127), 14.VI.19.
                 <u>Trans.</u>: Fr. 680000(1): 684–5.

190614   O polozhenie na Yuzhnom fronte. (The situation on the Southern Front.)
                 (230000(7).II.i: 206–9)
                 <u>Trans.</u>: Fr. 680000(1): 688–90.
                 [Report to Plenum Kharkov Soviet.]

190617   Bulat i zlato. (Steel and gold.) (<u>V Puti</u>, (54), 1919)
                 <u>Repr.</u>: 230000(7).II.i: 92–5; <u>Pr</u>, (137), 26.VI.19.
                 <u>Trans.</u>: Fr. 680000(1): 554–8.

190618   Prikaz, No. 112. (230000(7).II.i: 210)
                 <u>Trans.</u>: Fr. 680000(1): 691–2.
                 [Severe punishment for deserters, Makhno-ites, disorganizers and
                 traitors in the Workers and Peasants Red Army.]

190619   Prikaz, No. 113. (230000(7).II.i: 211–4)
                 <u>Trans.</u>: Fr. 680000(1): 692–6.
                 [For 13th Army.]

190626   [To Chairman, Council of Defence.] (640000(1): 576)
                 <u>Trans.</u>: Eng. 640000(1): 577.
                 [On loss of artillery on Southern Front.]

190627(1)   Prikaz, No. 118. (230000(7).II.i: 96)
                 <u>Trans.</u>: Fr. 680000(1): 558–9.

190627(2) Ugroza Voronezhu i Kursku. (The threat to Voronezh and Kursk.)
(V Puti, (55), 28.VI.19)
Repr.: 230000(7).II.i: 215-6; 260000(18).II: 188-90; Iz, (143), 3.VII.19.
Trans.: Fr. 680000(1): 696-8.

[190628(1)] Shtatnye sovetskie dezertiry. (Soviet Staff deserters.) (V Puti, (55),
28.VI.19)
Repr.: 230000(7).II.i: 139.
Trans.: Fr. 680000(1): 610-1.

190628(2) Eshche raz ukrainskie uroki. (Once more, Ukrainian lessons.) (V Puti,
(56), 1919)
Repr.: 230000(7).II.i: 217-9.
Trans.: Fr. 680000(1): 698-702.

190629 Prikaz, No. 119. (230000(7).II.i: 220)
Trans.: Fr. 680000(1): 702-3.

190700 THE HISTORY OF THE RUSSIAN REVOLUTION TO BREST-LITOVSK.
[Trans. Eng. See 180000(5) for all trans., repr., notes. 2nd ed.]

*190703 [*Speech to CC.]
[c. 640000(1): 585]

190705 [Offer to resign from Revolutionary Council of War.]
[c. 410000(1): Ch. X.]

190708(1) Prichiny neudach na Yuzhnom fronte. (Reasons for failure on the
Southern Front.) (230000(7).II.i: 221-3)
Trans.: Fr. 680000(1): 703-7.

190708(2) Vnimanie k ranenym i bol´nym voinam! (Attention to the wounded and
sick servicemen!) (230000(7).II.ii: 291-2)

190709 Prikaz, No. 121. (230000(7).II.i: 97)
Trans.: Fr. 680000(1): 559-60.

190710 Glubokomyslennoe pustoslovie. (Profound drivel.) (Iz, (161), 24.VII.19)
Repr.: 230000(7).II.i: 143-8; Voennoe Delo, (23-24), 1919.
Trans.: Eng. p.q. Workers Dreadnought, (VI.38), 13.XII.19;
Fr. 680000(1): 615-21;
It. p.q. Ordine Nuovo, (I.120), 1.V.21.

190711(1)   Zelenyi i belyi. (The Green and White.) (<u>V Puti</u>, (59), 1919)

<u>Repr</u>.: 230000(7).II.i: 224-5.

<u>Trans</u>.: Fr. 680000(1): 707-8.

190711(2)   Prikaz, No. 122. (230000(7).II.i: 226)

<u>Trans</u>.: Fr. 680000(1): 709.

190711(3)   [To Sklyansky.] (640000(1): 596)

<u>Trans</u>.: Eng. 640000(1): 597.

[On conference of political workers of the 8th **Army**.]

190712   Ocherednye voprosy voennogo stroitel´stva. (The next problems in military construction.) (230000(7).II.i: 53-6)

<u>Trans</u>.: Fr. 680000(1): 508-15.

[Letter to Revolutionary Soviets of Army and Fronts.]

190714   [To Sklyansky.] (640000(1): 598)

<u>Trans</u>.: Eng. 640000(1): 599.

190715   Vostok i Yug. (East and South.) (<u>V Puti</u>, (61), 1919)

<u>Repr</u>.: 230000(7).II.i: 227-8.

<u>Trans</u>.: Fr. 680000(1): 709-10.

190716   Do zimy zakonchit! (The end by winter!) (<u>V Puti</u>, (61), 1919)

<u>Repr</u>.: 230000(7).II.i: 229-30; <u>Iz</u>, (156), 18.VII.19.

<u>Trans</u>.: Eng. <u>Call</u>(Ln), 23.XII.19; <u>Soc</u>(G), (XVIII.245), 24.XII.19;
     Fr. 680000(1): 711-3.

190717   Prestupnaya demagogiya. (Criminal demagogy.) (230000(7).II.i: 231-4)

<u>Trans</u>.: Fr. 680000(1): 713-8.

190718(1)   Komandiry dolzhny umet povinovat´sya. (Commanders must know how to obey.) (<u>V Puti</u>, (64), 1919)

<u>Repr</u>.: 230000(7).II.i: 96-9.

<u>Trans</u>.: Fr. 680000(1): 560-2.

190718(2)   Prikaz, No. 126. (<u>Krasnaya Gazeta</u>, 30.VII.19)

<u>Repr</u>.: 230000(7).II.i: 235.

<u>Trans</u>.: Am. <u>Soviet Russia</u>, 14.II.20;
     Fr. 680000(1): 718-9.

[To servicemen on the Southern Front. Strike at the enemy, spare the prisoners.]

190719(1)   Deistvitel´nost i "kriticheskaya" boltovnya. (Reality and "critical" chatter.) (V Puti, (65), 1919)
Repr.: 230000(7).II.i: 237-9; Iz, (160), 23.VII.19.
Trans.: Fr. 680000(1): 720-4.

190719(2)   Urozhai i voina. (The harvest and the war.) (V Puti, (66), 19.VII.19)
Repr.: 230000(7).II.i: 236; 260000(18).II: 190-1; Pr, (170), 3.VIII.19.
Trans.: Fr. 680000(1): 719-20.

[190719(3)]   Nuzhen poryadok. (The need is for order.) (V Puti, (66), 19.VII.19)
Repr.: 230000(7).II.i: 241-2.
Trans.: Fr. 680000(1): 725-7.

190721   Prikaz, No. 129. (230000(7).II.i: 240)
Trans.: Fr. 680000(1): 724-5.

190722(1)   Prikaz, No. 130. (230000(7).II.i: 243)
Trans.: Fr. 680000(1): 727-8.

190722(2)   Prikaz, No. 131. (230000(7).II.i: 244)
Trans.: Fr. 680000(1): 728.
[To 14th Army.]

190723   Den ranenogo. (A day for the wounded.) (230000(7).II.ii: 295)

190724   T.: Partizanstvo i regulyarnaya armiya. (Partisanism and a regular army.) (Voennoe Delo, (25:54), 1919)
Repr.: 230000(7).II.i: 59-64; Iz, (187), 24.VIII.19.
Trans.: Fr. 680000(1): 515-22.

190726   Prikaz, No. 132. (230000(7).II.i: 245-6)
Trans.: Fr. 680000(1): 729-30.
[To 12th and 14th Armies.]

190727(1)   [To Lenin.] (640000(1): 604)
Trans.: 410000(1): Ch. X;
        Eng. 640000(1): 605.
[On Yegorev and a plan of attack for the Southern Front. T321.]

190727(2)   [To Sklyansky.] (640000(1): 608)
Trans.: Eng. 640000(1): 609.

190728   Krasnaya Armiya. (The Red Army.) (<u>DSP</u>, 7.IX.19)

        <u>Repr.</u>: 230000(7).II.ii: 258-9.

190729(1)   [To Sklyansky.] (640000(1): 612)

        <u>Trans</u>.: 410000(1): Ch. X;

            Eng. 640000(1): 613.

        [On Southern Front.]

190729(2)   Prikaz, No. 134. (230000(7).II.i: 247-8)

        <u>Repr.</u>: p.q. 300000(1): Ch. XXXVI.

        <u>Trans</u>.: p.q. 300000(1): Ch. XXXVI;

            Fr. 680000(1): 730-3.

190729(3)   Nashi fronty i mezhdunarodnoe polozhenie. (Our Fronts and the

        international situation.) (<u>Iz</u>(Penza), 31.VII.19)

        <u>Repr.</u>: 260000(18).II: 191-9.

        [Report to meeting of Party workers in Penza.]

[190730(1)] Na pomoshch bol'nomu i ranenomu krasnoarmeitsu. (To the help of

        sick and wounded Red Army Men.) (230000(7).II.ii: 296)

        [Letter to the Committee for Aid to Sick and Wounded Red Army Men.]

[190800]   Slovo ukrainskim soldatam, obmanutym banditami. (A word to the

        Ukrainian soldiers deceived by the bandits.) (230000(7).II.i: 257-8)

        <u>Trans</u>.: Fr. 680000(1): 739-41.

190801(1)   Prikaz, No. 135. (230000(7).II.i: 249)

        <u>Trans</u>.: Fr. 680000(1): 732-3.

190801(2)   Brestskii etap. (The Brest stage.) (260000(18).I: 144-51)

        <u>Repr.</u>: Joffe: i-vi.

190801(3)   [To Lenin.] (640000(1): 618)

        <u>Trans</u>.: Eng. 640000(1): 619.

        [On the situation in the Ukraine.]

190802(1)   Prikaz, No. 136. (230000(7).II.i: 250)

        <u>Trans</u>.: Fr. 680000(1): 733.

190802(2)   Vozvrati vintovku! (Surrender rifles!) (<u>V Puti</u>, (73), 1919)

        <u>Repr.</u>: 230000(7).II.i: 251.

        <u>Trans</u>.: Fr. 680000(1): 734.

190802(3)   [To Sklyansky.] (640000(1): 618)
              Trans.: Eng. 640000(1): 619.

190803   Kto predal Poltavu? (Who betrayed Poltava?) (V Puti, (74), 1919)
              Repr.: 230000(7).II.i: 252-3.
              Trans.: Fr. 680000(1): 735-6.

190804   Makhno i drugie. (Makhno and [his] friends.) (V Puti, (75), 1919)
              Repr.: 230000(7).II.i: 254-5.
              Trans.: Fr. 680000(1): 737-8.

190805(1)   [Memorandum to CC CPR.] (640000(1): 620)
              Trans.: Am. p.q. Lerski: 161-2;
                      Eng. 640000(1): 621; p.q. Deutscher, PA: 456.
              [On 'Eastern Front' orientation.]

190805(2)   [Proposal to overhaul the Southern Front.]
              [c. Deutscher, PA: 457.]

190805(3)   [2nd proposal to overhaul the Southern Front.]
              [c. Deutscher, PA: 457.]

190805(4)   Programma militsii i ee akademicheskii kritik. (A programme for a
              militia and its academic critics.) (Voennoe Delo, (25:54): 1919)
              Repr.: 230000(7).II.i: 115-21.
              Trans.: Fr. 680000(1): 581-9.

190805(5)   [To Lenin.] (640000(1): 628)
              Trans.: Eng. 640000(1): 629.
              [On military measures in the Ukraine.]

190806(1)   [To Lenin.] (640000(1): 632)
              Trans.: Eng. 640000(1): 633.
              [On military measures in the Ukraine.]

190806(2)   [To Lenin.] (640000(1): 638)
              Trans.: Eng. 640000(1): 639.
              [On military measures in the Ukraine.]

190807(1)   Prikaz, No. 140. (230000(7).II.ii: 260)

190807(2)   [To Rakovsky.] (640000(1): 640)
              Trans.: Eng. 640000(1): 641.
              [On military measures in the Ukraine.]

190807(3)   [To Sklyansky.] (640000(1): 642)
              Trans.: Eng. 640000(1): 643.
              [On interpretation of T's telegram by CC.]

190807(4)   [Telegram to RVS, 12th Army.] (640000(1): 642)
              [Trans. Eng.]

190808   Prikaz, No. 142. (230000(7).II.i: 256)
              Trans.: Fr. 680000(1): 738-9.

190809(1)   Instruktsiya otvetstvennym rabotnikam 14-i Armii. (Instructions to
              responsible workers in the 14th Army.) (230000(7).II.i: 259-63)
              Trans.: Fr. 680000(1): 742-7.

190809(2)   14-ya Armiya i ee komanduyushchii. (The 14th Army and its
              commanders.) (230000(7).II.i: 264-5)
              Trans.: Fr. 680000(1): 747-9.

190809(3)   [To Lenin.] (640000(1): 646)
              Trans.: Eng. 640000(1): 647.
              [On interpretation by CC of T's telegram.]

190811   [To CC CPR.] (640000(1): 650)
              Trans.: Eng. 640000(1): 651.
              [On military situation in the Ukraine. T342.]

[190812]   Ukrainskii avgust. (August in the Ukraine.) (V Puti, (80), 12.VIII.19)
              Repr.: 230000(7).II.i: 266-7.
              Trans.: Fr. 680000(1): 749-51.

190813   Prikaz, No. 143. (230000(7).II.i: 270)
              Trans.: Fr. 680000(1): 754-5.

190816   Neobkhodimo osvezhit apparat snabsheniya. (Revvoensovetam.) (It is
              necessary to renew the Supply Administration: To Revolutionary
              Military Soviets.) (230000(7).II.ii: 261-2)

190818(1)   10-ya Armiya. (The 10th Army.) (V Puti, (83), 1919)
              Repr.: 230000(7).II.i: 268-9.
              Trans.: Fr. 680000(1): 752-4.

190818(2)   Na oblavu! (Chase them!) (DerevKom, (210), 18.IX.19; V Puti, (84),
              19.VIII.19)   ++++

190818(2)   ++++   Repr.: *190000(13); 230000(7).II.i: 271-2; DerevKom, (210), 18.IX.19.

Trans.: Fr. 680000(1): 757-8.

[190819]   Khrabost ot otchayaniya. (Bravery from despair.) (V Puti, (84),
19.VIII.19)

Repr.: 230000(7).II.i: 273-5; DerevKom, (190), 24.VIII.19; Pr,
(185), 22.VIII.19.

Trans.: Fr. 680000(1): 759-61.

190824   Kavaleristam korpusa Mamontova. (To the Cavalrymen of Mamontov's
corps.) (Iz, (188), 26.VIII.19)

Repr.: *190000(7); *190000(18); 230000(7).II.i: 276-7.

Trans.: Fr. 680000(1): 762-3.

190826(1)   Polozhenie na fronte. (The situation at the front.) (Iz, (189),
27.VIII.19)

Repr.: 230000(7).II.i: 65-9; 260000(18).II: 199-205.

Trans.: Fr. 680000(1): 523-9.

[Interview with Soviet press.]

190826(2)   Denikin budet unichtozhen! (Denikin will be destroyed!) (Iz, (189),
27.VIII.19; Pr, (189), 27.VIII.19)

Repr.: 260000(18).II: 206-13.

[Speech to Joint-session of Moscow Soviet and trade union and factory-
committee representatives.]

190829   Cherchil ugrozhaet, no nam ne strashno. (Chruchill threatens but we
are not afraid.) (260000(18).II: 239-40)

[Interview. Archives.]

[190900]   Nuzhno perevooruzhit´sya! (We must re-arm!) (Voennoe Delo, (26:55),
IX.19)

Repr.: 230000(7).II.i: 149-51.

Trans.: Fr. 680000(1): 622-5.

[Reply to some military specialists.]

[190901(1)]   Finlyandiya i trinadtsat drugikh. (Finland and the thirteen others.)
(Iz, (194), 3.IX.19; Pr, (194), 1.IX.19)

Repr.: 230000(7).II.i: 379-82; 260000(18).II: 241-5; p.q. 300000(1):
XXXV.

Trans.: p.q. 300000(1): Ch. XXXV;

Eng. Soc(G), (XIX.24), 1.VII.20;

Fr. 680000(1): 869-73.

[Warning to Finnish bourgeoisie against intervention.]

190901(2) Petrogradskii front v tsentre vnimaniya. (The Petrograd Front is the centre of attention.) (p.q. DerevKom, (196), 2.IX.19)
Repr.: 260000(18).II: 245-64; STENOTCHPETSOV, 1.IX.19.
[Speech at Extraordinary session of Petrograd Soviet.]

190901(3) Pis'mo k frantsuzskim tovarishcham. (Letter to French comrades.) (KI, (5), IX.19)
Repr.: 230000(8): 23-6; 260000(10): 123-6.
Trans.: Eng. Call(Ln), 4.XII.19; CI, (5), IX.19; Glasgow Worker, 6.XII.19;
    Fr. IC, (5), 1919; VieOuv, 21.XI.19; Lévy: 144-8;
    Ger. Kom(B), (III.1), 3.I.20; KomInt, (5), IX.19;
    Port. 200000(106).
[To Loriot, Rosmer, Monatte and Péricat.]

190902 Dobit Kolchaka, unichnoshit Denikina! (Finish off Kolchak, destroy Denikin!) (260000(18).II: 213-5)
[Interview.]

190904(1) Prikaz, No. 146. (230000(7).II.i: 278-9)
Trans.: Fr. 680000(1): 763-5.
[Fight against Mamontov's robber gang.]

190904(2) Prikaz, No. 147. (230000(7).II.i: 280-1)
Trans.: Fr. 680000(1): 766-7.
[On Southern Front.]

190904(3) Rabochie i krest'yane, vykhodite na oblavu! (Workers and peasants, make chase!) (V Puti, (86), 1919)
Repr.: 230000(7).II.i: 282.
Trans.: Fr. 680000(1): 767-8.

190904(4) [To Lenin.] (640000(1): 662)
Trans.: Eng. 640000(1): 663.
[On productivity of Tula factories.]

190906(1) Nuzhny li nam partizany? (Do we need partisans?) (V Puti, (88), 1919)
Repr.: 230000(7).II.i: 283-4; DerevKom, (207), 14.IX.19; Iz, (203), 13.IX.19.
Trans.: Fr. 680000(1): 769-70.

190906(2)   Plan operatsii na Yuzhnom fronte. (An operational plan for the
Southern Front.) (230000(7).II.i: 301-3)
Repr.: 260000(18).II: 556-9; p.q. 320000(2): 210; 640000(1): 664.
Trans.: Am. p.q. 370000(14): 223; p.q. 620000(3): 223;
      Eng. 640000(1): 665; p.q. Deutscher, PA: 441;
      Fr. 680000(1): 786-9.
[Notes from secret Archives.]

190906(3)   [& others: Telegram, No. 364. (p.q. 320000(2): 219-20)
Trans.: p.q. 410000(1): Ch. X;
      Am. p.q. 370000(14): 223-4; p.q. 620000(3): 223-4.
[Proposal to modify S.S.Kamenev's plan for Southern Front. T355.]

190906(4)   Pref. I.G. i R.Berzin, OB OBYAZANNOSTYAKH POLITICHESKIKH KOMISSAROV.
[Postface, 190906(5). Loc NYPL.]

190906(5)   Postface, I.G. i R.Berzin, OB OBYAZANNOSTYAKH POLITICHESKIKH KOMISSAROV.
[Pref., 190906(4).]

190908   Avantyuristam, kareristam, prokhodimtsam vkhoda net! (To adventurers
and careerists -- no admittance!) (V Puti, (90), 1919)
Repr.: 230000(7).II.i: 285-6.
Trans.: Fr. 680000(1): 771-3.

190910   Strel'ba ili treskotnya? (Gunfire or crackling?) (DerevKom, (216),
25.IX.19)
Repr.: 230000(7).II.ii: 263-4)

190911(1)   Proletarii, na konya! (Proletariat, to horse!) (V Puti, (93), 12.IX.19)
Repr.: 230000(7).II.i: 287-8; Pr, (209), 20.IX.19.
Trans.: Fr. 680000(1): 773-5.

190911(2)   Mestnoe sovetskoe opolchenie. (Places for soviet volunteers.)
(V Puti, (93), 12.IX.19)
Repr.: 230000(7).II.i: 289-90.
Trans.: Fr. 680000(1): 775-7.

190912(1)   Prikaz, No. 149. (230000(7).II.i: 291)
Trans.: Fr. 680000(1): 777-8.

190912(2)   Prikaz, No. 150. (230000(7).II.i: 292)
Trans.: Fr. 680000(1): 778.

190913   Polkovnik Mironov. (Colonel Mironov.) (<u>V Puti</u>, (94), 1919)
            <u>Repr</u>.: 230000(7).II.i: 293-5.
            <u>Trans</u>.: Fr. 680000(1): 778.

190914   Oktyabr′skaya revolyutsiya. (The October Revolution.) (<u>KI</u>, (6), X.19)
            <u>Repr</u>.: 240000(32).II: 81-6.
            <u>Trans</u>.: Cz. Rude Pravo, (40), 7.XI.20;
                 Eng. <u>CI</u>, (6), X.19;
                 Fr. <u>BulCom</u>, (I.3), 1.IV.20; <u>IC</u>, (6), 1919; <u>Revue Com</u>, (I.9),
                    XI.20;
                 Ger. <u>Inprekor</u>, (I.18), 3.XI.21; <u>KomInt</u>, (6), X.19; <u>RusKor</u>,
                    (I.ii.14-16), X.20.
            [cf. 211107.]

190916(1)   Urok Mironovshchiny. (The lesson of the Mironov affair.) (<u>V Puti</u>,
            (95), 17.IX.19)
           ·<u>Repr</u>.: 230000(7).II.i: 296-8; 260000(18).II: 215-8; <u>DerevKom</u>, (214),
                 23.IX.19; <u>Pr</u>, (210), 21.IX.19.
            <u>Trans</u>.: Fr. 680000(1): 782-4.

190916(2)   Rukovodyashchie nachala blizhaishei politiki na Donu. (Guiding
            principle for an immediate policy for the Don.) (230000(7).II.i:
            299-300)
            <u>Repr</u>.: 260000(18).II: 218-9.
            <u>Trans</u>.: Fr. 680000(1): 785-6.
            [Archives.]

190920   [To CC CPR.] (640000(1): 672)
            <u>Trans</u>.: Eng. 640000(1): 673.
            [On 'Eastern orientation.']

*190923   [*Speech at Alexeev Military School.]
            [c. 190924(1).]

190924(1)   Ne sdadimsya, vyderzhim, pobedim! (We shall not give up, we shall
            hold on and conquer!) (<u>Iz</u>(VTsIK), (214), 26.IX.19)
            <u>Repr</u>.: 260000(18).II: 219-24; p.q. <u>DerevKom</u>, (220), 30.IX.19.
            <u>Trans</u>.: Eng. 201200.
            [Speech to Moscow Conference CPR.]

190924(2)   Rezolyutsiya. (A resolution.) (260000(18): 224-6)
            [See 190924(1).]

⌊190927⌋   ⌊Letter to Politbureau.⌋   (p.q. 410000(1): Ch. X)

                 ⌊On plan for Souther Front.⌋

[190929]   Pokhorony pogibshikh pri vzryve kommunistov. (The funeral of the
                 communists killed in an explosion.) (<u>Pr</u>, (217), 30.IX.19)

190930   Rabotnitsa i voina. (The working woman and the war.) (<u>Pr</u>, (219),
                 2.X.19)

                 <u>Repr</u>.: 230000(7).II.ii: 297-8.

[191000]   O voenspetsakh. (Military specialists.) (230000(7).II.i: 101-3)

                 <u>Trans</u>.: Fr. 680000(1): 563-6.

                 ⌊Autumn, 1919. Archives.⌋

191004   Doklad. (A report.) (<u>Pr</u>, (223), 7.X.19)

                 <u>Repr</u>.: 240000(8): 157-67; p.q. 260000(18).II: 226-30; p.q. <u>MolGvard</u>,
                       1920: 19-20.

                 ⌊To 2nd Congress Russian Komsomol; fight against Denikin.⌋

191005   A.P.Nikolaev. Vechnaya pamyat Krasnomu Generalu. (A.P.Nikolaev.
                 To the eternal memory of a Red General.) (<u>V Puti</u>, (97) 16.X.19)

                 <u>Repr</u>.: 230000(7).II.i: 100; 260000(17): 257; <u>BoPr</u>, (2), 20.IX.19;
                       <u>KI</u>, (9), 22.III.20.

                 <u>Trans</u>.: Fr. 680000(1): 562; <u>BulCom</u>, (I.50-51), 23.XII.20; <u>IC</u>, (9),
                       1920;

                       Ger. <u>KomInt</u>, (II.9), 1920.

                 ⌊Note peculiarity of date in <u>BoPr</u>.⌋

191006   Tul´skaya stal. (Tual steel.) (<u>V Puti</u>, (96), 6.X.19)

                 <u>Repr</u>.: 230000(7).II.i: 304.

                 <u>Trans</u>.: Fr. 680000(1): 790-1.

191010   ⌊To Smilga.⌋ (640000(1): 684)

                 <u>Trans</u>.: Eng. 640000(1): 685.

                 ⌊On policy towards Don Cossacks.⌋

191013   Krasnaya Armiya v osveshchenii belogvardeitsam. (The Red Army as seen
                 by the White Guards.) (<u>Iz</u>, (231), 16.X.19)

                 <u>Repr</u>.: 230000(7).II.i: 104-13.

                 <u>Trans</u>.: Fr. 680000(1): 566-79.

191014(1)   Proekt pis´mo. (Draft letter.) (230000(7).II.ii: 265)   ++++

191014(1)   ++++   [To Party members of Revolutionary Military Soviets of Armies, Army Groups, and to Heads of Political Departments.]

191014(2)   Prikaz, No. 1692. (230000(7).II.ii: 266)

191014(3)   Zaklyuchitel´noe slovo. (Summary speech.) (230000(7).II.i: 70-5)
Trans.: Fr. 680000(1): 529-36.
[At conference of representatives of the Central Administration of Military Schools and Commanders Training Courses.]

191015(1)   [To Politbureau; not to abandon Petrograd.] (c. 300000(1): Ch. XXXV)

191015(2)   [Resolution of the Politbureau; on the situation at the front.]
(300000(1): Ch. XXXV)

191015(3)   [13 decrees proposed to CC, and accepted.] (c. 410000(1): Ch. X)

[191016(1)]   Udar po Petrogradu. (A blow at Petrograd.) (V Puti, (97), 16.X.19)
Repr.: 200000(2): 184-5; 230000(7).II.i: 385; 260000(18).II: 264-5.
Trans.: Fr. 680000(1): 875-6.

191016(2)   Petrograd oboronyaetsya i vnutri. (Petrograd is being defended and from within.) (Iz, (233), 18.X.19; Pr, (233), 18.X.19; V Puti, (98), 18.X.19)
Repr.: 200000(2): 186-8; 230000(7).II.i: 383-4; 260000(18).II: 265-7.
Trans.: Eng. p.q. Deutscher, PA: 413;
Fr. 680000(1): 873-5; V, (3), 15.III.39.

191017(1)   i Zinov´ev: Na pomoshch Krasnomu Petrogradu! (To the help of Red Petrograd!) (200000(2): 183)

191017(2)   [To Lenin.] (p.q. 300000(1): Ch. XXXV)
Repr.: 640000(1): 696.
Trans.: p.q. 300000(1): Ch. XXXV;
Eng. 640000(1): 697.
[On Yudenich and Esthonia. T369.]

191017(3)   [To Sklyansky.] (640000(1): 698)
Trans.: Eng. 640000(1): 699.

191018(1) Prikaz, No. 155. (230000(7).II.i: 400-2)

    Repr.: p.q. 300000(1): Ch. XXXV.

    Trans.: p.q. 300000(1): Ch. XXXV;

       Fr. 680000(1): 893-6.

    [For 7th Army; on false communiques.]

191018(2) Pered perelomom. (Before the crisis.) (Iz, (234), 19.X.19; Pr, (234),

    19.X.19)

    Repr.: 200000(2): 196-8; 230000(7).II.i: 403-4; 260000(18).II: 268-70.

    Trans.: Fr. 680000(1): 896-9.

191019 BOI ZA PETERBURG (THE BATTLE FOR PETROGRAD), 200000(1).

    Repr.: 200000(2): 210-27; 230000(7).II.i: 386-99; 260000(18).II:

       270-87; BoPr, (38), 21.X.19.

    Trans.: Fr. 680000(1): 877-93.

    [Archives.]

191020(1) Prikaz, No. 156-157. (BoPr, (38), 21.X.19; Iz, (236), 22.X.19; Pr,

    (236), 22.X.19)

    Repr.: 200000(2): 234; 230000(7).II.i: 405.

    Trans.: Fr. 680000(1): 899.

    [For Red Army Commanders, Commissars defending Petrograd: an appeal.]

191020(2) [To Lenin.] (640000(1): 704)

    Trans.: Eng. 640000(1): 705.

    [On Yudenich and Esthonia.]

191021(1) Perelom. (The Crisis.) (DerevKom, (239), 22.X.19; Iz, (236), 22.X.19;

    Pr, (236), 22.X.19; V Puti, (99), 22.X.19)

    Repr.: 200000(2): 237; 230000(7).II.i: 406; 260000(18).II: 287-8.

    Trans.: Fr. 680000(1): 900.

191021(2) i Zinov'ev: Prikaz. (200000(2): 233)

    [On battle for Petrograd.]

[191022] [Peredvizhnye sredstva: I.] (Means of communication: I.)

    (200000(2): 238)

    [On battle for Petrograd.]

191023 Pervyi udar. (The first blow.) (BoPr, (41), 24.X.19; Iz, (238),

    24.X.19; V Puti, (100), 24.X.19)

    Repr.: 200000(2): 240-1; 230000(7).II.i: 407; 260000(18).II: 288-9.

    Trans.: Fr. 680000(1): 901-2.

191024(1)   Prikaz, No. 158. (Iz, (239), 25.X.19; Pr, (239), 25.X.19)
             Repr.: 230000(7).II.i: 408.
             Trans.: Fr. 680000(1): 902-3.
             [On prisoners.]

191024(2)   Prikaz, No. 159. (Iz, (239), 25.X.19; Pr, (239), 25.X.19)
             Repr.: 200000(2): 243; 230000(7).II.i: 409; p.q. 300000(1): Ch. XXXV.
             Trans.: p.q. 300000(1): Ch. XXXV;
                     Fr. 680000(1): 903-4; Commune, (92), 24.II.38; QI, (14-15),
                        I-II.45; Lévy: 143.
             [For Red Army and Red Fleet; the two Britains.]

191024(3)   Prikaz, No. 160. (200000(2): 291)
             Repr.: 230000(7).II.i: 410.
             Trans.: Fr. 680000(1): 904-5.

191024(4)   [To Lenin.] (640000(1): 728)
             Trans.: Eng. 640000(1): 729.
             [On defence of Petrograd.]

191025(1)   Tanki. (Tanks.) (V Puti, (101), 1919)
             Repr.: 200000(2): 244-5; 230000(7).II.i: 411-2; Iz, (240), 26.X.19.
             Trans.: Fr. 680000(1): 905-7.

191025(2)   Velikaya pobeda. (A great victory.) (V Puti, (102), 26.X.19)
             Repr.: 200000(2): 246-7; 230000(7).II.i: 306; Iz, (241), 28.X.19.
             Trans.: Fr. 680000(1): 791-2.

191025(3)   [To Butov.] (640000(1): 730)
             Trans.: Eng. 640000(1): 731.
             [On Yudenich and Esthonia.]

191025(4)   [To Sklyansky.] (640000(1): 732)
             Trans.: Eng. 640000(1): 733.
             [On S.S.Kamenev's request to be consulted.]

[191026]   Privetstvie Revvoensovetu Yuzhnogo fronta po povodu razgroma konnykh
             korpusov belykh pod Voronezhom. (Greetings to the Revolutionary
             Military Soviet of the Southern Front on the occasion of the rout of
             the White Cavalry Corps near Voronezh.) (V Puti, (102), 26.X.19)
             Repr.: 230000(7).II.i: 305; Iz, (241), 28.X.19.
             Trans.: Fr. 680000(1): 791.

191027(1) [To Lenin.] (640000(1): 740)

Trans.: Eng. 640000(1): 741.

[On Yudenich and Esthonia.]

191027(2) [To Commander, 7th Army.] (640000(1): 744)

Trans.: Eng. 640000(1): 745.

[On Yudenich and 7th Army.]

191028(1) Prikaz, No. 161. (Iz, (244), 31.X.19)

Repr.: 230000(7).II.i: 413.

Trans.: Fr. 680000(1): 907-8.

191028(2) Prikaz, No. 162. (Iz, (247), 4.XI.19)

Repr.: 230000(7).II.i: 414-5.

Trans.: Fr. 680000(1): 908-10.

[Redoubled vigilance!]

191029 Vmeshaetsya li Finlyandiya? (Is Finland intervening?) (Iz, (242), 29.X.19)

Repr.: 260000(18).II: 289-90.

Trans.: Am. Soviet Russia, 6.III.20.

191030(1) Prikaz, No. 162a. (230000(7).II.i: 416)

Trans.: Fr. 680000(1): 911.

191030(2) Petrograd. (Oktyabr 1917-1919 g.g.) (Petrograd: October 1917-1919.) (Pr, (250), 7.XI.19)

Repr.: 200000(2): 36-40; [200000(47)]; 230000(7).II.i: 417-20; 240000(32).II: 86-90; 260000(18).II: 290-4; KRASNYI PETROGRAD: 27-32.

Trans.: Fr. 200000(63); 680000(1): 911-6; BulCom, (I.11), 27.V.20; Ger. 200000(64); Nor. 200000(105).

191030(3) [To Butov.] (640000(1): 746)

Trans.: Eng. 640000(1): 747.

[On reported assistance to Yudenich from Finns.]

191031 Interview.

Trans.: Am. Chicago Daily News, 7.XI.19; Eng. p.q. ManGuard, 30.XII.19; Workers Dreadnought, (VI.41), 3.I.20; Fr. Lévy: 148-55; Nor. p.q. NyTid, 29.XII.19.

191102(1)   Prikaz, No. 163. (<u>DerevKom</u>, (250), 4.XI.19)
Repr.: 230000(7).II.i: 421.
Trans.: Fr. 680000(1): 916.
[Death to traitors.]

191102(2)   [To Lenin.] (640000(1): 752)
Trans.: Eng. 640000(1): 753.
[On position on Ural Front.]

191103(1)   Vmeshayutsya li Finny? (Are the Finns intervening?)
(230000(7).II.i: 422)
Repr.: 260000(18).II: 294-5.
Trans.: Fr. 680000(1): 917.
[Interview with Soviet press.]

191103(2)   Soldatam armii generala Yudenicha. (To the soldiers of General
Yudenich's army.) (<u>V Puti</u>, (103), 1919)
Repr.: 230000(7).II.i: 423.
Trans.: Fr. 680000(1): 918.

191103(3)   Prikaz, No. 164. (230000(7).II.i: 424-5)
Trans.: Fr. 680000(1): 919-20.

191103(4)   Prikaz, No. 165. (230000(7).II.i: 426)
Trans.: Fr. 680000(1): 920-1.

191103(5)   Prikaz, No. 166. (230000(7).II.i: 427-8)
Trans.: Fr. 680000(1): 921-3.
[For 7th Army; Small fry to be arrested!]

191103(6)   [To Lenin.] (640000(1): 754)
Trans.: Eng. 640000(1): 755.
[On supplies for Petrograd Front.]

191104(1)   Prikaz, No. 167. (230000(7).II.i: 429-30)
Trans.: Fr. 680000(1): 923-4.

191104(2)   Prikaz, No. 169. (<u>Iz</u>, (249), 6.XI.19)
Repr.: 230000(7).II.i: 431.
Trans.: Fr. 680000(1): 924.

191104(3)   Prikaz, No. 170. (Iz, (249), 6.XI.19)
             Repr.: 230000(7).II.i: 432.
             Trans.: Fr. 680000(1): 925.

191104(4)   Chto nuzhno dlya razgroma band Yudenicha. (What is needed for routing
             Yudenich's band.) (Pr, (249), 6.XI.19)

191104(5)   [At Politbureau CC CPR.]
             [c. 640000(1): 423.]

191107(1)   Da zdravstvuet pobeda! (Hail the victory!) (260000(18).II: 230)
             [On 2nd anniversary of the October Revolution. Archives.]

191107(2)   Oborona Petrograda. (The defence of Petrograd.) (Iz, (251), 9.XI.19;
             Pr, (251), 9.XI.19)
             Repr.: 200000(2): 273-86; 230000(7).II.i: 433-43; 260000(18).II:
                     297-310.
             Trans.: Fr. 680000(1): 926-38.
             [Report to All-Russian CEC.]

[191113]   Pust Moskva posmeetsya. (Moscow may chuckle.) (Pr, (254), 13.XI.19)

191114   [At CC; on terms with Poland.]
             [c. 300000(1): Ch. X.]

[191116]   Parlamentarizm. (Parliamentarism.) (Pr, (257), 16.XI.19)

191120   Frantsuzskii sotsializm nakanune revolyutsii. (French socialism is on
             the eve of revolution.) (Pr, (260), 26.XI.19)
             Repr.: 230000(8): 26-37; 240000(29): 43-53; 260000(10): 126-38.
             Trans.: Am. 451000: 64-75;
                     Fr. 670306: 55-66.

191130   Prikaz, No. 174. (Pr, (270), 2.XII.19)
             Repr.: 230000(7).II.i: 307.
             Trans.: Am. Soviet Russia, 31.I.20;
                     Fr. 680000(1): 793;
                     Pol. Swit, 13.XII.19.

[191200]   [A secret order.] (p.q. Majstrenko: 181)
             [Quoted from *Tyutyunyk Zymovyi pokhid 1919-1920 rr (The Winter
             Campaign of 1919-1920).]

191203(1) Pod znamenem prostykh, no velikikh zadach. (Under the banner of simple but great tasks.) (<u>Pr</u>, (271), 3.XII.19)

 Repr.: 260000(18).II: 317-8.

191203(2) |At 8th Conference, CPR.| (PROTOKOLY: 103)

191205(1) K s"ezdu Sovetov. (The Soviet Congress.] (<u>Pr</u>, (274), 6.XII.19)

 [7th Soviet Congress.]

191205(2) Itogi dvukh let grazhdanskoi voiny. (Balance sheet of two years of civil war.) (<u>Iz</u>, (274,276), 6,9.XII.19; <u>Pr</u>, (274), 6.XII.19)

 Repr.: 260000(18).II: 319-20; K 7-mu S"EZDU SOVETOV: 35-47; p.q. <u>DerevKom</u>, (280), 10.XII.19.

 [To 7th Soviet Congress.]

191206 Rech. (A speech.) (<u>Pr</u>, (276,278,279), 9,11,12.XII.19)

 Trans.: Eng. [200000(93)].

 [To 7th Soviet Congress; on foreign policy.]

191207 Nasha voennoe stroitel'stvo i nashi fronty. (Our military construction and our fronts.) (<u>Iz</u>, (276-9), 9-12.XII.19; p.q. <u>Krasnaya Gazeta</u>, (282), 9.XII.19; <u>Pr</u>, (276-9), 9-12.XII.19)

 Repr.: 190000(17); 230000(7).II.ii: 3-30; 260000(18).II: 320-55; p.q. 270000(4): 209-13.

 Trans.: Eng. 200000(61).

191208 Rech. (A speech.) (<u>Pr</u>, (277), 10.XII.19)

 [To 7th Soviet Congress.]

[191209] i Lenin: Postanovlenie Sovnarkom. (A regulation of the Sovnarkom.) (<u>Iz</u>, (276), 9.XII.19)

 [On help for people of Ural region.]

191211(1) Prikaz, No. 180. (<u>Iz</u>, (281), 14.XII.19)

 Repr.: 230000(7).II.i: 308-10.

 Trans.: Fr. 680000(1): 794-7.

 [On measures taken by partisans.]

191211(2) Prikaz, No. 181. (<u>Iz</u>, (279), 12.XII.19)

191211(3) See 191217(3).

191212(1) Nashi ocherednye voprosy. (Our immediate problems.) (<u>Pr</u>, (280), 13.XII.19)

 Repr.: 230000(7).II.i: 76-82. ++++

191212(1)   ++++ <u>Trans</u>.: Fr. 680000(1): 537-45.

[Speech to Conference of Political Workers in the Red Army.]

191212(2)   i S.S.Kamenev: Prikaz, No. 341. (<u>Iz</u>, (281), 14.XII.19)

191213   Alternative for 191217(2).

191216   Perekhod ko vseobshchei trudovoi povinnosti v svyazi s militsionnoi sistemoi. (The transition to universal labour service linked with a militia system.) (<u>Pr</u>, (283), 17.XII.19)

<u>Repr</u>.: 230000(7).II.ii: 33-6; 270000(4): 10-4.

<u>Trans</u>.: Eng. p.q. Deutscher, PA: 487; LABOUR CONDITIONS: 146-9.

[Theses to CEC; on the economic transition from war to peace.]

191217(1)   Po povodu dvukh dokumentov. (Concerning two documents.) (230000(7).II.ii: 267)

[To Red Army; reply to Potyaev and Luganovsky, on centralization.]

191217(2)   Prikaz, No. 183. (<u>BoPr</u>, (91), 19.XII.19; <u>Iz</u>, (284), 18.XII.19; <u>Pr</u>, (284), 18.XII.19)

<u>Repr</u>.: 230000(7).II.ii: 268.

[We shall carry the matter through to the end.]

191217(3)   [Definition of Borot'bist (Workers) Party.] (640000(1): 784)

<u>Trans</u>.: Eng. 640000(1): 785.

191217(4)   [Memorandum on Borot'bist (Workers) Party.] (640000(1): 786)

<u>Trans</u>.: Eng. 640000(1): 787.

191218   Zhan Longe. (<u>KI</u>, (7-8), XI-XII.19)

<u>Repr</u>.: 230000(8): 37-44; 240000(29: 54-60; 260000(10): 138-45.

<u>Trans</u>.: Am. 451000: 76-83;

     Fr. 670306: 67-74; <u>BulCom</u>, (I.12), 3.VI.20;

     Ger. <u>KomInt</u>, (7-8), XI-XII.19.

[CPFrance.]

191220   Kazaki, v Sovetskuyu kolonnu stroisya! (Cossacks, line up in the Soviet ranks!) (<u>Pr</u>, (4), 6.I.20)

<u>Repr</u>.: 230000(7).II.ii: 269-70.

[On the occasion of the forthcoming Cossack Congress.]

191222(1)   Petrograd, bud na strazhe! (Petrograd, stay on guard!) (Iz, (288),
23.XII.19; Pr, (288), 23.XII.19; V Puti, (104), 22.XII.19)
Repr.: 230000(7).II.i: 444-5; 260000(18).II: 310-2.
Trans.: Fr. 680000(1): 938-40.

191222(2)   Gotov'tes k nedele fronta! (Prepare for Front Week!) (Iz, (289),
24.XII.19; Pr, (289), 24.XII.19)
Repr.: 230000(7).II.ii: 299-300.

191222(3)   [To Lenin.] (640000(1): 800)
Trans.: Eng. 640000(1): 801.
[On policy of interventionists.]

191227(1)   Zhenshchinam rabotnitsam! Po povodu nedeli fronta. (To women workers!
Concerning Front Week.) (Pr, (293), 28.XII.19)
Repr.: 230000(7).II.ii: 301.

191227(2)   Privetstvie komanduyushchemu vos'moi armii tovarishchu Sokol'nikovu.
(Greetings to the Commander of the 8th Army, cde. Sokolnikov.) (Iz,
(293), 28.XII.19; Pr, (293), 28.XII.19)

191230   Obshchii plan ucheta rabochei sily. (A general plan for calculating
the labour force.) (270000(4): 253-4)
[Resolution No. 1 of a conference on the question of introducing
universal labour service and mobilizing labour resources. Archives.]

191231   [At CC.]
[c. 640000(1): 804.]

200000(1)   BOI ZA PETERBURG. (THE BATTLE FOR PETROGRAD.)
              [See 191019 for all repr., trans.]

200000(2)   i Zinov´ev: † BOR´BA ZA PETROGRAD. (THE STRUGGLE FOR PETROGRAD.)

*200000(3)   *BUDTE NA STRAZHE! (STAY ON GUARD!)
              [See 200510(5) for all repr.]

*200000(4)   *VOZRODIM TRANSPORT! (REVIVE TRANSPORT!)
              [See 200530 for all repr.]

200000(5)   VOINA S POL´SHEI. (THE WAR WITH POLAND.)
              [See 200505(1) for all repr., trans., notes.]

*200000(6)   *VOINA S POL´SHEI. (THE WAR WITH POLAND.)
              [See 200505(1) for all repr., trans., notes.]

*200000(7)   *VOINA S POL´SHEI. (THE WAR WITH POLAND.)
              [See 200505(1) for all repr., trans., notes.]

*200000(8)   *VOR V DOME. (A THIEF IN THE HOUSE.)
              [See 200430(2) for all repr.]

*200000(9)   *GORE NE DOVODYASHCHIM DO KONTSA! (OUR CUP OF SORROW HAS NOT YET
              BEEN DRAINED!)
              [See 200616(1) for all repr., trans.]

*200000(10)   *"DAITE FRONTU KRASNYKH KOMANDIROV." ("SEND RED COMMANDERS TO THE
              FRONT.")
              [See 200605 for all repr.]

*200000(11)   *"DAITE FRONTU KRASNYKH KOMANDIROV." ("SEND RED COMMANDERS TO THE
              FRONT.")
              [See 200605 for all repr.]

*200000(12)   *"DAITE FRONTU KRASNYKH KOMANDIROV." ("SEND RED COMMANDERS TO THE
              FRONT.")
              [See 200605 for all repr.]

*200000(13)   *DOLGOVECHNYE I NEDOLGOVECHNYE PRAVITEL´STVA. (ESTABLISHED AND
              TEMPORARY GOVERNMENTS.)
              [See 201008(1) for all repr., notes.]

*200000(14)   *"ZAPADNYI FRONT ZOVET." ("THE WESTERN FRONT IS CALLING.")
                 [See ⌊200917⌋ for all repr.]

*200000(15)   *KRASNOMU VOINU POL'SKOGO FRONTA. (TO THE RED ARMY MEN ON THE POLISH
                 FRONT.)
                 [See 200501(1) for all repr.]

200000(16)   MIR S POL'SHEI DOSTIGNUT. (PEACE ACHIEVED WITH POLAND.)
                 [See 201013(1) for all repr.]

200000(17)   MOBILIZATSIYA TRUDA. (THE MOBILIZATION OF LABOUR.)
                 [See 200124(1) for all repr., trans., notes.]

*200000(18)   *O ZADACHAKH PROIZVODSTVENNYKH SOYUZOV. (PRODUCTION TASKS OF THE
                 UNIONS.)
                 [See 201224(1) for all repr., notes.]

200000(19)   OB ORGANIZATSII TRUDA. (THE ORGANIZATION OF LABOUR.)
                 [See 200409(1) for all repr., trans., notes.]

200000(20)   ORGANIZATSIYA TRUDA. (THE ORGANIZATION OF LABOUR.)
                 [See 200404(1) for all repr., trans., notes.]

*200000(21)   *OTKRYTOE PIS'MO. (AN OPEN LETTER.)
                 [See 201031 for all repr, trans.]

*200000(22)   *OCHEREDNYE ZADACHI KHOZYAISTVENNOGO STROITEL STVA. (IMMEDIATE TASKS
                 OF ECONOMIC CONSTRUCTION.)
                 [See 200330 for all repr., trans.]

200000(23)   PAMYATKA KRASNOARMEITSA YUZHNOGO FRONT. (INSTRUCTIONS FOR RED ARMY MEN
                 ON THE SOUTHERN FRONT.)
                 [See 201008(2) for all repr.]

*200000(24)   *PAMYATKA KRASNOARMEITSA YUZHNOGO FRONT. (INSTRUCTIONS FOR RED ARMY MEN
                 ON THE SOUTHERN FRONT.)
                 [See 201008(2) for all repr.]

*200000(25)   *PAMYATKA KRASNOARMEITSA YUZHNOGO FRONT. (INSTRUCTIONS FOR RED ARMY MEN
                 ON THE SOUTHERN FRONT.)
                 [See 201008(2) for all repr.]

*200000(26)   *PAMYATKA KRASNOARMEITSA YUZHNOGO FRONT. (INSTRUCTIONS FOR RED ARMY MEN
                 ON THE SOUTHER FRONT.)
                 [See 201008(2) for all repr.]

*200000(27)   *PARIZHSKAYA KOMMUNA I SOVETSKAYA ROSSIYA. (THE PARIS COMMUNE AND SOVIET RUSSIA.)

[Separate print of Ch. V of TERRORIZM I KOMMUNIZM, 200000(37) which see for all repr., trans., notes.]

*200000(28)   *PIS'MO REVOLYUTSIONNYM VOENNYM SOVETAM FRONTOV, ARMII I KO VSEM OTVETSTVENNYM RABOTNIKAM KRASNOI ARMII I KRASNOGO FLOTA. BOL'SHE RAVENSTVA.) (LETTER TO REVOLUTIONARY MILITARY SOVIETS OF THE FRONT AND ARMIES, AND TO ALL RESPONSIBLE WORKERS OF THE RED ARMY AND RED NAVY. MORE EQUALITY.)

[See 201031 for all repr., trans.]

200000(29)   PUT K EDINOMU KHOZYAISTVENNOMU PLANU. (THE WAY TO A UNIFIED ECONOMIC PLAN.)

[See 201108 for all repr., trans., notes.]

200000(30)   RECH NA MITINGE V GOMELE. (SPEECH TO MEETING IN GOMEL.)

[See 200510(4) for all repr., trans., notes.]

200000(31)   RECH NA III VSEROSSIISKOM S"EZDE SOVETOV NARODNOGO KHOZYAISTVA. (SPEECH TO 3rd ALL-RUSSIAN CONGRESS OF PEOPLE'S ECONOMIC SOVIET.)

[See 200124(1) for all repr., trans., notes.]

*200000(32)   *RECH T. TROTSKOGO NA MASSOVOM MITINGE V GOR. GOMELE. (SPEECH OF CDE. TROTSKY TO MASS MEETING IN GOMEL.)

[See 200510(4) for all repr., trans., notes.]

*200000(33)   *SLOVO ZHELEZNODORZHNIKAM PO POVODU POL'SKOGO NASTUPLENIYA. (A WORD TO THE RAILWAYMEN CONCERNING THE POLISH ATTACK.)

[See 200501(2) for all repr., notes.]

*200000(34)   *SMERT POL'SKOI BURZHUAZII! (DEATH TO THE POLISH BOURGEOISIE!)

[See 200429(2) for all repr.]

200000(35)   SOVETSKAYA ROSSIYA I BURZHUAZNAYA POL'SHA. (SOVIET RUSSIA AND BOURGEOIS POLAND.)

[See 200510(4) for all repr., trans., notes.]

*200000(36)   *SOVETSKAYA ROSSIYA I BURZHUAZNAYA POL'SHA. (SOVIET RUSSIA AND BOURGEOIS POLAND.)

[See 200510(4) for all repr., trans., notes.]

200000(37)   TERRORIZM I KOMMUNIZM.   (TERRORISM AND COMMUNISM.)

Repr.: p.q. 200000(2): 313-7; p.q. *200000(27); p.q. 230000(7).II:
71-88; 230000(18); 250000(8); *250000(10); p.q. KI, (10,11),
11.V, 14.VI.20; p.q. Levin i Yurgens: 80-2.

Trans.: Am. 220000(21); 610000(8); 630000(13); p.q. 640800: 111-6;
p.q. 650900: 142-59; 690000(18); p.q. Soviet Russia,
27.XI.20, 15,29.I, 5,12.II, 26.III, 2.IV.21;

Arab. 640000(8);

Bul. *210000(9);

Ch. *310000(37);

Cz. *250000(35); p.q. SocDem, (II.36-40), 5.XI-3.XII.20;

Den. p.q. SocInf, III-IV.70;

Eng. 210000(27); 350000(4); p.q. 550900; p.q. 640000(5):
142-59; p.q. 640000(10): 142-59;

Fin. 210000(60); 210000(61);

Fr. p.q. 200000(74); 200000(75); 200000(76); p.q. 210000(26);
360000(1); p.q. ⌊580000(7)⌋; 630608; p.q. 680000(4):
passim; p.q. BulCom, (I.23-24, 50-51, II.3, V.21), 12.VIII,
23.XII.20, 20.I.21, 23.V.24; p.q. Contre LeC, (II.18-19),
26.XI.28; p.q. IC, (II.11), VI.20; p.q. Rev, (III.30),
15.V.36;

Ger. p.q. 200000(51); p.q. *200000(52); 200000(56); 200000(79);
200800(2); 210000(42); 210000(57); 230000(27); 230000(28);
230000(35); ⌊670000(3)⌋; p.q. *Aktion, 1920; p.q. Inprekor
(II.66), 13.V.22; p.q. Jugend-Int, (II.7), III.21; p.q.
KomInt, (II.10,11), 1920; p.q. RusKor, (I.ii.12-13),
IX.20; p.q. ALMANACH: 88-105, 147-52;

It. *210000(41); 640100; p.q. 680200(2): 91-8; p.q. Ordine
Nuovo, (I.77,236), 18.III, 25.VIII.21;

Jap. *620120: 640330(4); p.q. 681125: 118-24;

Lith. Komunaras, (6), VI.22;

Scand. p.q. KaI, (1), 1920; KeI, (1), 1920;

Serb. p.q. PARTIJA: 242-55;

Sin. p.q. 510000;

Sp. *200000(77); *651000(2); p.q. 670000(5): 111-6; p.q.
El Com, (II.31), 26.III.21;

Swed. *210000(35); 270000(19); 280000(4); p.q. 691100(2):
96-101; p.q. FI(S), (1), 1969; p.q. Rote Ryssland,
7.XI.20;

Yid. p.q. *⌊220000(36)⌋.

⌊Pref. 200529(1); Postface 200617; nPref 350110, 360628.⌋

200000(38) CHTO NUZHNO SDELAT KREST´YANAM, CHTOBY VYVESTI KHOZYAISTVO IZ
RAZORENIYA. (WHAT THE PEASANTRY MUST DO; HOW SAVE THE ECONOMY
FROM RUIN.)
[See 200212(1) for all repr., trans., notes.]

*200000(39) *CHTO NUZHNO SDELAT KREST´YANAM, CHTOBY VYVESTI KHOZYAISTVO IZ
RAZORENIYA. (WHAT THE PEASANTRY MUST DO; HOW SAVE THE ECONOMY
FROM RUIN.)
[See 200212(1) for all repr., trans., notes.]

*200000(40) *CHTO NUZHNO SDELAT KREST´YANAM, CHTOBY VYVESTI KHOZYAISTVO IZ
RAZORENIYA. (WHAT THE PEASANTRY MUST DO; HOW SAVE THE ECONOMY
FROM RUIN.)
[See 200212(1) for all repr., trans., notes.]

*200000(41) *CHTO NUZHNO SDELAT KREST´YANAM, CHTOBY VYVESTI KHOZYAISTVO IZ
RAZORENIYA. (WHAT THE PEASANTRY MUST DO; HOW SAVE THE ECONOMY
FROM RUIN.)
[See 200212(1) for all repr., trans., notes.]

*200000(42) *CHTO OZNACHAET PEREKHOD MAKHNO NA STORONU SOVETSKOI VLASTI. (THE
SIGNIFICANCE OF MAKHNO'S COMING OVER TO THE SIDE OF THE SOVIET STATE
POWER.)
[See 201010(1) for all repr.]

*[200000(43)] *DOLGOVECHNYE I NEDOLGOVECHNYE PRAVITEL´STVA. (ESTABLISHED AND
TEMPORARY GOVERNMENTS.)
[See 201008(1) for all repr., notes.]

*[200000(44)] *DOBROVOL´TSY NA POL´SKII FRONT! (VOLUNTEERS, TO THE POLISH FRONT!)
[See [200525] for all repr.]

*[200000(45)] *K PERVOMU MAYA. (MAY DAY.)
[See [200501(3)] for all repr., trans.]

*[200000(46)] *PAMYATKA KRASNOARMEITSA YUZHNOGO FRONT. (INSTRUCTIONS TO RED ARMY MEN
ON THE SOUTHERN FRONT.)
[See 201008(2) for all repr.]

[200000(47)] PETROGRAD (Oktyabr 1919-1919 g.g.) (PETROGRAD: October 1917-1919.)
[See 191030(2) for all repr., trans.]

*[200000(48)]   *RECH K TEKUSHCHEMU MOMENTU V PERIOD NASTUPLENIYA KRASNYKH VOISK
NA DENIKINA. (SPEECH ON THE CURRENT SITUATION AT THE TIME OF THE
ATTACK BY THE RED FORCES ON DENIKIN.)
[See 201020 for all repr., trans., notes.]

*[200000(49)]   *SMERT POL´SKOI BURZHUAZII! (DEATH TO THE POLISH BOURGEOISIE!)
[See 200429(2) for all repr.]

*[200000(50)]   *CHTO OZNACHAET PEREKHOD MAKHNO NA STORONU SOVETSKOI VLASTI. (THE
SIGNIFICANCE OF MAKHNO'S COMING OVER TO THE SIDE OF THE SOVIET STATE
POWER.)
[See 201010(1) for all repr.]

200000(51)   DIE ARBEITERKLASSE UND IHRE SOWJETPOLITIK.
[Trans. Ger. p.q. 200000(37).]

*200000(52)   *DIE ARBEITERKLASSE UND IHRE SOWJETPOLITIK.
[Trans. Ger. p.q. 200000(37).]

200000(53)   L'AVÈNEMENT DU BOLCHEVISME.
[Trans. Fr. See 180000(5) for all trans., repr., notes.]

200000(54)   IL BOLSCEVISMO DINNANZI ALLA GUERRA E ALLA PACE DEL MONDO.
[Trans. It. See [140000(3)] for all trans., notes.]

200000(55)   DALLA RIVOLUZIONE D'OTTOBRE AL TRATTATO DI PACE DI BREST-LITOWSK.
[Trans. It. See 180000(5) for all trans., repr., notes.]

200000(56)   TERRORISMUS UND KOMMUNISMUS.
[Trans. Ger. See 200000(37) for all trans., repr., notes.]

200000(57)   LEON TROTZKI'S ANTWORT AUF KARL KAUTSKY'S 'TERRORISMUS UND KOMMUNISMUS'.
[Trans. Ger. See 200000(37) for all trans., repr., notes.]

200000(58)   —: LE MONDE CAPITALISTE ET L'INTERNATIONALE COMMUNISTE.
[Trans. Fr. See 200807(1) for all trans., repr., notes.]

200000(59)   —: LE MONDE CAPITALISTE ET L'INTERNATIONALE COMMUNISTE.
[Trans. Fr. See 200807(1) for all trans., repr., notes.]

200000(60)   DIE ORGANISIERUNG DER ROTEN ARMEE.
[Trans. Ger. See 180710(1) for all trans., notes. Printed with
Lenin, DER ROTEN ARMEE.]

200000(61)   OUR MILITARY CONSTRUCTION AND OUR FRONTS.
              [Trans. Eng. See 191207.]

200000(62)   A PARADISE IN THIS WORLD.
              [Trans. Eng. See 180414 for all trans., repr., notes.]

200000(63)   PÉTROGRAD (1917-1919).
              [Trans. Fr. See 191030(2) for all trans., repr., notes.]

200000(64)   PETROGRAD (1917-1919).
              [Trans. Ger. See 191030(2) for all trans., notes.]

*200000(65)   *ŘÍJNOVA REVOLUCE.
              [Trans. Cz. See 180000(5) for all trans., repr., notes.]

*200000(66)   *ROSJA SOWIECKA A POLSKA BURZUAZYJMA.
              [Trans. Pol. See 200510(4) for all trans., repr., notes.]

200000(67)   DIE RUSSISCHE SOZIALISTISCHE ROTE ARMEE.
              [Trans. Ger. See 180422(1) for all trans., repr., notes.]

200000(68)   LES SOVIETS ET L'IMPÉRIALISME MONDIAL.
              [Trans. Fr. See 180421 for all trans., repr.]

200000(69)   LES SOVIETS ET L'IMPÉRIALISME MONDIAL.
              [Trans. Fr. See 180421 for all trans., repr.]

200000(70)   DE SOWJETMACHT EN HET INTERNATIONALE IMPERIALISME.
              [Trans. Hol. See 180421 for all trans.]

200000(71)   SOWJET-RUSSLAND UND DAS BÜRGERLICHE POLEN.
              [Trans. Ger. See 200510(4) for all trans., repr., notes.]

*200000(72)   *SOWJET-RUSSLAND UND DAS BÜRGERLICHE POLEN.
              [Trans. Ger. See 200510(4) for all trans., repr. notes.]

200000(73)   u.a.: SOWJET-RUSSLAND UND POLEN.
              [Trans. Ger. See 200505(1) for all trans., notes.]

200000(74)   LE TERRORISME.
              [Trans. Fr. p.q.200000(37).]

200000(75)   TERRORISME ET COMMUNISME.
              [Trans. Fr. See 200000(37) for all trans., repr., notes.]

200000(76) TERRORISME ET COMMUNISME. L'ANTI-KAUTSKY.
[Trans. Fr. See 200000(37) for all trans., repr., notes.]

*200000(77) *TERRORISMO Y COMUNISMO.
[Trans. Sp. See 200000(37) for all trans., repr., notes.]

200000(78) —: THE CAPITALIST WORLD AND THE COMMUNIST INTERNATIONAL.
[Trans. Eng. See 200807(1) for all trans., repr., notes.]

200000(79) TERRORISMUS UND KOMMUNISMUS. (ANTI-KAUTSKY.)
[Trans. Ger. See 200000(37) for all trans., repr., notes.]

200000(80) EL TRIUNFO DEL BOLCHEVISMO.
[Trans. Sp. See 180000(5) for all trans., repr., notes. 2nd ed.]

200000(81) DIE WIRTSCHAFT IN SOWJET-RUSSLAND UND IN WESTEUROPA.
[Trans. Ger. See 200124(1) for all trans., repr. Catalogued under
A.Rykow und T.]

200000(82) DIEWIRTSCHAFT IN SOWJET-RUSSLAND UND IN WESTEUROPA.
[Trans. Ger. See 200124(1) for all trans., repr. This ed. includes
speech by Lenin.]

[200000(83)] ARBEID, DISCIPLINE EN ORDE ZULLEN DE SOCIALISTIESE SOWJET-REPUBLIEK
REDDEN.
[Trans. Hol. See 180328(1) for all trans.]

[200000(84)] —: LE MONDE CAPITALISTE ET L'INTERNATIONALE COMMUNISTE.
[Trans. Fr. See 200807(1) for all trans., repr., notes.]

[200000(85)] EL TRIUNFO DEL BOLCHEVISMO.
[Trans. Sp. See 180000(5) for all trans., repr., notes.]

*[200000(86)] *TRABAJO, DISCIPLINA Y ORDEN.
[Trans. Sp. See 180328(1) for all trans., notes.]

[200000(87)] Voprosy, podlezhashchie rassmetreniyu Komissii po trudovoi povinnosti.
(Questions submitted for consideration by the Commission on Labour
Service.) (270000(4): 254-5)
[Archives.]

[200000(88)] O zadachakh politicheskoi agitatsii v 1-i Armii truda. (Tasks of
political agitation in the 1st Labour Army.) (270000(4): 322)
[Telegram to cde. Mylin. Archives.]

[200000(89)]   Partiya i transport. (The Party and transport.) (270000(4): 380-3)
                [Draft of appeal to all local organizations of CPR(b). Archives.]

200000(90)   [Urges peace with Baltic states.]
                Trans.: Eng. p.q. Deutscher, PA: 464.
                [Harvard Archives.]

[200000(91)]   Pref. A CONSTITIÇÃO POLITICA DA REPUBLICA DOS SOVIETS.
                [Trans. Port. LocBDIC. Russian original not traced.]

*200000(92)   *TRUD, DISTSIPLINA, PORYADOK SPASUT SOTSIALISTICHESKU SOVETSKUYU
                RESPUBLIKU. (WORK, DISCIPLINE AND ORDER WILL SAVE THE SOCIALIST
                SOVIET REPUBLIC.)
                [See 180328(1) for all repr., trans., notes.]

[200000(93)]   THE FOREIGN POLICY OF SOVIET RUSSIA.
                [Trans. Eng. See 191206.]

200000(94)   —: DIE KAPITALISTISCHE WELT UND DIE KOMMUNISTISCHE INTERNATIONALE.
                [Trans. Ger. See 200807(1) for all trans., repr.]

*[200000(95)]   *Pref. to report by Potyaev.
                [c. 640000(1): 798.]

*[200000(96)]   *[THE OCTOBER REVOLUTION.]
                [Trans. Ch. See 180000(5) for all trans.]

*200000(97)   *OD PRZEWROTU LISTOPADOWEGO DO POKOJU BRZESKIEGO.
                [Trans. Pol. See 180000(5) for all trans.]

*200000(98)   *CZEGO ONI CHCA.
                [Trans. Pol. See 200509(2) for all trans., notes.]

*200000(99)   *WOJNA S POLSZEJ.
                [Trans. Pol. See 200505(1) for all trans.]

*[200000(100)] *MANIFEST KOMMUNISTICHESKOGO INTERNATSIONALA. (THE MANIFESTO OF
                THE COMMUNIST INTERNATIONAL.)
                [See 190306(1) for all repr., trans. Advert.]

*[200000(101)] *MANIFEST KOMMUNISTICHESKOGO INTERNATSIONALA. (THE MANIFESTO OF
                THE COMMUNIST INTERNATIONAL.)
                [See 190306(1) for all repr., trans. Advert.]

*200000(102)   *VOINA S POL´SHEI. (THE WAR WITH POLAND.)
                 [See 200505(1) for all repr., trans.]

*200000(103)   *ROSJA SOWIECKA A BURZUAZYJNA POLSKA.
                 [Trans. Pol. See 200510(4) for all trans., repr., notes.]

*200000(104)   *PIS´MO KREST´YANNU PERMSKOI GUB. IVANU ANDREEVICHU SIGUNOVU.
                 (LETTER TO A PEASANT OF THE PERM PROVINCE, IVAN ANDREEVICH SIGUNOV.)
                 [See 200212(1) for all repr.]

200000(105)   og Zinoviev: PETROGRAD: 1917-1919.
                 [Trans. Nor. See 191030(2) for all trans., notes.]

200000(106)   EL ADVENIMIENTO DEL BOLSHEVIKISMO.
                 [Trans. Port. See 180000(5), 190901(3) for all trans.]

200101(1)   Zadachi Komissii po vseobshchei trudovoi povinnosti. (Tasks of the
                 Commission on Universal Labour Service.) (EkZhizn, (29), 3.I.20;
                 Iz, (2), 3.I.20)
                 Repr.: 270000(4): 251-2.

200101(2)   Pis´mo tov. Bonch-Bruevichu. (Letter to cde. Bonch-Bruevich.)
                 (270000(4): 256-7)
                 [Archives.]

[200103]   Geroi truda. Pamyati Pavla Spiridonovicha Vasileva. (A labour hero.
                 In memory of Pavel Spiridonovich Vasilev.) (Iz, (2), 3.I.20; Pr, (2),
                 3.I.20)

200106   Osnovnye zadachi i trudnosti khozyaistvennogo stroitel´stva.
                 (Fundamental tasks and the difficulties of economic construction.)
                 (270000(4): 83-103)
                 [Report to Moscow Committee CPR(b). Archives.]

200109(1)   Telefonogramma predsedatelyu moskovskogo Gubsovnarkhoza. (Telegram
                 phoned to Chairman Moscow Provincial Economic Soviet.) (270000(4):
                 213-4)
                 [Archives.]

200109(2)   et al: [Letter to CPItaly.] (Ordine Nuovo, (I.13), 13.I.20)
                 [Trans. It.]

200111   Telegramma Revvoensovetu 3-i Armii, No. 162. (Telegram, No. 162, to
                 Revolutionary Military Soviet of 3rd Army.) (230000(7).II.ii: 37)

200112   Khozyaistvennoe polozhenie respubliki i osnovnye zadachi
          vosstanovleniya promyshlennosti. (The economic situation of the
          Republic and the fundamental tasks of restoring the economy.)
          (270000(4): 27-52)
          Trans.: Eng. p.q. Farbman: 45.
          [Report to fraction of All-Russian Central Soviet of Trade Unions.
          Archives.]

200113   Telegramma Revvoensovetu Turkfronta. (Telegram to Revolutionary
          Military Soviet of the Turkestan Front.) (270000(4): 263-6)
          [Archives.]

[200114] Proekt postanovleniya Soveta Oborony o 1-i Armii truda. (Draft of
          regulation of Defence Soviet on the 1st Labour Army.)
          (270000(4): 267-8)
          [Archives.]

200115(1) Pochto-telefonogramma nachal´niku Vseroglavshtaba. (Telegram to Head
          of All-Russian General Staff.) (270000(4): 257-8)
          [Archives.]

200115(2) Prikaz-pamyatka po 3-i Krasnoi Armii -- 1-i Revolyutsionnoi Armii
          Truda. (Instruction to 3rd Red Army, the 1st Revolutionary Labour
          Army.) (Iz, (10), 16.I.20; Pr, (10), 16.I.20)
          Repr.: 230000(7).II.ii: 38-40; 270000(4): 269-72; Levin i Yurgens; 82-4.
          Trans.: Eng. p.q. Deutscher, PA: 495; p.q. LABOUR CONDITIONS: 158.

200115(3) Telegramma v Revvoensovet 3-i armii. (Telegram to Revolutionary
          Military Soviet of 3rd Army.) (270000(4): 272)
          [Archives.]

200115(4) Telefonogram tov. Rykovu. (Telegram to cde. Rykov.) (270000(4): 517)
          [Copy to Lenin. Archives.]

200115(5) Prikaz, No. 50. (Pr, (10), 16.I.20)

200119   Postanovlenie zasedaniya Mezhduvedomstvennoi Komissii po vvedeniyu
          vseobshchei trudovoi povinnosti. (Regulation of Inter-departemntal
          Commission on introduction of universal labour service.)
          (270000(4): 513-5)

[200122(1)] O mobilizatsii industrial'nogo proletariata, trudovoi povinnosti,
militarizatsii khozyaistva i primenenii voinskikh chastei dlya
khozyaistvennykh nuzhd. (The mobilization of the industrial
proletariat, labour service, militarization of the economy and the
employment of military units for economic needs.) (Pr, (14), 22.I.20)
Repr.: p.q. 200000(37): Ch. VIII; 230000(7).II.ii: 43-9; 270000(4):
          107-14; PROTOKOLY: 81-4; 98-123; PetPr, (17), 25.I.20.
Trans.: Fr. Bulletin d'Information de la IIIe Internationale
            Communiste, (2), 12.III.20;
          Ger. RusKor, (I.i.4), II.20.
[Other Russian brochure eds. not traced. Other p.q. trans. 200000(37):
Ch. VIII. Theses.]

200122(2) [To Lenin, Zinoviev and Krestinsky; on Pilsudski's preparations for
war.]
[c. Deutscher, PA: 459. T422.]

200123 Revvoensovet III Sovtrudarm. (The Revolutionary Military Soviet of
the 3rd Soviet Labour Army.) (270000(4): 517-8)
[Archives.]

200124(1) Mobilizatsiya truda. (The mobilization of Labour.) (EkZhizn, (17-19),
27-29.I.20; Iz, (18), 28.I.20; Pr, (18,19), 28,29.I.20)
Repr.: 200000(17); 200000(31); 270000(4): 52-78.
Trans.: Am. Living Age, 15.V, 26.VI.20;
          Eng. p.q. New Russia, (I.6), 2.III.20; p.q. Deutscher, PA: 493;
          Fr. Bulletin d'Information, (1), 20.II.20;
          Ger. 200000(81); 200000(82); RusKor, (I.i.8-9), VI.20.
[Report to joint-meeting of 3rd session of Sovnarkhoz and Moscow Soviet.]

200124(2) Zaklyuchitel'noe slovo. (Summary speech.) (270000(4): 78-83)
[See 200124(1).]

200128 i dr.: Pravitel'stvu Pol'shi i pol'skomu narodu. (To the Polish
government and people.) (Iz, (20), 30.I.20; PetPr, (21), 30.I.20;
Pr, (20), 30.I.20; ZhiznNats, (4:61), 1.II.20)
Repr.: 260000(18).II: 615-6; DKVS(1957): 331-3.
Trans.: Ger. Bulletin des Petrograder Büros, (6), 15.VI.20;
          Hol. Tribune, (296), 18.IX.20.

200200(1)   Osnovnye voprosy prodovol´stvennoi i zemel´noi politiki. (Fundamental problems of food and land policy.) (V Puti, 1920)
Repr.: *210000(12); 240000(22): 57-8; 260000(18).II: 543-4.
Trans.: 240000(22).

200200(2)   Zadachi osoboupolnomochennykh Soveta trudovoi armii na boevykh uchastkakh trudovogo fronta. (Tasks of special plenipotentiaries of the Labour Army Soviet in the military units of the labour front.) (270000(4): 320)
[Archives.]

200201   [To Lenin; on taking over transport.]
[c. Deutscher, PA: 498. Harvard Archives.]

200203(1)   Zadachi trudovoi mobilizatsii. (Tasks of labour mobilization.) (Iz, (24), 4.II.20; Pr, (24), 4.II.20)
Repr.: 270000(4): 4-8.
Trans.: Eng. p.q. LABOUR CONDITIONS: 150.

200203(2)   & Lenin: [To Stalin; on moving him to the Caucasus.]
Trans.: 410000(1): Ch. X.

200204(1)   & Lenin: [To Stalin; on moving him to the Caucasus.]
Trans.: 410000(1): Ch. X.

200204(2)   Trudyashchimsya. (To the working people.) (230000(7).II.ii: 41-2)
Repr.: 270000(4): 8-10.
[Appeal of All-Russian CEC.]

200208   Za khlebom dlya golodnykh! Za toplivom dlya kholodnykh! (Bread for the hungry! Fuel for the cold!) (V Puti, (106), 8.II.20)
Repr.: 230000(7).II.ii: 50-1; 270000(4): 323-5; DerevKom, (47), 29.II.20; Trudovaya Nedelya, 19.II.20.
Trans.: Am. Soviet Russia, 12.VI.20.

200209(1)   Voprosy khozyaistvennogo raionirovaniya v svyazi s primeneniem sil 1-i Armii truda. (Problems of economic regionalization linked with the use of the forces of the 1st Labour Army.) (270000(4): 273-5)
[Letter to Pyatakov. Archives.]

200209(2)   Kto gubit transport? Kto razrushaet zheleznuyu? Kto obrekaet
naselenie na golod i vsyakie drugie lisheniya? (Who is ruining the
transport? Who is breaking down the railways? Who is driving the
populace to hunger and every other kind of misery?) (V Puti, (107), 16.II
16.II.20)
Repr.: 230000(7).II.ii: 52-4; 270000(4): 361-4.

200211(1)   Telegramma. (A telegram.) (270000(4): 258-9)
[To Commander Turkestan Front. Archives.]

200211(2)   Telegramma. (A telegram.) (270000(4): 518)
[To Lenin & Rykov. Archives. T431.]

200212(1)   Chto nuzhno sdelat krest'yanam. (What the peasantry must do.)
(DerevKom, (59,60), 16,17.III.20)
Repr.: 200000(38); *200000(39); *200000(40); *200000(41); *200000(104);
270000(4): 14-23.
Trans.: Eng. p.q. New Russia, (I.12), 22.IV.20.
[Letter to Ivan Andreevich Sigunov.]

200212(2)   Bor'ba so snezhnymi zanosami. (The struggle against snowdrifts.)
(270000(4): 364-5)
[Telegram to the body responsible for removing snow from roads, the
People's Commissariat for Roads, and Commander-in-Chief of All-Russian
Armed Forces. Archives.]

200217   Rech. (A speech.) (Ural'skii Rabochii, (39), 19.II.20)
Repr.: 270000(4): 275-82.
[At celebration joint-meeting of Party and workers in Ekaterinburg.]

200219(1)   Rech. (A speech.) (270000(4): 282-5)
Trans.: Ger. RusKor, (I.i.6-7), IV-V.20.
[To Revolutionary Military Soviet of 1st Labour Army, in Ekaterinburg.
Archives.]

200219(2)   [To the D.M.S.]
Trans.: Eng. McCullagh.
[To the District Medical Superintendent at Ekaterinburg; on the
fight against typhus.]

200220(1)   Ochered za temi, kotorye rodilis v 1901 godu. (The turn of those
born in 1901.) (270000(4): 311-5)

200220(2) Soyuz molodezhi — na trudovoi front! (Youth League — into the
labour front!) (270000(4): 315)
[Telegram to Party Organizations of the Urals.]

200220(3) Bor´ba za chistotu. (The struggle for cleanliness.) (270000(4): 318-9)
[Order of the Day, No. 45, of Revolutionary Military Soviet of 1st
Labour Army.]

200220(4) [To Lenin.] (p.q. 270000(4): 525)
[On reorganization of 3rd Army.]

200221 Rech. (A speech.) (240000(28): 168-73)
[At celebration of Comintern Youth Section, in Ekaterinburg.]

200222 Organizatsiya remontykh artelei. (The organization of repair workshops.)
(270000(4): 327-8)
[Telegram to Provincial Executive Committee of Urals. Archives.]

200223 Interview with Lincoln Eyre.
Trans.: Am. NYWorld, 1920;
Eng. Daily News, 25.II.20.

200224(1) Prikaz, No. 194. (230000(7).II.ii: 55)

200224(2) Mobilizatsiya rabotnikov na khozyaistvennyi front. (The mobilization
of labour for the economic front.) (270000(4): 325)
[Telegram to Party Organizations in the Urals. Archives.]

200225(1) Telegramma, No. 205. (Telegram No. 205) (230000(7).II.ii: 56)

200225(2) Osnovnye polozheniya. (The fundamental situation.) (230000(7).II.ii:
58-60)
Repr.: 270000(4): 285-9.

200226(1) Prikaz, No. 195. (230000(7).II.ii: 57)

200226(2) Zadachi 1-i Armii truda. (Tasks of 1st Labour Army.) (230000(7).II.ii:
61-3)
Repr.: 270000(4): 289-92.
[Theses of report to Communist Red Army Men, in Ekaterinburg. Archives.]

200227 Obshchie usloviya perevogo perioda raboty. (General conditions of the
first period of work.) (Iz, (47), 2.III.20)
Repr.: 270000(4): 330-1.

200228(1)   Obshchee polozhenie Respubliki i zadachi 1-i Armii truda. (The
general situation of the Republic and the tasks of the 1st Labour Army.)
(<u>Krasnyi Nabat</u>, (55,56), 28,29.II.20)
<u>Repr</u>.: 270000(4): 292-311.
<u>Trans</u>.: Eng. p.q. Deutscher, PA: 465.
[Speech in Ekaterinburg.]

200228(2)   Tezisy o perekhode k militsionnoi sisteme. (Theses on the transition
to a militia system.) (230000(7).II.i: 133-4)
<u>Repr</u>.: p.q. 270000(4): 546; PROTOKOLY: 405-18; PRODOVOL´STVENNAYA: 131-4.
<u>Trans</u>.: Eng. p.q. <u>Call</u>(Ln), 15.IV.20;
        Fr. 680000(1): 603-5;
        Ger. <u>RusKor</u>, (I.i.6-7), IV-V.20.

200302   O vyvoze metallov. (The output of metal.) (270000(4): 328-9)
[Archives.]

200303   Prikaz, No. 7. (230000(7).II.ii: 64-5)
<u>Repr</u>.: 270000(4): 316-8.
[Struggle against labour-desertion.]

200304   Prikaz, No. 198. (230000(7).II.ii: 66)
[To All-Ural Commission for organization of subbotniks.]

[200305]   Molodezh gotovit smena. (Youth fills the breach.) (<u>DerevKom</u>, (51),
5.III.20)
<u>Trans</u>.: Am. <u>Mil</u>, 20.II.70;
       Ger. <u>Jug-Int</u>, (I.22), VII-VIII.20.

200308   Uvelichivaite proizvoditel´nost truda. (Increase labour productivity.)
(270000(4): 321)
[To Party Organizations in the Urals. Archives.]

[200309]   [Secret debate at 10th Congress; on Poland.]
[c. 410000(1): Ch. X.]

200310(1)   Chto takoe khoroshii polk i chto takoe plokhoi polk? (What is a good
and what a bad regiment?) (230000(7).II.ii: 271-2)

200310(2)   Svyashchennaya zadacha Krasnoi Armii. (Sacred tasks of the Red Army.)
(230000(7).II.ii: 273-4)

200312   K voprosu o lesnykh zagotovkakh. (The problem of timber supplies.)
(270000(4): 326-7)
[Archives.]

200316   ⌊Rebuttal of opposition at 4th All-Ukrainian Party Conference.⌋
       ⌊c. 410000(1): Ch. VIII.⌋

[200323(1)]   Protsent rabotnikov i proizvoditel'nost truda. (The percentage of
       workers and labour productivity.) (Pr, (63,65), 23,25.III.20)
       Repr.: 230000(7).II.ii: 67-70; 270000(4): 331-5.
       ⌊Interview on Labour Army.⌋

200323(2)   1-i Armiya truda kak oblastnoi organ. (The 1st Labour Army as a
       Provincial organ.) (270000(4): 335-8)
       ⌊Interview on Labour Army. Archives.⌋

200323(3)   K organizatsii Vseural'skogo subbotnika. (The organization of All-Ural
       subbotniks.) (270000(4): 320-1)

[200324]   Iz tezisov ob ocherednykh zadachakh khozyaistvennogo stroitel'stva.
       (From theses on the immediate tasks of economic construction.)
       (PetPr, (65), 24.III.20)
       ⌊For 9th Party Congress. See 200330. cf. PROTOKOLY(1960): 533-8⌋

200325   Partiya pered litsom novykh khozyaistvennykh zadach. (The Party faced
       with new economic tasks.) (Iz, (68), 26.III.20)
       Repr.: 260000(18).II: 355-71; p.q. 270000(4): 103-6.
       ⌊Report to 16th All-Moscow District Conference CPR.⌋

200330   Ocherednye zadachi khozyaistvennogo stroitel'stva. (The immediate
       tasks of economic construction.) (p.q. DerevKom, (72), 1.IV.20;
       EkZhizn, (70,71), 31.III, 1.IV.20; Iz, (70), 31.III.20; PetPr, (71),
       31.III.20; Pr, (70), 31.III.20)
       Repr.: *200000(22); 270000(4): 114-28; PROTOKOLY: 200-13, 214;
           PROTOKOLY(1960): 75-7.
       Trans.: Eng. p.q. Deutscher, PA: 499;
           Ger. p.q. RusKor, (I.i.10), VII.20.
       ⌊To 9th Party Congress. See also ⌊200324⌋, 200331(1).⌋

200331(1)   Rech. (A Speech.) (PROTOKOLY(1960): 188-201)
       ⌊See 200330.⌋

200331(2)   i S.S.Kamenev: Prikaz, No. 506. (Iz(N), (81), 15.IV.20)

200331(3)   i S.S.Kamenev: Prikaz, No. 508. (Iz(N), (81), 15.IV.20)

200331(4)   Prikaz, No. 559. (<u>Iz</u>(N), (84), 18.IV.20)

200404(1)   Organizatsiya truda. (The organization of labour.) (<u>Iz</u>, (75), 6.IV.20;
             <u>PetPr</u>, (76), 6.IV.20; <u>Pr</u>, (75), 6.IV.20)
             <u>Repr</u>.: 200000(20); 270000(4): 129-63; PROTOKOLY(1960): 384-96.
             <u>Trans</u>.: Eng. p.q. Fischer: 161-2;
                       Ger. <u>RusKor</u>, (I.i.10), VII.20; p.q. Bergmann: 85-92.
             [Report to 9th Congress CPR.]

200404(2)   Zaklyuchitel'noe slovo. (Summary speech.) (270000(4): 163-77)
             <u>Trans</u>.: Eng. p.q. <u>Call</u>(Ln), 29.IV.20.
             [See 200404(1).]

200404(3)   i S.S.Kamenev: Prikaz, No. 504. (<u>Iz</u>(N), (81), 15.IV.20)

200404(4)   Prikaz, No. 728. (<u>Iz</u>(N), (107), 16.V.20)

200408   Prikaz, No. 553. (<u>Iz</u>(N), (83), 17.IV.20)

200409(1)   Ob organizatsii truda. (On the organization of labour.) (<u>EkZhizn</u>, (78),
             14.IV.20; <u>Iz</u>, (78), 14.IV.20)
             <u>Repr</u>.: 200000(19); 270000(4): 178-96.
             <u>Trans</u>.: Eng. p.q. Carr, BR.II: 206, 215-6.
             [Report to 3rd All-Russian Trade Union Congress.]

200409(2)   Zaklyuchitel'noe slovo. (Summary speech.) (<u>PetPr</u>, (79), 14.IV.20)
             <u>Repr</u>.: 270000(4): 196-204.
             [See 200409(1). Archives.]

200409(3)   Proletarii vsekh stran, tovarishchi rabochie! (Proletarians of all
             lands, comrade-workers!) (230000(7).II.ii: 275-6)
             <u>Repr</u>.: 270000(4): 205-6.
             [Appeal of 3rd All-Russian Trade Union Congress.]

[200414]   Telegramma. (A telegram.) (<u>Iz</u>, (78), 14.IV.20)
             [To Pyatakov.]

200415   Pervomaiskii subbotnik na transporte. (May Day subbotniks for transport.)
             (<u>EkZhizn</u>, (89), 22.IV.20)
             <u>Repr</u>.: 270000(4): 380.
             [Telegram No. 313. Archives.]

[200416] Pis'mo k redaktsiyu. (Letter to Editorial Board.) (*Iz*, (80), 16.IV.20)

200418 Kak borotsya s progulami. (How to fight against shriking.)
(270000(4): 374-6)
Trans.: Ger. RusKor, (I.ii.17-18), XI.20.
[Résumé. Archives.]

200419(1) Armiya — na pomoshch transportu! Prikaz, No. 204. (Army — to the
help of transport! Order of the Day, No. 204.) (*Iz*, (85), 22.IV.20;
Pr, (84), 21.IV.20)
Repr.: 270000(4): 372-3.

200420 Trud — osnova zhizni. (Work — the basis of life.) (PetPr, '94),
1.V.20)
Repr.: 230000(7).II.ii: 277; 270000(4): 3.
[Archives.]

[200422] Chto dolzhen znat kazhdyi. (What everyone should know.) (DerevKom,
(86:492), 22.IV.20)

200423 O pyatidesyatiletnem. (On his [i.e. Lenin's] 50th birthday.) (Pr,
(86), 23.IV.20)
Repr.: 240000(14); 240000(15); 240000(24): 145-50.
Trans.: 240000(24);
           Am. 640800: 205-8; Current History, III.24;
           Cz. Rude Pravo, (V.21), 24.I.24;
           Den. 310000(25);
           Eng. 680200(1): 1-6;
           Ger. p.q. Der Kom, (I.2), V.30; RusKor, (I.i.8-9), VI.20;
                ALMANACH: 181-4;
           Heb. Kuntras, 1924;
           Jap. 681125: 308-11;
           Sp. 670000(5): 298-304;
           Swed. 691100(2): 264-8;
           Yid. KomFon, (22), 27.I.24.

[200425] i dr.: Polozhenie. (A regulation.) (*Iz*, (88), 25.IV.20)
Trans.: Hol. Tribune, (180), 6.V.20.

200428 Polozhenie o Komissii po bor'be s trudovym dezertirstvom na zheleznykh dorogakh. (Regulation on the Commission for struggle against labour-desertion, on the railways.) (Iz, (96), 6.V.20)
Repr.: 270000(4): 376-9.
[Prikaz, No. 990.]

200429(1) Trud i voina. (Work and the war.) (Pr, (93), 1.V.20)
Repr.: 230000(7).II.ii: 278-9; 260000(18).II: 384-6; KI, (10), 11.V.20.
Trans.: Ger. KI, (10), 1920; RusKor, (I.i.8-9), VI.20.

200429(2) Smert pol'skoi burzhuazii! (Death to the Polish bourgeoisie!) (Iz, (93), 1.V.20; PetPr, (94), 1.V.20)
Repr.: *200000(34); *[200000(49)]; 230000(7).II.ii: 91; 260000(18).II: 375-6.

200429(3) Krasnomu voinu pol'skogo fronta. (To a Red fighter on the Polish front.) (Iz, (93), 1.V.20)
Repr.: 230000(7).II.ii: 92.

200429(4) i dr.: Ko vsem rabochim, krest'yanam i chestnym grazhdanam Rossii. (To all workers, peasants and honourable citizens of Russia.) (BoPr, (94), 1.V.20; Iz, (92), 30.IV.20; Pr, (92), 30.IV.20; ZhiznNats, (13:70), 29.IV.20)
Repr.: 230000(7).II.ii: 97-100; 260000(18).II: 376-80; DerevKom, (101), 11.V.20; DVPS: 492-5.
Trans.: Eng. p.q. New Russia, (II.17), 27.V.20;
    Fr. Bulletin du Bureau d'Information, (6), 15.VI.20; RevCom, (I.6,7), VIII,IX.20;
    Ger. Bulletin des Petrograder Büros, (6), 15.VI.20; RusKor, (I.i.8-9), VI.20;
    Nor. Ny Tid, 14.V.20.

200430(1) Pol'skii front i nashi zadachi. (The Polish front and our tasks.) (230000(7).II.ii: 93-6)
Repr.: 260000(18).II: 380-3.
Trans.: p.q. 410000(1): Ch. X.

200430(2) Vor v dome. (A thief in the house.) (PetPr, (95), 4.V.20; Pr, (94), 4.V.20)
Repr.: *200000(8); 260000(18).II: 384.

200430(3)   [Letter to CC; on Poland.]
               [c. 410000(1): Ch. X.]

200500   Po povodu rechi Bonar Lou. (On a speech by Bonar Law.) (<u>Iz</u>, (127),
               13.VI.20)
               <u>Repr</u>.: 230000(7).II.ii: 143-4; 260000(18).II: 417-8.
               [Archives.]

200501(1)   Prikaz, No. 209. (<u>Pr</u>, (94), 4.V.20)
               <u>Repr</u>.: *200000(15); 230000(7).II.ii: 101.

200501(2)   Slovo zheleznodorozhnikam po povodu pol´skogo nastupleniya. (A word
               to the railwaymen concerning the Polish attack.) (<u>Glavpolitput</u>, (3),
               1920; <u>PetPr</u>, (95), 5.V.20; <u>Pr</u>, (94), 4.V.20)
               <u>Repr</u>.: *200000(33); 270000(4): 371-2.
               [Prikaz, No. 994.]

[200501(3)]   K PERVOMU MAYA. (MAY DAY.), *[200000(45)].
               <u>Trans</u>.: Am. <u>Soviet Russia</u>, 5.VI.20;
                          Ger. <u>RusKor</u>, (I.i.8-9), VI.20.

200501(4)   Prikaz, No. 693. (<u>Iz</u>(N), (102), 11.V.20)

200502(1)   Pol´skii front. (The Polish front.) (<u>Iz</u>, (96), 6.V.20)
               <u>Repr</u>.: 230000(7).II.ii: 102-5; 260000(18).II: 386-90.
               <u>Trans</u>.: p.q. 410000(1): Ch. X;
                          Fr. <u>Bulletin du Bureau d'Information</u>, (6), 15.VI.20;
                          Ger. <u>Bulletin des Petrograder Büros</u>, (6), 15.VI.20.
               [Interview.]

200502(2)   i dr.: Prikaz, No. 718. (<u>Pr</u>, (95), 5.V.20)
               <u>Repr</u>.: 260000(18).II: 617-8.
               <u>Trans</u>.: Fr. <u>Bulletin du Bureau d'Information</u>, (6), 15.VI.20.

200503   Prikaz, No. 731. (<u>Iz</u>(N), (105), 14.V.20)

200504   Formirovanie kommunisticheskogo bataliona. (The formation of a
               communist battalion. (<u>Pr</u>, (97), 7.V.20)
               <u>Trans</u>.: Ger. <u>Bulletin des Petrograder Büros</u>, (6), 15.VI.20.

200505(1) Voina s Pol'shei. (The war with Poland.) (Iz, (96), 6.V.20; PetPr,
(97), 6.V.20)
Repr.: 200000(5); 200000(6); 200000(7); *200000(102); 230000(7).II.ii:
106-17; 260000(18).II: 390-404.
Trans.: p.q. 410000(1): Ch. X;
Ger. 200000(73): 11-24;
Pol. *200000(99).
[See 200510(4) for repr. with supplementary pars. Report to joint-meeting
of All-Russian CEC, Moscow Soviet and heads of trade unions and factory
committees.]

[200505(2)] i S.S.Kamenev: Prikaz, No. 718. (Iz, (95), 5.V.20)

200505(3) Prikaz, No. 735. (Iz(N), (107), 16.V.20)

[200505(4)] i S.S.Kamenev: Prikaz, No. 741. (Iz, (98), 8.V.20)

200505(5) Rech. (A speech.) (Pr, (96), 6.V.20)
[To Red Army parade.]

200506 Prikaz, No. 741. (Iz(N), (102), 11.V.20)

200507(1) Po povodu sozdaniya osobogo soveshchaniya pri Glavnokomanduyushchem.
(Concerning the establishment of a special advisory body attached to
the Supreme Commander.) (230000(7).II.ii: 119-20)
Repr.: 260000(18).II: 407-8.
Trans.: Eng. p.q. Deutscher, PA: 460.
[Archives. ?T511.]

200507(2) Bor'ba s razrukoi transporta. (The struggle against the destruction
of transport.) (Iz, (104), 15.V.20)
[Prikaz, No. 1008, of People's Commissar for Communications.]

200507(3) Prikaz, No. 224. (Iz(N), (112), 23.V.20)

200508(1) Prikaz, No. 210. (DerevKom, (101), 11.V.20; Pr, (100), 11.V.20)
Repr.: 230000(7).II.ii: 121-2.

200508(2) Kiev v rukakh pol'skikh panov! (Kiev is in the hands of the Polish
gentry!) (V Puti, (110), 8.V.20)
Repr.: 230000(7).II.ii: 123-4; 260000(18).II: 408-9; Iz, (104),
15.V.20.

200508(3)   i Glazorov: O bor´be s trudovym dezertirstvom. (The struggle against labour-desertion.) (Glavpolitput, (3), 1920; Pr, (106), 18.V.20)

Repr.: 270000(4): 379-80.

[Prikaz, No. 1017.]

200509(1)   Udvoite bditel´nost! (Redouble vigilance!) (Pr, (101), 12.V.20)

[Prikaz, No. 212A; on transport.]

200509(2)   Chego oni khotyat? (What do they want?) (V Puti, (112), 10.V.20)

Repr.: 230000(7).II.ii: 130-1; 260000(18).II: 409-11; PetPr, (106), 16.V.20; Pr, (104), 15.V.20.

Trans.: Eng. p.q. New Russia, (II.19), 10.VI.20; Pol. *200000(98).

200509(3)   Prikaz, No. 213. (Iz, (100), 11.V.20)

Repr.: 230000(7).II.ii: 125-9.

Trans.: p.q. 410000(1): Ch. X.

[On Poland.]

200510(1)   Prikaz, No. 214. (230000(7).II.ii: 132)

200510(2)   Prikaz, No. 215. (230000(7).II.ii: 133)

[Fight against deserters.]

200510(3)   Prikaz, No. 217. (DerevKom, (102), 12.V.20; Iz, (101), 12.V.20; Iz(NKVD), (104), 13.V.20; PetPr, (101), 11.V.20; Pr, (101), 12.V.20)

Repr.: 230000(7).II.ii: 134.

[Generosity to prisoners and wounded.]

200510(4)   VOINA S POL´SHEI (THE WAR WITH POLAND), 200000(30).

Repr.: *200000(32); 200000(35); *200000(36); 230000(7).II.ii: 117-8; 260000(18).II: 404-6.

Trans.: Ger. 200000(71); 200000(72); RusKor, (I.i.11), VIII.20; Pol. *200000(66); *200000(103).

[Speech in Gomel. Originally pubd. from train. See also 200505(1); 230000(7).II.ii: 117-8 has supplementary pars.]

200510(5)   Budte na strazhe! (Stay on guard!) (PetPr, (101), 11.V.20; Pr, (100), 11.V.20)

Repr.: *200000(3).

200511(1)   Za Sovetskuyu Ukrainu! (For a Soviet Ukraine!) (V Puti, (114), 12.V.20)
Repr.: 230000(7).II.ii: 135-7; 260000(18).II: 411-3.

200511(2)   K vtoroi godovshchine Gudka. (The second anniversary of Gudok.)
(Iz, (101), 12.V.20)
Repr.: 270000(4): 4D7.

200511(3)   [Message to CC; appointment of Stalin to Southern Army in Poland.]
Trans.: Eng. p.q. Deutscher, PA: 466.
[T516.]

200513   V chadu i khmelyu. (Dazed and dizzy.) (V Puti, (115), 14.V.20)
Repr.: 230000(7).II.ii: 138-9; 260000(18).II: 414-5.

200515(1)   Sovetskaya i shlyakhetskaya. (Soviet power and the Polish gentry.)
(V Puti, (116), 16.V.20)
Repr.: 230000(7).II.ii: 140-1; 260000(18).II: 415-7.

200515(2)   Prikaz, No. 220. (230000(7).II.ii: 142)

200518   Nashi uspekhi na zapadnom fronte. (Our successes on the Western Front.)
(Iz, (107), 19.V.20; Pr, (107), 19.V.20)
Repr.: 260000(18).II: 418-20; DerevKom, (110), 22.V.20.

200522   Prikaz, No. 1042. (Iz, (115), 29.V.20; Pr, (115), 29.V.20)
Repr.: 270000(4): 345-7; EkZhizn, (238), 24.X.20.
Trans.: Eng. p.q. New Russia, (II.24), 15.VII.20.
[On transport.]

[200525]   Dobrovol´tsy, na pol´skii front! (Volunteers, to the Polish front!)
(Pr, (114), 25.V.20)
Repr.: *[200000(44)]; DerevKom, (115), 28.V.20; Iz, (114), 28.V.20;
        PetPr, (115), 28.V.20.

[200527]   Udvoim usiliya! (Redoubled efforts!) (Iz, (113), 27.V.20; Pr, (113),
27.V.20)

200528   Gudok. Prikaz, No. 1049/bis. (Iz, (115), 29.V.20; Pr, (115),
29.V.20)
Repr.: 270000(4): 405-6.

200529(1)   Pref. TERRORIZM I KOMMUNIZM (TERRORISM AND COMMUNISM), 200000(37).
[See 200000(37) for all repr., trans.]

200529(2)   Proizvodstvenno-transportnyi plan No. 1042 i edinstvo khozyaistvennogo
            plana. (Transport-production plan, No. 1042 and the unity of the
            economic plan.) (270000(4): 348-50)

200530   Vozrodim transport! (Revive the transport!) (PetPr, (119), 3.VI.20)
            Repr.: *200000(4).

200531   Prikaz, No. 505. (Iz(NKVD), (107), 16.V.20)

[200600]   [Historical introduction to theses on Communist Parties and Parliament.]
            Trans.: Eng. Degras, DOCCI.I: 150-2; CI, (I.11-12), VI-VII.20;
                    Fr. : THÈSES: 66-7; IC, (II.11), VI.20;
                    Ger. PROTOKOLL: 466-9.

200602   i Lenin: Obrashchenie Soveta Narodnykh Komissarov k belym ofitseram.
            (Appeal of the Sovnarkom to White Officers.) (DerevKom, (120),
            4.VI.20; PetPr, (119), 3.VI.20)

[200603]   Po povodu byvshikh ofitserov, eshche ostayushchikhsya v lagere belykh.
            (Concerning ex-officers still in the White camp.) (Iz, (118), 3.VI.20)
            Repr.: 230000(7).II.i: 114.
            Trans.: Fr. 680000(1): 579-80.

*200604   *[Memorandum on attitude to Poland.]
            [c. Deutscher, PA: 462. T533.]

200605   Daite frontu Krasnykh komandirov. (Send Red commanders to the front.)
            (Iz, (121), 6.VI.20; PetPr, (122), 6.VI.20; Pr, (121), 6.VI.20)
            Repr.: *200000(10); *200000(11); *200000(12).

200612   Pochto-telegramma, No. 2886b. (Telegram, No. 2886b.) (230000(7).II.ii:
            147)
            [To cdes. Lenin, Chicherin, Karakhan, Krestinsky, Radek and Kamenev.]

200614   Prikaz, No. 1051. (Pr, (128), 15.VI.20)

200615   Prikaz, No. 229. (PetPr, (131), 17.VI.20)
            Repr.: 230000(7).II.ii: 280.
            Trans.: Am. Soviet Russia, 4.IX.20;
                    Ger. p.q. Kommunismus, (I.41-42), 26.X.20.
            [On Persia.]

200616(1) Gore ne dovodyashchim do kontsa! (Woe to those who do not carry matters to a finish!) (Iz, (130), 17.VI.20; PetPr, (131), 17.VI.20; Pr, (130), 17.VI.20)
Repr.: *200000(9); 230000(7).II.ii: 183-4; 260000(18).II: 420-1.
Trans.: Eng. p.q. New Russia, (II.23), 8.VII.20.

200616(2) i S.S.Kamenev: Prikaz, No. 222. (Iz, (129), 16.VI.20; PetPr, (130), 16.VI.20)
[Death to deserters and traitors.]

200617 Vmesto poslesloviya. (In place of a Postface.) (200000(37)
[See 200000(37) for all repr., trans.]

[200618(1)] K pol´skim rabochim, krest´yanam i legioneram. (To the Polish workers, peasants and legionaries.) (Pr, (131), 18.VI.20)
Repr.: 260000(18).II: 421-3.
Trans.: Pol. Pochodnia, [1920].

200618(2) Po povodu spetsialistov i komissarov. (Concerning specialists and commissars.) (Gudok, (32), 1920)
Repr.: 270000(4): 407-8.

200621 O trudovoi distsipline. (On labour discipline.) (230000(7).II.ii: 148-52)
Repr.: 270000(4): 365-71.
Trans.: Eng. p.q. Deutscher, PA: 501.
[Speech to meeting of Muromsk railwaymen. Archives.]

200629 Zakleimit varvarov! (Brand the barbarians!) (230000(7).II.ii: 145-6)
Repr.: 260000(18).II: 423-4.
[Telegram, No. 2886a, to cdes. Chicherin, Lenin, Karakhan, Krestinsky, Radek and Kamenev. Archives.]

200630 Prikaz, No. 230. (Iz, (142), 1.VII.20; Pr, (142), 1.VII.20)
Repr.: 230000(7).II.ii: 153.
[Closing down Voennoe Delo because of the chauvinism and incapacity of its editorial board.]

[200700(1)] K voprosu ob okruzhnoi sisteme NKPS. (On the question of the turn-round system of the People's Commisariat for Communications.) (270000(4): 384-5)
[Notes for Railwaymen's Congress. Archives.]

[200700(2)]   Na puti k proizvodstvennomu soyuzu. (The way to a production union.)
(270000(4): 386-7)
[Note for Railwaymen's Congress.]

[200700(3)]   K voprosu o zadachakh vosstanovleniya transporta. (The problem of
the tasks of repairing transport.) (270000(4): 347-8)
[Pref., Shatunovsky. See 210503.]

[200702]   i dr.: Obrashchenie VTsIK, Sovnarkom i Revvoensoveta: Na pomoshch
ranenym i bol'nym Krasnoarmeitsam. (Appeal of All-Russian CEC, the
Sovnarkom and the Revolutionary Military Soviet: Help the wounded
and sick Red Army men.) (Iz, (143), 2.VII.20; Pr, (143), 2.VII.20)
Repr.: DerevKom, (160), 22.VII.20.

200707   i dr.: Bor'ba so shkurnikami. Prikaz. (The struggle against self-
seekers. Order of the Day.) (Pr, (150), 10.VII.20)

200711(1)   Neobkhodimaya popravka. (A necessary correction.) (230000(7).II.ii:
154)
[On bourgeois lies about Red Army on Polish front.]

200711(2)   i dr.: Rabochim, krest'yanam i vsem chestnym grazhdanam Sovetskoi
Rossii i Sovetskoi Ukrainy. (To the workers, peasants and all honest
citizens of Soviet Russia and Soviet Ukraine.) (Iz, (159), 21.VII.20;
PetPr, (159), 21.VII.20; Pr, (159), 21.VII.20)
Repr.: 230000(7).II.ii: 157-61; 260000(18).II: 424-30; DVPS(1959):
55-60.
[Appeal of the Sovnarkom.]

200713(1)   [Urges acceptance of British mediation in Poland.]
[c. Deutscher, PA: 463. T544.]

200713(2)   [Again urges acceptance of British mediation in Poland.]
[c. Deutscher, PA: 463. T545.]

200717   Prikaz, No. 231. (Iz, (157), 18.VII.20; Pr, (157), 18.VII.20)
Repr.: 230000(7).II.ii: 155-6; DerevKom, (161), 23.VII.20; PetPr,
(160), 22.VII.20.
[Spare the prisoners.]

200721   Doklad. (A report.) (270000(4): 388-405)
[To Railwaymen's Congress. Archives.]

[200722]   O frantsuzskoi sotsialisticheskoi partii. (The French Socialist Party.)
           (KI, (12), 20.VII.20; Pr, (160), 22.VII.20)
           Repr.: 230000(8): 44-53; 240000(29): 60-70; 260000(10): 145-56.
           Trans.: Am. 451000: 84-94;
                   Eng. CI, (11-12), VI-VII.20;
                   Fr. 670306: 75-86; BulCom, (I.30-31), 16.IX.20; IC, (II.12),
                       30.VII.20; p.q. Kriegel: TOURS: 249-53;
                   Ger. KomInt, (II.12), 1920;
                   Sp. El Com, (II.33), 9.IV.21.
           [Conditions of admission to Comintern.]

200723   Rech. (A speech.) (Pr, (171), 5.VIII.20)
           Repr.: 240000(9): 73-6; 260000(10): 49-53; BoPr, (163), 25.VII.20.
           Trans.: Am. 451000: 97-101;
                   Fr. BulCom, (I.36), 14.X.20;
                   Ger. PROTOKOLL: 91-5.
           [To 2nd Congress Comintern; on Zinoviev's report on role of Party.]

200726   [Conversation with Frosaard and Cachin.]
           Trans.: Fr. p.q. Kriegel.I: 643.

[200728]   Revolyutsiya obnimet vse chelovechestvo. (Revolution embarces all
           mankind.) (DerevKom. (165), 28.VII.20)

200731(1) Dvurushnikov — von iz strany! Prikaz, No. 232. (Double-dealers,
           leave the country! Order of the Day, No. 232.) (BoPr, (170), 3.VIII.20;
           Iz, (168), 1.VIII.20; PetPr, (170), 3.VIII.20; Pr, (169), 2.VIII.20)
           Repr.: 230000(7).II.ii: 162-3; 260000(18).II: 430-1.
           [The expulsion of the French Deputy, Lafont.]

200731(2) Pis'mo frantsuzskomu sindikalistu o kommunisticheskoi partii. (Letter
           to a French syndicalist on the Communist Party.) (KI, (13), 28.IX.20)
           Repr.: 230000(8): 55-62; 260000(10): 156-64.
           Trans.: Eng. CI, (13), 1920;
                   Fr. 670306: 87-95; BulCom, (I.46), 2.XII.20; VieOuv, 26.XI.20;
                   Ger. KomInt, (II.13), 1920;
                   Scand. KeI, (2), XII.20;
                   Sp. El Com, (II.32), 2.IV.21.

200800   Proletariat i krest´yanstvo v revolyutsii i v sovetsko-pol´skoi voine.
(The proletariat and the peasantry in the Revolution and in the
Soviet-Polish war.)   (260000(18).II: 544-8)
Trans.: Ger. RusKor, (I.ii.11), VIII.20.
[Archives.]

200807(1)   Manifest vtorogo kongressa Kommunisticheskogo Internatsionala.
(Manifesto of the 2nd Congress of the Communist International.)
(KI, (13), 28.IX.20)
Repr.: *[210000(52)]; 240000(29): 76-103; 260000(10): 53-83; p.q.
      Kom(Gruzii), (5), 24.X.20.
Trans.: Am. 451000: 102-32;
      Cz. p.q. Rude Pravo, (48), 17.XI.20;
      Eng. 200000(78); p.q. Degras, DOCCI.I: 173-83; CI, (13), 1920;
      Fr. THÈSES: 70-81;
      Ger. 200000(94); KomInt, (II.13), 1920; p.q. ALMANACH: 5-14;
      Hol. 210000(33); p.q. Tribune, (74), 27.XII.20.

200807(2)   [Speech, on Manifesto of 2nd Congress Comintern.]
Trans.: Am. p.q. Eudin & Fisher: 41-4;
      Eng. p.q. Deutscher, PA: 467;
      Fr. RevCom, (I.6), VIII.20;
      Ger. PROTOKOLL: 676-702.

[200810(1)]   Frantsuzskie rabochie, sprosite Lafona!   (French workers, ask Lafont!)
(Iz, (175), 10.VIII.20)
Repr.: 260000(18).II: 431-2.

200810(2)   Chem dolzhen byt Gudok?   (What must Gudok be?)   (270000(4): 406)
[Archives.]

200811   Tezisy voenno-politicheskoi kampanii po povodu zaklyucheniya mira s
Pol´shei. (Theses of a military-political campaign for concluding
peace with Poland.)   (230000(7).II.ii: 164-5)

[200812]   Provokatsiya frantsuzskikh imperialistov.   (A provocation by French
imperialists.)   (BoPr, (179), 13.VIII.20; Iz, (177), 12.VIII.20;
Pr, (177), 12.VIII.20)
Repr.: 260000(18).II: 432-5.
[Interview.]

200814   Prikaz, No. 233. (<u>BePr</u>, (182), 17.VIII.20; <u>DerevKom</u>, (181), 15.VIII.20;
<u>Pr</u>, (180), 15.VIII.20)
<u>Repr</u>.: 230000(7).II.ii: 166; 260000(18).II: 435.
<u>Trans</u>.: Eng. <u>ManGuard</u>, 16.VIII.20.
[On to Warsaw.]

200816   Oproverzhenie. (A refutation.) (230000(7).II.ii: 167)
<u>Repr</u>.: 260000(18).II: 436.
[On Poland.]

200817(1)   O vrangelevskom fronte. (The Wrangel front.) (<u>PetPr</u>, (183), 18.VIII.20;
<u>Pr</u>, (182), 18.VIII.20)
<u>Repr</u>.: 230000(7).II.ii: 185-92; 260000(18).II: 436-45.
[Report to Moscow Soviet. Archives.]

200817(2)   Na puti k ob"edineniyu sukhoputnogo i vodnogo transporta. (The way
to a unification of land and water transport.) (270000(4): 385-6)
[Archives.]

200817(3)   [To Politbureau; refusal to go to Poland.]
[c. Deutscher, PA: 468. T565.]

200818   Prikaz, No. 234. (230000(7).II.ii: 193)
[On Wrangel.]

200819   [& Stalin: Report to Politbureau on the military situation.]
[c. Deutscher, PA: 468. Harvard Archives.]

[200823]   Nam nuzhna yuzhnaya granitsa. (We need a southern frontier.) (<u>V Puti</u>,
(117), 23.VIII.20)
<u>Repr</u>.: 230000(7).II.ii: 194-5; 260000(18).II: 445-7; <u>PetPr</u>, (214),
25.IX.20.
<u>Trans</u>.: Eng. p.q. <u>New Russia</u>, (III.38), 21.X.20.

200825   Posledysh. (An epigone.) (<u>V Puti</u>, (119), 25.VIII.19)
<u>Repr</u>.: 230000(7).II.ii: 196-7; 260000(18).II: 447-8.
[On Wrangel.]

200826   Prikaz, No. 236. (<u>PetPr</u>, (195), 3.IX.20)
<u>Repr</u>.: 230000(7).II.ii: 198.
[Don't drive them away; destroy them! On Wrangel.]

200828   Kuban ne podnyalas. (The Kuban has not risen.) (<u>V Puti</u>, (120), 29.VIII.20)

Repr.: 230000(7).II.ii: 199-200; 260000(18).II: 448-50; <u>BoPr</u>, (197) 5.IX.20; <u>PetPr</u>, (196), 4.IX.20.

200830(1)   Prikaz, No. 237. (230000(7).II.ii: 201)

[Reading 237 for 239. cf. 200903.]

200830(2)   Prevoskhodnyi udar. (A most excellent blow.) (<u>BoPr</u>, (192), 31.VIII.20; <u>Iz</u>, (191), 31.VIII.20; <u>PetPr</u>, (192), 31.VIIİ.20; <u>V Puti</u>, (121), 30.VIII.20)

Repr.: 230000(7).II.ii: 202-3; 260000(18).II: 450-1.

200830(3)   Tovarishchi zheleznodorozhniki! (Comrade railwaymen!) (230000(7). II.ii: 204)

200830(4)   Kubanskii desant Vrangelya unichtozhen. (Wrangel's Kuban force has been destroyed.) (<u>Pr</u>, (191), 31.VIII.20)

[Telegram.]

200831   K rabote po remontu parovozov. (The work of repairing locomotives.) (270000(4): 350-1)

[Archives.]

200901   Desant Vrangelya. (Wrangel's force.) (<u>BoPr</u>, (195), 3.IX.20)

Repr.: 230000(7).II.ii: 205; 260000(18).II: 452-3.

[Interview with Soviet press. Archives.]

200903   Prikaz, No. 239. (<u>Pr</u>, (196), 5.IX.20)

Repr.: 230000(7).II.ii: 168.

200908(1)   Prikaz, No. 240. (230000(7).II.ii: 169)

[Issued from Smolensk. Issued as Prikaz, No. 235 from Kharkov.]

[200908(2)]   Nuzhen vtoroi urok? (Is a second lesson needed?) (<u>V Puti</u>, (122), 8.IX.20)

Repr.: 230000(7).II.ii: 170-1; 260000(18).II: 453-4.

[200908(3)]   Remont parovozov. (The repair of locomotives.) (<u>Pr</u>, (198,199), 8,9.IX.20)

Repr.: 270000(4): 351-60.

[Order of the Day, No. 1042.]

200909 Prikaz, No. 241. (230000(7).II.ii: 172)

    [Severe punishment for agents of the Polish gentry.]

200910 My sil'nee chem byli. (We are stronger than we were.) (V Puti, (124),

    11.IX.20)

    Repr.: 230000(7).II.ii: 173-4; 260000(18).II: 454-6; Iz, (203)

      14.IX.20; Pr, (203), 14.IX.20.

200911 Pany ne khotyat mira. (T$_h$e [Polish] gentry don't want peace.)

    (V Puti, (125), 12.IX.20)

    Repr.: 230000(7).II.ii: 175-6; 260000(18).II: 456-9; BoPr, (206),

      16.IX.20; DerevKom, (206), 18.IX.20; Pr, (204), 15.IX.20.

[200912] i dr.: Vozzvanie k ofitseram armii bar. Vrangelya. (An appeal to

    the officers of Baron Wrangel's army.) (Iz, (202), 12.IX.20; Pr,

    (202), 12.IX.20)

    Repr.: 260000(18).II: 459-60.

    Trans.: Nor. Ny Tid, 20.IX.20.

[200917] Zapadnyi front zovet. (The Western Front is calling.) (Iz, (206),

    17.IX.20; Pr, (206), 17.IX.20)

    Repr.: *200000(14); 260000(18).II: 460-2.

200922 Prikaz, No. 1907. (Iz(NKVD), (223), 5.X.20)

200924(1) Prikaz, No. 242. (Iz, (213), 25.IX.20; Iz(NKVD), (216), 26.IX.20;

    Krasnaya Gazeta, (214), 25.IX.20; Pr, (213), 25.IX.20)

    Repr.: 230000(7).II.ii: 177; 260000(18).II: 462-3.

    [Poland again offered peace.]

200924(2) Interv'yu. (An interview.) (230000(7).II.ii: 281-2)

    Repr.: 260000(18).II: 463-5.

    Trans.: Eng. ManGuard, 27.IX.20.

    [We want peace, but are prepared for war.]

200924(3) Interv'yu. (An interview.) (230000(7).II.ii: 283-4)

    Repr.: 260000(18).II: 465-7.

    Trans.: Eng. p.q. Carr, BR.III: 280.

    [The war against Poland and the over-all position of the Soviet

    Republic.]

200926   Prikaz, No. 1946. (Iz(NKVD), (225), 7.X.20)

200928   Budem pomnit o nashikh krasnoarmeitsakh v Germanii. (We must remember
                our Red Army men in Germany.) (DerevKom, (218), 30.IX.20; Iz, (216),
                29.IX.20; Iz(NKVD), (219), 30.IX.20; PetPr, (218), 30.IX.20; Pr, (216),
                29.IX.20)

201002   Rech. (A speech.) (Iz, (220), 3.X.20)
                Repr.: 230000(7).II.ii: 285-7; 260000(18).II: 468-70; BoPr, (222),
                        5.X.20; PetPr, (222), 5.X.20.
                [In Red Square. In honour of Red Commanders.]

201008(1)   Dolgovechnye i nedolgovechnye pravitel'stva. (Established and temporary
                governments.) (BoPr, (228), 12.X.20)
                Repr.: *200000(13); *[200000(43)].
                [On Pilsudski's regime in Poland.]

201008(2)   Pamyatka krasnoarmeitsa yuzhnogo fronta. (Instructions to Red Army men
                on the Southern Front.) (Iz, (227), 12.X.20)
                Repr.: 200000(23); *200000(24); *200000(25); *200000(26); *[200000(46)];
                        230000(7).II.ii: 206-9; BoPr, (231), 15.X.20.

201010(1)   Chto oznachaet perekhod Makhno na storonu Sovetskoi vlasti. (The
                significance of Makhno's coming over to the side of the Soviet State
                Power.) (V Puti, (132), 11.X.20)
                Repr.: *200000(42); *[200000(50)]; 230000(7).II.ii: 210-2;
                        260000(18).II: 470-4.

201010(2)   Lettre aux camarades yougo-slaves.
                Trans.: Fr. BulCom, (I.47-48), 9.XII.20.

201013(1)   Mir s Pol'shei dostignut. (Peace achieved with Poland.) (V Puti,
                (134), 1920)
                Repr.: 200000(16); 230000(7).II.ii: 178-80; 260000(18).II: 474-6.

201013(2)   Prikaz, No. 246. (Iz, (230), 15.X.20)
                Repr.: 230000(7).II.ii: 213.

201014(1)   Makhno i Vrangel. (Makhno and Wrangel.) (230000(7).II.ii: 214)

201014(2)   Prikaz, No. 247. (230000(7).II.ii: 215)

[201014(3)]   Dovol´no terdet Vrangelya. (There has been enough trouble from
               Wrangel.) (DerevKom, (230), 14.X.20)

201015(1)   Kak organizovan otryad Makhno? (How is Makhno's detachment organized?)
               (230000(7).II.ii: 216-7)

201015(2)   Zadacha na chetvertyi god. (Tasks for the fourth year.)
               (230000(7).II.ii: 288)

[201015(3)]   Prikonchim s Vrangelam. (Let's be done with Wrangels.) (DerevKom,
               (231), 15.X.20)

[201016]   L.T.: Petlyura, rimskii papa i frantsuzskie frank-masony. (Petlyura,
               the Roman Pope and French free-masonry.) (Iz, (231), 16.X.20; Pr,
               (231), 16.X.20)

201017   Yuzhnyi front i zimnyaya kampaniya. (The Southern Front and the winter
               campaign.) (Iz, (233), 19.X.20; Pr, (233), 19.X.20)
               Repr.: 230000(7).II.ii: 218-9; 260000(18).II: 476-8.

201020   O tekushchem momente. (The current situation.) (Iz, (236), 22.X.20)
               Repr.: *[200000(48)].
               Trans.: Am. p.q. Eudin & Fisher: 62;
                       Eng. p.q. Soc(G), (XIX.43), 25.XI.20;
                       Sp. p.q. El Com, (I.26), 20.XI.20.
               [Speech to Congress of Committees of Disabled and Wounded Red Army Men,
               at time of Denikin's attack.]

[201023]   L.T.: Martov — retsidivist. (Martov is a recidivist.) (Pr, (237),
               23.X.20)

201027(1)   Da budet poslednim! (It will be the last!) (V Puti, (135), 1920)
               Repr.: 230000(7).II.ii: 220; p.q. 300000(1): Ch. XXXIV.
               Trans.: p.q. 300000(1): Ch. XXXIV.

201027(2)   Ne vypuskat! (Don't let go!) (V Puti, (136), 27.X.20)
               Repr.: 230000(7).II.ii: 221-2; 260000(18).II: 478-80; BoPr, (249),
                       5.XI.20.

201027(3)   Privet vozrozhdayushcheisya Ukraine! (Greetings to the renascent
               Ukraine!) (Gudok, (149), 5.XI.20; PetPr, (251), 7.XI.20)
               Repr.: 270000(4): 501.

201031   BOL´SHE RAVENSTVA! (MORE EQUALITY!), *200000(21).

Repr.: *200000(28); 230000(7).II.i: 83-7.

Trans.: Fr. 680000(1): 545-50.

[Letter to Revolutionary Military Soviets of the Front and the Armies, and to all responsible workers of the Red Army and Red Fleet.]

[201100(1)]   Osnovnoe postanovlenie Polnomochnoi Komissii Soveta Narodnykh Komissarov po Donetskomu Basseinii. (Proekt.) (Fundamental regulation of the Plenipotentiary Commission of the Sovnarkom for the Donets Basin: Draft.) (270000(4): 489-92)

[Archives.]

[201100(2)]   Mery po okhrane truda rabochikh Donbassa. (Proekt.) (Measures for labour protection for Donbas workers.: Draft.) (270000(4): 498-500)

[Archives.]

[201102]   Reshayushchie dni na yuzhnom fronte. (Decisive days on the Southern Front.) (BoPr, (247), 3.XI.20; Iz, (245), 2.XI.20)

Repr.: 260000(18).II: 480-1.

201106(1)   Tre goda bor´by i ucheby. (Three years of struggle and study.) (PetPr, (252), 10.XI.20; Pr, (250), 7.XI.20)

Repr.: 260000(18).II: 481-5.

[Speech at celebration meeting of Plenum of Moscow Soviet, Moscow Committee CPR, and Moscow trade unions jointly with District Committees, leaders of trade unions, factory committees; in honour of the anniversary of the Russian Revolution. Archives.]

201106(2)   Pis´mo v Tsektran. (Letter to CC Transport Union.) (270000(4): 409-10)

[Archives.]

201107   Vospominaniya ob oktyabr´skom perevorote. (Reminiscences of the October Revolution.) (ProlRev, (10), 1922)

Repr.: 240000(32).II: 90-100.

Trans.: Am. NI, I.38; Soviet Russia, 22.I.21;
        Cz. Slavik: 239-49;
        Fr. BulCom, (VI.3), 6.XI.25.

201108   Put k edinomu khozyaistvennomu planu. (The way to a unified economic plan.) (EkZhizn, (251-3), 9-11.XI.20)

Repr.: 200000(29); 270000(4): 215-32; p.q. Krasnaya Gazeta, (265), 25.XI.20; K VIII S"EZDU. ++++

201108   ++++   Trans.: Am. Soviet Russia, 5,12.III.21;
                Ger. RusR, (*13,14), *8,15.XII.20.
                [To 8th Congress Soviets.]

201109   Professional'nye soyuzy i ikh dal'neishaya rol. (The trade unions and
                their future role.) (X S"EZD RKP(1963): 815-9)
                [Preliminary draft of theses.]

201112   i dr.: Dlya chego sozdana Polnomochnoi Komissiya. (Why the
                Plenipotentiary Commission has been set up.) (270000(4): 493-5)
                [From the Sovnarkom; on the Donbas. Archives.]

201115   Sevastopol vzyat -- na Donbass! (Sebastopol has been freed -- On to
                the Donbas!) (BoPr, (266), 26.XI.20; Krasnaya Gazeta, (265), 25.XI.20)
                Repr.: 270000(4): 502-3.
                [Archives.]

201116   Prikaz, No. 250. (Pr, (260), 19.XI.20)

201117   Rossiya, na pomoshch Donetskomu shakhteru! (Russia, help the Donets
                miners!) (EkZhizn, (263), 23.XI.20: Iz, (263), 23.XI.20; PetPr, (264),
                24.XI.20; Pr, (263), 23.XI.20)
                Repr.: 270000(4): 503-4.

201118   i dr.: Osnovnye zadachi Polnomochnoi Komissii. (Fundamental tasks of
                the Plenipotentiary Commission.) (270000(4): 495-7)
                [Archives.]

201119   Neobkhodimye meropriyatiya. (Indispensible measures.) (270000(4):497-8)
                [To cdes. Lenin and Krestinsky. Archives. T623.]

201120   Polozhenie i zadachi Sovetskoi Respubliki posle okonchaniya grazhdanskoi
                voiny. (The position and tasks of the Soviet Republic after the
                conclusion of the civil war.) (260000(18).II: 492-4)
                [Interview.]

201122   Rech. (A speech.) (PetPr, (264), 24.XI.20)
                [At All-Ukrainian Party Conference.]

201124   O politike KAPD. (On the policy of the KAPD.) (KI, (17), 7.VI.21)

Repr.: 240000(29): 137-52; 260000(10): 101-15.

Trans.: Am. 451000: 137-52;

         Eng. CI, (III.16-17), 1921;

         Fr. BulCom, (II.34), 18.VIII.21;

         Ger. KomInt, (II.17), 1921;

         Scand. KeI, (6), IX.21.

[Reply to Gorter; on CPGermany.]

201126(1)   Frontov bol´she net! (No Fronts left!) (Pr, (269), 30.XI.20)

Repr.: 260000(18).II: 489-92.

Trans.: Am. Soviet Russia, 5.II.21.

[Speech to Moscow cells CPR.]

[201126(2)]   Vnimanie Donbassu! (Attention to the Donbas!) (Byulleten Vseukrainskoi Konf. KP(b), (5), 26.XI.20)

Repr.: 270000(4): 505-9.

[Speech at Conference CPUkraine.]

201128   Stroitel´stvo krasnoi vooruzhennoi sily. (Building up the Red Armed Forces.) (230000(7).II.i: 122-32)

Trans.: Fr. 680000(1): 589-603.

[Speech at discussion on research into and for utilization of the experiences of World War of 1914-1918. Archives.]

201129   Soobshchenie. (A communique.) (230000(7).II.ii: 289-30)

[To Soviet press; on Red Army.]

201200   ON MANY FRONTS.

[Trans. Eng. See 190924(1) for all trans.]

201202(1)   Rech. (A speech.) (Iz, (273,275), 4,7.XII.20; PetPr, (274), 5.XII.20; Pr, (273-5), 4-7.XII.20)

Repr.: 270000(4): 410-26; EkZhizn, (272), 12.XII.20.

Trans.: Fr. p.q. BulCom, (II.4), 27.I.21;

         Ger. RusKor, (II.i.1-2), I-II.21; p.q. RusR, (14), 15.XII.20.

[To Enlarged Plenum Tsektran. On tasks of trade unions.]

201202(2)   Zaklyuchitel´noe slovo. (Summary speech.) (270000(4): 426-38)

Trans.: Ger. p.q. RusR, (18), 14.I.21.

[See 201202(1).]

201208(1)   Rezolyutsiya. (A resolution.) (270000(4): 438-42)
              [See 201202(1).]

201208(2)   Na put stroitel´stva sotsializma! (On the road to building socialism!)
              (BoPr, (277-9), 9-11.XII.20; Iz, (276-8), 8-10.XII.20; PetPr, (278,279),
              10,11.XII.20; Pr, (276-8), 8-10.XII.20)
              Repr.: 260000(18).II: 495-506.
              Trans.: Eng. p.q. The Com, 13.I.21;
                      Fr. p.q. BulCom, (II.2), 13.I.21;
                      Ger. RusR, (14,15), 15,22.XII.20;
                      It. p.q. Ordine Nuovo, (I.169), 16.VI.21.
              [Speech to All-Russian conference of heads of Women's Provincial
              Sections.]

201209(1)   Dlya Donbassa! (Concerning the Donbas!) (DerevKom, (278:684), 10.XII.20;
              Iz, (278), 10.XII.20; PetPr, (278), 10.XII.20; Pr, (278), 10.XII.20)
              Repr.: 270000(4): 509-10.

201209(2)   Prikaz, No. 251. (BoPr, (278), 10.XII.20; Pr, (279), 11.XII.20)

201215   Rech. (A speech.) (BoPr, (283), 16.XII.20; Iz, (283), 16.XII.20;
              PetPr, (283), 16.XII.20)
              [To 2nd Moscow District Congress of Soviets.]

[201219]   Novyi period -- novye zadachi. (A new period -- new tasks.) (PetPr,
              (287), 21.XII.20; Pr, (286), 19.XII.20)
              Trans.: Fr. BulCom, (II.5), 3.II.21;
                      Ger. RusKor, (II.i.1-2), I-II.21; RusR, (16), 29.XII.20.

[201220]   Tezisy o transporte. (Theses on transport.) (EkZhizn, (287), 21.XII.20;
              Iz, (288), 22.XII.20)
              Repr.: 270000(4): 443-51; PetPr, (290), 24.XII.20.
              [For 8th Congress of Soviets. Possibly i Emshanov.]

201222(1)   Ob itogakh raboty na transportu. (Results of work in transport.)
              (270000(4): 452-77)
              [Report to 8th Congress of Soviets.]

201222(2)   Zaklyuchitel´noe slovo. (Summary speech.) (270000(4): 477-83)
              Trans.: Ger. RusKor, (II.i.1-2), I-II.21.
              [See 201222(1).]

201222(3) Rezolyutsiya. (A resolution.) (270000(4): 483-5)
[See 201222(1).]

*201224(1) *O ZADACHAKH PROIZVODSTVENNYKH SOYUZOV. (PRODUCTION TASKS OF THE
TRADE UNIONS), *200000(18).
Repr.: *210000(8).
[Speech to meeting of activists in the unions and of delegates to 8th
Congress of Soviets.]

*201224(2) *Zaklyuchitel´noe slovo. (Summary speech.)
[See *201224(1). c. Lenin, SOCH. XXVI: 530.]

201224(3) et al: [Telegram to Tours Congress of CPFrance.]
Trans.: Fr. Kriegel: TOURS: 140-1;
   Ger. RusR, (16), 29.XII.20.

201225(1) Pref. ROL I ZADACHI PROFESSIONAL´NYKH SOYUZOV (THE ROLE AND TASKS OF
THE TRADE UNIONS), 210000(13).

201225(2) i dr.: Proekt postanovleniya. (Draft regulation.) (PetPr, (293),
28.XII.20)
Repr.: KI, (16), 31.III.21; X S"EZD(1963): 674-85.
Trans.: Ger. RusKor, (II.i.3-4), III-IV.21.
[For 10th Congress of CPR; on role and tasks of trade unions.]

201227 Doklad. (A Report.) (EkZhizn, (293), 28.XII.20; Iz, (293), 28.XII.20;
PetPr, (293), 28.XII.20; Pr, (293,294), 28,29.XII.20)
Repr.: OTCHET: 154-75.
Trans.: Ger. p.q. RusKor, (II.i.1-2), I-II.21.
[To 8th Congress of Soviets.]

201229(1) Soobshchenie o demobilizatsii. (Communique on demobilization.)
(Iz, (296), 31.XII.20; PetPr, (296), 31.XII.20; Pr, (296), 31.XII.20)
Repr.: 230000(7).III.i: 3-6; 260000(18).II: 506-10.
Trans.: Ger. RusR, (18), 14.I.21.

201229(2) Zaklyuchitel´noe slovo. (Summary speech.) (Iz, (296), 31.XII.20;
PetPr, (296), 31.XII.20; Pr, (296), 31.XII.20)
Repr.: OTCHET: 236-40.
[See 201227.]

201230(1)   Rol profsoyuzov v proizvodstve. (The role of the trade unions in production.) (Iz, (1), 1.I.21; Krasnaya Gazeta, (296), 31.XII.20) Repr.: 210000(9); *210000(16).
[Speech to joint-session of delegates to 8th Congress of Soviets, VTsSPS and MGSPS and members of CPR.]

201230(2)   Zaklyuchitel'noe slovo. (Summary speech.)
[See 201230(1). c. Lenin, SOCH. XXVI: 530.]

210000(1)   VOENNAYA DOKTRINA ILI MNIMO-VOENNOE DOKTRINSTVO. (MILITARY DOCTRINE OR PSEUDO-MILITARY DOCTRINAIRISM.)
[See 211205 for all repr., trans.]

210000(2)   2 PIS'MA PETROGRADSKOI ORGANIZATSII RKP I OTVET T. TROTSKOGO. (2 LETTERS FROM THE PETROGRAD ORGANIZATION, CPR, AND CDE. TROTSKY'S REPLY.)
[See [210115(1) for all repr.]

*210000(3)   *MIROVOE EKONOMICHESKOE POLOZHENIE I NASHI ZADACHI. (THE WORLD ECONOMIC SITUATION AND OUR TASKS.)
[See 210613(2) for all repr., trans.]

210000(4)   i Varga: MIROVOE POLOZHENIE I NASHI ZADACHI. (THE WORLD SITUATION AND OUR TASKS.)
[See 210704 for all repr., trans.]

*210000(5)   *MIROVOE POLOZHENIE I TRETII KONGRESS KOMMUNISTICHESKOGO INTERNATSIONALA. (THE WORLD SITUATION AND THE THIRD CONGRESS OF THE COMINTERN.)
[See 210623 for all repr., trans.]

210000(6)   NA PROIZVODSTVENNYI PUT. (THE WAY TO PRODUCTION.)
[See 210104 for all repr., notes.]

210000(7)   † NOVYI ETAP. MIROVOE POLOZHENIE I NASHI ZADACHI. (A NEW STAGE. THE WORLD SITUATION AND OUR TASKS.)
Trans.: Am. Soviet Russia, 1.III-15.IV.22;
       Fr. 220000(26); p.q. BulCom, (III.22), 1.IV.22; p.q. Vie Ouv, 2.VI.22;
       Ger. 210000(36);
       Sp. *210000(49);
       Swed. 230000(25); 270000(8); 270000(14);
       Ukr. p.q. Nash Styag, (II.4), 1922;
       Yid. *220000(35).
[Pref. 210819.]

*210000(8)   *O ZADACHAKH PROIZVODSTVENNYKH SOYUZOV. (PRODUCTION TASKS OF THE TRADE UNIONS.)
[See *201224(1) for all repr., notes.]

210000(9)   O ZADACHAKH PROFSOYUZOV. (TASKS OF THE TRADE UNIONS.)
[See 201230(1) for all repr., notes.]

210000(10) O ROLI PROFESSIONAL´NYKH SOYUZOV. (THE ROLE OF THE TRADE UNIONS.)
[See 210000(13) for all repr., trans., notes.]

210000(11) O ROLI PROFESSIONAL´NYKH SOYUZOV. (THE ROLE OF THE TRADE UNIONS.)
[See 210000(13) for all repr., trans., notes.]

*210000(12) *OSNOVNYE VOPROSY PRODOVOL´STVENNOI I ZEMEL´NOI POLITIKI.
(FUNDAMENTAL PROBLEMS OF FOOD AND LAND POLICY.)
[See 200200(1) for all repr., note.]

210000(13) ROL I ZADACHI PROFESSIONAL´NYKH SOYUZOV. (ROLE AND TASKS OF THE TRADE
UNIONS.)
Repr.: 210000(10); 210000(11); *210000(14); 210000(15); *210000(53);
*210000(54); *210000(57); *220000(40); *220000(42).
Trans.: Ger. RusKor, (II.i.3-4), III-IV.21; p.q. RusR, (19), 21.I.21.
[Pref. 201225(1). Speech to meeting of trade unions and delegates to
10th Party Congress.]

*210000(14) *ROL I ZADACHI PROFESSIONAL´NYKH SOYUZOV. (ROLE AND TASKS OF THE TRADE
UNIONS.)
[See 210000(13) for all repr., trans., notes.]

210000(15) ROL I ZADACHI PROFESSIONAL´NYKH SOYUZOV. (ROLE AND TASKS OF THE TRADE
UNIONS.)
[See 210000(13) for all repr., trans., notes.]

*210000(16) *ROL PROFSOYUZOV V PROIZVODSTVE. (THE ROLE OF THE TRADE UNIONS IN
PRODUCTION.)
[See 201230(1) for all repr., note.]

*210000(17) *SVETOVNATA STOPANSKA KRIZA I REVOLYUTSIYATA. (THE WORLD ECONOMIC
CRISIS AND REVOLUTION.)
[Trans. Bul See 210613(2) for all repr., trans.]

*210000(18) *SVETOVNATA STOPANSKA KRIZA I REVOLYUTSIYATA. (THE WORLD ECONOMIC
CRISIS AND REVOLUTION.)
[Trans. Bul. See 210613(2) for all repr., trans.]

*210000(19) *TERORIZM I KOMUNIZM. (TERRORISM AND COMMUNISM.)
[Trans. Bul. See 200000(37) for all trans.]

*[210000(20)] *VNIMANIE K MELOCHAM! (ATTENTION TO TRIFLES!)
[See [211001] for all repr., trans.]

*[210000(21)]   *K MOLODEZHI. (TO THE YOUTH.)
                  [See 210714(2) for all repr., trans., notes.]

*[210000(22)]   *O PROEKTE DESYATI. (THE PROJECT OF THE DECEMISTS.)
                  [See [210217(2) for all repr.]

[210000(23)]   i dr.: SHIROKAYA KONFERENTSIYA FABRICHNO-ZAVODSKIKH KOMITETOV.
                  (A BROAD CONFERENCE OF FACTORY COMMITTEES.)
                  [See 211028 for T's contribution to explanatory meeting on NEP.]

210000(24)   u.a. AN DIE MITGLIEDER DES KAPD.
                  [Trans. Ger. From ECCI. See [210813(3)] for all trans.]

210000(25)   § DER CHARAKTER DER RUSSISCHEN REVOLUTION.
                  [Trans. Ger. See 170000(5) for all trans.]

210000(26)   LA COMMUNE DE PARIS ET LA RUSSIE DES SOVIETS.
                  [Trans. Fr. See *200000(27) for all trans., note.]

210000(27)   THE DEFENCE OF TERRORISM.
                  [Trans. Eng. See 200000(37) for all repr., trans., notes.]

210000(28)   L'ESERCITO ROSSO DELLA RUSSIA.
                  [Trans. It. See 180421 for all trans., note.]

*210000(29)   *IL FALLIMENTO DELLA SECONDA INTERNAZIONALE.
                  [Trans. It. See [140000(3)] for all trans., notes.]

210000(30)   u.a.: DIE HELDEN DER WIENER KONFERENZ.
                  [Trans. Ger. Contribution to an anthology; trans. from Rus.]

210000(31)   DAS HUNGERNDE RUSSLAND UND DAS SATTE EUROPA.
                  [Trans. Ger. See 210830 for all repr., trans.]

210000(32)   DIE WELTLAGE UND DIE AUFGABEN DER KOMMUNISTISCHEN INTERNATIONALE.
                  [Trans. Ger. See 210623 for all repr., trans.]

210000(33)   —: DE KAPITALISTISCHE WERELD EN DE COMMUNISTISCHE INTERNATIONALE.
                  [Trans. Hol. See 200807(1) for all trans.]

*210000(34)   *DI KINDER WEGN DER OKTYABR REVOLJUTSJE.
                  [Trans. Yid. Russian orig. not traced.]

210000(35)   KOMMUNISMEN OCH TERRORN.
                  [Trans. Swed. See 200000(37) for all repr., trans., notes.]

210000(36)   § DIE NEUE ETAPPE.
              [Trans. Ger. See 210000(7) for all trans.]

*210000(37)   *DI OKTJABR REVOLJUTSJA.
              [Trans. Yid. See 180000(5) for all trans., notes.]

*210000(38)   *PROBLÉMY ORGANISACE PRÁCE.
              [Trans. Cz. Russian original not traced.]

210000(39)   A REVIEW AND SOME PERSPECTIVES.
              [Trans. Eng. See 060600, 190312 for all repr., trans., notes.]

*210000(40)   *SVĚTOVÁ HOSPODÁŘSKÁ KRISE A NOVE UKOLY KOMUNISTICKÉ INTERNACIONÁLY.
              [Trans. Cz. See 210623 for all trans.]

*210000(41)   *TERRORISMO E COMMUNISMO.
              [Trans. It. See 200000(37) for all repr., trans., notes.]

210000(42)   TERRORISMUS UND KOMMUNISMUS. ANTI-KAUTSKY.
              [Trans. Ger. See 200000(37) for all repr., trans., notes.]

210000(43)   u Varga: THESEN ZUR WELTLAGE UND DIE AUFGABEN DER KOMMUNISTISCHEN
              INTERNATIONALE.
              [Trans. Ger. See 210704 for all trans., repr., notes.]

210000(44)   et a.: THÈSES SUR LA TACTIQUE.
              [Trans. Fr. See 210702 for all trans.]

210000(46)   u.a.: ZU NEUER ARBEIT, ZU NEUER KÄMPFEN.
              [Trans. Ger. See 210717 for all trans.]

[210000(47)] DE GROOTE CONGRESSREDE. DE ECONOMISCHE WERELDCRISIS EN DE NIEUWE
              TAAK DER COMMUNISTISCHE INTERNATIONALE.
              [Trans. Hol. See 210623 for all trans.]

[210000(48)] & Varga: THE INTERNATIONAL SITUATION: A STUDY OF CAPITALISM IN DECLINE.
              [Trans. Eng. See 210704 for all trans.]

*[210000(49)] *NUEVA ETAPA.
              [Trans. Sp. See 210000(7) for all trans.]

210000(50)   & others: The world Congress of the Communist International.
             Trans.: Eng. CI, (III.14-15, 16-17), 1921;
                     Ger. PROTOKOLL: 4-11; RusR, (35), 10.V.21; Flugschriften, (6);
                     It. Ordine Nuovo, (I.145), 26.V.21;
                     Scand. KeI, (6), IX.21;
                     Sp. El Com, (II.31), 26.III.21.
             [Manifesto of ECCI, addressed to all the proletarian organizations
             affiliated to, or who desire to belong to, the Comintern.]

210000(51)   § UNZER REVOLJUTSION.
             [Trans. Yid. See 190000(68), note.]

*[210000(52)]   *KAPITALISTICHESKII MIR I KOMMUNISTICHESKII INTERNATSIONAL. (THE
             CAPITALIST WORLD AND THE COMMUNIST INTERNATIONAL.)
             [See 200807(1) for all repr., trans.]

*210000(53)   *K DISKUSSII O PROFSOYUZOV. (THE DISCUSSION ON THE TRADE UNIONS.)
             [See 210000(13) for all repr., trans.]

*210000(54)   *O ROLI PROFESSIONAL´NYKH SOYUZOV. (THE ROLE OF THE TRADE UNIONS.)
             [See 210000(13) for all repr., trans.]

*210000(55)   *EL BOLCHEVIQUISMO ANTE LA GUERRE Y LA PAZ DEL MUNDO.
             [Trans. Sp. See [140000(3)] for all repr., trans., notes.]

210000(56)   THESEN ZUR WELTLAGE UND DIE AUFGABEN DER KOMMUNISTISCHEN INTERNATIONALE.
             [Trans. Ger. See 210704 for all repr., trans.]

*210000(57)   *THÈSES SUR LA SITUATION MONDIALE ET NOS TÂCHES.
             [Trans. Fr. See 210613(2) for all repr., trans.]

*210000(58)   *NA PROIZVODSTVENNYI PUT! (THE WAY TO PRODUCTION!)
             [See 210104 for all repr.]

*210000(59)   *ROL I ZADACHI PROFESSIONAL´NYKH SOYUZOV. (THE ROLE AND TASKS OF THE
             TRADE UNIONS.)
             [See 201225(1) for all repr., trans., notes.]

210000(60)   TERRORISMI JA KOMMUNISMI.
             [Trans. Fin. See 200000(37) for all repr., trans., notes.]

210000(61)   TERRORISMI JA KOMMUNISMI.
             [Trans. Fin. See 200000(37) for all repr., trans., notes.]

210000(62)   RÍJNOVA REVOLUCE.
               [Trans. Cz. See 180000(5) for all repr., trans., notes.]

210104   NA PROIZVODSTVENNYI PUT! (THE WAY TO PRODUCTION!), 210000(6).
               Repr.: p.q. 230000(7).III.i: 7-9; p.q. 260000(18).II: 510-4;
                       270000(4): 232-48.
               [Speech to meeting of CPR(b) members of Moscow district. Archives.]

[210111]   Proizvodstvennaya demokratiya. (Industrial democracy.) (Pr, (5),
               11.I.21)

[210114]   Tsektran. (Pr, (8), 14.I.21)

[210115(1)]   Otvet petrogradskim tovarishcham. (A reply to Petrograd comrades.)
               (PetPr, (11), 18.I.21; Pr, (9), 15.I.21)
               Repr.: 210000(2); STENOTCHET X S"EZD (1963): 834-5.
               [On trade union discussion.]

210115(2)   i dr.: O "Dvukhapolovinnom internationale". (The "2 1/2 International".)
               (KI, (16), 31.III.21)
               Trans.: Ger. KomInt, (II.16), VI.21; RusR, (22), 8.II.21;
                       Scand. KeI, (5), VII.21.
               [In the case of all documents issued by the ECCI only those have been
               recorded which contain, in one trans. or other, the name of T.]

210116   Rol i zadachi professional'nykh soyuzov. (The role ans tasks of the
               trade unions.) (PetPr, (12), 19.I.21)
               Trans.: Ger. KomInt, (II.16), VI.21;
                       Sp. p.q. El Com, (II.36), 23.IV.21.
               [Theses for 10th Party Congress. cf. 210000(13).]

[210119]   Deistvitel'nost protiv kazenshchiny. (Reality against conventionalism.)
               (Pr, (12), 19.I.21)

*210124   *Rech. (A speech.) (Byulleten 2-go Vserossiiskogo s"ezda
               Gornorabochikh, (1), 25.I.21)
               [To Communist fraction at 2nd All-Russian Miners Congress. c. Lenin,
               SOCH. XXVI: 530.]

210125   u.a.: Der fünfzigste Jahrestag des Pariser Kommune.
               Trans.: Ger. KomInt, (II.16), VI.21; RusR, (22), 8.II.21.

[210126]   Zaklyuchitel'noe slovo. (Summary speech.) (Byulleten 2-go Vserossiiskogo s"ezda Gornorabochikh, (2), 26.I.21)
Repr.: p.q. 320000(2): 43.
Trans.: Am. p.q. 370000(14): 31; p.q. 620000(3): 31;
       Ger. p.q. 320000(18);
       Jap. p.q. 680320.
[See *210124.]

210127   et al.: Télégram au Comité directeur, Paris.
Trans.: Fr. L'I.C. ET SA SECTION FRANÇAISE: 36-7.

[210129]   Est raznoglasiya no k chemu putanitsa? (There are differences, but why confusion?) (Pr, (19), 29.I.21)

210201(1)   i Krestinskii: Vsem gubkoman RKP, vsem politodelam Krasnoi Armi i Flota. (To all District Bureaus CPR, to all concerned with politics in the Red Army and Fleet.) (PetPr, (23), 3.II.21; Pr, (21), 1.II.21)

[210201(2)]   Ustalyi putnik na molochnoi diete. (A tired traveller on a milk diet.) (Pr, (21), 1.II.21)
[Reply to Zinoviev.]

210204   Pref. C.Tales: LA COMMUNE DE PARIS.
Trans.: Am. NI, III.35;
       Fr. [580000(7)]; p.q. 680000(4): 266-7; 690700(1): 11-9;
       Ger. Arbeiter-Lit, (1), 1924: 106-18.

210212(1)   Khozyaistvennoe polozhenie Urala i zadachi Polnomochnoi komissii. (The economic situation in the Urals and the tasks of the Plenopotentiary Commission.) (270000(4): 339-41)

[210212(2)]   Za toplivom (For fuel.) (270000(4): 341-2)
[An appeal to peasants, workers, and Soviet office-workers.]

[210213]   K voprosu o srashchivanii. (The question of fusion.) (EkZhizn, (32), 13.II.21)

210217(1)   Rech. (A speech.) (230000(7).III.i: 10-4)
Trans.: Eng. p.q. Deutscher, PA: 480.
[At meeting of military workers in Ekaterinburg; on militia system. Archives.]

[210217(2)]   O proekte desyati. (The project of the Decemists.) (<u>EkZhizn</u>, (35),
                   17.II.21)
                   <u>Repr.</u>: *[210000(22)].

210221   [To Sklyansky.]
                   <u>Trans</u>.: 410000(1): Ch. VIII.
                   [On Georgia. T637.]

210226   Verzha — Lepti — Lefevr. (Vergeat, Lepetit, Lefevre.) (230000(8):
                   63-5)
                   <u>Repr.</u>: 260000(10): 164-7.
                   <u>Trans</u>.: Fr. MÉMOIRE: 12-5.
                   [3 French delegates to Comintern who died en route to Congress.]

210302   i Lenin: Myatezh byvshego generala Kozlovskogo i korablya
                   "Petropavlovsk". (The mutiny of ex-General Kozlovsky and the
                   battleship "Petropavlovsk".) (<u>DerevKom</u>, (47), 3.III.21; <u>Gudok</u>, (244),
                   4.III.21; <u>Iz</u>, (47), 3.III.21; <u>PetPr</u>, (47), 3.III.21; <u>Pr</u>, (47), 3.III.21;
                   <u>Trud</u>, (11), 3.III.21)
                   <u>Repr.</u>: 230000(7).III.i: 201; 260000(18).II: 517-8.

210305   Poslednee preduprezhdenie. (A last warning.) (<u>DerevKom</u>, (50), 6.III.21;
                   <u>Krasnaya Gazeta</u>, (50), 6.III.21; <u>Iz</u>, (51), 8.III.21; <u>Iz</u>(Vre), (5),
                   7.III.21; <u>Pr</u>, (51), 8.III.21)
                   <u>Repr.</u>: 230000(7).III.i: 202; 260000(18).II: 518; <u>Narodnoe Delo</u>, (53),
                             9.III.21.
                   <u>Trans</u>.: Am. <u>Soviet Russia</u>, 23.IV.21;
                             Eng. <u>Chamberlin</u>.II: 443;
                             Ger. <u>RusR</u>, (27), 15.III.21;
                             Nor. <u>Ny Tid</u>, 8.III.21.
                   [On Kronstadt.]

210312   Alternative for[210313].

[210313]   O sobytiyakh v Kronshtadte. (The events in Kronstadt.) (<u>Pr</u>, (57),
                   16.III.21)
                   <u>Repr.</u>: 230000(7).III.i: 203-4; 260000(18).II: 518-20.
                   <u>Trans</u>.: Eng. <u>Daily Herald</u>, 17.III.21;
                             Nor. <u>Ny Tid</u>, 16.III.21;
                             Sp. <u>El Com</u>, (II.36), 23.IV.21.
                   [Interview with foreign press on suggested foreign inspiration of the
                   Kronstadt rising.]

210314(1)   Rech. (A speech.) (Pr, (58), 17.III.21)
             Repr.: STENOTCHET X S"EZD: 191-6.
             Trans.: Eng. p.q. Deutscher, PA: 508.
             [At 10th Party Congress; on Workers Opposition.]

210314(2)   Rech. (A speech.) (PetPr, (60), 17.III.21; Pr, (58), 17.III.21)
             Repr.: STENOTCHET X S"EZD: 146-51; 213-6.
             Trans.: Ger. RusKor, (II.i.5), V.21.
             [At 10th Party Congress; on trade union question.]

210314(3)   Proekt zayavlenie. (Draft statement.) (STENOTCHET X S"EZD: 352-3)
             Repr.: STENOTCHET X S"EZD(1963): 674-85.
             [For 10th Party Congress; on trade union question.]

[210315]   i dr.: Obrashchenie X s"ezda RKP k piterskim rabochim. (Appeal of the
             10th Congress CPR to the workers of Petrograd.) (Iz, (56), 15.III.21)

210321   [Exchange of notes with Lenin; on Red Navy.]
             [c. Deutscher, PU: 56. T661.]

210323(1)   L.T.: Kronshtadt i birzha. (Kronstadt and the Stock Exchange.)
             (Krasnaya Gazeta, (66), 25.III.21; Pr, (63), 24.III.21)
             Repr.: 230000(7).III.i: 205-6; 260000(18).II: 521-3.
             Trans.: Am. Soviet Russia, 14.V.21;
                     Sp. El Com, (II.37), 27.IV.21.

210323(2)   i dr.: K krest'yanstvu Rossiiskoi Sotsialisticheskoi Sovetskoi
             Respubliki. (To the peasantry of the RSFSR.) (Gudok, (258), 23.III.21;
             Krasnaya Gazeta, (65), 24.III.21; Pr, (62), 23.III.21)
             Trans.: Eng. Chamberlin.II: 501-3.
             [Tax in kind in place of requisitioning of agricultural products.]

[210400(1)] Martovskoe revolyutsionnoe dvizhenie v Germanii. (The March
             revolutionary movement in Germany.) (260000(10): 116-20)
             [Private notes.]

[210400(2)] Nado za eto privlekat k sudu. (People should be brought to trial
             for this.) (270000(2): 244)
             [On quality of book production.]

210403   Rech. (A speech.) (<u>Iz</u>, (73), 5.IV.21)

Repr.: 230000(7).III.i: 207; 260000(18).II: 523.

Trans.: Eng. p.q. Deutscher, PA: 514;

         Sp. p.q. <u>El Com</u>, (II.35), 20.IV.21.

⌊At parade in honour of Kronstadt heroes.⌋

⌊210404⌋   i dr.: O poryadke ot komandirovaniya voennykh kommunistov. (The procedure for sending Army Communists on missions.) (<u>Iz</u>(TsIK), (30), 4.IV.21)

210407   ⌈Note on Kopp's report on Germany rebuilding Russian armaments.⌉

⌊c. Carr, BR.III: 362. Harvard Archives.⌋

210418   Martovskoe dvizhenie v Germanii. (The March movement in Germany.) (<u>PetPr</u>, (140), 6.VII.21)

Repr.: 260000(10): 115-6.

⌊210421⌋   i dr.: Pervomaiskoe vozzvanie Ispolkoma Kominterna. (May Day appeal of ECCI.) (<u>Pr</u>, (86), 21.IV.21)

Repr.: 260000(10): 83-7.

Trans.: Eng. <u>Keep Left</u>, (XIX.4), IV.70.

⌊210426⌋   Polozhenie nashego izdatel´skogo dela. (The position in our publishing work.) (<u>Iz</u>, (90), 26.IV.21; <u>Krasnaya Gazeta</u>, (93), 27.IV.21)

Repr.: 270000(2): 244-6.

⌊Interview.⌋

210429   & others: ECCI statement on expulsion of Paul Levi.

Trans.: Eng. Degras, DOCCI.I: 219-20;

        Ger. <u>KomInt</u>, (II.17), 1921;

        Hol. <u>Tribune</u>, (182), 7.V.21.

⌊210500⌋   Bezrabotnye i professional´nye soyuzy. (The unemployed and the trade unions.) (260000(10): 87-8)

210503   ⌊Letter to Lenin; on a book by I.Shatunovsky.⌋

⌊c. Deutscher, PU: 42. See 200700(3). T671.⌋

210600   ⌊Interview.⌋

Trans.: Fr. Morizet: 102-9; <u>Huma</u>, 24.VIII.21.

⌊On Red Army.⌋

210613(1)   Krasnaya Armiya shtabu revolyutsii. (The Red Army to the General
              Staff of the Revolution.) (Iz, (128), 14.VI.21; PetPr, (126),
              15.VI.21; Pr, (128), 14.VI.21)
              Repr.: 240000(29): 137.
              Trans.: Am. 451000: 173; 640800: 109-10; FI, VIII.45;
                      Jap. 681125: 117-8;
                      Sp. 670000(5): 109-10;
                      Swed. 691100(2): 95-6.

210613(2)   MIROVOE EKONOMICHESKOE POLOZHENIE I NASHI ZADACHI (THE WORLD ECONOMIC
              SITUATION AND OUR TASKS), *210000(3).
              Trans.: Bul. *210000(17); *210000(18);
                      Cz. p.q. Rude Pravo, (II.146), 24.VI.21;
                      Fr. *210000(57); BulCom, (II.26,30), 23.VI, 21.VII.21;
                      Ger. 210000(36).
              [Speech to Moscow members CPR(b), communist fraction Moscow Soviet,
              and Moscow activists. Pref. 210615.]

210615   Pref. MIROVOE EKONOMICHESKOE POLOZHENIE I NASHI ZADACHI (THE WORLD
              ECONOMIC SITUATION AND OUR TASKS), 210613(2). (p.q. Trud, (91), 17.VI.21)

210616   Taktika partii po otnosheniyu k levomu bloku. (The Party's tactic in
              relation to the Left Bloc.) (230000(8): 69-80)
              Repr.: p.q. 240000(6): 141.
              [On CPFrance.]

210623   Doklad o mirovom khozyaistvennom krizise i novykh zadachakh
              Kommunisticheskogo Internatsionala. (Report on the world economic
              crisis and the new tasks of the Communist International.) (Iz, (136,137),
              25,26.VI.21; Krasnaya Gazeta, (133), 25.VI.21; Pr, (136), 25.VI.21)
              Repr.: *210000(5); 210000(7); 240000(29): 138-96; PetPr, (148),
                      16.VII.21; Trud, (91), 17.VII.21.
              Trans.: Am. 451000: 174-226;
                      Cz. *210000(40); p.q. Rude Pravo, (II.150,173), 29.VI, 26.VII.21;
                      Eng. p.q. The Com, 16.VII.21;
                      Fr. 220000(26): 9-71; p.q. 680000(4): 115-6; BulCom, (II.26,29,
                          30), 23.VI, 14,21.VII.21; Bulletin du IIIème Congrès, (2),
                          25.VI.21;
                      Ger. 210000(36): 3-47; 210000(32); PROTOKOLL: 48-90; Bulletin
                          des III. Kongresses, (2), 27.VI.21; p.q. ALMANACH: 122-6;

++++

210623   ++++   <u>Trans</u>.: Hol. [210000(47)];

It. p.q. <u>Ordine Nuovo</u>, (I.190), 10.VII.21;

Nor. TIL: 3-13; p.q. <u>Ny Tid</u>, 5.VII.21;

Sp. *210000(49);

Swed.: 230000(25): 9-56;

Yid. *220000(35).

210624   Zaklyuchitel´noe slovo. (Summary speech.) (<u>PetPr</u>, (134), 28.VI.21;
<u>Pr</u>, (137), 26.VI.21)

<u>Repr</u>.: 240000(29): 187-96.

<u>Trans</u>.: Am. 451000: 227-37;

Cz. p.q. <u>Rude Pravo</u>, (II.193), 19.VIII.21;

Ger. PROTOKOLL: 125-37; <u>Bulletin des III. Kongresses</u>, (3),
28.VI.21;

Hol. p.q. <u>Tribune</u>, (236), 11.VII.21.

[See 210623.]

210625   i dr.: Tsentral´nomu komitetu frantsuzskoi kommunisticheskoi partii
ot Ispolkoma Kominterna. (To the CC CPFrance from the ECCI.)
(230000(8): 90-6)

<u>Repr</u>.: 240000(29): 306-12.

<u>Trans</u>.: Am-Eng. 530700: 44-51;

Fr. 670306: 124-30; L'I.C. ET SA SECTION FRANÇAISE: 7-16.

[Variant dates. May be 210726.]

210629   Rech po ital´yanskom voprosu. (Speech on the Italian question.)
(<u>Iz</u>, (141), 1.VII.21)

<u>Repr</u>.: 240000(29): 217-22.

<u>Trans</u>.: Am. 451000: 262-8;

Ger. PROTOKOLL: 391-8; <u>Bulletin des III. Kongresses</u>, (9),
4.VII.21.

[At 3rd Congress Comintern.]

210700   Shkola revolyutsionnoi strategii. (A school of revolutionary strategy.)
(210000(7))

<u>Repr</u>.: 240000(29): 266-305.

<u>Trans</u>.: Am-Eng. 530700: 1-43;

Bul. *220000(10); *220000(11);

Fr. 220000(26): 73-139; p.q. 670306: 105-12; p.q. 680000(4):
passim;   ++++

210700   ++++   <u>Trans.</u>: Ger. 210000(36): 51-98; p.q. <u>Gegner</u>, (II.12), 1921;

                Sp. *210000(49);

                Swed. 230000(25): 61-109.

         [Speech to Party members, Moscow organization CPR(b).]

210702   Rech po dokladu tov. Radeka "O taktike Kominterna". (Speech on cde.
Radek's report "On the tactics of the Comintern.") (<u>Pr</u>, (146), 7.VII.21)

         <u>Repr.</u>: 240000(29): 222-33; <u>Byulleten III Kongressa KI</u>, (14), 11.VII.21.

         <u>Trans.</u>: Am. 451000: 269-81;

                Cz. p.q. <u>Rude Pravo</u>, (II.176), 29.VII.21;

                Fr. 210000(44);

                Ger. PROTOKOLL: 637-50; <u>Bulletin des III. Kongresses</u>, (14),

                     10.VII.21.

210704   i Varga: TEZISY III KONGRESSA O MIROVOM POLOZHENIE I ZADACHAKH
KOMMUNISTICHESKOGO INTERNATSIONALA (THESES OF THE 3rd CONGRESS ON
THE WORLD SITUATION AND THE TASKS OF THE COMMUNIST INTERNATIONAL),
210000(4).

         <u>Repr.</u>: 240000(29).

         <u>Trans.</u>: Am. 451000: 238-61;

                Eng. 210000(48); p.q. <u>Labour Monthly</u>, VIII.21; p.q. Degras,

                     DOCCI.I: 229-39; MATERIAL: 77-96;

                Fr. <u>BulCom</u>, (II.29), 14.VII.21; p.q. <u>Huma</u>, 24.VII.21; <u>Vie Ouv</u>,

                     15.VII.21 ff;

                Ger. 210000(36); 103-28; 210000(43); 210000(56);

                Hol. p.q. <u>Tribune</u>, (11), 13.X.21;

                It, p.q. <u>Ordine Nuovo</u>, (I.204,206), 24,26.VII.21;

                Sp. <u>El Com</u>, (II.61,63,64,66), 23,30.VII, 3,13.VIII.21.

         [See Ger. <u>Bulletin des III.Kongresses</u>, (16), 12.VII.21 for corrections
to theses.]

210705   Rech. (A speech.) (<u>Pr</u>, (149), 10.VII.21)

         <u>Repr.</u>: 240000(29): 233-40; <u>Byulleten III Kongressa</u>, (17), 14.VII.21.

         <u>Trans.</u>: Am. 451000: 282-9;

                Eng. p.q. <u>The Com</u>, 16.VII.21;

                Ger. PROTOKOLL: 781-9; <u>Bulletin des III. Kongresses</u>, (17),

                     13.VII.21.

         [At 3rd Congress Comintern; on Lenin's report "On tactics of the CPR."]

210706 & others: Revolutionary tactics.

    Trans.: Cz. Rude Pravo, (II.194,195,197, 198, 202-4), 20,21,24,25,
            30.VIII-1.IX.21;
            Eng. p.q. ComRev, (4), VIII.21;
            Ger. THESEN; Kommunismus, (II.27-28), 1.VIII.21;
            Nor. Ny Tid, 8.VII.21 ff.

[210712] Glavnyi urok III Kongressa. (Main lessons of the 3rd Congress.)
    (Pr, (150), 12.VII.21)
    Repr.: 240000(29): 243-6.
    Trans.: Am. 451000: 293-6;
            Cz. p.q. Rude Pravo, (II.169), 21.VII.21;
            Eng. The Com, 6.VIII.21;
            Fr. EM, (2), II.69; Huma, 10.VIII.21;
            Hol. p.q. Tribune, (243), 19.VII.21;
            It. Ordine Nuovo, (I.226), 15.VIII.21;
            Sp. El Com, (II.66), 13.VIII.21.

210713(1) Pis'mo tov. Monatu. (Letter to cde. Monatte.) (230000(8): 80-3)
    Repr.: 240000(29): 124-6; 260000(10): 167-9.
    Trans.: Am. 451000: 158-61;
            Fr. 670306: 113-5; Maitron & Chambelland: 295-7.
    [On CPFrance.]

210713(2) Alternative for [210712].

210714(1) Pis'mo t.t. Kashemu i Frossaru. (Letter to cdes. Cachin and Frossard.)
    (230000(8): 83-6)
    Repr.: p.q. 240000(6): 141-2; 240000(29): 127-30.
    Trans.: Am. 451000: 162-5;
            Fr. [220000(31)]; 670306: 116-9.
    [On CPFrance.]

210714(2) Doklad ob itogakh III Kongressa Kommunisticheskogo Internatsionala
    molodezhi. (Report on the balance sheet of the 3rd Congress of the
    Communist International to the Youth.) (Pr, (154), 16.VII.21)
    Repr.: *[210000(21)]; 240000(28): 174-89; 240000(29): 246-60.
    Trans.: Am. 451000: 297-312;
            Cz. p.q. Rude Pravo, (II.185), 9.VIII.21.
    [At 2nd Congress of Communist Youth International.]

210714(3)   Zaklyuchitel´noe slovo. (Summary speech.) (240000(28): 190-4)
             Repr.: 240000(29): 260-6.
             Trans.: Am. 451000: 313-20;
                        Cz. p.q. Rude Pravo, (II.204), 1.IX.21.
             [See 210714(2).]

210715   Rech. (A speech.) (240000(29): 120-3)
             Trans.: Am. 451000: 153-8;
                        Cz. p.q. Rude Pravo, (II.173), 26.VII.21.
             [To 2nd World Conference of Communist women.]

210717(1)   i dr.: Vozzvanie III Kongressa Kominterna k rabochim i rabotnitsam
             vsekh stran. (Appeal of 3rd Congress of the Comintern to the working
             men and women of all lands.) (Iz, (159), 22.VII.21; PetPr, (154),
             23.VII.21; Pr, (159), 22.VII.21)
             Trans.: Fr. THÈSES: 139-42; Huma, 4.VIII.21;
                        Ger. 210000(46); Bulletin des EKKI, (1), 8.IX.21; Moskau,
                           (48), 22.VII.21; Flugschriften, (1); THESEN;
                        Nor. TIL: 77-80.

210717(2)   u.a.: An das Proletariat aller Nationen der Tschechoslowakei.
             Trans.: Eng. Bulletin of the ECCI, (1), 8.IX.21;
                        Ger. Bulletin des EKKI, (1), 8.IX.21.

[210717(3)] u.a.: An die Arbeiter und Arbeiterinnen italiens.
             Trans.: Eng. Bulletin of the ECCI, (1), 8.IX.21;
                        Ger. Bulletin des EKKI, (1), 8.IX.21;
                        It. Ordine Nuovo, (I.225), 14.VIII.21.

210717(4)   et al.: A resolution on the White Russian question.
             Trans.: Eng. Bulletin of the ECCI, (2), 20.IX.21.

210720   Zadachi krasnoarmeitskoi gazety. (Tasks of a Red Army newspaper.)
             (270000(2): 238-9)

210723   O tsentral´nom organe partii l'Humanité. (On l'Humanité, central
             organ of the Party.) (230000(8): 86-9)
             Repr.: 240000(29): 130.
             Trans.: Am. 451000: 166-9;
                        Fr. [220000(31)]; 670306: 120-3.
             [On CPFrance.]

210726   Alternative for 210625.

210730   u.a.: Proletarische Hilfe für Sowjetrussland.
                 <u>Trans</u>.: Eng. <u>Bulletin of the ECCI</u>, (1), 8.IX.21;
                       Ger. <u>Bulletin des EKKI</u>, (1), 8.IX.21;
                       Nor. <u>Ny Tid</u>, 4.VIII.21.

[210800(1)]   et al.: For the unity of the world proletariat against the union of
                 social traitors.
                 <u>Trans</u>.: Eng. <u>Bulletin of the ECCI</u>, (2), 20.IX.21.

[210800(2)]   et al.: To the workers and soldiers of all countries.
                 <u>Trans</u>.: Eng. <u>Bulletin of the ECCI</u>, (2), 20.IX.21.

[210800(3)]   et al.: To new work, to new struggles.
                 <u>Trans</u>.: Eng. <u>Bulletin of the ECCI</u>, (1), 8.IX.21;
                       Cz. <u>Rude Pravo</u>, (II.183), 6.VIII.21.

[210800(4)]   i Milyutin: Tsirkular. (A circular letter.) (<u>Iz</u>(NKSO), (7), 13.III.22)
                 [To various bodies; on help for families of Red Army men.]

210805   Prikaz, No. 254. (230000(7).III.i: 154-6)
                 <u>Trans</u>.: Eng. p.q. Deutscher, PA: 481.

210807   [Memorandum to CC; on planning.]
                 [c. Carr, BR.II: 377. See also 220823, 230120. T774.]

210813(1)   u.a.: An den Kongress der V.K.P.D. in Jena.
                 <u>Trans</u>.: Ger. <u>Bulletin des EKKI</u>, (1), 8.IX.21.

[210813(2)]   u.a.: An das Proletariat Jugoslaviens.
                 <u>Trans</u>.: Eng. <u>Bulletin of the ECCI</u>, (1), 8.IX.21;
                       Ger. <u>Bulletin des EKKI</u>, (1), 8.IX.21.

[210813(3)]   u.a. An die Mitglieder der Kommunistische Arbeiterpartei Deutschlands.
                 <u>Trans</u>.: Eng. <u>Bulletin of the ECCI</u>, (1), 8.IX.21;
                       Ger. <u>Bulletin des EKKI</u>, (1), 8.IX.21;
                       Scan. <u>KeI</u>, (6), IX.21.

210819   Pref. NOVYI ETAP (THE NEW STAGE), 210000(7).
                 <u>Trans</u>.: Am. <u>Soviet Russia</u>, 15.II.22.
                 [See 210000(7) for other trans.]

210825   Pis'mo. (A letter.) (Sverchkov: 5-9)
          Repr.: 250000(6). I: 515-8.
          [To Istpart; on 1905 revolution.]

210830   Golod i mirovoe polozhenie. (Famine and the world situation.)
          (KomTrud, (426), 1.IX.21)
          Repr.: 230000(7).III.i: 211-29; STENOTCHET MOSSOV, (6), 1921.
          Trans.: Cz. p.q. Rude Pravo, (II.229), 30.IX.21;
                  Ger. 210000(31); 220000(24); RusKor, (II.ii.10-11), X-XI.21;
                  Hol. p.q. Tribune, (18), 21.X.21.

210902   Privet Ukrainskomu Pravoberezh'yu! (Greetings to the right-bank
          Ukraine!) (V Puti, (142), 1921)
          Repr.: 230000(7).III.i: 230-1.

210905(1) Prikaz, No. 256. (230000(7).III.i: 163)

210905(2) Prikaz, No. 257. (230000(7).III.i: 262-3)

210905(3) Prikaz, No. 259. (230000(7).III.i: 157)

210905(4) Prikaz, No. 260. (230000(7).III.i: 158)

210905(5) Rech. (A speech.) (230000(7).III.i: 232-41)
          [At Zhitomir city Soviet. Archives.]

210907(1) Birzhevaya respublika i ee Nulans. (The stock-exchange republic and
          its Noulens.) (V Puti, (145), 1921; Pr, (201), 10.IX.21)
          Repr.: 230000(7).III.i: 242-3.
          Trans.: Am. Nation, 9.X.21;
                  Hol. Tribune, (2), 3.X.21.

210907(2) Petlya vmesto khleba. (Spying instead of food.) (Iz(Odessa), (529),
          9.IX.21)
          Repr.: MISSII GUVERA: 9-12.
          [Speech to Odessa city Soviet.]

210910(1) Prikaz, No. 261. (230000(7).III.i: 264)

210910(2) Prikaz, No. 262. (230000(7).III.i: 159)

210911   Prikaz, No. 263. (Iz, (203), 13.IX.21; Pr, (203), 13.IX.21)
          Repr.: 230000(7).III.i: 160-1.
          [More attention to the disabled of the civil war.]

210912(1) Zaklyuchitel'naya rech. (Summary speech.) (230000(7).III.i: 18-23)
[Analysis of the manoeuvres at Kotyuzhan.]

210912(2) Prikaz, No. 264. (230000(7).III.i: 162)

210913(1) Pochto-telegramma. (Telegram.) (230000(7).III.i: 163-4)
[To cde. Zabelsky, Chairman of Revolutionary Military Tribunal; on Kozlov affair. See 210905(1).]

210913(2) Prikaz, No. 265. (KomTrud, (440), 17.IX.21; Pr, (209), 20.IX.21)
Repr.: 230000(7).III.i: 265.
[On banditry.]

[210916] Etomu nado polozhit konets! (We must put a stop to this!) (Iz, (206), 16.IX.21; Pr, (206), 16.IX.21)
Trans.: Am. Soviet Russia, XI.21;
    Cz. Rude Pravo, (II.237), 9.X.21;
    Ger. RusKor, (II.ii.10-11), X-XI.21.
[On banditry.]

210920 Rech. (A speech.) (Iz, (211), 22.IX.21)
Repr.: 230000(7).III.i: 247-61; STENOTCHET MOSSOV, (8), 1921.
[At 2nd annual Plenum Moscow Soviet.]

210921 Rech. (A speech.) (230000(7).III.ii: 15-31)
Repr.: 240000(28): 195-216.
Trans.: Cz. p.q. Rude Pravo, (II.230), 1.X.21;
    Ger. p.q. Jug-Int, (III.3), XI.21;
    Hol. p.q. Tribune, (100), 26.I.22.
[At 4th All-Russian Congress of Komsomol.]

210926 Iz rechi. (From a speech.) (KomTrud, (448), 27.IX.21; Pr, (215), 27.IX.21)
Repr.: 230000(7).III.ii: 32.
[At parade of Moscow garrison on day of 1st graduation of officers from Red General Staff.]

[210929] [Banditry and counter-revolution.] (Novyi Put, 29.IX.21)
Trans.: Am. Soviet Russia, XII.21.

[211001] Vnimanie k melocham! (Attention to trifles!) (PetPr, (205), 4.X.21; Pr, (219), 1.X.21)
Repr.: *210000(20); 230000(4): 29-33; 230000(7).III.i: 15-7;

++++

⌊211001⌋   ++++   Repr.: 240000(28): 127-30; 250000(1): 31-5; 270000(2): 13-6.
Trans.: It. Ordine Nuovo, (I.309), 6.XI.21.

211011   i dr.: Prikaz, No. 2252. (Iz, (228), 12.X.21; Pr, (229), 12.X.21)
Repr.: 230000(7).III.i: 165-6.
Trans.: Cz. Rude Pravo, (III.40), 16.II.22.
⌊A week of care for the property of Red Army men.⌋

211020   Rech. (A speech.) (Iz, (239-42), 25-28.X.21; Pr, (240-3), 25-28.X.21)
Repr.: 230000(7).III.i: 24-37.
Trans.: Cz. p.q. Rude Pravo, (II.274), 23.XI.21.
⌊At 2nd Congress of Departments of Political Education. Archives.⌋

211021   Pis'mo. (A letter.) (230000(7).III.i: 167)
⌊To Ed. Board, Journal of Military Studies of XIth Petrograd Rifle
Division.⌋

211024   Alternative for 211025.

211025   Zadachi Krasnoi Armii. (Tasks of the Red Army.) (230000(7).III.i:
38-56)
Trans.: Cz. p.q. Rude Pravo, (III.3), 4.I.22;
        Fr. p.q. CorInt, (I.11), 17.XI.21; p.q. Morizet;
        Ger. p.q. Inprekor, (I.25), 19.XI.21; RusKor, (II.ii.12),XII.21;
        Nor. p.q. Ny Tid, 29.X.21.
⌊Report to Commanders and political commissars of Moscow Military
Area. Archives.⌋

211028   et al.: SHIROKAYA KONFERENTSIYA FABRICHNO-ZAVODSKIKH KOMITETOV, PRAVLENII
SOYUZOV I PLENUMA MGSPS. (⌊SPEECH TO⌋ A BROAD CONFERENCE OF FACTORY
COMMITTEES, TRADE UNION LEADERS AND THE PLENUM OF THE MOSCOW PROVINCIAL
SOVIET OF TRADE UNIONS.), 210000(23.
Repr.: p.q. 261209.
⌊On NEP.⌋

211029   Zaklyuchitel'noe slovo. (Summary speech.)
⌊See 211028.⌋

⌊211100⌋   Lettre à Rosmer.
Trans.: Fr. ⌊220000(31)⌋; 14-8; 670306: 131-4.
⌊See 670306 for analysis of problem of date.⌋

[211101(1)]   Prikaz, No. 2458. (230000(7).III.i: 168-70)

211101(2)   Vstupitel'noe slovo na diskussii o voennoi doktrine. (Opening speech at discussion on military doctrine.) (Krasnaya Armiya, (7-8), 1921)
Repr.: 230000(7).III.ii: 201.
Trans.: Am. 690000(11): 19-20; FI, I.44;
     Eng. 690400(1): 5-6.
[At Society for Military Studies attached to the Red Army Military Academy.]

211101(3)   Zaklyuchitel'noe slovo. (Summary speech.) (230000(7).III.ii: 202-9)
Trans.: Am. 690000(11): 20-30; FI, I.44;
     Eng. 690400(1): 6-15.
[See 211101(2). Archives.]

211102   Rech. (A speech.) (230000(7).III.i: 57-71)
[To Cadets of All-Russian CEC 1st Unified Military School. Archives.]

211107   Prazdnovanie 4-i godovshchiny. (Celebration of the 4th anniversary.) (Pr, (254), 11.XI.21)
Trans.: Fr. BulCom, (II.51), 17.XI.21; CorInt, (I.9), 9.XI.21.
[Evening celebration of the anniversary of the October Revolution at Elektrosila Factory, No. 3; Lenin also in attendance. cf. 190914.]

211109   Frantsuzskii sindikalizm i Sovetskaya Rossiya. (French syndicalism and Soviet Russia.) (230000(8): 96-8)

211110(1)   Prikaz, No. 267. (Iz, (253), 11.XI.21; PetPr, (235), 11.XI.21; Pr, (254), 11.XI.21)
Repr.: 230000(7).III.i: 266-7.
Trans.: Am. Soviet Russia, 1.II.22.
[A new provocation of the Polish military clique.]

211110(2)   [Speech to CPSU members.] (p.q. 261209)
[At Moscow district of Sokolniki.]

211113   Frantsuzskii sindikalizm i Sovetskaya Rossiya. (French syndicalism and Soviet Russia.) (Pr, (256), 13.XI.21)
Repr.: 230000(8): 98-104.

211118   Tula ostaetsya velikoi kuznitsei Krasnoi Armii. (Tula is still the great forge of the Red Army.) (<u>Iz</u>, (262), 22.XI.21; <u>PetPr</u>, (246), 24.XI.21; <u>Pr</u>, (263), 22.XI.21)

<u>Repr</u>.: 230000(7).III.i: 72-3.

211120   Diviziya Tul´skogo soveta. (The Tula Soviet Division.) (<u>Iz</u>, (263), 23.XI.21; <u>Pr</u>, (264), 23.XI.21)

<u>Repr</u>.: 230000(7).III.i: 74-5.

211122   See 211205.

211200(1)   Rech. (A speech.) (240000(29): 318-25)

<u>Trans</u>.: Am-Eng. 530700: 59-67.

[On Zinoviev's report on tactics of the Comintern.]

[211200(2)]   Zaklyuchitel´noe slovo. (Summary speech.) (240000(29): 325-9)

<u>Trans</u>.: Am-Eng. 530700: 68-73.

[See 211200(1).]

211205   Voennaya doktrina ili mnimo-voennoe doktrinstvo. (Military doctrine or pseudo-military doctrinairism.) (<u>KI</u>, (19), 17.XII.21)

<u>Repr</u>.: 210000(1); *220000(2); 230000(7).III.ii: 210-40; VOENNAYA NAUKA I REVOLYUTSIYA, (2), 1921.

<u>Trans</u>.: p.q. 361013: Ch. VIII;

      Am. 690000(11): 31-69; <u>FI</u>, II-IV.44;

      Eng. 690400(1): 17-52; <u>CI</u>, (III.19), [1922]; p.q. Deutscher, PA: 484;

      Ger. <u>KomInt</u>, (III.19), 1922.

211206   Pis´mo Ol´minskomu. (Letter to Olminsky.) (<u>Iz</u>, (282), 10.XII.24)

<u>Repr</u>.: <u>BO</u>, (28), VII.32; Safarov.

<u>Trans</u>.: Am. <u>Mil</u>, 5.XI.32;

      Eng. <u>Inprecor</u>, 23.I.25;

      Fr. TROTSKI ET: 61-3;

      Ger. <u>Inprekor</u>, (IV.52), 23.XII.24;

      It. [660000(2)]: 39-40; TROTSKI ED: 61-3;

      Pol. Kamieniew, *LENINIZM CZY TROCKIZM?

[T714.]

212108   Alternative for 211206.

211209 Ne nedelya, a pyat´desyat dve nedeli! (Not one but fifty-two weeks!) (Iz, (278), 10.XII.21)
Repr.: 230000(7).III.i: 76.
⌊On Red Army wounded and invalid.⌋

211210(1) Zaklyuchitel´noe slovo. (Summary speech.) (230000(7).III.i: 80-92)
⌊At 2nd conference of communist cells in Higher Institutions of Military Training. Archives.⌋

⌊212110(2)⌋ Nado uchit´sya pisat! (We must learn how to write ⌊for young people⌋!) (Pr, (279), 10.XII.21)
Repr.: 230000(7).III.i: 77-9; 240000(28): 64-6; 270000(2): 239-42.

211211 Prikaz, No. 268. (Iz, (280), 13.XII.21; PetPr, (263), 14.XII.21; Pr, (281), 13.XII.21)
Repr.: 230000(7).III.i: 266-9.
⌊We must stay strong!⌋

211212 Doklad. (A report.) (Pr, (286,287), 18,20.XII.21)
Repr.: 230000(7).III.i: 93-100; Voennyi Vestnik, (1), 1922.
⌊To conference of Party cells of Military Training Institutions of Moscow Army.⌋

⌊211215⌋ Marsel´skomu s"ezdu frantsuzskoi kompartii. (To the Marseilles Congress of the CPFrance.) (230000(8): 107-13)
Repr.: 240000(29): 312-8.
Trans.: Am-Eng. 530700: 52-8;
   Eng. Degras, DOCCI.I: 303-6;
   Fr. 670306: 135-40; L'I.C. ET SA SECTION FRANÇAISE: 20-7.
⌊Open letter from ECCI.⌋

⌊211216⌋ Au comité directeur du parti communiste français.
Trans.: Fr. 670306: 141-3.

⌊211218⌋ Invalidy grazhdanskoi voiny. (The invalids of the civil war.) (Iz, (285), 18.XII.21)
Repr.: 230000(7).III.i: 104-5.

211219 Alternative for ⌊211215⌋.

211221   Priliv. (Flood-tide.) (<u>Pr</u>, (292), 25.XII.21)

Repr.:   240000(29): 330-9.

Trans.: Am-Eng. 530700: 74-84;

       Cz. p.q. <u>Rude Pravo</u>, (22,24), 26,28.I.22;

       Fr. <u>CorInt</u>, (II.5), 18.I.22;

       Ger. <u>Inprekor</u>, (II.4), 16.I.22;

       It, <u>Ordine Nuovo</u>, (II.27), 27.I.22.

[The economic situation and the international workers movement.]

[211223]   Ekh, ne khvataet nam tochnosti! (Alas, we are not thorough enough!) (<u>Iz</u>, (289), 23.XII.21)

Repr.:   230000(7).III.i: 101-3; 270000(2): 359-62.

[Archives.]

[211225]   Alternative for 211221.

211226   Frontov net, — opasnost est. (There are no fronts, but danger remains.) (<u>Iz</u>, (293), 28.XII.21; <u>PetPr</u>, (276), 29.XII.21; <u>Pr</u>, (294), 28.XII.21)

Repr.:   *220000(14); 220000(15); *[220000(17)]; *220000(41); 230000(7).III.i: 273-300.

Trans.: Am. p.q. <u>Living Age</u>, 18.III.22;

       Eng. p.q. <u>Soc</u>(G), (XXI.4), 26.I.22;

       Fr. p.q. Morizet;

       Ger. 220000(27).

[Report to 9th Congress of Soviets.]

211227   Rech. (A speech.) (<u>Iz</u>, (293), 28.XII.21; <u>Pr</u>, (295), 29.XII.21)

Trans.: Ger. p.q. <u>Inprekor</u>, (IV.4), 10.I.24;

       Hol. p.q. <u>Tribune</u>, (80), 3.I.22;

       It. p.q. <u>Ordine Nuovo</u>, (II.4), 4.I.22.

[At 9th Congress of Soviets; on fundamental problems of industrial construction.]

[211229]   Postanovlenie. (A regulation.) (<u>Iz</u>, (294), 29.XII.21; <u>Pr</u>, (295), 29.XII.21)

Trans.: Cz. <u>Rude Pravo</u>, (III.5), 6.I.22.

*220000(1) *VESENNIE PROISKI VRAGOV. (SPRING INTRIGUES OF THE ENEMY.)
    [See 220312 for all repr., notes.]

*220000(2) *VOENNAYA DOKTRINA ILI MNIMO-VOENNOE DOKTRINSTVO. (MILITARY DOCTRINE
    OR PSEUDO-MILITARY DOCTRINAIRISM.)
    [See 211205 for all repr., trans.]

220000(3) § VOINA I REVOLYUTSIYA. (WAR AND REVOLUTION.)
    Repr.: 230000(2).
    [Pref. 1st ed. 220424(1); Pref. Vol. II 220522(1); Pref. 2nd ed.
    230616(1). This ed. contains material omitted from 2nd ed. 230000(2).]

*220000(4) *DNEVNIK LVA TROTSKOGO. TETRAD SEDMAYA. (LEON TROTSKY'S DIARY.
    SEVENTH NOTEBOOK.)

220000(5) MEZHDU IMPERIALIZMOM I REVOLYUTSIEI. (BETWEEN IMPERIALISM AND
    REVOLUTION.) (Iz, (50,51), 3,4.III.22; Pr, (45), 25.II.22)
    Repr.: 220000(6); 230000(18): 207-333; 250000(8): 183-296; p.q. KI,
      (20), 14.III.22.
    Trans.: Am. 630000(6);
      Cz. *250000(35);
      Eng. 220000(18); The Com, (88-94), 8.IV-20.V.22; p.q. Daily
        Herald, 28.III-3.IV.22;
      Fr. 220000(22); p.q. 680000(4): passim; 700603; p.q. BulCom,
        (II.21), 25.V.22; p.q. CorInt, (II.22,40,42), 22.III,
        24,31.V.22;
      Ger. 220000(30); 230000(27); 230000(28); 230000(36); [670000(3)];
        p.q. Inprekor, (II.29,33,34), 11,21,23.III.22; p.q.
        RusKor, (III.i.4-5), IV-V.22.
    [Pref. 220220. Written specially for The Com. Iz, and Pr. are p.q.]

220000(6) MEZHDU IMPERIALIZMOM I REVOLYUTSIEI. (BETWEEN IMPERIALISM AND
    REVOLUTION.)
    [See 220000(5) for all repr., trans., notes.]

*220000(7) *OSNOVNAYA VOENNAYA ZADACHA MOMENTA. (BASIC MILITARY TASKS OF THE
    MOMENT.)
    [See 220401(1) for all repr., trans.]

220000(8) § i Rakovskii: OCHERKI POLITICHESKOI RUMYNII. (RUMANIAN POLITICAL
    SKETCHES.)
    [Pref. 220612; 2nd ed. 230000(20); 230430(1) Pref. 2nd ed.]

*220000(9)   *V GODOVSHCHINA OKTYABR´SKOI REVOLYUTSII I IV KONGRESS KOMINTERNA.
(THE 5th ANNIVERSARY OF THE OCTOBER REVOLUTION AND THE 4th CONGRESS
OF THE COMINTERN.)
[See 221020 for all repr., trans.]

*220000(10)   *REVOLYUTSIONNA STRATEGIYA. (REVOLUTIONARY STRATEGY.)
[Trans. Bul. See 210700 for all trans., repr.]

*220000(11)   *REVOLYUTSIONNA STRATEGIYA. (REVOLUTIONARY STRATEGY.)
[Trans. Bul See 210700 for all repr., trans.]

220000(12)   ‡ 1905.
Repr.: 220000(13); 240000(33); [250000(11)].
Trans.: Am. p.q. 650900: 43-61; p.q. NI(WP), XI.42;
       Eng. p.q. 640000(5): 43-61; p.q. 640000(10): 43-61;
       Fr. 230000(29); p.q. 680000(4): passim; 690415; p.q. Clarté,
          (II.30), 1.II.23;
       Ger. 230000(33);
       It. 480000(1); 690610;
       Ukr, 250000(36).
[Expanded version of 100000(2). Pref. 1st ed. 220112; Pref. 2nd ed.
220710(1). Fr. ed. lacks 220628. It. eds. differ in appendices.]

220000(13)   § 1905.
[2nd ed. See 220000(12) for all repr., trans., notes.]

*220000(14)   *FRONTOV NET, — OPASNOST EST. (THERE ARE NO FRONTS, BUT DANGER
REMAINS.)
[See 211226 for all repr., trans.]

220000(15)   FRONTOV NET, — OPASNOST EST. (THERE ARE NO DRONTS, BUT DANGER
REMAINS.)
[See 211226 for all repr., trans.]

*[220000(16)]   *MIROVAYA REVOLYUTSIYA I IV KONGRESS KOMINTERNA. (WORLD REVOLUTION
AND THE 4th CONGRESS OF THE COMINTERN.)
[See 221228 for all repr., trans.]

*[220000(17)]   *POCHEMU NAM NUZHNA SIL´NAYA ARMIYA? (WHY DO WE NEED A STRONG ARMY?)
[See 211226 for all repr., trans.]

220000(18)   BETWEEN RED AND WHITE.
[Trans. Eng. See 220000(5) for all repr., trans., notes.]

220000(19) § LE COMMUNISME EN FRANCE ET L'INTERNATIONALE.
Trans.: Ger. 220000(23); 220000(29).
[Trans. Fr. See 220226(1), 220302(1), 220304 for all repr., trans.]

220000(20) LA CRISE DU PARTI COMMUNISTE FRANÇAIS.
[Trans. Fr. See 220519(1), 220519(2) for all repr., trans.]

220000(21) DICTATORSHIP VS DEMOCRACY.
[Trans. Am. See 200000(37) for all repr., trans., notes.]

220000(22) ENTRE L'IMPÉRIALISME ET LA RÉVOLUTION.
[Trans. Fr. See 220000(5) for all repr., trans., notes.]

220000(23) § DIE FRAGEN DER ARBEITERBEWEGUNG IN FRANKREICH UND DIE KOMMUNISTISCHE
INTERNATIONALE.
[Trans. Ger. See 220000(19) for all repr., trans., notes.]

220000(24) DAS HUNGERNDE RUSSLAND UN DAS "SATTE" EUROPA.
[Trans. Ger. See 210830 for all repr., trans.]

220000(25) MEINE FLUCHT AUS SIBIRIEN.
[Trans. Ger. See 070000(3) for all trans., notes.]

220000(26) § NOUVELLE ÉTAPE.
[Trans. Fr. See 210000(7) for all trans.]

220000(27) DIE ROTE ARMEE DER SOWJET-REPUBLIK AUF DER WACHT!
[Trans. Ger. See 211226 for all trans.]

*220000(28) *LE SALUT DU PARTI COMMUNISTE FRANÇAIS.
Repr.: 670000(9).
[Trans. Fr. See 220608, 220610 for all repr., trans.]

220000(29) DIE TAKTIK DER KOMMUNISTISCHE INTERNATIONALE GEGEN DIE OFFENSIV DES
KAPITALS.
[Trans. Ger. See 220226(1), 220302(1) for all repr., trans.]

220000(30) ZWISCHEN IMPERIALISMUS UND REVOLUTION.
[Trans. Ger. See 220000(5) for all repr., trans., notes.]

[220000(31)] § LETTRES A QUELQUES CAMARADES FRANÇAIS (1921-1922).
[Trans. Fr. Processed. LocBN.]

220000(32) O kul´ture budushchego. (The culture of the future.) (270000(2):446-9)
Trans.: Heb. Bamifne, (III.6), 10.XII.37.
[Draft. Incorporated with slight variation in 230929. Archives.]

220000(33)   PS 170512/. (220000(3).II: 508-9/481-2)
              Trans.: Am. FI, IX.44.
              [See 170512/ for other trans.]

*220000(34)   *[Dictatorship, where is thy whip?]
              [p.q. Slonim: 278. Russian original not traced.]

*220000(35)   *DER NEUER ETAP. DI VELT-LAGE UN UNZERE OJFGABEN.
              [Trans. Yid. See 210000(7) for all trans.]

*[220000(36)] *TERORIZM UN REVOLJUTSJA.
              [Trans. Yid. p.q. 200000(37).]

*220000(37)   i dr.: *KARL LIBKNEKHT, ROZA LYUKSEMBURG I LEO YUGIKHES.
              [Trans. Bul. See 190118 for all trans.]

220000(38)   EL BOCHEVIQUISMO ANTE LA GUERRA Y LA PAZ DEL MUNDO.
              [Trans. Sp. See [140000(3)] for all repr., trans., notes.]

*220000(39)   i dr.: *DOKLADY. (REPORTS.)
              [See 221114(1) for all repr., trans.]

*220000(40)   *ROL I ZADACHI PROFESSIONAL'NYKH SOYUZOV. (ROLE AND TASKS OF THE
              TRADE UNIONS.)
              [See 210000(13) for all repr., trans., notes.]

*220000(41)   *KRASNAYA ARMIYA I POLITICH. PERSPEKTIVY. (THE RED ARMY AND POLITICAL
              PERSPECTIVES.)
              [See 211226 for all repr., trans., notes.]

*220000(42)   *ROL I ZADACHI PROFESSIONAL'NYKH SOYUZOV. (ROLE AND TASKS OF THE
              TRADE UNIONS.)
              [See 210000(13) for all repr., trans., notes.]

[220104(1)]   Soveshchanie. (A conference.) (PetPr, (5), 6.I.22; Pr, (3), 4.I.22)
              Repr.: 230000(7).III.i: 106-10; 240000(28): 101-4; Pref. *SOVESHCHANIE.
              [To military delegates to 9th Soviet Congress.]

220104(2)   Pavel Levi i koi-kakie "levye". (Paul Levi and some "Leftists".)
              (Pr, (5), 6.I.22)
              Repr.: 240000(29): 339-44.
              Trans.: Am-Eng. 530700: 85-90;
                      Fr. CorInt, I.22; p.q. (VIII.115), 16.XI.27;
                      Ger. Inprekor, (II.6), 14.I.22.
              [On CPGermany and Comintern.]

220112   Pref. 1905, 220000(12). (p.q. Iz, (29), 7.II.22)

Trans.: Eng. p.q. Inprecor, (36), 9.V.23;
         Fr. BulCom, (IV.12), 22.III.23;
         Ger. 5. JAHRSTAG.

[See 220000(12) for all repr., trans., notes.]

220113(1)   Zaboda ob Armii. (Care for the Army.) (Iz, (10), 14.I.22)

Repr.: 230000(7).III.i: 111-2.

220113(2)   Prikaz, No. 101. (Iz, (13), 18.I.22)

220113(3)   i dr.: Nedelya dostoyanie Krasnoarmeitsa. (Red Army gift week.)
(Iz, (13), 18.I.22)

220116   Rech. (A speech.) (Iz, (12), 17.I.22; Pr, (12,13), 17,18.I.22)

Repr.: 230000(7).III.ii: 33-42; *STENMOSSOV.

Trans.: Am. p.q. NYTimes, 19.I.22;
         Cz. p.q. Rude Pravo, (III.67), 19.III.22;
         Eng. p.q. Daily Herald, 19.I.22; p.q. Dennis: 477.

[At Plenum of Moscow Soviet; on Genoa and The Hague conferences.]

220117   Pis'mo v Narkomsobes i Vserokompom. (Letter to the Narkom of Social
Security and the All-Russian Committee for Help.) (Iz(NKSO), (2),
4.II.22)

[On aid to Army invalids.]

220121   Iz rechi. (From a speech.) (Pr, (16), 22.I.22)

Repr.: 240000(28): 67.

[At conference of Moscow non-Party young workers.]

[220125]   Spasibo rabochiei Moskva! (Thank you, Moscow workers!) (Iz, (18),
25.I.22)

Repr.: 230000(7).III.i: 113.

[220131(1)]   Nado polozhit konets rastocheniyu bumagi. (We must put a stop to the
squandering of paper.) (Iz, (23), 31.I.22; PetPr, (28), 2.II.22)

Repr.: 270000(2): 247.

[220131(2)]   Rech. (A speech.) (Iz, (23), 31.I.22)

[At Moscow Soviet; on relations with France, Poland and Rumania.]

220202   [Address at dedication of new Tank Brigade.]

Trans.: Eng. Morning Post, 11.II.22.

220211   Prikaz, No. 365. (PetPr, (35), 14.II.22)
                Repr.: 230000(7).III.i: 270.

220218   Rech. (A speech.) (Voennaya Nauka i Revolyutsiya, (1), 1922)
                Repr.: 230000(7).III.ii: 43-8.
                [At celebration of 4th anniversary of the Red Army, at Training School
                for Higher Commanding Staff; organized by Military Academy.]

220220   Pref. MEZHDU IMPERIALIZMOM I REVOLYUTSIEI (BETWEEN IMPERIALISM AND
                REVOLUTION), 220000(5).
                Trans.: Ger. KomInt, (III.20), 1922.
                [See 220000(5) for other repr., trans., notes.]

[220223(1)]   Pyaty god — god ucheby. (The fifth year a year of study.) (PetPr,
                (43), 23.II.22; Pr, (43), 23.II.22)
                Repr.: 230000(7).III.i: 114-6; 270000(2): 291-3.
                Trans.: Ger. RusKor, (III.i.4-5), IV-V.22.
                [On Red Army.]

220223(2)   Rech. (A speech.) (Iz, (44), 24.II.22)
                Repr.: 230000(7).III.i: 117-8.
                Trans.: Eng. p.q. ComRev, VI.22; p.q. Newsletter, 22.II.58.
                [At parade in Red Square.]

220223(3)   "Slushai, gotov'sya, Krasnaya Armiya!" ("Listen, be ready, Red Army!")
                (230000(7).III.ii: 49-55)
                Trans.: Am. p.q. NYTimes, 26.II.22;
                        Cz. p.q. Rude Pravo, (II.53), 3.III.22.
                [Speech at celebration meeting of Moscow Soviet in honour of 4th
                anniversary of Red Army.]

220225   Rech. (A speech.) (PetPr, (49), 2.III.22)
                [At Plenum ECCI.]

220226(1)   Edinyi front. (The united front.) (230000(8): 113-29)
                Trans.: Am. NI, VII,VIII.38;
                        Eng. p.q. MYJ, (I.2), [XII.69]; p.q. Young Socialist(Ceylon),
                            (III.2), [XI.64];
                        Fr. 220000(19); 670306: 147-63; BulCom, (III.13,14), 30.III,
                            6.IV.22; p.q. V, (63), 21.XI.30;
                        Ger. 220000(23): 3-18; 220000(29); Inprekor, (II.29), 11.III.22;
                            TAKTIK: 78-83.
                        Cz. p.q. Rude Pravo, (III.64), 16.III.22.

220226(2)   et Zinoviev: Lettre du CC du PC de Russie à l'Exécutif élargi de l'I.C.
         <u>Trans</u>.: Fr. <u>BulCom</u>, (III.20), 11.V.22;
                Ger. TAKTIK: 111-2.

220227   Vnimanie k teorii. (Attention to theory.) (<u>Pod ZnamMarks</u>, (1-2),
         I-II.22)
         <u>Repr</u>.: 240000(28): 78-80; 270000(2): 257-9.
         <u>Trans</u>.: Am. <u>YS</u>(NY), (XII.9), IX.69;
                Ger. <u>Jug-Int</u>, (IV.1), IX.22.

220228(1)   Prikaz, No. 515. (230000(7).III.i: 171-3)

220228(2)   Prikaz, No. 268a. (<u>Iz</u>, (48), 1.III.22; <u>Pr</u>, (48), 1.III.22)
         <u>Repr</u>.: 230000(7).III.ii: 56.
         <u>Trans</u>.: Cz. <u>Rude Pravo</u>, (56), 7.III.22.
         [On postponement of Genoa Conference.]

220302(1)   O edinom fronte. (The united front.) (<u>Pr</u>, (49,50), 2,3.III.22)
         <u>Repr</u>.: 230000(8): 130-48; p.q. 240000(6): 142; 240000(29): 344-62.
         <u>Trans</u>.: Am-Eng. 530700: 91-109; <u>FI</u>, III.41;
                Fr. 220000(19); 700000(6): 14-28; <u>BulCom</u>, (III.13,14), 30.III,
                     8.IV.22; <u>CorInt</u>, (II.20,21), 15,18.III.22;
                Ger. 220000(23): 19-28; 220000(29);
                It, p.q. <u>Ordine Nuovo</u>, (II.92), 2.IV.22.
         [Material for report to Fr. Commission of ECCI on the Fr. question.]

220302(2)   Nachalo krizisa. (The beginning of the crisis.) (230000(8): 148-63)
         <u>Trans</u>.: Fr. 220000(19): 27-48; 670306: 164-77;
                Ger. 220000(23): 19-28.
         [On CPFrance.]

220303(1)   Pis'mo tov. Morizet. (Letter to cde. Morizet.) (<u>Iz</u>, (57), 11.III.22)
         <u>Repr</u>.: 230000(8): 163-6; Morizet.
         <u>Trans</u>.: Am. <u>Soviet Russia</u>, 15.V.22;
                Fr. <u>CorInt</u>, (II.25), 1.IV.22; <u>Huma</u>, 7.V.22; Pref. Morizet;
                Ger. <u>Inprekor</u>, (II.44), 8.IV.22; <u>RusKor</u>, (III.i.4-5), IV-V.22;
                It. <u>Ordine Nuovo</u>, (II.98), 8.IV.22.

220303(2)   Alternative for 220302(2).

220304	Rezolyutsiya. (A resolution.)
	Russian: 240000(29): 362-4.
	<u>Trans</u>.: Am-Eng. 530700: 110-2;
	       Eng. Degras, DOCCI.I: 324-6;
	       Fr. 220000(19);
	       Ger. 220000(23): 29-31; TAKTIK: 139-40.
	[At Enlarged Plenum ECCI; on CPFrance. See 220302(2). Date of adoption.]

220308	O zadachakh militsii. (Tasks of the militia.) (<u>Iz</u>, (55), 9.III.22; <u>PetPr</u>, (57), 11.III.22) <u>Trans</u>.: Cz. <u>Rude Pravo</u>, (III.61), 12.III.22. [At All-Russian Congress of militia.]
220309	Alternative for 220303(1).
220312	Vesennie proiski vragov. (Spring intrigues of the enemy.) (<u>Iz</u>, (59), 14.III.22; <u>PetPr</u>, (60), 15.III.22; <u>Pr</u>, (59), 14.III.22; <u>Trud</u>, (57), 14.III.22) <u>Repr</u>.: *220000(1); 230000(7).III.i: 301-18. [At Moscow Soviet celebration of anniversary of February revolution.]
220314	To, chto nuzhno ponyat. (What we must understand.) (<u>PetPr</u>, (65), 22.III.22; <u>Pr</u>, (64), 21.III.22) [On Poland.]
220316	Pochto-telegramma. (A telegram.) (230000(7).III.i: 174) [To cde. Polonsky; on war propaganda. Archives.]
[220321]	Iz besedy. (From an interview.) (<u>Iz</u>, (64), 21.III.22) <u>Repr</u>.: 230000(7).III.ii: 241. [American press. Archives.]
220324	Pochto-telegramma. (A telegram.) (230000(7).III.i: 174-5) [To cde. Polonsky; on war propaganda. Archives.]
220327	Rech. (A speech.) (PROTOKOLY(1961).) [To 11th Congress CPR(b).]
220328	Doklad. (A report.) (<u>Pr</u>, (71), 29.III.22) <u>Repr</u>.: 230000(7).III.i: 119-29; p.q. 240000(28): 18-9;104-6,112-4; PROTOKOLY: 135-44; PROTOKOLY(1961). <u>Trans</u>.: It. p.q. <u>Ordine Nuovo</u>, (II.92), 2.IV.22. [To 11th Congress CPR(b); on Red Army.]

220329(1)   Rech. (A speech.) (Iz, (72), 30.III.22; PetPr, (73), 31.III.22;
Pr, (73), 31.III.22)
Repr.: PROTOKOLY: 284–90; PROTOKOLY(1961).
Trans.: Cz. p.q. Rude Pravo, (III.79), 4.IV.22.
[To 11th Congress CPR(b); on trade union question.]

220329(2)   Iz rechi na XI s"ezde RKP. (From a speech to the 11th Congress CPR)
(Trud, (71), 31.III.22)
Repr.: p.q. 240000(28): 112–4,115–7; PROTOKOLY: 299–311.
[On Red Army. cf. 220328.]

220329(3)   Prenya po dokladu o profdvizheniya. (Intervention in debate on trade
union report.) (Pr, (73), 29.III.22)
[cf. 220329(1).]

220331   Voennye Akademii i bespartiinye. (MilitaryAcademies and non-Party men.)
(Iz, (74), 1.IV.22)
Repr.: 230000(7).III.i: 176.
[Letter to Ed.]

220400(1)   f.n. to 140812. (220000(3).I: 59)

220400(2)   f.n. to 141031. (220000(3).I: 100)

220400(3)   f.n. to [151022(1)]. (22000(3).II: 25)

220400(4)   f.n. to [151022(2)]. (220000(3).II: 32)

220400(5)   f.n. to [160100]. (220000(3).I: 317)

220400(6)   f.n. to [160930]. (220000(3).I: 288)

220400(7)   f.n. to [170205]. (260000(17): 35–6)

220401(1)   DOKLAD (A REPORT), *220000(7).
Repr.: 230000(7).III.ii: 242–58.
Trans.: p.q. 361013: Ch. VIII;
Am. 690000(11): 70–91; FI, V,VI.44;
Eng. 690400(1): 53–72.
[To conference of military delegates at 11th Party Congress.]

220401(2)   Zaklyuchitel'noe slovo. (Summary speech.) (230000(7).III.ii: 258-70)

Trans.: Am. 690000(11): 91-108; FI, VI,VII.44;

Eng. 690400(1): 72-87.

[See 220401(1).]

220401(3)   Rech. (A speech.) (230000(7).III.i: 130-2)

[At conference of All-Russian sailors. Archives.]

220403   K voprosu o voennoi propagande. (The question of war propaganda.)
(Iz, (76), 4.IV.22)

220411(1)   Yaponia v Genue i Vladivostoke. (Japan at Genoa and in Vladivostok.)
(Iz, (82), 12.IV.22; PetPr, (83), 13.IV.22)

Repr.: 230000(7).III.ii: 57.

220411(2)   [At Politbureau; refuses post of Deputy Premier.]
[c. Deutscher, PU: 35. Harvard Archives.]

220413(1)   Prikaz, No. 271. (230000(7).III.ii: 58)

[220413(2)]   La grève dans l'état ouvrier.

Trans.: Fr. BulCom, (III.15), 13.IV.22.

220414   Prikaz, No. 272. (Iz, (85), 19.IV.22)

Repr.: 230000(7).III.ii: 59.

Trans.: Cz. Rude Pravo, (III.93), 21.IV.22;

Fr. Huma, 17.IV.22;

Nor. Ny Tid, 19.V.22.

[Keep your powder dry!]

220418   [Secret memorandum; on Rabkrin.] (p.q. Lenin, SOCH.XXVII : 542-3)

Trans.: p.q. 410000(1): Ch. XI.

[T746.]

*220419   *[To Politbureau; on unified economic authority.]
[c. Daniels: 475 n.124. T747.]

220424(1)   Pref. VOINA I REVOLYUTSIA (WAR AND REVOLUTION), 220000(3).

220424(2)   Gazeta Chernova. (Chernov's paper.) (220000(3).I: 29-31)

220424(3)   Nado znat vcherashnii den. (We must know the past.) (240000(28): 92-3)

220424(4)   PS 190318(7). (260000(17): 48)

220424(5)   PS 190318(5). (260000(17): 49)

220424(6)   PS 190318(6). (260000(17): 68)

220424(7)   G.I.Chudnovskii. (220000(3).I: 28-9)
                   Repr.: 260000(17): 247-8.

220425   Beglye mysli o Plekhanove. (Cursory thoughts on Plekhanov.)
                   (Pod ZnamMarks, (5-6), 1922)
                   Repr.: 220000(3).I: 17-22; 240000(28): 86-91; 260000(17): 56-61.
                   Trans.: Am. FI, III.43;
                           Eng. 490700; [610000(18)]; Free Expression, XI.42; Keep Left,
                               (XIX.7), VII-VIII.70;
                           Fr. [620000(6)]; BulCom, (IV.51), 20.XII.23; QI, XII.56.

220426   Pamyati E.A.Litkensa. (In memory of E.A.Litkens.) (Pr, (92), 27.IV.22)
                   Repr.: 260000(17): 258-61.
                   Trans.: Ger. Inprekor, (II.61), 6.V.22.

220429   Kommunisty i krest´yanstvo vo Frantsii. (Communists and peasantry in
                   France. (Pr, (95), 30.IV.22)
                   Repr.: 230000(8): 166-71; 240000(29): 365-70.
                   Trans.: Am-Eng. 530700: 113-8;
                           Eng. p.q. Inprecor, (II.44), 1922;
                           Fr. Huma, 22.V.22;
                           Ger. p.q. Inprekor, (II.69), 18.V.22.
                   [Contribution to discussion on united front in France.]

220500   Pis´mo Krasnoarmeitsu. (Letter to a Red Army man.) (Krasnoarmeets,
                   (47), V.22)
                   Repr.: 230000(7).III.i: 177.

220501(1)   Rech. (A speech.) (Iz, (96), 3.V.22; Trud, (94), 3.V.22)
                   Repr.: 230000(7).III.ii: 60-1.
                   Trans.: Eng. p.q. Russian Information Review, 8.VI.22.
                   [To parade in Red Square.]

220501(2)   PS [161025]. (220000(3).II: 302/293)

[220504]   O genuezskoi konferentsii. (The Genoa Conference.) (Pr, (100), 7.V.22)
                   Trans.: Am. p.q. NYTimes, 5.V.22.
                   [See also [220507], [220518], [220827] for others in series.]

[220507]   Iz beseda. (From an interview.) (<u>Pr</u>, (100), 7.V.22)

Repr.: 230000(7).III.ii: 62-3.

Trans.: Eng. <u>The Com</u>, (112), 23.IX.22.

[With foreign press; on Genoa and The Hague Conferences. See [220504]
for series.]

220508(1)   Voennoe znanie i marksizm. (Military knowledge and Marxism.)
(230000(7).III.ii: 271-4)

Trans.: Am. 690000(11): 109-13; <u>FI</u>, XII.43;
        Eng. 690400(1): 89-92.

[Speech to session of Military Scientific Institute.]

220508(2)   Zaklyuchitel´noe slovo. (Summary speech.) (230000(7).III.ii: 274-89)

Trans.: Am. 690000(11): 113-33; <u>FI</u>, XII.43;
        Eng. 690400(1): 92-111.

[See 220508(1).]

220508(3)   Primechanie k nastoyashchemu izdaniyu. (Note to the present edition.)
(220000(3).II: 283-4/274-5)

[See [161006].]

220508(4)   Discours au CE élargi.

Trans.: Fr. <u>BulCom</u>, (III.33), 10.VIII.22.

[On CPFrance.]

220508(5)   Uroki pervomaiskogo prazdnovaniya. (Lessons of the May Day celebrations.)
(<u>Pr</u>, (102), 10.V.22)

Repr.: 240000(29): 370-4.

Trans.: Am-Eng. 530700: 119-23;
        Cz. <u>Rude Pravo</u>, (III.114), 17.V.22;
        Eng. <u>ComReview</u>, VI.22;
        Fr. <u>CorInt</u>, (II.38), 17.V.22; <u>Huma</u>, 12.VI.22;
        Lith. <u>Komunaras</u>, (6), VI.22.

220512(1)   Ispolkom Kominterna Tsentral´nomu komitetu FKP. (ECCI to CC CPFrance.)
(230000(8): 172-80)

Repr.: 240000(29): 374-82.

Trans.: Am-Eng. 530700: 124-32;
Fr. <u>BulCom</u>, (III.37), 7.IX.22; L'I.C. ET SA SECTION FRANÇAISE: 46-56.

220512(2)   Télégramme aux éditeurs, <u>Clarté</u>.

Trans.: Fr. <u>Huma</u>, 13.V.22.

220513   Kto i chemu izmenyaet. (Who is a traitor and to whom?) (<u>Pr</u>, (107), 16.V.22)

<u>Repr</u>.: Pref. PROTSESS.

<u>Trans</u>.: Am. <u>Soviet Russia</u>, 15.VII.22;

     Ger. <u>Inprekor</u>, (II.80), 30.V.22;

     It. <u>Ordine Nuovo</u>, (II.158), 8.VI.22;

     Pol. <u>NPrzeglad</u>, (I.3-4), VIII-IX.22.

[Trial of SRs.]

220515   Pref. M.Martinet, NOCH. (NIGHT.) (<u>Iz</u>, (107), 16.V.22)

<u>Repr</u>.: 230000(8): 304-14.

<u>Trans</u>.: Eng. <u>Labour Monthly</u>, VIII.22;

     Fr. 250000(13); 250000(14); 640911: 258-68; <u>Clarté</u>, (22), 1.X.22;

     Gr. 660000(6): 232-43;

     It. 680000(6): 37-50;

     Sp. 690000(8).II: 103-13;

     Swed. p.q. 690600(1): 232-3.

[PS 220801.]

[220516]   Privet slavnoi divizii! (Greetings to a famous Division!) (<u>Iz</u>, (108), 17.V.22; <u>Pr</u>, (107), 16.V.22)

<u>Repr</u>.: 230000(7).III.i: 178.

[Telegram to Kikvidze Division.]

[220518]   Iz beseda. (From an interview.) (<u>Iz</u>, (109), 18.V.22; <u>Pr</u>, (109), 18.V.22; <u>Trud</u>, (107), 18.V.22)

<u>Repr</u>.: 230000(7).III.ii: 63-5.

<u>Trans</u>.: Am. p.q. <u>NYTimes</u>, 31.V.22;

     Cz. p.q. <u>Rude Pravo</u>, (142,144), 21,23.VII.22;

     Eng. p.q. Dennis: 437;

     Hol. Vaderland, 1922;

     It. <u>Ordine Nuovo</u>, (II.142), 23.V.22;

     Pol. <u>NPrzeglad</u>, (I.5), X.22.

[With foreign press; on Genoa and The Hague Conferences. See [220504] for series.]

220519(1)   Krizis frantsuzskoi Kommunisticheskoi Partii. (The crisis of the CPFrance.) (230000(8): 180-98)

<u>Trans</u>.:Fr. 220000(20); 670000(8); <u>BulCom</u>, (III.28), 6.VII.22.

[To ECCI.]

220519(2)   Zaklyuchitel´noe slovo. (Summary speech.)

Russian: 230000(8): 198-207.

<u>Trans</u>.: Fr. 220000(20); 670000(8); <u>BulCom</u>, (III.34,35), 17,24.VIII.22.
[See 220519(1).]

220520   Prikaz, No. 1247. (230000(7).III.i: 179-80)

220521   Put Krasnoi Armii. (The Way of the Red Army.) (<u>EzhKom</u>, (8), 21.V.22)

<u>Repr</u>.: 230000(7).I: 13-21.

<u>Trans</u>.: Am. p.q. Bunyan & Fisher: 569-72; p.q. <u>FI</u>, VIII.41;

        Fr. 680000(1): 31-41; <u>V</u>, (144,145), 2,9.III.33;

        Ger. 240000(40): 7-16; <u>RusKor</u>, (III.ii.7-10), VII-X.22;

           JAHRBUCH: 256-68.

220522(1)   Pref. Vol. II, VOINA I REVOLYUTSIYA (WAR AND REVOLUTION), 220000(3).

<u>Repr</u>.: 230000(2); 260000(17): 71-4.

220522(2)   Pis´mo tov. Rosmeru. (Letter to cde. Rosmer.)

Russian: 230000(8): 207-10.

<u>Trans</u>.: Fr. [220000(31)]; 670306: 178-81.
[On CPFrance.]

220523   Frantsuzskii kommunizm i pozitsiya t. Rappoporta. (French communism
and the position of cde. Rappoport.)

Russian: 230000(8): 210-4; 240000(29): 382-6.

<u>Trans</u>.: Am-Eng. 530700: 133-7;

        Fr. <u>BulCom</u>, (III.26), 22.VI.22; <u>CorInt</u>, (II.45), 10.VI.22;

        Ger. <u>Inprekor</u>, (II.92), 13.VI.22.

220526   Naivnost khitresov. (The naivety of sly people.) (<u>Pr</u>, (117), 28.V.22)

<u>Trans</u>.: Fr. <u>BulCom</u>, (III.30), 20.VII.22; <u>CorInt</u>, (II.46), 14.VI.22;

        Ger. <u>Inprekor</u>, (II.84), 8.VI.22; <u>RusKor</u>, (III.i.6), VI.22;

           AN DEN PRANGER!: 44-58;

        It. <u>Ordine Nuovo</u>, (II.165), 15.VI.22.

[Some explanations to cdes. Vandervelde, Rosenfeld, T.Libknecht and
others; on trial of SRs.]

220600(1)   f.n. to [120304]. (230000(9): 255)

<u>Trans</u>.: Ger. 680800(2): 288;

        Jap. 611225.II: 168.

220600(2)   f.n. to [140316]. (230000(9): 305)
           Trans.: Ger. 680800(2): 346;
                 Jap. 611225.II: 152.

220600(3)   PS [080629]. (230000(9): 318)
           Trans.: Ger. 680800(2): 359;
                 Jap. 611225.II: 168.

220600(4)   f.n. to 080412. (260000(12): 267)

220600(5)   Résolutions et messages de l'Exécutif de juin 1922.
           Trans.: Fr. 670306: 187-95; L'INTERNATIONALE COMMUNISTE ET SA SECTION
                 FRANÇAISE: 58-69.

220606   Pis'mo tov. Ker. (Letter to cde. Ker.) (230000(8): 214-8)
           Repr.: 240000(29): 386-90.
           Trans.: Am-Eng. 530700: 138-42;
                 Fr. 670306: 182-6; Humbert Droz: 71-6.
           [On CPFrance.]

220608   Edinyi front i levyi blok. (The united front and the Left Bloc.)
           (Pr, (127), 10.VI.22)
           Repr.: 230000(8): 218-48.
           Trans.: Fr. *220000(28); 670000(9): 3-35; BulCom, (III.36), 31.VIII.22;
                 Ger. Inprekor, (II.94), 14.VI.22; KomInt, (III.21), 1922.
           [At ECCI; on CPFrance.]

220609   Alternative for 220610.

220610   Zaklyuchitel'noe slovo. (Summary speech.) (Pr, (128), 11.VI.22)
           Repr.: 230000(8): 249-60; KI, (21), 19.VII.22.
           Trans.: Fr. *220000(28); 670000(9): 36-48; BulCom, (III.37), 7.IX.22;
                 Ger. Inprekor, (II.100), 17.VI.22; KomInt, (III.21), 1922.
           [See 220608.]

220611   Rezolyutsiya. (A resolution.) (230000(8): 260-9)
           Repr.: 240000(29): 398.
           Trans.: Am-Eng. 530700: 143-51;
                 Fr. p.q. 580000(7): 30.
           [See 220608.]

220612   Pref. i Rakovskii: OCHERKI POLITICHESKOI RUMYNII (RUMANIAN POLITICAL
                SKETCHES), 220000(8).
                [1st ed.]

[220618]   Predatel´stvo i revolyutsionnyi dolg. (Treachery and revolutionary
                duty.) (Pr, (134), 18.VI.22)
                Trans.: Ger. Inprekor, (II.112), 24.VI.22; RusKor, (III.i.6), VI.22;
                    It. Ordine Nuovo, (II.184), 4.VII.22.

220623   Illyuzii i deistvitel´nost. (Illusions and reality.) (Pr, (138),
                24.VI.22)
                Trans.: Ger. Inprekor, (II.121), 29.VI.22.

220628   Ob osobennostyakh istoricheskogo razvitiya Rossii. (On the peculiarities
                of the historical development of Russia.) (Pr, (144,145), 1,2.VII.22)
                Repr.: 220000(12): 294-309; 220000(13); p.q. 310000(1): App. I.
                Trans.: p.q. 310000(1): App. I.
                [See further [220707].]

220700   See 220900.

[220707]   Parokhod — ne parokhod, a barzha. (The steamer isn't a steamer; it's
                a barge.) (Pr, (149), 7.VII.22)
                [Reply to Pokrovsky's reply to 220628.]

220708(1)   Privetstvie glavnokomanduyushchemu S.S.Kamenevu. (Greetings to C-in-C
                S.S.Kamenev.) (Iz, (151), 9.VII.22)
                Repr.: 230000(7).III.i: 181.

220708(2)   Bditel´noe vnimanie. (Vigilant attention.) (Pr, (150), 8.VII.22)

220710(1)   Pref. 1905, 220000(12).
                [2nd ed. See 220000(12) for all repr., trans., notes.]

[220710(2)]   Privetsvennaya telegramma. (Greetings telegram.) (Iz(NKSO), (26),
                10.VII.22)
                [To peasant committee helping Red Army invalids.]

220712   PS [130903]. (230000(20): 116)
                Repr.: 260000(1): 432.

220718   "Ty" i "vy" v Krasnoi Armii. ("Thou" and "you" in the Red Army.)
                (Iz, (159), 19.VII.22)
                Repr.: 230000(7).III.i: 133; 270000(2): 58-9.

220722   Alternative for 220725.

220725   Geroyu karandasha i kisti. Prikaz, No. 1764. (To a hero of pencil
                and paint.) (Iz, (166), 27.VII.22; RabM, (140), 27.VII.22)
                Repr.: 230000(7).III.i: 182; 270000(2): 242.
                [The cartoonist Moor.]

[220727]   O tekushchem momente. (The current situation.) (Iz, (168), 29.VII.22;
                Pr, (168), 29.VII.22; Trud, (167), 28.VII.22)
                [Interview with correspondent of Corriere della Sera.]

220728   Pis'mo tov. Trenu. (Letter to cde. Treint.)
                Russian: 230000(8): 269-72; 240000(29): 399-402.
                Trans.: Am-Eng. 530700: 152-5;
                        Fr. [220000(31)]: 32-8; 670306: 202-6.
                [On CPFrance. Russian omits PS.]

220731   Alternative for 220728.

220801   PS 220515.
                Russian: 230000(8): 314.
                Trans.: Fr. Huma, 7.X.22.

220802   [Message to Politbureau; on planning.]
                [c. Deutscher, PA: 498. cf. 220823.]

220823   [To CC; on economic planning.]
                [See also 210807, 230120. T774.]

220826   Otvety inostrannym korrespondentam. (Replies to foreign correspondents.)
                (Iz, (193), 30.VIII.22; PetPr, (194), 31.VIII.22; Trud, (191,192),
                27,30.VIII.22)
                Repr.: 230000(7).III.ii: 66-7,67-9.
                Trans.: Am. p.q. NYTimes, 27.VIII.22;
                        Eng. p.q. Dennis: 481;
                        Ger. p.q. Inprekor, (II.175), 2.IX.22;
                        Nor. Ny Tid, 7.IX.22.
                [On relations with Europe and USA.]

[220827]   Iz beseda. (From an interview.) (<u>Iz</u>, (192), 27.VIII.22)
             <u>Repr.</u>: 230000(7).III.ii: 65-6.
             <u>Trans</u>.: Am. p.q. <u>NYTimes</u>, 27.VIII.22;
                     Cz. <u>Rude Pravo</u>, (III.210), 8.IX.22;
                     Eng. p.q. Dennis: 446; <u>Inprecor</u>, (II.76), 1922.
             [On Genoa and The Hague Conferences. See [220504].]

220900   Pis´mo Ispolkoma Kominterna senskoi Federatsii. (Letter from ECCI
             to the Seine Federation.) (230000(8): 273-8)
             <u>Trans</u>.: Am-Eng. 530700: 156-61;
                     Fr. 670306: 196-201; L'I.C. ET SA SECTION FRANÇAISE: 69-76.
             [On CPFrance.]

220912   [Again refuses appointment as Deputy Premier.]
             [c. Deutscher, PU: 66.]

220913   S"ezdu frantsuzskoi kommunisticheskoi partii. (To Congress of CPFrance.)
             (230000(8): 278-94)
             <u>Repr.</u>: 240000(29): 408-25.
             <u>Trans</u>.: Am-Eng. 530700: 162-80.
             [A letter.]

220916(1)   Ssylka v Verkholensk. (Exile in Verkholensk.) (<u>Katorga i Ssylka</u>, (5),
             1923: 91-5)
             <u>Repr.</u>: SBORNIK ISTPART, (1), 1923: 3-4.

220916(2)   Vne-oktyabr´skaya literatura. (Pre-October literature.) (<u>PetPr</u>, (210),
             19.IX.22; <u>Pr</u>, (209,210,221,222,224), 17,19.IX, 1,3,5.X.22)
             <u>Repr.</u>: 230000(9): 15-40.
             <u>Trans</u>.: 230000(9).
             [Revised from <u>Pr</u> for 230000(9).]

221006   Parizhskomu s"ezdu FKP. (To the Paris Congress of CPFrance.)
             (230000(8): 296-7)
             <u>Repr.</u>: 240000(29): 425-6.
             <u>Trans</u>.: Am-Eng. 530700: 181-2;
                     Eng. Degras, DOCCI.I: 373-4;
                     Fr. L'I.C. ET SA SECTION FRANÇAISE: 102-3.
             [From ECCI.]

221010   Iz rechi. (From a speech.) (<u>Iz</u>, (229,230), 11,12.X.22; <u>Pr</u>, (230),

12.X.22; <u>Trud</u>, (228), 11.X.22)

<u>Repr</u>.: 230000(7).III.i: 134-5; p.q. 240000(28): 118.

<u>Trans</u>.: Cz. <u>Rude Pravo Vecernik</u>, (242), 24.X.22;

Eng. <u>Inprecor</u>, (II.91), 1922;

Ger. <u>Inprekor</u>, (II.202), 15.X.22; <u>RusKor</u>, (III.ii.7-10), VII-X.22.

⌊At Textile Workers Congress; on pre-conscription age-group of 1901.⌋

221011   Rech. (A speech.) (<u>Iz</u>, (231), 13.X.22; <u>PetPr</u>, (231,232), 13,14.X.22;

<u>Pr</u>, (231), 13.X.22; <u>Trud</u>, (229), 12.X.22)

<u>Repr</u>.: 240000(28): 217-39; 270000(2): 294-317; <u>Byulleteni V</u>

<u>Vserossiiskogo S"ezda RKSM</u>, 1923.

<u>Trans</u>.: Ger. p.q. <u>Inprekor</u>, (II.204,206), 24,26.X.22; <u>RusKor</u>,

(III.ii.7-10), VII-X.22.

⌊At 5th All-Russian Congress of Komsomol; on tasks of young workers.⌋

[221012]   Kusochek sovetskoi demokratii. (A glimpse of soviet democracy.)

(<u>PetPr</u>, (230), 12.X.22; <u>Pr</u>, (230), 12.X.22)

<u>Repr</u>.: 270000(2): 74-5.

<u>Trans</u>.: Cz. <u>Rude Pravo</u>, (247), 21.X.22;

Eng. <u>Inprecor</u>, (II.92), 1922;

Ger. <u>Inprekor</u>, (II.201), 17.X.22;

Swed. <u>Röde Ryssland</u>, (44), 4.XI.22.

[221015]   Interview.

<u>Trans</u>.: Am. <u>NYTimes</u>, 15.X.22.

⌊With Paxton Hibben; on Soviet economy.⌋

221016   Rech. (A speech.) (<u>Iz</u>, (234), 17.X.22)

<u>Repr</u>.: 230000(7).III.i: 136-41; 240000(28): 240-7; KRASNYI VOENNYI FLOT:

121-9.

⌊At 5th All-Russian Congress of Komsomol.⌋

[221017]   Tov. Trotskii privetstvuet shefa Krasnogo Flota. (Cde. Trotsky greets

chief of Red Fleet.) (<u>Pr</u>, (234), 17.X.22)

[cf. ⌊221029⌋.]

221020   Pyataya godovshchina oktyabr'skoi revolyutsii i IV Kongress Kominterna.

(The 5th anniversary of the October Revolution and the 4th Comintern

Congress.) (<u>Pr</u>, (238), 21.X.22)

<u>Repr</u>.: *220000(9); p.q. 240000(6): 143-4; p.q. 240000(28): 16-7,77;

240000(29): 429-57; PYAT LET: 11-8.   ++++

221020   ++++   Trans.: Am-Eng. 530700: 185-216;
                          Cz. p.q. <u>Rude Pravo</u>, (III.256,257), 2,3.XI.22;
                          Eng. <u>Inprecor</u>, (II.95,110), 1922; p.q. Degras, DOCCI.I: 316,417;
                          Fr. p.q. <u>BulCom</u>, (III.45), 9.XI.22;
                          Ger. p.q. <u>Jug-Int</u>, (IV.6), II.23.

221021   Interview.
                  <u>Trans</u>.: Eng. <u>ManGuard</u>, 23.X.22;
                          Hol. <u>Tribune</u>, (139), 15.III.23.
                  [With Arthur Ransome; on world affairs.]

221024(1)   Prikaz, No. 273. (<u>Iz</u>, (243), 27.X.22; <u>Pr</u>, (243), 27.X.22)
                  <u>Repr</u>.: 230000(7).III.i: 183; 240000(28): 119.
                  [Military training of 1901 class completed.]

221024(2)   Prikaz, No. 274. (<u>Iz</u>, (242), 26.X.22; <u>PetPr</u>, (243), 27.X.22)
                  <u>Repr</u>.: 230000(7).III.i: 184.
                  [The occupation of Vladivostok.]

221025   Pronitsal´nyi glaz. (A penetrating eye.) (270000(2): 247-50)
                  [Archives.]

221028   Zum zweiten Auflage: Pref. ZWISCHEN IMPERIALISMUS UND REVOLUTION, in
                  230000(28): 227-8.
                  [Trans. Ger.]

[221029]   Telegramma. (A telegram.) (<u>Iz</u>, (245), 29.X.22)
                  <u>Repr</u>.: 230000(7).III.i: 185.
                  [To Revolutionary Military Soviet of Black Sea Fleet. cf. [221017].]

221031   Interv´yu. (An interview.) (<u>Iz</u>, (253), 9.XI.22; <u>Pr</u>, (253), 9.XI.22;
                  <u>Trud</u>, (252), 9.XI.22)
                  <u>Repr</u>.: 230000(7).III.ii: 70-2.
                  <u>Trans</u>.: Eng. <u>ManGuard</u>, 1.III.23; Degras, SOVDOC.I: 375.
                  [With M.S.Farbman.]

221100(1)   [Interview with Bedacht, Cannon and Eastman.]
                  [c. Draper; ROOTS: 384.]

[221100(2)]   i dr.: K proektu programmy ital´yanskoi Kommunisticheskoi Partii. (A draft
                  programme of CPItaly.) (KI, (23), 1922)

[221100(3)]   i dr.: S"ezdu frantsuzskoi Kommunisticheskoi Partii. (To the Congress
                  of CPFrance.) (<u>KI</u>, (23), 1922)

221101   Interview.

Trans.: Eng. Observer, 5.XI.22; p.q. Degras, SOVDOC.I: 345.

[On Lausanne Conference.]

221102(1)   Prikaz, No. 275. (Iz, (253), 9.XI.22; Krasnaya Gazeta, (255), 10.XI.22)

Repr.: 230000(7).III.i: 186.

[Fight against illiteracy.]

221102(2)   Alternative for 221103(1).

221103(1)   "Protivorechiya" sovetskoi politiki. ("Contradictions" of Soviet

policy.) (Iz, (250), 4.XI.22)

Repr.: 230000(8): 297-304; p.q. 240000(6): 144.

Trans.: Eng. ComReview, XII.22; Inprecor, (II.101). 21.XI.22;

         Fr. 670306: 207-13; BulCom, (III.48), 30.XI.22; Lutte desC,(14),

            30.XI.22; Vie Ouv, 24.XI.22;

         Ger. Inprekor, (II.220), 18.XI.22; RusKor, (III.ii.7-10,11-12),

            VII-X, XI-XII.22.

[221103(2)]   Otvet. (A reply.) (Krasnaya Gazeta, (250), 3.XI.22; Trud, (248),

3.XI.22)

[To greetings to Red Army from International Conference of Communist

Co-operatives.]

221105   Pis'mo. (A letter.) (Pr, (253), 9.XI.22)

Trans.: Eng. Bulletin 4th Congress CI, (1), 16.XI.22;

         Ger. Bulletin des IV. Kongresses, (1-2), 11.XI.22; Inprekor,

            (II.223), 23.XI.22.

[To Petrograd Soviet. Also described as telegram.]

221107   Rech. (A speech.) (Iz, (253), 9.XI.22; Pr, (253), 9.XI.22)

Repr.: 240000(29): 458-60.

Trans.: Am-Eng. 530700: 217-9.

[At parade in Red Square; in honour of Comintern.]

221113   Rezolyutsiya. (A resolution.) (IV Vsemirnyi Kongress KI: 411-2)

Trans.: Am. p.q. FI, VIII.45;

         Fr. THÈSES: 167-9.

[On Versailles Treaty; at Comintern Congress.]

221114(1)   Novaya ekonomicheskaya politika Sovetskoi Rossii i perspektivy
mirovoi revolyutsii. (The new economic policy of Soviet Russia and the
perspectives of world revolution.) (Iz, (259), 16.XI.22; Krasnaya
Gazeta, (260), 16.XI.22; Pr, (259), 16.XI.22; Trud, (258), 16.XI.22)

     Repr.: *220000(39); 230000(11); 230000(18): 337-87; p.q. 240000(6):
         145-6; 240000(29): 460-500; 250000(8): 301-45; IV KONGRESS:
         74-111.

     Trans.: Am-Eng. 530700: 220-63;
         Eng. Bulletin of 4th Congress, (10), 18.XI.22; p.q. The Com,
            (124), 16.XII.22;
         Cz. *250000(35);
         Fr. 230000(32); p.q. BulCom, (IV.16), 19.IV.23; p.q. Huma,
            23.XI.22; p.q. Vie Ouv, 11.V.23;
         Ger. 230000(27); 230000(28); 230000(31); ⌊670000(3)⌋;
            Bulletin des IV. Kongresses, (10), 17.XI.22; RusKor,
            (III.ii.7-10), VII-X.22; PROTOKOLL: 268-95;
         Sp. Antorcha, (III.59-63), 12.I-9.II.23; p.q. Batalla, (I.11),
            8.III.23.

     ⌊Report to 4th Congress Comintern. See 230000(11) for notes.⌋

221114(2)   Rech. (A speech.) (PetPr, (258), 16.XI.22)
     Trans.: Eng. The Com, (125), 23.XII.22.
     ⌊In reply to discussion on 221112(1).⌋

221115   Popravka k proektu takticheskoi rezolyutsii 4-go Kongressa Kominterna.
(Correction to draft resolution on tactics of 4th Congress Comintern.)
(240000(6): 144-5)

221121   & others: ⌊Statement of Russian delegation to 4th Congress Comintern.⌋
     Trans.: Cz. Rude Pravo, (290), 12.XII.22;
         Eng. Bulletin 4th Congress, (18), 28.XI.22;
         Ger. Inprekor, (II.230), 7.XII.22.

221125   Kommunizm i ... frank-masonstvo. (Communism and ... freemasonry.)
(Iz, (269), 28.XI.22; Bol, 1922)
     Repr.: 230000(8): 317-21.
     Trans.: Eng. p.q. Inprecor, (II.115), 19.XII.22;
         Fr. CorInt, 9.XII.22; Drapeau Rouge, 30.XII.22; Huma, 24.XII.22;
            Lutte deC, (6), IV.64; QI, (16), IV.39.
     ⌊On CPFrance.⌋

[221130(1)]   Politicheskie perspektivy. (Political prospects.) (Iz, (271),
               30.XI.22)
               Repr.: p.q. 240000(6): 75-6/146-7; p.q. 240520.
               Trans.: Am. p.q. 451000: 9-10.

[221130(2)]   Politicheskie perspektivy. (Political prospects.)
               Russian: 230000(11); 230000(18): 388-95; 240000(29): 531-7.
               Trans.: Am-Eng. 530700: 297-303;
                       Eng. Bolschewik, (20), 30.XI.22;
                       Fr. 230000(32); Bolschewik, (20), 30.XI.22;
                       Ger. Bolschewik, (20), 30.XI.22.

221130(3)   See 221205.

221200(1)   [Third refusal to accept post of Deputy Premier.] (300000(1): Ch.XXXIX)

221200(2)   u.a.: Aufruf der KI an das italienische Proletariat.
               Trans.: Ger. Inprekor, (II.241), 21.XII.22.

221201(1)   Khozyaistvennoe sostoyanie sovetskoi Rossii s tochki zreniya
               sotsialisticheskoi revolyutsii. (The economic situation of Soviet Russia
               from the standpoint of socialist revolution.) (Pr, (276), 6.XII.22)
               Repr.: 230000(18): 396-408; 240000(29): 500-10; 250000(8): 346-56.
               Trans.: Am-Eng. 530700: 264-75;
                       Cz..p.q..Rude Pravo, (IV.88), 17.IV.23;
                       Eng. p.q. Inprecor, (III.3), 9.I.23;
                       Fr. BulCom, (IV.4), 25.I.23; p.q. CorInt, (III.1), 15.I.23;
                       Ger. 230000(27): 457-71; 230000(28): 457-71; [670000(3)]:
                            457-71; p.q. Inprekor, (II.237,241), 16,21.XII.22;
                            RusKor, (III.ii.11-12), XI-XII.22.
               [Theses to 4th Congress Comintern.]

221201(2)   FKP na IV Kongresse Kominterna. (The CPFrance at the 4th Congress of
               the Comintern.) (Iz, (274), 3.XII.22; PetPr, (273,274), 3,5.XII.22;
               Pr, (275), 5.XII.22; Trud, (272), 2.XII.22)
               Repr.: 230000(8): 321-62; IV Vsemirnyi Kongreee KI, 1922: 317-54.
               Trans.: Cz. p.q. Rude Pravo, (III.290), 12.XII.22;
                       Eng. Bulletin 4th Congress CI, (28), 8.XII.22;
                       Fr. 670306: 220-60; BulCom, (IV.2-3), 18.I.23; p.q. CorInt,
                            (III.1), 15.I.23;
                       Ger. p.q. Inprekor, (II.237), 16.XII.22; PROTOKOLL: 838-73.
               [Report of Fr. Commission.]

221202(1)   Zaklyuchitel'noe slovo. (Summary speech.) (<u>Iz</u>, (274), 3.XII.22; <u>Trud</u>, (273), 3.XII.22)

                <u>Repr</u>.: <u>IV Vsemirnyi Kongress KI</u>, 1922: 354-6.

                <u>Trans</u>.: Eng. <u>Bulletin 4th Congress CI</u>, (29), 8.XII.22;

                        Ger. PROTOKOLL: 878-80.

                [See 221201(2).]

221202(2)   Rezolyutsiya. (A resolution.) (230000(8): 363-72)

                <u>Repr</u>.: 240000(29): 510-9.

                <u>Trans</u>.: Am-Eng. 530700: 275-84;

                        Eng. p.q. Degras, DOCCI.I: 403-5.

                [See 221201(2).]

221202(3)   Rezolyutsiya. (A resolution.) (<u>Pr</u>, (275), 5.XII.22)

                <u>Repr</u>.: 230000(8): 378-81; 240000(29): 525-8.

                <u>Trans</u>.: Am-Eng. 530700: 291-4.

                [See 221201(2).]

221205   Rabochaya i boevaya programma frantsuzskoi Kommunisticheskoi Partii. (A workers and militant programme for CPFrance.)

                Russian: 230000(8): 372-8; 240000(29): 519-25.

                <u>Trans</u>.: Am-Eng. 530700: 285-90;

                        Fr. 670306: 214-7; <u>BulCom</u>, (IV.7), 15.II.23;

                        Hol. p.q. <u>Tribune</u>, (68), 19.XII.22.

                [Date of adoption.]

221207   Rech. (A speech.) (<u>Iz</u>, (278), 8.XII.22)

                <u>Repr</u>.: 230000(7).III.ii: 73-81; <u>Krasnye Zori</u>, (1), I.23.

                [At celebration meeting at Military Academy; on 4th anniversary of Academy.]

221212   [Reply to Lenin.]

                [c. 271021. On monopoly. T764.]

[221218]   Krest'yanskii molodnyak pod ruzhem. (The peasant youth under arms.) (<u>Pr</u>, (286,287), 17,20.XII.22)

                <u>Repr</u>.: p.q. 240000(8): 107-9.

                [Speech at conference of Institutes of Higher Learning.]

221220(1)   Pref. NOVAYA EKONOMICHESKAYA POLITIKA SOVETSKOI ROSSII I PERSPEKTIVY MIROVOI REVOLYUTSII (THE NEW ECONOMIC POLICY OF SOVIET RUSSIA AND THE PROSPECTS OF WORLD REVOLUTION), 230000(11). ++++

221220(1) ++++ Repr.: 230000(18): 335; 250000(8): 299.

Trans.: Ger. 230000(27): vii-viii; 230000(28): vii-viii; [670000(3)]:
vii-viii.

[See 221114(1) for other trans., notes.]

221221 Prikaz, No. 2846. (Iz, (6), 16.I.23; PetPr, (8), 12.I.23)
Repr.: 230000(7).III.i: 187.
[On Navy.]

221222 Prikaz, No. 2848. (Pr, (292), 24.XII.22)
Repr.: 230000(7).III.i: 188-9.

221225 Privetsvie. (A greeting.) (Iz(NKSO), (50), 25.XII.22)
[To National Commissariat of Social Security for help to Red Army
invalids.]

221227 [Correspondence with Lenin, begun 10.XII.22.]
[c. Deutscher, PU: 67. T764.]

221228 Doklad. (A report.) (Iz, (296), 29.XII.22; Trud, (295), 29.XII.22)
Repr.: *[220000(16)]; p.q. 240000(28): 13-5; 240000(29): 537-63;
p.q. 260000(7): 89-90.
Trans.: Am. FI, VIII,IX.43;
Am-Eng. 530700: 304-33;
Fr. p.q. 260000(22): 111-4.
[To communist fraction of 10th Soviet Congress with non-Party delegates
attending. See 260000(7) for other p.q. trans.]

*230000(1)   *AVIATSIYA — ORUDIE BUDUSHCHEGO. (AVIATION, WEAPON OF THE FUTURE.)
[See 230530 for all repr.]

230000(2)   ‡ VOINA I REVOLYUTSIYA. (WAR AND REVOLUTION.)
[2nd ed. See 220000(3) for all repr. Pref. 230616(1). Omits some items.]

230000(3)   § VOPROSY BYTA. (PROBLEMS OF LIFE.)
Repr.: 230000(4); 250000(1); 270000(2): 3-43.
Trans.: Am. 240000(28);
        Eng. 240000(29); 621100(1);
        Ger. 230000(26);
        Jap. *250710; 250720; *251028; 270901.
[Pref. 1st ed. 230704; Letter 230717; Pref. 2nd ed. 230909. Contents of repr. and trans. vary. Supplement (Questions and Answers) in Rabochaya Moskva, (166-78), 28.VII-12.VIII.23)

230000(4)   ‡ VOPROSY BYTA. (PROBLEMS OF LIFE.)
[2nd enlarged ed. See 230000(3) for all repr., trans., notes.]

230000(5)   § ZADACHI XII S"EZDA RKP. (TASKS OF 12th CONGRESS CPR.)
[See 230405(3) for all repr., trans., notes.]

230000(6)   ZADACHI KOMMUNISTICHESKOGO VOSPITANIYA. (TASKS OF COMMUNIST EDUCATION.)
[See 230618 for all repr., trans., notes.]

230000(7)   ‡ KAK VOORUZHALAS REVOLYUTSIYA. (HOW THE REVOLUTION WAS ARMED.)
Trans.: Fr. p.q. 680000(1);
        Ger. p.q. 240000(40); p.q. *240000(41).
[3 vols. in 5 parts. Pref. Vol. I 230227; Pref. Vol. II 240108; Pref. Vol. III.ii 241015(1). Fr. 680000(1) trans. Vols. I, II.i.]

230000(8)   ‡ KOMMUNISTICHESKOE DVIZHENIE VO FRANTSII. (THE COMMUNIST MOVEMENT IN FRANCE.)
[Pref. 230325.]

230000(9)   ‡ LITERATURA I REVOLYUTSIYA. (LITERATURE AND REVOLUTION.)
Repr.: 240000(18); p.q.
Trans.: Am. 250000(22); 570900(2); 600000(5); 680000(10);
        Ch. *[300000(31)];
        Fr. 640911; p.q. Clarté, (II.46), 1.XI.23; p.q. Huma, 1.IV.23;
           p.q. QI, (XI.5-7,8-10), VII, XI.53;   ++++

230000(9)   ++++ <u>Trans</u>.: Ger. p.q. 240000(44); 680800(2);
                            Gr. 660000(6);
                            It. p.q. 581000; p.q. 680000(6): 53-71;
                            Jap. 250720; *310601; 641225;
                            Sp. ⌊240000(45)⌋]; 640900(1); 690000(8) p.q. <u>Batalla</u>, (I.17),
                                4.V.23.
                    ⌊Dedication 230814; Pref. 230919; Pref. in 2nd ed. 240509; Pref. 2nd ed.
                    240709(2). Ger. 680800(2) and Jap. 641225 are the only complete trans.
                    Most Pref. in trans. are inaccurately dated, confusing 1st and 2nd ed.,
                    and are incomplete. Some trans. include additional material.⌋

*230000(10)   *NA POSTU. (TO YOUR POSTS.)
                  [Anniversary Journal of Kharkov militia.]

230000(11)   NOVAYA EKONOMICHESKIYA POLITIKA SOVETSKOI ROSSII I PERSPEKTIVY MIROVOI
                  REVOLYUTSII. (THE NEW ECONOMIC POLICY OF SOVIET RUSSIA AND THE
                  PROSPECTS OF WORLD REVOLUTION.)
                  ⌊See 221114(1) for all repr., trans., notes. Pref. 221220; ⌊231100(2)⌋.⌋

230000(12)   OSNOVNYE VOPROSY PROMYSHLENNOSTI. (FUNDAMENTAL PROBLEMS OF
                  PRODUCTION.)
                  ⌊See 230401(1) for all repr., trans., notes; 230425(1) Pref.⌋

*230000(13)   *OSNOVNYE VOPROSY PROMYSHLENNOSTI. (FUNDAMENTAL PROBLEMS OF
                  PRODUCTION.)
                  ⌊See 230401(1) for all repr., trans., notes; 230425(1) Pref.⌋

*230000(14)   *OSNOVNYE VOPROSY PROMYSHLENNOSTI. (FUNDAMENTAL PROBLEMS OF
                  PRODUCTION.)
                  ⌊See 230401(1) for all repr., trans., notes; 230425(1) Pref.⌋

*230000(15)   *OSNOVNYE VOPROSY PROMYSHLENNOSTI. (FUNDAMENTAL PROBLEMS OF
                  PRODUCTION.)
                  ⌊See 230401(1) for all repr., trans., notes; 230425(1) Pref.⌋

*230000(16)   *OSNOVNYE VOPROSY PROMYSHLENNOSTI. (FUNDAMENTAL PROBLEMS OF
                  PRODUCTION.)
                  ⌊See 230401(1) for all repr., trans., notes; 230425(1) Pref.⌋

*230000(17)   *OSNOVNYE VOPROSY PROMYSHLENNOSTI. (FUNDAMENTAL PROBLEMS OF
                  PRODUCTION.)
                  ⌊See 230401(1) for all repr., trans., notes; 230425(1) Pref.⌋

230000(18)   § OSNOVNYE VOPROSY REVOLYUTSII. (FUNDAMENTAL PROBLEMS OF REVOLUTION.)

Repr.: 250000(8).

Trans.: Cz. *250000(35);

        Ger. 230000(27); 230000(28); [670000(3)].

[Pref. 230504(1). 250000(8) varies in appendices only. Details of trans. at 250000(8).]

230000(19)   i Kabakchiev: † OCHERKI POLITICHESKOI BULGARII. (POLITICAL SKETCHES OF BULGARIA.)

[Pref. 230319(1); PS 230619.]

230000(20)   i Rakovskii: † OCHERKI POLITICHESKOI RUMYNII. (POLITICAL SKETCHES OF RUMANIA.)

[2nd ed. See 220000(8) for all repr. Pref. 230430(1).]

*230000(21)   *PERSPEKTIVY I ZADACHI VOENNOGO STROITEL'STVA. (PROSPECTS AND TASKS OF MILITARY CONSTRUCTION.)

[See 230210 for all repr., trans.]

*230000(22)   i dr.: *CHTO NUZHNO ZNAT O GERMANSKOI REVOLYUTSII. (WHAT MUST BE KNOWN ABOUT THE GERMAN REVOLUTION.)

[Co-authors Zinoviev and Larin.]

*[230000(23)]   * ARMIYA BUDUSHCHEGO. (THE ARMY OF THE FUTURE.)

[? 230530.]

*[230000(24)]   i Rakovskii: *PERSPEKTIVI I ZAVDANNYA NOVOGO ETANU. (PROSPECTS AND TASKS OF THE NEW STAGE.)

[Trans. Ukr. To 7th All-Ukrainian Conference CPUkraine.]

230000(25)   ARBETARKLASSEN OCH VÄRLDSLÄGET. (DEN NYA ATAPPEN.)

[Trans. Swed. See 210000(7) for all trans.]

230000(26)   § FRAGEN DES ALLTAGSLEBENS.

[Trans. Ger. See 230000(3) for all trans., notes.]

230000(27)   § DIE GRUNDFRAGEN DER REVOLUTION.

[Trans. Ger. See 230000(18) for all repr., trans., notes.]

230000(28)   § DIE GRUNDFRAGEN DER REVOLUTION.

[Trans. Ger. See 221028 Pref.; 230000(18) for all repr., trans., notes.]

230000(29)   § 1905.

[Trans. Fr. See 220000(12) for all repr., trans., notes.]

230000(30)   MY FLIGHT FROM SIBERIA.
               [Trans. Am. See 070000(3) for all repr., trans., notes.]

230000(31)   DIE NEUE ÖKONOMISCHE POLITIK SOWJETRUSSLANDS UND DIE WELTREVOLUTION.
               [Trans. Ger. See 221114(1) for all repr., trans., notes.]

230000(32)   LA NOUVELLE POLITIQUE ÉCONOMIQUE DES SOVIETS ET LA RÉVOLUTION MONDIALE.
               [Trans. Fr. See 221114(1) for all trans., notes.]

230000(33)   DIE RUSSISCHE REVOLUTION 1905.
               [Trans. Ger. See 220000(12) for all trans., notes.]

230000(35)   TERRORISMUS UN KOMMUNISMUS. ANTI-KAUTSKY.
               [Trans. Ger. See 200000(37) for all repr., trans., notes. 3rd ed.]

230000(36)   ZWISCHEN IMPERIALISMUS UND REVOLUTION.
               [Trans. Ger. See 220000(5) for all repr., trans., notes; 221028 Pref.
               2nd ed. in 230000(28): 227-8.]

230000(37)   [Talk with Nansen.]
               Trans.: Eng. p.q. Carr, BR.III: 371.

230000(39)   Pis'mo. (A letter.) (KRASNYI VOENNYI FLOT, 1923)
               [To Presidium 2nd All-Russian Communist Sailors Conference.]

*230000(40)   *ZADACHI XII S"EZD RKP. (TASKS OF 12th CONGRESS CPR.)
               [See 230405(3) for all repr., trans., notes.]

230000(41)   i Stalin: MILLIYET MESSELESI TURINDA.
               [Trans. Tatar. See 230419 for all notes.]

*230000(42)   *OT OKTYABR'SKOI REVOLYUTSII DO BRESTSKOGO MIRA. (FROM THE OCTOBER
               REVOLUTION TO THE PEACE OF BREST.)
               [See 180000(5) for all repr., trans., notes.]

[230101]   Novgodnei pozhelanie yaponskomu narodu. (New Year wishes to the
               Japanese people.) (Pr, (1), 3.I.23)
               Trans.: Am. p.q. NYTimes, 2.I.23.

230106   Prikaz, No. 59. (230000(7).III.i: 190)

230115   [Letter to Politbureau.]
               [On Stalin's letter on planning. c. Deutscher, PU: 49. T773.]

230120   [Letter to Politbureau.]
           [On planning. c. Deutscher, PU: 49. T774. See 210807, 220823.]

[230121]   Interview.
           Trans.: Am. NYTimes, 21.I.23.
           [With Savel Zeinand; on Red Army.]

230125   [Letter to CC.]
           Trans.: Eng. p.q. Carr, BR.II: 380.
           [On Gosplan. T775.]

230127(1)   Predislovie k knige A.L.Strong. (Pref. to A.L.Strong's book.) (Iz, (19),
           28.I.25)
           Trans.: Eng. Strong, THE FIRST TIME IN HISTORY;
                     Fr. BulCom, (IV.9), 1.III.23; CorInt, (III.6), 16.II.23;
                     Ger. Inprekor, (III.30), 16.II.23.
           [On NEP.]

230127(2)   & others: [On the split in the leadership of CPR.] (p.q. 250701)

230129   [Annotations to discussion in Orgburo.]
           [c. Carr, SinOC.II: 198. Harvard Archives.]

230200   [Conversation with Lenin.]
           Trans.: 410000(1): Ch. XII.
           [On forthcoming 12th Congress CPR.]

230205(1)   Polk imeni germanskogo proletariata. Prikaz, No. 277. (The "German
           Proletariat" Regiment.) (Iz, (26), 6.II.23; PetPr, (27), 6.II.23)

230205(2)   Prikaz, No. 279. (Iz, (41), 23.II.23; PetPr, (42), 23.II.23; Pr, (41),
           23.II.23)
           Repr.: 230000(7).III.ii: 3-6.
           Trans.: Eng. Inprecor, (III.20), 27.II.23;
                     Ger. Inprekor, (III.33), 21.II.23.
           [On 5th anniversary of Red Army.]

230210   Pered vtorym pyatiletiem Krasnoi Armii. (Before the second five-years
           of the Red Army.) (Iz, (34), 15.II.23; PetPr, (35), 15.II.23; Pr, (34),
           15.II.23; Rabochaya Moskva, (34), 15.II.23)
           Repr.: 230000(7).III.ii: 7-9; *230000(21); p.q. 240000(28): 110-1.
           Trans.: Cz. Rude Pravo, (IV.43,44), 22,23.II.23;

                                                       ++++

230210   ++++   Trans.: Eng. p.q. Inprecor, (III.20), 27.II.23;

                  Fr. BulCom, (IV.11), 15.III.23; p.q. CorInt, (III.8), 2.III.23.

230213   [Note to Politbureau.]

                 [On enlarged credits. c. Carr, INTER: 15. T778, T2962.]

[230215]   Otvety tovarishchu Klod Makkei. (Replies to cde. Claude McKay.)

                 (Iz, (34), 15.II.23; Pr, (34), 15.II.23)

                 Trans.: Am. p.q. 670600: 58; p.q. 690400(2): 58; p.q. 700800: 58;

                       SocAp, 20.IX.39;

                   Am-Eng. 530700: 354-6;

                   Eng. Inprecor, 13.III.23;

                   Fr. BulCom, (IV.11), 15.III.23; CorInt, (III.9), 9.III.23;

                   Ger. Inprekor, (III.38), 28.II.23;

                   Jap. p.q. 681010: 107-8;

                   Sp. Antorcha, (III.85), 13.VII.23.

                 [On negro question.]

230218   Eshche o zadachakh voennogo stroitel'stva. (Again on the tasks of

                 military construction.) (Iz, (38), 20.II.23; PetPr, (39), 28.II.23;

                 Pr, (38), 20.II.23; Trud, (41), 23.II.23)

                 Repr.: 230000(7).III.ii: 10-12.

                 [See 230210.]

230221(1)   [Discussion on Lenin's illness.]

                 Trans.: 410000(1): Ch. XII.

                 [At Politbureau.]

[230221(2)]   Kommunisticheskaya ucheba prezhde vsego. (Communist education before

                 all else.) (Rabochaya Moskva, (39), 21.II.23)

230223(1)   [Letter to Politbureau.]

                 Trans.: Eng. p.q. Deutscher, PU: 89.

                 [On reorganization of CC. T2963.]

[230223(2)]   i dr.: Prikaz. (Rabochaya Moskva, (41), 23.II.23)

[230223(3)]   Prikaz pod Kazan'yu. (Order issued in the neighbourhood of Kazan.)

                 (Rabochaya Moskva, (41), 23.II.23)

[230223(4)]   Prikaz. Gotov'sya Petrograd! (Order. Get ready, Petrograd!)

                 (Rabochaya Moskva, (41), 23.II.23)

230227   Pref. KAK VOORUZHALAS REVOLYUTSIYA (HOW THE REVOLUTION WAS ARMED),
          230000(7).I. (PetPr, (50), 4.III.23; Pr, (48), 3.III.23)
          Trans.: Fr. 680000(1): 25-9.

230304   Vozhdushnyi flot — v poryadke dnya. (An Air Force is on the order
          of the day.) (Iz, (50), 6.III.23; PetPr, (51), 6.III.23; Pr, (50),
          6.III.23; Rabochaya Moskva, (50), 6.III.23)
          Repr.: 230000(7).III.ii: 181-4; p.q. 240000(28): 121-2.

230306(1) Tezisy o promyshlennosti. (Theses on industry.) (Pr, (78), 11.IV.23;
          Rabochaya Moskva, (78,79), 12,13.IV.23)
          Repr.: PROTOKOLY(1968): 810-5.
          Trans.: Eng. [560000(6)]; Labour Monthly, VII,VIII.23;
                  Fr. p.q. BulCom, (IV.18), 3.V.23.
          [T2964.]

230306(2) Pis'mo. (A letter.) (SotsV, (23-24), 17.XII.23)
          [To CC, enclosing letter and art. on national question received from
          Lenin's secretary.]

230307   [Conversation with Lenin's secretaries.] (p.q. 300000(1): Ch. XXXIX)

230313   Mysli o partii. (Thoughts about the Party.) (Pr, (56), 14.III.23)
          Repr.: 240000(28): 20-8.
          Trans.: Fr. BulCom, (IV.50), 13.XII.23;
                  Sp. ∅ Antorcha, (IV.115,118), 8,29.II.24.
          [See also 230319(2), 230430(2). For anniversary of CPR. On youth.]

230319(1) Pref. i Kabakchiev: OCHERKI POLITICHESKOI BULGARII (POLITICAL SKETCHES
          OF BULGARIA), 230000(19).
          [PS 230619.]

230319(2) Mysli o partii. (Thoughts about the Party.) (Pr, (61), 20.III.23)
          Repr.: 240000(28): 28-37.
          Trans.: Fr. BulCom, (IV.50), 13.XII.23.
          [See 230313 for series. On youth and the national question.]

230321   Neobkhodimoe ob"eyasnenie s sindikalistami-kommunistami. (A necessary
          discussion with syndicalist-communists.) (PetPr, (65,66), 23,24.III.23;
          Pr, (64), 23.III.23)
          Repr.: 230000(8): 285-92.

++++

230321   ++++   <u>Trans</u>.: Am. 310300(1): 9–18; 690000(13): 6–12;

        Eng. [380000(21)]; 680300(2): 19–29; <u>Inprecor</u>, (III.35),

          3.V.23;

        Fr. 670306: 261–8; <u>BulCom</u>, (IV.15), 12.IV.23; <u>CorInt</u>, (III.13,14),

          7,13.IV.23;

        Ger. <u>Inprekor</u>, (III.66,67), 20,23.IV.23.

    [On CPFrance.]

230323   Alternative for 230321.

230325   <u>Pref</u>. KOMMUNISTICHESKOE DVIZHENIE VO FRANTSII (THE COMMUNIST MOVEMENT

    IN FRANCE), 230000(8). (<u>Pr</u>, (67), 27.III.23)

    <u>Repr</u>.: 240000(29): 563–9.

    <u>Trans</u>.: Am-Eng. 530700: 334–40;

        Eng. p.q. <u>Inprecor</u>, (III.23), 19.IV.23;

        Fr. 670306: 269–75; <u>BulCom</u>, (IV.40), 4.X.23; p.q. <u>CorInt</u>,

          (III.14,15), 13,20.IV.23.

*230328   *[Letter to Party Secretariat.]

    |Challenging accuracy of Minutes. c. Daniels: 472 n.42. T792.|

230403   Vnimatel'nost i vezhlivost, kak neobkhodimaya smazka bytovykh

    otnoshenii. (Civility and politeness as a necessary lubricant in

    daily relations.) (<u>Pr</u>, (74), 4.IV.23)

    <u>Repr</u>.: 230000(3); 230000(4): 62–6; 240000(28): 146–9; 250000(1): 64–9;

        270000(2): 60–4.

    <u>Trans</u>.: Am. 240000(48): 68–77;

        Eng. 240000(49): 68–77; 621100(1): 33–6;

        Fr. <u>CorInt</u>, (III.15), 20.IV.23;

        Jap. 250720: 53–8; 270901: 85–95.

230405(1)   Otvet delegatsii bespartiinykh rabochikh. (Reply to non-Party workers

    delegates.) (240000(28): 67–70)

    <u>Trans</u>.: Cz. <u>Rude Pravo</u>, (106), 9.V.23;

        Eng. p.q. <u>CI</u>, (25), 1923.

    [Address of welcome to 7th All-Ukrainian Conference CPUkraine. Eng.

    trans. in article by E.Yaroslavsky.]

230405(2)   O bol'nom. (The wounded [Lenin].) (240000(24): 159–66)

    [p.q. of 230405(3). For trans. see 240000(24). f.n. in Eng. trans.

    inaccurate.]

230405(3) Zadachi XII s"ezda RKP. (Tasks of 12th Congress CPR.) (Pr, (78,79),
11,12.IV.23)
Repr.: 230000(5); *230000(40).
Trans.: Fr. CorInt, (III.15,16), 20,27.IV.23;
Ger. p.q. Inprekor, (III.69), 23.IV.23;
Gr. 660000(9);
Ukr. p.q. RobVis, (III.9), 15.XII.35.
[Speech to conference CPUkraine. See 230405(2) note.]

230412 Privet konferentsii VVUZ. (Greetings to conference of Institutes of
Higher Learning.) (Iz, (79), 12.IV.23)

230416 Alternative for 230417.

230417 [Letter to CC.]
Trans.: 410000(1): Ch. XI;
Am. NYTimes, 1.VII.56;
Eng. MOSCOW TRIALS: 51.
[Not in all trans. of 410000(1). T795, T795.]

230418 [Letter to Stalin.]
Trans.: 410000(1): Ch. XI.
[Re 230417. T796.]

230419 i Stalin: MILLIYET MESSELESI TURINDA, 230000(41).
[Trans. Tat. Theses on the national question, adopted by 12th Congress
CPR. T. on pages 16-29.]

230420(1) Doklad o promyshlennosti. (Report on production.) (EkZhizn, (88-90),
22-25.IV.23; Pr, (88), 22.IV.23; Rabochaya Moskva, (86), 21.IV.23;
Trud, (87), 22.IV.23)
Repr.: 230000(12); *230000(13-17); PROTOKOLY: 282-322; PROTOKOLY(1968):
309-52; p.q. Levin i Yurgens:211-5.
Trans.: Fr. p.q. BulCom, (IV.19), 10.V.23; p.q. CorInt, (III.17),
5.V.23.
[See 230425(1). To 12th Congress CPR. For interventions in debate
see PROTOKOLY.]

230420(2) [At Politbureau.]
[c. 410000(1): Ch. XI. On Lenin's request for poison.]

230421   Zaklyuchitel'noe slovo. (Summary speech.) (EkZhizn, (90), 25.IV.23;
            Pr, (89), 24.IV.23; Rabochaya Moskva, (87), 22.IV.23)
            Repr.: PROTOKOLY: 365-83; PROTOKOLY(1968): 398-417.
            [See 230420(1).]

230422(1)   Prikaz, No. 278. (230000(7).III.i: 191-2)

230422(2)   Prikaz, No. 279. (Pr, (89), 24.IV.23)
            Repr.: 230000(7).III.i: 193.

230425(1)   Pref. OSNOVNYE VOPROSY PROMYSHLENNOSTI (FUNDAMENTAL PROBLEMS OF
            PRODUCTION), 230000(12).
            Repr.: p.q. 240000(22): 85-6.

[230425(2)] Pis'mo. (A letter.) (Iz, (9o), 25.IV.23; Pr, (90), 25.IV.23)
            Repr.: 230000(7).III.i: 194.
            [To 2nd All-Russian Conference of Communists in the Navy.]

230425(3)   Rech. (A speech.) (PROTOKOLY(1968): 628-35)

230426   Rech. (A speech.) (230000(7).III.ii: 185-90)
            [At meeting of Friends of the Air Force.]

230427   [Attack on Bogdanov.]
            [c. Carr, INTER: 27. cf. XII S"EZD RKP: 370-2.]

230430(1)   Pref. i Rakovskii: OCHERKI POLITICHESKOI RUMYNII (POLITICAL SKETCHES OF
            RUMANIA), 230000(20).
            [2nd ed.]

230430(2)   Mysli o partii. (Thoughts about the Party.) (PetPr, (95-7), 1-4.V.23;
            Pr, (95), 1.V.23)
            Repr.: 240000(28): 37-47; 270000(2): 317-26.
            Trans.: Am. ISR, Summer, 1958.
            [See 230313 for series.]

230501   Rech. (A speech.) (Iz, (96), 3.V.23; Pr, (96), 3.V.23)
            Repr.: 230000(7).III.ii: 82-4.
            [At parade in Red Square.]

230502   Pis'mo v redaktsiyu. (Letter to Editorial Board.) (EkZhizn, (97),
            4.V.23)
            Repr.: 230000(7).III.ii: 191.

230503(1)   Doklad. (A report.) (EkZhizn, (97), 4.V.23; Iz, (97), 4.V.23)
[To 4th State Conference of Textile Workers.]

230503(2)   Zaklyuchitel'noe slovo. (Summary speech.) (Iz, (97), 4.V.23)
[See 230503(1).]

[230503(3)]   Tverzhe, krepche i sil'nee! (Be harder, firmer and more strong!)
(Rabochaya Moskva, (94), 3.V.23)
[On the international political situation.]

230504(1)   Pref. OSNOVNYE VOPROSY REVOLYUTSII (FUNDAMENTAL PROBLEMS OF REVOLUTION),
230000(18). (Pr, (99), 6.V.23)
Repr.:   240000(28): 81-5; 250000(8): 1-6.
Trans.: Eng. p.q. Inprecor, (III.64), 4.X.23;
        Ger. 230000(27); 230000(28); [670000(3)]; p.q. Inprekor,
           (III.145), 12.IX.23.
[PS 241020.]

230508   Eshche raz ob anarkho-sindikalistskikh predrassudkakh. (Once again on
the anarcho-syndicalist prejudices.) (Pr, (103), 11.V.23)
Trans.: Am. 310300(1): 19-22; 690000(13): 12-5;
        Eng. 680800(2): 30-4; Inprecor, (III.43), 14.VI.23;
        Fr. CorInt, (III.20), 29.V.23.
[Reply to Louzon; on French workers movement.]

230512(1)   Rech. (A speech.) (Iz, (105), 13.V.23; PetPr, (105), 13.V.23; Pr,
(105), 13.V.23; Rabochaya Moskva, (103,104), 13,15.V.23; Trud, (104),
13.V.23)
Repr.:   230000(7).III.ii: 85-7.
Trans.: Am. p.q. Eudin & Fisher: 166,187;
        Cz. p.q. Rude Pravo Večerna, (124), 2.VI.23;
        Eng. p.q. Glasgow Worker, 23.VI.23; Inprecor, (III.41), 7.VI.23;
           p.q. Workers Weekly, 23.VI.23;
        Ger. Inprekor, (III.87), 25.V.23/ 21,26.V.23.
[At Extraordinary Plenum Moscow Soviet; on Curzon ultimatum. Archives.]

[230512(2)]   O mezhdunarodnom polozhenii. (On the international situation.)
(Rabochaya Moskva, (102), 12.V.23)
[In reply to a letter sent him on 5.V.23.]

230515   Bor'ba za kul'turnost. (The struggle for culture.) (PetPr, (107),
16.V.23; Pr, (107), 16.V.23)

++++

230515   ++++   <u>Repr</u>.:   230000(3): 53-8; 230000(4): 67-72; 240000(8): 150-4; 250000(1):
         67-72; 270000(2): 26-31.

        <u>Trans</u>.: Am. 240000(48): 78-87; 640800: 300-4;

            Eng. 240000(49): 78-87; 621100(1): 37-40;

            Ger. 230000(26): 76-84;

            Hol. p.q. <u>Tribune</u>, (108), 6.II.24;

            It. 680200(2): 162-7;

            Jap. 250720: 58-64; 270901: 96-107; 681125: 312-8;

            Sp. 670000(5): 304-8;

            Swed. 691100(2): 270-4.

        [PS 240000(8): 153-4.]

[230516]   Divizii imeni Kikvidze. (The Kikvidze Division.) (<u>Iz</u>, (107), 16.V.23)
        <u>Repr</u>.: 230000(7).III.ii: 88.

230518   Perspektivy i zadachi voennogo stroitel´stva. (Prospects and tasks of
        military construction.) (<u>Pr</u>, (114), 25.V.23)
        <u>Repr</u>.: 230000(7).III.i: 142-53; *VOENNAYA MYSLI.II, 1923.

230526   Krasnaya Armiya — rassadnitsa prosv"eshcheniya. (The Red Army is a
        seed-bed of education.) (<u>Iz</u>, (116), 27.V.23; <u>Pr</u>, (116), 27.V.23;
        <u>Rabochaya Moskva</u>, (114), 27.V.23)
        <u>Repr</u>.: 230000(7).III.i: 195; 270000(2): 100-1.
        [Prikaz, No. 280.]

230529   Ne razbrasyvat´sya! (Don't try to do several things at once!)
        (<u>Pr</u>, (118), 31.V.23)
        <u>Repr</u>.: 240000(28): 97-8; 270000(2): 340-1.
        [Letter to Kiev cdes.]

230530   Orudie budushchego. (The weapon of the future.) (<u>Pr</u>, (121), 3.VI.23)
        <u>Repr</u>.: *230000(1); 230000(7).III.ii: 192-5; p.q. 240000(28): 122.
        [For forthcoming Air Week. ? [230000(23)].]

230601   Sotrudnikam i chitatelyam <u>Molodoi Gvardii</u>. (To contributors and
        readers of Molodaya Gvardiya.) (<u>Iz</u>, (123), 6.VI.23; <u>MolGvard</u>, (4-5),
        1923; <u>Pr</u>, (123), 6.VI.23)
        <u>Repr</u>.: 240000(28): 95-6; 270000(2): 213-5.

230605(1)   Iz doklada. (From a report.) (230000(7).III.ii: 89-95)
        <u>Trans</u>.: Eng. p.q. <u>Inprecor</u>, (III.48), 5.VII.23;
             Ger. p.q. <u>Inprekor</u>, (III.107), 27.VI.23.
        [To Moscow District Conference of Metal Workers. Archives.]

230605(2)   Aviatsiya i metallisty. (Aviation and metal-workers.) (230000(7).
              III.ii: 196-7)
              [From report to Moscow District Conference of Metal Workers. Archives.]

[230612]   Partiya i molodezh ostal´nykh narodov. (The Party and the youth of
              the rest of the people.) (p.q. 240000(28): 48-9)
              [From speech to CC CPR.]

230616(1)   Pref. VOINA I REVOLYUTSIYA (WAR AND REVOLUTION), 230000(2).
              [2nd ed.]

230616(2)   Letter to ARA, on its departure from Russia.
              Trans.: Am. p.q. NYTimes, 18.VI.23.

230616(3)   Doklad. (A report.) (Iz, (134), 19.VI.23; Pr, (136), 21.VI.23;
              Trud, (132), 17.VI.23)
              Repr.: 230000(7).III.ii: 96-105.
              [To All-Russian Congress of Metal Workers.]

230618   Zadachi kommunisticheskogo vospitaniya. (Tasks of communist education.)
              (Iz, (135), 20.VI.23; Pr, (139,140), 24,26.VI.23)
              Repr.: 230000(6); 240000(5); 240000(28): 50-63; 270000(2): 327-40.
              Trans.: Am. FI, VIII.44;
                      Eng. 621100(1): 52-5; ComReview, XI.23; Inprecor, (III.56),
                          16.VIII.23;
                      Fr. QI, VII-VIII.47;
                      Ger. Jug-Int, (IV.12), VIII.23;
                      Hol. Int(H), (XII.6-7), 1969; p.q. Tribune, (254), 2.VIII.23;
                      Heb. Ketuvim, 1923.
              [Speech on 5th anniversary of J.M.Sverdlov University.]

230619   PS 230319(1).

230621   O krivoi kapitalisticheskogo razvitiya. (The curve of capitalist
              development.) (Vestnik SotsAkad, (4-5), IV-VI.23)
              Repr.: 250000(8): 357-63.
              Trans.: Am. FI, V.41;
                      Eng. Perspectives, (52), V-VI.69; Workers' Republic, (20),
                          Winter, 1967-8;
                      Sp. Perspectiva Mundial, (24-25), I.68.
              [Letter in place of promised article.]

230625 Iz rechi. (From a speech.) (Pr, (140), 26.VI.23)

Repr.: 230000(7).III.ii: 106-13.

[At meeting of representatives of the Party, trade unions, Komsomol and other organizations in the Krasnaya Presnya District. Archives.]

230628 Kogda zhe nastupit peremena? (When will there be a change?) (Iz, (143), 29.VI.23; Pr, (143), 29.VI.23)

Repr.: 270000(2): 250-1.

[Question to Mospoligraf.]

230629(1) Gazeta i ee chitateli. (The newspaper and its readers.) (PetPr, (145), 1.VII.23; Pr, (145), 1.VII.23)

Repr.: 230000(3): 5-14; 230000(4): 18-28; 250000(1): 19-30; 270000(2): 171-80.

Trans.: Ger. 230000(26): 1-16.

230629(2) Rech. (A speech.) (Iz, (144), 30.VI.23; Rabochaya Moskva, (142), 30.VI.23)

[The need for an air force.]

230630 O svoevremennosti lozunga "Soedinennye shtaty Evropy". (The timeliness of the slogan "The United States of Europe.") (Pr, (144), 30.VI.23)

Repr.: 230000(18); 240000(29): 569-75; 250000(8): 367-72; 260000(7): 81-3.

Trans.: Am. FI, VII.42;

    Am-Eng. 530700: 341-6;

    Cz. Rude Pravo, (IV.161), 13.VII.23;

    Eng. [460000(14)]; [590000(5)]; ComReview, X.23; Inprecor, (III.50), 12.VII.23;

    Fr. [620000(4)]; 680000(4): 357; BulCom, (IV.30), 26.VII.23; CorInt, (III.26), 7.VII.23;

    Ger. Inprekor, (III.114), 6.VII.23;

    Heb. Kuntras, (146), 1924;

    Hol. Tribune, (234), 10.VII.23;

    Sp. Batalla, (I.20), 17.VIII.23.

[For international discussion. See 260000(7) for other trans.]

230704 Pref. VOPROSY BYTA (PROBLEMS OF LIFE), 230000(3).

Repr.: 230000(4): 5; 250000(1): 5.

[230710]   Ne o "politike" edinoi zhiv chelovek. "Man does not live by
"politics" alone.) (<u>PetPr</u>, (152), 10.VII.23; <u>Pr</u>, (152), 10.VII.23)
<u>Repr</u>.: 230000(3): 15-24; 230000(4): 7-17; p.q. 240000(28): 94;
250000(1): 7-18; 270000(2): 3-12.
<u>Trans</u>.: Am. 240000(48): 1-21;
Eng. 240000(49): 1-21; 621100(1): 7-17; <u>Labour Monthly</u>, XI.23;
Fr. 640911: 269-77; <u>BulCom</u>, (IV.36), 6.IX.23; <u>Clarté</u>, (II.41),
15.VIII.23; <u>CorInt</u>, (III.30), 4.VIII.23;
Ger. 230000(26): 17-32;
Jap. 250720: 9-22; 270901: 1-26;
Sp. 690000(8).II: 93-101;
Swed. 690600(1): 234-42.
[See 241029(2).]

[230711]   Chtoby perestroit byt, nado poznat ego. (To re-build life we must be
acquainted with it.) (<u>PetPr</u>, (153), 11.VII.23; <u>Pr</u>, (153), 11.VII.23)
<u>Repr</u>.: 230000(3): 32-7; 230000(4): 34-40; p.q. 240000(28): 131-2;
250000(1): 36-42; 270000(2): 16-21.
<u>Trans</u>.: Am. 240000(48): 22-33; p.q. <u>FI</u>, VIII.45;
Eng. 240000(49): 22-33; 621100(1): 14-8; p.q. <u>Inprecor</u>, (III.67),
18.X.23; <u>New Russia</u>(Shanghai), (II.35), 29.XI.23; p.q.
<u>WIN</u>, VI-VII.46;
Fr. 640911: 278-83; <u>CorInt</u>, (III.35), 8.IX.23; <u>QI</u>, (XII.6-8),
VI-VIII.54;
Ger. 230000(26): 33-43; <u>Inprekor</u>, (III.150), 24.IX.23;
Jap. 250720: 22-30; 270901: 27-41;
Sp. 690000(8).II: 43-8; <u>Antorcha</u>, (III.95), 21.IX.23; p.q.
<u>Batalla</u>, (I.25), 28.IX.23;
Swed. 690600(1): 243-8.

[230712]   Vodka, tserkov i kinematograf. (Vodka, the church, and the cinema.)
(<u>PetPr</u>, (154), 12.VII.23; <u>Pr</u>, (154), 12.VII.23)
<u>Repr</u>.: 230000(3): 48-52; 230000(4): 41-6; 240000(28): 133-7;
250000(1): 43-8; 270000(2): 22-6; Lebedev.
<u>Trans</u>.: Am. 240000(48): 34-43;
Eng. 240000(49): 34-43; 621100(1): 19-22;
Fr. <u>CorInt</u>, (III.29), 28.VII.23; 640911: 284-8;
Ger. 230000(26): 44-52; <u>Inprekor</u>, (III.123), 25.VII.23;
Hol. p.q. <u>Tribune</u>, (253), 1.VIII.23;
Jap. 250720: 30-6; 270901: 42-53;
Sp. 690000(8).II: 49-53;   ++++

[230712]   ++++ <u>Trans</u>.: Swed. 690600(1):249-53.

[230713]   Ot staroi sem´i — k novoi. (From the old family to the new.) (<u>Pr</u>,
             (155), 13.VII.23)
             <u>Repr</u>.: 230000(3): 38-47; 230000(4): 47-56; p.q. 240000(8): 138-41;
                      250000(1): 49-58; 270000(2): 31-9.
             <u>Trans</u>.: Am. 240000(48): 44-61;
                      Eng. 240000(49): 44-61; 621100(1): 23-9; p.q. <u>New Russia</u>
                          (Shanghai), (II.35), 29.XI.23;
                      Fr. <u>CorInt</u>, (III.36), 15.IX.23;
                      Ger. 230000(26): 53-67;
                      Jap. 250720: 37-48; 270901: 54-74.

[230714]   Sem´ya i obryadnost. (The family and ceremonial.) (<u>PetPr</u>, (156),
             14.VII.23; <u>Pr</u>, (156), 14.VII.23)
             <u>Repr</u>.: 230000(3): 48-52; 230000(4): 57-61; 240000(28): 142-5;
                      250000(1): 59-63; 270000(2): 39-43.
             <u>Trans</u>.: Am. 240000(48): 62-9; 650900: 338-42;
                      Eng. 240000(49): 62-9; 621100(1): 30-2; 640000(5): 338-42;
                          640000(10): 338-42;
                      Ger. 230000(26): 68-75;
                      Jap. 250720: 48-53; 270901: 75-84.

230717   Pis´mo. (A letter.) (<u>Iz</u>, (159), 18.VII.23; <u>PetPr</u>, (159), 18.VII.23;
             <u>Rabochaya Moskva</u>, (157), 18.VII.23; <u>Trud</u>, (158), 18.VII.23)
             [To Ed.; on VOPROSY BYTA, 230000(3).]

230719   Formal´naya shkola poezii i marksizma. (The formalist school of
             poetry and marxism.) (<u>Pr</u>, (166), 26.VII.23)
             <u>Repr</u>.: 230000(9): 119-35.
             <u>Trans</u>.: 230000(9).

230806   Protiv prosveshchennogo byurokratizma (a takzhe i neprosveshchennogo).
             (Against enlightened bureaucratism — and also the unenlightened
             kind.) (<u>PetPr</u>, (181,182), 14,15.VIII.23; <u>Pr</u>, (181), 14.VIII.23)
             <u>Repr</u>.: 230000(4): 73-82; 250000(1): 76-86; 270000(2): 66-74.
             <u>Trans</u>.: Am. 240000(48): 88-99;
                      Eng. 240000(49): 88-99; 621100(1): 41-5;
                      Jap. 250720: 65-73; 270901: 108-23.

230808   O kakogo ugla podoit? (From which angle should we approach?) (PetPr,
(184,186), 18,21.VIII.23; Pr, (183), 17.VIII.23)

Repr.: 230000(4): 83–91; 250000(1): 87–96; 270000(2): 206–13.

Trans.: Am. 240000(48): 100–14;

         Eng. 240000(49): 100–14; 621100(1): 46–51;

         Jap. 250720: 73–82; 270901: 124–41.

230814   [Dedication of LITERATURA I REVOLYUTSIYA (LITERATURE AND REVOLUTION),
230000(9).]

[To Christian George Rakovsky.]

230828   Alternative for 230621.

230908(1)   Proletarskaya kul´tura i proletarskoi iskusstvo. (Proletarian culture
and proletarian art.) (PetPr, (207–9), 14–16.IX.23; Pr, (207,208),
14,15.IX.23)

Repr.: 230000(9): 136–58; Krasnaya Nov, (7), 1926.

Trans.: 230000(9);

         Fr. p.q. CorInt, (III.38), 29.IX.23;

         Ger. p.q. Bjedny.

230908(2)   Partiinaya politika v iskusstve. (The Party's policy in art.)
(Pr, (209), 16.IX.23)

Repr.: 230000(9): 159–68.

Trans.: 230000(9);

         Fr. p.q. CorInt, (III.38), 29.IX.23.

230909   Pref. VOPROSY BYTA (PROBLEMS OF LIFE), 230000(4).

Repr.: 250000(1): 3; 270000(2): 43–4.

[2nd ed.]

230916   Futurizm. (Futurism.) (PetPr, (216,218,220,221), 25,27,29,30.IX.23;
Pr, (216,217), 25,26.IX.23)

Repr.: 230000(9): 91–118.

Trans.: 230000(9).

230919   Pref. LITERATURA I REVOLYUTSIYA (LITERATURE AND REVOLUTION), 230000(9).
(Iz, (219), 28.IX.23)

Trans.: 230000(9);

         Am. p.q. 640800: 315–20;

         Eng. p.q. Marxist Outlook, (I.2), III.66;

         Jap. p.q. 681125: 328–36;

         Sp. p.q. 670000(5): 319–23;

         Swed. p.q. 691100(2): 283–8.

230923(1)   Pis´mo. (A letter.) (<u>Pr</u>, (222), 2.X.23)

[To Ed.; on criticism of 230000(9).]

[230923(2)]   Mozhno li kontr-revolyutsiya ili revolyutsiya sdelat v srok? (Can counter-revolution or revolution be made on schedule?) (<u>PetPr</u>, (215), 23.IX.23; <u>Pr</u>, (215), 23.IX.23)

<u>Repr</u>.: 240000(29): 575-80; 250000(8): 373-8; <u>SputnikKom</u>, 1924.

<u>Trans</u>.: Am. <u>FI</u>, VII-VIII.47, <u>NI</u>(WP), X.46;

      Am-Eng. 530700: 347-53;

      Eng. 680501; <u>BMS</u>(E), (I.2), Autumn 1968; <u>Inprecor</u>, (III.66), 11.X.23; <u>Labour Monthly</u>, I.24;

      Fr. <u>CorInt</u>, (III.40), 13.X.23; <u>Vie Ouv</u>, 10.X.23;

      Ger. <u>Inprekor</u>, (III.152), 26.IX.23; VOM BÜRGERKRIEG.

230927   Pis´mo Akademiku I.P.Pavlovu. (Letter to Academician I.P.Pavlov.) (270000(2): 260)

<u>Trans</u>.: Fr. 640911: 304-5; <u>QI</u>, XII.56;

      It. 690500(2): 51-2;

      Sp. 690000(8).II: 90-1;

      Swed. 690600(1): 270-1.

[Archives.]

230929   Iskusstvo revolyutsii i sotsialisticheskoe iskusstvo. (Revolutionary art and socialist art.) (<u>Pr</u>, (220,221), 29,30.IX.23)

<u>Repr</u>.: 230000(9): 169-90.

<u>Trans</u>.: 230000(9);

      Am. p.q. 640800: 320-6;

      Jap. p.q. 681125: 336-40;

      Sp. p.q. 670000(5): 323-9;

      Swed. p.q. 691100(2): 288-93.

[See 220000(32) note.]

[230930]   Beseda senatora King. (Interview with Senator King.) (<u>Iz</u>, (221), 30.IX.23; <u>Pr</u>, (221), 30.IX.23; <u>Rabochaya Moskva</u>, (219), 30.IX.23; <u>Trud</u>, (220), 30.IX.23)

<u>Repr</u>.: 230000(7).III.ii: 114-7.

<u>Trans</u>.: Am. p.q. <u>NYTimes</u>, 3.X.23;

      Eng. p.q. <u>Russian Information Review</u>, 20.X.23.

[231005]   Pis´mo. (A letter.) (<u>Iz</u>, (226), 5.X.23)

<u>Repr</u>.: 230000(7).III.ii: 118.

[Reply to greetings; on Germany.]

231008 [First letter to CC and CCC.] (p.q. <u>SotsVestnik</u>, (11), 28.V.24)

Trans.: Am. p.q. Eastman, L: 142-3; p.q. Shachtman, THE STRUGGLE: 153-8;
     Eng. p.q. Carr, INTER: 105; p.q. Deutscher, PU: 109-11; p.q.
       REPORT OF 13th CONFERENCE CPR: p.q. <u>CI</u>, (IV.16), 15.XI.27;
     Jap. p.q. 631130: 9-11.

[See 231023(2).]

231016 Pref. POKOLENIE OKTYABRYA (THE GENERATION OF OCTOBER), 240000(28).
(<u>PetPr</u>, (236), 18.X.23; <u>Pr</u>, (236), 18.X.23)
Repr.: p.q. 270000(2): 341-6.

[231017] Pis'mo v redaktsiyu <u>Rote Fane</u>. (Letter to Ed. Board <u>Rote Fahne</u>.)
(<u>PetPr</u>, (235), 17.X.23; <u>Rabochaya Gazeta</u>, (234), 17.X.23)
Repr.: 230000(7).III.ii: 119.

231019(1) Doklad. (A report.) (<u>Iz</u>, (241), 21.X.23; <u>PetPr</u>, (239), 21.X.23; <u>Pr</u>,
(239), 21.X.23; <u>Trud</u>, (238), 21.X.23)
Repr.: 230000(7).III.ii: 120-5.
Trans.: Am. p.q. Eudin & Fisher: 180, 217-8;
     Cz. p.q. <u>Rude Pravo</u>, (IV.266), 13.XI.23;
     Eng. p.q. <u>Workers Weekly</u>, (40), 9.XI.23.
[To 3rd Moscow District Congress of Metal Workers; on Germany. Archives.]

231019(2) O Krasnoi Armii. (The Red Army.) (<u>Iz</u>, (241), 21.X.23)
[Speech to Plenum CC.]

231020 Doklad. (A report.) (STENOTCHET VIII VSEROSS. S"EZDA SOYUZA SVYAZI.)
Repr.: 230000(7).III.ii: 126-45.
[To 8th All-Russian Congress of Communications Workers.]

231021 Sovremennoe polozhenie i zadachi voennogo stroitel'stva. (The current
situation and the tasks of military construction.) (<u>EkZhizn</u>, (240),
23.X.23; <u>Iz</u>, (242), 23.X.23)
Repr.: 230000(7).III.ii: 146-69; 240000(31).
Trans.: Am. p.q. <u>Worker</u>, 1.XII.23;
     Eng. p.q. <u>Russian Information Review</u>, 10.XI.23.
[Report to Conference of Political Workers in Red Army and Fleet.]

231022 Zaklyuchitel'noe slovo. (Summary speech.) (<u>Iz</u>, (242), 23.X.23)
Repr.: 230000(7).III.ii: 169-72.
[See 231021.]

231023(1)   Pis′mo. (A letter.) (<u>Pr</u>, (240), 23.X.23)

Repr.: 270000(2): 215.

[To State Institute of Journalism; on its anniversary.]

231023(2)   [2nd letter to CC.] (<u>SotsVestnik</u>, (11), 28.V.24)

Repr.: p.q. 271021.

Trans.: Eng. p.q. Carr, INTER: 295-7,299.

[See 231008.]

231023(3)   Vragi i soyuzniki germanskoi revolyutsii. (Enemies and allies of the German revolution.) (<u>PetPr</u>, (241), 24.X.23)

[Answers at a meeting. See 231021.]

231024   Alternative for 231023(2).

231029(1)   Prikaz, No. 281. (<u>Iz</u>, (248), 30.X.23; <u>PetPr</u>, (246), 30.X.23; <u>Pr</u>, (246), 30.X.23)

Repr.: 230000(7).III.i: 196.

[Greetings to Komsomol from Red Army and Navy.]

231029(2)   Pyat let Komsomola. (5 years of the Komsomol.) (<u>Pr</u>, (246), 30.X.23)

Repr.: 230000(7).III.ii: 173-6; 240000(28): 248-52.

[On Germany.]

231030   Prikaz, No. 282. (<u>Iz</u>, (249), 31.X.23; <u>PetPr</u>, (247), 31.X.23; <u>Pr</u>, (247), 31.X.23)

Repr.: 230000(7).III.ii: 177.

[Peace demonstrations and war preparations.]

[231101]   i dr.: Zabota o detyakh sovetskoi strany. (Care for Soviet children.) (<u>Iz</u>, (250), 1.XI.23)

231102   Pref. Bezymenskii, KAK PAKHNET ZHIZN (THE SMELL OF LIFE).

[LocBM/NYPL.]

231105   God sed′moi. (The 7th year.) (<u>PetPr</u>, (253), 7.XI.23; <u>Pr</u>, (253), 7.XI.23)

Repr.: <u>MolGvard</u>, (9-10), 1923: 3-5.

Trans.: Am. p.q. <u>NYTimes</u>, 8.XI.23.

[On 6th anniversary of Russian Revolution.]

[231121]   Nach. Glavvozdukh flota SSSR tov. Rosengol′ts. (To cde. Rosengolts, Head of the Soviet Navy.) (<u>Pr</u>, (264), 21.XI.23)

[231123(1)]   Prikaz, No. 2545. (<u>Iz</u>, (268), 23.XI.23)

<u>Repr</u>.: 230000(7).III.ii: 198.

[On Red Navy.]

231123(2)   Pis'mo. (A letter.) (<u>Iz</u>, (269), 24.XI.23; <u>PetPr</u>, (267), 24.XI.23;

<u>Pr</u>, (267), 24.XI.23; <u>Trud</u>, (266), 24.XI.23)

<u>Repr</u>.: 240000(4): 9-19; p.q. 250000(5); 270000(2): 261-8.

<u>Trans</u>.: Eng. p.q. <u>Newsletter</u>, 16.IX.61;

          Fr. p.q. 680000(4): 339-40; <u>BulCom</u>, (IV.49), 6.XII.23.

[To 1st All-Russian Congress of Scientific Workers.]

[231123(3)]   Otvet. (A reply.) (<u>Iz</u>, (268), 23.XI.23)

[To letter from Dagestan workers.]

[231128]   Pis'mo. (A letter.) (<u>Pr</u>, (270), 28.XI.23)

<u>Repr</u>.: 270000(2): 64-5.

<u>Trans</u>.: Am. <u>IP</u>, (VIII.12), 30.III.70.

[To celebration meeting of Moscow women workers.]

[231200(1)]   Obshchestvennyi sostav partii. (The social composition of the Party.)

(240000(22): 15-21)

<u>Trans</u>.: 240000(22);

          Fr. p.q. 680000(4): 310-1 <u>BulCom</u>, (V.6), 8.II.24; LE PARTI

            BOLCHÉVIK: 78-85.

231200(2)   Byurokratizm i revolyutsiya. (Bureaucratism and the revolution.)

(240000(22): 32-9)

<u>Trans</u>.: 240000(22);

          Am. 650900: 170-7; <u>NI</u>, I.35;

          Eng. 640000(5): 170-7; 640000(10): 170-7.

231200(3)   Traditsiya i revolyutsionnaya politika. (Tradition and revolutionary

policy.) (240000(22): 40-9)

<u>Trans</u>.: 240000(22);

          Am. p.q. 680000(4): 98-9; <u>NI</u>(WP), IV.41;

          Eng. p.q. <u>Red Mole</u>, (I.2), 1.IV.70;

          Fr. <u>Clarté</u>, (III.58), 1.V.24; p.q. <u>Le Com</u>, (II.23), 25.VIII.29;

          Sp. <u>Antorcha</u>, (IV.128), 16.V.24.

231200(4) "Nedootsenka" krest'yanstva. (The "under-estimation" of the peasantry.)
(Pr, (277), 6.XII.23)
Repr.: 240000(22): 50-8.
Trans.: 240000(22);
    Eng. Inprecor, (IV.1), 4.I.24;
    Fr. BulCom, (V.11), 14.III.24;
    Ger. Inprekor, (III.184), 27.XII.23.

231200(5) Planovoe khozyaistvo. ("No. 1042.") (Planned economy: "No. 1042.")
(240000(22): 59-74)
Trans.: 240000(22).

231200(6) [Interview with A.L.Strong.]
Trans.: Eng. Strong: passim.

231203 O kazenshchine, voennoi i vsyakoi inoi. (Red tape, military and
otherwise.) (Pr, (275), 4.XII.23)
Repr.: 240000(22): 87-92; 270000(2): 75-80.
Trans.: 240000(22);
    Am. 690000(11): 154-8.

231205 & others: [Resolution to Politbureau and CCC.]
[c. 410000(1): Ch. XII; on "workers democracy" in the Party.]

[231206(1)] Alternative for 231200(4).

[231206(2)] O smychke. (The alliance [between town and country].) (PetPr, (277),
6.XII.23; Pr, (277), 6.XII.23)
Repr.: 240000(22): 93-9.
Trans.: 240000(22);
    Eng. Red Flag, (n.s.5), I.37;
    Hol. p.q. Tribune, (86), 11.I.24.

231207 Vsesoyuznomu soveshchaniyu komitetov pomoshchi bol'nym i ranenym
krasnoarmeitsam i invalidam voiny. (To the All-Union Conference of
Committees for aiding sick and wounded Red Army men and war disabled.)
(Pr, (280), 9.XII.23)
[A letter.]

231208(1) Novyi kurs. (the new course.) (PetPr, (282), 12.XII.23; Pr, (281),
11.XII.23)
Repr.: 240000(22): 77-83; IZ MATERIALOV PARTIINOI DISKUSSII.

++++

231208(1)   ++++ <u>Trans</u>.: 240000(22);

           Am. 640800: 137-41; Eastman, L: 145-51;

           Eng. <u>Inprecor</u>, (IV.12), 15.II.24;

           Fr. <u>CorInt</u>, (IV.8), 31.I.24; <u>Vie Ouv</u>, 8.II.24; LE PARTI
              BOLCHÉVIK: 13-23;

           Ger. <u>Inprekor</u>, (IV.8), 21.I.24; Bukharin: NIEDER;

           Jap. 631130: 12-21; 681125: 145-9;

           Sp. 670000(5): 137-41;

           Swed. 691100(2): 121-5.

      [PS 231210.]

[231208(2)]   Prikaz, No. 2656. (<u>Iz</u>, (281), 8.XII.23; <u>Pr</u>, (279), 8.XII.23)
      <u>Repr</u>.: 230000(7).III.i: 197-8.
      [On 5th anniversary of Red Army.]

231210   PS 231208(1). (240000(22): 83-6)
      <u>Trans</u>.: 240000(22);

           Am. Eastman, L: 151-3;

           Ger. <u>Inprekor</u>, (IV.8), 21.I.24.

231217   Pis´mo v otvet zaprosy. (Letter in reply to enquiries.) (<u>Pr</u>, (287),
      18.XII.23)
      <u>Trans</u>.: Am. Eastman, L: 79.
      [Attitude to slanders.]

231222   Gruppirovki i fraktsionnye obrazovaniya. (Groups and factional
      organizations.) (240000(22): 22-31)
      <u>Trans</u>.: 240000(22);

           Eng. <u>Inprecor</u>, (IV.16), 29.II.24;

           Fr. p.q. 680000(4): 324; <u>BulCom</u>, (V.3), 18.I.24; <u>CorInt</u>,
              (IV.13), 19.II.24; LE PARTI BOLCHÉVIK: 55-67;

           Ger. <u>Inprekor</u>, (IV.13), 28.I.24;

231223   Vopros o partiinykh pokoleniyakh. (The question of the Party
      generations.) (<u>PetPr</u>, (295), 29.XII.23; <u>Pr</u>, (295), 29.XII.23)
      <u>Repr</u>.: 240000(22): 7-14.
      <u>Trans</u>.: 240000(22);

           Fr. <u>BulCom</u>, (V.4), 25.I.24; <u>CorInt</u>, (IV.13), 19.II.24;
              LE PARTI BOLCHÉVIK: 68-77;

           Ger. <u>Inprekor</u>, (IV.13), 28.I.24.

      [See Ed. note in <u>Pr</u>. following this article.]

*240000(1)   *VOPROSY BYTA. (PROBLEMS OF LIFE.)
Repr.: *240000(2).
[Possibly 240428.]

*240000(2)   *VOPROSY BYTA. (PROBLEMS OF LIFE.)
[See *240000(1).]

*240000(3)   *VOPROSY GRAZHDANSKOI VOINY. (PROBLEMS OF CIVIL WAR.)
[See 240729(1) for all repr., trans.]

240000(4)   ‡ VOPROSY KUL′TURNOI RABOTY. (PROBLEMS OF CULTURAL WORK.)
[Pref. 240920.]

240000(5)   ZADACHI KOMMUNISTICHESKOGO VOSPITANIYA. (TASKS OF COMMUNIST EDUCATION.)
[See 230618 for all repr., trans., notes.]

240000(6)   ‡ ZAPAD I VOSTOK. (WEST AND EAST.)
[Pref. 240715.]

*240000(7)   *KRASNAYA PAMYATKA. (RED ARMY HANDBOOK.)
Repr.: *240000(8); *240000(9); *240000(10); *240000(12).
Trans.: Am. p.q. 640800: 109;
       Eng. p.q. Deutscher, PU: 26;
       Ger. *240000(58);
       Jap. p.q. 681125: 117;
       Sp. 370000(8); p.q. 670000(5): 109;
       Swed. p.q. 691100(2): 95;
       Tat. *240000(11).

*240000(8)   *KRASNAYA PAMYATKA. (RED ARMY HANDBOOK.)
[See *240000(7) for all repr., trans.]

*240000(9)   *KRASNAYA PAMYATKA. (RED ARMY HANDBOOK.)
[See *240000(7) for all repr., trans.]

*240000(10)   *KRASNAYA PAMYATKA. (RED ARMY HANDBOOK.)
[See *240000(7) for all repr., trans.]

*240000(11)   *KRASNAYA PAMYATKA. (RED ARMY HANDBOOK.)
[Trans. Tat. See *240000(7) for all trans.]

*240000(12)   *KRASNAYA PAMYATKA. (RED ARMY HANDBOOK.)
[See *240000(7) for all repr., trans.]

240000(13)   LENIN I STARAYA ISKRA. (LENIN AND THE OLD ISKRA.)
[See 240305 for all repr., trans.]

240000(14)   LENIN KAK NATSIONAL'NYI TIP. (LENIN AS A NATIONAL TYPE.)
[See 200423 for all repr., trans., notes.]

240000(15)   LENIN KAK NATSIONAL'NYI TIP. (LENIN AS A NATIONAL TYPE.)
[See 200423 for all repr., trans., notes.]

*240000(16)   *LENINIZM I BIBLIOTECHNAYA RABOTA. (LENINISM AND THE WORK OF
LIBRARIANS.)
[See 240703 for all repr., notes.]

*240000(17)   *LENINIZM I RABOCHIE KLUBY. (LENINISM AND WORKERS CLUBS.)
[See 240717 for all repr.]

240000(18)   § LITERATURA I REVOLYUTSIYA. (LITERATURE AND REVOLUTION.)
Trans.: Jap. 651225.
[2nd enlarged ed. See 230000(9) for all repr., trans., notes.]

*240000(19)   *MOLODEZH, UCHIS POLITIKE. (YOUNG PEOPLE, STUDY POLITICS.)
[See 240429(2) for all repr., trans., notes.]

240000(20)   NA PUTYAKH K EVROPEISKOI REVOLYUTSII. (ON THE ROAD TO EUROPEAN
REVOLUTION.)
[See 240411 for all repr., trans., notes.]

*240000(21)   *NA PUTYAKH K EVROPEISKOI REVOLYUTSII. (ON THE ROAD TO EUROPEAN
REVOLUTION.)
[See 240411 for all repr., trans., notes.]

240000(22)   ‡ NOVYI KURS. (THE NEW COURSE.)
Trans.: Am. 430900; 650000(5);
            Cz. *240000(47);
            Eng. 561000;
            Fr. 240000(39); 570000(1); 630419:27-99;
            Ger. [240000(52)];
            It. 670315;
            Jap. p.q. 631130; 660427;
            Sp. *280000(3); *[310000(31)].
[Pref. 240100(1); Pref. Gr. ed. 330128(1).]

240000(23) O ZADACHAKH DEREVENSKOI MOLODEZHI. (TASKS OF THE COUNTRYSIDE YOUTH.)
[See 240428 for all repr., notes.]

240000(24) ‡ O LENINE. (LENIN.)
Repr.: 240000(25)
Trans.: Am. 250000(17); 340000(18); 590000(4); 620000(9);
        Eng. 250000(18); 250000(19); p.q. 510300;
        Fr. 250000(20); 700600(7); p.q. BulCom, (VI.5), 20.XI.25; p.q.
            Vie Ouv, 6.XI.25;
        Ger. 240000(50); 321200(5); 640000(2); [680000(8)]; p.q.
            Arbeiter-Lit, (1), 1924;
        Hol. 670000(14);
        It. *[430000(3)]; 640110; 670310;
        Jap. 251016; *620000(19);
        Sp. 270000(9).
[Pref. 240421. See separate items for other trans.]

240000(25) § O LENINE. (LENIN.)
[See 240000(24) for all repr., trans., notes.]

*240000(26) *OT OKTYAB'SKOI REVOLYUTSII DO BRESTSKOGO MIRA. (FROM THE OCTOBER
REVOLUTION TO THE BREST PEACE.)
[See 180000(5) for all repr., trans.]

*240000(27) *PAMYATI IL'ICHA. (IN MEMORY OF ILYICH [LENIN].)
Repr.: *[240000(36)].
[Possibly 240423.]

240000(28) ‡ POKOLENIE OKTYABRYA. (THE GENERATION OF OCTOBER.)
[Pref. 231016.]

240000(29) ‡ PYAT LET KOMINTERNA. (FIVE YEARS OF THE COMINTERN.)
Repr.: 250000(9).
Trans.: Am. 451000 +
        Am-Eng. 530700;
        Jap. *621130; 660228.
[Pref. 240520.]

*240000(30) *RECHI. (SPEECHES.)
[Collection of speeches made during journey from Crimea to Leningrad.]

240000(31)   SOVREMENNOE POLOZHENIE I ZADACHI VOENNOGO STROITEL'STVA. (THE
             CURRENT SITUATION AND THE AIMS OF MILITARY CONSTRUCTION.)
             [See 231021 for all repr., trans., notes.]

240000(32)   ‡ 1917.
             [Pref. 240915.]

240000(33)   i dr.: 1917. UROKI OKTYABRYA. (1917. LESSONS OF OCTOBER.)
             [See 240915 for all repr., trans.]

240000(34)   § 1905.
             [See 220000(12) for all repr., trans., notes.]

240000(35)   UROKI OKTYABRYA. (LESSONS OF OCTOBER.)
             [See 240915 for all repr., trans.]

*[240000(36)]   *VOZHD ZHELEZNOI KOGORTY. PAMYATI IL'ICHA. (THE LEADER OF THE IRON
             COHORTS. IN MEMORY OF ILYICH.)
             [See *240000(27) for all repr., notes.]

[240000(37)]   O NOVOM BYTE. (THE NEW LIFE.)
             [Printed with O ZADACHAKH DEREVENSKOI MOLODEZHI, 240000(23) as Part II
             but the 2 parts are treated as a single report.]

*[240000(38)]   *POUKITE OT OKTOMBRI 1917. (LESSONS OF OCTOBER, 1917.)
             [Trans. Bul. See 240915 for all trans., notes.]

240000(39)   § COURSE NOUVEAU.
             [Trans. Fr. See 240000(22) for all repr., trans.]

240000(40)   § DIE GEBURT DER ROTEN ARMEE.
             [Trans. Ger. Excerpts from 230000(7).]

*240000(41)   *DIE GEBURT DER ROTEN ARMEE.
             [Trans. Ger. See note 240000(40).]

*240000(42)   *JAUNATNEI. (Podolnenie: KAS IS LENINISMUS.)
             [Trans. Latv. Possibly 240522.]

240000(43)   JEAN JAURÈS.
             [Trans. Fr. See 170000(1) for all repr., trans.]

240000(44)   LITERATUR UND REVOLUTION.
             [Trans. Ger. Abr. See 230000(9) for all repr., trans., notes.]

[240000(45)]   LITERATURA Y REVOLUCIÓN.

        [Trans. Sp. See 230000(9) for all repr., trans., notes. Pref. dated correctly.]

240000(46)   MIN FLYKT FRÅN SIBIRIEN.

        [Trans. Swed. See 070000(3) for all trans., notes.]

*240000(47)   *NOVÝ KURS.

        [Trans. Cz. See 240000(22) for all trans.]

240000(48)   § PROBLEMS OF LIFE.

        [Trans. Am. See 230000(3) for all trans., notes.]

240000(49)   § PROBLEMS OF LIFE.

        Trans.: Eng.;
                Jap. 250720: 1-82, 270901.

        [See 230000(3) for all trans., notes.]

240000(50)   ÜBER LENIN.

        [Trans. Ger. See 240000(24) for all repr., trans., notes.]

[240000(52)]   § DER NEUE KURS.

        [Trans. Ger. See 240000(22) for all trans.]

240000(54)   Pref. D.Bjedny, DIE HAUPSTRASSE.

        [Trans. Ger. p.q. 230908(1).]

*240000(55)   Pref. A.Bezymenskii, KOMSOMOLYA.

        [CatKL.]

240000(56)   LENIN YOK! YOKDIR INDI LENIN!

        [Trans. Turc. See 240122(1) for all trans.]

*240000(58)   *ROTES MERKBLATT FÜR DIE KRIEGER DER ARBEITER- UND BAUERNARMEE UND DER ROTEN FLOTTE ÜBER DIE WICHTIGSTEN FRAGEN DES KRIEGSHANDWERKS.

        [Trans. Ger. See *240000(7) for all trans.]

*240000(59)   *LENIN I STARAYA ISKRA. (LENIN AND THE OLD ISKRA.)

        [See 240305 for all repr., trans.]

240100(1)   Pref. NOVYI KURS (THE NEW COURSE), 240000(22).
                [See 240000(22) for all trans.]

240100(2)   [Projet de thèses de Trotsky et Radek et Piatakov.]
                [c. CorInt, 1924: 936.]

[240103]   Nuzhno shire, prochnee, pravil'ne postavit delo pomoshchi invalidam.
                (We need to give wider, solid, direct aid to the disabled.) (Iz, (2),
                3.I.24)

240108   Pref. KAK VOORUZHALAS REVOLYUTSIYA (HOW THE REVOLUTION WAS ARMED),
                230000(7).II.i: 3-4.
                Trans.: Fr. 680000(1): 451-2.

240122(1)   Lenin net! (Lenin is no more!) (EkZhizn, (94), 24.I.24; Iz, (19),
                24.I.24; Krasnyi Mir, 1924; Pr, (19), 24.I.24; Trud, (19), 24.I.24)
                Repr.: 240000(24): 166-8; U VELIKOI MOGILY: 27.
                Trans.: Am. FI, I-II.51; Labor Challenge, (III.1), I.47; SocAp,
                      24.VIII.40;
                    Bul. Osvob, (5), I.31;
                    Eng. 680200(1): 21-3; CI, (V.30), 1924; Inprecor, (IV.8),
                      31.I.24; Workers Weekly, (52), 1.II.24;
                    Fr. Drapeau Rouge, (I.22), 26.I.24; Huma, 25.I.24;
                    Ger. Aktion, (XII.3-4), V.29; Fahne desKom, (III.3), 18.I.29;
                      Inprekor, (IV.14), 28.I.24; (IV.5), 2.II.24;
                    Hol. Baan, (II.40), 24.I.31; Tribune, (90), 26.I.24;
                    It. Prometeo, (II.13), 15.II.29;
                    Sp. Antorcha, (IV.114), 1.II.24;
                    Turc. 240000(56);
                    Yid. KomFon, (20), 25.I.24.
                [See 240000(24) for other trans.]

240122(2)   [Telegram to Moscow; on date of Lenin's funeral.] (410000(1): Ch. XII)
                Trans.: 410000(1): Ch. XII.

[240200]   [Special letter to delegation of CPR.]
                [c. 301100(1): 203; on France.]

240223   6 let Krasnoi Armii. (The Red Army after 6 years.) (Pr, (44), 23.II.24)
                Trans.: Am. Current History, V.24;
                      Eng. Inprecor, (IV.19), 13.III.24;

++++

240223 ++++ Trans.: Fr. BulCom, (VI.5), 20.XI.25; CorInt, (IV.17), 12.III.24;
              Ger. Inprekor, (IV.10)/(IV.30), 8.III/4.III.24;
              Hol. Tribune, (137), 11.III.24.

240305 LENIN I STARAYA ISKRA. (LENIN AND THE OLD ISKRA.)
        Repr.: 240000(24): 3-45; 240000(25); *240000(59); p.q. 300000(1):
              Ch. XI.
        Trans.: 240000(24); p.q. 300000(1): Ch. XI.

240319 Novaya kniga F.Engelsa. (A new book by F.Engels.) (Pr, (71), 28.III.24)
        Trans.: Am. 690000(11): 34-47; NI(WP), V.44;
              Eng. 690400(1): 113-25;
              Fr. QI, (13), VII.58; Que Faire, (3-4), V.70;
              Ger. Arbeiter-Lit, (1), 1924: 199-213.
        [Pref. F.Engels, NOTES ON WAR, 1870-1871.]

[240323] Otvety na voprosy predstavitelya amerikanskogo gazetnogo Tresta Khersta.
          (Replies to questions from representative of American Hurst Newspaper
          Trust.) (Iz, (68), 23.III.24; Trud, (67), 23.III.24)

240400 [To I.N.Smirnov.]
        Trans.: 410000(1): Supp. I.
        [On Stalin.]

240406 Vokrug oktyabrya. (Around October.) (Iz, (88), 16.IV.24; Pr,
        (87,89,91,93), 16,18,20,23.IV.24; Trud, (87), 16.IV.24)
        Repr.: 240000(24): 45-142; 240000(25); p.q. U VELIKOI MOGILY: 480-1,
              528-30.
        Trans.: 240000(24);
              Am. p.q. FI, I-II.52; p.q. Mil, 1.V.70; p.q. SocAp, 25.I.41;
              Eng. p.q. Inprecor, (IV.30), 22.V.24; p.q. Labour Monthly,
                  VII.24;
              Fr. p.q. CorInt, (IV.26,28), 14,28.V.24;
              Ger. p.q. Inprekor, (IV.19)/(IV.52), 10.V/6.V.24;
              Yid. p.q. Emes, (87,94,95), 16,24,25.IV.24; p.q. KomFon,
                  (19,75), 24.I, 22.IV.24.

240411 Na putyakh k evropeiskoi revolyutsii. (On the road to European
        revolution.) (Iz, (86), 13.IV.24; Pr, (90), 19.IV.24)
        Repr.: 240000(6): 5-29; 240000(20); 240000(21); p.q. 260000(7): 91-3.
        Trans.: Am. IP, (VII.16,17), 28.IV, 5.V.69;
              Eng. 690000(9); p.q. Inprecor, (IV.35), 19.VI.24;
              Ger. Inprekor, (IV.53), 9.V.24/(IV.19), 10.V.24.

240412(1)   Rech. (A speech.) (<u>Iz</u>, (87), 15.IV.24; <u>Pr</u>, (86), 15.IV.24)
[In Tiflis. Briefest extracts.]

240412(2)   Interv´yu. (An interview.) (<u>Iz</u>, (92), 20.IV.24)
<u>Trans</u>.: Am. <u>NYTimes</u>, 13.IV.24.

240412(3)   Pis´mo partiinoe konferentsii tifliskogo garnizona. (Letter to a
Party Conference of the Tiflis garrison.) (<u>Pr</u>, (86), 15.IV.24)

240413   Rech. (A speech.) (<u>Iz</u>, (87), 15.IV.24; <u>Pr</u>, (86), 15.IV.24)
[In Tiflis. Briefest extracts.]

240414   Rech. (A speech.) (<u>Iz</u>, (87), 15.IV.24; <u>Pr</u>, (86), 15.IV.24)
[In Baku. Briefest extracts.]

240415(1)   Pis´mo Komsomolu Gruzii. (Letter to Georgian Komsomol.) (<u>Pr</u>, (88),
17.IV.24)
<u>Repr</u>.: 270000(2): 346-7.

240415(2)   Rech. (A speech.) (<u>Pr</u>, (88), 17.IV.24)
[In Rostov. Briefest extracts.]

[240416]   See 240406.

[240418]   See 240406.

240419(1)   Rech. (A speech.) (<u>Krasnaya Zvezda</u>, (91), 20.IV.24)
<u>Repr</u>.: 270000(2): 101-6.
<u>Trans</u>.: Am. p.q. <u>NYTimes</u>, 19.V.24;
      Eng. p.q. <u>Newsletter</u>, 16.IX.61.
[At Congress of Councils of Physical Culture.]

240419(2)   Rech. (A speech.) (<u>Iz</u>, (93), 22.IV.24; <u>Pr</u>, (92), 22.IV.24; <u>Trud</u>,
(92), 22.IV.24)
[At 7th Railwaymen's Congress.]

[240420]   Otvety na voprosy korrespondenta United Press. (Replies to questions
from United Press correspondent.) (<u>Iz</u>, (92), 20.IV.24)

240421(1)   Pref. O LENINE (LENIN), 240000(24).
<u>Trans</u>.: 240000(24).

240421(2) Perspektivy i zadachi na vostoke. (Prospects and tasks in the East.)
(Pr, (98), 1.V.24)
Repr.: 240000(6): 30-41; p.q. 260000(7): 93-4.
Trans.: Am. 570000(2); 640800: 229-40; 690000(4); FI, XII.42;
        Eng. 700100; p.q. Inprecor, (IV.31), 29.V.24; RevCom, VIII.45;
        Fr. QI(OSPE), (3), I.44;
        Ger. p.q. Inprekor, (IV.22/IV.59), 31.V/37.V.24;
        Jap. 681125: 241-52;
        Sp. 670000(5): 226-36;
        Swed. 691100(2): 205-15.
[See 260000(7) for other p.q. trans. Speech to Communist University
of Working People of the East, in Tiflis (Tbilsi).]

240423 Rech. (A speech.) (Iz, (96), 25.IV.24; Pr, (95), 25.IV.24; Trud,
(95), 25.IV.24)
Repr.: Possibly *240000(27); possibly*[240000(36)].
[To Railwaymen's Congress; on Lenin.]

[240424] SSSR i Yaponiya. (The USSR and Japan.) (Iz, (95), 24.IV.24)
[Interview with Osaka Mainichi correspondent.]

240428 Komsomol, na front khozyaistvennoi i kul´turnoi smychki. (Komsomol!
to the front of an economic and cultural alliance.) (Iz, (98),
30.IV.24; Krasnaya Zvezda, (97), 30.IV.24)
Repr.: 240000(23); p.q. 270000(2): 362-5.
[Report to Moscow District Komsomol Conference. Possibly *240000(1),
*240000(2).]

240429(1) Pervoe maya na zapade i na vostoke. (May Day in the West and in the
East.) (Pr, (97), 30.IV.24)
Repr.: 240000(6): 42-65.
Trans.: Am. p.q. NYTimes, 1.V.24.

240429(2) Molodezh, uchis politike! (Young people, study politics!) (KI, (3-4),
V-VI.24)
Repr.: *240000(19); 270000(2): 347-53.
Trans.: Eng. 660800(2); FI(Ln), (III.1), I.66.
[Speech on 5th anniversary of Communist Young Workers Hostels.]

240429(3) Prikaz, No. 591. (Iz, (98), 30.IV.24; Pr, (97), 30.IV.24)

240507   Nashi voennye zadachi. (Our military tasks.) (Pr, (103), 9.V.24)
[Basic thoughts of report to Red Army Military Academy. See further
240729(1).]

240509   Rech. O politike partii v khudozhestvennoi literature. (A speech.
Party policy on artistic literature.) (VOPROSY KUL´TURY: 93-110)
Repr.: 240000(18): 195-203.
Trans.: Eng.680300(1); FI(Ln), (IV.2), VII.67;
         Fr. Lettres Nouvelles, V-VI.67;
         Jap. 641225.I: 237-60;
         Sp. 690000(8).II: 1-18;
         Swed. 690600(1): 180-96.
[Repr. is slight modification. At Conference organized by Press
Dept., CC CPR(b).]

240510(1)   Zadachi voennoi pechati. (Tasks of the military press.) (Krasnaya
Zvezda, (105), 11.V.24)
Repr.: 240000(4): 20-43; 270000(2): 219-35.
[Speech to Congress of Military Press Workers.]

[240510(2)]   Interv´yu. (An interview.) (Pr, (104), 10.V.24)
[With correspondent of Popolo d'Italia.]

240511   Pokhorony tov. Yu.Kh.Lutovinova. (The funeral of cde. Yu.Ch. Lutovinov.)
(Trud, (105), 11.V.24)

240512   Pis´mo v redaktsiyu Molodoi Gvardii. (Letter to Ed. Board Molodoi
Gvardiya.) (Pr, (108), 15.V.24)
Repr.: 270000(2): 216.

240513(1)   O konflikte s germanskim pravitel´stvom. (On the conflict with the
German government.) (Gudok, (1193), 13.V.24; Pr, (106), 13.V.24;
Trud, (106), 13.V.24)

[240513(2)   VII moskovskoi gubs"ezda khimikov. (The 7th Moscow District Congress
of Chemical Workers.) (Trud, (106), 13.V.24)

[240514(1)]   Nam nado organizovyatsya. (We need organization.) (Gudok, (1194),
14.V.24)
Trans.: Fr. p.q. CorInt, (IV.29), 4.VI.24.
[On War Chemical Industry.]

[240514(2)]   Pis'mo v TsIK MROP. (Letter to CC MROP.) (Iz, (108), 14.V.24; Pr, (107), 14.V.24)

240518   Pis'mo. (A letter.) (Kniga o knigakh, (3), V.24)
[On bibliography.]

240519(1)   Organizatsiya khimicheskoi oborony. (The organization of chemical defence.) (Pr, (112), 20.V.24)
Trans.: Eng. p.q. Carr, SinOC.II: 1013.

240519(2)   Zaklyuchitel'noe slovo. (Summary speech.) (Pr, (112), 20.V.24)
[See 240519(1).]

240520   Pref. PYAT LET KOMINTERNA (FIVE YEARS OF THE COMINTERN), 240000(29).
Repr.: 240000(6): 66-80; p.q. 260000(7): 94-5.
Trans.: Am. FI, VIII.44;
        Fr. p.q. 680000(4): 117-8.
[See 240000(29) for all trans.; f.n. 240604.]

240522   Predislovie k knige tov. Averbakha, VOPROSY YUNOSHESKOGO DVIZHENIYA I LENIN. (Pref. to cde. Averbakh's book, PROBLEMS OF THE YOUTH MOVEMENT AND LENIN.) (270000(2): 354-5)
[Possibly trans. Latv. *240000(42).]

240523   Rech. (A speech.) (Pr, (118), 27.V.24)
Repr.: XIII S"EZD RKP(b): 629-33.
Trans.: Am. p.q. Eastman, L: 87;
        Eng. Inprecor, (IV.33), 10.VI.24; p.q. Carr, INTER: 363; p.q.
            Deutscher, STALIN: 278;
        Fr. CorInt, (IV.33), 19.VI.24;
        Ger. Inprekor, (IV.65), 10.VI.24.
[To 13th Congress CPR(b); on Left Opposition.]

240524   Alternative for 240523.

240525   V.P.Nogin. (Iz, (119), 27.V.24; Pr, (118), 27.V.24)
Repr.: 260000(17): 261-2.
[Funeral oration.]

240526
Preniya po dokladam TsK. (Discussion of CC report.) (Iz, (119), 27.V.24; Pr, (118), 27.V.24; Trud, (118), 27.V.24)
Repr.: PROTOKOLY: 154-68; PROTOKOLY(1963): 146-59.
Trans.: Eng. p.q. Deutscher, PU: 139;
        Ger. p.q. Inprekor, (IV.62), 4.VI.24.
[On Left Opposition, at 13th Party Congress.]

[240530]
Rech. (A speech.) (Iz, (122), 30.V.24)
[After 13th Party Congress. cf. PROTOKOLY: Appendix.]

[240531(1)]
Prikaz, No. 592. (Iz, (123), 31.V.24)

240531(2)
Rech. (A speech.) (Iz, (127), 5.VI.24)
[At Artillery Conference.]

240600
[On America and Britain.]
Trans.: Eng. p.q. [310328].

240601
Peredacha eskadrili imeni Lenina XIII S"ezda RKP(b). ([Speech at] handing over of Lenin Air Squadron.) (Iz, (125), 3.VI.24)

240604
f.n. to 240520.

[240605]
Slovo na "Dobrokhimom". (A word to the "Society of Friends of Chemical Defence.) (EkZhizn, (201), 5.VI.24; Iz, (127), 5.VI.24; Pr, (126), 5.VI.24)

240606
Pyat let sovetskoi knigi. (Five years of Soviet books.) (Krasnaya Zvezda, (128), 7.VI.24; Iz, (128), 7.VI.24)
Repr.: 270000(2): 251-2.

240607
Amsterdamskii Internatsional i voina. (The Amsterdam International and war.) (Pr, (128), 8.VI.24)
Repr.: 240000(6): 81-9.
Trans.: Eng. Inprecor, (IV.35,36), 19,26.VI.24;
        Fr. BulCom, (V.27), 4.VII.24; CorInt, (IV.36), 24.VI.24;
        Ger. Inprekor, (IV.69), 17.VI.24/(IV.25), 21.VI.24.

240609
[Discussion with Count Brockdorff-Rantzau.]
Trans.: Eng. Freund: 254-8.
[On Russo-German relations.]

240610(1) My i vostok. (We and the East.) (<u>Iz</u>, (131), 11.VI.24; <u>Pr</u>, (133), 14.VI.24)
<u>Repr</u>.: 240000(6): 90-107.
⌊Speech to celebration meeting of Educational Workers; at Sokolniki.⌋

240610(2) O torgovom flote. (The merchant fleet.) (<u>Iz</u>, (160), 16.VII.24)
⌊Speech at a meeting.⌋

240610(3) K pyatiletiyu voennogo izdatel´stva. (The fifth anniversary of military publishing.) (Pref. PYAT LET VOENNOI KNIGI)

240618(1) ⌊Note to Krassin.⌋
<u>Trans</u>.: Eng. Carr, SinOC.I: 469.
⌊On Anglo-American relations. T3490.⌋

⌊240618(2)⌋ Sovetskaya Rossiya i Yaponiya. (Soviet Russia and Japan.) (<u>Iz</u>, (135), 18.VI.24; <u>Pr</u>, (135), 18.VI.24)
<u>Trans</u>.: Fr. p.q. <u>CorInt</u>, (IV.39), 2.VII.24.
⌊Interview with Tomizi Naito, correspondent of <u>Nichiro Soofukai</u>.⌋

240621 Cherez kakoi etap my prokhodim? (Through what stage are we passing?) (<u>Iz</u>, (158), 13.VII.24; <u>Pr</u>, (157), 13.VII.24)
<u>Repr</u>.: 240000(6): 108-38; p.q. 260000(7): 97-8.
<u>Trans</u>.: Eng. 650000(10); <u>FI</u>(Ln), Summer, 1964.
⌊Speech to 5th All-Russian Congress of Medical and Veterinary Workers.⌋

240624 Neskol´ko slov o vospitanii cheloveka. (A few words about the upbringing of a human being.) (240000(4): 77-88)
<u>Repr</u>.: 270000(2): 106-13.

240629 ⌊Reply to Kolarov's invitation to address 5th Congress Comintern.⌋
<u>Trans</u>.: Eng. <u>Inprecor</u>, (IV.48), 12.VIII.24.

240630 Rech. (A speech.) (270000(2): 365-8)
⌊At graduation party for District Party Secretaries, held under the auspices of CC CPR(b). Archives.⌋

[240700] Rede zum Jubiläumsmanifest in der Sitzung der kommunistischen Fraktion
des Zentralsexekutivkomitees des Sowjets.
Trans.: Ger. Fahne desKom, (I.36), 18.XI.27.

240702 [Exchange of notes with Piatakov and Krassin, at STO.]
[c. Carr, SinOC.I: 475. T818.]

240703 Leninizm i bibliotechnaya rabota. (Leninism and the work of librarians.)
(Iz, (155), 10.VII.24; Pr, (154), 10.VII.24)
Repr.: 240000(4): 89-117; *240000(16); 270000(2): 114-32.
[Speech at 1st All-Union Congress of Librarians.]

240705 --: Manifest V Kongressa Kominterna. (Manifesto of 5th Congress
Comintern.) (Iz, (153), 8.VII.24; KI, (5-6), VII-VIII.24; Pr, (151),
6.VII.24)
Repr.: p.q. 260000(7): 95-7.
Trans.: p.q. 260000(7);
        Eng. p.q. Degras, DOCCI.II: 107-13;
        Fr. p.q. 680000(4): 119-21; CorInt, (IV.45), 17.VII.24;
        Ger. Inprekor, (IV.92), 29.VII.24.
[On 10th anniversary of World War I.]

[240711] Trotsky responde a un calumniador.
Trans.: Sp. Antorcha, (IV.136), 11.VII.24.
[Reply to Lord Hailsham.]

240715 Pref. ZAPAD I VOSTOK (WEST AND EAST), 240000(6).
Repr.: p.q. 260000(7): 98-9.
Trans.: p.q. 260000(7).

240717 Leninizm i rabochie kluby. (Leninism and workers' clubs.) (Iz, (166),
23.VII.24; Pr, (165), 23.VII.24; Trud, (166), 24.VII.24)
Repr.: 240000(4): 118-63; *240000(17); 270000(2): 133-63.
Trans.: Am. p.q. Davis;
        Eng. p.q. 660800(1); p.q. FI(Ln), (III.1), I.66.
[See further, 240827.]

240720 Pref., B.Efimov, KARIKATURII. (Iz, (167), 24.VII.24)
[Brochure locNYPL.]

240723   Rabkor i ego kul´turnaya rol. (The worker-correspondent and his cultural role.) (<u>Pr</u>, (183), 14.VIII.24)
Repr.: 240000(4): 44-76; 270000(2): 180-201.

240727   Rech. (A speech.) (<u>Iz</u>, (171), 29.VII.24)
[On anniversary of founding of Moscow.]

240728   Doklad. (A report.) (<u>Iz</u>, (177), 5.VIII.24; <u>Pr</u>, (176), 5.VIII.24; <u>Trud</u>, (176), 5.VIII.24)
Repr.: 260000(7): 5-40.
Trans.: Am. p.q. 640800: 208-12; p.q. Eudin & Fisher: 244-9; <u>FI</u>, VII-VIII.45;
     Eng. <u>Workers Press</u>, (151,152), 29,30.IV.70;
     Fr. p.q. 680000(4): passim; <u>Cahiers duBol</u>, (I.3,4), 5,12.XII.24;
         p.q. <u>QI</u>, (3), I.44; p.q. <u>RévProl</u>, (I.1), I.25; p.q. <u>V</u>, (4), 5.V.39;
     Jap. p.q. 681125: 218-23;
     Nor. p.q. <u>Ny Tid</u>, 27.X.24;
     Sp. p.q. 670000(5): 206-10;
     Swed. p.q. 691100(2): 185-9.
[To meeting of Society of Friends of the Physics and Mathematics Faculties; on perspectives of world development. See 260000(7) for other trans.]

240729(1)   Voprosy grazhdanskoi voiny. (Problems of civil war.) (<u>Iz</u>, (192,193,195), 24,26,28.VIII.24; <u>Pr</u>, (202), 6.IX.24)
Repr.: *240000(3); 250000(8): 379-402.
Trans.: Am. p.q. 360500(1): 143-6; p.q. 570500: 143-6; 700600; <u>ISR</u>, III-IV.70;
     Eng. p.q. <u>Free Expression</u>, I.45;
     Fr. 260900; p.q. 301100(1): 237-40; p.q. 690000(1).I: 256-9;
         <u>Initiative Socialiste</u>, (17), VI.68; ∉ <u>VoixCom</u>, (V.8-10,12,13), 24.II-10.III,24,31.III.35;
     Ger. p.q. 290000(4): 132-4;
     Sp. 310000(5): 107-52.
[Speech to Board of Military Science Society. See also 240507.]

240729(2)   Pref. LITERATURA I REVOLYUTSIYA (LITERATURE AND REVOLUTION), 240000(18).
[2nd ed. See 230000(9), notes.]

240731(1)   Chetvertomu vypusku voennoi akademii RKKA. (To 4th Graduation from the Military Academy of the Red Army.) (<u>Iz</u>, (174), 1.VIII.24)

240731(2)   Nel´zya zabyvat. (It is impossible to forget.) (Iz, (175), 2.VIII.24)

240812   [Verifies a Lenin manuscript.] (Krasnyi Arkhiv, (V.7), 1924)
       Trans.: Eng. Vulliamy.

240818   SSSR na storone ugnetennogo Kitaya. (The USSR is on the side of
       oppressed China.) (Iz, (217), 23.IX.24; Pr, (190), 23.VIII.24)
       Trans.: Eng. Inprecor, (IV.72), 9.X.24; Newsletter, 28.V.60;
              Ger. Inprekor, (IV.40), 4.X.24.

[240821]   Neskol´ko zamechanii v otvet t. Semashko. (A few remarks in reply to
       cde. Semashko.) (Iz, (189), 21.VIII.24)
       Repr.: 270000(2): 80-1.

240827   Eshche, o rabochikh klubakh. (Once more, on workers clubs.) (Pr, (193),
       27.VIII.24)
       Repr.: 240000(4): 164-71; 270000(2): 163-7.
       [See 240717.]

[240831]   Dobro pozhalovat, pyat tysyach vzvodnytch! (Greetings, 5,000 Platoons!)
       (Pr, (197), 31.VIII.24)

240906   Pamyati M.S.Glazmana. (In memory of M.S.Glazman.) (260000(17): 262-5)
       [Archives.]

240915   Pref. 1917, 240000(32).
       Repr.: 240000(33); 240000(35); 250000(12); OB UROKAKH; TROTSKII PERED
              SUDOM; UROKI OKTYABRYA.
       Trans.: Am. 370000(6); 630000(8): 115-77;
              Bul. *240000(38);
              Ch. *400000(15); *470000(1);
              Cz. *250000(28);
              Den. 250000(31);
              Eng. 250000(21); 630000(9): 115-77; Inprecor, (V.16), 26.II.25;
                 ERRORS: 29-119;
              Fr. p.q. 680000(4): 447-52; Cahiers duBol, (I.5,6), 19,26.XII.24;
                 Procacci: 31-82;
              Ger. 250000(26); 290000(7); Aktion, (XV.2-3), 15.II.25;
                 Inprekor, (V.15), 1.I.25/(V.16), 29.I.25; OKTOBERREVOLUTION:
                 8-76; UM DEN OKTOBER;
              It. *250000(15); [660000(2)]: 3-38; Procacci: 33-89; p.q.
                 Prometeo, (I.9, III.40), 15.XI.28, 1.XI.30;   ++++

240915   ++++   <u>Trans</u>.: Jap. *610805; 661130: 69-143;
                 Nor. 250000(31);
                 Sp. 310000(5): 3-104; *530000(4);
                 Swed. 250000(30).

         [Correction 241014. Eng. 250000(21) and Swed. 250000(30) omit last
         2 pages of Russian text. Procacci omits last 3 pars, in Fr.]

240920   Pref. VOPROSY KUL´TURNOI RABOTY (PROBLEMS OF CULTURAL WORK), 240000(4).

240922   Kabardino-Balkarskaya avtonomnaya oblast i ee zadachi. (The Kabardino-
         Balkarsk Autonomous Region and its tasks.) (<u>Iz</u>, (238), 17.X.24; <u>Pr</u>,
         (237), 17.X.24)
         <u>Trans</u>.: Eng. p.q. <u>Inprecor</u>, (IV.72), 9.X.24;
                Kar. 250000(29).
         [Speech in Nalchik; on soviet power as an instrument of independence
         and cultural advance.]

240928   Vernoe i fal´shivoe o Lenine. (Truth and falsehood about Lenin.)
         (<u>Iz</u>, (229), 7.X.24; <u>Pr</u>, (228), 7.X.24; <u>Trud</u>, (228), 7.X.24)
         <u>Trans</u>.: Den. 310000(25);
                Eng. <u>ComRev</u>, XII.24;
                Fr. <u>CorInt</u>, (IV.74), 4.XI.24; <u>DrapR</u>, (I.273), 14.XI.24;
                Hol. 670000(14): 193-208.
         [See 240000(24), note, for other trans. On Gorki´s brochure on Lenin.]

240930   Malen´kie o bol´shom. (The little ones on the great man.) (<u>Iz</u>, (230),
         8.X.24; <u>Pr</u>, (229), 8.X.24; <u>Trud</u>, (229), 8.X.24)
         [See 240000(24), note, for other trans. On Lenin.]

241014   Neobkhodimaya popravka. (A necessary correction.) (240000(32).I: lxvii)
         [See 240915.]

241015(1)   Shag a shagom. (Step by step.) (<u>Iz</u>, (251), 1.XI.24; <u>Pr</u>, (250), 1.XI.24)
         <u>Repr</u>.: Pref. 230000(7).III.ii.
         <u>Trans</u>.: p.q. 361013.

241015(2)   O perevyborakh angliiskogo parlamenta. (The British general election.)
         (<u>Iz</u>, (237), 16.X.24)
         [p.q. speech in Pyatagorsk.]

241018   Kalenym utyugom! (With a red-hot iron!) (<u>Iz</u>, (240), 19.X.24;
           <u>Pr</u>, (239), 19.X.24)
           <u>Repr</u>.: 270000(2): 201-6.

241020(1)   PS to 230504(1). (250000(8): 6)

[241020(2)]   Izbytok userdiya. (Excessive zeal.) (<u>Bol</u>, (12-13), 20.X.24)
           [Reply to Vardin's review of O LENINE, 240000(24).]

241023   Pyatsya godovshchina "Yudenishkikh den". (The 5th anniversary of
           "Yudenich Day.") (<u>Iz</u>, (246), 26.X.24; <u>Krasnaya Gazeta</u>, (245),
           26.X.24)
           <u>Repr</u>.: 260000(18).II: 312-3.
           <u>Trans</u>.: Fr. <u>CorInt</u>, (IV.74), 4.XI.24.
           [Letter to <u>Krasnaya Gazeta</u>.]

241025   Rost mirovogo militarizma i nashi voennye zadachi. (The growth of world
           militarism and our military tasks.) (<u>Iz</u>, (254), 5.XI.24)
           <u>Repr</u>.: 260000(7): 99-102.
           <u>Trans</u>.: Fr. p.q. <u>CorInt</u>, (IV.77), 19.XI.24; p.q. <u>DrapR</u>, (I.281),
                23-24.XI.24.
           [Speech at Red Army Conference. See 260000(7) for other trans.]

241027   O stenografii. (Shorthand.) (VOPROSY STENOGRAFII, 1924)
           <u>Repr</u>.: 270000(2): 216-8.

241029(1)   Oni obrecheny na porozhenie. (They are doomed to defeat.) (<u>Iz</u>, (249),
           30.X.24)

241029(2)   Pis'mo. (A letter.) (270000(2): 453)
           [Note to [230710]. To Central Publishers of the Peoples of the East,
           on publication of his book in Tatar.]

241031   Pref. O DEVYATOM YANVARYA (JANUARY 9th), 250000(7).

241102   Pref. Ya.Shafir, OCHERKI GRUZINSKOI ZHIRONDY (SKETCHES OF THE GEORGIAN
           GIRONDE).
           [LocHIS/NYPL.]

[241107]   Oktyabr zhivet. (October lives.) (<u>Iz</u>, (256), 7.XI.24; <u>Pr</u>, (255),
           7.XI.24)

[241117] V chem zadachi <u>Krest´yanskoi Gazety</u>? (What are the tasks of
<u>Krestyanskaya Gazeta</u>?) (<u>KrestGaz</u>, (51), 17.XI.24)
<u>Repr</u>.: 270000(2): 368.

241130 [The purposes of this explanation: Our differences.]
<u>Trans</u>.: Eng. p.q. Carr, SinOC.II: 28-9.
[T2969.]

250000(1)   § VOPROSY BYTA. (PROBLEMS OF LIFE.)
[3rd ed. Repr. of 230000(4). See 230000(3) for all repr., trans., notes.]

*250000(2)   *D.I.MENDELEEV I MARKSIZM. (D.I.MENDELEYEV AND MARXISM.)
[See 250917 for all repr., trans.; 380418(1) Pref. Am. ed.]

250000(3)   K SOTSIALIZMU ILI K KAPITALIZMU? (TOWARDS SOCIALISM OR CAPITALISM?)
[See 250828(2) for all repr., trans., notes.]

*250000(4)   *KACHESTVO PRODUKTSII I SOTSIALISTICHESKII KHOZYAISTVO. (THE QUALITY OF PRODUCTION AND SOCIALIST ECONOMY.)

250000(5)   KUDA IDET ANGLIYA? (WHERE IS BRITAIN GOING?) (Pr, (120,125,130,135), 28.V, 4,11,17.VI.25)
Trans.: Am. 250000(32); p.q. 640800: 196-205;
        Eng. 260200; 261000(1); 261000(2); 600200; 700500(2);
           p.q. Red Flag, (9), V-VI.34; p.q. WIN, I-II.49;
        Fr. 260000(25); p.q. 680000(4): passim; p.q. Vie Ouv, 19.III, 4.VI.25;
        Ger. 250000(33); 260000(28);
        Jap. 260915; 260930; p.q. 681125: 205-16;
        Sp. 270000(6); p.q. 670000(5): 194-203;
        Swed. p.q. 691100(2): 174-82.
[Pref. 250524; 2nd instalment 260000(11); Pref. Eng. ed. [260000(33)]; Pref. Ger. ed. 260506; Pref. 260000(11), 260519. Fr. 260000(25) includes 260000(11) without Pref. 260519.]

250000(6)   † NASHA PERVAYA REVOLYUTSIYA. (OUR FIRST REVOLUTION.)
Trans.: Am. p.q. 180000(40);
        Eng. p.q. 531200; p.q. 540300;
        Yid. p.q. 190000(68); p.q. 210000(51).
[Pref. 250319. Soch. II.]

250000(7)   † O DEVYATOM YANVARYA. (JANUARY 9th.)
[Repr. of 050000(1) with supplementary material. Pref. 241031.]

250000(8)   † OSNOVNYE VOPROSY PROLETARSKOI REVOLYUTSII. (FUNDAMENTAL PROBLEMS OF PROLETARIAN REVOLUTION.)
[Pref. 230504(1); PS to 230504(1), 241020. Reprint of 230000(18) with different appendices. Soch. XII.]

250000(9)   § PYAT LET KOMINTERNA. (FIVE YEARS OF THE COMINTERN.)
[Repr. of 240000(29).]

*250000(10)   *TERRORIZM I KOMMUNIZM. (TERRORISM AND COMMUNISM.)
[See 200000(37) for all repr., trans.]

250000(11)   § 1905.
[See 220000(12) for all repr., trans., notes.]

250000(12)   UROKI OKTYABRYA. (LESSONS OF OCTOBER.)
[See 240915 for all repr., trans.]

250000(13)   LE DRAME DU PROLÉTARIAT FRANÇAIS.
[Trans. Fr. See 220515 for all repr., trans.]

250000(14)   LE DRAME DU PROLÉTARIAT FRANÇAIS.
[Trans. Fr. See 220515 for all repr., trans.]

*250000(15)   *GL'INSEGNAMENTI DELL' OTTOBRE.
[Trans. It. See 240915 for all repr., trans.]

250000(16)   KAPITALISMUS ODER SOZIALISMUS.
[Trans. Ger. See 251107, Pref.; 250828(2) for all repr., trans.]

250000(17)   § LENIN.
[Trans. Am. See 240000(24) for all repr., trans., notes.]

250000(18)   § LENIN.
[Trans. Eng. See 240000(24) for all repr., trans., notes.]

250000(19)   § LENIN.
[Trans. Eng. See 240000(24) for all repr., trans., notes.]

250000(20)   § LÉNINE.
[Trans. Fr. See 240000(24) for all repr., trans., notes.]

250000(21)   THE LESSONS OF OCTOBER, 1917.
[Trans. Eng. See 240915 for all trans., notes.]

250000(22)   § LITERATURE AND REVOLUTION.
[Trans. Am. See 230000(9) for all repr., trans., notes.]

250000(23)   § LITERATURE AND REVOLUTION.
[Trans. Eng. See 230000(9) for all trans., notes.]

250000(25)   § MY FLIGHT FROM SIBERIA.
[Trans. Am. See 070000(3) for all repr., trans., notes.]

250000(26)   1917: DIE LEHREN DER REVOLUTION.
[Trans. Ger. See 240915 for all repr., trans., notes.]

*250000(28) *POUČENI Z ŘÍJNA. Predml. Lev Trocký, ČEMU NÁS UČE ŘÍJEN.
[Trans. Cz. See 240915 for all trans., notes.]

250000(29)   QABARTY BYLA MALQARNY AFTONOMNY OBLASTARY BYLA ANY NE DAT ETERGE
KEREKLI BULGANYNY HAQQYNDAR.
[Trans. Kar. See 240922.]

250000(30)   REVOLUTIONENS LÄRDOMAR (1917).
[Trans. Swed. See 240915 for all trans., notes.]

250000(31)   1917.
[Trans. Den. See 240915 for all trans., notes.]

250000(32)   WHITHER ENGLAND?
[Trans. Am. See 250000(5) for all trans., notes; 250524 Pref.]

250000(33)   WOHIN TREIBT ENGLAND?
[Trans. Ger. See 250000(5) for all repr., trans., notes.]

*250000(34) *OT OKTYABR'SKOI REVOLYUTSII DO BRESTSKOGO MIRA. (FROM THE OCTOBER
REVOLUTION TO THE PEACE OF BREST.)
[See 180000(5) for all repr., trans., notes.]

*250000(35) § *ZÁKLADNI OTÁZKY REVOLUCE: TERORISMUS A KOMUNISMUS; MEZI IMPERIALISMEM
A REVOLUCE; NOVA HOSPODAŘ SOV. RUSKA A VYHLIDKY SVĚT REVOL.
[Trans. Cz. See 230000(18) for all trans.]

250000(36)   § 1905 rik.
[Trans. Ukr. See 220000(12) for all trans., notes.]

250115   Pis'mo Plenumu TsK RKP(b). (Letter to Plenum CC CPR(b).) (EkZhizn,
(16), 20.I.25; Iz, (16), 20.I.25; Pr, (16), 20.I.25; Trud, (16), 20.I.25)
Trans.: Am. Eastman, L: 153-8;
    Eng. ComRev, III.25; Inprecor, (-), 7.II.25; ERRORS: 372-7;
    Fr. CorInt, (V.7), 30.I.25; EuropeN, 7.II.25; RevProl, (I.2),
        II.25;
    Ger. Inprekor, (V.18), 29.I.25; Int, (VIII.2), II.25.
[Resignation.]

250313   Pamyati Sverdlova. (In memory of Sverdlov.) (260000(17): 248-55)
Trans.: Am. FI, XI.46.

250319   Pref. NASHA PERVAYA REVOLYUTSIYA (OUR FIRST REVOLUTION), 250000(6).

250320   Telegramma. (A telegram.) (Iz, (70), 27.III.25)
⌊Condolence on death of cde. Narimanov.⌋

250327   Pamyati t.t. Myasnikova, Mogilevskogo i Atarbekova. (In memory of
cdes. Myasnikov, Mogilevsky and Atarbekov.) (Iz, (73), 31.III.25;
Pr, (73), 31.III.25)
⌊Speech at funeral meeting, in Sukhum.⌋

250403   Telegramma na zapros redaktsii Sunday Worker. (Telegram in reply to
an inquiry from Ed. Sunday Worker.) (Iz, (104), 9.V.25; Pr, (104),
9.V.25)
Trans.: Eng. Sunday Worker, 10.V.25;
        Fr. CorInt, (V.54), 23.V.25; DrapR, (II.126), 29.V.25;
        Ger. Inprekor, (V.34), 22.VIII/(V.123), 21.VIII.25.
⌊See further 250701. On Eastman, LEON TROTSKY: PORTRAIT OF A YOUTH.⌋

250501   See 250506.

250506   [Statements, en route to Moscow.]
Trans.: Am. p.q. NYTimes, 7.V.25;
        Eng. p.q. Morning Post, 12.V.25.

250522   ⌊On Eastman, SINCE LENIN DIED.⌋
Trans.: Eng. Inprecor, (V.60), 30.VII.25;
        Fr. CorInt, (V.72,82), 22.VII, 22.VIII.25;
        Ger. Inprekor, (V.34), 22.VIII/(V.111), 21.VII.25.
⌊p.q. 250701.⌋

250524   Pref. KUDA IDET ANGLIYA? (WHERE IS BRITAIN GOING?), 250000(5).
Repr.: p.q. 260000(7): 102-6.
Trans.: Am. 250000(32); p.q. 690600(3): 115;
        Eng. 600200; WIN, XII.45;
        Fr. 260000(25): 5-8;
        Sp. 270000(6): 16-9.

250525   Stabilizatsiya mirovogo kapitalizma. (The stabilization of world capitalism.) (<u>Iz</u>, (119), 27.V.25; <u>PlanKhoz</u>, (6), VI.25)

<u>Repr</u>.: p.q. 260000(7): 107-9.

<u>Trans</u>.: p.q. 260000(7).

[Contribution to a discussion led by Radek and Varga.]

250531   Rech. (A speech.) (<u>Iz</u>, (123), 2.VI.25; <u>Pr</u>, (123), 2.VI.25; <u>Trud</u>, (124), 3.VI.25)

<u>Trans</u>.: Am. p.q. <u>NYTimes</u>, 2.VI.25.

[At opening of Thermo-technical Institute; on scientific-technical thinking and socialism.]

[250606]   Moskovskii dukh. (The Moscow spirit.) (<u>Pr</u>, (127), 6.VI.25)

<u>Trans</u>.: Am. p.q. <u>NYTimes</u>, 7.VI.25;
       Eng. <u>Inprecor</u>, (V.51), 18.VI.25;
       Fr. <u>CorInt</u>, (V.62), 17.VI.25; <u>DrapR</u>, (II.140), 16.VI.25;
          <u>Vie Ouv</u>, 10.VII.25;
       Ger. <u>Inprekor</u>, (V.93), 12.VI.25/(V.24), 13.VI.25.

[In memory of murdered workers and students of Shanghai.]

250612(1)   Voprosy elektrokhozyaistva. (Problems of the economics of electricification.) (<u>EkZhizn</u>, (166), 23.VII.25; <u>Pr</u>, (166), 23.VII.25)

<u>Repr</u>.: VOPROSY ELEKTROPROMYSHLENNOSTI I ELEKTROFIKATSII: 3-15.

[Brochure LocNYPL.]

250612(2)   [Letter to Dzerzhinsky.]

[c. 300207(2).]

250624   [Letter to Piatakov.]

[c. 300207(2).]

[250630]   Rezolyutsiya. (A resolution.) (<u>Iz</u>, (147), 1.VII.25)

[At Conference under auspices of Head of Administration of Electrical Enterprises [i.e. Trotsky].]

250701   Po povodu knigi Istmena 'Posle smerti Lenina'. (On Eastman's book 'Since Lenin Died'.) (<u>Bol</u>, (16), 1.IX.25)

<u>Trans</u>.: Eng. <u>Inprecor</u>, (V.68), 3.IX.25; <u>Sunday Worker</u>, 19.VII.25;
       Fr. <u>CorInt</u>, (V.82), 22.VIII.25;
       Ger. <u>Inprekor</u>, (V.123), 21.VIII/(V.34), 22.VIII.25.

250706   Ob upushchenii kachestva produktsii promyshlennosti. (Improving the quality of industrial products.) (Iz, (152), 7.VII.25; Pr, (161), 17.VII.25)

*250710   *ROSHIA KAKUMEI-KA NO SEIKATSU-RON.
[Trans. Jap. from 240000(49). See 230000(3) for all repr., trans., notes.]

250712   Pis'mo. (A letter.) (Iz, (163), 19.VII.25; Pr, (163), 19.VII.25)
[Welcome to delegation from Germany.]

250716   Budem okhranyat elektroprovoda! (We must protect electrical wiring!) (Iz, (162), 18.VII.25)

250720   BUNGAKU TO KAKUMEI + TENKAN-KI NO BUNKA.
[Trans. Jap. See 230000(9) + 230000(3) for all repr., trans., notes.]

250729   Na voprosu nemetskikh gostei. (Questions from German visitors.)
(EkZhizn, (171), 29.VII.25; Iz, (171), 29.VII.25; Trud, (171), 29.VII.25)
[On concessions policy of USSR.]

250730(1)   Interv'yu. (An interview.) (Iz, (172, 30.VII.25; Pr, (172), 30.VII.25)
Trans.: Am. Current History, II.26;
         Ger. NFreie Presse, 11.X.25.
[With Chamberlin, of UP.]

[250730(2)]   Kachestvo tovarov. (The quality of goods.) (EkZhizn, (172), 30.VII.25)

250804   Mogut li nashego proizvodstva kokurirovat s Avstriiskimi? (Is our production able to compete with Austria's?) (EkZhizn, (189), 21.VIII.25)

250817   Bor'ba za kachestvo produktsii. (The struggle for quality in production.) (EkZhizn, (186), 18.VIII.25; Iz, (186,194,195), 18,27,28.VIII.25; Pr, (194,195), 27,28.VIII.25)
Repr.: Possibly *260000(36).
[Speech at NTO, special conference on quality in production.]

250828(1)   Sklyanskii pogib! (Sklyanskii is dead!) (Iz, (196), 29.VIII.25; Pr, (196), 29.VIII.25)
Repr.: 260000(17): 272-4.
Trans.: Fr. CorInt, (V.87), 5.IX.25.

250828(2)   K sotsializmu ili k kapitalizmu? (Towards socialism or capitalism?)
             (EkZhizn, (211,212,215,216), 16,17,20,22.IX.25; Iz, (198,199,211,212,215,
             216), 1,2,16,17,20,22.IX.25; Pr, 198,199,211,212,215,216), 1,2,16,17,20,
             22.IX.25)
             Repr.: 250000(3); *260000(9).
             Trans.: Am. 260000(27); p.q. 640800: 132-6;
                     Eng. 260000(26); p.q. Labour Monthly, XI,XII.25;
                     Fr. 280000(6); *670000(18); p.q. 680000(4): 140-4; Clarté,
                         (14-16), 15.X,XI,XII.27-I.28; p.q. Lutte deC, (1), II-III.28;
                         p.q. VieOuv, 18.XII.25;
                     Ger. 250000(16); 260000(24);
                     Jap. *270000(18); p.q. 681125: 140-4;
                     Sp. p.q. 670000(5): 132-6; *280000(12);
                     Swed. p.q. 691100(2): 116-20.
             ⌊PS 250912; dated instalment 250915(1); Pref. 2nd ed. 251107(1). Eng.
             260000(26) lacks final par. and supplementary tables.⌋

250901   Rech. (A speech.) (Iz, (200), 3.IX.25)
             Repr.: *260000(14).
             ⌊To meeting of workers in VEK Factory, Kharkov.⌋

250902   Alternative for 250901.

250903   Dneprostroi. (Iz, (204), 8.IX.25; Pr, (204), 8.IX.25)
             ⌊On the journey of the Dnieperstroi Commission to Zaporozh.⌋

250908   Réponse au Comité Central du PCR à la question posée par le CC du PCF
             concernant le journal de Monatte-Rosmer.
             Trans.: Fr. Huma, 1.X.25; RévProl, (I.10), X.25;
                     Ger. Inprekor, (V.41), 10.X.25.

250910   Pamyati t.t. Sklyanskogo i Khurgina. (In memory of cdes. Sklyansky
             and Khurgin.) (Iz, (216), 22.IX.25; Pr, (216), 22.IX.25)

250911   Pamyati E.M.Sklyanskogo. (In memory of E.M.Sklyansky.) (Iz, (217),
             23.IX.25; Pr, (217), 23.IX.25)
             Repr.: 260000(17): 274-81.
             Trans.: Fr. CorInt, (V.87), 5.IX.25.

250912   PS to 250828(2). (EkZhizn, (212), 17.IX.25)

[250913]   Problema kachestvennykh izmeritelei. (Problems of quality standards.)
                (EkZhizn, (209), 13.IX.25)

250915(1)   See 250828(2), note.

250915(2)   O Dneprostroe. (On Dnieperstroi.) (EkZhizn, (210), 15.IX.25; Iz, (210),
                15.IX.25)
                [Reply to R.E.Klasson.]

250917   D.I.Mendeleev i marksizm. (D.I.Mendeleyev and marxism.) (EkZhizn,
                (213,221,222), 18,27,29.IX.25)
                Repr.: *250000(2); 270000(2): 268-88.
                Trans.: Am. p.q. 640800: 342-52; NI, II.40;
                        Eng. 491000;
                        It. 581000: 173-94; 690500(2): 9-34;
                        Jap. p.q. 681125: 357-66;
                        Sp. 640900: 242-68; p.q. 670000(5): 345-54; 690000(8).II: 55-75;
                            Babel, (15-16), I-IV.41;
                        Swed. p.q. 691100(2): 308-17.
                [Pref. Am. ed. 380418(1). Speech to Mendeleyev Congress.]

250920   Alternative for 250910.

250923   Sel'skokhozyaistvennye mashiny i orudiya -- v tsentre vnimaniya!
                (Agricultural machinery and tools in the centre of attention!)
                (EkZhizn, (220), 26.IX.25; Iz, (223), 30.IX.25; Pr, (223), 30.IX.25)

250925   Nasha khozyaistvennaya orientirovka na mirovoi rynok. (Our economic
                orientation to the world market.) (EkZhizn, (220), 26.IX.25; Trud,
                (221), 27.IX.25)

250929   Pref. MOI POBEG IZ SIBIRII (MY FLIGHT FROM SIBERIA), 260000(13).

250930   Bor'ba za kachestvo produktsii. (The struggle for quality in
                production.) (Iz, (224), 1.X.25)
                Trans.: Fr. p.q. CorInt, (V.111), 11.XI.25;
                        Ger. p.q. Inprekor, (V.45), 7.XI.25.

251002   Vsesoyuznyi s"ezd kozhevennoi promyshlennosti. (At the All-Union
                Congress of the Leather Industry.) (Iz, (226), 3.X.25)

251005   Uchastie profsoyuzov v bor'be za kachestvo. (The participation of
                the trade unions in the struggle for quality.) (Iz, (228), 6.X.25)

251016   LENIN KAISO-KI.
              [Trans. Jap. See 240000(24) for all repr., trans., notes.]

251025   [Rech.] [A speech.] (Pr, (253), 5.XI.25)
              Trans.: Eng. p.q. Deutscher, PU: 214.

*251028   *MUSANSHA BUNKA-RON.
              [Trans. Jap. from 240000(49). See 230000(3) for all repr., trans.,
              notes.]

251031   Telegramma. (A telegram.) (Iz, (251), 1.XI.25; Pr, (251), 1.XI.25)
              [To CC CPR; on Frunze's death.]

251102   Pamyati M.V.Frunze. (In memory of M.V.Frunze.) (Iz, (259), 13.XI.25;
              Pr, (259), 13.XI.25)
              Repr.: 260000(17): 281-5.

251107(1)   Pref. K SOTSIALIZMU ILI K KAPITALIZMU? (TOWARDS SOCIALISM OR
              CAPITALISM?), *260000(9). (Iz, (261), 15.XI.25; Pr, (261), 15.XI.25)
              Trans.: Am. 260000(27);
                      Eng. 260000(26);
                      Fr. 280000(6);
                      Ger. 260000(24).

251107(2)   Za kachestvo -- za kul´turu. (For quality -- for culture.) (Pr, (255),
              7.XI.25)
              Repr.: 270000(2): 369-84.
              Trans.: Eng. p.q. Inprecor, (V.81), 19.XI.25;
                      Fr. p.q. CorInt, (V.111), 11.XI.25.

251108   Vosem let. Itogi i perspektivy. (8 years. Results and prospects.)
              (Iz, (272), 28.XI.25; Pr, (272), 28.XI.25)
              Repr.: 260000(3); *260000(4).
              [Speech at celebration meeting of Kislovodsk Soviet; on anniversary of
              the October Revolution.]

251109   Pref. POLITICHESKAYA KHRONIKA (POLITICAL CHRONICLES), 260000(16).

251119   Telegramma. (A telegram.) (EkZhizn, (265), 20.XI.25; Iz, (265),
              20.XI.25)
              [Greetings to Congress of Metal Workers.]

251123(1)   Pref. KOMMUNISTICHESKII INTERNATSIONAL (THE COMMUNIST INTERNATIONAL),
              260000(10).

251200 Stroit sotsializm — znachit osvobozhdat zhenshchinu i okhranyat mat.
(Building socialism means freeing the woman and protecting the mother.)
(Za Novyi Byt, XII.25)
Repr.: *260000(15); 270000(2): 55-8.
Trans.: Ger. NRussland, (III.3-4), 1926.

251205 K voprosu o sel´skokhozyaistvennykh kommunakh. (The problem of
agricultural communes.) (Pr, (278), 5.XII.25)

251207(1) Rech. (A speech.) (Iz, (288), 17.XII.25; Pr, (288), 17.XII.25)
Repr.: *260000(15); 270000(2): 44-55.
[To 3rd All-Union Conference for the Protection of Mothers and Children.]

251207(2) Privetstvie. (Greetings.) (EkZhizn, (280), 8.XII.25; Iz, (280),
8.XII.25)
[On opening of Shaturka Electrical Power Station.]

251208 Novaya stranitsa. (A new page.) (Iz, (281), 9.XII.25)
Repr.: *260000(8); 270000(2): 384-96.
[Speech to All-Union District Medical Workers.]

251215 Pref. SOVETSKAYA RESPUBLIKA I KAPITALISTICHESKII MIR (THE SOVIET
REPUBLIC AND THE CAPITALIST WORLD), 260000(18).

251218 [At 14th All-Russian Congress CPR(b).]
Trans.: Am. p.q. NYTimes, 30.XII.25.

251222(1) [Note on 14th All-Russian Congress CPR(b).]
[c. Deutscher, PU: 255. T2975.]

251222(2) See 260513.

251225 See 260513.

251226 Cherez dvadtsat let. 1905g. (Twenty years later. 1905.) (Iz, (6),
8.I.26; Pr, (6), 8.I.26)
Repr.: 250000(6).II: 223-36; *260000(19).
[Speech to 2nd All-Union Congress of the Society of Political Prisoners
and Deportees.]

251228 See 260513.

260000(1) ‡ BALKANY I BALKANSKAYA VOINA. (THE BALKANS AND THE BALKAN WAR.)
[Pref. 260619. Soch. VI.]

*260000(2) *BOR´BA ZA KACHESTVO PRODUKTSII I RABOCHI KORRESPONDENT. (THE STRUGGLE
FOR QUALITY IN PRODUCTION AND THE WORKER-CORRESPONDENT.)
[See 260113(2) for all repr., trans.]

260000(3) VOSEM LET. (8 YEARS.)
[See 251108 for all repr., notes.]

*260000(4) VOSEM LET. (8 YEARS.)
[See 251108 for all repr., notes.]

260000(5) ‡ DELO BYLO V ISPANII. (WHAT HAPPENED IN SPAIN.)
Repr.: 270000(1): 251-323; *270000(5).
Trans.: Sp. 290000(5); 680000(9).
[Pref. [260000(29)]; Pref. Sp. 290600(2). See individual items for
other trans.]

*260000(6) *DOKLAD O MEZHDUNARODNOM I VNUTRENNEM POLOZHENII. (REPORT ON THE
INTERNATIONAL AND INTERNAL SITUATION.)
[See 260129 for all repr., notes.]

260000(7) ‡ EVROPA I AMERIKA. (EUROPE AND AMERICA.)
Trans.: Cz. *260000(23);
      Eng. 500400; 510100: 1-35;
      Fr. 260000(22);
      Ger. 260000(21);
      Hol. 270000(7);
      Sp. p.q. 270000(6): 229-70; ¢ Antorcha, (VI.250-65), 17.IX.26-
        7.I.27.
[Pref. 260225(1). Eng. and Sp. Antorcha lack appendices.]

*260000(8) *ZADACHI RABOTNIKOV KUL´TURNOGO STROITEL´STVA. (TASKS OF WORKERS IN
CULTURAL CONSTRUCTION.)
[See 251208 for all repr., notes.]

*260000(9) *K SOTSIALIZMU ILI K KAPITALIZMU? (TOWARDS SOCIALISM OR CAPITALISM?)
[See 250828(2) for all repr., trans., notes.]

260000(10) ‡ KOMMUNISTICHESKII INTERNATSIONAL. (THE COMMUNIST INTERNATIONAL.)
[Pref. 251123(1). Soch. XIII.]

260000(11)   ‡ KUDA IDET ANGLIYA?   (WHERE IS BRITAIN GOING?)

Trans.: Fr. 260000(25);

Sp. 270000(6).

[2nd instalment of 250000(5). Pref. 260519, lacking in Fr. and Sp. See individual items for other trans.]

260000(12)   ‡ KUL´TURA STAROGO MIRA. (THE CULTURE OF THE OLD WORLD.)

[Soch. XX.]

260000(13)   § MOI POBEG IZ SIBIRII. (MY FLIGHT FROM SIBERIA.)

[See 070000(3) for all repr., trans., notes. Pref. 250929.]

*260000(14)   *O NASHIKH NOVYKH ZADACHAKH. (OUR NEW TASKS.)

[See 250901 for all repr., notes.]

*260000(15)   *OKHRANA MATERINSTVA I BOR´BA ZA KUL´TURU. (THE DEFENCE OF MOTHERHOOD AND THE STRUGGLE FOR CULTURE.)

[See 251207(1) for all repr., notes. 251200 is printed with this.]

260000(16)   ‡ POLITICHESKAYA KHRONIKA. (POLITICAL CHRONICLES.)

[Pref. 251109. Soch. IV.]

260000(17)   ‡ POLITICHESKIE SILUETY. (POLITICAL SKETCHES.)

[Pref. [260507]. Soch. VIII.]

260000(18)   ‡ SOVETSKAYA RESPUBLIKA I KAPITALISTICHESKII MIR. (THE SOVIET REPUBLIC AND THE CAPITALIST WORLD.)

[Pref. 251215. Soch. XVII.]

*260000(19)   *1905. CHEREZ DVADTSAT LET. (1905. TWENTY YEARS LATER.)

[See 251226 for all repr., notes.]

*260000(20)   § *PROLETARIAT I LITERATURA. (THE PROLETARIAT AND LITERATURE.)

[A collection of articles. Advert.]

260000(21)   § EUROPA UND AMERIKA.

[Trans. Ger. See 260000(7) for all trans., notes.]

260000(22)   § EUROPE ET AMÉRIQUE.

[Trans. Fr. See 260000(7) for all trans., notes.]

*260000(23)   *EVROPA A AMERIKA.

[Trans. Cz. See 260000(7) for all trans., notes.]

260000(24) KAPITALISMUS ODER SOZIALISMUS?
            [Trans. Ger. See 250000(3) for all repr., trans., notes.]

260000(25) § OÙ VA L'ANGLETERRE?
            [Trans. Fr. See 250000(5), 260000(11), 260506 for all trans., notes.]

260000(26) TOWARDS SOCIALISM OR CAPITALISM?
            [Trans. Eng. See 250000(3) for all repr., trans., notes.]

260000(27) WHITHER RUSSIA? TOWARDS SOCIALISM OR CAPITALISM?
            [Trans. Am. See 250000(3) for all trans., notes.]

260000(28) WOHIN TREIBT ENGLAND?
            [Trans. Ger. See 250000(5) for all repr., trans., notes.]

[260000(29)] Pref. DELO BYLO V ISPANII (WHAT HAPPENED IN SPAIN), 260000(5).

260000(30) Itogi 1905 g. (A review of 1905.) (250000(6).II: 236-49)
            [Archives.]

[260000(31)] Lenin.
            Trans.: Eng. Encyclopedia Britannica, 14th ed.;
                    Fr. 580000(9); Critique Sociale, (3), X.31;
                    Hol. NWeg, (VIII.1), I.33.

*260000(32) *[Unpublished note on agriculture.]
            [c. Carr, SinOC.I: 310, note. Harvard Archives.]

[260000(33)] Pref. WHERE IS BRITAIN GOING?, 260200.
            Trans.: Eng. 261000(1); 600200;
                    Fr. Cahiers duBol, (II.45), 25.III.26.

260000(34) A WORLD SURVEY.
            [Trans. Eng. p.q. 260215.]

*260000(35) *EL EJERCITO ROJO.
            [Trans. Sp. Advert.]

[260101]   Nasha Gazeta. (Nasha Gazeta, (1), 1.I.26)
            Repr.: 270000(2): 396-7.

260105   See 260513.

260106   See 260513.

260107   See 260513.

260108   Letter to Bukharin.

Trans.: Am. FI, X.41;
        Eng. WIN, XI-XII.42.
T2976.]

260112   See 260513.

260113(1)   See 260513.

260113(2)   Ocherednye zadachi rabkorov. (The next tasks of the worker-correspondents.) (Iz, (16), 20.I.26; Pr, (16), 20.I.16; Trud, (14), 17.I.26)

Repr.: *260000(2); 270000(2): 397-405.

Trans.: Am. p.q. NYTimes, 6.II.26;
        Eng. p.q. Newsletter, 15.VII.61.

[Speech to All-Union Conference of Worker-Correspondents.]

[260117]   Predstoyashchie peregovory s Frantsiei, i chego ot nikh mozhno ozhidat. (The forthcoming negotiations with France and what might be expected from them.) (Pr, (14), 17.I.26)

Trans.: Ger. p.q. Inprekor, (VI.4), 30.I/(VI.19), 26.I.26.

260118   K voprosu o tendentsiyakh razvitiya mirovogo khozyaistva. (On the problem of tendencies in the development of world economy.) (PlanKhoz, (1), I.26)

Repr.: p.q. 260000(7): 109-11.

Trans.: p.q. 260000(7).

260119   Pamyati Sergei Esenina. (In memory of Sergei Esenin.) (Pr, (15), 19.I.26)

Trans.: Am. New Masses, (I.2), VI.26;
        Eng. FI(P), Autumn 1958;
        Fr. Clarté, (V.1), 15.VI.26; 640911: 218-21;
        Gr. 660000(6): 205-8;
        It. 680000(6): 75-9; 680200(2): 179-83;
        Sp. 690000(8).II: 125-8;
        Swed. 690000(1): 197-200.

[T2978.]

260129   Doklad. (A report.) (Iz, (25,26), 31.I, 2.II.26; Pr, (25,26), 31.I,
           2.II.26; Trud, (24), 30.I.26)
           Repr.: *260000(6).
           Trans.: Fr. DrapR, (III.31,32), 31.I, 1.II.26.
           [To 6th Moscow Congress of Textile Workers.]

260130   Alternative for 260129.

260200   WHERE IS BRITAIN GOING?
           [Trans. Eng. See 250000(5) for all repr., trans., notes.]

260203   Kŭl'tura i sotsializm. (Culture and socialism.) (Krasnaya Nov, (6),
           1926)
           Repr.: 270000(2): 423-46; Novyi Mir, (1), I.27. .
           Trans.: Am. p.q. 640800: 305-14;
                   Eng. 630000(1); Labour Review, Autumn 1962; p.q. Deutscher, PU:2;
                   Fr. p.q. 640911: 303-4; p.q. QI, (XIV.10-12), XII.56;
                   Ger. NRussland, (IV.3-4,5-6), 1927;
                   Heb. Hashomer Hatzair(W), (III.9), 1929;
                   It. 680200: 167-79;
                   Jap. p.q. 681125: 318-28;
                   Sp. p.q. 670000(5): 308-18;
                   Swed. p.q. 691100(2): 274-83.

260209   Ne tol'ko stranno, no i chudovishchno! (Not only strange but monstrous!)
           (Iz, (33), 10.II.26; Pr, (33), 10.II.26)

260211   Kuda idet Angliya? O tempe i srokakh. (Where is Britain going? On
           the pace and intervals.) (Iz, (34), 11.II.26; Pr, (34), 11.II.26)
           Repr.: p.q. 260000(7): 111-2; 260000(11): 29-38.
           Trans.: Eng. Inprecor, (VI.19), 11.III.26;
                   Fr. 260000(25): 180-92; CorInt, (VI.32,34), 2,13.III.26;
                   Ger. Inprekor, (VI.9), 6.III/(VI.34), 2.III.26;
                   Sp. 270000(6): 171-82.
           [See 260000(7) for other p.q. trans.]

260212   Vystuplenie. (A statement.) (Iz, (37), 14.II.26)
           [At Congress of Dairy Co-operatives.]

260213(1) [Note on "Current problems of the international Communist movement."]
           [c. Carr, SinOC.I: 493. T2979.]

260213(2)   [Note on "Current problems of the International Communist Movement."]
[c. Carr, SinOC.I: 493. T2980.]

260215   Dva polyusa rabochego dvizheniya. (Two poles of the workers movement.)
(EkZhizn, (38), 16.II.26; Iz, (50-53), 2-5.III.26; Pr, (50-53),
2-5.III.26)
Repr.: 260000(7): 41-80.
Trans.: 260000(7);
        Am. FI,IV,V.43;
        Eng. p.q. 260000(34); 330715(5); 501000; 510000: 37-71;
            Workers Press, (154,155), 2,5.V.70;
        Fr. p.q. Cahiers duBol, (II.51), 15.VI.26; p.q. Clarté, (V.1),
            15.VI.26; p.q. QI(OSPE), I.44;
        Ger. p.q. Weltbühne, (12), 23.III.26;
        Jap. 260807;
        Sp. 270000(6): 229-70.

[260216]   [The murder of the Soviet couriers and the Home Secretary of Latvia.]
Trans.: Eng. Inprecor, (VI.13), 18.II.26;
        Fr. CorInt, (VI.22), 26.II.26;
        Ger. Inprekor, (VI.7), 20.II/(VI.26), 16.II.26.

260225(1)   Pref. EVROPA I AMERIKA (EUROPE AND AMERICA), 260000(7).

260225(2)   Rech. (A speech.) (270000(2): 405-9)
Trans.: Eng. 660800(2); FI(Ln), (III.1), I.66.
[On 5th anniversary of Soviet Georgia. Archives.]

260301   Radio, nauka, tekhnika i obshchestvo. (Radio, science, technique and
society.) (Krasnaya Nov, (2), 1927)
Repr.: 270000(2): 410-23.
Trans.: Am. p.q. 640800: 352-5;
        Eng. 570000(4); Labour Review, XII.57;
        Fr. 640911: 289-302; QI, (2), IV.58;
        Hol. Int. (III.12), 15.II.59;
        It. p.q. 680200(2): 187-92; 690500(2): 37-47;
        Jap. 681125: 367-70;
        Sp. p.q. 670000(5): 355-8; 690000(8).II: 77-90;
        Swed. p.q. 691100(2): 317-20.

260302   [Letter to Bordiga.]
Trans.: It. ANUALI: 271-3.
[On ILOpp; on Germany.]

260304   Letter to Bukharin.
Trans.: Am. FI, X.41;
        Eng. WIN, X-XI.42.
[T868.]

260305   See 260513.
[Lacking in Eng. trans.]

260310   Kuda idet Angliya? Brelsford i marksizm. (Where is Britain going?
Brailsford and marxism.) (Iz, (60), 14.III.26; Pr, (60), 14.III.26)
Repr.: 260000(11): 39-48.
Trans.: Fr. 260000(5): 193-204; p.q. 680000(4): 122;
        Sp. 270000(6): 189-93.
[On Brailsford's pref. to WHERE IS BRITAIN GOING?, 260200.]

260312   Rech. (A speech.)
[On China. c. Carr, SinOC.II: 764.]

260318   [At Politbureau.] (p.q. 271021, section 33)

260325   [Findings of the Special Commission on China.] (p.q. 290804)
[T870.]

260400(1)   Rech. (A speech.) (STENZAS APREL'SKOGO PLENUMA TsK: 373-4, 375-419)

260400(2)   [Marginal note to 'Voprosy nashei politiki v otnoshenii Kitaya i
Yaponii.']
[c. Brandt: Ch. IV, note 52. T870.]

*[260400(3)]   *O religii. (On religion.) (Antireligioznik, (4), 1926)

*260402   *[To Serebryakov.]
[c. Daniels: 485, note 11. T873.]

260412   [Against Rykov's resolution.] (STENZAS APREL'SKOGO PLENUMA TsK: 124)
Repr.: p.q. 271100.
Trans.: Fr. BulCom, (VIII.22-23), X-XI.27;
        Heb. Hapoel Hatzair, (XIX.14), 1926.
[T2983.]

260414   [Letter to Lunacharsky; on 1920–1921]
      [c. Deutscher, PA: 504. T875.]

260503   Kuda idet Angliya? Eshche raz o patsifizme i revolyutsii. (Where is
      Britain going? Once more on pacifism and revolution.) (Derites kak
      cherti, V.26)
      Repr.: 260000(11): 49–63.
      Trans.: Eng. p.q. Inprecor, (VI.45), 5.VI.26; p.q. Deutscher, PU: 222;
         Fr. 260000(25): 205–17; p.q. 680000(4): 101–2; Cahiers du Bol,
           (II.53), 15.VII.26; CorInt, (VI.67,69), 29.V, 2.VI.26;
         Ger. Inprekor, (VI.77), 26.V.26;
         Sp. 270000(6): 194–204.
      [Reply to Bertrand Russell.]

260506   Pref. WOHIN TREIBT ENGLAND?, 260000(28).
      Russian: 260519; KI, (5–6), V–VI.26.
      Trans.: Eng. 260000(12); 600200; CI, (22), 1926; Inprecor, (VI.46),
         10.VI.26;
         Fr. 260000(25): 9–15;
         Ger. Inprekor, (VI.78), 28.V.26; KomInt, (5–6), V–VI.26;
         Sp. 270000(6): 9–15.
      [Trans. Ger. See 250000(5) for other repr., trans., notes.]

[260507] Pref. POLITICHESKIE SILUETI (POLITICAL PROFILES), 260000(17).

260513   § Voprosy angliiskogo rabochego dvizheniya. (Problems of the British
      workers movement.) (KI, (5–6), V–VI.26; Pr, (118,119), 25,26.V.26)
      Repr.: 260519: 5–25.
      Trans.: Eng. CI, (22), 1926;
         Ger. KomInt, (5–6), V–VI.26.
      [Trans. Eng. lacks 260305.]

260519   Pref. KUDA IDET ANGLIYA? Vypusk vtoroi(WHERE IS BRITAIN GOING? 2nd
      instalment), 260000(11).
      [Comprises 260513 and other material.]

260528(1) Za kachestvo, protiv byurokratizma, za sotsializm! (For quality;
      against bureaucratism; for socialism!) (EkZhizn, (122), 29.V.26;
      Iz, (125), 2.VI.26; Pr, (125), 2.VI.26)
      Repr.: 270000(2): 81–96.
      [Speech at All-Union Conference of Agricultural Workers.]

260528(2)   [Letter to CI; on China.] (p.q. 270801)

260606   [Excerpts; concerning session of Politbureau.]
          [c. Deutscher, PU: 223. T2986.]

260609   [Memorandum on Britain.]
          [c. Carr, SinOC.I: 514. T2987.]

260619   Pref. BALKANY I BALKANSKAYA VOINA (THE BALKANS AND THE BALKAN WAR),
          260000(1).

*[260700(1)]   *[Speech to CC and CCC.]
                [c. Daniels: 486, note 26. T2989.]

260700(2)   The Russian Opposition: Questions and Answers.
             Trans.: Am. p.q. 280712; NI, V.38.
             [T3003.]

*[260700(3)]   *Dva slova ob armii. (Two words about the Army.)
                [c. Daniels: 485, note 9. T2990.]

260702   Rech v pol'skoi komissii Kominterna. (Speech to Comintern Polish
          Commission.) (BO, (29-30), IX.32)
          [T2995. cf. T3024, T3437.]

260711   [Memorandum; on Russian trade unions.]
          [c. Carr, SinOC.I: 585. T2993.]

260714   Alternative for 260723.

260721   F.Dzerzhinskomu. (On F.Dzerzhinsky.) (EkZhizn, (168), 24.VII.26;
          Iz, (168), 24.VII.26; Pr, (168), 24.VII.26)
          [Obituary.]

260723   [Declaration of Opposition to CC and CCC.] (p.q. 270600(1))
          [T881. ? T2996.]

260727   Alternative for 260702.

260807   YOROPPA TO AMERIKA.
          [Trans. Jap. See 260215 for all trans., notes.]

*260813(1)   *[To Politbureau.]
              [c. Daniels: 490, note 115. T2997.]

*260813(2)   Against expulsion of Ossovsky.
        [c. Daniels: 490, note 115. T2998.]

260814   Pref. KHOZYAISTVENNOE STROITEL'STVO SOVETSKOI RESPUBLIKI (THE
        ECONOMIC CONSTRUCTION OF THE SOVIET REPUBLIC), 270000(4).

260900   LES PROBLÈMES DE LA GUERRE CIVILE.
        [Trans. Fr. See 240729(1) for all repr., trans., notes.]

260915   EIKOKU NANSI WA DOKOE IKU?
        [Trans. Jap. See 250000(5) for all repr., trans., notes.]

260919   [Theses for 15th Conference CPSU.]
        [c. Degras, DOCCI.II: 336. T894, T3006.]

260923   Teoriya sotsializma v otdel'noi strane. (The theory of socialism in
        one country.)
        [c. Carr, SinOC.I: 303. See further [261212]. T3007.]

260926   [Speech at meeting of aviation workers.]
        [c. Scheffer.]

260927   [The CPChina and the Kuo Min Tang.]
        [c. Brandt: Ch. IV, note 27. T3008.]

260930   EIKOKU WA DOKOE IKU?
        [Trans. Jap. See 250000(5) for all repr., trans., notes.]

261000(1)   WHERE IS BRITAIN GOING?
        [Trans. Eng. See 250000(5) for all repr., trans., notes.]

261000(2)   WHERE IS BRITAIN GOING?
        [Trans. Eng. See 250000(5) for all repr., trans., notes.]

261000(3)   [To L.B.Kamenev; on Stalin.]
        [c. 410000(1): Supplement I.]

261004   [Joint appeal, with Zinoviev, to Stalin, for a truce.]
        [c. Deutscher, PU: 293.]

261016 i dr.: Zayavlenie. (A declaration.) (<u>Iz</u>, (240), 17.X.26; <u>Pr</u>, (240), 17.X.26)

Trans.: Am. 370000(14): 319, note 35; 620000(3): 319, note 35;
    Fr. <u>BulCom</u>, (VIII.18-19), IV-VI.27; <u>Cahiers duBol</u>, 20.XII.26;
    Ger. <u>Aktion</u>, (XVI.11-12), XII.26.
[From Left Opposition. ? T896.]

261101 Rech. (A speech.) (<u>Iz</u>, (257), 6.XI.26; <u>Pr</u>, (257), 6.XI.26)

Repr.: XV KONF. VKP(b): 505-35.

Trans.: Am. <u>NI</u>(WP), VIII,XI,XII.42;
    Eng. <u>Inprecor</u>, (VI.79), 25.XI.26; <u>CI</u>(Ln), (III.4), 30.XI.26;
     p.q. Deutscher, PU: 302;
    Fr. <u>Cahiers duBol</u>, 20.XII.26;
    Ger. <u>Aktion</u>, (XVIII.1), II.28.

261102 [On the views of the Opposition.] (p.q. 271100(2))

261125 Telegramma. (A telegram.) (<u>Iz</u>, (274), 26.XI.26; <u>Pr</u>, (274), 26.XI.26)
[On death of L.Krassin.]

261126 The inter-relation between revolution and counter-revolution.

Trans.: Am. 640800: 142-5; <u>FI</u>, X.41;
    Eng. <u>WIN</u>, X-XI.42;
    Jap. 681125: 14--53;
    Sp. 670000(5): 142-5;
    Swed. 691100(2): 125-8.

261208 Alternative for 261209.

261209 Rech. (A speech.) (<u>Iz</u>, (289), 14.XII.26; <u>Pr</u>, (289), 14.XII.26)

Repr.: p.q. 271021.

Trans.: Am. p.q. 280628; p.q. <u>Mil</u>, 11.VII.31;
    Eng. p.q. Campbell: 67; <u>Inprecor</u>, (VII.1), 7.I.27;
    Fr. <u>CorInt</u>, (VI.137), 18.XII.26/(VII.6), 14.I.27.
[T3016.]

[261212] [Later version of 260923.]
[c. Carr, SinOC.I: 303. T3017.]

261214(1) [& others: Letter to Stalin and Politbureau.]
[c. Deutscher, PU: 310. T908a.]

261214(2)   [& others: Declaration of the Opposition to the 7th Enlarged Plenum
             ECCI.] (p.q. 270903)
             Trans.: Fr. BulCom, (VIII.18-19), IV-VI.27.
             [T908b.]

270000(1) ‡ EVROPA V VOINE. (EUROPE IN THE WAR.)
[Pref. 270117. Soch. IX.]

270000(2) ‡ KUL´TURA PEREKHODNOGO PERIODA. (THE CULTURE OF THE TRANSITIONAL
PERIOD.)
[Pref. 270219. Soch. XXI.]

270000(3) O SIBIRI. (ON SIBERIA.)
[See 270228(1).]

270000(4) ‡ KHOZYAISTVENNOE STROITEL´STVO SOVETSKOI RESPUBLIKI. (THE ECONOMIC
CONSTRUCTION OF THE SOVIET REPUBLIC.)
[Pref. 260814. Soch. XV.]

*270000(5) *DELO BYLO V ISPANII. (WHAT HAPPENED IN SPAIN.)
[See 260000(5) for all repr., trans., notes.]

270000(6) ¿ A DÓNDE VA INGLATERRA?
[Trans. Sp. See 250000(5), 260215 for all trans., notes.]

270000(7) EUROPA EN AMERIKA.
[Trans. Hol. See 260000(7) for all trans., notes.]

270000(8) ARBETARKLASSEN OCH VÄRLDSLÄGET. (Den nya etappen.)
[Trans. Swed. See 210000(7) for all repr., trans., notes.]

270000(9) LENIN.
[Trans. Sp. See 240000(24) for all trans., notes.]

*270000(10) *VOR DEM THERMIDOR. REVOLUTION UND KONTERREVOLUTION IN SOWJETRUSSLAND.
(DIE PLATFORM DER LINKEN OPPOSITION.)
[Trans. Ger. See 270903 for all trans.]

[270000(11)] u.a.: ERKLÄRUNG DER FÜNFHUNDERT.
[Trans. Ger. Pref. 270526(1). See 270526(2) for all trans., notes.]

[270000(12)] —: § DER KAMPF UM DIE KOMMUNISTISCHE INTERNATIONALE.
[Trans. Ger. See 271000 for all trans., notes.]

*[270000(13)] *DOKUMENTY RUSKÉ OPOSICE g. 1927.
[Trans. Rum. See 271000 for all trans., notes.]

270000(14) ARBETARKLASSEN OCH VÄRLDSLÄGET. (Den nya etappen.)
[Trans. Swed. See 210000(7) for all repr., trans., notes.]

*[270000(15)]   *Die Frage der Tradition in der Kunst. (NBücherschau, (v), 1927)
[Trans. Ger.]

[270000(16)]   i dr.: PROEKT PLATFORMY BOL'SHEVIKOV-LENINTSEV (OPPOZITSII) K XV
S"EZDU VKP(b). (DRAFT PLATFORM OF THE BOLSHEVIK-LENINISTS (OPPOSITION)
TO 15th CONGRESS CPR(b).)
Repr.: *[270000(17)].
[See 270903 for all trans. Processed.]

*[270000(17)]   i dr.: *PROEKT PLATFORMY BOL'SHEVIKOV-LENINTSEV (OPPOZITSII) K XV
S"EZDU VKP(b). (DRAFT PLATFORM OF THE BOLSHEVIK-LENINISTS (OPPOSITION)
TO 15th CONGRESS CPR(b).)
[See 270903 for all repr., trans. Printed.]

*270000(18)   *ROSHIA WA DOKOE IKU?
[Trans. Jap. See 250828(2) for all trans.]

270000(19)   KOMMUNISMEN OCH TERRORN.
[Trans. Swed. See 200000(37) for all repr., trans., notes.]

270106   [Draft protest to Politbureau; against Stalin.]
[c. Deutscher, PU: 336. T913.]

270117   Pref. EVROPA V VOINE (EUROPE IN THE WAR), 270000(1).

270120   [Letter to Semashko; on Joffe.]
[c. Deutscher, PU: 380. T918.]

270200   [Speech at Plenary Session CC.] (p.q. 300715)

270219(1)   Tekushchi moment. (The current time.)
[c. Daniels: 489, note 103. T3028.]

270219(2)   Pref. KUL'TURA PEREKHODNOGO PERIODA (THE CULTURE OF THE TRANSITIONAL
PERIOD), 270000(2).

270221   [Letter to Ordjonikidze; on treatment of the International Opposition.]
[c. Deutscher, PU: 311. T928.]

270228(1)   O SIBIRI (ON SIBERIA), 270000(3).
Trans.: Ger. Frankische Tagepost, 23,24.XI.28.

270228(2)   [Speech; on China.]
Trans.: Am. p.q. NYTimes, 1.III.27.

[270300(1)]   et al: Résolution de l'opposition sur la Comité Anglo-Russe.
                Trans.: Fr. BulCom, (VIII.16-17), I-III.27;
                        Ger. [270000(12)]: 173.

[270300(2)]   Amendements à la résolution sur la situation en Angleterre.
                Trans.: Fr. 271000;
                        Ger. [270000(12)]: 138-42;
                        Rum. *[270000(13)].

270304   [Letter to Radek.]
                Trans.: Ch. 470427: 1-3.
                [T934.]

270318   [Letter to Ordjonikidze.]
                [c. Carr, SinOC.I: 488. T937.]

270322(2)   [A brief note.]
                Trans.: Ch. 470427: 5-6.
                [T3033.]

270325   Neketorye soobrazheniya otnositel'no kachestvo produktsii i tseny.
                (Some considerations regarding the quality of production and prices.)
                (Pr, (68), 25.III.27)
                [Contribution to the campaign to reduce prices.]

270329   [Letter to Alsky.]
                Trans.: Ch. 470427: 7-9.
                [T938.]

270331   [To Politbureau; on China.]
                [c. Brandt: Ch. VI, note 11. T3036.]

[270400]   Résolution sur la question chinoise.
                Trans.: Fr. BulCom, (VIII.18-19), IV-VI.27.

270403   Class relations in the Chinese revolution.
                Trans.: Am. 570000(2): 11-4; 690000(11): 11-4; NI, III,IV.38;
                        Ch. 470427: 10-7;
                        Jap. *610325; 640330(3): 1-16.
                [T3038.]

270405   [On the Chinese situation.]
                [c. Deutscher, PU: 331. T3039,3040.]

[270411]   [Speech in Moscow.]
             [c. Living Age, 1.VI.27 from Kölnische Ztg. 11.IV.27.]

270412   [Against Martynov's eulogy of the Kuomintang, in Pravda.]
             [c. Deutscher, PU: 331. T3041.]

270414   [Personal statement, at CC.]
             [c. Deutscher, PU: 332. T3042.]

270416   [On the slogan of soviets in China.]
             Trans.: Ch. 470427: 61-5.
             [T3047.]

270418   Druzhestvennyi obmen portretami Stalina i Chan-Kai-Shi. (The friendly
             exchange of portraits between Stalin and Chiang Kai-shek.) (BO, (28),
             VII.32)
             Trans.: Am. Mil, 17.IX.32;
                     Ger. PermRev, (II.20), VIII.32;
                     Yid. Unser Kampf, (I.14), 15.IX.32.
             [T946.]

270500   Déclaration des cdes. Trotsky et Vouyovitch au Plénum de l'Exécutif.
             Trans.: Fr. 271000;
                     Ger. [270000(12)]: 134-7;
                     Hol. Klassen, (II.9), IX.27;
                     Rum. *[270000(13)].

270505   et al.: [To the Politbureau.]
             [c. Daniels: 487, note 67. T955.]

270507   The Chinese revolution and the theses of cde. Stalin.
             Trans.: Am. 320600(2): 23-72; 620000(2): 23-72; 660000(4): 23-72;
                         670000(16): 17-66;
                     Ch. 470427: 19-39;
                     Cz. BOJ: 80-103;
                     Eng. 690500(4): 1-43;
                     Fr. 271000; BulCom, (VIII.24-25, IX.26), XII.27, I-III.28;
                         Broué: 139-76;
                     Ger. [270000(12)]: 102-9;
                     Jap. *610325; 640330(3): 17-58;
                     Rum. *[270000(13)].
             [Epilogue, 270517(1). T3053.]

270512   u.a.: AN DAS POLITBÜRO DES ZK DER WKP(B).

⌊Trans. Ger. Alternative for 270526(1). Printed with ⌊270000(11)⌋.⌋

270516   The struggle for peace and the Anglo-Russian Committee.

Trans.: Am. NI, X.35;

Ch. 470427: 67-71;

Cz. BOJ: 110-20;

Eng. WIN, IX.41;

Ger. ⌊270000(12)⌋: 110-25;

Hol. EENHEIDSFRONTTAKTIEK;

Rum. *⌊270000(13)⌋.

270517(1)   The speech of Tchen Du-Siu on the tasks of the Chinese Communist Party.

Trans.: Am. 320600(2): 72-82; 620000(2): 72-82; 660000(4): 72-82;

670000(16): 66-76;

Ch. p.q. 470427: 39-43;

Cz. BOJ: 104-9;

Eng. 690500(4): 44-52;

Fr. 271000; BulCom. (VIII.24-25, IX.26), XII.27, I-III.28;

Broué: 176-84;

Ger. ⌊270000(12)⌋: 102-9;

Jap. *610325; 640330(3): 58-67;

Rum. *⌊270000(13)⌋.

⌊Epilogue to 270507.⌋

270517(2)   ⌊Letter to Krupskaya.⌋

Trans.: Eng. p.q. Deutscher, PU: 333.

⌊On Left Opposition and "self-criticism". T950, 951.⌋

⌊270523⌋   Speech on the Chinese question.

Trans.: Am. 320600(2): 83-101; 620000(2): 83-101; 660000(4): 83-101;

670000(16): 77-95;

Ch. p.q. 470427: 48-9;

Eng. 690500(4): 53-69;

Ger. CHINESISCHE: 32-43;

Jap. *610325; 640330(3): 68-85;

Rum. ? *⌊270000(13)⌋.

⌊At 8th Plenum ECCI. Ger. gives date as "between 23 and 26 May, 1927."⌋

270524   Speech on the Chinese question.

    Trans.: Am. 320600(2): 102-11; 620000(2): 102-11: 660000(4): 102-11;
             670000(16): 96-105;

        Ch. 470427: 51-9;

        Eng. 690500(4): 70-8;

        Fr. 271000; Broué: 191-8;

        Ger. ⌊270000(12)⌋: 126-33;

        Jap. *610325; 640330(3): 86-94;

        Rum. ? * 270000(13)⌋.

    ⌊Second speech at Plenum ECCI.⌋

270526(1)   Pref. ⌊Declaration of the 83⌋, 270526(2).

    Trans.: Cz. BOJ: 121-2;

        Ger. ⌊270000(11)⌋; ⌊270000(12)⌋: 149-51;

        Hol. Klassen, (II.12), XII.27;

        Rum. ? *⌊270000(13)⌋.

270526(2)   ⌊Declaration of the 83.⌋

    Trans.: Cz. BOJ: 122-32;

        Eng. p.q. Rosenberg;

        Fr. 271000; p.q. 680000(4): 181; BulCom, (VIII.20-21),
          VII-IX.27;

        Ger. ⌊270000(11)⌋; 270000(12)⌋: 151-64;

        Hol. Klassen, (II.12), XII.27;

        Rum. ? *⌊270000(13)⌋.

    ⌊To Politbureau. Later knows as "of the 500", and later again
    signed by thousands.⌋

270527(1)   The sure road.

    Trans.: Am. 320600(2): 112-9; 620000(2): 112-9; 660000(4): 112-9;
          670000(16): 106-13;

        Ch. 470427: 73-6;

        Eng. 690500(4): 79-85;

        Fr. 271000; BulCom, (VIII.20-21), VII-IX.27; Broué: 199-205;

        Ger. ⌊270000(12)⌋: 165-70;

        Jap. *610325; 640330(3): 95-101;

        Rum. ? *⌊270000(13)⌋.

270527(2)   It is time to understand and correct.

    Trans.: Ch. 470427: 77.

    ⌊T3064.⌋

270528(1)   Hankow and Moscow.

                <u>Trans</u>.: Am. 320600(2): 120-2; 620000(2): 120-2; 660000(4): 120-2;

                            670000(16): 114-6;

                     Ch. 470427: 80;

                     Eng. 690500(4): 86-8;

                     Fr. 271000; <u>BulCom</u>, (VIII.20-21), VII-IX.27;

                     Ger. ⌊270000(12)⌋: 147-8;

                     Jap. *610325; 640330(3): 102-4;

                     Rum. ❓ *⌊270000(13)⌋.

        ⌊T3065,3066.⌋

270528(2)   Is it not time to understand?

                <u>Trans</u>.: Am. 320600(2): 123-7; 620000(2): 123-7; 660000(4): 123-7;

                            670000(16): 117-21;

                     Ch. 470427: 78-9;

                     Eng. 690500(4): 89-92;

                     Fr. 271000; <u>BulCom</u>, (VIII.20-21), VII-IX.27;

                     Ger. ⌊270000(12)⌋: 143-6;

                     Jap. *610325; 640330(3): 105-8;

                     Rum. ? *⌊270000(13)⌋.

        ⌊T3062.⌋

270600(1)   Rech. (A speech.) (320000(2): 133-53)

                <u>Trans</u>.: Am. 370000(14): 126-48; 620000(3): 126-48;

                     Bul. <u>Osvob</u>, (2), III.31;

                     Fr. 290600(3): 110-32; 630419: 173-90;

                     Ger. 320000(18);

                     Jap. *611005; 640330(2): 257-80;

                     Sp. ? *⌊290000(12)⌋; 690500(3): 130.

        ⌊To CCC. T3071.⌋

270600(2)   Rech. (A speech.) (320000(2): 154-64)

                <u>Trans</u>.: Am. 370000(14): 148-59; 620000(3): 148-59;

                     Bul. <u>Osvob</u>, (3), IV.31;

                     Fr. 290600(3): 132-43; 630419: 190-211;

                     Ger. 320000(18);

                     Jap. *611005; 640330(2): 280-91;

                     Sp. ? *⌊290000(12)⌋; 690500(3): 158.

        ⌊2nd speech to CCC. T3071.⌋

270600(3)   Alternative for 270500.

270604   [Letter to Presidium ECCI.]
                [c. Degras, DOCCI.II: 367. T958.]

270609(1)   [Letter to Presidium ECCI.]
                [c. Degras, DOCCI.II: 367. T959.]

270609(2)   Kompartii i Gomindan. (The CPs and the Kuomintang.)
                [c. Carr, SinOC.II: 718. T3055.]

[270612]   [Speech, at railway station, on Smilga's departure.]
                [c. Deutscher, PU: 339.]

270623   Pochemu my ne trebovali do sikh por vykhoda iz Gomindana? (Why have
                we not withdrawn from the Kuomintang yet?)
                [c. Brandt: Ch. V, note 87. T3072.]

270625   et al.: [Letter to Politbureau.]
                [c. Brandt: Ch. V, note 87. T3073.]

270627   [Letter to CC.]
                [c. Deutscher, PU: 339. T3074.]

270628(1)   [To Ordjonikidze.]
                [c. Daniels: 488, note 87. T965.]

270628(2)   [Letter to CC.]
                [c. Deutscher, PU: 340. T966, T3075.]

270702   Alternative for 270900(1).

270711   [Letter to Ordjonikidze; on "Clemenceau" thesis.] (p.q. Stalin: 675-6)
                Trans.: Eng. p.q. CI, (IV.15), 15.X.27; p.q. Deutscher, PU: 349.

270713   [Letter to an Oppositionist.]
                [c. Deutscher, PU: 334. T979.]

[270719]   Politika dal'nego pritsela. (A long-range policy.) (Pr, (161),
                19.VII.27)
                [On July Days, 1917.]

270800   & Zinoviev: VERKEERDE EINHEIDSFRONTTAKTIEK.
                [Trans. Hol. See 270801 for T's speech.]

270801   Voennaya opasnost, politika oborony i Oppozitsiya. (The war danger;
         the defence policy and the Opposition.) (p.q. 290907)
         Repr.: 320000(2): 165-79.
         Trans.: Am. 370000(14): 161-77; 620000(3): 161-77;
                 Bul. Osvob. (4), IX.31;
                 Fr. 290600(3): 147-63; 630419: 199-211;
                 Ger. 320000(18);
                 Hol. 270800;
                 It. Prometeo, (II.21,22), 15.IX, 1.X.29;
                 Jap. *611005; 640330(2): 292-307; 680320: 41-55;
                 Sp. *[290000(12)]; 690500(3): 173.
         [T3080.]

270802   [Note on "Clemenceau" thesis.]
         Trans.: Eng. p.q. Deutscher, PU: 351.
         [T3081.]

270804   i dr.: Zayavlenie. Po povodu rechi t. Molotova o 'povstanchestve'
         oppozitsii. (Declaration [to CCC]. On cde. Molotov's speech on the
         "insurrection" of the Opposition.)
         [c. Daniels: 488, note 80. T993.]

270806   [Speech to CC and CCC.]
         [c. Daniels: 488, note 79. T3085.]

270808   i dr.: Zayavlenie. (A statement.) (Pr, (180,181), 10,11.VIII.27;
         Trud, (180,181), 10,11.VIII.27)
         Trans.: Am. p.q. Nation, 14.IX.27;
                 Eng. p.q. NOT GUILTY: 381; CI, (IV.14), 30.IX.27; Inprecor,
                     (VII.49), 18.VIII.27;
                 Fr. BulCom, (VIII.20-21), VII-IX.27; Cahiers duBol, (III.79),
                     1.IX.27.
         [T994.]

270819   SSSR i SShSA. (The USSR and the USA.) (Pr, (191), 24.VIII.27)
         Trans.: Am. Nation, 5.X.27;
                 Eng. Inprecor, (VII.52), 8.IX.27;
                 Fr. CorInt, (VII.93), 7.IX.27;
                 Ger. Inprekor, (VII.87), 30.VIII.27.
         [Interview with American workers delegation.]

270830   [Letter from Trotsky group to Zinoviev and Kamenev.]
[c. Inprecor, (VIII.7), 9.II.28. See letter of Zinoviev and Kamenev.]

270900(1)   Novye vozmozhnosti kitaiskoi revolyutsii, novye zadachi, novye oshibki.
(New opportunities of the Chinese revolution; new tasks; new mistakes.)
Trans.: Ch. 470427: 81-96.
[T3089.]

270900(2)   [Conversation with Menzhinsky; on treatment of the Opposition.]
Trans.: 410000(1): Supplement I.
[T1009.]

[270900(3)]   Kak oni borutsia s oppozitsiei. (How they fight the Opposition.)
[c. Daniels: 491, note 151. T1001.]

270901   TENKAN-KI NO BUNKA.
[Trans. Jap. See 230000(3) for all repr., trans., notes. Trans. from
240000(49).]

270903   i dr.: Proekt platformy bol'shevikov-lenintsev (oppozitsii) k XV
s"ezdu VKP(b). (Draft programme of the bolshevik-leninists (Opposition)
to 15th Congress CPR(b).)
Russian: [270000(16)]; *[270000(17)].
Trans.: Am. [280000(9)]: 23-195;
      Eng. [280000(10)]: 23-195; 630100;
      Fr. 271100(1); 570000(1);
      Ger. *270000(10); 280000(7): 21-159; [280000(8)];
        [300000(28)]: 21-159;
      Hol. p.q. Klassen, (III.2,4,7), II,IV,VII.28;
      Jap. *611005; 640330(2): 16-127; 700130: 154-284;
      Sp. *280000(5): 25-180.
[T1007.]

270906   & others: [Approach to the Politbureau and CC.]
[c. Deutscher, PU: 357. T1010.]

270912   & others: Appeal to the Comintern.
Trans.: [280000(10)]: 354-7;
      Ger. Fahne desKom, (II.3), 20.I.28.
[T1015.]

270917   Alternative for 270927.

270923   Alternative for 270925.

270924   The "Clemenceau" thesis and the Party regime.
Trans.: Am. NI, VII.34.
[T3092.]

270925   What we gave and what we got.
Trans.: Am. NI, IX-X.34;
      Fr. p.q. 301100(1): 134.
[T3093.]

270927   [Speech to Presidium ECCI.]
Trans.: Am. p.q. 280700; p.q. FI, XI.41;
      Eng. p.q. Deutscher, PU: 359-60;
      Fr. p.q. 301100(1): 199.
[T3094.]

270930   [Letter to Rakovsky.]
[c. Deutscher, PU: 362. T1018.]

271000(1)   § DOCUMENTS DE L'OPPOSITION DE GAUCHE DE L'INTERNATIONALE COMMUNISTE.
No. 1.
Trans.: Fr.;
      Ger. [270000(12)];
      Rum. *[270000(13)].
[9 items.]

[271000(2)]   [Collective Declaration.]
[c. Daniels: 493, note 201. T1030.]

271001   & others: The Opposition and the Wrangel officer.
Trans.: Am. NI, XI.34;
      Fr. Contre leC, (I.5-6), 30.XII.27.
[T1019.]

271004   & others: Appeal to Party members.
Trans.: Am. NI, XI.34;
      Eng. p.q. NOT GUILTY: 379-80.
[T1021.]

271006   [Article submitted to Pravda, but not published.]
[c. Deutscher, PU: 349. T1023.]

271021　　Pis'mo v Istpart TsK VKP(b). (Letter to the Bureau of Party History.)
(320000(2): 13-100)
Trans.: Am. [280000(9)]: 199-315; 370000(14): 1-88; 620000(3): 1-88;
　　　　p.q. 630000(8): 183-243; p.q. Mil, 8,22.III.30;
　　　Eng. [280000(10)]: 199-315; p.q. 630000(9): 183-243;
　　　Fr. 290600(3): 25-106; 630419: 113-72; BulCom, (IX.29-30),
　　　　VIII-XII.28; Contre leC, (I.5-6), 30.XII.27;
　　　Ger. 280000(2); 280000(7): 160-252; [300000(28)]: 160-252;
　　　　320000(18); Aktion, (XIX.1-2), III.29; p.q. Arbeiter-
　　　　Stimme, (37), XI.28; p.q. Prager Presse, 4.XI.28;
　　　　￠ Volks, (159-86), 7.IX-29.X.28;
　　　Hun. p.q. 300700(3);
　　　Jap. *611005; 640330(2): 128-209; 680320: 56-126;
　　　Sp. *280000(5): 181-266; *[290000(12)]; 690500(3): 23;
　　　Yid. Unser Kampf, (I.1-4,6-11,14,16), 1.II-15.III,15.IV-1.VIII,
　　　　15.IX, 15.XI.32.
[See [280000(9)], 290600(3) for other trans. Supplementary insertions,
from 1932 on, are fuller. T3099.]

271022　　[Speech at CC and CCC meeting.]
Trans.: Eng. p.q. Seibert: 116.
[T3100.]

271023　　Rech. (A speech.) (Pr, (251), 2.XI.27)
Trans.: Am. [280000(9)]: 3-19;
　　　Bul. Osvob, (5), XII.31;
　　　Eng. [280000(10)]: 3-19; p.q. ManGuard, 16.XI.27; p.q.
　　　　Seibert: 118;
　　　Fr. 290600(3): 168-79; 630419: 212-20; Contre leC, (I.1,2),
　　　　20.XI, 2.XII.27; p.q. DrapR, (IV.334,335), 1,2.XII.27;
　　　Ger. 280000(7): 7-20; [300000(28)]: 7-20;
　　　Jap. *611005; 640330(2): 3-15;
　　　Sp. *280000(5): 9-24; 690500(3): 197.
[For Pr. see Diskussionyi listok, 2. See [280000(9)], 290600(3) for
other trans. T3102.]

271024　　[Letter to Secretariat CC.]
[c. Deutscher, PU: 367. T1032.]

[271030]   et a.: Une infamie.
            Trans.: Fr. Contre leC, (I.4), 19.XII.27.
            [Reply to Huma, 27.X.27.]

271100(1)   et al.: LA PLATE-FORME POLITIQUE DE L'OPPOSITION RUSSE.
            [Trans. Fr. See 270903 for all repr., trans., notes.]

271100(2)   i dr.: Kontr-tezisy trotskistoi oppozitsii o rabote v derevne.
            (Counter-theses of the Trotskyist Opposition on work in the countryside.)
            (Pr, (254,263), 5,17.XI.27)
            Trans.: Eng. p.q. 280712; Inprecor, (VII.70), 12.XII.27;
                        Fr. BulCom, (VIII.22-23), X-XI.27; Contre leC, (I.2), 2.XII.27;
                            CorInt, (VII.124), 11.XII.27.
            [For Pr see Diskussionyi listok, 3,5. T1039.]

271102(1)   [Appeal to Oppositionists.]
            [c. Deutscher, PU: 369. T3101.]

271102(2)   Alternative for 271111.

271108(1)   [Balance of the anniversary.]
            [c. Deutscher, PU: 378. T3098.]

271108(2)   [Asks Politbureau for official inquiry into events of 7.XI.27.]
            [c. Deutscher, PU: 378. T3103.]

271109   [?] et al.: [To Politbureau.]
            [c. Daniels: 491, note 149. T1048.]

271111   [Supplementary insertions to 271021, Section 16.] (320000(3))
            Trans.: Am. [280000(9)]: 222-3; 370000(14): 14-5; 620000(3): 14-5;
                        Eng. [280000(10)]: 222-3.
            [See [280000(9)] for other trans.]

271113   Zapiska. (A note.)
            [c. Deutscher, PU: 378. T3104.]

271115   [Note to CE of Soviets; on change of address, etc.]
            [c. Deutscher, PU: 379. T1053.]

271117   'Zayavlenie' oppozitsii i polozhenie v partii. ("The Declaration" of
            the Opposition and the situation in the Party.)
            [c. Daniels: 493, note 208. 2 parts; see 211120. T3105.]

271118   [Note; in reply to rumours.]
                 [c. Deutscher, PU: 384. T3107.]

271119(1)   [On Joffe's suicide.]
                 Trans.: Am. p.q. NYTimes, 20.XI.27;
                         Eng. p.q. Deutscher, PU: 383-4.
                 [T3106.]

271119(2)   [An obituary on Joffe.]
                 [c. Deutscher, PU: 384. T3108.]

271120   See 271117.

271121   See 280103.

271203(1)   i dr.: Zayavlenie. (A statement.) (Trud, (290), 20.XII.27)
                 Repr.: PROTOKOLY(1961-2): 1596-8.
                 Trans.: Eng. REPORT OF 15th CONGRESS: 386-9; Seibert: Appendix III.
                 [To 15th Congress CPR. Signed by 121.]

271203(2)   i dr.: Obrashchenie XV s"ezdu VKP(b). (Addressed to 15th CPR(b)
                 Congress.) (PROTOKOLY(1961-2): 1598-9)

271213   i dr.: Zayavlenie. (A statement.) (Trud, (290), 20.XII.27)

271215   [On the new stage.]
                 Trans.: Am. p.q. Shachtman: 202-3;
                         Fr. p.q. 280712;
                         Ger. Fahne desKom, (II.51,52), 21,28.XII.28.

271218   Declaration of the Trotsky-Radek group to the 15th Party Congress.
                 Trans.: Eng. Seibert: Appendix V.
                 [T1061.]

*[271220]   *E. 1/2 stde. bei Trotzki.
                 Trans.: Ger. NWien Journal, 20.XII.27.

*280000(1)   *NASHI POLITICHESKIE ZADACHI. (OUR POLITICAL TASKS.)
[See 040000 for all repr., trans., notes.]

280000(2)   DIE FÄLSCHUNG DER GESCHICHTE DER RUSSISCHENREVOLUTION.
[Trans. Ger. See 271021 for all repr., trans., notes.]

*280000(3)   *NUEVO RUMBO. ¿A DÓNDE VA RUSIA?
[Trans. Sp. See 240000(22) for all repr., trans., notes.]

280000(4)   KOMMUNISMEN OCH TERRORN.
[Trans. Swed. See 200000(37) for all repr., trans., notes.]

*280000(5)   § *LA SITUACIÓN REAL DE RUSIA.
[Trans. Sp. See ⌊280000(9)⌋ for all trans., notes.]

280000(6)   VERS LE CAPITALISME OU VERS LE SOCIALISME?
[Trans. Fr. See 250000(3) for all trans., notes.]

280000(7)   § DIE WIRKLICHE LAGE IN RUSSLAND.
[Trans. Ger. See ⌊280000(9)⌋ for all repr., trans., notes;
dissociation ⌊290600(7)⌋.]

280000(8)   ENTWURF EINER PLATFORM DER RUSSISCHEN OPPOSITION. ZUM 15. PARTEITAG
DER WKP(B).
[Trans. Ger. See 270903 for all trans., notes.]

⌊280000(9)⌋   ‡ THE REAL SITUATION IN RUSSIA.
Trans.: Am.;
        Cz. *300000(30);
        Eng. ⌊280000(10)⌋;
        Fr. 290600(3);
        Ger. 280000(7); ⌊300000(28)⌋;
        Jap. *290621; ? 300000(8); *611005; 640330(2);
        Pol. *290000(15);
        Sp. *280000(5);
        Swed. 290000(10);
        Tur. p.q. 290000(9);
        Yid. *290000(3).
[See note to Fr. 290600(3). For other trans. see separate items.]

⌊280000(10)⌋   § THE REAL SITUATION IN RUSSIA.
[Trans. Eng. See ⌊280000(9)⌋ for other trans., notes.]

[280000(11)]   [Correspondence with Ryazanov on translations and editions of Marx, Engels and Hodgskin.]

[c. Deutscher, PU: 400-1. T1401,1578.]

*280000(12)   *¿A DÓNDE VA RUSIA?

[Trans. Sp. See 250828(2) for all repr., trans.]

280100   [Letter to CC; on negotiations with Stalin.]

[c. Deutscher, PU: 390. Harvard Archives.]

280103   § K voprosu o proiskhozhdenii legendii o "trotskizme". (On the origins of the legend of "trotskyism".) (BO, (9), II-III.30)

Repr.: 320000(2): 101-11.

Trans.: Am. 370000(14): 89-101; 620000(3): 89-101; Mil, 1.III.29;

Fr. p.q. Le Com, (II.2), 31.III.29; Contre leC, (III.25-26), 1929;

Ger. 320000(18); Aktion, (XIX.1-2), III.29; Fahne desKom, (III.2), 11.I.29;

It. Prometeo, (II.19), 15.IV.29;

Jap. 680320: 157-66.

[Includes 271121; 300207(1) in later versions. T3122.]

280114(1)   Pis'mo. (A letter.) (Pr, (13), 15.I.28)

Trans.: Eng. CI(Ln), 5.II.28; Inprecor, (VIII.3), 19.I.28;

Fr. Contre leC, (II.7), 22.I.28;

Ger. Aktion, (XVIII.2-3), III-IV.28.

[See note to 280114(2).]

280114(2)   Pis'mo. (A letter.) (Pr, (13), 15.I.28)

Trans.: Eng. CI(Ln), 5.II.28; Inprecor, (VIII.3), 19.I.28;

Fr. Contre leC, (II.7), 22.I.28;

Ger. Aktion, (XVIII.2-3), III-IV.28.

[To Peter. 2 letters intercepted; on international Opposition.]

280115   Interview, with Paul Scheffer.

Trans.: Eng. p.q. Glasgow Herald, 18.I.28;

Ger. Berliner Tageblatt, 1928; NWien Journal, 18.I.28.

280117   [Telegram to Kalinin and Menzhinsky; on treatment by GPU.]

[c. Deutscher, PU: 294-5.]

280125   [Certificate of good conduct to GPU escort.]
           [c. Deutscher, PU: 396.]

280200   Letter of protest, to Kalinin, Ordjonikidze and Menzhinsky.
           Trans.: Eng. p.q. Deutscher, PU: 398.
           [T1108.]

280228   [Letter from exile, to friends in Siberia.] (p.q. 291004)
           Repr.: p.q. 300000(1): Ch. XLIII.
           Trans.: p.q. 300000(1): Ch. XLIII.
           [T1161.]

[280300(1)]   [Telegram to daughter Zina.]
           [c. Deutscher, PU: 429.]

280300(2)   [Letter to Rakovsky.]
           [c. 300000(1): Ch. XLIII. On family matters.]

280302   [3 letters to Preobrazhensky.]
           Trans.: Am. 570000(2): 19-23; 690000(4): 19-23; NI, IV.36;
                  Ch. 470427: 159-70;
                  Fr. QI, (VII.1-2), I-II.49; Broué: 319-38.
           [Date of the first only is established; but see 280400(1). On China.
           T1189; cf. T1516.]

280305   [Letter to Sosnovsky.]
           [c. Deutscher, PU: 405. T1197.]

280310   Letter to I.N.Smirnov.
           Trans.: Eng. p.q. Deutscher, PU: 77;
                  Fr. Contre leC, (II.13), 5.VIII.28; Lutte deC, (6), VIII-IX.28;
                  Ger. Fahne desKom, (II.38), 21.IX.28.
           [T1179.]

280317   [Letter to Byeloborodov.]
           Trans.: Eng. p.q. THE CASE: 118.

280400(1)   [Letter to Preobrazhensky.] [T1189]

280400(2)   See 281000(2).

280401   [Letter; on life in Alma Ata.]
           [c. Deutscher, PU: 399. Harvard Archives.]

[280500]   [Letter; on the declaration of Krestinsky and Antonov-Ovseenko.]
            [c. Deutscher, PU: 406-7. Against capitulation.]

280509   Letter.
            Trans.: Eng. p.q. THE CASE: 111-2.
            [T3112.]

280523   [Letter to Byeloborodov.]
            [c. Deutscher, PU: 412. T1509.]

280524   [Letter to Preobrazhensky.] (p.q. 300000(1): Ch. XLIII)
            Trans.: p.q. 300000(1): Ch. XLIII.
            [T1516.]

280525   **Alternative for** 280526(1).

280526(1)   [Letter to Yudin.]
            [c. Deutscher, PU: 412. T1530/1541.]

280526(2)   Letter to Okudzhava; on capitulations. (p.q. 290907)
            Repr.: p.q. 300000(1): Ch. XLIII.
            Trans.: p.q. 300000(1): Ch. XLIII;
                    Am. p.q. FI, XII.46;
                    Eng. p.q. THE CASE: 112;
                    Fr. p.q. 371116(2): 111-2.
            [For other trans. see Fr. 371116(2). T1738.]

*[280600]   *[A letter.]
            [c. Daniels: 495, note 22. T1588.]

280602   Letter to a comrade, from exile.
            Trans.: Am. FI, VII.41.
            [T1613.]

280624   Letter to a friend.
            [c. Deutscher, PU: 418. T1770.]

280628   THE DRAFT PROGRAM OF THE COMMUNIST INTERNATIONAL.

Trans.: Am. 290000(2); 360500(1): 1-230; 570500: 1-230; p.q. 6408::
        145-50, 241-6; Mil, 15.XI.28-1.VIII.29; p.q. NMil, 26.X.35;

Bul p.q. Osvob, (5), 10.XII.31;

Ch. *300000(5); p.q. 470427: 171-99;

Den. p.q. 4I, (I.1), II.37;

Eng. 540000(1); p.q. WIReview, (II.3), VI-VII.57;

Fr. 301100(1): 168-380; 690000(1): 81-366; p.q. Contre leC,
    (II.20-21), 15.XII.28;

Ger. 290000(4); p.q. Aktion, (XVIII,10-12), XII.28; ¢ Volks,
    (209,211,215-9,221, II.5-9,14,36), 8,12,19-29,31.XII.28,
    9-16,26.I, 6.III.29;

It. 570400: 103-289; p.q. 680200(2): 101-7,126-32; 690500(1);

Jap. *610515; *620925; 640330(1): 2-228; p.q. 681125: 153-8,
    252-8;

Sp. *300000(10); *650000(12); p.q. 670000(5): 145-50,237-42;

Swed. p.q. 691100(2): 128-33,216-20.

[Appendix to Section III 281004. See Fr. 301100(1) for other trans.
Some trans. are limited to one section only. T3115-7.]

280700   The Canton insurrection.

Trans.: Am. 320600(2): 128-57; 620000(2): 128-57; 660000(4): 128-57;
        670000(16): 122-51;

Eng. 690500(4): 93-119;

Jap. *610325; 640330(3): 109-34.

280712   Et maintenant?

Trans.: Fr. 301100(1): 19-90; 690000(1): 13-77; Le Com, (34-8,II.2),
        11.XI.28-31.III.29; Contre leC, (II.15-16), 25.X.28; p.q. V,
        (57), 10.X.30;

Ger. Aktion, (XVIII.10-12), XII.28; p.q. Arbeiter-Stimme,
    (37), XI.28; Fahne desKŏm, (II.43), 26.X.28;

Jap. *610515; *620925; 640330(1): 231-306.

[Postface 280723. See Fr. 301100(1) for other trans. T3118-3121.]

280714   [Letter to Rakovsky.] (p.q. 300000(1): Ch. XLIII)

Trans.: p.q. 300000(1): Ch. XLlII.

[T1943.]

280715   [Letter; on differences with Decemists.]

[c. Deutscher, PU: 433. T3124.]

280717(1)   Po povodu tezisov t. Radeka. (The theses of cde. Radek.) (<u>BO</u>, (1-2), VII.29)

                <u>Trans</u>.: Am. <u>Mil</u>, 1.VIII.29;

                          Fr. <u>Contre leC</u>, (III.31-32), 10.VI.29;

                          Ger. <u>Fahne desKom</u>, (III.22), 21.VI.29.

                [T3125.]

280717(2)   [Circular letter.]

                [c. Deutscher, PU: 425. T1968.]

280723   The July Plenum and the Right danger.

                <u>Trans</u>.: Am. <u>Mil</u>, 15.XII.28;

                          Fr. <u>Contre leC</u>, (II.15-16), 25.X.28;

                          Ger. <u>Aktion</u>, (XVIII.10-12), XII.28; <u>Fahne desKom</u>, (II.44),

                              2.XI.28.

                [Postface to 280712. T3126.]

280800   [Letter to comrades; on the Opposition.] (p.q. 300000(1): Ch. XLIII)

                <u>Trans</u>.: 300000(1): Ch. XLIII.

                [T2148.]

280820   [Letter to S.A.; on differences with Decemists.]

                [c. Deutscher, PU: 433,445. T3127.]

280830(1)   Letter to V.D.; on Zinoviev and Kamenev.

                <u>Trans</u>.: Eng. THE CASE: 112.

280830(2)   [Letter to Palatnikov.]

                [c. Deutscher, PU: 447. T2418.]

[280900]   Who is leading the CI today?

                <u>Trans</u>.: Am. <u>Mil</u>, 15.VIII-30.XI.29;

                          Fr. 301100(1): 397-434; 690000(1): 469-94; p.q. <u>Le Com</u>, (II.14),

                              23.VI.29; <u>Contre leC</u>, (III.31-32), 10.VI.29;

                          Ger. 300100; <u>Fahne desKom</u>, (III.18-23), 17.V-28.VI.29;

                          Hol. <u>Baan</u>, (II.32-37), 29.XI.30-3.I.31.

                [Pref. to Ger. 300100, 291107. T3128,3129.]

280909(1)   Some remarks on the 6th Congress Comintern.

                <u>Trans</u>.: Am. <u>Mil</u>, 15.III.29;

                          Fr. <u>Le Com</u>, (33), 4.XI.28; <u>Contre leC</u>, (II.15-16), 25.X.28;

                          Ger. <u>Aktion</u>, (XVIII.10-12), XII.28; <u>Fahne desKom</u>, (II.40), 5.X.28

              [T3130.]

280909(2)   ⌊Letter to a comrade.⌋ (p.q. ⌊290900(1)⌋)

280911   Pis´mo N.I.Muralovu. (A letter to N.I.Muralov.) (<u>BO</u>, (19), III.31)
             <u>Trans</u>.: Am. <u>NI</u>, XI.34.
             ⌊On Max Eastman. T2538.⌋

280912   Réponse à un contradicteur bienveillant.
             <u>Trans</u>.: Fr. 290600(3): 183-214 630419: 221-43; p.q. 680000(4): 312-3;
                     Sp. 690500(3): 213.
             ⌊See 290600(3) for other trans. T3131,3132.⌋

280922   ⌊Circular letter on the Decemists.⌋
             ⌊c. Deutscher, PU: 432. T2642, ?T3136.⌋

280929   Lettre sur le Programme.
             <u>Trans</u>.: Fr. <u>Contre leC</u>, (III.29-30), 6.V.29.
             ⌊T3136.⌋

281000(1)   PERMANENTNAYA REVOLYUTSIYA. (THE PERMANENT REVOLUTION.)
             Russian: 300000(3).
             <u>Trans</u>.: Am. 310500; p.q. 640800: 62-5; 650000(3); 690000(13);
                     700000(8); ⌊700000(12)⌋;
                 Arab. 650000(4);
                 Bul. p.q. <u>Osvob</u>, (I.7,8), 13,20.V.32;
                 Ch. *⌊380000(17)⌋;
                 Cz. *⌊320000(25)⌋; p.q. ⌈330000(33)⌉;
                 Eng. p.q. 400000(3); 470300; 620700(1);
                 Fin. 700000(15);
                 Fr. 320810; p.q. 610000(5) 630419: 277-439; 640627; p.q.
                     680000(4): passim;
                 Ger. 300000(21) 651100; 680000(7); 691000;
                 It. 670121; p.q. <u>Prometeo</u>, (IV.52,55-7), 15.V,5.VII-2.VIII.31;
                 Jap. *610805; 661130: 147-314;
                 Nor. ⌊690000(10)⌋;
                 Sp. *310000(17); 610501; 631126; p.q. 670000(5): 63-6;
                     690700(2).
             ⌊Introd. 291130(1); Epilogue 291130(2); Pref. to foreign eds. 300329.
             291130(2) reprinted separately. Fr.,It., and Sp. have appendices.⌋

281000(2)   *⌊800 political letters, 550 telegrams, from IV to X.28.⌋
             ⌊c. Deutscher, PU: 401.⌋

281002(1) [Letter; on differences with Decemists.]
           [c. Deutscher, PU: 433. T2712. ? T3140.]

281002(2) [Letter to Elzin; on rumour of deportation from Alma Ata.]
           <u>Trans</u>.: Eng. p.q. Deutscher, PU: 454.
           [T2713.]

281004   The Chinese question after the 6th Congress C.I.
           <u>Trans</u>.: Am. 320600(2): 158-231; 620000(2): 158-231; 660000(4): 158-231;
                      670000(16): 152-225 p.q. <u>Mil</u>, 28.XII.31;
                 Ch. 470427: 203-32;
                 Eng. 690500(4): 120-84;
                 Fr. 301100(1): 329-94; 690000(1): 369-445; <u>Contre leC</u>, (III.27-28),
                      12.IV.29;
                 It. 570000(7): 185-239;
                 Jap. *610325; 640330(3): 135-95;
                 Sp. *300000(10); *650000(12).
           [T3141,3142.]

281013   [Letter to Rakovsky.]
           [c. Degras, DOCCI.II: 452. T2766.]

281014   [Telegram to deportees of Enisseisk.]
           <u>Trans</u>.: Eng. p.q. Deutscher, PU: 453.
           [T2768.]

281020   [Letter to Radek.]
           [c. Deutscher, PU: 452. T2819,2820.]

281021   On the situation in Russia.
           <u>Trans</u>.: Am. <u>Mil</u>, 1.II.29;
                 Eng. p.q. Deutscher, PU: 128,447,458;
                 Fr. <u>Contre leC</u>, (III.22), 28.I.29; <u>Lutte deC</u>, (8), II.29;
                 Ger. p.q. <u>Arbeiter-Stimme</u>, (39), I.29; <u>Fahne desKom</u>, (III.1),
                      4.I.29.
           [Letter to friends. T3145,3146.]

281100   Crisis in the Right-Center Bloc.
           <u>Trans</u>.: Am. <u>NI</u>(WP), XII.41, II.42;
                 Fr. <u>Contre leC</u>, (III.25-26), 1929;
                 Ger. <u>Fahne desKom</u>, (III.11-16), 15.III-26.IV.29.
           [T3143,3144.]

281107   ⌊Letter to Sosnovsky.⌋
           ⌊c. Deutscher, PU: 402. T2868.⌋

281110   Une lettre.
           Trans.: Fr. Contre leC, (III.29-30), 6.V.29.
           ⌊On differences with Decemists. T2874.⌋

281111   Letter to Borodai.
           Trans.: Am. NI(WP), IV.43; p.q. Shachtman: 218;
                   Ger. Fahne desKom, (III.4), 25.I.29.

281124   Une lettre.
           Trans.: Fr. p.q. ⌊320400⌋; 640911: 323-4.
           ⌊On literature. T2899.⌋

281200(1)   Na zloby dnya. (News of the day.)
           ⌊c. Deutscher, PU: 448. T3154,3155.⌋

281200(2)   La Chine et la Constituante.
           Trans.: Fr. Contre leC, (III.27-28), 12.IV.29.

281215   See 360606.

281216(1)   Pis´mo. (A letter.) (290000(1): 57-65)
           Repr.: p.q. 300000(1): Ch. XLIV.
           Trans.: p.q. 300000(1): Ch. XLIV;
                 Am. Mil, 1.IV.29;
                 Fr. Contre leC, (III.24), 9.III.29; RévProl, (V.79), 1.V.29;
                 It. Prometeo, (II.14), 15.III.29.
           ⌊To CC CPSU and Presidium of Comintern on the demand he abandon
           politics. See 290225 for other trans. T2912.⌋

281216(2)   "Takov khod sobytii." ("That's how things went.") (290000(1): 7-15)
           Trans.: Den. Politiken(D), 26.II.29;
                 Ger. Aktion, (XIX.3-4), V.29.
           ⌊Dated in Fr. See 290000(1) for all trans., notes.⌋

290000(1)   ‡ CHTO I KAK PROIZOSHLO? (WHAT HAPPENED AND HOW?)
             [See 290225 for all trans.]

290000(2)   THE DRAFT PROGRAM OF THE COMMUNIST INTERNATIONAL.
             [Trans. Am. See 280628 for all repr., trans., notes.]

*290000(3)   *DER EMES WEGN RATNRUSLAND.
             [Trans. Yid. See [280000(9)] for all trans., notes.]

290000(4)   § DIE INTERNATIONALE REVOLUTION UND DIE KOMMUNISTISCHE INTERNATIONALE.
             [Trans. Ger. See 301100(1) for all trans., notes.]

290000(5)   § MIS PERIPECIAS EN ESPAÑA.
             [Trans. Sp. See 260000(5) for all repr., trans. Pref. 290600(2).]

290000(6)   § MON EXIL.
             [Trans. Fr. See 290225 for all trans., notes.]

290000(7)   1917: DIE LEHREN DER REVOLUTION.
             [Trans. Ger. See 240915 for all repr., trans., notes.]

290000(8)   DIE ÖSTERREICHISCHE KRISE, DIE SOZIALDEMOKRATIE UND DER KOMMUNISMUS.
             [Trans. Ger. See 291113 for all trans.]

290000(9)   RUSYADA HAKIKÎ VAZIYET.
             [Trans. Tur. See [280000(9)] for all trans., notes.]

290000(10)   DET VERKLIGA LÄGET I RYSSLAND.
             [Trans. Swed. See [280000(9)] for all trans., notes.]

290000(11)   DIE VERTEIDIGUNG DER SOWJET-REPUBLIK UND DIE OPPOSITION.
             [Trans. Ger. See 290907 for all trans.]

*[290000(12)]   *LA REVOLUCIÓN DESFIGURADA.
             [Trans. Sp. See 290600(3) for all repr., trans., notes.]

*[290000(13)]   *LA RIVOLUZIONE SFIGURATA.
             [Trans. It. See 290600(3) for all trans., notes.]

290000(14)   Lettre à Gourget.
             Trans.: Fr. p.q. LA CRISE.II: 40.

*290000(15) *PRAWDA O ROSJI SOWIECKIEJ.
             [Trans. Pol. See [280000(9)] for all trans., notes.]

290110   Réponse à deux conciliateurs.

<u>Trans</u>.: Fr. <u>Contre leC</u>, (III.27-28), 12.IV.29.

[On ILOpp.]

290120   [Declaration on expulsion from Russia.] (300000(1): Ch. XLIII)

<u>Trans</u>.: 300000(1): Ch. XLIII;

        Eng. <u>Daily Express</u>, 27.II.29.

[T2945.]

290200   [Interview with German social-democratic press.] (p.q. 290422)

<u>Russian</u>: p.q. 300000(1): Ch. XLV.

<u>Trans</u>.: p.q. 300000(1): Ch. XLV;

        Ger. <u>Arbeiterztg</u>, 3.III.29; <u>Danziger Ztg</u>. 24.II.29; <u>Dresdner</u>

          <u>Nach</u>, 23.II.29.

290212   [Declaration on entry into Turkey.] (290000(1))

<u>Repr</u>.: 300000(1): Ch. XLIV.

<u>Trans</u>.: 290000(1); 300000(1): Ch. XLIV;

        Fr. <u>RévProl</u>, (V.79), 1.V.29;

        Ger. <u>Volks</u>, (II.41), 15.III.29.

[T2950.]

290215   [On being tricked re entry into Germany. (p.q. 300000(1): Ch. XLV)

<u>Trans</u>.: p.q. 300000(1): Ch. XLV.

290217   Telegramma. (A telegram.) (p.q. 290422)

<u>Repr</u>.: 300000(1): Ch. XLV.

<u>Trans</u>.: 300000(1): Ch. XLV.

[To Lobe.]

290225   ‡ CHTO I KAK PROIZOSHLO? (WHAT HAPPENED AND HOW?), 290000(1).

<u>Trans</u>.: Am. p.q. <u>NRep</u>, 22.V.29; p.q. <u>NYTimes</u>, 26-28.II, 1.III.29;

        Den. p.q. <u>Politiken</u>(D), 26.II-1.III.29;

        Eng. p.q. <u>Daily Express</u>, 27,28.II, 1.III.29;

        Fr. 290000(6); 551115: 19-70; p.q. 680000(4): 309; p.q. <u>Le Com</u>,

          (II.10), 26.V.29; p.q. <u>Lutte deC</u>, (9), III.29; p.q. <u>RévProl</u>,

          (V.79), 1.V.29;

        Ger. *[300000(29)]; <u>Aktion</u>, (XIX.3-4), V.29; p.q. <u>Arbeiterztg</u>,

          (62), 3.III.29; p.q. <u>NBuch</u>, (7), 1929; p.q. <u>NFreie Presse</u>,

          19.IV.29; <u>Tagebuch</u>, (9,10), 2,9.III.29;

                            +++

290225   ++++ Trans.: Heb. p.q. <u>Davar</u>, (1152,1154,1156), 1929;
            Nor. p.q. <u>Arbeiderbladet</u>, 3,21.VIII, 3,4.IX.29;
            Sp. 310000(5): 155-215; *310000(13).
     ⌊6 articles for the bourgeois press of which only some appeared.
     Russian 290000(1) combines articles 3 and 4. The trans. in <u>NRep</u> is
     expanded. See 281216(2) note. Suppl. 290327. T3173.⌋

290227   Sur le vote secret.
     <u>Trans</u>.: Fr. p.q. <u>Contre leC</u>, (III.24), 9.III.29;
            Ger. <u>Fahne desKom</u>, (III.19), 24.V.29.
     ⌊Extract from a letter.⌋

*⌊290229⌋   *⌊Interview.⌋
     <u>Trans</u>.: Tur. <u>Milliet</u>, 29.II.29.
     ⌊c. <u>Inprecor</u>, (17), 5.IV.29.⌋

⌊290300(1)⌋   Amerikanskim bol´shevikam-lenintsam (oppozitsii) redaktsiya gazety
     <u>The Militant</u>. (To the American Bolshevik-Leninists (Opposition)
     Editorial Board, <u>The Militant</u>.) (<u>BO</u>, (1-2), VII.29)
     <u>Trans</u>.: Am. <u>Mil</u>, 1.VI.29; p.q. 12.IV.30; <u>NI</u>(WP), IX.40;
            Fr. 551115: 352-6; <u>Contre leC</u>, (III.29-30), 6.V.29;
            Jap. 631130: 109-14.
     ⌊T3210.⌋

290300(2)   See 290422.

290300(3)   G.Gurov: Protiv pravoi oppozitsii. (Against the right opposition.)
     (<u>BO</u>, (1-2), VII.29)
     <u>Trans</u>.: Am. <u>FI</u>, V.46.

290304   Kh.: V chem neposredstvennaya tsel vysylki Trotskogo? (What is the
     immediate purpose in exiling Trotsky?) (<u>BO</u>, (1-2), VII.29)
     <u>Trans</u>.: p.q. 360820(2);
            Eng. p.q. NOT GUILTY: 382;
            Fr. <u>Contre leC</u>, (III.23), 25.II.29; p.q. Sedov: 18.
     ⌊Signed V in <u>Contre leC</u>. T3176.⌋

290305   ⌊To Minsk GPU official.⌋
     ⌊c. Deutscher, PO: 7. T3177.⌋

290308 ⌊To Minsk GPU official.⌋
        ⌊c. Deutscher, PO: 7. T3178.⌋

*290312 *⌊Interview.⌋
         Trans.: Ger. Rhenische-Westfälische Ztg, 21.III.29;
                 Tur. Aksham, 20.III.29; Jumruriet, 20.III.29.
         ⌊c. Inprecor, (26), 14.VI.29.⌋

290316   Interview.
         Trans.: Eng. Daily Express, 18.III.29.

290319(1) Telegramma. (A telegram.) (300000(1): Ch. XLV.)
           Trans.: 300000(1): Ch. XLV.
           ⌊To Rosenfeld; on entry into Germany.⌋

290319(2) Telegramma. (A telegram.) (300000(1): Ch. XLV)
           Trans.: 300000(1): Ch. XLV.
           ⌊To Rosenfeld; on entry into Germany.⌋

290320   ⸺: Vnutri pravo-tsentristskogo bloka. (Inside the Right-Centrist bloc.)
         (BO, (1-2), VII.29)
         ⌊Authorship from Daniels: 498, note 113. T3179.⌋

290323(1) "Mr. Churchill is wrong."
           Trans.: Am. NI(WP), IX.42;
                   Eng. John O'London, 20.IV.29.
           ⌊T3183.⌋

*⌊290323(2)⌋ *Ein Interview.
             Trans.: Ger. Sächsische Staats Ztg, 23.III.29 Schlessische Ztg,
                     23.III.29; ThurAllgemZtg, 26.III.29.
             ⌊T3185.⌋

290327   Pis'mo rabochim SSSR. (A letter to the workers of the USSR.)
         (BO, (1-2), VII.29)
         Repr.: 290000(1): 74-83.
         Trans.: Am. Mil, 1,15.V.29; Nation, 29.V.29;
                 Fr. 551115: 53-9; Contre leC, (III.27-28), 12.IV.29;
                 Ger. Aktion, (XIX.3-4), V.29; Volks, (II.54), 10.IV.29;
                 Hol. NWeg, (IV.5), V.29;
                 It. Prometeo, (II.16), 1.V.29;
                 Sp. 310000(5): 219-29;
                 Yid. Unser Kampf, (I.4), 15.III.32.
         ⌊T3186.⌋

290329   Alternative for 290327.

290331(1)   O gruppirovakh v kommunisticheskoi oppozitsii. (Groupings in the
                 communist opposition.) (BO, (1-2), VII.29)
                 Trans.: Am. FI, VI.40; V.46;
                      Fr. 551115: 335-41; p.q. 670306: 312-21; p.q. 680000(4): 344-5;
                          p.q. Le Com, (II.7), 5.V.29; Contre leC, (III.27-28),
                          12.IV.29; Freymond: 144-8;
                      Ger. Fahne desKom, (III.16), 26.IV.29;
                      Hol. ⌊450000(5)⌋;
                      Jap. 631130: 87-94.
                 ⌊T3188.⌋

290331(2)   Telegramma. (A telegram.) (290422)
                 Repr.: 300000(1): Ch. XLV.
                 Trans.: 300000(1): Ch. XLV;
                      Fr. 551115: 64.
                 [To Rosenfeld; on entry into Germany.]

290400(2)   Telegramma. (A telegram.) (290422)
                 ⌊On delay in receiving a visa to enter Germany.⌋

⌊290400(3)⌋   ⌊Interview with S.Saenger.⌋
                 ⌊c. Living Age, VII.29 from Präger Tagblatt, 1929.⌋

290413   Telegramma. (A telegram.) (290422)
                 Repr.: 300000(1): Ch. XLV.
                 Trans.: 300000(1): Ch. XLV.
                 [To Lobe; on refusal of visa to enter Germany.⌋

290415(1)   Pref. L'INTERNATIONALE COMMUNISTE APRÈS LÉNINE, 301100(1).
                 Repr.: 690000(1).

⌊290415(2)⌋   Interview with Maurice Paz.
                 Trans.: Am. Mil, 15.IV.29;
                      Fr. Contre leC, (III.25-26), 1929.
                 ⌊T3174.⌋

290422   Demokraticheskii urok, kotorogo ya ne poluchil. (Istoriya odnoi vizy.)

(A lesson in democracy I did not receive; the story of a visa.)

(BO, (1-2), VII.29)

Trans.: Fr. 551115: 60-67; Contre leC, (III.29-30), 6.V.29;

        Ger. Aktion, (XIX.5-6), IX.29;

        Nor. Arbeiderbladet, 27.VII.29.

[Substantially included in 300000(1): Ch. XLV. T3193.]

290424   Otvety na voprosy korrespondenta yaponskoi gazety Osaka Mainichi.

(Replies to questions from the correspondent of the Japanese newspaper

Osaka Mainichi.) (BO, (1-2), VII.29)

Trans.: Esp. Contre leC, (III.33-34), 19.VII.29;

        Fr. 551115: 68-70; Contre leC, (III.29-30), 6.V.29.

[By letter. T3195.]

290425   Pis'mo t. Suvarinu. (A letter to cde. Souvarine.) (BO, (1-2), VII.29)

Trans.: Am. FI, V.46; Mil, 15.VIII.29;

        Fr. p.q. 680000(4): passim; Freymond: 149-52;

        Ger. Fahne desKom, (III.23), 28.VI.29.

[T3197.]

290501   Pref. LA RÉVOLUTION DÉFIGURÉE, 290600(3).

Repr: 290600(3); p.q. 680000(4): 236-8.

Trans.: 290600(3).

[Trans. Fr.]

290510   Lettre à Souvarine.

Trans.: Fr. Freymond: 152-3.

290516   Alternative for 290526.

290522(1)   Pis'mo. (A letter.) (BO, (1-2), VII.29)

Trans.: Am. Mil, 1.VII.29;

        Fr. 551115: 157-9;

        Ger. Aktion, (XIX.5-6), IX.29;

        Jap. 631130: 22-6.

[To Russian comrades. T3198.]

[290522(2)]   [Interview.]

Trans.: Den Politiken(D), 22.V.29.

[At Sisli.]

290523   Sur certaine défections.
               Trans.: Fr. Contre leC, (III.31-32), 10.VI.29;
                       It. Prometeo, (II.18), 15.VI.29.
               [Letter to Treint.]

290526   Radek i oppozitsiya. (Radek and the Opposition.) (BO, (1-2), VII.29)
               Trans.: Am. Mil, 1.VIII.29;
                       Fr. 551115: 160-3; Le Com, (II.13), 16.VI.29; Contre leC,
                           (III.31-32), 10.VI.29;
                       Ger. Volks, (II.85), 7.VI.29;
                       Jap. 631130: 27-30.
               [PS 290707. T3200.]

290600(1)   —: Politicheskaya obstanovka v Kitae i zadachi bol´shevikov-lenintsev
               (oppozitsii). (The political situation in China and the tasks of the
               Bolshevik-Leninists (Opposition).) (BO, (1-2), VII.29)
               Trans.: Ch. 470427: 240-2;
                       Fr. Le Prol, 1.VII.30;
                       Ger. Aktion, (XIX.5-8), IX.29; Fahne desKom, (III.24), 5.VII.29.
               [T3202.]

290600(2)   Pref. MIS PERIPECIAS EN ESPAÑA, 290000(5).
               [See 290000(5) for all repr., trans. T3168, T3169.]

290600(3)   † LA RÉVOLUTION DÉFIGURÉE.
               Repr.: 630419: 103-243.
               Trans.:It. *[290000(13)];
                      Sp. *[290000(12)]; 690500(3).
               [Pref. 290501. Overlaps [280000(9)] and includes 280912. T3160,T3161.]

290600(4)   [Application for visa to enter Britain.]
               [c. 300000(1): Ch. XLV.]

290600(5)   [Telegram to Snowden.]
               [c. 300000(1): Ch. XLV.]

290600(6)   [Telegram to Snowden.]
               [c. 300000(1): Ch. XLV.]

290600(7)   [Statement.]
               Trans.: Nor. Monde(Verden), (I.9), VI.29.
               [Non-association with publication of 280000(7).]

⌊290600(8)⌋ ⌊Lettre à Gourget.⌋

Trans.: Fr. LA CRISE.II: 40.

⌊Fr. section ILOpp.⌋

290601 Bol´shevikam-oppozitsioneram nuzhna pomoshch. (The Bolshevik
Opposition needs help.) (BO, (1-2), VII.29)

Trans.: Fr. 551115: 164; Contre leC, (III.31-32), 10.VI.29;

RevProl, (V.84), 19.VII.29;

Jap. 631130: 33.

⌊T3204.⌋

290611 Why I want to come to London.

Trans.: Eng. Daily Express, 19.VI.29.

⌊T3205.⌋

290612 Vidal: On Brandler-Thalheimer.

Trans.: Am. p.q. 350228; FI, VIII.46; Mil, 1.X.29;

Fr. 551115: 342-7; Contre leC, (III.33-34), 19.VII.29;

Freymond: 154-8;

Ger. Aktion, (XIX.5-8), IX.29; Fahne desKom, (III.24),

5.VII.29;

Jap. 631130: 95-103.

⌊See 290425, 290712. T3206.⌋

290614 Vyderzhka, vyderzhka, vyderzhka! (Hold on, hold on, hold on!)
(BO, (1-2), VII.29)

Trans.: Eng. p.q. THE CASE: 528;

Fr. 551115: 165-8; Le Com, (II.19), 28.VII.29; Contre leC,
(III.33-34), 19.VII.29;

Ger. Aktion, (XIX.5-8), IX.29;

Jap. 631130: 34-8.

⌊Against capitulation. T3207.⌋

290615 Alternative for 290614.

*290621 *ROSHIA NO SHINSO.

⌊Trans. Jap. See ⌊280000(9)⌋ for all trans.⌋

⌊290626⌋ Red. internatsional´nogo zhurnala oppozitsiya: Chto gotovit den 1-go
avgusta? (What will the 1st of August bring?) (BO, (1-2), VII.29)

Trans.: Am. Mil, 1.VIII.29;

Fr. p.q. Le Com, (II.17), 14.VII.29;

Ger. Arbeiter Stimme, (45), VII.29; Fahne desKom, (III.25),

12.VII.29.

⌊See further ⌊290726⌋. On Comintern's "International Anti-War Day".
T3209.⌋

[290700]   Ot izdatel´stva. (From the Publisher.) (BO, (1-2), VII.29.
       |T3213, T3214.]

290701   Diplomatiya ili revolyutsionnaya politika? (Diplomacy or a revolutionary
       policy?) (BO, (1-2), VII.29)
       Trans.: Cz. Jiskra, (III.5(14)), X.36;
           Ger. Aktion, (XIX.5-8), IX.29; Fahne desKom, (III.26), 19.VII.29;
           Pol. Prol, (1), V.32.
       [Letter to Czech comrades; on capitulations. T3215.]

290703   Lettre à Souvarine.
       Trans.: Fr. 670306: 322-3; Lutte deC, (46-47), I-II.33; Freymond: 208-9.

290707   PS, 290526. (BO, (1-2), VII.29)
       Trans.: Eng. p.q. THE CASE: 528;
           Fr. 551115: 163; Contre leC, (III.33-34), 19.VII.29;
           Jap. 631130: 31-2.

290711   Lettre à Maurice Paz.
       Trans.: Fr. 670306: 324-8; V, (4), 5.V.39.

290712   Eshche raz o Brandlere-Tal´heimere. (Once more on Brandler-Thalheimer.)
       (BO, (1-2), VII.29)
       [See 290612.]

290715   Letter to Daily Herald.
       Trans.:Eng. Daily Herald, 22.VII.29.
       [T3216.]

290722   See 290727(2), note.

[290726]   —: Nochmals: Der 1. August. Die Komintern in eigenen Spiegel.
       Trans.: Ger. Fahne desKom, (III.27), 26.VII.29.
       |See [290626], T3211, T3212.]

290727(1)   Zhalkii dokument. (A disgraceful document.) (BO, (3-4), IX.29)
       Trans.: Ch. 470427: 235-7;
           Fr. 551115: 169-83;
           Ger. Aktion, (XIX.5-8), IX.29; Fahne desKom, (III.30-2),
             16-30.VIII.29; NMahnruf, (V.20), X.32;
           It. 620000(20): 87-103; *680900(3); 681100: 105-22;
           Jap. 631130: 39-56.
       |On China. T3218.]

290727(2)   [Answers to questions from American Press Agency.] (p.q. 290804)
            [T3217 dates this 22.VII.29.]

[290800(1)] Red.: Zasedanie peterburgskogo komiteta RSDRP(b) 1/14 noyabrya 1917 g.
            (Minutes of Petersburg Committee, RSDLP(b), 1/14 November, 1917.)
            (BO, (7), XI-XII.29)
            Repr.: 320000(2): 112-31.
            Trans.: Am. 370000(14): 101-23; 620000(3): 101-23; Mil. 12.XI.32;
                    Fr. Contre leC, (III.33-34), 19.VII.29;
                    Ger. 320000(18); Fahne desKom, (III,29,30,32), 9,16,30.VIII.29;
                    Hol. NWeg, (VIII.1), I.33;
                    Jap. 680320: 171-97.
            [Ed. pref. and the Minutes.]

290800(2)   --: Déclaration.
            Trans.: Fr. 670306: 342-51; V, (1), 13.IX.29.
            [Rédigé par L.T. -- PN. Note there are 2 issues of V numbered (1)
            LocBM.]

290804   Sovetsko-kitaiskii konflikt i zadachi oppozitsii. (The Sino-Soviet
            conflict and the tasks of the Opposition.) (BO, (3-4), IX.29)
            Trans.: Am. Mil, 15.IX.29;
                    Ch. 470427: 313-8;
                    Fr. 551115: 213-22; Le Com, (II.24), 1.IX.29; Contre leC,
                        (III.36-37), 21.IX.29; V, (1), 13.IX.29;
                    Ger. Aktion, (XIX.5-8), IX.29; Fahne desKom, (III.31), 23.VIII.29.
            [Reply to Louzon. T3233.]

290806   Otkrytoe pis'mo redaktsii ezhenedel'nika frantsuzskoi kommunisticheskoi
            oppozitsii Pravda. (Open letter to La Vérité, weekly of the French
            Communist Opposition.) (BO, (3-4), IX.29)
            Trans.: Am. FI, VIII.46;
                    Fr. 551115: 348-51; 670306: 338-41; V, (3), 27.IX.29;
                    Jap. 631130: 104-8.
            [With undated PS. T3219.]

290811   Redaktsii Bor'ba Klassov. (Letter to Lutte de Classes.) (BO, (3-4),
            IX.29)
            Trans.: Am. FI, IX.46;
                    Fr. 670306: 329-37; Lutte deC, (12), 10.IX.29.
            [T3220.]

290824　　　　　Iz pis´ma oppozitsioneru v Rossii. (From a letter to an Oppositionist in Russia.) (BO, (3-4), IX.29)
[T3223,3224.]

⌊290900(1)⌋　　Red.: K psikhologii kapitulyanstva. (The psychology of capitulation.) (BO, (3-4), IX.29)
[See also note in BO, (5), X.29. T3227.]

⌊290900(2)⌋　　Red.: O pis´makh tov. Sosnovskogo. (Cde. Sosnovsky's letters.) (BO, (3-4), IX.29)
[T3228.]

⌊290900(3)⌋　　Ot izdatel´stva. (From the publisher.) (BO, (3-4), IX.29)
[T3229.]

⌊290900(4)⌋　　--: Pobeg iz ssylki G.I.Myasnikova i ego mytarstva. (G.I.Myasnikov's flight from exile and his harassment.) (BO, (3-4), IX.29)
Trans.: Fr. V, (1), 13.IX.29.
[T3231.]

⌊290900(5)⌋　　--: Radek i burzhuaznaya pechat. (Radek and the bourgeois press.) (BO, (3-4), IX.29)
[T3232.]

290907　　　　　Zashchita sovetskoi respubliki i oppozitsiya. (The defence of the Soviet Republic and the Opposition.) (BO, (5), X.29)
Trans.: Am. FI, X,XII.46,III.47; Mil, 21.XII.29-25.I.30;
Ch. *300000(12); 470427: 319-28;
Fr. 300000(9); 551115: 223-67; p.q. 680000(4): passim;
Ger. 290000(11);
It. 620000(20): 109-54; *680900(3); 681100: 129-77;
Jap. 631030: 7-63;
Sp. *300000(7).
[Against the Leninbund policy. T3234.]

290910　　　　　Alternative for 290907.

290914　　　　　Pref. MOYA ZHIZN (MY LIFE), 300000(1).
Trans.: 300000(1).
[Lacking in Eng. 300000(20).]

290925(1)　　　Pis´mo ital´yanskim levym kommunistam. (Storonnikam tov. Amadeo Bordiga.)

++++

290925(1) ++++ (Letter to Italian Left Communists: To adherents of cde. Amadeo Bordiga.) (BO, (6), X.29)

Trans.: Am. FI, VI.47; Mil, 22.III.30;

Ger. Fahne desKom, (III.37), 11.X.29;

It. Prometeo, (II.25), 1.XII.29.

[T3240.]

290925(2) Otkrytoe pis'mo bol'shevikam-lenintsam (oppozitsioneram), podpisavshim zayavlenie v TsK i TsKK tov. V.Kassiora, M.Okudzhava i Kh. Rakovskogo. (Open letter to the Bolshevik-Leninists (Oppositionists) who signed the declaration to the CC and CCC of cdes. V.Kassior, M.Okudzhava and Ch. Rakovsky.) (BO, (6), X.29)

Trans.: Bul. Osvob, (3), IV.31;

Fr. 551115: 190-4; V, (5), 11.X.29;

Ger. Fahne_desKom, (III.41), 22.XI.29;

Jap. 631130: 63-7.

[Against capitulation. T3239.]

290930 Kitaisko-sovetskii konflikt i pozitsiya bel'giiskikh levykh kommunistov. (The Sino-Soviet conflict and the position of the Belgian Left Communists.) (BO, (6), X.29)

Trans.: Fr. 551115: 268-73; Le_Com, (II.27), 19.X.29.

[Reply to Overstraaten. T3232.]

[291000(1)] Red.: Chto dal'she? Levaya oppozitsiya v VKP. (What next? The Left Opposition in the CPSU.) (BO, (6), X.29)

Trans.: Am. Mil, 28.XII.29, 4.I.30;

Fr. Lutte_deC, (15), XI.29.

[T3242.]

[291000(2)] Red.: Otpoved kapitulyantu. (Reply to a capitulator.) (BO, (6), X.29)

[Pref. to extracts from letters of F.Dingelshtedt.]

291004 Razoruzhenie i Soedinennye Shtaty Evropy. (Disarmament and the United States of Europe.) (BO, (6), X.29)

Trans.: Am. FI, V.45; Mil. 7.XII.29;

Fr. 551115: 279-90; p.q. Le_Com, (II.30), 17.XI.29; V, (7), 25.X.29;

Ger. Aktion, (XIX.5-8), IX.29; Fahne desKom, (III.39), 25.X.29;

Hol. Baan, (I.29-31), 9-23.XI.29;

It. 620000(20): 155-67; *680900(3); 681100: 178-90; Prometeo,

++++

291004 ++++ Trans.: It. <u>Prometeo</u>, (II.24), 15.XI.29.
⌊<u>Aktion</u> was published after printed date of issue. T3243.⌋

291012 Lettre à G.Rosenthal.
Trans.: Fr. p.q. Naville: 84.

291014 Kommunizm i sindikalizm. (Vvedenie k diskussiyu.) (Communism and syndicalism: Introduction to a discussion.) (<u>BO</u>, (7), XI-XII.29)
Trans.: Am. 310300(1): 23-37; 690000(13): 15-23; <u>Mil</u>, 14.XII.29;
        Eng. 380000(21) 680300(2): 35-50;
        Fr. <u>V</u>, (8), 1.XI.29; 700000(6): 30-9;
        Hol. p.q. <u>Kompass</u>, XI.47; III.48; <u>NWeg</u>, (IV.11), XI.29.
[T3244.]

291017 K 12-i godovshchine oktyabrya. (the 12th anniversary of October.) (<u>BO</u>, (7), XI-XII.29)
Trans.: Am. <u>Mil</u>, 30.XI.29;
        Fr. 551115: 73-80; p.q. <u>Le Com</u>, (II.30), 17.XI.29; <u>V</u>, (9), 8.XI.29;
        Ger. <u>Fahne desKom</u>, (III.40), 8.XI.29;
        It. 620000(20): 5-13; *680900(3); 681100: 19-28;
        Jap. 700130: 99-109.
⌊T3245.⌋

291019 Greetings to weekly <u>Militant</u>.
Trans.: Am. <u>Mil</u>, 30.XI.29.

291021 Printsipal'nye oshibki sindikalizma. (K diskussii s Monattom i ego edinomyshlennikami.) (The errors in principle of syndicalism. For the discussion with Monatte and his co-thinkers.) (<u>BO</u>, (7), XI-XII.29)
Trans.: Am. 310300(1): 37-45; 690000(13): 24-9; <u>Mil</u>, 15.II.30;
        Eng. 380000(21); 680300(2): 51-60;
        Fr. 670306: 355-62; <u>Lutte deC</u>, (17), I.30; <u>V</u>, (64), 28.XI.30.
⌊T3247.⌋

⌊291100(1)⌋ L.T.: O sotsializme v otdel'noi strane i ob ideinoi prostratsii. (On socialism in one country and ideological prostration.) (<u>BO</u>, (7), XI-XII.29)
⌊T3249.⌋

⌊291100(2)⌋ Red.: My trebuem sodeistviya. O zadachakh <u>Byulletenya</u>. (We call for help. The tasks of the <u>Bulletin</u>.) (<u>BO</u>, (7), XI-XII.29)
Trans.: Am. <u>Mil</u>, 1.VIII.31.
[T3250.]

291104   [Letter to Sobolevicius and Well.]
             [c. Deutscher, PO: 28.]

291107   Pref. WER LEITET HEUTE DIE KOMMUNISTISCHE INTERNATIONALE, 300100.
             [Trans. Ger. T3253.]

291109   Chto proiskhodit v Kitae? (What is happening in China?) (BO, (7),
             XI-XII.29)
             Trans.: Am. 320600(2): 232-6; 620000(2): 232-6; 660000(4): 232-6;
                         670000(16): 226-30; Mil, 30.XII.29;
                  Ch. 470427: 243-5;
                  Eng. 690500(4): 185-9;
                  Fr. 551115: 307-10; Le Com, (II.31), 1.XII.29;
                  Ger. Fahne desKom, (III.42), 6.XII.29;
                  Hol. p.q. Ban, (I.34), 14.XII.29;
                  It. Prometeo, (II.25), 1.XII.29;
                  Jap. *610325; 640330(3): 196-200.
             [T3254.]

291110   Alternative for 291109.

291113   Avstriiskii krizis i kommunizm. (The Austrian crisis and Communism.)
             (BO, (7), XI-XII.29)
             Trans.: Am. Mil, 4,11.I.30;
                  Fr. 310000(12): 50-61; 551115: 293-306; Le Com, (II.32,III.1),
                         22.XII.29, 5.I.30; V, (14,15), 13,20.XII.29;
                    Ger. Fahne desKom, (III.42,43), 6,20.XII.29;
                    Hol. Ban, (I.34), 14.XII.29; NWeg, (V.3), III.30;
                     It. Prometeo, (II.27,28), 1.II, 1.III.30.
             ["Third period" of the Comintern. See also 300108.]

[291126]   Druzyam v SSSR. (To friends in the USSR.)
             [c. Deutscher, PO: 28-9. T3255.]

291130(1)   Introduction, PERMANENTNAYA REVOLYUTSIYA (THE PERMANENT REVOLUTION),
             281000(1).
             Trans.: Am. p.q. 640800: 62-5; p.q. Lerski: 267-8;
                  It. p.q. 680200(2): 51-5;
                  Jap. p.q. 681125: 68-71;
                  Sp. p.q. 670000(5): 63-6;
                  Swed. p.q. 691100(2): 52-5.
             [See 281000(1) for other trans., notes. Often erroneously dated.]

291130(2)   Epilogue, PERMANENTNAYA REVOLYUTSIYA (THE PERMANENT REVOLUTION),
             281000(1).
             Trans.: Am. Mil, 1.III.30; Calverton: 421-6;
                     Den. ANTOLOGI: 31-8;
                     Eng. MarxOut, (I.10), XI.66;
                     Fr. Lutte deC, (18), II.30;
                     Viet. *480000(11).
             [See 281000(1) for other repr., trans. T3256.]

291205   [Reply to Myasnikov.]
             Trans.: Fr. p.q. [300500(2)].

291218   See 300108.

291220   Otvet na pis´ma druzei. (Reply to a letter from a friend.) (BO, (10),
             IV.30)
             [See 291228, 300207(2). T3258.]

291221   On the "revelations" of Bessedovsky.
             Trans.: Am. Mil, 18.I.30;
                     Fr. 551115: 274-5; V, (17), 3.I.30.
             [T3259,T3260.]

291222(1)   Otvet tov. Trotskogo kitaiskim oppzitsioneram. (Reply to Chinese
             Oppositionists.) (BO, (9), II-III.30)
             Trans.: Am. Mil, 1.II.30;
                     Ch. 470427: 246-8;
                     Fr. V, (18), 10.I.30;
                     Ger. Fahne desKom, (IV.1), 10.I.30.
             [T3261.]

291222(2)   See 300108.

[291225]   Red.: [Note to] Kak i za chto Stalin rasstrelyal Blyumkina? (How and
             why did Stalin shoot Blumkin?) (BO, (9), II-III.30)
             Trans.: Am. Mil, 22.II.30;
                     Eng. p.q. THE CASE: 529;
                     Fr. Le Com, (III.3), 2.II.30; V, (21), 31.I.30.

291227   See 300108.

291228   L.T.: Otvet na pis´ma druzei. (Reply to a letter from a friend.)

(<u>BO</u>, (10), IV.30)

<u>Trans</u>.: Fr. 551115: 183-5;

It. 620000(20): 103-4; *680900(3); 681100: 122-4;

Jap. 631130: 57-8.

[See 291220, 300207(2). T3262.]

291229   Alternative for 291228.

300000(1)   MOYA ZHIZN. (MY LIFE.)

               Repr.: *300000(2).

               Trans.: Am. 300000(19); *310000(18); 600000(8); p.q. 640800: 206-8;
                        p.q. 650900: 67-76, 111-9; 700000(4);

                 Bul. *[310000(4)]; p.q. Osvob, (I.3-5,12), 15,22.IV, 1.V,
                      17.VI.32;

                 Ch. *310000(36); *[320000(36)]; *[320000(37)]; *470000(3);

                 Cz. *300000(18);

                 Den. p.q. Politiken(D), 9.VII-15.X.29;

                 Eng. 300000(20); p.q. 640000(5): 67-76,111-9; p.q. 640000(10):
                      67-76,111-9; p.q. 680200(1): 6-9; p.q. Marxist Outlook,
                      (II.10), XI.67;

                 Fr. 300522; p.q. 340000(4); p.q. 470615; 531130; 660000(5);
                      p.q. 680000(4): passim; 680331; p.q. V, (62), 14.XI.30;

                 Ger. 300000(13); 610000(3); p.q. Frankfurter Ztg, 11.VI.31;
                      p.q. NFreie Presse, 12.VI.31; p.q. Tagebuch, (46), 16.XI.29;

                 Gr. 670000(15);

                 Heb. 300000(6);

                 Hol. 300000(17);

                 Ice. p.q. 360000(20);

                 It. 300300(1); *330000(14); 610400;

                 Jap. *300723 *310614; *370814; *610000(16); 661031; p.q.
                      681125: 216-8;

                 Nor. 350000(9);

                 Pol. *300000(32);

                 Port. *430000(1);

                 Sp. *300000(15); 360000(27); *460000(11); 600730; p.q. 670000(5):
                      204-5; p.q. Batalla, (II.69), 21.X.36; p.q. POUM, (I.7),
                      7.X.36;

                 Swed. 370000(9); p.q. 691100(2): 183-5;

                 Yid. *300000(14).

            [Pref. 290914; Pref. Fr. abr. 331204(1). Additional information in Am.
600000(8), 700000(4), Fr. 531130, 660000(5), 680331, Ger. 610000(3).
See individual entries for abridged eds. T3264.]

*300000(2)   *MOYA ZHIZN. (MY LIFE.)

               [See 300000(1) for all repr., trans., notes.]

300000(3)	PERMANENTNAYA REVOLYUTSIYA. (THE PERMANENT REVOLUTION.)
	[See 281000(1) for all trans., notes.]
300000(4)	POLOZHENIE PARTII I ZADACHI LEVOI OPPOZITSII. (THE STATE OF THE PARTY AND THE TASKS OF THE LEFT OPPOSITION.)
	[See 300323 for all repr., trans.]
*300000(5)	[CRITIQUE OF THE DRAFT PROGRAMME OF THE COMINTERN.]
	[Trans. Ch. See 280628 for all repr., trans. c. BO, (17-18), XI-XII.30.]
300000(6)	CHAYAI.
	[Trans. Heb. See 300000(1) for all trans., notes.]
*300000(7)	*COMO HICIMOS LA REVOLUCIÓN DE OCTUBRE.
	[Trans. Sp. See 180000(5) for all trans. See also 290907.]
*300000(8)	*BAKURO SARETARU SOBETO ROSHIA.
	[Trans. Jap. See [280000(9)] for all repr., trans.]
300000(9)	LA DÉFENSE DE L'URSS ET L'OPPOSITION.
	[Trans. Fr. See 290907 for all repr., trans.]
*300000(10)	*EL GRAN ORGANIZADOR DE DERROTAS. LA INTERNACIONAL COMUNISTA DESPUÉS DE LENIN.
	[Trans. Sp. See 301100(1) for all repr., trans., notes.]
300000(11)	DIE LAGE DER PARTEI UND DIE AUFGABEN DER LINKEN OPPOSITION. Offener Brief an die Mitglieder der WKP(b).
	[Trans. Ger. See 300323 for all trans.]
*300000(12)	*[DEFENCE OF THE SOVIET UNION AND THE OPPOSITION.]
	[Trans. Ch. See 290807 for all trans. c. BO, (17-18), XI-XII.30.]
300000(13)	MEIN LEBEN.
	[Trans. Ger. See 300000(1) for all repr., trans., notes.]
*300000(14)	*MEJN LEBEN.
	[Trans. Yid. See 300000(1) for all trans., notes.]
*300000(15)	*MI VIDA.
	[Trans. Sp. See 300000(1) for all repr., trans., notes.]
*300000(16)	*LA MIA PRIMA EVASIONE.
	[Trans. It. See 070000(3) for all trans., notes.]
300000(17)	MIJN LEVEN.
	[Trans. Hol. See 300000(1) for all trans., notes.]
*300000(18)	*MOJE PAMĚTI.
	[Trans. Cz. See 300000(1) for all trans., notes.]
300000(19)	MY LIFE.
	[Trans. Am. See 300000(1) for all repr., trans., notes.]
300000(20)	MY LIFE.
	[Trans. Eng. See 300000(1) for all trans., notes.]

300000(21)   DIE PERMANENTE REVOLUTION.

⌊Trans. Ger. See 281000(1) for all repr., trans., notes.⌋

300000(22)   LA RÉVOLUTION ESPAGNOLE ET LES TÂCHES COMMUNISTES.

⌊Trans. Fr. See 300525(1) for all repr., trans., notes.⌋

*⌊300000(23)⌋   *⌊ON THE CHINESE REVOLUTION.⌋

⌊Trans. Ch. 2 vol. c. BO, (17-18), XI-XII.30.⌋

300000(24)   LA "TROISIÈME PÉRIODE" D'ERREURS DE L'INTERNATIONALE COMMUNISTE.

⌊Trans. Fr. See 300108 for all repr., trans., notes.⌋

300000(25)   DIE WENDUNG DER KOMINTERN UND DIE LAGE IN DEUTSCHLAND.

⌊Trans. Ger. See 300926(1) for all trans., notes.⌋

⌊300000(28)⌋   DIE WIRKLICHE LAGE IN RUSSLAND.

⌊Trans. Ger. See ⌊280000(9)⌋ for all repr., trans., notes.⌋

*⌊300000(29)⌋   *ANKLAGEN AUS VERBANNUNG UND EXIL.

⌊Trans. Ger. See 290225 for all trans., notes.⌋

*300000(30)   *ZFALŠOVANÁ REVOLUCE.

⌊Trans. Cz. See ⌊280000(9)⌋ for all trans., notes.⌋

*⌊300000(31)⌋   *⌊LITERATURE AND REVOLUTION.⌋

⌊Trans. Ch. See 230000(9) for all trans., notes.⌋

*300000(32)   *MOJE ŻYCIE.

⌊Trans. Pol. See 300000(1) for all trans., notes.⌋

300000(33)   ⌊Letter to friends in USSR.⌋

⌊c. Daniels: 468, note 45. T3279.⌋

300100   WER LEITET HEUTE DIE KOMMUNISTISCHE INTERNATIONALE?

⌊Trans. Ger. See ⌊280900⌋ for all trans. Pref. 291107.⌋

300103(1)   Nekotorye itogi sovetsko-kitaiskogo konflikta. (Some results of the sino-soviet conflict.) (BO, (9), II-III.30)

Trans.: Am. Mil, 8.II.30;

Ch. 470427: 330;

Fr. V, (19), 17.I.30.

⌊T3282.⌋

300103(2)   See 300108.

300104   —: Ya.G.Blumkin rasstelyan stalinym. (J.G.Blumkin shot by the stalinists.) (BO, (9), II-III.30)

Repr.: p.q. 350118.

⌊On ILOpp. Authorship established from 350118.⌋

300105(1)   Opposition serves the Bolshevik-Leninists.

Trans.: Am. p.q. Mil, 1.III.30.

300105(2)   See 300108.

300108   "Tretii period" oshibok Kominterna. (The "third period" of the errors of the Comintern.) (BO, (8), I.30)

     Trans.: Am. Mil, 25.I-22.II.30;
         Fr. 300000(24); p.q. 670306: 291-8, 301-14; p.q. 680000(4): passim; p.q. Le Com, (III.3,4,5), 2,16.II, 2.III.30; V, (20-25), 24.I-22.II.30;
         Ger. p.q. Der Kom, (I.1), 1V.30;
         Ukr. RobVis, (II.12-17), 15.VI-1.IX.34;
         Yid. Klorkeit, (1-6), IV-IX.30.

     ⌊Instalments dated 291218, 291222(2), 291227, 300103(2), 300105(2). Addition ⌊300109⌋. See also 291113. T3280,3285.⌋

⌊300109⌋   Neobkhodimoe dopolnenie. (A necessary addition.) (BO, (8), I.30)

     Trans.: Fr. 670306: 298-300; V, (21), 31.I.30.

     ⌊See 300108. T3280.⌋

300120   Ot redaktsii. (From the Editorial Board.) (BO, (8), I.30)

     Trans.: Fr. V, (21), 31.I.30.

     ⌊T3298,3299.⌋

300122   —: Novyi shag vpered. (A new step forward.) (BO, (11), V.30)

     Trans.: Am. p.q. Mil, 29.III.30.

     ⌊On unification of International Left Opposition. T3290,3310.⌋

300130   See 300427.

300206   Otkrytoe pis'mo vsem chlenam Leninbunda. (Open letter to all members
          of the Leninbund.) (BO, (9), II-III.30)
          Trans.: Am. FI, IV.47; Mil, 29.III.30;
                  Ger. Der Kom, (I.1), IV.30.
          [T3293.]

300207(1) K voprosu o proiskhozhdenii legendy o "trotskizme". (On the question
          of the origins of the legend of "trotskyism.") (BO, (9), II-III.30)
          Repr.: 320000(2): 101-11.
          Trans.: Am. 370000(14): 89-99; 620000(3): 89-99;
                  Bul. Osvob, (I.23,24), 2,9.IX.32;
                  Ger. 320000(18);
                  Jap. 680320: 157-70;
                  Yid. Klorkeit, (4), VII.30.
          [Comprising 271121, 280103, 300207(1). T3122,T3295-7.]

300207(2) L.T.: Otvety na pis'ma druzei. (Replies to letters from friends.)
          (BO, (10), IV.30)
          Trans.: Fr. 551115: 185-9;
                  It. 620000(20): 105-8; *680900; 681100: 124-8;
                  Jap. 631130: 58-62.
          [See 291220, 291228. Fr. trans., followed by It. and Jap. rearranges
          the material. T3294.]

300208   G./Red.: [Pref. to] Ob internatsional'nom ob"edinenii levoi oppozitsii.
          (Po povodu predlozhenii Vérité.) (On the unification of the Left
          Opposition, internationally; concerning the proposal of La Vérité.)
          (BO, (10), IV.30)
          Trans.: Am. Mil,29.III.30;
                  Fr. V, (45), 18.VII.30.
          [See 300122. T3301.]

300209   —: Stalin vstupil v soyuz s Shumanom i Kerenskim protiv Lenina i
          Trotskogo. (Stalin has taken to the road of alliance with Schuman and
          Kerensky against Lenin and Trotsky.) (BO, (9), II-III.30)
          [See also [300400(3)]. T3298,T3299.]

300212   [Letter to Gorkin.]
          [c. Gorkin in Mil, 5.IV.30/V, (25), 28.II.30.]

300213   Novyi khozyaistvennyi kurs v SSSR. (The new course in the economy of the USSR.) (BO, (9), II-III.30)

Trans.: Am. Mil, 15.III.30;

        Fr. V, (26,27), 7,14.III.30; VoixCom, (I.2-4,7,8), 25.I-22.II, 5,19.IV.31;

        Ger. Fahne desKom, (IV.13-15), 23,30.V, 6.VI.30; p.q. Frankfurter Ztg, 29.IV.30; Der Kom, (I.3,4,6), V,VI,VII.30;

        Hol. NWeg, (VI.1,2), I,II.31;

        It, Prometeo, (III.30), 1.V.30.

[T3300.]

[300215]   Interview, with Emil Ludwig.

Trans.:Am. p.q. Living Age, 15.II.30;

        Ger. p.q. Berliner Tagblatt, [1930].

300228   Alternative for 300208.

300300(1)   LA MIA VITA.

[Trans. It. See 300000(1) for all repr., trans., notes.]

[300300(2)] Al'fa: Uroki kapitulyatsii. (Nekrologicheskie razmyshleniya.) (Lessons of the capitulations; Obituary reflections.) (BO, (9), II-III. 30)

Trans.: Am. Mil, 19.IV.30;

        Fr. Lutte deC, (20), IV.30.

[T3292.]

300301   —: Da ili net? (Yes or No?) (BO, (10), IV.30)

Trans.: Am. Mil, 29.III.30;

        Fr. V, (27), 14.III.30.

[On Blumkin's assassination. T3302.]

300314   Pyatiletka i mirovaya bezrabotitsa. (The Five-Year Plan and world unemployment.) (BO, (10), IV.30)

Trans.: Am. 310000(25); Mil, 12.IV.30;

        Eng. 520900(1);

        Fr. V, (29), 28.III.30;

        Ger. Fahne desKom, (IV.11), 9.V.30; Der Kom, (I.2), V.30;

        Hol. NWeg, (V.6,7), VI,VII.30;

        Sp. 310000(10).

[Brochure eds. include 300821.]

300323   Otkrytoe pis′mo chlenam VKP(b). (Open letter to members of the
CPSU(b).) (<u>BO</u>, (10), IV.30)
<u>Repr.</u>: 300000(4).
<u>Trans.</u>: Am. <u>Mil</u>, 24.V, 7,14.VI.30;
        Fr. <u>Lutte deC</u>, (20), IV.30;
        Ger. 300000(11).

300326   [& others: Telegram to Rakovsky family.]
[c. [300400(2)].]

300329   Dve kontsentsii. (Two theories.) (<u>BO</u>, (12-13), VI-VII.30)
<u>Repr.</u>: 300000(3).
<u>Trans.</u>: Am. <u>FI</u>, Winter, 1955; <u>Mil</u>, 10,17.V.30;
        Eng. [541100(2)];
        Fr. 551115: 141-53; 630419: 247-59; <u>QI</u>, VI.55;
        It. 620000(20): 74-86; *680900; 681100: 91-104.
[Corrections in <u>BO</u>, (14), VIII.30. Pref. to foreign ed. 281000(1).
See 281000(1) for other repr., trans. T3303.]

[300400(1)]   Al′fa: "Chist i prozrachen, kak kristall." ("As pure and transparent
as crystal.") (<u>BO</u>, (10), IV.30)
<u>Trans.</u>: Am. <u>Mil</u>, 26.IV.30;
        Fr. <u>V</u>, (33), 25.IV.30.
[On Stalin's speech on the American question. T3304.]

[300400(2)]   Red.: Rasstrely oppozitsionerov; Khristian Georgievich Rakovskii v
opasnosti!; Nashim druz′yam zagranitsei. (The shooting of the
Oppositionists; Christian Georgievich Rakovsky in danger!; To our
friends abroad.) (<u>BO</u>, (10), IV.30)

[300400(3)]   —: Oni ne znali. (<u>BO</u>, (10), IV.30)
[See 300209. T3305.]

300402   Lozung natsional′nogo sobraniya v Kitae. (The slogan of a National
Assembly in China.) (<u>BO</u>, (11), V.30)
<u>Trans.</u>: Am. <u>Mil</u>, 14.VI.30;
        Ch. 470427: 249-51.
[Reply to Chinese comrades. T3306.]

300413(1)   Skrip v apparate. (BO, (11), V.30)
              Trans.: Am. Mil, 21,28.VI.30;
                      Fr. Lutte deC, (23), VII.30;
                      Ger. Der Kom, (I.7-9), VIII-IX.30;
                      Yid. p.q. Klorkeit, (3), VI.30.
              [Corrections in BO, (12-13), VI-VII.30. A popular explanation of Right
              and Left. T3307.]

300413(2)   Une lettre.
              Trans.: Fr. p.q. Naville: 87.

300416   Why does Lovestone not answer?
              Trans.: Am. Mil, 26.VII.30.

300422   Otkrytoe pis'mo ital'yanskim kommunistam, ob"edinennym vokrug Prometeo.
              (Open letter to Italian communists united around Prometeo.) (BO, (11),
              V.30)
              Trans.: Am. FI, VI.47; Mil, 14.VI.30;
                      Fr. Lutte deC, (23), VII.30;
                      It, Prometeo, (III.31), 1.VI.30.
              [T3308.]

300425   K kapitalizmu ili k sotsializmu? (Towards capitalism or socialism?)
              (BO, (11), V.30)
              Trans.: Fr. Lutte deC, (21-22,23), V-VI, VII.30;
                      Hol. NWeg, (V.9,10), IX, X.30.
              [T3309.]

300427   [6 letters to Olberg, from 30.I.30 to 27.IV.30.]
              Trans.: Eng. p.q. NOT GUILTY: 104.
              [D10, PCB, 1.]

[300500(1)]   T.: Samoubiistvo V.Mayakovskogo. (V.Mayakovsky's suicide.)
              (BO, (11), V.30)
              Trans.: Am. ISR, I-II.70;
                      Fr. 640911: 222-4; Lutte deC, (21-22), V-VI.30; V, (35), 9.V.30;
                      Ger. Aktion, (XX.1-2), VIII.30;
                      Gr. 660000(6): 209-11;
                      It. 680000(6): 83-7;
                      Sp. 690000(8).II: 131-3;
                      Swed. 690600: 201-3.
              [T3311.]

⌊300500(2)⌋ N.M.: Zabyvchivyi Myasnikov. (The forgetful Myasnikov.)
(BO, (11), V.30)
Trans.: Fr. V, (36), 16.V.30;
   Ger. Aktion, (XX.1-2), VIII.30.
⌊N.M. = N.Markin = Leon Sedov. 'Extraits d'une correspondance entre
Myasnikov et LT'; includes ⌊291205⌋. Rédigé par L.Sedov sur un
canevas de L.T. -- PN.⌋

⌊300500(3)⌋ --: Krupnyi shag vpered. (A great step forward.) (BO, (11), V.30)
⌊T3310.⌋

300510 ⌊Letter to Klorkeit and to Jewish workers in France.⌋
Trans.: Am. 700700: 14;
   Yid. Klorkeit, (3), V.30.

300514 Otvet tovarishcham iz ital'yanskoi oppozitsii. (Answer to comrades
of the Italian Opposition.) (BO, (15-16), IX-X.30)
Trans.: Am. Mil, 7.VIII.30; NI(WP), I/VII.44;
   Eng. SocAp(Ln), X.43; WIN, X.44;
   Fr. Lutte deC, (23), VII.30; p.q. V, (44), 11.VII.30;
   It. Prometeo, (III.34), 1.VIII.30; ANUALI: 1061-6.
⌊T3312.⌋

300516 ⌊Letter to a local organization of the Leninbund.⌋
Trans.: Am. p.q. CLO(5), VIII.31;
   Fr. BInt, (5), III.31; OCG, (5), III.31.
⌊In OCG, (5), see "Urbahns et l'opposition de gauche internationale".⌋

300522 MA VIE.
⌊Trans. Fr. See 300000(1) for all repr., trans., notes.⌋

300523 Alternative for 300528.

300525(1) Zadachi ispanskikh kommunistov. (Tasks of the Spanish Communists.)
(BO, (12-13), VI-VII.30)
Trans.: 310528(1);
   Fr. 300000(22); 590600: 403-10; p.q. Le Com, (III.13),
    22.VI.30; V, (40), 13.VI.30;
   Gr. 630000(10): 3-11;
   Hol. 310000(21);
   Jap. *630430; 650430: 161-9;
   Sp. 680000(9): 87.
⌊Letter to Contra la Corriente. T3315.⌋

300525(2) See 310528(1).

300528   Chto takoe tsentrizm? (What is centrism?) (BO, (12-13), VI-VII.30)

           Trans.: Fr. Commune, (128,129), 24,28.V.38; V, (42), 27.VI.30;

                 Ger. Aktion, (XX.1-2), VIII.30.

           [T3316.]

300530   —: Revolyutsiya v Indii, ee zadachi i opasnosti. (The revolution in India; its tasks and dangers.) (BO, (12-13), VI-VII.30)

           Trans.: Am. Mil, 12.VII.30;

                 Hol. NWeg, (V.8), VIII.30.

           [T3317.]

[300600(1)]   L.T.: Otvet tov. K. (Reply to cde. K[ote Zinzadze].) (BO, (12-13), VI-VII.30)

           Trans.: Fr. Lutte deC, (24), VIII.30.

300600(2)   Al'fa: Zametki zhurnalista. (Notes of a journalist.) (BO, (12-13), VI-VII.30)

           Trans.: Am. Mil, 26.VII, 15.VIII.30;

                 Fr. V, (46,55,56), 25.VII, 26.IX, 3.X.30.

           [T3319-3321.]

[300600(3)]   [Ed. note to article by F.Dingel'shtedt.] (BO, (12-13), VI-VII.30)

           Trans.: Fr. Lutte deC, (III.24), [VIII.30].

300610   O "zashchitnikakh" Oktyabr'skoi revolyutsii. (On "the defenders" of the October Revolution.) (BO, (14), VIII.30)

           Trans.: Am. Mil, 26.VII.30;

                 Fr. V, (46), 25.VII.30;

                 Ger. NYVolksztg, 1930.

           [Letter to New Masses.]

300612   Alternative for 300707.

300619   Pis'mo v redaktsiyu ital'yanskoi kommunisticheskoi gazety Prometeo. (Letter to Ed. Board of the Italian Communist paper Prometeo.) (BO, (15-16), IX-X.30)

           Trans.: Am. FI, IX-X.47;

                 Fr. Lutte deC, (III.23), VII.30;

                 It. Prometeo, (III.33), 15.VII.30.

300626   Lettre à Naville.

           Trans.: Fr. p.q. CRISE.II: 40.

           [On Fr. section ILOpp.]

[300700(1)]   A.: Stalin i ego Agabekov. (Stalin and his Agabekov.) (BO, (14),
                VIII.30)
                Trans.: Am. Mil, 15.VIII.30;
                        Fr. V, (46), 25.VII.30;
                        Ger. Der Kom, (I.9), IX.30.
                [Agabekov, head of the GPU, defected. T3330.]

[300700(2)]   D.: Istochniki Manuil'skogo i kompanii. (The sources of Manuilsky and
                company.) (BO, (14), VIII.30)
                Trans.: Am. Mil, 26.VII.30.
                [T3326.]

300700(3)   LENIN VÉGRENDELETE. Levele a part történelmi intézetéhez.
                [Trans. Hun. of sections 61-66 of 271021.]

300707   [Letter to EC German Opposition, sent via Mueller. (p.q. 310131(2))

300715   Stalin, kak teoretik. (Stalin as a theoretician.) (BO, (14), VIII.30)
                Trans.: Am. ISR, Fall, 1956, Winter, 1957; Mil, 15.IX-1.XII.30; NI(WP),
                        X, XI.41;
                        Fr. 551115: 81-108; Lutte deC, (25-26), IX-XII.30;
                        It. 620000(20): 14-43; *680900; 681100: 29-59;
                        Jap. *590000(6); 700130: 59-98.
                [T3324.]

*300723   *WAGA SEIKATSU.
                [Trans. Jap. See 300000(1) for all repr., trans., notes.]

[300800(1)]   —: K politicheskoi biografii Stalina. (A political biography of
                Stalin.) (BO, (14), VIII.30)
                Repr.: 320000(2): 180-200.
                Trans.: Am. 370000(14): 179-98; 620000(3): 179-98; Mil, 25.VI, 2.VII.32;
                        Bul. Osvob, (I.29-31), 14-28.X.32;
                        Fr. Lutte deC, (46-47), I-II.33;
                        Ger. Arbeiter Stimme, (102,103), V, VI.32; PermRev, (I.3,5, II.1),
                            IX,XII.31, I.32;
                        Jap. 680320: 199-221.
                [T3327.]

[300800(2)] Al´fa: Zametki zhurnalista. (Notes of a journalist.) (BO, (14),
             VIII.30)
             Trans.: Am. Mil, 15.IX.30.
             [T3318,T3331.]

[300800(3)] —: Kto kogo? (Who will prevail?) (BO, (14), vIII.30)
             Trans.: Am. Mil, 1.IX.30;
                     Fr. Le Com, (III.15), 20.VII.30; V, (47,48), 1,8.VIII.30.
             [T3328,T3330.]

300801   Pis´mo vengerskim tovarishcham. (Letter to Hungarian comrades.)
             (BO, (15-16), IX-X.30)
             [T3332.]

300821   Mirovaya bezrabotitsa i sovetskaya pyatiletka. (World unemployment
             and the Soviet Five-Year Plan.) (BO, (15-16), IX-X.30)
             Trans.: Am. 310200;
                     Eng. 520900;
                     Fr. p.q. V, (78), 6.III.31;
                     Ger. PermRev, (II.13,14), VII,VIII.32;
                     Sp. 310000(10); Comunismo, (I.9), X.31.
             [Letter to Czech workers. Also in brochure ed. of 300314. T3333.]

300825   Privet Vérité. (Greetings to La Vérité.) (BO, (15-16), IX-X.30)
             Trans.: Bul. p.q. Osvob, (I.4), 22.IV.32;
                     Fr. 670306: 369-75; V, (53), 12.IX.30.
             [T3334.]

300826   Stalin i kitaiskaya revolyutsiya. (Stalin and the Chinese revolution.)
             (BO, (15-16), IX-X.30)
             Trans.: Am. 320600: 267-310; 620000(2): 267-310; 660000(4): 267-310;
                         670000(16): 261-304; Mil, 26.XII.31, 2.I.32;
                     Ch. 470427: 252-73;
                     Eng. 690500(4): 216-52;
                     Jap. *610325; 640330(3): 227-67.
             [Facts and documents. T3335.]

300900(1)   i dr.: K kommunistam Kitaya i vsego mira. (To the Communists of China and of the whole world.) (<u>BO</u>, (15-16), IX-X.30)

                <u>Trans</u>.: Am. <u>Mil</u>, 1.X.30;

                        Bul. <u>Osvob</u>, (2), III.31;

                        Ch. 470427: 274-80;

                        Fr. <u>Lutte deC</u>, (III.25-26), IX-XII.30; <u>V</u>, (53), IX.30; Broué: 339-50;

                        It. <u>Prometeo</u>, (III.37), 15.IX.30;

                        Yid. <u>Klorkeit</u>, (6), IX.30.

        [Rédigé intégralement par LT. — PN. T3338.]

[300900(2)]   Al´fa: Zametki zhurnalista. (Notes of a journalist.) (<u>BO</u>, (15-16), IX-X.30)

                <u>Trans</u>.: Am. p.q. <u>Mil</u>, 1.X.30;

                        Ger. p.q. <u>Arbeiter Stimme</u>, (59), IX.30; p.q. <u>Der Kom</u>, (I.10), IX.30.

        [T3337,T3341,T3343.]

300913   See 330400(1).

300917   Pis´mo konferentsii nemetskoi levoi oppozitsii. (Letter to Conference of German Left Opposition.) (<u>BO</u>, (17-18), XI-XII.30)

        <u>Trans</u>.: Am. <u>Mil</u>, 1.II.31.

        [T3346.]

300918   Alternative for 300917.

300926(1)   Povorot Kominterna i polozhenie v Germanii. (The turn in the Comintern and the situation in Germany.) (<u>BO</u>, (17-18), XI-XII.30)

        <u>Trans</u>.: Am. 301000(1); p.q. 690400(3): 9-12;

                        Eng. 580200; <u>IntSoc</u>, (38-39), VIII.69;

                        Fr. 310000(12): 31-49; 590600: 23-46; p.q. <u>Le Com</u>, (III.21), 19.X.30; <u>V</u>, (57,59,60), 10,24,31.X.30;

                        Ger. 300000(25);

                        Hol. <u>NWeg</u>, (V.11,12), XI,xII.30;

                        It. <u>Prometeo</u>, (III.41-43), 15.XI-15.XII.30;

                        Jap. *520000(4); 620530: 1-28.

300926(2)   —: Otstuplenie v besporyadke: Manuil'skii o "demokraticheskoi diktature". (A flight in full disorder: Manuilsky on the "democratic dictatorship".) (BO, (17-18), XI-XII.30)
Trans.: Am. 320600(2): 237-43; 620000(2): 237-43; 660000(4): 237-43;
670000(16): 231-7; Mil, 15.I.31;
Ch. 470427: 281-3;
Eng. 690500(4): 190-5;
Fr. V, (55,56), 26.IX, 3.X.30;
Jap. *610325; 640330(3): 201-6.

300929   To Professor Kaun. On Sukhanov's account of meeting with Gorky.
(310000(1): AppendixIII)
Trans.: 310000(1): Appendix III;
Am. p.q. Kaun: 602-7.

301000(1)   THE TURN IN THE COMINTERN AND THE GERMAN SITUATION.
[Trans. Am. See 300926(1) for all repr., trans.]

[301000(2)]   —: Krestintern i Antiimperialisticheskaya Liga. (The Krestintern and the Anti-Imperialist League.) (BO, (15-16), IX-X.30)
Trans.: Am. p.q. Mil, 15.XI.30;
Bul. Osvob, (2), III.31.
[T3339.]

[301000(3)]   —: Nuzhna razrabotka istorii vtoroi kitaiskoi revolyutsii. (We need a working-up of a history of the second Chinese revolution.)
(BO, (15-16), IX-X.30)
[T3340.]

[301000(4)]   T.: Prosperiti Molotova v naukakh. (Molotov's prosperity in science.)
(BO, (15-16), IX-X.30)
Trans.: Am. Mil, 15.XI.30.
[T3341.]

301004   [Letter to Bulgarian comrades.]
Trans.: Am. p.q. CLO(2), 1.III.31;
Fr. p.q. OCG, (2), XI.30;
Ger. p.q. KLO, (2), XI.30.
[T3345.]

301009   [On RM's membership of the ILOpp.]
Trans.: Fr. p.q. CRISE.I: 52.

301010 Alternative for 301004.

301012 Alternative for 301013.

301013 Pis'mo Ispolitel'nomu byuro bel'giiskoi oppozitsii. (Letter to EC of the Belgian [Left] Opposition.) (BO, (17-18), XI-XII.30)
Trans.: Am. CLO, (2), 1.III.31;
Fr. Le Com, (III.22), 16.XI.30;
Ger. KLO, (2), XI.30.

301022 [Pref. to] Zayavlenie tov. Rakovskogo i drugikh. (Statement of cde. Rakovsky and others.) (BO, (17-18), XI-XII.30)
Trans.: Am. Mil, 15.I.31;
Eng. p.q. NOT GUILTY: 39;
Fr. Lutte deC, (III.25-26), IX-XII.30; V, (61), 7.XI.30.

301100(1) ‡ L'INTERNATIONALE COMMUNISTE APRÈS LÉNINE. (Le grand organisateur de la défaite.)
Repr.: 690000(1).
Trans.: Am. 360500(1); 570500;
Bul. p.q. 330000(1);
Fr. p.q. Lutte deC, (19,21-22), III,V-VI.30; p.q. QI, (22-24), IX-XI.45;
Ger. 290000(4);
It. 570400;
Jap. *610515; *620925; 640330(1);
Sp. *300000(10); p.q. 611025: 60-1; *650000(12); p.q. 690700(2).
[Trans. Fr. See separate items for other trans. Pref. 290415(1). Contents of book-trans. vary. T3192.]

[301100(2)] —: Chto dal'she? (What next?) (BO, (17-18), XI-XII.30)
Trans.: Am. Mil, 1.I.31.
[On the campaign against the Right, in the Soviet Union.]

[301100(3)] —: Chemu uchit protsessa vreditelei? (What is to be learned from the trial of the wreckers?) (BO, (17-18), XI-XII.30)
Trans.: Am. Mil, 1.I.31;
Fr. V, (65), 5.XII.30;
It. Prometeo, (III.42), 1.XII.30.
[T3350.]

301100(4)	THE STRATEGY OF THE WORLD REVOLUTION.
	<u>Trans</u>.: 301100(1);
	Am. 301100(4);
	Eng. 670800.
	⌊Addressed to 6th Congress Comintern, with 280628.⌋
301100(5)	Alternative for 300926(2).
⌊301100(6)⌋	On Thermidor and Bonapartism.
	<u>Trans</u>.: Am. <u>CLO</u>, (2), 1.III.31; <u>Class Struggle</u>(NY), (I.1), V.31.
	⌊Reply to Weil, for German comrades. See further 301126.⌋
301114	Pref. foreign eds. ISTORIYA RUSSKOI REVOLYUTSII (THE HISTORY OF THE RUSSIAN REVOLUTION), 310000(1).
301121(1)	--: Blok levykh i pravykh. (The bloc of the Left and Right.) (<u>BO</u>, (17-18), XI-XII.30)
	<u>Trans</u>.: Am. <u>Mil</u>, 1.I.31.
	⌊T3349.⌋
301121(2)	See 310528(1)/330400(1).
	⌊On Spanish revolution.⌋
301126	O termidorianstvo i bonapartizme. (Thermidor and Bonapartism.) (<u>BO</u>, (17-18), XI-XII.30)
	<u>Trans</u>.: Am. <u>Mil</u>, 15.I.31; <u>CLO</u>, (2), 1.III.31;
	Bul. <u>Osvob</u>, (1), I.31;
	Fr. <u>Lutte deC</u>, (28-29), I⊥-III.31; <u>OCG</u>, (2), XI.30;
	Ger. <u>KLO</u>, (2), XI.30;
	It. <u>Prometeo</u>, (III.43, IV.51), 15.XII.30, 1.V.31;
	Sp. <u>Comunismo</u>, (I.1), 15.V.31.
301129(1)	Letter to Marxist Workers Group "Osvobozhdenie".
	<u>Trans</u>.: Am. <u>CLO</u>, (3), 1931;
	Bul. <u>Osvob</u>, (1), I.31;
	Fr. <u>OCG</u>, (3), I.31;
	Ger. <u>KLO</u>, (3), I.31.
301129(2)	See 330400(1).
	⌊On Spanish revolution.⌋

[301200(1)]   —: Uspekhi sotsializma i opasnosti avantyurizma. (The successes of socialism and the dangers of adventurism.) (BO, (17-18), XI-XII.30)

Trans.: Am. Mil, 15.III, 1,15.IV.31;
        Bul. Osvob, (1), I.31;
        Cz. *[310000(33)];
        Fr. p.q. Le Com, (IV.1), 8.I.31; V, (66-69), 12.XII.30-2.I.31;
        Ger. Aktion, (XXI.1-2), IV.31;
        It. Prometeo, (IV.44), 1.I.31.

[301200(2)]   Al´fa: Zametki zhurnalista. (Notes of a journalist.) (BO, (17-18), XI-XII.30)

Trans.: Am. Mil, 1.II.31.

[301200(3)]   —: Novaya zhertva Stalina. (A fresh Stalin victim.) (BO, (17-18), XI-XII.30)

Trans.: Bol. Osvob, (1), I.31.
[On Kote Zinzadze.]

301205   Monatte a franchi le Rubicon.

Trans.: Am. 310300(1): 46-52; 690000(13): 29-34;
        Eng. 680300(2): 61-8;
        Fr. 670306: 363-8; RevProl, (VII.114), 5.III.31; V, (67), 19.XII.30.
[T3352.]

301210   [Letter to Shachtman; on China.]

Trans.: Am. p.q. 320600(2): 19-20; p.q. 620000(2): 19-20; p.q. 660000(4): 19-20; p.q. 670000(16): 13-4.

301212   See 310528(1).
[On Spanish revolution.]

301215   Alternative for 301205.

310000(1)   ISTORIYA RUSSKOI REVOLYUTSII. (THE HISTORY OF THE RUSSIAN REVOLUTION.)

Trans.: Am. 320000(10); 360000(3); 370000(27); 570000(3); 590000(7);
600000(29); 610000(1); 640000(7); p.q. 640800: 84-96,
100-8; p.q. 650900: 77-110; p.q. 670600: 59-60; p.q.
690400(2): 59-60; p.q. 700800(1): 59-60; p.q. SatEvening Post,
25.IV-30.V.30, 27.VIII, 3.IX.32;

Bul. *[310000(2)]; p.q. 330000(1);

Ch. *400000(2);

Cz. *340000(3);

Eng. 320600(1): 340900(1); 360400(1) p.q. 640000(5): 77-110;
p.q. 640000(10): 77-110; 651000(1): 670000(11); p.q.
680200(1): 9-21;

Fr. 330100(3); p.q. 340000(19); 500000(1); 620000(1);
670000(17); p.q. 680000(4): passim; p.q. 690000(1): 497-567;
p.q. Europe, 15.III, 15.IV.34; p.q. Voie de Lénine, (IV.5),
11.IX.44;

Ger. 310000(7); 600000(3); 670000(1); p.q. Aussiger Tageblatt,
13.VII.31; p.q. Deutsche Algemeine Ztg, 7.IX.30; p.q.
NRundschau, 1930, 1931, 1932; p.q. Pester Lloyd, 26.IV.31;

Gr. 610000(19)+650000(9); p.q. Diesthenes, (11,12), XI,XII.65;

Heb. 310000(24); 410000(4);

Hol. 360000(2);

It. *360000(8); *390000(9); *460000(9); *600000(31); *640600;
641200; p.q. 680200(2): 73-86; 671100(4);

Jap. *500000(3); *540215; 660730; p.q. 681010: 109-11; p.q.
681125: 91-103,107-16;

Nor. p.q. Okt, (7), XI.37;

Pol. *320000(30);

Sin. 570200;

Sp. *310000(8); *540123; p.q. 611025: 57-9; 620000(16); p.q.
670000(5): 84-96,100-8; p.q. 690700(2): 227; p.q. Perspectiva
Mundial, (I.11-12), 2.XII.66;

Swed. p.q. 691100(2): 72-83,86-94;

Yid. *320000(34).

[301114, Pref. to foreign eds.; 310225 Pref.; 320513 Pref. to Vol. II
[and Vol. III]; 400700(1) Pref. Ch. ed. Undated appendices and
Supplements. See various eds. for abridgements.]

*[310000(2)]   *ISTORIYA NA RUSKATA REVOLYUTSIYA. (THE HISTORY OF THE RUSSIAN REVOLUTION.)
[Trans. Bul. from Ger. Vol. I only. See 310000(1) for all trans., notes.]

[310000(3)]   K ISTORII OKTYABR´SKOI REVOLYUTSII. (THE HISTORY OF THE OCTOBER REVOLUTION.)
[See 180000(5) for all repr., trans., notes.]

*[310000(4)]   *MOYA ZHIVOT. (MY LIFE.)
[Trans. Bul. See 300000(1) for all trans., notes.]

310000(5)   § DE OCTUBRE ROJO A MI DESTIERRO.
[Trans. Sp. Comprising 240915,240729(1),290225,290327. Unauthorized ed.]

310000(6)   GEGEN DEN NATIONALKOMMUNISMUS.
[Trans. Ger. See 310825 for all repr., trans.]

310000(7)   GESCHICHTE DER RUSSISCHEN REVOLUTION.
[Trans. Ger. See 310000(1) for all repr., trans., notes.]

*310000(8)   *HISTORIA DE LA REVOLUCIÓN RUSA.
[Trans. Sp. See 310000(1) for all repr., trans., notes. This ed. omits 7 chaps.]

310000(9)   § LA REVOLUÇÃO ESPANHOLA.
[Trans. Port. See 310124,310405,310528(1) for all repr., trans., notes.]

310000(10)   EL PLAN QUINQUENAL.
[Trans. Sp. See 300821 for all trans.]

310000(11)   PROBLEME DER ENTWICKLUNG DER USSR.
[Trans. Ger. See 310404 for all trans.]

310000(12)   ‡ LES PROBLÈMES DE LA RÉVOLUTION ALLEMANDE.
[Trans. Fr.]

*310000(13)   *QUE HA PASSAT.
[Trans. Sp. See 290000(1) for all repr., trans., notes.]

*310000(14)   *LA REVOLUCIÓN ESPAÑOLA.
[Trans. Sp. See 310124 for all repr., trans., notes.]

310000(15)   LA REVOLUCIÓN ESPAÑOLA Y LAS TACTICA DE LOS COMUNISTAS.
               [Trans. Sp. See 310124 for all repr., trans., notes.]

310000(16)   § LA REVOLUCIÓN ESPAÑOLA Y SUS PELIGROS.
               [Trans. Sp. See 310528(1) for all repr., trans., notes.]

*310000(17)   *LA REVOLUCIÓN PERMANENTE.
               [Trans. Sp. See 300000(3) for all repr., trans., notes.]

*310000(18)   *MY LIFE.
               [Trans. Am. See 300000(1) for all repr., trans., notes.]

*310000(19)   *LA SITUACIÓN REAL DE RUSIA. (LA PLATAFORMA DE LA OPOSICIÓN.)
               [Trans. Sp. See 270903 for all repr., trans., notes.]

310000(20)   SOLL DER FASCHISMUS WIRKLICH SIEGEN?
               [Trans. Ger. See 311126 for all repr., trans., notes.]

310000(21)   § DE SPAANSCHE REVOLUTIE EN DE GEVAREN DIE HAAR BEDREIGEN.
               [Trans. Hol. See 310528(1) for all trans., notes.]

310000(22)   DIE SPANISCHE REVOLUTION.
               [Trans. Ger. See 310124 for all repr., trans. Includes 310415.]

310000(23)   § DIE SPANISCHE REVOLUTION UND DIE IHR DROHENDEN GEFAHREN.
               [Trans. Ger. See 310528(1) for all repr., trans., notes.]

310000(24)   TOLDOT HAMAHAPEICHA HARUSIT.
               [Trans. Heb. See 310000(1) for all repr., trans., notes.]

310000(25)   Gorki og T.: LENIN.
               [Trans. Den. See 200423 for all trans. of T.]

[310000(26)]   § LETTRES A LA CONFÉRENCE DE LA LIGUE COMMUNISTE FRANÇAISE.
               [Trans. Fr.]

[310000(28)]   ZAL HET FASCISME WERKELIJK OVERWINNEN?
               [Trans. Hol. See 311126 for all repr., trans., notes.]

[310000(29)]   ZAL HET FASCISME WERKELIJK OVERWINNEN?
               [Trans. Hol. See 311126 for all repr., trans., notes.]

*[310000(30)] *MOET HET DUITSCHE FASCISME ZEGEVIEREN?
               [Trans. Hol. See 311208 for all repr., trans., notes.]

*[310000(31)]   *NUEVA RUTA.
                    [Trans. Sp. See 240000(22) for all repr., trans., notes.]

*[310000(32)]   *ŠPANELSKÁ REVOLUCE.
                    [Trans. Cz. See 310124 for all trans., notes.]

*[310000(33)]   *ÚSPĚCHY SOCIALISMU A NEBEZPEČI AVANTURISMU.
                    [Trans. Cz. See [301200(1)] for all trans.]

[310000(34)]   [Introduction to] Martovskoe partiinoe soveshchanie 1917 g. (The March
                    1917 Party Conference.) (320000(2): 225-90)
                    Trans.: 320000(2).
                    [T3162.]

*310000(35)   *DOJTSHLAND DER SHLISSEL ZU DER INTERNATIONALER LAGE.
                    [Trans. Yid. See 311126 for all trans., notes.]

*310000(36)   *[MY LIFE.]
                    [Trans. Ch. Vol. 1 [of 2] published. See 300000(1) for all trans.,
                    notes.]

*310000(37)   *[TERRORISM AND COMMUNISM.]
                    [Trans. Ch. See 200000(37) for all trans., notes.]

310000(38)   [Interview, with Fritz von Unruh.] (von Unruh)
                    Trans.: Jug. Socijalna Misso, (VI), IX.33.
                    [Trans. Ger.]

310000(39)   [Interview, with Georg Lukacs.]
                    [c. Lukacs, Survey, (47), IV.63. Trans. from It. Nuovi Argumenti, 1962.]

310100   The Five-Year Plan and the world; America discovers the world.
                    Trans.: Am. Living Age, V.31;
                            Eng. ManGuard, 27,28.III.31;
                            Ger. NMahn, (III.18), IX.31; Volks, (IV.17-22), 1.V-5.VI.31.
                    [Interview. T3378.]

310104   Oshibki pravykh elementov frantsuzskoi kommunisticheskoi Ligi v
                    sindikal'nom voprose. (The mistakes of the Right elements of the French
                    Communist League in the trade union question.) (BO, (1a), III.31)
                    Trans.: Am. 310300(1): 53-63; 690000(13): 34-41;
                            Eng. [380000(21)]; [420000(6)]; [600000(20)]; 680300(2): 69-79;
                            Fr. 670306: 379-89; V, (71), 16.I.31.
                    [T3356.]

310107   --: Pamyati druga: Nad svezhei mogiloi Koté Tsintsadze. (In memory of
          a friend: At the fresh grave of Kote Tzinzadze.) (BO, (19), III.31)
          Trans.: Am. Mil, 15.II.31;
                       Fr. 551115: 195-8; V, (71), 16.I.31;
                       It. Prometeo, (IV.46), 15.II.31;
                       Jap. 631130: 68-72.
          ⌊T3357.⌋

310108   Kitaiskoi levoi oppozitsii. (To the Chinese Left Opposition.)
          (BO, (19), III.31)
          Trans.: Am. CLO, (5), VIII.31;
                       Ch. 470427: 284-9;
                       Fr. BInt, (5), III.31; OCG, (5), III.31.

310112   See 310528(1)/330400(1).
          ⌊On Spanish revolution.⌋

310113   See 330400(1).
          ⌊On Spanish revolution.⌋

310115   Über die Bordigisten. Kritische Bemerkungen anlasslich der Resolution
          der Gruppe Prometheo über den Kampf für demokratische Losungen.
          Trans.: Am. CLO, (17), I.33;
                       Fr. OCG, (17), VI.32;
                       Ger. KLO, (17), VI.32.

310124   Ispanskaya revolyutsiya. (The Spanish revolution.) (BO, (19), III.31)
          Trans.: Am. 310300(2); p.q. 650900: 223-33; CLO, (2), ⌊1931⌋;
                       Cz. *⌊310000(32)⌋;
                       Eng. 520900(2); p.q. 640000(5): 223-33; p.q. 640000(10): 223-33;
                       Fr. 320810; 590600: 411-34; 630419: 387-406; p.q. 680000(4):
                            256-7; V, (74-76), 6-20.II.31; VoixCom, (I.5-10), 8.III-
                            17.V.31;
                       Ger. 310000(22); KLO, (4), II.31; NMahn, (III.6,7), III-IV,V.31;
                       Gr. 630000(10): 12-44;
                       Hol. p.q. NWeg, (VI.5), V.31;
                       It. 620000(20): 183-205; *680900; 681100: 205-29; Prometeo,
                            (IV.47-50), 1.III-15.IV.31;
                       Jap. *630430; 650430: 170-95;
                       Sp. *310000(14); 310000(15); *330300(4); p.q. Antorcha(Madrid),
                            (I.2), 30.VI.34.
          ⌊Pref. to Cz. ed. ⌊310615⌋. T3358,T3390.⌋

310126   —: Monatte -- advokat sotsial-patriotov. (Monatte, advocate of the social-patriots.) (<u>BO</u>, (19), III.31)
  Trans.: Fr. <u>V</u>, (74), 6.II.31.

310131(1)   See 310528(1)/330400(1).
  ⌊On Spanish revolution.⌋

310131(2)   Lettre au Secrétariat administratif.
  Trans.: Am. <u>CLO</u>, (5), VIII.31;
     Fr. <u>OCG</u>, (5), III.31.
  ⌊On German section ILOpp.⌋

310200   WORLD UNEMPLOYMENT AND THE FIVE-YEAR PLAN.
  ⌊Trans. Am. See 300821 for all trans., notes.⌋

310205   See 310528(1)/330400(1).
  ⌊On Spanish revolution.⌋

310207   Alternative for 310217.

310209   Zadushennaya revolyutsiya. (A strangled revolution.) (<u>BO</u>, (20-21), V-VI.31)
  Trans.: Am. 320600(2): 244-58; 620000(2): 244-58; 660000(4): 244-58;
     670000(16): 238-52; <u>Mil</u>, 15.VI.31;
   Ch. 470427: 290-5;
   Eng. 690500(4): 196-208;
   Fr. 320810: 313-30; ⌊600000(22)⌋; 630419: 372-81; 640911:
     306-15 <u>Lutte deC</u>, (31), VI.31; <u>NRF</u>, IV.31; <u>V</u>, (81),
     27.III.31;
   It. 670000(10): 133-41;
   Jap. *610325; 640330(3): 207-19;
   Sp. 640900(1): 225-36; 690000(8).II: 139-47;
   Swed. 690600(1): 272-81.
  ⌊Review of Malraux, LES CONQUÉRANTS. See further 310613.⌋

310213   See 310528(1)/330400(1).
  ⌊On Spanish revolution.⌋

310215   See 310528(1)/330400(1).
  ⌊On Spanish revolution.⌋

310217   The crisis in the German Left Opposition. Open letter to the Landau group.
  Trans.: Am. <u>CLO</u>, (6), 1931;   ++++

310217 ++++   Trans.: Fr. BInt, (6), IV.31; OCG, (6), IV.31;
           Ger. KLO, (6), IV.31.
       ⌊T3364.⌋

310225   Pref. ISTORIYA RUSSKOI REVOLYUTSII (THE HISTORY OF THE RUSSIAN
        REVOLUTION), 310000(1).
        Trans.: 310000(1);
           Hol. p.q. NWeg, (VI.12), XII.31.

310300(1)   ‡ COMMUNISM AND SYNDICALISM.
        Trans.: Am. 310300(1); 690000(13);
           Eng. ⌊380000(21)⌋.
        ⌊See individual entries for other trans.⌋

310300(2)   THE REVOLUTION IN SPAIN.
        ⌊Trans. Am. See 310124 for all trans., notes.⌋

⌊310300(3)⌋   Al′fa: Zametki zhurnalista. (Notes of a journalist.) (BO, (19), III.31)
        Trans.: Am. Mil, 15.IV.31;
           Fr. V, (79), 13.III.31.
        ⌊T3366,T3367,T3369,T3371.⌋

⌊310300(4)⌋   --: N.V.Vorovskaya. (BO, (19), III.31)
        ⌊T3368.⌋

⌊310300(5)⌋   --: Pyatiletka v chetyre goda? (The Five-Year Plan in four?)
        (BO, (19), III.31)
        ⌊T3370.⌋

310304   See 330400(1).
        ⌊On Spanish revolution.⌋

310308   L.T.: Delo t. Ryazanova. (The case of cde. Ryazanov.) (BO, (21-22),
        V-VI.31)
        Trans.: Am. Mil, 1.V.31;
           Fr. V, (80), 20.III.31;
           Ger. Aktion, (XXI.1-2), IV.31;
           Hol. NWeg, (VI.7), VII.31.
        ⌊T3373.⌋

310311   Deistvitel′noe raspolozhenie figur na politicheskoi doske. (The real
        disposition of pieces on the political chessboard.) (BO, (21-22),
        V-VI.31)
              ++++

310311   ++++   <u>Trans</u>.: Am. <u>Mil</u>, 1.V.31;

                Bul. <u>Osvob</u>, (2), III.31;

                Fr. <u>V</u>, (81), 27.III.31;

        [T3375.]

310313   See 310528(1).

        [On Spanish revolution.]

310315   See 330400(1).

        [On Spanish revolution.]

310325   K diskussii o sindikal'nom edinstve. (On trade union unity discussion.)
        (<u>BO</u>, (21-22), V-VI.31)

        <u>Trans</u>.: Am. 690000(13): 45-53; <u>Mil</u>, 15.V.31;

                Bul. <u>Osvob</u>, (3), IV.31;

                Fr. 700000(6): 40-5; <u>Lutte deC</u>, (45), III.32; <u>V</u>, (84), 17.IV.31;

                Yid. <u>Unser Kampf</u>, (I.2), 15.II.32.

        [T3377.]

310329   See 330400(1).

        [On Spanish revolution.]

310401   See 330400(1).

        [On Spanish revolution.]

310404   Problemy razvitiya SSSR. (Problems of the development of the USSR.)
        (<u>BO</u>, (20), IV.31)

        <u>Trans</u>.: Am. 310600(1);

                Bul. <u>Osvob</u>, (I.22-24), 26.VIII-9.IX.32;

                Fr. <u>V</u>, (88-90,93), 15.V-5,26.VI.31; <u>VoixCom</u>, (I.11,12,18),

                    31.V, 14.VI, 6.IX.31;

                Ger. 310000(11); <u>Aktion</u>, (XXI.3-4), VII.31;

                It. <u>Prometeo</u>, (IV.58-64), 23.VIII-29.IX.31.

        [T3379.]

310405   Alternative for 310415.

*[310411]   *Lenin's Heimkehr.

        <u>Trans</u>.: Ger. <u>Frankfurter Ztg</u>, 11.IV.31; <u>NFreie Presse</u>, 12.IV.31.

        [? p.q. 300000(1), ? 310000(1).]

310412   Letter to <u>Comunismo</u>/Nin.

Trans.: Fr. 330400(1); 590600: 435-8; <u>Lutte deC</u>, (III.30), IV.31;

Gr. 630000(10): 44-5;

Jap. *630430; 650430: 196-7;

Sp. <u>Comunismo</u>, (I.1), 15.V.31.

[T3380.]

310414(1)   See 310528(1).

[On Spanish revolution.]

310414(2)   Thaelmann and the "People's Revolution".

Trans.: Am. <u>Mil</u>, 11.VII.31.

310414(3)   A proposito di un libro del comp. Trotsky in lingua italiana.

Trans.: It. <u>Prometeo</u>, (IV.60), 27.IX.31.

[See also 310528(2).]

310415   Desyat zapovedei ispanskogo kommunista. (Ten commandments for the
Spanish communists.) (<u>BO</u>, (21-22), V-VI.31)

Trans.: Am. 310600(2); <u>Class Struggle</u>(NY), (I.2), VI.31; <u>Mil</u>, 1.VI.31;

Bul. <u>Osvob</u>, (3), IV.31;

Fr. 590600: 439-44; <u>Lutte deC</u>, (30), IV.31; <u>V</u>, (87), 8.V.31;
<u>VoixCom</u>, (I.10), 17.V.31;

Ger. 310000(22); <u>Volks</u>, (IV.19), 15.V.31;

Gr. 630000(10): 46-50;

Hol. <u>Baan</u>, (III.4), 23.V.31;

It. <u>BOC</u>, (2), 15.VI.31; <u>OCI</u>, (2), VI.31; <u>Prometeo</u>, (IV.53),
7.VI.31;

Jap. *630430; 650430: 198-201;

Sp. 680000(9): 157; <u>Comunismo</u>, (I.2), 15.VI.31.

[T3381.]

310420   See 310528(1)/330400(1).

[On Spanish revolution.]

310422   See 330400(1).

[On Spanish revolution.]

310423   See 310528(1).

[On Spanish revolution.]

310424   Pis'mo v Politbyuro VKP(b). (Letter to the Politbureau CPSU(b).)
(BO, (21-22), V-VI.31)

Trans.: Am. 310600(2); Mil, 4.VII.31;
        Fr. 590600: 445-8; V, (91), 12.VI.31; VoixCom, (I.13), 28.VI.31;
        Ger. 310000(23);
        Gr. 630000(10): 50-2;
        Hol. 310000(21);
        Jap. *630430; 650430: 202-3.

[See 310528(1), Appendices for other trans. On Spain.]

310500   THE PERMAMENT REVOLUTION.
[Trans. Am. See 281000(1) for all repr., trans., notes.]

310501   —: Dopolnitel'naya kleveta na D.B.Ryazanova. (A new slander against
D.B.Ryazanov.) (BO, (21-22), V-VI.31)

Trans.: Am. Mil, 4.VII.31;
        Fr. V, (91), 12.VI.31;
        Ger. PermRev, (I.1), VII.31.
[T3384.]

310517   See 310528(1).
[On Spanish revolution.]

310520   See 310528(1).
[On Spanish revolution.]

310523(1)   [Letter to Treint.]
[c. 310913(1). T3385.]

310523(2)   Letter to Shachtman.
Trans.: Am. p.q. CLA, (2), VII.32.
[On Spain.]

310526   See 330400(1).
[On Spanish revolution.]

310528(1)   § Ispanskaya revolyutsiya i ugrozhayushchie ei opasnosti. (The Spanish
revolution and the dangers threatening it.) (BO, (21-22), V-VI.31)

++++

310528(1) ++++ Trans.: Am. 310600(2);

Fr. 320810; 590600: 451-73,483-510; 630419: 407-27; p.q.
   680000(4): passim; p.q. Lutte deC, (31), V.31; p.q.
   OCG, (2-3), IV.33; V, (91,92), 12,19.VI.31;

Ger. 310000(23); Aktion, (XXI.3-4), VII.31; p.q. UnserW, (II.35),
   XI.34;

Gr. 630000(10): 53-88; 630000(11): 3-21;

Hol. 310000(21);

It. 310700(1); 620000(20): 206-30,231-44; *680900(3); 681100:
   230-55,256-87; Prometeo, (IV.60), 27.IX.31;

Jap. *630430; 650430: 204-32;

Sp. *310000(14); 310000(16); *330300(4); 680000(9): 113;
   Comunismo, (I.3), 1.VIII.31.

[The Appendix, Voprosy ispanskoi revolyutsii izo dnya v den (Problems of
the Spanish revolution from day to day) = 17 items. See 310609, Pref. to
It. ed. 310700(1). T3383.]

310528(2)   **Alla frazione di sinistra italiana.**
Trans.: It, Prometeo, (IV.60), 27.IX.31.
[See also 310414(3).]

310530   See 330400(1).
[On Spanish revolution.]

310531   [On Spanish revolution.] (310708(1))
Trans.: Fr. 590600: 495; BInt, (9-10), VII-VIII.31; OCG, (4), IV.33;
   Gr. 630000(11): 21-2;
   It. 620000(2): 243-4; *680900(3); 681100: 269-70;
   Jap. *630430; 650430: 253-4;
   Sp. 680000(9): 139; Comunismo, (I.5), X.31.

310600(1)   PROBLEMS OF THE DEVELOPMENT OF THE USSR.
[Trans. Am. See 310404 for all trans.]

310600(2)   THE SPANISH REVOLUTION IN DANGER.
[Trans. Am. See 310528(1) for all trans., notes.]

[310600(3)] Al'fa: Zametki zhurnalista. (Notes of a journalist.) (BO, (21-22),
V-VI.31)
Trans.: Am. Mil, 1,8.III.31;
   Fr. Lutte deC, (III.32-33), VI-VII.31.

*310601   *SHAKAI SHISO ZENSHU.
                 [Trans. Jap. See 250720, *251028 for all repr., trans., notes.]

310607   Lettre.
                 Trans.: Fr. CRISE.II: 40-1.
                 [On Fr. section ILOpp.]

310609   Pref. LA RIVOLUZIONE SPAGNUOLA E I PERICOLI CHE LA MINACCIANO,
                 310700(1).
                 Trans.: Am. CLO(8), 1931;
                         Fr. BInt, (8), VI.31; OCG, (8), VI.31;
                         It. BOC, (3), 15.VIII.31; OCI, (3), [VIII.] 1931.
                 [T3387.]

310612   O platforme katalanskogo "Raboche-krest´yanskogo bloka". (The platform
                 of the Catalan "Workers and Peasants Bloc".) (BO, (23), VIII.31)
                 Trans.: Am. Mil, 1.VIII.31;
                         Fr. 590600: 475-80; Lutte deC, (31), VI.31;
                         Gr. 630000(10): 89-94;
                         Jap. *630430; 650430: 233-7;
                         Sp. Comunismo, (I.3), 1.VIII.31.
                 [T3388.]

310613   L.T.: Ob udushennoi revolyutsii i ee udushitelyakh. (A strangled
                 revolution and its stranglers.) (BO, (23), VIII.31)
                 Trans.: Am. 320600(2): 259-66; 620000(2): 259-66; 660000(4): 259-66;
                         670000(16): 253-60;
                         Ch. 470427: 297-300;
                         Fr. 320810: 223-32; 630419: 382-6; 640911: 316-21; Lutte deC,
                         (32-33), VI-VII.31;
                         It. 670121: 142-6;
                         Jap. *610325; 640330(3): 220-6;
                         Sp. 640900(1): 236-42; 690000(8).II: 157-61;
                         Swed. 691100(1): 282-7.
                 [See also 310209. For other Fr. repr. see 281000(1). On China. T3389.]

*310614   *WAGA SEIKATSU KARA.
                 [Trans. Jap. See 300000(1) for all repr., trans., notes. Abgd.]

[310615]   Pref. *SPANĚLSKÁ REVOLUCE, *[310000(32)].
                 [Trans. Cz. T3390.]

310618   Letter on the Spanish revolution; for the Left Opposition.

Trans.: Am. FI, X.43; Mil, 18.VII.31;
            Fr. 590600: 495-9; BInt, (9-10), VII-VIII.31;
            Gr. 630000(11): 22-7;
            It. 620000(20): 244-8; *680900(3); 681100: 270-4;
            Jap. *630430; 650430: 254-8;
            Sp. 680000(9): 140; Comunismo, (I.5), X.31.
[See also 310708(1), note. T3394.]

310624   [On Spanish revolution.] (310708(1))

Trans.: Am. FI, X.43; Mil, 25.VII.31;
            Fr. 590600: 502-3; BInt, (9-10), VII-VIII.31;
            Gr. 630000(11): 27-33;
            Hol. p.q. Baan, (III.17), 22.VIII.31;
            It. 620000(20): 248-52; *680900(3) 681100: 274-8;
            Jap. *630430; 650430: 258-62;
            Sp. 680000(9): 149; Comunismo, (I.5), X.31.
[T3392.]

310628   Alternative for 310629.

310629   [On Spanish revolution.] (310708(1))

Trans.: Am. Mil, 5.IX.31;
            Fr. 330400(1); 590600: 502-3; BInt, (9-10), VII-VIII.31;
                OCG, (4), IV.33;
            Gr. 630000(11): 33-4;
            It. 620000(20): 252-3; *680900(3); 681100: 278-9;
            Jap. *630430; 650430: 262-3;
            Sp. 680000(9): 143,153; Comunismo, (I.6), XI.31.

310700(1)   § LA RIVOLUZIONE SPAGNUOLA E I PERICOLI CHE LA MINACCIANO.
            [Trans. It. See 310528(1) for all repr., trans., notes. Pref. 310609.]

[310700(2)] —: Bukharin o permanente revolyutsii. (Bukharin on the permanent
            revolution.) (BO, (23), VIII.31)

Trans.: Am. Mil, 1.VIII.31;
            Fr. Lutte deC, (III.32-33), VI-VII.31;
            Ger. PermRev, (I.1), VII.31.

310701   [On Spanish revolution.] (310708(1))

Trans.: Am. FI, X.43; Mil, 25.VII.31;

        Fr. 590600: 504-7;

        Gr. 630000(11): 34-40;

        It. 620000(20): 253-7; *680900(3); 681100: 279-83;

        Jap. *630430; 650430: 264-8.

[T3393.]

310702   [On Spanish revolution.] (310708(1))

Trans.: Fr. 590600: 507-10; p.q. BInt, (9-10), VII-VIII.31; OCG, (4),

        IV.33;

        Gr. 630000(11): 40-5;

        It. 620000(20): 257-60; *680900(3); 681100: 283-7;

        Jap. *630430; 650430: 268-72.

[To Nin.]

310708(1)   —: § Voprosy ispanskoi revolyutsii izo dnya v den. (Problems of the
Spanish revolution from day to day.) (BO, (23), VIII.31)
[Includes 310531, 310618, 310624; 310629, 310701, 310702, 310713.
Repr. as appendices to 310528(1). T3394.]

310708(2)   O prokhvostakh i ikh pomoshchnikakh. (Blackguards and their aides.)
(BO, (23), VIII.31)

Trans.: Am. Mil, 8.VIII.31;

       Bul. Osvob, (I.15), 8.VII.32;

       Fr. V, (95), 17.VII.31;

       Ger. PermRev, (I.2), VIII.31.

[See also 310708(3), 310715(2). T3395.]

310708(3)   Pis'mo v redaktsiyu Vossische Zeitung. (Letter to Ed. Vossische
Zeitung.) (BO, (23), VIII.31)

Trans.: Ger. Vossische Ztg, 12.VII.31.

[Included in 310708(2). See also 310715(2). On slanders.]

310708(4)   Discours du camarade Seipold prononcé au Landtag de Prusse.

Trans.: Fr. V, (96), VIII.31;

       Ger. PermRev, (II.7), IV.32.

[Rédigé par LT. — PN.]

310713   Eshche o tekushchikh voprosakh ispanskoi revolyutsii. (Again on
current problems of the Spanish revolution.) (BO, (23), VIII.31)

Trans.: Am. Mil, 19.IX.31;   ++++

310713   ++++   <u>Trans</u>.: Fr. <u>V</u>, (98), 1.IX.31.
[On Maurin, Catalonia. See 310708(1). T3397.]

310714   Otvety na voprosy predstavitelya Associated Press America. (Replies to questions from Associated Press America correspondent.) (<u>BO</u>, (23), VIII.31)
<u>Trans</u>.: Am. <u>NYTimes</u>, 19,26.VII.31;
       Fr. <u>V</u>, (98), 1.IX.31.
[T3400.]

310715(1)   --: Novye zigzag i novye opasnosti. (New zigzags and new dangers.) (<u>BO</u>, (23), VIII.31)
<u>Trans</u>.: Am. <u>Mil</u>, 15,22.VIII.31;
       Bul. <u>Osvob</u>, (4), IX.31;
       Fr. <u>V</u>, (96), 1.VIII.31; <u>VoixCom</u>, (I.16,17), 9,23.VIII.31;
       Ger. <u>NMahn</u>, (III.16,22,23), VIII,IX-X,XI.31; <u>PermRev</u>, (I.2), VIII.31;
       Hol. <u>NWeg</u>, (VI.10), X.31;
       It. p.q. <u>BOC</u>, (4), 20.XI.31;
       Sp. 330000(36): 41-55;
       Yid. p.q. <u>Unser Kampf</u>, (I.6), 15.IV.32.
[On Soviet economy. T3399.]

310715(2)   V redaktsiyu <u>Pravdy</u>. (To Ed. Board <u>Pravda</u>.) (<u>BO</u>, (23), VIII.31)
<u>Trans</u>.: Am. <u>Mil</u>, 22.VIII.31;
       Fr. <u>V</u>, (96), 1.VIII.31; <u>VoixCom</u>, (I.16), 9.VIII.31;
       Sp. <u>Comunismo</u>, (I.4), 1.IX.31.
[See also 310708(2), 310708(3). On slanders. T3398.]

[310716]   Complaint of falsifying.
<u>Trans</u>.: Eng. <u>ManGuard</u>, 16.VII.31.
[Letter to Ed.]

310719   Greetings to weekly <u>Militant</u>.
<u>Trans</u>.: Am. <u>Mil</u>, 15.VIII.31.

310722   Alternative for 310702.

310727   [On Spanish revolution.] (330400(1))

310728   G.Gourov: Some ideas on the position and the tasks of the Left
                Opposition.
                <u>Trans</u>.: Am. <u>CLA</u>, 1931.
                [T3401.]

310730   —: Pis´mo ob ispanskoi revolyutsii. (Letter on the Spanish
                revolution.) (<u>BO</u>, (24), IX.31)
                <u>Trans</u>.: Am. <u>Mil</u>, 26.IX.31.
                [T3402.]

310802   —: Pis´mo ob ispanskoi revolyutsii. (Letter on the Spanish
                revolution.) (<u>BO</u>, (24), IX.31)
                <u>Trans</u>.: Am. <u>FI</u>, X.45.
                [T3403.]

310820(1)   O rabochem kontrole nad proizvodstvom. (Workers control of production.)
                (<u>BO</u>, (24), IX.31)
                <u>Trans</u>.: Am. <u>Mil</u>, 17,24.X.31; <u>NI</u>(WP), V-VI.51; <u>World Outlook</u>, (VI.4),
                        2.II.68;
                    Eng. [600000(28)]; 690000(3);
                    Fr. 310000(12): 23-30; 590600: 49-58;
                    Ger. 310000(6); p.q. <u>PermRev</u>, (I.3), IX.31; p.q. <u>Volks</u>, (IV.38),
                        25.IX.31;
                    It. 620000(20): 263-71; *680900(3); 681100: 291-300;
                    Jap. *520000(4); 620530: 29-39;
                    Sp. p.q. <u>Comunismo</u>, (I.6), XI.31.
                [See also 310912.]

310820(2)   Lettre au CC de la Ligue Communiste.
                <u>Trans</u>.: Fr. <u>GBL</u>, (4), [VIII.31]; p.q. CRISE.II: 40.
                [Fr. section ILOpp.]

310820(3)   Lettre à Collinet.
                <u>Trans</u>.: Fr. <u>GBL</u>, (4), [VIII.31].
                [Fr. section ILOpp.]

310825   Protiv natsional-kommunizma! (Uroki "krasnogo" referenduma.) (Against
                national-communism! Lessons of the "red" referendum.) (<u>BO</u>, (24), IX.31)
                <u>Trans</u>.: Am. <u>Mil</u>, 19,26.IX, 10.X.31;
                        Bul. <u>Osvob</u>, (I.17-20), 22.VII-12.VIII.32;

                                                                    ++++

310825   ++++   <u>Trans</u>.: Fr. 310000(12): 3-22; 590600: 59-84; p.q. 680000(4): 208-9;
                         <u>V</u>, (99), 15.IX.31; p.q. <u>VoixCom</u>, (I.20), 4.X.31;
                         Ger. 310000(6); 320000(7); 320000(8); p.q. <u>PermRev</u>, (I.3),
                              IX.31; <u>Volks</u>, (IV.45.,46), 13,20.XI.31;
                         Hol. [400000(6)];
                         Jap. *520000(4); 620530: 41-71.

310826   [On Spanish revolution.]   (330400(1))

[310900(1)]   A.: Mnogoznachitel'nye fakty. (Very significant facts.) (<u>BO</u>, (24),
                  IX.31)
                  <u>Trans</u>.: Am. <u>Mil</u>, 14.XI.31;
                         Fr. <u>V</u>, (106), 28.XI.31; <u>VoixCom</u>, (I.25), 13.XII.31.

310900(2)   Lettre ouverte à l'organisation bolchevique-léniniste de Grèce
                  (Archiomarxiste).
                  <u>Trans</u>.: Fr. <u>OCG</u>, (10), X.31.

[310900(3)]   Red.: Chitatelyam-druzym, chitatelyam-sochuvstvuyushchim, chitatelyam-
                  kolebyushimsya, chitatelyam-zadumavshimsya, chitatelyam-protivnikam.
                  (To friendly, sympathetic, vacillating, thoughtful and antagonistic
                  readers.) (<u>BO</u>, (24), IX.31)
                  [T3405.]

310901   The Catalonian Separatists, Soviets and Communists.
                  <u>Trans</u>.: Am. p.q. <u>FI</u>, X.43; <u>Mil</u>, 19.XII.31;
                         Fr. p.q. 330400(1).
                  [Letter to Nin; on Spain.]

310902   Ob"eyasneniya v krugu druzei. (Explanation to a circle of friends.)
                  (<u>BO</u>, (24), IX.31)
                  [On the elements of dual power in the USSR. T3406.]

310912   Gegen der Widersacher der Losung Kontrolle der Produktion. (Neuer Brief
                  an die Well-Gruppe.)
                  <u>Trans</u>.: Am. <u>Mil</u>, 21.XI.31;
                         Eng. [600000(28)];
                         Ger. <u>Volks</u>, (IV.43), 30.X.31;
                         Jap. *630430; 650430: 273-4.
                  [See 310820(1).]

310913(1)   On the German October.

            <u>Trans</u>.: Am. <u>NI</u>, II.38.

            [Letter to Treint. T3409.]

310913(2)   Pref. STALINSKAYA SHKOLA FAL´SIFIKATSIYA. (THE STALIN SCHOOL OF

            FALSIFICATION), 320000(2).

            <u>Trans</u>.: 320000(2).

310922   Lettre au camarade Treint.

            [Trans. Fr. Processed. LocHIS.]

310925(1)   A few remarks apropos the internal difficulties and frictions in the

            Ligue.

            <u>Trans</u>.: Am. <u>IIM</u>, 1932.

            [Only part I of the text. T3410.]

310925(2)   Lettre à la conférence de la Ligue Communiste française.

            [Trans. Fr. Processed. LocHIS.]

310927   On Opposition and the Party in Spain.

            <u>Trans</u>.: Am. <u>Mil</u>, 14.XI.31;

                  Fr. 330400(1); <u>OCG</u>, (4), IV.33.

310929   Greetings to <u>El Soviet</u>.

            <u>Trans</u>.: Am. <u>Mil</u>, 31.X.31;

                  Fr. 590600: 511-4; <u>OCG</u>, (12), X.31;

                  Ger. <u>KLO</u>, (12), XI.31;

                  Gr. 630000(11): 45-7;

                  Jap. *630430; 650430: 273-4.

311010   Reply to Weisbord.

            <u>Trans</u>.: Am. <u>Class Struggle</u>(NY), (I.5), XII.31; <u>Mil</u>, 28.XI.31.

311017   Zadachit"ena L"evata Oppozitsiya v B´lgariya. (Tasks of the Left

            Opposition in Bulgaria.)

            <u>Trans</u>.: Bul. <u>Osvob</u>, (5), 10.XII.31.

311107   Tasks of the Left Opposition in Britain and India. Some critical

            remarks on an unsuccessful thesis.

            <u>Trans</u>.: Am. <u>Mil</u>, 12.XII.31;

                  Eng. p.q. <u>Communist</u>(B), (2), IX.32;

                  Fr. <u>BInt</u>, (13), XI.31; <u>OCG</u>, (13), I.32.

            [T3412.]

311110   The British elections and the Communists.

Trans.: Am. p.q. Mil, 5.XII.31;

Eng. p.q. Red Flag, (II.1), XI.34; p.q. Marxist Review, [1949];

Fr. p.q. V, (108), 26.XII.31; p.q. VoixCom, (II.2), 24.I.32;

Ger. p.q. NMahn, (IV.3), II.32; p.q. PermRev, (II.2), I.32.

311114   Russo-German relations.

Trans.: Am. Mil, 21.XI.31.

311115   What is fascism?

Trans.: Am. p.q. 690400(3): 5; p.q. FI, X.43; p.q. Mil, 16.I.32;

Eng. p.q. 620900.

[Extract from a letter to a British comrade.]

311117   What is a revolutionary situation? The decisive importance of the C.P.

Trans.: Am. Mil, 19.XII.31;

Fr. OCG, (13), I.32.

[On Germany. T3413.]

311118   Lettre à Molinier.

Trans.: Fr. p.q. CRISE.II: 41.

311119   [On Spanish revolution.] (330400(1))

311126   Klyuch k mezhdunarodnomu polozheniyu — v Germanii. (The key to the
international situation is in Germany.) (BO, (25-26), XI-XII.31)

Trans.: Am. 320000(9); 650900: 245-56; p.q. Mil, 19.III.32;

Bul. Osvob, (I.1,2), 1,8.IV.32;

Cz. 320000(12);

Eng. 440000(2); 581100; 640000(5): 245-56; 640000(10): 245-56;
700500: 1-24; Communist(B), (1), V.32; p.q. IntSoc, (38-39),

Fr. 590600: 85-106; V, (107), 12.XII.31; VoixCom, (I.26),
27.XII.31;

Ger. 310000(20); 320000(16); 320000(32); Arbeiter Stimme, (91),
XII.31; p.q. NMahn, (25), XII.31;

Hol. [310000(28)]; [310000(29)];

It. 620000(20): 271-93; *680900(3); 681100: 301-23; BOC, (5),
15.XII.31; OCI, (5), 1931; Prometeo, (IV.66, V.67,68),
27.XII.31, 17,31.I.32;

++++

311126   ++++   <u>Trans</u>.: Jap. *520000(4); 620530: 73-95;

                Pol. *320000(31); <u>Prol</u>, (1), V.32;

                Sp. ⌊320000(22)⌋;

                Yid. *310000(35).

    ⌊PS 311228. T3414.⌋

⌊311200⌋   Zayavlenie bol′shevikov-lenintsev (levoi oppozitsii) po povodu podgotovki belogvardeitsami terroristicheskogo akta protiv t. Trotskogo. (Statement of the Bolshevik-Leninists (Left Opposition) on the attempted White Guard terrorist act against cde. Trotsky.) (<u>BO</u>, (27), III.32)

    <u>Trans</u>.: Bul. <u>Osvob</u>, (I.17), 22.VII.32;

              Fr. p.q. <u>V</u>, (109), 9.I.32;

              Ger. <u>PermRev</u>, (I.5), XII.31;

              It. <u>BOC</u>, (7), 15.II.32;

              Sp. <u>Comunismo</u>, (II.9), II.32.

    ⌊T3421.⌋

311208   V chem sostoit oshibochnost segodnyashnei politiki germanskoi kompartii? (What is the error in today's policy of the CPGermany?) (<u>BO</u>, (27), III.32)

    <u>Trans</u>.: Am. 320000(9); 650900: 245-56; <u>Mil</u>, 9.I.32;

              Bul. <u>Osvob</u>, (I.6), 6.V.32;

              Eng. 440000(2); 581100; 640000(5): 245-56; 640000(10): 245-56; 700500: 25-38; <u>Communist</u>(B), (2), IX.32;

              Fr. 330000(13); <u>V</u>, (108), 26.XII.31; <u>VoixCom</u>, (II.1), 10.I.32;

              Ger. 320000(16); 320000(21); 320000(32); <u>NMahn</u>, (IV.2), I.32; p.q. <u>PermRev</u>, (II.1, III.5), I.32, II.33; p.q. <u>Volks</u>, (VI.3), 1.II.33;

              Hol. *310000(30); ∅ <u>Klassen</u>(A), (1,2), ⌊1932⌋; <u>NWeg</u>, (VII.1), I.32;

              It. <u>BOC</u>, (6), 15.I.32;

              Pol. <u>Prol</u>, (1), V.32;

              Sp. <u>Comunismo</u>, (II.8), I.32.

    ⌊T3416.⌋

311216   ⌊On Spanish revolution.⌋ (330400(1))

311222   Letter to the national sections.
                Trans.: Am. p.q. Mil, 13.II.32; p.q. DCL, 1932;
                        Fr. p.q. GBL, 10.IV.32;
                        Yid. p.q. Unser Kampf, (I.3), 1.III.32.
                [On ILOpp. The 2 American p.q. give the complete text. T3417.]

311225(1)   Letter to National Committee, Communist League of America.
                Trans.: Am. CLA, (2), VII.32.

311225(2)   Letter to Shachtman.
                Trans.: Am. p.q. CLA, (2), VII.32.
                [Am. section ILOpp.]

311228   PS 311126.
                Trans.: 311126;
                        Fr. BInt, (14), III.32; OCG, (14), III.32.

320000(1)   NEMETSKAYA REVOLYUTSIYA I STALINSKAYA BYUROKRATIYA. (THE GERMAN
              REVOLUTION AND THE STALINIST BUREAUCRACY.)
              Repr.: p.q. BO, (27), III.32.
              Trans.: Am. 320900(1); p.q. 640800: 163-5, 167-71; p.q. 650900: 234-44;
                      p.q. 690400(3): 6-9,12-13; Mil. 26.III-18.VI.32;
                  Eng. p.q. [600000(28)]; p.q. 620900; p.q. 640000(5): 234-44;
                      p.q. 640000(10): 234-44; 700500: 45-213; p.q. IntSoc,
                      (38-39), VIII-IX.69; p.q. WIN, (VII.1), I-II.47; p.q.
                      MIR, (2), 1970;
                  Fr. 320000(6); 590600: 107-230; p.q. Lutte deC, (III.36),
                      VIII-IX.31;
                  Ger. 320000(19); 320000(20); p.q. Arbeiter Stimme, (102,103),
                      V,VI.32; p.q. Gegner, (415), 1932; p.q. Leipziger Volksztg,
                      3.III.32; p.q. NMahn, (IV.6,7), III,IV.32; p.q.
                      Weltbühne, (9), 1.III.32;
                  Hol. NWeg, (VII.9-12), IX-XII.32;
                  It. 620000(20): 299-420; *680900; 681100; p.q. BOC, (7),
                      15.II.32;
                  Jap. *520000(4); 620530: 99-299; p.q. 681125: 171-3, 175-9;
                  Pol. *320000(29); p.q. Prol, (1), V.32;
                  Sp. *[320000(28)]; p.q. 670000(5): 162-4,166-70; p.q.
                      Comunismo, (II.11-14), IV-VII.32;
                  Swed. p.q. 691100(2): 144-6,147-51;
                  Yid. p.q. *320000(33); p.q. 330000(44); p.q. Unser Kampf,
                      (I.7,8,16), 1,15.V, 15.XI.32.
              [Pref. 320127.]

320000(2)   ‡ STALINSKAYA SHKOLA FAL'SIFIKATSII. (THE STALIN SCHOOL OF
              FALSIFICATION.)
              Trans.: Am. 370000(14); 620000(3);
                  Ger. 320000(18);
                  Jap. 680320.
              [Pref. 310913(2); Pref. Am. ed. 370303(1). Supplementary material
              in Am. and Jap. eds.]

*320000(3)   *AZ EGYETLEN ÚT.
              [Trans. Hun. See 330400(2) for all trans.]

320000(5)   § DER EINZIGE WEG.
              [Trans. Ger. See 330400(2) for all repr., trans.]

320000(6) ET MAINTENANT?
[Trans. Fr. See 320000(1) for all repr., trans.]

320000(7) GEGEN DEN NATIONALKOMMUNISMUS. (Lehren des "roten" Volksentscheids.)
[Trans. Ger. See 310825 for all repr., trans.]

320000(8) GEGEN DEN NATIONALKOMMUNISMUS. (Lehren des "roten" Volksentscheids.)
[Trans. Ger. See 310825 for all repr., trans.]

320000(9) GERMANY -- THE KEY TO THE INTERNATIONAL SITUATION.
[Trans. Am. See 311126, 311208 for all repr., trans.]

320000(10) THE HISTORY OF THE RUSSIAN REVOLUTION.
[Trans. Am. See 310000(1) for all repr., trans., notes. 3 vols.]

*320000(11) *LDARKO SHEL MA-AMAD HAPOALIM BGERMANYA.
[Trans. Heb. p.q. 330400(2).]

320000(12) NĚMECKO KLÍČEM K MEZINÁRODNI SITUACI.
[Trans. Cz. See 311126 for all trans.]

*320000(14) *LA RÉVOLUTION RUSSE.
[Trans. Fr. See 321127 for all repr., trans., notes.]

320000(15) § LA SEULE VOIE.
[Trans. Fr. See 330400(2) for all repr., trans., notes.]

320000(16) SOLL DER FASCISMUS WIRKLICH SIEGEN?
[Trans. Ger. See 311126,311208 for all repr., trans.]

320000(18) § DIE STALINISCHE SCHULE D. FÄLSCHUNG.
[Trans. Ger. See 320000(2) for all trans., notes.]

320000(19) WAS NUN?
[Trans. Ger. See 320000(1) for all repr., trans.]

320000(20) WAS NUN?
[Trans. Ger. See 320000(1) for all repr., trans.]

320000(21) WIE WIRD DER NATIONALSOZIALISMUS GESCHLAGEN?
[Trans. Ger. See 311208 for all repr., trans.]

[320000(22)] ALEMANIA, CLAVE DE LA SITUACIÓN INTERNACIONAL.
[Trans. Sp. See 311126 for all repr., trans.]

[320000(23)]   OFFENER BRIEF AN DAS ZENTRAL-EXEKUTIVKOMITEE DER SOWJET-UNION.
               [Trans. Ger. See 320301 for all repr., trans.]

[320000(24)]   § LA ÚNICA SALIDA DE LA SITUACIÓN ALEMAÑA.
               [Trans. Sp. See 330400(2) for all trans.]

*[320000(25)] § *JEDINÁ CESTA.
               [Trans. Cz. See 330400(2) for all trans.]

*[320000(26)] § *⌊JEDINÁ CESTA.⌋
               [Trans. Hun. See 330400(2) for all trans.]

*[320000(27)] *PERMANENTNÍ REVOLUCE.
               [Trans. Cz. See 281000(1) for all trans.]

*[320000(28)] * ¿ Y AHORA? FASCISMO I COMUNISMO EN ALEMAÑA.
               [Trans. Sp. See 320000(1) for all repr., trans.]

*320000(29)   *A CO DALEJ?
               [Trans. Pol. See 310000(1) for all trans.]

*320000(30)   *HISTORIA REWOLUCJI ROSYJSKIEJ.
               [Trans. Pol. See 310000(1) for all trans., notes.]

*320000(31)   *O SYTUACJI MIĘDZYNARODOWEJ. KLUCZ DO SYTUACJI MIĘDZYNARODOWEJ W
               NIEMCZECH.
               [Trans. Pol. See 311126 for all trans.]

320000(32)   SOLL DER FASCHISMUS WIRKLICH SIEGEN?
               [Trans. Ger. See 311126,311208 for all repr., trans.]

*320000(33)   *WOS WAJTER? (Lebnsfragen fun dajczn proletarjat.)
               [Trans. Yid. p.q. 320000(1).]

*320000(34)   *DI GESHICHTE FUN DER RUSISHE REVOLJUTSJA.
               [Trans. Yid. Vol. 1 only. See 310000(1) for all trans., notes.]

320000(35)   FARVOS STALIN NEMT AVEK MEJN BIRGER RECHT.
               [Trans. Yid. See 320301 for all trans.]

*[320000(36)] *[MY LIFE.]
               [Trans. Ch. See 300000(1) for all repr., trans., notes. 3 vols.]

*[320000(37)]   *[MY LIFE.]
                [Trans. Ch. See 300000(1) for all repr., trans. Only Vol. 1 of
                2 projected.]

320102   —: "Vosstanie" 7 noyabrya 1927 goda. (The "uprising" of November 7,
                1927.) (BO, (27), III.32)
                Trans.: Am. Mil, 6.II.32;
                        Fr. V, (110), 23.I.32;
                        Ger. PermRev, (II.2), I.32;
                        Hol. p.q. Baan, (III.40), 30.I.32;
                        Sp. Comunismo, (II.9), II.32.
                [T3422.]

320104   Letter to the Politbureau, from Turkey.
                Trans.: Am. p.q. FI, VI.41;
                        Fr. p.q. 371115.
                [T3423.]

320105   Letter to the National Committee, Communist League of America.
                Trans.: Am. CLA, (2), VII.32.

320115   Reply to Jewish Group in the Communist League of France.
                Trans.: Am. CLA, (2), VII.32.

320117   See 330400(1).

320123   Denies asking German government for a visa.
                Trans. :Am. p.q. NYTimes, 24.I.32.

320127   Pref. NEMETSKAYA REVOLYUTSIYA I STALINSKAYA BYUROKRATIYA (THE GERMAN
                REVOLUTION AND THE STALINIST BUREAUCRACY), 320000(1).
                Trans.: Fr. Lutte deC, (37), 15.III.32; V, (112), 1.III.32;
                        Ger. PermRev, (II.4), II.32;
                        Sp. Comunismo, (II.11-14), IV-VII.32.
                [See 320000(1) for other trans.]

[320130]   The Left Opposition and the Brandlerites. Letter to a comrade.
                Trans.: Am. Mil, 30.I.32;
                        Ger. PermRev, (II.2), I.32;
                        Yid. Unser Kampf, (I.3), 1.III.32.

320210   Letter to Shachtman.
                Trans.: Am. CLA, (2), VII.32)

320215(1)   Otvety na voprosy redaktsii New York Times. (Replies to questions
            from Ed. New York Times.) (BO, (28), VII.32)
            Trans.: Am. p.q. 690825: 9; Mil, 12.III.32; NYTimes, 5.III.32;
                    Fr. V, (114), 8.IV.32;
                    Ger. PermRev, (II.9), V.32;
                    Hol. Baan, (IV.3), 21.V.32.

320215(2)   Une interview à la presse américaine au sujet de sa privation de la
            nationalité soviétique.
            Trans.: Am. NYTimes, 27.II.32;
                    Bul. Osvob, (I.21), 19.VIII.32;
                    Fr. V, (113), 15.III.32.

[320226(1)] Letter to American publishers, Simon & Schuster.
            Trans.: Am. p.q. NYTimes, 27.II.32.

[320227]   Why Russia does not fight Japan.
            Trans.: Am. Liberty, 27.II.32.

320229   Interv'yu. (An interview.) (BO, (28), VII.32)
            Trans.: Ger. PermRev, (III.2), I.33.
            [With American United Press Association.]

320301   Otkrytoe pis'mo prezidiumu TsIK"a Soyuza SSR. (Open letter to the
            Presidium CC Soviet Union.) (BO, (27), III.32)
            Trans.: Am. Mil, 2,9.IV.32;
                    Bul. Osvob, (I.2), 8.IV.32;
                    Fr. Lutte deC, (38), 15.IV.32; V, (114), 8.IV.32; VoixCom,
                        (II.8), 17.IV.32;
                    Ger. [320000(23)]; NMahn, (IV.8), IV.32; PermRev, (II.6),
                        III.32;
                    Hol. NWeg, (VII.7), VII.32;
                    It. BOC, (8), 15.IV.32; OCI, (8), 1932; Prometeo, (V.75,76),
                        22.V, 19.VI.32;
                    Pol. Prol, (1), V.32;
                    Sp. *[350000(23)];
                    Yid. 320000(35); Unser Kampf, (I.5), 1.IV.32.
            [On Germany.]

320307(1)   To the Central Committee of the Left Opposition in Spain.
            Trans.: Am. IIM, 1932.

320307(2)   An die Konferenz der spanischen Links-Opposition.
            Trans.: Ger. KLO, (15), III.32.

320315   An die Redaktion des "Internationalen Bulletin".
Trans.: Ger. OCG, (15), III.32; PermRev, (II.7), IV.32.
[On Rakovsky.]

320329   K´m b´lgarskit"e drugari. (To Bulgarian friends.)
Trans.: Bul. Osvob, (I.3), 15.IV.32.

[320400]   L'opinion de Léon Trotsky sur la littérature "prolétarienne".
Trans.: Fr. 640911: 322-31; Humbles, (XVII.7-8), VII-VIII.32;
         Lutte deC, (38-39), 15.VI.32;
     Sp. 690000(8).II: 115-23;
     Swed. 690600(1): 288-96.

320412   L"evi sotsialdemokrati. (Left social-democracy.)
Trans.: Bul. p.q. Osvob, (I.4), 22.IV.32.

320413   [A letter.]
Trans.: Ger. Neumann: Pref.
[Protest against being associated with author's views.]

[320415]   I see war with Germany.
Trans.: Am. Forum, IV.32; Mil, 16.VII.32; Modern Thinker, (II), VI.32;
     Fr. 590600: 231-40; Lutte deC, (42), II.32;
     Ger. Aktion, (XXII.1-4), VIII.32; PermRev, (II.17,18), VIII.32;
     Jap. *520000(4); 620530: 261-70.

320423   Otvety na voprosy predstavitelya Chicago Daily News. (Answers to
questions from Chicago Daily News correspondent.) (BO, (28), VII.32)
Trans.: Am. Chicago Daily News, 18.V.32; Mil, 4.VI.32;
     Bul. Osvob, (I.19,21), 5,19.VIII.32;
     Fr. V, (116), 18.V.32;
     Ger. NFreie Presse, 15.V.32; PermRev, (II.10), V.32; Pester
         Lloyd, 1932;
     Heb. Bamifne, 1932.
[On disarmament; world war. T3427.]

[320500]   T.: "Fundament sotsializma." Nesereznyi chelovek o sereznom voprose.
("Fundamentals of socialism." A light-minded man on a weighty
problem.) (BO, (28), VII.32)
Trans.: Am. Mil, 30.VII.32;
     Eng. p.q. NOT GUILTY: 40-1;
     Bul. Osvob, (I.26), IX.32;
     Ger. PermRev, (II.22), IX.32; ++++

[320500] ++++   Trans.: Yid. Unser Kampf, (I.12), 15.VIII.32.
      [On Radek.]

320504   Otgovor na maiskit"e pozdravi. (Reply to May Day greetings.)
      Trans.: Bul. Osvob, (I.7), 13.V.32.

[320508]   Is Stalin weakening or the Soviets?
      Trans.: Am. p.q. NYTimes, 8.V.32;
           Eng. Political Quarterly, VII-IX.32; p.q. NOT GUILTY: 264;
           Nor. SOVIETUNIONEN: 95-100.
      |T3428.]

320509   Greetings to Unser Kampf.
      Trans.: Am. 700700: 15-7; Mil, 11.VI.32;
         Fr. OCG, (17), VI.32;
         Ger. KLO, (17), VI.32;
         Yid. Unser Kampf, (I.9), 1.VI.32.

320512   Interview with Montag Morgen.
      Trans.: Am. Mil, 18.VI.32;
         Bul. Osvob, (I.16), 15.VII.32;
         Fr. 590600: 243-4; V, (117), 1.VI.32; VoixCom, (II.12), 12.VI.32;
         Ger. Montag Morgen, 1932; PermRev, (II.11), VI.32; Volks,
             (V.17), 27.V.32;
         Jap. *520000(4); 620530: 271-2.
      [On fascism in Germany.]

320513   Pref. Vol.II, ISTORIYA RUSSKOI REVOLYUTSII (THE HISTORY OF THE
      RUSSIAN REVOLUTION), 310000(1).
      Trans.: 310000(1).

320519(1)   Letter to National Committee, Communist League of America.
      Trans.: Am. [620000(15)]; 690825: 6-9; Class Struggle(NY), (II.7),
           VIII.32; CLA, (2), VII.32; EB, V.48; Mil, 11.VI.32;
         Fr. Lutte deC, (43), X.32;
         Yid. Unser Kampf, (I.10), 1.VII.32.
      [On Labor Party question in USA. T3429.]

320519(2)   Letter to National Committee, Communist League of America.
      Trans.: Am. p.q. CLA, (2), VII.32.

320520(1)   Alternative for 320512.

320520(2) Gourov: Au Secrétariat international administratif.

    <u>Trans</u>.: Fr. <u>DocSI</u>.

    [On ILOpp. LocPer.]

320522(1) 2nd letter to Weisbord.

    <u>Trans</u>.: Am. <u>Class Struggle</u>(NY), (II.7), VIII.32;

       Fr. <u>OCG</u>, (17), VI.32.

    [PS 320524(1). On ILOpp in USA.]

320522(2) Alternative for 320512.

320524(1) PS 2nd letter to Weisbord, 320522(1).

    <u>Trans</u>.: Am. <u>Class Struggle</u>(NY), (II.7), VIII.32; <u>Mil</u>, 10.IX.32;

       Fr. <u>OCG</u>, (17), VI.32.

320524(2) Do edin b´lgarski rabotnik. (To a Bulgarian worker.)

    <u>Trans</u>.: Bul. <u>Osvob</u>, (I.12), 17.VI.32.

320600(1) THE HISTORY OF THE RUSSIAN REVOLUTION.

    [Trans. Eng. See 310000(1) for all repr., trans., notes. 3 vols.]

320600(2) † PROBLEMS OF THE CHINESE REVOLUTION.

    <u>Trans</u>.: Am. 320600(2); 620000(2); 660000(4); 670000(16);

       Ch. 470427;

       Jap. *460000(12); *610325; 640330(3).

    [Ch. ed. 470427 not fully identical. See entries for other trans.]

320613(1) Blizhe k proletariyam "tsvetnykh" ras! (Closer to the proletarians

    of the "coloured" races!) (<u>BO</u>, (28), VII.32)

    <u>Trans</u>.: Am. p.q. 670600: 60-1; p.q. 690400: 60-1; p.q. 700800: 60-1;

       <u>FI</u>, VIII.45; <u>Mil</u>, 2.VII.32;

      Bul. <u>Osvob</u>, (I.17), 22.VII.32;

      Eng. <u>FI</u>(P), Autumn 1958;

      Fr. <u>QI</u>, (22-24), IX-XI.45; (6), V.59; <u>V</u>, (122), 1.VIII.32;

      Ger. <u>PermRev</u>, (II.13), VII.32;

      Jap. p.q. 681010: 111-3;

      Sp. 611025: 54-6; 690700(2): 223.

    [T3432.]

320613(2)   Pis´mo o kongresse protiv voiny. (Letter on the Anti-War Congress.)
(BO, (28), VII.32)

Trans.: Am. Mil, 16.VII.32;
        Fr. 590600: 245-51; Lutte deC, (38-39), 15.VI.32;
        Ger. Aktion, (XXII.1-4), VII.32; NMahn, (IV.14), VII.32;
            PermRev, (II.13), VI.32;
        Jap. *520000(4); 620530: 273-8;
        Yid. Unser Kampf, (I.11), 1.VIII.32.
[T3433.]

320613(3)   Letter to Spanish Youth.

Trans.: Am. Young Spartacus, III.33;
        Bul. Osvob, (I.13), 24.VI.32;
        Fr. 330400(1); OCG, (2-3), IV.33; V, (143), 23.II.33.
[T3434.]

320614   On the German October.
Trans.: Am. p.q. NI, II.38.
[Letter to Neurath.]

320615   Alternative for 320616.

320616   Stalinskaya byurokratiya v tiskakh, levaya oppozitsiya na podeme.
(The Stalin bureaucracy in straits; the Left Opposition on the upsurge.)
(BO, (28), VII.32)

Trans.: Am. Mil, 9.VII.32;
        Fr. V, (120), 1.VII.32; VoixCom, (II.14), 10.VII.32;
        Ger. NMahn, (IV.14), VII.32; PermRev, (II.13), VII.32;
        Yid. Unser Kampf, (I.11), 1.VIII.32.

320625   Pis´mo tsyurikhskim rabochim. (Letter to Zurich workers.) (BO, (28),
VII.32)

Trans.: Am. Mil, 20.VIII.32;
        Bul. Osvob, (I.14), 1.VII.32;
        Fr. V, (121), 15.VII.32; VoixCom, (II.15), 24.VII.32;
        Ger. PermRev, (II.14), VII.32;
        Yid. Unser Kampf, (I.12), 15.VIII.32.
[Against slanders.]

320628   Ruki proch ot Rozy Lyuksemburg! (Hands off Rosa Luxemburg!)
(BO, (28), VII.32)   ++++

320628   ++++   Trans.: Am. Mil, 6,13.VIII.32;

                  Bul. Osvob, (I.20–2), 12–26.VIII.32;

                  Fr. 551115: 321–3; Lutte deC, (40–41), VII–VIII.32;

                  Ger. PermRev, (II.15), 23.VII.32;

                  Hol. NWeg, (VII.8), VIII.32; RodeOkt, (3), XII.46;

                  It. 620000(20): 168–79; *680900(3); 681100: 191–202;

                  Sp. Comunismo, (II.16), IX.32.

[320700(1)]   Al´fa: O Dem´yane Bednom. (Demyan Biedny.) (BO, (28), VII.32)

[320700(2)]   Ot redaktsii i izdatel´stva. (From the Editorial Board and Publisher.)
                  (BO, (28), VII.32)
                  [T3431.]

320725   —: Zayavlenie bol´shevikov-lenintsev (mezhdunarodnoi levoi oppozitsii
                  Kommunisticheskogo Internatsionala) kongressu protiv voiny v
                  Amsterdame. (Declaration of the Bolshevik-Leninists (International
                  Left Opposition of the Communist International) to the Anti-War Congress
                  in Amsterdam.) (BO, (29–30), IX.32)
                  Trans.: Am. Mil, 27.VIII.32;
                        Ger. Arbeiter Stimme, (108), VIII.32;
                        Sp. Comunismo, (II.17), X.32.
                  [T3436.]

320800   Das deutsche Rätsel.
                  Trans.: Ger. Weltbühne, (45), 8.XI.32.

320802   Bonapartizm i fashizm. (Bonapartism and fascism.) (BO, (29–30), IX.32)
                  Trans.: Am. Mil, 20.VII.32;
                      Bul. Osvob, (I.29), 14.X.32;
                      Eng. IntSoc, (38–39), VIII–IX.69;
                      Fr. V, (123), 15.VIII.32; VoixCom, (II.18), 14.VIII.32;
                      Hol. NWeg, (VII.9), IX.32;
                      It. BOC, (11), 15.IX.32; OCI, (11), 1932;
                      Sp. Comunismo, (II.15), VIII.32;
                      Yid. Unser Kampf, (I.13), 1.IX.32.
                  [See 330400(2) for other trans.]

320804(1)   Pilsudchina, fashizm i kharakter nashei epokhi. (Pilsudski-ism,
                  fascism, and the character of our epoch.) (BO, (29–30), IX.32)
                  [T2993, 3024, 3437.]

320804(2) **Burzhuaziya, melkaya burzhuaziya i proletariat.** (The bourgeoisie, the
petty-bourgeoisie, and the proletariat.) (<u>BO</u>, (29-30), IX.32)
Trans.: 330400(2);
      Am. p.q. 440800(2); p.q. 690400(2): 14-7; <u>Mil</u>, 3.IX.32;
      Bul. <u>Osvob</u>, (I.27), 30.IX.32;
      Eng. p.q. 620900; <u>IntSoc</u>, (38-39), VIII-IX.69;
      Fr. p.q. 680000(4): 148-9; <u>VoixCom</u>, (II.23), 18.IX.32;
      Ger. <u>PermRev</u>, (II.19), VIII.32;
      Hol. <u>NWeg</u>, (VII.9), IX.32;
      Sp. <u>Comunismo</u>, (II.16), IX.32;
      Yid. <u>Unser Kampf</u>, (I.14), 15.IX.32.

320806 **Usilim nastuplenie!** (Intensify the offensive!) (<u>BO</u>, (29-30), IX.32)
Trans.: Am. <u>Mil</u>, 27.VIII.32;
      Bul. <u>Osvob</u>, (I.29), 14.X.32;
      Fr. 590600: 253-7; 670306: 390-3; <u>V</u>, (123), 15.VIII.32;
      Ger. <u>PermRev</u>, (II.19), VIII.32;
      Jap. *520000(4); 620530: 279-82;
      Yid. <u>Unser Kampf</u>, (I.13), 1.IX.32.
[T3438.]

320809 **Soyuz sotsial-demokratii s fashizmom ili bor´ba mezhdu nimi?** (Alliance
or struggle between social democracy and fascism?) (<u>BO</u>, (29-30), IX.32)
Trans.: 330400(2);
      Am. <u>Mil</u>, 10.IX.32;
      Bul. <u>Osvob</u>, (I.23,24), 2,9.IX.32;
      Eng. <u>IntSoc</u>, (38-39), VIII-IX.69;
      Fr. <u>V</u>, (124), 5.IX.32; <u>VoixCom</u>, (II.24), 25.IX.32;
      Ger. <u>PermRev</u>, (II.20), VIII.32;
      Hol. <u>NWeg</u>, (VII.10), X.32;
      Sp. <u>Comunismo</u>, (II.17), X.32.

320810 § LA RÉVOLUTION PERMANENTE.
[Trans. Fr. See 281000(1) for all repr., trans., notes.]

[320815] Earlier version of 320917.

320817   Thaelmann's twenty-one mistakes.
            Trans.: 330400(2);
                        Am. Mil, 24.IX.32;
                        Bul. Osvob, (I.25), 16.IX.32;
                        Fr. V, (125), 22.IX.32; VoixCom, (II.25,26), 2,9.X.32;
                        Ger. p.q. PermRev, (II.20), VIII.32;
                        Hol. NWeg, (VII.10), X.32.

320818(1)   Perspectives of the upturn.
            Trans.: Am. Mil, 12.VIII.32; CLA, (4), 1932.
            [PS in CLA, (4). T3441.]

320818(2)   The checking of the Stalin-Thaelmann policy against their own experience.
            Trans.: 330400(2);
                        Am. Mil, 17.IX.32;
                        Bul. Osvob, (I.26), 23.IX.32;
                        Fr. V, (126), 29.IX.32; VoixCom, (II.28), 23.X.32;
                        Ger. PermRev, (II.21), IX.32;
                        Hol. NWeg, (VII.10), X.32.

320823   Alternative for 321030(1).

320825   Gespräch mit Trotzki.
            Trans.: Ger. Linke Front, (II.1-2), 1.XII.32.
            [Interview with SAP member.]

320831   L.T.: Privet pol'skoi levoi oppozitsii! (Greetings to the Polish Left
            Opposition!) (BO, (29-30), IX.32)
            Trans.: Bul. Osvob, (I.30), 21.X.32;
                        Yid. Unser Kampf, (I.15), 15.X.32.
            [T3444.]

320900(1)   WHAT NEXT?
            [Trans. Am. See 320000(1) for all trans.]

[320900(2)] —: Iz arkhiva. (From the archives.) (BO, (29-30), IX.32)

            [T3450.]

320902   Chto govoryat po povodu edinogo fronta v Prage? (What do they say
about the United Front in Prague?) (BO, (32), XII.32)
Trans.: 330400(2);
         Am. Mil, 22,29.X.32;
         Hol. NWeg, (VII.11), XI.32.

320910   The road to socialism.
Trans.: 330400(2);
         Am. Mil, 15.X.32;
         Bul. Osvob, (I.31), 28.X.32;
         Eng. IntSoc, (38-39), VIII-IX.69;
         Hol. NWeg, (VII.12), XII.32.

320912   The only road.
Trans.: 330400(2);
         Am. Mil, 12.XI.32;
         Eng. IntSoc, (38-39), VIII-IX.69;
         Hol. NWeg, (VII.12), XII.32.

320913   Pref. THE ONLY ROAD, 330400(2).
Trans.: 330400(2);
         Eng. IntSoc, (38-39), VIII-IX.69;
         Fr. V, (127), 6.X.32.

320914   Afterword, THE ONLY ROAD, 330400(2).
Trans.: 330400(2);
         Eng. IntSoc, (38-39), VIII-IX.69;
         Hol. NWeg, (VII.12), XII.32.

320917   Is Soviet Russia fit to recognize?
Trans.: Am. p.q. Class Struggle(NY), (IV.6-7), VI-VII.34; Liberty,
         14.I.33;
         Bul. ¢ Osvob, (I.35,36), 6,13.I.33;
         Ger. PermRev, (II.33), XII.32;
         Ukr. RobVis, (II.18), 15.IX.34.
[T3439.]

320920   Ispanskie kornilovtsy i ispanskie stalintsy. (Spanish kornilovists and
Spanish stalinists.) (BO, (31), XI.32)
Trans.: Fr. 330400(1); 590600: 515-22; OCG, (2-3), IV.33; V, (131),
         10.XI.32;   ++++

320920   ++++   Trans.: Ger. PermRev, (II.28), XI.32;
                        Gr. 630000(11): 47-55;
                        Jap. *630430; 650430: 275-81;
                        Sp. 680000(9): 169; Comunismo, (II.19), XII.32.
                  [T3452.]

320922(1)   Krest'yanskaya voina v Kitae i proletariat. (Peasant war in China and
                  the proletariat.) (BO, (32), XII.32)
                  Trans.: Am. 570000(2); 690000(4): 15-8; FI, I-II.50; Mil, 15.X.32;
                        Ch. 470427: 301-5;
                        Fr. 551115: 311-8; Lutte deC, (43), X.32;
                        Jap. *610325; 640330(3): 298-308.
                  [PS 320926. T3453.]

320922(2)   Do v Osvobozhdenie. (To Osvobozhdenie.)
                  Trans.: Bul. Osvob, (I.27), 30.IX.32.

320926   PS to 320922(1). (BO, (32), XII.32)
                  Trans.: Am. 570000(2); 690000(4): 18; FI, I-II.50; Mil, 22.X.32;
                        Ch. 470427: 305-6;
                        Fr. 551115: 318-20; Lutte deC, (43), X.32;
                        Jap. *610325; 640330(3): 308-11.
                  [T3453.]

[321000]   Letter to Symposium.
                  Trans.: Am. Symposium, (III.4), X.32.
                  [Reply to criticisms of THE HISTORY OF THE RUSSIAN REVOLUTION.]

321003   Strategiya deistviya, a ne spekulyatsii. (A strategy of action and not
                  of speculation.) (BO, (32), XII.32)
                  Trans.: Am. Class Struggle(NY), (III.6), VI.33;
                        Ch. 470427: 307-12;
                        Fr. Lutte deC, (46-47), I-II.33;
                        Ger. PermRev, (II.29), XI.32;
                        Hol. NWeg, (VIII.5), VIII.33.
                  [On China. T3456.]

321006   Predislovie k pol´skomu izdaniyu DETSKOI BOLEZNI LEVIZNY V
KOMMUNIZME. (Pref. ⌊Lenin,⌋ LEFT-WING COMMUNISM: AN INFANTILE
DISEASE.) (BO, (32), XII.32)

                 Trans.: Bul. Osvob, (I.31), 28.X.32;
                         Eng. Communist(B), (3,5), I,V.33;
                         Fr. 590600: 321-30; V, (132), 17.XI.32;
                         Ger. PermRev, (II.26), 29.XI.32;
                         Jap. *520000(4); 620530: 359-67;
                         Pol. *Lenin(W.I.).

321007   Redaktsii Oktyabr´skikh Pisem. (To the Ed. Board of Oktyabr´skie Pis´ma.)
(BO, (32), XII.32)

         ⌊On the SAP. T3457.⌋

321013(1)   --: 15 let! (15 years!) (BO, (31), XI.32)

                 Trans.: Am. Mil, 12.XI.32;
                         Bul. Osvob, (I.31), 28.X.32;
                         Fr. V, (130), 3.XI.32; VoixCom, (II.30), 6.XI.32;
                         Ger. PermRev, (II.26), XI.32;
                         Port. Luta de Classe, (III.9), I.33;
                         Sp. Comunismo, (II.18), XI.32;
                         Yid. Unser Kampf, (I.16), 15.XI.32.

         ⌊Anniversary of October Revolution.⌋

321013(2)   L.T.: Sentyabr´skii plenum IKKI. (Beglye primechaniya na polyakh.)
(The ECCI September Plenum: Hasty marginal notes.) (BO, (31), XI.32)

                 Trans.: Am. Mil, 5.XI.32;
                         Bul. Osvob, (I.31), 28.X.32;
                         Eng. Communist(B), (5), V.33;
                         Fr. V, (130), 3.XI.32; VoixCom, (II.29), 30.X.32;
                         Ger. PermRev, (II.24), X.32;
                         Hol. Baan, (IV.29), 19.XI.32;
                         Sp. Comunismo, (II.18), XI.32;
                         Yid. Unser Kampf, (I.16), 15.XI.32.

321013(3)   Letter to Weisbord.

         Trans.: Am. Mil, 31.XII.32.

         ⌊On ILOpp in USA. See further 321022(3).⌋

321017   ⌊Letter to Sedov.⌋

         Trans.: Eng. p.q. Deutscher, PO: 174.

321019   L.T.: Stalintsy prinimayut mery. (The stalinists take measures.)
          (BO, (31), XI.32)
          Trans.: Am. 330200(1); Mil, 12-26.XI.32;
                  Fr. 551115: 199-210; Lutte deC, (45), XII.32;
                  Ger. 321100(2);
                  Heb. Haarets, (4043,4044), 1933;
                  Jap. 631130: 73-86.
          [The expulsion of Zinoviev and Kamenev.]

321020(1) Letter to CLA.
          Trans.: Am. CLA, (4), 1932.

[321020(2)] G.G.: Mil k kachestve "boevogo" stalintsa. (Mil as a "militant"
          stalinist.) (BO, (31), XI.32)
          Trans.: Am. Mil, 12.XI.32;
                  Fr. V, (129), 20.X.32; VoixCom, (II.29), 30.X.32;
                  Ger. PermRev, (II.24), X.32.
          [See 321013(4). On German section ILOpp.]

321022(1) Sovetskoe khozyaistvo v opasnosti! (Soviet economy in danger!)
          (BO, (31), XI.32)
          Trans.: Am. 330200(1); Mil, 12,19.XI, 3,17,31.XII.32, 7.I.33;
                  Bul. *[330000(4)];
                  Cz. 330000(21);
                  Fr. 551115: 109-37; Lutte deC, (44), XI.32; VoixCom, (II.36:
                      Suppl.), 18.XII.32;
                  Ger. 321100(2);
                  Hol. Baan, (IV.31-38-*39), 3.XII.32-21,*28.I.33;
                  Hung. DEMOKRATIKUS;
                  It. 620000(20): 44-6,46-73; *680900(3); 681100: 60-2,62-90;
                  Jap. 700130: 111-50;
                  Pol. *330000(41);
                  Sp. *330000(9); 330000(36);
                  Yid. 330100(1).
          [Pref. to foreign eds. 321022(2) lacking in Yid. 330100(1).]

321022(2) Pref. foreign eds. 321022(1). (BO, (32), XII.32)
          Trans.: 321022(1).

321022(3) Letter to National Committee, Communist League of America.
          Trans.: Am. CLA, (4), 1932; Mil, 31.XII.32.
          [Suspension of negotiations with Weisbord group. On ILOpp in USA.
          See 321013(3).]

321024(1)   [Letter to Sedov.]
              Trans.: Eng. p.q. Deutscher, PO: 174.

321024(2)   [A letter.]
              Trans.: Ger. Linke Front, (II.1-2), 1.XII.32.
              [On SAP.]

321030(1)   Nemetskii bonapartizma. (German bonapartism.) (BO, (32), XII.32)
              Trans.: Am. Mil, 24.XII.32;
                      Fr. 590600: 331-8; V, (131), 10.XI.32;
                      Ger. PermRev, (II.27), XI.32;
                      Jap. *520000(4); 620530: 368-75.
              [T3443.]

321030(2)   [Letter to Sedov.]
              Trans.: Eng. p.q. Deutscher, PO: 174.

321100(1)   Letter to Wicks.
              Trans.: Eng. THE CASE: 274-5.
              [Used at Dewey Commission investigation to illustrate "conspiratorial"
              character of T's activities.]

321100(2)   SOWJETWIRTSCHAFT IN GEFAHR!
              [Trans. Ger. See 321022(1) for all trans. Includes 321019.]

321101   Greetings to weekly Militant.
              Trans.: Am. Mil, 26.XI.32.

321104   Perspektivy amerikanskogo marksizma. (Perspectives of American marxism.)
              (BO, (32), XII.32)
              Trans.: Am. FI, Fall 1954; Mil, 31.XII.32; Modern Monthly, III.33;
                      Fr. Lutte deC, (46-47), I-II.33;
                      Ger. PermRev, (III.1), I.33;
                      Hol. NWeg, (VIII.4), IV.33.
              [Open letter to V.P.Calverton. T3463.]

321105   Frankfurtskim druz´yam! (To Frankfurt friends!) (BO, (32), XII.32)

321113   Letter to CLA.
              Trans.: Am. CLA, (4), 1932.

321114   See 330400(1).
              [On Spanish revolution.]

321122   Earlier version of 321200(3).
              [T3466.]

321123(1)   Newsreel, radio message to USA.

        Trans.: Am. Mil, 3.XII.32;

              Eng. p.q. THE CASE: 170;

              Fr. VoixCom, (II.34), 4.XII.32.

       [Also recorded on disc. Summary of 321127. T3462.]

321123(2)   Press statement; on visit to Copenhagen.

        Trans.: Am. NYTimes, 12.XII.32;

              Eng. p.q. THE CASE: 171.

[321123(3)]   Interview.

        Trans.: Den. Politiken(D), 24.XI.32.

[321123(4)]   Interview.

        Trans.: Den. SocDemok, 24.XI.32.

321127   IN DEFENSE OF THE RUSSIAN REVOLUTION.

        Trans.: Am. 330200(3); p.q. 640800: 363-5; p.q. FI, VII-VIII.47; Mil,
           21.I.33;

           Bul. *[330000(6)]; p.q. Osvob, (I.36), 13.I.33;

           Cz. *[340000(16)];

           Den. p.q. [350000(15)]; p.q. Politiken(D), 28.XI.32; p.q.
             SocDemok, 28.XI.32;

           Eng. 330000(19); 490800; 500000(2); 620500; WIN, XI.45; p.q.
             Workers Fight(M/r), (1), X.67;

           Fr. *320000(14); 670000(2); 690900(1): 37-56; QI, (XV.7-10),
             X-XI.57; V, (133), 8.XII.32; VoixCom, (III.1), 1.I.33;

           Ger. PermRev, (II.34), XII.32;

           Gr. 660000(7);

           It. p.q. BOC, (12), 15.XII.32;

           Jap. p.q. 681125: 378-80;

           Mal. 621031;

           Pol. *330000(43);

           Sp. *330000(4); 610622; p.q. 670000(5): 366-8; 671100(1): 3-39;
             Comunismo, (III.20), I.33; RepAm, (XXVII.12,16), 23.IX,
             28.X.33;

           Swed. p.q. 691100(2): 328-30;

           Yid. Unser Kampf, (II.2), II.33.

       |Copenhagen speech. T3469-72.|

[321200(1)]   Al´fa: Stalin snova svidetel´stvuet protiv Stalina. (Stalin again
testifies against Stalin.) (BO, (32), XII.32)
[cf. 370303(2).]

[321200(2)]   —: "Obeimi rukami." ("With both hands.") (BO, (32), XII.32)
Trans.: Am. Mil, 7.I.33;
        Bul. Osvob, (I.37,39), 20.I, 23.III.33;
        Fr. V, (138), 19.I.33;
        Ger. PermRev, (II.31), XII.32;
        Yid. Unser Kampf, (II.1), 15.I.33.
[Stalin and relations with USA. See further 330114. Authorship
established from V, (149), 2.II.33.]

321200(3)   Zayavlenie bol´shevikov-lenintsev po povodu poezdki t. Trotskogo.
(Statement by the Bolshevik-Leninists on cde. Trotsky's journey.)
(BO, (32), XII.32)
Trans.: Bul. Osvob, (I.37,38), 20,27.I.33;
        Fr. V, (133), 8.XII.33;
        Ger. PermRev, (II.33), XII.32;
        It. Prometeo, (V.83), 1.I.33;
        Sp. Comunismo, (III.20), I.33;
        Yid. Unser Kampf, (II.1), 15.I.33.
[Some trans. follow earlier version 321122. T3475.]

321200(4)   Iz arkhiva. (From the archives.) (BO, (32), XII.32)
Trans.: Am. ISR, V.70;
        Fr. V, (136), 5.I.33.

*321200(5)   *ÜBER LENIN.
[Trans. Ger. See 240000(24) for all repr., trans., notes.]

[321200(6)]   —: International´naya levaya oppozitsiya, ee zadachi i metody.
(The International Left Opposition: its tasks and methods.) (BO, (33),
III.33)
Trans.: Am. p.q. FI, VIII.44; Mil, 6.III.33;
        Fr. OCG, II.33; V, (142), 16.II.33;
        Sp. Comunismo, (III.22,23), III,IV.33.
[Rédigé par LT. -- PN. T3505.]

321203(1)   [Letter to Sedov.]
Trans.: Eng. p.q. NOT GUILTY: 84.

321203(2)   Otvety na voprosy zhurnalistov. (Answers to questions from
journalists.) (BO, (32), XII.32)
[On trip to Copenhagen.]

321205   Otkrytoe pis'mo g-nu Vanderveld. (An open letter to Mr. Vandervelde.)
                (BO, (32), XII.32)
                Trans.: Am. Class Struggle(NY), (III.1), I.33; Mil, 7.I.33;
                        Fr. 610000(2); V, (134), 15.XII.32; VoixCom, (II.36), 18.XII.32;
                        Ger. PermRev, (III.1), I.33;
                        Hung. Miscarea Sociala, (IV.1), I.33;
                        Pol. *330000(43);
                        Sp. Comunismo, (III.20), I.33; RepAm, (XXVII.12), 23.IX.33;
                        Yid. Unser Kampf, (II.1), 15.I.33.
                [T3476.]

321208(1)   [Declaration to the press.]
                [c. Deutscher, PO: 193. T3479.]

[321208(2)]   Telegram to Herriot, Chautemps, De Monzie. Copies to Blum and Thorez.
                Trans.: Am. Mil, 14.I.33;
                        Fr. V, (133), 8.XII.32.

321209   Danske studenter intervjuer Leo Trotski.
                Trans.: Den. 4I, (I.2), III.37)

321211   Press statement; on journey to Copenhagen.
                Trans.: Am. NYTimes, 12.XII.32.
                [T3480.]

321216   Gourov: On the situation of the Left Opposition.
                Trans.: Am. CLA, (9), 1933;
                        Fr. OCG, (19), XII.32.
                [Letter to sections ILOpp. T3481.]

321219   Do Osvobozhdenie. (To Osvobozhdenie.)
                Trans.: Bul. Osvob, (I.35), 6.I.33.

321220(1)   Sur l'opposition communiste belge et son journal.
                Trans.: Fr. VoixCom, (III.1), 1.I.33.
                [T3484.]

321220(2)   Alternative for 321228(2).

321221   See 321231.

321228(1)   To the leadership of the German Left Opposition.

Trans.: Am. CLA, (8), 28.I.33.

[See further 321228(2), 330104(2).]

321228(2)   On those who have forgotten the ABC.

Trans.: Am. CLA, (8), 28.I.33; Class Struggle(NY), (III.3-4), III-IV.33;

Bul. Osvob, (I.38), 27.I.33;

Ger. PermRev, (III.1), I.33.

[See also 321228(1), 330104(2). T3486.]

321231   The testament of Lenin.

Trans.: Am. 350000(10); 461100(1); 700000(1); NI, VII,VIII.34;

Eng. 530000(3); 541100(1);

Fr. QI, VII.56;

Hol. Int, (I.2-5), 1.IV-1.X.57;

Jap. *611005; 640330(2): 213-54;

Sp. *400000(13); 650000(1);

Ukr. 340000(26); RobVis, (II.19-22), 1.X-18.XI.34.

[T3487.]

330000(1) SOTSIALIZM V OTD´ELNA STRANA. (SOCIALISM IN ONE COUNTRY.)
[Trans. Bul. See 310000(1), Suppl. III to Vol. II [/III in trans.]
for all trans.]

[330000(2)] SIGNAL TREVOGI. (ALARM SIGNAL.)
[See 330303(2) for all repr., trans.]

*[330000(3)] *REDT NA AVSTRIYA. (IT IS NOW AUSTRIA'S TURN.)
[Trans. Bul. See 330323(1) for all trans.]

*[330000(4)] *SVETSKOTO STOPANSTVO V OPASNOSTA. (SOVIET ECONOMY IN DANGER.)
[Trans. Bul. See 321022(1) for all trans.]

*[330000(5)] *TRAGEDIYATA NA GERMANSKAYA PROLETARIAT. (THE TRAGEDY OF THE GERMAN
PROLETARIAT.)
[Trans. Bul. See 330314 for all trans.]

*[330000(6)] *SHCHO E OKTOMBRIISKATA REVOLYUTSIYA. (WHAT THE OCTOBER REVOLUTION IS.)
[Trans. Bul. See 321127 for all trans.]

330000(7) § DECLARAȚILE OPOZIȚIEI COMUNISTE INTERNACIONALE DE STINGA (BOLȘEVICI-
LENINIȘTI).
[Trans. Rum. See 330000(8) for all trans.]

330000(8) § DÉCLARATIONS POUR LE CONGRÈS ANTIFASCISTE EUROPÉEN DE PARIS.
Trans.: Fr;
Rum. 330000(7).

*330000(9) *LA ECONOMIÁ SOVIÉTICA EN PELIGRO.
[Trans. Sp. See 321022(1) for all repr., trans.]

330000(10) L´ÉCONOMIE SOVIÉTIQUE EN DANGER: SIGNAL D'ALARME.
[Trans. Fr. See 330303(2) for all repr., trans.]

330000(11) O QUE É A REVOLUCAO DE OUTUBRO.
[Trans. Port. See 321127, 321205 for all repr., trans., notes.]

330000(13) LA LUTTE CONTRE LE FASCISME EN ALLEMAGNE.
[Trans. Fr. See 311208 for all repr., trans.]

*330000(14) *LA MIA VITA.
[Trans. It. See 300000(1) for all repr., trans., notes.]

330000(15)   § ÖSTERREICH AN DER REIHE.

[Trans. Ger. Extracts from 1929-33; Anhang 330319.]

330000(17)   QU'EST-CE QUE LE NATIONAL-SOCIALISME?

[Trans. Fr. See 330610 for all repr., trans.]

*330000(18)   *REVOLUÇÃO E CONTRA-REVOLUÇÃO NA ALEMANTIA.

[Trans. Port. See 330400(2) for all trans.]

330000(19)   THE RUSSIAN REVOLUTION.

[Trans. Eng. See 321127 for all repr., trans.]

330000(21)   SOVĚTSKÉ HOSPODÁŘSTVI V NEBEZPEČI.

[Trans. Cz. See 321022(1), 321022(2) for all trans.]

330000(25)   DIE 4. INTERNATIONALE UND DIE USSR.

[Trans. Ger. See 331001 for all repr., trans.]

330000(26)   WHAT HITLER WANTS.

[Trans. Am. See 330602 for all repr., trans.]

[330000(27)]   —: DÉCLARATION DES QUATRE.

[Trans. Fr. See 330827 for all repr., trans., notes.]

[330000(28)]   DIALOGO CON UN OBRERO SOCIALISTA.

[Trans. Sp. See 330223 for all trans.]

[330000(31)]   4de INTERNATIONALE EN DE USSR.

[Trans. Hol. See 330826, 331001 for all repr., trans.]

[330000(32)]   4de INTERNATIONALE EN DE USSR.

[Trans. Hol. See 330826, 331001 for all repr., trans.]

*[330000(33)]   *CO JE PERMANENTNI REVOLUCE?

[Trans. Cz. See 291130(2) for all trans., notes.]

*[330000(34)]   *SEÑAL DE ALARMA.

[Trans. Sp. See 330303(2) for all trans.]

*330000(35)   *ENTRETIEN AVEC UN OUVRIER SOCIAL-DÉMOCRATE.

[Trans. Fr. See 330223 for all repr., trans.]

330000(36)   EL FRACASO DEL PLAN QUINQUENAL.

[Trans. Sp. See 310715(1), 321022(1), 321022(2) for all repr., trans.]

*330000(37)   *BESEDA SE SOCIÁL DEMOKRATICKÝM DĚLNIKEM.
               [Trans. Cz. See 330223 for all trans.]

*330000(38)   *PŘED ŘEŠENÍM.
               [Trans. Cz. See 330105 for all trans.]

[330000(39)]   A LETTER TO A SOCIAL-DEMOCRATIC WORKER. A thesis on the United Front.
               [Trans. Eng. See 330223 for all trans.]

*330000(41)   i Stalin: *GOSPODARKA SOWIECKA U POROGU 2-giej PIATILETKI.
               [Trans. Pol. See 321022(1) for all trans.]

*330000(42)   *NIEMCY NA PRZELOMIE.
               [Trans. Pol. See 330105 for all trans.]

*330000(43)   *OSTATNIE PRZEMÓWIENIE W KOPENHADZE.
               [Trans. Pol. See 321127 for all trans.]

*330000(44)   *DER PROBLEM FUN AJNHAJTLECHEN FRONT.
               [Trans. Yid. p.q. 320000(1).]

330100(1)   SOVJETISHE VIRKSHAFT IN GEFAR.
               [Trans. Yid. See 321022(1) for all trans.]

[330100(2)]   Über den Krieg in China.
               Trans.: Ger. PermRev, (III.2), I.33.
               [An interview.]

330100(3)   L'HISTOIRE DE LA RÉVOLUTION RUSSE.
               [Trans. Fr. See 310000(1) for all repr., trans., notes. 4 vol.]

[330101]   Lettera.
               Trans.: It. Prometeo, (VI.83), 1.I.33.
               [Break with Bordigists.]

330103   See 330104(1).

330104(1)   M.Istman i marksizm. (M.Eastman and marxism.) (BO, (33), III.33)
               Trans.: Am. Mil, 28.I.33;
                       Eng. Red Flag, (7), I.34;
                       Fr. Lutte deC, (46-47), I-II.33.

330104(2)   G.Gourov: To the International Secretariat and to all sections of the
              International Left Opposition.
              Trans.: Am. CLA, (8), 28.I.33.
              [See also 321228(1), 321228(2), 330128(2). ILOpp in Germany.]

330105   See 330205.

330111(1)   Danger of Thermidor.
              Trans.: Am. Mil, 4.II.33;
                      Eng. p.q. THE CASE: 256;
                      Fr. V, (139), 26.I.33; VoixCom, (III.5), 29.I.33;
                      Ger. PermRev, (III.3), I.33;
                      Hol. Baan, (IV.40-42), 4-18.II.33;
                      It. BOC, (13), 1.II.33;
                      Sp. Comunismo, (III.21), II.33.
              [On Soviet Union. T3498.]

330111(2)   Po povodu smerti Z.L.Volkovoi. (On the death of Z.L.Volkov.)
              (BO, (33), III.33)
              Trans.: Am. Mil, 11.II.33;
                      Fr. p.q. 340000(4): 250-2; p.q. 470615: 212-3; V, (138), 19.I.33;
                          VoixCom, (III.5), 29.I.33;
                      Ger. PermRev, (III.3), I.33;
                      Hol. Baan, (IV.38), 21.I.33;
                      Ice. p.q. 360000(20);
                      Nor. p.q. 350000(9): 238-40;
                      Sp. Comunismo, (III.21), II.33.
              [Letter to CC CPSU on death of his daughter Zinaida. T3500.]

330114   L.T.: Stalinskoe oproverzhenie. (Stalin's denial.) (BO, (33), III.33)
              Trans.: Am. Mil, 11.II.33;
                      Fr. V, (139), 26.I.33;
                      Ger. PermRev, (III.3), I.33.
              [See also [321200(2)]. T3501.]

330126   Soviet economy in danger.
              Trans.: Am. Mil, 3.III.33;
                      Fr. V, (143), 23.II.33;
                      Ger. PermRev, (III.7), II.33.
              [Letter to Socialistische Arbeiterztg. T3502.]

330128(1)   Predislovie k grecheskomu izdaniyu "Novyi kurs". (Pref. Greek edition of THE NEW COURSE.) (BO, (33), III.33)
[See 240000(22).]

330128(2)   Serious lessons from an inconsequential thing.
Trans.: Am. Class Struggle(NY), (III.3-4), III-IV.33;
        Ger. PermRev, (III.5), II.33.
[See 321228(1) for series. On capitulation of Wels-Senin group in Germany.]

330200(1)   SOVIET ECONOMY IN DANGER.
[Trans. Am. See 321022(1), 321022(2). Includes 321019.]

330200(3)   IN DEFENSE OF THE RUSSIAN REVOLUTION.
[Trans. Am. See 321127 for all repr., trans.]

330205   Pered resheniem. (Before the decision.) (BO, (33), III.33)
Trans.: Am. Mil, 24.II.33;
        Cz. *330000(38);
        Fr. 590600: 341-50; V, (142), 16.II.33;
        Ger. PermRev, (III.7), II.33;
        Jap. *520000(4); 620530: 376-87;
        Pol. *330000(42);
        Sp. Comunismo, (III.22), III.33;
        Yid. Unser Kampf, (II.3), IV.33.
[PS 330206. On Germany.]

330206   PS 330205. (BO, (33), III.33)
Trans.: Fr. OCG, (6), VI.33.

330221 Pref. EXTRAITS DE LA CORRESPONDANCE DE NIN A TROTSKY ET DE TROTSKY
A NIN, 330400(1).

⌊Trans. Fr. See 330400(1) for all repr., trans.⌋

330223 The United Front for defense. Letter to a social-democratic worker.
Trans.: Am. Mil, 1,15.IV.33;
Cz. *330000(37);
Eng. ⌊330000(39)⌋; Communist(B), (4-5), IV-V.33;
Fr. *330000(35); 590600: 351-74; V, (145,146), 9,16.III.33;
VoixCom, (III.12,13), 19,26.III.33;
Ger. UWort, (I.2,3), IV,IV.33;
Hol. NWeg, (VIII.5,6), V,VI.33;
It. 620000(20): 421-43; *680900; 681100: 458-81;
Jap. *520000(4); 620530: 388-416;
Sp. ⌊330000(28)⌋.

⌊On Germany. T3509.⌋

330228 Minutes of discussion on the Negro Question.
Trans.: Am. 670600: 109; 690600: 10-9; 700800(1): 10-9; EYS, (4),
VII.62; CLA, (12), 19.IV.33;
Eng. p.q. IntSoc, (43), IV-V.70;
Jap. 681010: 22-37.

⌊T3511.⌋

⌊330300(1)⌋ Bol'shoi uspekh. (A great achievement.) (BO, (33), III.33)
⌊On Pre-Conference of ILOpp. T3516.⌋

⌊330300(2)⌋ Al'fa: Molotov o Zinov'ev. (Molotov on Zinoviev.) (BO, (33), III.33)

⌊330300(3)⌋ Alternative for ⌊330400(3)⌋.
⌊Declaration of the ILOpp delegation to the Paris Anti-Fascist
Congress. Redigé par LT. — PN. T3512.⌋

*330300(4) *LA REVOLUCIÓN ESPAÑOLA.
⌊Trans. Sp. See 290600(2), 310124, 310528(1) for all repr.,
trans.⌋

330303(1)   See 330503.

330303(2)   Signal trevogi. (Alarm signal.) (BO, (33), III.33)
       Repr.: [330000(2)].
       Trans.: Am. Mil, 18,25.III.33;
          Eng. Communist(B), (6), VI.33;
          Fr. 330000(10); p.q. 680000(4): 317-8; V, (146), 16.III.33;
          Ger. UWort, (I.3,4,5), IV,V,V.33;
          Hol. Fak, (II.53,54,61,65,67,74,76), 6,13,27.V, 9,16.VI, 11,18.
            VII.33;
          Hung. DEMOKRATIKUS;
          Sp. *[330000(34)].
       [On Soviet economy. T3514.]

330306   Nuzhna nemedlennaya pomoshch; vsem druzyam oktyabr'skoi revolyutsii.
       (Help is needed at once; To all friends of the October Revolution.)
       (BO, (34), V.33)
       Trans.: Am. Mil, 15.IV.33.
       [T3517.]

330307   G.Gourov: On the question of the situation of the American League.
       Trans.: Am. CLA, (13), 29.IV.33.
       [T3518.]

330310   On the new Germany.
       Trans.: Am. Mil, 29.IV.33;
          Eng. ManGuard, 22.III.33;
          Fr. V, (148), 31.III.33;
          Ger. UWort, (I.2), IV.33;
          Hol. Fak. (II.45), 15.IV.33;
          Yid. 330400(4).
       [T3519.]

330312   G.Gourov: PCA ou nouveau parti. Au Secrétariat international.
       Trans.: Fr. OCG, (4), IV.33.
       [On Germany. T3520.]

330314   Tragediya nemetskogo proletariata. Nemetskie rabochie podminutsya,
stalinizm — nikogda! (The tragedy of the German proletariat. The
German workers will rise again, stalinism — never!) (BO, (34), V.33)
Trans.: Am. 440800(2); p.q. 640800: 171-3; Mil, 8.IV.33;
        Bul. *[330000(5)];
        Cz. *[340000(17)];
        Eng. 620900; Red Flag, (1), V.33;
        Fr. 590600: 375-87; V, (147), 24.III.33; VoixCom, (III.14),
           2.IV.33;
        Ger. UWort, (I.2), IV.33;
        Hol. NWeg, (VIII.4), IV.33;
        It. 570400: 243-52;
        Jap. *520000(4); 620530: 417-30; p.q. 681125: 179-82;
        Jug. Socijalne Misao, (VI), IX.33;
        Sp. p.q. 670000(5): 171-2; Comunismo, (III.23), IV.33;
        Swed. p.q. 691100(2): 151-3;
        Yid. 330400(4).

330315   [Letter to Politbureau.]
[c. 330513. T3502.]

330317(1)   G—off: Germany and the USSR. Letter to the sections.
Trans.: Am. CLA, (11), 31.III.33.
[T3523.]

330317(2)   Interview.
Trans.: Am. p.q. NYTimes, 18.III.33.
[On USA.]

330319   Brief an einen österreichischen Genossen.
Trans.: Ger. 330000(15); Bauer;
        Hol. Bauer.
[? T3524.]

330321   L.T.: Gitler i krasnaya armiya. (Hitler and the Red Army.) (BO, (34),
V.33)
Trans.: Am. Mil, 8.IV.33;
        Bul. Osvob, (I.41), 6.XI.33;
        Fr. V, (148), 31.III.33; VoixCom, (III.15), 9.IV.33;
        Sp. Comunismo, (III.23), IV 33.
[T3526.]

330323(1)   Avstriya na ocheredi. (It is now Austria's turn.) (BO, (34), V.33)
    Trans.: Am. Mil, 15,29.IV.33; 17.II.34;
       Bul. *[330000(3)];
       Eng. Red Flag, (2), VI.33;
       Fr. V, (149,150), 7,14.IV.33; VoixCom, (III.16,17), 16,23.IV.33;
       Ger. 330000(15).
    [T3527.]

330323(2)   On Rakovsky.
    Trans.: Am. Mil, 8.IV.33;
       Eng. Red Flag, (2), VI.33;
       Fr. V, (149), 7.IV.33; VoixCom, (III.16), 16.IV.33.

330329(1)   G.Gurov: KPG ili novaya partiya? (The CPGermany or a new party?)
    (BO, (34), V.33)
    Trans.: Am. CLA, (12), 19.IV.33;
       Fr. OCG, (4), IV.33.
    [T3530.]

330330 Nuzhno chestnoe vnutripartiinoe soglashenie. (Honest inter-party
    agreement is needed.) (BO, (34), V.33)
    Trans.: Bul. Osvob, (II.43), 14.XII.33;
       Yid. Unser Kampf, (II.5), 15.VI.33.
    [ILOpp and CPSU. T3531.]

330400(1)   † Extraits de la correspondance de Nin à Trotsky et de la correspondance
    de Trotsky à Nin.
    Trans.: Am. CLO, (2-3), III.33;
       Fr. OCG, (4), IV.33; LA RÉVOLUTION ESPAGNOLE: 85-94.
    [Pref. 330221.]

330400(2)   † THE ONLY ROAD.
    Trans.: Am.;
       Cz.*[320000(5)];
       Eng. 590100; 700500: 217-300;
       Fr. 320000(15); 590600: 259-320;
       Ger. 320000(5); p.q. Arbeiter Stimme, (108,109,111), VIII,IX,
        Heb.X*320000(11);
       Hung. *320000(26);
       Jap. *520000(4); 620530: 288-357;
       Port. *330000(18);

++++

330400(2)   ++++   Trans.: Sp. ⌊320000(24)⌋.

⌊Pref. 320913; Afterword 320914. For other trans. see individual entries.⌋

⌊330400(3)⌋   —: Zayavlenie delegatov, prinadlezhashchikh k Internatsional noi Levoi Oppozitsii (Bol´sheviki-lenintsy), k kongressu bor´by protiv fashizma. (Declaration of delegates, members of the International Left Opposition (Bolshevik-Leninists) to the Congress for struggle against fascism.) (BO, (34), V.33)

Trans.: Am. Mil, 20.V.33;

Fr. 330000(8); V, (150), 14.IV.33; VoixCom, (III.23), 4.VI.33;
Ger. UWort, (I.4), V.33;
Rum. 330000(7);
Sp. Comunismo, (III.24), V.33.

⌊See note to ⌊330300(3)⌋. T3532.⌋

330400(4)   DIE TRAGEDIJE FUN DEUTSHEN PROLETARIAT.

⌊Trans. Yid. See 330310, 330314 for all trans.⌋

⌊330400(5)⌋   G.Gourov: A tous les membres de l'O.G. espagnole.

Trans.: Fr. CCG, (5), V.33.

⌊On Spain.? T3540.⌋

330401   Chto takoe istoricheskaya ob"ektivnost? (What is historical objectivity (BO, (35), VII.33)

Trans.: Am. Mil, 15.VII.33;

Fr. QI, (2), 11.37;
Sp. 671100(1): 40-7; Babel, (15-16), I-IV.41; Batalla, (XXIV. 163,164), II,III.68; RepAm, (XXVII.18), 11.XI.33.

⌊T3533.⌋

330406   Pref. O.Fischer, LENINISMUS GEGEN STALINISMUS.

Trans.: Am. Mil, 15.XII.33;

Fr. VoixCom, (III.24), 11.VI.33; V, (156), 26.V.33.
Ger. Fischer(0).

330409   Krushenie germanskoi kompartii i zadachi oppozitsii. (The collapse of the CP Germany and the tasks of the Opposition.) (BO, (34), V.33)

Trans.: Am. Mil, 6,13.V.33;

Fr. V, (151), 21.IV.33; VoixCom, (III.19), 7.V.33;
Ger. UWort, (I.4), V.33;
Gr. ¢ Pali, (302), 18.VII.33;

330409   ++++   Trans.: Yid. Unser Kampf, (II.4), 1.VI.33.
                  [T3534.]

330410   —: Po povodu yunosheskogo dvizheniya. (On the Youth movement.)
                  (BO, (34), V.33)
                  Trans.: Am. Mil, 8.VII.33;
                          Fr. V, (151), 21.IV.33.
                  [Declaration of ILOpp. delegation to Prague [? Copenhagen] Youth
                  Conference. T3536.]

330413   Un saludo.
                  Trans.: Sp. ICE, (I.2), 1.VIII.33.
                  [To comrades in Chile.]

[330415]   Interview, with B.J.Field.
                  Trans.: Am. Mil, 15.IV.33.
                  [Reply to Louis Fischer.]

330417   L.D.: To the International Secretariat.
                  Trans.: Am. CLA, (13), 29.IV.33;
                          Fr. p.q. OCG, (4), IV.33.
                  [Letter on the German situation.]

330421   G.G.: Discussion on the German tasks. Reply to National Committee of
                  the German Opposition.
                  Trans.: Am. Mil, 1.VII.33;
                          Fr. V, (158), 9.VI.33; VoixCom, (III.22), 28.V.33; BISI, (4),
                              V.33.
                  [T3538.]

330427   The Left Opposition and the SAP.
                  Trans.: Eng. Red Flag, (4), VIII.33;
                          Fr. BISI, (4), V.33.
                  [On German section ILOpp. T3541.]

[330428]   —: Sur un article de Heckert.
                  Trans.: Fr. V, (152,153), 28.IV, 5.V.33.
                  [See also [330512(2)].]

330429   —: Problemy sovetskogo rezhima. (Teoriya pererozhdeniya i pererozhdenie teorii.) (Problems of the Soviet regime; The thoery of degeneration and the degeneration of theory.) (<u>BO</u>, (34), V.33)
Trans.: Am. <u>Mil</u>, 27.V, 3.VI.33;
        Eng. p.q. <u>Red Flag</u>, (3), VII.33;
        Fr. <u>V</u>, (154), 12.V.33; <u>VoixCom</u>, (III.21), 21.V.33;
        Ger. <u>UWort</u>, (I.6), VI.33;
        Hol. <u>NWeg</u>, (VIII.7,8), VII,VIII.33;
        Sp. <u>Comunismo</u>, (III.25), VI.33.
[T3542.]

330430   [Letter to Parijanine.]
[c. NOT GUILTY: 214. D116.]

330503   To the Austrian social-democratic Opposition. Reply to some concrete questions.
Trans.: Am. <u>Mil</u>, 3.VI.33;
        Fr. <u>V</u>, (154), 12.V.33; <u>VoixCom</u>, (III.21), 21.V.33;
        Ger. <u>UWort</u>, (I.5), V.33;
        Yid. <u>Unser Kampf</u>, (II.6), 1.VII.33.
[T3543.]

330506   Pis´mo. (A letter.)
Trans.: Bul. 330000(1).

330507   T.: Posle 1-go maya v Avstrii. (After May Day in Austria.) (<u>BO</u>, (35), VII.33)
Trans.: Am. <u>Mil</u>, 3.VI.33;
        Fr. <u>V</u>, (155), 19.V.33; <u>VoixCom</u>, (III.22), 28.V.33;
        Ger. <u>UWort</u>, (I.5), V.33.
[T3544.]

330510   Novelist and Politician: Céline and Poincaré.
Trans.: Am. 650900: 345-55; <u>Atlantic</u>, X.35;
        Eng. 640000(5): 345-55; 640000(10): 345-55;
        Fr. 640911: 332-42; p.q. <u>L'Herne</u>, (5), 1965;
        Sp. 690000(8).II: 164-73;
        Swed. 690600(1): 297-307.
[T3546.]

330512(1) —: Po povodu vneshnei politiki stalinskoi byurokratii. (Concerning the foreign policy of the stalinist bureaucracy.) (BO, (35), VII.33)
Trans.: Am. Mil, 10.VI.33;
    Bul. Osvob, (I.40), 18.X.33;
    Fr. V, (155), 19.V.33; VoixCom, (III.22), 28.V.33;
    Ger. UWort, (I.6), VI.33;
    Sp. Comunismo, (III.25), VI.33;
    Yid. Unser Kampf, (II.5), 15.VI.33.
[T3547.]

[330512(2)] —: Comment le fascisme est-il venu au pouvoir en Allemagne.
Trans.: Fr. V, (154), 12.V.33.
[See also [330428].]

330513 Raz"yasnenie. (An explanation.) (BO, (35), VII.33)
[To foreign press on letter of 15.III.33. T3522 makes this 330510.
Date printed in BO, (35), VII.33 taken.]

330519 Greetings to Red Flag.
[Trans.: Am. Mil, 22.VII.33.
[Organ of Br. section of ILOpp. T3548.]

330522 Platforma gruppy Brandlera. (The platform of the Brandler group.)
(BO, (35), VII.33)
Trans.: Am. Mil, 17.VI.33;
    Fr. V, (158), 9.VI.33; VoixCom, (III.25), 18.VI.33;
    Ger. UWort, (I.6), VI.33.
[T3550.]

330523 L.T.: Zinov'ev i Kamenev. (BO, (35), VII.33)
Trans.: Am. Mil, 10.VI.33;
    Eng. Red Flag, (4), VIII.33;
    Fr. V, (157), 2.VI.33; VoixCom, (III.24), 11.VI.33;
    Hol. Baan, (V.9), 1.VII.33;
    Sp. Comunismo, (III.25), VI.33;
    Yid. Unser Kampf, (II.5), 15.VI.33.
[T3551.]

330525   —: O Khristiane Georgieviche Rakovskom. (On Christian Georgevich
Rakovsky.) (BO, (35), VII.33)
Trans.: Am. Mil, 10.VI.33;
         Fr. V, (157), 2.VI.33; VoixCom, (III.24,25), 11,18.VI.33;
         Ger. UWort, (I.6), VI.33;
         Hol. Baan, (V.7), 16.VI.33;
         Sp. Comunismo, (III.25), VI.33;
         Yid. Unser Kampf, (II.5), 15.VI.33.
[T3552.]

330528   —: Nemetskaya katastrofe. Otvetstvennost rukovodstva. (The German
catastrophe. The responsibility of the leadership.) (BO, (35), VII.33)
Trans.: Am. 650900: 257-66; Mil, 15.VII.33; NRep, 5.VII.33;
         Eng. 640000(5): 257-66; 640000(10): 257-66;
         Ger. NWeltbühne, (23), 8.VI.33;
         Hol. Fakkel, (II.69,70), 23,27.VI.33.
[T3553.]

330531   [Letter to Guernut.]
[c. NOT GUILTY: 214. D167.]

330602   Gitler i razoruzhenie. (Hitler and disarmament.) (BO, (35), VII.33)
Trans.: Am. 330000(26); Class Struggle(NY), (IV.4-5), IV-V.34;
         Harpers, IX.33; Mil, 2,9.IX.33;
         Eng. ManGuard, 21,22.VI.33;
         Fr. Europe, 1933;
         Ger. NWeltbühne, (25,26), 22,29.VI.33;
         Nor. Samtiden, (XLIV.7), 1933.
[T3554.]

330604   "4-e avgusta." ("August 4.") (BO, (35), VII.33)
Trans.: Am. Mil, 8.VII.33;
         Fr. V, (159), 16.VI.33; VoixCom, (III.26), 25.VI.33;
         Ger. UWort, (I.7), VI.33;
         It. BOC, (16), 15.VI.33.
[T3555.]

330607(1)   Interview, avec M.Simenon.
Trans.: Fr. Paris-Soir, 15,16.VI.33;
         Hol. NWeg, (VIII.9), IX.33.
[T3556.]

330607(2)   [Letter to Parijanine.]

Trans.: Eng. p.q. NOT GUILTY: 214.

[D168.]

[330609(1)]   Al´fa: Poslednyaya fal´sifikatsiya stalintsev. (The latest falsification of the stalinists.) (BO, (35), VII.33)

Trans.: Am. Mil, 17.VI.33;

        Fr. V, (158), 9.VI.33;

        Ger. UWort, (I.6), VI.33;

        It. BOC, (16), 15.VI.33.

[T3564.]

[330609(2)]   Pour la renaissance du communisme en Allemagne.

Trans.: Fr. V, (158), 9.VI.33.

[Resolution adopted by Plenum International Opposition. Adoptée après discussion avec LT. -- PN.]

330610   What is National Socialism?

Trans.: Am. 640800: 173-82; Class Struggle(NY), (IV.1), I.34; FI, II.43;

        Modern Thinker, (III.6), X.33; Yale Review, XII.33;

     Eng. IntSoc, (38-39), VIII-IX.69; WIN, IV.43;

     Fr. 330000(17); [450000(4)]; [570000(9)]; 590600: 389-99; p.q.

        ActSoc, (II.7), 17,24.II, 3.III.34; NRF, III.34;

     Ger. NWeltbühne, (28), 13.VII.33;

     Heb. Hashomer Hatzair, (2), X-XI.33;

     It. 570400: 253-62;

     Jap. *520000(4); 620530: 431-41; 681125: 182-91;

     Sp. *340700(5); 670000(5): 172-80;

     Swed. 691100(2): 153-61.

[PS 331102. T3557.]

330613(1)   Diplomaticheskii i parlamentskii kretinizm. (Diplomatic and parliamentary cretinism.) (BO, (35), VII.33)

Trans.: Am. Mil, 8.VII.33;

        Fr. 670306: 413-6; V, (160), 23.VI.33; VoixCom, (III.26), 25.VI.33;

        Ger. UWort, (I.7), VI.33;

        Hol. Baan, (V.11), 15.VII.33;

        Yid. Unser Kampf, (II.7), 15.VII.33.

[Austria. T3558.]

330613(2) Interv'yu predstavitel'nitse New York World Telegram. (Interview with
New York World Telegram correspondent.) (BO, (35), VII.33)
Trans.: Mil, 17.VI.33; ? New York World Telegram, 4.VII.33.
|T3565.|

330615 G.Gurov: Levye sotsialisticheskie organizatsii i nashi zadachi.
(Left socialist organizations and our tasks.) (BO, (35), VII.33)
Trans.: Am. Mil, 5.VIII.33;
　　　　Eng. CLB, (8), |VI.33|;
　　　　Fr. V, (163), 14.VII.33.
|T3559.|

330616 O politike partii v oblasti iskusstva i filosofii. (The Party's policy
in the sphere of art and philosophy.) (BO, (35), VII.33)
Trans.: Am. Mil, 22.VII.33;
　　　　Sp. 640900(1): 208-11; 690000(8).II: 179-81; Comunismo, (III.27),
　　　　　　VIII.33.
[Reply to Am. comrades Glee, Ross and Morris. T3560.]

330617 O trudnostyakh nashei raboty. (On the difficulties of our work.)
(BO, (35), VII.33)
|To Austrian comrades. T3561.|

330618 "Mise au point."
Trans.: Fr. V, (160), 23.VI.33.

330622 How long can Hitler stay?
Trans.: Am. 440800(2); AmMercury, I.34; Class Struggle(NY), (III.9,10),
　　　　　　IX-X,XI.33;
　　　　Cz. *[340000(14)];
　　　　Eng. 620900;
　　　　Fr. V, (168,169), 18,25.VIII.33; VoixCom, (III.37,38),
　　　　　　10,17.IX.33;
　　　　Ger. NWeltbühne, (30,31), 27.VII, 3.VIII.33;
　　　　It. 570400: 263-72;
　　　　Sp. Comunismo, (III.28), IX.33.
|T3563.|

330700 |Unpublished diary.|
Trans.: Eng. p.q. Deutscher, PO: 13.

330704 Alternative for 330613(2).

330706	—: Zinov'ev o rezhime VKP. (Zinoviev on the regime of the CPSU.)
	(BO, (38-39), II.34)
	Trans.: Am. Mil, 29.VII.33.
	⌊T3566.⌋
330707	Letter to H.Molinier.
	Trans.: Eng. p.q. NOT GUILTY: 214-5.
	⌊D173,175.⌋
330712	Yaponiya dvizhetsya v katastrofe. (Japan advances to catastrophe.)
	(BO, (38-39), II.34)
	Trans.: Am. p.q. FI, II.44; Liberty, 18.XI.33; p.q. Mil. 29.I.34
	⌊T3567.⌋
330714	Fascism and democratic slogans.
	Trans.: Am. Mil, 26.VIII.33; NI(WP), VII.43;
	Eng. Red Flag, (5), IX.33;
	Fr. V, (167), 11.VIII.33;
	Ger. UWort, (I.10), VIII.33;
	Hol. Fakkel, (II.97), 29.IX.33;
	Sp. Batalla, (XXI.149), III.65; Comunismo, (III.28), IX.33
	⌊T3568.⌋
330715(1)	Eleven principles of the I.L.O. (as amended).
	Trans.: Am. Mil, 30.IX.33; IP, (VIII.16), 27.IV.70;
	Eng. CLB, (11), 12.VIII.33;
	Yid. Unser Kamf, (II.8), XI.33.
330715(2)	G.Gurov: Nuzhno stroit zanovo kommunisticheskie partii i Internatsional.
	(The Communist Parties and the International must be built again.)
	(BO, (36-37), X.33)
	Trans.: Am. CLA, (13), 29.IV.33; FI, VII.43; Mil, 14.X.33;
	Bul. Osvob, (II.39-40), 16.XI.33;
	Eng. CLB, (11), 12.VIII.33; WIN, I.44;
	Fr. OCG, (7), VIII.33; VoixCom, (III.41), 8.X.33;
	Ger. UWort, (I.11), VIII.33;
	Hung. DEMOKRATIKUS;
	Jap. 631130: 117-28;
	Port. 340000(6).
330715(3)	Pered otezdom. (Before the removal.)
	Trans.: Am. Modern Monthly, III.34;
	Eng. p.q. Deutscher, PO: 216-7.
	⌊T3569.⌋

330715(4)   A.: Samoubiistvo Skrypnika. (Skrypnik's suicide.) (BO, (36-37), X.33)

Trans.: Am. Mil, 12.VIII.33;

Fr. V, (163), 14.VII.33; VoixCom, (III.30), 23.VII.33;

Ger. UWort, (I.10), VIII.33.

⌊T3570.⌋

330715(5)   EUROPE AND AMERICA.

⌊Trans. Eng. See 260215 for all repr., trans.⌋

330719(1)   Fontamara. (BO, (36-37), X.33)

Trans.: Am. Mil, 26.VIII.33; NI, XII.34;

Fr. 640911: 343; V, (166), 4.VIII.33; VoixCom, (III.35), 8.X.33;

Sp. 640900(1): 211-2; 690000(8).II: 174; Comunismo, (III.28),

IX.33;

Swed. 690600(1): 308.

⌊Review of Silone, FONTAMARA. T3572.⌋

330719(3)   N.N.: Stalin uspokaivaet Gitlera. (Stalin reassures Hitler.)

(BO, (36-37), X.33)

Trans.: Am. Mil, 26.VIII.33;

Fr. V, (167), 11.VIII.33;

Ger. UWort, (I.10), VIII.33.

⌊On possibility of T's return to the Soviet Union. T3573.⌋

330720(1)   G.G./G.Gourov: Nel´zya bol´she ostavat´sya v odnom "Internatsionale" so

Stalinym, Manuil´skim, Lozovskim i Ko. (It is impossible to remain in

the same "International" with the Stalins, Manuilskys, Lozovskys, and

Co.) (BO, (36-37), X.33)

Trans.: Am. CLA, (13), 29.IV.33; Mil, 21.X.33;

Eng. Red Flag, (6), X-XI.33;

Fr. OCG, (7), VIII.33; V, (171), 8.IX.33;

Ger. UWort, (I.13), X.33;

Hol. Baan, (V.18-20), 2-16.IX.33;

Port. 340000(6);

Sp. ClarProl, (5), I.34;

Ukr. RobVis, (I.3), 15.XII.33.

⌊Interview. T3574.⌋

330720(2)   Alternative for 330719(1).

330726   Une mise au point nécessaire. Un démenti à l'Humanité.
              Trans.: Fr. V, (166), 4.VIII.33.
              ⌊T3575.⌋

330727   L.D.: On the new Communist Parties and the new International.
              Trans.: Am. CLA, (13), 29.IV.33;
                        Eng. CLB, (12), 28.VIII.33.
              ⌊Minutes of discussion. V46.⌋

⌊330728⌋   "Déclaration" de la Commission exécutive de la Ligue Communiste sur
              le séjour de L.T. en France.
              Trans.: Fr. V, (165), 28.VII.33.

330730(1)   ⌊Letter to Paris.⌋
              ⌊c. NOT GUILTY: 227. D209.⌋

330731(1)   ⌊Letter to Naville.⌋
              ⌊c. NOT GUILTY: 224,227. D211.⌋

330731(2)   ⌊Letter to Paris.⌋
              ⌊c. NOT GUILTY: 227. D212.⌋

330731(3)   ⌊Letter to Paris.⌋
              ⌊c. NOT GUILTY: 227. D213.⌋

⌊330800(1)⌋   Letter to Independent Labour Party.
              Trans.: Am. Class Struggle(NY), (III.10), XI.33;
                        Eng. NLeader, 25.VIII.33.
              ⌊On Maxton's Pref. to THE RUSSIAN REVOLUTION, 330000(19). T3579.⌋

330805   G.G.: Dashe kleveta dolzhna imet mysl. (Even slander needs meaning.)
              (BO, (38-39), II.34)
              Trans.: Am. Mil, 16.IX.33;
                        Fr. V, (167), 11.VIII.33; VoixCom, (III.34), 20.VIII.33;
                        Sp. Comunismo, (III.29), X.33;
                        Ukr. RobVis, (II.5), 1.III.34.
              ⌊T3576.⌋

330813   —: Organ finansovogo kapitala o "trotskizme". (An organ of finance capital on "trotskyism".) (<u>BO</u>, (36-37), X.33)
     <u>Trans</u>.: Am. <u>Mil</u>, 2.IX.33;
            Fr. <u>V</u>, (168), 18.VIII.33;
            Ger. <u>UWort</u>, (I.11), VIII.33.
     ⌊cf. 350214. T3593.⌋

330817(1)   ⌊Letter to Naville.⌋
     ⌊c. NOT GUILTY: 224.⌋

330817(2)   See 330820.

330817(3)   —: Declaration of ILOpp to the Left Socialist Conference.
     <u>Trans</u>.: Am. <u>Mil</u>, 23.IX.33;
            Fr. <u>V</u>, (170), 1.IX.33;
            Ger. <u>UWort</u>, (I.12), IX.33;
            Hol. <u>Baan</u>, (V.20), 16.IX.33; <u>NWeg</u>, (VIII.9), IX.33;
            Yid. <u>Unser Kampf</u>, (II.8), XI.33.
     ⌊Rédigée par LT. -- PN. T3584.⌋

330818(1)   Lettre.
     <u>Trans</u>.: Fr. <u>Commune</u>, (148), 21.X.38; CRISE.II: iv-v.
     ⌊To Frank. On ILOpp. in France.⌋

330818(2)   Brief.
     <u>Trans</u>.: Ger. <u>LKI</u>, (1), I.34.
     ⌊To Schwab. On German section ILOpp.⌋

⌊330813(3)⌋   Lettre à <u>Vérité</u>.
     <u>Trans</u>.: Fr. <u>V</u>, (168), 18.VIII.33; <u>VoixCom</u>, (III.34), 20.VIII.33.
     ⌊Refusing offer of financial help for himself.⌋

330820   Conversations with Schwab and Sneevliet.
     <u>Trans</u>.: Eng. p.q. NOT GUILTY: 312.
     ⌊From 17 to 20.VIII.33. On ILOpp.⌋

330821   ⌊Letter to Naville.⌋
     ⌊c. NOT GUILTY: 224.⌋

330825   ⌊Letter to Naville.⌋
     ⌊c. NOT GUILTY: 224.⌋

330826 i dr.: Rezolyutsiya o neobkhodimosti novogo Internatsionala i ego printsipakh. (Resolution on the need for a new International and its principles.) (BO, (36-37), X.33)

 Trans.: Am. Mil, 23.IX.33;
    Eng. Red Flag, (6), X-XI.33;
    Fr. ⌊330000(27)⌋; V, (170), 1.IX.33;
    Hol. ⌊330000(27)⌋; ⌊330000(32)⌋; Baan, (V.20), 16.IX.33;
     NWeg, (VIII.9), IX.33.
 ⌊Red Flag has revised text. Rédigé par LT. -- PN. T3589.⌋

330827 Alternative for 330826.

330828 Whither the ILP?

 Trans.: Am. Mil, 23.IX.33;
    Eng. Red Flag, (6), X-XI.33;
    Fr. V, (172), 15.IX.33;
    Ger.UWort, (I.12), IX.33;
    Hol. Baan, (V.23,24), 7,14.X.33.
 ⌊On Britain. T3590.⌋

330829 Interview with C.A.S⌊mith⌋.

 Trans.: Am. Living Age, VI.34;
    Eng. NLeader, 13.X.33.
 ⌊On ILP, Britain.⌋

330831(1) Rezolyutsiya Plenuma Internatsional'n. Levoi Oppozitsii (b-1). (Resolution of the Plenum of the International Left Opposition (B-L),) (BO, (36-37), X.33)

 Trans.: Am. Mil, 7.X.33.
 ⌊On the Conference of the Left Socialist and Opposition Communist organizations in Paris, 27-28, August, 1933. See 330913 note.⌋

330831(2) ⌊Interview with Paton and Schmidt.⌋
 ⌊c. NOT GUILTY: 226. On ILOpp.⌋

330831(3) Alternative for 330826.

330901(1) G.Gourov: Left Socialist Conference -- nucleus for a new International.

 Trans.: Am. Mil, 23.IX.33;
   Fr. OCG, (9), IX.33;
   Hol. Fakkel, (II.93), 15.IX.33; NWeg, (VIII.9), IX.33.
 T3592.⌋

⌊330901(2)⌋ Onken: Stalin prepares a treacherous blow.

 Trans.: Am. Mil, 23.IX.33;
   Fr. V, (170), 1.IX.33; VoixCom, (III.36), 3.IX.33.
 ⌊T3587.⌋

330903(2)   L.D.: A letter on the ILOpp and the ILP.
             Trans.: Eng. p.q. CLB, (15-16), 24.X.33.

330904   The ILP and the new International.
             Trans.: Am. p.q. 690000(13): 53-7; Mil, 30.IX.33;
                     Fr. p.q. 700000(6): 50-3; V, (174), 6.X.33; VoixCom, (III.40),
                         8.X.33;
                     Ger. UWort, (II.36), XII.34.
             ⌊On ILP trade unions. T3593.⌋

330910   G.G./G.Gourov: More on the Paris Conference.
             Trans.: Am. Mil, 30.IX.33;
                     Fr. V, (172), 15.IX.33.
             ⌊On ILOpp. T3595.⌋

330913   ⌊Date of adoption of 330831(1).⌋
             ⌊Text loc. HIS is signed G.Gourov. T3591.⌋

330916   G.Gourov: Letter on the ILOpp and the ILP.
             Trans.: Eng. CLB, (15-16), 24.X.33.
             ⌊T3597.⌋

330918   G.Gourov: Il faut en finir.
             Trans.: Fr. GBL, (5), 22.IX.33.
             ⌊On Fr. section ILOpp. T3599.⌋

330920   L.T.: Edinyi front s Grzhezinskim. (The united front with Grzezinsky.)
             (BO, (36-37), X.33)
             Trans.: Am. Mil, 7.X.33;
                     Fr. V, (174), 6.X.33;
                     Ger. UWort, (I.13), X.33;
                     Hol. Baan, (V.25), 21.X.33;
                     Sp. Comunismo, (III.29), X.33.

330925   Letter on the ILOpp and the ILP.
             Trans.: Eng. CLB, (15-16), 24.X.33.
             ⌊T3603.⌋

331000   LA QUATRIÈME INTERNATIONALE ET L'URSS.

                  [Trans. Fr. See 331001 for all repr., trans.]

331001   Klassovaya priroda sovetskogo gosudarstva. (The class nature of the
                  Soviet State.) (BO, (36-37), X.33)

                  Trans.: Am. 340200(2); Mil, 6,20.I.34;
                          Cz. 340000(2);
                          Eng. 340000(7); 521200; 580000(10); 620000(11); 680800(1): 3-34;
                                680900(2);
                          Fr. 331000; p.q. 680000(4): passim; p.q. V, (175), 13.X.33;
                          Ger. 330000(25); 340000(10); *340000(23); UWort, (I.14), XI.33;
                          Hol. [330000(31)]; [330000(32)]; p.q. Baan, (V.25), 21.X.33;
                                Klassen(A), (I.6-8), 6.III-1.V.37;
                          Hung. [360000(19)];
                          Jap. 631030: 64-9;
                          Port. *[340000(12)];
                          Sp. *[350000(22)];
                          Ukr. 340000(24); RobVis, (II.5-7), 1,15.III, 1.IV.34;
                          Yid. 340000(20).

                [T3607.]

331002(1)   Letter to New Leader.
                  Trans.: Am. Mil, 21.X.33.
                  [On Britain. T3608.]

331002(2)   Letter to British section, Bolshevik-Leninists.
                  Trans.: Eng. CLB, (15-16), 24.X.33.

331003(1)   Letter to Spartacus Youth Club, Canada.
                  Trans.: Am. October Youth, (5), X-XI.33.

331003(2)   Letter to Adelante.
                  Trans.: Eng. p.q. NOT GUILTY: 41.
                  [On Spain. D411.]

331008   Letter to the International Secretariat.
                  Trans.: Am. CLA, (15), VI.34.
                  [On ILOpp.]

331100   Interview, with Guerin.
                  [c. Guerin: 42-4.]

[331101]   Russia and world revolution.

                Trans.: Am. NRep, 1.XI.33;

                      Ger. Weltbühne, (49), 7.XII.33.

331102   PS, What is National Socialism?, 330610.

                Trans.: Am. Mil, 16.XII.33;

                      Eng. Red Flag, (7), I.34;

                      Fr. NRF, III.34.

              [See 330610 for other trans. T3557.]

331103   See [340200(1)].

[331104]   On the Saar question.

                Trans.: Am. Mil, 4.XI.33;

                      Ger. UWort, (I.13), X.34.

331107   L.T.: Zadachi segodnyashnego dnya. (Our present tasks.) (BO, (38-39), II.34)

                Trans.: Am. Mil, 9.XII.33; NI(WP), VII.43;

                      Cz. 340000(2);

                      Eng. Red Flag, (7), I.34;

                      Fr. 670306: 419-23; ActSoc, (II.3), 20.I.34; V, (180), 17.XI.33;

                          VoixCom, (III.49), 3.XII.33; p.q. (IV.42), 21.X.34; Pref.

                          *LA SITUATION POLITIQUE APRÈS LES PLEINS POUVOIRS;

                      Ger. UWort, (I.15), XI.33;

                      Hol. Baan, (V.31), 2.XII.33; Fakkel, (II.117), 8.XII.33;

                      Ukr. RobVis, (II.4), 1.I.34.

              [T3613.]

331110   L.T.: Mariya Reeze i Komintern. (Maria Reese and the Comintern.)
                (BO, (38-39), II.34)

                Trans.: Am. Mil, 25.XI.33; Pref. M.Reese;

                      Bul. Osvob, (II.41-42), 18.XII.33;

                      Eng. Communist(B), (7), [XII.33];

                      Fr. V, (180), 17.XI.33; VoixCom, (III.49), 3.XII.33;

                      Ger. UWort, (I.15), XI.33;

                      Hol. Baan, (V.29), 18.XI.33; Fakkel, (II.112), 21.XI.33; Pref.

                          M.Reese;

                      Port. 340000(6);

                      Sp. Comunismo, (IV.31), I.34;

                      Ukr, RobVis, (II.4), 1.I.34.

              [T3614,3654,3655.]

331116   Gurow: Lettre à la section belge des B–L.

Trans.: Fr. LCA, (2), XI.33; OCG, (10), XII.33;
        Ger. IKD, (I.9), 20.XII.33.

331123   Hitler the pacifist.

Trans.: Am. Mil, 30.XII.33, 6.I.34;
        Fr. V, (183), 8.XII.33; VoixCom, (III.52), 24.XII.33;
        Ger. NWeltbühne, (48), 30.XI.33.

[T3625.]

331130   Nationalism and economic life.

Trans.: Am. Class Struggle(NY), (IV.9-10), X.34; Foreign Affairs, IV.34;
        FI, IX.45; Winter 1956; Armstrong: 237-40;
        Fr. OCG, (10), XII.33;
        Ger. NWeltbühne, (52), 28.XII.33;
        Hol. NWeg, (IX.5), V.34.

[T3636.]

331200   Lettre au sujet des dirigeants de la section espagnole de l'opposition
de gauche.

Trans.: Fr. LA RÉVOLUTION ESPAGNOLE: 94-5.

331204(1)   Pref. MA VIE, 340000(4).

[See 340000(4) for all repr., trans., notes. T3622.]

331204(2)   Zur Diskussion über die grundlegenden theoretischen Auffassungen der
LKI.

Trans.: Am. ICL, (2), IX.34;
        Ger. LKI, (1), I.34.

331212   Al'fa: Zametki zhurnalista. (Notes of a journalist.) (BO, (38-39),
II.34)

Trans.: Am. Mil, 20,27.I.34;
        Fr. p.q. V, (184), 22.XII.33;
        Ger. UWort, (II.1), I.34;
        Sp. Comunismo, (IV.32), II.34.

[331214]   Politics in the Reichstag trial.

Trans.: Am. NRep, 3.I.34;
        Ger. NWeltbühne, (50), 14.XII.33;
        Pol. Lidove Noviny, (XLI.631), 17.XII.33.

331230 —: Predlozhenie delegatsii kommunistov-internatsionalistov.
(Proposal of the International-Communist delegation.) (<u>BO</u>, (38-39), II.34)
<u>Trans</u>.: Port. 340000(6).
⌊Call for Fourth International. See 340120(2). T3634.⌉

340000(1) CHETVERTYI INTERNATSIONAL I VOINA. (WAR AND THE FOURTH INTERNATIONAL.)
[See 340610 for all trans.]

340000(2) IV. INTERNACIONÁLA A SSSR.
[Trans. Cz. See 331001 for all trans.; 331107, 340120(1).]

*340000(3) *DĚJINY RUSKÉ REVOLUCE.
[Trans. Cz. See 310000(1) for all trans., notes.]

340000(4) MA VIE.
Repr.: 470615.
Trans.: Ch. *[380000(16)];
        Nor. 350000(9).
[Authorized abr. of Fr. See 300000(1) for full text. Pref. 331204(1).
Postface n.d.]

340000(5) —: LA QUATRIÈME INTERNATIONALE ET LA GUERRE.
[Trans. Fr. See 340610 for all trans.]

340000(6) § RUMO À IV INTERNACIONAL!
[Trans. Port. 4 items; 2 signed G.Gurov.]

340000(8) THE SOVIET UNION AND THE FOURTH INTERNATIONAL.
[Trans. Eng. See 331001, 340120(1) for all repr., trans.]

340000(9) —: DIE VIERTE INTERNATIONALE UND DER KRIEG.
[Trans. Ger. See 340610 for all repr., trans.]

340000(10) DIE 4. INTERNATIONALE UND DIE USSR.
[Trans. Ger. See 331001, 340120(1) for all trans.]

[340000(11)] ON CENTRISM.
[Trans. Eng. See 340222 for all repr., trans.]

*[340000(12)] *A IV INTERNACIONAL E A U.R.S.S.
[Trans. Port. See 331001 for all trans.]

*[340000(13)] *LA IV INTERNACIONAL Y LA GUERRA.
[Trans. Sp. See 340610 for all repr., trans.]

*[340000(14)] *NĚMECKÉ PERSPEKTIVY.
[Trans. Cz. See 330622 for all trans.]

[340000(15)]   —: DE 4. INTERNATIONALE EN DE OORLOG.

                [Trans. Hol. See 340610 for all repr., trans.]

*[340000(16)]   *RÍJNOVA REVOLUCE. (Reč v Kodani.)

                [Trans. Cz. See 321127 for all trans.]

*[340000(17)]   *TRAGEDIA NĚMECKÉHO PROLETARIATU.

                [Trans. Cz. See 330314 for all trans.]

340000(18)   § LENIN.

                [Trans. Am. See 240000(24) for all repr., trans., notes.]

340000(19)   CINQ JOURNÉES DE LA RÉVOLUTION RUSSE.

                [Trans. Fr. p.q. 310000(1).]

340000(20)   DER SOVJETEN FARBAND UN DER 4ter INTERNATSIONAL.

                [Trans. Yid. See 331001 for all trans.]

340000(21)   [WAR AND THE FOURTH INTERNATIONAL.]

                [Trans. Ch. See 340610 for all trans.]

*[340000(22)]   *DIE VIERTE INTERNATIONALE UND DER KRIEG.

                [Trans. Ger. See 340610 for all repr., trans.]

*340000(23)   *DIE VIERTE INTERNATIONALE UND DIE USSR.

                [Trans. Ger. See 331001 for all repr., trans.]

340000(24)   SSSR I IV. INTERNATSIONAL. (THE USSR AND THE 4th INTERNATIONAL.)

                [Trans. Ukr. See 331001 for all trans.]

340000(25)   [Conversation with Fritz Sternberg.]

                Trans.: Eng. Sternberg.

340000(26)   ZAPOVIT LENINA. (LENIN'S TESTAMENT.)

                [Trans. Ukr. See 321231 for all repr., trans.]

340101   L.T.: Anatolii Vasil'evich Lunacharskii. (BO, (38-39), II.34)

                Trans.: Fr. 640911: 225-9;

                      Ger. Weltbühne, (2), 11.I.34;

                      Gr. 660000(6): 213-7;

                      Hol. NWeg, (IX.1), I-II.34;

                      It. 680000(6): 91-6;

                      Nor. Mot Dag, (XII.1), 26.I.34;

                                           ++++

340101   ++++   <u>Trans</u>.: Sp. 690000(8).II: 175-8;

                   Swed. 690600(1): 204-8.

           [Obituary. T3635.]

340105   For the Fourth International.

           <u>Trans</u>.: Am. <u>Mil</u>, 27.I.34;

                 Eng. <u>Communist</u>(B), (9), [1934];

                 Fr. <u>VoixCom</u>, (IV.6), 11.II.34;

                 Ger. <u>UWort</u>, (II.2), I.34.

           [Letter to ILP member. T3637.]

340109   G.G.: Revisionism and planning.

           <u>Trans</u>.: Am. <u>NI</u>(WP), III.45;

                 Fr. <u>VoixCom</u>, (IV.4), 28.I.34.

           [On the De Man plan. To Belgian section ILOpp. T3638.]

340111   Die SAP, die LKI und die Vierte Internationale.

           <u>Trans</u>.: Ger. <u>LKI</u>, (1), I.34.

           [T3641.]

340118   ---: Gde granitsy nadeniya? (Are there no limits to the fall?)

           (<u>BO</u>, (38-39), II.34)

           <u>Trans</u>.: Am. <u>Mil</u>, 10.III.34;

                Fr. <u>V</u>, (188,193), 2,16.II.34;

                Ger. <u>UWort</u>, (II.3), II.34;

                Hol. <u>Baan</u>, (V.41-43), 10-24.II.34; <u>Fakkel</u>, (III.14,16),

                    20,27.II.34;

                Sp. <u>Comunismo</u>, (IV.33), III.34;

                Ukr. <u>RobVis</u>, (II.10,11), 15.V, 1.VI.34.

           [On 13th Plenum ECCI. T3642.]

340120(1)   ---: Nakanune s"ezda. (Bolshevik Congresses -- once and now.)

           (<u>BO</u>, (38-39), II.34)

           <u>Trans</u>.: Am. 340200(2); <u>Mil</u>, 10.II.34;

                Cz. 340000(2);

                Eng. 340000(8); 520000(1); <u>WIReview</u>, (II.2), IV-V.57;

                Fr. <u>V</u>, (187), 26.I.34; <u>VoixCom</u>, (IV.4), 28.I.34;

                Ger. 340000(10); <u>NWeltbühne</u>, (7), 15.II.34;

                Pol. <u>Nowe Pismo</u>, (III.15), 11.III.34;

                Sp.*[350000(22)]; <u>Comunismo</u>, (III.33), III.34.

           [T3643.]

340120(2)   ---: Soveshchanie bloka chetyrekh. (The deliberations of the Bloc of Four.) (BO, (38-39), II.34)

Trans.: Port. 340000(6).

[On the Fourth International. See 331220. T3645.]

340123   Alternative for 340124.

340124   A real achievement -- Unser Wort.

Trans.: Am. Mil, 10.II.34;

         Fr. V, (188), 2.II.34;

         Ger. UWort, (II.3), II.34.

[On Ger. section ILOpp. T3647.]

[340200(1)]   On the Jewish problem.

Trans.: Am. Class Struggle(NY), (IV.2), II.34;

         Eng. Workers Voice, (V.1), III.46;

         Hol. NWeg, (IX.1), I-II.34.

[? T3618.]

340200(2)   THE SOVIET UNION AND THE FOURTH INTERNATIONAL.

[Trans. Am. See 331001 for all repr., trans.]

340220   Lettre à Parijanine.

Trans.: Fr. Humbles, (XIX.5-6), V-VI.34.

340222   Centrism and the Fourth International.

Trans.: Am. Class Struggle(NY), (IV.8), VIII.34; Mil, 17.III.34;

         Spartacist, (9), I-II.67;

         Eng. [340000(11)]; Red Flag, (8), II-IV.34; An Solas, (15-16),

           Autumn-Winter, 1966;

         Fr. V, (195), 2.III.34; VoixCom, (IV.10), 11.III.34;

         Ger. UWort, (II.7), III.34;

         Hol. Baan, (V.44), 3.III.34;

         Sp. Comunismo, (IV.34), IV.34;

         Ukr, RobVis, (II.8), 15.IV.34.

[T3649.]

340223   Alternative for 340222.

[340300]   For the Fourth International.

                Trans.: Am. Mil, 31.III.34;

                        Fr. 670306: 424-32; LCI, (5), VII.34; V, (196), 9.III.34;

                        Ger. UWort, (II.8), III.34;

                        Hol. Baan, (V.49), 7.IV.34;

                        Ukr. RobVis, (II.9), 1.V.34.

        [Appeal of the Communist-Internationalists to the workers of the world. Rédigé par LT. -- PN. V104-6.]

[340304]   On the Rakovsky case.

                Trans.: Am. p.q. Mil, 10.III.34;

                        Eng. p.q. ManGuard, 10.III.34;

                        Fr. VoixCom, (IV.9), 4.III.34;

                        Ukr. RobVis, (II.7), 1.IV.34.

        [Interview.]

340313   The Red Army.

                Trans.: Am. SatEvening Post, 26.V.34.

        [T3651-3.]

340316   A centrist attack on marxism.

                Trans.: Am. Mil, 14.IV.34;

                        Fr. V, (198), 23.III.34; VoixCom, (IV.15), 15.IV.34;

                        Ger. UWort, (II.10), III.34;

                        Hol. Baan, (V.48), 31.III.34; NWeg, (IX.4), IV.34.

        [T3656,3657.]

340323   Once more on centrism.

                Trans.: Am. Class Struggle(NY), (IV.8), VIII.34; Mil, 21.IV.34;

                        Fr. V, (202), 20.IV.34;

                        Ger. UWort, (II.11), IV.34;

                        Hol. Baan, (V.49), 7.IV.34.

        [Reply to Fakkel. T3662.]

340325   Alla Redazione della Verità.

                Trans.: It. Verità, (1), III.34.

        [On It. section ILOpp. T3660.]

340331   Chto oznachaet kapitulyatsiya Rakovskogo? (What is the meaning of
Rakovsky's capitulation?) (<u>BO</u>, (40), X.34)
Trans.: Am. <u>Mil</u>, 28.IV.34;
         Fr. <u>V</u>, (200), 6.IV.34; <u>VoixCom</u>, (IV.15), 15.IV.34;
         Ger. <u>UWort</u>, (II.12), IV.34;
         Sp. <u>Antorcha</u>(Madrid), (I.1), 1.V.34.

340405   G.Gourov: To the Greek section of the League of Communist
Internationalists.
Trans.: Am. <u>CLA</u>, (15), IV.34;
         Fr. <u>LCI</u>, (4), VI.34.

340419   —: The real significance of Rakovsky's capitulation.
Trans.: Am. <u>Mil</u>, 19.V.34;
         Fr. <u>V</u>, (207), 27.IV.34.

⌊340427⌋   —: Doloi povyazki a glaz! (Remove the bandages from the eyes!)
(<u>BO</u>, (40), X.34)
Trans.: Fr. <u>V</u>, (203), 27.IV.34;
         Hol. <u>Baan</u>, (VI.4), 26.V.34.
⌊On slander by <u>l'Humanité</u>. Rédigée par LT. — PN.⌋

340501   Alternative for 340610.

⌊340513⌋   Parabellum: Les "révolutionnaires" de <u>l'Humanité</u> et le "contre-
révolutionnaire" Trotsky.
Trans.: Fr. <u>VoixCom</u>, (V.17), 13.V.34.
⌊cf. ⌊340427⌋.⌋

⌊340600(1)⌋   —: A program of action for France.
Trans.: Am. <u>FI</u>, X.42; <u>Mil</u>, 30.VI.34;
         Fr. <u>EM</u>, (2), II.69; <u>QI</u>, VI-VII.46; <u>V</u>, (211), VI.34.

⌊340608(1)⌋   —: Conversation avec un camarade du rayon de Saint-Denis.
Trans.: Am. <u>Mil</u>, 30.VI.34;
         Fr. <u>V</u>, (209), 8.VI.34; <u>VoixCom</u>, (IV.25), 24.VI.34.

⌊340608(2)⌋   —: Arguments et ripostes.

Trans.: Fr. V, (209), 8.VI.34.

⌊Rédigé par LT. — PN.⌋

340610   CHETVERTYI INTERNATSIONAL I VOINA. (WAR AND THE FOURTH INTERNATIONAL),
340000(1).

Trans.: Am. 340700(1);

       Ch. 340000(21);

       Eng. ⌊400000(17)⌋;

       Fr. 340000(5); p.q. 680000(4): 240-1; p.q. V, (228), 15.XII.34;

       Ger. 340000(9); *⌊340000(22)⌋;

       Hol. ⌊340000(15)⌋; ⌊350000(20); p.q. Baan, (VI.11), 14.VII.34;

       Jap. 631130: 129-72;

       Sp. *⌊340000(13)⌋; IV Int, (I.5,8-13), III,IV-VIII.37;

       Ukr. RobVis, (II.23-III.3), 1.XII.34-1.II.35.

⌊Unsigned in all eds. See also ⌊340600(2)⌋. D350. ? T3632.⌋

⌊340616⌋   **Sympathizer: The foreign policy of the Soviet Union.**

Trans.: Am. Mil, 16.VI.34.

⌊Identical with an Eng. doc. signed G., On the new policy of the
CPFrance; not otherwise listed.⌋

340700(1)   —: WAR AND THE FOURTH INTERNATIONAL.

⌊Trans. Am. See 340610 for all trans., notes.⌋

340700(2)   Vidal: The League in face of the turn.

Trans.: Am. CLA, (16), IX.34;

⌊On entrist tactic in France. See further, 340700(3), 340922, 340806,
341216. V111.⌋

340700(3)   Vidal: The French League faced with a decisive turn.

Trans.: Am. CLA, (17), X.34;

       Fr. VoixCom, (IV.35), 2.IX.34.

⌊See 340700(2) for series. V112.⌋

⌊340700(4)⌋   Greetings to New International.

Trans.: Am. NI, VII.34.

*340700(5)   *RETRATO DEL NACIONAL-SOCIALISMO.

⌊Trans. Sp. See 330610 for all repr., trans.⌋

340710   —: Evolyutsiya sotsialisticheskoi partii (S.F.I.O.). (The evolution of the Socialist Party (S.F.I.O.).) (<u>BO</u>, (40), X.34)

Trans.: Am. <u>NI</u>, IX-X.34;

         Eng. <u>Red Flag</u>, (II.1), XI.34; <u>WIN</u>, VII-VIII.45;

         Fr. <u>V</u>, (218), 17.VIII.34; <u>VoixCom</u>, (IV.34), 26.VIII.34;

         Ger. <u>UWort</u>, (II.31), VIII.34.

⌊On France. See further 340800(3).⌋

340715   —: Bonapartizm i fashizm. (Bonapartism and fascism.) (<u>BO</u>, (40), X.34)

Trans.: Am. <u>NI</u>, VIII.34;

         Eng. 680900(1);

         Fr. <u>V</u>, (216), 3.VIII.34; <u>VoixCom</u>, (IV.32), 12.VIII.34;

         Ger. <u>UWort</u>, (II.27), VII.34;

         Ukr. <u>RobVis</u>, (II.18), 15.IX.34.

⌊V114.⌋

340800(3)   —: Put vykhoda: S.F.I.O. i S.F.I.C. (The way out: The S.F.I.O. and the S.F.I.C.) (<u>BO</u>, (40), X.34)

Trans.: Am. <u>NI</u>, IX-X.34;

         Eng. <u>WIN</u>, VII-VIII.45;

         Fr. 670306: 433-41; <u>V</u>, (220), IX.34;

         Ger. <u>UWort</u>, (II.33,34), IX, X.34;

         Hol. <u>NWeg</u>, (IX.10), X.34;

         Ukr. <u>RobVis</u>, (II.18), 15.IX.34.

⌊See also 340710.⌋

340806   Vidal: Summary of the discussion.

Trans.: Am, <u>CLA</u>, (17), X.34;

         Fr. <u>VoixCom</u>, (IV.38), 23.IX.34.

⌊See 340700(2) for series. V120.⌋

340808   ⌊Discussion with Doumanget, Aulas and Serret.⌋

⌊c. 670306: 441, fn.⌋

340810   Lettre à Maurice Doumanget.

Trans.: Fr. 670306: 442-7.

⌊On France.⌋

⌊340817(1)⌋   Bol'shevikam-lenintsam v SSSR. (To the Bolshevik-Leninists in the USSR.) (<u>BO</u>, (40), X.34)

Trans.: Am. <u>Mil</u>, 8.IX.34;

         Eng. <u>Red Flag</u>, (11), X.34;

         Fr. <u>V</u>, (218), 17.VIII.34; <u>VoixCom</u>, (IV.34), 26.VIII.34;

         Ger. <u>UWort</u>, (II.33), IX.34.

340817(2) If America should go communist.

Trans.: Am. 570900(1); 640800: 212-21; FI, III-IV.51; Liberty,
        23.III.35;

    Fr. [530000(5)]; [560000(5)]; 690900(2): 17-23;

    Jap. 681125: 223-32;

    Sp. 670000(5): 210-8;

    Swed. 691100(2): 189-97.

[T3665.]

340900(1) THE HISTORY OF THE RUSSIAN REVOLUTION.

[Trans. Eng. See 310000(1) for all repr., trans., notes. 1 vol.]

[340900(2)] G.Gourov: On our attempt to fuse with the Hennaut group.

Trans.: Am. ICL, (2), IX.34.

[On Belgium; ILOpp.]

[340900(3)] Gourov: A letter.

Trans.: Am. ICL, (2), IX.34.

[On Belgium; ILOpp.]

340922 Crux: Een voorstander neemt stelling in de Fransche discussie.

Trans.: Hol. NWeg, (IX.10), X.34.

[Identified from incomplete, unidentified Am. text signed Crux.]

341000(1) Où va la France?

Trans.: Am. 360000(11): 7-48; p.q. 650900: 267-77; 680612(2): 7-48;
        p.q. 690400(3): 17-20;

    Eng. 460000(13); 610600: 3-42; p.q. 620900; p.q. 640000(5):
        267-77; p.q. 640000(10): 267-77;

    Fr. 360000(6); 580900: 5-38; 670306: 448-75; p.q. 680000(4):
        passim; V, (226), 9.XI.34; VoixCom, (IV.46-8), 18.XI-
        2.XII.34;

    Ger. 360000(12): 5-29;

    Gr. 660000(10);

    Hol. p.q. Klassen(A), (I.3), 19.XII.36;

    It. 620000(20): 449-83; *680900(3); 681100: 485-523;

    Jap. 630430; 650430: 4-49;

    Sp. ¢ Octubre, (I.1,2), 1.X, XI.35.

[T3666.]

341000(2) On Birobidjan.

     Trans.: Am. 700700: 19.

     ⌊On Jewry in Soviet Union.⌋

341020 Ukrainskim tovarishcham v Kanadi. (To Ukrainian comrades in Canada.)

     Trans.: Ukr. RobVis, (II.23), 1.XII.34.

341101 Crux: To the International Secretariat and the leadership of the

     Belgian section.

     Trans.: Am. DocE; IntNews, (I.3), [X.35].

     [On entrist tactic, extended internationally.]

[341102] —: Objection et réponses. La milice du peuple.

     Trans.: Fr. 670306: 476–84; V, (225), 2.XI.34.

     ⌊Rédigé par LT. — PN.⌋

341109 See 341000(1).

[341200] Crux: Unity and the Youth.

     Trans.: Am. IntNews, (I.3), ⌊X.35⌋.

     [On Fr. youth and ILOpp. T3664.]

[341201] —: A propos du Bonapartisme. Le marxisme a ses avantages.

     Trans.: Fr. V, (227), 1.XII.34.

     ⌊Rédigé par LT. — PN.⌋

341216 Crux: Encore une fois sur notre tournant.

     Trans.: Fr. DocF.

     ⌊See 340700(2) for series.⌋

341228 Stalinskaya byurokratiya i ubiistvo Kirova. (The Stalin bureaucracy

     and the assassination of Kirov.) (BO, (41), I.35)

     Trans.: Am. 350200(1); 560501;

        Cz. *[360000(22)];

        Eng. MOSCOW TRIALS: 137–47;

        Fr. 350000(1); *350000(2); p.q. 680000(4): 320–1; VoixCom,

         (V.2,3), 13,20.I.35;

        Ger. 360000(23);

        Hol. ⌊350000(21)⌋;

        Ukr. 350000(24); RobVis, (III.4,5), 15.II, 1.III.35.

341230(1)   Obvintel´nyi akt. (The indictment.) (<u>BO</u>, (41), I.35)

Trans.: Am. 350200(1); 560501; <u>NMil</u>, 19.I.35;
Cz. *[360000(22)];
Eng. MOSCOW TRIALS: 148-50;
Fr. 350000(1); *350000(2); <u>V</u>, (229), 5.I.35; <u>VoixCom</u>, (V.1),
6.I.35;
Ger. 360000(23); <u>UWort</u>, (III.1), II.35;
Ukr. 350000(24); <u>RobVis</u>, (III.3), 1.II.35.

341230(2)   Press statement.

Trans.: Am. p.q. <u>NYTimes</u>, 13.I.35;
Eng. p.q. <u>ManGuard</u>, 1.I.35;
Fr. <u>VoixCom</u>, (V.1), 6.I.35;
Ger. <u>UWort</u>, (III.1), II.35;
Hol. <u>Baan</u>, (VI.37), 12.I.35.

[<u>NYTimes</u> from <u>Seven Days</u> [? <u>7 Dnei v illyustratsiyakh</u>, Paris].]

350000(1)   § LA BUREAUCRATIE STALINIENNE ET L'ASSASSINAT DE KIROV.
            <u>Trans.</u>: Fr, 350000(1); *350000(2);
                    Cz. *[360000(22)];
                    Ger. 360000(23.
            [5 entries.]

*350000(2) *LA BUREAUCRATIE STALINIENNE ET L'ASSASSINAT DE KIROV.
            [Trans. Fr. See 350000(1) for all repr., trans.]

350000(3)   CARTA AL PROLETARIADO FRANCES.
            [Trans. Sp. See 350610(1) for all repr., trans.]

350000(4)   THE DEFENCE OF TERRORISM.
            [Trans. Eng. nPref. 350110. See 200000(37) for all repr., trans.,
            notes.]

350000(5)   ---: DU PLAN DU CGT A LA CONQUÊTE DU POUVOIR.
            [Trans. Fr. See [350405(2)].]

350000(6)   L'ÉTAT OUVRIER: THERMIDOR ET BONAPARTISME.
            [Trans. Fr. See 350201 for all repr., trans.]

350000(8)   LETTRE OUVERTE AUX OUVRIERS FRANÇAIS.
            [Trans. Fr. See 350610(1) for all repr., trans.]

350000(9)   MITT LIV.
            [Trans. Nor. See 340000(4) for all trans., notes; Pref. 351001.]

350000(10) ON LENIN'S TESTAMENT.
            [Trans. Am. See 321231 for all repr., trans.]

350000(11) ONCE AGAIN: THE ILP.
            [Trans. Eng. See 351100(1) for all trans. Interview.]

350000(12) ROSA LUXEMBOURG ET LA IVe INTERNATIONALE.
            [Trans. Fr. See 350624(1) for all repr., trans.]

350000(13) STALIN BEGRAAFT DE 3e INTERNATIONALE.
            [Trans. Hol. See 350525(2) for all trans.]

[350000(14)] DE ARBEIDERSTAAT, THERMIDOR EN BONAPARTISME.
            [Trans. Hol. See 350201 for all repr., trans.]

[350000(15)]   ET FORSVAR FOR DEN RUSSISKE REVOLUTION.
               [Trans. Den. p.q. 321127.]

[350000(16)]   ENCORE UNE FOIS, OÙ VA LA FRANCE?
               [Trans. Fr. See [350328] for all repr., trans.]

[350000(17)]   THE ILP AND THE STRUGGLE FOR THE FOURTH INTERNATIONAL. THE MIDDLE OF
               THE ROAD.
               [Trans. Am. See 350918 for all trans.]

[350000(18)]   SECTARIANISM, CENTRISM AND THE FOURTH INTERNATIONAL.
               [Trans. Eng. See 351022 for all repr., trans.]

[350000(19)]   STALIN'S TREASON AND THE WORLD REVOLUTION. + Crux and others: FOR
               THE FOURTH INTERNATIONAL.
               [Trans. Eng. See 350610(1) and 350700(1) for all trans.]

[350000(20)]   —: DE VIERDE INTERNATIONALE EN DE OORLOG.
               [Trans. Hol. See 340610 for all repr., trans.]

[350000(21)]   DE ZAAK KIROV EN DE STALINISTISCHE BUREAUCRATIE.
               [Trans. Hol. See 341228 for all trans.]

*[350000(22)] *LA IV INTERNACIONAL Y LA U.R.S.S.
               [Trans. Sp. See 331001 for all trans.]

*[350000(23)] *EL ULTIMO PLATO PICANTE DEL COCINERO STALIN.
               [Trans. Sp. See 320301 for all trans.]

350000(24)   § STALINS'KA BYUROKRATIYA I UBIISTVO KIROVA. (THE STALIN BUREAUCRACY
               AND THE ASSASSINATION OF KIROV.)
               [Trans. Ukr. 4 items.]

350000(25)   ROBITNICHA DERZHAVA, TERMIDOR I BONAPARTIZM. + SHCHO DO PITANNYA PRO
               BONAPARTIZM. (THE WORKERS STATE: THERMIDOR AND BONAPARTISM. + ONCE
               MORE ON BONAPARTISM.)
               [Trans. Ukr. See 350201, 350300 for all trans.]

[350000(26)]   ON SOUTH AFRICAN PROBLEMS.
               [Trans. Eng. See 350420.]

350110   Pref. THE DEFENCE OF TERRORISM, 350000(4).

Trans.: Am. 610000(8); 630000(13); 690000(18);
            Ar. p.q. ⌊660000(3)⌋;
            Eng. 350000(4);
            Fr. 360000(1); p.q. 630608: 312-5;
            Jap. *620120; 640330(4): 21-33.
[T3669.]

350112   Neketorye itogi stalinskoi amal'gamy. (Some results of the Stalin
amalgam.) (BO, (42), II.35)
Trans.: Am. NMil, 9.II.35;
            Cz. *⌊360000(22)⌋;
            Fr. 350000(1); V, (230), 20.I.35;
            Ger. 360000(23);
            Ukr. 350000(24); RobVis, (III.6), 15.III.35.

350116   See 350118.

350117   See 350118.

350118   Delo Zinov'eva, Kameneva i dr. (The affair of Zinoviev, Kamenev and the
others.) (BO, (42), II.35)
Trans.: Cz. *⌊360000(22)⌋;
            Fr. 350000(1);
            Ger. 360000(23).

350126   L.T.: Vse stanovit'sya postepenno na svoe mesto. (Everything gradually
falls into its place.) (BO, (42), II.35)
Trans.: Cz. *⌊360000(22)⌋;
            Eng. p.q. THE CASE: 498; p.q. NOT GUILTY: 384;
            Fr. 350000(1); p.q. V, (231), 10.II.35;
            Ger. 360000(23);
            Hol. Baan, (VI.41), 9.II.35;
            Ukr. 350000(24); RobVis, (III.7), 1.IV.35.
[Letter to American friends.]

350130   --: Kuda stalinskaya byurokratiya vedet SSSR? (Where is the Stalin
bureaucracy leading the USSR?) (BO, (42), II.35)
Trans.: Am. NI, III.35;
            Fr. V, (234,235), 12,19.IV.35; ∅ VoixCom, (V.16,17), 21,28.IV.35;
            Ger. UWort, (III.2), III.35;
            Hol. Baan, (VI.44), 2.III.35;
            Ukr. RobVis, (III.8), 15.IV.35.
[V124.]

350200(1)   THE KIROV ASSASSINATION.

                 [Trans. Am. See 341228, 341230(1) for all repr., trans.]

⌊350200(2)⌋   Crux: Letter to Cannon.

                 Trans.: Am. WP, (1), 1935.

                 ⌊On ILOpp in USA.⌋

[350200(3)]   Crux: Zum London-Amsterdam Büro.

                 Trans.: Ger. DocH; UWort, (III.1), II.35.

                 [On a SAP thesis. V121.]

350201   Rabochee gosudarstvo, termidor i bonapartizm. (The workers state, thermidor and bonapartism.) (BO, (43), IV.35)

                 Trans.: Am. ISR, Summer 1956; NI, VII.35;

                      Cz. p.q. Jiskra, (III.4), IX.36;

                      Eng. ⌊610000(11)⌋; 680800(1): 38-64;

                      Fr. 350000(6); ⌊600000(12)⌋; p.q. 680000(4): passim; 690900(2): 27-42; p.q. QI(OSPE), (8-10), VI-VIII.44; p.q. V, (238), 10.V.35; VoixCom, (V.14), 7.IV.35;

                      Ger. ⌊360000(15)⌋; UWort, (III.4,6,7), V,VI,VII.35;

                      Hol. ⌊350000(14)⌋; Int(H), (VIII), V.65; (XI.12), 1968;

                      Hung. ⌊360000(19)⌋;

                      Jap. 631030: 94-119;

                      Ukr. 350000(25); RobVis, (III.11,12-13), 1.VI, 1.VII.35.

                 ⌊See further 350300(1).⌋

350207   Pages from a diary.

                 Trans.: 580000(4);

                      Am. 650900: 400-2;

                      Eng. 640000(5): 400-2; 640000(10): 400-2.

350208   Pages from a diary.

                 Trans.: 580000(4).

350209   Pages from a diary.

                 Trans.: 580000(4).

350210   L.T.: "Soviet democracy."

                 Trans.: Am. NMil, 30.III.35;

                      Fr. Lutte deC, (51-52), IV-VI.35;

                      Ger. UWort, (III.2), III.35;

                      Hol. Baan, (VI.43), 23.II.35;

++++

350210 ++++   Trans.: Ukr. RobVis, (III.5), 1.III.35.
                    [V126,127.]

350211   Pages from a diary.
                    Trans.: 580000(4).

350212   Pages from a diary.
                    Trans.: 580000(4).

350213   Pages from a diary.
                    Trans.: 580000(4).

350214   Pages from a diary.
                    Trans.: 580000(4).
                    [cf. 330813.]

350215   Pages from a diary.
                    Trans.: 580000(4);
                            Am.650900: 402-3;
                            Eng. 640000(5): 402-3; 640000(10): 402-3.

350216   Pages from a diary.
                    Trans.: 580000(4).

350217   Pages from a diary.
                    Trans.: 580000(4);
                            Am. 650900: 403-4;
                            Eng. 640000(5): 403-4; 640000(10): 403-4.

350218   Pages from a diary.
                    Trans.: 580000(4);
                            Fr. p.q. 680000(4): 309-10.

350220   Pages from a diary.
                    Trans.: 580000(4).

350226   Crux: Letter to Sneevliet.
                    Trans.: Am. WP, (1), 1935.
                    [On ILOpp. in Holland.]

350228   Crux: Centrist combinations and marxist tactics.
                    Trans.: Am. WP, (1), 1935.
                    [To Polish comrade V. V128.]

350300(1)   Eshche k voprosu o bonapartizme. (Again on the question of bonapartism.) (BO, (43), IV.35)

Trans.: Fr. 690900(2): 24-6; QI, (2), II.37; (8-10), 1944;
        Ger. ⌊360000(15)⌋;
        Hol. p.q. NFakkel, (I.14), 26.IV.35;
        Ukr. 350000(25).

⌊Information from the sphere of marxist terminology. See 350201. T3670.⌋

350302   Crux: Lettre au SI.

Trans.: Am. p.q. Doc C;
        Fr. LCB, IV.35.

[On Belgian section ILOpp.]

350305   Crux: Lettre aux camarades de la Chine.

Trans.: Fr. p.q. LCA, (1), 1.V.35;
        Ger. p.q. LKI, (2), VI.35.

350306   Pages from a diary.

Trans.: 580000(4).

350307   Pages from a diary.

Trans.: 580000(4).

350309   Pages from a diary.

Trans.: 580000(4).

350310   Pages from a diary.

Trans.: 580000(4).

350318   Pages from a diary.

Trans.: 580000(4).

350321   Pages from a diary.

Trans.: 580000(4);
        Am. p.q. 650900: 404;
        Eng. p.q. 640000(5): 404; p.q. 640000(10): 404.

350322   Pages from a diary.

Trans.: 580000(4).

350323(1)   Crux: The situation in the Stockholm Youth Bureau.
             Trans.: Am. SYL, XI.35.
             [On ILOpp youth.]

350323(2)   Pages from a diary.
             Trans.: 580000(4).

350325   Pages from a diary.
             Trans.: 580000(4);
                     Fr. p.q. 680000(4): 347-8.

350326   Pages from a diary.
             Trans.: 580000(4).

350327   Pages from a diary.
             Trans.: 580000(4);
                     Am. 650900: 404-6;
                     Eng. 640000(5): 404-6; 640000(10): 404-6.

[350328]   Encore une fois, Où va la France?
             Trans.: Am. 360000(11): 49-118; 680612: 49-118; NI, V.35;
                     Eng. 610600: 43-114;
                     Fr. [350000(16)]; 360000(6); 580900: 41-99; p.q. 680000(4):
                         passim; QI, II.69; V, (232), 28.III.35; ¢ VoixCom, (V.16,17),
                         21,28.IV.35;
                     Ger. 360000(12): 30-72;
                     Hol. p.q. De Int, (I.2), V.35;
                     Jap. *630430; 650430: 50-129.
             [Hol. gives pseudonym Opmerker. T3671.]

350329   Pages from a diary.
             Trans.: 580000(4).

350331(1)   Novaya petlya stalinskoi amal´gamy. (A new noose in the stalinist
             amalgam.) (BO, (43), IV.35)
             Trans.: Am. NMil, 4.V.35;
                     Fr. p.q. V, (234), 12.IV.35;
                     Ger. UWort, (III.3), IV.35;
                     Ukr. RobVis, (III.10), 15.V.35.
             [V130.]

350331(2)   Pages from a diary.

       <u>Trans</u>.: 580000(4).

[350400]   Al'fa: Zametki zhurnalista. (Notes of a journalist.) (<u>BO</u>, (43), IV.35)

       <u>Trans</u>.: Am. p.q. <u>NMil</u>, 15.VI.35;

           Eng. p.q. THE CASE: 533;

           Fr. <u>V</u>, (237), 3.V.35;

           Ger. <u>UWort</u>, (III.4), V.35;

           Hol. p.q. <u>NFakkel</u>, (I.16), 3.V.35;

           Ukr. <u>RobVis</u>, (III.10), 15.V.35.

       [On Red Army. V131.]

350402   Pages from a diary.

       <u>Trans</u>.: 580000(4);

           Am. p.q. 650900: 406;

           Eng. p.q. 640000(5): 406; p.q. 640000(10): 406.

350403   Pages from a diary.

       <u>Trans</u>.: 580000(4).

350404   Pages from a diary.

       <u>Trans</u>.: 580000(4);

           Am. p.q. 650900: 406-7;

           Eng. p.q. 640000(5): 406-7); p.q. 640000(10): 406-7.

350405(1)   Pages from a diary.

       <u>Trans</u>.: 580000(4);

           Am. p.q. 650900: 407;

           Eng. p.q. 640000(5): 407; p.q. 640000(10): 407.

[350405(2)] Du plan de la CGT.

       <u>Trans</u>.: Fr. 350000(5); 670306: 485-98; <u>V</u>, (233), 5.IV.35.

       [Speech by A.Bardin, delegate to National Congress CGT. Rédigé par

       LT. — PN.]

350407   Pages from a diary.

       <u>Trans</u>.: 580000(4).

350409   Pages from a diary.

       <u>Trans</u>.: 580000(4);

           Am. p.q. 650900: 408;

           Eng. p.q. 640000(5): 408; p.q. 640000(10): 408.

350410   Pages from a diary.
           Trans.: 580000(4);
                   Am. 650900: 408-11;
                   Eng. 640000(5): 408-11; 640000(10): 408-11.

350411   Pages from a diary.
           Trans.: 580000(4).

350414   Pages from a diary.
           Trans.: 580000(4).

350415   --: Die Lage in Frankreich und die Aufgaben der Bolschevistischen-
           Leninistischen Gruppe der SFIO.
           Trans.: Ger. LKI, (2), VI.35.

350420   L.T.: Zamechaniya po povodu tezisov Kommunisticheskoi Ligi Yuzhnoi
           Afrika. (Remarks on the theses of the Communist League of South
           Africa.) (BO, (44), VII.35)
           Trans.: Am. p.q. 670600: 61-3; p.q. 690400(2): 61-3; p.q. 700700: 61-3;
                       p.q. FI, XI.45; ISR, Fall 1966;
                   Eng. ⌊350000(26)⌋; Workers Voice, XI.44;
                   Fr. p.q. LCA, (5), X.35;
                   Ger. p.q. LKI, (4), VIII.35;
                   Hol. De Int, (I.7), X.35;
                   Jap. p.q. 681010: 113-5.
           ⌊T3672.⌋

350424   --: Centrist alchemy or marxism.
           Trans.: Am. NI, VII.35;
                   Fr. LCA, (2), 1.VI.35;
                   Ger. UWort, (III.5), V.35.
           [V133.]

⌊350426⌋   --: La trahison staliniste établie par la seule lecture de l'Humanité.
           Trans.: Am. NMil, 18.V.35;
                   Fr. V, (236), 26.IV.35.

350427   Pages from a diary.
           Trans.: 580000(4).

350429   Pages from a diary.
           Trans.: 580000(4).

350502   Pages from a diary.
        Trans.: 580000(4).

350504   Pages from a diary.
        Trans.: 580000(4).

350505   Pages from a diary.
        Trans.: 580000(4).

350508   Pages from a diary.
        Trans.: 580000(4);
           Am. p.q. 650900: 411;
           Eng. p.q. 640000(5): 411; p.q. 640000(10): 411.

350509   Pages from a diary.
        Trans.: 580000(4).

350510   Pages from a diary.
        Trans.: 580000(4).

350513   Pages from a diary.
        Trans.: 580000(4).

350514   Pages from a diary.
        Trans.: 580000(4).

350515   Pages from a diary.
        Trans.: 580000(4).

350516(1)   Pages from a diary.
        Trans.: 580000(4);
           Am. 650900: 411-2;
           Eng. 640000(5): 411-2; 640000(10): 411-2.

350516(2)   [(Incomplete) Article on the interrelation between physiological
        determination and the "autonomy" of thought.]
        [c. 350516(1).]

350517   Pages from a diary.
        Trans.: 580000(4).

350523   Pages from a diary.
        Trans.: 580000(4).

350525(1)   Pages from a diary.
                   Trans.: 580000(4).

350525(2)   —: Stalin has signed the death certificate of the 3rd International.
                   Trans.: Am.NMil, 8.VI.35;
                             Fr. V, (240), 25.V.35;
                             Ger. UWort, (III.6), VI.35;
                             Hol. 350000(13);
                             Ukr. RobVis, (III.12-13), 1.VII.35.
                   [Open letter to world proletariat.]

350526   Pages from a diary.
                   Trans.: 580000(4).

350601   Pages from a diary.
                   Trans.: 580000(4).

350606   Pages from a diary.
                   Trans.: 580000(4).

350607(1)   A.: K VII kongressu Kominterna. (The 7th Comintern Congress.)
                   (BO, (44), VII.35)
                   Trans.: Am. NMil, 27.VII.35;
                             Fr. Spartacus, (V.24), 17.VIII.35;
                             Ger. UWort, (III.9), VIII.35;
                             Hol. NFakkel, (I.57), 27.IX.35;
                             Ukr. RobVis, (III.7), 1.XI.35.

350607(2)   To the students of Edinburgh University.
                   Trans.: 580000(4);
                             Am. NMil, 29.VI.35;
                             Fr. Spartacus, (V.24), 17.VIII.35;
                             Ger. UWort, (III.8), VIII.35;
                             Ukr. RobVis, (III.2), 15.VIII.35.
                   [T3674.]

350607(3)   Telegram to Minister of Justice, Norway.
                   Trans.: Nor. Lie: 65.

350608   Pages from a diary.
                   Trans.: 580000(4).

350609 Pages from a diary.
 Trans.: 580000(4).

350610(1) Pis'mo frantsuzskim rabochim: Izmena Stalina i nezhdunarodnaya
 revolyutsiya. (Letter to the workers of France: Stalin's treachery
 and world revolution.) (BO, (44), VII.35)
 Trans.: Am. NI, VIII.35; NI(WP), I.45;
   Eng. ⌊350000(19)⌋; Spark, VIII.35;
   Fr. 350000(8); 670306: 501-12; p.q. 680000(4): 324; Combat, (1),
    15.I.36; Humbles, (XX.6), VI.35; Spartacus, (V.21),
    29.VI.35; V, (243), 21.VI.35; V, (519), V-VI.60;
   Ger. UWort, (III.7), VII.35;
   Hol. NFakkel, (I.31), 28.VI.35;
   Sp. 350000(3); Octubre, (I.1), 1.X.35;
   Ukr. RobVis, (III.1), 1.VIII.35.

350610(2) Crux: Letter to the International Secretariat.
 Trans.: Am. IntNews, (I.2), X.35; WP, (2), 7.IX.35;
   Fr. 670306: 513-5; p.q. Braun: 5-6.
 [On Fr. section ILOpp. T3675.]

350611 Second telegram to Minister of Justice, Norway.
 Trans.: Nor. Lie: 65.

350612 Telegram to Minister of State of Norway, Nygaardsveld.
 Trans.: Nor. Lie: 66.

350613 Crux: Letter to the International Secretariat.
 Trans.: Am. WP, (2), 7.IX.35.
 [On fusion of Bolshevik-Leninists with Navile group, in France. T3675.]

350617 Pages from a diary.
 Trans.: 580000(4).

350620 Pages from a diary.
 Trans.: 580000(4).

350624(1) Luxemburg and the Fourth International.
 Trans.: Am. NI, VIII.35;
   Fr. 350000(12); 700228: 249-53; V, (245), 21.VII.35;
    RÉVOLUTION ALLEMANDE;
   Ger. UWort, (III.8), VIII.35.
 ⌊T3677.⌋

350624(2)   Pages from a diary.
                   Trans.: 580000(4).

350626   Pages from a diary.
                   Trans.: 580000(4).

350629   Pages from a diary.
                   Trans.: 580000(4).

350700(1)   Crux i dr.: Za Chetvertyi Internatsional. (For the Fourth International.)
                   (BO, (44), VII.35)
                   Trans.: Am. FI, VIII.35; NMil, 3.VIII.35;
                           Eng. [350000(19)]; Spark, IX.35;
                           Fr. LCA, (3), VII.35; Spartacus, (V.24), 17.VIII.35; V, (247),
                               23.VIII.35;
                           Ger. UWort, (III.8), VIII.35;
                           Hol. NFakkel, (I.37), 19.VII.35;
                           Sp. Octubre, (I.1), 1.X.35;
                           Ukr. RobVis, (III.2), 15.VIII.35.
                   [Rédigé par LT. — PN. T3673.]

350701   Pages from a diary.
                   Trans.: 580000(4).

350703   Crux: Lettre à Rous.
                   Trans.: Fr. GBL, (9), XII.35; p.q. Braun: 41.
                   [On Fr. section ILOpp.]

350704   Pages from a diary.
                   Trans.: 580000(4).

350711   Lettre.
                   Trans.: Fr. p.q. GBL, (9), XII.35.
                   [On Fr. section ILOpp.]

350713   Pages from a diary.
                   Trans.: 580000(4);
                           Am. 650900: 412-3;
                           Eng. 640000(5): 412-3; 640000(10): 412-3.

350718   Crux: Aux Bolcheviques-Léninistes de Pologne.
                   Trans.: Fr. LCB, (3), IX.35.
                   [See further 350728.]

350722(1) Address to young Communists and marxists who wish to think. War and
the Fourth International.
> Trans.: Am. Young Marxist, Fall 1948; Young Spartacus, XI-XII.35;
> > Eng. Spark, X.35;
> > > Fr. 670306: 516-20; Spartacus, (V.30), 19.X.35; V, (247),
> > > > 23.VIII.35;
> > > Ukr. RobVis, (III.3), 1.IX.35.

[T3682,3683.]

350722(2) Lettre.
> Trans.: Fr. p.q. GBL, (9), XII.35.

[On Fr. section ILOpp.]

350726(1) Interview.
> Trans.: Am. p.q. NYTimes, 27.VII.35;
> > Nor. Arbeiderbladet, (180), 26.VII.35.

350726(2) Crux: Lettre à Naville.
> Trans.: Fr. p.q. Braun: 41.

350728 Crux: Lettre aux Bolcheviques-Léninistes de Pologne.
> Trans.: Fr. LCB, (3), IX.35.

[See 350718.]

350729 L.T.: Who defends Russia? Who helps Hitler?
> Trans.: Am. NI, X.35;
> > Fr. ActSocRév, (III.35), 31.VIII.35; LCA, (4), 1.IX.35;
> > Ger. UWort, (III.9), IX.35;
> > Hol. De Int, (I.5), VIII.35;
> > Sp. Octubre, (I.2), XI.35.

[T3685,3686.]

360730(1) A propos d'expulsions.
> Trans.: Fr. GBL, (9), XII.35.

[On Fr. section of ILOpp.]

350730(2) Pages from a diary.
> Trans.: 580000(4).

350730(3) Crux: Letter to cde. Rous.
> Trans.: Am. WP, (2), 7.IX.35;
> > Fr. p.q. Braun: 9,12.

[On Fr. section ILOpp.]

350730(4) Crux: Télégram.
Trans.: Fr. Braun: 7.
[Fr. section ILOpp.]

350801 Lettre.
Trans.: Fr. GBL, (9), XII.35.
[Fr. section ILOpp.]

350807 "Labels" and "Numbers".
Trans.: Am. NMil, 7.IX.35;
Fr. 670306: 521-6; Spartacus, (V.26), 7.IX.35; V, (247),
23.VIII.35.
[On France. To Pivert. V140,141.]

350809 [Interview with Harold Isaacs.]
Trans.: Ch. 470427: 331-4.

350810 Crux: Lettre à Rous.
Trans.: Fr. p.q. Braun: 9,13,16; p.q. LA CRISE.II: 51.
[Fr. section ILOpp.]

350811(1) Pref., P.J.Schmidt, SUR LES RELATIONS DU RSAP(Hollande) AVEC LA LCI
ET LE BUREAU D'AMSTERDAM.
Trans.: Fr. LCA, (4), 1.IX.35;
Ger. UWort, (III.9), IX.35.

350811(2) Letter; on French youth.
Trans.: Am. WP, (2), 7.IX.35;
Fr. p.q. GBL, (9), XII.35; p.q. Braun: 7-8.
[T3687.]

350811(4) Letter to National Committee, Workers Party, USA.
Trans.: Am. WP, (2), 7.IX.35;
Fr. LCB, (3), IX.35.

350812 Letter to National Committee, Workers Party, USA.
Trans.: Am. IIB, IX.35; WP, (2), 7.IX.35;
Fr. LCB, (3), IX.35.

350813 See 350809.

350819   The Church struggle under fascism.

Trans.: Am. p.q. NI(WP), IX.46.

[From letter to German International Communists.]

350823(1)   L.T.: Likvidatsionnyi Kongress III Internatsionala. (The liquidation

Congress of the Comintern.) (BO, (46), XII.35)

[T3689,3690.]

350823(2)   Crux: A la rédaction de l'Action Socialiste Révolutionnaire.

Trans.: Fr. LCA, (4), 1.IX.35;

        Ger. LKI, (5), X.35.

350823(3)   Crux: Lettre à Schmidt.

Trans.: Fr. p.q. Braun: 37.

350829   L.T.: Na sud rabochikh organizatsii! Protiv vsekh vidov gangsterizma

v rabochem dvizhenii. (To the judgment seat of workers organizations!

Against all kinds of gangsterism in the working-class movement.)

(BO, (45), IX.35)

Trans.: Am. Mil, 5.X.35.

[On the murder of the Italian socialist Montanari. T3691, 3692.]

[350900(1)]   Al´fa: Kak oni pishut istoriya i biografiya. (How history and

biography are written.) (BO, (45), IX.35)

Trans.: Am. 690700(1): 20-4; NMil, 12.X.35;

       Ger. UWort, (III.10), X.35.

[Stalin on Engels' anniversary. T3695,3696.]

350900(2)   Lettre à Charleroi.

Trans.: Fr. LCB, 1935.

[Belgian section ILOpp.]

[350900(3)]   Ot redaktsii Byulletenya. (From the Ed. Board of the Bulletin.)

(BO, (45), IX.35)

Trans.: Fr. LCA, (5), X.35.

[T3693,3694.]

350900(4)   Parabellum: "Questions of the Italo-Ethiopian War."

Trans.: Am. NI, X.35; p.q. World Outlook, (VI.11), 22.III.68.

350906   Alternative for 350907(2).

350907(1) Lettre.
Trans.: Fr. p.q. GBL, (9), XII.35.
⌊On Fr. section ILOpp.⌋

350907(2) --: Pora organizovat pomoshch revolyutsioneram-internatsionalistam!
(The revolutionary-internationalists need help!) (BO, (45), IX.35)
Trans.: Am. NMil, 28.IX.35;
        Fr. Spartacus, (V.30), 19.X.35; V, (249), 11.X.35;
        Ger. UWort, (III.10), X.35;
        Sp. IV Int, (I.1), 3.IX.36.
⌊T3701,T3702.⌋

350907(3) See 350914.

350908 Pages from a diary.
Trans.: 580000(4).

350913 Crux: Lettre à Van.
Trans.: Fr. p.q. Braun: 11,13,17,37.
⌊On Fr. section ILOpp.⌋

350914 Po povodu VII Kongressa Kominterna. (On the 7th Congress Comintern.)
(BO, (45), IX.35)
Trans.: Am. NI, X.35;
        Fr. ActSocRev, (III.51), 22.XII.35; LCA, (5), X.35; p.q. V,
            (251), 8.XI.35;
        Hol. NFakkel, (I.57,60), 27.IX, 8.X.35;
        Sp. Octubre, (I.2), XI.35.
⌊2 articles; see 350907(3). T3699,T3700.⌋

350915 Crux: Lettre à Rous.
Trans.: Fr. p.q. Braun: 17.
⌊On Fr. section ILOpp.⌋

350916 Crux: Lettre à Rous.
Trans.: Fr. p.q. Braun: 13-4,17,18,21.
⌊On Fr. section ILOpp.⌋

350918 The ILP and the Fourth International. The Middle of the Road.
Trans.: Am. ⌊350000(17)⌋; NI, XII.35;
        Eng. 420000(2); 590700: 1-20; 700800(2): 1-14; Controversy, XII.35
            WIN, XII.41; p.q. Workers' Fight(M/r), (7), VI.68;
        Fr. LCA, (6), XII.35; p.q. V, (252), 20.XI.35;   ++++

350918   ++++   <u>Trans</u>.: Ger. <u>UWort</u>, (IV.3,4), II,II.36;

                   Hol. <u>De Int</u>, (I.8), XI.35;

                   Jap. 631130: 173-95;

                   Sin. p.q. 510400.

         ⌊PS 351020. T3703,3704.⌉

350926   —: Terror byurokraticheskogo samosokhraneniya. (The terror of bureaucratic self-preservation.) (<u>BO</u>, (45), IX.35)

         <u>Trans</u>.: Am. <u>NMil</u>, 2.XI.35;

                   Fr. <u>LCA</u>, (5), X.35;

                   Ger. <u>UWort</u>, (III.1), XI.35;

                   Ukr. <u>RobVis</u>, (III.6), 15.X.35.

         ⌊T3697,3698.⌉

351001   Pref. MITT LIV, 350000(9).

         ⌊Trans. Nor. See 300000(1) for full text of book. T3706,3707.⌉

351015   Engels' letter to Kautsky.

         <u>Trans</u>.: Am. 690700(1): 3-19; <u>NI</u>, VI.36.

         ⌊T3709,3710.⌉

351016   Lettre au camarade Theo van Driesten.

         <u>Trans</u>.: Fr. <u>LCA</u>, (6), XII.35; <u>LCB</u>, (4), XI.35-I.36;

                   Ger. <u>RoodGard</u>, (1), X-XI.35;

                   Hol. <u>RoodGard</u>, (1), X-XI.35.

         ⌊On ILOpp section in Holland. Ger. is photostat reproduction. T3714.⌉

351020   PS, The ILP and the Fourth International, 350918.

         <u>Trans</u>.: Fr. <u>LCA</u>, (6), XII.35.

         ⌊T3711.⌉

351022   Sectarianism, centrism and the Fourth International.

         <u>Trans</u>.: Am. <u>NMil</u>, 4.I.36;

                   Eng. ⌊350000(18)⌉; 450000(8); 651200;

                   Fr. <u>LCA</u>, (6), XII.35;

                   Ukr. <u>RobVis</u>, (III.8), 1.XII.35.

         ⌊T3712,3713.⌉

351024   Lettre à Molinier.

         <u>Trans</u>.: Fr. p.q. LA CRISE.II: 41.

         ⌊On Fr. section ILOpp.⌉

351026 Lettre au camarade van Driesten.

    Trans.: Fr. LCB, (4), XI.35-I.36.

    [On Fr. section ILOpp.]

351031 Romen Rollan vypolnyaet poruchenie. (Romain Rolland executes an

    assignment.) (BO, (46), XII.35)

    Trans.: Am. NI, XII.35;

      Fr. 610000(7); Humbles, (XX.12), XII.35; Spartacus, (V.34),

       14.XII.35; V, (252), 20.XI.35;

      Ger. UWort, (III.12), XII.35;

      Hol. NFakkel, (I.74), 26.XI.35;

      Ukr. RobVis, (IV.2), 15.I.36.

    [On a French defence of stalinism. T3715,3716.]

351100(1) Once again the ILP.

    Trans.: Am. NI, II.36;

      Eng. 350000(11); 441216; 590700: 21-34; 700800(2): 16-24;

      Jap. 631130: 197-215.

    [Interview with Robertson. T3740.]

351100(2) Al'fa: Mastityi Smerdyakov. (A venerable Smerdyakov.) (BO, (47), I.36)

    [Ironical reference to character in Dostoevsky, THE BROTHERS KARAMAZOV.

    T3717,3718.]

351104(1) Lessons of October.

    Trans.: Am. NMil, 30.XI.35;

      Fr. Rév, (II.16,17), XII,7.XII.35;

      Hol. De Int, (I.9), XII.35.

    [T3719,3720.]

351104(2) Crux: Au SI de la LCI(BL).

    Trans.: Fr. LCB, (4), XI.35-I.36; p.q. Braun: 44,45.

    [On Fr. section ILOpp.]

351107(1) Pref. Zeller, THE REVOLUTIONARY ROAD FOR SOCIALISTS.

    Trans.: Am. p.q. NMil, 30.XI.35; Zeller;

      Fr. 670306: 527-34; Rév, (IV.40), 15.IV.37;

      Ger. p.q. IJI, (II.2), III.36.

    [T3721,3722.]

351107(2)   Edouard Herriot: Politician of the golden mean.

Trans.: Am. FI, XII.41.

⌊T3723,3724.⌋

351112   Pochemu Stalin pobedil oppozitsiyu? (How did Stalin triumph over
the Opposition?) (BO, (46), XII.35)

Trans.: Fr. LOuv(Fr), (9,10), 22.VIII, 5.IX.36;

Ger, ⌊360000(15)⌋;

Heb. *370000(5);

Hol. RodeOkt, (I.10), X.36;

Hung. ⌊360000(19)⌋;

Sp. ⊄ IV Int, (I.2), 15.IX.36; p.q. POUM, (I.3), 9.IX.36;

Tribuna Socialista, (4), IV.63;

Ukr. RobVis, (IV.1), 1.I.36.

⌊T3725,3726.⌋

351113   Crux: Lettre à Rous.

Trans.: Fr. LCB, (4), XI.35-I.36; p.q. Braun: 45.

⌊On Fr. section ILOpp.⌋

351117   Crux: Lettre à Zeller.

Trans.: Fr. p.q. Braun: 31.

⌊On Fr. section ILOpp.⌋

351118   Crux: Letter to Vereecken.

Trans.: Am. WP, (3), 12.II.36; DocC;

Fr. GBL, (9), XII.35.

⌊T3688.⌋

351121   Crux: Lettre au Politbureau GB-L.

Trans.: Fr. GBL, (9), XII.35; p.q. Braun: 34.

⌊On Fr. section ILOpp.⌋

351125   Lettre au BP du GBL.

Trans.: Fr. GBL, (9), XII.35; p.q. Braun: 31,35.

⌊On Fr. section ILOpp.⌋

351126(1)   For Committees of Action not People's Front.

Trans.: Am. IP, (VI.21), 3.VI.68; NMil, 14.XII.35; Vanguard, 7.I.36;

Eng. 610600: 115-21;

Fr. 360000(6); 360000(7); 580900: 103-8; 670306: 535-41; p.q.

QI, (30), VI.68; II.69; V, (253), 26.XI.35;   ++++

351126(1)   ++++   Trans.: Ger. 360000(12): 85-8; UWort, (IV.1), I.36;
                           Gr. Diethnistes, (15), III.66;
                           Hol. De Int, (I.9), XII.35;
                           Jap. *630430; 650430: 130-6.
                [On France. T3728,3729.]

351126(2)   Crux: Télégramme à Rous.
                Trans.: Fr. Braun: 35.

351126(3)   Lettre à Theo van Driesten.
                Trans.: Fr. LCB, (4), XI.35-I.36.
                [On Fr. section ILOpp.]

351126(4)   Redaktsii Robitnichi Visti. (To the Ed. Board Robitnichi Visti.)
                Trans.: Ukr. RobVis, (III.9), 15.XII.35.
                [Organ of Canadian-Ukrainian speaking ILOpp.]

351128(1)   Crux: Lettre au SI.
                [c. Braun: 35.]

351128(2)   Crux: Déclaration.
                Trans.: Fr. Braun: 36.
                [Disassociating from La Commune.]

351128(3)   Crux: Lettre à Naville.
                Trans.: Fr. p.q. Braun: 39.
                [On Fr. section ILOpp.]

351129(1)   Crux: Lettre au B.P. GB-L/ à Rous.
                Trans.: Fr. GBL, (9), XII.35; p.q. Braun: 51.
                [On Fr. section ILOpp.]

351129(2)   Crux: Télégramme.
                Trans.: Fr. Braun: 36.
                [On Fr. section ILOpp.]

351130   Crux: Letter to members, Groupe Bolchevik-Léniniste.
                Trans.: Am. WP, (3), 12.II.36;
                           Fr. p.q. Braun: 43; LA CRISE.I: 75-6.
                [On Fr. section ILOpp.]

351203(1)   Crux: Lettre au CC GB-L.
                Trans.: Fr. GBL, (10), 13.XII.35; p.q. Braun: 30,37; LA CRISE.I: 75-6.
                [On Fr. section ILOpp.]

351203(2)   Crux: Résolution au SI.

Trans.: Fr. Braun: 36.

[On Fr. section ILOpp.]

351203(3)   Crux: Lettre au SI.

Trans.: Fr. p.q. Braun: 38; LA CRISE.I: 78-9.

[On Fr. section ILOpp.]

351204   Crux: Lettre aux camarades.

Trans.: Fr. GBL, (10), 13.XII.35; p.q. Braun: 32-3,39; LA CRISE.I: 79-81.

[On Fr. section ILOpp.]

351205   Crux: Lettre au BP GB-L.

Trans.: Fr. GBL, (10), 13.XII.35; p.q. Braun: 40.

[On Fr. section ILOpp.]

351206   L.T.: Lettre au C.C.

Trans.: Fr. GBL, (10), 13.XII.35.

[On Fr. section ILOpp.]

351209   Lettre à la Rédaction, Révolution.

Trans.: Fr. GBL, (10), 13.XII.35; LA CRISE.I: 76-8.

[On Fr. section ILOpp.]

351212(1)   Letter to Scheflo.

Trans.: Eng. p.q. NOT GUILTY: 189.

[On ILOpp.]

351212(2)   Alternative for 351209.

351213(1)   [Letter to Politbureau, GB-L.]

[c. NOT GUILTY: 189. On Fr. section ILOpp.]

351213(2)   [Letter to Biline.]

[c. NOT GUILTY: 189. On Fr. section ILOpp.]

351216   Lettre au BP, GB-L.

Trans.: Fr. p.q. Braun: 40; LA CRISE.I: 71-4.

[On Fr. section ILOpp.]

351220   Mise au point adressée au journal La Commune.

Trans.: Fr. V, (254), 27.XII.35.

[On Fr. section ILOpp.]

351226   Crux: Lettre à Rous.
              Trans.: Fr. p.q. Braun: 20.
              [On Fr. section ILOpp.]

351227   [Letter to Lyova [i.e. Leon Sedov].]
              [c. Deutscher, PO: 240.]

351228   Bemerkungen zur Dokumentensammlung Leo Trotzki's aus den Jahren
              1917-1923.
              Trans.: Ger. 640000(1): vii.

351230   Crux: Leçons de l'entrée dans la S.F.I.O.
              Trans.: Fr. p.q. LCB, (4), XI.35-I.36; p.q. Braun: 4.
              [On Fr. section ILOpp.]

360000(1)   DÉFENSE DU TERRORISME.
             [Trans. Fr. See 200000(37) for all repr., trans., notes; 350110;
             nPref. 360328.]

360000(2)   GESCHIEDENIS DER RUSSISCHE REVOLUTIE.
             [Trans. Hol. See 310000(1) for all trans., notes. 5 vol.]

360000(3)   THE HISTORY OF THE RUSSIAN REVOLUTION.
             [Trans. Am. See 310000(1) for all repr., trans., notes. 1 vol.]

360000(4)   LA NOUVELLE CONSTITUTION DE L'URSS.
             [Trans. Fr. See 360416 for all repr., trans.]

360000(6)   § OÙ VA LA FRANCE?
             Trans.: Am. 360000(11); p.q. 640800: 188-92; 680612(2);
                     Eng. p.q. 610600;
                     Fr. 360000(6); p.q. 360000(7); 580900; QI, II.69;
                     Ger. 360000(12);
                     Hol. *[390000(6)];
                     Jap. *630430; 650430: 1-158;
                     Sp. p.q. 670000(5): 181-9;
                     Swed. p.q. 691100(2): 162-70.
             [Pref. 360610. Other trans. see separate entries. Am. trans. lacks
             some items.]

360000(7)   POUR COMBATTRE LE FASCISME, IL FAUT UNE PUISSANTE MILICE OUVRIÈRE.
             [Trans. Fr. See 351126(1) for all repr., trans., notes.]

*360000(8)   *STORIA DELLA RIVOLUZIONE RUSSA.
             [Trans. It. See 310000(1) for all repr., trans., notes.]

360000(9)   VERRATENE REVOLUTION.
             [Trans. Ger. See 361013 for all repr., trans., notes.]

360000(10)   VIE DE LÉNINE: JEUNESSE.
             Trans.: Am. p.q. 650900: 325-37; p.q. FI, VII-VIII.50;
                     Eng. p.q. 640000(5): 325-37; p.q. 640000(10): 325-37;
                     Fr. 360000(10); p.q. Rév, (VI.55), I.39;
                     Ger. 690000(5);
                     Sp. *490000(2).

360000(11)   § WHITHER FRANCE?
             [Trans. Am. See 360000(6) for all repr., trans., notes.]

360000(12)　　§ WOHIN GEHT FRANKREICH?

[Trans. Ger. See 360000(6) for all trans., notes.]

*360000(13)　　*ZRAZENÁ REVOLUCE.

[Trans. Cz. See 361013 for all trans., notes.]

[360000(15)]　　§ ARBEIDERSTAAT, THERMIDOR UND BONAPARTISMUS.

[Trans. Ger. See 350201, 350300, 351112, 360111 for all repr., trans.]

[360000(17)]　　& others: THE NEW REVOLUTIONARY UPSURGE AND THE TASKS OF THE FOURTH
INTERNATIONAL.

[Trans. Eng. See 360700(1) for all trans.]

[360000(18)]　　DE NIEUWE GRONDWET VAN DE SOWJET UNIE.

[Trans. Hol. See 360416 for all repr., trans.]

[360000(19)]　　§ SZTALIN ROMBLÁSBA VISZI A SZOVJETUNIOT!

[Trans. Hung. See 351112, 360823(2), 360827, 350201 for all trans.]

360000(20)　　AEVI MÍN.

[Trans. Ice. Greatly abgd. trans from Nor. 350000(9). See 300000(1)
for full text, trans., notes.]

*[360000(22)]　　*PROCESY PROTI "TERORISTUM" V SSSR.

[Trans. Cz. See 360000(23) for possible contents.]

360000(23)　　§ DIE "TERRORISTEN"-PROZESSE IN DER U.S.S.R.

[Trans. Ger. See 350000(1), 360823(2), 360827 for all trans.]

*360000(24)　　*LA NOUVELLE CONSTITUTION DE L'URSS.

[Trans. Fr. See 360416 for all repr., trans.]

[360000(25)]　　AN OPEN LETTER TO AN ENGLISH COMRADE.

[Trans. Eng. See 360403 for all trans. On ILP.]

360000(27)　　MI VIDA.

[Trans. Sp. See 300000(1) for all repr., trans., notes. 5 vol.]

360101　　The class nature of the Soviet State.

Trans.: Am. NMil, 6.VI.36;

Fr. BIP, 2-3.V.36; Rév, (III.31), 22.V.36;

Ger. BIJ, 10.XI.[36].

360104   Crux: Lettre au CC du GB—L.

Trans.: Fr. p.q. Braun: 54.

[On Fr. section ILOpp.]

360107   Crux: Lettre à D.

Trans.: Fr. p.q. Braun: 55.

[On Fr. section ILOpp.]

360110   Al'fa: Zametki zhurnalista. (Notes of a journalist.) (BO, (48), II.36)

Trans.: Am. NI, II.36;

Fr. BIP, 2/3.V.36;

Ger. UWort, (IV.3), II.36; (IV.11), VI.36;

Ukr. RobVis, (IV.5,6), 1,15.III.36.

[T3892,3893.]

360111   —: Sovetskaya sektsiya IV Internatsionala. (The Soviet section of the 4th International.) (BO, (48), II.36)

Trans.: Am. NMil, 15.II.36;

Fr. Rév, (III.25), 28.II.36;

Ger. [360000(15)]; UWort, (IV.5), III.36;

Hol. RodeOkt, (I.1,2), I,II.36;

Ukr. RobVis, (IV.6), 15.III.36.

[See further 360400(2). Authorship from 361211. T3894,3895.]

360113   Karakteristiek der Colijnpolitiek.

Trans.: Hol. p.q. NFakkel, (III.40), 1.X.37.

[On Holland.]

360114   Lettre à D.

Trans.: Fr. p.q. Braun: 54,55,56.

[On Fr. section ILOpp.]

360115(1)   Revolyutsionnye plenniki Stalina i mirovoi rabochii klass. (Stalin's revolutionist prisoners and the world working class.) (BO, (48), II.36)

Trans.: Am. NMil, 1.II.36;

Eng. Spark, IV.36;

Fr. BIP, 2/3.V.36; Spartacus, (VI.11), 30.V.36;

Ger. UWort, (IV.4), I^1.36;

Ukr. RobVis, (IV.5), 1.III.36.

[T3896,3897.]

360116   See 360416.

360122   Alternative for 360123.

360123   The treachery of the Spanish POUM.
                Trans.: Am. NMil, 15.II.36;
                        Fr. LCA, (7-8), V.36; LCI, (7-8), V.36; LA RÉVOLUTION
                            ESPAGNOLE: 96-8;
                        Ger. UWort, (IV.4), II.36.
                [T3898,3899.]

360124(1)   L.T.: Confidential letter to Cannon and Shachtman.
                Trans.: Am. Class Struggle(NY), (VI.3-4), VIII.36; p.q. Venkataramani.
                [On Am. section ILOpp.]

360124(2)   [Telegram to Rose Karsen.]
                Trans.: Am.Venkataramani.
                [Quoted in 360124(1). On Am. section ILOpp.]

360128(1)   Denial to Associated Press of Daily Worker(USA) lies.
                Trans.: Am. NMil, 15.II.36;
                        Ukr. RobVis, (IV.5), 1.III.36.
                [T3900.]

360128(2)   Cable to Militant hits Hearst lies.
                Trans.: Am. NMil, 1.II.36.
                [T3900.]

360130   The Stalin frame-up mill at work.
                Trans.: Am. NMil, 22.II.36.
                [Letter to Scheflo.]

360131   Crux: Lettre à Rous.
                Trans.: Fr. p.q. Braun: 56.
                [On Fr. section ILOpp.]

360227   Statement to Associated Press.
                Trans.: Am. NYTimes, 28.II.36.
                [On Soviet regime.]

360304   Lettre à Fischer.
                Trans.: Fr. p.q. Braun: 50,56.
                [On Fr. section ILOpp.]

360309   Letter to Cannon.

Trans.: Am. p.q. Venkataramani.

[On Am. section ILOpp.]

360316   Crux: Letter à un camarade belge.

Trans.: Fr. p.q. Braun: 12.

[On Fr. section ILOpp.]

360318   Zayavlenie i otkroveniya Stalina. (Stalin's declarations and
revelations.) (BO, (49), IV.36)

Trans.: Am. NMil, 4.IV.36;

Cz. Jiskra, (III.2), V.36;

Eng. Red Flag, (1), V.36;

Fr. ActSocRév, (IV.14), 4.IV.36; Rév, (III.27), 27.III.36;

Ger. UWort, (IV.8), IV.36;

Hol. NFakkel, (II.97), 10.IV.36.

[On Stalin-Howard interview. T3903.]

360319   See [360400(3)].

360321   Po povodu knigi Al'freda Rosmera, RABOCHEE DVIZHENIE VO VREMYA VOINY.
(Alfred Rosmer's book, LE MOUVEMENT OUVRIER PENDANT LA GUERRE.)
(BO, (50), V.36)

Trans.: Am. NI, VI.36;

Fr. Rév, (III.30), 15.V.36;

Ger. UWort, (IV.8), IV.36.

[Review. T3906.]

360325   L.T.: Plan fizicheskogo istrebleniya bolsh.-lenintsev. (The Plan for
the physical extermination of the Bolshevik-Leninists.) (BO, (50), V.36)

Trans.: Am. NMil, 16.V.36;

Fr. BIP, 2/3.V.36;

Ger. UWort, (IV.10), V.36;

Hol. RevSoc, (II), 1936;

Ukr. RobVis, (IV.11), 15.VI.36.

[T3907,3908.]

360327   Lettre à Dauge.

Trans.: Fr. GBL, (15), 10.V.36.

[ILOpp section in Belgium.]

360328   Frantsiya na povorote. (France at the turning-point.) (BO, (50), V.36)

         Trans.: Am. 360000(11): 119-39; 610000(8); 630000(13); p.q. 640800:
                 183-92; 680612(2): 119-39; NMil, 25.IV, 2,9.V.36;

            Ar. 640000(8);

            Eng. 610600: 122-41; Red Flag, (2), VI-VII.36;

            Fr. 360000(1); 360000(6); 580900: 111-27; 630608: 286-311;
                 670306: 555-70; p.q. 680000(4): 349-50; ActSocRev, (IV.22,23),
                 30.V, 6.VI.36; Commune, (25), 22.V.36; QI, II.69;

            Ger. 360000(12): 73-84;

            Hol. RodeOkt, (I.6), VI.36;

            Jap. *620120; 640330(4): 1-20; p.q. 681125: 191-201;

            Sp. p.q. 670000(5): 181-9;

            Swed. p.q. 691100(2): 162-70.

         [Pref. 2nd ed. 360000(1). T3909-11.]

360400(1)   THE HISTORY OF THE RUSSIAN REVOLUTION.

         [Trans.Eng. See 310000(1) for all repr., trans., notes.]

[360400(2)]   L.T.: Eshche o sovetskoi sektsii IV Internatsionala. (Once again, on

         the Soviet section of the Fourth International.) (BO, (49), IV.36)

         Trans.: Am. NMil, 2.V.36;

            Fr. BIP, 2/3.V.36;

            Ger. UWort, (IV.9), V.36;

            Hol. RodeOkt, (I.10), X.36.

         [See 360111.]

[360400(3)]   Al'fa: "Tuda, otkuda net vozvrata." Zakas Stalina Dem'yanu Bednomu.

         ("The point of no return." Stalin's order to Demyan Byedny.)

         (BO, (49), IV.36)

         Trans.: Am. NMil, 11.IV.36;

            Ger. UWort, (IV.8), IV.36.

         [T3904,3905.]

360403   Open letter to an English comrade.

         Trans.: Eng. [360000(25)];

            Fr. LCA, (7-8), V.36; LCI, (7-8), V.36;

            Ger. UWort, (IV.9), V.36.

         [Reply to an article in New Leader(Ln). T3912.]

360412   Tasks of the Fourth International.

<u>Trans</u>.: Am. <u>NI</u>, IV.39; <u>NMil</u>, 2.V.36;

       Fr. <u>LCA</u>, (7-8), V.36; <u>LCI</u>, (7-8), V.36; LA RÉVOLUTION ESPAGNOLE: 101-3;

       Ger. <u>UWort</u>, (IV.9), V.36;

       Hol. <u>RevSoc</u>, (II.5,6), V,VI.36.

[On Spain. R3913.]

360416   —: Novaya konstitutsiya SSSR. (The new constitution of the USSR.) (<u>BO</u>, (50), V.36)

<u>Trans</u>.: Am. <u>NMil</u>, 9.V.36;

       Eng. <u>Spark</u>, II.37;

       Fr. 360000(4); *360000(24); p.q. 680000(4): 145-6; <u>ActSocRév</u>, (IV.25,26), 20,27.VI.36; p.q. <u>Spartacus</u>, (VI.11), 30.V.36;

       Ger. <u>UWort</u>, (IV.10), V.36;

       Hol. [360000(18)]; <u>RodeOkt</u>, (I.5), V.36;

       Sp. 360700(2);

       Ukr. <u>RobVis</u>, (IV.10,11), 1,15.VI.36.

[T3916,3917.]

360422   On dictators and the heights of Oslo.

<u>Trans</u>.: Am. <u>NI</u>, VI.36;

       Eng. 590700: 35-8; 700800(2): 25-7;

       Fr. <u>GBL</u>, (15), 10.V.36; <u>LCA</u>, (7-8), V.36;

       Ger. <u>UWort</u>, (IV.10), V.36;

       Jap. 631130: 216-20.

[On ILOpp. T3920,3921.]

360426   [Letter to Victor Serge.]

[c. 670306: 546 f.n.]

360427   Brief aan B.Spanjer.

<u>Trans</u>.: Ger. <u>Kompas</u>, I.52.

[ILOpp youth.]

360429   [Letter to Victor Serge.]

<u>Trans</u>.: Eng. p.q. Deutscher, PO: 270.

360500(1)   § THE THIRD INTERNATIONAL AFTER LENIN.

[Trans. Am. See 301100(1) for all repr., trans., notes.]

[360500(2)]   L.T.: Samye ostrye blyuda eshche vperedi! (The spiciest dishes are
              still to come!) (BO, (50), V.36)
              Trans.: Fr. p.q. Sedov: 21;
                      Ger. UWort, (IV.10), V.36.

[360500(3)]   A.: Po stol´tsam Pravdy. (In the columns of Pravda.) (BO, (50), V.36)
              Trans.: Am. NMil, 16.V.36;
                      Eng. p.q. THE CASE: 501;
                      Ger. UWort, (IV.14), IX.36.
              [T3914,3915.]

360522   La nouvelle Constitution et la repression en URSS.
              Trans.: Am. p.q. NYTimes, 19.VII.36;
                      Eng. 690321; Controversy, VII.36;
                      Fr. ActSocRév, (IV.31), 2.VIII.36; Spartacus, (VI.15), 18.VII.36;
                          SIP, 20.VI.36;
                      Ger. SIP, 20.VI.36;
                      Hol. NFakkel, (II.108), 26.VI.36;
                      Sp. IV Int, (I.1), 3.IX.36; Nueva Era, (I.6), VII.36.
              [Statement to Associated Press. T3922.]

360603   Red.: Po povodu statei tov. Tsiliga. (On cde. Ciliga's article.)
              (BO, (51), VII-VIII.36)
              [T3923.]

360605   L.T.: Reshayushchii étap. (The decisive stage.) (BO, (51), VII-VIII.36)
              Trans.: Am. 360000(11): 140-8; 680612: 140-8;
                      Eng. 610600: 142-9; Fight, (1), 10.X.36;
                      Fr. 360000(6); 580900: 129-37; 670306: 571-7; ActSocRév, (IV.25),
                          20.VI.36; LOuv(Fr), (1), 12.VI.36; QI, II.69;
                      Ger. 360000(12): 93-7; UWort, (IV.12), VI.36;
                      Hol. NFakkel, (II.107), 19.VI.36;
                      It. 620000(20): 484-91; *680900(3); 681100: 524-31;
                      Jap. *630430; 650430: 137-44.
              [On France. T3924,3925.]

360606   [84 articles, 12 books and pamphlets, on capitulations; beginning
              15.XII.28.]
              [c. THE CASE: 86.]

360607   Pref. N.Braun: L'ORGANE DE MASSE.
              Trans.: Fr. Braun; 670306: 542-5.

360609   L.T.: Frantsuzskaya revolyutsiya nachalas. (The French revolution has
begun.) (<u>BO</u>, (51), VII–VIII.36)

Trans.: Am. 360000(11): 149–55; 680612: 149–55; <u>Nation</u>, 4.VII.36;
Eng. 610600: 150–6; <u>Spark</u>, IX.36;
Fr. 360000(6); 580900: 139–46; 670306: 578–83; <u>ActSocRév</u>,
(IV.26), 27.VI.36; <u>LOuv</u>(Fr), (4), 18.VII.36; <u>QI</u>, II.69;
Ger. 360000(12): 93–7; <u>UWort</u>, (IV.12), VI.36;
Hol. <u>RodeOkt</u>, (I.7), VII.36;
Jap. *630430; 650430: 145–51.

⌊T3926,3927.⌋

360610   Pref. OÙ VA LA FRANCE?, 360000(6).

Repr.: 360000(6);
Trans.: 360000(6).

360700(1)   The new revolutionary upsurge and the tasks of the Fourth International.

Trans.: Cz. <u>Jiskra</u>, (III.4), IX.36;
Eng. ⌊360000(17)⌋;
Fr. <u>ActSocRév</u>, (IV.34), 22.VIII.36; <u>LOuv</u>(Fr), (7), 5.VIII.36;
<u>QI</u>, (1), X.36;
Ger. <u>UWort</u>, (IV.14), IX.36.

360700(2)   LA NUEVA CONSTITUCIÓN DE LA URSS.

⌊Trans. Sp. See 360416 for all trans.⌋

⌊360700(3)⌋   Interview, with Collins.

Trans.: Eng. <u>Internal Bulletin, Marxist Group</u>, 1936; <u>Internal Bulletin</u>,
<u>RCP</u>, 1945.

⌊On Br. section ILOpp. T3965.⌋

360701   Crux & others: On the United States of America.

⌊Thesis of Geneva Conference of the Fourth International. LocPer.⌋

360704   To the public opinion of the toilers of the whole world.

Trans.: Eng. <u>Fight</u>, (1), 10.X.36;
Hol. <u>NFakkel</u>, (II.115), 14.VIII.36; <u>RodeOkt</u>, (I.8), VIII.36.

⌊Theses of Geneva Conference of the Fourth International. T3934.⌋

360708   —: Chetvertyi Internatsional i SSSR. (The Fourth International and
the USSR.) (<u>BO</u>, (54–55), III.37)

Trans.: Eng. *430800(2); 560900(1); 690321; <u>Fight</u>, 12.XII.36; <u>Spark</u>,
II.37;   ++++

360708   +++   Trans.: Fr. QI, (1), X.36;
                        Hol. RevSoc, (II.7-8), VII-VIII.36;
                        Hung. ⌊360000(19)⌋.
                    [Theses. T3935,3936.]

360709(1)   Maksim Gor′kii. (BO, (51), VII-VIII.36)
                    Trans.: Am. IntReview, IX-X.36;
                        Hol. RodeOkt, (I.9), IX.36.
                    [Obituary. T3937,3938.]

360709(2)   L.T.: Pered vtorym étapom. (Before the second stage.) (BO, (51),
                    VII-VIII.36)
                    Trans.: Am. Nation, 8.VIII.36;
                        Eng. 610600: 157-63;
                        Fr. 360000(6); 580900: 149-54; 670306: 584-90; ActSocRév, (IV.30),
                            25.VII.36; QI, II.69;
                        Ger. 360000(12): 98-101;
                        Hol. NFakkel, (II.113), 31.VII.36;
                        Jap. *630430; 650430: 152-8.
                    ⌊On France. T3939,3940.⌋

360715   Letter to CC RSAP.
                    Trans.: Am. 690000(13): 57-8; SWP, (5), VIII.38;
                        Hol. IDB, (1), 1.VII.37.
                    [On ILOpp section in Holland. See further 360719.]

360716   Interview with Molinier and Desnots.
                    Trans.: Fr. LA CRISE.II: 25-7.
                    [On Fr. section ILOpp.]

360718   Alternative for 360715.

360719   Letter to CC RSAP.
                    Trans.: Am. SWP, (5), VIII.38;
                        Hol. IDB, (1), 1.VII.37. See also 360715.⌋
                    [On ILOpp section in Holland.

360727   Lettre.
                    Trans.: Cz. Jiskra, (III.4), IX.36;
                        Fr. 670306: 591-4; LOuv(Fr), (8), 15.VIII.36; LA RÉVOLUTION
                            ESPAGNOLE: 103-4.
                    [On Spain. T3942,3943.]

360730(1) The lesson of Spain.

 Trans.: Am. SocAp(C), IX.36;

    Eng. Red Flag, IX.36; Spark, X.36; Umlilo Mollo, (I.2), X.36;

    Fr. ActSocRév, (IV.33), 15.VIII.36; LOuv(Fr), (7), 8.VIII.36;

    Ger. UWort, (IV.14), IX.36;

    Hol. NFakkel, (II.116), 21.VIII.36;

    Hung. ⌊380000(9)⌋;

    Sp. 680000(9): 177; IV Int, (I.3), 15.X.36; p.q. Batalla,

     (II.22), 27.VIII.36; POUM, (I.3), 9.IX.36.

 ⌊T3944,3945.⌋

360730(2) Lettre à Victor Serge.

 Trans.: Fr. 670306: 546-52.

360803 Alternative for 360823(2).

360804 Pref. LA RÉVOLUTION TRAHIE, 361013.

 Trans.: 361013.

 ⌊See 360900(1), note.⌋

360815 Let us know the facts.

 Trans.: Am. NYTimes, 30.VIII.36; SocAp(C), IX.36;

    Eng. New Leader, 21.VIII.36; Red Flag, IX.36;

    Fr. LOuv(Fr), (9), 22.VIII.36;

    Ger. UWort, (IV.Sonder.), VIII.36;

    Hol. NFakkel, (II.118), 4.IX.36;

    Sp. IV Int, (I.2), 15.IX.36.

 ⌊Reply to Tass Agency. On Moscow Trials. T3954.⌋

360819(1) ⌊Letter to Chief of Police, Oslo.⌋

 Trans.: Fr. LOuv(Fr), (10), 5.IX.36;

    Hol. NFakkel, (II.120,121), 18,25.IX.36;

    Sp. POUM, (I.4), 16.IX.36.

 ⌊Autobiography; Moscow trials.⌋

360819(2) Statement on the trials.

 Trans.: Am. p.q. NYTimes, 20.VIII.36.

360819(3) Statement on the trials.

 Trans.: Am. p.q. NYTimes, 20.VIII.36.

360820(1)   Terreur individuelle et terreur de masse.

<u>Trans</u>.: Cz. <u>Jiskra</u>, (III.5), X.36;

Fr. <u>LOuv</u>(Fr), (10), 5.IX.36;

Ger. <u>UWort</u>, (IV.Sonder.), VIII.36;

Hol. <u>RodeOkt</u>, (I.9), IX.36.

⌊On Moscow trials.⌋

360820(2)   Interview, <u>Dagbladet</u>.

<u>Trans</u>.: Am. p.q. <u>NYTimes</u>, 2.IX.36; p.q. <u>SocAp</u>(C), 1.X.36; p.q.

Shachtman: 101-2;

Cz. <u>Jiskra</u>, (III.4), IX.36;

Eng. p.q. <u>Red Flag</u>, X.36;

Fr. <u>LOuv</u>(Fr), (10), 5.IX.36; <u>RévProl</u>, (230), 30.IX.36; p.q.

<u>SIP</u>, (8), 13.IX.36;

Hol. <u>NFakkel</u>, (II.121), 25.IX.36;

Nor. <u>Dagbladet</u>, 21.VIII.36.

⌊On Moscow trials; V.Olberg. T3955.⌋

360821   Interview.

<u>Trans</u>.: Nor. <u>Arbeiderbladet</u>, (194), 21.VIII.36;

Sp. <u>POUM</u>, (I.4), 16.IX.36.

⌊On Moscow trials. T3956.⌋

360823(1)   Première déclaration sur le procès.

<u>Trans</u>.: Fr. <u>LOuv</u>(Fr), (10), 5.IX.36;

Ger. <u>UWort</u>, (IV.15), X.36;

Hol. <u>NFakkel</u>, (II.117), 28.VIII.36;

Nor. <u>Arbeiderbladet</u>, (197), 25.VIII.36.

⌊T3958.⌋

360823(2)   Stalin is not everything.

<u>Trans</u>.: Am. p.q. <u>NYTimes</u>, 7.IX.36;

Eng. p.q. <u>Spark</u>, II.37;

Fr. <u>SIP</u>, (14), 1.XII.36;

Ger. 360000(23);

Hung. ⌊360000(19)⌋.

360823(4)   Reply to questions from La Comité pour le droit et la justice.

<u>Trans</u>.: Eng. <u>Spark</u>, II.37;

Fr. <u>SIP</u>, (14), 1.XII.36;

Ger. FÜR RECHT: 13-4.

⌊On Moscow trials.⌋

360824	Press statement.
	<u>Trans</u>.: Am. <u>NYTimes</u>, 25.VIII.36;
	Eng. <u>Times</u>, 25.VIII.36;
	Nor. <u>Arbeiderbladet</u>, (196), 24.VIII.36.
360825	Press statement.
	<u>Trans</u>.: Am. <u>NYTimes</u>, 26.VIII.36;
	Eng. <u>Times</u>, 26.VIII.36;
	Nor. <u>Arbeiderbladet</u>, (197), 25.VIII.36; <u>Dagbladet</u>, 1936.
	⌊On Moscow trials. T3962.⌋
360826(1)	Letter to Trygvie Lie, Norwegian Minister of Justice.
	<u>Trans</u>.: Am. <u>Nation</u>, 10.X.36;
	Eng. <u>Forward</u>, 26.IX.36; <u>ManGuard</u>, 17.IX.36;
	Fr. <u>LOuv</u>(Fr), (11), 12.IX.36; <u>SIP</u>, (8), 13.IX.36.
	⌊Autobiography; Moscow trials.⌋
360826(2)	Interview: Denies conspiracy charge.
	<u>Trans</u>.: Eng. <u>News Chronicle</u>, 27.VIII.36.
	⌊On Moscow trials. T3960.⌋
360827	Trials without end.
	<u>Trans</u>.: Cz. <u>Jiskra</u>, (III.4), IX.36;
	Eng. <u>Spark</u>, II.37;
	Fr. <u>Commune</u>, (36), 18.XII.36; <u>SIP</u>, (14), 1.XII.36;
	Ger. 360000(23);
	Hung. ⌊360000(19).⌋
360900(1)	PS, Pref. THE REVOLUTION BETRAYED, 360804.
	⌊Trans. Am. Not in all trans.⌋
360915(1)	Letter to Puntervold.
	<u>Trans</u>.: Eng. THE CASE: 218; NOT GUILTY: 385.
	⌊On Moscow trials.⌋
360915(2)	Declares 2nd trial was inevitable.
	<u>Trans</u>.: p.q. 371116(2);
	Fr. p.q. 371116(2): 141-2.
	⌊Confiscated message; on Moscow trials.⌋

360923   Les poursuites en Belgie.

Trans.: Fr. LOuv(Fr), (15), 10.X.36; SIP, (11), 2.X.36;

         Nor. Aftenposten, 24.IX.36.

[On trotskyists.]

361000(1)   [Letter to Sedov.]

[Confiscated. c. 371116(2): 35. Reply to Pritt's brochure on Moscow trials. T3966.]

361000(2)   Lettre à la Fédération Syndicale Internationale.

[Confiscated. c. 371116(2): 35. On Moscow trials.]

361012   Pis'mo. (A letter.) (BO, (52-53), X.36)

[To Sedov. Trans. from Fr. D119.]

361013   LA RÉVOLUTION TRAHIE.

Trans.: Am. 370000(12); 450000(3); 570000(6); [640000(4)]; p.q.

         640800: 150-62,275-9; 650000(7); p.q. 650900: 160-9,

         178-205,216-221; [690000(7)]; [700000(9)]; p.q. SatRevLit,

         (XV.18), 27.II.37;

   Ch. *380000(18);

Cz. *360000(13); p.q. BYROKRACIE: § 3;

Den. 600000(30);

Eng. 370500; p.q. 640000(5): 160-9,178-205,216-21; 640000(10):

         160-9,178-205,216-21; 670000(13); p.q. Red Flag, (6),

         II.37;

Fr. 361013; 370000(13); 610000(7); 630419: 443-640; p.q.

         680000(4): passim; 690000(15);

Ger. 360000(9); 370000(18); 571000; 680000(3); p.q. Int,

         (II.1.Sonder.), XI.56-III.57;

Gr. 450000(6); 450000(7);

Hung. p.q. [380000(9)];

It. 560900(2); p.q. 680200(2): 109-21,149-54; 681000;

Jap. 370726; *590000(9); 680610; p.q. 681125: 159-70,287-92;

Serb. p.q. BIROKRATIJA: 200-7;

Sp. *370000(19); *371100; p.q. 610622; 630501; 640617;

         p.q. 670000(5): 151-6,270-4; p.q. IV Int, (I.7), III.37;

Swed. 690600(2); p.q. 691100(2): 134-43,247-50.

[Pref. 360804; PS to 360804, 360900(1); Pref. Argentinian ed. 630501,

370900. 2 undated appendices. T3946-53.]

361022   Letter to League of Nations, Geneva.

⌊c. 380331. On Stalin as a terrorist.⌋

361030   Lettre à G.Rosenthal.

<u>Trans</u>.: Fr. p.q. Naville: 80.

⌊On Moscow trials.⌋

361126   ⌊Letter to Puntervold.⌋

⌊c. NOT GUILTY: 164. On Moscow Trials. D324.⌋

361202   Letter to Sedov.

<u>Trans</u>.: Eng. p.q. NOT GUILTY: 165.

⌊On Moscow trials.⌋

361211   ⌊Statement to Norwegian court.⌋

<u>Trans</u>.: Eng. p.q. THE CASE: 578;

     Fr. 371116(2): 36-76;

     Ger. 370000(17): 38-75;

     Gr. 620000(18): 34-64;

     It. *661200;

     Pol. *370000(28);

     Port. *440000(1);

     Sp. *380000(15); *470000(9); 620000(10): 41-64.

⌊On fascist raid on Norwegian residence.⌋

361218(1)   Pozor! (Shame!) (<u>BO</u>, (54-55), III.37)

<u>Trans</u>.: Eng. p.q. <u>Mil</u>(A), (IV.1), 19.IV.37; p.q. <u>Red Flag</u>, (7),

     III-IV.37; p.q. <u>Spark</u>, II.37;

     Fr. <u>LOuv</u>(Fr), (II.31-33), 12-26.II.37; <u>QI</u>, (3), III-IV.37;

     Nor. <u>Okt</u>, (1), IV.37.

⌊To La Comité pour le droit et pour la justice, on Rosenmark's report

in <u>Cahiers des Droits de l'Homme</u>. T3967.⌋

361218(2)   Letter to Sedov.

<u>Trans</u>.: Eng. p.q. Deutscher, PO: 353-4.

361228   Pages from a journal.

<u>Trans</u>.: Am. 700400: 7-9; <u>FI</u>, VI.41;

     Fr. 371116(2): 77-82;

     Ger. 370000(17): 65-8;

     Gr. 620000(18): 65-9;

     It. *661200;   ++++

361228 ++++ <u>Trans</u>.: Pol. *370000(28);
Port. *440000(1);
Sp. *380000(15); *470000(9); 620000(10): 65-8.

361230 Pages from a journal.
<u>Trans</u>.: Am. 700400: 9-10; <u>FI</u>, VI.41;
Fr. 371116(2): 82-8;
Ger. 370000(17): 80-6;
Gr. 620000(18): 69-74;
It. *661200;
Pol. *370000(28);
Port. *440000(1);
Sp. *380000(15); *470000(9); 620000(10): 68-72.

361231 On Zinoviev and Kamenev.
<u>Trans</u>.: Am. 700400: 11-2; <u>FI</u>, VIII.41;
Fr. 371116(2): 88-98;
Ger. 370000(17): 86-95;
Gr. 620000(18): 74-81;
It. *661200;
Pol. *370000(28);
Port. *440000(1);
Sp. *380000(15); *470000(9); 620000(10): 72-7.

370000(1)   I STAKE MY LIFE!

[Trans. Am. See 370209 for all repr., trans.]

370000(2)   I STAKE MY LIFE.

[Trans. Eng. See 370209 for all repr., trans.]

370000(3)   § IN DEFENSE OF THE SOVIET UNION.

[Trans. Am. 14 extracts.]

370000(4)   JEG INNESTÅR MED MITT LIV!

[Trans. Nor. See 370209 for all trans.]

*370000(5)   *KEITSAD NITSACH STALIN?

[Trans. Heb. See 351112 for all trans.]

370000(6)   LESSONS OF OCTOBER.

[Trans. Am. See 240915 for all trans., notes.]

370000(8)   MANUAL DEL SOLDATO ROJO.

[Trans. Sp. See *240000(7) for all trans.]

370000(9)   MITT LIV.

[Trans. Swed. See 300000(1) for all trans., notes.]

370000(10)   ‡ EL PROCESO DE MOSCÚ.

Trans.: Sp. 370000(10); [370000(23)]; IV Int, (I.6), II.37.

[See separate entries for other trans.]

370000(13)   LA RÉVOLUTION TRAHIE.

[Trans. Fr. See 361013 for all repr., trans., notes.]

370000(14)   § THE STALIN SCHOOL OF FALSIFICATION.

[Trans. Am. See 320000(2) for all repr., trans., notes; Pref. 370303(1).]

370000(15)   STALINISM AND BOLSHEVISM.

[Trans. Am. See 370828 for all repr., trans.]

370000(16)   STALINISME OG BOLSJEVISME.

[Trans. Nor. See 370828 for all trans.]

370000(17)   § STALINS VERBRECHEN.

[Trans. Ger. See 371116(2) for all trans., notes.]

370000(18) VERRATENE REVOLUTION.
[Trans. Ger. See 361013 for all repr., trans., notes.]

*370000(19) *LA REVOLUCIÓN TRAICIONADA.
[Trans. Sp. See 361013 for all repr., trans., notes.]

[370000(21)] I STAKE MY LIFE!
[Trans. Eng. See 370209 for all repr., trans., notes.]

[370000(22)] DET KOMMUNISTISKE MANIFEST.
[Trans. Den. See 371030 for all trans.]

[370000(23)] § EL PROCESO DE MOSCÚ.
[Trans. Sp. See 370000(10) for all repr., trans., notes.]

[370000(24)] DIE SPANISCHE LEHRE. EINE LETZTE WARNUNG.
[Trans. Ger. See 371217 for all repr., trans.]

370000(25) Review, J.London, THE IRON HEEL.
Trans.: Am. NI(WP), IV.45;
Eng. Young Socialist(Ceylon), (III.2/12), [1965];
Fr. 640911: 346-51;
Gr. 660000(6): 244-7;
It. 680000(6): 99-102;
Sp. 640900(1): 222-5; 690000(8).II: 74-7;
Swed. 690600(1): 311-3.
[Fr. and Gr. give date for 371016.]

370000(26) YO ACUSO.
[Trans. Sp. See 370209 for all trans., notes.]

370000(27) THE HISTORY OF THE RUSSIAN REVOLUTION.
[Trans. Am. See 310000(1) for all repr., trans., notes.]

*370000(28) *ZBRODNIE STALINA.
[Trans. Pol. See 371116(2) for all trans.]

370000(29) YA KLADU ZHITTYA!
[Trans. Ukr. See 370209 for all trans., notes.]

370000(30) YA ES TIEMPO DE PASAR A UNA OFENSIVA INTERNACIONAL CONTRA EL STALINISMO.
[Trans. Sp. See 371102 for all trans.]

370000(31)   NEGENTIG JAAR VAN DIE KOMMUNISTE-MANIFES.

[Trans. Afr. Pref., Marx & Engels, DIE KOMMUNISTE-MANIFES. See 371030 for all trans.]

370101   Pourquoi ils ont avoués des crimes qu'ils n'avaient pas commis.

<u>Trans</u>.: Am. 700400: 13-5;

        Fr. 371116(2): 98-108;

        Ger. 370000(17): 95-105;

        Gr. 620000(18): 81-9;

        It. *661200;

        Pol. *370000(28);

        Port. *440000(1);

        Sp. *380000(15); *470000(9); 620000(10): 78-84.

[On Moscow trials.]

370103   "La soif du pouvoir."

<u>Trans</u>.: Am. 700400: 15-6;

        Fr. 371116(2): 108-12;

        Ger. 370000(17): 105-8;

        Gr. 620000(18): 89-92;

        It. *661200;

        Pol. *370000(28);

        Port. *440000(1);

        Sp. *380000(15); *470000(9); 620000(10): 84-7.

370104   "La haine de Staline."

<u>Trans</u>.: Am. 700400: 16-8;

        Fr. 371116(2): 113-9;

        Ger. 370000(17): 108-15;

        Gr. 620000(18): 92-7;

        It. *661200;

        Pol. *370000(28);

        Port. *440000(1);

        Sp. *380000(15); *470000(9); 620000(10): 87-91.

370105   Notes, en route.

<u>Trans</u>.: Am. 700400: 18-9;

        Fr. 371116(2): 120-3;

        Ger. 370000(17): 115-8;

        Gr. 620000(18): 97-100;   ++++

370105   ++++   <u>Trans</u>.: It. *661200;
               Pol. *370000(28);
               Port. *440000(1);
               Sp. *380000(15); *470000(9); 620000(10): 91-3.
      [On Moscow trials.]

370106   L'envoi de terroristes en URSS.
          <u>Trans</u>.: Am. 700400: 19-20;
               Fr. 371116(2): 123-8;
               Ger. 370000(17): 118-23;
               Gr. 620000(18): 100-3;
               It. *661200;
               Pol. *370000(28);
               Port. *440000(1);
               Sp. *380000(15); *470000(9); 620000(10): 93-6.

370109(1)   Pages from a journal.
          <u>Trans</u>.: Am. 700400: 21-2; <u>FI</u>, VI.41;
               Fr. 371116(2): 128-32;
               Ger. 370000(17): 124-9;
               Gr. 620000(18): 104-8;
               It. *661200;
               Pol. *370000(28);
               Port. *440000(1);
               Sp. *380000(15); *470000(9); 620000(10): 97-100.
      [On Moscow trials. T3968.]

370109(2)   Interview, on arrival at Tampico, Mexico.
          <u>Trans</u>.: Am. 700400: 22-3; p.q. <u>NYTimes</u>, 10.I.37.

370111   Telegram to New York.
          <u>Trans</u>.: Am. 700400: 23.
      [On Moscow trials.]

370112(1)   Statement.
          <u>Trans</u>.: Am. p.q. <u>NYTimes</u>, 13.I.37.
      [On Spain. T3970.]

[370112(2)]   Interview, with Ola Apenes.
          <u>Trans</u>.: Nor. <u>Aftenposten</u>, (42), 27.I.37.

370116   Interview, with Julius Klyman.

Trans.: Am. 700400: 23-5; St Louis Post-Dispatch, 17.I.37.

⌊c. NYTimes, 17.I.37. T3971.⌋

370118   Interview, with Der Weg (El Camino).

Trans.: Am. 700700: 20-2; FI, XII.45; LabChal, (II.11), VII.46;

NIB, (II.1), III.37; Duker: IIIB: Item 126: 31-4;

Eng. Mil(A), (IV.3), 31.V.37; WIN, VI-VII.46;

Fr. 600000(10); PSR, (12), II.38; QI, (2), II.37; SIP, (18),

16.III.37; Léon: 183-5;

Hol. RodeOkt, (1), VIII.46;

Yid. Der Weg, 1937.

⌊On Jewry. Conducted in Fr. Duker gives other *sources. T3973.⌋

370120   Brands trial as new frame-up.

Trans.: Am. p.q. NYTimes, 21.I.37.

⌊T3975,3976.⌋

370121   Alternative for 370122.

370122   Novaya moskovskaya amal´gama. (A new Moscow amalgam.) (BO, (54-55),

III.37)

Trans.: Am. 700400: 26-30; Truth, IV.37;

Fr. 371116(2): 134-44;

Ger. 370000(17): 130-9;

Gr. 620000(18): 109-16;

Hol. NFakkel, (III.5), 28.I.37;

It. *661200;

Pol. *370000(28);

Port. *440000(1);

Sp. p.q. 370000(10): 5-7,26-8; p.q. ⌊370000(23)⌋: 5-7,26-8;

*380000(15); *470000(9); 620000(10): 100-6.

⌊T3978-81.⌋

370123(1)   Dictated statement, denying charges.

Trans.: Am. p.q. NYTimes, 24.I.37.

⌊On Moscow trials. T3987,3988.⌋

370123(2)   Derides charges at trial.

Trans.: Am. 700400: 31; NYTimes, 24.I.37.

⌊T3989,3990.⌋

370123(3)   Cable.

                Trans.: Am. 700400: 31-2; Labor Action(SF), 6.II.37;

                        Eng. ManGuard, 25.I.37.

                [On Moscow trials. T3992.]

370124(1)   Cable.

                Trans.: Am. 700400: 32-3; Labor Action(SF), 6.II.37;

                        Eng. ManGuard, 26.I.37.

                [On Moscow trials. T3993.]

370124(2)   Communiqué to the press; on Piatakov's flight to Oslo.

                Trans.: Eng. THE CASE: 215-6;

                        Fr. 371116(2): 297;

                        Ger. 370000(17): 291-2;

                        Gr. 620000(18): 246;

                        It. *661200;

                        Pol. *370000(28);

                        Port. *440000(1);

                        Sp. *380000(15); *470000(9); 620000(10): 203-4.

                [On Moscow trials. T3994,3995.]

370124(3)   On Romm.

                Trans.: Am. 700400: 32; NYTimes, 25.I.37.

                [On Moscow trials.]

370126(1)   La confessiones "voluntarias" de los acusados.

                Trans.: Sp. 370000(10): 12-3; [370000(23)]: 12-3.

                [On Moscow trials. T4008-10.]

370126(2)   Los recursos financieros de la conspiracion.

                Trans.: Sp. 370000(10): 13; [370000(23)]: 13.

                [On Moscow trials. T4011-3.]

370126(3)   Mouralow.

                Trans.: Sp. 370000(10): 13-4; [370000(23)]: 13-4.

                [On Moscow trials. T4014-6.]

370127(1)   Piatakov's phantom flight; My concrete propositions to the Moscow court.

                Trans.: Am. 700400: 33-4; ACD, (3), 3.II.37; Truth, IV.37;

                        Eng. p.q. Forward, 6.XI.37; Mil(A), (IV.5), 7.VII.37; THE CASE:

                          216-8,219;   ++++

370127(1)   ++++   Trans.: Fr. BMIP, (2-3), II-III.37;
                              Sp. 370000(10): 14-5; ⌊370000(23)⌋: 14-5.
                     ⌊On Moscow trials. T4019,4020.⌋

370127(2)   Statement; on arrest of son Sergei.
                     Trans.: Am. 700400: 34; p.q. NYTimes, 28.I.37.
                     [T4021-3.]

370128(1)   Vokrug protsessa 17-ti. (The trial of the 17.) (BO, (54-55), III.37)
                     Trans.: Am. 700400: 34-5;
                              Sp. 370000(10): 15-7; ⌊370000(23)⌋: 15-7.
                     ⌈T4029-31.⌋

370128(2)   See 370129(4)

370129(1)   El Fiscal Vishinsky.
                     Trans.: Sp. 370000(10): 20-1; ⌊370000(23)⌋: 20-1.
                     ⌊T4039-41.⌋

370129(2)   La peticion de mi extradicion.
                     Trans.: Sp. 370000(10): 21; ⌊370000(23)⌋: 21.
                     ⌊On Moscow trials. T4037,4038.⌋

370129(3)   Stalin in retreat.
                     Trans.: Am. 700400: 36; NYTimes, 30.I.37.
                     ⌊On Moscow trials. T4042-4.⌋

370129(4)   Interview, with Roy Howard.
                     Trans.: Am. San Francisco News, 1.II.37.
                     ⌊For NYWorld Telegram. T4024,4025,4033.⌋

370130   Poslednie slova podsudimykh. (The last words of the accused.)
                     (BO, (54-55), III.37)
                     Trans.: Am. 700400: 37; p.q. NYTimes, 31.I.37.
                     ⌊On Moscow trials. T4048-50.⌋

370131(1)   Pochemu GPU vybralo dekabr? (Why did the GPU choose December?)
                     (BO, (54-55), III.37)
                     Trans.: Am. 700400: 37;
                              Sp. 370000(10): 23; ⌊370000(23)⌋: 23.
                     ⌊On Moscow trials. T4061-3.⌋

370131(2)   Pochemu GPU vybralo Norvegiyu? (Why did the GPU choose Norway?)
(<u>BO</u>, (54-55), III.37)
<u>Trans</u>.: Am. 700400: 37-8;
         Sp. 370000(10): 23-4; ⌊370000(23)⌋: 23-4.
⌊On Moscow trials. T4064,4065.⌋

370131(3)   Kaganovich predice mi fin.
<u>Trans</u>.: Sp. 370000(10): 22; ⌊370000(23)⌋: 22.
⌊On Moscow trials. T4055-7.⌋

370131(4)   <u>El Pueblo</u> pide el castigo.
<u>Trans</u>.: Sp. 370000(10): 22-3; ⌊370000(23)⌋: 22-3.
⌊On Moscow trials. T4058-60.⌋

370131(5)   "Salvados."
<u>Trans</u>.: Sp. 370000(10): 21-2; ⌊370000(23)⌋: 21-2.
⌊On Moscow trials. T4066-8.⌋

370131(6)   Trece van a morir.
<u>Trans</u>.: Sp. 370000(10): 21; ⌊370000(23)⌋: 21.
⌊On Moscow trials. T4069,4070.⌋

370200(2)   ⌊Piatakov's⌋ Story vague on time, place.
<u>Trans</u>.: Am. 700400: 38; p.q. <u>Truth</u>, IV.37;
         Sp. 370000(10): 19-20; ⌊370000(23)⌋: 19-20.
⌊On Moscow trials. T4034-6.⌋

⌊370200(3)⌋   ⌊Letter to Walter Nelz.⌋
<u>Trans</u>.: Ger. <u>Trotz alledem!</u>, (II.3), II.37.
⌊On International Defence Committee; Moscow trials.⌋

370201(1)   Final? (The end?) (<u>BO</u>, (54-55), III.37)
<u>Trans</u>.: Am. 700400: 38-9;
         Eng. p.q. <u>ManGuard</u>, 2.II.37.
⌊On Moscow trials. T4074-6.⌋

⌊370203⌋   Hearst repudiated.
<u>Trans</u>.: Am. <u>ACD</u>, (3), II.37; 700400: 174.
⌊On Moscow trials.⌋

370204   Carta a los Bolcheviques-Leninistes de Mexico.
<u>Trans</u>.: Sp. <u>IV Int</u>, (I.6), II.37.
⌊On Mexican section ILOpp.⌋

370209 O protsesse. (On the trial.) (BO, (54-55), III.37)

     Trans.: Am. 370000(1); p.q. 640800: 264-8; 650900: 278-89;
        Ben. ⌊690000(12)⌋;
        Den. p.q. Politiken(D), 11.II.37;
        Eng. 370000(2); ⌊370000(21)⌋; 370500: 292-312; ⌊430000(2)⌋;
          501200; 640000(5): 278-89; 640000(10): 278-89;
        Fr. p.q. 371116(2): 144-60; p.q. Commune, (50), 2.IV.37;
         La Lutte, (VI.161-4), 1,4,8,11.VII.37; QI, (3), IV.37;
        Ger. p.q. 370000(17): 140-61;
        Gr. p.q. 620000(18): 117-29; 660000(8);
        Hol. p.q. Int, (II.9), 1.V.58;
        It. p.q. *661200;
        Jap. 680610: 324-48; p.q. 681125: 275-81;
        Mal. 570411;
        Nor. 370000(4);
        Pol. p.q. *370000(28);
        Port. p.q. *440000(1);
        Sp. 370000(26); p.q. *380000(15); p.q. *470000(9); p.q.
         620000(10): 107-16; p.q. 670000(5): 259-63;
        Swed. 370000(9): 265-86; p.q. 691100(2): 237-41;
        Ukr. 370000(29).
    ⌊T4084-90.⌋

370211 Interview avec Mme. Titayna.
    Trans.: Fr. Paris-Midi, 16.II.37; QI, (3), III-IV.37.
    ⌊On Moscow trials, etc. T4097-9.⌋

370214 Wire to meeting in Capitol Building, Chicago.
    Trans.: Am. 700400: 39-40; Labor Action(SF), 27.II.37;
       Eng. Mil(A), (V.7), 1.VII.38.
    ⌊On Moscow trials. T4093-6.⌋

370215 Romm frequented dark alleys.
    Trans.: Am. 700400: 40-1; NYTimes, 16.II.37; Truth, IV.37;
       Fr. BMIP, (2-3), II-III.37.
    ⌊On Moscow trials. T4100-2.⌋

370219   Answers to certain questions from the representative of Havas Agency.

            Trans.: Am. Labor Action(SF), 17.IV.37; NYEvening Post, 1937;

                    Den. 4I, (I.2), III.37;

                    Eng. THE CASE: 301-3; Red Flag, (7), III-IV.37; Spark, IV.37;

                    Fr. LOuv(Fr), (II.33), 26.II.37;

                    Ger. UWort, (V.2), V.37;

                    Hol. Klassen(A), (I.8), 1.V.37;

                    Nor. Okt, (1), IV.37;

                    Sp. IV Int, (I.7), III.37.

            [On Spain. T4103,4104.]

370219(2)   Letter.

            Trans.: Am. p.q. 700400: 174.

            [Against Hearst reprint of articles.]

370222   Thermidor and antisemitism.

            Trans.: Am. 650900: 206-15; 700700: 22-9; p.q. FI, XII.45; NI(WP), V.41;

                    Eng. 640000(5): 206-15; 640000(10): 206-15; p.q. WIN, VI-VII.46;

                    Hol. RodeOct, (1), VIII.46.

            [On Jewry in Soviet Union. T4105,4106.]

370303(1)   Pref. THE STALIN SCHOOL OF FALSIFICATION, 370000(14).

            Repr.: 370000(14);

            Trans.: 370000(14).

            [T4117,4118.]

370303(2)   How the Insurrection took place.

            Trans.: Am. 370000(14): 199-203; 620000(3): 199-203;

                    Jap. 680320: 223-7.

            [On October Revolution. cf. [331200(1)].]

370305   Lettre à Victor Serge. Réponse aux calomnies de Jacques Sadoul.

            Trans.: Fr. p.q. 670306: 595-7; LOuv(Fr), (II.37), 26.III.37.

            [T4119,4120.]

370306   Fenner Brockway — Pritt No. 2.

            Trans.: Am. 700400: 73-4;

                    Eng. BCD, (2), VII.37; New Leader, 3.IX.37;

                    Hol. IDB, (4), I.38.

            [On Moscow trials. T4121,4122.]

370308   On an interview of André Malraux.

<u>Trans</u>.: Am. 700400: 74; p.q. <u>Nation</u>, 27.III.37;

       Fr. 640911: 344-5; <u>LOuv</u>(Fr), (II.39), 9.IV.37;

       Sp. 690000(8).II: 161-3;

       Swed. 690600(1): 309-10.

[T4123,4124.]

370309   Letter to Cannon.

<u>Trans</u>.: Am. p.q. Venkataramani.

[On ILOpp section in USA.]

370310   [Deposition on the theft of his archives from Paris.]

[c. THE CASE: 340.]

370313(1)   Concrete questions to M.Malraux.

<u>Trans</u>.: Am. 700400: 74-5;

       Eng. <u>Mil</u>(A), (IV.3), 31.V.37; <u>Spark</u>, V.37;

       Fr. 670306: 598-601; <u>LOuv</u>(Fr), (II.37), 26.III.37;

       Hol. <u>NFakkel</u>, (III.14), 9.IV.37.

[T4125,4126.]

370313(2)   L.T.: Otel Bristol. (The Hotel Bristol.) (<u>BO</u>, (56-57), VII-VIII.37)

<u>Trans</u>.: Am. <u>Truth</u>, IV.37;

       Eng. <u>Mil</u>(A), (IV.3), 31.V.37; p.q. THE CASE: 519-22.

[On Moscow trials. T4127.]

370316   A mockery of justice.

<u>Trans</u>.: Am. 700400: 41-3; <u>Truth</u>, IV.37;

       Eng. <u>Forward</u>, 10.IV.37; <u>ManGuard</u>, 16.III.37; p.q. THE CASE:

         467-70;

       Ger. <u>UWort</u>, (V.2), V.37.

[On Moscow trials. T4128,4129.]

370320   Lund: The proposed Barcelona Conference.

<u>Trans</u>.: Am. <u>IBF</u>, VII.37.

[On Spain.]

370323   Lund: To the Editorial Board, <u>La Lutte Ouvrière</u>.

<u>Trans</u>.: Am. <u>IBF</u>, VII.37;

       Fr. <u>BII</u>, (1), IV.37; <u>SIP</u>, (19-20), VI.37;

       Hol. <u>IDB</u>, (1), 1.VII.37.

[On Spain. T4131.]

370410(1) At 1st session Dewey Commission.
Trans.: Eng. THE CASE: 1-34.

370410(2) At 2nd session Dewey Commission.
Trans.: Eng. THE CASE: 35-63.

370412(1) At 3rd session Dewey Commission.
Trans.: Eng. THE CASE: 64-108.

370412(2) At 4th session Dewey Commission.
Trans.: Eng. THE CASE: 109-50.

370413(1) At 5th session Dewey Commission.
Trans.: Eng. THE CASE: 151-91.

370413(2) At 6th session Dewey Commission.
Trans.: Eng. THE CASE: 192-226.

370414(1) At 7th session Dewey Commission.
Trans.: Eng. THE CASE: 227-66.

370414(2) At 8th session Dewey Commission.
Trans.: Eng. THE CASE: 267-300.

370415 At 9th session Dewey Commission.
Russian: p.q. BO, (62-63), II.38.
Trans.: Eng. THE CASE: 301-43.

370416(1) At 10th session Dewey Commission.
Trans.: Eng. THE CASE: 344-81;
Fr. p.q. La Lutte, (206), 28.VIII.38.

370416(2) At 11th session Dewey Commission.
Trans.: Eng. THE CASE: 382-414.

370417(1) At 12th session Dewey Commission.
Trans.: Eng. THE CASE: 415-43.

370417(2) At 13th session Dewey Commission.
Russian: p.q. BO, (56-57,56-59,84), VII-VIII, IX-X.37, VIII-X.40)
Trans.: Am. [500000(4)]; p.q. 640800: 268-73; p.q. 650900: 290-304;
p.q. FI, VII-VIII.47;
Eng. p.q. 640000(5): 290-304; 640000(10): 290-304; p.q. FI(P),
(11), Autumn 1960; THE CASE: 444-585; MOSCOW TRIALS:
66-130; ++++

370417(2) ++++ Trans.: Fr. 371116(2): 160–334; p.q. V, (2), VI.38;
Ger. 370000(17): 162–330;
Gr. 620000(18): 140–277;
Hol. p.q. IenP, (4–5), VIII–IX.37;
It. *661200;
Jap. 561123: 1–210; p.q. 681125: 281–6;
Pol. *370000(28);
Port. *440000(1);
Sp. *380000(15); *470000(9); 620000(10): 116–238; p.q.
670000(5): 263–8;
Swed. p.q. 691100(2): 241–5.

370423 --/Crux: Vozmozhna li pobeda v Ispanii? (Is victory possible in Spain?)
(BO, (56–57), VII–VIII.37)
Trans.: Eng. Fight, (I.3), VI.38; Spark, VII.37;
Fr. LOuv(Fr), (II.44,45), 14,21.V.37; LA RÉVOLUTION ESPAGNOLE:
129–32;
Hol. RevSoc, (III.2–3), VI.37;
Sp. IV Int, (I.11), VI.37.
⌊T4141,4142.⌋

370424 La cuestion agraria en Bolivia.
Trans.: Sp. 611025: 36–9; 690700(2): 203.
⌊Interview with Alfredo Sarifines G.⌋

370429 L.T.: Dantsigskii sud nad trotskistami. (The Danzig trial of the
trotskyists.) (BO, (56–57), VII–VIII.37)
Trans.: Am. 700400: 43–5; SocAp, 28.VIII.37;
Fr. LOuv(Fr), (II.54), 27.VIII.37;
Ger. Die Int, (III.2), 1970; UWort, (V.4), XI.37.
⌊T4145,4146.⌋

370500 THE REVOLUTION BETRAYED.
⌊Trans. Eng. See 361013 for all repr., trans., notes; 370209.⌋

370502 Alternative for 370522.

370512 Lund: The insurrection in Barcelona.
Trans.: Am. IBF, VII.37;
Fr. LOuv(Fr), (II.48), 10.VI.37; LA RÉVOLUTION ESPAGNOLE: 137–8.
⌊T4147.⌋

370518   Reply to Carlton Beals.

Trans.: Am. 700400: 66-7; NYTimes, 26.V.37;

        Eng. BCD, (2), VII.37;

        Fr. SIP, (21-22), VIII.37;

        Hol. IenP, (3), VII.37.

[On questions posed at Dewey Commission. T4148,4149.]

370522   To 3rd National Congress of JSR, France.

Trans.: Am. 700400: 84-5; Challenge of Youth, X.37;

        Fr. Rév, (IV.42), 15.VII.37.

[T4151,4152.]

370523   See 370601.

370525   On the BLs in the SP(USA).

Trans.: p.q. 400124.

370529   In re Copenhagen.

Trans.: Eng. THE CASE: 589-90.

[To Dewey Commission. D100.]

370600   Stalin on his own frame-ups.

Trans.: Am. 700400: 46-51; SocAp, 30.X,6.XI.37;

        Fr. 371116(2): 353-67;

        Ger. 370000(17): 348-61;

        Gr. 620000(18): 293-303;

        It. *661200;

        Pol. *370000(28);

        Port. *440000(1);

        Sp. *380000(15); *470000(9); 620000(10): 238-47; IV Int, (I.11),

           VI.37.

[On Moscow trials.]

370601   The Fourth International.

Trans.: Am. 700400: 83-4;

        Eng. Spark, VIII.37;

        Fr. LOuv(Fr), (II.50), 24.VI.37.

[Associated Press interview. cf. NYTimes, 24.V.37.]

370612   —: Nachalo kontsa. (The beginning of the end.) (BO, (58-59), IX-X.37)

Trans.: Am. 700400: 51-4; p.q. NYTimes, 13.VI.37; SocAp, 16.X.37;

Eng. Spark, XII.37; WIN, II.38;

Fr. 371116(2): 367-76; p.q. Lutte, (192,193), 7,14.IV.38;

Ger. 370000(17): 362-71;

Gr. 620000(18): 304-11;

It. *661200;

Pol. *370000(28);

Port. *440000(1);

Sp. *380000(15); *470000(9); 620000(10): 247-53.

[On Red Army; stalinism.]

370615   Wolfe: Letter to Burnham, Carter, Glotzer and Webber.

Trans.: Am. p.q. Venkataramani.

[On ILOpp in USA.]

370617(1)   Obezglavlenie Krasnoi armii. (The decapitation of the Red Army.)
(BO, (56-57), VII-VIII.37)

Trans.: Am. 700400: 55-60; IP, (VIII.9), 9.III.70; p.q. Mil, 4.X.41;

Den 4I, (I.4), IX.37;

Fr. 371116(2): 335-53; LOuv(Fr), (II.53), 6.VIII.37;

Ger. 370000(17): 331-47; p.q. UWort, (V.3), VIII.37;

Gr. 620000(18): 278-92;

It. *661200;

Nor. Okt, (4-5), VIII-IX.37;

Pol. *370000(28);

Port. *440000(1);

Sp. *380000(15); *470000(9); 620000(10): 227-38.

[T4157,4158.]

370617(2)   Cable to CEC, Soviet Union.

Trans.: Am. NYTimes, 18.VI.37.

[T4159.]

370625   Wolfe: Letter to Burnham.

Trans.: Am. p.q. Venkataramani.

[On ILOpp in USA.]

370629   Factual correction to Dewey Commission.

Trans.: Eng. THE CASE: 592-3.

[T4162,4163.]

370630   In re Copenhagen.

     <u>Trans</u>.: Eng. THE CASE: 590.

     [To Dewey Commission.]

370700   --: LA GUERRA Y LA IV INTERNACIONAL.

     [Trans. Sp. See 340610 for all trans.]

370705   Pref. LES CRIMES DE STALINE, 371116(2).

     <u>Trans</u>.: 371116(2);

         Am. 700400: 60-1.

370706   Otvety na voprosy Vendelina Tomasa. (Replies to Wendelin Thomas's questions.) (<u>BO</u>, (56-57), VII-VIII.37)

     <u>Trans</u>.: Am. 700400: 159-60; <u>SocAp</u>, 21.VIII.37;

         Eng. <u>Fight</u>, (10), IX.37;

         Fr. <u>Commune</u>, (66), 3.IX.37; <u>LOuv</u>(Fr), (II.55), 10.IX.37;
            <u>SIP</u>, (21-22), VIII.37.

     [T4176,4177.]

370726   STALIN SEIKEN O ABAKU.

     [Trans. Jap. See 361013 for all repr., trans., notes.]

370730   Yaponiya i Kitai. (Japan and China.) (<u>BO</u>, (58-59), IX-X.37)

     <u>Trans</u>.: Am. 700400: 101; p.q. <u>NYTimes</u>, 1.VIII.37;

         Ch. 470427: 335;

         Den. <u>4I</u>, (I.5), X.37;

         Fr. <u>LOuv</u>(Fr), (II.54), 27.VIII.37; <u>Rév</u>(G), (9), IX.37;

         Hol. <u>NFakkel</u>, (III.39), 24.IX.37;

         Nor. p.q. <u>Okt</u>, (4-5), VIII-IX.37;

         Sp. <u>Excelsior</u>, 10.VIII.37; <u>IV Int</u>, (I.13), VIII.37.

     [Interview. T4179,4180.]

370805   See 370900.

370808   L.T.: Ubiistvo Andreya Nina agentami G.P.U. (The murder of Andres Nin by agents of the GPU.) (<u>BO</u>, (58-59), IX-X.37)

     <u>Trans</u>.: Eng. <u>Spark</u>, X.37;

         Fr. <u>LOuv</u>(Fr), (II.54), 27.VIII.37;

         Hol. <u>Klassen</u>(G), (2), 26.IX.37; <u>NFakkel</u>, (III.39), 24.IX.37;

         Nor. <u>Okt</u>, (4-5), VIII-IX.37.

     [Trans. from Fr. T4183,4184.]

370809   Pered novoi mirovoi voinoi. (Before a new world war.) (BO, (58-59),
IX-X.37)

Trans.: Am. 700400: 150-3; p.q. Liberty, 13.XI.37; Yale Review, VI.38;
      Eng. 380000(4); Spark, (IV.8,9), VIII,IX.38; WIN, X.38; p.q.
          Workers Fight, (I.5), X.38;
      Fr. 380000(3); p.q. 700126: 23-43; LOuv(B), ∉ (III.21),
          21.V.38; LOuv(Fr), (II.54), 27.VIII.37; QI, (5,6-7),
          II,III-IV.38; Rév, (V.49,51), VI,VII.38;
      Hol. EB(A), 1945; Enige Weg, (I.10,11), 22.VI, 6.VII.38.
⌊T4185-90.⌋

370811   Crux: Discussion with Li Fu-jen.

Trans.: Am. 700400: 101-6; SPC, (3), XII.37;
      Ch. 470427: 336-44;
      Fr. PSR, (10), XII.37.
⌊Afterword, 370903. On China.⌋

*370814   *WAGA SHOGAI.

⌊Trans. Jap. See 300000(1) for all repr., trans., notes.⌋

370816   Réponse aux questions du journal Mexico al dia.

Trans.: Am. 700400: 176;
      Fr. LOuv(B), (III.8), 19.II.38; LOuv(Fr), (II.55), ₁0.IX.37;
         QI, (4), I.38.
⌊On Spain. See note to 370817. T4192-4.⌋

370817   Interview ⌊with Eric Baume⌋.

Trans.: Am. 700400: 153-4;
      Eng. Sunday Sun (Sydney, Australia), 21.XI.37; p.q. Baume: 9;
      Fr. QI, (4), I.38.
⌊The Sunday Sun version does not agree with Fr. text but seems to
follow 370816. T4195,4196.⌋

370824   Crux: The examination of ideas and individuals through the experience
of the Spanish revolution.

Trans.: Am. IIB, (2), IV.38; SPC, (1), X.37;
      Fr. PSR, (9), XI.37; LA RÉVOLUTION ESPAGNOLE: 145-51;
      Ger. IIB(G), (1), IV.38;
      Hol. VI(p), (1), 1938.
⌊T4199,4200.⌋

370826   Letter to Cannon.

         <u>Trans</u>.: Am. p.q. Venkataramani.

         ⌊On ILOpp section in USA.⌋

370828   Stalinizm i bol´shevizm. (Stalinism and Bolshevism.) (<u>BO</u>, (58-59), IX-X.37)

         <u>Trans</u>.: Am. 370000(15); 600000(9); 650900: 356-69; 700000(2); <u>SocAp</u>,

                 25.IX, 2.X.37;

              Eng. ⌊410000(2)⌋; 451100; 520400; 640000(5): 356-69;

                 640000(10): 356-69;

              Fr. ⌊530000(5)⌋; ⌊560000(5)⌋; 690000(2): 3-16; <u>Nouvelles Etudes</u>

                 <u>Marxistes</u>, (2), ⌊1970⌋; <u>QI</u>, (4), I.38;

              Ger. 470000(2): 9-28; <u>Banner</u>, X.37; <u>EWeg</u>, (1), XII.37;

              Gr. 460000(6);

              Hol. p.q. <u>EB</u>(A), 1945; <u>Enige Weg</u>, (I.5-7), 13.IV-11.V.38;

                 <u>IVe Int</u>, (I.1), XII.38; p.q. <u>Klassen</u>(G), (2), 26.IX.37;

              Jap. 631130: 222-42;

              Nor. p.q. <u>Okt</u>, (7), XI.37;

              Sin. 471001;

              Sp. 620000(17).

         ⌊T4201,4202.⌋

370829   Alternative for 370828.

370900(1)   Prefacio para la Edición Argentina, LA REVOLUCIÓN TRAICIONADA, 630501.

         ⌊Trans. Sp. T4181.⌋

370900(2)   ⌊Conversation with Wheeler-Bennet.⌋

         ⌊c. Wheeler-Bennet: 186 f.n. On Brest-Litovsk peace treay.⌋

370903   Afterword to 370811.

         <u>Trans</u>.: Am. <u>SFC</u>, (3), XII.37;

              Fr. <u>PSR</u>, (10), XII.37.

         ⌊On China. T4203.⌋

370905   London Bureau aids Stalin frame-ups. Once more on Fenner Brockway.

         <u>Trans</u>.: Am. 700400: 76-7; <u>SocAp</u>, 18.IX.37;

              Fr. <u>LOuv</u>(B), (III.1), 1.I.38; <u>LOuv</u>(Fr), (II.62), 9.XII.37.

         ⌊On Moscow trials. See 370306. T4204-6.⌋

370913   Answers to United Press, Mexico.

<u>Trans</u>.: Am. 700400: 154;

Fr. <u>QI</u>, (4), I.38.

[On China. T4207.]

370914   Crux: Answers to questions concerning the Spanish revolution. A concise summary.

<u>Trans</u>.: Am. <u>III</u>, 1938; <u>SPC</u>, (1), X.37;

Fr. <u>POI</u>, (4), 20.II.38;

Ger. <u>IIB</u>(G), (1), IV.38.

[T4208.]

370918   Letter to Glotzer.

<u>Trans</u>.: Am. p.q. Venkataramani.

[On ILOpp section in USA.]

370920(1)   Letter to Shachtman.

<u>Trans</u>.: p.q. 400124.

[On Spain.]

370920(2)   Interview, with J.P.McKnight of AP.

<u>Trans</u>.: Am. 700400: 106; <u>SocAp</u>, 9.X.37;

Ch. 470427: 348;

Fr. <u>QI</u>, (4), I.38.

[On Japan.]

370921   Tragicheskii urok. (A tragic lesson.) (<u>BO</u>, (60-61), XII.37)

<u>Trans</u>.: Am. 700400: 112-4; <u>SocAp</u>, 6.XI.37;

Fr. <u>Commune</u>, (74), 19.XI.37; <u>LOuv</u>(Fr), (II.61), 25.XI.37;

Poretski: 9-13;

Ger. <u>EWeg</u>, (1), XII.37;

Hol. <u>IDB</u>, (3), XI.37.

[On Ignace Reiss; GPU. T4209,4210.]

370922   Réponse à M.Rodman.

<u>Trans</u>.: Am. 700400: 176;

Fr. <u>QI</u>, (4), I.38.

[T4211.]

370923   On the Sino-Japanese war.

<u>Trans</u>.: Am. 700400: 107-8; <u>IP</u>, (VII.40), 1.XII.69; <u>SPC</u>, (1), X.37;

        Ch. 470427: 349-51;

        Fr. <u>LOuv</u>(B), (II.43), 23.X.37; <u>LOuv</u>(Fr), (II.59), 4.XI.37;

            <u>Lutte</u>, (178), 28.XI.37;

        Ger. <u>EWeg</u>, (1), XII.37;

        Hol. <u>NFakkel</u>, (III.44), 29.X.37;

        Sp. 611025: 41-6; 690700(2): 209; <u>Octubre</u>(BA), (II.4), III-V.47.

[Letter to Diego Rivera. T4212.]

370925   Pacifism and China.

<u>Trans</u>.: Am. 700400: 109; <u>SocAp</u>, 16.X.37;

        Ch. 470427: 353-4;

        Fr. <u>QI</u>, (4), I.38.

[Answers to journalist Roger Devlin. T4213.]

370928   The ultra-lefts in general and the incurable ultra-lefts in particular.

<u>Trans</u>.: Am. <u>SPC</u>, (1), X.37;

        Fr. 590600: 523-9; <u>QI</u>, (4), I.38;

        Ger. <u>EWeg</u>, (3), III.38;

        Gr. 630000(11): 56-63;

        Hol. <u>IDB</u>, (3), XI.37;

        Jap. *630430; 650430: 282-8,288.

[PS 370929(1). On Spain. T4214.]

370929(1)   PS 370928.

<u>Trans</u>.: 370928.

370929(2)   Heny: Cable to Sneevliet.

<u>Trans</u>.: 370930(2).

[On Reiss.]

370930(1)   Statement on Reiss's widow.

<u>Trans</u>.: Am. 700400: 115; p.q. <u>NYTimes</u>, 1.X.37; <u>SocAp</u>, 9.X.37;

        Hol. <u>NFakkel</u>, (III.41), 8.X.37.

370930(2)   Letter to New York.

<u>Trans</u>.: Am. 700400: 114.

[On Reiss.]

371001   Crux: Answers to questions.

<u>Trans</u>.: Am. 700400: 154-8; <u>III</u>(3), 1938; <u>SWP</u>, (3), VIII.38;

Ch. 470427: 355.

[On world affairs. T4215.]

371003   Letter.

<u>Trans</u>.: p.q. 400124.

371006   Letter.

<u>Trans</u>.: Am. <u>SocAp</u>, 23.X.37.

[To Carlos Tresca; on aid to Spain. T4216.]

371010   Letter to Cannon.

<u>Trans</u>.: p.q. 400124.

371014   To Cannon, Shachtman and Warde.

<u>Trans</u>.: p.q. 400124.

371015   Letter to Ed. <u>Modern Monthly</u>.

<u>Trans</u>.: Am. 700400: 78; <u>SocAp</u>, 11.XII.37.

371016   See 370000(25), note.

371019   On arrest of assassins of Ignace Reiss.

<u>Trans</u>.: Am. 700400: 115-6; <u>SocAp</u>, 30.X.37.

371022   Crux: On the revolutionary calendar.

<u>Trans</u>.: Am. <u>SWP</u>, (5), VIII.38;

Fr. <u>POI</u>, (1), 15.XI.37.

[On Spain. T4221.]

371027   To the International Secretariat; concerning the resolution on the

Sino-Japanese war.

<u>Trans</u>.: Am. 700400: 110-1; <u>SPC</u>, (3), XII.37;

Ch. 470427: 370-2;

Fr. <u>PSR</u>, (10), XII.37.

[T4222.]

371030   90 years of the Communist Manifesto.

Trans.: Afr. 370000(31);

Am. 631101; p.q. 640800: 285-95; p.q. 670600: 63; p.q.
671100(3); p.q. 690400(2): 63; 700200(1); p.q. 700800: 63;
FI, I-II.48; NI, I.38; II.38;

Ben. [700000(3)];

Den. [370000(22)];

Eng. 480200; 550700; 620000(21); Left Review, IV,V.38; Spark,
(IV.5), V.38;

Fr. 450300; 480300; [620000(7)]; 690900(1): 3-10; LO(C),
(V.1), I-II.69; QI, (6-7), III-IV.38; V, (2), VI.38;

Ger. EWeg, (2), I.38;

Hol. NFakkel, (IV.7,8), 19,25.II.38;

Jap. p.q. 681010: 116; p.q. 681125: 298-307;

Sp. p.q. 670000(5): 289-98;

Swed. p.q. 691100(2): 256-64.

[Written as Pref to Afrikaans trans. of Marx & Engels, THE COMMUNIST
MANIFESTO. Am. NI, II.38 is corrected version of NI, I.38. T4223-5.]

*371100   *LA REVOLUCIÓN TRAICIONADA.

[Trans. Sp. See 361013 for all repr., trans., notes.]

371102   Pora pereiti v mezhdunarodnoe nastuplenie protiv stalinizma! (It is
time to launch an international offensive against stalinism!)
(BO, (60-61), XII.37)

Trans.: Am. 700400: 117-9; SocAp, 20.XI.37;

Eng. Forward, 11.XII.37; Mil(A), (V.2,3), 24.I, 7.II.38; WIN,
18.XII.37; IX.40;

Fr. LOuv(B), (II.48), 27.XI.37; LOuv(Fr), (II.61), 25.XI.37;

Ger. EWeg, (1), XII.37; UWort, (VI.2), III.38;

Hol. IDB, (4), I.38; Klassen(G), (3), 5.XII.37;

Nor. Okt, (II.1), I.38; p.q. Tidens Tegn, (19), 24.I.38;

Sp. 370000(30).

[T4226,4227.]

371104   Once again: The USSR defense.

Trans.: Am. 700400: 86-90; FI, VII-VIII.51; SPC, (2), XI.37;

Eng. [570000(5)];

Fr. Commune, (82-84), 14-28.I.38; Lutte, (182,183), 9,16.I.38;
PSR, (11), I.38; QI, VI.38;

Hol. Enige Weg, (I.15), 31.VIII.38.

[To Craipeau. T4229,4230.]

371107   Alternative for 371104.

371116(1)   Coming trials to reveal secret plans of GPU.

                Trans.: Am. 700400: 120; SocAp, 27.XI.37;

                      Eng. Mil(A), (V.1), 10.I.38; WIN, I.38.

371116(2)   † LES CRIMES DE STALINE.

                Trans.: Am. p.q. 700400: passim;

                      Fr. 371116(2); p.q. QI, (XIV.1-3), III.56;

                      Ger. 370000(17);

                      Gr. 620000(18);

                      Hol. p.q. RodeOct, (II), 1937: 127-41,227-37,249-62;

                      It. *661200;

                      Nor. p.q. Okt, (II.2), II.38;

                      Pol. *370000(28);

                      Port. *440000(1);

                      Sp. *380000(15); *470000(9); 620000(10).

          [Pref. 370705. Fr. text in many eds. of same date. Sub-titled in Fr. LA RÉVOLUTION TRAHIE.II. For other trans. see separate entries. T4164-75.]

371117   Letter to friends.

                Trans.: Am. 700400: 174; p.q. Challenge of Youth, 20.IX.40.

371125(1)   Bertram Wolfe on the Moscow trials.

                Trans.: Am. 700400: 78-80; SocAp, 4.XII.37.

          [T4233,4234.]

371125(2)   Nerabochee i neburzhuaznoe gosudarstvo? (Neither a workers not a bourgeois state?) (BO, (62-63), II.38)

                Trans.: Am. 700400: 90-4; FI, VII-VIII.51; SPC, (3), XII.37;

                      Eng. [570000(5)]; 690321; SocVan, (I.2), IV.52; WIN, IX-X.46;

                      Fr. PSR, (13), IV.38; QI, (9), VI.38;

                      Ger. EWeg, (2), I.38;

                      Hol. Enige Weg, (I.16), 14.IX.38.

          [T4235,4236.]

371127(1)   Telegram to Chautemps.

                Trans.: Am. 700400: 120; SocAp, 27.XI.37;

                      Eng. Mil(A), (V.1), 10.I.38.

          [On Reiss.]

371127(2)   Alternative for 371125(2).

371129(1)   On the Pioneer Press.
             Trans.: Am. 700400: 95; Mil, 27.XI.50; SocAp, 1.I.38.
             ⌊On ILOpp in USA. T4237,4238.⌋

371129(2)   Moscow-Amsterdam unity.
             Trans.: Am. 700400: 177; SocAp, 11.XII.37;
                     Fr. LOuv(B), (II.52), 25.XII.37; LOuv(Fr), (II.63), 23.XII.37;
                     Ger. UWort, (VI.1), I.38;
                     Sp. El Universal, 1937.
             ⌊T4239.⌋

371202   Letter to Sneevliet.
             Trans.: Am. p.q. 690000(13): 58-9; 700400: 96-7; SWP, (5), VIII.38;
                     Fr. BI, (3), V.38; PSR, (14), V.38.
             ⌊On ILOpp in Holland.⌋

371203   Letter to Ed. New York Times.
             Trans.: Am. 700400: 111; NYTimes, 7.XII.37.
             ⌊On China. T4240,4241.⌋

371208   To the Editors, Socialist Appeal.
             Trans.: Am. 700400: 98-9; SPC, (5), XII.37; SWP, (VII.2), IV.45.
             ⌊On SWP, USA. T4244,4245.⌋

371213(1)   Kratkie komentarii k verdiktu. (Brief commentary on the verdict.)
             (BO, (62-63), II.38)
             Trans.: Am. 700400: 68-9;
                     Eng. Forward, 15.I.38; Mil(A), (V.3), 7.II.38;
                     Fr. LOuv(B), (III.2), 8.I.38;
                     Ger. EWeg, (3), III.38;
                     Hol. NFakkel, (III.52), 24.XII.38;
                     Sp. IV Int, (II.17), XII.37.
             ⌊Spoken to journalists in Sp. On Dewey Commission. T4250-2.⌋

371213(2)   Otvety na voprosy zhurnalistov po povodu verdikta Mezhdunarodnoi
             Komissii. (Answers to questions from journalists on the verdict of
             the International Commission.) (BO, (62-63), II.38)
             Trans.: Am. 700400: 69-71; SocAp, 25.XII.37;
                     Eng. Forward, 15.I.38;
                     Sp. IV Int, (II.17), XII.37.
             ⌊Dewey Commission findings. T4253,4254.⌋

371213(3) Telegram to Dewey Commission.

  Trans.: Am. 700400: 72; NYTimes, 14.XII.37; SocAp, 18.XII.37;

    Nor. Okt, (II.1), I.38.

  ⌊T4255.⌋

371214 Letter to Emrys Hughes.

  Trans.: Am. 700400: 177;

    Eng. p.q. Forward, 31.VIII.40.

371217 Ispanskii urok -- poslednee predosterezhenie. (The lesson of Spain --

  The last warning.) (BO, (62-63), II.38)

  Trans.: Am. p.q. 640800: 192-5; FI, IV.45; SocAp, 8,15.I.38;

    Eng. 380000(6); 480000(6); 560700;⌊690000(17)⌋; 691115; Spark,

     III,IV.38;

    Fr. 460000(3); 590600: 531-52; LOuv(B), (III.3-5), 15-29.I.38;

     LOuv(Fr), (III.65,66), 20.I, 3.II.38; Lutte, (191-3),

     27.III-14.IV.38; QI, (5), II.38;

    Ger. ⌊370000(24)⌋; EWeg, (3), III.38;

    Gr. 630000(1₁): 64-92;

    Hol. EB(A), 1945; Enige Weg, (I.1), 18.II.38; VI(p), (2), 1938;

    It. 570400: 275-96;

    Jap. *630430; 650430: 289-313; p.q. 681125: 201-4;

    Nor. Okt, (II.2,3,5), II,III,V.38;

    Sp. 390000(1); p.q. 670000(5): 191-3; Claridad, (328), VIII.38;

     Clave, (1), 1.X.38;

    Swed. p.q. 691100(2): 170-3.

  ⌊T4257,4258.⌋

371219 En hilsen fra Mexico.

  Trans.: Nor. Okt, (II.1), I.38; p.q. Tidens Teg, (19), 24.I.38.

371223 Letter to Australian comrades.

  Trans.: Am. 700400: 111; FI, VII.42.

380000(1) APRÈS MUNICH: UNE LEÇON TOUTE FRAÎCHE.
      [Trans. Fr. See 381010 for all repr., trans.]

380000(2) APRÈS MUNICH: UNE LEÇON TOUTE FRAÎCHE.
      [Trans. Fr. See 381010 for all repr., trans.]

380000(3) AVANT LA NOUVELLE GUERRE MONDIALE.
      [Trans. Fr. See 370809, 381010 for all repr., trans.]

380000(4) THE COMING WORLD WAR.
      [Trans. Eng. See 370809 for all repr., trans.]

380000(5) THE DEATH AGONY OF CAPITALISM AND THE TASKS OF THE WORKING CLASS:
      THE TRANSITIONAL PROGRAMME.
      [Trans. Eng. See 380500(1) for all repr., trans.]

380000(6) THE LESSONS OF SPAIN -- THE LAST WARNING.
      [Trans. Eng. 371217 for all repr., trans.]

380000(7) ¿QUÉ SIGNIFICA LA LUCHA CONTRA EL "TROTSKISMO"?
      [Trans. Sp. See 381009 for all notes.]

[380000(8)] DISCUSSION SUR LE PROGRAMME DE TRANSITION.
      [Trans. Fr. See 380607 for all trans.]

[380000(9)] A SPANYOL TANULSÁG.
      [Trans. Hung. See 360730(1); p.q. 361013 for all trans.]

[380000(10)] L'AGONIE DU CAPITALISME.
      [Trans. Fr. See 380500(1) for all repr., trans.]

380000(13) Conversation with a British sympathizer.
      Trans.: p.q. 391215(2).

380000(14) Lettre.
      Trans.: Am. Warde;
        Fr. p.q. 680000(4): 204-5; Naville: 122-4.
      [To Denise Naville -- PN.]

*380000(15) *LOS CRÍMENES DE STALIN.
      [Trans. Sp. See 371116(2) for all repr., trans., notes.]

*380000(16) *[MY LIFE.]
      [Trans. Ch. Abr. See 340000(4) for all trans.]

*⌊380000(17)⌋   *⌊THE PERMANENT REVOLUTION.⌋
                  ⌊Trans. Ch. See 281000(1) for all trans.⌋

*⌊380000(18)⌋   *⌊THE REVOLUTION BETRAYED.⌋
                  ⌊Trans. Ch. See 361013 for all trans.⌋

380000(19)   ⌊THE DEATH AGONY OF CAPITALISM AND THE TASKS OF THE FOURTH INTERNATIONAL:
                  THE TRANSITIONAL PROGRAM.⌋
                  ⌊Trans. Ch. See 380500(1) for all trans.⌋

*380000(20)   *POUR UN ART RÉVOLUTIONNAIRE INDÉPENDANT.
                  ⌊Trans. Fr. See 380725(2) for all repr., trans.⌋

⌊380000(21)⌋   § COMMUNISM AND SYNDICALISM.
                  ⌊Trans. Eng. See 310300(1) for all repr., trans.⌋

380102   Reply to Van.
                  Trans.: Am. 700400: 99-100; IIB, (2), IV.38; III, (3), 1938; SWP, (3),
                          VIII.38;
                      Fr. BI, (2), IV.38; POI, (4), 20.II.38;
                      Ger. IIB(G), (1), IV.38.
                  ⌊ILOpp section in Holland. T4260.⌋

380105   Revolyutsiya i voina v Kitae. (Revolution and war in China.)
                  (BO, (72), XII.38)
                  Trans.: Am. 570000(2); 690000(4): 2-6; FI, X.45;
                      Ch. 470427: 358-66;
                      Eng. Pref. Isaacs (1st ed. only.);
                      Jap. *610325; 640330(3): 312-29.
                  ⌊T4261,4262,4451,4452.⌋

380108   Za stenami Kremlya. (Behind the Kremlin walls.) (BO, (73), I.39)
                  Trans.: Am. 700400: 165-9; NI, III.39.
                  ⌊T4263-5.⌋

380113   Prodolzhaet li eshche sovetskoe pravitel´stvo sledovat printsipam,
                  usvoennym 20 let tomu nazad? (Does the Soviet government still follow
                  the principles adopted 20 years ago?) (BO, (66-67), V-VI.38)
                  Trans.: Am. 700400: 169-72; FI, III.45;
                      Eng. Forward, 12,19.II.38; Spark, (IV.6), VI.38; WIN, VII.38;
                      Hol. EB(A), 1945; Enige Weg, (I.8), 25.V.38; IVe Int, (I.5),
                          VIII.39.
                  ⌊T4266,4267.⌋

380115   Shumikha vokrug Kronshtadta. (Hue and cry over Kronstadt. (<u>BO</u>, (66-67),
            V-VI.38)
            <u>Trans</u>.: Am. 700400: 160-4; <u>NI</u>, IV.38;
                        Eng. [610000(9)];
                        Fr. <u>EM</u>, (1), I.69; <u>LOuv</u>(B), (III.8,9), 19,26.II.38; <u>LOuv</u>(Fr),
                            (III.67), 17.II.38; <u>QI</u>, (5), II.38;
                        Hol. <u>EB</u>(A), 1945; <u>Enige Weg</u>, (I.3,4), 10,30.III.38.
            [Anarchism; Kronstadt. See further 380706. T4268,4269.]

380117   Alternative for 380127(1).

380120   Letter to Dwight MacDonald.
            <u>Trans</u>.: Am. <u>FI</u>, III-IV.50.
            [World affairs.]

380121(1)   To the Editorial Board, <u>De Nieuwe Fakkel</u> and of <u>De Internationale</u>.
            <u>Trans</u>.: Am. 700400: 97; <u>SWP</u>, (5), VIII.38;
                        Fr. <u>BI</u>, (3), V.38; <u>PSR</u>, (14), V.38; <u>QI</u>, (6-7), III-IV.38;
                        Hol. <u>Enige Weg</u>, (I.1), 18.II.38.
            [ILOpp section in Holland. T4270,4271.]

380121(2)   Letter to IS.
            <u>Trans</u>.: Am. p.q. 690000(13), 59; 700400: 97-8; <u>SWP</u>, (5), VIII.38;
                        Fr. <u>BI</u>, (3), V.38; <u>PSR</u>, (14), V.38.
            [On FI.]

380126   A caricature of defeatism.
            <u>Trans</u>.: Am. 700400: 100; <u>IIB</u>, (2), IV.38; <u>III</u>, (3), 1938; <u>SWP</u>, (3),
                        VIII.38;
                        Fr. <u>BI</u>, (2), IV.38; <u>PSR</u>, (13), IV.38;
                        Ger. <u>IIB</u>(G), (1), IV.38.
            [On ILOpp section in Holland. T4272.]

380127(1)   The fifth wheel.
            <u>Trans</u>.: Am. 700400: 177-8; <u>SocAp</u>, 12.II.38;
                        Fr. <u>Commune</u>, (147), 7.X.38;
                        Hol. <u>Enige Weg</u>, (I.4), 30.III.38;
                        Sp. <u>IV Int</u>, (II.19), VIII.38.
            [On anarchism. T4273,4374.]

380127(2)   Lettre.
            <u>Trans</u>.: Fr. <u>POI</u>, (4), 20.III.38.
            [On ILOpp.]

380204   Letter to a young student.

Trans.: Am. 700400: 174; Challenge of Youth, III.38.

[On Moscow trials. T4282.]

380212   Carta retratto a Espinosa.

Trans.: Fr. Babel, (15-16), I-IV.41.

380216   Ikh moral i nasha. (Their morals and ours.) (BO, (68-69), IX.38)

Trans.: Am. [420000(7)]; 420800; p.q. 640800: 331-41; p.q. 650900:
370-99; 660800(1): p.q. 670600: 63-5; 690000(14); p.q.
690400(2): 63-5; p.q. 700800(1): 63-5; NI, VI.38;
Eng. [620000(14)]; p.q. 640000(5): 370-99; p.q. 640000(10):
370-99; 680700: 5-47;
Fr. 390320; [600000(19)]; [650000(14)]; 660510: 17-103; p.q.
680000(4): passim; p.q. Voie de Lénine, (1), IV.39;
Ger. 671000; UWort, (VI.4-5), X.38;
Gr. 650000(2);
Hol. 460000(2); 690000(16); Enige Weg, (II.6-9), 26.IV-8.VI.39;
It. 581000; 670831;
Jap. p.q. 681010: 117-9; p.q. 681125: 346-56;
Sin. 631200;
Sp. 390000(3); *390000(8); 620719; p.q. 670000(5): 334-44;
Swed. p.q. 691100(2): 298-307.

[PS undated. T4275-7.]

380218   Leon Sedoff. Sees possibilities of foul play.

Trans.: Am. 691100(1): 67; SocAp, 26.II.38;
Eng. Forward, 5.III.38; Mil(A), (V.6), 11.IV.38.

[T4278,T4279.]

380220   Lev Sedov: syn, drug, borets. (Leon Sedov -- Son, friend, fighter.)
(BO, (64), III.38)

Trans.: Am. 380300(1); 691100(1): 68-73; p.q. Labor Challenge, (II.4),
III.46;
Ch. *[390200(3)];
Eng. 620000(13); 671200;
Fr. 530000(2); LOuv(Fr), (III.70-72), 17-31.III.38; Rév(G),
(II.5), V.38; V, (2), VI.38.

[Obituary. T4280,T4281.]

380224   Nails fresh attack on his asylum.
                Trans.: Am. 700400: 178-80; SocAp, 5.III.38;
                        Eng. WIN, IV.38.
                [T4284-6.]

380228   Moskovskii protsess 21-go: novaya rasprava. (The Moscow trial of the
                21: A new massacre.) (BO, (64), III.38)
                Trans.: Am. 700400: 123-4; SocAp, 12.III.38.

300300(1)   LEON SEDOFF, SON — FRIEND — FIGHTER.
                [Trans. Am. See 380220 for all trans.]

[380300(2)]   —: Zametki na polyakh otchetov Pravdy o protsesse 21-go. (Notes
                in the margin of Pravda's report on the trial of the 21.)
                (BO, (64), III.38)
                Trans.: Am. 700400: 145-6.
                [T4326,4327.]

380301(1)   Eight ministers.
                Trans.: Am. 700400: 124; NYTimes, 3.III.38; SocAp, 12.III.38;
                        Eng. WIN, IV.38;
                        Fr. LOuv(Fr), (III.70), 17.III.38; V, (2), VI.38.

[380301(2)]   De russiske "tilståelser" og Russlands utenrikspolitikk.
                Trans.: Nor. Tidens Tegn, (73), 28.III.38.
                [On Moscow trials.]

380302   Sees trial as reply to Dewey.
                Trans.: Am. 700400: 128-9; NYTimes, 3.III.38.
                [On Moscow trials. T4291,4292.]

380303(1)   Did Soviet doctors murder Maxim Gorky?
                Trans.: Am. 700400: 130-1; NYTimes, 4.III.38;
                        Eng. Forward, 26.III.38.
                [On Moscow trials. T4293,4294.]

380303(2)   On Hearst.
                Trans.: Am. 700400: 174; SocAp, 19.III.38.

380303(3)   To the attention of thinking people.
                Trans.: Am. 700400: 130.
                [On Moscow trials. T4297.]

380304(1)   Popravki i primechaniya k pokazaniyam podsudimykh. (Corrections and notes to the evidence of the accused.) (BO, (65), IV.38)

Trans.: Am. 700400: 132-3.

[On Moscow trials. T4301.]

380304(2)   Forecasts Vyshinsky's tactics.

Trans.: Am. 700400: 131-2; NYTimes, 5.III.38.

380305   Denies receipt of Soviet funds.

Trans.: Am. 700400: 133-4; p.q. NYTimes, 6.III.38.

[T4302.]

380306(1)   Sees army opposed to Stalin.

Trans.: Am. 700400: 134-5; NYTimes, 7.III.38.

[T4303.]

[380306(2)]   Behind the Moscow trials.

Trans.: Am. 700400: 125-8; IP, (VIII.9), 9.III.70;

Eng. Sunday Express, 6.III.38;

Nor. Tidens Tegn, (55), 7.III.38.

[T4305.]

380307   L.T.: Rol Genrikha Yagody. (The role of Heinrich Yagoda.) (BO, (65), IV.38)

Trans.: Am. 700400: 136-7; NYTimes, 8.III.38;

Fr. Commune, (126), 19.V.38.

[On Moscow trials. T4308,4309.]

380308(1)   Diplomaticheskie plany Moskvy v zerkale protsessa. (Moscow's diplomatic plans in the light of the trials.) (BO, (65), IV.38)

Trans.: Am. 700400: 138-9; NYTimes, 9.III.38;

Eng. p.q. 690321; Controversy, VII.38; WIN, VI.38;

Fr. Commune, (132), 10.VI.38;

Ger. UWort, (VI.87), V.38;

Hol. EB(A), 1945; Enige Weg, (I.9), 8.VI.38.

380308(2)   Anachronisms.

Trans.: Am. 700400: 137.

[On Moscow trials. T4311.]

[380308(3)]   Eine Erklaerung.

Trans.: Ger. UWort, 8.III.38 [processed inset. LocIISG.]

380309   Statya Stalina o mirovoi revolyutsii i nyneshnii protsess. (Stalin's article on world revolution and the current trial.) (<u>BO</u>, (65), IV.38)
<u>Trans</u>.: Am. 700400: 139-41;
         Fr. <u>Commune</u>, (96/131), 9.III/3.VI.38;
         Ger. <u>UWort</u>, (VI.3), V.38.
[Stalin's letter to Ivanov. T4315,4316.]

380310(1)   Itogi protsessa. (Review of the trial.) (<u>BO</u>, (65), IV.38)
<u>Trans</u>.: Am. 700400: 141-3;
         Eng. <u>Forward</u>, 16.IV.38;
         Fr. <u>V</u>, (2), VI.38.
[On Moscow trials. 2 parts. T4317,4318.]

380310(2)   L.T.: Sluchai s prof. Pletnevya. (The case of Prof. Pletnev.) (<u>BO</u>, (65), IV.38)
<u>Trans</u>.: Am. 700400: 143-4; <u>SocAp</u>, 26.III.38.
[T4319,4320.]

380310(3)   Lettre à Jeanne Martin.
<u>Trans</u>.: Fr. <u>V</u>, (4), 5.V.38.
[On family matters.]

380311   L.T.: Podsudimye Zelenskii i Ivanov. (The accused Zelensky and Ivanov.) (<u>BO</u>, (65), IV.38)
<u>Trans</u>.: Am. 700400: 144-5.
[On Moscow trials. T4321,4322.]

380312   L.T.: Stalin i Gitler. (Stalin and Hitler.) (<u>BO</u>, (65), IV.38)
<u>Trans</u>.: Am. 700400: 146-7; <u>SocAp</u>, 26.III.38;
         Fr. <u>Commune</u>, (118), 30.IV.38; <u>LOuv</u>(B), (III.20), 14.V.38;
         Hol. <u>RodeOct</u>, (III.6), VI.38.
[On Vyshinsky's concluding speech at Moscow trial. T4323,4324.]

380313   Letter to Kirchwey.
<u>Trans</u>.: Am. 700400: 80; <u>SocAp</u>, 26.III.38.
[On Moscow trials. T4325.]

380317(1)   --: Novye nevozvrashchentsy. (New defectors.) (<u>BO</u>, (65), IV.38)
<u>Trans</u>.: Am. 700400: 180-1.
[On Soviet Union. T4330,4331.]

380317(2)   [Reply to letter to Editor, from Bilamnis, Latvian Minister in
                Washington.]
                <u>Trans</u>.: Am. 700400: 147-8; <u>NYTimes</u>, 21.III.38.
                [On Moscow trials. T4332.]

380319   The priests of half-truth.
                <u>Trans</u>.: Am. 700400: 81-2; <u>SocAp</u>, 16.IV.38;
                        Eng. <u>WIN</u>, V.38;
                        Fr. <u>QI</u>, (10), VII.38.
                [On USA. T4333,4334.]

380321   Alternative for 380331.

380331   Letter to League of Nations.
                <u>Trans</u>.: Am. 700400: 121-2; <u>SocAp</u>, 23.IV.38;
                        Eng. <u>WIN</u>, V.38;
                        Fr. <u>LOuv</u>(B), (III.20), 14.V.38; <u>LOuv</u>(Fr), (III.77), 5.V.38;
                        Ger. <u>UWort</u>, (VI.3), V.38.
                [Demanding trial of Stalin as a terrorist. T4337,4338.]

[380400(1)]   —: Kain Dzhugashvili idet do kontsa. (Cain Djugashvili goes the
                whole way.) (<u>BO</u>, (65), IV.38)
                <u>Trans</u>.: Am. 700400: 148;
                        Fr. <u>Commune</u>, (120), 3.V.38.
                [T4328,4329.]

380400(2)   Crux: Labor Party discussion.
                <u>Trans</u>.: Am. [620000(15)]; 690825: 10-21; <u>EB</u>, V.48.
                [T4339.]

380410   Lettre à Jeanne Martin.
                <u>Trans</u>.: Fr. p.q. <u>V</u>, (4), 5.V.39.
                [On family matters.]

380415   Letter to Cannon/to New York.
                <u>Trans</u>.: Am. p.q. 400124.

380418(1)   Pref. MARXISM AND SCIENCE, 491000.
                <u>Trans</u>.:Am. 491000.
                [See 250917 for all trans. T4343,4344.]

380418(2)   Lettre à Jeanne Martin.
                <u>Trans</u>.: Fr. p.q. <u>V</u>, (4), 5.V.39.
                [On family matters.]

380422   Fair play for Mexico.
              Trans.: Am. 691100(1): 84; SocAp, 14.V.38;
                      Eng. Forward, 7.V.38;
                      Sp. 611025: 16-9; 690700(2): 183; BIM, (3), VII.38;
                          El Universal, 23.IV.38.
              [Letter to Daily Herald(Ln), T4345.]

380423   Alternative for 380422.

380500(1)   --: Agoniya kapitalizma i zadachi Chetvertogo Internatsionala. (The
              death agony of capitalism and the tasks of the Fourth International.)
              (BO, (66-67), V-VI.38)
              Trans.: Am. 460501; 640000(9); p.q. 640800: 254-60,279-81; 700200(2);
                          SocAp, 22.X.38; FOUNDING CONFERENCE: 15-53;
                      Ch. 380000(19);
                      Den. [680000(5)];
                      Eng. 380000(5); 420000(1); 560000(1); 630000(2); WIN, IV.39;
                      Fr. [380000(10)]; 440800(1); 460800; 680612(1); 690900(3);
                          p.q. 700000(6): 54-6; QI, (8,12-13), V, IX-X.38; p.q.
                          Voie de Lénine, (V.14), 21-28.I.45;
                      Gr. 630000(12); Diethnistes, (11-12), XI-XII.65;

                      Hol. [470000(4)]; [630000(3)]; IIB(G), V.38;
                      It. p.q. 680200(2): 135-42; p.q. MARXISMO: 100-3;
                      Jap. *[600000(18)]; 631130: 243-98; p.q. 681125: 266-72,292-3;
                          700831: 17-44;
                      Nor. Okt, (II.6-7), XI-XII.38;
                      Sin. 640200: 13-81;
                      Sp. p.q. 381100; *640000(6); [650000(11)]; p.q. 670000(5):
                          274-6; Clave, (I.3,4), XII.38,I.39; ⌀ Obrero Militante,
                          VIII-IX.62; Presente, XI.38;
                      Swed. p.q. 681100(2): 228-33,251-2; 691100(3).
              [Transitional Programme. See also 380415,380519,380607. T4340-2.]

380519   Crux: Remarks on the Transitional Program.
              Trans.: Am. 690300(2): 1-4; 691100(1): 43; SWP, (2), 1938;
                      Fr. [480000(9)]; QI, VI-VII.46.
              [See 380500(1). T4346.]

380522   Learn to think.

Trans.: Am. 691100(1): 5; <u>NI</u>, VII.38;

         Eng. <u>WIN</u>, VIII.38; I.43;

         Fr. <u>QI</u>, (10), VII.38;

         Hol. <u>Enige Weg</u>, (I.13), 3.VIII.38.

[Fourth International and war. T4348,4349.]

380531(1)   Crux: Discussion upon the Labor Party(USA).

Trans.: Am. [620000(15)]; 690300(2): 5-10; 690825: 21-7; <u>EB</u>, V.38;

         <u>SWP</u>, (2), 1938.

[T4352,4353.]

380531(2)   "For" the Fourth International? No! The Fourth International.

Trans.: Am. 691100(1): 45; <u>III</u>, (3), 1938; <u>SWP</u>, (3), VIII.38.

[T4354,4355.]

380600   Nationalized industry and workers' management.

Trans.: Am. 691100(1): 87; <u>FI</u>, VIII.46;

         Eng. 690300(1); <u>WIN</u>, VIII.48;

         Fr. <u>QI</u>, X-XI.46;

         Gr. <u>Marxistiko Deltio</u>, (VII.43), IX.66;

         Sp. 611025: 25-9; 690700(2): 193.

380601(1)   Letter to Shachtman.

Trans.: p.q. 400124.

380601(2)   A la conférence internationale de la IVe Internationale.

Trans.: Am. 691100(1): 47; <u>IP</u>, (VII.30), 22.IX.69;

         Fr. 640911: 349-51.

[On Art and Literature. T4356.]

380602   Crux: Conversation on Czecho-Slovakia.

Trans.: Am. 691100(1): 6; <u>III</u>, (3), 1938; <u>SWP</u>, (3), VIII.38;

         Eng. <u>RSL</u>, X.38.

[On coming world war.]

380605   Meksika i britanskii imperializm. (Mexico and British imperialism.)

(<u>BO</u>, (70), X.38)

Trans.: Am. 691100(1): 85; <u>SocAp</u>, 25.VI.38;

         Eng. <u>Forward</u>, 25.VI.38;

         Fr. <u>Lutte</u>, (205), 14.VIII.38; <u>QI</u>, X-XI.46;

         Ger. <u>UWort</u>, (VI.4-5), X.38;

++++

380605   +++   Trans.: Hol. Enige Weg, (I.18), 12.X.38;

                  Sp. 611025: 16-9; 670000(5): 690700(2): 187; BIM, (3), VII.38;

                      Presente, XI.61; El Universal, 7.VI.38.

        [T4358,4359.]

380606   Alternative for 380605.

380607   Crux: Discussion on the Transitional Program.

        Trans.: Am. 690300(2): 11-20; 691100(1): 48; FI, II.46; SWP, (I.6),

                VIII.38;

              Fr. ⌊380000(8)⌋; EM, (2), II.69;

              Sp. BAO, (3), X.38.

        [See 380500(1). T4357.]

380610   La bureaucratie totalitaire et l'Art.

        Trans.: Fr. 640911: 352-3; LOuv(Fr), (III.86), 22.VII.38;

              It. 680000(6): 131-3;

              Sp. 690000(8).II: 183-4;

              Swed. 690600(1): 314-5.

        [T4360.]

380612   Letter to IS: on Diego Rivera.

        Trans.: Eng. p.q. Deutscher, PO: 444.

380617   See 380618(1).

380618(1)   Iskusstva i revolyutsiya. (Art and revolution.) (BO, (77-78), V-VII.39)

        Trans.: Am. FI, III-IV.50; Partisan Review, VIII.38;

              Eng. WIN, IV.39;

              Fr. 640911: 354-63; LOuv(Fr), (III.86), 22.VII.38; QI, (11),

                VIII.38;

              Gr. 660000(6): 248-57;

              It. 680000(6): 115-27;

              Sp. 640900(1): 197-208; 690000(8).II: 185-94; Clave, (I.5), II.39.

        ⌊T4365,4366.⌋

380618(2)   No, it is not the same.

        Trans.: Am. 691100(1): 137; SocAp, 2.VII.38.

        [On Lovestone, Moscow trials. T4367,4368.]

380619   See 380618(1).

380703(1) K.: Iz sovetov dolzhny byt izgnany byurokratiya i novaya sovetskaya aristokratiya. (It is necessary to drive out the bureaucracy and the new Soviet bureaucracy from the soviets.) (BO, (68-69), VIII-IX.38)
Trans.: Am. 691100(1): 53; FI, Winter, 1954; SWP, (I.6), VIII.38.
[Contribution to a discussion. T4370,4371.]

380703(2) --: Totalitarnye porazhentsy. (Totalitarian defeatists.) (BO, (68-69), VIII-IX.38)
Trans.: Fr. QI, (14-15), XI-XII.38;
            Hol. Enige Weg, (II.5), 13.IV.39;
            Nor. Okt, (III.2), V.39.
[On Soviet Union. cf. [381126]. T4372,4373.]

380704 Alternative for 380703(1).

380705 --: Stalin i ego soobshchiki osuzhdeny. (Stalin and his accomplices condemned.) (BO, (68-69), VIII-IX.38)
Trans.: Am. 700400: 72.
[T4362-4,4374.]

380706 Eshche ob usmirenii Kronshtadta. (More on the suppression of Kronstadt.) (BO, (70), X.38)
Trans.: Am. 700400: 164; NI, VIII.38;
            Fr. QI, (11), VIII.38.
[See 380115. T4376,4377.]

380710 Declaracion al periodico Vida.
Trans.: Sp. IV Int, (II.19), VIII.38.
[T4379.]

380717 K godovshchine gibeli Raissa. (The anniversary of Reiss's death.)
(BO, (68-69), VIII-IX.38)
Trans.: Am. 700400: 122;
            Fr. LOuv(Fr), (III.95), 21.X.38;
            Gr. UWort, (VI.6-7), XII.38.
[T4380,4381.]

380718 Fears Klement's fate.
Trans.: Am. 691100(1): 74; SocAp, 30.VII.38.
[T4384,4385.]

380719(1)   On my conspiracy.
             <u>Trans</u>.: Am. 691100(1): 88; <u>SocAp</u>, 30.VII.38;
                  Sp. <u>IV Int</u>, (II.19), VIII.38.
             [On stay in Mexico. T4386,4387.]

380719(2)   Sledstvie po delu o smerti moego syna L'va Sedova. (The investigation
             into the case of the death of my son, Leon Sedov.) (<u>BO</u>, (68-69),
             VIII-IX.38)
             <u>Trans</u>.: Am. 691100(1): 74; <u>SocAp</u>, 13.VIII.38;
                  Eng. 671200: 39-46; <u>WIN</u>, IX.38;
                  Fr. <u>Commune</u>, (142), 26.VIII.38; <u>QI</u>, (14-15), XI-XII.38;
                  Hol. <u>NFakkel</u>, (IV.36), 9.IX.38.
             [T4388,4389.]

380720   Crux: Conversation on the Labor Party(USA).
             <u>Trans</u>.: Am. [620000(15)]; 690825: 27-31; <u>EB</u>, V.48; <u>SWP</u>, (7), VIII.38.
             [T4390.9.]

380723   —: Pokhishchenie tov. Klementa. (The kidnapping of cde. Klement.)
             (<u>BO</u>, (68-69), VIII-IX.38)
             [T4390,4391.]

380724   L.T.: Predstoyashchii protsess diplomatov. (The forthcoming trial
             of the diplomats.) (<u>BO</u>, (68-69), VIII-IX.38)
             <u>Trans</u>.: Am. 691100(1): 99;
                  Eng. <u>Forward</u>, 20.VIII.38; <u>Mil</u>(A), (I.2), 1.X.38.
             [Moscow trials. T4392,4393.]

380725(1)   Alternative for 380724.

380725(2)   André Breton & Diego Rivera: Manifesto: Towards a free revolutionary Art.
             <u>Trans</u>.: Am. <u>Partisan Review</u>, Fall, 1938; <u>World Outlook</u>, (IV.31), 14.X.66;
                  Eng. 630000(1): 34-9; <u>Art & Artists</u>, (IV.5), VIII.69; <u>Black
                       Dwarf</u>, (XIV.27), 30.I.70; SURREALISM AND REVOLUTION: 27-30;
                  Fr. *380000(20); 640911: 364-6; <u>Contre leC</u>, (1), X.38;
                  Ger. 680800(2): 440-6;
                  Hol. <u>RodeOct</u>, (IV), 1939: 69-72;
                  It. 581000: 111-6; 680000(6): 105-11;
                  Sp. 640900(1): 268-75; 690000(8).II: 195-200; <u>Clave</u>, (I.1),
                       1.X.38;
                  Swed. 690600(1): 326-31.
             [See Breton, LA CLÉ DES CHAMPS: 41, n. 1 on authorship. T4394.]

380729   Conversation on the slogan "For a Workers and Farmers Government."
<u>Trans</u>.: Am. 691100(1): 54; <u>SWP</u>, (7), VIII.38.
[On USA. T4395.]

380801   Tells of a "letter" from victim of GPU.
<u>Trans</u>.: Am. 691100(1): 77; <u>SocAp</u>, 13.VIII.38;
         Fr. <u>Commune</u>, (142), 26.VIII.38;
         Hol. <u>NFakkel</u>, (IV.34), 26.VIII.38.
[On Klement. T4400,4401.]

380803   Po povodu sud´by Rudol´fa Klementa. (On the fate of Rudolf Klement.)
(<u>BO</u>, (68-69), VIII-IX.38)
<u>Trans</u>.: Am. 691100(1): 77; <u>SocAp</u>, 20.VIII.38;
         Fr. <u>LOuv</u>(Fr), (III.88), 2.IX.38;
         Hol. <u>NFakkel</u>, (IV.33), 19.VIII.38.
[PS 380804. T4402,4403.]

380804   PS to 380803.
<u>Trans</u>.: Am. 691100(1): 80; <u>SocAp</u>, 20.VIII.38;
         Eng. <u>WIN</u>, IX.38.
[T4402,4403.]

380811   L.T.: SSSR i Yaponiya. (The USSR and Japan.) (<u>BO</u>, (70), X.38)
<u>Trans</u>.: Am. 691100(1): 8; <u>SocAp</u>, 27.VIII.38;
         Eng. <u>Forward</u>, 3.IX.38;
         Fr. <u>LOuv</u>(Fr), (III.89), 16.IX.38.
[T4406,4407.]

380824   Sledstvie po delu o smerti L´va Sedova. (The investigation into the
case of the death of Leon Sedov.) (<u>BO</u>, (70), X.38)
<u>Trans</u>.: Am. 691100(1): 8; <u>SocAp</u>, 10.IX.38;
         Fr. <u>Commune</u>, XII.38; <u>QI</u>, (14-15), XI-XII.38.
[T4412,4413.]

380830   —: Krupnyi uspekh. (A great achievement.) (<u>BO</u>, (70), X.38)
<u>Trans</u>.: Am. 691100(1): 56; <u>NI</u>, X.38;
         Den. <u>4I</u>, (III.1), I.39;
         Fr. <u>QI</u>, (12-13), IX-X.38;
         Ger. <u>UWort</u>, (VI.6-7), XII.38;
         Hol. <u>Enige Weg</u>, (I.17), 28.IV.38; <u>IVe Int</u>, (I.2), [I.39];
         Nor. <u>Okt</u>, (II.6-7), XI-XII.38;

++++

380830   ++++   <u>Trans</u>.: Sp. <u>BAO</u>, (3), X.38.

[On founding of Fourth International. T4415,4416.]

380900   Lettre à Sieva.

<u>Trans</u>.: Fr. p.q. <u>V</u>, (4), 5.V.39.

[On family matters.]

380903   --: Manifest konferentsii Chetvertogo Internatsionala k rabochim

vsego mira. (Manifesto of the Fourth International to the workers

of the whole world.) (<u>BO</u>, (72), XII.38)

<u>Trans</u>.: Am. <u>SocAp</u>, 22.X.38; FOUNDING CONFERENCE: 56-62;

Hol. <u>Enige Weg</u>, (II.13), 7.IX.39;

Sp. p.q. 611025: 47-50; <u>Clave</u>, (I.2), XI.38; <u>IV Int</u>, (II.24),

VIII.39.

[Against imperialist war.]

380915   Alternative for 380903.

380917   "Navstrenu resheniyu." ("Towards a decision.") (<u>BO</u>, (70), X.38)

<u>Trans</u>.: Am. 691100(1): 57; <u>NI</u>, XI.38.

[Review of Czerny, TOWARDS A DECISION [a Cz. book]. T4421,4422.]

380919(1)   Frazy i real'nost. (Phrases and reality.) (<u>BO</u>, (70), X.38)

<u>Trans</u>.: Am. 691100(1): 9; <u>SocAp</u>, 1.X.38;

Fr. [600000(26)]; <u>LOuv</u>(Fr), (III.95), 21.X.38;

Ger. <u>UWort</u>, (VI.6-7), XII.38;

Hol. <u>Enige Weg</u>, (I.21), 23.XI.38; <u>IVe Int</u>, (I.1), XII.38;

Sp. <u>Clave</u>, (I.1), 1.X.38.

[PS 380922. T4423,4424.]

380919(2)   --: Totaliternoe "pravo ubezhishcha". (The totalitarian "right of

asylum".) (<u>BO</u>, (70), X.38)

<u>Trans</u>.: Am. 700400: 181;

Sp. <u>Clave</u>, (I.1), 1.X.38.

[On Toledano's attacks. T4425.]

380919(3)   Letter to Seva.

<u>Trans</u>.: Eng. p.q. Deutscher, PO: 405.

[On family matters.]

380920   Au sujet de l'assassinat de Rudolf Klement.

<u>Trans</u>.: Am. 691100(1): 83;

++++

380920   ++++   Trans.: Fr. LOuv(Fr), (III.92), 30.IX.38.
[T4426.9.]

380921   Iz inter'vyu s predstavitelyami yuzhno-amerikanskoi pressy. (From an
interview with a representative of the South American press.)
(BO, (74), II.39)
Trans.: Am. 691100(1): 89; SocAp, 8.X.38.
[To El Pais, Cuba. Fight against imperialism. T4427,4428.]

380922   PS to 380919(1).

380923   Iz besedy s argentinskim delegatom tov. Fossa. (From a talk with an
Argentian delegate, cde. Fossa.) (BO, (70), X.38)
Trans.: Am. 691100(1): 90; SocAp, 5.XI.38;
       Fr. QI, (14-15), XI-XII.38;
       Hol. Enige Weg, (I.21), 23.XI.38;
       Sp. p.q. 611025: 32-4; p.q. 670000(5): 279-81; p.q. 690700(2):
           199; Accion Obrera, 1941; Clave, (I.2), XI.38.
[Fight against imperialism. T4429,4430.]

380925   Alternative for 380922.

380926   Alternative for 380923.

380929   Kruks: Beseda o zadachakh amerikanskikh professional'nykh soyuzov.
(Talk on the tasks of the American trade unions.) (BO, (71), XI.38)
Trans.: Am. 690000(13): 62-8; SocAp, 29.X.38.
[T4431,4432.]

381006   On the Party press.
Trans.: p.q. 400124.

381007   After Munich, Stalin will seek accord with Hitler.
Trans.: Am. 691100(1): 11; SocAp, 8.X.38;
       Fr. 700126: 65-6; p.q. CES, (4), 30.X.39;
       Hol. NFakkel, (IV.43), 28.X.38; IVe Int, (I.5), VIII.39.

381009   ¿QUÉ SIGNIFICA LA LUCHA CONTRA EL "TROTSKISMO"?
[Trans. Sp. T4433,4434.]

381010   Svezhii urok. (A fresh lesson.) (BO, (71), XI.38)
            Trans.: Am. 691100(1): 17; p.q. FI, VIII.45; NI, XII.38;
                    Eng. 430800(1); Spark, (V.2,3), II,III.39; WIN, I,II.39;
                    Fr. 380000(1); 380000(2); 380000(3); p.q. 680000(4): 124-8;
                        p.q. 700126: 47-68; LOuv(Fr), (III.100,101), 25.XI, 2.XII.38;
                        p.q. Guerin: 275-6;
                    Hol. Enige Weg, (I.24,25), 4,18.I.39; IVe Int, (I.3), [II.39];
                    Sp. Babel, (5), 1939; Clave, (I.2), XI.38.
            [On the character of the coming war. See 381014 note. T4435,4436.]

381014   Social-patriotic sophistry.
            Trans.: Am. NI, XI.38;
                    Fr. LOuv(Fr), (III.97), 4.XI.38;
                    Hol. Enige Weg, (I.20), 9.XI.38.
            [New trans. of p.q. 381010 with re-arrangement of sentences.]

381018   Rech: na gramofonnoi plastnike (na angliiskom yazyke). (Speech, in
            English, on gramophone disc.) (BO, (71), XI.38)
            Trans.: Am. 691100(1): 58; FI, X.40; Labor Challenge, (II.18), X.46;
                    SocAp, 5.XI.38;
                    Eng. [430000(4)]; SocAp(Ln), (V.12), VI.43.
            [On founding of Fourth International and on 10th anniversary of the
            American section of the ILOpp. T4440-2.]

381022(1)   V redaktsii Byulletenya Oppozitsiya, Lutte Ouvrière i IVe Internationale.
            (To the Eds. Byulleten Oppozitsii, Lutte Ouvrière(Fr) and IVe
            Internationale.) (BO, (72), XII.38)
            Trans.: Am. 700400: 177.
            [T4443,4444.]

381022(2)   Red.: Lozhnyi vzglyad. (A false view.) (BO, (72), XII.38)
            Trans.: Am. 700400: 158.
            [On stalinism. T4447,4448.]

381022(3)   --: Predateli v roli obvinitelei. (Traitors in the role of accusers.)
            (BO, (72), XII.38)
            Trans.: Sp. Clave, (I.2), XI.38.
            [On stalinism, Spain. T4449,4450.]

381027   Lettre à G.Rosenthal.
            Trans.: Fr. p.q. Naville: 101.

381028   Greetings to Antoinette Konikow.

               Trans.: Am. <u>Mil</u>, 13.VII.46.

               [See photograph.]

*381100   *LA URSS Y LOS PROBLEMAS DE LA EPOCA DE TRANSICIÓN.

               [Trans. Sp. p.q. 380500(1).]

381108   Karl Kautskii. (<u>BO</u>, (73), I.39)

               Trans.: Am. 690700(1): 25-6; <u>NI</u>, II.39;

                     Fr. <u>LOuv</u>(Fr), (III.102), 16.XII.38;

                     Ger. <u>UWort</u>, (VII.1), II.39;

                     Sp. <u>Clave</u>, (I.4), I.39.

               [Obituary. T4456,4457.]

381110   Defends asylum. In reply to Toledano.

               Trans.: Am. 691100(1): 93; <u>SocAp</u>, 19.XI.38.

381114   —: 21-ya godovshchina. (The 21st anniversary.) (<u>BO</u>, (73), I.39)

               Trans.: Am. 700400: 172-3;

                     Fr. <u>LOuv</u>(Fr), (III.102), 16.XII.38;

                     Hol. <u>NFakkel</u>, (V.3), 20.I.39.

               [On October Revolution. T4465.]

[381126]   Why Russia is powerless.

               Trans.: Am. 691100(1): 100; <u>Liberty</u>, 26.XI.38.

               [cf. 380703(2).]

381128   Telegraph reply to Father Coughlin.

               Trans.: Am. p.q. <u>NYTimes</u>, 29.XI.38.

               [On slanders. T4473.]

381201   Po povodu ubiistva Rudol′fa Klementa. (On the murder of Rudolf Klement.)

               (<u>BO</u>, (73), I.39)

               [T4474,4475.]

381202   Red.: Viktor Serzh i IV Internatsional. (Victor Serge and the Fourth

               International.) (<u>BO</u>, (73), I.39)

               Trans.: Am. 691100(1): 138.

               [T4478,4479.]

[381213]   Interview, with Wm.R.Mathews.

               Trans.: Am. 691100(1): 138, <u>Arizona Daily Star</u>, 13.XII.38; 13.XII.42;

                     p.q. <u>NYTimes</u>, 13.XII.38.

381214 **Chas resheniya blizitsya.** (The decisive hour.) (BO, (74), II.39)

  <u>Trans</u>.: Am. 691100(1): 117; <u>SocAp</u>, 24.XII.38;

    Eng. <u>Workers Fight</u>, (II.2), I.39; <u>WIN</u>, II.39;

    Fr. 670306: 602-11; <u>LOuv</u>(Fr), (IV.103), 6.I.39;

    Ger. <u>UWort</u>, (VII.1), II.39;

    Hol. <u>Enige Weg</u>, (I.26), 1.II.39; <u>RodeOct</u>, (IV), 1939: 33-40;

    Nor. <u>Okt</u>, (III.1), II.39;

    Sp. <u>Clave</u>, (I.4), I.39.

  [On France. T4484,4485.]

381218 Alternative for 381214.

381220 L.T.: **Politicheskii dialog.** (A political dialogue.) (BO, (75-76), III-IV.39)

  <u>Trans</u>.: Am. 691100(1): 59; p.q. <u>FI</u>, XI.44; <u>IP</u>, (VII.33), 13.X.69;

    Eng. <u>Workers Fight</u>, (4), IX.39;

    Ger. 470000(2): 3-8; <u>UWort</u>, 1939;

    Hol. <u>Enige Weg</u>, (II.11), 6.VII.39; <u>IVe Int</u>, (I.5), VIII.39.

  [On Fourth International. T4486,4487.]

381222(1) Where is the PSOP going?

  <u>Trans</u>.: Am. 691100(1): 121; <u>NI</u>, V.39;

    Fr. 670306: 615-7; <u>BQI</u>, (1), VI.39;

    Sp. <u>Clave</u>, (I.9), 1.VI.39.

  [On France; to Pivert. T4488,4489.]

381222(2) Letter.

  <u>Trans</u>.: Am. 700700: 29-30; <u>FI</u>, XII.45; <u>Labor Challenge</u>, (II.18), VII.46;

    Eng. <u>WIN</u>, VI-VII.46;

    Hol. <u>RodeOct</u>, (1), VIII.46.

  [On Jewish problem. T4490,4491.]

381222(3) **Za svobodu iskusstva.** (For the freedom of Art.) (BO, (74), II.39)

  <u>Trans</u>.: Am. <u>Partisan Review</u>, Winter, 1939;

    Fr. <u>Clé</u>, (2), II.39;

    Hol. <u>Enige Weg</u>, (II.4), 29.III.39;

    Nor. <u>Okt</u>, (III.1), III.39.

  [Letter to Breton. T4492,4493.]

381228 **Otvet na voprosy predstavitelya** <u>Daily News</u>. (Reply to questions from <u>Daily News</u>(USA) correspondent.) (BO, (74), II.39) ++++

381228   ++++   <u>Trans</u>.: Am. 691100(1): 94; <u>Mil</u>, 18.IV.60; <u>SocAp</u>, 14.I.39;

               Fr. <u>LOuv</u>(Fr), (IV.107), 3.II.39.

        [Pasley slanders answered. T4494,4495.]

381230   Lenin i imperialisticheskaya voina. (Lenin and imperialist war.)

        (<u>BO</u>, (74), II.39)

        <u>Trans</u>.: 410000(1): Ch. VI;

               Am. 410000(1): Ch. VI; 691100(1): 142; <u>FI</u>, I.42;

               Eng. 430800(1); 680200: 24-32; <u>Bolshevik-Leninist</u>, VIII.42;

                  <u>PermRev</u>(India), (—), I.43.

        [Trans. differ in Am. texts. T4496.]

390000(1)   ESPAÑA, ÚLTIMA ADVERTENCIA: la leccion de España, la ultima
            Advertencia.
            [Trans. Sp. See 371217 for all repr., trans.]

[390000(2)]   L'URSS DANS LA GUERRE.
              [Trans. Fr. See 390925 for all repr., trans.]

390000(3)   SU MORAL Y LA NUESTRA.
            [Trans. Sp. See 380216 for all repr., trans.]

390000(4)   THE USSR IN WAR.
            [Trans. Eng. See 390925 for all repr., trans.]

*[390000(5)]   *LA QUESTION UKRAINIENNE.
               [See 390422(1) for all repr., trans.]

*[390000(6)]   *WAARHEEN GAAT FRANKRIJK?
               [Trans. Hol. See 360000(6) for all trans.]

390000(7)   Pref. THE LIVING THOUGHTS OF KARL MARX.
            [Trans. Am. See 390418 for all repr., trans., notes.]

*390000(8)   *SU MORAL Y LA NUESTRA.
             [Trans. Sp. See 380216 for all repr., trans.]

*390000(9)   *STORIA DELLA RIVOLUZIONE RUSSA.
             [Trans. It. See 310000(1) for all repr., trans., notes.]

390000(10)   § VINGT LETTRES.
             [Trans. Fr. See 190600 for all repr., trans.]

390111   [Statement to Mexican press.]
         [c. Deutscher, PO: 445. T4504.]

[390114]   --: [Message to Stein.]
           Trans.: Am. SocAp, 14.I.39.
           [Authorship from Levine: Ch. III. On attempted assassination.]

390115   A M. le Président du Tribunal civil de la Seine.
         Trans.: Fr. p.q. V, (4), 5.V.39.
         [On family matters.]

390116   Lettre à Sieva.

Trans.: Fr. p.q. <u>V</u>, (4), 5.V.39.

[On family matters.]

390120   Letter to Shachtman.

Trans.: Am. p.q. 400107, p.q. 400124.

390121   [Letter to Enrique Espinoza.]

Trans.: Fr. <u>Babel</u>, (15-16), I-IV.41.

390130(1)   Clave: Clarity or confusion.

Trans.: Am. 691100(1): 96; <u>NI</u>, III.39;

         Eng. p.q. Deutscher, PO: 445;

         Sp. <u>Clave</u>, (I.5), II.39.

[Addressed to <u>Trinchera Aprista</u>; on Diego Rivera. T4509,4510.]

390130(2)   —: Stalin, Skoblin i Ko. (Stalin, Skoblin and Co.) (<u>BO</u>, (74), II.39)

Trans.: Sp. <u>Clave</u>, (I.6), 1.III.39.

[T4511.]

[390200(1)]   —: Ispanskaya tragediya. (The tragedy of Spain.) (<u>BO</u>, (74), II.39)

Trans.: Am. <u>SocAp</u>, 10.II.39;

         Den. <u>4I</u>, (III.2), III-IV.39;

         Eng. <u>WIN</u>, III.39;

         Fr. 590600: 553-7; <u>LOuv(Fr)</u>, (IV.3), 3.III.39;

         Gr. 630000(11): 52-5;

         Hol. <u>Enige Weg</u>, (II.3), 15.III.39; <u>IVe Int</u>, (I.3), [II.39];

         Jap. *630430; 650430: 314-6;

         Sp. 680000(9): 199.

[T4507,4508.]

[390200(2)]   —: Za Grinshpana — protiv fashistskikh pogromshchikov i stalinskikh begodyaev. (For Grynszpan — against fascist pogroms and stalinist villanies.) (<u>BO</u>, (74), II.39)

Trans.: Am. 691100(1): 144; <u>SocAp</u>, 14.II.39;

         Eng. <u>WIN</u>, III.39;

         Fr. <u>LOuv(Fr)</u>, (IV.3), 3.III.39;

         Hol. <u>Enige Weg</u>, (II.3), 15.III.39;

         Sp. <u>Clave</u>, (I.6), 1.III.39.

[T4513,4514.]

*[390200(3)]   *[LEON SEDOFF — SON — FRIEND — FIGHTER.]
                 [Trans. Ch. c. "Letter from Shanghai", BO, (74), II.39. See
                 380220 for all trans.]

390214   Letter to a friend in France.
                 Trans.: Am. 691100(1): 122; NI, V.39;
                         Fr. 670306: 618-22; BQI, (1), VI.39;
                         Sp. Clave, (I.9), 1.VI.39.
                 [To Rosmer. Sp. says to Pivert. T4517,4518.]

[390217]   —: Eks-radikal´naya intelligentsiya i mirovaya reaktsiya. (Ex-radical
                 intellectuals and world reaction.) (BO, (74), II.39)
                 Trans.: Am. 691100(1): 145; SocAp, 17.II.39;
                         Fr. QI, (16), IV.39;
                         Hol. Enige Weg, (II.6), 26.IV.39;
                         Sp. Clave, (I.5), II.39.
                 [See further 390307(1). T4505,4506.]

390304(1)   L.T.: Ispaniya, Stalin i Ezhov. (Spain, Stalin and Yezhov.)
                 (BO, (75-76), III-IV.39)
                 Trans.: Am. SocAp, 21.IV.39;
                         Sp. Clave, (I.6), 1.III.39.
                 [T4534,4535.]

390304(2)   —: Misterii imperializma. (Mysteries of imperialism.) (BO, (75-76),
                 III-IV.39)
                 Trans.: Sp. Clave, (I.6), 1.III.39.
                 [T4536,4537.]

390304(3)   L.T.: Umerla Krupskaya. (Krupskaya is dead.) (BO, (75-76), III-IV.39)
                 Trans.: Am. 691100(1): 102; NI, IV.39;
                         Fr. QI, (16), IV.39;
                         Nor. Okt, (III.2), V.39;
                         Sp. Babel, (5), 1939; Clave, (I.6), 1.III.39.
                 [T4540,4541.]

390306   L.T.: Gitler i Stalin. (Hitler and Stalin.) (BO, (75-76), III-IV.39)
                 Trans.: Am. 691100(1): 20; SocAp, 28.III.39;
                         Eng. WIN, IV.39;
                         Fr. p.q. CES, (4), 30.X.39; LOuv(Fr), (IV.115), 7.IV.39;
                         Hol. Enige Weg, (II.5), 13.IV.39.
                 [T4542,4543.]

390307(1)   T.: Eshche o "krizise marksizma". (Once again on the "crisis of marxism.") (BO, (75-76), III-IV.39)

Trans.: Am. 691100(1): 146; 700300(1): 45-7; NI, V.39;
      Ger. EWeg, (6), VII.39;
      Hol. Enige Weg, (II.11), 6.VII.39;
      Sp. Clave, (I.7), 1.IV.39.
[See [390217]. T4544,4545.]

390307(2)   Red.: **Shag v storonu** sotsial-patriotizma. (A step towards social-patriotism.) (BO, (75-76), III-IV.39)

Trans.: Am. 691100(1): 22; NI, VII.39;
      Sp. Clave, (II.1), 1.IX.39.
[On ILOpp in Palestine. T4546,4547.]

390307(3)   Al´fa: "Uchites rabotat po-stalinski!" ("Learn to work in the Stalin manner.") (BO, (75-76), III-IV.39)

Trans.: Am. 691100(1): 102; NI, V.39.
[T4548,4549.]

390309   Letter to Shachtman.

Trans.: p.q. 391215(2).

390310   L.T.: Tsentrizm i IV Internatsional. (Centrism and the Fourth International.) (BO, (75-76), III-IV.39)

Trans.: Am. 691100(1): 124; NI, V.39;
      Fr. p.q. 670306: 623-30; BQI, (1), VI.39;
      Sp. Clave, (I.9), 1.VI.39.
[To Guerin. T4550,4551.]

390311   L.T.: Kapitulyatsiya Stalina. (Stalin's capitulation.)
(BO, (75-76), III-IV.39)

Trans.: Am. 691100(1): 25; SocAp, 7.IV.39;
      Eng. Mil(A), (II.5), VII.39; WIN, VI.39; Workers Fight, (2),
         V.39;
      Fr. p.q. 700126: 69-72; p.q. CES, (4), 30.X.39; LOuv(Fr),
         (IV.117), 21.IV.39;
      Hol. Enige Weg, (II.7), 10.V.39; NFakkel, (V.42), 20.X.39;
      Sp. Clave, (I.7), 1.IV.39.
[PS 390324(1). T4552,4553.]

390318   Otvety na voprosy Miss Sybil Vincent, predstavitel'nitsy londonskogo
          Daily Herald. (Reply to questions from Miss Sybil Vincent,
          correspondent of the London Daily Herald.) (BO, (75-76), III-IV.39)
          Trans.: Am. 691100(1): 28; SocAp, 4.IV.39;
                  Eng. Daily Herald, 27.V.39;
                  Fr. p.q. 700216: 73-8; LOuv(Fr), (IV.117), 21.IV.39;
                  Hol. Rode Oct, (IV), 1939: 117-20;
                  Nor. Okt, (III.2), V.39;
                  Sp. Clave, (I.8), 1.V.39.
          [Fight against war. T4555.]

390320   LEUR MORALE ET LA NÔTRE.
          [Trans. Fr. See 380216 for all repr., trans.]

[390321] --: Eshche raz o prichinakh porazheniya ispanskoi revolyutsii.
          Izobretateli zontika. (Once again on the causes of the defeat of the
          Spanish revolution. The inventors of the umbrella.) (BO, (75-76),
          III-IV.39)
          Trans.: Am. SocAp, 21.III.39;
                  Sp. Clave, (I.6), 1.III.39.
          [T4532,4533.]

390324(1) PS 390311. (BO, (75-76), III-IV.39)
          Trans.: Am. SocAp, 7.IV.39;
                  Eng. Mil(A), (II.5), VII.39; WIN, VI.39; Workers Fight, (2);
                      V.39;
                  Fr. 700126: 79-80; LOuv(Fr), (IV.117), 21.IV.39;
                  Hol. Enige Weg, (II.7), 10.V.39;
                  Sp. Clave, (I.7), .IV.39.

390324(2) Their friend Miaja.
          Trans.: Am. SocAp, 31.III.39;
                  Hol. Enige Weg, (II.7), 10.V.39;
                  Sp. Clave, (I.7), IV.39.
          [T4557.]

390400(1) See 390409,390411.

390400(2)   Crux: Fighting against the stream: Interview with Johnson.
Trans.: Am. 691100(1): 61,63; FI, I.41, p.q. V.41; SWP, (II.7), I.40;
        Eng. p.q. ⌊600000(21)⌋; p.q. 651200;
        Fr. p.q. 670306: 631-8.
⌊Discussion of James, WORLD REVOLUTION. On ILOpp. T4559,4560.⌋

390402   See 390422(1).

390404   See 390409.

390405   See 390409.

390409   Self-determination for the American Negroes.
Trans.: Am. 670600: 24-37; 690400(2): 24-37; 700800(1): 24-37;
        FI, V,IX.48,II.49; BMS, (4), ⌊1962⌋; SWP, (I.9), VI.39;
        Eng. p.q. IntSoc, (43), IV-V.70;
        It. QI(It), (I.1), XII.67;
        Jap. 681010: 47-73.
⌊See also 390411. 3 discussions. T4561,4562.⌋

390411   Crux: Plans for the Negro organization.
Trans.: Am. 670600: 38-48; 690400(2): 38-48; 700800(1): 38-48;
        SWP, (I.9), VI.39;
        Jap. 681010: 74-92.
⌊See also 390409. T4563.⌋

390418   Marxism in our time.
Trans.: Am. 390000(7); *400000(7); 470100; 630200; p.q. 640800:
        221-5; 700300(1);
        Eng. 400000(8); 420600; 461100(2);
        Fr. 460000(5); 470910; 600000(6); p.q. 680000(4): passim;
        700129;
        Ger. 470600;
        Hol. 400000(9); 510000(2);
        It. *400000(10); *490000(3);
        Jap. p.q. 681125: 232-7; 700130: 10-57;
        Sp. *400000(11); *430625; *480000(5); p.q. 611025: 51-3;
        *620700(2); p.q. 670000(5): 218-23; p.q. 690700(2): 215;
        Swed. p.q. 691100(2): 197-201.
⌊Abr. when printed as Pref. LIVING THOUGHTS OF KARL MARX and trans.
Eng. lists 14 countries for Pref. T4519,4523-30.⌋

390419   Greets Tresca.

        Trans.: Am. 691100(1): 147; FI, II.43; SocAp, 21.IV.39.

390422(1)   Ob ukrainskom voprose. (The Ukrainian question.) (BO, (77-78),
        V-VII.39)

        Trans.: Am. 690600(3): 71-3; FI, XI.49; NI(WP), VIII.48; SocAp, 9.V.39;
           Eng. WIN, VI.39;
           Fr. *[390000(5)]; 560000(3); 700603: 183-92; BQI, (1), VI.39;
             QI, (25-26), XII.45-I.46; V, (6), VIII.39;
           Hol. Enige Weg, (II.8), 25.V.39; RodeOct, (IV), 1939: 164-6;
           Nor. Oktober, (III.3), IX.39;
           Sp. Clave, (II.1), 1.IX.39.
        [See further 390730, 390805. T4564,4565.]

390422(2)   Letter to Emrys Hughes.

        Trans.: Am. 691100(1): 147;
           Eng. Forward, 31.VIII.40.

390501   Bonapartistskaya filosofiya gosudarstva. (The bonapartist philosophy
        of the State.) (BO, (77-78), V-VII.39)

        Trans.: Am. 691100(1): 103; NI, VI.39;
           Fr. BQI, (1), VI.39;
           Ger. 470000(2): 29-38;
           Hol. Enige Weg, (II.9), 8.VI.39; NFakkel, (V.32,33),
             11,18.VIII.39;
           Sp. Clave, (I.8), 1.V.39; Voz, (2), VII.39.
        [T4567,4568.]

390527   V.T.O'Brien: Letter on the Socialist Appeal.

        Trans.: Am. p.q. 400124.

390607   Istoriya bol′shevizma v zerkale Tsentral′nogo komiteta. (A history of
        bolshevism in the mirror of the Central Committee.) (BO, (77-78),
        V-VII.39)

        Trans.: Am. 691100(1): 106; NI, VIII.39;
           Eng. WIN, VI.43;
           Fr. BQI, (2), VIII.39.
         [T4570,4571.]

390609   Moralisty i sikofanty protiv marksizma. (The moralists and sycophants against marxism.) (<u>BO</u>, (77-78), V-VII.39)
Trans.: Am. [420000(7)]; 420800; 660800(1); 690000(14); <u>NI</u>, VIII.39;
       Eng. [620000(14)]; 680700: 48-62;
       Fr. 660510: 109-23; <u>BQI</u>, (2), VIII.39;
       Hol. <u>Enige Weg</u>, (II.13), 7.IX.39;
       It. 670831;
       Sin. 631200: 65-81;
       Sp. 390000(3).
[See 390907. T4572,4573.]

360610(1)   A.: "Sovetskie plutarkhi." ("Soviet Plutarchs".) (<u>BO</u>, (77-78), V-VII.39)
Trans.: Am. 700400: 181.
[T4584,4585.]

390610(2)   Red.: Desyat let. (Ten years.) (<u>BO</u>, (77-78), V-VII.39)
Trans.: Am. 691100(1): 65; <u>NI</u>, VIII.39.
[Anniversary of <u>Byulleten Oppozitsii</u>. T4574,4575.]

390610(3)   M.N.: K itogam chistok. (Balance sheet of the purges.) (<u>BO</u>, (77-78), V-VII.39)
Trans.: Am. 700400: 149.
[On Moscow trials. T4576,4577.]

390610(4)   —: 1917-1939 g.g. (<u>BO</u>, (77-78), V-VII.39)
Trans.: Am. 700400: 173.
[Prognoses. T4580,4581.]

390610(5)   —: Prognozy 1931 goda. (Prognoses of 1931.) (<u>BO</u>, (77-78), V-VII.39)
[T4582,4583.]

390616   On skepticism in the SWP.
Trans.: p.q. 400124.
[Letter to Cannon.]

390621   Zagadka SSSR. (The riddle of the USSR.) (<u>BO</u>, (79-80), VIII-X.39)
[T4586-8.]

390701   The Kremlin in world politics.
Trans.: Am. 691100(1): 29; <u>NI</u>(WP), X.42;
       Fr. p.q. 700126: 81-4.
[T4589.]

390715   "Trotskyism" and the PSOP.

        Trans.: Am. 691100(1): 129; NI, X.39;

                Fr. SDS, (42), XI-XII.67; Guérin: 278-97.

        [On France. T4594-6.]

390717   See 390921.

390723(1)   Lettre à la rédaction de Juin 36.

        Trans.: Fr. Guérin: 277-8.

        [On France. T4597.]

390723(2)   Interview.

        Trans.: Am. 691100(1): 33; IP, (VII.28), 8.IX.69;

                Eng. [700000(10)]

        [On world affairs.]

390725   Indiya pered imperialistskoi voinoi. (India faced with imperialist war.)

        (BO, (79-80), VIII-X.39)

        Trans.: Am. 640800: 247-52; 691100(1): 37; NI, IX.39; Lerski: 177-84;

                Ben. 690000(6);

                Eng. 670000(4); Young Socialist, (III.3/13), VI.65;

                Fr. QI, (20-21), VII-VIII.45; QI(OSPE), (2), XII.43;

                Gr. Diethnistes, (13), I.66;

                Jap. 681125: 258-62;

                Sp. 670000(5): 243-8; Clave, (II.1), 1.IX.39;

                Swed. 691100(2): 221-6.

        [T4598-4600.]

390729   "Progressivnyi paralich." ("Progressive paralysis.") (BO, (79-80),

        VIII-X.39)

        Trans.: Am. 691100(1): 39; FI, V.40;

                Sp. Clave, (II.3-4), XI-XII.39.

        [Second International and the coming war. T4601,4602.]

390730   Nezavisimost Ukrainy i sektanskaya putanitsa. (Ukrainian independence

        and sectarian muddleheads.) (BO, (79-80), VIII-X.39)

        Trans.: Am. 690600(3): 74-8; FI, XII.49; SocAp, 15,18.IX.39;

                Fr. BI, XI.39; CIste, (9), 5.XI.39.

        [See also 390422(1), 390805. T4603-5.]

390800   Three conceptions of the Russian Revolution.

Trans.: 410000(1): Appendix;

      Am. 650100; 650900: 123-41; FI, XI.42; NI(WP), XI.45;

      Eng. 520600: 99-111; 640000(5): 123-41; 640000(10): 123-41;

         WIN, IV.43;

      Fr. 690900(1): 20-36; QI, (16-19), III-VI.45;

      Ger. Int, (2,3), XII.48, II-III.49.

[Not in all trans. of 410000(1). T4782.]

390805   L.T.: Demokraticheskie krepostniki i nezavisimost Ukrainy. (Democratic feudalists and Ukrainian independence.) (BO, (79-80), VIII-X.39)

Trans.: Am. 690600(3): 79; SocAp, 31.X.39.

[See also 390422(1), 390730. T4606,T4607.]

390807   A new great writer: Malaquais.

Trans.: Am. FI, I.41;

      Sp. 640900(1): 212-22; 690000(8).II: 149-56; Babel, (15-16),

        I-IV.41.

[T4608-10.]

390902   Stalin -- intendant Gitlera. (Stalin is Hitler's quarter-master.) (BO, (79-80), VIII-X.39)

Trans.: Am. 690600(3): 5-6; SocAp, 11.IX.39;

      Eng. Daily Express, 18.XI.39;

      Fr. 700126: 91-8;

      Hol. RodeOct, (IV), 1939: 239-42.

[T4611,T4612.]

390904   Germano-sovetskii soyuz. (The German-Soviet alliance.) (BO, (79-80), VIII-X.39)

Trans.: Am. 690600(3): 7-8; SocAp, 9.IX.39;

      Eng. WIN, X.39;

      Fr. 700126: 99-102; CES, (4), 30.X.39;

      Hol. NFakkel, (V.40), 6.X.39;

      Sp. IV Int, (II.25-26), VIII-IX.39.

[T4613,T4614.]

390905   Who is guilty of starting the second World War?

Trans.: Am. 690600(3): 8-9; SocAp, 11.IX.39;

      Fr. 700126: 103-6.

[T4615,T4616.]

390906   Stalin — the temporary holder of the Ukraine.
<u>Trans</u>.: Am. 690600(3): 80; <u>SocAp</u>, 24.X.39;
       Sp. <u>IV Int</u>, (II.25-26), VIII-IX.39.
[T4617,4618.]

390907   Ocherednoe oproverzhenie Viktora Serzha. (Victor Serge's usual denial.)
(<u>BO</u>, (78-79), VIII-X.39)
<u>Trans</u>.: Am. 660800: 76; 690000(14): 76.
[See 390609. T4620,4621.]

390911   Moskva mobilizuet. (Moscow is mobilizing.) (<u>BO</u>, (79-80), VIII-X.39)
<u>Trans</u>.: Am. 690600(3): 9; <u>SocAp</u>, 15.IX.39;
       Fr. 700126: 107-9;
       Hol. p.q. <u>NFakkel</u>, (V.38), 22.IX.39.
[T4622,4623.]

390912   V.T.O.: Letter to Cannon.
<u>Trans</u>.: Am. 421200: 1-2; [640000(3)]: 1-2; 650000(6): 1-2; 700000(11):1-2;
       Eng. 661100: 1-2;
       It. 690224: 35;
       Jap. 631030: 142-3.
[On SWP, USA.]

390914   Sees closer Hitler-Stalin ties.
<u>Trans</u>.: Am. 690600(3): 10; <u>SocAp</u>, 20.IX.39;
       Fr. 700126: 111-2.
[T4624,4625.]

390918   Le mystère est levé.
<u>Trans</u>.: Fr. 700126: 113-6.
[On world war. T4626,4627.]

390921   K godovshchine ubiistva I.Raissa. (For the anniversary of the murder
of I.Reiss.) (<u>BO</u>, (79-80), VIII-X.39)
<u>Trans</u>.: Am. 690600(3): 10; <u>SocAp</u>, 27.X.39.

390922   Stalin.
<u>Trans</u>.: Am. <u>Life</u>, 2.X.39;
       Eng. <u>News Chronicle</u>, 16.III.40;
       Fr. p.q. 700126: 85-9; p.q. <u>SDS</u>, (41), X-XI.67.
[Eng. <u>News Chronicle</u> is abr. T4629-31.]

390925   SSSR v voine. (The USSR in war.) (<u>BO</u>, (79-80), VIII-X.39)

         <u>Trans</u>.: Am. 421200: 3-21; ⌊640000(3)⌋: 3-21; 650000(6): 3-21; p.q.
                650900: 305-14; 700000(11): 3-21; <u>NI</u>, XI.39; <u>SWP</u>, (II.1),
                10.X.39;

              Den. <u>Clarte</u>(D), (V), 1940; <u>Klasse Kamp</u>, (3), 1939;

              Eng. 390000(4); p.q. 640000(5): 305-14; p.q. 640000(10):
                305-14; 661100: 3-26; <u>Class Struggle</u>(Ln), (1), ⌊1939⌋;

              Fr. ⌊390000(2)⌋; ⌊610000(10)⌋; p.q. 700126: 117-25; <u>CIste</u>,
                (11,12-13), 20.XI, 8.XII.39; p.q. <u>QI</u>, II.46;

              Hol. p.q. <u>Enige Weg</u>, (II.16), 16.XI.39; <u>RSP</u>, I.40; <u>DocH</u>;

              It. 570400: 299-320; 690224: 39-64;

              Jap. 631030: 144-66;

              Sp. p.q. <u>Clave</u>, (II.2), X.39.

         ⌊T4632,4633.⌋

391001   La politique du Kremlin: L'accord de septembre Hitler-Staline.

         <u>Trans</u>.: Fr. 700126: 127-31.

         ⌊T4634-5.⌋

391003   The United States will participate.

         <u>Trans</u>.: Am. 690000(3): 11; <u>NYTimes</u>, 4.X.39;

              Fr. <u>CIste</u>, (10), 12.XI.39.

391008   Crux: Letter to Stanley.

         <u>Trans</u>.: Am. 421200: 22-3; ⌊640000(3)⌋: 22-3; 650000(6): 22-3;
                700000(11): 22-3;

              Eng. 661100: 27-8;

              It. 690224: 65-7;

              Jap. 631030: 166-9.

         ⌊On SWP, USA.⌋

391018   Eshche i eshche raz o prirode SSSR. (Again and once more again on
         the nature of the USSR.) (<u>BO</u>, (81), I.40)

         <u>Trans</u>.: Am. 421200: 24-32; ⌊640000(3)⌋: 24-32; 650000(6): 24-32; p.q.
                690600(3): 12; 700000(11): 24-32; <u>NI</u>, II.40; p.q.
                <u>SocAp</u>, 14.XI.39; <u>SWP</u>, (II.2), 6.XI.39;

              Eng. 661100: 29-39; <u>WIN</u>, IV.40;

              Fr. ⌊600000(17)⌋; p.q. 700126: 133-5; p.q. <u>QI</u>, (VIII.8-10),
                VIII-X.50;

              Hol. <u>DocB</u>;

              It. 690224: 68-79;

              Jap. 631030: 172-84;

              Sp. 580130: 35-46; <u>Clave</u>, (II.3-4), XI-XII.39.

         ⌊T4641,4642.⌋

391021 The referendum and democratic centralism.

   <u>Trans</u>.: Am. 421200: 33; ⌊640000(3)⌋: 33; 650000(6): 33; 700000(11):
     33; <u>SWP</u>, (II.2), 6.XI.39;

     Eng. 661100: 40-1;

     It. 690224: 80-1;

     Jap. 631030: 185-6.

   ⌊On SWP, USA. T4643,4644.⌋

391022 Crux: Letter to Stanley.

   <u>Trans</u>.: Am. 421200: 34-6; ⌊640000(3)⌋: 34-6; 650000(6): 34-6;
     700000(11): 34-6; <u>SWP</u>, (II.2), 6.XI.39;

     Eng. 661100: 42-4;

     It. 690224: 82-7;

     Jap. 631030: 187-90.

   ⌊On SWP, USA.⌋

391023 Cables <u>Daily Herald</u> he will not write for it.

   <u>Trans</u>.: Am. 690600(3): 12; <u>SocAp</u>, 3.XI.39;

     Den.<u>Klasse Kamp</u>, (4), ⌊1939⌋.

391028 J,Hansen: Letter to Cannon.

   <u>Trans</u>.: Am. Cannon: 98-9;

     Eng. 661100: 45-7;

     It. 690224: 88.

   ⌊On SWP, USA.⌋

391106 Lund: Letter to Shachtman.

   <u>Trans</u>.: Am. 421200: 37-41; ⌊640000(3)⌋: 37-41; 650000(6): 37-41;
     700000(11): 37-41;

     Eng. 661100: 48-53;

     It. 690224: 91-7;

     Jap. 631030: 191-7.

   ⌊On SWP, USA.⌋

391117 Pis´mo redaktsiyu <u>New York Times</u>. (Letter to Ed. <u>New York Times</u>.)
   (<u>BO</u>, (81), X.40)

   <u>Trans</u>.: Am. 690600(3): 13; <u>NYTimes</u>, 23.XI.39.

   ⌊On Soviet Union. T4647-50.⌋

391120 Alternative for 391117.

391124   Letter to an Indian comrade.

Trans.: Am. 690600(3): 14; <u>SWP</u>, (II.5), XII.39; Lerski: 187-9;

Eng. <u>PermRev</u>, (I.3), IX.43;

Fr. 700126: 137-9.

391128   Letter to Political Committee, SWP.

Trans.: Am. 690600(3): 125-6.

[On Dies Committee; SWP, USA.]

391204(1)   Pis'mo v redaktsiyu <u>New York Times</u>. (Letter to Ed., <u>NYTimes</u>.)

(<u>BO</u>, (81), I.40)

Trans.: Am. 690600(3): 18-9; <u>SocAp</u>, 23.XII.39.

[See further, 391204(2). On Soviet Union and the war. T4651,4652.]

391204(2)   Dvoinaya zvezda: Gitler-Stalin. (The twin-star: Hitler-Stalin.)

(<u>BO</u>, (81), I.40)

Trans.: Am. 690600(3): 14-7; <u>Liberty</u>, 27.I.40;

Fr. p.q. 700126: 141-55;

Sp. <u>Clave</u>, (II.5), I.40; <u>IV Int</u>, (II.29), I.40.

[See 391204(1). T4653-5.]

391206   Alternative for 391204(1).

391207   The Dies Committee.

Trans.: Am. 690600(3): 51; <u>NYTimes</u>, 18.XII.39; <u>SocAp</u>, 16.XII.39.

[Press statement. T4656.]

391211   Pochemu ya soglasilsya vystupit pered Komissiei Daiesa? (Why have I

consented to appear before the Dies Committee.) (<u>BO</u>, (81), I.40)

Trans.: Am. 690600(3): 51-3; <u>SocAp</u>, 30.XII.39;

Sp. <u>Clave</u>, (II.5), I.40.

[T4657,4658,4665.]

391212   Dies backing down.

Trans.: Am. 690600(3): 53; <u>SocAp</u>, 23.XII.39.

[T4659,4660.]

391215(1)   Letter to Cannon.

Trans.: Am. 421200: 42; [640000(3)]: 42; 650000(6): 42; 700000(11): 42;

Eng. 661100: 54-5;

It. 690224: 98;

Jap. 631030: 198-9.

[On SWP, USA. T4661.]

391215(2)   Melko-burzhuaznaya oppozitsiya v Rabochei Sotsialisticheskoi Partii
            Soedinennykh Shtatov. (A petty-bourgeois opposition in the Socialist
            Workers Party, USA.) (BO, (82-83), II-IV.40)
            Trans.: Am. 421200: 43-62; ⌊640000(3)⌋: 43-62; p.q. 640800: 355-9;
                    650000(6): 43-62; 700000(11): 43-62; p.q. Labor Challenge,
                    (V.8), VIII.49; NI, III.40; SWP, (II.7), I.40;
                Eng. 661100: 56-80;
                Fr. p.q. QI, (VIII.8-10), VIII-X.50;
                It. p.q. 680200(2): 192-6; 690224: 100-31;
                Jap. 631030: 200-26; p.q. 681125: 370-4;
                Sp. 580130: 47-73; p.q. 670000(5): 358-63; Babel, (11), 1940;
                    p.q. Clave, (II.6), II.40;
                Swed. p.q. 691100(2): 320-4.
            ⌊T4662-4.⌋

391217   See 391211.

391219   Letter to Wright.
            Trans.: Am. 421200: 63; ⌊640000(3)⌋: 63; 650000(6): 63; 700000(11): 63;
                    SWP, (II.6), I.40;
                Eng. 661100: 81;
                It. 690224: 132-4;
                Jap. 631030: 227-8.
            ⌊On SWP, USA.⌋

391220   Letter to Shachtman.
            Trans.: Am. 421200: 64; ⌊640000(3)⌋: 64; 650000(6): 64; 700000(11): 64;
                    SWP, (II.6), I.40;
                Eng. 661100: 82;
                It. 690224: 135;
                Jap. 631030: 229.
            ⌊On SWP, USA.⌋

391226(1)   ⌊Denies rumour of reconciliation with Stalin.⌋
            ⌊c. NYTimes, 27.XII.39. Based on rumour in Mexican press. T4666.⌋

391226(2)   W.Rork: Letter to National Committee Majority, SWP.

Trans.: Am. 421200: 65-6; ⌊640000(3)⌋: 65-6; 650000(6): 65-6;
                700000(11): 65-6;
          Eng. 661100: 83-4;
          It. 690224: 136-8;
          Jap. 631030: 231-2.

⌊On SWP, USA. T4667.⌋

391227   W.Rork: Letter to National Committee Majority, SWP.

Trans.: Am. 421200: 66-7; ⌊640000(3)⌋: 66-7; 650000(6): 66-7;
                700000(11): 66-7;
          Eng. 661100: 84-6;
          It. 690224: 138-40;
          Jap. 631030: 233-5.

⌊On SWP, USA. T4667.⌋

400000(1)　　　　‡ LOS GANGSTERS DE STALIN.
　　　　　　　　　　[Trans. Sp.]

*[400000(2)]　　　*[THE HISTORY OF THE RUSSIAN REVOLUTION.]
　　　　　　　　　　[Trans. Ch. See 310000(1) for all trans.; Pref. Ch. ed. 400700(1).]

400000(3)　　　　THE PERMANENT REVOLUTION.
　　　　　　　　　　[Trans. Eng. See 281000(1) for all repr., trans., notes.]

[400000(4)]　　　—: MANIFESTO OF THE FOURTH INTERNATIONAL. IMPERIALIST WAR AND THE
　　　　　　　　　　WORLD PROLETARIAN REVOLUTION.
　　　　　　　　　　[Trans. Eng. See 400526 for all trans.]

400000(5)　　　　MANIFÈSTE DE LA IVe INTERNATIONALE AUX TRAVAILLEURS DU MONDE.
　　　　　　　　　　[Trans. Fr. See 400526 for all trans. Underground publ.]

[400000(6)]　　　TEGEN HET NATIONALCOMMUNISME.
　　　　　　　　　　[Trans. Hol. See 310825 for all trans.]

400000(7)　　　　Pref. THE LIVING THOUGHTS OF KARL MARX.
　　　　　　　　　　[Trans. Am. See 390418 for all repr., trans., notes.]

400000(8)　　　　Pref. THE LIVING THOUGHTS OF KARL MARX.
　　　　　　　　　　[Trans. Eng. See 390418 for all repr., trans., notes.]

400000(9)　　　　Pref. DE LEVENDE GEDACHTEN VAN KARL MARX.
　　　　　　　　　　[Trans. Hol. See 390418 for all repr., trans., notes.]

*400000(10)　　　*Pref. CARLO MARX.
　　　　　　　　　　[Trans. It. See 390418 for all trans., notes.]

*400000(11)　　　*Pref. EL PENSAMIENTO VIVO DE MARX.
　　　　　　　　　　[Trans. Sp. See 390418 for all repr., trans., notes.]

*400000(13)　　　*EL TESTAMENTO DE LENIN.
　　　　　　　　　　[Trans. Sp. See 321231 for all trans.]

400000(14)　　　MANIFESTO OF THE FOURTH INTERNATIONAL ON THE IMPERIALIST WAR AND THE
　　　　　　　　　　WORLD PROLETARIAN REVOLUTION.
　　　　　　　　　　[Trans. Am. See 400526 for all trans.]

*400000(15)　　　*[LESSONS OF OCTOBER.]
　　　　　　　　　　[Trans. Ch. See 240915 for all trans.]

*400000(16)   *MANIFESTO SOBRE LA GUERRA DE LA IV INTERNACIONAL.
               [Trans. Sp. See 400526 for all repr., trans.]

[400000(17)]   WAR AND THE FOURTH INTERNATIONAL.
               [Trans. Eng. See 340610 for all trans.]

400000(18)   Interview.
               [c. Etiemble. On relations with the Surrealists.]

400103   W.Rork: Letter to National Committee Majority, SWP. Burnham and
               dialectics.
               Trans.: Am. 421200: 68; [640000(3)]: 68; 650000(6): 68; 700000(11): 68;
                        SWP, (II.6), I.40;
                    Eng. 661100: 86-7;
                    It. 690224: 140-2;
                    Jap. 631030: 236-7.
               [On SWP, USA.]

400104   W.Rork: Letter to National Committee Majority, SWP.
               Trans.: Am. 421200: 69; [640000(3)]: 69; 650000(6): 69; 700000(11): 69;
                        SWP, (II.6), I.40;
                    Eng. 661100: 88;
                    It. 690224: 142;
                    Jap. 631030: 238.
               [On SWP, USA.]

400105   Letter to Joe.
               Trans.: Am. 421200: 70-1; [640000(3)]: 70-1; 650000(6): 70-1;
                        700000(11): 70-1; SWP, (II.6), I.40;
                    Eng. 661100: 89-90;
                    It. 690224: 143-4;
                    Jap. 631030: 239-40.
               [On SWP, USA.]

400107   An open letter to comrade Burnham.
               Trans.: Am. 421200: 72-94; [640000(3)]: 72-94; 650000(6): 72-94;
                        700000(11): 72-94; FI, V.40; SWP, (II.9), I.40;
                    Eng. 661100: 91-119;
                    It. 690224: 145-76;
                    Jap. 631030: 241-71;
                    Sp. 580130: 75-105.
               [On SWP, USA. T4819-21.]

400109   W.Rork: Letter to Cannon.

       <u>Trans</u>.: Am. p.q. 421200: 95; p.q. ⌊640000(3)⌋: 95; p.q. 650000(6):
          95; p.q. 700000(11): 95;

         Eng. p.q. 661100: 120;

         It. p.q. 690224: 177;

         Jap. p.q. 631030: 272.

       ⌊On SWP, USA.⌋

400110   Letter to Dobbs.

       <u>Trans</u>.: Am. 421200: 96-7; ⌊640000(3)⌋: 96-7; 650000(6): 96-7;
          700000(11): 96-7;

         Eng. 661100: 121-2;

         It. 690224: 178-80;

         Jap. 631030: 273-4.

       ⌊On SWP, USA.⌋

400112   Nota a la <u>Prensa</u>.

       <u>Trans</u>.: Sp. 400000(1): 159-60.

       ⌊On GPU.⌋

400113   Letter to Wright.

       <u>Trans</u>.: Am. 421200: 98; ⌊640000(3)⌋: 98; 650000(6): 98;
          700000(11): 98;

         Eng. 661100: 123;

         It. 690224: 181;

         Jap. 631030: 276-7.

       ⌊On SWP, USA.⌋

400116(1)   L.T.: Letter to Cannon.

       <u>Trans</u>.: Am. p.q. 421200: 99; p.q. ⌊640000(3)⌋: 99; p.q. 650000(6): 99;
          p.q. 700000(11): 99;

         Eng. p.q. 661100: 124;

         It. p.q. 690224: 182;

         Jap. p.q. 631030: 277.

       ⌊On SWP, USA.⌋

400116(2)   L.T.: Letter to Warde.

       <u>Trans</u>.: Am. p.q. 421200: 100; p.q. ⌊640000(3)⌋: 100; p.q. 650000(6):
          100; p.q. 700000(11): 100;

         Eng. p.q. 661100: 125;

         It. p.q. 690224: 183-4;

         Jap. p.q. 631030: 278.

       ⌊On SWP, USA.⌋

400118 Cornell: Letter to Hansen.

 <u>Trans</u>.: Am. p.q. 421200: 101-2; p.q. ⌊640000(3)⌋: 101-2; p.q.
    650000(6): 101-2; p.q. 700000(11): 101-2;

   Eng. p.q. 661100: 126-7;

   It. p.q. 690224: 185-6;

   Jap. p.q. 631030: 279-80.

 ⌊On SWP, USA.⌋

400124 Ot tsarapiny -- k opasnosti gangreny. (From a scratch to the
 danger of gangrene.) (<u>BO</u>, (82-83), II-IV.40)

 <u>Trans</u>.: Am. 421200: 103-48; ⌊640000(3)⌋: 103-48; 650000(6): 103-48;
    700000(11): 103-48; <u>NI</u>, III.40; <u>SWP</u>, (II.11), II.40;

   Eng. ⌊420000(5)⌋; 661100: 128-87;

   Fr. ⌊500000(5)⌋; p.q. <u>QI</u>, (VIII.8-10), VIII-X.50;

   It. 690224: 187-252;

   Jap. 631030: 281-344;

   Sp. 580130: 107-69; <u>Clave</u>, (II.8), IV-V.40.

 ⌊On SWP, USA. Russian is p.q. T4822,4823.⌋

400129 Letter to Abern.

 <u>Trans</u>.: Am. 421200: 149-50; ⌊640000(3)⌋: 149-50; 650000(6): 149-50;
    700000(11): 149-50;

   Eng. 661100: 188-9;

   It. 690224: 253-4;

   Jap. 631030: 345-6.

 ⌊On SWP, USA.⌋

400210 Letter to Goldman.

 <u>Trans</u>.: Am. 421200: 151; ⌊640000(3)⌋: 151; 650000(6): 151;
    700000(11): 151;

   Eng. 661100: 190;

   It. 690224: 255-6;

   Jap. 631030: 347-8.

 ⌊On SWP, USA.⌋

400214 Mirovoe polozhenie i perspektivy. (The world situation and
 perspectives.) (<u>BO</u>, (82-83), II-IV.40)

 <u>Trans</u>.: Am. p.q. 640800: 225-8; 690500(3): 20-7; <u>FI</u>, VIII,IX.42;
    <u>St Louis Post-Dispatch</u>, 10,17,24.III.40;

   Eng. <u>News Chronicle</u>, 19,20,21,23,25,26.III.40;

   Fr. p.q. 700126: 157-77; p.q. <u>CIste</u>, (2), 25.IV.40;

   Jap. p.q. 681125: 237-40;

   Sp. p.q. 670000(5): 223-5;

   Swed. 691100(2): 201-4.

 ⌊T4824-6.⌋

400219   Letter to Goldman.
                <u>Trans</u>.: Am. 421200: 152; ⌊640000(3)⌋: 152; 650000(6): 152;
                          700000(11): 152;
                      Eng. 661100: 191;
                      It. 690224: 256-7;
                      Jap. 631030: 349-50.
                ⌊On SWP, USA.⌋

400221(1)   Back to the Party!
                <u>Trans</u>.: Am. 421200: 153-5; ⌊640000(3)⌋: 153-5; 650000(6): 153-5;
                          700000(11): 153-5;
                      Eng. 661100: 192-5;
                      It. 690224: 258-62;
                      Jap. 631030: 351-4.
                ⌊On SWP, USA. T4827.⌋

⌊400221(2)⌋   Imperialismo y revolucion nacional.
                <u>Trans</u>.: Sp. 611025: 12-4; 690700(2): 179; <u>Critica</u>, 21.II.40.

400223   Reply to Burnham: Science and Style.
                <u>Trans</u>.: Am. 421200: 156-7; ⌊640000(3)⌋: 156-7; 650000(6): 156-7;
                          700000(11): 156-7;
                      Eng. 661100: 196-9;
                      It. 690224: 263-4;
                      Jap. 631030: 355-6.
                ⌊On SWP, USA.⌋

400227(1)   Testament (A).
                <u>Trans</u>.: 580000(4);
                      Am. 640800: 360-1;
                      Eng. <u>FI</u>(P), (7), Autumn, 1959; <u>Socialist Worker</u>, (183),
                          22.VIII.70;
                      Fr. <u>QI</u>, (7), IX-X.59;
                      Ger. <u>Int</u>, (IV.3-4), XII.59;
                      Jap. 681125: 375-6;
                      Sp. 670000(5): 363-4;
                      Swed. 691100(2): 325-6.
                ⌊See also 400227(2), 400303. T4828a.⌋

400227(2)   Testament (B).

       Trans.: 580000(4);

          Am. 640800: 361;

          Eng. FI(P), (7), Autumn 1959;

          Fr. QI, (7), IX-X.59;

          Ger. Int, (IV.3-4), XII.59;

          Jap. 681125: 376;

          Sp. 670000(5): 364;

          Swed. 691100(2): 326.

       [See also 400227(1), 400303. T4828b.]

400227(3)   W.Rork: Letter to Cannon.

       Trans.: Am. 421200: 158; [640000(3)]: 158; 650000(6): 158;

          700000(11): 158;

          Eng. 661100: 198;

          It. 690224: 265-6;

          Jap. 631030: 357-8.

       [On SWP, USA.]

400229   W.Rork: Letter to Joseph Hansen.

       Trans.: Am. 421200: 159-60; [640000(3)]: 159-60; 650000(6): 159-60;

          700000(11): 159-60;

          Eng. 661100: 199-200;

          It. 690224: 267-9;

          Jap. 631030: 359-60.

       [On SWP, USA.]

400303   Testament (C).

       Trans.: 580000(4);

          Am. 640800: 361-2;

          Eng. FI(P), (7), Autumn 1959;

          Fr. QI, (7), IX-X.59;

          Ger. Int, (IV.3-4), XII.59;

          Jap. 681125: 376-7;

          Sp. 670000(5): 364-5;

          Swed. 691100(2): 326-7.

       [See also 400227(1), 400227(2). T4828c.]

400304   W.Rork: Letter to Dobbs.

Trans.: Am 421200: 161-3; ⌊640000(3)⌋: 161-3; 650000(6): 161-3;
700000(11): 161-3;

Eng. 661100: 201-3;

It. 690224: 270-2;

Jap. 631030: 362-5.

⌊On SWP, USA. T4830.⌋

400313   Stalin posle finlyandskoi opyta. (Stalin after the Finnish
experience.) (BO, (82-83), II-IV.40)

Trans.: Am. 690600(3): 28-9;

Eng. Sunday Express, 17.III.40;

Fr. p.q. 700126: 179-84.

⌊Eng. trans. is shorter than Am. T4833-5.⌋

400404   W.Rork: Letter to Dobbs.

Trans.: Am. 421200: 163-4; ⌊640000(3)⌋: 163-4; 650000(6): 163-4;
700000(11): 163-4;

Eng. 661100: 204-5;

It. 690224: 272-5;

Jap. 631030: 366-8.

⌊On SWP, USA.⌋

400416   W.Rork: Letter to Dobbs.

Trans.: Am. p.q. 421200: 165; p.q. ⌊640000(3): 165; p.q. 650000(6):
165; 700000(11): 165;

Eng. p.q. 661100: 206;

It. p.q. 690224: 276-7;

Jap. p.q. 631030: 369-70.

⌊On SWP, USA.⌋

400423(1)   Petty-bourgeois moralists and the proletarian party.

Trans.: Am. 421200: 166-9; ⌊640000(3)⌋: 166-9; 650000(6): 166-9;
700000(11): 166-9;

Eng. 661100: 207-11;

It. 690224: 278-82;

Jap. 631030: 371-5.

⌊On SWP, USA. T4837,4838.⌋

400423(2)   To the workers of the USSR.

Trans.: Am. 640800: 281-4 690600(3): 30; FI, X.40; Mil, 23.VII.56;
SocAp, 11.V.40;

Fr. p.q. 700126: 185;

Gr. Diethnistes, (10), X.65;

It. 680200(2): 154-8;   ++++

400423(2) ++++<u>Trans</u>.: Jap. 681125: 294-7;

Sp. 670000(5): 276-8;

Swed. 691100(2): 252-5.

⌊T4839,T4840.⌋

400425   Balance sheet of the Finnish events.

<u>Trans</u>.: Am. 421200: 170-8; ⌊640000(3)⌋: 170-8; 650000(6): 170-8;

700000(11): 170-8; <u>FI</u>, VI.40;

Eng. 661100: 212-22; <u>WIN</u>, VII.40;

It. 690224: 283-94;

Jap. 631030: 376-87;

Sp. 580130: 177-88; <u>Clave</u>, (II.8), IV-V.40.

⌊T4841,T4842.⌋

400500   The Tanaka Memorial.

<u>Trans</u>.: Am. 690600(3): 109-11; <u>FI</u>, VI.41.

⌊On Japan. T4815.⌋

400501   Letter to Chris. On Japan's plans for expansion.

<u>Trans</u>.: Am. 690600(3): 116; <u>FI</u>, X.40;

Fr. <u>QI</u>, VIII-IX.46.

400514(1) Letter to LaFollette -- On Brailsford.

<u>Trans</u>.: Am. 690600(3): 116; <u>FI</u>, X.40;

Fr. <u>QI</u>, VIII-IX.46.

⌊On world war.⌋

400514(2) Una proposicion a los calumniadores professionales de <u>Futuro</u> y de

<u>El Popular</u>.

<u>Trans</u>.: Sp. 400000(1): 161-2.

⌊On GPU. T4845,T4846.⌋

400519   See 400526.

400526   Manifest Chetvertogo Internatsionala. Imperialistskaya voina i

proletarskaya revolyutsiya. (Manifesto of the Fourth International.

Imperialist war and proletarian revolution.) (<u>BO</u>, (84), VIII-X.40)

<u>Trans</u>.: Am. 400000(14); p.q. 640800: 252-3,260-2; p.q. 670600: 65-6;

p.q. 690400(2): 65-6; 690600(3): 31-46; p.q. 700800(1): 65-6;

<u>SocAp</u>, 29.VI.40;

Ch. p.q. 470427: 360;

Eng. ⌊400000(4)⌋;   ++++

400526   ++++   <u>Trans</u>.: Fr. 400000(5); 700126: 187-243;

                 Gr. p.q. <u>Diethnistes</u>, (13), I.66;

                 It. p.q. 680200(2): 142-5;

                 Jap. *610000(17); 631130: 299-351; p.q. 681010: 119-20; p.q.

                     681125: 264-5,272-4;

                 Sp. *400000(16); p.q. 611025: 30-31; p.q. 670000(5): 255-7,

                     287-8; p.q. 690700(2): 197; <u>Clave</u>, (II.10-13), VI-IX.40;

                 Swed. p.q. 691100(2): 226-7,233-5.

⌊Date of adoption by Emergency Conference of FI. See 400528(2).
T4847-76.⌋

400527   Ocurso al Procurador de Justicia.

                 <u>Trans</u>.: Sp. 400000(1): 163-72.

                 ⌊On GPU. T4876.1.⌋

400528(1)   W.R.: Letter to Cannon.

                 <u>Trans</u>.: Am. p.q. 421200: 179; p.q. ⌊640000(3)⌋: 179; p.q. 650000(6): 179;

                     p.q. 700000(11): 179;

                     Eng. p.q. 661100: 223;

                     It. p.q. 690224: 295;

                     Jap. p.q. 631030: 388.

                 ⌊On SWP, USA.⌋

400528(2)   Letter to comrades. On the Manifesto of the Fourth International.

                 <u>Trans</u>.: Am. 690600(3): 116; <u>FI</u>, X.40;

                     Fr. <u>QI</u>, VIII-IX.46.

                 ⌊See 400526.⌋

400528(3)   ¿Acusadores o Acusados?

                 <u>Trans</u>.: Sp. 400000(1): 172-3.

                 ⌊On GPU. T4905,T4906.⌋

400531   ⌊Letter to President Cardenas; for release of associates.⌋

                 ⌊c. Serge: 313. After attempted assassination of May 24, 1940. T4876.⌋

400601   Letter to Attorney-General, Mexico. The May 24 attempt.

                 <u>Trans</u>.: Am. 690600(3): 81-2; <u>FI</u>, X.40; p.q. <u>SocAp</u>, 15.VI.40.

                 ⌊On GPU. T4880,T4881.⌋

400602   El Diputado Toledano lanza una nueva calumnia.

                 <u>Trans</u>.: Sp. 400000(1): 173-5.

                 ⌊On slanders. T4882.⌋

400605   Letter to Goldman. Dialectics catches up with Burnham and Shachtman.
     Trans.: Am. 421200: 180; [640000(3)]: 180; 650000(6): 180; 700000(11):
         180; p.q. SocAp, 15.VI.40;
       Eng. 661100: 224;
       It. 690224: 296;
       Jap. 631030: 389.
     [On SWP, USA.]

400608   Stalin seeks my life. The May 24 attempt.
     Trans.: Am. 690600(3): 83-9; FI, VIII.41;
       Fr. L'ASSASSINAT: 7-19;
       Sp. 400000(1): 17-39.
     [T4884-9.]

400612   See 400615.

400615   Lund: Discussion with Cannon.
     Trans.: Am. p.q. 670600: 66; p.q. 690400(2): 66; 690600(3): 54-66;
       p.q. 700800(1): 66; PDB, (1,2), VIII,IX.40; SWP, (III.1),
       VIII.40; (IV.10), IV.53;
       Eng. [660000(1); FI(Ln), (II.2), VIII.65;
       Fr. p.q. 700126: 245-55;
       Jap. p.q. 681010: 120.
     [See further 400807. T4891.]

400617   Alternative for 400618(1).

400618(1)   L.T.: Rol Kremlya v evropeiskoi katastrofe. (The Kremlin's role in
     the European catastrophe.) (BO, (84), VIII-X.40)
     Trans.: Am. 690600(3): 47; FI, X.40; SocAp, 22.VI.40;
       Eng. WIN, IX.40;
       Fr. 700126: 257-9.
     [T4894,T4895.]

400618(2)   The reptile breed of the Nation.
     Trans.: Am. 690600(3): 89; FI, X.40; SocAp. 6.VII.40.
     [Social-patriotism in the USA. T4896-8.]

400813(3)   Joseph Hansen: Who is the author of the Nation's article?
     Trans.: Am. 690600(3): 89; FI, X.40; SocAp, 6.VII.40.
     [See 400618(2).]

400625(1)   GPU tries to cover murder with slander.
             Trans.: Am. 690600(3): 90; SocAp, 6.VII.40;
                     Sp. 400000(1): 175-7.
             [On Shelden Harte; GPU. T4899.]

400625(2)   & Others: [Message of sympathy to Mr. Harte.]
             Trans.: Am. 690600(3): 90; SocAp, 29.VI.40.
             [On Shelden Harte. T4900-2.]

400630   Chto dal'she? My ne menyaem kursa. (What next? We do not change
             course.) (BO, (84), VIII-X.40)
             Trans.: Am. 690600(3): 48-9. FI, X.40; SocAp, 6.VII.40;
                     Fr. 700126: 261-6;
                     Hol. Kompas, III.46;
                     Sp. Clave, (II.10-13), VI-IX.40.
             [Also signed L.Lund. T4903,T4904.]

400700(1)   Pref. [THE HISTORY OF THE _USSIAN REVOLUTION], *400000(2).
             Trans.: Am. 690600(3): 114; FI, XII.41; XII.45;
                     Ch. *400000(2); 470427: 367-8.
             [Ch. ed. of 310000(1).]

400700(2)   On the Jewish problem.
             Trans.: Am. 690600(3): 115; p.q. FI, XII.41; XII.45;
                     Eng. p.q. WIN, VI-VII.46;
                     Hol. p.q. RodeOct, (1), VIII.46.

400702(1)   [Declaration to Mexican court.]
             [c. 400703.]

400703   Declaracion suplementaria a la diligencia del 2 de julio.
             Trans.: Sp. 400000(1): 181-3.
             [On GPU. T4911,T4912.]

400705	Futuro, El Popular, La Voz de Mexico y los agentes de la GPU.
	Trans.: Sp. 400000(1): 133-55.
	[T4908-10.]
400709	Letter to Al; on conscription.
	Trans.: Am. 690600(3): 117; FI, X.40;
	Eng. WIN, XII.40; I.43;
	Fr. QI, VIII-IX.46.
400711	Alternative for 400727(2).
400726	El Sr. Pavon Flores, abogado de la GPU.
	Trans.: Sp. 400000(1): 177-81.
	[T4917,T4918.]
400727(1)	Letter to Herald-Tribune; on May 24 attempt.
	Trans.: Am. 690600(3): 91; FI, X.40; SocAp, 10.VIII.40;
	Sp. 400000(1): 184-7.
	[On GPU. T4919,T4920.]
400727(2)	Apelacion a la Prensa.
	Trans.: Sp. 400000(1): 183-4.
	[On GPU. T4913,T4914.]
400729	Letter to Al. Misfortune of an intellectual.
	Trans.: Am. 690600(3): 117; FI, X.40;
	Fr. QI, VIII-IX.46.
400802(1)	Statement to United Press.
	Trans.: Am. FI, X.40;
	Fr. 700126: 267-8.
	[On the world war. T4923.]
400802(2)	Letter to Charles. Nipping a new GPU lie.
	Trans.: Am. 690600(3): 117; FI, X.40;
	Fr. QI, VIII-IX.46.
400802(3)	Stalin still Hitler's vassal.
	Trans.: Am. 690600(3): 49; SocAp, 10.VIII.40.
400803(1)	Letter to generous friends.
	Trans.: Am. 690600(3): 117-8; FI, X.40;
	Fr. QI, VIII-IX.46.

400803(2)   Letter to generous friends.
              Trans.: Am. 690600(3): 118; FI, X.40;
                      Fr. QI, VIII-IX.46.

400806   Foresaw assassin would use trotskyist label.
              Trans.: Am. 690600(3): 91-2; p.q. SocAp, 31.VIII.40;
                      Fr. p.q. QI, VIII-IX.46;
                      Sp. El Universal, 1940.

400807   Some questions on American problems.
              Trans.: Am. p.q. 421200: 181-3; p.q. ⌊640000(5)⌋: 181-3; p.q. 650000(6):
                      181-3; p.q. 690400(3): 27-8; 690600(3): 67-70; p.q.
                      700000(11): 181-3; FI, X.40; SWP, (III.2), IX.40;
                      Eng. 620900; p.q. 661100: 225-8; WIN, III.41;
                      Fr. QI, VIII-IX.46;
                      It. p.q. 690224: 297-301;
                      Jap. p.q. 631030: 390-4.
              ⌊Alternative title: Discussion with Lund. T4924,T4925.⌋

400809   Letter to Goldman. On a petty-bourgeois philistine.
              Trans.: Am. p.q. 421200: 184-5; p.q. ⌊640000(3)⌋: 184-5; p.q. 650000(6):
                      184-5; p.q. 690600(3): 118; 700000(11): 184-5; p.q. FI,
                      X.40; p.q. SocAp, 17.VIII.40;
                      Eng. p.q. 661100: 229-30;
                      Fr. p.q. QI, VIII-IX.46;
                      It. p.q. 690224: 302-3;
                      Jap. p.q. 631030: 395-6.
              ⌊On Dwight MacDonald.⌋

⌊400810⌋   Did Stalin poison Lenin?
              Trans.: 410000(1): Ch. XII;
                      Am. Liberty, 10.VIII.40.

400812   Letter to a friend. How to defend ourselves.
              Trans.: Am. 690600(3): 118; FI, X.40;
                      Fr. QI, VIII-IX.46.
              ⌊On Fourth International.⌋

400813   Letter to friends. How to really defend democracy.
              Trans.: Am. 690600(3): 118-9; FI, X.40;
                      Eng. WIN, XII.40.

400816(1)   Letter to C.Charles.
            Trans.: Am. 690600(3): 119; FI, X.40;
                    Fr. QI, VIII-IX.46.

400816(2)   Letter to Gerland. On Dewey's philosophy.
            Trans.: Am. 690600(3): 119; FI, X.40.

400817(1)   Komintern i GPU. (The Comintern and the GPU.) (BO, (85,86), III,VI.41)
            Trans.: Am. 690600(3): 92-107; FI, XI.40;
                    Sp. 400000(1): 43-129.
            [T4926-8.]

400817(2)   Your Old Man: Letter to Chris. Another thought on conscription.
            Trans.: Am. p.q. 421200: 186; p.q. [640000(3)]: 186; p.q. 650000(6): 186;
                    p.q. 690600(3): 119; p.q. 700000(11): 186; p.q. FI, X.40;
                    Eng. p.q. 661100: 231; p.q. WIN, XII.40;
                    Fr. p.q. QI, VIII-IX.46;
                    It. p.q. 690224: 304-5;
                    Jap. p.q. 631030: 397.

400818   Letter to R. "Welcome to our small garrison."
            Trans.: Am. 690600(3): 120; FI, X.40;
                    Fr. QI, VIII-IX.46.

400820(1)   Letter to class-war prisoner, Edward.
            Trans.: Am. 690600(3): 120; FI, X.40;
                    Fr. QI, VIII-IX.46.

400820(2)   Letter to class-war prisoner, Max.
            Trans.: Am. 690600(3): 120; FI, X.40;
                    Fr. QI, VIII-IX.46.

[400820(3)] The class, the party, and the leadership. Why was the Spanish
            proletariat defeated? Questions of marxist theory.
            Trans.: Am. FI, XII.40;
                    Eng. [570000(8)]; WIN, XI.41;
                    Fr. QI, VIII-IX.46 LA RÉVOLUTION ESPAGNOLE: 153-9;
                    Sp. *[650000(13)].
            [T4816.]

400820(4)   Trade unions in the epoch of imperialism.

               Trans.: Am. 620200; FI, II.41 Labor Challenge, (II.12,13),
                       VII,VIII.46;
                    Eng. ⌊410000(3)⌋; 480000(7); 680300(2): 5-17; WIN, V.41;
                       Workers Republic, (25), Autumn 1969;
                    Fr. ⌊480000(10)⌋; ⌊620000(8)⌋; ⌊690000(19)⌋; 700600: 57-65;
                       Avant-Garde, (I.2), ⌊--⌋; Rouge, (26), 2.VII.69;
                    Ger. Spartacus, (12-13), IV-V.70; Was Tun, (III.12), ⌊VI⌋.70;
                    Gr. *470000(6); *560000(2);
                    Hol. Kompas, IX.46; RodeOkt, (2), X.46;
                    It. MARXISMO: 104-12;
                    Jap. *490000(4); 631001; 700831: 1-7;
                    Sin. 650500;
                    Sp. p.q. 611025: 14-5; *611100; *640900(2); *⌊650000(13)⌋;
                       p.q. 670000(5): 285-7; p.q. 690700(2): 181.

⌊400820(5)⌋   On the future of Hitler's armies.
               Trans.: Am. 690600(3): 113; Mil, 10.V.41;
                    Fr. p.q. 700126: 270-1.
               ⌊Fragment from archives.⌋

⌊400820(6)⌋   Bonapartizm, fashizm i voina. (Bonapartism, fascism and war.)
               (BO, (84), VIII-X.40)
               Trans.: Am. p.q. 640800: 166-7; 690400(3): 28-30; 690600(3): 120-3;
                       FI, X.40;
                    Eng. 620900; WIN, II.41;
                    Fr. p.q. 700126: 268-70; Avant-Garde, (I.2), ⌊--⌋; QI,
                       VIII-IX.46; V(OCE), (20), 15.IX.41; Voie de Lénine, (11),
                       15.I.42;
                    Jap. p.q. 681125: 174-5;
                    Sp. p.q. 670000(5): 165;
                    Swed. p.q. 691100(2): 147.
               ⌊Unfinished article.⌋

400820(7)   Letter to Hank.
               Trans.: Am. 690600(3): 120; FI, X.40.

⌊400820(8)⌋   On ulitiarianism.
               Trans.: Am. p.q. FI, I.42;
               ⌊Fragment.⌋

400821   ⌊Last words.⌋ (BO, (87), VIII.41)
               Trans.: Am. SocAp, 24.VIII.40.
               ⌊See article by J.Hansen.⌋

410000(1)   § STALIN.

Trans.: Am. 410000(1); 460315; 580000(2); p.q. 640800: 66-70;
        670000(12);

    Eng. 470000(7); 680000(2); 690000(2);

    Fr. 480508; p.q. 680000(4): passim;

    Ger. 520000(3); 530000(6);

    Hol. 490000(1);

    It. *480000(3); 620404;

    Jap. 670115; p.q. 681125: 72-6;

    Sp. 470400; *480000(4); *560000(8); *600000(32); p.q. 611025:
        62-3; 630000(4); p.q. 670000(5); 67-70; 670900; p.q.
        690700(2): 233;

    Swed. p.q. 691100(2): 55-9.

⌊Distribution withheld until 1946. T4668-4814.⌋

⌊410000(2)⌋   STALINISM AND BOLSHEVISM.

⌊Trans. Eng. See 370828 for all repr., trans.⌋

⌊410000(3)⌋   TRADE UNIONS IN THE EPOCH OF IMPERIALIST DECAY.

⌊Trans. Eng. See ⌊400820(4)⌋ for all repr., trans.⌋

410000(4)   TOLDOT HAMAHAPEICHA HARUSIT.

⌊Trans. Heb. See 310000(1) for all repr., trans., notes. This 2nd
ed. omits Appendices.⌋

420000(1) THE DEATH AGONY OF CAPITALISM AND THE TASKS OF THE WORKING CLASS.
      [Trans. Eng. See 380500(1) for all repr., trans.]

[420000(2)] THE ILP AND THE STRUGGLE FOR THE FOURTH INTERNATIONAL: THE MIDDLE OF
      THE ROAD.
      [Trans. Eng. See 350918 for all repr., trans.]

[420000(5)] FROM A SCRATCH TO THE DANGER OF GANGRENE.
      [Trans. Eng. See 400124 for all repr., trans.]

[420000(6)] THE MISTAKES OF THE RIGHT ELEMENTS ON THE TRADE UNION QUESTION.
      [Trans. Eng. See 310104 for all repr., trans.]

[420000(7)] THEIR MORALS AND OURS.
      [Trans. Am. See 380216,390609 for all repr., trans.]

420600   Pref. THE LIVING THOUGHTS OF KARL MARX.
      [Trans. Eng. See 390418 for all repr., trans., notes.]

420800   THEIR MORALS AND OURS.
      [Trans. Am. See 380216,390609 for all repr., trans.]

421200   † IN DEFENSE OF MARXISM.
      Trans.: Am. 421200; [640000(3)]; 650000(6); 700000(11);
         Eng. 661100;
         Jap. 631030;
         Sp. 580130.
      [Sp. omits the correspondence. See separate items for other repr.,
      trans.]

*430000(1)   *MINHA VIDA.

                [Trans. Port. See 300000(1) for all trans., notes.]

[430000(2)]   I STAKE MY LIFE.

                [Trans. Eng. See 370209 for all repr., trans.]

[430000(3)]   § LENIN.

                [Trans. It. See 240000(24) for all repr., trans.]

[430000(4)]   TROTSKY SPEAKS.

                [Trans. Eng. See 381018 for all trans.]

*430625   Pref. *EL PENSAMIENTO VIVO DE MARX.

                [Trans. Sp. See 390418 for all repr., trans., notes.]

430800(1)   IMPERIALIST WAR AND REVOLUTIONARY PERSPECTIVES. + LENIN ON IMPERIALISM.

                [Trans. Eng. See 381010, 381230 for all repr., trans.]

*430800(2)   *THE FOURTH INTERNATIONAL AND THE SOVIET UNION.

                [Trans. Eng. See 360708 for all repr., trans.]

430900   § THE NEW COURSE.

                [Trans. Am. See 240000(22) for all repr., trans.]

*440000(1)   *DA NORUEGA AO MÉXICO. (Memorias.)

[Trans. Port. See 371116(2) for all trans.]

440000(2)   GERMANY — THE KEY TO THE INTERNATIONAL SITUATION.

[Trans. Eng. See 311126 for all repr., trans., notes.]

440800(1)   L'AGONIE DU CAPITALISME ET LES TÂCHES DE LA IVe INTERNATIONALE.

[Trans. Fr. See 380500(1) for all repr., trans.]

440800(2)   § FASCISM -- WHAT IT IS: HOW TO FIGHT IT.

Trans.: Am. 440800(2);

           Eng. 620900.

[See 690400(3) for further excerpts.]

441216   ONCE AGAIN -- ON THE ILP.

[Trans. Eng. See 351100(1) for all repr., trans.]

*450000(1)   *DALLA RIVOLUZIONE D'OTTOBRE AL TRATTATO DI PACE DI BREST-LITOWSK.
[Trans. It. See 180000(5) for all repr., trans.]

450000(3)   THE REVOLUTION BETRAYED.
[Trans. Am. See 361013 for all repr,, trans., notes.]

[450000(4)]   QU'EST-CE QUE LE NATIONAL-SOCIALISME?
[Trans. Fr. See 330610 for all repr., trans.]

[450000(5)]   GROEPERINGEN IN DE COMMUNISTISCHE OPPOSITIE.
[Trans. Hol. See 290331 for all trans.]

450000(6)   E PRODOMENE EPANASTASE.
[Trans. Gr. See 361013 for all repr., trans., notes.]

450000(7)   E PRODOMENE EPANASTASE.
[Trans. Gr. See 361013 for all repr., trans., notes.]

450000(8)   SECTARIANISM, CENTRISM AND THE FOURTH INTERNATIONAL.
[Trans. Eng. See 351022 for all repr., trans.]

450300   MANIFESTE COMMUNISTE.
[Trans. Fr. See 371030 for all repr., trans.]

451000   § THE FIRST FIVE YEARS OF THE COMMUNIST INTERNATIONAL.
[Trans. Am. Vol. I. See 530700 for Vol. II. See 240000(29) for all trans.]

451100   STALINISM AND BOLSHEVISM.
[Trans. Eng. See 370828 for all repr., trans.]

460000(2) HUN MORAAL EN DE ONZE.
[Trans. Hol. See 380216 for all repr., trans.]

460000(3) § LEÇON D'ESPAGNE: DERNIER AVERTISSEMENT.
[Trans. Fr. See 371217 for all repr., trans. p.q. 310124, 310528(1) passim.]

460000(5) LE MARXISME ET NOTRE ÉPOQUE.
[Trans. Fr. See 390418 for all repr., trans., notes.]

460000(6) MPOLSEVIKISMOS KAI STALINISMOS.
[Trans. Gr. See 370828 for all trans.]

460000(8) ON LENIN'S TESTAMENT.
[Trans. Am. See 321231 for all repr., trans.]

*460000(9) *STORIA DELLA RIVOLUZIONE RUSSA.
[Trans. It. See 310000(1) for all repr., trans., notes.]

*[460000(10)] *WAS NUN?
[Trans. Ger. See 320127 for all repr., trans.]

*460000(11) *MI VIDA.
[Trans. Sp. See 300000(1) for all repr., trans., notes.]

*460000(12) *CHUGOKU KAKUMEIRON.
[Trans. Jap. See 320600(2) for all repr., trans., notes.]

460000(13) WHITHER FRANCE?
[Trans. Eng. See 341109 for all repr., trans.]

[460000(14)] THE UNITED STATES OF EUROPE.
[Trans. Eng. See 230630 for all repr., trans.]

460315 STALIN.
[Trans. Am. See 410000(1) for all repr., trans., notes.]

460501 THE DEATH AGONY OF CAPITALISM AND THE TASKS OF THE FOURTH INTERNATIONAL.
[Trans. Am. See 380500(1) for all repr., trans.]

460800 L'AGONIE DU CAPITALISME ET LES TÂCHES DE LA IVᵉ INTERNATIONALE.
[Trans. Fr. See.380500(1) for all repr., trans.]

461100 Pref. THE LIVING THOUGHTS OF KARL MARX.
[Trans. Eng. See 390418 for all repr., trans., notes.]

*470000(1)   *[LESSONS OF OCTOBER.]
              [Trans. Ch. See 240915 for all trans.]

470000(2)   § KOMMUNISMUS ODER STALINISMUS.
              [Trans. Ger. See 370828,381220,390501 for all repr., trans.]

*470000(3)   *[MY LIFE.]
              [Trans. Ch. See 300000(1) for all repr., trans., notes.]

[470000(4)]   OVERGANGSPROGRAM VAN DE VIERDE INTERNATIONALE.
              [Trans. Hol. See 380500(1) for all repr., trans.]

*470000(6)   *TA SINDIKATA STEN EPOKHE TES IMPERIALISKHES PARAKHMES.
              [Trans. Gr. See [400820(4)] for all trans.]

470000(7)   STALIN.
              [Trans. Eng. See 410000(1) for all repr., trans., notes.]

*470000(9)   *STALIN Y SUS CRÍMENES.
              [Trans. Sp. See 371116(2) for all repr., trans., notes.]

470100   MARXISM IN THE UNITED STATES: MARXISM IN OUR TIMES.
              [Trans. Am. See 390418 for all repr., trans., notes.]

470300   THE PERMANENT REVOLUTION.
              [Trans. Eng. See 281000(1) for all repr., trans., notes.]

470400   STALIN.
              [Trans. Sp. See 410000(1) for all repr., trans., notes.]

470427   ‡ [PROBLEMS OF THE CHINESE REVOLUTION.]
              [Trans. Ch. Not fully identical with Am. 320600(2).]

470600   DER MARXISMUS UND UNSERE EPOCHE.
              [Trans. Ger. See 390418 for all trans., notes.]

470615   MA VIE.
              [Trans. Fr. See 340000(4) for all repr., trans., notes.]

470910   Pref. PAGES IMMORTELLES DE KARL MARX.
              [Trans. Fr. See 390418 for all repr., trans., notes.]

471001   STALINVADAYA SAHA BOLSHEVIKVADAYA.
              [Trans. Sin. See 370828 for all trans.]

480000(2) § ON THE LABOR PARTY IN THE USA.
Trans.: Am. 480000(2); [620000(15)]; EB, V.48.

480000(3) STALIN.
[Trans. It. See 410000(1) for all repr., trans., notes.]

*480000(4) *STALIN.
[Trans. Sp. See 410000(1) for all repr., trans., notes.]

*480000(5) Pref. *EL PENSAMIENTO VIVO DE MARX.
[Trans. Sp. See 390418 for all repr., trans., notes.]

480000(6) THE LESSON OF SPAIN.
[Trans. Eng. See 371217 for all repr., trans.]

480000(7) TRADE UNIONS IN THE EPOCH OF IMPERIALIST DECAY.
[Trans. Eng. See [400820(4)] for all repr., trans.]

[480000(9)] DISCUSSION SUR LE PROGRAMME TRANSITOIRE.
[Trans. Fr. See 380519 for all trans.]

[480000(10)] LES SYNDICATS A L'ÉPOQUE DE LA DÉCADENCE IMPÉRIALISTE.
[Trans. Fr. See [400820(4)] for all repr., trans.]

[480000(11)] *CACH-MANG THUONG-TRUC.
[Trans. Viet. See 291130(2) for all trans., notes.]

480103 MILLENOVECENTO CINQUE.
[Trans. It. See 100000(2) for all repr., trans., notes. This ed. lacks some Appendices.]

480200 90 YEARS OF THE COMMUNIST MANIFESTO.
[Trans. Eng. See 371030 for all repr., trans., notes.]

480300 90 ANNÉES DE MANIFESTE COMMUNISTE.
[Trans. Fr. See 371030 for all repr., trans., notes.]

480508 STALINE.
[Trans. Fr. See 410000(1) for all trans., notes. Editorial links do not trans. Am. version, 410000(1). Includes book list.]

490000(1)   STALIN.

[Trans. Hol. See 410000(1) for all trans., notes. Omits Appendix 390800.]

*490000(2)   *VIDA DE LENIN: JUVENTUD.

[Trans. Sp. See 360000(10) for all trans.]

*490000(3)   Pref. *CARLO MARX.

[Trans. It. See 390418 for all trans., notes.]

*490000(4)   *TEIKOKUSHUGI-JIDAI NO RODO-KUMIAI.

[Trans. Jap. See [400000(4)] for all trans.]

490700   GEORGE VALENTINOVICH PLEKHANOV.

[Trans. Eng. See 220425 for all repr., trans.]

490800   IN DEFENCE OF OCTOBER.

[Trans. Eng. See 321127 for all repr., trans.]

491000   MARXISM AND SCIENCE.

[Trans. Eng. See 250917, 380418(1) for all repr., trans.]

500000(1)   L'HISTOIRE DE LA RÉVOLUTION RUSSE.
[Trans. Fr. See 310000(1) for all repr., trans., notes. Revised trans.]

500000(2)   THE RUSSIAN REVOLUTION.
[Trans. Eng. See 321127 for all repr., trans.]

*500000(3)   *ROSHIYA KAKUMEI-SHI.
[Trans. Jap. See 310000(1) for all repr., trans., notes.]

[500000(4)]   STALIN'S FRAME-UP SYSTEM AND THE MOSCOW TRIALS.
[Trans. Am. See 370417(2) for all trans.]

[500000(5)]   D'UNE ENGRATIGNURE AU DANGER DE GANGRÈNE.
[Trans. Fr. See 400124 for all trans.]

500400   EUROPE AND AMERICA.
[Trans. Eng. See 240728 for all repr., trans., notes.]

501000   WHITHER EUROPE? PERSPECTIVES OF WORLD DEVELOPMENT.
[Trans. Eng. See 260215 for all repr., trans.]

501200   I STAKE MY LIFE.
[Trans. Eng. See 370208 for all repr., trans.]

510000(1)   Lenin & T.: PARIS COMMUNYA.
             [Trans. Sin. See [170317(1)] for all repr., trans.]

510000(2)   Pref. DE LEVENDE GEDACHTEN VAN KARL MARX.
             [Trans. Hol, See 390418 for all repr., trans., notes.]

510100   EUROPE AND AMERICA.
             [Trans. Eng. See 240728, 260215 for all repr., trans.]

510300   § LENIN.
             [Trans. Eng. Abr. See 240000(24) for all repr., trans. Revised trans.]

510400   GENERAL STRIKAYATA YUDDAYA NAVATVIYA HAKIDA?
             [Trans. Sin. p.q. 350918.]

510900   THE ZIMMERWALD MANIFESTO.
             [Trans. Eng. See 150915 for all trans.]

520000(3)   STALIN.

                 [Trans. Ger. See 410000(1) for all repr., trans.]

*520000(4)   *TSUGI WA NANI KA? FASCISM RON.

                 [Trans. Jap. See 650430 for possible contents.]

520300   AN OPEN LETTER TO JULES GUESDE.

                 [Trans. Eng. See 161011 for all repr., trans., notes.]

520400   STALINISM AND BOLSHEVISM.

                 [Trans. Eng. See 370828 for all repr., trans.]

520600   THE OCTOBER REVOLUTION.

                 [Trans. Eng. See 180000(5), 390800 for all repr., trans., notes.]

520900(1)   WORLD UNEMPLOYMENT AND THE FIVE-YEAR PLAN.

                 [Trans. Eng. See 300314 for all trans.]

520900(2)   THE REVOLUTION IN SPAIN.

                 [Trans. Eng. See 310124 for all repr., trans.]

521200   THE CLASS NATURE OF THE SOVIET STATE.

                 [Trans. Eng. See 331001 for all repr., trans.]

530000(2)   LÉON SEDOV.
              [Trans. Fr. See 380220 for all repr., trans.]

530000(3)   ON LENIN'S TESTAMENT.
              [Trans. Eng. See 321231 for all trans.]

*530000(4)   *¿QUÉ FUÉ LA REVOLUCIÓN DE OCTUBRE?
              [Trans. Sp. See 240915,321127 for all repr., trans.]

[530000(5)]   BOLCHÉVISME ET STALINISME. + LE RÉGIME COMMUNISTE AUX USA.
              [Trans. Fr. See 350323(1), 370828 for all repr., trans.]

530000(6)   STALIN.
              [Trans. Ger. See 410000(1) for all repr., trans., notes.]

530700   § THE FIRST FIVE YEARS OF THE COMMUNIST INTERNATIONAL.
              [Trans. Am-Eng. Vol. II. See 451000 for Vol. I; 240000(29) for all
              trans.]

531130   MA VIE.
              [Trans. Fr. See 300000(1) for all repr., trans., notes. Supplementary
              material by A.Rosmer. Revised trans.]

531200   § 1905: BEFORE AND AFTER.
              [Trans. Eng. Together with 540300 comprises 180000(40).]

540000(1)   THE DRAFT PROGRAMME OF THE COMMUNIST INTERNATIONAL.
[Trans. Eng. See 280628 for all repr., trans.]

*540123   *HISTORIA DE LA REVOLUCIÓN RUSA.
[Trans. Sp. See 310000(1) for all repr., trans., notes. Only 1 of 4 volumes published.]

*540215   *ROSHIYA KAKUMEI-SHI.
[Trans. Jap. See 310000(1) for all repr., trans., notes. 6 vols.]

540300   § 1905: RESULTS AND PERSPECTIVES.
Trans.: Eng. 540300;
          Jap. *610805; 661130: 6-54; 671031.
[See 531200, note.]

541000   IN DEFENCE OF INSURRECTION.
[Trans. Eng. See 061004 for all trans.]

541100(1)   ON LENIN'S TESTAMENT.
[Trans. Eng. See 321231 for all repr., trans.]

[541100(2)]   TWO CONCEPTIONS OF SOCIALISM.
[Trans. Eng. See 300329 for all trans.]

550700   NINETY YEARS OF THE COMMUNIST MANIFESTO.

[Trans. Eng. See 371030 for all repr., trans., notes.]

550900   THE PARIS COMMUNE.

[Trans. Eng. See *200000(27) for all trans., notes.]

551115   † ECRITS. I.

[Trans Fr. See further in series 580900, 590600.]

560000(1) THE DEATH AGONY OF CAPITALISM AND THE TASKS OF THE WORKING CLASS.
[Trans. Eng. See 380500(1) for all repr., trans., notes.]

560000(3) LA QUESTION UKRAINIENNE.
[Trans. Fr. See 390422(1) for all repr., trans.]

560000(4) STALINISM AND BOLSHEVISM.
[Trans. Eng. See 370828 for all repr., trans.]

[560000(5)] BOLCHEVISME ET STALINISME. + LE RÉGIME COMMUNISTE AUX USA.
[Trans. Fr. See 350323(1), 370828 for all repr., trans.]

[560000(6)] THESES ON INDUSTRY.
[Trans. Eng. See 230306 for all repr., trans.]

*560000(8) *STALIN.
[Trans. Sp. See 410000(1) for all repr., trans., notes.]

560501 THE KIROV ASSASSINATION.
[Trans. Am. See 350200(1) for all repr., trans., notes.]

560600 § WHAT IS A PEACE PROGRAMME?
[Trans. Eng.]

560700 THE LESSONS OF SPAIN — THE LAST WARNING.
[Trans. Eng. See 371217 for all repr., trans.]

560900(1) THE FOURTH INTERNATIONAL AND THE USSR.
[Trans. Eng. See 360708 for all repr., trans., notes.]

560900(2) LA RIVOLUZIONE TRADITA.
[Trans. It. See 361013 for all repr., trans.]

561000 § THE NEW COURSE.
[Trans. Eng. See 240000(22) for all trans.]

561123 STALIN NO ANKOKU SAIBAN.
[Trans. Jap. See 370417(2) for all trans.]

570000(1)   et a.: § LES BOLCHEVIKS CONTRE STALINE.
[Trans. Fr. See 240000(22), 270903 for all repr., trans.]

570000(2)   § THE CHINESE REVOLUTION: PROBLEMS AND PERSPECTIVES.
Trans.: Am. 570000(2); 690000(4).
[6 items.]

570000(3)   THE HISTORY OF THE RUSSIAN REVOLUTION.
[Trans. Am. See 310000(1) for all repr., trans., notes.]

570000(4)   RADIO, SCIENCE, TECHNIQUE AND SOCIETY.
[Trans. Eng. See 260301 for all repr., trans.]

[570000(5)]   THE CLASS NATURE OF THE SOVIET STATE.
[Trans. Eng. See 371104, 371125(2) for all repr., trans.]

570000(6)   THE REVOLUTION BETRAYED.
[Trans. Am-Eng. See 361013 for all trans.]

[570000(8)]   THE CLASS, THE PARTY AND THE LEADERSHIP.
[Trans. Eng. See [400820(3)] for all repr., trans.]

[570000(9)]   QU'EST-CE QUE LE NAZISME.
[Trans. Fr. See 330610 for all repr., trans.]

570200   RUSSIAN VIPLAVAYA.
[Trans. Sin. Abr. See 310000(1) for all trans., notes.]

570400   § LA TERZA INTERNATIONALE DOPO LENIN.
[Trans. It. See 301100(1) for all repr., trans., notes.]

570411   ANTE JEEVAN PANTHAYAM VEKKUNNU.
[Trans. Mal. See 370209 for all trans.]

570500   § THE THIRD INTERNATIONAL AFTER LENIN.
[Trans. Am. See 301100(1) for all repr., trans., notes.]

570900(1)   IF AMERICA SHOULD GO COMMUNIST.
[Trans. Am. See 350323(1) for all repr., trans.]

570900(2)   LITERATURE AND REVOLUTION.
[Trans. Am. See 230000(9) for all repr., trans., notes.]

570900(3)   A PARADISE IN THIS WORLD.

[Trans. Eng. See 180414 for all repr., trans.]

571000   VERRATENE REVOLUTION.

[Trans. Ger. See 361013 for all repr., trans., notes.]

580000(2) STALIN.
[Trans. Am. See 410000(1) for all repr., trans., notes.]

580000(4) § TROTSKY'S DIARY IN EXILE: 1935.
Trans.: Am. 580000(4); 630000(5);
    Eng. 590000(8);
    Fr. 600210;
    Ger. 600000(11); 621100;
    Gr. 590000(1);
    It. 600100;
    Jap. 680430; 690831.
[See separate entries for other trans.]

[580000(7)] LA COMMUNE DE PARIS ET LA RUSSIE DES SOVIETS.
[Trans. Fr. See *200000(27) for all repr., trans., notes.]

[580000(8)] LETTRE A JULES GUESDE.
[Trans. Fr. See 161011 for all repr., trans., notes.]

580000(9) LÉNINE.
[Trans. Fr. See [260000(31)] for all trans.]

580000(10) THE CLASS NATURE OF THE SOVIET UNION.
[Trans. Eng. See 331001 for all repr., trans., notes.]

580130 § EN DEFENSA DEL MARXISMO.
[Trans. Sp. See 421200 for all trans. Omits all correspondence in Am.]

580200 THE TURN IN THE COMMUNIST INTERNATIONAL AND THE GERMAN SITUATION.
[Trans. Eng. See 300926(1) for all repr., trans.]

580225 LENINTE ANTYA LEKHANAM.
[Trans. Mal. See 321231 for all trans.]

580900 ‡ ECRITS. II.
[Trans. Fr. See 360000(6) for all repr., trans.]

581000 § LETTERATURA, ARTE E LIBERTA.
[Trans. It. p.q. 230000(9); 080915;230919;250917;380216;380725(2).]

581100 GERMANY — THE KEY TO THE INTERNATIONAL SITUATION.
[Trans. Eng. See 311126, 311208 for all repr., trans.]

590000(1)   § EMEROLOGIO TES EKSORIAS.

[Trans. Gr. See 580000(4) for all trans.]

590000(4)   § LENIN.

[Trans. Am. See 240000(24) for all repr., trans., notes.]

590000(5)   UNITED STATES OF EUROPE.

[Trans. Eng. See 230630 for all repr., trans., notes.]

*590000(6)   *RIRONKA TOSHITEHO STALIN.

[Trans. Jap. See 300715 for all trans.]

590000(7)   THE RUSSIAN REVOLUTION.

[Trans. Am. See 310000(1) for all repr., trans., notes. Abr.]

590000(8)   § TROTSKY'S DIARY IN EXILE: 1935.

[Trans. Eng. See 580000(4) for all trans., notes.]

*590000(9)   *URAGIRARETA KAKUMEI.

[Trans. Jap. See 361013 for all repr., trans.]

590100   § THE ONLY ROAD.

[Trans. Eng. See 330400(2) for all trans.]

590600   ‡ ECRITS. III.

Trans.: Fr. 590600;

It. p.q. 620000(20);

Jap. p.q. 620530; p.q. *630430; 650430: 161-316.

590700   § THE ILP AND THE STRUGGLE FOR THE FOURTH INTERNATIONAL: THE MIDDLE
OF THE ROAD.

[Trans. Eng. See 350918, 351100(1), 360422 for all repr., trans.]

600000(2)   L'ÉTAT OUVRIER, THERMIDOR ET BONAPARTISME.

[Trans. Fr. See 350201 for all repr., trans.]

600000(3)   GESCHICHTE DER RUSSISCHEN REVOLUTION.

[Trans. Ger. See 310000(1) for all repr., trans., notes. Abr.]

600000(4)   JEAN JAURÈS.

[Trans. Fr. See 170000(1) for all repr., trans.]

600000(5)   LITERATURE AND REVOLUTION.

[Trans. Am. See 230000(9) for all repr., trans., notes.]

600000(6)   LE MARXISME ET NOTRE EPOQUE.

[Trans. Fr. See 390418 for all repr., trans., notes.]

600000(8)   MY LIFE.

[Trans. Am. See 300000(1) for all repr., trans., notes.]

600000(9)   STALINISM AND BOLSHEVISM.

[Trans. Am. See 370828 for all repr., trans.]

600000(10)   SUR LA QUESTION JUIVE.

[Trans. Fr. See 370118 for all repr., trans.]

600000(11)   TAGEBUCH IM EXIL.

[Trans. Ger. See 580000(4) for all repr., trans., notes.]

[600000(12)]   BONAPARTISME BOURGEOIS ET BONAPARTISME SOVIÉTIQUE.

[Trans. Fr. See 350201 for all repr., trans.]

[600000(17)]   ENCORE UNE FOIS SUR LA NATURE DE L'URSS.

[Trans. Fr. See 391018 for all repr., trans.]

*[600000(18)]   *KATOTEKI KORYO.

[Trans. Jap. See 380500(1) for all trans., repr.]

600000(19)   LEUR MORALE ET LA NÔTRE.

[Trans. Fr. See 380216 for all repr., trans., notes.]

[600000(20)]   THE MISTAKES OF THE RIGHT ELEMENTS ON THE TRADE UNION QUESTION.

[Trans. Eng. See 310104 for all repr., trans.]

[600000(21)]   ON THE HISTORY OF STALINISM.

[Trans. Eng. See 390400(2) for all repr., trans.]

[600000(22)]   LA RÉVOLUTION ÉTRANGLÉE.
                [Trans. Fr. See 310209 for all repr., trans.]

[600000(26)]   LE TRAITÉ DE VERSAILLES.
                [Trans. Fr. See 380919(1), 380922 for all repr., trans.]

600000(29)   THE HISTORY OF THE RUSSIAN REVOLUTION.
                [Trans. Am. See 310000(1) for all repr., trans., notes.]

600000(30)   REVOLUTIONEN FORRÅDT.
                [Trans. Den See 361013 for all trans.]

*600000(31)   *STORIA DELLA RIVOLUZIONE RUSSA.
                [Trans. It. See 310000(1) for all repr., trans., notes.]

*600000(32)   *STALIN.
                [Trans. Sp. See 410000(1) for all repr., trans., notes.]

600100   § DIARIO D'ESILIO: 1935.
                [Trans. It. See 580000(4) for all trans., notes.]

600200   WHERE IS BRITAIN GOING?
                [Trans. Eng. See 250000(5) for all repr., trans., notes.]

600210   § JOURNAL D'EXIL: 1935.
                [Trans. Fr. See 580000(4) for all trans., notes.]

600730   MI VIDA.
                [Trans. Sp. See 300000(1) for all repr., trans., notes.]

610000(1) THE HISTORY OF THE RUSSIAN REVOLUTION.
    [Trans. Am. See 310000(1) for all repr., trans., notes.]

610000(2) LETTRE OUVERTE A VANDERVELDE.
    [Trans. Fr. See 321205 for all trans.]

610000(3) MEIN LEBEN.
    [Trans. Ger. See 300000(1) for all repr., trans., notes.]

610000(5) LA RÉVOLUTION PERMANENTE: THÈSES.
    [Trans. Fr. See 291130(2) for all repr., trans., notes.]

610000(6) LA RÉVOLUTION TRAHIE.
    [Trans. Fr. See 361013 for all repr., trans.]

610000(7) ROMAIN ROLLAND REMPLIT SA MISSION.
    [Trans. Fr. See 351031 for all repr., trans.]

610000(8) TERRORISM AND COMMUNISM.
    [Trans. Am. See 200000(37) for all repr., trans., notes.]

[610000(9)] HUE AND CRY OVER KRONSTADT.
    [Trans. Eng. See 380115 for all repr., trans.]

[610000(10)] L'URSS ET LA GUERRE.
    [Trans. Fr. See 390925 for all repr., trans.]

[610000(11)] THE WORKERS STATE AND THE QUESTION OF THERMIDOR AND BONAPARTISM.
    [Trans. Eng. See 350201 for all repr., trans.]

*610000(16) *WAGA SHOGAI.
    [Trans. Jap. See 300000(1) for all repr., trans., notes.]

*610000(17) *INTANASHIONARU TO SENSO.
    [Trans. Jap. See 400526 for all trans.]

[610000(18)] GEORGE VALENTINOVICH PLEKHANOV.
    [Trans. Eng. See 220425 for all repr., trans.]

610000(19) ISTORIA TES ROSIKES EPANASTASI.
    [Trans. Gr. See 310000(1) for all trans., notes. Vol. II at 650000(9).]

*610325 *CHUGOKU KAKUMEIRON.
    [Trans. Jap. See 320600(2) for all repr., trans. Not fully identical.]

610400   LA MIA VITA.
                [Trans. It. See 300000(1) for all repr., trans., notes.]

610501   LA REVOLUCIÓN PERMANENTE.
                [Trans. Sp. See 281000(1) for all repr., trans., notes.]

*610515   *LENIN SHIGO NO DAISAN INTANASHONARU.
                [Trans. Jap. See 301100(1) for all repr., trans., notes.]

610600   § WHITHER FRANCE?
                [Trans. Eng. See 360000(6) for all repr., trans., notes.]

610622   LA REVOLUCIÓN RUSA Y LA BUROCRATIA SOVIÉTICA.
                [Trans. Sp. See 321127, p.q. 361013 for all repr., trans.]

*610805   *EIZOKU KAKUMEIRON.
                [Trans. Jap. See 661130. On permanent revolution.]

*611005   *SAYOKU HANTAIHA NO KORYO.
                [Trans. Jap. See 640330(2).]

611025   § POR LOS ESTADOS UNIDOS SOCIALISTAS DE AMÉRICA LATINA.
                [Trans. Sp.]

*611100   *LOS SINDICATOS EN LA EPOCA DEL IMPERIALISMO.
                [Trans. Sp. See ⌊400820(4)⌋ for all repr., trans.]

620000(1)   L'HISTOIRE DE LA RÉVOLUTION RUSSE.

[Trans. Fr. See 310000(1) for all repr., trans., notes.]

620000(2)   § PROBLEMS OF THE CHINESE REVOLUTION.

[Trans. Am. See 320600(2) for all repr., trans., notes.]

620000(3)   § THE STALIN SCHOOL OF FALSIFICATION.

[Trans. Am. See 320000(2) for all repr., trans., notes.]

[620000(4)]   DE L'OPPORTUNITÉ DU MOT D'ORDRE DES ETATS—UNIS SOCIALISTES D'EUROPE.

[Trans. Fr. See 230630 for all repr., trans.]

[620000(5)]   LES ETATS—UNIS SOCIALISTES D'EUROPE.

[Trans. Fr. p.q. 170512.]

[620000(6)]   GEORGES VALENTINOVITCH PLEKHANOV.

[Trans. Fr. See 220425 for all trans.]

[620000(7)]   90 ANNÉES DE MANIFÈSTE COMMUNISTE.

[Trans. Fr. See 371030 for all repr., trans., notes.]

[620000(8)]   LES SYNDICATS A L'ÉPOQUE DE LA DÉCADENCE IMPÉRIALISTE.

[Trans. Fr. See [400820(4)] for all repr., trans.]

620000(9)   § LENIN.

[Trans. Am. See 240000(24) for all repr., trans., notes.]

620000(10)   § LOS CRÍMENES DE STALIN.

[Trans. Sp. See 371116(2) for all repr., trans., notes.]

620000(11)   THE CLASS NATURE OF THE SOVIET STATE.

[Trans. Eng. See 331001 for all repr., trans.]

620000(12)   THE PROGRAMME OF PEACE.

[Trans. Eng. See 170000(4) for all repr., trans., notes.]

620000(13)   LEON SEDOFF — SON, FRIEND, FIGHTER.

[Trans. Eng. See 380220 for all repr., trans.]

[620000(14)]   THEIR MORALS AND OURS. + MORALISTS AND SYCOPHANTS AGAINST MARXISM.

[Trans. Eng. See 380216, 390609 for all repr., trans., notes.]

[620000(15)]   § THE LABOR PARTY IN AMERICA.

[Trans. Am. See 480000(2) for all repr.]

620000(16)   HISTORIA DE LA REVOLUCIÓN RUSA.
               [Trans. Sp. See 310000(1) for all repr., trans., notes. Lacks 3
               Appendices.]

620000(17)   BOLCHEVISMO Y STALINISMO.
               [Trans. Sp. See 370828 for all repr., trans.]

620000(18)   TA EGKLAMATA TOU STALIN.
               [Trans. Gr. See 371116(2) for all trans.]

*620000(19)   *LENIN.
               [Trans. Jap. See 240000(24) for all repr., trans., notes.]

620000(20)   § SCRITTI.
               [Trans It. p.q. Fr. 551115.]

620000(21)   THE COMMUNIST MANIFESTO TO-DAY.
               [Trans. Eng. See 371030 for all repr., trans., notes.]

*620120   *TERORIZUMU TO KOMUNIZUMU.
               [Trans. Jap. See 200000(37) for all repr., trans., notes.]

620200   TRADE UNIONS IN THE EPOCH OF IMPERIALIST DECAY.
               [Trans. Am. See ⌊400820(4)⌋ for all repr., trans.]

620404   STALIN.
               [Trans. It. See 410000(1) for all repr., trans., notes. Omits 390800.]

620500   IN DEFENCE OF OCTOBER.
               [Trans. Eng. See 321127 for all repr., trans.]

620530   SHAKAI FASHIZUMU RON HIHAN.
               [Trans. Jap. See Fr. 590600: 23-399 for all trans.]

620700(1)   THE PERMANENT REVOLUTION. + RESULTS AND PROSPECTS.
               [Trans. Eng. See 060600, 281000(1) for all repr., trans., notes.]

*620700(2)   Pref. *EL PENSAMIENTO VIVO DE MARX.
               [Trans. Sp. See 390418 for all repr., trans., notes.]

620719   SU MORAL Y LA NUESTRA.
               [Trans. Sp. See 380216 for all repr., trans., notes.]

620900   § FASCISM — WHAT IT IS — AND HOW TO FIGHT IT.
               [Trans. Eng. See 440800(2), note.]

*620915   *LENIN SHIGO NO DAISAN INTANASHONARU.
               [Trans. Jap. See 301100(1) for all repr., trans., notes.]

621031   RUSSIAN VIPLAVAM. Copenhagen prasangam.
               [Trans. Mal. See 321127 for all trans.]

621100(1)   § PROBLEMS OF LIFE.
               [Trans. Eng. See 230000(3) for all trans., notes.]

621100(2)   § TAGENBUCH IM EXIL.
               [Trans. Ger. See 580000(4) for all repr., trans., notes.]

*621130   *KOMUNISTO INTANASHONARU NO SAISHO NO GOKANEN.
               [Trans. Jap. See 451000 for all trans., note; 530700 for all repr.]

630000(1)   CULTURE AND SOCIALISM. + ART AND REVOLUTION.
[Trans. Eng. See 260203, 380725(2) for all repr., trans.]

630000(2)   THE DEATH AGONY OF CAPITALISM AND THE TASKS OF THE FOURTH INTERNATIONAL.
[Trans. Eng. See 380500(1) for all repr., trans., notes.]

[630000(3)]   OVERGANGSPROGRAM VAN DE VIERDE INTERNATIONALE.
[Trans. Hol. See 380500(1) for all repr., trans., notes.]

630000(4)   STALIN.
[Trans. Sp. See 410000(1) for all repr., trans., notes.]

630000(5)   § TROTSKY'S DIARY IN EXILE: 1935.
[Trans. Am. See 580000(4) for all repr., trans., notes.]

630000(6)   BETWEEN RED AND WHITE.
[Trans. Am. See 220000(5) for all trans.]

*630000(7)   § *THE BASIC WRITINGS OF TROTSKY.
Trans.: Am. *630000(7); 650900;
        Eng. 640000(5); 640000(10).
[Am. *630000(7) ignored in cross-references.]

630000(8)   § THE ESSENTIAL TROTSKY.
Trans.: Am. 630000(8);
        Eng. 630000(9).
[See 180000(5), 240915, p.q. 271021 for all repr., trans.]

630000(9)   § THE ESSENTIAL TROTSKY.
[Trans. Eng. See 630000(8).]

630000(10)   § O EMPHULOS POLEMOS STEN ISPANIA.
[Trans. Gr. See 630000(11), Part II.]

630000(11)   § E TRAGODIA TES ISPANIE.
[Trans. Gr. See 630000(10), Part I.]

630000(12)   THANASIME AGONIA TOU KAPITALISMOU.
[Trans. Gr. See 380500(1) for all trans., notes.]

630000(13)   TERRORISM AND COMMUNISM.
[Trans. Am. See 200000(37) for all repr., trans., notes.]

630100   & others: THE PLATFORM OF THE LEFT OPPOSITION (1927).
[Trans. Eng. See [270000(16)], 270903 for all repr., trans., notes.]

630200   Pref. THE LIVING THOUGHTS OF KARL MARX.
[Trans. Am. See 390418 for all repr., trans., notes.]

630419   § DE LA RÉVOLUTION.
[Trans. Fr. See 240000(22), 290600(3), 300000(3), 361013 for all
repr., trans., notes.]

*630430   *FURANSU WA DOKO E IKU.
[Trans. Jap. See 650430.]

630501   LA REVOLUCIÓN TRAICIONADA.
[Trans. Sp. See 361013 for all repr., trans., notes; Pref. 370900(1).]

630608   TERRORISME ET COMMUNISME.
[Trans. Fr. See 200000(37) for all repr., trans., notes.]

631001   TEIKOKUSHUGI NO BOTSURAKUKI NIOKERU KODOKUMIAI.
[Trans. Jap. See [400820(4)] for all trans.]

631030   § SOBIETO KOKKARON.
[Trans. Jap. See 290907, 331001, 350201, 421200 for all trans.]

631101   THE COMMUNIST MANIFESTO TODAY.
[Trans. Am. See 371030 for all repr., trans., notes.]

631126   LA REVOLUCIÓN PERMANENTE.
[Trans. Sp. See 281000(1) for all repr., trans., notes.]

631130   § DAIYON INTANASHONARU.
[Trans. Jap. On the Fourth International.]

631200   UNGE SADACHARAYA HA APAGE SADACHARAYA.
[Trans. Sin. See 380216 for all trans.]

640000(1) † THE TROTSKY PAPERS.
[Vol. I: 1917-1919. Russian and Eng. See 351228, note. See Contre leC, (III.29-30), 6.V.29 for item on "Publications envisagées".]

640000(2) ÜBER LENIN.
[Trans. Ger. See 240000(24) for all repr., trans., notes.]

[640000(3)] § IN DEFENSE OF MARXISM.
[Trans. Am. See 421200 for all repr., trans., notes.]

[640000(4)] THE REVOLUTION BETRAYED.
[Trans. Am. See 361013 for all repr., trans., notes.]

640000(5) § THE BASIC WRITINGS OF TROTSKY.
[See *630000(7) for all repr., notes. Trans. Eng.]

*640000(6) *LA AGONIA DEL CAPITALISMO Y LA IV INTERNACIONAL.
[Trans. Sp. See 380500(1) for all repr., trans.]

640000(7) THE HISTORY OF THE RUSSIAN REVOLUTION.
[Trans. Am. See 310000(1) for all repr., trans., notes.]

640000(8) AL IRHAB WAL CHIOUÏA.
[Trans. Arab. See 200000(37) for all trans., notes. Trans. from Fr.]

640000(9) THE DEATH AGONY OF CAPITALISM AND THE TASKS OF THE FOURTH INTERNATIONAL.
[Trans. Am. See 380500(1) for all repr., trans., notes.]

640000(10) § THE BASIC WRITINGS OF TROTSKY.
[Trans. Eng. See *630000(7) for all repr., trans., notes.]

640100 TERRORISMO E COMUNISMO.
[Trans. It. See 200000(37) for all repr., trans., notes.]

640110 § LENIN.
[Trans. It. See 240000(24) for all repr., trans., notes.]

640200 & Lenin: PARLIMENTHUVA SAHA VIPLAVAYA.
[Trans. Sin. See 380500(1) for all T. trans.: 13-81.]

640330(1) LENIN SHIGO NO DAISAN INTANASHONARU.
[Trans. Jap. See 301100(1) for all repr., trans., notes.]

640330(2)   SAYOKU HANTAIHA NO KONYO.
             [Trans. Jap. See 280000(9): 5-252; 321231; 370000(14): 125-77 for all
             repr., trans.]

640330(3)   § CHUGOKU KAKUMEIRON.
             [Trans. Jap. See 320600(2) for all repr., trans. Not fully identical.]

640330(4)   TERORIZUMU TO KOMUNIZUMU.
             [Trans. Jap. See 200000(37) for all repr., trans., notes.]

*640600   *STORIA DELLA RIVOLUZIONE RUSSA.
             [Trans. It. See 310000(1) for all repr., trans., notes. Lacks
             Appendices to Vol. II[/III].]

640617   LA REVOLUCIÓN TRAICIONADA.
             [Trans. Sp. See 361013 for all repr., trans., notes.]

640627   LA RÉVOLUTION PERMANENTE.
             [Trans. Fr. See 281000(1) for all repr., trans., notes.]

640800   § THE AGE OF PERMANENT REVOLUTION.
             Trans.: Am. 640800;
                     Jap. 681125;
                     Sp. 670000(5);
                     Swed. 691100(2).
             [Sp. 670000(5) includes additional material.]

640900(1)   § LITERATURA Y REVOLUCIÓN. + ESCRITOS DIVERSOS ... SOBRE PROBLEMAS
             DEL ARTE, LA CULTURA Y LA CIENCIA.
             [Trans. Sp.   230000(9) and other items.]

*640900(2)   *LOS SINDICATOS EN LA EPOCA DE LA DECADENCIA IMPERIALISTA.
             [Trans. Sp. See [400820(4)] for all repr., trans.]

640911   § LITTÉRATURE ET RÉVOLUTION.
             Trans.: Fr. 640911;
                     Swed. 690600(1).
             [230000(9) and other items.]

641200   STORIA DELLA RIVOLUZIONE RUSSA.
             [Trans. It. See 310000(1)ffor all repr., trans., notes. Lacks
             Appendices to Vol. II[/III].]

641225 § BUNGAKU TO KAKUMEI.

[Trans. Jap. See 230000(9) for all trans. of Parts I and II. The last 3 chaps. were included in a Lenin Anthology, published by Kawadeshobo, Tokyo, 1962; not listed in this catalogue.]

650000(1)   EL TESTAMENTO DE LENIN.
              [Trans. Sp. See 321231 for all repr., trans.]

650000(2)   E ETHIKE TOUS KAI E ETHIKE MAS.
              [Trans. Gr. See 380216 for all trans.]

650000(3)   THE PERMANENT REVOLUTION. + RESULTS AND PROSPECTS.
              [Trans. Am. See 060600, 190312, 281000(1) for all repr., trans., notes.]

650000(4)   [THE PERMANENT REVOLUTION. + RESULTS AND PROSPECTS.]
              [Trans. Iran. See 060600, 281000(1) for all trans., notes.]

650000(5)   § THE NEW COURSE.
              [Trans. Am. See 240000(22) for all repr., trans., notes.]

650000(6)   § IN DEFENSE OF MARXISM.
              [Trans. Am. See 421200 for all repr., trans., notes.]

650000(7)   THE REVOLUTION BETRAYED.
              [Trans. Am. See 361013 for all repr., trans., notes.]

650000(8)   THE HISTORY OF THE RUSSIAN REVOLUTION.
              [Trans. Eng. See 310000(1) for all repr., trans., notes.]

650000(9)   ISTORIA TES ROSIKES EPANASTASE.
              [Trans. Gr. Vol. II. See 310000(1) for all trans., notes. Vol. I
              at 610000(19).]

650000(10)   THROUGH WHAT STAGE ARE WE PASSING?
              [Trans. Eng. See 240621 for all repr., trans.]

[650000(11)] LA AGONIA DEL IMPERIALISMO Y LAS TAREAS DE LA IV INTERNACIONAL.
              [Trans. Sp. See 380500(1) for all repr., trans., notes.]

*650000(12)   *EL GRAN ORGANIZADOR DE DEROTTAS.
              [Trans. Sp. See 301100(1) for all repr., trans., notes.]

*[650000(13)] *LOS SINDICATOS EN LA EPOCA DE LA DECADENCIA DEL IMPERIALISMO. +
              CLASE, PARTIDO Y DIRECCION.
              [Trans. Sp. See [400820(3)], [400820(4)] for all repr., trans., notes.]

[650000(14)] LEUR MORALE ET LA NÔTRE.
              [Trans. Fr. See 380216 for all repr., trans., notes.]

650100   WHAT IS THE PERMANENT REVOLUTION?
                [Trans. Am. See 390800 for all repr., trans., notes.]

650430   § SUPEIN KAKUMEI TO JINMIN SENSKI.
                [Trans Jap. See 580900; 590600: 403-537 for all repr., trans., notes.]

650500   VURTHIYA SAMITHI SAHA RAJAYA.
                [Trans. Sin. See [400820(4)] for all trans., notes.]

650900   § THE BASIC WRITINGS OF TROTSKY.
                [Trans. Am. See *630000(7) for all repr., trans.]

651000(1)   THE HISTORY OF THE RUSSIAN REVOLUTION.
                [Trans. Eng. See 310000(1) for all repr., trans., notes.]

*651000(2)   *TERRORISMO Y COMUNISMO.
                [Trans. Sp. See 200000(37) for all repr., trans., notes.]

651100   DIE PERMANENTE REVOLUTION.
                [Trans. Ger. See 281000(1) for all repr., trans., notes.]

651200   AGAINST THE STREAM!
                [Trans. Eng. See 351002, 390400(2) for all trans., notes.]

[660000(1)] ON STALINISM AND TROTSKYISM IN THE U.S.A.
     [Trans. Eng. See 400615 for all trans.]

[660000(2)] GLI INSEGNAMENTI DELL'OTTOBRE. + LETTERA A OLMINSKI.
     [Trans. It. See 211206, 240915 for all repr., trans.]

660000(4) § PROBLEMS OF THE CHINESE REVOLUTION.
     [Trans. Am. See 320600(2) for all repr., trans., notes.]

660000(5) MA VIE.
     [Trans. Fr. See 300000(1) for all repr., trans., notes.]

660000(6) § LOGOTEKNIA KAI EPANASTASE.
     [Trans. Gr. See 230000(9) for all trans., notes. From Fr. 640911.]

660000(7) E OKTOBRIANE EPANASTASE.
     [Trans. Gr. See 321127 for all trans.]

660000(8) OI DIKES TES MOSKHAS.
     [Trans. Gr. See 370209 for all trans.]

660000(9) O LENIN ENANTION TES GRAFEIKRATIAS.
     [Trans. Gr. See 230405(3) for all trans.]

660000(10) § POU PEGAINEI E GALLIA.
     [Trans. Gr. See 361009 for all trans.]

660100 THE INTELLIGENTSIA AND SOCIALISM.
     [Trans. Eng. See [101100] for all repr., trans.]

660228 § KOMUNISTO INTANASHONARU NO SAISHO NO GOKANEN.
     [Trans. Jap. See 451000, 530700 for all repr., trans.]

660427 THE NEW COURSE.
     [Trans. Jap. See 240000(22) for all trans. Omits appendices. Title in
     Jap. and Eng.]

660500 THE STRUGGLE FOR STATE POWER.
     [Trans. Eng. See [180000(53)]: 170-203 for all trans.]

660510 LEUR MORALE ET LA NÔTRE. + LES MORALISTES ET SYCOPHANTES CONTRE LE
     MARXISME.
     [Trans. Ft. See 380216, 390609 for all repr., trans.]

660730   ROSHIYA KAKUMEI-SHI.

                 [Trans. Jap. See 310000(1) for all repr., trans., notes. 10th ed.]

660800(1)   THEIR MORALS AND OURS. + THE MORALISTS AND SYCOPHANTS AGAINST MARXISM.

                 [Trans. Am. See 380216, 390609, 390907 for all repr., trans. With supplementary essays by other hands.]

660800(2)   § THE FIGHT FOR MARXISM.

                 [Trans. Eng. See 240429(2), 240717, 260225(2) for all trans.]

661031   WAGA SHOGAI.

                 [Trans. Jap. See 300000(1) for all repr., trans., notes. 2 vol.]

661100   § IN DEFENCE OF MARXISM.

                 [Trans. Eng. See 391028, 421200 for all trans.]

661130   § EIZOKU KAKUMEIRON.

                 [Trans. Jap. See 240915, 281000(1), 540300 for all repr., trans.]

*661200   § *I CRIMINI DI STALIN.

                 [Trans. It. See 371116(2) for all trans., notes.]

670000(1)   GESCHICHTE DER RUSSISCHEN REVOLUTION.

[Trans. Ger. See 310000(1) for all repr., trans., notes. Abr.]

670000(2)   LA RÉVOLUTION RUSSE.

[Trans. Fr. See 321127 for all repr., trans.]

[670000(3)]   GRUNDFRAGEN DER REVOLUTION.

[Trans. Ger. See 230000(18) for all repr., trans., notes.]

670000(4)   AN OPEN LETTER TO THE WORKERS OF INDIA.

[Trans. Eng. See 390725 for all trans.]

670000(5)   § LA ERA DE LA REVOLUCION PERMANENTE.

[Trans. Sp. See 640800 ≠ 380605; p.q. 380923† p.q. [400820(4)] for all repr., trans.]

670000(6)   ERGEBNISSE UND PERSPEKTIVEN.

[Trans. Ger. See 060600; [151017(1)]; 190312 for all repr., trans.]

670000(8)   LA CRISE DU PARTI COMMUNISTE FRANÇAIS.

[Trans. Fr. See 220000(20) for all repr., trans.]

670000(9)   LE SALUT DU PARTI COMMUNISTE FRANÇAIS.

[Trans. Fr. See *220000(28) for all repr., trans.]

670000(11)   THE HISTORY OF THE RUSSIAN REVOLUTION.

[Trans. Eng. See 310000(1) for all repr., trans., notes.]

670000(12)   STALIN.

[Trans. Am. See 410000(1) for all repr., trans., notes.]

670000(13)   THE REVOLUTION BETRAYED.

[Trans. Eng. See 361013 for all repr., trans., notes.]

670000(14)   en Maksim Gorkij: HERINNERINGEN AAN LENIN.

[Trans. Hol. See 240000(24) for all trans., notes.]

670000(15)   E ZON MOU.

[Trans. Gr. See 300000(1) for all trans. Vol. I [of II] only.]

670000(16)   § PROBLEMS OF THE CHINESE REVOLUTION.

[Trans. Am. See 320600(2) for all repr., trans., notes.]

670000(17)   HISTOIRE DE LA RÉVOLUTION RUSSE.

[Trans. Fr. See 310000(1) for all repr., trans., notes.]

*670000(18)   *VERS LE CAPITALISME OU VERS LE SOCIALISME?
                    [Trans. Fr. See 250828(2) for all repr., trans., notes.]

670115   STALIN.
                    [Trans. Jap. See 410000(1) for all trans., notes.]

670121   LA RIVOLUZIONE PERMANENTE.
                    [Trans. It. See 281000(1) for all repr., trans., notes.]

670131   1905. KEKKA TO TEMBA.
                    [Trans. Jap. See 060600, [151017(1)], 190312 for all trans.]

670306   § LE MOUVEMENT COMMUNISTE EN FRANCE.
                    [Trans. Fr.]

670310   § LENIN.
                    [Trans. It. See 240000(24) for all repr., trans., notes.]

670315   § NUOVO CORSO.
                    [Trans. It. See 240000(22) for all trans., notes.]

670600   § ON BLACK NATIONALISM.
                    Trans.: Am. 670600; 690400(2); 700800(1);
                          Jap. 681010.

670800   STRATEGY AND TACTICS IN THE IMPERIALIST EPOCH.
                    [Trans. Eng. See 301100(4) for all trans., notes.]

670831   LA LORO MORALE E LA NOSTRA.
                    [Trans. It. See 380216, 390609 for all trans., notes.]

670900   STALIN.
                    [Trans. Sp. See 410000(1) for all repr., trans., notes.]

671000   IKH MORAL UND UNSERE.
                    [Trans. Ger. See 380216 for all repr., trans., notes.]

671100(1)   LA REVOLUCIÓN RUSA.
                    [Trans. Sp. See 321127, 330401 for all trans.]

671100(2)   WHAT NEXT?
                    [Trans. Eng. See 170000(5), 170919/ for all trans.]

671100(3)   THE COMMUNIST MANIFESTO.
                    [Trans. Am. See 371030 for all repr., trans., notes.]

671100(4)   STORIA DELLA RIVOLUZIONE RUSSA.
             [Trans. It. See 310000(1) for all repr., trans., notes. Lacks
             Appendices.]

671200   LEON SEDOV: SON — FRIEND — FIGHTER.
             [Trans. Eng. See 380220, 380719(2) for all repr., trans.]

680000(1) ECRITS MILITAIRES.

[Trans. Fr. See 230000(7).I, II.i for all trans.]

680000(2) STALIN.

[Trans. Eng. See 410000(1) for all repr., trans., notes.]

680000(3) VERRATENE REVOLUTION.

[Trans. Ger. See 361013 for all repr., trans., notes.]

680000(4) § POLITIQUE DE TROTZKY.

[Trans. Fr. Excerpts with comments.]

[680000(5)] KAPITALISMENS DØDSKAMP OG IV. INTERNATIONALES OPGAVEN.

[Trans. Den. See 380500(1) for all trans.]

680000(6) § SCRITTI LETTERARI.

[Trans. It. 11 items.]

680000(7) DIE PERMANENTE REVOLUTION.

[Trans. Ger. See 281000(1) for all repr., trans., notes.]

[680000(8)] ÜBER LENIN.

[Trans. Ger. See 240000(24) for all repr., trans., notes.]

680000(9) § MIS PERIPECIAS EN ESPAÑA.

[Trans. Sp. See 260000(5), 300525(1), 310528(1) for all repr., trans.]

680000(10) LITERATURE AND REVOLUTION.

[Trans. Am. See 230000(9) for all repr., trans., notes.]

680200(1) § ON LENIN.

[Trans. Eng. 5 items.]

680200(2) § SCELTA DI SCRITTI.

[Trans. It. p.q. 551115.]

680300(1) CLASS AND ART.

[Trans. Eng. See 240509 for all repr., trans.]

680300(2) MARXISM AND THE TRADE UNIONS.

[Trans. Eng. See 310300(1), [400820(4)] for all repr., trans., notes.]

680320 § [THE STALIN SCHOOL OF FALSIFICATION.]

[Trans. Jap. See 320000(2) for all trans., notes.]

680321 MA VIE.

[Trans. Fr. See 300000(1) for all repr., trans., notes.]

680430   § BOMEI NIKKI.

          [Trans. Jap. See 580000(4) for all repr., trans., notes.]

680501   SCHEDULE FOR A REVOLUTION.

          [Trans. Eng. See ⌊230923(2)⌋ for all repr., trans.]

680610   [THE REVOLUTION BETRAYED.]

          [Trans. Jap. See 361013 for all repr., trans., notes.]

680612(1)   L'AGONIE DU CAPITALISME ET LES TÂCHES DE LA IVe INTERNATIONALE.

          [Trans. Fr. See 380500(1) for all repr., trans., notes.]

680612(2)   WHITHER FRANCE?

          [Trans. Am. See 360000(6) for all repr., trans., notes.]

680700   THEIR MORALS AND OURS. + THE MORALISTS AND SYCOPHANTS AGAINST MARXISM.

          [Trans. Eng. See 380216, 390609 for all repr., trans., notes.]

680800(1)   THE CLASS NATURE OF THE SOVIET STATE. + THE WORKERS STATE AND THE
          QUESTION OF THERMIDOR AND BONAPARTISM.

          [Trans. Eng. See 331001, 350201 for all repr., trans., notes.]

680800(2)   § LITERATUR UND REVOLUTION.

          [Trans. Ger. See 230000(9) [Parts I and II], 380725(2) for all
          repr., trans., notes.]

680900(1)   BONAPARTISM AND FASCISM.

          [Trans. Eng. See 340715 for all repr., trans.]

680900(2)   THE CLASS NATURE OF THE SOVIET STATE.

          [Trans. Eng. See 331001 for all repr., trans., notes.]

*680900(3)   § *SCRITTI.

          [Trans. It. See 620000(28) for all repr., note.]

*680920   § *SOVIET KEIZAI NO SHOMONDAI.
          Trans.:Jap. *680920; 700130.
          [On Soviet economic problems.]

681000   LA RIVOLUZIONE TRADITA.

          [Trans. It. See 361013 for all repr., trans., notes. Lacks Pref.]

681010   § KOKUJIN KAKUMEI RON.
                [Trans. Jap. See 670600 for all repr., trans.]

681100   § SCRITTI.
                [Trans. It. See 620000(20) for all repr., note.]

681125   § [THE AGE OF PERMANENT REVOLUTION.]
                [Trans. Jap. See 640800 for all trans.]

690000(1)   L'INTERNATIONALE COMMUNISTE APRÈS LÉNINE.
[Trans. Fr. See 301100(1) for all repr., trans. New trans.]

690000(2)   STALIN.
[Trans. Eng. See 410000(1) for all repr., trans., notes.]

690000(3)   WORKERS CONTROL OF PRODUCTION.
[Trans. Eng. See 310820(1) for all repr., trans., notes.]

690000(4)   § THE CHINESE REVOLUTION: Problems and perspectives.
[Trans. Am. See 570000(2) for all repr., trans.]

690000(5)   DER JUNGE LENIN.
[Trans. Ger. See 360000(10) for all trans.]

690000(6)   BHARATIYA SRAMIKDER PRTOTI KHOLA CHITHI.
[Trans. Ben. See 390725 for all trans.]

[690000(7)]   THE REVOLUTION BETRAYED.
[Trans. Am. See 361013 for all repr., trans., notes.]

690000(8)   § LITERATURA Y REVOLUCION. + OTROS ESCRITOS SOBRE LA LITERATURA Y
EL ARTE.
[Trans. Sp. See 230000(9) for all repr., trans., notes. With other
items.]

690000(9)   ON THE ROAD TO THE EUROPEAN REVOLUTION.
[Trans. Eng. See 240411 for all repr., trans.]

[690000(10)]   DEN PERMANENTE REVOLUSJON.
[Trans. Nor. See 281000(1) for all trans., notes.]

690000(11)   § MILITARY WRITINGS.
[Trans. Am. 10 items.]

[690000(12)]   AMAR JIBON PON.
[Trans. Ben. See 370209 for all trans.]

690000(13)   ON THE TRADE UNIONS.
[Trans. Am. See 310300(1) for all repr., trans., notes.]

690000(14)   THEIR MORALS AND OURS. + THE MORALISTS AND SYCOPHANTS AGAINST MARXISM.
[Trans. Am. See 380216, 390609, 390907 for all repr., trans., notes.]

690000(15)   LA RÉVOLUTION TRAHIE.
              [Trans. Fr. See 361013 for all repr., trans., notes.]

690000(16)   HUN MORAAL EN DE ONZE.
              [Trans. Hol. See 380216 for all repr., trans., notes.]

[690000(17)] THE LESSONS OF SPAIN.
              [Trans. Eng. See 371217 for all repr., trans., notes.]

690000(18)   TERRORISM AND COMMUNISM.
              [Trans. Am. See 200000(37) for all repr., trans., notes.]

[690000(19)] LES SYNDICATS A L'ÉPOQUE DE LA DÉCADENCE IMPÉRIALISTE.
              [Trans. Fr. See [400820(4)] for all repr., trans., notes.]

690000(20)   THE PERMANENT REVOLUTION. + RESULTS AND PROSPECTS.
              [Trans. Am. See 060600, 190312, 281000(1) for all repr., trans., notes.]

690100   § FLIGHT FROM SIBERIA.
              [Trans. Eng. See 070000(3) for all trans., notes.]

690224   § IN DIFESA DEL MARXISMO.
              [Trans. It. See 421200 for all trans.]

690300(1)   NATIONALIZED INDUSTRY AND WORKERS MANAGEMENT.
              [Trans. Eng. See 380600 for all trans.]

690300(2)   § DISCUSSIONS ON THE TRANSITIONAL PROGRAM.
              [Trans. Am. See 380519, 380531(1), 380607 for all repr., trans.]

690321   § ON SOVIET STATE POWER: 1934-1938.
              [Trans. Eng. 6 items.]

690400(1)   § MARXISM AND MILITARY AFFAIRS.
              [Trans. Eng. 8 items.]

690400(2)   § ON BLACK NATIONALISM.
              [Trans. Am. See 670600 for all repr., trans.]

690400(3)   § FASCISM: WHAT IT IS: HOW TO FIGHT IT.
              Trans.: Am. 690400(3); 700300(2).
              [11 items. See also 440800(2).]

690415   § 1905. + BILAN ET PERSPECTIVES.
              [Trans. Fr. See 060600, 190312, 220000(12) for all repr., trans., notes.]

690500(1)   LA TERZA INTERNAZIONALE DOPO LENIN.
             [Trans. It. See 280628 for all repr., trans., notes.]

690500(2)   § MARXISMO E SCIENZA.
             [Trans. It. See 230927, 250917, 260301 for all repr., trans.]

690500(3)   LA LUCHA CONTRA LA BUROCRACIA.
             [Trans. Sp. See 290600(3) for all trans.]

690500(4)   § PROBLEMS OF THE CHINESE REVOLUTION.
             [Trans. Eng. See 320600(1) for all trans., notes.]

690600(1)   § LITTERATUR OCH REVOLUTION.
             [Trans. Swed. From Fr. 640911 with 2 variations.]

690600(2)   DEN FÖRRÅDDA REVOLUTIONEN.
             [Trans. Swed. See 361013 for all trans., notes.]

690600(3)   § WRITINGS: 1939-40.
             [Trans. Am.]

690610   1905.
             [Trans. It. See 220000(12) for all repr., trans., notes.]

690700(1)   § ON ENGELS AND KAUTSKY.
             [Trans. Am. See [350900(1)], 351015, 381108 for all repr., trans.]

690700(2)   § LA REVOLUCIÓN PERMANENTE.
             [Trans. Sp. See 611025, 631126 for all repr., trans.]

690825   § ON THE LABOR PARTY IN THE UNITED STATES.
             [Trans. Am. 5 items.]

690831   § BOMEI NIKKI.
             [Trans. Jap. See 580000(4) for all repr., trans., notes.]

690900(1)   § LA RÉVOLUTION PERMANENTE EN RUSSIE.
             [Trans. Fr. 4 items.]

690900(2)   § SUR LA NATURE DE L'ÉTAT SOVIÉTIQUE.
             [Trans. Fr. 4 items.]

690900(3)   L'AGONIE DU CAPITALISME ET LES TÂCHES DE LA IVe INTERNATIONALE.
             [Trans. Fr. See 380500(1) for all repr., trans., notes.]

691000   PERMANENTE REVOLUTION.

[Trans. Ger. See 281000(1) for all repr., trans., notes.]

691100(1)   § WRITINGS: 1938-9.

[Trans. Am.]

691100(2)   § DEN PERMANENTE REVOLUTIONENS EPOK.

[Trans. Swed. See 640800 for all trans.]

691100(3)   KAPITALISMENS DÖDSKAMP OCH IV INTERNATIONALENS UPPGIFTER.

[Trans. Swed. See 380500(1) for all trans., notes.]

691115   THE LESSONS OF SPAIN.

[Trans. Eng. See 371217 for all repr., trans.]

700000(1)   ON THE SUPPRESSED TESTAMENT OF LENIN.
               [Trans. Am. See 321231 for all repr., trans., notes.]

700000(2)   STALINISM AND BOLSHEVISM.
               [Trans. Am. See 370829 for all repr., trans., notes.]

[700000(3)]   BARTOMAN COMMUNIST ISTAHAR.
               [Trans. Ben. See 371030 for all trans.]

700000(4)   MY LIFE.
               [See 300000(1) for all repr., trans., notes,]

700000(5)   RAPPORT DE LA DÉLÉGATION SIBIRIENNE.
               [Trans. Fr. See 030700 for all trans.]

700000(6)   § CLASSE OUVRIÈRE, PARTI ET SYNDICAT.
               [Trans. Fr. 6 items.]

700000(7)   § LÉNINE.
               [Trans. Fr. See 240000(24) for all repr., trans., notes.]

70000(8)   THE PERMANENT REVOLUTION. + RESULTS AND PROSPECTS.
               [Trans. Am. See 060600, 190312, 281000(1) for all repr., trans.,
               notes.]

[700000(9)]   THE REVOLUTION BETRAYED.
               [Trans. Am. See 361013 for all repr., trans., notes.]

[700000(10)]   ON THE EVE OF WORLD WAR II.
               [Trans. Eng. See 390723(2) for all trans.]

700000(11)   § IN DEFENSE OF MARXISM.
               [Trans. Am. See 421200 for all repr., trans., notes.]

[700000(12)]   THE PERMANENT REVOLUTION. + RESULTS AND PROSPECTS.
               [Trans. Am. See 060600, 190312, 281000(1) for all repr., trans.,
               notes.]

[700000(13)]   [THE HISTORY OF THE RUSSIAN REVOLUTION.]
               [Trans. Ch. See 310000(1) for all repr., trans., notes.]

700000(14)   § ON LITERATURE AND ART.
               [Trans. Am. More than 20 items.]

700000(15)   JATKUVA VALLANKUMOUS.

           [Trans. Fin. See 281000(1) for all trans., notes.]

700000(16)   IL BOLSCEVISMO DINNANZI ALLA GUERRA E **ALLA** PACE DEL MONDO.

           [Trans. It. See [140000(3)] for all repr., trans., notes.]

700000(17)   DALLA RIVOLUZIONE D'OTTOBRE **AL** TRATTATO DI PACE DI BREST-LITOWSK.

           [Trans. It. See 180000(5) for all repr., trans., notes.]

700000(18)   LAVORO, DISCIPLINA E ORDINE SALVERANNO LA REPUBLICA SOCIALISTA
           DEI SOWJET.

           [Trans. It. With Lenin, LA LOTTA PER IL PANE. See 180328(1) for
           all repr., trans.]

700100   TO THE TOILERS OF THE EAST.

           [Trans. Eng. See 240421(2) for all repr., trans., notes.]

700126   § SUR LA DEUXIÈME GUERRE MONDIALE.

           [Trans. Fr. 28 items including 390918, 391001 in first publication.]

700129   MARX VU PAR TROTZKY.

           [Trans. Fr. See 390418 for all repr., trans., notes.]

700130   § SOVIET KEIZAI NO SHOMONDAI.

           [Trans. Jap. See *680920 for all repr., notes.]

700200(1)   THE COMMUNIST MANIFESTO.

           [Trans. Am. See 371030 for all repr., trans., notes.]

700200(2)   THE DEATH AGONY OF CAPITALISM AND THE TASKS OF THE FOURTH INTERNATIONAL

           [Trans. Am. See 380500(1) for all repr., trans., notes.]

700228   NOS TÂCHES POLITIQUES.

           [Trans. Fr. See 040000 for all trans.]

700300(1)   MARXISM IN OUR TIMES.

           [Trans. Am. See 390307(1), 390418 for all repr., trans., notes.]

700300(2)   § FASCISM: WHAT IT IS: HOW TO FIGHT IT.

           [Trans. Am. See 690400(3) for all repr., notes.]

700400   § WRITINGS: 1937-8.

           [Trans. Am.]

700500(1)   § GERMANY 1931-1932.
             [Trans. Eng. 4 items.]

700500(2)   WHERE IS BRITAIN GOING?
             [Trans. Eng. See 250000(5) for all repr., trans., notes.]

700600   PROBLEMS OF CIVIL WAR.
             [Trans. Am. See 240729(1) for all repr., trans.]

700603   ENTRE L'IMPÉRIALISME ET LA RÉVOLUTION.
             [Trans. Fr. See 220000(5), 390422(1) for all repr., trans., notes.]

700700   § ON THE JEWISH QUESTION.
             [Trans. Am. 8 items.]

700800(1)   § ON BLACK NATIONALISM.
             [Trans. Am. See 670600 for all repr., trans., notes.]

700800(2)   IN THE MIDDLE OF THE ROAD.
             [Trans. Eng. See 350918 for all repr., trans., notes.]

700831   KATOTEKI KORYO. + TEIKOKUSHUGI NO BOTSURAKUKI NIOKERU KODOKUMIAI.
             [Trans. Jap. See 380500(1), [400820(4)] for all repr., trans., notes.]

PART II

BOOK LIST

Cyrillic script

*ARMIYA BUDUSHCHEGO. (Biblioteka Vseobshch. No. 3), 1923. 16.   *⌊230000(23)⌋
   (LocHIS)

*AVIATSIYA -- ORUDIE BUDUSHCHEGO. Uralkniga: Ekaterinburg, 1923. 8.   *230000(1)
   (CatBibEzh)

† BALAKANY I BALKANSKAYA VOINA. Gosizdat: M-L, 1926. 503.   260000(1)
   ⌊Soch. VI⌋
   (LocBDIC/BM/BN/HIS/NYPL/SEES)

† BELGIYA I SERBIYA V VOINE. Kommunist: M-P, 1919. 128.   190000(1)
   (LocBDIC/LC/ULH)

BLAGOCHESTIV"EISHII, SAMODERZHAVN"EISHII! ... See Domov i T,
   YUBILEI POZORA NASHEGO (1613-1913).

Zinov´ev i T, BOI ZA PETERBURG. Gosizdat: Pet, 1920. 53.   200000(1)
   (LocBDIC/HIS/KBS/ULH)

*BOL´SHEVIKIT"E I SV"ETSKIYA MIR. Siuznata sots. knizhariyatsa   *180000(1)
   i pechatiyatsam: Granite City, Ill., USA, 1918. 134.
   (LocNYPL)

*BOR´BA ZA KACHESTVO. Plannovoe Khozyaistvo: L, 1926. 84.   *260000(36)
   (CatBibEzh)

*BOR´BA ZA KACHESTVO PRODUKTSII I RABOCHII KORRESPONDENT. Gosizdat: *260000(2)
   M-L, 1926. 48.
   (CatPostnikov)

Zinov´ev i T, † BOR´BA ZA PETROGRAD. Gosizdat: Pet, 1920. 318.   200000(2)
   (LocBDIC/GDS/HIS)

*BUDTE NA STRAZHE! M, 1920.   *200000(3)
   (CatKL)

CHEMU UCHAT SOTSIALISTYI-REVOLYUTSIONERY? Novy Mir: StP, 1905.   050000(2)
   (LocHIS)

*CHERZ POBEDY K MIRU. Prikaz. Pet, 1919.   *190000(29)
   (CatKL)

CHETVERTYI INTERNATSIONAL I VOINA. Geneva, 1934. 38.   340000(1)
   ⌊Printed in USA.⌋
   (LocIISG)

† CHTO I KAK PROIZOSHLO? Imp. Navarre: P, 1929. 84.   290000(1)
    (LocAAS/BDIC/BM/BN/IISG/LSE/NYPL/O)

CHTO NUZHNO SDELAT KREST´YANAM, CHTOBY VYVESTI KHOZYAISTVO IZ   200000(38)
    RAZORENIYA. Gosizdat: Gomol´skov Otdelenie, 1920. 15.
    (LocBDIC/BM/HIS)

*CHTO NUZHNO SDELAT KREST´YANAM, ... Gosizdat: Kubansko-Chernomorskii   *200000(39)
    Obl. Otdel: Ekatinograd, 1920. 15.
    (CatKL)

*CHTO NUZHNO SDELAT KREST´YANAM, ...   *200000(40)
    (CatKL)

*CHTO NUZHNO SDELAT KREST´YANAM, ... Gosizdat: M, 1920. 16.   *200000(41)
    ⌊Rabochie-krest´yanskie listok No. 44)
    (LocHIS/KBS)

i dr., *CHTO NUZHNO ZNAT O GERMANSKOI REVOLYUTSII. Chita, 1923.   *230000(22)
    (CatKL)

*CHTO OZNACHAET PEREKHOD MAKHNO NA STORONU SOVETSKOI VLASTI. M, 1920.   *200000(42)
    (CatPLVK)

*CHTO OZNACHAET PEREKHOD MAKHNO NA STORONU SOVETSKOI VLASTI.   *⌊200000(50)⌋
    (CatKL)

§ CHTO ZHE DAL´SHE? (ITOGI I PERSPEKTIVY.) Priboi: Pet, 1917. 30.   170000(5)
    (LocHIS/ULH)

*DAITE FRONTU KRASNYKH KOMANDIROV. Vyatka, 1920.   *200000(10)
    (CatKL)

*DAITE FRONTU KRASNYKH KOMANDIROV. M, 1920.   *200000(11)
    (CatKL)

*DAITE FRONTU KRASNYKH KOMANDIROV. Tula, 1920.   *200000(12)
    (CatKL)

† DELO BYLO V ISPANII. Artel Pisateli Krug: M, 1926. 131.   260000(5)
    (LocHIS)

§ DELO BYLO V ISPANII. Priboi: L, 1927. 136.   270000(5)
    (CatKL)

*DEZERTIRY -- POMOSHCHNIKI KOLCHAKA. Kargopol, 1919.   *190000(4)
    (CatKL)

*D.I.MENDELEEV I MARKSIZM. M-L, 1925.   *250000(2)

    (CatKL)

*DNEVNIK L´VA TROTSKOGO. Tetrad sedmaya.   Constantinople, 1922. 16.   *220000(4)

    (Poddelka soch. L.Trotskogo)

    (CatPostnikov)

*DOBROVOL´TSY NA POL´SKII FRONT! M, ⌊1920⌋.   *⌊200000(44)⌋

    (CatKL)

DO DEVYATAGO YANVARYA. Tip. Partii: Geneva, 1905. 64.   050000(1)

    (LocBDIC/BM/BN/HIS/LC/NYPL)

DOKLAD. See Secondary Sources: DEKRETY, POLOZHENIYA I PRIKAZY PO KRASNOI ARMII.

*DOKLAD O MEZHDUNARODNOM I VNUTRENNEM POLOZHENII. ⌊M⌋, 1926.   *260000(6)

    (CatKL)

*DOKLADY tt. LENINA, TROTSKOGO. Proletarii: ⌊Kharkov⌋, 1922. 204.   *220000(39)

    (CatKL)

*DOLGOVECHNYE I NEDOLGOVECHNYE PRAVITEL´STVA. M, 1920.   *200000(13)

    (CatPLVK)

*DOLGOVECHNYE I NEDOLGOVECHNYE PRAVITEL´STVA. Briansk, ⌊1920⌋.   *⌊200000(43)⌋

    (CatKL)

2 PIS´MA PETROGRADSKOI ORGANIZATSII RKP I OTVET t. TROTSKOGO.   210000(2)

    Gosizdat: Pet, 1921. 8.

    (LocHIS/NYPL)

† EVROPA I AMERIKA. Gosizdat: M-L, 1926. 112.   260000(7)

    (LocBM/HIS/NYPL/O(T))

† EVROPA V VOINE. Gosizdat: M-L, 1927. 420.   270000(1)

    ⌊Soch. IX⌋

    (LocBDIC/BN/HIS/KBS/NYPL/SEES)

*FRONTOV NET, — OPASNOST EST. Izd. Vys. Voen. Rev. Soveta: *220000(14)

    M, 1922. 32.

    (CatPLVK)

FRONTOV NET, — OPASNOST EST. Izd. Vys. Voen. Rev. Soveta: 220000(15)

    M, 1922. 47. 2 izd.

    (LocBDIC)

§*GODY VELIKAGO PERELOMA. Kommunist: M-Pet, N.Novgorod, 1919.   *190000(3)

    ⌊3 vols. in 1⌋

    (LocLC)

*GORE NE DOVODYASHCHIM DO KONTSA! M, 1920.   *200000(9)

    (CatKL)

GOSPODIN PETR STRUVE V POLITIKE. Novy Mir: StP, 1906. 72.   060000(1)

    ⌊N.Trotskii⌋

    (LocBDIC/BM/HIS/O/CatZ)

GOSPODIN PETR STRUVE V POLITIKE. Novy Mir: StP, 1906. 72. 2 izd.   060000(2)

    ⌊N.Trotskii⌋

    (LocBDIC/ULH)

*ISTORIYA NA RUSKATA REVOLYUTSIYA. Siuznata sots. knizharnisa   *190000(5)

    i pechatnitsa: Granite City, Ill., USA, 1919. 137.

    (LocNYPL)

*ISTORIYA NA RUSKATA REVOLYUTSIYA. Sofia, ⌊1931⌋.   *⌊31000C(2)⌋

    ⌊Advert.⌋

ISTORIYA OKTYABR´SKOI REVOLYUTSII. 1918.   180000(5)

    (LocBM/HIS/SEES)

ISTORIYA RUSSKOI REVOLYUTSII. Granit: B, 1931-3. 2 Vols.   310000(1)

    (LocBDIC/BM/BN/HIS/LC/NYPL/O/SEES/ULH)

ISTORIYA SOVETA RABOCHIKH DEPUTATOV G. S-PETERBURGA. Glagolev: 060000(3)

    StP, ⌊1906⌋. 323.

    (LocCU/HIS/SEES)

ITOGI I PERSPEKTIVY. Dvizhushchie sily revolyutsii. Sovetskii Mir: 190000(6)

    M, 1919. 86.

    (LocBM/HIS/KBS/NYPL)

ITOGI SUDA NAD SOVETOM RABOCHIKH DEPUTATOV. Tip. V.Ivanovna: 060000(4)

    Kazan, 1906. 8.

    (LocBDIC/HIS)

IZ ISTORIII ODNOGO GODA....II. INTELLIGENTSIYA. Novyi Mir: ⌊060000(8)⌋

    StP, ⌊1906⌋. 96.

    (LocHIS/IISG/CatZ)

Y.M.Steklov i T, IZ RABOCHAGO DVIZHENIYA V ODESSE I NIKOLAEVE.   000700

    R.S.D.R.P.: Geneva, 1900. 33.

    (LocBDIC/BM/NYPL)

*KACHESTVO PRODUKTSII I SOTSIALISTICHESKII KHOZYAISTVO.   *250000(4)

     Plannovoe Khozyaistvo: M-L, 1925. 13.

     (CatBibEzh/CatILO)

‡ KAK VOORUZHALAS REVOLYUTSIYA. Vysshi Voennyi Redaktsionnyi Soveta: 230000(7)

     M, 1923-5. 3 Vols. in 5.

     (LocBDIC/BM/BN/HIS/LC/LSE/NYPL/O/SEES/ULH)

*KAPITALISTICHESKII MIR I KOMMUNISTICHESKII INTERNATSIONAL. MANIFEST   *⌈210000(52)⌉

     II-go KONGRESSA KOMM. INTERN. Izd. Komm. Intern.:

     Pet, ⌊1921⌋. 56.

     (CatIK)

 Zinov´ev i T, KARL LIBKNEKHT I ROZA LYUKSEMBURG. Izd. Petr. Soveta: 190000(8)

     Pet, 1919. 32.

     (LocBDIC/BM/HIS/KBS)

Zinov´ev i T,*KARL LIBKNEKHT I ROZA LYUKSEMBURG. Soyuza Kommun   *190000(81)

     Severnoi Oblasti: Pet, 1919. 32.

     (CatPostnikov)

i dr., *KARL LIBKNEKHT, ROZA LYUKSEMBURG I LEO YUGIKHES.   *220000(37)

     (CatGB)

*KAVALERISTAM KORPUSA MAMONTOVA. M, 1919.   *190000(7)

     (CatPLVK)

*K DISKUSSII O PROFSOYUZAKH. Izd. Tsektran: Pet, 1921. 16.   *210000(53)

     (CatIK)

‡ KHOZYAISTVENNOE STROITEL´STVO SOVETSKOI RESPUBLIKI. Gosizdat: 270000(4)

     M-L, 1927. 600.

     ⌊Soch. XV⌋

     (LocBDIC/BN/HIS/KBS/NYPL/SEES)

K ISTORII OKTYABR´SKOI REVOLYUTSII. Russkaya Sotsialisticheskaya   ⌊310000(3)⌋

     Federatsiya: NY, ⌊1931⌋. 115.

     (LocHIS/NYPL)

*K MOLODEZHI. Zarnisk, ⌊1921⌋.   *⌊210000(21)⌋

     (CatKL)

KOGDA ZHE KONETS PROKLYATOI BOIN"E? Izd. Voennoi Organizatsii pri   ⌊170000(2)⌋

     Yur´evskom"e Komitet"e R.S.-D.R.P.: Yur´ev"e, ⌊1917⌋. 16.

     (LocIISG)

*KOGDA ZHE KONETS PROKLYATOI BOINI. Priboi: Pet, 1917.   170000(3)

    ⌊Advert.⌋

† KOMMUNISTICHESKOE DVIZHENIE VO FRANTSII. Moskovskii Rabochii: 230000(8)

    M, 1923. 456.

    (LocBN/LC/NYPL)

† KOMMUNISTICHESKII INTERNATSIONAL. Gosizdat: M-L, 1926. 247.   260000(10)

    ⌊Soch. XIII⌋

    (LocBDIC/BM/BN/HIS/KBS/NYPL/SEES)

*KOMMUNISTAM NA VOSTOCHNOM FRONTA. 1919.   *190000(9)

    (LocLC)

KONSTITUTSIYA "OSVOBOZHDENTSEV". Novyi Mir/Alekseev: StP, ⌊1906⌋. 19.   ⌊060000(9)⌋

    ⌊N.Trotskii⌋

    (LocBDIC/BN/HIS/ULH)

*K PERVOMU MAYA. ⌊1920⌋.   *⌊200000(45)⌋

    (CatZ)

KRASNAYA ARMIYA. Vserossiiskoi Tsentral´nyi Ispolitel´nyi Komitet   180000(6)

        Sovetov R., S., K., i K. Deputatov, Voennyi otdel: M, 1918. 32.

    (LocBDIC/HIS/LC/NYPL/O/ULH)

KRASNAYA ARMIYA. VTsIK: M, 1918. 30.   180000(7)

    (LocBDIC)

*KRASNAYA ARMIYA. Budapeshtskaya Gruppa Rossiiskoi Kommunisticheskoi   *190000(67)

    Partii: Budapest, 1919. 32.

    (LocHIS)

*KRASNAYA ARMIYA I POLITICH. PERSPEKTIVY. 1922.   *220000(41)

    (CatBibEzh)

*KRASNAYA PAMYATKA. Krasnaya Zvezda: M, 1924.   *240000(7)

    (CatKL)

*KRASNAYA PAMYATKA. Tula, 1924.   *240000(8)

    (CatKL)

*KRASNAYA PAMYATKA. Zlatoust, 1924.   *240000(9)

    (CatKL)

*KRASNAYA PAMYATKA. Tashkent, 1924.   *240000(10)

    (CatKL)

*KRASNAYA PAMYATKA. M, 1924.   *240000(11)

    ⌊Tatar⌋

    (CatKL)

*KRASNOMU VOINU POL´SKOGO FRONTA. M, 1920.   *200000(15)
    (CatKL)

*KRATKAYA PAMYATKA. M-L, 1924. 2oe dop. izd.   *240000(12)
    (CatKL)

K SOTSIALIZMU ILI K KAPITALIZMU? Plannovoe khozyaistvo Gosplan SSSR: 250000(3)
    M-L, 1925. 61.
    (LocBDIC/LC)

*K SOTSIALIZMU ILI K KAPITALIZMU? Plannovoe khozyaistvo Gosplan SSSR: *260000(9)
    M-L, 1926. 67
    (CatKL)

KUDA IDET ANGLIYA? Gosizdat: M-L, 1925. 171.   250000(5)
    (LocBDIC/BM/HIS/LnL/NYPL)

KUDA IDET ANGLIYA? 2 vypusk. Gosizdat: M-L, 1926. 96.   260000(11)
    (LocBDIC/HIS/LnL)

✝ KUL´TURA PEREKHODNOGO PERIODA. Gosizdat: M-L, 1927. 520.   270000(2)
    (Soch. XXI)
    (LocBDIC/HIS/KBS/NYPL/SEES)

✝ KUL´TURA STAROGO MIRA. Gosizdat: M-L, 1926. 579.   260000(12)
    (Soch. XX)
    (LocBDIC/HIS/KBS/NYPL/SEES)

*K VIII S"EZDU SOVETOV. See PUT K EDINOMU KHOZYAISTVENNOMU PLANU.

*LENINIZM I BIBLIOTECHNAYA RABOTA. Krasnaya Nov: M, 1924. 72.   *240000(16)
    (CatBibEzh/CatKL)

*LENINIZM I RABOCHIE KLUBY. M, 1924.   *240000(17)
    (CatKL)

LENIN I STARAYA ISKRA. Gosizdat: M, 1924. 48.   240000(13)
    (LocHIS/CatZ)

*LENIN I STARAYA ISKRA. Istpart: M, 1924.   *240000(59)
    [Advert.]

LENIN KAK NATSIONAL´NYI TIP. Gosizdat: Pet, 1924. 8.   240000(14)
    (LocBM)

LENIN KAK NATSIONAL´NYI TIP. Gosizdat: L, 1924. 8. 2 izd.   240000(15)
    (LocBM)

✝ LITERATURA I REVOLYUTSIYA. Krasnaya Nov: M, 1923. 394.   230000(9)
    (LocBDIC/BM/CU/LnL/LSE/ULO)

§ LITERATURA I REVOLYUTSIYA. Gosizdat: M, 1924. 422. 2oe dop. izd.　240000(18)
　　(LocHIS/IISG/LC/NYPL/SEES)

† LYUDI STAROI I NOVOI EPOKH. Kommunist: M, 1919. 151.　　190000(10)
　　(LocBM/HIS/LC/NYPL)

*MANIFEST KOMMUNISTICHESKOGO INTERNATSIONALA K PROLETARIAM　　*190000(71)
　　VSEGO MIRA. Izd. Komm. Inter.: M, 1919. 14.
　　(CatIK)

*MANIFEST KOMMUNISTICHESKOGO INTERNATSIONALA K PROLETARIAM　　*⌊200000(100)⌋
　　VSEGO MIRA.
　　⌊Advert.⌋

*MANIFEST KOMMUNISTICHESKOGO INTERNATSIONALA K PROLETARIAM VSEGO MIRA.　　*⌊200000(101)⌋
　　Izd. Otdela Pechati: Kazan, ⌊1920⌋. 2 izd.
　　Advert.⌋

MEZHDU IMPERIALIZMOM I REVOLYUTSIEI. Gosizdat: M, 1922. 131.　　220000(5)
　　(LocBDIC/HIS/LC/NYPL)

MEZHDU IMPERIALIZMOM I REVOLYUTSIEI. Novyi Mir: B, 1922. 144.　　220000(6)
　　(LocBDIC/BM/HIS/IISG/LSE/NYPL/ULH)

MEZHDUNARODNOE POLOZHENIE I KRASNAYA ARMIYA. Vserossiiskoi Tsentral′nyi　180000(9)
　　Ispolitel′nyi Komitet Sovetov R., S., K. i K. deputatov:
　　M, 1918. 24.
　　(LocAAS/BDIC/HIS)

MEZHDUNARODNOE POLOZHENIE I KRASNAYA ARMIYA. VTsIK: M, 1918. 16.　　180000(8)
　　(LocBDIC/BM/HIS/LnL/NYPL/0)

MEZHDUNARODNOE POLOZHENIE I KRASNAYA ARMIYA. Ispol. Kom. Khark. Sov.　190000(11)
　　Rab. Dep. Tsentrpechat: Kharkov, 1919. 24.

MEZHDUNARODNOE POLOZHENIE I KRASNAYA ARMIYA. Byuro Kommunistov　　180000(10)
　　musul′man Sev. oblasti: Pet, 1918. 48.
　　(LocBDIC)

*MIROVAYA REVOLYUTSIYA I IV KONGRESS KOMINTERNA. Izd. VTsIk:　　*220000(16)
　　M, 1922. 20.
　　(CatBibEzh/CatKL)

MIROVOE EKONOMICHESKOE POLOZHENIE I NASHI ZADACHI. Gosizdat:　　210000(3)
　　M, 1921. 30.
　　(LocBM/HIS)

i Varga, MIROVOE POLOZHENIE I NASHI ZADACHI. Otdel Pechati Kominterna: 210000(4)
    M, 1921. 11.
    (LocBM/HIS)

*MIROVOE POLOZHENIE I TRETYI KONGRESS KOMMUNISTICHESKOGO INTERNATSIONALA. *210000(5)
    Tul´skoe Gubernskoe Upravlenie izdatel´skim delam: Tula, 1921. 94.
    (LocHIS)

MIR S POL´SHEI DOSTIGNUT. M, 1920.   200000(16)
    (LocBDIC)

MOBILIZATSIYA TRUDA. Gosizdat: M, 1920. 48.   200000(17)
    (LocBDIC/HIS/KBS)

§ MOI POBEG IZ SIBIRI. Molodaya Gvardiya: M-L, 1926. 80.   260000(13)
    (LocBM/HIS)

*MOLODEZH, UCHIS POLITIKE. Izd. Moskprofobra: M, 1924. 8.   *240000(19)
    (CatBibEzh/CatKL)

*MOYA ZHIVOT.   *⌊310000(4)⌋
    ⌊Advert.⌋

MOYA ZHIZN. Granit: B, 1930. 2 Vols.   300000(1)
    (LocBDIC/BM/BN/HIS/IISG/KBC/LC/LnL/LSE/NYPL/SEES/ULH)

*MOYA ZHIZN. Berey: Riga, 1930.   *300000(2)
    (LocNYPL)

NA BOR´BU S GOLODOM! Kommunist: M-Pet, 1918. 63.   180000(12)
    (LocHIS/LC/LnL/O/SEES/ULH)

NA BOR´BU S GOLODOM! Khark. Gub. prod. Komiteta: ⌊Kharkov⌋, 1919. 63.   190000(12)
    (LocBDIC)

NA FRONTAKH. Sovetskii Mir: M, 1919. 31.   190000(16)
    (LocHIS/KBS/LC/NYPL)

*NA OBLAVU! Penza, 1919.   *190000(13)
    (CatKL)

*NA POSTU. Kharkov, 1923.   *230000(10)
    (CatKL)

NA PROIZVODSTVENNYI PUT! Gosizdat: M, 1921. 22.   210000(6)
    (LocBDIC/BM/HIS/KBS/LC)

*NA PROIZVODSTVENNYI PUT! Tsektran: M, 1921. 20.   *210000(58)
    (CatPostnikov)

*NA PUTYAKH K EVROPEISKOI REVOLYUTSII. Tiflis, 1924.   *240000(21)
    (CatKL)

NA PUTYAKH K EVROPEISKOI REVOLYUTSII. Krasnaya Nov: M, 1924. 26.   240000(20)
    (LocHIS/ULH)

† NASHA PERVAYA REVOLYUTSIYA. Gosizdat: M-L, 1925-6. 2 Vols.   250000(6)
    ⌊Soch. II⌋
    (LocBDIC/HIS/NYPL/SEES)

*NASHA POLITIKA V DELE SOZDANIYA ARMII. TEZISY. ⌊Pubd. from train⌋   *180000(13)
    1918. 14.
    (LocNYPL)

† NASHA REVOLYUTSIYA. Glagolev: StP, 1906. 286.   060000(6)
    (LocBDIC/BM/HIS/IISG/KBC/LSE/O)

NASHA TAKTIKA V BOR´BE ZA UCHREDITEL´NOE SOBRANIE. + REVOLYUTSIYA   060000(5)
    I EE SILY. Novaya Volna: M, 1906. 32.
    ⌊L.T—tii⌋
    (LocLnL)

NASHE VOENNOE STROITEL´STVO I NASHI FRONTY. Liter.-izdat. otdel.   190000(17)
    upravl. Revol. voen. sov. respubliki: M, 1919. 32.
    (LocBDIC)

*NASHI POLITICHESKIE ZADACHI. M, 1928.   *280000(1)
    (LocLC)

† NASHI POLITICHESKIYA ZADACHI. (Unsere politische Aufgabe.)   040000
    Tip.-partii: Geneva, 1904. 107.
    (LocBDIC/BM/BN/HIS/IISG/LC/ULH)

NA STRAZHE MIROVOI REVOLYUTSII. Sovetskii Mir: M, 1919. 31.   190000(14)
    (LocBDIC)

*NA URAL! Samara, 1919.   *190000(15)
    (CatKL)

NEMETSKAYA REVOLYUTSIYA I STALINSKAYA BYUROKRATIYA. Grylewicz: 320000(1)
    B, 1932. 160.
    (LocBDIC/BM/CU/HIS/IISG/NYPL/O/ULH)

NOVAYA EKONOMICHESKAYA POLITIKA SOVETSKOI ROSSII I PERSPEKTIVY   230000(11)
    MIROVOI REVOLYUTSII. Moskovskii Rabochii: M, 1923. 70.
    (LocBDIC/HIS/NYPL/ULH)

† NOVYI ETAP. MIROVOE POLOZHENIE I NASHI ZADACHI.   210000(7)
     Gosizdat: M, 1921. 160.
     (LocBDIC/BM/BN/HIS/IISG/KBS/LnL/LSE/NYPL/SEES/ULH)

† NOVYI KURS. Krasnaya Nov: M, 1924. 104.   240000(22)
     (LocBDIC/BM/CU/HIS/IISG/LSE/NUC/NYPL/SEES)

OB ORGANIZATSII TRUDA. 1920.   200000(19)
     (LocHIS)

*OBRASHCHENIE K KAVALERISTAM KORPUSA MAMONTOVA.   *190000(18)
     (CatKL)

*OCHEREDNYE ZADACHI KHOZYAISTVENNOGO STROITEL´STVA. Rostov, 1920.   *200000(22)
     (CatKL)

i Kabakchiev, † OCHERKI POLITICHESKOI BOLGARII. Gosizdat: 230000(19)
     M-Pet, 1923. 204.
     (LocBDIC/BM/HIS/NYPL)

i Rakovskii, § OCHERKI POLITICHESKOI RUMYNII. Gosizdat; M, 1922. 151. 220000(8)
     (LocBM/BN/HIS/NYPL)

i Rakovskii, † OCHERKI POLITICHESKOI RUMYNII. Gosizdat: 230000(20)
     M-Pet, 1923. 169. 2 izd.
     (LocBM)

‡ O DEVYATOM YANVARYA. Gosizdat: M-L, 1925. 141.   250000(7)
     (LocHIS/LC)

ODNA ILI DVE PALATY? Novyi Mir: StP, 1906. 32.   060216
     ⌊L.Takhotskii⌋
     (LocO/ULH)

*O GERMANSKOI SOTSIALDEMOKRATII. M, 1908. 60.   *080000(1)
     (CatPostnikov)

*OKHRANA MATERINSTVA I BOR´BA ZA KUL´TURU. N.Z.K.: M, 1926. 32. *260000(15)
     (LocLC)

OKTYABR´SKAYA REVOLYUTSIYA. Kommunist: M-Pet, 1918. 126.   180000(15)
     (LocBDIC/HIS/LC/LSE/SEES/ULH)

† O LENINE. Gosizdat: M, 1924. 168.   240000(24)
     (LocBM/LC/LSE/NYPL/SEES/CatZ)

§ O LENINE. Gosizdat: M, 1924. 168. 2 izd.   240000(25)
     (LocBDIC/BM/BN/HIS/KBS/LOV/O/SEES/ULH)

Zinov'ev i T, O MYATEZH"E LEVYKH S.-R. Petrogradskii Sovet: 180000(14)
     Pet, 1918. 47.
     (LocBDIC/BM/GDS/HIS/KBS/LnL/NUC/NYPL/O)

*O NASHIKH NOVYKH ZADACHAKH. Gosizdat: M-L, 1926. 19.   *260000(14)
     (CatPostnikov)

*O PROEKTE DESYATI. M, ⌊1921⌋.   *⌊210000(22)⌋
     (CatKL)

ORGANIZATSIYA KRASNOI ARMII. Vserossiiskii Tsentral'nii Ispolitel'nyi   180000(16)
     Komitet Sovetov R., S., K. i K. deputatov: Voennyi otdel:
     M, 1918. 24.
     (LocBDIC/BM/BN/HIS/LC/ULH)

ORGANIZATSIYA TRUDA. Izd. PUR'a: M, 1920.   200000(20)
     (LocBM)

O ROLI PROFESSIONAL'NYKH SOYUZOV. 1-ya Obraztsovaya tip. M.S.N.Kh.:   210000(10)
     M, 1921. 78.
     (LocBM/HIS)

*O ROLI PROFESSIONAL'NYKH SOYUZOV. 2 izd.   *210000(54)
     ⌊Not loc.⌋

O ROLI PROFESSIONAL'NYKH SOYUZOV. Gosizdat: Pet, 1921. 71. 3 izd.   210000(11)
     (LocBDIC)

O SIBIRI. Mospoligraf: M, 1927. 15.   270000(3)
     (LocNYPL)

*OSNOVNAYA VOENNAYA ZADACHA MOMENTA. Vysshii voennyi redaktsionnyi   *220000(7)
     sovet R.S.F.S.R.: M, 1922. 128.
     (LocBDIC)

*OSNOVNYE VOPROSY PRODOVOL'STVENNOI I ZEMEL'NOI POLITIKI. 1921.   *210000(12)
     (LocBM)

† OSNOVNYE VOPROSY PROLETARSKOI REVOLYUTSII. Gosizdat: M-L, 1925. 475.   250000(8)
     ⌊Soch. XII⌋
     (LocBDIC/BM/HIS/LC/NYPL/SEES/ULH)

*OSNOVNYE VOPROSY PROMYSHLENNOSTI. Krasnaya Nov: M, 1923. 114.   *230000(13)
     (CatKL)

OSNOVNYE VOPROSY PROMYSHLENNOSTI. M, 1923. 67. 2 izd.   230000(12)
     (LocHIS/LC/NYPL)

*OSNOVNYE VOPROSY PROMYSHLENNOSTI. Nov. Derevnya: M, 1923. 87.   *230000(14)
    3 izd.
    (CatKL)

*OSNOVNYE VOPROSY PROMYSHLENNOSTI. M, 1923. 87. 4 izd.   *230000(15)
    (CatKL)

*OSNOVNYE VOPROSY PROMYSHLENNOSTI. Devyatoe Yanvarya: M, 1923. 64.   *230000(16)
    (CatKL)

*OSNOVNYE VOPROSY PROMYSHLENNOSTI. Pechati Gubkoma RKP: Saratov,   *230000(17)
    1923. 77.
    (CatKL)

† OSNOVNYE VOPROSY REVOLYUTSII. Gosizdat: M-Pet, 1923. 429.   230000(18)
    (LocHIS/LC/NYPL/SEES)

*OTKRYTOE PIS´MO. Irkutsk, 1920.   *200000(21)
    (CatKL)

*OT OKTYABR´SKOI REVOLYUTSII DO BRESTSKOGO MIRA. Proletarii: *⌊190000(31)⌋
    Kremenchug, ⌊1919⌋.
    (CatZ)

*OT OKTYABR´SKOI REVOLYUTSII DO BRESTSKOGO MIRA. Proletarii: *230000(42)
    Kharkov, 1923.
    ⌊Advert.⌋

*OT OKTYABR´SKOI REVOLYUTSII DO BRESTSKOGO MIRA. Proletarii: *240000(26)
    Kharkov, 158. 2 izd.
    ⌊Advert.⌋

*OT OKTYABR´SKOI REVOLYUTSII DO BRESTSKOGO MIRA. Proletarii: *250000(34)
    Kharkov, 1925. 158.
    (LocLC)

O ZADACHAKH DEREVENSKOI MOLODEZHI. Novaya Moskva: M, 1924. 23.   240000(23)
    (LocHIS)

O ZADACHAKH PROFSOYUZOV. Gosizdat: M, 1921. 22.   210000(9)
    (LocBDIC/BM/HIS/KBS/LC/NYPL)

*O ZADACHAKH PROIZVODSTVENNYKH SOYUZOV. M, 1920. 51.   *200000(18)
    (CatPostnikov)

*O ZADACHAKH PROIZVODSTVENNYKH SOYUZOV. Krasnoadar, 1921.   *210000(8)
    (CatKL)

*PAMYATI IL"ICHA. Orel, 1924. *240000(27)
    (CatKL)

PAMYATKA KRASNOARMEITSA YUZHNOGO FRONT. Liter.-izdat. otdel 200000(23)
    polit. upravl. Revvoensoveta respubliki: M, 1920. 8.
    (LocBDIC)

*PAMYATKA KRASNOARMEITSA YUZHNOGO FRONT. Archangel, 1920. *200000(24)
    (CatKL)

*PAMYATKA KRASNOARMEITSA YUZHNOGO FRONT. Vyatka, 1920. *200000(25)
    (CatKL)

*PAMYATKA KRASNOARMEITSA YUZHNOGO FRONT. Samara, 1920. *200000(26)
    (CatKL)

*PAMYATKA KRASNOARMEITSA YUZHNOGO FRONT. Tula, 1920. *200000(46)
    (CatKL)

*PARIZHSKAYA KOMMUNA I SOVETSKAYA ROSSIYA. Kharkov, 1920. *200000(27)
    (CatKL)

PERMANENTNAYA REVOLYUTSIYA. Granit: B, 1930. 169. 300000(3)
    (LocBDIC/BM/CU/HIS/IISG/LC/LSE/NYPL/ULH)

i Rakovskii, *PERSPEKTIVI I ZAVDANNYA NOVOGO ETAPU. *230000(24)
    (CatKL)

*PERSPEKTIVYI I ZADACHI VOENNOGO STROITEL'STVA. Izd. VVRS: *230000(21)
    M, 1923. 31.
    (CatBibEzh/CatPLVK)

PERSPEKTIVYI RUSSKOI REVOLYUTSII. Ladyschnikow: B, 1917. 84. 171200(3)
    (LocBM/HIS/KBC/LC/NYPL/ULH/ULO/CatZ)

Zinov'ev i T, PETROGRAD (Oktyabr 1917-1919 g.g.) Pet, ⌊1920⌋. ⌊200000(47)⌋
    (LocBM/HIS/IISG)

i Lenin, *PIS'MO K KREST'YANAM-SEREDNYAKAM. Kharkov, 1919. 15. *190000(19)
    (CatPostnikov)

i Lenin, PIS'MO K KREST'YANAM-SEREDNYAKAM. Tver, ⌊1919⌋. *⌊190000(32)⌋
    (CatKL)

i Lenin, PIS'MO K KREST'YANAM-SEREDNYAKAM. Zadonsk, ⌊1919⌋. *⌊190000(33)⌋
    (CatKL)

*PIS'MO KREST'YANAM-SEREDNYAKAM OT NARODNOGO KOMISSARA PO VOENNYM *190000(79)
    I MORSKIM DELAM. M, 1919.
    ⌊Advert.⌋

*PIS´MO K REVOLYUTSIONNYM VOENNYM SOVETAM, SOVETAM FRONTOV, ARMII   *200000(28)
     I KO VSEM OTVETSTVENNYM RABOTNIKAM KRASNOI ARMII I KRASNOGO FLOTA.
     Pet, 1920.
     (CatKL)

*POCHEMU NAM NUZHNA SIL´NAYA ARMIYA?   Pet, ⌊1922⌋.   *⌊220000(17)⌋
     (CatKL)

† POKOLENIE OKTYABRYA.   Molodaya Gvardiya: Pet i M, 1924.   260.   240000(28)
     ⌊Fakt. 1923 g. -- BibEzh.⌋
     (LocLSE/SEES)

† POLITICHESKAYA KHRONIKA.   Gosizdat: M-L, 1926.   647.   260000(16)
     ⌊Soch. IV⌋
     (LocBDIC/BM/HIS/KBS/NYPL/SEES)

† POLITICHESKIE SILUETY.   Gosizdat: M-L, 1926.   373.   260000(12)
     ⌊Soch. VIII⌋
     (LocBDIC/BM/HIS/NYPL/SEES⌋

POLOZHENIE PARTII I ZADACHI LEVOI OPPOZITSII.   Byulleten Oppozitsii: 300000(4)
     P, 1930.   4.
     (LocPer)

PORYADOK IZ KHAOSA.   Izdanie Dal´nevostochnogo Krasvogo Komiteta   190000(20)
     Rossiiskoi Kommunisticheskoi partii (bol´shevikov)
     Vladivostok, 1919.   16.
     (LocHIS)

*PORAYDOK IZ KHAOSA.   VTsIK: M, 1919.   *190000(49)
     ⌊Advert.⌋

*POUKITIE OT OKTOMBRI 1917.   Granite City, Ill., USA, ⌊1924⌋.   72.   *⌊240000(38)⌋
     (LocNYPL)

i dr., PROEKT PLATFORMY BOL´SHEVIKOV-LENINTSEV (OPPOZITSII)   ⌊270000(16)⌋
     K XV S"EZDU VKP(b). ⌊1927⌋. 140.   ⌊Processed⌋
     (LocBDIC/IISG)

i dr., PROEKT PLATFORMY BOL´SHEVIKOV-LENINTSEV (OPPOZITSII)   ⌊270000(17)⌋
     K XV S"EZDU VKP(b). ⌊1927⌋. 80.
     ⌊Some surviving pages checked.⌋

PROGRAMMA MIRA.   Kniga: Pet, 1917.   30.   170000(4)
     (LocBDIC/BM)

*PROLETARIAT I LITERATURA.   *260000(20)
     ⌊Advert.⌋

PUT K EDINOMU KHOZYAISTVENNOMU PLANU. Izd. Politodela 7-e armii: 200000(29)
    Pet, 1920. 23.
    (LocHIS)

† PYAT LET KOMINTERNA. Gosizdat: M, 1924. 612.   240000(29)
    (LocBDIC/HIS/LC/NYPL)

§ PYAT LET KOMINTERNA. Gosizdat: M, 1925. 660. 2 izd.   250000(9)
    (LocBM/LC/SEES)

*V GODOVSHCHINA OKTYABR'SKOI REVOLYUTSII I IV KONGRESS KOMINTERNA.   *220000(9)
    MKRKP: M, 1922. 32.
    (CatBibEzh/CatKL)

*RECH. M, 1919.   *190000(21)
    (CatPLVK)

*RECHI, PROIZNESENNYE NA TEREZHE V 1924 g. Pyatigorsk, 1924.   *240000(30)
    (CatKL)

*RECH K TEKUSHCHEMU MOMENTU V PERIOD NASTUPLENIYA KRASNYKH VOISK   *⌊200000(48)⌋
    NA DENIKINA. Smolensk, ⌊1920⌋.
    (CatKL)

RECH NA MITINGE V GOMELE. 1920. 16.   200000(30)
    ⌊Published from train⌋
    (LocPer)

*RECH NA SOEDINENNOM ZASEDANII SAMARSKOGO SOVETA RABOCHIKH I   *190000(24)
    KRASNOARMEISKIKH DEPUTATOV. Samara, 1919.
    (CatKL)

RECH NA III VSEROSSIISKOM S"EZDU SOVETOV NARODNOGO KHOZYAISTVA.   200000(31)
    Vysshi sovet narodnogo khozyaistvo. Otdel redaktsionno-
    izdatel'skii: M, 1920. 14.
    (LocHIS/LnL/LSE/NYPL/SEES)

RECH NA ZASEDANII VSEUKRAINSKOGO TsIK. 1919.   190000(23)
    (LocHIS)

*RECH, PROIZNESSENAYA NA GORODSKIM MITINGE. 1919.   *190000(25)
    (CatKL)

*RECH PROIZNESENNAYA NA MITINGE V G. VYATKE. Vyatka, ⌊1919⌋.   *⌊ 0000(36)⌋
    (CatKL)

*RECH, PROIZNESENNAYA V MOSKOVSKOGO SOVETA. Vladimir, ⌊1919⌋.   *⌊190000(35)⌋
    (CatKL)

*RECH T. TROTSKOGO NA MASSOVOM MITINGE V GOR. GOMELE. Homel, 1920.   *200000(32)
    (CatKL)

*RECH V ZASEDANII MOSKOVSKOGO SOVETA. ⌊M⌋, ⌊1919⌋.   *⌊190000(34)⌋
    (CatKL)

*RECH V ZASEDANII MOSKOVSKOGO SOVETA. Samara, 1919.   *190000(22)
    (CatKL)

*RED"ET E NA AVSTRIYA. ⌊Sofia⌋,⌊1933⌋.   *⌊330000(3)⌋
    ⌊Advert.⌋

REVOLYUTSIONNAYA STRATEGIYA. Osvobozhdenie: Sofia, 1922. 66.   220000(10)
    (LocIISG)

*REVOLYUTSIONNAYA STRATEGIYA. Sofia, 1922.   *220000(11)
    (CatBNS)

REVOLYUTSIYA I EE SILY. See NASHA TAKTIKA V BOR´BE ZA UCHREDITEL´NOE
    SOBRANIE, 060000(5).

ROBITNICHA DERZHAVA, TERMIDOR I BONAPARTIZM. Nakladom "Robitnichikh   350000(25)
    Vistei": Toronto, 1935. 28.
    (LocPer)

ROL I ZADACHI PROFESSIONAL´NYKH SOYUZOV. Gosizdat: M, 1921. 32.   210000(13)
    (LocBDIC/BM/HIS)

*ROL I ZADACHI PROFESSIONAL´NYKH SOYUZOV. M, 1921. 24.   *210000(59)
    (CatPostnikov)

*ROL I ZADACHI PROFESSIONAL´NYKH SOYUZOV. Pet, 1921.   *210000(14)
    (CatKL)

ROL I ZADACHI PROFESSIONAL´NYKH SOYUZOV. Gosizdat Ural´skoe Oblastnoe   210000(15)
    Otdelenie: Ekaterinburg, 1921. 12.
    (LocKBS)

*ROL I ZADACHI PROFESSIONAL´NYKH SOYUZOV. Pereizd. Polit. Upr. Balt.   *220000(40)
    Flota v Petr., 1922.
    (CatBibEzh)

*ROL I ZADACHI PROFESSIONAL´NYKH SOYUZOV. Pereizd.... v Minske, 1922.   *220000(42)
    (CatBibEzh)

*ROL PROFSOYUZOV V PROIZVODSTVE. 1921.   *210000(16)
    (LocBM)

RUSKATA REVOLYUTSIYA. Part. Sots. kn--a i pechat: Sofia, 1910. 32.   100000(1)
    (LocIISG)

*SHCHO E OKTOMBRIISKATA REVOLYUTSIYA. ⌊Sofia⌋, ⌊1933⌋.   *⌊330000(6)⌋
  ⌊Advert.⌋

i dr., SHIROKAYA KONFERENTSIYA FABRICHNO-ZAVODSKIKH KOMITETOV. 210000(23)
  Gosizdat: M, 1921. 91 + 2.
  (LocBM)

SIGNAL TREVOGI. Byulleten Oppozitsii: P, 1933.   330000(2)
  (LocIISG)

*SLOVO K RABOCHIM I KRASNOARMEITSAM. Petr. Soveta: Pet, 1918. 35. *180000(11)
  (CatIK)

SLOVO RUSSKIM RABOCHIM I KREST´YANAM O NASHAKH DRUZ´YAKH I VRAGAKH 180000(17)
  I O TOM, KAK UBERECH I UPROCHIT SOVETSKUYU RESPUBLIKU.
  Zhizn i Znanie: M, 1918. 64.
  (LocBDIC/BM/HIS/IISG/LC/NYPL)

*SLOVO RUSSKIM RABOCHIM I KREST´YANAM.... Kommunist: M, 1918. 64. *180000(18)
  (LocULO)

SLOVO RUSSKIM RABOCHIM I KREST´YANAM.... Pet. Sov. Dep.: 180000(23)
  Pet, 1918. 39. 2 izd.
  (LocKBS)

*SLOVO RUSSKIM RABOCHIM I KREST´YANAM.... Pet. Sov. Dep.: *180000(19)
  Pet, 1918. 31. 5 izd.
  (LocHIS/NYPL)

*SLOVO ZHELEZNODOROZHNIKAM PO POVODU POL´SKOGO NASTUPLENIYA. *200000(33)
  Pet, 1920.
  (CatKL)

*SMERT POL´SKOI BURZHUAZII! M, 1920.   *200000(34)
  (CatKL)

*SMERT POL´SKOI BURZHUAZII! Kazan, ⌊1920⌋.   *⌊200000(49)⌋
  (CatKL)

SOCHINENIYA:

II	NASHA PERVAYA REVOLYUTSIYA.	250000(6)
III	1917.	240000(32)
IV	POLITICHESKAYA KHRONIKA.	260000(16)
VI	BALKANY I BALKANSKAYA VOINA.	260000(1)
VIII	POLITICHESKIE SILUETY.	260000(12)
IX	EVROPA V VOINE.	270000(1)
XII	OSNOVNYE VOPROSY PROLETARSKOI REVOLYUTSII.	250000(8)
XIII	KOMMUNISTICHESKII INTERNATSIONAL.	260000(10)
XV	KHOZYAISTVENNOE STROITEL´STVO SOVETSKOI RESPUBLIKI.	270000(4)
XVII	SOVETSKAYA RESPUBLIKA I KAPITALISTICHESKII MIR.	260000(18)
XX	KUL´TURA STAROGO MIRA.	260000(12)
XXI	KUL´TURA PEREKHODNOGO PERIODA.	270000(2)

SOTSIALIZM V OTD"ELNA STRANA. Nachalo: Sofia, 1933. 64.   330000(1)
    (LocIISG)

† SOVETSKAYA RESPUBLIKA I KAPITALISTICHESKII MIR.   260000(18)
    Gosizdat: M-L, 1926. 2 vols.
    ⌊Soch. XVII⌋
    (LocAAS/BDIC/HIS/KBS/NYPL)

SOVETSKAYA ROSSIYA I BURZHUAZNAYA POL´SHA. Literaturno-izdatel´skii   200000(35)
    otdel Politicheskogo upravleniya Revvoensoveta respubliki:
    M, 1920. 15.
    (LocBDIC/KBS/LC/ULH)

*SOVETSKAYA ROSSIYA I BURZHUAZNAYA POL´SHA. Pravda: Prague, 1920. 16.   *200000(36)
    (LocHIS)

SOVETSKAYA VLAST I MEZHDUNARODNYI IMPERIALIZM. VTsIK: M, 1918. 24.   180000(20)
    (LocBDIC/BM/HIS/LnL/O)

SOVETSKAYA VLAST I MEZHDUNARODNYI IMPERIALIZM. Priboi: M, 1918. 24.   180000(21)
    (LocBM)

SOVETSKAYA VLAST I MEZHDUNARODNYI IMPERIALIZM. PGR: Pet, 1918. 20.   180000(22)
    (LocBDIC/HIS/KBS/NYPL)

SOVREMENNOE POLOZHENIE I ZADACHI VOENNOGO STROITEL´STVA.　　　240000(31)

　　　Izd. VVRS: M, 1924. 35.

　　　(LocNYPL)

SOZDANIE RABOCHIE I KREST´YANSKOI KRASNOI ARMII. [M], [1918].　　　[180000(27)]

　　　(LocBM/HIS)

SSSR I IV INTERNATSIONAL. Nakladam "Robitnichikh Vistei": Toronto,　　　340000(24)

　　　1934. 40.

　　　(LocPer)

STALINS´KA BYUROKRATIYA I UBIISTVO KIROVA. Nakladam "Robitnichikh　　　350000(24)

　　　Vistei": Toronto, 1935. 51.

　　　(LocPer)

† STALINSKAYA SHKOLA FAL´SIFIKATSII. Granit: B, 1932. 290.　　　320000(2)

　　　(LocBDIC/BM/BN/CU/HIS/IISG/LC/NYPL/O/ULH)

*STROIT SOTSIALIZM -- ZNACHIT OSVOBOZHDAT ZHENSHCHINU I OKHRANYAT MAT.

　　　See *OKHRANA MATERINSTVA, *260000(15).

*SVETOVNATA STOPANSKA KRIZA I REVOLYUTSIATA. Sofia, 1921.　　　*210000(17)

　　　(CatBNS)

*SVETOVNATA STOPANSKA KRIZA I REVOLYUTSIATA. Sofia, 1921.　　　*210000(18)

　　　(CatBNS)

*SVETSKOTO STOPANSTVO V OPASNOSTA. [Sofia], [1933].　　　*[330000(4)]

　　　[Advert.]

*TERORIZM I KOMUNIZM. Sofia, 1921.　　　*210000(19)

　　　(CatBNS)

TERRORIZM I KOMMUNIZM. Gosizdat: Pet, 1920. 178.　　　200000(37)

　　　(LocBDIC/HIS/IISG/KBS/LC/LSE/NYPL/ULH)

*TERRORIZM I KOMMUNIZM. Gosizdat: M-L, 1925. 2 izd.　　　*250000(10)

　　　(CatKL)

*TRAGEDIYATA NA GERMANSKAYA PROLETARIAT. [Sofia], [1933].　　　*[330000(5)]

　　　[Advert.]

TRUD, DISTSIPLINA, PORYADOK SPASUT SOTSIALISTICHESKUYU SOVETSKUYU　　　180000(24)

　　　RESPUBLIKU. Vserossiiskii Tsentral´nyi Ispolitel´nyi Komitet

　　　sovetov R., S., K. i K. deputatov: M, 1918. 32.

　　　(LocBDIC/BM/HIS/NYPL/O/ULH/ULO)

TRUD, DISTSIPLINA, PORYADOK... Petr. sov.: Pet, 1918. 32.   180000(25)
    (LocBDIC/BM/KBS/LC/NYPL)

TRUD, DISTSIPLINA, PORYADOK... Kommunist: M, 1918. 32.   180000(59)
    (LocBDIC)

*TRUD, DISTSIPLINA, PORYADOK... Zhizn i Znanie: M, 1918.   *180000(62)
    ⌊Advert.⌋

TRUD, DISTSIPLINA, PORYADOK... Kommunisticheskaya partiya bol´shevikov 190000(26)
    Ukrainy: Ekaterinoslav, 1919. 20.
    (LocBDIC)

*TRUD, DISTSIPLINA, PORYADOK... Ukr. Tsentr. agenstva po snabzheniyu *190000(27)
    i rasprostraneniyu proiznedenii pechati: Kharkov, 1919. 31.
    (LocNUC)

*TRUD, DISTSIPLINA, PORYADOK... Tashkent, 1920.   *200000(92)
    (CatKL)

§ TUDA I OBRATNO. Shipovnik: StP, 1907. 123.   070000(3)
    (LocIISG/LC/NYPL/ULH)

§ TUDA I OBRATNO. Petrogr. sov.: Pet, 1919. 63.   190000(28)
    (LocBM/HIS/KBS/LC/NYPL/SEES)

1905. Gosizdat: M, 1922. 417.   220000(12)
    (LocBDIC/HIS/LC/LSE/ULH)

1905. Gosizdat: M, 1922. 417. 2 izd.   220000(13)
    (LocAAS/BDIC/BM/GDS/SEES)

1905. Gosizdat: M-L, 1924. 427. 3 izd.   240000(34)
    (LocBM)

1905. Gosizdat: M-L, 1925. 427. 4 izd.   ⌊250000(11)⌋
    (LocHIS/NYPL/0)

*1905. CHEREZ DVADTSAT LET. M-L, 1926.   *260000(19)
    (CatKAB)

1905 RIK. Derzh. vid. Ukraini: Kharkov, 1925. 275.   250000(36)
    (LocLOV)

1917. Gosizdat: M, 1924-5. 2 Vols.   240000(32)
    ⌊Soch. III⌋
    (LocBDIC/HIS/IISG/KBS/LSE/NYPL/0/SEES/ULH)

1917. UROKI OKTYABRYA. Berlinskoe Knigoizdatel´stvo: B, 1924. 59. 240000(33)
    (LocBDIC/BM/BN/CU/HIS/LnL/NUC/NYPL/SEES/ULH)

UROKI OKTYABRYA. L, 1924. 240000(35)
    (LocO/CatZ)

UROKI OKTYABRYA. B, 1925. 59. 250000(12)
    (LocBDIC/BM)

*VESENNIE PROISKY VRAGOV. Vys. Voen. Redakts. Soveta: M, 1922. 31. *220000(1)
    (CatPLVK)

*VESNA KOTORAYA RESHAET. Samara, ⌊1919⌋. *⌊190000(30)⌋
    (CatKL)

*VNIMANIE K MELOCHAM! Pet, ⌊1921⌋. *⌊210000(20)⌋
    (CatKL)

*VNUTRENNIE I VNESHNIE ZADACHI SOVETSKOI VLAST. ⌊1918⌋. *⌊180000(26)⌋
    ⌊Advert.⌋

VOENNAYA DOKTRINA ILI MNIMO-VOENNOE DOKTRINSTVO. Gosizdat: 210000(1)
    M, 1921. 35.

*VOENNAYA DOKTRINA ILI MNIMO-VOENNOE DOKTRINSTVO. Polit. Upr. P.V.O.: *220000(2)
    Pet, 1922. 52.
    (CatKL)

§ VOINA I REVOLYUTSIYA. Gosizdat: Pet, 1922-3. 2 Vols. 220000(3)
    (LocBM/HIS/LC/NYPL)

‡ VOINA I REVOLYUTSIYA. Gosizdat: M-Pet, 1923-4. 2 izd. 2 Vols. 230000(2)
    (LocBM/BDIC/LC)

† VOINA I TEKHNIKA. Kommunist: M-Pet, 1919. 164. 190000(2)
    (LocBDIC/BM/HIS/KBS/LC/ULH)

VOINA S POL´SHEI. Literaturno-izdatel´skii otdel politicheskogo 200000(5)
    upravleniya revolyutsionnogo voennogo soveta respubliki:
    M, 1920. 15.
    (LocBDIC/HIS/KBS/ULH)

*VOINA S POL´SHEI. M, 1920. 15. 2 izd. *200000(6)
    (CatKL)

*VOINA S POL´SHEI. Saratov, 1920. *200000(7)
    (CatKL)

*VOINA S POL´SHEI. Izd. Politotdela Zapfronta, 1920. *200000(102)
    ⌊Advert.⌋

† VOPROSY BYTA. Krasnaya Nov: M, 1923. 117.   230000(3)
  (LocBN/LC/NYPL)

§ VOPROSY BYTA. Krasnaya Nov: M, 1923. 2 dop. izd.   230000(4)
  (LocHIS/IISG/LC/LSE/NYPL)

§ VOPROSY BYTA. Gosizdat: M, 1925. 167. 3 izd.   250000(1)
  (LocBDIC/BM/HIS/NYPL/O/SEES)

*VOPROSY BYTA. Krasnyi Mir: Kostroma, 1924. 6.   *240000(1)
  (CatKL)

*VOPROSY BYTA. Baku, 1924. 6.   *240000(2)
  (CatKL)

*VOPROSY GRAZHDANSKOI VOINY. Priboi: Pet, 1924. 38. *240000(3)
  (CatPostnikov)

† VOPROSY KUL´TURNOI RABOTY. Gosizdat: M, 1924. 171. 240000(4)
  (LocBDIC/BN/HIS/LC/MU/NYPL/SEES)

*VOR V DOME. M, 1920.   *200000(8)
  (CatKL)

VOSEM LET. Gosizdat: M-L, 1926. 21.   260000(3)
  (LocNYPL)

*VOSEM LET. Kislovodsk, 1926.   *260000(4)
  (CatKL)

*VOZHD ZHELEZNOI KOGORTY. PAMYATI IL"ICHA. Rostov, ⌊1924⌋. *⌊240000(36)⌋
  (CatKL)

*VOZRODIM TRANSPORT! Pet, 1920.   *200000(4)
  (CatKL)

V PL"ENU U ANGLICHAN. Vsiga: Pet, ⌊1917⌋. 15.   170000(6)
  (LocAAS/NYPL/ULH)

V PLENU U ANGLICHAN. Vserossiiskii Tsentral´nyi Ispolitel´nyi 180000(2)
  Komitet Sovetov R., S. i K. deputatov: M, 1918. 14.
  (LocBDIC/HIS)

VTOROI S"EZD ROS. SOTS. DEM. R.P. OTCHET SIBIRSKOI DELEGATSII. 030700
  R.S.D.R.P.: Geneva, 1903. 36.
  (LocBDIC/BM/BN/IISG/LnL/NYPL/ULH/CatZ)

V ZASHCHITU PARTII. Tip. Partii: StP, 1907. 148.   070000(1)
  (LocBM/IISG/SEES/CatZ)

YA KLADU ZHITTYA! Vidavnistvo "Robitnichi Visti": Toronto, 1937. 32.   370000(2)
    (LocPer)

Domov i T., YUBILEI POZORA NASHEGO (1613-1913). Pravda: Vienna, 1912.   120000(2)
    27.
    (LocBM/IISG)

§ ZADACHI XII S"EZDA RKP. Krasnaya Nov: M, 1923. 71.   230000(5)
    (LocPer)

*ZADACHI XII S"EZDA RKP. Izd. "Devyatoe Yanvarya" Transposektsii: *230000(40)
    M, 1923. 64.
    (LocHIS)

ZADACHI KOMMUNISTICHESKOGO VOSPITANIYA. Krasnaya Nov: M, 1923. 29.   230000(6)
    (LocNYPL)

ZADACHI KOMMUNISTICHESKOGO VOSPITANIYA. Krasnaya Nov: M, 1924. 29.   240000(5)
    2 izd.
    (LocLSE)

*ZADACHI RABOTNIKOV KUL´TURNOGO STROITEL´STVA. M, 1926.   *260000(8)
    (CatKL)

† ZAPAD I VOSTOK. Krasnaya Nov: M, 1924. 149.   240000(6)
    (LocBM/HIS/LC/NYPL/SEES)

*"ZAPADNYI FRONT ZOVET!" Ekaterinburg, 1920.   *200000(14)
    (CatKL)

ZAPOVIT LENINA. Robitnichi Visti: Toronto, 1934. 62.   340000(26)
    (LocPer)

*ZHAN ZHORES. Kniga: Pet, 1917. 15.   *170000(1)
    (L₀cLC)

ZHAN ZHORES. Vserossiiskii Tsentral´nyi Ispolitel´nyi Komitet   180000(4)
    Sovetov R., S., K. i K. deputatov: M, 1918. 16. 2 izd.
    (LocAAS/BDIC/BM/HIS/ULH)

CONCORDANCE TO BOOKS

Cyrillic script

260000(1)   BALKANY I BALKANSKAYA VOINA
            (THE BALKANS AND THE BALKAN WAR)

v   260619

I.   U POROGA VOINY
      (ON THE THRESHHOLD OF WAR)

      1.   Balkansky vopros
           (The Balkan Question)

3-6   ⌊081217(3)⌋
6-13   ⌊090103⌋
13-26   081014

      2.   Balkanskie strany i sotsializm
           (The Balkan Countries and
           Socialism)

27-35   ⌊120000(1)⌋
36-41   ⌊100801(1)⌋
41-5   ⌊100801(2)⌋

      3.   Zagadka bolgarskoi demokratii
           (The Enigma of Bulgarian
           Democracy)

46-50   ⌊121118⌋
50-2   ⌊121119(1)⌋
52-4   ⌊121119(2)⌋

II.   VOINA
      (WAR)

      1.   Serbiya v voine
           (Serbia at War)

57-61   ⌊121004(1)⌋
61-4   ⌊121004(2)⌋
64-8   ⌊121003(1)⌋
68-73   ⌊121213⌋
73-8   ⌊121005(1)⌋
79-82   ⌊121005(2)⌋
82-9   ⌊121219⌋
89-97   ⌊121214⌋

97-104   ⌊121120(3)⌋
105-12   ⌊121230⌋
112-5   ⌊121221⌋
115-27   ⌊121225⌋
127-9   ⌊121024⌋
129-33   ⌊121229⌋

      2.   Bolgariya v voine. Pervyi period —
           S soyuznikami protiv Turssii
           (Bulgaria at War. The first Period —
           With Allies against Turkey)

134-9   ⌊121013⌋
140-4   ⌊121014⌋
144-53   ⌊121019(1)⌋
153-60   ⌊121015⌋
160-5   ⌊121129⌋
165-74   ⌊121100(1)⌋
174-9   ⌊121019(2)⌋

      3.   Rasskazy uchastnikov
           (Stories of Participants)

180-5   ⌊121031⌋
185-91   ⌊121104⌋
191-4   ⌊121100(1)⌋
194-9   ⌊130129⌋
199-204   ⌊121200⌋

      4.   Otgoloski voiny
           (Echoes of the War)

205-7   ⌊121100(2)⌋
207-11   ⌊130402⌋
211-7   ⌊121109⌋

      5.   Makedoniya i Armeniya

218-25   ⌊121022⌋
225-35   121112
235-43   ⌊130719⌋

723

190000(1)	BELGIYA I SERBIYA V VOINE (BELGIUM AND SERBIA AT WAR)	290000(1)	CHTO I KAK PROIZOSHLO? (WHAT HAPPENED AND HOW?)

5-6	181204
7-19	150200
20-32	141226
33-68	[150300]
69-92	150216
92-127	160500

7-15	281216(2)
16-24	
25-31	
31-6	
37-46	
47-56	290225

Prilozheniya (Appendices)

57-65	281216(1)
74-83	290327

200000(2) Zinov'ev i T,
BOR'BA ZA PETROGRAD
(THE STRUGGLE FOR PETROGRAD)

260000(5) DELO BYLO V ISPANII
(WHAT HAPPENED IN SPAIN)

36-40	191030(2)
183	191017(1)
184-5	[191016(1)]
186-8	191016(2)
196-8	191018(2)
210-27	191019
233	191021(2)
234	191020(1)
237	191021(1)
238	[191022]
240-1	191023
243	191024(2)
244-5	191025(1)
246-7	191025(2)
273-86	191107(2)
291	191024(3)

Prilozheniya (Appendix)

313-7	200000(37)

5	260000(29)
7-12	
13-4	
15-25	
26-40	161110
41-9	161111
50-3	161112
54-62	
63-80	161114(3) 161115(2)
81-5	
86-90	
91-7	161126
98-104	
105-7	161208
108-14	161216
115-20	161221
121-6	161231(1)
127-32	170101 170113(2)

GRAZHDANSKAYA VOINA V RSFSR

V 1918 G.

(THE CIVIL WAR IN THE RFSSR, 1918)

1. Pervye akty soyuznicheskoi
    interventsii
    (First Acts of Allied
    Intervention)

199–200	[180622(1)]
201	180701(1)
202–4	180701(3)
205	180717(1)
206	180722(3)
207	180723(2)
208	180806(5)
209	180822

2. Chekho-Slovatskii myatezh
    (The Czechoslovak
    Insurrection)

210–1	180529(1)
212–5	180531(1)
216	180604(3)
217	180613(1)
218	180613(2)
219–29	180729(1)
229	180729(2)
230–1	180814(2)

3. Bor´ba za Kazan
    (The Fight for Kazan)

232–3	180808(10)
234	180813(1)
235	[180814(1)]
236	180815(1)
237–8	180819
239	180824(1)
240	180826
241	180827(1)
242	[180828(1)]

243	180830(1)
244	[180830(2)]
245	[180830(3)]
246	[180831(1)]
247	180900(3)
248	180900(4)
249	180910
250	180911(1)
251–6	180911(3)
257	180912(3)
258	180913(1)
259	180913(2)
260	180913(3)
261	[180914(1)]
262–3	180912(2)
264	181103
265	181115

4. Myatezh Levykh Es-Erov,
    6–8 iyulya 1918 g. v Moskve
    (The Insurrection of the Left-
    SRs in Moscow, 6–8 July, 1918)

266–9	180704(1)
269–74	180704(2)
274	180704(3)
275	[180707]
276–87	180709(1)
287–95	180709(2)
295–6	180709(3)
297	180708(1)
298–9	[180708(2)]
300	180715(2)

KRASNAYA ARMIYA V GRAZHDANSKOI VOINE

(THE RED ARMY IN THE CIVIL WAR)

303–17	180710(1)
317–9	180710(2)
320–4	180902(1)
325–9	180900(5)
330–1	180903(2)
332–41	181109
342–3	181130

249	190801(1)
250	190802(1)
251	190802(2)
252-3	190803
254-5	190804
256	190808
257-8	[190800]
259-63	190809(1)
264-5	190809(2)
266-7	[190812]
268-9	190818(1)
270	190813

3.   Reid Mamontova.
Mironovshchina. Vtoroe
nastuplenie Krasnoi Armii
na Ukrainu
(Avgust-dekabr 1919 g.)
(Mamontov's Raid. The
Mironov Affair. The Red
Army's second Advance
into the Ukraine: August -
December, 1919)

271-2	190818(2)
273-5	[190819]
276-7	190824
278-9	190904(1)
280-1	190904(2)
282	190904(3)
283-4	190906(1)
285-6	190908
287-8	190911(1)
289-90	190911(2)
291	190912(1)
292	190912(2)
293-5	190913
296-8	190916(1)
299-300	190916(2)
301-3	190906(2)

304	191006
305	[191026]
306	191025(2)
307	191130
308-10	191211(1)

VOSTOCHNYI FRONT
(THE EASTERN FRONT)
Nastuplenie Kolchaka
(Mart-aprel 1919 g.)
(Kolchak's Advance:
March-April, 1919)

313-5	190324(1)
316	190326
317-33	190406(2)
334-6	190407(1)
337-9	190409
340-2	190410(1)
343-5	190412(2)
346-7	190413
348-50	190414
351-2	[190418(1)]
353-5	190423(2)
356	190424(1)
357-8	[190424(2)]
359	190426
360-1	190427
362-3	[190428]
364-6	190420(2)
367-8	190430
369	190501(1)
370	190504
371	190505
372	190506
373-4	190507(1)

BOR'BA ZA PETROGRAD
(THE STRUGGLE FOR PETROGRAD)

377-8	190211(1)
379-82	[190901(1)] ++++

YUZHNYI FRONT
(THE SOUTHERN FRONT)

Bor´ba s Vrangelem
(The Struggle against Wrangel)

NA RAZNYE TEMY
(VARIOUS TOPICS)

(Stati, Zametki, Prikazy, Vozzvaniya)
(Articles, Notes, Orders of the Day, Appeals)

114-6	[220223(1)]
117-8	220223(2)
119-29	220328
130-2	220401(3)
133	220718
134-5	221010
136-41	221016
142-53	230518

2. Prikazy, Tsirkulyarii,
    Telegrammy i dr.
    (Orders of the Day,
    Circulars, Telegrams,
    &c.)

154-6	210805
157	210905(3)
158	210905(4)
159	210910(2)
160-1	210911
162	210912(2)
163	210905(1)
163-4	210913(1)
165-6	211011
167	211021
168-70	[211101(1)]
171-3	220228(1)
174	220316
174-5	220324
176	220331
177	220500
178	[220516]
179-80	220520
181	220708(1)
182	220725
183	221024(1)
184	221024(2)
185	[221029]
186	221102(1)
187	221221

188-9	221222
190	230106
191-2	230422(1)
193	230422(2)
194	[230425(2)]
195	230526
196	231029(1)
197-8	[231208(2)]

KRONSTADTSKII MYATEZH
(THE CRONSTADT INSURRECTION)

201	210302
202	210305
203-4	[210313]
205-6	210323(1)
207	210403

BANDITIZM I GOLOD
(BANDITRY AND FAMINE)

1. Rechi, Stati
    (Speeches, Articles)

211-29	210830
230-1	210902
232-41	210905(5)
242-3	210907(1)
244-6	[210916]
247-61	210920

2. Prikazy
    (Orders of the Day)

262-3	210905(2)
264	210910(1)
265	210913(2)
266-7	211110(1)
268-9	211211
270	220211

270000(4)   KHOZYAISTVENNOE STROITEL'STVO
SOVETSKOI RESPUBLIKI
(THE ECONOMIC CONSTRUCTION OF
THE SOVIET REPUBLIC)

NOVYI KURS   ++++

77-104	PRILOZHENIYA (APPENDICES)
77-83	231208(1)
83-6	231210
87-92	231203
93-9	231206(2)
100-4	

=========================

230000(19)   Kabakchiev i T,
OCHERKI POLITICHESKOI
BOLGARII
(POLITICAL SKETCHES OF
BULGARIA)

vii-viii	230319(1)
viii	230619

POLITICHESKIE OTNOSHENIYA
(POLITICAL RELATIONS)

9-18	[120000(1)]

Zagadka bolgarskoi demokratii
(The Riddle of Bulgarian Democracy)

19-24	[121118]
24-5	[121119(1)]
25-7	[131102]
28-34	[130710]
34-43	[131102]

BOLGARIYA V BALKANSKOI VOINE
(BULGARIA IN THE BALKAN WAR)

47-57	[121013]

OKOLO KIRKILISSE
(AROUND KIRKILISSE)

58-67	[121100(1)]

IZNANKA POBEDY
(SHAME OF VICTORY)

68-73	[121019(2)]
73-7	[121110(1)]
77	[121110(2)]
78-80	[121100(2)]
80-3	[121100(1)]
83-5	[121120(2)]

ARMIYA POBEDITELEI
(VICTORIOUS ARMY)

86-91	[121206]

PRESTUPLENIYA SHOVINIZMA I DEMOKRATIYA
(THE CRIMES OF CHAUVINISM AND DEMOCRACY)

92-5	:121019(4)]
95-100	[121019(3)]
100-6	121127

CHETNICHESTVO I VOINA
(CHETNIK-ISM AND THE WAR)

107-15	[121022]

=========================

230000(20)	Rakovski i T,
	OCHERKI POLITICHESKOI
	RUMYNII
	(POLITICAL SKETCHES OF
	RUMANIA)
5-7	220612
9-10	230430(1)
11-8	130707
19-25	[130728]
26-32	[130731]
33-44	[130809]
45-52	[130917]
53-62	[130921]
63-71	[130912]
72-81	[130827]
82-92	[130817]
93-116	[130903]
116	220712
117-22	[131017]

====================

250000(7)	O DEVYATOM YANVARYA
	(ON JANUARY 9th)
3	241031
5-59	041220
59-71	050120
72-80	050303(1)
81-2	[050600(1)]
83-92	220000(12): 74-82
93-4	[100101(4)]
97-105	PRILOZHENIYA (APPENDICES)
107-41	PRIMECHANIYA (NOTES)

====================

240000(24)	O LENINE
	(LENIN)
v-vii	240421(1)
3-45	240305
45-142	240406
	PRILOZHENIYA (APPENDICES)
145-50	200423
151-8	180902(2)
159-66	230405(2)
166-8	240122(1)

====================

250000(8)	OSNOVNYE VOPROSY PROLETARSKOI
	REVOLYUTSII
	(FUNDAMENTAL PROBLEMS OF
	PROLETARIAN REVOLUTION)
1-6	230504(1)
6	241020(1)
I.	TERRORIZM I KOMMUNIZM
	(TERRORISM AND COMMUNISM)
9-15	200529(1)
16-177	200000(37)
178-80	200617
II.	MEZHDU IMPERIALIZMOM I
	REVOLYUTSIEI
	(BETWEEN IMPERIALISM AND
	REVOLUTION)
183-296	220000(5)

==

POKOLENIE OKTYABRYA   ++++

  III.   VOORUZHENNYI SOYUZ MOLODEZHI
        (ARMING THE YOUTH ALLIANCE)

Armiya -- shkola
(The Army -- a School)

101-4	[220104(1)]
104-6	[220328]
107-9	[221218]
110-1	230210
112-4	220329(2)

Molodye kommunistii -- v armiyu!
(Communist Youth -- Into the Army!)

| 115 | [220104(1)] |
| 115-7 | 220329(2) |

Doprizyv 1901 g
(The 1901 Call-up)

| 118 | 221010 |
| 119 | 221024(1) |

Orudie budushchego
(The Weapon of the Future)

120-1	
121-2	230504
122	230530

  IV.   ZA NOVOI BYT
       (FOR A NEW LIFE)

125-6	180328(1)
127-30	[211001]
131-2	[230711]
133-7	[230712]
138-41	[230713]
142-5	[230714]
144-9	230403
150-4	230515

  V.   KOMSOMOLSTAM
   (TO KOMSOMOL MEMBERS)

  (Doklady i rechi)
  (Reports and Speeches)

157-67	191004
168-73	200221
174-89	210714(2)
190-4	210714(3)
195-216	210921
217-39	221011
240-7	221016
248-52	231029(2)

==============================

260000(16)	POLITICHESKAYA KHRONIKA
	(POLITICAL CHRONICLES)
v	251109

  I.   PERED 1905 GODOM
    (BEFORE 1905)

   1. Stat'i iz Vostochnogo Obozreniya
     (Articles from Vostochnoe Obozrenie)

3-7	[001015]
7-12	[001223]
12-6	[010214]
17-20	[010329]
20-6	[010530]
26-31	[010804]
32-5	[010809]
35-42	[010926]
42-3	[010902]

POLITICHESKAYA KHRONIKA   ++++

II.   PERIOD REAKTSII

(PERIOD OF THE REACTION)

2.   Kanun revolyutsii

(Eve of Revolution)

1.   Vokrug pervoi Dumy

(At the Time of the first Duma)

44-5	[021101(1)]
45-8	[021115]
48-50	[021101(2)]
51-6	[021201]
56-9	[021215]
59-61	[030215(1)]
61-3	[030201(1)]
63	[030201(2)]
64-5	[030201(3)]
65-7	[030215(2)]
67-70	[030701(1)]
70-7	[030701(2)]
77-84	[031125]
84-7	[031215]
87-94	[040210]
94-102	[040225]
102-6	[040305]
107-12	[041005]
112-9	[041020(1)]
119-23	[041020(2)]
124-8	[040101]

| 153-69 | 060212 |
| 169-74 | [070000(5)] |

2.   Vokrug vtoroi Dumy

(At the Time of the second Duma)

175-207	[070000(4)]
179-81	[070000(6)]
207-18	[070600]

3.   Vokrug tretei Dumy

(At the Time of the third Duma)

219-29	[080400(2)]
230-8	[080400(3)]
238-44	[080600(1)]
245	[081003]
246-50	[081217(1)]
250-5	[081217(2)]
256-60	[090327(1)]
261-3	[090327(3)]
263-5	[090327(2)]
266-71	[090602]
271-2	[090920(3)]
272-8	[090920(2)]
278-84	[090920(1)]
284-6	[091208(5)]
286-7	[091208(2)]
287-90	[091121(2)]
290-5	[100318(2)]
296-9	[100515]
299-302	[100624(2)]
302-5	[101120(2)]
305-10	[120302]

3.   Protiv Sotsialistov-Revolyutsionerov

(Against the Social-Revolutionaries)

129-32	[030101]
133-7	[030301]
138-41	[030201(4)]
141-6	[030315]
146-50	[030601]

260000(18)   SOVETSKOI RESPUBLIKA I
             KAPITALISTICHESKII MIR
             (THE SOVIET REPUBLIC AND
             THE CAPITALIST WORLD)

             TOM I
             (VOLUME ONE)

             Chast I
             (Part One)

PERVONACHAL'NYI PERIOD ORGANIZATSII
SIL
(THE INITIAL PERIOD OF THE
ORGANIZATION OF FORCES)

v   251215

I.   BREST

1.   Vtoroi period mirnykh
     peregovorov
     9 yan.-10 fev. 1918 g.
     (The second Period of Peace
     Negotiations
     9 Jan.-10 Feb. 1918)

3   171227/
3-11   171228(1)/
11   171228(2)/
11-2   171231(1)/
12-4   171230(1)
14   180101/
15-6   171228(3)/
16-24   171229(1)/
24-8   171229(2)/
28-32   171230(2)/
33-8
38-44   180102(1)/
44-9   180102(2)/
49-50   180105(1)/
51-3   180105(2)/

2.   V pereryve
     (In the Interval)

53-62   180113(1)/
62-5   180113(2)/
66   180114(1)/
67-9   180117(1)/
69-71   171228(4)/
71-2   171230(3)/
72-3   180102(3)/
73-6   180117(2)/
76-8   180118(1)/
78-80
80-4
84-5   180118(2)/
85-9   180203(1)
89-91   180207(1)
91-2   180116/
92   180202(1)
92-3   ⌊180203(2)⌋
94-6   180207(2)
96-7   180131
97-102   180209
102-5   180210(1)
106   180210(2)

II. POSLE RAZYVA
     (AFTER THE BREAK)

107-11   180214
111-6   180216(1)
116   180217(2)
116-7   180218
117-20   180220
120-1   180221
121-4   180222(2)
124   ⌊180222(1)⌋
125   180304
125-6   ⌊180310⌋
128-30   ⌊180319(3)⌋
130-1   180318
132-4   180328(2)   ++++

SOVETSKAYA RESPUBLIKA I
KAPITALISTICHESKII MIR
(THE SOVIET REPUBLIC AND
THE CAPITALIST WORLD)

Chast II
(Part Two)

GRAZHDANSKAYA VOINA
(THE CIVIL WAR)

I.   OT OBORONY K NASTUPLENIYU
     (FROM DEFENCE TO ATTACK)

3–6	180930(1)
6–16	181003
16–8	181030
19–31	181109
31–58	181118
58–60	181130
60–4	190107(1)
64–7	190109(2)
67–96	190224

II. NASTUPLENIE KOLCHAKA
     (KOLCHAK'S ATTACK)

99–112	190401
112–32	190406(2)
132–5	190407(1)
135–8	190412(1)
138–40	190412(2)
140–3	190409
143–8	190412(3)
148–50	190414
150–60	190424(3)
160–3	190420(2)

III. DEVYATYI VAL
     (THE NINTH WAVE)

1.   Nastuplenie Denikina
     (Denikin's Attack)

Edinym frontom Rossii i Ukrainy —
na vraga!
(A United Front of Russia and the
Ukraine — against the Enemy!)

167–74	190519
174–9	190520
179–82	190521(1)
182–4	190601(1)
184–8	190604(1)
188–90	190627(2)
190–1	190719(2)
191–9	190729(3)
199–205	190826(1)
206–13	190826(2)
213–5	190902
215–8	190916(1)
218–9	190916(2)
219–24	190924(1)
224–6	190924(2)
226–30	191004
230	191107(1)

2.   Bor´ba za Petrograd
     (The Struggle for Petrograd)

231–5	190211(1)
235–9	190219
239–40	190829
241–5	[190901(1)]
245–64	190901(2)
264–5	191016(1)
265–7	191016(2)
268–70	191018(2)
270–87	191019
287–8	191021(1)
288–9	191023
289–90	191029
290–4	191030(2)
294–5	191103(1)
295–7	191103(5) ++++

(x)   Dating where possible.

1917 ++++

61–9	⌊170602(2)/⌉	154–8	⌊170627/⌉
		158–9	⌊170708/⌉
2.	Voprosy mira	159–61	⌊170820(1)/⌉
	(Peace Problems)		
		2.	Iyul´skie dni
70–93	170512/		(The July Days)
92–3	220000(2)		
94–9	⌊170615/⌉	162	170706/
99–106	⌊170617/⌉	163–5	⌊170709/⌉
		165–6	170710/
3.	I S"ezd sovetov	167–70	170717/
	The first Soviet Congress)		
		3.	Kapitulyatsiya melkoburzhuaznoi
107–8	170601/		demokratii pered kontr-
109–12	⌊170607/⌉		revolyutsiei
113–22	170605(1)/		(The Capitulation of petty-
122	170605(2)/		bourgeois Democracy to the
122–4	170609(1)/		Counter-revolution)
124–32	170609(2)/		
133–5	170612/	171	170720(1)/
		172–4	170721/
4.	Vokrug iyunskogo nastupleniya	174–6	170725(1)/
	(Around the June	177–92	⌊170725(2)/⌉
	Demonstration)		
		4.	Iz tyurmy
136–7	170604/		(From Prison)
138–40	170628(1)/		
141–4	170628(2)/	193–200	⌊170901(3)/⌉
		201–2	170725(3)/
5.	K voprosu ob ob"edinenii	203	⌊170802/⌉
	Internatsionalistov	204–5	170808/
	(The Question of the	206–11	⌊170815(2)/⌉
	Unification of the	211–2	⌊170820(2)/⌉
	Internationalists)	212–3	⌊170901(3)/⌉
144–9	170628(3)/	213–5	170901(1)/
149	⌊170702/⌉		

IV. NAPOR KONTR–REVOLYUTSII
(COUNTER–REVOLUTION'S
PRESSURE)

1. Protiv burzhuaznoi klevety
(Against bourgeois Slanders)

153–4   170623/

———————————

1917

Chast II
(Part Two)

OT OKTYABRYA DO BRESTA
(FROM OCTOBER TO BREST)

VII.   OKTYABR'SKOE VOSSTANIE
        (THE OCTOBER INSURRECTION)

VOINA I REVOLYUTSIYA.I   ++++

IX.   RUSSKII SOTSIAL-PATRIOTIZM
      (RUSSIAN SOCIAL-PATRIOTISM)

127-9/123-5	⌊150516⌋
129-34/126-30	⌊151110⌋
134-9/130-4	⌊151212⌋
139-44/135-9	⌊151111⌋
144-8/139-44	⌊151219⌋
149-52/144-7	⌊151229(1)⌋
152-6/147-51	⌊160114⌋
156-77/151-71	⌊160210⌋
173-7	⌊160210⌋
177-81/172-5	⌊160409⌋
181-4/175-8	⌊160420⌋
184-8/178-82	⌊160504⌋
188-90/182-4	⌊160629⌋
190-7/184-91	⌊160719⌋
197-200/191-3	⌊160729⌋
200-4/194-7	160800(1)
204-7/197-201	⌊160903⌋
207-11/201-4	⌊161103⌋

X.   KRIZIS FRANTSUZSKOGO SOTSIALIZMA
    (THE CRISIS OF FRENCH SOCIALISM)

215-20/207-12	151222
220-1/212-3	⌊160803(1)⌋
221-3/213-5	⌊160813(1)⌋
223-6/215-8	⌊160808(1)⌋
227-8/218-9	⌊160808(2)⌋
228-31/219-22	⌊160818(1)⌋
231-41/222-32	⌊160914(2)⌋
241-8/232-9	⌊160900(1)⌋

XI.   V GERMANSKOI SOTSIAL-
      DEMOKRATII
      (IN THE GERMAN SOCIAL-
      DEMOCRACY)

251-2/243-4	⌊150331⌋
253-6/245-8	⌊150613⌋

256-8/248-50	⌊150711(1)⌋
258-62/250-3	⌊150717(1)⌋
262-4/254-6	⌊151117⌋
264-7/256-8	⌊151228(1)⌋
267-71/259-63	⌊160802⌋
271-83/263-74	⌊161006⌋
283-4/274-5	220508(3)

XII.   V AVSTRIISKOI SOTSIAL-DEMOKRATII
      (IN THE AUSTRIAN SOCIAL-DEMOCRACY)

287-90/279-82	⌊160521(2)⌋
290-4/282-6	⌊160604⌋
294-6/286-8	⌊160624⌋
297-302/288-93	⌊161025⌋
303/293	220501(2)

XIII.   TRAVLYA RAKOVSKOGO
        (THE PERSECUTION OF RAKOVSKY)

305-6/297-8	⌊150417⌋
307-10/299-302	⌊150505⌋
310-1/302-3	⌊150505⌋
311-5/303-7	⌊150930⌋
316-7/307-9	⌊160704(2)⌋

XIV.   V MIRE MERZOSTI I RASTLENIYA
        (IN A WORLD OF ABOMINATION
        AND CORRUPTION)

321-4/313-6	⌊150401⌋
324-7/316-9	⌊151203⌋
327-30/319-22	⌊151218⌋
330-3/322-5	⌊160813(2)⌋
334-5/325-6	⌊160910⌋
335-6/327-8	⌊160912⌋
336-7/328-9	⌊161022⌋

XV.   VYSYLKA IZ FRANTSY
      (EXILED FROM FRANCE)

341-8/333-40	⌊170210⌋
348-55/340-7	161011

240000(6)   ZAPAD I VOSTOK
             (WEST AND EAST)

3-4   240715
5-29   240411
30-41   240421(2)
42-65   240429(1)
66-80   240520
81-9   240607
90-107   240610(1)
108-38   240621

141-7   PRILOZHENIYA (APPENDICES)

141   210616
141-2   210714(1)
142   220302(1)
142-3   220608
143-4   221020
144   221103(1)
144-5   221115
145-6   221114(1)
146-7   [221130(1)]

BOOK LIST

Other scripts

Pol	*A CO DALEJ? Nowa Era: Warsaw, 1930. 116. (CatIT)	*300000(29)
Sp	¿A DONDE VA INGLATERRA? Ediciones Biblos: Madrid, 1927. 270. (LocUCB)	270000(6)
Sp	*¿A DONDE VA RUSIA? Oriente: Madrid, 1928. (CatBE)	*280000(12)
Port	EL ADVENIMIENTO DEL BOLSHEVIKISMO. Documentos del Progresso: Buenos Aires, 1920. 160. (LocIISG)	200000(106)
Ice	AEVI MÍN. Steindórsprent H.F.: Reikjavik, 1936. 189. (LocKBC)	360000(20)
Eng	AGAINST SOCIAL PATRIOTISM. See AN OPEN LETTER TO JULES GUESDE, 520300.	
Eng	AGAINST THE STREAM! Perspectives Pamphlet: Ln, 1965. 15. (LocPer)	651200
Am	THE AGE OF PERMANENT REVOLUTION. Dell: NY, 1964. 384. (LocLC)	640800
Jap	⌊THE AGE OF PERMANENT REVOLUTION⌋ Kawade World Books: Tokyo, 1968. 404. (LocPer)	681125
Sp	*LA AGONIA DEL CAPITALISMO Y LA IV INTERNACIONAL. Liga Obrera Marxista: Mexico, 1964. ⌊Advert.⌋	*640000(6)
Sp	LA AGONIA DEL IMPERIALISMO Y LAS TAREAS DE LA IV INTERNACIONAL. Quarta Internacional: Santiago de Chile, ⌊1965⌋. 32. (LocPer)	⌊650000(11)⌋
Fr	L'AGONIE DU CAPITALISME. Parti Socialiste Révolutionnaire: Charleroi, ⌊1938⌋. 28. (LocPer)	⌊380000(10)⌋
Fr	L'AGONIE DU CAPITALISME ET LES TÂCHES DE LA IVe INTERNATIONALE. ⌊P⌋, 1944. 28. (LocPer)	440800(1)
Fr	L'AGONIE DU CAPITALISME ET LES TÂCHES DE LA IVe INTERNATIONALE. ⌊P⌋, 1946. 38. (LocHIS/IISG)	460800
Fr	L'AGONIE DU CAPITALISME ET LES TÂCHES DE LA IVe INTERNATIONALE. Société Internationale d'Editions, P, 1968. 38. (LocPer)	680612

Fr   L'AGONIE DU CAPITALISME ET LES TÂCHES DE LA IVe   690900(3)
         INTERNATIONALE. La Vérité: P, 1969. 45.
         (LocPer)

Sp   ALEMANIA, CLAVE DE LA SITUACIÓN INTERNACIONAL. Comunismo: ⌊320000(22)⌋
         Madrid, ⌊1932⌋. 31.
         (LocPer)

Ger   u. Lenin, *ALLEN KRIEGSVÖLKERN. ⌊1917⌋   *⌊170000(10)⌋
         ⌊Advert.⌋

Ben   AMAR JIBON PON. The Merit Publishers: Calcutta, ⌊1969⌋.   ⌊690000(12)⌋
         32.
         (LocPer)

Ger   *AN ALL VÖLKER. ⌊1918⌋   *⌊180123(1)⌋
         ⌊Advert.⌋

Ger   u.a., AN DAS POLITBÜRO DES ZK DER WKP(B). See ERKLÄRUNG
         DER FÜNFHUNDERT, ⌊270000(11)⌋.

Ger   u. Lenin, AN DIE DEUTSCHEN SOLDATEN. Pet, ⌊1917⌋.   ⌊170000(9)⌋
         (LocHIS/IISG)

Ger   u.a., AN DIE MITGLIEDER DES KAPD. Hamburg, 1921.   210000(24)
         (LocPer)

Swed   DEN ANKLAGADE ANKLAGAR. See MITT LIV, 370000(9).

Ger   *ANKLAGEN AUS VERBANNUNG UND EXIL.   *⌊300000(29)⌋
         ⌊Advert.⌋

Mal   ANTE JEEVAN JNAN PANTHAYAM VERKUNNU. Theenalam Publications: 570411
         Nadavaramba, Irinjalakuda, 1957. 52.
         (LocPer)

Fr   APRÈS"LA PAIX" IMPÉRIALISTE DE MUNICH. See AVANT LA
         NOUVELLE GUERRE MONDIALE, 380000(3).

Fr   APRÈS MUNICH: UNE LEÇON TOUTE FRAÎCHE. Bibliothèque   380000(1)
         Marxiste: ⌊P⌋, 1938. 17.
         (LocBN/HIS)

Fr   APRÈS MUNICH: UNE LEÇON TOUTE FRAÎCHE. Publications   380000(2)
         Populaires: P, 1938. 24.
         (LocBN/HIS)

Fr   A QUAND LA FIN DE CE MAUDIT CARNAGE? Commissariat des   180000(28)
         Affaires étrangères: ⌊Pet⌋, 1918. 18.
         (LocHIS)

Hol   ARBEID, DISCIPLINE EN ORDE ZULLEN DE SOCIALISTIESE   ⌊200000(83)⌋
         SOWJET-REPUBLIK REDDEN. Bos: Amsterdam, ⌊1920⌋. 16.
         (LocAAS/IISG)

Hol	DE ARBEIDERSTAAT: THERMIDOR EN BONAPARTISME. + NOGMAALS DE KWESTIE VAN HET BONAPARTISME. De Vlam: Amsterdam, [1935]. 23. (LocAAS/IISG)	⌊350000(14)⌋
Ger	ARBEIT, DISZIPLIN UND ORDNUNG WERDEN DIE SOZIALISTISCHE SOWJET-REPUBLIK RETTEN! Verlag Buchhandlung des Arbeiterbundes: Basle, 1918. 29. (LocAAS/ABC/BM/BN/HIS/IISG/NYPL/O)	180000(29)
Ger	ARBEIT, DISZIPLIN UND ORDNUNG ... Verlag Gesellschaft und Erzietung: B, 1919. 23. (LocBDIC/BM/LC/LSE/NYPL)	190000(37)
Ger	ARBEIT, DISZIPLIN UND ORDNUNG ... KPDeutschösterreichs: Vienna, 1919. 31. (LocBDIC/NYPL)	190000(38)
Ger	ARBEIT, DISZIPLIN UND ORDNUNG ... Hoffman: B, [1919]. 18. (LocIISG)	⌊190000(60)⌋
Ger	DIE ARBEITERKLASSE UND IHRE SOWJET-POLITIK. Seehof:B, 1920. 54. (LocAAS/ABC/BDIC/HIS/IISG/NYPL)	200000(51)
Ger	*DIE ARBEITERKLASSE UND IHRE SOWJET-POLITIK. Stuttgart, 1920. (CatDB)	*200000(52)
Ger	ARBEITERSTAAT, THERMIDOR UND BONAPARTISMUS. + WARUM HAT STALIN ÜBER DIE OPPOSITION GESIEGT? + DIE SOWJET= SECTION DER IV. INTERNATIONALE. Unser Wort: P, [1936]. 40. (LocAAO/AAS/ABC/BN/BRB/IISG)	⌊360000(15)⌋
Den	ARBEJDE, DISCIPLIN OG ORDEN KAN REDDE SOVJETREPUBLIKEN. Europaeisk Forlag: Copenhagen, [1918]. 24. (LocAAS/ABC/KBC/ULO)	⌊180000(49)⌋
Swed	ARBETARKLASSEN OCH VÅRLDSLÄGET. (DEN NYA ETAPPEN.) Frams Forlag: Stockholm, 1923. 109. (LocAAS/ABC/KBS/ULH)	230000(25)
Swed	ARBETARKLASSEN OCH VÅRLDSLÄGET. (DEN NYA ETAPPEN.) Frams Forlag: Stockholm, 1927. 121. [2nd ed.] (LocAAS)	270000(8)
Swed	ARBETARKLASSEN OCH VÅRLDSLÄGET. (DEN NYA ETAPPEN.) Socialistiskt Bibliotek. VII: Stockholm, 1927. 121. (LocAAS)	270000(14)

Yid *ARBET, DISTSIPLIN UND ORDNUNG WELN RATEVEN DIE RATYEN   *180000(30)
     REGIERUNG. Comisariat far idische inyonim in
     Peterburg: Pet, 1918. 29.
     (LocLC)

Rum ARMATA ROSIE. Editure grupuhi din partidul comunist rus.:   190000(39)
     [M], 1919. 16.
     (LocBDIC)

Eng Breton & Rivera, ART AND REVOLUTION. See CULTURE AND
     SOCIALISM, 630000(1).

Yid DER ARTIKEL IN MANSHESTER GARDIEN. See DI TRAGEDJA FUN
     DEUTSHEN PROLETARIAT, 330400(4).

Fr et a., AUX MASSES LABORIEUSES DE FRANCE, D'ANGLETERRE,   [180000(31)]
     D'AMÉRIQUE ET DU JAPON. [Pet], [1918]. 2.
     (LocHIS)

Fr AVANT LA NOUVELLE GUERRE MONDIALE. + APRÈS "LA PAIX"   380000(3)
     IMPÉRIALISTE DE MUNICH. Parti socialiste révolutionnaire:
     Brussels, 1938. 51.
     (LocBRB/HIS/PSB)

Fr L'AVÈNEMENT DU BOLCHEVISME. Chiron; P, 1919. 142.   190000(40)
     (LocAAS/BDIC/BN/BRB/IISG/LnL/LSE/ULH/CatZ)

Fr L'AVÈNEMENT DU BOLCHEVISME. Chiron: P, 1920. 142. [2nd ed.]200000(53)
     (LocBM/BN/KBC/NYPL/PSB/ULO)

Jap *BAKURO SARETARU SOBETO ROSHIA. [Tokyo], 1930.   *300000(8)
     (LocNDL)

Ben BARTOMAN COMMUNIST ISTAHAR. Chitta Mitra: Calcutta,   [700000(3)]
     [1970]. 16.
     (LocPer)

Am *THE BASIC WRITINGS OF TROTSKY. Random House: NY, 1963.   *630000(7)
     (LocNUC)

Am THE BASIC WRITINGS OF TROTSKY. Vintage Russian Library: 650900
     NY, 1965. 428.
     (LocPer)

Eng THE BASIC WRITINGS OF TROTSKY. Secker & Warburg: Ln,   640000(5)
     1964. 428.
     (LocAAO/AAS/BM/KBS)

Eng THE BASIC WRITINGS OF TROTSKY. Mercury Books: Ln, 1964.   640000(10)
     428.
     (LocPer)

Cz   *BESEDA SE SOCIÁLNĚ-DEMOKRATICKÝM DĚLNIKEM. MLO frakce   *330000(37)
         Bolševikulenincu v K.S.Č.: Ostrava, 1933. 31.
         (CatBK)

Eng   BETWEEN RED AND WHITE. Communist Party of Great Britain: 220000(18)
         Ln, 1922. 104.
         (LocAAS/BM/CU/HIS/LSE/NYPL/O)

Eng   BETWEEN RED AND WHITE. University Microfilms: Ann Arbor,   630000(6)
         1963. 104. [Processed]
         (LocPer)

Ben   BHARATIYA SRAMIKDER PROTI KHOLA CHITHI. The Merit   690000(6)
         Publishers: Calcutta, 1969. 8.
         (LocPer)

Fr   BILAN ET PERSPECTIVES. See 1905, 690415.

Fr   et a., LES BOLCHEVIKS CONTRE STALINE. Quatrième   570000(1)
         Internationale: P, 1957. 163.
         (LocBN/NUC)

Sp   EL BOLCHEVIQUISMO ANTE LA GUERRA Y LA PAZ DEL MUNDO.   190000(41)
         Editorial Cervantes: Valencia, 1919. 192.
         (LocLC/NYPL)

Sp   *EL BOLCHEVIQUISMO ANTE LA GUERRA... Editorial Cervantes: *190000(42)
         Valencia, 1919. 268. [2 ed. notablemente aumentada.]
         (CatIT)

Sp   *EL BOLCHEVIQUISMO ANTE LA GUERRA... Editorial Cervantes: *210000(55)
         Barcelona, 1921. 202. [3 ed.]
         [Advert.]

Sp   EL BOLCHEVIQUISMO ANTE LA GUERRA... Cervantes: Barcelona,   220000(38)
         1922. 202. [4 ed.]
         (LocPer)

Fr   BOLCHEVISME ET STALINISME. + LE RÉGIME COMMUNISTE AUX   [530000(5)]
         USA. [--]: P, [1953]. 20. [Processed]
         (LocAAS)

Fr   BOLCHEVISME ET STALINISME. + LE RÉGIME COMMUNISTE AUX   [560000(5)]
         USA. [S.P.E.L.]: P, [1956]. 30.
         (LocAAS)

Sp   BOLCHEVISMO Y STALINISMO. Ediciones Mariategui: Santiago   620000(17)
         de Chile. 1962. 40.
         (LocPer)

It   IL BOLSCEVISMO DINNANZI ALLA GUERRA E ALLA PACE DE MUNDO.   200000(54)
         [--]: Milano, 1920. 95.
         (LocBDIC)

It   IL BOLSCEVISMO... Edizioni Reprint: [--], 1970. 95.   700000(16)
         (LocPer)

Eng	BOLSHEVIK CONGRESSES -- ONCE AND NOW. See THE SOVIET UNION AND THE FOURTH INTERNATIONAL, 340000(8).	
Am	THE BOLSHEVIKI AND WORLD PEACE. Boni & Livewright: NY, 1918. 238. (LocAAS/ABC/BDIC/BM/BN/CU/HIS/IISG/KBC/KBS/LnL/LSE/NYPL)	180000(32)
Jap	BOMEI NIKKI. Gendai Shiso-sha: Tokyo, 1968. 478. (LocPer)	680430
Jap	BOMEI NIKKI. Gendai Shiso-sha: Tokyo, 1969. 478. ⌊2nded.⌋ (LocPer)	690831
Eng	BONAPARTISM AND FASCISM. International Marxist Group: Ln, 1968. 6. ⌊Processed⌋ (LocPer)	680900(1)
Fr	BONAPARTISME BOURGEOIS ET BONAPARTISME SOVIÉTIQUE. ⌊--⌋: ⌊P⌋, ⌊1960⌋. 4. ⌊Processed⌋ (LocPer)	⌊600000(12)⌋
Ger	BRIEF AN EINEN ÖSTERREICHEN GENOSSEN. See ÖSTERREICH AN DER REIHE, 330000(15)	
Jap	BUNGAKU TO KAKUMEI. Gendai Shiche-sha: Tokyo, 1964. ⌊2 vol.⌋ (LocPer)	641225
Jap	BUNGAKU TO KAKUMEI. + TENKAN-KI NO BUNKA. Knizo-sha: Tokyo, 1925. 360. (LocNDL)	250720
Fr	LA BUREAUCRATIE STALINIENNE ET L'ASSASSINAT DE KIROV. Librairie du Travail: P, 1935. 42. (LocAAS/ABC/BDIC/BN/HIS/IISG/NYPL/PSB/ULO)	350000(1)
Fr	*LA BUREAUCRATIE STALINIENNE ET L'ASSASSINAT DE KIROV. ⌊--⌋: P. 1935. 32. ⌊Advert.⌋	*350000(2)
Viet	*CACH-MANG THUONG-TRUC. Groupe Bolchevik-Léniniste vietnamien en France: P, 1948. ⌊Processed⌋ ⌊Private notice⌋	*480000(11)
Eng	--: THE CAPITALIST WORLD AND THE COMMUNIST INTERNATIONAL. Publishing Office of the III International: M, 1920. 32. (LocABC)	200000(78)
It	*CARLO MARX. Mondadori: Milan, 1940. (CatLI)	*400000(10)

It	*CARLO MARX. Mondadori: Milan, 1949. (CatIT)	*490000(3)
Port	CARTA ABERTA A VANDERVELDE. See O QUÉ E A REVOLUÇÃO DE OUTUBRO, 330000(11).	
Sp	CARTA AL PROLETARIADO FRANCES. Editorial Socialismo: Puerto Rico, 1935. 14. (LocPer)	350000(3)
Eng	CENTRISM AND THE FOURTH INTERNATIONAL. See ON CENTRISM, [340000(11)].	
Am	§ CHAPTERS FROM MY DIARY. Revolutionary Age: Boston, 1918. 32. (LocNYPL/UCB)	180000(33)
Ger	DER CHARAKTER DER RUSSISCHEN REVOLUTION. Arbeiter- Buchhandlung: Vienna, 1921. 53. (LocAAS/BDIC/BN/HIS/IISG/LnL/LSE/NYPL)	210000(25)
Heb	CHAYAI. Mizpah: Jerusalem-Tel Aviv, 1930. 3 vols. (LocLC/NYPL)	300000(6)
Am	THE CHINESE REVOLUTION: PROBLEMS AND PERSPECTIVES. Bulletin of Marxist Studies, No. 1: NY, 1957. 22. (LocIISG/NUC)	570000(2)
Am	THE CHINESE REVOLUTION: PROBLEMS AND PERSPECTIVES. Merit Publishers: NY, 1969. 23. (LocPPA)	690000(4)
Jap	*CHUGOKU KAKUMEIRON. Chukoronsha: Tokyo, 1946. (CatIT)	*460000(12)
Jap	*CHUGOKU KAKUMEIRON. Gendai Shicho-sha: Tokyo, 1961. 341. (CatIT)	*610325
Jap	CHUGOKU KAKUMEIRON. Gendai Shicho-sha: Tokyo, 1964. 341. (LocPer)	640330(3)
Fr	CINQ JOURNÉES DE LA RÉVOLUTION RUSSE. Ligue Communiste Internationaliste: [P], 1934. 15. (LocPer)	340000(19)
Sp	*CLASE, PARTIDO Y DIRECCIÓN. See *LOS SINDICATOS EN LA EPOCA DE LA DECADENCIA DEL IMPERIALISMO, *[650000(13)].	
Eng	CLASS AND ART. New Park Publications: Ln, 1968. 27. (LocPer)	680300
Eng	THE CLASS NATURE OF THE SOVIET STATE. Lanka Samasamaja: Colombo, Ceylon, 1952. 22.	521200

Eng THE CLASS NATURE OF THE SOVIET STATE. WIR Publications: Ln, ⌊570000(5)⌋
    [1957], 17. ⌊Processed⌋
    (LocPer)

Eng THE CLASS NATURE OF THE SOVIET STATE. International 680900(2)
    Marxist Group: Ln, 1968. 20. ⌊Processed⌋
    (LocPer)

Eng THE CLASS NATURE OF THE SOVIET STATE. + THE WORKERS 680800(1)
    STATE AND THE QUESTION OF THERMIDOR AND BONAPARTISM.
    New Park Publications: Ln, 1968. 64.
    (LocNUC)

Eng THE CLASS NATURE OF THE SOVIET UNION. WIR: Ln, 1958. 17. 580000(10)
    ⌊Processed⌋
    (LocPer)

Eng THE CLASS NATURE OF THE SOVIET UNION. International 620000(11)
    Bookshop: Nottingham, 1962. 20. ⌊Processed⌋
    (LocPer)

Eng THE CLASS, THE PARTY AND THE LEADERSHIP. Workers ⌊570000(8)⌋
    International Review: Ln, ⌊1957⌋. 12.
    (LocPer)

Fr CLASSE OUVRIÈRE, PARTI ET SYNDICAT. Classique Rouge: 700000(6)
    P, 1970. 67.
    (LocPer)

Cz *CO JE PERMANENTNI REVOLUCI? *⌊330000(33)⌋
    [Advert.]

Eng THE COMING WORLD WAR. J.R.Strachan: Ln, 1938. 32. 380000(4)
    (LocBM/CU/IISG/0)

Fr LA COMMUNE DE PARIS ET LA RUSSIE DES SOVIETS. Humanité: 210000(26)
    P, 1921. 36.
    (LocAAS/BDIC/BM/BN/BRB/HIS/IISG/PSB)

Fr LA COMMUNE DE PARIS ET LA RUSSIE DES SOVIETS. + LES ⌊580000(7)⌋
    LEÇONS DE LA COMMUNE. La Vérité: P, ⌊1958⌋. 30.
    (LocPer)

Am COMMUNISM AND SYNDICALISM. Communist League of America: 310300(1)
    NY, 1931. 63.
    (LocAAS/BN/HIS/LC/LSE/NYPL)

Am COMMUNISM AND SYNDICALISM. See ON THE TRADE UNIONS,
    690000(13).

Eng COMMUNISM AND SYNDICALISM. [Revolutionary Socialist ⌊380000(21)⌋
    League]: [Ln], ⌊1938⌋. 25. ⌊Processed⌋
    (LocPer)

Fr	LE COMMUNISME EN FRANCE ET L'INTERNATIONALE. Humanité: P, 1922. 74. (LocBDIC/BN/HIS)	220000(19)
Am	THE COMMUNIST MANIFESTO. Vanguard Publications: Toronto, 1967. 72. (LocPer)	671100(3)
Am	THE COMMUNIST MANIFESTO. Pathfinder Press Inc.: NY, 1970. 47. (LocPer)	700200(1)
Am	THE COMMUNIST MANIFESTO TODAY. Workers Vanguard Publishing Association: [Toronto], 1963. 13. [Processed] (LocPer)	631101
Eng	THE COMMUNIST MANIFESTO TO-DAY. International Bookshop: Nottingham, 1962. 9. [Processed] (LocPer)	620000(21)
Sp	*COMO HICIMOS LA REVOLUCIÓN DE OCTUBRE. Nosotros: Madrid, 1930. 252. (CatBE/CatLEHA)	*300000(7)
Fr	COURS NOUVEAU. [--]: Courbevoie, 1924. 125. (LocAAS/ABC/BDIC/BN/HIS/IISG)	240000(39)
Sp	*LOS CRIMENES DE STALIN. Zig-Zag: Santiago de Chile, 1938. (CatIT)	*380000(15)
Sp	LOS CRIMENES DE STALIN. Zig-Zag: Santiago de Chile, 1962. 253. (LocPer)	620000(10)
Fr	LES CRIMES DE STALINE. Grasset: P, 1937. 378. (LocAAO/AAS/BDIC/BN/BRB/HIS/IISG/PSB)	371116
It	*I CRIMINI DI STALIN. Casini: Rome, 1966. 336. [Advert.]	*661200
Fr	LA CRISE DU PARTI COMMUNISTE FRANÇAIS. Humanité: P, 1922. 32. (LocBDIC/HIS/IISG)	220000(20)
Fr	LA CRISE DU PARTI COMMUNISTE FRANÇAIS. Feltrinelli Reprint: Milan, 1967. 32. (LocPer)	670000(8)
Cz	IV. INTERNACIONÁLA A SSSR. + DNEŠNI NAŠE ÚKOLY. Kopp: Prague, 1934. 23. (LocBN)	340000(2)

Port	*A IV INTERNACIONAL E A U.R.S.S. [--]: [--], [1934]. [Advert.]	*[340000(12)]
Sp	*LA IV INTERNACIONÁL Y LA GUERRA. Nueva Etapa: Rosario, Argentine, [1934]. 29. [Advert.]	*[340000(13)]
Sp	*LA IV INTERNACIONÁL Y LA U.R.S.S. [--]: [--], [1935]. [Advert.]	*[350000(22)]
Eng	CULTURE AND SOCIALISM. + MANIFESTO TOWARDS A FREE REVOLUTIONARY ART. New Park: Ln, 1963. 39. (LocPer)	630000(1)
Rum	*CUVANT CATRE TARANII SI MUNCITORII RUSI. [--]: Rumania, 1918. [Advert.]	*180000(56)
Pol	*CZEGO ONI CHCA. [--]: Smolensk-Briansk, 1920. (CatZK)	*200000(98)
Jap	DAIYON INTANASHONARU. Gendai Shicho-sha: Tokyo, 1963. 354. (LocPer)	631130
It	DALLA RIVOLUZIONE D'OTTOBRE AL TRATTATO DI PACE DI BREST-LITOWSK. Avanti!: Milan, 1919. 95. [3 ed.] (LocIISG)	190000(43)
It	DALLA RIVOLUZIONE D'OTTOBRE ... Avanti!: Milan, 1920. 85. [5 ed.] (LocBDIC)	200000(55)
It	*DALLA RIVOLUZIONE D'OTTOBRE ... Atlantica: Milan, 1945. 156. (CatLI)	*450000(1)
It	DALLA RIVOLUZIONE D'OTTOBRE ... Edizioni Reprint: [--], 1970. 95. (LocPer)	700000(17)
Port	*DA NORUEGA AO MÉXICO. (MEMORIAS). Epasa: Rio de Janeiro, 1944. 486. (CatBB)	*440000(1)
Am	THE DEATH AGONY OF CAPITALISM AND THE TASKS OF THE FOURTH INTERNATIONAL. Pioneer Publishers: NY, 1946. 66. (LocIISG)	460501
Am	THE DEATH AGONY OF CAPITALISM ... Pioneer Publishers: NY, 1964. 66. (LocPPA)	640000(9)
Am	THE DEATH AGONY OF CAPITALISM ... Pathfinder Press: NY, 1970. 46. (LocPPA)	700200(2)

Ch	[THE DEATH AGONY OF CAPITALISM]... Communist League of China: Shanghai, 1938. (LocPer)	380000(19)
Eng	THE DEATH AGONY OF CAPITALISM ... Socialist Labour League: Ln, 1956. 55. (LocPer)	560000(1)
Eng	THE DEATH AGONY OF CAPITALISM ... Socialist Labour League: Ln, 1963. 59. (LocPer)	630000(2)
Eng	THE DEATH AGONY OF CAPITALISM AND THE TASKS OF THE WORKING CLASS. WIN, Special Issue: Ln, 1938. 47. (LocAAS/IISG/LSE)	380000(5)
Eng	THE DEATH AGONY OF CAPITALISM ... WIL: Ln, 1942. 47. (LocBM)	420000(1)
Rum	DECLARAȚILE OPOZITIEI COMUNISTE INTERNATIONALE DE STINGA (BOLȘEVICI-LENINISȚI). Tipografia Art Voltaire: P, 1933. 39. (LocPer)	330000(7)
Fr	DÉCLARATION DES QUATRES. [--]: Neuves-Maisons, [1933]. 7. [Processed] (LocPer)	[330000(27)]
Fr	DÉCLARATIONS POUR LE CONGRÈS ANTIFASCISTE EUROPÉEN DE PARIS. Ligue Communiste: P, 1933. 24. (LocPer)	330000(8)
Eng	THE DEFENCE OF TERRORISM. Labour Publishing Co. & Geo. Allen & Unwin: Ln, 1921. 176. (LocABC/BM/BN/CU/HIS/LC/LnL/O)	210000(27)
Eng	THE DEFENCE OF TERRORISM. Geo. Allen & Unwin: Ln, 1935. 176. [2 ed.; new Pref.] (LocBM/CU/IISG/LC/LnL/LSE/O)	350000(4)
Ch	*[THE DEFENCE OF THE SOVIET UNION AND THE OPPOSITION.] [See note in text.]	*300000(12)
Fr	LA DÉFENSE DE L'URSS ET L'OPPOSITION. Librairie du Travail: P, 1930. 61. (LocAAS/BDIC/BM/BN/HIS/IISG/LSE/NYPL/PSB)	300000(9)
Fr	DÉFENSE DU TERRORISME. Nouvelle Revue Critique: P, 1936. 189. (LocAAS/BDIC/BN/BRB/KBS/NYPL/PSB)	360000(1)

Cz	*DĚJINY RUSKÉ REVOLUCE. Fr. Borovy: Prague, 1934-6. 3 vol (CatBK)	*340000(3)
Fr	DE LA RÉVOLUTION. Editions de Minuit: P, 1963. 654. (LocAAS/BN/BRB/KBS)	630419
Fr	DE LA RÉVOLUTION D'OCTOBRE A LA PAIX DE BREST-LITOVSK. Demain: Geneva, 1918. 158. (LocBDIC/BM/BN/IISG/LnL/LSE/NYPL/PSB)	180000(34)
Fr	DE L'OPPORTUNITÉ DU MOT D'ORDRE DES ETATS-UNIS SOCIALISTES D'EUROPE. S.P.E.L.: P, [1962]. 8. [Processed] (LocPer)	[620000(4)]
Sp	DE OCTUBRE ROJO A MI DESTIERRO. Zeus: Madrid, 1931. 229. (LocPer)	310000(5)
Ger	Lenin u. T., *DEUTSCHE DESERTEURE BERICHTEN. [--]. 1918. [Advert.]	*[180000(50)]
Sp	DIALOGO CON UN OBRERO SOCIALISTA. Comunismo: Madrid, [1933]. 31. (LocPer)	[330000(28)]
It	DIARIO D'ESILIO. Il Saggiatore: Milan, 1960. 187. (LocIISG/NUC)	600100
Am	DICTATORSHIP VS DEMOCRACY. Workers Party of America: NY, 1922. 191. (LocHIS/LC/NYPL)	220000(21)
Gr	OI DIKES TES MOSXAS. Neon Bibliopoleion: Athens, 1966. 16. (LocPer)	660000(8)
Eng	D.I.MENDELYEV AND MARXISM. See MARXISM AND SCIENCE, 491000.	
Rum	DISCURSUL. See Lenin i T, PUTERA SOVIETELOR SI CRIZA SOCIALA DIN GERMANIA (LocBDIC) [Not otherwise indexed in this section.]	
Am	DISCUSSIONS ON THE TRANSITIONAL PROGRAM. Education for Socialists; Socialist Workers Party: NY, 1969. 20. (LocPPA)	690300(2)
Fr	DISCUSSION SUR LE PROGRAMME DE TRANSITION. [--]: P, 1938. (LocPer)	[380000(8)]
Fr	DISCUSSION SUR LE PROGRAMME TRANSITOIRE. [--]: [P], [1948]. 7. [Processed] (LocPer)	[480000(9)]

Fr   90^e ANNIVERSAIRE DU MANIFESTE COMMUNISTE. See MANIFESTE
          COMMUNISTE, 370000(7).
Cz   DNEŠNI NAŠ ÚKOLY. See IV. INTERNACIONÁLA A SSSR, 340000(2).
Fr   DOCUMENTS DE L'OPPOSITION DE GAUCHE DE L'INTERNATIONALE   271000(1)
          COMMUNISTE. No. 1. Imp. Centrale de la Bourse:
          P, 1927. 69.
          (LocBN)

Fr   DOCUMENTS DE L'OPPOSITION ... No. 2. See LA PLATE-FORME
          POLITIQUE ... 271100(1).
Jap   *DOITSU WA DOKO E YUKU.   *520000(4)
          [Private notice.]
Yid   *DOJTSHLAND DER SHLISSEL ZU DER INTERNATIONALER LAGE.   *310000(35)
          Klorheit: P, 1931. 15.
          (LocJ)
Rum   *DOKUMENTY RUSKÉ OPOSICE g 1927.   *[270000(13)]
          [Advert.]
Hol   DE DOODSTRIJD VAN HET KAPITALISME ... See OVERGANGSPROGRAM,...470000(4)
Am   THE DRAFT PROGRAM OF THE COMMUNIST INTERNATIONAL. The Militant:
          NY, 1929. 139.   290000(2)
          (LocAAS/HIS/LC/LSE/NYPL)
Ch   *[THE DRAFT PROGRAM OF THE COMMUNIST INTERNATIONAL.]   *300000(5)
          [See note in text.]
Eng   THE DRAFT PROGRAMME OF THE COMMUNIST INTERNATIONAL.   540000(1)
          New Park: Ln, 1954. 63.
          (LocIISG)
Fr   LE DRAME DU PROLÉTARIAT FRANÇAIS. Librairie du Travail: 250000(13)
          P, 1925. 16.
          (LocBDIC/HIS/IISG)
Fr   LE DRAME DU PROLÉTARIAT FRANÇAIS. Librairie du Travail: 250000(14)
          P, 1925. 16. [2 ed.]
          (LocAAS/BN)
It   *UN DRAMMA GIUDIZARIO. IL PROCESSO BEYLIS. Avanti!: Milan,   *[180000(51)]
          [1918]. 15.
          (CatLI)
Hol   DUITSCHLAND, DE SLEUTEL TOT DEN INTERNATIONALEN TOESTAND.
          See ZAL HET FASCISME WERKELIK OVERWINNEN?, [310000(28)].
Fr   D'UNE EGRATIGNURE AU DANGER DE GANGRÈNE. Secrétariat   [500000(5)]
          international de la IVe Internationale: P, [1950].
          40. [Processed]
          (LocAAS)

Fr	--: DU PLAN DE LA CGT A LA CONQUÈTE DU POUVOIR. La Brèche syndicale: P, 1935. (LocBN)	350000(5)
Sp	*LA ECONOMÍA SOVIÉTICA EN PELIGRO. Bergua: Madrid, 1933. 85. (CatIT)	*330000(9)
Fr	L´ÉCONOMIE SOVIÉTIQUE EN DANGER: SIGNAL D'ALARME. Ligue Communiste: P, 1933. 30. (LocBDIC/BN/HIS/PSB)	330000(10)
Hol	DE ECONOMISCHE WERELDCRISIS EN DE NIEUWE TAAK DER COMMUNISTISCHE INTERNATIONALE. See DE GROOTE CONGRESREDE, ⌊210000(17)⌋	
Fr	ECRITS. I. Rivière et Cie: P, 1955. 372. (LocAAS/BDIC/BM/BN/IISG/KBS/LSE/NUC/ULO)	551115
Fr	ECRITS. II. Quatrième Internationale: P, 1958. 156. (LocAAS/BDIC/IISG/KBS/LSE/NUC/ULO)	580900
Fr	ECRITS. III. Quatrième Internationale: P, 1959. 575. (LocAAS/BDIC/IISG/KBS/LSE/NUC)	590400
Fr	ECRITS MILITAIRES. L'Herne: P, 1968. 1,000. (LocBN/ULO)	680000(1)
Gr	TA EGKLEMATA TOU STALIN. Prometheas: Athens, 1962. 311. (LocPer)	620000(18)
Hun	*AZ EGYETLEN ÚT. Typ. Typographis: Bratislava, 1932. 71. (CatBK)	*320000(3)
Jap	EIKOKU NANJI DOKOE IKU? Kokusai-sha: Tokyo, 1926. 248. (LocNDL)	260915
Jap	EIKOKU WA DOKOE IKU? Dojin-sha: Tokyo, 1926. 217. (LocNDL)	260930
Ger	DER EINZIGE WEG. Grylewicz: B, 1932. 64. (LocAAS/BN/IISG)	320000(5)
Jap	*EIZOKU KAKUMEIRON. Gendai Shichosha: Tokyo, 1961. 336. (LocPer)	*610805
Jap	EIZOKU KAKUMEIRON. Gendai Shicho-sha: Tokyo, 1966. 336. (LocPer)	661130
Sp	*EL EJERCITO ROJO. Biblioteca Internacional: ⌊--⌋, 1926. ⌊Advert.⌋	*260000(35)
Gr	EMEROLOGO TES EXORIAS. Dialechta Keimena: Athens, 1959. 212. (LocPer)	590000(1)

Yid	*DER EMES VEGEN RATNRUSLAND. [--]: Warsaw-NY, 1929. 302. (LocLC/NYPL)	*290000(3)
Fr	ENCORE UNE FOIS, OÙ VA LA FRANCE? La Vérité: P, [1935]. 24. (LocPer)	[350000(16)]
Fr	ENCORE UNE FOIS SUR LA NATURE DE L'URSS. [--]: P, [1960]. 12. [Processed] (LocAAS)	[600000(17)]
Sp	EN DEFENSA DEL MARXISMO. Editorial Amerindia: Buenos Aires, 1958. 188. (LocPer)	580130
Fr	ENTRE L'IMPÉRIALISME ET LA RÉVOLUTION. Humanité: P, 1922. 177. (LocAAS/BDIC/BM/BN/BRB/HIS/IISG/NYPL/PSB)	220000(22)
Fr	ENTRE L'IMPÉRIALISME ET LA RÉVOLUTION. Taupe: Brussels, 1970. 192. (LocPer)	700603
Fr	ENTRETIEN AVEC UN OUVRIER SOCIAL-DÉMOCRATE. Ligue Communiste: P, 1933. 14. (LocHIS)	330000(35)
Ger	ENTWURF EINER PLATFORM DER RUSSISCHEN OPPOSITION. ZUM 15. PARTEITAG DER WKP(B). Fahne des Kommunismus: B, [1928]. 72. (LocPer)	[280000(8)]
Sp	LA ERA DE LA REVOLUCION PERMANENTE. Saeta: Mexico, 1967. 383. (LocPer)	670000(5)
Ger	ERGEBNISSE UND PERSPEKTIVEN. Verlag Neue Kritik: Hamburg, 1967. 136. (LocABC)	670000(6)
Ger	u.a., ERKLÄRUNG DER FÜNFHUNDERT. Fahne des Kommunismus: B, [1927]. 16. (LocBN)	[270000(11)]
It	L'ESERCITO ROSSO DELLA RUSSIA. Il Solco: Città di Castello, 1921. 43. (LocNYPL/SEES)	210000(28)
Sp	ESPAÑA, ÚLTIMA ADVERTENCIA: LA LECCION DE ESPAÑA. Grupo internacionalista obrero: Santiago de Chile, 1939. 36. (LocBN)	390000(1)

Am	THE ESSENTIAL TROTSKY. Barnes & Noble: NY, 1963. 251. (LocNUC)	630000(8)
Eng	THE ESSENTIAL TROTSKY. Geo. Allen & Unwin: Ln, 1963. 251. (LocAAS/BM/KBS)	630000(9)
Fr	L'ÉTAT OUVRIER: THERMIDOR ET BONAPARTISME. Librairie du Travail: P, 1935. 28. (LocAAS/BDIC/BN/HIS/IISG/PSB)	350000(6)
Fr	L'ÉTAT OUVRIER: THERMIDOR ET BONAPARTISME. Union communiste: P, 1960. 22. [Processed] (LocPer)	600000(2)
Fr	LES ETATS-UNIS SOCIALISTES D'EUROPE. S.P.E.L.: P, [1962], 14. [Processed] (LocPer)	[620000(5)]
Gr	E ETHIKE TOUS KAI E ETHIKE MAS. Neo Bibliopoleion: [Athens], 1965. 52. (LocPer)	650000(2)
Fr	ET MAINTENANT? Rieder: P, 1932. 67. (LocAAS/BN/HIS/LC/LSE/NYPL/PSB)	320000(6)
Hol	EUROPA EN AMERIKA. De Proletarier: Gent, 1927. 142. (LocAAS/IISG)	270000(7)
Ger	EUROPA UND AMERIKA. Neuer Deutscher Verlag: B, 1926. 137. (LocAAS/BM/HIS/IISG/LC/LSE)	260000(21)
Eng	EUROPE AND AMERICA. [--]: Ln, 1933. 24. [Processed] (LocGDS)	330715(5)
Eng	EUROPE AND AMERICA. Bolshevik Samasamaja Publications: Colombo, Ceylon, 1950. 35. (LocBM)	500400
Eng	EUROPE AND AMERICA. + WHITHER EUROPE? Lanka Samasamaja: Colombo, Ceylon, 1951. 71. (LocBM/IISG)	510100
Fr	EUROPE ET AMÉRIQUE. Humanité: P, 1926. 142. (LocAAO/BDIC/BN/HIS/IISG/NYPL)	260000(22)
Cz	*EVROPA A AMERIKA. Komunisticke nakl., typ. "Svoboda": Prague, 1926. 48. (CatBK)	*260000(23)
Fr	L'EXPULSION DE LÉON TROTZKY. Lettre à Jules Guesde. La Vie Ouvrière: P, [1916]. 36. (LocIISG)	[160000(1)]
Am	THE EXPULSION OF ZINOVIEV. See SOVIET ECONOMY IN DANGER, 330200(1).	

It   *IL FALLIMENTO DELLA SECONDA INTERNAZIONALE. Il Solco: *210000(29)
         Città di Castello, 1921. 126.
         (LocNYPL)

Ger.   DIE FÄLSCHUNG DER GESCHICHTE DER RUSSISCHEN REVOLUTION.   280000(2)
         Volkswille: B, 1928. 72.
         (LocAAS/ABC/BDIC/BM/NYPL)

Fr   LA FAMILLE DECLERC. See LETTRE A JULES GUESDE, ⌊580000(9)⌋.

Yid   FARVOS STALIN NEMT AVEK MEJN BIRGER RECHT. Communist   320000(35)
         League of America(Opposition): NY, 1932. 16.
         (LocPer)

Am   FASCISM –– WHAT IT IS: HOW TO FIGHT IT. Pioneer Publishers: 440800(2)
         NY, 1944. 47.
         (LocBM/IISG/NYPL)

Am   FASCISM: WHAT IT IS: HOW TO FIGHT IT. Merit: NY, 1969. 30.   690400(3)
         (LocPer)

Am   FASCISM: WHAT IT IS: HOW TO FIGHT IT. Merit: NY, 1970. 30.   700300(2)
         (LocPer)

Eng   FASCISM –– WHAT IT IS: HOW TO FIGHT IT. International   620900
         Bookshop: Nottingham, 1962. 24. ⌊Processed⌋
         (LocPer)

Eng   THE FI AND THE USSR. Lanka Samasamaja: Colombo, Ceylon,   560900(1)
         1956. 9.
         (LocPer)

Eng   *THE FI AND THE USSR. ⌊Ln⌋, ⌊1943⌋.   *430800(3)
         ⌊Advert.⌋

Eng   THE FIGHT FOR MARXISM. New Park: Ln, 1966. 30.   600800(2)
         (LocPer)

Am   THE FIRST FIVE YEARS OF THE COMMUNIST INTERNATIONAL. Vol.I.   451000
         Pioneer Publishers: NY, 1945. 374.
         (LocAAS/ABC/BM/CU/HIS/IISG/KBS/LC/LSE/NLS/NYPL/O)

Am-Eng THE FIRST FIVE YEARS.... Vol. II. Pioneer Publishers: 530700
         NY-Ln, 1953. 384.
         (LocAAS/ABC/BM/CU/HIS/IISG/KBS/LC/LSE/NLS/NYPL/O)

Eng   FLIGHT FROM SIBERIA. Young Socialist Publications: 690100
         Colombo, Ceylon, 1969. 56.
         (LocPer)

Am   FOR A UNITED FRONT AGAINST FASCISM. See GERMANY –– KEY TO
         THE INTERNATIONAL SITUATION, 320000(9).

Eng   FOR A UNITED FRONT AGAINST FASCISM. See GERMANY –– KEY TO
         THE INTERNATIONAL SITUATION, 440000(2)

Eng	THE FOREIGN POLICY OF SOVIET RUSSIA. B.S.P.: Ln, ⌊1920⌋. 32. (LocBM)	⌊200000(93)⌋
Swed	DEN FÖRRÅDA REVOLUTIONEN. Partisan Förlaget: Mölndal, 1969. 234. (LocPer)	690600(2)
Den	ET FORSVAR FOR DEN RUSSISKE REVOLUTION. Danske Sektion af Internationale Kommunister (Bolschewiker-Leninister): ⌊Copenhagen⌋, ⌊1935⌋. 23. ⌊Processed⌋ (LocKBC)	⌊350000(15)⌋
Eng	*THE FOURTH INTERNATIONAL AND THE SOVIET UNION. Bolshevik-Leninist Party of India: ⌊--⌋, 1943. ⌊Advert.⌋	*430800(2)
Sp	EL FRACASO DEL PLAN QUINQUENAL. + NUEVO ZIGZAG Y NUEVOS PELIGROS. Nueva Epoca: Santiago de Chile, 1933. 55. (LocPer)	330000(36)
Ger	DIE FRAGEN DER ARBEITERBEWEBUNG IN FRANKREICH UND DIE KOMMUNISTISCHE INTERNATIONALE. Carl Hoym: Hamburg, 1922. 31. (LocAAS/ABC/IISG/LC/LnL)	220000(23)
Ger	FRAGEN DES ALLTAGSLEBENS. C.Hoym: Hamburg, 1923. 169. (LocAAS/BDIC/BM/HIS/IISG/KBC/LSE/NYPL/ULH)	230000(26)
Den	FRA NOVEMBERREVOLUTIONEN TIL BREST-LITOWSK-FREDEN. Europaisk Forlag: Copenhagen, ⌊1919⌋. 150. (LocABC/IISG/KBC/LC/ULO)	⌊190000(61)⌋
Eng	FROM A SCRATCH TO THE DANGER OF GANGRENE. ⌊--⌋: Ln, ⌊1942⌋. ⌊Processed⌋ (LocPer)	⌊420000(5)⌋
Am	FROM OCTOBER TO BREST-LITOVSK. Socialist Publishing Society: NY, 1919. 100. (LocBDIC/BM/IISG/NYPL)	190000(44)
Jap	*FURANSU WA DOKO E IKU. Gendai Shicho-sha: Tokyo, 1963. 326. (CatIT)	*630430.
Sp	LOS GANGSTERS DE STALIN. Editorial America: Mexico, 1940. 191. (LocPer)	400000(1)

Ger	DIE GEBURT DER ROTEN ARMEE. Verlag für Literatur und Politik: Vienna, 1924. 216. (LocAAS/ABC/BDIC/BM/BN/HIS/IISG/LC/LSE/NYPL/ULH)	240000(40)
Ger	*DIE GEBURT DER ROTEN ARMEE. [—]: Leipzig, 1924. 216. (CatDB)	*240000(41)
Ger	GEGEN DEN NATIONALKOMMUNISMUS. + ÜBER ARBEITERKONTROLLE DER PRODUKTION. Grylewicz: B, 1931. 36. (LocBN/IISG/LSE)	310000(6)
Ger	GEGEN DEN NATIONALKOMMUNISMUS. Grylewicz: B, 1932. 24. 2nd ed. (LocAAS/ABC/BN/HIS/IISG/PSB)	320000(7)
Ger	GEGEN DEN NATIONALKOMMUNISMUS. Grylewicz: B, 1932. 24. 3rd ed. (LocAAS/NYPL)	320000(8)
Sin	GENERAL STRIKAYATA YUDDAYA NAVATVIYA HAKIDA? Lanka Samasamaja: Colombo, Ceylon, 1951. 8. (LocPer)	510400
Fr	GEORGES VALENTINOVITCH PLEKHANOV. S.P.E.L.: P, [1962]. 12. [Processed] (LocPer)	[620000(6)]
Eng	GEORGE VALENTINOVICH PLEKHANOV. Fight Pamphlet: Colombo, Ceylon, 1949. 5. (LocIISG)	490700
Eng	GEORGE VALENTINOVICH PLEKHANOV. International Bookshop: Nottingham, [1961]. 5. [Processed] (LocPer)	[610000(18)]
Am	GERMANY — THE KEY TO THE INTERNATIONAL SITUATION. + FOR A UNITED FRONT AGAINST FASCISM. Pioneer Publishers: NY, 1932. 45. (LocHIS/NYPL)	320000(9)
Eng	GERMANY — THE KEY TO THE INTERNATIONAL SITUATION. + FOR A UNITED FRONT AGAINST FASCISM. Revolutionary Communist Party: Ln, 1944. 47. (LocAAS/BM/CU/IISG/LSE)	440000(2)
Eng	GERMANY — THE KEY TO THE INTERNATIONAL SITUATION. + FOR A UNITED FRONT AGAINST FASCISM. Lanka Samasamaja: Colombo, Ceylon, 1958. 33. (LocBM/IISG/NUC)	581100
Eng	GERMANY: 1931-1932. New Park: Ln, 1970. 304 (LocPer)	700500

Ger	GESCHICHTE DER RUSSISCHEN REVOLUTION. S.Fischer Verlag: B, 1931. 2 vol. (LocAAS/ABC/BM/BN/HIS/IISG/KBC/KBS/LC/NYPL/ULH)	310000(7)
Ger	GESCHICHTE DER RUSSISCHEN REVOLUTION. S.Fischer Verlag: Frankfurt, 1960. 759. (LocIISG)	600000(3)
Ger	GESCHICHTE DER RUSSISCHEN REVOLUTION. S.Fischer Verlag: Frankfurt, 1967. 759. (LocPer)	670000(1)
Hol	GESCHIEDENIS DER RUSSISCHE REVOLUTIE. Querido: Amsterdam, 1936. 5 vol. (LocBRB/IISG)	360000(2)
Yid	*DI GESHICHTE FUN DER RUSISHER REVOLJUTSJA. [--]: Warsaw-B, 1932. (LocJ)	*320000(34)
Pol	i Stalin, *GOSPODARKA SOWIECKA U PROGU 2-giej PIATILETKI. Nowa Era: Warsaw, 1933. 64. (CatIT)	*330000(41)
Sp	*EL GRAN ORGANIZADOR DE DERROTAS. Hoy: Madrid, 1930. 348. (CatBE/CatLEHA)	*300000(10)
Sp	*EL GRAN ORGANIZADOR DE DERROTAS. Olimpo: Buenos Aires, 1965. [Advert.]	*650000(12)
Hol	GROEPERINGEN IN DE COMMUNISTISCHE OPPOSITIE. [--]: Amsterdam, :1945]. 5. Processed. (LocPer)	[450000(4)]
Hol	DE GROOTE CONGRESREDE VAN TROTSKY. DE EKONOMISCHE WERELDCRISIS EN DE NIEUWE TAAK DER COMMUNISTISCHE INTERNATIONALE. Communistische Partij: Amsterdam, [1921]. 61. (LocIISG)	[210000(47)]
Ger	GRUNDFRAGEN DER REVOLUTION. Carl Hoym: Hamburg, 1923. 475. (LocAAO/AAS/ABC/LSE/NYPL/PSB/CatZ)	230000(27)
Ger	GRUNDFRAGEN DER REVOLUTION. Carl Hoym: Hamburg, 1923. 475. 2nd ed. (LocHIS/LC/NYPL)	230000(28)
Ger	GRUNDFRAGEN DER REVOLUTION. Feltrinelli: Milan, [1967]. 475. [Processed reprint of 230000(28).] (LocPer)	[670000(3)]

Sp	—: LA GUERRA Y LA IV INTERNACIONAL. Publicaciones LCI: Mexico, 1937. 32. (LocPer)	370700
Ger	u.a., DIE HELDEN DER WIENER KONFERENZ. [—]: Vienna, 1921. (LocIISG)	210000(30)
Hol	en Maksim Gorkij, HERINNERINGEN AAN LENIN. N.V. de Arbeiderspers: Amsterdam, 1967. 200. (LocPer)	670000(14)
Fr	HISTOIRE DE LA RÉVOLUTION RUSSE. Rieder: P, 1933. 4 vols. (LocAAS/BDIC/BRB/CU/HIS/IISG/PSB/CatZ)	330100(3)
Fr	HISTOIRE DE LA RÉVOLUTION RUSSE. Editions du Seuil: P, 1950. 2 vols. (LocBN/ULH)	500000(1)
Fr	HISTOIRE DE LA RÉVOLUTION RUSSE. Editions du Seuil: P, 1110. (LocBDIC/BN)	620000(1)
Fr	HISTOIRE DE LA RÉVOLUTION RUSSE. Editions du Seuil: P, 2 vols. (LocPer)	670000(17)
Sp	HISTORIA DE LA REVOLUCIÓN RUSA. Editorial Cervantes: Valencia, 1919. 218. (LocBM/LC)	190000(45)
Sp	*HISTORIA DE LA REVOLUCIÓN RUSA. Editorial Cervantes: Valencia, 1919. 2nd ed. (LocLC)	*190000(89)
Sp	*HISTORIA DE LA REVOLUCIÓN RUSA. Cenit: Madrid, 1931. 2 vols. (Vol. I LocNYPL)	*310000(8)
Sp	*HISTORIA DE LA REVOLUCIÓN RUSA. Ed. Indoamérica: Buenos Aires, 1954. 288. [Vol. 1 of 4] (CatBBA/CatIT)	*540123
Sp	HISTORIA DE LA REVOLUCIÓN RUSA. Tilcara: Buenos Aires, 1962. 2 vol. (LocPer)	620000(16)
Pol	*HISTORJA REWOLUCJI ROSYJSKIEJ. Bibljon: Warsaw, 1932. 3 vols. (CatIT)	*320000(30)

Am	THE HISTORY OF THE RUSSIAN REVOLUTION. Simon & Schuster: NY, 1932. 3 vols. (LocHIS/LC/NYPL)	320000(10)
Am	THE HISTORY OF THE RUSSIAN REVOLUTION. Simon & Schuster: NY, 1936. 1 vol. [Pagination as in 1st ed.] (LocCU/LC/NYPL)	360000(3)
Am	THE HISTORY OF THE RUSSIAN REVOLUTION. Simon & Schuster: NY, 1937. (LocPer)	370000(27)
Am	THE HISTORY OF THE RUSSIAN REVOLUTION. Ann Arbor: Univ. of Michigan, 1957. (LocBM/KBS/LC/LSE)	570000(3)
Am	THE HISTORY OF THE RUSSIAN REVOLUTION. Ann Arbor: Univ. of Michigan, 1960. 2nd ed. (LocBM)	600000(29)
Am	THE HISTORY OF THE RUSSIAN REVOLUTION. Ann Arbor: Univ. of Michigan, 1961. 3rd ed. (LocPer)	610000(1)
Am	THE HISTORY OF THE RUSSIAN REVOLUTION. Ann Arbor: Univ. of Michigan, 1964. 4th ed. (LocPer)	640000(7)
Ch	*[THE HISTORY OF THE RUSSIAN REVOLUTION.] Communist League of China: Shanghai, 1940. 3 vols. [Private notice.]	*[400000(2)]
Ch	[THE HISTORY OF THE RUSSIAN REVOLUTION.] [Society of Historical Studies]: [? Hong Kong], [1970]. 3 vols. (LocPer)	[700000(13)]
Eng	THE HISTORY OF THE RUSSIAN REVOLUTION. Gollancz: Ln, 1932. 3 vols. (LocAAO/BM/BN/CU/LC/LnL/LSE/NYPL/O)	320600(1)
Eng	THE HISTORY OF THE RUSSIAN REVOLUTION. Gollancz: Ln, 1934. 1295. (LocABC/BM/LnL/O)	340900
Eng	THE HISTORY OF THE RUSSIAN REVOLUTION. Gollancz: Ln, 1936. 1295. (LocPer)	360400(1)
Eng	THE HISTORY OF THE RUSSIAN REVOLUTION. Gollancz: Ln, 1965. 1295. (LocBRB)	650000(8)

Eng	THE HISTORY OF THE RUSSIAN REVOLUTION. Gollancz: Ln, 1965. 1295. (LocULO)	651000
Eng	THE HISTORY OF THE RUSSIAN REVOLUTION. Sphere Books: Ln, 1967. 3 vols. (LocPer)	670000(11)
Eng	THE HISTORY OF THE RUSSIAN REVOLUTION TO BREST-LITOVSK. Geo. Allen & Unwin: Ln, 1919. 153. (LocBDIC/BM/BN/CU/IISG/KBS/LC/LnL/LSE/NYPL/O/SEES/ULO)	190400(2)
Eng	THE HISTORY OF THE RUSSIAN REVOLUTION TO BREST-LITOVSK. Socialist Labour Party: Glasgow, 1919. 153. (LocPer)	190700
Eng	HUE AND CRY OVER KRONSTADT. Socialist Labour League: Ln, [1961]. 10. [Processed] (LocAAS)	[610000(9)]
Ger	DAS HUNGERNDE RUSSLAND UND DAS "SATTE" EUROPA. Malik: B, 1921. 30. (LocAAS/ABC/HIS/IISG/LSE/NYPL/ULO)	210000(31)
Ger	DAS HUNGERNDE RUSSLAND UND DAS "SATTE" EUROPA. Malik: B, 1922. 30. 2nd ed. (LocBM)	220000(24)
Hol	HUN MORAAL EN DE ONZE. Prometheus: Amsterdam, 1946. 31. (LocIISG)	460000(2)
Hol	HUN MORAAL EN DE ONZE. Politeia: Amsterdam, 1969. 79. (LocIISG)	690000(16)
Am	IF AMERICA SHOULD GO COMMUNIST. Pioneer Publishers: NY, 1957. 21. (LocBM/NUC)	570900(1)
Ger	IHRE MORAL UND UNSERE. Voltaire Verlag: B, 1967. 84. (LocPer)	671000
Eng	THE ILP AND THE FOURTH INTERNATIONAL: IN THE MIDDLE OF THE ROAD. WIL: Ln, [1942]. 16. (LocCU/IISG/LSE)	[420000(2)]
Eng	THE ILP AND THE FOURTH INTERNATIONAL: IN THE MIDDLE OF THE ROAD. Lanka Samasamaja: Colombo, Ceylon. 1959. 38. (LocAAS/IISG/NUC)	590700

| Am | THE ILP AND THE STRUGGLE FOR THE FOURTH INTERNATIONAL: IN THE MIDDLE OF THE ROAD. [Reprinted from <u>New International</u>]: NY, [1935]. 15. (LocPer) | [350000(17)] |

Am THE ILP AND THE STRUGGLE FOR THE FOURTH INTERNATIONAL: IN
THE MIDDLE OF THE ROAD. [Reprinted from <u>New
International</u>]: NY, [1935]. 15.
(LocPer)   [350000(17)]

Eng IMPERIALIST WAR AND REVOLUTIONARY PERSPECTIVES. + LENIN   430800(1)
ON IMPERIALISM. Bolshevik-Leninist Party of India:
Calcutta, 1943. 50.
(LocPer)

Am IMPERIALIST WAR AND THE WORLD PROLETARIAN REVOLUTION.
See MANIFESTO OF THE FOURTH INTERNATIONAL, 380903(1).

Eng IN DEFENCE OF INSURRECTION. Lanka Samasamaja: Colombo,   541000
Ceylon, 1954. 16.
(LocAAS/BM/IISG)

Eng IN DEFENCE OF MARXISM. New Park: Ln, 1966. 263.   661100
(LocPer)

Eng IN DEFENCE OF OCTOBER. [--]: Colombo, Ceylon, 1949. 27.   490800
(LocPer)

Eng IN DEFENCE OF OCTOBER. Young Socialist: Colombo, Ceylon,   620500
1962. 23.
(LocABC)

Am IN DEFENSE OF MARXISM. Pioneer Publishers: NY, 1942. 211.   421200
(LocAAS/BM/HIS/IISG/LC/LSE/NYPL)

Am IN DEFENSE OF MARXISM. Pioneer Publishers: NY,[1964]. 211.   [640000(3)]
(LocPer)

Am IN DEFENSE OF MARXISM. Merit: NY, 1965. 211.   650000(6)
(LocPer)

Am IN DEFENSE OF MARXISM. Pathfinder: NY, 1970. 211.   700000(11)
(LocPer)

Am IN DEFENSE OF THE RUSSIAN REVOLUTION. Pioneer Publishers   330200(3)
for the Communist League of America (Opposition):
NY, 1933. 45.
(LocAAS/HIS/LC/LSE/NYPL)

Am IN DEFENSE OF THE SOVIET UNION. Pioneer Publishers: NY,   [370000(3)]
[1937]. 40.
(LocBM/BN/HIS/NYPL)

Am THE INDICTMENT. See THE KIROV ASSASSINATION, 350200(1).

It IN DIFESA DEL MARXISMO. Samona i Savelli: Rome, 1969. 364.   690224
(LocPer)

It *GL'INSEGNAMENTI DELL'OTTOBRE. Avanti!: Milan, 1925. 65.   *250000(15)
(LocAAS)

It   GL'INSEGNAMENTI DELL'OTTOBRE. + LETTERA A OLMINSKI.   ⌊660000(2)⌋
            Feltrinelli Reprint: Milan, ⌊1966⌋. 51.
            (LocPer)

Jap   *INTANASHIONARU TO SENSO. Gendai Shicho-sha: Tokyo, 1961.   *610000(17)
            ⌊Advert.⌋

Eng   THE INTELLIGENTSIA AND SOCIALISM. 'Fourth International':   660100
            Ln, 1966. 16.
            (LocPer)

Fr   L'INTERNATIONALE COMMUNISTE APRÈS LÉNINE. Rieder: P,   301100(1)
            1930. 438.
            (LocAAS/ABC/BDIC/BN/BRB/HIS/IISG/KBC/KBS/LC/LSE/NYPL/SEES)

Fr   L'INTERNATIONALE COMMUNISTE APRÈS LÉNINE. Presses   690000(1)
            Universitaires de Paris: P, 1969. 2 vol.
            (LocNUC)

Ger   DIE INTERNATIONALE REVOLUTION UND DIE KOMMUNISTISCHE   290000(4)
            INTERNATIONALE. E.Laub'sche: B, 1929. 208.
            (LocAAS/ABC/BDIC/BM/HIS/IISG/KBC/LC/LnL/LSE/NYPL)

Eng   & Varga: THE INTERNATIONAL SITUATION. Communist Party of   ⌊210000(48)⌋
            Great Britain: Ln, ⌊1921⌋. 20.
            (LocBM/CU/HIS/O)

Eng   IN THE MIDDLE OF THE ROAD. International Perspectives   700800(2)
            Publication: Brighton, 1970. 27.
            (LocPer)

Arab   AL IRHAB WAL CHIOUÏA. Institut de Damas: Damascus,   ⌊640000(8)⌋
            ⌊1964⌋. 313.
            (LocPer)

Am   I STAKE MY LIFE! Pioneer Publishers: NY, 1937. 24.   370000(1)
            (LocAAS/BM/BN/CU/HIS/IISG/LSE/NYPL)

Eng   I STAKE MY LIFE! Socialist Labour Party of Australia: 370000(2)
            Sydney, 1937.
            (LocNYPL)

Eng   I STAKE MY LIFE. British Committee for the Defence of   ⌊370000(21)⌋
            Leon Trotsky: Ln, ⌊1937⌋. 15.
            (LocBM/IISG)

Eng   I STAKE MY LIFE. WIL: Ln, ⌊1943⌋. 24.   ⌊430000(2)⌋
            (LocPer)

Eng   I STAKE MY LIFE. Lanka Samasamaja: Colombo, Ceylon,   501200
            1950. 20.
            (LocIISG)

Gr   ISTORIA TES ROSIKES EPANASTASE. Prometheas: Athens, 1961.   610000(19) +
            (LocPer)   650000(9)

Fin	JATKUVA VALLANKUMOUS. Tammi: Helsinki, 1970. 139.	700000(15)
	(LocPer)	
Lat	*JAUNATNEI. [Podolenie: KAS IS LENINISMUS.] M, 1924.	*240000(42)
	(CatKL)	
Fr	JEAN JAURÈS. Vs. Tsentrs. Ispol. Kom. R., S., Kr., i	180000(36)
	K. Dep.: M, 1918. 16.	
	(LocBDIC/BM/HIS)	
Fr	JEAN JAURÈS. Humanité: P, 1924. 16.	240000(43)
	(LocHIS)	
Fr	JEAN JAURÈS. S.P.E.L.: P, 1960. 15.	600000(4)
	(LocBDIC)	
Yid	*JEAN JAURÈS. Pet, 1919.	*190000(46)
	(Per Ch.A.)	
Cz	*JEDINÁ CESTA. [--]: [--], [1932].	*[320000(25)]
	[Advert.]	
Hun	*JEDINÁ CESTA. [--]: [--], [1932].	*[320000(26)]
	[Advert.]	
Nor	JEG INNESTÅR MED MITT LIV! Tidsskrift: Oslo, 1937. 23.	370000(4)
	(LocAAO/AAS/ULO)	
Fr	JOURNAL D'EXIL: 1935. Gallimard: P, 1960. 223.	600210
	(LocAAS/BDIC/BN/KBS/NUC)	
Ger	DER JUNGE LENIN. Molden: Vienna, 1969. 271.	690000(5)
	(LocNUC)	
Ger	u.a.: DER KAMPF UM DIE KOMMUNISTISCHE INTERNATIONALE.	[270000(12)]
	Fahne des Kommunismus: [B], [1927]. 175.	
	(LocBM/IISG)	
Swed	KAPITALISMENS DÖDSKAMP OCH IV INTERNATIONALENS UPPGIFTER.	691100(3)
	Partisan Förlag AB: Mölndal, 1969. 53.	
	(LocPer)	
Den	KAPITALISMENS DØDSKAMP OG IV. INTERNATIONALES OPGAVER.	[680000(5)]
	Revolutionaere Socialister: Copenhagen, [1968].	
	28. [Processed]	
	(LocPer)	
Ger	KAPITALISMUS ODER SOZIALISMUS? Neuer Deutscher Verlag:	250000(16)
	B, 1925. 109.	
	(LocAAS/IISG/LSE/NYPL/ULO)	
Ger	KAPITALISMUS ODER SOZIALISMUS? Neuer Deutscher Verlag:	260000(24)
	B, 1926. 109. 2 ed.	
	(LocBM)	

| Ger | —; DIE KAPITALISTISCHE WELT UND DIE KOMMUNISTISCHE INTERNATIONALE. Verlag der Kommunistische Internationale: [Pet], 1920. 32. (LocABC) | 200000(94) |

Ger   —; DIE KAPITALISTISCHE WELT UND DIE KOMMUNISTISCHE   200000(94)
         INTERNATIONALE. Verlag der Kommunistische Internationale:
         [Pet], 1920. 32.
         (LocABC)

Hol   —; DE KAPITALISTISCHE WERELD EN DE COMMUNISTISCHE   210000(33)
         INTERNATIONALE. Communistische Partij: [Amsterdam],
         1921. 48.
         (LocPer)

Cz   *KAPITOLY Z MÉHO DENNIKU. [—]: Chicago, [1919]. 30.   *[190000(63)]
         (CatBK/CatSCL)

Fr   KARL LIEBKNECHT ET ROSA LUXEMBOURG. Editions de   190000(47)
         l'Internationale Communiste: Pet, 1919. 30.
         (LocBM/HIS/LSE)

Ger   KARL LIEBKNECHT UND ROSA LUXEMBURG. Verlag der   190000(48)
         Kommunistische Internationale: Pet, 1919. 32.
         (LocABC/BM/LnL/LSE)

Jap   *KATOTEKI KORYO. [—]: Tokyo, [1960].   *[600000(18)]
         [Advert.]

Jap   KATOTEKI KORYO. + TEI KOKUSHUGI NO BOTSURAKUKI NIOKEKU   700831
         KODOKUMIAI. Shinjidaisha: Tokyo, 1970. 50.
         (LocPer)

Heb   *KEITSAD NITSACH STALIN? [—]: Jerusalem, 1937.   *370000(5)
         (LocJ)

Yid   *DI KINDER WEGEN DER OKTYABR REVOLUTIE. [—]: Zhitomir,   *210000(34)
         1921.
         (Per Ch.A.)

Am   THE KIROV ASSASSINATION. + THE INDICTMENT. Pioneer   350200(1)
         Publishers: NY, 1935. 32.
         (LocAAS/HIS/LC/LSE/NYPL)

Am   THE KIROV ASSASSINATION. + THE INDICTMENT. Pioneer   560501
         Publishers: NY, 1956. 32.
         (LocIISG)

Jap   KOKUJIN KAKUMEI RON. Nagoya: Fubaisha, 1968. 154.   681010
         (CatIT)

Swed   KOMMUNISMEN OCH TERRORN. Fram: Stockholm, 1921. 271.   210000(35)
         (LocAAO/AAS/ABC/IISG/KBS/ULH/ULO)

Swed   KOMMUNISMEN OCH TERRORN. Fram: Stockholm, 1927. 256.   270000(19)
         (LocAAS)

Swed   KOMMUNISMEN OCH TERRORN. Boklagret: Stockholm, 1928. 256.   280000(4)
         (LocAAS)

Ger	KOMMUNISMUS ODER STALINISMUS? 4. Internationale: [--], 1947. 38. (LocPer)	470000(2)
Hun	*A KOMMUNISTA INTERNACIONALE KIALTVÁNYA A VILÁG PROLETÁRJAINOZ. Közokt. Nepbizt.: Budapest, 1919. 12. (CatGV)	*190000(73)
Den	DET KOMMUNISTISKE MANIFEST. Leninistisk Arbejdgruppe: Copenhagen, ⌊1937⌋. 15. ⌊Processed⌋ (LocABC/BN)	⌊370000(22)⌋
Jap	*KOMUNISTO INTANASHONARU NO SAISHO NO GOKANEN. Gendai Shicho-sha: Tokyo, 1962. 2 vol. (CatIT)	*621130
Jap	KOMUNISTO INTANASHONARU NO SAISHO NO GOKANEN. Gendai Shich-sha: Tokyo, 1966. 2 vol. 2nd ed. (LocPer)	660228
Ger	DER KRIEG UND DIE INTERNATIONALE. Borba: ⌊Zurich⌋,⌊1914⌋. 61. (LocIISG)	⌊140000(3)⌋
Ger	DER KRIEG UND DIE INTERNATIONALE. [--]: Zurich, 1914. 61. (LocAAS/ABC/BDIC/BM/BN/HIS/IISG/LC/LSE/CatZ)	140000(1)
Ger	DER KRIEG UND DIE INTERNATIONALE. Kommissionsverlag der Buchhandlung des Schweizes Grütlivereins: Zurich, 1914. 61. (LocIISG)	140000(2)
Ger	*DER KRIEG UND DIE INTERNATIONALE. ⌊--⌋: B, 1917. (LocNYPL)	*170000(7)
Ger	DER KRIEG UND DIE INTERNATIONALE. Sozialistischen Partei der Vereinigten Staaten: Chicago, ⌊1918⌋. 85. (LocLC/NYPL)	⌊180000(52)⌋
Ger	DER KRIEG UND DIE INTERNATIONALE. J.Borchardt: B, 1919. 64. (LocAAS/BDIC/IISG/LSE)	190300(4)
Ger	DER KRIEG UND DIE INTERNATIONALE. Futurus-Verlag: Munich, ⌊1919⌋. 87. (LocIISG)	⌊190000(63)⌋
Ger	Lenin u. T, KRIEG UND REVOLUTION. Kommissionsverlag der Grütlibuchhandlung: Zurich, 1918. 168. (LocBDIC/BN/KBC/NYPL/O/ULO)	180000(37)

Am	THE LABOR PARTY IN AMERICA. Vanguard: Toronto, [1962]. 37.		[620000(15)]
	(LocPer)		
Ger	DIE LAGE DER PARTEI UND DIE AUFGABEN DER LINKEN OPPOSITION.		300000(11)
	A.Müller: B, 1930. 15.		
	(LocBN/HIS/LSE)		
It	LAVORO, DISCIPLINA E ORDINE SALVERANNO LA REPUBLICA		190000(50)
	SOCIALISTA DEI SOWJET. Avanti!: Milan, 1919. 47.		
	(LocBDIC/HIS)		
It	LAVORO ... Edizioni Reprint: [--], 1970. 47.		700000(18)
	(LocPer)		
Heb	*LDARKO SHEL MA-AMAD HAPOALIM BGERMANJA. [--]: Merchavja,		*320000(11)
	Israel, 1932.		
	(Per Ch.A.)		
Sp	LECCIONES DE OCTUBRE. See ¿QUÉ FUÉ LA REVOLUCIÓN DE		
	OCTUBRE?, 530000(4).		
Fr	LEÇON D'ESPAGNE: DERNIER AVERTISSEMENT. Pionniers:		460000(3)
	P, 1946. 73.		
	(LocAAS/ABC/BDIC/BN/HIS)		
Fr	LES LEÇONS DE LA COMMUNE. See LA COMMUNE DE PARIS ET		
	LA RUSSIE DES SOVIETS, [580000(7)].		
Am	LENIN. Minton, Balch & Co.: NY, 1925. 216.		250000(17)
	(LocABC/BDIC/HIS/LC/NYPL)		
Am	LENIN. Blue Ribbon: NY, 1934. 216.		340000(18)
	(LocPer)		
Am	LENIN. Garden City: NY, 1959. 216.		590000(4)
	(LocNUC)		
Am	LENIN. Capricorn: NY, 1962. 216.		620000(9)
	(LocPer)		
Den	Gorki og T., LENIN. Mondes Forlag: Copenhagen, 1931. 32.		310000(25)
	(LocABC/KBC/ULO)		
Eng	LENIN. Harrap: Ln, 1925. 247.		250000(18)
	(LocBM/CU/LnL/LSE/O/SEES/ULO)		
Eng	LENIN. Plebs-Harrap: Ln, 1925. 247.		250000(19)
	(LocPer)		
Eng	LENIN. Lanka Samasamaja: Colombo, Ceylon, 1951. 20.		510300
	(LocIISG)		
It	LENIN. Rinascita: Milan, [1943]. 223.		[430000(5)]
	(LocPer)		
It	LENIN. Samonà e Savelli: Rome, 1964. 258.		640110
	(LocPer)		

It	LENIN. Samonà e Savelli: Rome, 1967. 256. (LocPer)	670310
Jap	*LENIN. Shikomashobo: Tokyo, 1962. (CatIT)	*620000(19)
Sp	LENIN. Libreria Beltran: Catalonia-Barcelona, 1927. 209. (LocAAS)	270000(9)
Fr	LÉNINE. Librairie du Travail: P, 1925. 229. (LocAAS/BDIC/BN/HIS/IISG/NYPL/PSB/ULH/CatZ)	250000(20)
Fr	LÉNINE. Union Communiste: P, 1958. 9. ⌊Processed⌋ (LocPer)	580000(9)
Fr	LÉNINE. Presses Universitaires: P, 1970. 298. (LocPer)	700000(7)
Gr	O LENIN ENANTION TES GRAPHEIOKRATIAS. Neon Bibliopoleion: Athens, 1966. 64. (LocPer)	660000(9)
Jap	LENIN KAISO-KI. Erunosu: Tokyo, 1925. 266. (LocNDL)	251016
Eng	LENIN ON IMPERIALISM. See IMPERIALIST WAR AND REVOLUTIONARY PERSPECTIVES, 430800(1).	
Jap	*LENIN SHIGO NO DAISAN INTANASHONARU. Gendai Shicho-sha: Tokyo, 1961. 361. (CatIT)	*610515
Jap	*LENIN SHIGO NO DAISAN INTANASHONARU. Gendai Shich-sha: Tokyo, 1962. ⌊Advert.⌋	*620925
Jap	LENIN SHIGO NO DAISAN INTANASHONARU. Gendai Shicho-sha: Tokyo, 1964. 361. (LocPer)	640330(1)
Mal	LENINTE ANTYA LEKHANAM. Theenalam Publications: Madavaramba, Irinjalakanda, 1958. 63. (LocPer)	580225
Hun	LENIN VÉGRENDELETE. Levele a pàrt torténelmi intézetéhez: P, 1930. 16. (LocBN)	300700(3)
Turc	LENIN YOK! Yokdir indi Lenin! Sredno-aziatskoe gosudarstvennoe izdatel´stvo: Tashkent, 1924. 7. (LocLOV)	240000(56)
Am	LEON SEDOFF, SON -- FRIEND -- FIGHTER. Young People's Socialist League: NY, 1938. 27. (LocAAS/BM/HIS/IISG/NYPL)	380300(1)

Ch	*[LEON SEDOFF -- SON -- FRIEND -- FIGHTER.] [See BO, (74), II.39): Letter from Shanghai.]	*[390200(3)]
Eng	LEON SEDOFF, SON -- FRIEND -- FIGHTER. International Bookshop: Nottingham, 1962. 11. [Processed] (LocPer)	620000(13)
Eng	LEON SEDOV, SON -- FRIEND -- FIGHTER. A Young Socialist Pamphlet: Ln, 1967. 48. (LocPer)	671200
Fr	LÉON SEDOV. S.P.E.L.: P, 1953. 18. [Processed] (LocAAS)	530000(2)
Ger	LEON TROTSKI'S ANTWORT AUF KARL KAUTSKY'S "TERRORISMUS UND KOMMUNISMUS". Arbeiter Bildung's Zentrale für die Vereinigten Staaten:NY, 1920. 74. (LocBM/NYPL)	200000(57)
Am	LESSONS OF OCTOBER. Pioneer Publishers: NY, 1937. 125. (LocAAS/BM/LC/LSE/NUC/NYPL/0)	370000(6)
Ch	*[LESSONS OF OCTOBER.] Communist League of China: Shanghai, 1940. [Private notice.]	*400000(15)
Ch	*[LESSONS OF OCTOBER.] Communist League of China: Shanghai, 1947. [Private notice.]	*470000(1)
Eng	THE LESSONS OF OCTOBER 1917. Labour Publishing Co.: Ln, 1925. 80. (LocBM/CU/HIS/LC/LSE/NYPL/0)	250000(21)
Eng	THE LESSONS OF SPAIN. -- THE LAST WARNING. J.R.Strachan: Ln, 1938. 32. (LocBM/BN/CU/LC/LnL/LSE/0/IISG)	380000(6)
Eng	THE LESSONS OF SPAIN. Spark Syndicate: Bombay, 1948. 37. (LocPer)	480000(6)
Eng	THE LESSONS OF SPAIN. Lanka Samasamaja: Colombo, Ceylon, 1956. 21. (LocAAS/ABC/NUC)	560700
Eng	THE LESSONS OF SPAIN. International Publications: Balmain, Australia, [1969]. 21. [Processed] (LocPer)	[690000(17)]
Eng	THE LESSONS OF SPAIN. The Merit Publishers: Calcutta, 1969. 25. (LocPer)	691115
Eng	THE LESSONS OF THE PARIS COMMUNE. See THE PARIS COMMUNE, 550900.	

It	LETTERATURA, ARTE, LIBERTÀ. Schwarz: Milan, 1958. 194. (LocPer)	581000
Eng	A LETTER TO A SOCIAL-DEMOCRATIC WORKER. [—]: [Ln], [1933]. 18. [Processed] (LocPer)	⌊330000(39)⌋
Am	A LETTER TO THE COMMUNIST WORKERS OF CZECHO-SLOVAKIA. See WORLD UNEMPLOYMENT AND THE FIVE-YEAR PLAN, 310200.	
Fr	LETTRE A JULES GUESDE. + LA FAMILLE DECLERC. S.P.E.L.: [1958]. 6. (LocPer)	⌊580000(8)⌋
Fr	LETTRE AU CAMARADE TREINT. [—]: [P], [1931]. [Processed] (LocHIS)	310922
Fr	LETTRE OUVERTE AUX OUVRIERS FRANÇAIS. La Vérité: P, 1935. 2. (LocBDIC/BN)	350000(8)
Fr	LETTRE OUVERTE A VANDERVELDE. Union Communiste: P, 1961. 3. [Processed] (LocPer)	610000(2)
Fr	LETTRES A LA CONFÉRENCE DE LA LIGUE COMMUNISTE. [—]: [P], [1931]. [Processed] (LocPer)	⌊310000(26)⌋
Fr	LETTRES A QUELQUES CAMARADES FRANÇAIS (1921-1922). [—]: [M], [1922]. [Processed] (LocBN)	⌊220000(31)⌋
Fr	LEUR MORALE ET LA NÔTRE. Sagittarius: P, 1939. 87. (LocAAS/BDIC/BN/HIS/LC/SEES)	390320
Fr	LEUR MORALE ET LA NÔTRE. [—]: P, 1960. 36. [Processed] (LocHIS)	600000(19)
Fr	LEUR MORALE ET LA NÔTRE. La Méthode: Cannes, [1965]. 23. (LocPer)	⌊650000(14)⌋
Fr	LEUR MORALE ET LA NÔTRE. + MORALISTES ET SYCOPHANTES CONTRE LE MARXISME. Pauvert: P, 1966. 132. (LocBN)	660510
Hol	DE LEVENDE GEDACHTEN VAN KARL MARX. Servire: Hague, 1940. 191. (LocBRB/IISG)	400000(9)
Hol	DE LEVENDE GEDACHTEN VAN KARL MARX. Servire: Hague, 1951. 182. (LocPer)	510000(2)

Pol	LIST OTWARTY DO VANDERWELDEGO. See OSTATNIE PRZEMÓNIENIE V KOPENHADZE, 330000(43).	
Sp	LITERATURA Y REVOLUCIÓN. M.A.Aguilar: Madrid, [1924], 257. (LocHIS)	[240000(45)]
Sp	LITERATURA Y REVOLUCIÓN. Jorge Alvarez Ed.: Buenos Aires, 1964. 293. (LocPer)	640900(1)
Sp	LITERATURA Y REVOLUCIÓN. + OTROS ESCRITOS ... Ruedo Ibérico: Colombes, France, 1969. 2 vols. (LocPer)	690000(8)
Am	LITERATURE AND REVOLUTION. International Publishers: NY, 1925. 256. (LocAAO/BM/HIS/LC)	250000(22)
Am	LITERATURE AND REVOLUTION. Russell & Russell: NY, 1957. 256. (LocBRB/IISG/LSE/NUC)	570900(2)
Am	LITERATURE AND REVOLUTION. Ann Arbor: Univ. of Michigan, 1960. 256. (LocNUC/O)	600000(5)
Am	LITERATURE AND REVOLUTION. Ann Arbor: Univ. of Michigan, 1968. 256. (LocPer)	680000(10)
Ch.	*[LITERATURE AND REVOLUTION.] Communist League of China: Shanghai, 1930. [Private notice.]	*[300000(31)]
Eng	LITERATURE AND REVOLUTION. George Allen & Unwin: Ln, 1925. 256. (LocAAS/BM/CU/LnL/NYPL)	250000(23)
Ger	LITERATUR UND REVOLUTION. Verlag für Literatur und Politik: Vienna, 1924. 179. (LocABC/BDIC/BM/IISG/KBC/LC/NYPL/ULH)	240000(44)
Ger	LITERATUR UND REVOLUTION. Gerhardt Verlag: B, 1968. 461. (LocNUC)	680800(2)
Fr	LITTÉRATURE ET RÉVOLUTION. Julliard: P, 1964. 366. (LocAAS/BN/BRB/KBC/KBS)	640911
Swed	LITTERATUR OCH REVOLUTION. Partisan Förlaget: Mölindäl, 1969. 361. (LocPer)	690600(1)
Am	Pref. THE LIVING THOUGHTS OF KARL MARX. Longmans, Green & Co. Inc.: NY, 1939. 184. (LocLC)	390000(7)

Am	Pref. *THE LIVING THOUGHTS OF KARL MARX. Longmans, Green & Co. Inc.: NY, 1940. (LocLC)	*400000(7)
Am	Pref. THE LIVING THOUGHTS OF KARL MARX. Fawcett: NY, 1963. 175. (LocNUC)	630200
Eng	Pref. THE LIVING THOUGHTS OF KARL MARX. Cassell: Ln, 1940. 189. (LocBM)	400000(8)
Eng	Pref. THE LIVING THOUGHTS OF KARL MARX. Cassell: Ln, 1942. 189. [2 ed.] (LocPer)	420600
Eng	Pref. THE LIVING THOUGHTS OF KARL MARX. Cassell: Ln, 1946. 189. [3 ed.] (LocPer)	461100
Gr	LOGOTEKHNIA KAI EPANASTASE. Prometheas: Athens, 1966. 270. (LocPer)	660000(6)
It	LA LORO MORALE E LA NOSTRA. De Donato: Bari, 1967. 118. (LocPer)	670831
It	Lenin e T, LA LOTTA PER IL PANE. For T see LAVORO....	
Sp	LA LUCHA CONTRA LA BUROCRACIA. Ediciones Coyoacan: Buenos Aires, 1969. 250. (LocPer)	690500(3)
Fr	LA LUTTE CONTRE LE FASCISME: ENTRETIEN AVEC UN OUVRIER SOCIAL-DÉMOCRATE. La Vérité: P, 1933. 14. (LocBDIC)	330000(13)
Ger	*MANIFEST DER KOMMUNISTISCHEN INTERNATIONALE. Volkskommissariat für Unterrichtswesen: Budapest, 1919. (CatGV)	*190000(74)
Fr	MANIFESTE COMMUNISTE. Parti Communiste Révolutionnaire: Brussels, 1945. 31. (LocBN/BRB/IISG/LC)	450300
Fr	MANIFESTE DE LA IVe INTERNATIONALE AUX TRAVAILLEURS DU MONDE. La Voie de Lénine: [Belgium], 1940. 31. (LocPer)	400000(5)
Sp	*MANIFESTIO SOBRE LA GUERRA DE LA IV INTERNACIONÁL. IV Internacionál: Argentine, 1940. [Advert.]	*400000(16)

Eng	MANIFESTO OF THE FIRST CONGRESS OF THE COMMUNIST INTERNATIONAL. Ln, 1919. (LocBM)	190000(51)
Eng	--: MANIFESTO OF THE FOURTH INTERNATIONAL: IMPERIALIST WAR AND THE WORLD PROLETARIAN REVOLUTION. WIL: Ln, [1940]. 45. (LocBM/BN/IISG)	[400000(4)]
Am	--: MANIFESTO OF THE FOURTH INTERNATIONAL: ON THE IMPERIALIST WAR AND THE WORLD PROLETARIAN REVOLUTION. Socialist Workers Party: NY, 1940. 46. (LocPPA)	400000(14)
Eng	MANIFESTO: TOWARDS A FREE REVOLUTIONARY ART. See ART AND REVOLUTION, 630000(1).	
Hol	MANIFEST VAN DE COMMUNISTISCHE INTERNATIONALE. See DE KAPITALISTISCHE WERELD EN DE COMMUNISTISCHE INTERNATIONALE, 210000(33).	
Sp	MANUAL DEL SOLDATO ROJO. Editorial Marxista: Barcelona, 1937. 20. (LocHIS)	370000(8)
Eng	MARXISM AND MILITARY AFFAIRS. Young Socialist: Colombo, Ceylon, 1969. 136. (LocPer)	690400
Am	MARXISM AND OUR TIMES. See MARXISM IN THE UNITED STATES, 470100.	
Am	MARXISM AND OUR TIMES. Pathfinder: NY, 1970. 47. (LocPPA)	700300
Eng	MARXISM AND SCIENCE. Lanka Samasamaja: Colombo, Ceylon, 1949. 20. (LocPer)	491000
Eng	MARXISM AND THE TRADE UNIONS. Socialist Labour League: Ln, [1968]. 80. (LocPer)	[680300(2)]
Fr	LE MARXISME ET NOTRE EPOQUE. Pionniers: P, 1946. 38. (LocAAS/BDIC/BN/HIS)	460000(5)
Fr	LE MARXISME ET NOTRE EPOQUE. S.P.E.L.: P, 1960. 29. (LocIISG)	600000(6)
Am	MARXISM IN THE UNITED STATES. Workers Party Publications: NY, 1947. 44. (LocAAS/HIS/LC/NYPL)	470100
It	MARXISMO E SCIENZA. Samonà e Savelli: Rome, 1969. 55. (LocPer)	690500(2)

Ger	DER MARXISMUS UND UNSERE EPOCHE. IV. Internationale: [--], 1947. 32. ⌊Processed⌋ (LocIISG)	470600
Fr	MARX VU PAR TROTZKY. Buchet Chastel: P, 1970. 283. (LocPer)	700129
Fr	MA VIE. Rieder: P, 1930. 3 vols. (LocBDIC/BM/BN/BRB/HIS/IISG/LC/LnL/SEES)	300522
Fr	MA VIE. Rieder: P, 1934. 256. (LocAAS/BN/SEES/ULO)	340000(4)
Fr	MA VIE. Pionniers: P, 1947. 220. (LocBN/BRB)	470615
Fr	MA VIE. Gallimard: P, 1953. 658. (LocBDIC/BN/BRB/LSE/CatZ)	531130
Fr	MA VIE. Gallimard: P, 1966. 692. (LocPer)	660000(5)
Fr	MA VIE. NRF-Gallimard: P, 1968. 658. (LocPer)	680331
Ger	MEINE FLUCHT AUS SIBIRIEN. Verlag der Jugend-Internationale: B, 1922. 87. (LocBM/IISG/LnL/NYPL)	220000(25)
Ger	MEIN LEBEN. S.Fischer Verlag: B, 1930. 572. (LocAAS/ABC/BN/IISG/KBC/KBS/LC/LSE/NYPL/ULO)	300000(13)
Ger	MEIN LEBEN. S.Fischer Verlag: Frankfurt, 1961. 558. (LocLSE)	610000(3)
Yid	*MEJN LEBEN. Biblion: Warsaw, 1930. 2 vol. (LocNYPL)	*300000(14)
It	*LA MIA PRIMA EVASIONE. Academia: Rome, 1930. 98. (CatLI)	*300000(16)
It	LA MIA VITA. Mondadori: Milan-Verona, 1930. 526. (LocPer)	300300(1)
It	*LA MIA VITA. Mondadori: Milan-Verona, 1933. 2nd ed. (CatLI)	*330000(14)
It	LA MIA VITA. Mondadori: Verona, 1961. 570. (LocPer)	610400
Hol	MIJN LEVEN. Querido: Amsterdam, 1930. 512. (LocIISG)	300000(17)
Am	MILITARY WRITINGS. Merit: NY, 1969. 158. (LocNUC)	690000(11)
Fr	1905. Humanité: P, 1923. 381. (LocBDIC/BM/BN/BRB/HIS/IISG/PSB/CatZ)	230000(29)

Fr	1905. + BILAN ET PERSPECTIVES. Editions de Minuit: P, 1969. 476. (LocNUC)	690415
It	MILLENOVECENTOCINQUE. Istituto Editoriale Italiano: Milan, 1948. 364. (LocLC/O)	480000(1)
It	1905. Samonà e Savelli: Rome, 1969. 276. (LocPer)	690610
Tat	i Stalin: MILLIYET MESELESI TURINDE. Edition Centrale des Peuples de l'U.R.S.S.: M, 1923. 29. (LocLOV)	230000(41)
Swed	MIN FLYKT FRÅN SIBIRIEN. ⌊--⌋: Stockholm, 1924. 78. (LocAAS/ABC/KBS/ULH)	240000(46)
Port	*MINHA VIDA. Jose Olympio: Rio de Janeiro, ⌊1943⌋. 572. (CatBB)	*⌊430000(1)⌋
Sp	MIS PERIPECIAS EN ESPAÑA. Editorial España: Madrid, 1929. 224. (LocHIS)	290000(5)
Sp	MIS PERIPECIAS EN ESPAÑA. Editorial del Pucara: Buenos Aires, 1968. 211. (LocPer)	680000(9)
Eng	THE MISTAKES OF THE RIGHT ELEMENTS ON THE TRADE UNION QUESTION. ⌊Revolutionary Communist Party⌋: ⌊Ln⌋, ⌊1942⌋. ⌊Processed⌋ (LocPer)	⌊420000(6)⌋
Eng	THE MISTAKES OF THE RIGHT ELEMENTS ON THE TRADE UNION QUESTION. Socialist Labour League: Ln, ⌊1960⌋. 10. ⌊Processed⌋ (LocPer)	⌊600000(20)⌋
Nor	MITT LIV. Tiden Norsk: Oslo, 1935. 244. (LocAAO/AAS/ABC/KBC/ULO)	350000(9)
Swed	MITT LIV. + DEN ANKLAGADE ANKLAGAR. Natur och Kultur: Oslo, 1937. 286. (LocAAS/KBS)	370000(9)
Sp	*MI VIDA. Cenit: Madrid, 1930. 612. (CatBE/CatLEHA)	*300000(15)
Sp	MI VIDA. Ercilla: Santiago de Chile, 1936. 5 vols. (LocPer)	360000(27)
Sp	*MI VIDA. Editorial Colón: Mexico, 1946. ⌊Advert.⌋	*460000(11)

Sp	MI VIDA. Com. General de Ediciones: Mexico, 1960. 616. (LocPer)	600730
Hol	*MOET HET DUITSCHE FASCISME ZEGEVIEREN? ⌊--⌋: ⌊--⌋, ⌊1931⌋ ⌊Advert.⌋	*⌊310000(30)⌋
Cz	*MOJE PAMĚTI. ⌊--⌋: Prague, 1930. (CatBK)	*300000(18)
Pol	*MOJE ZYCIE. Biblion: Warsaw, 1930. (CatZK)	*300000(32)
Fr	--: LE MONDE CAPITALISTE ET L'INTERNATIONALE COMMUNISTE. Internationale Communiste: Pet, 1920. 47. (LocPer)	200000(58)
Fr	--: LE MONDE CAPITALISTE.... Bibliothèque Communiste: P, 1920. 45. (LocIISG)	200000(59)
Fr	--: LE MONDE CAPITALISTE.... ⌊--⌋: Switzerland, ⌊1920⌋. 36. (LocPer)	⌊200000(84)⌋
Fr	MON EXIL. Editions du Groupe communiste d'Opposition Belge: Brussels, 1929. 45. (LocBN/HIS)	290000(6)
Sp	MORALISTAS Y SICOFANTES CONTRA EL MARXISMO. See SU MORAL Y LA NUESTRA, 390000(4).	
Fr	MORALISTES ET SYCOPHANTES CONTRE LE MARXISME. See LEUR MORALE ET LA NÔTRE, 660510.	
Am	THE MORALISTS AND SYCOPHANTS AGAINST MARXISM. See THEIR MORALS AND OURS, ⌊420000(7)⌋/420800/660800.	
Fr	LE MOUVEMENT COMMUNISTE EN FRANCE (1919-1939). Editions de Minuit: P, 1967. 723. (LocBRB/ULH)	670306
Gr	MPOLSEVIKISMO KAI STALINISMO. Ergatikes Pales: Athens, ⌊1946⌋. 24. (LocPer)	⌊460000(6)⌋
Cz	*MUJ ŽIVOT (PAMĚTI). See *MOJE PAMĚTI, *300000(18).	
Hun	*MUNKA, FEGYELEM ÉS REND MENTIK MEG A PROLETÁRSÁGOT. Kozokt Nepbizt: Budapest, 1919. 16. (CatGV)	*190000(75)
Hun	*MUNKA, FEGYELEM ÉS REND MENTIK MEG A PROLETÁRSÁGOT. J.Rigler: Budapest, 1919. 16. (CatGV)	*190000(76)

Hun	*MUNKA, FEGYELEM ÉS REND MENTIK MEG A SZOVJET KÖZTÁSASÁGOT. [--]: [Budapest], [1919]. 32. (CatGV)	*[190000(77)]
Jap	*MUSANSHA MUNKA-RON. Shuho Kaku: Tokyo, 1925. 179. (LocNDL)	*251028
Am	MY FLIGHT FROM SIBERIA. Young International: B, 1923. 80. (LocBM)	230000(30)
Am	MY FLIGHT FROM SIBERIA. American Library Service: NY, 1925. 60. (LocHIS/LC/NYPL)	250000(25)
Am	MY LIFE. C.Scribner's Sons: NY, 1930. 599. (LocBM/HIS/LC/NYPL)	300000(19)
Am	*MY LIFE. C.Scribner's Sons: NY, 1931. 599. 2nd ed. (LocWiener Library, Harvard)	*310000(18)
Am	MY LIFE. Grosset & Dunlap: NY, 1960. 599. (LocNUC)	600000(8)
Am	MY LIFE. Pathfinder Press Inc.: NY, 1970. 602. (LocPer)	700000(4)
Ch	*[MY LIFE.] [--]: Shanghai, 1931. [1 vol.] [Private notice]	*310000(36)
Ch	*[MY LIFE.] [--]: Shanghai, [1932]. 3 vol. [Private notice]	*[320000(36)]
Ch	*[MY LIFE.] [--]: Shanghai, [1932]. [1 vol of 2] [Private notice]	*[320000(37)]
Ch	*[MY LIFE.] [--]: Shanghai, [1938]. [abr.] [Private notice]	*[380000(16)]
Ch	*[MY LIFE.] [--]: Shanghai, 1947. [Private notice]	*470000(3)
Eng	MY LIFE. Thornton Butterworth: Ln, 1930. 512. (LocBM/CU/IISG/LC/LSE/O)	300000(20)
Swed	NÄR SKALL DET FÖRBANNADE KRIGET SLUTA? [--]: Stockholm, 1918. 19. (LocAAS/ABC/KBS)	180000(38)
Eng	NATIONALIZED INDUSTRY AND WORKERS MANAGEMENT. International Marxist Group: Ln, 1969. 3. [Processed] (LocPer)	690300(1)

Afr	NEGENTIG JAAR VAN DIE KOMUNISTE-MANIFEST. Werkersparty van Suid-Afrika: Cape Town, ⌊1937⌋. 48. (LocPer)	370000(31)
Cz	NĚMECKÉ KLÍČEM K MEZINÁRODNÍ SITUACI. + V CEM JE NESPRÁVNÁ POLITIKA NĚMECKÉ KOMUNISTICKÉ STRANY. V.Palána: Prague, 1932. 46. (LocIISG)	320000(12)
Ger	DIE NEUE ETAPPE. Carl Hoym: Hamburg, 1921. 167. (LocAAO/AAS/ABC/BDIC/HIS/IISG/LnL/LSE/NYPL/O)	210000(36)
Ger	—: DAS NEUE KOMMUNISTISCHE MANIFEST. Verlag Willaschek & Co.: Hamburg, ⌊1919⌋. 16. (LocABC)	⌊190000(64)⌋
Her	DER NEUE KURS. [—]: [B], ⌊1924⌋. (LocHIS/LSE)	⌊240000(52)⌋
Ger	DIE NEUE ÖKONOMISCHE POLITIK SOWJETRUSSLAND UND DIE WELTREVOLUTION. C.Hoym: Hamburg, 1923. 38. (LocBDIC/BM/HIS/IISG/LC/NYPL/ULH)	230000(31)
Ger	1917: DIE LEHREN DER REVOLUTION. E.Laubsche Verlags== buchhandlung: B, 1925. 79. (LocAAS/ABC/HIS/IISG/KBS/LC/LSE/NYPL/O/PSB/ULH)	250000(26)
Ger	1917: DIE LEHREN DER REVOLUTION. E.Laub'sche Verlagsbuchhandlung: B, 1929. 79. (LocBDIC/HIS)	290000(7)
Yid	*DER NEUER ETAP. DI VELT-LAGE UN UNZERE OJFGABEN. [—]: Homel, 1922. 156. (LocNYPL)	*220000(35)
Fin	NEUVOSTOVALTA JA YLEISMAAILMALLINEN VALLANKUMOUS. Suomalaisen Kommunistisen Puolueen Keskuskomites: Pietari, 1918. 48. (LocBDIC/ULH)	180000(39)
Am	THE NEW COURSE. New International Publishing Co.: NY, 1943. 265. (LocAAS/HIS/LC/LSE/NYPL)	430900
Am	THE NEW COURSE. Ann Arbor: Univ. of Michigan, 1965. 265. (LocNUC)	650000(5)
Eng	THE NEW COURSE. New Park: Ln, 1956. 111. (LocNUC)	561000
Jap	THE NEW COURSE. Jap. Section, Fourth International: Kyoto, 1966. 61. [Processed] (LocPer)	660427

Eng   & others: THE NEW REVOLUTIONARY UPSURGE AND THE TASKS   ⌊360000(17)⌋
          OF THE FOURTH INTERNATIONAL. ⌊--⌋: Ln, ⌊1936⌋.
          ⌊Processed. Part of an unidentified document.⌋
          (LocPer)

Pol   *NIEMCY NA PRZEŁOMIE. Era: Warsaw, 1933. 16.   *330000(42)
          (CatIT/CatZK)

Hol   DE NIEUWE GRONDWET VAN DE SOWJET UNIE. De Vlam: ⌊360000(18)⌋
          Amsterdam, ⌊1936⌋. 14.
          (LocIISG)

Eng   1905: BEFORE AND AFTER. Lanka Samasamaja: Colombo,   531200
          Ceylon, 1953. 34.
          (LocBM)

Eng   1905: RESULTS AND PERSPECTIVES. Lanka Samasamaja: 540300
          Colombo, Ceylon, 1954. 48.
          (LocIISG)

Eng   *90 YEARS OF THE COMMUNIST MANIFESTO. Lanka Samasamaja: *480200
          Colombo, Ceylon, 1948. 9.
          ⌊Advert.⌋

Eng   90 YEARS OF THE COMMUNIST MANIFESTO. Lanka Samasamaja: 550700
          Colombo, Ceylon, 1955. 9. 2nd ed.
          (LocAAS/IISG)

Nor   1917. Det Norske Arbeiderspartei: Oslo, 1925. 59.   250000(31)
          (LocAAO/ABC/ULH)

Hol   NOGMAALS DE KWESTIE VAN HET BONAPARTISME. See DE
          ARBEIDERSTAAT: THERMIDOR EN BONAPARTISME,
          ⌊350000(14)⌋.

Fr   NOS TÂCHES POLITIQUES. Pierre Belfond: P, 1970. 256.   700228
          (LocPer)

Fr   LA NOUVELLE CONSTITUTION DE L'URSS. Librairie du   360000(4)
          Travail: P, 1936. 18. ⌊Processed⌋
          (LocBN/HIS)

Fr   *LA NOUVELLE CONSTITUTION DE L'URSS. ⌊--⌋: ⌊P⌋, 1936. 22.   *360000(24)
          (LocAAS/HIS)

Fr   NOUVELLE ETAPE. Humanité: P, 1922. 142.   220000(26)
          (LocAAS/BDIC/BM/BN/BRB/HIS/IISG/PSB)

Fr   LA NOUVELLE POLITIQUE ECONOMIQUE DES SOVIETS ET LA   230000(32)
          RÉVOLUTION MONDIALE. Humanité: P, 1923. 78.
          (LocBDIC/HIS/O/PSB)

Cz	*NOVÝ KURS. Kommunist.knihkup. a nakladat: Prague, 1924. 74. (CatBK)	*240000(47)
Sp	LA NUEVA CONSTITUTICIÓN DE LA URSS. LCI: Mexico, 1936. 15. (LocBN)	360700(2)
Sp	*NUEVA ETAPA. [--]: Madrid, ⌊1921⌋. ⌊Documentos Politicos.I: 15: 1-76⌋ (LocNYPL)	*⌊210000(49)⌋
Sp	*NUEVA RUTA. [--]: [--], ⌊1931⌋. ⌊Advert.⌋	*⌊310000(31)⌋
Sp	*NUEVO RUMBO. ¿A DÓNDE VA RUSIA? Ediciones Oriente: Madrid, 1928. 265. (CatBE/CatLEHA)	*280000(3)
It	NUOVO CORSO. Samonà e Savelli: Rome, 1967. 144. (LocPer)	670315

Sp	OBJETIVIDAD HISTORICA. See LA REVOLUCIÓN RUSA, 671100.	
Ch	*⌊THE OCTOBER REVOLUTION.⌋ Communist Party of China: Shanghai, ⌊1920⌋. ⌊Private notice.⌋	*⌊200000(96)⌋
Eng	THE OCTOBER REVOLUTION. Modern India Publications: Bombay, 1952. 111. (LocNYPL)	520600
Pol	*ODGLOSY PODRÓŻY TROCKIEGO DO KOPENHAGI. See *OSTATNIE PRZEMÓWIENIE W KOPENHADZE, *330000(43).	
Pol	*OD PRZEWROTU LISTOPADOWEGO DO POKOJU BRZESIEGO. Ksiazka: Warsaw, 1920. 107. (CatZK)	*200000(97)
Gr	O EMPHULIOS POLEMOS STEN ISPANIA. Ergatikes Pales: Athens, 1963. 94. (LocPer)	630000(10)
Ger	OFFENER BRIEF AN DAS ZENTRAL EXEKUTIV-KOMITEE DIE SOWJET-UNION. Thoma: ⌊Vienna⌋, ⌊1932⌋. 12. (LocIISG)	⌊320000(23)⌋
Ger	*OFFIZIELES TELEGRAM DER RUSSISCHEN VOLKSKOMISSARE. [--]: [--], ⌊1918⌋. ⌊Advert.⌋	*180123(2)/
Yid	DI OKTJOBR REVOLJUTSIJE. Kommissariat po delam natsional´nostei yevreiskaia sektsiia: Pet, 1921. 110. (LocNYPL)	*210000(37)

Gr	E OKTOBRIANE EPANASTASE. Neo Bibliopoleion: Athens, 1966. 36.	660000(7)
	(LocPer)	
Esth	*OKTOBRIREVOLUTSION. [--]: Pet, 1919.	*190000(52)
	(CatKL)	
Am	ON BLACK NATIONALISM AND SELF-DETERMINATION. Merit: NY, 1967. 66.	670600
	(LocABC)	
Am	ON BLACK NATIONALISM ... Merit: NY, 1969. 66. [2 ed.]	690400(2)
	(LocPer)	
Am	ON BLACK NATIONALISM ... Pathfinder: NY,[1970]. 63. [3 ed.]	700800(1)
	(LocPer)	
Eng	ONCE AGAIN -- ON THE ILP. F.Maitland: Edinburgh, 1944. 10. [Processed]	441216
	(LocPer)	
Eng	ONCE AGAIN: THE ILP. WIL: Ln, 1935. 7. [Processed]	350000(11)
	(LocLSE)	
Eng	ON CENTRISM. Acton ILP: Ln, [1934]. 4. [Processed]	[340000(11)]
	(LocPer)	
Am	ON ENGELS AND KAUTSKY. Merit: NY, 1969. 30.	690700
	(LocPPA)	
Eng	ON LENIN. The Merit Publishers: Calcutta, 1968. 32.	680200(1)
	(LocPer)	
Am	ON LENIN'S TESTAMENT. Pioneer Publishers: NY, 1935. 47.	350000(10)
	(LocBM/HIS/LSE/NYPL)	
Am	ON LENIN'S TESTAMENT. Pioneer Publishers: NY, 1946. 48.	461100(1)
	(LocAAS/ABC/BM/IISG/NYPL)	
Am	ON LENIN'S TESTAMENT. Pioneer Publishers: NY, 1953. 48.	530000(3)
	(LocNYPL)	
Eng	ON LENIN'S TESTAMENT. New Park: Ln, 1954. 32.	541100(1)
	(LocPer)	
Am	ON LITERATURE AND ART. Pathfinder: NY, 1970. 248.	700000(14)
	(LocPer)	
Am	THE ONLY ROAD. Communist League of America + Pioneer Publishers: NY, 1933. 93.	330400(2)
	(LocAAS)	
Eng	THE ONLY ROAD. Lanka Samasamaja: Colombo, Ceylon, 1959. 88.	590100
	(LocAAS/BM/IISG)	
Eng	ON MANY FRONTS. [--]: M, 1920. 43.	201200
	(LocAAS/IISG)	
Eng	ON SOUTH AFRICAN PROBLEMS. [--]: [--], [1935]. 9.	[350000(26)]
	(LocPer)	

Eng	ON SOVIET STATE POWER: 1934-1938. Richardson: Ln, 1969. 40. [Processed] (LocPer)	690321
Eng	ON STALINISM AND TROTSKYISM IN THE USA. New Park: Ln, [1966]. 23. (LocPer)	[660000(1)]
Ch	*[ON THE CHINESE REVOLUTION.] [See note in text.]	*300000(23)
Eng	ON THE EVE OF WORLD WAR II. Samasamaj Prakashan: Calcutta, [1970]. 8. (LocPer)	[700000(10)]
Eng	ON THE HISTORY OF STALINISM. Socialist Labour League: Ln, [1960]. 10. (LocPer)	[600000(21)]
Am	ON THE JEWISH QUESTION. Merit: NY, 1970. 31. (LocPer)	700700
Am	ON THE LABOR PARTY IN THE USA. Socialist Workers Party: NY, 1948. 23. [Processed] (LocHIS)	480000(2)
Am	ON THE LABOR PARTY IN THE USA. Merit: NY, 1969. 35. (LocPer)	690825
Eng	ON THE ROAD TO THE EUROPEAN REVOLUTION. Roberts: Ln, 1969. 17. [Processed] (LocPer)	690000(9)
Am	ON THE SUPPRESSED TESTAMENT OF LENIN. Pathfinder: NY, 1970. 48. (LocPer)	700000(1)
Am	ON THE TRADE UNIONS. Merit: NY, 1969. 80. (LocNUC)	690000(13)
Hol	DE OORLOG EN DE INTERNATIONALE. J.Emmerling: Amsterdam, 1915. 93. (LocBN/IISG)	150000(1)
Eng	AN OPEN LETTER TO ALL REVOLUTIONARY PROLETARIAN ORGANISATIONS AND GROUPINGS. See STALIN'S TREASON ... [350000(19)].	
Eng	OPEN LETTER TO AN ENGLISH COMRADE. Clapham ILP: Ln, [1936]. 6. [Processed] (LocPer)	[360000(25)]
Eng	AN OPEN LETTER TO JULES GUESDE. Lanka Samasamaja: Colombo, Ceylon, 1952. 8. (LocBM)	520300

| Eng | AN OPEN LETTER TO THE WORKERS OF INDIA. The Merit Publishers: Calcutta, 1967. 8. (LocPer) | 670000(4) |

Eng   AN OPEN LETTER TO THE WORKERS OF INDIA. The Merit   670000(4)
        Publishers: Calcutta, 1967. 8.
        (LocPer)

Port   O QUE É A REVOLUÇÃO DE OUTUBRO. + CARTA ABERTA A   330000(11)
        VANDERVELDE. Luta de classe: S.Paulo, 1933.
        61.
        (LocPer)

Ger   DIE ORGANISIERUNG DER ROTEN ARMEE. [---]: Vienna, 1920.   200000(60)
        (LocIISG/LnL/NYPL)

Pol   *OSTATNIE PRZEMÓWIENIE W KOPENHADZE. ODGLOSY PODRÓZY   *330000(43)
        TROCKIEGO DO KOPENHAGI. + LIST OTWARTY DO
        VANDERWELDEGO. Nowa Era: Warsaw, 1933. 47.
        (CatIT)

Ger   ÖSTERREICH AN DER REIHE. + BRIEF AN EINEN OESTERREICHISCHE   330000(15)
        GENOSSEN. Links-opposition der K.P.O.E.
        (Bolschewiki-Leninisten): Vienna, 1933. 15.
        (LocAAS/BN/IISG)

Ger   DIE ÖSTERREICHISCHE KRISE, DIE SOZIALDEMOKRATIE UND DER   290000(8)
        KOMMUNISMUS. Thoma: Vienna, 1929. 18.
        (LocHIS/IISG/LSE)

Pol   *O SYTUACJI MIEDZYNARODOWEJ. KLUCZ DO SYTUACJI   *320000(31)
        MIEDZYNARODOWEJ W NIEMCZECH. Era: Warsaw, 1932. 23.
        (CatIT)

Eng   OUR MILITARY CONSTRUCTION AND OUR FRONTS. Executive   200000(61)
        Committee of the Communist International: M, 1920.
        39.
        (LocLSE/ULO)

Am   OUR REVOLUTION. Henry Holt & Co.: NY, 1918. 220.   180000(40)
        (LocAAS/BDIC/BM/HIS/LC/NYPL/SEES/CatZ)

Fr   OÙ VA LA FRANCE? Librairie du Travail: P, 1936. 193.   360000(6)
        (LocAAS/BDIC/BM/HIS/IISG/NYPL)

Fr   OÙ VA LA FRANCE? See ECRITS.II, 580900.

Fr   OÙ VA L'ANGLETERRE? Humanité: P, 1926. 246.   260000(25)
        (LocAAS/BN/HIS/IISG/NYPL)

Hol   OVER ARBEIDERSCONTROLE DER PRODUCTIE. See TEGEN HET
        NATIONALCOMMUNISME, ⌊400000(7)⌋.

Hol   OVERGANGSPROGRAM VAN DE VIERDE INTERNATIONALE. Revolutionnair
        Communistische Partij: Amsterdam, ⌊1947⌋. 31.   ⌊470000(4)⌋
        3rd ed. ⌊Processed⌋
        (LocPer)

Hol   OVERGANGSPROGRAM VAN DE VIERDE INTERNATIONALE.   [630000(3)]

         Nederlande Sektie van de Vierde Internationale:
         Amsterdam, [1963]. 32. [Processed]
         (LocPer)

Fr   LES PAGES IMMORTELLES DE MARX. Editions Corrêa: P, 1947.   470910

         283.
         (LocBN)

Eng   A PARADISE IN THIS WORLD. BSP: Ln, 1920. 30.   200000(62)

         (LocBM/HIS/LSE)

Eng   A PARADISE IN THIS WORLD. Lanka Samasamaja: Colombo,   570900(3)

         Ceylon, 1957. 29.
         (LocAAS/BM/IISG/NUC)

Eng   THE PARIS COMMUNE. + LESSONS OF THE PARIS COMMUNE.   550900

         Lanka Samasamaja: Colombo, Ceylon, 1955. 14.
         (LocAAS)

Sin   & Lenin, PARIS COMMUNYA. Lanka Samasamaja: Colombo,   510000

         Ceylon, 1951. 13.
         (LocPer)

Sin   & Lenin, PARLIMENTHUVA SAHA VIPLAVAYA. International   640200

         Publishers: Colombo, Ceylon, 1964. 86.
         (LocPer)

Ger   DER PAZIFISMUS IM DIENSTE DES IMPERIALISMUS. [--]:   170000(8)

         Pet, 1917.
         (LocBM/HIS/LSE/NYPL)

Sp   *EL PENSAMIENTO VIVO DE MARX. Losada: Buenos Aires,   *400000(11)

         1940.
         [Advert.]

Sp   *EL PENSAMIENTO VIVO DE MARX. Losada: Buenos Aires,   *430625

         1943.
         [Advert.]

Sp   *EL PENSAMIENTO VIVO DE MARX. Losada: Buenos Aires,   *480000(5)

         1948. 327.
         (CatIT)

Sp   *EL PENSAMIENTO VIVO DE MARX. Losada: Buenos Aires,   620700(2)

         1962. 242.
         (LocNUC)

Swed   DEN PERMANENTA REVOLUTIONENS EPOK. Partisan: Mölndäl,   691100(2)

         1969. 332.
         (LocPer)

Nor	DEN PERMANENTE REVOLUSJON. Pax Forlag: Oslo, [1969]. 142. (LocAAS)	[690000(10)]
Ger	DIE PERMANENTE REVOLUTION. Die Aktion: B, 1930. 168. (LocABC/BDIC/IISG/LSE/NYPL)	300000(21)
Ger	DIE PERMANENTE REVOLUTION. Verlag Neue Kritik: Frankfurt, 1965. 168§ (LocBRB)	651100
Ger	DIE PERMANENTE REVOLUTION. Verlag Neue Kritik: Frankfurt, 1968. 168. 2nd ed. (LocPer)	680000(7)
Ger	DIE PERMANENTE REVOLUTION. Fischer Bücherei: Frankfurt, 1969. 154. (LocPer)	691000
Cz	*PERMANENTNÍ REVOLUCE. [--]: [--], [1932]. [Advert.]	*[320000(27)]
Am	THE PERMANENT REVOLUTION. Pioneer Publishers: NY, 1931. 157. (LocAAS/HIS/LC/LSE/NYPL)	310500
Am	THE PERMANENT REVOLUTION. + RESULTS AND PROSPECTS. Pioneer Publishers: NY, 1965. 254. (LocPer)	650000(3)
Am	THE PERMANENT REVOLUTION. + RESULTS AND PROSPECTS. Merit: NY, 1969. 281. (LocNUC)	690000(20)
Am	THE PERMANENT REVOLUTION. + RESULTS AND PROSPECTS. Merit ⌐ NY, 1970. 281. (LocPer)	700000(8)
Am	THE PERMANENT REVOLUTION. + RESULTS AND PROSPECTS. Pathfinder: NY, 1970. 281. (LocPer)	[700000(12)]
Ch	*[THE PERMANENT REVOLUTION.] Communist League of China: Shanghai, [1938]. [Private notice.]	*[380000(17)]
Eng	THE PERMANENT REVOLUTION. Workers International Press: Ln, 1940. 218. [Processed] (LocCU/LC/0)	400000(3)
Eng	THE PERMANENT REVOLUTION. Gupta Rahman & Gupta: Calcutta, 1947. 175. (LocPer)	470300

Eng	THE PERMANENT REVOLUTION. + RESULTS AND PROSPECTS.	620700(1)
	New Park: Ln, 1962. 254.	
	(LocLSE)	
Eng	PERSPECTIVES OF WORLD DEVELOPMENT. See WHITHER EUROPE?	
	PERSPECTIVES OF WORLD DEVELOPMENT, 501000.	
Fr	PÉTROGRAD (1917-1919). Editions de l'Internationale	200000(63)
	Communiste: Pet, 1920. 16.	
	(LocBM/BN/HIS/IISG/LSE)	
Ger	PETROGRAD (1917-1919). Verlag der Kommunistische	200000(64)
	Internationale: Pet, 1920. 16.	
	(LocABC/BM/LSE/NYPL)	
Nor	og Zinoviev, PETROGRAD: 1917-1919. [--]: Kristiania,	200000(105)
	1920.	
	(LocULO)	
Sp	EL PLAN QUINQUENAL. Comunismo: Madrid, 1931. 15.	310000(10)
	(LocPer)	
Sp	PLATAFORMA DE LA OPOSICIÓN. See LA SITUACIÓN REAL DE	
	RUSIA (LA PLATAFORMA DE LA OPOSICIÓN), *310000(19).	
Fr	LA PLATE-FORME DE L'OPPOSITION RUSSE. L'Opposition de	271100(1)
	Gauche de l'Internationale Communiste: P, 1927. 48.	
	(LocBN/NYPL)	
Eng	& others, THE PLATFORM OF THE LEFT OPPOSITION (1927).	630100
	New Park: Ln, 1963. 115.	
	(LocPer)	
Fr	POLITIQUE DE TROTSKY. Armand Colin: P, 1968. 399.	680000(4)
	(LocPer)	
Sp	POR LOS ESTADOS UNIDOS SOCIALISTAS DE AMÉRICA LATINA.	611025
	Ediciones Coyoacan: Buenos Aires, 1961. 71.	
	(LocNUC)	
Cz	*POUČENI Z ŘÍJNA. PREDML. LEV TROCKÝ. CEMU NÁS UČE	*250000(28)
	ŘÍJEN. Kommunist. knihkup. a nakladat: Prague,	
	1925. 133.	
	(CatSČL)	
Fr	POUR COMBATTRE LE FASCISME, IL FAUT UNE PUISSANTE MILICE	360000(7)
	OUVRIÈRE. Parti Socialiste Révolutionnaire:	
	[Brussels], 1936. 24.	
	(LocBDIC/HIS/PSB)	
Fr	*POUR UN ART RÉVOLUTIONNAIRE INDÉPENDANT. [--]: P, 1938.	*380000(20)
	4.	
	(LocBN)	

Gr	POU PEGAINEI E GALLIA. Neon Bibliopoleion: Athens, 1966. 56. (LocPer)	660000(10)
Pol	*PRAWDA O ROSJI SOWISCKIEJ. Polska Ajencja Wydawnicza: Warsaw, 1929. 238. (CatZK)	*290000(15)
Cz	*PŘED ŘEŠENÍM. M.L.O. frakce bolševiku-lenincu v K.S.Č: Ostrawa, 1933. 31. (CatBK)	*330000(38)
Ger	PROBLEME DER ENTWICKLUNG DER USSR. A.Grylewicz: B, 1931. 31. (LocAAS/BDIC/BN/HIS/LSE/NYPL)	310000(11)
Fr	LES PROBLÈMES DE LA GUERRE CIVILE. Librairie du Travail: P, 1926. 38. (LocAAS/BDIC/BN/HIS/NYPL/PSB)	260900
Fr	LES PROBLÈMES DE LA RÉVOLUTION ALLEMANDE. Ligue Communiste (Opposition): P, 1931. 61. (LocBN/HIS/IISG/PSB)	310000(12)
Yid	*DER PROBLEM FUN AJNHAJTLECHE FRONT. Naje Era: Warsaw, 1933. (CatIT)	*330000(44)
Am	PROBLEMS OF CIVIL WAR. Merit: NY, 1970. 23. (LocPer)	700600
Am	PROBLEMS OF LIFE. George H.Doran Co.: NY, 1924. 114. (LocHIS/LC/NYPL)	240000(48)
Eng	PROBLEMS OF LIFE. Methuen: Ln, 1924. 114. (LocAAO/BM/CU/HIS/IISG/KBC/LC/O)	240000(49)
Eng	PROBLEMS OF LIFE. Young Socialist: Colombo, Ceylon, 1962. 59. (LocPer)	621100(1)
Am	PROBLEMS OF THE CHINESE REVOLUTION. Pioneer Publishers: NY, 1932. 432. (LocABC/HIS/IISG/LC/LSE/NYPL/SEES)	320600(2)
Am	PROBLEMS OF THE CHINESE REVOLUTION. Paragon Book Gallery: NY, 1962. 432. (LocKBC/KBS)	620000(2)
Am	PROBLEMS OF THE CHINESE REVOLUTION. Paragon Reprint Book Corporation: NY, 1966. 432. (LocAAS)	660000(4)

Am	PROBLEMS OF THE CHINESE REVOLUTION. Ann Arbor: Univ. of Michigan, 1967. 441. (LocPer)	670000(16)
Ch	⌊PROBLEMS OF THE CHINESE REVOLUTION.⌋ Communist League of China: Shanghai, 1947. 372. (LocPer)	470427
Eng	PROBLEMS OF THE CHINESE REVOLUTION. New Park, Ln, 1969. 354. (LocPer)	690500(4)
Am	PROBLEMS OF THE DEVELOPMENT OF THE USSR. Communist League of America (Opposition): NY, 1931. 48. (LocBN/HIS/LC/NYPL)	310600(1)
Cz	*PROBLÉMY ORGANISACE PRÁCE. ⌊—⌋: Chicago, 1921. 48. (CatBK/CatSCL)	*210000(38)
Sp	EL PROCESO DE MOSCÚ. Nueva Era: Mexico, 1937. 28. (LocBN/HIS/NYPL)	370000(10)
Sp	EL PROCESO DE MOSCÚ. Ediciones de la Liga Comunista: Mexico, ⌊1937⌋. 28. (LocPer)	⌊370000(23)⌋
Cz	*PROCESY PROTI "TERORISTUM" V SSSR. ⌊—⌋: ⌊—⌋, ⌊1936⌋. ⌊Advert.⌋	*⌊360000(22)⌋
Gr	E PRODOMENE EPANASTASE. Ergatikes Pales: Athens, 1945. 2 vol. (LocBN)	450000(6)
Gr	E PRODOMENE EPANASTASE. Bibliothiki "Trotski": Athens, 1945. 326. (LocPer)	450000(7)
Fr	PROGRAMME DE TRANSITION. See L'AGONIE DU CAPITALISME ET LES TÂCHES DE LA QUATRIÈME INTERNATIONALE, 440800.	
Eng	THE PROGRAMME OF PEACE. International Bookshop: NOTTINGHAM, ⌊1962. 26. (LocPer)	620000(12)
Fr	et a: PROJET DE PLATE-FORME DES BOLCHEVIKS-LÉNINISTES (OPPOSITION). See LA PLATE-FORME POLITIQUE DE L'OPPOSITION RUSSE, 271100(1).	
Am	Lenin & T., THE PROLETARIAN REVOLUTION. The Communist Press: NY, ⌊1918⌋. 453. (LocAAO/HIS)	⌊180000(53)⌋

Kar   QABARTY BYLA MALQARNY AFTONOMNY OBLASTARY BYLA ANY NE   250000(29)
        DAT ETERGE KEREKLI BULGANYNY HAQQYNDAR. [--]:
        M, 1925. 35.
        (LocLOV)

Fr   90 ANNÉES DE MANIFESTE COMMUNISTE. Bibliothèque Marxiste: .480300
        [P], 1948. [Processed]
        (LocPer)

Fr   90 ANNÉES DE MANIFESTE COMMUNISTE. S.P.E.L.: P, [1962].   [620000(7)]
        13. [Processed]
        (LocPer)

Fr   90ème ANNIVERSAIRE DU MANIFESTE COMMUNISTE. See
        MANIFESTE COMMUNISTE, 450300.

Fr   --: LA QUATRIÈME INTERNATIONALE ET LA GUERRE. Ligue   340000(5)
        Communiste Internationaliste (Bolchevik-Léniniste):
        P, 1934. 48.
        (LocBN)

Fr   LA QUATRIÈME INTERNATIONALE ET L'URSS. Ligue Communiste   331000
        (Bolchevik-Léniniste): P, 1933. 31.
        (LocBDIC/BN/HIS/IISG)

Sp   *¿QUE FUÉ LA REVOLUCIÓN DE OCTUBRE? + LECCIONES DE
        OCTUBRE. Ed. Indoamérica: Argentine, 1953-4. 228.   *530000(4)
        (CatBBA)

Sp   *QUÉ HA PASSAT. [--]: Barcelona, 1931. 61.   *310000(13)
        (CatLEHA)

Sp   ¿QUÉ SIGNIFICA LA LUCHA CONTRA EL "TROTSKISMO"? Seccion   380000(7)
        Mexicana de la IV Internacional: Mexico, 1938. 15.
        (LocBN/HIS)

Fr   QU'EST-CE QUE LE NATIONAL-SOCIALISME? Parti Communiste   [450000(4)]
        Internationaliste: P, [1945]. 10.
        (LocPer)

Fr   QU'EST-CE QUE LE NAZISME? La Vérité: P, [1957]. 16.   [570000(9)]
        (LocAAS)

Fr   *LA QUESTION UKRAINIENNE. [--]: P, 1939.   *390000(5)
        [Advert.]

Fr   LA QUESTION UKRAINIENNE. S.P.E.L.: P, 1956. 6.   560000(3)
        [Processed]
        (LocAAS)

Eng	RADIO, SCIENCE, TECHNIQUE AND SOCIETY. Labour Review Pamphlet: Ln, 1957. 19. (LocAAS)	570000(4)
Fr	RAPPORT DE LA DÉLÉGATION SIBIRIENNE. Spartacus: P, 1970. 96. (LocPer)	700000(5)
Am	THE REAL SITUATION IN RUSSIA. Harcourt, Brace & Co.: NY, [1928]. 364. (LocHIS/LC/LSE/NYPL/ULH)	[280000(9)]
Eng	THE REAL SITUATION IN RUSSIA. George Allen & Unwin: Ln, [1928]. 364. (LocAAO/ABC/BM/BRB/CU/IISG/KBC/LC/LnL/LSE/SEES)	[280000(10)]
Fr	LE RÉGIME COMMUNISTE AUX USA. See BOLCHEVISME ET STALINISME, 530000(5).	
Fr	RÉPONSE AU GROUPE SOCIALISTE PARLEMENTAIRE. [See POUR L'ACTION: 16-22. LocIISG]	[180000(57)]
Am/Eng	RESULTS AND PROSPECTS. See THE PERMANENT REVOLUTION, 650000(3)/ 620700.	
Sp	*RETRATO DEL NACIONAL-SOCIALISMO. [--]: Santiago de Chile, 1934. [Advert.]	*340700(1)
Eng	A REVIEW AND SOME PERSPECTIVES. Communist International: M, 1921. 90. (LocAAS/HIS/ULH)	210000(39)
Port	*REVOLUÇÃO E CONTRA-REVOLUÇÃO NA ALEMANTIA. [--]: San Paulo, 1933. (CatBT)	*330000(18)
Port	A REVOLUÇÃO ESPANHOLA. Empresa Editora Unitas: S. Paulo, 1931. 127. (LocPer)	310000(9)
Sp	*LA REVOLUCIÓN DESFIGURADA. [--]: Madrid, [1929]. (LocWiener Library, Harvard)	*[290000(12)]
Sp	*LA REVOLUCIÓN ESPAÑOLA. Publicaciones Teivos: Madrid, 1931. 70. (LocLC)	*310000(14)
Sp	*LA REVOLUCIÓN ESPAÑOLA. Ed. Fénix: Madrid, 1933. 102. (CatLEHA)	*330300(4)
Sp	LA REVOLUCIÓN ESPAÑOLA Y LA TACTICA DE LOS COMUNISTAS. [--]: Barcelona, 1931. 40. (LocPer)	310000(15)

Sp	LA REVOLUCIÓN ESPAÑOLA Y SUS PELIGROS. Comunismo: Madrid, 1931. 32. (LocPer)	310000(16)
Sp	*LA REVOLUCIÓN PERMANENTE. Cenit: Madrid, 1931. 235. (CatBE/CatLEHA)	*310000(17)
Sp	LA REVOLUCIÓN PERMANENTE. Indice Rojo: Mexico, 1961. 274. (LocPer)	610501
Sp	LA REVOLUCIÓN PERMANENTE. Editorial Coyoacan: Mexico, 1963. 2 vols. (LocPer)	631126
Sp	LA REVOLUCIÓN PERMANENTE. Editorial Coyoacan: Buenos Aires, 1969. 236. (LocPer)	690700(2)
Sp	LA REVOLUCIÓN RUSA. + OBJETIVIDAD HISTORICA. Perspectiva Mundial: Mexico, 1967. 47. (LocPer)	671100(1)
Sp	LA REVOLUCIÓN RUSA Y LA BUROCRATIA SOVIETICA. Ed. Coyoacan: Buenos Aires, 1961. 76. (LocNUC)	610622
Sp	*LA REVOLUCIÓN TRAICIONADA. Editorial Claridad: Buenos Aires, 1937. 254. (LocLC)	*371100
Sp	*LA REVOLUCIÓN TRAICIONADA. Ediciones Ercilla: Santiago de Chile, 1937. 284. [Private notice]	*370000(19)
Sp	LA REVOLUCIÓN TRAICIONADA. Ed. Indice Rojo: Mexico, 1963. 252. (LocPer)	630501
Sp	LA REVOLUCIÓN TRAICIONADA. ProcesO: Argentine, 1964. 264. (LocPer)	640617
Fr	LA RÉVOLUTION ALLEMANDE ET LA BUREAUCRATIE STALINIENNE: ET MAINTENANT? See ET MAINTENANT?, 320000(6).	
Am	THE REVOLUTION BETRAYED. Doubleday, Doran & Co.: NY, 1937. 308. (LocABC/BM/HIS/KBC/LC/NYPL/O)	370000(12)
Am	THE REVOLUTION BETRAYED. Pioneer Publishers: NY, 1945. 308. (LocBM/IISG/NYPL)	450000(3)

Am	THE REVOLUTION BETRAYED. Pioneer Press: NY, [1964]. 308. (LocPer)	⌊640000(4)⌋
Am	THE REVOLUTION BETRAYED. Merit: NY, 1965. 308. (LocPer)	650000(7)
Am	THE REVOLUTION BETRAYED. Merit: NY, [1969]. 308. (LocPer)	[690000(7)]
Am	THE REVOLUTION BETRAYED. Merit: NY, [1970]. 308. (LocPer)	⌊700000(9)⌋
Am-Eng	THE REVOLUTION BETRAYED. Pioneer Publishers: NY-Ln, 1957. 308. (LocPer)	570000(6)
Ch	*⌊THE REVOLUTION BETRAYED.⌋ Communist League of China: Shanghai, 1938. ⌊Private notice⌋	*380000(18)
Eng	THE REVOLUTION BETRAYED. + I STAKE MY LIFE. Faber & Faber: Ln, 1937. 312. (LocAAS/BM/CU/LnL/O/SEES)	370500
Eng	THE REVOLUTION BETRAYED. New Park: Ln, 1967. 308. (LocPer)	670000(13)
Jap	[THE REVOLUTION BETRAYED.] Gendai Shicho-sha: Tokyo, 1968. 350. (LocPer)	680610
Fr	LA RÉVOLUTION DÉFIGURÉE. Rieder: P, 1929. 215. (LocAAS/BDIC/BN/BRB/HIS/IISG/LnL/NYPL/O/PSB/ULH)	290600(3)
Den	REVOLUTIONEN FORRÅDT. Bergen: Copenhagen, 1960. 208. (LocAAO/AAS/ABC/KBS)	600000(30)
Swed	REVOLUTIONENS LÄRDOMAR (1917). Dagens Förlag: Stockholm, 1925. 83. (LocAAS/KBS/ULH)	250000(30)
Fr	LA RÉVOLUTION ESPAGNOLE ET LES TÂCHES COMMUNISTES. Editions Communistes: P, 1930. 7. (LocPer)	300000(22)
Fr	LA RÉVOLUTION ETRANGLÉE. [--]: P. [1960]. 12. [Processed] (LocAAS)	[600000(22)]
Am	THE REVOLUTION IN SPAIN. Communist League of America (Opposition): NY, 1931. 32. (LocBM/BN/HIS/LC/NYPL)	310300(2)

Eng	THE REVOLUTION IN SPAIN. Lanka Samasamaja: Colombo, Ceylon, 1952. 25. (LocIISG)	520900(2)
Eng	THE REVOLUTION IN SPAIN. Lanka Samasamaja: Colo bo, Ceylon, ⌊1967⌋. 25. ⌊Photoprint⌋ (LocPer)	⌊670000(10)⌋
Fr	LA RÉVOLUTION PERMANENTE. Rieder: P, 1932. 352. (LocBDIC/BN/BRB/HIS/IISG/KBC/O/PSB)	320810
Fr	LA RÉVOLUTION PERMANENTE. Gallimard: P, 1964. 382. (LocPer)	640627
Arab	⌊LA RÉVOLUTION PERMANENTE. + BILAN ET PERSPECTIVES.⌋ Daratellia: Beyrut, 1965. 312. (LocPer)	650000(4)
Fr	LA RÉVOLUTION PERMANENTE EN RUSSIE. Maspero: P, 1969. 56. (LocPer)	690900(1)
Fr	LA RÉVOLUTION PERMANENTE: THÈSES. U.C.I.: P, 1961. 6. ⌊Processed⌋ (LocPer)	610000(5)
Fr	*LA RÉVOLUTION RUSSE. ⌊Advert.⌋	*320000(14)
Fr	LA RÉVOLUTION RUSSE. La lutte Ouvrière: Montreal, 1967. 16. (LocPer)	670000(2)
Fr	LA RÉVOLUTION TRAHIE. Grasset: P, 1936. 346. (LocBM/BN/BRB/HIS/IISG/KBC/ULH/ULO)	361013
Fr	LA RÉVOLUTION TRAHIE. Grasset: P, 1937. 346. 18th ed. (LocBDIC/KBS/NYPL/CatZ)	370000(13)
Fr	LA RÉVOLUTION TRAHIE. Quatrième Internationale: P, 1961. 268. (LocPer)	610000(7)
Fr	LA RÉVOLUTION TRAHIE. Union Général d'Editions: P, 1969. 313. (LocPer)	690000(15)
Cz	*RÍJNOVA REVOLUCE. Rejman: Prague, 1920. 111. (CatSČL)	*200000(65)
Cz	RÍJNOVA REVOLUCE. Rude Pravo: Prague, 1921. 108. (LocPer)	210000(62)
Cz	*RÍJNOVA REVOLUCE. ⌊Reč v Kodani.⌋ ⌊Advert.⌋	*⌊340000(16)⌋

Jap	*RIRONKA TOSHITEHO STALIN. [--]: Tokyo, 1959. 222.	*590000(6)
	[Private notice]	
It	LA RIVOLUZIONE PERMANENTE. Einaudi: Turin, 1967. 206.	670121
	(LocPer)	
It	*LA RIVOLUZIONE SFIGURATA. [--]: [Italy], [1929].	*[290000(13)]
	[Advert.]	
It	LA RIVOLUZIONE SPAGNUOLA E I PERICOLI CHE LA	310700(1)
	MINACCIANO.	
	(LocIISG)	
It	LA RIVOLUZIONE TRADITA. Schwarz: Milan, 1956. 239.	560900(2)
	(LocIISG)	
It	LA RIVOLUZIONE TRADITA. Samonà e Savelli: Rome, 1968. 266.	681000
	(LocNUC)	
Yid	*DI ROJTE ARMEJ. [--]: M, 1919.	*190000(54)
	(Per Ch.A.)	
Fr	ROMAIN ROLLAND REMPLIT SA MISSION. U.C.I.: P, 1961. 5.	610000(7)
	[Processed]	
	(LocPer)	
Fr	*ROSA LUXEMBOURG ET LA IVe INTERNATIONALE. [--]: P, 1935.	*350000(12)
	[Advert.]	
Jap	*ROSHIA KAKUMEI-KA NO SEIKATSU-RON. Jigyo no Nihon-sha:	*250710
	Tokyo, 1925. 192.	
	(LocNDL)	
Jap	*ROSHIA KAKUMEI-SHI. Kôbundô: Tokyo, 1950. 5 vols.	*500000(3)
	(CatIT)	
Jap	*ROSHIA KAKUMEI-SHI. Kadokawa Shoten: Tokyo, 1954. 6 vols.	*540215
	(CatIT)	
Jap	ROSHIA KAKUMEI-SHI. Kadokawa Shoten: Tokyo, 1966. 6 vols.	660730
	10th ed.	
	(LocPer)	
Jap	*ROSHIA NO SHINSHO. Fuji Shobo: Tokyo, 1929. 270.	*290621
	(LocNDL)	
Jap	*ROSHIA WA DOKOE IKU? Dojin-sha: Tokyo, 1927.	*270000(18)
	(LocNDL)	
Pol	ROSJA SOWIECKA A POLSKA BURZUAZYJMA. Minsk, 1920. 15.	200000(66)
	(LocBDIC/NYPL)	
Pol	*ROSJA SOWIECKA A BURZUAZYJMA POLSKA. [--]: Homel, 1920.	*200000(103)
	31.	
	(CatZK)	

Ger	DIE ROTE ARMEE. [—]: Basel, 1919.	190000(53)
	(LocIISG)	
Ger	DIE ROTE ARMEE DER SOWJET-REPUBLIK AUF DER WACHT! C.Hoym:	220000(27)
	Hamburg, 1922. 46.	
	(LocAAS/ABC/CU/HIS/IISG/LnL/NYPL/CatZ)	
Ger	*ROTES MERKBLATT FÜR DIE KRIEGER DER ARBEITER- UND	*240000(58)
	BAUERNARMEE UND DER ROTEN FLOTTE ÜBER DIE WICHTIGSTEN	
	FRAGEN DES KRIEGSHANDWERKS. C.Hoym: Hamburg, 1924. 28.	
	[Advert.]	
Port	RUMO À IV INTERNACIONAL! Luta de Classe: San Paulo,	340000(6)
	1934. 62.	
	(LocBN)	
Am	THE RUSSIAN REVOLUTION. Doubleday & Co.: NY, 1959. 524.	590000(7)
	(LocNUC)	
Eng	THE RUSSIAN REVOLUTION. Labour Literature Department: Ln,	330000(19)
	1933. 40.	
	(LocAAS/BM/CU/IISG/LSE/NYPL/O/SEES)	
Eng	THE RUSSIAN REVOLUTION. New Park: Ln, 1950. 16.	500000(2)
	(LocPer)	
Eng	THE RUSSIAN REVOLUTION. See THE HISTORY OF THE RUSSIAN	
	REVOLUTION TO BREST-LITOVSK, 190400(2).	
Mal	RUSSIAN VIPLAVAM. Copenhagen prasangam. The Marxist	621031
	Publications: Madavaramba, Irinjakaluda, 1962. 44.	
	(LocPer)	
Sin	RUSSIAN VIPLAVAYA. Lanka Samasamaja: Colombo, Ceylon,	570200
	1957. 105.	
	(LocPer)	
Am	RUSSIA: PROBLEMS OF THE DEVELOPMENT OF THE USSR. See	
	PROBLEMS OF THE DEVELOPMENT OF THE USSR, 310600(1).	
Ger	DIE RUSSISCHE REVOLUTION 1905. Vereinigung Internationaler	230000(33)
	Verlangsanstalten: B, 1923. 334.	
	(LocAAS/HIS/LC/LSE/NYPL/PSB/ULH)	
Ger	u.a., DIE RUSSISCHE SOZIALISTISCHE ROTE ARMEE. [—]: B,	190000(55)
	1919.	
	(LocLSE; see under H.Bergmann.]	
Ger	u.a., DIE RUSSISCHE SOZIALISTISCHE ROTE ARMEE. Internationaler	
	Verlag: Zurich, 1920. 94.	200000(67)
	(LocBDIC/HIS/IISG/LSE)	

Nor DEN RUSSISKE ARBEIDERREVOLUTION. Norges soc. dem.   190000(56)
      ungdomsforbundets Forlag: Kristiania, 1919. 127.
      (LocAAO/AAS/LC/ULO)

Ger RUSLLAND IN DER REVOLUTION. Verlag Kaden & Comp.: Dresden,   100000(2)
      [1910]. 359.
      (LocAAS/ABC/BDIC/BM/IISG/KBS/SEES/CatZ)

Tur RUSYADA HAKIKÎ VAZIYET. Sonne: B, 1929. 54.   290000(9)
      (LocLOV)

Swed DEN RYSKA ARBETARE OCH REVOLUTIONEN. See DEN RYSKA
      ARBETARREVOLUTIONEN, 180000(41).

Swed DEN RYSKA ARBETARREVOLUTIONEN. Fram: Stockholm, 1918.   180000(41)
      108.
      (LocAAS/ABC/IISG/KBC/KBS/ULH)

Fr LE SALUT DU PARTI COMMUNISTE FRANCAIS. Humanité: P, 1922.   220000(28)
      48.
      (LocBDIC)

Fr LE SALUT DU PARTI COMMUNISTE FRANCAIS. Feltrinelli Reprint: 670000(9)
      Milan, 1967. 48.
      (LocPer)

Jap *SAYOKU HANTAIHA NO KÔRYÔ. Gendai Shicho-sha: Tokyo, 1961.   *611005
      320.
      (CatIT)

Jap SAYOKU HANTAIHA NO KÔRYÔ. Gendai Shicho-sha: Tokyo, 1964.   640330(2)
      320.
      (LocPer)

It SCELTA DI SCRITTI. Samonà e Savelli: Rome, 1968. 197.   680200(2)
      (LocPer)

Eng SCHEDULE FOR A REVOLUTION. The Merit Publishers: Calcutta,   680501
      1968. 16.
      (LocPer)

It SCRITTI: 1929-36. Einaudi: Turin, 1962. 498.   620000(20)
      (LocPer)

It *SCRITTI: 1929-36. Mondadori: Milan, 1968. 543.   *680900(3)
      [Advert.]

It SCRITTI: 1929-36. Mondadori: Milan, 1968. 543.   681100
      (LocPer)

It SCRITTI LETTERARI. Samonà e Savelli: Rome, 1968. 139.   680000(6)
      (LocPer)

Eng SECTARIANISM, CENTRISM AND THE FOURTH INTERNATIONAL. WIL: ⌊350000(18)⌋
    Ln, ⌊1935⌋. 6. ⌊Processed⌋
    (LocLSE)

Eng SECTARIANISM, CENTRISM AND THE FOURTH INTERNATIONAL. W.Tait: 450000(8)
    Edinburgh, 1945. 8. ⌊Processed⌋
    (LocPer)

Sp *SEÑAL DE ALARMA. Ed. Lucha de clases: Santiago de Chile: *⌊330000(34)⌋
    ⌊1933⌋. 52.
    ⌊Advert.⌋

Jap SEN KYUHKAYU GONEN KAKUMEI. KEKKA TO TEMBA. Gendai 670131
    Shicho-sha: Tokyo, 1967. 206.
    ⌊Alternative title: ICHICHI KUMOMO ITSUNEN KAKUMEI.
    KEKKA TO TEMBA.⌋
    (LocPer)

Fr LA SEULE VOIE. Ligue Communiste: P, 1932. 32. 320000(15)
    (LocBDIC/BN/HIS/LC)

Jap SHAKAI FASHIZMU RON HIHAN. Gendai Shicho-sha: Tokyo, 620530
    1962. 446.
    (LocPer)

Jap *SHAKAI SHISO ZENSHU. Heibon-sha: Tokyo, 1931. *310601
    (LocNDL)

Fr SIGNAL D'ALARME. See L'ÉCONOMIE SOVIÉTIQUE EN DANGER,
    330000(10).

Gr *TA SINDIKATA STEN EPOKHE TES IMPERIALISKHES PARAKHMES. *470000(6)
    Philogiki Hetairia: Athens, 1947. 16.
    (CatBABH)

Sp *LOS SINDICATOS EN LA EPOCA DE LA DECADENCIA DEL IMPERIALISMO.
    + CLASE, PARTIDO Y DIRECCION. Merit: NY, ⌊1965⌋. *⌊650000(13)⌋
    ⌊Advert.⌋

Sp *LOS SINDICATOS EN LA EPOCA DE LA DECADENCIA IMPERIALISTA. *640900(2)
    Liga Obrera Marxista: Mexico, 1964.
    ⌊Advert.⌋

Sp *LOS SINDICATOS EN LA EPOCA DEL IMPERIALISMO. Editorial *611110
    Presente: Buenos Aires, 1961.
    ⌊Advert.⌋

Sp *LA SITUACIÓN REAL DE RUSIA. M.Aguilar: Madrid, 1928. 285. *280000(5)
    (CatBE)

Sp *LA SITUACIÓN REAL DE RUSIA. Apolo: Barcelona, 1931. 241. *310000(19)
    (CatBE/CatLEHA)

Jap	SOBIETO KOKKARON. Gendai Shicho-sha: Tokyo, 1963. 402. (LocPer)	631030
Fr	[Loriot et T.], LES SOCIALISTES DE ZIMMERWALD ET LA GUERRE. Comité pour la Reprise des Relations Internationales: P, [1915]. 29. (LocBDIC)	151100(2)
Ger	SOLL DER FASCHISMUS WIRKLICH SIEGEN? Grylewicz: B, 1931. 16. (LocBN/IISG/LSE)	310000(20)
Ger	SOLL DER FASCISMUS WIRKLICH SIEGEN? + WIE WIRD DER NATIONALSOZIALISMUS GESCHLAGEN? Grylewicz: B, 1932. 23. (LocAAS/ABC/HIS/IISG/LSE)	320000(16)
Ger	SOLL DER FASCISMUS WIRKLICH SIEGEN? + WIE WIRD DER NATIONALSOZIALISMUS GESCHLAGEN? Grylewicz: B, 1932. 23. [Another ed.; not 320000(16).] (LocO)	320000(32)
Cz	SOVĚTSKÉ HOSPODÁŘSTVI V NEBEZPEČI. Edice Dělnické Politiky: [--], 1933. 20. (LocBN)	330000(21)
Am	SOVIET ECONOMY IN DANGER. + THE EXPULSION OF ZINOVIEV. Communist League of America-Pioneer Press: NY, 1933. 67. (LocHIS/LC/LSE/NYPL)	330200(1)
Jap	*SOVIET KEIZAI NO SHOMONDA. Gendai Shicho-sha: Tokyo, 1968. 294. (CatIT)	*680920
Jap	SOVIET KEIZAI NO SHOMONDA. Gendai Shicho-sha: Tokyo, 1970. 294. 2nd ed. (LocPer)	700130
Fr	LES SOVIETS ET L'IMPÉRIALISME MONDIAL. Editions de l'Internationale Communiste: Pet, 1920. 36. (LocHIS/LSE)	200000(68)
Fr	LES SOVIETS ET L'IMPÉRIALISME MONDIAL. Humanité: P, 1920. 30. (LocBM/BRB/LSE/ULO)	200000(69)
Am	THE SOVIET UNION AND THE FOURTH INTERNATIONAL. Pioneer Press: NY, 1934. 31. (LocBN/LC/NYPL)	340200(2)

Eng	THE SOVIET UNION AND THE FOURTH INTERNATIONAL. + BOLSHEVIK CONGRESSES, ONCE AND NOW. Aldred: Glasgow, 1934. 24. (LocAAS/BM/HIS/LSE/NYPL)	340000(8)
Yid	DER SOVJETEN FARBAND UN DER 4ter INTERNATIONAL. Unser Kampf: NY, 1934. 30. (LocNYPL)	340000(20)
Yid	SOVJETISHE VIRTSHAFT IN GEFAR. Yid. Grupe bai der Komligue frankreich (Internats. linke Opositsje): P, 1933. 23. (LocBN)	330100(1)
Hol	DE SOWJETMACHT EN HET INTERNATIONALE IMPERIALISME. J.J.Bos & Co.: Amsterdam, 1920. 26. (LocAAS/IISG)	200000(70)
Ger	DIE SOWJET-MACHT UND DER INTERNATIONALE IMPERIALISMUS. Promachos: Belp-Bern, 1918. 48. (LocAAS/BDIC/BM/IISG)	180000(42)
Ger	SOWJET-RUSSLAND UND DAS BÜRGERLICHE POLEN. A.Seehof: B, 1920. 24. (LocAAS/ABC/BDIC/NYPL)	200000(71)
Ger	*SOWJET-RUSSLAND UND DAS BÜRGERLICHE POLEN. ⌊--⌋: Stuttgart, 1920. (CatDB)	*200000(72)
Ger	u.a., SOWJETRUSSLAND UND POLEN. Russische Korrespondenz: B, 1920. 39. (LocBDIC/HIS/LnL/NYPL)	200000(73)
Ger	SOWJETWIRTSCHAFT IN GEFAHR! A.Grylewicz: B, 1932. 40. (LocAAS/BN/LSE/O)	321100(2)
Hol	DE SPAANSCHE REVOLUTIE EN DE GEVAREN DIE HAAR BEDREIGEN. Revolutionaar Socialistische Partij: Amsterdam, 1931. ⌊30⌋ (LocAAS/IISG)	310000(21)
Cz	*SPANĚLSKÁ REVOLUCE. ⌊Advert.⌋	*⌊310000(32)⌋
Ger	DIE SPANISCHE LEHRE. EINE LETZTE WARNUNG. Lee: Antwerp, ⌊1937⌋. 42. (LocAAS/IISG)	⌊370000(24)⌋
Ger	DIE SPANISCHE REVOLUTION. + ZEHN GEBOTE DES SPANISCHEN KOMMUNISTEN. F.Büchner: Leipzig, 1931. 20. (LocBN/IISG/LC/LSE/NYPL)	310000(22)

Ger	DIE SPANISCHE REVOLUTION UND DIE IHR DROHENDEN GEFAHREN!
	     A.Grylewicz: B, 1931. 32.
	     (LocABC/BN/LSE/NYPL)
		310000(23)

Am	THE SPANISH REVOLUTION IN DANGER. Pioneer Publishers: NY,
	     1931. 62.
	     (LocBN/HIS/LC/LSE/NYPL)
		310600(2)

Hun	A SPANYOL TANULSÁG! [--]: Bratislava, [1938]. 16. (LocPer)	[380000(9)]
Am	STALIN. Harper: NY, 1941. 516. (LocPer)	410000(1)

Am	STALIN. Harper: NY, 1946. 516. 2nd ed.
	     (LocAAS/ABC/BDIC/BM/BN/HIS/KBC/KBS/LC/LnL/NYPL/
	     SEES/ULO/CatZ)
		460315

Am	STALIN. Grosset & Dunlap: NY, 1958. 516. (LocLnL/NUC)	580000(2)
Am	STALIN. Stein & Day: NY, 1967. 516. (LocPer)	670000(12)
Eng	STALIN. Hollis & Carter: Ln, 1947. 516. (LocBDIC/BM/BN/BRB/CU/O/ULH)	470000(7)
Eng	STALIN. MacGibbon & Kee: Ln, 1968. 516. (LocPer)	680000(2)
Eng	STALIN. Panther Books: Ln, 1969. 2 vols. (LocPer)	690000(2)
Ger	STALIN. Kiepenhauer & Witsch: Cologne-B, 1952. 579. (LocIISG)	520000(3)
Ger	STALIN. Verlag Rote Weissbücher: [--], 1953. 579. (LocPer)	530000(6)
Hol	STALIN. Brill: Leiden, 1949. 503. (LocBRB/IISG)	490000(1)
It	*STALIN. Garzanti: Milan, 1948. (CatLI)	*480000(3)
It	STALIN. Garzanti: Milan, 1962. 465. (LocPer)	620404
Jap	STALIN. Godo Shuppan: Tokyo, 1967. 3 vols. (LocPer)	670115
Sp	STALIN. José Janés: Barcelona, 1947. 533. (LocPer)	470400
Sp	*STALIN. José Janés: Barcelona, 1948. 538. 2nd ed. (CatLEHA)	*480000(4)

Sp	*STALIN. José Janés: Barcelona, 1956. 3rd ed. (CatLEHA)	*560000(8)
Sp	*STALIN. Plaza & Janés: Barcelona, 1960. 541. (CatLEHA)	*600000(32)
Sp	STALIN. Plaza & Janés: Barcelona, 1963. 541. (LocPer)	630000(4)
Sp	STALIN. Plaza & Janés: Barcelona, 1967. 574. (LocPer)	670900
Hol	STALIN BEGRAAFT DE 3e INTERNATIONALE. De Vlam: Amsterdam, 1935. 12. (LocIISG)	350000(13)
Fr	STALINE. Grasset: P, 1948. 621. (LocBDIC/BN/LC/PSB)	480508
Ger	DIE STALINISCHE SCHULE D. FÄLSCHUNG. [--]: B, 1932. (LocHIS)	320000(18)
Am	STALINISM AND BOLSHEVISM. Pioneer Publishers: NY, 1937. 29. (LocAAS/BM/HIS/IISG/LC/NYPL)	370000(15)
Am	STALINISM AND BOLSHEVISM. Pioneer Publishers: NY, 1960. 27. (LocNUC)	600000(9)
Am	STALINISM AND BOLSHEVISM. Pathfinder Press Inc.: NY, 1970. 29. (LocPer)	700000(2)
Eng	STALINISM AND BOLSHEVISM. Pioneer Publishing Assoc.: Glasgow, [1941]. 16. (LocPer)	[410000(2)]
Eng	STALINISM AND BOLSHEVISM. Gupta Rahman & Gupta: Calcutta, 1945. 20. (LocPer)	451100
Eng	STALINISM AND BOLSHEVISM. Modern India Publications: Bombay, 1952. 26. (LocPer)	520400
Eng	STALINISM AND BOLSHEVISM. New Park: Ln, 1956. 19. (LocPer)	560000(4)
Nor	STALINISME OG BOLSJEVISME. Tidskrifter Oktober: Oslo, 1937. 26. (LocAAS/ABC/BN)	370000(16)
Ger	DIE STALINISTEN ENGREIFEN MASSNAHMEN. See SOWJET WIRTSCHAFT IN GEFAHR, 321100(2).	

Jap	STALIN NO ANKOKU SAIBAN. Tôyô keiza shimpo-sha: Tokyo, 1956. 222. (LocPer)	561123.
Am	THE STALIN SCHOOL OF FALSIFICATION. Pioneer Publishers: NY, 1937. 326. (LocBM/HIS/LC/LSE/NYPL)	370000(14)
Am	THE STALIN SCHOOL OF FALSIFICATION. Pioneer Publishers: NY, 1962. 326. (LocAAS/NUC/ULH)	620000(3)
Jap	[THE STALIN SCHOOL OF FALSIFICATION.] Gendai Shicho-sha: Tokyo, 1968. 378. (LocPer)	680320
Jap	STALIN SEIKEN O ABAKU. Shincho-sha: Tokyo, 1937. 273. (LocNDL)	370726
Am	STALIN'S FRAME-UP SYSTEM AND THE MOSCOW TRIALS. Pioneer Publishers: NY, [1950]. 144. (LocPPA)	[500000(4)]
Eng	STALIN'S TREASON AND THE WORLD REVOLUTION. + Crux & others, OPEN LETTER TO ALL REVOLUTIONARY PROLETARIAN ORGANIZATIONS AND GROUPINGS. ILP Marxist Group: Ln,[1935]. [Processed] (LocPer)	[350000(19)]
Ger	STALIN'S VERBRECHEN. Jean Christophe-Verlag: Zurich, 1937. 371. (LocAAS/ABC/IISG/KBC/SEES/ULO)	370000(17)
Sin	STALINVADAYA SAHA BOLSHEVIKVADAYA. Voice of Revolution: Moratuwa, Ceylon, 1947. 31. (LocPer)	471001
Sp	*STALIN Y SUS CRIMENES. Graf Valera: Madrid, 1947. 304. (CatLEHA)	*470000(9)
It	*STORIA DELLA RIVOLUZIONE RUSSA. Treves: Milan, 1936. 2 vols. (CatLI)	*360000(8)
It	*STORIA DELLA RIVOLUZIONE RUSSA. Garzanti: Milan, 1939. 3 vols. (CatLI)	*390000(9)
It	*STORIA DELLA RIVOLUZIONE RUSSA. Garzanti: Milan, 1946. 3 vols. (CatZ)	*460000(9)

| It | *STORIA DELLA RIVOLUZIONE RUSSA. Garzanti: Milan, 1960. (CatIT) | *600000(31) |

| It | *STORIA DELLA RIVOLUZIONE RUSSA. Sugar: Milan, 1964. 1270. [Advert.] | *640600 |

| It | STORIA DELLA RIVOLUZIONE RUSSA. Sugar: Milan, 1964. 1270. 2nd ed. (LocPer) | 641200 |

| It | STORIA DELLA RIVOLUZIONE RUSSA. Sugar: Milan, 1967. 768. (LocPer) | 671100(4) |

| Eng | STRATEGY AND TACTICS OF THE IMPERIALIST EPOCH. New Park: Ln, 1967. 78. (LocPer) | 670800 |

| Am | THE STRATEGY OF THE WORLD REVOLUTION. Communist League of America (Opposition): The Militant Press: NY, 1930. 86. (LocBM/BN/HIS/IISG/LC/LSE/NYPL) | 301100(4) |

| Eng | THE STRUGGLE FOR STATE POWER. Young Socialist: Colombo, Ceylon, 1966. 52. (LocPer) | 660500 |

| Sp | SU MORAL Y LA NUESTRA. + MORALISTAS Y SICOFANTES CONTRA EL MARXISMO. Ediciones de Clave: Mexico, 1939. 111. (LocPer) | 390000(3) |

| Sp | SU MORAL Y LA NUESTRA. + MORALISTAS Y SICOFANTES CONTRA EL MARXISMO. Ediciones de Clave: Mexico, 1962. 111. (LocPer) | 620719 |

| Sp | *SU MORAL Y LA NUESTRA. Ediciones Ercilla: Santiago de Chile, 1939. 92. (LocHIS) | *390000(8) |

| Jap | SUPEIN KAKUMEI TO JINKIN SENSEI. Gendai Shicho-sha: Tokyo, 1965. 446. (LocPer) | 650430 |

| Am | THE SUPPRESSED TESTAMENT OF LENIN. See ON LENIN'S TESTAMENT, 350000(10). | |

| Fr | SUR LA DEUXIÈME GUERRE MONDIALE. La Taupe: Brussels, 1970. 275. (LocPer) | 700126 |

| Fr | SUR LA NATURE DE L'ÉTAT SOVIÉTIQUE. Maspero: P, 1969. 45. (LocPer) | 690900(2) |

Fr	SUR LA QUESTION JUIVE. Union Communiste: P, 1960. 4.	600000(10)
	⌊Processed⌋	
	(LocPer)	
Cz	*SVĚTOVÁ HOSPODÁŘSKÁ KRISE A NOVE ÚKOLY KOMMUNISTICKÉ	*210000(40)
	INTERNACIONÁLY. Rejman: Prague, 1921. 38.	
	(CatSČL)	
Fr	LES SYNDICATS A L'ÉPOQUE DE LA DÉCADENCE IMPÉRIALISTE.	⌊480000(10)⌋
	Ecole du Militant: ⌊P⌋, ⌊1948⌋. 14. ⌊Processed⌋	
	(LocAAS)	
Fr	LES SYNDICATS A L'ÉPOQUE DE LA DÉCADENCE IMPÉRIALISTE.	⌊620000(8)⌋
	S.P.E.L.: P, ⌊1962⌋. 12. ⌊Processed⌋	
	(LocPer)	
Fr	LES SYNDICATS A L'ÉPOQUE DE LA DÉCADENCE IMPÉRIALISTE.	⌊690000(19)⌋
	Ligue Communiste: "Rouge": P, ⌊1969⌋. 8.	
	(LocPer)	
Hun	SZTALIN ROMBLÁSBA VISZI A SZOVJETUNIOT! K.Terebessy:	⌊360000(19)⌋
	Bratislava, ⌊1936⌋. 20.	
	(LocBN)	
Ger	TAGEBUCH IM EXIL. Kiepenheuer & Witsch: Cologne-B,	600000(11)
	1960. 255.	
	(LocAAS/KBS/NUC)	
Ger	TAGEBUCH IM EXIL. Deutscher Taschenbuch Verlag: Munich,	621100(2)
	1962, 193.	
	(LocPer)	
Ger	DIE TAKTIK DER KOMMUNISTISCHEN INTERNATIONALE GEGEN	220000(29)
	DIE OFFENSIVE DES KAPITALS. C.Hoym: Hamburg, 1922.	
	(LocPer)	
Hol	TEGEN HET NATIONAL COMMUNISME. + OVER ARBEIDERSCONTROLE	⌊400000(6)⌋
	DER PRODUCTIE. ⌊--⌋: ⌊Amsterdam⌋, ⌊1940⌋. 25.	
	⌊Processed⌋	
	(LocIISG)	
Jap	*TEIKOKUSHUGI-JIDAI NO RODO-KUMIAI. Hakubunsha: Tokyo,	*490000(4)
	1949.	
	(Private notice)	
Jap	TEIKOKUSHUGI NO BOTSURAKUKI NIOKERU RODOKUMIAI.	631001
	International Youth League: Kansai, Japan, 1963.	
	8. ⌊Processed⌋	
	(LocPer)	

Jap	TENKAN-KI NO BUNKA. Chugai Bunka Kyokai: Tokyo, 1927. 293. (LocNDL)	270901
Jap	TENKAN-KI NO BUNKA. See BUNGAKU TO KAKUMEI, 250720.	
Yid	*TERORIZM UN REVOLJUTSJE. Jewish Socialist Federation of America: NY, ⌊1922⌋. 31. (LocNYPL)	*⌊220000(36)⌋
Jap	*TERORIZUMU TO KOMUNIZUMU. Gendai Shicho-sha: Tokyo, 1962. ⌊Advert.⌋	*620120
Jap	TERORIZUMU TO KOMUNIZUMU. Gendai Shich-sha: Tokyo, 1964. 243. (LocPer)	640330(4)
Am	TERRORISM AND COMMUNISM. Ann Arbor: Univ. of Michigan, 1961. 1919 (LocKBS/NUC/O)	610000(8)
Am	TERRORISM AND COMMUNISM. Ann Arbor: Univ. of Michigan, 1963. 191. (LocPer)	630000(13)
Am	TERRORISM AND COMMUNISM. Ann Arbor: Univ. of Michigan, 1969. 191. (LocPer)	690000(18)
Ch	*⌊TERRORISM AND COMMUNISM.⌋ Communist League of China: Shanghai, 1931. ⌊Private notice⌋	*310000(37)
Fr	LE TERRORISME. Bibliothèque Communiste: P, 1920. 24. (LocBDIC/BN/PSB)	200000(74)
Fr	TERRORISME ET COMMUNISME. Editions de l'Internationale Communiste: Pet, 1920. 241. (LocAAO/GDS/IISG/PSB/ULO)	200000(75)
Fr	TERRORISME ET COMMUNISME. Bibliothèque Communiste: P, 1920. 253. (LocBDIC/BM/HIS/IISG)	200000(76)
Fr	TERRORISME ET COMMUNISME. Union Générale d'Editions: 1963. 316. (LocAAS/BN/KBS)	630608
Fin	TERRORISMI JA KOMMUNISMI. V.K.P.: n suom. järjestöjen keskustoimisto: Pietari, 1921. 212. (LocULH)	210000(60)

Fin	TERRORISMI JA KOMMUNISMI. Savon kansan kirjpaino oy: Kuopio, 1921. 208. (LocULH)	210000(61)
It	*TERRORISMO E COMUNISMO. Avanti!: Milan, 1921. 179. (LocNYPL)	*210000(41)
It	TERRORISMO E COMUNISMO. Sugar: Milan, 1964. 207. (CatIT)	640100
Sp	*TERRORISMO Y COMUNISMO. Biblioteca Nueva: Madrid, 1920. 274. (LocNYPL)	*200000(77)
Sp	*TERRORISMO Y COMUNISMO. Politica Obrera: Buenos Aires, 1965. [Advert.]	*651000(2)
Ger	TERRORISMUS UND KOMMUNISMUS. K.I.: Pet, 1920. 166. (LocAAO/AAS/ABC/ULO)	200000(56)
Ger	TERRORISMUS UND KOMMUNISMUS. K.P.Österreich, Arbeiter Buchhandlung: Vienna, 1920. 166. (LocBDIC/BM/HIS/IISG/LC/LnL/LSE)	200000(79)
Ger	TERRORISMUS UND KOMMUNISMUS. ANTI-KAUTSKY. Carl Hoym: Hamburg, 1920. 159. (LocAAS/BDIC/IISG/KBC/NYPL/CatZ)	200800(2)
Ger	TERRORISMUS UND KOMMUNISMUS. ANTI-KAUTSKY. Carl Hoym: Hamburg, 1921. 161. 2nd ed. (LocABC/BDIC/BN/CU/IISG/LC/LSE/CatZ)	210000(42)
Ger	TERRORISMUS UND KOMMUNISMUS. ANTI-KAUTSKY. Carl Hoym, Hamburg, 1923. 161. 3rd ed. (LocNYPL)	230000(35)
Ger	DIE "TERRORISTEN"-PROZESSE IN DER U.S.S.R. W.Salus: Prague, 1936. 31. (LocAAS/BRB)	360000(23)
It	LA TERZA INTERNAZIONALE DOPO LENIN. Schwarz: Milan, 1957. 327. (LocIISG)	570400
It	LA TERZA INTERNAZIONALE DOPO LENIN. Samonà e Savelli: Rome, 1969. 249. (LocPer)	690500(1)
Sp	*EL TESTAMENTO DE LENIN. Ediciones Progreso: Buenos Aires, 1940. [Advert.]	*400000(13)

| Sp | EL TESTAMENTO DE LENIN. Merit: NY, 1965. 115. (LocPPA) | 650000(1) |

Sp   EL TESTAMENTO DE LENIN. Merit: NY, 1965. 115.   650000(1)
        (LocPPA)

Gr   THANASIME AGONIA TOU KAPITALISMOU. Ergatikes Pales: 630000(12)
        Athens, 1963. 70.
        (LocPer)

Am   THEIR MORALS AND OURS. + THE MORALISTS AND SYCOPHANTS   420800
        AGAINST MARXISM. Pioneer Publishers: NY, 1942. 48.
        (LocBM/HIS/IISG/LC/NYPL)

Am   THEIR MORALS AND OURS. + THE MORALISTS AND SYCOPHANTS   ⌊420000(7)⌋
        AGAINST MARXISM. Pioneer Publishers Co.: Mexico,
        ⌊1942⌋. 64.
        (LocAAS/ULO)

Am   THEIR MORALS AND OURS. + THE MORALISTS AND SYCOPHANTS   660800(1)
        AGAINST MARXISM. Merit: NY, 1966. 80.
        (LocABC)

Am   THEIR MORALS AND OURS. THE MORALISTS AND SYCOPHANTS   690000(14)
        AGAINST MARXISM. Merit: NY, 1969. 80.
        (LocPer)

Eng   THEIR MORALS AND OURS. + THE MORALISTS AND SYCOPHANTS   ⌊620000(14)⌋
        AGAINST MARXISM. International Bookshop:
        Nottingham, ⌊1962⌋. 30. ⌊Processed⌋
        (LocPer)

Eng   THEIR MORALS AND OURS. + MORALISTS AND SYCOPHANTS   680700
        AGAINST MARXISM. New Park Publications Ltd.,
        Ln, 1968. 62.
        (LocPer)

Ger   u. Varga, THESEN ZUR WELTLAGE UND DIE AUFGABEN DER   210000(43)
        KOMMUNISTISCHEN INTERNATIONALE. ⌊--⌋: Hamburg, 1921.
        15.
        (LocPer)

Ger   u. Varga: THESEN ZUR WELTLAGE.... Pressebüro der   210000(56)
        Komintern: M, 1921. 15.
        (LocABC)

Eng   THESES ON INDUSTRY. New Park: Ln, ⌊1956⌋. 16.   ⌊560000(6)⌋
        ⌊Processed⌋
        (LocIISG)

Fr   *THÈSES SUR LA SITUATION MONDIALE ET NOS TÂCHES. Section   *⌊210000(57)⌋
        de la Presse de l'Internationale Communiste: M,
        1921. 15.
        ⌊Advert.⌋

Fr   et a., THÈSES SUR LA TACTIQUE. Section de la Presse de   210000(44)
         la Presse de l'Internationale Communiste: M, 1921. 20.
         (LocIISG)

Am   THE THIRD INTERNATIONAL AFTER LENIN. Pioneer Publishers: 360500(1)
         NY, 1936. 357.
         (LocAAS/BM/HIS/IISG/NYPL/O/SEES)

Am   THE THIRD INTERNATIONAL AFTER LENIN. Pioneer Publishers: 570500
         NY, 1936. 400.
         (LocNUC/NYPL)

Eng   THROUGH WHAT STAGE ARE WE PASSING? New Park Publications   650000(10)
         Ltd.: Ln, 1965. 43.
         (LocPer)

Heb   TOLDOT HAMAHAPEICHA HARUSIT. Mizpah: Tel Aviv, 1931. 3 vols.310000(24)
         (LocJ)

Heb   TOLDOT HAMAHAPEICHA HARUSIT. Mizpah: Tel Aviv, 1941.   410000(4)
         3 vols. 2nd ed.
         (LocPer)

Eng   TO THE TOILERS OF THE EAST. The Merit Publishers: 700100
         Calcutta, 1970. 14.
         (LocPer)

Eng   TOWARDS SOCIALISM OR CAPITALISM? Methuen: Ln, 1926. 128.   260000(26)
         (LocBM/CU/HIS/LC/LnL/LSE/NYPL/O/SEES)

Sp   *TRABAJO, ORDEN Y DISCIPLINA SALAVARÁN A LA REPÚBLICA   *[200000(86)]
         SOCIALISTA. Documentos del Progreso: Buenos Aires,
         [1920].
         [Advert.]

Am   TRADE UNIONS IN THE EPOCH OF IMPERIALIST DECAY. Workers'   620200
         Vanguard Publishing Association: Toronto, 1962.
         13. [Processed]
         (LocPer)

Eng   TRADE UNIONS IN THE EPOCH OF IMPERIALIST DECAY. WIL: Ln,   [410000(3)]
         [1941]. 16. 4th imp.
         (LocCU/HIS/IISG/LSE/SEES)

Eng   *TRADE UNIONS IN THE EPOCH OF IMPERIALIST DECAY. Spark   *480000(7)
         Syndicate: Bombay, 1948.
         [Advert.]

Cz   *TRAGEDIA NEMECKÉHO PROLETARIATU. [--]: [--], [1934].   *[340000(17)]
         [Advert.]

Yid	DI TRAGEDJE FUN DEUTSHEN PROLETARIAT. + DER ARTIKEL IN MANSHESTER GARDIEN. Yid. grupe bei der Komligue Frankreich: P, 1933. 16. (LocBN)	330400(4)
Gr	E TRAGODIA TES ISPANIA. Ergatikes Pales: Athens, 1963. 95. (LocPer)	630000(11)
Fr	LE TRAITÉ DE VERSAILLES. [--]: P, [1960]. 9. [Processed] (LocPer)	[600000(26)]
Am	THE TRANSITIONAL PROGRAM. See THE DEATH AGONY OF CAPITALISM...., 380000(5).	
Ch	[THE TRANSITIONAL PROGRAM.] Communist League of China: Shanghai, 1938. 47. (LocPer)	380000(19)
Sp	*EL TRIUNFO DEL BOLSHEVISMO. Biblioteca Nueva: Madrid, 1919. [Advert.]	*190000(66)
Sp	EL TRIUNFO DEL BOLSHEVISMO. Biblioteca Nueva: Madrid, 1920. 268. 2nd ed. (LocBDIC/HIS/NYPL)	200000(80)
Sp	EL TRIUNFO DEL BOLSHEVISMO. Biblioteca Nueva: Madrid, [1920]. 272. 3rd ed.	[200000(85)]
Fr	LA "TROISIÈME PÉRIODE" D'ERREURS DE L'INTERNATIONALE COMMUNISTE. Librairie du Travail: P, 1930. 64. (LocAAS/BDIC/BM/BN/HIS/IISG/LC/NYPL/PSB)	300000(24)
Eng	THE TROTSKY PAPERS: 1917-1922. Vol. I: 1917-1919. Mouton: The Hague, 1964. 858. (LocAAS/BN/BRB/KBC/KBS/PSB/ULO)	640000(1)
Am	TROTSKY'S DIARY IN EXILE: 1935. Harvard: Cambridge, U.S.A. 1958. 218. (LocAAS/ABC/BDIC/BM/BRB/KBC/KBS/LSE/NUC/NYPL/ULO)	580000(4)
Am	TROTSKY'S DIARY IN EXILE: 1935. Athenaeum: NY, 1963. 164. (LocNUC)	630000(5)
Eng	TROTSKY'S DIARY IN EXILE: 1935. Faber & Faber: Ln, 1959. 176. (LocBM/CU/LSE/NUC/O/SEES)	590000(8)
Eng	TROTSKY SPEAKS. WIL: Birmingham, [1943]. 9. [Processed] (LocPer)	[430000(4)]

Jap	*TSUGI WA NANI KA? Gendai Shicho-sha: Tokyo, 1952. 283. (CatIT)	*520000(4)

Am	THE TURN IN THE COMMUNIST INTERNATIONAL AND THE GERMAN
	    SITUATION. Communist League of America (Opposition):
	    NY, 1930. 30.
	    (LocBM/BN/HIS/LSE/NYPL)
		301000(1)

Eng	THE TURN IN THE COMMUNIST INTERNATIONAL AND THE GERMAN
	    SITUATION. Lanka Samasamaja: Colombo, Ceylon,
	    1958. 24.
	    (LocIISG)
		580200

Eng	TWO CONCEPTIONS OF SOCIALISM. Socialist Labour League:
	    Ln, 1954. 14. [Processed]
	    (LocPer)
		[541100(2)]

Fin	TYÖ, KURI JA JÄRJESTYS PELASTAVAT SOSIALISTISEN
	    NEUVOSTOTASAVALLAN. [--]: Pietari, 1918. 23.
	    (LocULH)
		180000(61)

Ger	ÜBER ARBEITERKONTROLLE DES PRODUKTION. See GEGEN DEN NATIONALKOMMUNISMUS, 310000(6).	

Ger	Sinowjew u. T, ÜBER DIE ROTE ARMEE. Buchhandlung des
	    Arbeiterbundes: Basel, 1919. 57.
	    (LocHIS/IISG)
		190000(57)

Ger	ÜBER LENIN. Neues Deutscher Verlag: B, 1924. 174. (LocAAO/BM/IISG/NYPL)	240000(50)
Ger	ÜBER LENIN. Offentliches Leben: B, 1932. 170. (LocAAS/LC)	321200(5)

Ger	ÜBER LENIN. Europaische Verlangsanstalt: Frankfurt,
	    1964. 152.
	    (LocPer)
		640000(2)

Ger	ÜBER LENIN. Europaische Verlangsanstalt: Frankfurt,
	    1964[/1968], 152.
	    (LocNUC)
		[680000(8)]

Sp	EL ULTIMO PLATO PICANTE DEL COCINERO STALIN. [--]: [--],
	    [1935]. 15.
	    (LocPer)
		[350000(23)]

Ger	DIE ULTRALINKEN UND DER MARXISMUS. WELCHEN WEG GEHT DER
	    LENINBUND? See DIE VERTEIDIGUNG DES SOWJET-REPUBLIK
	    UND DIE OPPOSITION, 290000(11).	

Sin	UNGE SADACHARAYA SAHA APAGE SADACHARAYA. International Publishers: Colombo, Ceylon, 1963. 144. (LocPer)	631200
Sp	LA ÚNICA SALIDA DE LA SITUACIÓN ALEMAÑA. El Hogar del Libro: Barcelona, ⌊1932⌋. 104. (LocIISG)	⌊320000(24)⌋
Eng	THE UNITED STATES OF EUROPE. Revolutionary Communist Party: Ln, [1946]. 5. ⌊Processed⌋ (LocPer)	⌊460000(14)⌋
Eng	UNITED STATES OF EUROPE. W.I.R. Publications: Ln, [1959], 6. ⌊Processed⌋ (LocPer)	⌊590000(5)⌋
Yid	UNZER REVOLJUTSION. Vanguard Publishing: NY, 1919. 238. (LocPer)	190000(68)
Yid	UNZER REVOLJUTSION. Op-tu-dait Publishing Co.: NY, 1921. 238. (LocPer)	210000(51)
Jap	*URAGIRARETA KAKUMEI. Ronsho-sha: Tokyo, 1959. 387. (CatIT)	*590000(5)
Fr	L'URSS DANS LA GUERRE. Presses Universitaires: La Louvière, ⌊1939⌋. 31. (LocPer)	⌊390000(2)⌋
Fr	L'URSS EN GUERRE. [--]: ⌊P⌋, [1961]. 26. ⌊Processed⌋ (LocPer)	⌊610000(10)⌋
Sp	*LA URSS Y LOS PROBLEMAS DE LA EPOCA DE TRANSICIÓN. [--]: [--], 1938. ⌊Advert.⌋	*381100
Cz	*ÚSPĚCY SOCIALISMU A NEBEZPEČI AVANTURISMU. [--]: [--], ⌊1931⌋. ⌊Advert.⌋	*⌊310000(33)⌋
Eng	THE USSR IN WAR. David Gray: Ln, 1939. 14. (LocHIS)	390000(4)
Swed	Domov och T., VÅR VANHEDERS JUBILUEUM (1613-1913). Fram: Stockholm, 1913. 28. (LocAAS/IISG)	130000
Cz	V CEM NESPRÁVNÁ POLITIKA NĚMECKÉ KOMUNISTICKÉ STRANY. See NĚMECKO KLÍČEM K MEZINÁRODNI SITUACI, 320000(12).	

Fin	VENÄJAN TYÖVÄEN VALLANKUMOUSEN HISTORIAA. Amerikan Suomalaisten Sosialististen Kustannus Lukkeiden Kustantama: Fitchburg, Mass., USA, (1919]. 144. (LocULH)	[190000(72)]
Hol	en Zinoviev, VERKEERDE EINHEIDSFRONTTAKTIEK. National Arbeids-Sekretariat: Amsterdam, 1927. 48. (LocIISG)	270800
Swed	DET VERKLIGA LAGET I RYSSLAND. Bonniers: Stockholm, 1929. 256. (LocAAO/AAS/KBC/KBS)	290000(10)
Ger	VERRATENE REVOLUTION. Lee: Antwerp-Zurich-Prague, 1936. 308. (LocAAO/AAS/ABC/BRB/IISG)	360000(9)
Ger	VERRATENE REVOLUTION. Lee: Antwerp-Zurich-Prague, 1937. 305. (LocIISG/LC/NYPL/SEES)	370000(18)
Ger	VERRATENE REVOLUTION. Veritas: Zurich, 1957. 305. (LocIISG)	571000
Ger	VERRATENE REVOLUTION. Verlag Neue Kritik: Frankfurt, 1968. 305. (LocPer)	680000(3)
Fr	VERS LE CAPITALISME OU VERS LE SOCIALISME? Lutte de Classes: P, 1928. 73. (LocAAS/BDIC/BN/HIS/IISG/KBC/LC/PSB)	280000(6)
Fr	*VERS LE CAPITALISME OU VERS LE SOCIALISME? Feltrinelli Reprint: Milan, 1967. 73. [Advert.]	*670000(18)
Ger	DIE VERTEIDIGUNG DER SOWJET-REPUBLIK UND DIE OPPOSITION. A.Grylewicz: B, 1929. 40. (LocAAS/BN/IISG/LSE/NYPL)	290000(11)
Sp	*VIDA DE LENIN: JUVENTUD. Edit. Indo-Americana: Argentine, 1949. 270. (CatIT)	*490000(2)
Fr	VIE DE LÉNINE: JEUNESSE. Rieder: P, 1936. 303. (LocAAO/AAS/BDIC/BRB/HIS/KBC/NYPL/SEES)	360000(10)
Hol	--: DE VIERDE INTERNATIONALE EN DE OORLOG. RSP: [Zandam], [1934]. 38. (LocAAS)	[340000(15)]
Hol	--: DE VIERDE INTERNATIONALE EN DE OORLOG. De Roode Vlag: Zandam, [1935]. 38. (LocIISG)	[350000(20)]

Hol	4de INTERNATIONALE EN DE USSR. Rev. Soc. Partij: Zaandam, [1933], 32. (LocIISG)	⌊330000(31)⌋
Hol	4de INTERNATIONALE EN DE USSR. Rev. Soc. Partij: Zaandam, [1933]. 32. (LocPer. Identical with ⌊330000(31)⌋ but for cover.⌋	⌊330000(32)⌋
Ger	—: DIE VIERTE INTERNATIONALE UND DER KRIEG. G.Vereecken: Brussels, 1934. 40. (LocBN/IISG)	340000(9)
Ger	—: *DIE VIERTE INTERNATIONALE UND DER KRIEG. Lee: Antwerp, ⌊1934⌋. ⌊Advert.⌋	*⌊340000(22)⌋
Ger	DIE VIERTE INTERNATIONALE UND DIE USSR. G.Kopp: Prague, 1933. 24. (LocAAS/ABC/BM/BN/HIS/IISG)	330000(25)
Ger	DIE VIERTE INTERNATIONALE UND DIE USSR. G.Kopp: Prague, 1934. 24. (LocIISG/NYPL)	340000(10)
Ger	*DIE VIERTE INTERNATIONALE UND DIE USSR. Lee: Antwerp, ⌊Advert.⌋	*⌊340000(23)⌋
Hun	et al., *VILÁGHABORU ÉS VILAGFORRADALOM. [—]: ⌊Budapest⌋, ⌊1919⌋. 29. (CatGV)	*⌊190000(78)⌋
Fr	VINGT LETTRES. La Vie ouvrière: P, 1919. 34. (LocBDIC/BN/HIS/IISG/NYPL/PSB/CatZ)	190600
Fr	VINGT LETTRES. Parti Ouvrier Internationaliste: ⌊P⌋, 1939. 26. ⌊Processed⌋ (LocPer)	390000(10)
Serb	*VLAST SOVJETA I INTERNACIONALNI IMPERIJALIZAM. ⌊—⌋: Pet, 1919. 32. (LocBN)	*190000(80)
Ger	VON DER OKTOBER REVOLUTION BIS ZUM BRESTER FRIEDENSVERTRAG. Promachos: Belp-Bern, 1918. 120. (LocAAO/BDIC/BM/BN/IISG/LnL/NYPL)	180000(43)
Ger	VON DER OKTOBER REVOLUTION BIS ZUM BRESTER FRIEDENSVERTRAG. Hoffmans Verlag: B,⌊1918⌋. 120. (LocAAS/ABC/BM/IISG/KBS)	⌊180000(44)⌋

Ger	VON DER OKTOBER REVOLUTION BIS ZUM BRESTER FRIEDENSVERTRAG. Futurus-Verlag: Munich, [1918]. 87. (LocIISG/LSE/CatZ)	[180000(54)]
Ger	VON DER OKTOBER REVOLUTION BIS ZUM BRESTER FRIEDENSVERTRAG. Vulkan-Verlag: Leipzig, 1919. 91. (LocBDIC/IISG/NYPL/O)	190000(58)
Ger	VON DER OKTOBER REVOLUTION BIS ZUM BRESTER FRIEDENSVERTRAG. Franks Verlag: Leipzig, 1919. 92. (LocBDIC/IISG/NYPL/O)	190000(70)
Ger	VON DER OKTOBER REVOLUTION BIS ZUM FRIEDEN VON BREST-LITOVSK. Rote Fahne: B, 1919. (LocIISG)	190000(65)
Ger	*VON OKTOBER BIS NACH BREST-LITOVSK. Deutsche Sprachgruppe der Socialist Party of the United States: Chicago, [1919]. 128. (LocKBC/KBS/LC/NYPL/ULH/ULO)	*[190000(59)]
Ger	*VOR DEM THERMIDOR. REVOLUTION UND KONTRREVOLUTION IN SOWJETRUSSLAND. (DIE PLATFORM DER LINKEN OPPOSITION). [--]: Hamburg, 1927. (CatPostnikov)	*270000(10)
Sin	VURTHIYA SAMITHI SAHA RAJAYA. Young Socialist: Colombo, Ceylon, 1965. 29. (LocPer)	650500
Hol	*WAARHEEN GAAT FRANKRIJK? [--]: [--], [1939]. [Advert.]	*[390000(6)]
Jap	*WAGA SEIKATSU. Arusu: Tokyo, 1930. 2 vols. (LocNDL)	*300723
Jap	*WAGA SEIKATSU KARA. Shun'yo-do: Tokyo, 1931. 170. (LocNDL)	*310614
Jap	*WAGA SHOGAI. Kaizo-sha: Tokyo, 1937. 3 vols. (LocNDL)	*370814
Jap	*WAGA SHOGAI. Gendai Shicho-sha: Tokyo, [1961]. 3 vols. (CatIT)	*[610000(16)]
Jap	WAGA SHOGAI. Kadokawa Shoten: Tokyo, 1966. 2 vols. (LocPer)	661031
Am	--: WAR AND THE FOURTH INTERNATIONAL. Communist League of America: NY, 1934. 35. (LocIISG)	340700(1)

Ch	--: [WAR AND THE FOURTH INTERNATIONAL.] Bolshevik-Leninist Group: [Shanghai], 1934. 78. (LocPer)	340000(21)
Eng	--: WAR AND THE FOURTH INTERNATIONAL. D.Gray: Nottingham, [1940]. 20. [Processed] (LocPer)	[400000(17)]
Am	WAR AND THE FOURTH INTERNATIONAL. See MANIFESTO OF THE FOURTH INTERNATIONAL, [400000(4)].	
Eng	WAR OR REVOLUTION. Socialist Labour Press: Glasgow, 1918. 29. (LocBM)	180000(45)
Ger	WAS IST EIN FRIEDENSPROGRAMM? Herold: Pet, 1918. 43. (LocAAO/AAS/BDIC/BM/HIS/IISG/LSE/NYPL/ULH/ULO)	180000(46)
Ger	WAS NUN? A.Grylewicz: B, 1932. 116. (LocAAS/BN/HIS/IISG)	320000(19)
Ger	WAS NUN? A.Grylewicz: B, 1932. 116. 2nd ed. (LocHIS/IISG/LnL/LSE/NYPL)	320000(20)
Ger	WAS NUN? Revolutionary Communist Party: Ln, [1946]. 120. [Processed] (LocHIS)	[460000(10)]
Ger	DIE WELTLAGE UND DIE AUFGABEN DER KOMMUNISTISCHEN INTERNATIONALE. Tipografiya III Internatsional: M, 1921. 20. (LocABC)	210000(32)
Ger	DIE WELTLAGE UND UNSERE AUFGABEN. See DIE NEUE ETAPPE, 210000(36).	
Ger	DIE WENDUNG DER KOMINTERN UND DIE LAGE IN DEUTSCHLAND. Der Kommunist: B, 1930. 16. (LocAAS/BDIC/BN/HIS/IISG/LSE)	300000(25)
Ger	WER LEITET HEUTE DIE KOMMUNISTISCHE INTERNATIONALE? Die Aktion: B, 1930. 51. (LocAAS/ABC/BDIC/HIS/IISG/LC/LSE/NYPL)	300100
Am	WHAT HITLER WANTS. Harper: NY, 1933. 31. (LocHIS/LC/LSE/NYPL)	330000(26)
Am	WHAT IS A PEACE PROGRAMME? Herold: Pet-The People's Institute: San Francisco, 1918. 24. (LocBN)	180000(48)
Eng	WHAT IS A PEACE PROGRAMME? Bureau of International Propaganda attached to the Commissariat for Foreign Affairs of the Provisional Workmen's and Peasants' Government of the Russian Republic: Pet, 1918. 24. (LocABC/BDIC/BM/HIS/KBC/LnL/NYPL/O/ULH)	180200

Eng	WHAT IS A PEACE PROGRAMME? Bureau of International Revolutionary Propaganda attached to the Commissariat for Foreign Affairs of the Provisional Workmen's and Peasants' Government of the Russian Republic: Pet, 1918. 24. (LocHIS/LC)	180000(58)
Eng	WHAT IS A PEACE PROGRAMME? Lanka Samasamaja: Colombo, Ceylon, 1956. 38. (LocAAS/BM/IISG)	560600
Am	WHAT IS THE PERMANENT REVOLUTION? Pinetree Publications: Berkeley, California, 1965. 13. (LocIISG)	650100
Am	WHAT NEXT? Pioneer Publishers: NY, 1932. 192. (LocAAS/HIS/LC/LSE/NYPL)	320900(1)
Eng	WHAT NEXT? Young Socialist Publication: Colombo, Ceylon, 1967. 59. (LocPer)	671100(2)
Eng	WHERE IS BRITAIN GOING? George Allen & Unwin: Ln, 1926. 178. (LocBDIC/BM/BN/LC/LnL/LSE/O/ULH)	260200
Eng	WHERE IS BRITAIN GOING? George Allen & Unwin: Ln, 1926. 178. 2nd ed. (LocBM/CU/HIS/IISG/LC/O)	261000(1)
Eng	WHERE IS BRITAIN GOING? Communist Party of Great Britain: Ln, 1926. 178. (LocNLS)	261000(2)
Eng	WHERE IS BRITAIN GOING? Socialist Labour League: Ln, 1960. 136. (LocPer)	600200
Eng	WHERE IS BRITAIN GOING? New Park: Ln, 1970. 136. (LocPer)	700500(2)
Am	WHITHER ENGLAND? International Publishers: NY, 1925. 192. (LocBM/HIS/LC/NYPL)	250000(32)
Eng	WHITHER EUROPE? See EUROPE AND AMERICA, 510100.	
Eng	WHITHER EUROPE? Lanka Samasamaja: Colombo, Ceylon, 1950. 35. (LocBM/IISG)	501000
Am	WHITHER FRANCE? Pioneer Publishers: NY, 1936. 160. (LocAAS/BM/HIS/LC/LSE/NYPL)	360000(11)
Am	WHITHER FRANCE? Merit Publishers: NY, 1968. 160. (LocPPA)	680612

Eng	WHITHER FRANCE? Revolutionary Communist Party: Ln, 1946. 28. ⌊Part I only.⌋ ⌊Processed⌋ (LocPer)	460000(13)
Eng	WHITHER FRANCE? Lanka Samasamaja: Colombo, Ceylon, 1961. 166. (LocNUC)	610600
Am	WHITHER RUSSIA? International Publishers: NY, 1926. 150. (LocHIS/LC/NYPL)	260000(27)
Ger	WIE WIRD DER NATIONALSOZIALISMUS GESCHLAGEN? + ARBEITER-EINHEITSFRONT GEGEN DEN FASCHISMUS. A.Grylewicz: B, 1932. 16. (LocAAS/ABC/BN/IISG/LSE)	320000(21)
Ger	DIE WIRKLICHE LAGE IN RUSSLAND. Avalun Verlag: Hellerau, 1928. 288. (LocAAO/AAS/ABC/BDIC/BM/BN/IISG/KBS/LC/LSE/NYPL/ SEES/ULH/ULO)	280000(7)
Ger	DIE WIRKLICHE LAGE IN RUSSLAND. Avalun Verlag: Hellerau, 1928. 288. (LocLC/O)	⌊300000(28)⌋
Ger	Rykow u. T., DIE WIRTSCHAFT IN SOWJET-RUSSLAND UND IN WESTEUROPA. Seehof: B, 1920. 48. (LocBDIC/HIS/IISG/LnL/NYPL/ULO)	200000(81)
Ger	Rykow u. T., DIE WIRTSCHAFT IN SOWJET-RUSSLAND UND IN WESTEUROPA. Seehof: B, 1920. 48. 2nd ed. (LocIISG)	200000(82)
Ger	WOHIN GEHT FRANKREICH? Lee: Antwerp, 1936. 103. (LocAAO/AAS/ABC/IISG/O/ULO)	360000(12)
Ger	WOHIN TREIBT ENGLAND? Deutsche Verlagsgesellschaft für Politik und Geschichte: B, 1925. 143. (LocAAS/ABC/BDIC/IISG/ULO)	250000(33)
Ger	WOHIN TREIBT ENGLAND? Volksausgabe Neuer Deutsche Verlag: B, 1926. 143. 2nd ed. (LocAAO/ABC/BDIC/CU/IISG/CatILO)	260000(28)
Pol	*WOJNA S POLSZEJ. ⌊--⌋: M, 1920. 16. (CatZK)	*200000(99)
Eng	WORKERS' CONTROL OF PRODUCTION. Socialist Labour League: Ln, ⌊1960⌋. 19. ⌊Processed⌋ (LocLSE)	⌊600000(28)⌋
Eng	WORKERS CONTROL OF PRODUCTION. International Marxist Group: Ln, 1969. 8. ⌊Processed⌋ (LocPer)	690000(3)

Eng	THE WORKERS STATE AND THE QUESTION OF THERMIDOR AND BONAPARTISM. Socialist Labour League: Ln, ⌊1961⌋. 22. ⌊Processed⌋ (LocPer)	⌊610000(11)⌋
Eng	A WORLD SURVEY. SLP Australia: Sydney, 1926. 22. (LocIISG/NYPL)	260000(34)
Am	WORLD UNEMPLOYMENT AND THE FIVE-YEAR PLAN. + A LETTER TO THE COMMUNIST WORKERS OF CZECHO-SLOVAKIA. Communist League of America (Opposition): NY, 1931. 22. (LocBM/BN/HIS/LSE/NYPL)	310200
Eng	WORLD UNEMPLOYMENT AND THE FIVE-YEAR PLAN. + A LETTER TO THE COMMUNIST WORKERS OF CZECHO-SLOVAKIA. Lanka Samasamaja: Colombo, Ceylon, 1952. 20. (LocIISG)	520900(1)
Yid	*WOS WAJTER? Naje Era: Warsaw, 1932. 32. (LocJ)	*320000(33)
Am	WRITINGS: 1939-40. Merit: NY, 1969. 128. (LocNUC)	690600(3)
Am	WRITINGS: 1938-9. Merit: NY, 1969. 152. (LocNUC)	691100(1)
Am	WRITINGS: 1937-38. Pathfinder Press: NY, 1970. 184. (LocNUC)	700400
Sp	YA ES TIEMPO DE PASAR A UNA OFENSIVA INTERNACIONAL CONTRA EL STALINISMO. LCI: Mexico, 1937. 14. (LocPer)	370000(30)
Sp	¿Y AHORA? Comunismo: Madrid, ⌊1932⌋. ⌊Advert.⌋	*⌊320000(28)⌋
Sp	YO ACUSO. Nueva Era: Mexico, 1937. 53. (LocHIS)	370000(26)
Jap	YOROPPA TO AMERIKA. Nichi-Ro Kyokai: Tokyo, 1926. 72. (LocNDL)	260807
Eng	YOUNG PEOPLE, STUDY POLITICS! New Park: Ln, 1966. 30. (LocPer)	660800(2)
Hol	DE ZAAK KIROV EN DE STALINISTISCHE BUREAUCRATIE. ⌊--⌋: Zaandam, ⌊1935⌋. 22. (LocIISG)	⌊350000(21)⌋

Cz   *ZÁKLADNÍ OTÁZKY REVOLUCE: TERORISMUS A KOMMUNISMUS; MEZI   *250000(35)
       IMPERIALISMEM A REVOLUCE; NOVA HOSPODÁŘ. POLITIKA
       SOV. RUSKA A VYHLIDKY SVĚT REVOL. Komunist. knihkup.
       a nakladat lex.: Prague, 1925. 294.
       (CatSCL)

Hol   ZAL HET FASCISME WERKELIJK OVERWINNEN? De Vooruit: ⌊310000(28)⌋
       Amsterdam, ⌊1931⌋. 16.
       (LocAAS/IISG)

Hol   ZAL HET FASCISME WERKELIJK OVERWINNEN? Prometheus: ⌊310000(29)⌋
       [Amsterdam], ⌊1931⌋. 16.
       (LocAAS/IISG)

Pol   *ZBRODNIE STALINA. Bibliotheka Polska: Warsaw, 1937. 572.   *370000(28)
       (CatIT)

Ger   ZEHN GEBOTE DES SPANISCHEN KOMMUNISTEN. See DIE SPANISCHE
       REVOLUTION, 310000(22).

Cz   *ZFALŠOVANA REVOLUCE. Typ. Grafika: Prague, 1930. 206.   *300000(30)
       (CatBK)

Eng   THE ZIMMERWALD MANIFESTO. Lanka Samasamaja: Colombo,   510900
       Ceylon, 1951. 6.
       (LocPer)

Gr   E ZON MOU. [—]: Athens, 1967. ⌊Vol. I only.⌋   670000(15)
       (LocPer)

Cz   *ZRAZENÁ REVOLUCE. Ladislav Sotek: Prague, 1936. 285.   *360000(13)
       (CatBK)

Ger   u.a., ZU NEUER ARBEIT, ZU NEUER KÄMPFEN. [—]: Hamburg,   210000(46)
       (LocPer)

Ger   ZUR FRAGE DER EINHEITSFRONT. See DIE FRAGE DER
       ARBEITERSBEWEGUNG IN FRANKREICH UND DIE
       KOMMUNISTISCHE INTERNATIONALE, 220000(23).

Ger   ZWISCHEN IMPERIALISMUS UND REVOLUTION. C.Hoym: Hamburg,   220000(30)
       1922. 154.
       (LocAAO/ABC/BDIC/BM/IISG/LC/NYPL/ULH/ULO)

Ger   ZWISCHEN IMPERIALISMUS UND REVOLUTION. C.Hoym: Hamburg,   230000(36)
       1923. 153. 2nd ed.
       (LocHIS/IISG/LC/NUC/NYPL)

CONCORDANCE TO BOOKS

Other scripts

310300(1)	COMMUNISM AND SYNDICALISM	551115	ECRITS. I.

9-18	230321
19-22	230508
23-37	291014
37-45	291021
46-52	301205
53-63	310104

================================

L'EXIL

19-25	281216(2)
25-31	
31-5	
35-9	
39-45	
45-52	290225

_____

371116(2)	LES CRIMES DE STALINE

7-14	370705
15-36	
36-76	
77-82	361228
82-8	361230
88-98	361231
98-108	370101
108-12	370103
113-9	370104
120-3	370105
123-8	370106
128-33	370109(1)
134-44	370121
144-60	370209
160-73	
173-334	370417(2)
335-53	370617(1)
353-67	370600
367-75	370612

================================

53-9	290327
60-7	290422
64	290331(2)
65	290400(2)
65	290413
68-70	290424

LES PROBLÈMES ECONOMIQUES
DE L'UNION SOVIÉTIQUE

73-80	291017
81-108	300715
109-37	321022(1)
109-11	321022(2)

SOCIALISME DANS UN SEUL PAYS
OU RÉVOLUTION PERMANENTE

141-53	300329

LA LUTTE DES BOLCHEVIKS-
LÉNINISTES EN U.R.S.S.

157-9	290522(1)
160-3	290526
163	290707
164	290601
165-8	290615
169-83	290727(1)
183-5	291229
185-9	300207(2)

++++

ECRITS.III   ++++

330400(1)   EXTRAITS DE LA CORRESPONDENCE
DE NIN A TROTSKY ET DE LA
CORRESPONDENCE DE TROTSKY
A NIN

330221

300913	310526
301121(2)	310530
301129(2)	310531
301212	310629
310112	310702
310131(1)	310727
310205	310826
310213	310901
310215	310927
310215	311119
310304	311128
310315	311216
310329	320117
310401	320613(3)
310412	320920
310420	321114
310422	

⌊NOTE: This is not a pamphlet but the
relevant portion of OCG, (4), IV.33.⌋

330400(2)	THE ONLY ROAD
7-12	320913
13-20	320802
21-8	320804(2)
29-35	320809
36-47	320817
48-54	320818(2)
55-66	320902
67-76	
77-84	320910
85-91	320912
92-3	320914

===============

180000(40)	OUR REVOLUTION
29-44	041220
51-61	050120
69-144	060600
151-61	[061200(1)]
165-8	070408/
171-7	[170120]
181-5	[170313(1)]
189-97	[170317(2)]
201-4	[170319]
207-12	[170320(1)]

===============

310000(12)	LES PROBLÈMES DE LA RÉVOLUTION ALLEMANDE
3-22	310825
23-30	310820(1)
31-49	300926(1)
50-61	291113

===============

320600(2)	PROBLEMS OF THE CHINESE REVOLUTION
19-20	301210
23-72	270507
72-82	270517(1)
83-101	[270523]
102-11	270524
112-9	270527(1)
120-2	270528(1)
123-7	270528(2)
128-57	280700
158-231	281004
232-6	291109
237-43	300926(2)
244-58	310209
259-66	310613
267-310	300826

===============

470427	[PROBLEMS OF THE CHINESE REVOLUTION]
I.	Period of the Opposition Bloc, 1926-1927
1-3	270304
5-6	270322(2)
7-9	270329
10-7	270403
19-39	270507
39-43	270517(1)
48-9	[270523]
51-9	270524
61-5	270416
67-71	270516
73-6	270527(1)
77	270527(2)
78-9	270528(2)
80	270528(1)

[PROBLEMS OF THE CHINESE....++++

⌊180000(53)⌋ Lenin & T.,
　　　　THE PROLETARIAN REVOLUTION
　　　　IN RUSSIA

6	041220
163-4	170605(1)/
168	⌊170802/⌋
179-84	⌊170600(1)/⌋
185-92	⌊170602(2)/⌋
193-200	⌊170617/⌋
201-3	⌊170709/⌋

WHAT NEXT?

239-40	170907/
241-6	⌊170813/⌋
247-54	⌊170815(1)/⌋
255-62	⌊170820(3)/⌋
263-7	⌊170817/⌋
268-74	⌊170822/⌋
275-9	⌊170823/⌋

315-8	171120/
323-4	171209(3)/

WHAT IS A PEACE PROGRAM?

328	171212/
328-47	170512/

348-54	180214
428-9	180801

==========

⌊280000(10)⌋　　THE REAL SITUATION IN RUSSIA

3-19	271023
23-195	270903
199-315	271021
222-3	271111
	SUPPLEMENTS
354-7	270912

==========

290600(3)　　LA RÉVOLUTION DÉFIGURÉE

11-22	290501
25-106	271021
110-32	270600(1)
132-43	270600(2)
147-63	270801
168-79	271023
183-214	280912

==========

640000(1)　　THE TROTSKY PAPERS
　　　　⌊Pagination for Russian text⌋

vii	351228
2	171105/
8	180126/
10	180131(1)/
14	180131(2)/
24	180202(2)
64	180806(4)
68	180809(3)
70	180800
72	180809(1)
74	180812(2)
78	180813(2)
78	180814(4)
80	180815(2) ╫╫╫╫

86	180817(11)	182	181125(2)
86	180817(12)	184	181129(1)
98	180821(1)	186	181129(2)
100	180821(2)	192	181201(2)
100	180821(3)	192	181201(3)
104	180823(2)	196	181214(1)
106	180823(3)	198	181214(2)
108	180824(2)	204	181225(2)
112	180825(2)	210	181226(2)
112	180827(2)	212	181226(3)
114	180827(3)	214	181226(4)
114	180828(2)	218	181227(1)
116	180829(3)	218	181227(2)
118	180831(2)	220	181228
126	180911(2)	224	181229
128	180912(1)	224	181230(2)
130	180914(2)	226	181231(3)
132	180926(3)	226	181231(4)
134	180926(4)	228	190101
134	181004(2)	230	190102(2)
140	181005(2)	234	190102(3)
140	181005(4)	236	190102(4)
146	181011	238	190103(1)
146	181013(1)	240	190103(2)
148	181013(2)	240	190104(2)
150	181015	246	190107(2)
150	181020	246	190110(1)
152	181023(1)	248	190111(2)
156	181023(2)	251	181226(1)
158	181023(3)	252	190111(3)
162	181025	254	190112
164	181027	254	190119
166	181101	256	190112
168	181104(2)	258	190123
170	181104(3)	260	190125
174	181108(2)	262	190126
178	181124(3)	266	190100(1)
182	181023(4)	268	190212
182	181125(1)	270	190215 ++++

THE TROTSKY PAPERS   ++++

296	190316	450	190521(6)
302	190317(3)	454	190522(3)
302	190317(4)	456	190522(4)
304	190318(9)	458	190522(5)
306	190320	460	190523
306	190321(1)	464	190524
308	190321(2)	466	190526(2)
310	190322(1)	470	190527(1)
312	190323(2)	472	190527(2)
314	190324(2)	498	190601(3)
316	190324(3)	500	190601(4)
318	190324(4)	502	190601(5)
322	190325	504	190601(6)
324	190300(2)	506	190601(7)
338	190405(2)	516	190603
340	190407(2)	528	190605(2)
340	190407(3)	530	190605(3)
342	190407(4)	534	190605(4)
344	190410(2)	536	190605(5)
356	190415	536	190605(6)
358	190416	542	190607
364	190418(3)	576	190626
386	190501(3)	596	190711(3)
394	190502(1)	598	190714
396	190502(2)	604	190727(1)
398	190503(3)	608	190727(2)
402	190507(2)	612	190729(1)
404	190507(3)	618	190801(3)
412	190512(4)	618	190802(3)
416	190513	620	190805(1)
420	190514	628	190805(5)
428	190516(3)	632	190806(1)
430	190516(4)	638	190806(2)
430	190517(1)	640	190807(2)
432	190517(2)	642	190807(3)
444	190521(2)	642	190807(4)
446	190521(3)	646	190809(3)
448	190521(4)	650	190811
448	190521(5)	662	190904(4) ++++

664	190906(2)
672	190920
684	191010
696	191017(2)
698	191017(3)
704	191020(2)
728	191024(4)
730	191025(3)
732	191025(4)
740	191027(1)
744	191027(2)
746	191030(3)
752	191102(2)
754	191103(6)
758	191114
784	191217(3)
786	191217(4)
798	[200000(95)]
800	191222(3)
804	191231

================================

190600   VINGT LETTRES

	170103
9	161114(1)
10	161113(2)
10-1	161114(2)
11	161115(1)
11-4	161115(2)
14	161119
14-5	161122(1)
15-6	161122(2)
16-7	161129
17-20	⌊161130⌋
20-2	⌊161201⌋
22-3	161202
23-4	161209
24-7	161211
27-8	161213
28-30	⌊161214(1)⌋
30-1	⌊161214(2)⌋
31-2	161215
32-3	161217
33	161231(2)
34	170102(1)

================================

PERIODICALS LIST

Cyrillic script

	*ANTIRELIGIOZNIK			
AiF	ARMIYA I FLOT	(∅ LocBM)	Iz(NKSO)	IZVESTIYA
AiFSvobRos	ARMIYA I FLOT			NARODNOGO
	SVOBODNOI ROSSII	(∅ LocBM)		KOMISSARIATA
				SOTSIAL'NOGO
Bed	BEDNOTA	(∅ LocIISG)		OBESPECHENIYA	(∅ LocIISG)
BoPr	BOEVAYA PRAVDA	(∅ LocULH)	Iz(NKVD)	IZVESTIYA
Bol	BOL'SHEVIK	(LocGDS)		NARODNOGO
	BOR'BA	(LocIISG)		KOMISSARIATA PO
BO	BYULLETEN			VOENNYM DELAM	(∅ LocULH)
	OPPOZITSII	(LocBM)		*IZVESTIYA(Odessa)
				*IZVESTIYA(Pensa)
	*DEN		Iz(Pet)	*IZVESTIYA
DSP	DEN SOVETSKOI			PETROGRADSKOGO
	PROPAGANDY	(LocBM)		GORODSKOGO
DerBed	DEREVENSKAYA			OBSHCHESTVENNOGO
	BEDNOTA	(∅ LocBM)		UPRAVLENIYA
DerKom	DEREVENSKAYA		Iz(SRD)	*IZVESTIYA(1905)
	KOMMUNA	(∅ LocULH)	Iz(Vre)	IZVESTIYA
	DERITES KAK			VREMENNOGO
	CHERTI	(LocGDS)		REVOLYUTSIONNOGO
				KOMITETA	(LocCU)
EkZhizn	EKONOMICHESKAYA		Iz(VTsIK)	IZVESTIYA
	ZHIZN	(LocHIS)		VTsIK	(∅ LocBM)
				*IZVESTIYA
GazVR-KP	GAZETA VREMENNAGO			VSEUKRAINSKOGO
	RABOCHAGO I			TsIK KP
	KREST'YANSKAGO			
	PRAVITEL'STVA	(∅ LocKBS)		KATORGA I SSYLKA	(LocNYPL)
	*GLAVPOLITPUT		KM	*KIEVSKAYA MYSL
	GOLOS	(LocHIS)		KNIGA O KNIGAKH	(∅ LocIISG)
	*GRAZHDANSKOI		Kom	*KOMMUNIST
	VOINA		Kom	
	GUDOK	(∅ LocULH)	(Gruzii)	*KOMMUNIST
				(Gruzii)	(∅ LocIISG)
	ISKRA	(LocBM)	KI	KOMMUNISTICHESKII
Iz	IZVESTIYA	(LocHIS)		INTERNATSIONAL	(LocHIS)
Iz(H)	IZVESTIYA		KomTrud	KOMMUNISTICHESKII
	HEL'SINGSFORSKAGO			TRUD	(∅ LocIISG)
	SOVETA DEPUTATOV	(∅ LocIISG)	KrA	KRASNAYA ARMIYA	(∅ LocULH)
			KrGaz	KRASNAYA GAZETA	(∅ LocBM)

	*KRASNAYA NIVA			*ODESSKI NOVOSTI	
	KRASNAYA NOV	(∉LocNYPL)	OmV	OMSKII VESTNIK	(∉ LocKBS)
	*KRASNAYA ZVEZDA		Osvob	OSVOBOZHDENIE	(∉ LocIISG)
	*KRASNOARMEETS				
	*KRASNYE ZORI		PetPr	PETROGRADSKAYA	
	KRASNYI ARKHIV	(LocO)		PRAVDA	(LocHIS)
	*KRASNYI NABAT		PetGol	PETROGRADSKII	
	KRASNYI SEVER			GOLOS	(∉ LocKBS)
	(Vologda)		PlanKhoz	PLANNOVOE	
KrestGaz	*KREST´YANSKAYA			KHOZYAISTVO	(LocCU)
	GAZETA		PodZnam	POD ZNAMENEM	
			Marks	MARKSIZMA	(LocSEES)
	LUCH	(∉ LocIISG)	Pr	PRAVDA	(LocHIS)
			Pr(V)	PRAVDA(Vienna)	(LocBM)
MolGvard	MOLODAYA GVARDIYA	(LocNYPL)	Prol(1908)	*PROLETARII(1908)	
MosPech	*MOSKOVSKII		Prol(1917)	PROLETARII(1917)	(LocBM)
	PECHATNIK		ProlRev	PROLETARSKAYA	
				REVOLYUTSIYA	(LocCU)
N(05)	NACHALO(1905)	(LocHIS)			
Nach	NACHALO		RabGaz	*RABOCHAYA GAZETA	
	(Paris)	(LocHIS)	RabM	RABOCHAYA MOSKVA	(∉ LocULH)
	NARODNOE DELO	(∉ LocIISG)	Rab	RABOCHII	(LocBM)
	*NASHA GAZETA		RabiSol	*RABOCHII I SOLDAT	
NashaPr	NASHA PRAVDA	(∉ LocKBS)	RabPut	RABOCHII PUT	(LocBM)
	NASHA ZARYA	(∉ LocIISG)		*RANNEE UTRO	
	*NASHE DELO		RobVis	ROBOTNICHI VISTI	(LocPer)
NS	NASHE SLOVO	(∉ LocHIS)	RussG	*RUSSKAYA GAZETA	
	NASH STYAG	(∉ LocIISG)		RUSSKAYA VOLYA	(LocO)
	*NAUCHNOE				
	OBOZRENIE			SEVERNAYA KOMMUNA	(∉ LocKBS)
	*NIZHNOGORODSKAYA			*SEVERNAYA RABOCHAYA	
	KOMMUNA			GAZETA	
NZh	*NOVAYA ZHIZN(1905)		SotsDem	SOTSIALDEMOKRAT	(LocHIS)
NZhizn	NOVAYA ZHIZN(1917)		Sots-Dem	SOTSIAL-DEMOKRAT	(∉ LocKBS)
		(∉ LocIISG)	SotsVestnik		
NLuch	NOVYI LUCH	(∉ LocIISG)		SOTSIALISTICHESKOI	
NM	NOVYI MIR	(LocGDS)		VESTNIK	(LocIISG)
NM(NY)	NOVYI MIR(NY)	(LocNYPL)	SputnikKom	*SPUTNIK KOMMUNISTA	
	*NOVYI PUT(Riga)		SvobRos	*SVOBODA ROSSIYA	

```
            *TOVARISHCH
            TRUD                 (LocSHL)
            *TRUDOVAYA NEDELYA


            *URALSKII RABOCHII

VechPochta  VECHERNAYA POCHTA (∅ LocO)
VestnikKVD  VESTNIK KOMISSARIATA
              VNUTRENNIKH DEL (∅ LocBM)
VPS         VESTNIK PUTEI
              SOOBSHCHENIE     (∅ LocIISG)
Vestnik     VESTNIK
  SotsAkad    SOTSIALISTICHESKOI
              AKADEMII         (LocNYPL)
            *VESTNIK ZHIZNI
            *VOENNAYA NAUKA I
              REVOLYUTSIYA
            *VOENNOE DELO
VOb         *VOSTOCHNOE OBOZRENIE
            VPERED               (LocIISG)
            *V PUTI


            *ZA NOVYI BYT
ZhiDel      ZHIVOE DELO      (∅ LocIISG)
ZhiznNats   ZHIZN
              NATSIONAL'NOSTEI(LocHIS)
ZnamyaTrudKom
            *ZNAMYA TRUDOVOI
              KOMMUNY
ZT          ZNAMYA TRUDA     (∅ LocBM)
            ZVEZDA           (∅ LocBM)
```

CONCORDANCE TO PERIODICALS

Cyrillic script

ANTIRELIGIOZNIK

| (4) | 1926 | *⌊260400(3)⌋ |

================================

ARMIYA I FLOT

(1)	21.XI.17	171114(2)/
		171118(1)/
(3)	23.XI.17	171120/
		171121/
(4)	24.XI.17	171123/
(5)	25.XI.17	171124(5)/
(6)	26.XI.17	⌊171125(5)/⌋
(7)	28.XI.17	171124(1)/
		171125(6)/
		⌊171128(4)/⌋
		⌊171128(5)/⌋
		⌊171128(6)/⌋
(8)	30.XI.17	171126(2)/
		171128(3)/
(9)	1.XII.17	171126(3)/
(12)	5.XII.17	171203(1)/
		171203(6)/
(16)	9.XII.17	171206(5)/
		⌊171208(3)/⌋
(18)	12.XII.17	171203(5)/
(23)	17.XII.17	⌊171217(2)/⌋
(25)	20.XII.17	⌊171218(2)/⌋
(27)	22.XII.17	171219(1)/
(29)	24.XII.17	171222(1)/

================================

ARMIYA I FLOT SVOBODNOI ROSSII

| (215) | 20.XI.17 | 170918(1)/ |

================================

BEDNOTA

| (505) | 9.XII.17 | 171206(5)/ |
| (86) | 11.VI.18 | 180607(1) |

================================

BOEVAYA PRAVDA

(12)	20.IX.19	191005
(38)	21.X.19	191019
		191020(1)
(41)	24.X.19	191023
(91)	19.XII.19	191217(2)
(94)	1.V.20	200429(4)
(163)	25.VII.20	200723
(170)	3.VIII.20	200731(1)
(179)	13.VIII.20	⌊200812⌋
(182)	17.VIII.20	200814
(192)	31.VIII.20	200₈30(2)
(195)	3.IX.20	200901
(197)	5.IX.20	200828
(206)	16.IX.20	200911
(222)	5.X.20	201002
(228)	12.X.20	201008(1)
(231)	15.X.20	201008(2)
(247)	3.XI.20	⌊201102⌋
(248)	5.XI.20	201027(2)
(266)	26.XI.20	201115
(277)	9.XII.20	201208(2)
(278)	10.XII.20	201208(2)
		201209(2)
(279)	11.XII.20	201208(2)
(283)	16.XII.20	201215

================================

*BOL´SHEVIK

| | 1922 | 221125 |
| | | ⌊221130(2)⌋ |

===============================

BOL´SHEVIK

| (12-13) | 20.X.24 | ⌊241020(2)⌋ |
| (16) | 1.IX.25 | 250701 |

===============================

BOR´BA

(1)	22.II.14	⌊141022(1)⌋
		⌊141022(2)⌋
		⌊141022(3)⌋
		⌊141022(4)⌋
(2)	18.III.14	⌊140318⌋
(3)	9.IV.14	140315
		⌊140409⌋
(4)	28.IV.14	140414
		⌊140428⌋
(5)	16.V.14	⌊140516(1)⌋
		⌊140516(2)⌋
		⌊140516(3)⌋

===============================

BYULLETEN OPPOZITSII

(1-2)	VII.29	280717(1)
		⌊290300(1)⌋
		290300(2)
		290304
		290320
		290329
		290331(1)
		290422
		290424
		290425
		290522(1)

		290526
		290600(1)
		290601
		290614
		⌊290626⌋
		⌊290700⌋
		290701
		290707
		290712
(3-4)	IX.29	290727(1)
		290804
		290806
		290811
		290824
		⌊290900(1)⌋
		⌊290900(2)⌋
		⌊290900(3)⌋
		⌊290900(4)⌋
		⌊290900(5)⌋
(5)	X.29	290907
(6)	X.29	290925(1)
		290925(2)
		290930
		⌊291000(1)⌋
		⌊291000(2)⌋
		⌊291004⌋
(7)	XI-XII.29	⌊290800(1)⌋
		291014
		291017
		291021
		⌊291100(1)⌋
		291100(2)
		291109
		291113
(8)	I.30	300108
		⌊300109⌋
(9)	II-III.30	291222(1)
		⌊291225⌋
		300103(1)
		300104 ++++

BYULLETEN OPPOZITSII   ++++

(9)	II-III.30	300206	(15-16)	IX-X.30	300514
		300207(1)			300619
		300209			300801
		300213			300821
		⌊300300(2)⌋			300825
(10)	IV.30	291220			300826
		291228			300900(1)
		300207(2)			⌊300900(2)⌋
		300208			⌊301000(2)⌋
		300301			⌊301000(3)⌋
		300314			⌊301000(4)⌋
		300323	(17-18)	XI-XII.30	300918
		⌊300400(1)⌋			300926(1)
		⌊300400(2)⌋			300926(2)
		⌊300400(3)⌋			301013
(11)	V.30	300122			301022
		300402			⌊301100(2)⌋
		300413(1)			⌊301100(3)⌋
		300422			301121(1)
		300425			301126
		⌊300500(1)⌋			⌊301200(1)⌋
		⌊300500(2)⌋			⌊301200(2)⌋
		⌊300500(3)⌋			⌊301200(3)⌋
(12-13)	VI-VII.30	300329	(19)	III.31	280911
		300525(1)			310104
		300528			310107
		300530			310108
		⌊300600(1)⌋			310124
		⌊300600(2)⌋			310126
		⌊300600(3)⌋			⌊310300(3)⌋
(14)	VIII.30	300329			⌊310300(4)⌋
		300610			⌊310300(5)⌋
		⌊300700(1)⌋	(20)	IV.31	310404
		⌊300700(2)⌋	(21-22)	V-VI.31	300525(2)
		300715			301121(2)
		⌊300800(1)⌋			301212
		⌊300800(2)⌋			310112 ++++
		⌊300800(3)⌋			

BYULLETEN OPPOZITSII   ++++

(21-22)	V-VI.31	310131(1)
		310205
		310209
		310213
		310215
		310308
		310311
		310313
		310325
		310414(1)
		310415
		310420
		310423
		310424
		310501
		310517
		310520
		310528(1)
		⌊310600(3)⌋
(23)	VIII.31	310531
		310612
		310613
		310624
		310629
		⌊310700(2)⌋
		310701
		310708(1)
		310708(2)
		310708(3)
		310713
		310714
		310715(1)
		310715(2)
(24)	IX.31	310730
		310802
		310820(1)
		310825

		⌊310900(1)⌋
		⌊310900(3)⌋
		310902
(25-26)	XI-XII.31	310902
		311126
		311128
(27)	III.32	⌊311200⌋
		311208
		320000(1)
		320102
		320301
(28)	VII.32	211206
		270418
		320215(1)
		320229
		320423
		⌊320500⌋
		320613(1)
		320613(2)
		320616
		320625
		320628
		⌊320700(1)⌋
		⌊320700(2)⌋
(29-30)	IX.32	260702
		320725
		320802
		320804(1)
		320804(2)
		320806
		320809
		320831
		⌊320900(2)⌋
(31)	XI.32	320920
		321013(1)
		321013(2)
		321019
		⌊321020(2)⌋
		321022(1) ++++

BYULLETEN OPPOZITSII   ++++

(32)	XII.32	320902			330513
		320922(1)			330522
		320926			330523
		321003			330525
		321006			330528
		321007			330602
		321022(2)			330604
		321030(1)			⌊330609(1)⌋
		321104			330613(1)
		321105			330613(2)
		⌊321200(1)⌋			330615
		⌊321200(2)⌋			330616
		321200(3)			330617
		321200(4)	(36-37)	X.33	330715(2)
		321203(2)			330715(4)
		321205			330719(1)
(33)	III.33	⌊321200(6)⌋			330719(3)
		330104(1)			330720(1)
		330105			330813
		330111(2)			330826
		330114			330913
		330128(1)			330920
		330206			331001
		⌊330300(1)⌋	(38-39)	II.34	330706
		330303(2)			330712
(34)	V.33	330306			330805
		330314			331107
		330321			331110
		330323(1)			331212
		330329(1)			331230
		330330			340101
		⌊330400(3)⌋			340118
		330409			340120(1)
		330410			340120(2)
		330429	(40)	X.34	340331
(35)	VII.33	330401			⌊340427⌋
		330507			340710
		330512(1)			340715
					340817(1)
					340922 ++++

BYULLETEN OPPOZITSII   ++++

(41)	I.35	341228
		341230(1)
(42)	II.35	350112
		350118
		350126
		350130
(43)	IV.35	350201
		350300(1)
		350331(1)
		⌊350400⌋
(44)	VII.35	350420
		350607(1)
		350610(1)
		350700(1)
(45)	IX.35	350829
		⌊350900(1)⌋
		350900(3)
		350907(2)
		350907(3)
		350914
		350926
(46)	XII.35	350823(1)
		351031
		351112
(47)	I.36	351100(2)
(48)	II.36	360110
		360111
		360115(1)
(49)	IV.36	360318
		⌊360400(2)⌋
		⌊360400(3)⌋
(50)	V.36	360321
		360325
		360328
		360416
		⌊360500(2)⌋
		⌊360500(3)⌋

(51)	VII-VIII.36	360603
		360605
		360609
		360709(1)
		360709(2)
(52-53)	X.36	361012
(54-55)	III.37	360708
		361218(1)
		370122
		370128(1)
		370130
		370131(1)
		370131(2)
		370201
		370209
(56-57)	VII-VIII.37	370313(2)
		370417(2)
		370423
		370429
		370617(1)
		370706
(58-59)	IX-X.37	370417(2)
		370612
		370730
		370808
		370809
		370828
(60-61)	XII.37	370921
		371102
(62-63)	II.38	370415
		371125(2)
		371213(1)
		371213(2)
		371217
(64)	III.38	380220
		380228
		⌊380300(2)⌋ ++++

BYULLETEN OPPOZITSII   ++++

(65)	IV.38	380304(1)			⌊380903(3)⌋
		380307			381022(1)
		380308			381022(2)
		380309			381022(3)
		380310(1)	(73)	I.39	380108
		380310(2)			380903(4)
		380311			381108
		380312			381114
		380317(1)			381201
		⌊380400(1)⌋			381202
(66-67)	V-VI.38	380113	(74)	II.39	380921
		380115			381214
		380500(1)			381222(3)
(68-69)	VIII-IX.38	380216			381228
		380703(1)			381230
		380703(2)			390130(2)
		380705			⌊390200(1)⌋
		380717			⌊390200(2)⌋
		380719(2)			⌊390217⌋
		380723	(75-76)	III-IV.39	380903(4)
		380724			381220
		380803			390304(1)
		380804			390304(2)
(70)	X.38	380605			390304(3)
		380706			390306
		380811			390307(1)
		380824			390307(2)
		380830			390307(3)
		380917			390310
		380919(1)			390311
		380919(2)			390318
		380922			⌊390321⌋
		380923			390324(2)
(71)	XI.38	380929	(77-78)	V-VI-VII.39	380618(1)
		381010			390422(1)
		381018			390501
(72)	XII.38	380105			390607
		380903(1)			390609
		⌊380903(2)⌋			390610(1) ++++

BYULLETEN OPPOZITSII		++++
(77-78)	V-VI-VII.39	390610(2)
		390610(3)
		390610(4)
		390610(5)
(79-80)	VIII-IX-X.39	390621
		390725
		390729
		390730
		390805
		390902
		390904
		390907
		390911
		390921
		390925
(81)	I.40	391018
		391117
		391204(1)
		391204(2)
		391211
(82-83)	II-III-IV.40	391215(2)
		400124
		400214
		400313
(84)	VIII-IX-X.40	400526
		400618(1)
		400630
		400820(6)
(85)	III.41	400817(1)
(86)	VI.41	400817(1)

=====================================

DEN

(3)	4.X.12	⌊121004(1)⌋
		⌊121004(2)⌋
(4)	5.X.12	⌊121005(1)⌋
(12)	13.X.12	⌊121013⌋
(18)	19.X.12	⌊121019(3)⌋
(38)	9.XI.12	⌊121109⌋
(49)	20.XI.12	⌊121120(3)⌋
(51)	22.XI.12	⌊121120(3)⌋
(84)	25.XII.12	⌊121225⌋
(86)	29.XII.12	⌊121225⌋
(87)	30.XII.12	⌊121230⌋

=====================================

DEN SOVETSKOI PROPAGANDY

	7.IX.19	190728

=====================================

DEREVENSKAYA BEDNOTA

(16)	31.X.17	171026(1)/
(31)	17.XI.17	171115(2)/
(37)	24.XI.17	⌊171124(6)/⌋
		⌊171124(7)/⌋
(38)	25.XI.17	171114(3)/
(39)	26.XI.17	171124(1)/
(42)	1.XII.17	⌊171130/⌋
(49)	9.XII.17	171206(5)/

=====================================

DEREVENSKAYA KOMMUNA

(84)	15.IV.19	190410(1)
(190)	24.VIII.19	⌊190819⌋
(196)	2.IX.19	190901(2)
(207)	14.IX.19	190906(1)
(210)	18.IX.19	190818(2)
(214)	23.IX.19	190916(1)

++++

DEREVENSKAYA KOMMUNA		++++	EKONOMICHESKAYA ZHIZN		
(216)	25.IX.19	190910	(2)	3.I.20	200101(1)
(220)	30.IX.19	190924(1)	(17)	27.I.20	200124(1)
(239)	22.X.19	191021(1)	(18)	28.I.20	200124(1)
(250)	4.XI.19	191102(1)	(19)	29.I.20	200124(1)
(280)	10.XII.19	191205(2)	(70)	31.III.20	200330
			(71)	1.IV.20	200330
(47)	29.II.20	200208	(78)	14.IV.20	200409(1)
(51)	5.III.20	⌊200305⌋	(85)	22.IV.20	200415
(59)	16.III.20	200212(1)	(238)	24.X.20	200522
(60)	17.III.20	200212(1)	(251)	9.XI.20	201108
(72)	1.IV.20	200330	(252)	10.XI.20	201108
(86)	22.IV.20	⌊200422⌋	(253)	11.XI.20	201108
(101)	11.V.20	200429(4)	(263)	23.XI.20	201117
		200508(1)	(272)	2.XII.20	201202(1)
(102)	12.V.20	200510(3)	(287)	21.XII.20	⌊201220⌋
(110)	22.V.20	200518	(293)	28.XII.20	201227
(115)	28.V.20	⌊200525⌋			
(120)	4.VI.20	200602	(32)	13.II.21	⌊210213⌋
(160)	22.VII.20	⌊200702⌋	(35)	17.II.21	⌊210217(2)⌋
(161)	23.VII.20	200717			
(165)	28.VII.20	⌊200728⌋	(88)	22.IV.23	230420(1)
(181)	15.VIII.20	200814	(89)	24.IV.23	230420(1)
(206)	18.IX.20	200911	(90)	25.IV.23	230420(1)
(218)	30.IX.20	200928			230421
(230)	14.X.20	⌊201014(3)⌋	(97)	4.V.23	230502
(231)	15.X.20	⌊201015(3)⌋			230503(1)
(278)	10.XII.20	201209(1)	(240)	23.X.23	231021
			(94)	24.I.24	240122(1)
(47)	3.III.21	210302	(201)	5.VI.24	⌊240605⌋
(50)	6.III.21	210305			
			(16)	20.I.25	250115
			(166)	23.VII.25	250612(1)
			(171)	29.VII.25	⌊250729⌋
DERITES KAK CHERTI			(172)	30.VII.25	⌊250730(2)⌋
			(186)	18.VIII.25	250817
	V.26	260503	(189)	21.VIII.25	250804
			(209)	13.IX.25	⌊250913⌋
			(210)	15.IX.25	⌊250915(2)⌋
			(211)	16.IX.25	250828(2) ++++

EKONOMICHESKAYA ZHIZN   ++++

(212)	17.IX.25	250828(2)
		250912
(213)	18.IX.25	250917
(215)	20.IX.25	250828(2)
(216)	22.IX.25	250828(2)
(220)	26.IX.25	250923
		250925
(221)	27.IX.25	250917
(222)	29.IX.25	250917
(265)	20.XI.25	251119
(280)	8.XII.25	251207(2)
(38)	16.II.26	260215
(122)	29.V.26	260528(1)
(168)	24.VII.26	260721

==============================

EZHEGODNIK KOMINTERNA

(8)	21.V.22	220521

==============================

GAZETA VREMENNAGO RABOCHAGO I
  KREST´YANSKAGO PRAVITEL´STVA

(8)	11.XI.17	[171111(1)/]
(19)	26.XI.17	171108(1)/
		171110(1)/
		[171111(1)/]
		[171126(1)/]
(23)	2.XII.17	171201(3)/
(40)	23.XII.17	[171222(4)/]

==============================

GLAVPOLITPUT

(3)	1920	200501(2)
(-)	1920	200508(3)

==============================

GOLOS

(59)	20.XI.14	[140000(3)]
(60)	21.XI.14	[140000(3)]
(62)	24.XI.14	[141124]
(63)	25.XI.14	[141125]
(65)	27.XI.14	[141127]
(66)	28.XI.14	[141127]
(76)	10.XII.14	[141210]
(79)	13.XII.14	[140000(3)]
(93)	30.XII.14	[141230]
(100)	8.I.15	[150108]
(106)	15.I.15	[150115(2)]
(108)	17.I.15	[150115(2)]

==============================

GRAZHDANSKOI VOINA

(2)	28.VIII.18	[180828(1)]

==============================

GUDOK

(-)	1920	200511(2)
(32)	1920	200618(2)
(-)	1920	200810(2)
(149)	5.XI.20	201027(3)
(244)	4.III.21	210302
(258)	23.III.21	210323(2)
(1193)	13.V.24	[240513(1)]
(1194)	14.V.24	[240514(1)]

==============================

ISKRA

(27)	1.XI.02	⌊021101(1)⌋
		⌊021101(2)⌋
(28)	15.XI.02	⌊021115⌋
(29)	1.XII.02	⌊021201⌋
(30)	15.XII.02	⌊021215⌋
(31)	1.I.03	⌊030101⌋
(33)	1.II.03	⌊030201(1)⌋
		⌊030201(2)⌋
		⌊030201(3)⌋
		⌊030201(4)⌋
(34)	15.II.03	⌊030215(1)⌋
		⌊030215(2)⌋
(35)	1.III.03	⌊030301⌋
(36)	15.III.03	⌊030315⌋
(38)	15.IV.03	⌊030415⌋
(41)	1.VI.03	⌊030601⌋
(43)	1.VII.03	⌊030701(1)⌋
		⌊030701(2)⌋
(53)	25.XI.03	⌊031125⌋
(55)	15.XII.03	⌊031215⌋
(56)	1.I.04	⌊040101⌋
(59)	10.II.04	⌊040210⌋
(60)	25.II.04	⌊040225⌋
(61)	5.III.04	⌊040305⌋
(62)	15.III.04	⌊040315⌋
(68)	25.VI.04	⌊040625⌋
(75)	5.X.04	⌊041005⌋
(76)	20.X.04	⌊041020(1)⌋
		⌊041020(2)⌋
(90)	3.III.05	⌊050303(2)⌋
(92)	10.III.05	⌊050310⌋
(93)	17.III.05	⌊050317⌋

======================================

IZVESTIYA

(60)	7.V.17	170505/
(76)	27.V.17	170526/
(82)	3.VI.17	⌊170602(2)/⌋

(85)	7.VI.17	170605(1)/
(86)	8.VI.17	170605(2)/
(88)	10.VI.17	170609(1)/
(112)	8.VII.17	170706/
		⌊170708/⌋
(121)	19.VII.17	170717/
(124)	22.VII.17	170720(1)/
(125)	23.VII.17	170721/
(168)	10.IX.17	170909(1)/
(169)	13.IX.17	170911
(176)	20.IX.17	170918(1)/
		170919/
(177)	21.IX.17	170920(1)/
		170920(2)/
(180)	24.IX.17	170923(1)/
(181)	26.IX.17	170923(2)/
(191)	7.X.17	171006(1)/
		171006(2)/
(192)	8.X.17	171007(2)/
(193)	10.X.17	171009(1)/
(195)	12.X.17	171011(1)/
(201)	19.X.17	171018(4)/
(204)	22.X.17	171021(1)/
(205)	24.X.17	171023(1)/
		171024(2)/
(206)	25.X.17	171024(4)/
(207)	26.X.17	171024(3)/
		⌊171025(1)/⌋
		171025(2)/
(208)	27.X.17	171024(5)/
		171025(5)/
		171026(1)/
		⌊171027(1)/⌋
(209)	28.X.17	171025(5)/
		171026(1)/
(210)	29.X.17	171027(2)/
		⌊171028(1)/⌋
		171029(2)/
(211)	30.X.17	171028(1)/
		171029(1)/ ++++

IZVESTIYA   ++++

(212)	31.X.17	171029(3)/	(234)	24.XI.17	171116(2)/
		171030(1)/			171123/
		171030(2)/			⌊171124(3)/⌋
(213)	1.XI.17	171031/	(235)	25.XI.17	171124(1)/
(214)	2.XI.17	171102(2)/			171124(2)/
(215)	3.XI.17	⌊171103(1)/⌋			171124(4)/
(216)	4.XI.17	171103(2)/	(236)	26.XI.17	171125(3)/
		⌊171104(1)/⌋	(237)	27.XI.17	⌊171125(5)/⌋
(217)	5.XI.17	171104(2)/			171125(6)/
		171104(4)/			⌊171126(1)/⌋
(218)	7.XI.17	171104(2)/			171126(3)/
		⌊171107(1)/⌋	(238)	28.XI.17	⌊171128(1)/⌋
(220)	9.XI.17	171108(1)/			⌊171128(2)/⌋
		171108(2)/			⌊171128(4)/⌋
(221)	10.XI.17	171108(1)/	(239)	29.XI.17	171128(3)/
		171108(3)/			⌊171129(1)/⌋
		171109/	(240)	30.XI.17	171126(3)/
(222)	11.XI.17	171110(1)/			⌊171130/⌋
(223)	12.XI.17	171111(2)/	(241)	1.XII.17	171201(3)/
(225)	14.XI.17	171113(2)/	(243)	3.XII.17	171203(1)/
		⌊171114(1)/⌋			⌊171203(2)/⌋
(227)	16.XI.17	171115(1)/	(244)	6.XII.17	171202(1)/
		⌊171116(1)/⌋			171202(2)/
(228)	17.XI.17	171114(3)/			171202(3)/
		171116(3)/			171202(4)/
		⌊171117(3)/⌋			171204(1)/
(229)	18.XI.17	171117(1)/			⌊171206(4)/⌋
		171118(1)/	(245)	7.XII.17	171203(3)/
		171118(2)/			171203(4)/
		171118(4)/			⌊171207(1)/⌋
		⌊171118(5)/⌋	(246)	8.XII.17	⌊171208(1)/⌋
(230)	19.XI.17	171117(4)/			⌊171208(3)/⌋
		171118(3)/	(247)	9.XII.17	171206(5)/
		171118(4)/			171207(3)/
(232)	22.XI.17	⌊171122(1)/⌋			171208(2)/
(233)	23.XI.17	171121/			⌊171209(1)/⌋
		171122(2)/	(248)	10.XII.17	171208(4)/
					171209(3)/ ++++

IZVESTIYA ++++

(249)	12.XII.17	171203(5)/		(30)	21.II.18	180220
		171208(4)/		(31)	22.II.18	180221
(250)	13.XII.17	⌊171213/⌋		(33)	24.II.18	180222(2)
(253)	16.XII.17	171214(1)/		(34)	26.II.18	180223
		⌊171216/⌋		(36)	28.II.18	180226
(254)	17.XII.17	⌊171217(2)/⌋				⌊180228(1)⌋
(255)	18.XII.17	⌊171218(1)/⌋				⌊180228(2)⌋
		⌊171218(2)/⌋		(40)	5.II.18	180304
		⌊171218(3)/⌋				⌊180305(3)⌋
(256)	20.XII.17	⌊171220/⌋		(41)	6.II.18	180216(2)
(257)	21.XII.17	171219(1)/				⌊180306(2)⌋
		⌊171221/⌋		(51)	19.II.18	180318
(258)	22.XII.17	⌊171222(3)/⌋				⌊180319(3)⌋
(259)	23.XII.17	171222(1)/		(52)	20.II.18	180319(1)
		171222(2)/		(53)	21.III.18	180319(1)
(260)	24.XII.17	⌊171224/⌋		(55)	23.III.18	180322
(4)	6.I.18	171229(1)/		(56)	24.III.18	180321(1)
(5)	7.I.18	180102(1)/				⌊180324(1)⌋
		180105(1)/		(57)	26.III.18	180324(2)
(6)	9.I.18	180102(1)/		(61)	30.III.18	⌊180330(1)⌋
(8)	12.I.18	180110/		(63)	2.IV.18	180330(2)
(10)	14.I.18	180113(1)/		(65)	4.IV.18	180401(1)
		180113(3)/				180401(3)
(11)	16.I.18	180112/		(70)	10.IV.18	180403(2)
		180113(1)/				180404
		180114(1)/				180405(1)
		180114(2)/				180408(1)
		180116/		(71)	11.IV.18	180401(2)
(15)	20.I.18	180202(1)				180403(1)
(20)	26.I.18	180117(2)/				180405(2)
(21)	27.I.18	180118(1)/		(73)	13.IV.18	180408(2)
(25)	1.II.18	180128(2)/		(74)	14.IV.18	180408(3)
(26)	15.II.18	180214		(75)	16.IV.18	180410
(27)	17.II.18	180216(1)				180411(1)
(28)	19.II.18	180216(1)		(76)	17.IV.18	180416(1) ++++
		180217(2)				
(29)	20.II.18	180219(1)				
		180219(2)				
		180219(3)				

IZVESTIYA   ++++

(78)	20.IV.18	180409
		180411(2)
		180411(3)
		180413
		180415(1)
		180415(2)
		180417(1)
(79)	21.IV.18	180417(3)
		180420(1)
(80)	23.IV.18	180416(3)
		180417(2)
		180422(1)
		180422(2)
(81)	24.IV.18	180422(1)
		180422(2)
(82)	25.IV.18	180420(6)
		⌊180425(1)⌋
(83)	26.IV.18	180420(10)
		180423(2)
(84)	27.IV.18	⌊180427(1)⌋
(85)	28.IV.18	180416(2)
		180418
		180420(3)
		180420(4)
		180423(3)
		180424(2)
		180425(3)
		180425(4)
(86)	30.IV.18	180420(5)
		180420(7)
		180420(8)
		180420(9)
		180422(7)
		180423(5)
		180423(6)
		180424(1)

(87)	1.V.18	180422(5)
		180423(4)
		180426
		⌈180501(1)⌉
		⌈180501(2)⌋
(89)	4.V.18	180427(2)
		180503(1)
(-)^x	8.V.18	180508(2)
(90)	9.V.18	180503(2)
		180507(1)
		180507(2)
		⌊180509(1)⌋
		⌈180509(2)⌋
(91)	10.V.18	180422(6)
		180425(2)
		180503(5)
		180508(14)
		180508(15)
		180508(16)
		180508(17)
(92)	11.V.18	180507(3)
		180507(4)
		180508(4)
		180508(5)
		180508(6)
		180508(7)
		180508(8)
		180508(9)
		180508(10)
		⌊180511⌋
(93)	12.V.18	180507(5)
		180508(1) ++++

---

^{x} Ekstrenny vypusk (LocBM)

IZVESTIYA ++++

(94)	14.V.18	180507(6)			180524(2)
(95)	15.V.18	⌊180515(1)⌋			180524(3)
(100)	21.V.18	180518(1)			180524(4)
(101)	22.V.18	180508(9)			180524(5)
		180508(13)			⌊180526⌋
		180508(15)	(108)	30.V.18	180521(4)
		180509(5)			180529(1)
		180509(6)	(109)	31.V.18	180529(3)
		180509(7)			180529(4)
		180509(8)			180529(5)
		180509(9)			180530(1)
		180509(10)			180530(2)
		180512(4)			180530(3)
(102)	23.V.18	180504			⌊180530(4)⌋
		180518(2)			⌊180530(5)⌋
(103)	24.V.18	180512(2)			⌊180531(6)⌋
		180513(1)	(110)	1.VI.18	180601(1)
		180513(5)	(111)	2.VI.18	180522(1)
		180514(1)	(112)	4.VI.18	⌊180604(6)⌋
		180515(2)	(113)	5.VI.18	180604(1)
		180515(4)			180604(3)
		180517	(115)	7.VI.18	180524(6)
		180520(4)	(116)	8.VI.18	180607(1)
		180521(1)	(117)	9.VI.18	180531(3)
		180521(2)			180531(4)
(104)	25.V.18	⌊180525(5)⌋			180531(5)
(105)	26.V.18	⌊180526⌋			180601(2)
(106)	28.V.18	180508(1)			180601(3)
		180508(3)	(118)	11.VI.18	180531(5)
		180520(2)			180601(4)
		180520(3)			180605(2)
		180521(3)			180606(1)
		⌊180526⌋			180606(3)
(107)	29.V.18	180523(2)			180606(5)
		180523(3)			180610(4)
		180523(4)	(119)	12.VI.18	180611(1) ++++
		180523(5)			
		180524(1)			

IZVESTIYA   ++++

(121)	15.VI.18	180613(1)			180617(3)
		180613(2)			180618(2)
		180613(3)			180618(3)
		180614(2)			180618(4)
		180614(8)	(127)	22.VI.18	180615(8)
(122)	16.VI.18	180613(4)			180615(9)
		[180616(2)]			180615(10)
(123)	18.VI.18	180603(1)			180615(11)
		180603(2)			180615(12)
		180603(3)			180618(6)
		180604(5)			180618(8)
		180615(1)			180618(9)
		180617(1)			[180622(1)]
		[180618(1)]	(130)	26.VI.18	180510
(124)	19.VI.18	180524(8)			180606(4)
		180525(1)			180618(5)
		180525(2)			180618(7)
		180525(3)	(131)	27.VI.18	180618(10)
		180525(4)			180618(11)
		180602			180624(2)
		180604(7)			180626(2)
		180605(1)	(132)	28.VI.18	180624(4)
		180607(3)			180625(3)
		180607(4)			180628
		180607(5)	(134)	30.VI.18	180629(1)
		180610(1)	(135)	2.VII.18	180625(1)
		180614(4)			180625(2)
		180614(5)			180629(2)
		180614(6)			180629(3)
		180614(7)			180629(4)
		180615(2)			180629(5)
		180615(3)			180701(1)
		180615(6)			180701(4)
(125)	20.VI.18	180615(7)	(136)	3.VII.18	180623(2)
		180615(14)			180624(6)
(126)	21.VI.18	180615(4)			180625(4)
		180615(5)	(137)	4.VII.18	180701(3)
		180617(2)	(138)	5.VII.18	180704(1)
					180704(2) ++++

IZVESTIYA ++++

(140)	7.VII.18	180625(3)	(149)	17.VII.18	180717(1)
		⌊180707⌋			180717(2)
(141)	8.VII.18	180625(4)			⌊180717(3)⌋
		⌊180708(2)⌋	(150)	18.VII.18	180715(1)
(143)	10.VII.18	180605(6)	(151)	19.VII.18	180610(3)
		180606(7)			180716(2)
		180606(9)	(153)	21.VII.18	180623(1)
		180709(1)			180701(2)
		180709(2)			180712(3)
(144)	11.VII.18	180710(1)			180712(5)
(145)	12.VII.18	180626(1)			180712(6)
		180710(3)			180716(3)
		⌊180712(1)⌋			180716(4)
		⌊180712(2)⌋			180717(4)
(146)	13.VII.18	180621			180719(3)
		180622(2)			⌊180721⌋
		180622(3)	(154)	23.VII.18	180711(3)
		180624(1)			180717(5)
		180629(6)			180717(6)
		180630(6)			180717(7)
(147)	14.VII.18	180630(1)			180717(8)
		180630(2)			180717(9)
		180630(3)			180717(10)
		180630(4)			180717(11)
		180630(5)			180717(12)
(148)	16.VII.18	180620(2)			180717(13)
		180623(2)			180718(1)
		180624(4)			180718(2)
		180625(6)			180719(1)
		180630(6)			180719(2)
		180701(1)			180722(3)
		180701(2)			⌊180723(1)⌋
		180703(1)	(155)	24.VII.18	180723(2)
		180710(3)			180724(1) ++++
		180710(4)			
		180711(1)			
		180712(3)			
		180712(4)			
		180716(1)			

IZVESTIYA   ++++

(156)	25.VII.18	180723(2)	
		180723(4)	
		180723(5)	
(157)	26.VII.18	180718(3)	
		180720(1)	
		180720(2)	
		180722(1)	
		180723(9)	
		180726(1)	
		⌊180726(2)⌋	
		⌊180726(3)⌋	
		⌊180726(4)⌋	
		⌊180726(5)⌋	
(158)	27.VII.18	180725	
(160)	30.VII.18	180717(14)	
		180723(11)	
		180724(4)	
		180727(1)	
		180727(2)	
		⌊180730(1)⌋	
		⌊180730(2)⌋	
		⌊180730(3)⌋	
		⌊180730(4)⌋	
		⌊180730(5)⌋	
		⌊180730(6)⌋	
		⌊180730(7)⌋	
		⌊180730(8)⌋	
		⌊180730(9)⌋	
(163)	2.VIII.18	180723(7)	
(164)	3.VIII.18	180719(4)	
		180722(2)	
		180723(6)	
		180723(8)	
		180723(9)	
		180723(10)	
		180723(12)	
		180724(2)	
		180724(3)	
		180727(8)	

		180727(9)
		180802(1)
(165)	4.VIII.18	180704(4)
		180727(10)
		180730(10)
		180802(3)
		180802(4)
		180803(1)
		180803(2)
		180803(3)
		180803(5)
		180803(6)
		180803(7)
		180804(1)
		⌊180804(2)⌋
		⌊180804(3)⌋
		⌊180804(4)⌋
		⌊180804(5)⌋
		⌊180804(6)⌋
		180804(8)
		180805(1)
(166)	6.VIII.18	180802(3)
		180803(1)
		⌊180804(5)⌋
(167)	7.VIII.18	180805(3)
		180805(4)
		180805(8)
		180805(9)
		⌊180807(1)⌋
(168)	8.VIII.18	180729(3)
		180802(3)
		180804(8)
		180805(2)
		180805(5)
		180805(6)
		180805(7)
		⌊180808(1)⌋
		⌊180808(2)⌋ ++++

IZVESTIYA ++++

(170)	10.VIII.18	180806(2)	(181)	23.VIII.18	⌊180822⌋
		180806(3)	(184)	27.VIII.18	180825(1)
		180807(3)	(189)	3.IX.18	180902(1)
(171)	11.VIII.18	180808(10)	(190)	4.IX.18	180829(1)
(172)	13.VIII.18	180805(11)			180903(1)
		180807(4)	(195)	10.IX.18	180803(4)
		180807(5)			180829(2)
		180807(6)	(197)	12.IX.18	180911(1)
		180807(7)	(199)	14.IX.18	180910
		180807(8)			180912(2)
		180807(9)			180912(3)
		180807(10)			⌊180914(1)⌋
		180808(3)	(201)	17.IX.18	180913(1)
		180808(4)			180913(3)
		180810(1)			⌊180917(1)⌋
		180810(2)			⌊180917(2)⌋
		180811(2)	(206)	22.IX.18	180913(2)
(173)	14.VIII.18	⌊180814(1)⌋	(209)	26.IX.18	⌊180926(1)⌋
(174)	15.VIII.18	180809(2)			*⌊180926(2)⌋
(175)	16.VIII.18	180807(11)	(210)	27.IX.18	⌊180926(1)⌋
(176)	17.VIII.18	180806(1)	(213)	2.X.18	180930(1)
		180808(5)	(215)	4.X.18	181003
		180808(6)	(216)	5.X.18	⌊181004(1)⌋
		180808(7)			⌊181005(3)⌋
		180808(8)	(217)	6.X.18	⌊181006⌋
		180809(1)	(221)	11.X.18	181004(3)
		180814(3)	(229)	20.X.18	181018
		⌊180817(1)⌋	(230)	22.X.18	181005(1)
		⌊180817(2)⌋			181007(1)
		⌊180817(3)⌋			181007(2)
		⌊180817(4)⌋	(236)	29.X.18	181028
		⌊180817(5)⌋	(245)	10.XI.18	181109
		⌊180817(6)⌋	(250)	16.XI.18	181113
		⌊180817(7)⌋	(258)	26.XI.18	181123
		⌊180817(8)⌋	(283)	25.XII.18	⌊181225(1)⌋
		⌊180817(9)⌋	(284)	26.XII.18	⌊181226(1)⌋
		⌊180817(10)⌋	(286)	28.XII.18	⌊181226(1)⌋ ++++
(178)	20.VIII.18	180808(9)			
		180812(1)			
		180814(2)			

IZVESTIYA   ++++

(4)	5.I.19	190103(3)		(189)	27.VIII.19	190826(1)
(5)	10.I.19	181231(1)				190826(2)
(6)	11.I.19	190102(1)		(194)	3.IX.19	⌊190901(1)⌋
(7)	12.I.19	181231(2)		(203)	13.IX.19	190906(1)
(8)	14.I.19	190109(1)		(214)	26.IX.19	190924(1)
(10)	16.I.19	190109(3)		(231)	16.X.19	191013
(11)	17.I.19	190110(3)		(233)	18.X.19	191016(2)
(16)	24.I.19	190124		(234)	19.X.19	191018(2)
(20)	29.I.19	190128		(236)	22.X.19	191020(1)
(28)	6.II.19	⌊190206⌋				191021(1)
(32)	12.II.19	190204		(238)	24.X.19	191023
(33)	13.II.19	181203		(239)	25.X.19	191024(1)
(43)	25.II.19	190220				191024(2)
(45)	27.II.19	⌊190226⌋		(240)	26.X.19	191025(1)
(46)	28.II.19	190224		(241)	28.X.19	191025(2)
(51)	6.III.19	⌊190306(2)⌋				⌊191026⌋
(52)	7.III.19	190306(1)		(242)	29.X.19	191029
		190306(3)		(244)	31.X.19	191028(1)
(53)	9.III.19	190304		(247)	4.XI.19	191102(1)
(54)	11.III.19	190309(2)		(249)	6.XI.19	191104(2)
(59)	18.III.19	⌊190317(1)⌋				191104(3)
(64)	25.III.19	190318(1)		(251)	9.XI.19	191107(2)
		190318(2)		(274)	6.XII.19	191205(2)
		190318(4)		(276)	9.XII.19	191205(2)
(65)	26.III.19	190318(3)				191207
(70)	1.IV.19	190330				⌊191209⌋
(73)	4.IV.19	190403		(277)	10.XII.19	191207
(79)	12.IV.19	190412(1)		(278)	11.XII.19	191207
(90)	29.IV.19	⌊190429⌋		(279)	12.XII.19	191207
(92)	1.V.19	⌊190429⌋				191211(2)
(99)	10.V.19	190507(1)⌋		(281)	14.XII.19	191211(1)
(115)	29.V.19	190526(1)				191212(2)
(126)	13.VI.19	190604(1)		(284)	18.XII.19	191217(2)
(143)	3.VII.19	190627(2)		(288)	23.XII.19	⌊191222(1)⌋
(156)	18.VII.19	190716		(289)	24.XII.19	191222(2)
(160)	23.VII.19	190719(1)		(293)	28.XII.19	191227(2) ++++
(161)	24.VII.19	190710				
(187)	24.VIII.19	190724				
(188)	26.VIII.19	190824				

IZVESTIYA   ++++

(2)	3.I.20	200101(1)	(142)	1.VII.20	200630
		⌊200103⌋	(143)	2.VII.20	⌊200702⌋
(10)	16.I.20	200115(2)	(157)	18.VII.20	200717
(18)	28.I.20	200124(1)	(159)	21.VII.20	200711(2)
(20)	30.I.20	200128	(168)	1.VIII.20	200731(1)
(24)	4.II.20	200203(1)	(175)	10.VIII.20	⌊200810(1)⌋
(47)	2.III.20	200227	(177)	12.VIII.20	⌊200812⌋
(68)	26.III.20	200325	(191)	31.VIII.20	200830(2)
(70)	31.III.20	200330	(202)	12.IX.20	⌊200912⌋
(75)	6.IV.20	200404(1)	(203)	14.IX.20	200910
(78)	14.IV.20	200409(1)	(206)	17.IX.20	⌊200917⌋
		⌊200414⌋	(213)	25.IX.20	200924(1)
(80)	16.IV.20	⌊200416⌋	(216)	29.IX.20	200928
(85)	22.IV.20	200419(1)	(220)	3.X.20	201002
(88)	25.IV.20	⌊200425⌋	(227)	12.X.20	201008(2)
(92)	30.IV.20	200429(4)	(230)	15.X.20	201013(2)
(93)	1.V.20	200429(2)	(231)	16.X.20	⌊201016⌋
		200429(3)	(233)	19.X.20	201017
(95)	5.V.20	⌊200505(2)⌋	(236)	22.X.20	201020
(96)	6.V.20	200428	(245)	2.XI.20	⌊201102⌋
		200502(1)	(263)	23.XI.20	201117
		200505(1)	(273)	4.XII.20	201202(1)
(98)	8.V.20	200505(4)	(275)	7.XII.20	201202(1)
(100)	11.V.20	200509(3)	(276)	8.XII.20	201208(2)
(101)	12.V.20	200510(3)	(277)	9.XII.20	201208(2)
		200511(2)	(278)	10.XII.20	201208(2)
(104)	15.V.20	200507(2)			201209(1)
		⌊200508(2)⌋	(283)	16.XII.20	201215
(107)	19.V.20	200518	(288)	22.XII.20	⌊201220⌋
(113)	27.V.20	⌊200527⌋	(293)	28.XII.20	201227
(114)	28.V.20	⌊200525⌋	(296)	31.XII.20	201229(1)
(115)	29.V.20	200522			201229(2)
		200528	(1)	1.I.21	201230(1)
(118)	3.VI.20	⌊200603⌋	(47)	3.III.21	210302
(121)	6.VI.20	200605	(51)	8.III.21	210306
(127)	13.VI.20	200500	(56)	15.III.21	⌊210315⌋
(129)	16.VI.20	200616(2)	(73)	5.IV.21	210403
(130)	17.VI.20	200616(1)	(90)	26.IV.21	⌊210426⌋ ++++

IZVESTIYA   ++++

(128)	14.VI.21	210613(1)
(136)	25.VI.21	210623
(137)	26.VI.21	210623
(141)	1.VII.21	210629
(159)	22.VII.21	210717(1)
(203)	13.IX.21	210911
(206)	16.IX.21	[210916]
(211)	22.IX.21	210920
(228)	12.X.21	211011
(239)	25.X.21	211020
(240)	26.X.21	211020
(241)	27.X.21	211020
(242)	28.X.21	211020
(253)	11.XI.21	211110(1)
(262)	22.XI.21	211118
(263)	23.XI.21	211120
(278)	10.XII.21	211209
(280)	13.XII.21	211211
(282)	15.XII.21	211206
(285)	18.XII.21	[211218]
(289)	23.XII.21	[211223]
(293)	28.XII.21	211226
		211227
(294)	29.XII.21	[211229]
(10)	14.I.22	220113(1)
(12)	17.I.22	220116
(13)	18.I.22	220113(2)
		220113(3)
(18)	25.I.22	[220125]
(23)	31.I.22	[220131(1)]
		[220131(2)]
(29)	7.II.22	220112
(44)	24.II.22	220223(2)
(48)	1.III.22	220228(2)
(50)	3.III.22	220220
(51)	4.III.22	220220
(55)	9.III.22	220308
(57)	11.III.22	220303(1)

(59)	14.III.22	220312
(64)	21.III.22	[220321]
(72)	30.III.22	220329(1)
(74)	1.IV.22	220331
(76)	4.IV.22	220403
(82)	12.IV.22	220411(1)
(85)	19.IV.22	220414
(96)	3.V.22	220501(1)
(107)	16.V.22	220515
(108)	17.V.22	[220516]
(109)	18.V.22	[220518]
(151)	9.VII.22	220708(1)
(159)	19.VII.22	220718
(166)	27.VII.22	220725
(168)	29.VII.22	[220727]
(192)	27.VIII.22	[220827]
(193)	30.VIII.22	220826
(229)	11.X.22	221010
(230)	12.X.22	221010
(231)	13.X.22	221011
(234)	17.X.22	221016
(242)	26.X.22	221024(2)
(243)	27.X.22	221024(1)
(245)	29.X.22	[221029]
(250)	4.XI.22	[221103(1)]
(253)	9.XI.22	221031
		221102
		221107
(259)	16.XI.22	221114(1)
(269)	28.XI.22	221125
(271)	30.XI.22	[221130(1)]
(274)	3.XII.22	221201(2)
		221202(1)
(278)	8.XII.22	221207
(296)	29.XII.22	221228
(6)	16.I.23	221221
(19)	28.I.23	230127(1)
(26)	6.II.23	230205(1) ++++

IZVESTIYA ++++

(34)	15.II.23	230210	(87)	15.IV.24	240412(1)
		⌊230215⌋			240413
(38)	20.II.23	230218			240414
(41)	23.II.23	230205(2)	(88)	16.IV.24	240406
(50)	6.III.23	230304	(92)	20.IV.24	240412(2)
(79)	12.IV.23	⌊230412⌋			⌊240420⌋
(90)	25.IV.23	⌊230425(2)⌋	(93)	22.IV.24	240419(2)
(96)	3.V.23	230501	(95)	24.IV.24	⌊240424⌋
(97)	4.V.23	230503(1)	(96)	25.IV.24	240423
		230503(2)	(98)	30.IV.24	⌊240426⌋
(105)	13.V.23	230512(1)			240428
(107)	16.V.23	⌊230516⌋			240429(3)
(116)	27.V.23	230601	(108)	14.V.24	⌊240514(2)⌋
(123)	6.VI.23	230601	(119)	27.V.24	240525
(134)	19.VI.23	230616(3)			240526
(135)	20.VI.23	230618	(122)	30.V.24	⌊240530⌋
(143)	29.VI.23	230628	(123)	31.V.24	240531(1)
(144)	30.VI.23	230629(2)	(125)	3.VI.24	240601
(159)	18.VII.23	230717	(127)	5.VI.24	240531(2)
(219)	28.IX.23	230919			⌊240605⌋
(221)	30.IX.23	⌊230930⌋	(128)	7.VI.24	240606
(226)	5.X.23	⌊231005⌋	(131)	11.VI.24	240610(1)
(241)	21.X.23	231019(1)	(136)	18.VI.24	⌊240618(2)⌋
		231019(2)	(153)	8.VII.24	240705
(242)	23.X.23	231021	(155)	10.VII.24	240703
		231022	(158)	13.VII.24	240621
(248)	30.X.23	231029(1)	(160)	16.VII.24	240610(2)
(249)	31.X.23	231030	(166)	23.VII.24	240717
(250)	1.XI.23	⌊231101⌋	(167)	24.VII.24	240720
(268)	23.XI.23	⌊231123(1)⌋	(171)	29.VII.24	240727
		⌊231123(3)⌋	(174)	1.VIII.24	240731(1)
(269)	24.XI.23	231123(2)	(175)	2.VIII.24	240731(2)
(281)	8.XII.23	⌊231208(2)⌋	(177)	5.VIII.24	240728
(2)	3.I.24	⌊240103⌋	(189)	21.VIII.24	⌊240821⌋
(19)	24.I.24	240122(1)	(192)	24.VIII.24	240729(1)
(68)	23.III.24	⌊240323⌋	(193)	26.VIII.24	240729(1)
(86)	13.IV.24	240411	(195)	28.VIII.24	240729(1)
			(217)	23.IX.24	240818 ++++

IZVESTIYA ++++

(229)	7.X.24	240928		(223)	30.IX.25	250923
(230)	8.X.24	240930		(224)	1.X.25	250930
(237)	16.X.24	241015(2)		(226)	3.X.25	251002
(238)	17.X.24	240922		(228)	6.X.25	251005
(240)	19.X.24	241018		(251)	1.XI.25	251031
(246)	26.X.24	241023		(259)	13.XI.25	251102
(249)	30.X.24	241029(1)		(261)	15.XI.25	251107(1)
(251)	1.XI.24	241015(1)		(265)	20.XI.25	251119
(254)	5.XI.24	241025		(272)	28.XI.25	251108
(256)	7.XI.24	⌊241107⌋		(280)	8.XII.25	251207(2)
(282)	10.XII.24	211206		(281)	9.XII.25	251208
				(288)	17.XII.25	251207(1)
(16)	20.I.25	250115				
(70)	27.III.25	250320		(6)	8.I.26	251226
(73)	31.III.25	250327		(16)	20.I.26	260113(2)
(104)	9.V.25	250403		(25)	31.I.26	260129
(119)	27.V.25	250525		(26)	2.II.26	260129
(123)	2.VI.25	250531		(33)	10.II.26	260209
(147)	1.VII.25	⌊250630⌋		(34)	11.II.26	260211
(152)	7.VII.25	250706		(37)	14.II.26	260212
(162)	18.VII.25	250716		(50)	2.III.26	260215
(163)	19.VII.25	250712		(51)	3.III.26	260215
(171)	29.VII.25	⌊250729⌋		(52)	4.III.26	260215
(172)	30.VII.25	⌊250730(1)⌋		(53)	5.III.26	260215
(186)	18.VIII.25	250817		(60)	14.III.26	260310
(194)	27.VIII.25	250817		(125)	2.VI.26	260528(1)
(195)	28.VIII.25	250817		(168)	24.VII.26	260721
(196)	29.VIII.25	250828(1)		(240)	17.X.26	261016
(198)	1.IX.25	250828(2)		(257)	6.XI.26	261101
(199)	2.IX.25	250828(2)		(274)	26.XI.26	261125
(200)	3.IX.25	250902		(289)	14.XII.26	261208
(204)	8.IX.25	250903				
(210)	15.IX.25	⌊250915(2)⌋				
(211)	16.IX.25	250828(2)				
(212)	17.IX.25	250828(2)				
(215)	20.IX.25	250828(2)				
(216)	22.IX.25	250828(2)				
		250910				
(217)	23.IX.25	250911				

IZVESTIYA(H)

(215)	1.XII.17	171128(3)/
		[171129(1)/]
		[171130/]

=================================

IZVESTIYA(NKSO)

(2)	4.II.22	220117
(7)	13.III.22	[220313]
(26)	10.VII.22	[220710(2)]
(50)	25.XII.22	[221225]

=================================

IZVESTIYA(NKVD)

(8)	1.V.18	180429(1)
		180429(2)
		180429(3)
(9)	3.V.18	[180425(1)]
(10)	9.V.18	180430
		180503(2)
		180503(3)
		180503(4)
		180503(5)
		180507(1)
		180507(2)
		180507(3)
		180507(4)
(11)	10.V.18	180330(2)
		180503(2)
		180507(5)
		180507(6)
		180508(1)
		180508(3)
		180508(4)
		180508(5)
		180508(6)
		180508(7)
		180508(8)
		180508(9)

		180508(10)
		180508(11)
		180508(12)
		180508(13)
		180508(14)
		180508(15)
		180508(16)
		180508(17)
		180508(18)
(11)	10.V.18	[180509(2)]
		[180510(1)]
(12)	11.V.18	180330(2)
		180507(6)
		180509(4)
		180509(5)
		180509(6)
		180509(7)
		180509(8)
		180509(9)
		180509(10)
		180509(11)
		180509(12)
		180509(13)
		180509(14)
(13)	12.V.18	180330(2)
		180507(6)
		180510(2)
(14)	14.V.18	180507(6)
		180510(2)
		180512(1)
		180512(3)
		180512(4)
		180512(5)
		180513(1)
		180513(2)
		180513(3)
		180513(4)
		180513(5)
(15)	16.V.18	180512(2)

IZVESTIYA(NKVD) ++++

(15)	17.V.18	180515(4)	(25)	30.V.18	180528(1)
		180516(1)			180528(2)
(16)	17.V.18	180515(3)			180529(1)
		180515(4)			180529(3)
		180516(1)			180529(4)
(17)	18.V.18	180504			180529(5)
		180516(2)			180529(6)
		180517			[180530(5)]
(19)	21.V.18	180518(1)			[180530(6)]
		180520(1)	(26)	31.V.18	180529(7)
(20)	22.V.18	180518(1)			180530(7)
		180520(2)	(27)	1.VI.18	180531(3)
		180520(3)			180531(4)
		180520(4)			180531(8)
(21)	23.V.18	180320(3)	(28)	2.VI.18	180531(7)
		180518(1)	(29)	4.VI.18	180601(4)
		180521(1)			180601(5)
		180521(2)	(30)	5.VI.18	180601(2)
(22)	24.V.18	180518(1)			180601(3)
		180518(2)			180602
		180521(3)			180603(1)
(23)	26.V.18	180523(2)			180603(2)
		180523(3)			180603(3)
		180523(4)			180604(5)
		180523(5)			180604(7)
		180524(1)	(32)	7.VI.18	180605(2)
		180524(2)			180606(1)
		180524(3)			180606(3)
		180524(4)	(33)	8.VI.18	180605(1)
		180524(5)			180606(2)
(24)	28.V.18	180514(2)			180606(4)
		180516(4)			180606(5)
		180516(5)	(34)	9.VI.18	180607(1)
		180516(6)			180607(3)
		180521(4)			180607(4)
		180522(2)	(35)	11.VI.18	180606(4)
		180524(6)			180607(5)
		180524(7)			180610(1) ++++
		180527(2)			
		180527(3)			

IZVESTIYA(NKVD)   ++++

(36)	12.VI.18	180524(8)			180618(5)
		180525(1)			180618(6)
		180525(2)			180618(7)
		180525(3)			180618(8)
		180525(4)			180618(10)
		180611(2)			180618(11)
(37)	13.VI.18	180611(3)			180618(12)
(38)	14.VI.18	180614(2)	(44)	22.VI.18	180621
		180614(15)	(46)	25.VI.18	180622(2)
(39)	16.VI.18	180613(4)			180622(3)
(40)	18.VI.18	180606(3)			180622(4)
		180613(3)	(47)	26.VI.18	⌊180623(3)⌋
		180614(3)	(48)	27.VI.18	180624(1)
		180614(4)			180624(2)
		180614(5)			180624(3)
		180614(6)			180624(4)
		180614(7)	(49)	28.VI.18	180624(5)
		180615(8)			180625(1)
		180615(9)			180625(2)
		180615(10)			180625(3)
		180615(11)			180626(1)
		180615(12)	(50)	29.VI.18	180618(12)
		180615(13)			180627(1)
(41)	19.VI.18	180615(2)			180627(2)
		180615(3)			180627(3)
		180615(4)			180627(4)
		180615(5)			180627(5)
		180615(6)			180627(6)
		180617(1)			180627(7)
(42)	20.VI.18	180601(1)			180627(8)
		180615(7)			180627(9)
		180615(14)			180627(10)
		180615(15)			180627(11)
		180617(2)			180627(12)
		180617(3)			180627(13)
		180618(2)			180627(14)
		180618(3)			180627(15)
		180618(4)			180627(16) ++++

IZVESTIYA(NKVD)   ++++

(50)	29.VI.18	180627(17)			180716(4)
		180627(18)			180716(6)
		180627(19)			180717(2)
		180627(20)			180717(4)
		180627(21)	(68)	20.VII.18	180711(3)
		180627(22)			180717(5)
		180627(23)			180717(6)
		180627(24)			180717(7)
		180627(25)			180717(8)
		180627(26)			180717(9)
		⌊180629(7)⌋			180717(10)
(51)	30.VI.18	180625(4)			180717(11)
		180625(5)			180717(12)
(52)	2.VII.18	180629(2)			180717(13)
(53)	3.VII.18	180629(3)			180718(1)
(58)	9.VII.18	⌊180708(2)⌋			180718(2)
(59)	10.VII.18	180706(1)	(70)	23.VII.18	180719(1)
		180706(2)			180719(2)
		180706(3)			180719(3)
		180706(4)			⌊180723(1)⌋
(61)	12.VII.18	180708(1)	(71)	24.VII.18	180718(3)
(63)	14.VII.18	180620(2)			180718(6)
		180708(3)			180718(7)
		180710(1)			180722(3)
		180710(4)	(72)	25.VII.18	180717(14)
		180711(1)			180722(2)
		180711(2)			180723(2)
		180712(3)			180723(4)
		180712(4)			180723(5)
		180712(5)			180723(6)
		180712(6)			180723(7)
(66)	18.VII.18	180625(7)			180723(8)
		180703(2)			180723(9)
		180715(1)			180723(10)
		⌊180717(1)⌋			180724(2)
		⌊180718(4)⌋	(73)	26.VII.18	180711(3)
		⌊180718(5)⌋			180717(13)
(67)	19.VII.18	180716(2)			180718(1)
		180716(3)			180723(14) ++++

IZVESTIYA(NKVD)   ++++

(74)	27.VII.18	180719(4)			180805(3)
(75)	28.VII.18	180723(11)			180806(5)
(76)	30.VII.18	180722(5)	(83)	7.VIII.18	180803(8)
		180723(12)			180805(4)
		180723(15)			180805(5)
		180727(2)			180805(6)
		180727(3)			180805(7)
		180727(4)			180805(8)
		180727(5)			180805(9)
		180727(6)			180805(10)
		180727(7)			180806(1)
		⌊180730(4)⌋			⌊180807(1)⌋
(77)	31.VII.18	180727(1)	(84)	8.VIII.18	180807(12)
		180727(8)	(85)	9.VIII.18	180805(11)
		180727(9)			180806(1)
		⌊180731⌋			180806(2)
(78)	1.VIII.18	180717(15)			180806(3)
		180729(4)			180806(6)
		180729(5)			180806(7)
		180729(6)			180806(8)
		180729(7)			180806(9)
		⌊180801(2)⌋			180806(10)
(80)	3.VIII.18	180727(10)			180806(11)
(82)	6.VIII.18	180601(6)			180806(12)
		180607(6)			180806(13)
		180729(3)			180806(14)
		180802(2)			180806(15)
		180802(3)			180807(2)
		180802(4)			180807(3)
		180802(5)			180807(8)
		180803(1)			180807(9)
		180803(5)			180808(3)
		180803(6)			180808(4)
		180803(7)			180808(5)
		180804(1)			180808(6)
		180804(7)			180808(7)
		180804(8)			180808(8)
		180805(1)	(86)	10.VIII.18	180807(11)
		180805(2)	(87)	11.VIII.18	180810(3) ++++

IZVESTIYA(NKVD)   ++++

(88)	13.VIII.18	[180813(3)]		(102)	11.V.20	200501(4)
(90)	15.VIII.18	180808(9)				200506
		180809(1)		(104)	13.V.20	200510(3)
(95)	22.VIII.18	180810(3)		(105)	14.V.20	200503
(96)	23.VIII.18	180810(3)		(107)	16.V.20	200404(4)
(97)	24.VIII.18	180822				200505(3)
(101)	30.VIII.18	[180830(4)]				200531
(135)	11.X.18	181007(1)		(112)	23.V.20	200507(3)
		181007(2)		(216)	26.IX.20	200924(1)
		181007(3)		(219)	30.IX.20	200928
(137)	13.X.18	181009(1)		(223)	5.X.20	200922
		181009(3)		(225)	7.X.20	200926
(139)	16.X.18	181009(4)				
		181009(5)				
		181009(6)				
		181011(2)		IZVESTIYA(Odessa)		
		181011(3)				
		181011(4)		(529)	9.IX.21	210907(2)
		181011(5)				
		181011(6)				
		181011(7)		IZVESTIYA(Penza)		
		181011(8)				
		181012			31.VII.19	190729(3)
(140)	17.X.18	181009(2)				
		181014				
(149)	27.X.18	181021(1)		IZVESTIYA(Pet)		
		181021(2)				
		181021(3)		(26)	20.IV.18	180408(2)
		181022(1)		(50)	17.VII.18	180712(2)
		181022(2)		(59)	17.VIII.18	180808(10)
		181022(3)				
		181022(4)				
				IZVESTIYA(SRD)		
(81)	15.IV.20	200331(2)				
		200331(3)		(2)	18.X.05	⌊051018(1)⌋
		200404(3)				⌊051018(2)⌋
(83)	17.IV.20	200408				⌊051018(3)⌋
(84)	18.IV.20	200331(4)		(3)	20.X.05	⌊051018(4)⌋
						051019
						⌊051020(1)⌋
						⌊051020(2)⌋ ++++

IZVESTIYA(SRD)   ++++

(4)	30.X.05	051022(1)
		051022(2)
		[051030]
(5)	3.XI.05	051028
		051101(1)
		051101(2)
(6)	5.XI.05	051103
		[051105(1)]
(7)	7.XI.05	051105(2)
		051105(3)

=========================

IZVESTIYA(Vre)

(5)	7.III.21	210305

=========================

IZVESTIYA(VTsIK)

	19.XII.17	[171218(2)/]
(154)	13.VII.18	180722(3)
(166)	6.VIII.18	180806(5)
(30)	4.IV.21	[210404]

=========================

IZVESTIYA VSEUKRAINSKOGO TsIK KP

	20.V.19	190519
	22.V.19	190520
	25.V.19	190521(1)

=========================

KATORGA I SSYLKA

(5)	1923	220916(1)

=========================

KIEVSKAYA MYSL

(178)	29.VI.08	[080629]
(216)	6.VIII.08	[080806]
(218)	8.VIII.08	[080806]
(228)	18.VIII.08	[080818]
(295)	24.X.08	[081024]
(308)	6.XI.08	[081106]
(325)	23.XI.08	[081123]
(327)	25.XI.08	[081125]
(358)	30.XII.08	[081230]
(3)	3.I.09	[090103]
(9)	9.I.09	[090109]
(27)	27.I.09	[090127]
(29)	29.I.09	[090129]
(30)	30.I.09	[090130]
(37)	6.II.09	[090130]
(39)	8.II.09	[090208]
(63)	3.III.09	[090130]
(109)	21.IV.09	[090421]
(118)	30.IV.09	[090430]
(126)	8.V.11	[110508]
(137)	19.V.11	[110519]
(140)	22.V.11	[110519]
(145)	27.V.11	[110527]
(64)	4.III.12	[120304]
(72)	12.III.12	[120304]
(87)	29.III.12	[120329]
(129)	10.V.12	[120510]
(130)	11.V.12	[120510]
(136)	18.V.12	[120518]
(143)	25.V.12	[120525]
(274)	3.X.12	[121003(1)]
(276)	5.X.12	[121005(2)]
(285)	14.X.12	[121014]
(286)	15.X.12	[121015]
(290)	19.X.12	[121019(2)]
(293)	22.X.12	[121022]
(295)	24.X.12	[121024] ++++

KIEVSKAYA MYSL   ++++

(302)	31.X.12	[121031]		(252)	12.IX.13	[130912]
(306)	4.XI.12	[121104]		(253)	13.IX.13	[130903]
(312)	10.XI.12	[121110(1)]		(257)	17.IX.13	[130917]
(320)	18.XI.12	[121118]		(261)	21.IX.13	[130921]
(322)	19.XI.12	[121119(1)]		(276)	6.X.13	[131006]
		[121119(2)]		(285)	15.X.13	[131015]
(331)	29.XI.12	[121129]		(287)	17.X.13	[131017]
(332)	30.XI.12	[121120(4)]		(289)	19.X.13	[131019]
(334)	2.XII.12	121127		(295)	25.X.13	[131025]
(338)	6.XII.12	[121206]		(313)	2.XI.13	[131102]
(345)	13.XII.12	[121213]		(337)	6.XII.13	[131206]
(346)	14.XII.12	[121214]		(343)	12.XII.13	[131206]
(349)	17.XII.12	[121214]				
(353)	21.XII.12	[121221]		(14)	10.I.14	[140110]
(355)	23.XII.12	[121223]		(40)	9.II.14	[140209]
(360)	29.XII.12	[121229]		(46)	15.II.14	[140215]
				(50)	19.II.14	[140219]
(39)	8.II.13	[130208(2)]		(51)	20.II.14	[140220]
(66)	7.III.13	[130307]		(60)	1.III.14	[140301]
(137)	16.V.13	[130516]		(75)	16.III.14	[140316]
(171)	23.VI.13	[130623]		(78)	19.III.14	[140316]
(172)	24.VI.13	[130623]		(158)	2.VI.14	[140602]
(181)	3.VII.13	[130703]		(166)	19.VI.14	[140619]
(188)	10.VII.13	[130710]		(168)	21.VI.14	[140621]
(191)	13.VII.13	[130713]		(328)	28.XI.14	141120
(197)	19.VII.13	[130719]		(334)	4.XII.14	[141204]
(206)	28.VII.13	[130728]		(344)	14.XII.14	[141214]
(209)	31.VII.13	[130731]				
(211)	2.VIII.13	[130731]		(6)	6.I.15	[150106]
(218)	9.VIII.13	[130809]		(13)	13.I.15	[150113]
(226)	17.VIII.13	[130817]		(20)	20.I.15	[150120]
(229)	20.VIII.13	[130817]		(63)	4.III.15	150216
(230)	21.VIII.13	[130817]		(65)	6.III.15	150216
(236)	27.VIII.13	[130827]		(81)	22.III.15	[150322]
(238)	29.VIII.13	[130827]		(191)	12.VII.15	[150712]
(243)	3.IX.13	[130903]		(196)	17.VII.15	[150717(2)]
(245)	5.IX.13	[130903]		(252)	11.IX.15	[150911]
(246)	6.IX.13	[130903]		(261)	20.IX.15	[150920]
				(262)	21.IX.15	[150920] ++++

KIEVSKAYA MYSL   ++++

(294)	23.X.15	[151023]
(296)	25.X.15	[151025]
(306)	4.XI.15	151001
(353)	21.XII.15	[151221]
(1)	1.I.16	151222

==============================

KNIGA O KNIGAKH

(3)	V.24	240518

==============================

KOMMUNIST

(1)	20.IV.18	[180420(2)]

==============================

KOMMUNIST(Gruzii)

(5)	24.X.20	200807(1)

==============================

KOMMUNISTICHESKII INTERNATSIONAL

(1)	1.V.19	190304
		190306(1)
		190306(2)
		190420(3)
		[190429]
(3)	1.VII.19	190302(1)
(5)	IX.19	190901(3)
(6)	X.19	190914
(7-8)	XI-XII.19	191218
(9)	22.III.20	191005
(10)	11.V.20	200000(37)
		200429(1)
(11)	14.VI.20	200000(37)
(12)	20.VII.20	200722

(13)	28.IX.20	200731(2)
		200807(1)
(16)	31.III.21	201225(2)
		210115(2)
(17)	7.VI.21	201124
(19)	17.XII.21	211205
(20)	14.III.22	220000(5)
(21)	19.VII.22	220608
		220610
(23)	1922	[221100(2)]
(1)	1924	190124
(3-4)	V-VI.24	240429(2)
(5-6)	VII-VIII.24	240705
(5-6)	V-VI.26	251222(2)
		251225
		251228
		260105
		260106
		260107
		260112
		260113(1)
		260305
		260506
		260513
		260519

==============================

KOMMUNISTICHESKII TRUD

(426)	1.IX.21	210830
(440)	17.IX.21	210913(2)
(448)	27.IX.21	210926

==============================

KRASNAYA ARMIYA

(116)	6.XI.18	181105
(119)	12.XI.18	181109
(123)	16.XI.18	181113
(124)	17.XI.18	181116
(7-8)	1921	211101(2)

KRASNAYA GAZETA

(115)	12.VII.18	[180712(2)]
(166)	13.VIII.18	180808(10)
(195)	19.IX.18	180913(3)
(223)	20.X.18	181019
(--)	30.VII.19	190718(2)
(282)	9.XII.19	191207
(214)	25.IX.20	200924(1)
(265)	25.XI.20	201108
		201115
(296)	31.XII.20	201230(1)
(50)	6.III.21	210305
(65)	24.III.21	210323(2)
(66)	25.III.21	210323(1)
(93)	27.IV.21	[210426]
(133)	25.VI.21	210623
(250)	3.XI.22	[221103(2)]
(255)	10.XI.22	221102(1)
(260)	16.XI.22	221114(1)
(245)	26.X.24	241023

KRASNAYA NIVA

(1)	I.23	[160800(2)]

KRASNAYA NOV

(7)	1922	[161227]
(6)	1926	260301
(7)	1926	230908(1)

KRASNAYA ZVEZDA

(91)	21.IV.24	240419(1)
(97)	30.IV.24	240428
(105)	11.V.24	240510(1)
(128)	7.VI.24	240606

KRASNOARMEETS

(47)	V.22	220500

KRASNYE ZORI

(1)	I.23	221207

KRASNYI ARKHIV

(V.vii)	1924	240812

KRASNYI NABAT

(--)	27.IV.19	190424(3)
(55)	28.II.20	200228
(56)	29.II.20	200228

KRASNYI SEVER

(--)	7.V.19	190419

KREST´YANSKAYA GAZETA

(51)	17.XI.24	[241117]

=====================================

LUCH

(2)	18.IX.12	[120918]
(3)	19.IX.12	[120918]
(6)	22.IX.12	[120922]
(7)	23.IX.12	[120922]
(8)	25.IX.12	[120918]
(9)	26.IX.12	[120926]
(15)	3.X.12	[121003(2)]
(16)	4.X.12	[121004(3)]
(26)	16.X.12	[121016]
(23)	29.I.13	[130129]
(24)	30.I.13	[130130]
(27)	2.II.13	[130202(1)]
		[130202(2)]
(29)	5.II.13	[130205]
(32)	8.II.13	[130208(1)]
(41)	19.II.13	[130219]
(43)	21.II.13	[130219]
(44)	22.II.13	[130219]
(46)	24.II.13	[130224]
(53)	5.III.13	[130305]
(54)	6.III.13	[130306]
(56)	8.III.13	[130306]
(60)	13.III.13	[130313(1)]
		[130313(2)]
(61)	14.III.13	[130314]
(62)	15.III.13	[130315]
(66)	20.III.13	[130306]
(67)	21.III.13	[130321]
(69)	23.III.13	[130313(1)]
(71)	26.III.13	[130313(1)]
(72)	27.III.13	[130313(1)]
(73)	28.III.13	[130313(1)]
(76)	31.III.13	[130331]

(77)	2.IV.13	[130402]
(78)	3.IV.13	[130313(1)]
(82)	7.IV.13	[130313(1)]
(111)	16.V.13	[130516]

=====================================

MOLODAYA GVARDIYA

(--)	1920	191004
(4-5)	1923	230601
(9-10)	1923	231105
(--)	1924	240512

=====================================

MOSKOVSKII PECHATNIK

(49)	12.XII.25	251123(2)

=====================================

NACHALO(1905)

(1)	13.XI.05	[051113(1)]
		[051113(2)]
(2)	15.XI.05	[051113(2)]
		[051115(2)]
(3)	16.XI.05	[051116(1)]
		[051116(3)]
(4)	17.XI.05	[051117(1)]
		[051117(2)]
(5)	18.XI.05	[051118(1)]
		[051118(2)]
(6)	19.XI.05	[051119(1)]
		[051119(2)]
(7)	20.XI.05	[051120]
(8)	23.XI.05	[051123(1)]
		[051123(2)]
(9)	24.XI.05	[051124]
(10)	25.XI.05	[051125]	++++

NACHALO(1905)   ++++

| (11) | 26.XI.05 | [051126] |
| (12) | 27.XI.05 | [051127(3)] |

==

NACHALO(Paris)

(1)	30.IX.16	[160930]
(2)	1.X.16	[161001]
(6)	6.X.16	[161006]
(9)	12.X.16	[161012]
(16)	18.X.16	[161006]
(20)	22.X.16	[161022]
(21)	24.X.16	[161006]
(22)	25.X.16	[161025]
(29)	3.XI.16	161103
(31)	5.XI.16	[161105]
(54)	2.XII.16	161121
(74)	27.XII.16	[161227]

==

NARODNOE DELO

| (53:176) | 9.III.21 | 210305 |

==

NASHA GAZETA

| (1) | 1.I.26 | [260101] |

==

NASHA PRAVDA

(4)	12.I.19	[190105(1)]
(30)	14.II.19	190110(2)
(31)	15.II.19	190110(2)

==

NASHA ZARYA

| (II.11) | 1911 | [111100] |
| (III.5) | 1912 | [120500] |

==

NASHE DELO

| | 1897 | [970000] |

==

NASHE SLOVO

(14)	13.II.15	[150213]
(15)	14.II.15	[150214]
(22)	23.II.15	[150223]
(23)	24.II.15	[150223]
(28)	1.III.15	[150301]
(35)	10.III.15	[150301]
(41)	17.III.15	[150301]
(48)	25.III.15	[150325]
(53)	31.III.15	[150331]
(54)	1.IV.15	[150401]
(60)	9.IV.15	150115(1)
		[150409]
(62)	11.IV.15	[150411]
(66)	16.IV.15	[150416]
(67)	17.IV.15	[150417]
(74)	25.IV.15	[150425]
(77)	29.IV.15	[150429]
(79)	1.V.15	[150501]
(81)	5.V.15	[150505]
(82)	6.V.15	[150506]
(89)	15.V.15	[150515]
(90)	16.V.15	[150516]
(100)	29.V.15	[150515]
		[150529]
(102)	1.VI.15	[150601]
(105)	4.VI.15	[150604]
(106)	5.VI.15	[150515]
(107)	6.VI.15	[150515] ++++

NASHE SLOVO ++++

(113)	13.VI.15	[150613]	(218)	19.X.15	[151019]
(116)	17.VI.15	[150617]	(221)	22.X.15	[151022(1)]
(117)	18.VI.15	[150617]	(223)	24.X.15	[151024]
(118)	19.VI.15	[150617]	(224)	26.X.15	[151024]
(121)	23.VI.15	[150623]	(225)	27.X.15	[151027]
(122)	24.VI.15	[150624]	(227)	29.X.15	[151029]
(130)	3.VII.15	[150703]	(228)	30.X.15	[151030(1)]
(135)	8.VII.15	[150703]			[151030(2)]
(137)	11.VII.15	[150711(1)]	(229)	31.X.15	[151031]
		[150711(2)]	(232)	5.XI.15	[151031]
(141)	17.VII.15	[150717(1)]			[151105]
(142)	18.VII.15	[150718(1)]	(233)	6.XI.15	[151106]
		[150718(2)]	(236)	10.XI.15	[151110]
(143)	20.VII.15	[150718(2)]	(237)	11.XI.15	[151111]
(145)	22.VII.15	[150722]	(239)	13.XI.15	[151113]
(146)	23.VII.15	[150723]	(240)	14.XI.15	[151031]
(147)	24.VII.15	[150723]	(242)	17.XI.15	[151117]
(156)	4.VIII.15	[150804]	(244)	19.XI.15	[151031]
(166)	15.VIII.15	[150815]			[151119]
(167)	18.VIII.15	[150818]	(248)	24.XI.15	[151124]
(174)	26.VIII.15	[150826]	(249)	25.XI.15	[151124]
(175)	27.VIII.15	[150827]	(251)	27.XI.15	[151127]
(179)	1.IX.15	[150826]	(252)	28.XI.15	[151128]
(180)	2.IX.15	[150826]	(253)	30.XI.15	[151130]
(181)	3.IX.15	[150826]	(256)	3.XII.15	[151203]
(182)	4.IX.15	[150826]	(258)	5.XII.15	[151205]
(204)	30.IX.15	[150930]	(264)	12.XII.15	[151212]
(207)	3.X.15	[151003]	(269)	18.XII.15	[151218]
(208)	5.X.15	[151005]	(270)	19.XII.15	[151219]
(209)	6.X.15	[151006]	(273)	22.XII.15	151222
(210)	7.X.15	[151007(1)]	(275)	25.XII.15	[151225]
		[151007(2)]	(276)	28.XII.15	[151228(1)]
(212)	9.X.15	[151009]			[151228(2)]
(214)	12.X.15	[151012]	(277)	29.XII.15	[151229(1)]
(215)	13.X.15	[151013]			[151229(2)] ++++
(216)	14.X.15	[151013]			
		[151014]			
(217)	17.X.15	[151017(1)]			
		[151017(2)]			

NASHE SLOVO   ++++

(1:388)	1.I.16	⌊160101(1)⌋		(77:464)	31.III.16	⌊160331⌋
		⌊160101(2)⌋		(78:465)	1.IV.16	⌊160331⌋
(10:397)	13.I.16	⌊160113(1)⌋		(85:472)	9.IV.16	⌊160409⌋
		⌊160113(2)⌋		(86:473)	11.IV.16	160129
(11:398)	14.I.16	⌊160114⌋		(88:475)	13.IV.16	160129
(13:400)	16.I.16	⌊160116⌋		(89:476)	14.IV.16	⌊160414⌋
(20:407)	25.I.16	⌊160125⌋		(93:480)	19.IV.16	⌊160419⌋
(24:411)	29.I.16	⌊160129⌋		(94:481)	20.IV.16	⌊160420⌋
(25:412)	30.I.16	⌊160129⌋		(95:482)	21.IV.16	⌊160420⌋
(26:413)	1.II.16	⌊160201⌋		(97:484)	23.IV.16	⌊160423⌋
(28:415)	3.II.16	⌊160129⌋		(98:485)	26.IV.16	⌊160426⌋
(29:416)	4.II.16	⌊160129⌋		(102:488)	1.V.16	⌊160501(1)⌋
(32:419)[x]	8.II.16	⌊160208(1)⌋				⌊160501(2)⌋
		⌊160208(2)⌋		(104:490)	4.V.16	⌊160504⌋
(34:421)	10.II.16	⌊160210⌋		(106:492)	6.V.16	⌊160506(1)⌋
(35:422)	11.II.16	⌊160210⌋				⌊160506(2)⌋
		⌊160211⌋		(109:495)	10.V.16	⌊160510⌋
(39:426)	16.II.16	⌊160216⌋		(110:496)	11.V.16	⌊160511(1)⌋
(40:427)	17.II.16	⌊160217⌋				⌊160511(2)⌋
(43:430)	20.II.16	⌊160220⌋		(111:497)	12.V.16	⌊160511(2)⌋
(46:433)	24.II.16	⌊160224⌋		(112:498)	13.V.16	⌊160511(2)⌋
(50:437)	29.II.16	⌊160229⌋		(113:499)	14.V.16	⌊160511(2)⌋
(53:440)	3.III.16	⌊160210⌋		(114:500)	16.V.16	⌊160516(1)⌋
		⌊160303⌋				⌊160516(2)⌋
(54:441)	4.III.16	⌊160210⌋				⌊160516(3)⌋
(55:442)	5.III.16	⌊160305⌋		(119:505)	21.V.16	⌊160521(1)⌋
(56:443)	7.III.16	⌊160307⌋				⌊160521(2)⌋
(58:445)	9.III.16	⌊160309⌋		(121:507)	24.V.16	⌊160524⌋
(62:449)	14.III.16	⌊160210⌋		(124:510)	27.V.16	⌊160527⌋
(63:450)	15.III.16	⌊160210⌋		(130:516)	4.VI.16	⌊160604⌋
(69:456)	22.III.16	⌊160309⌋		(138:524)	15.VI.16	⌊160615⌋
(71:458)	24.III.16	⌊160324⌋		(143:529)	21.VI.16	⌊160621⌋
(72:459)	25.III.16	⌊160325⌋		(146:532)	24.VI.16	⌊160624⌋
(73:460)	26.III.16	⌊160326(1)⌋		(150:536)	29.VI.16	⌊160629⌋
				(152:538)	1.VII.16	⌊160701⌋
				(154:540)	4.VII.16	⌊160704(1)⌋
						⌊160704(2)⌋ ++++

---

[x] Corrected from (31:418)

NASHE SLOVO ++++

(156:542)	6.VII.16	[160706]
(161:547)	12.VII.16	[160712]
(162:548)	13.VII.16	[160713]
(165:551)	19.VII.16	[160719]
(166:552)	20.VII.16	[160719]
(172:558)	27.VII.16	[160727(1)]
		[160727(2)]
(173:559)	28.VII.16	[160728]
(174:560)	29.VII.16	[160729]
(177:563)	2.VIII.16	[160802]
(178:564)	3.VIII.16	[160802]
		[160803(1)]
		[160803(2)]
(179:565)	4.VIII.16	[160802]
		[160804]
(181:567)	6.VIII.16	[160806]
(182:568)	8.VIII.16	[160808(1)]
		[160808(2)]
(187:573)	13.VIII.16	[160813(1)]
		[160813(2)]
(188:574)	17.VIII.16	[160808(2)]
(189:575)	18.VIII.16	[160818(1)]
(191:577)	20.VIII.16	[160820]
(192:578)	22.VIII.16	[160822(1)]
		[160822(2)]
(193:579)	23.VIII.16	[160823]
(194:580)	24.VIII.16	[160823]
(197:583)	27.VIII.16	[160827]
(201:587)	1.IX.16	[160901]
(202:588)	2.IX.16	[160901]
(203:589)	3.IX.16	[160903]
(204:590)	5.IX.16	[160905]
(206:592)	7.IX.16	[160907(2)]
(207:593)	8.IX.16	[160908]
(209:595)	10.IX.16	[160910]
(210:596)	12.IX.16	[160912]
(212:598)	14.IX.16	[160914(1)]
		[160914(2)]
(213:599)	15.IX.16	[160914(2)]

NASH STYAG

(II.4)	1922	210000(7)

NAUCHNOE OBOZRENIE

	IV.02	[020400]

NIZHNOGORODSKAYA KOMMUNA

(--)	13.IV.19	190412(3)
(--)	15.IV.19	190412(3)

NOVAYA ZHIZN(1905)

(7)	7.XI.05	051103
(8)	8.XI.05	051106
(11)	12.XI.05	[051112(2)]
(13)	15.XI.05	051112(1)
		051114
(14)	16.XI.05	[051116(2)]
(26)	30.XI.05	051127(2)

NOVAYA ZHIZN(1917)

(18)	9.V.17	170507(1)/
		170507(2)/
		170507(3)/
(23)	14.V.17	170513/
(33)	27.V.17	170526/
(38)	2.VI.17	170601/
(41)	6.VI.17	170605(2)/
(56)	23.VI.17	[170623/]
(59)	27.VI.17	[170627/]
(69)	8.VII.17	[170708/]
(73)	13.VII.17	170710/
(88)	30.VII.17	170725(3)/ ++++

NOVAYA ZHIZN(1917)   ++++

(90)	2.VIII.17	[170802/]		(890)	20.I.17	[170120]
(122)	16.IX.17	170915/		(895)	26.I.17	[170126]
(134)	22.IX.17	170921(1)/		(900)	1.II.17	160907(1)
(138)	27.IX.17	170926(1)/		(901)	2.II.17	160907(1)
		170926(2)/		(902)	3.II.17	[170203]
(164)	27.X.17	171024(5)/		(903)	5.II.17	[170205]
(167)	30.X.17	171029(2)/		(904)	6.II.17	[170206]
(171)	3.XI.17	[171102(1)/]		(905)	7.II.17	[170207]
	9.XI.17	171108(3)/		(906)	8.II.17	[170208]
(LocIISG)				(908)	10.II.17	[170210]
(193:187)	5.XII.17	171203(3)/		(909)	12.II.17	[170210]
(207:201)	21.XII.17	171219(1)/		(910)	13.II.17	[170213]
				(913)	16.II.17	[170216]
(22:36)	12.II.18	180210(2)		(914)	17.II.17	[170217]
(112:327)	9.VI.18	180427(1)		(919)	23.II.17	[170223]
		180607(1)		(922)	27.II.17	[170227]
(114:329)	12.VI.18	180610(2)		(926)	3.III.17	[170303(1)]
(135:350)	11.VII.18	180709(1)				[170303(2)]
				(928)	6.III.17	[170217]
						[170306(1)]
						[170306(2)]

NOVYI LUCH

				(929)	7.III.17	[170307]
(2)	21.II.07	[070221]		(930)	8.III.17	[170308(1)]
(6)	25.II.07	[070225]				[170308(2)]
(7)	27.II.07	[070227]				[170308(3)]
				(931)	9.III.17	[170309(1)]
						[170309(2)]

NOVYI MIR

						[170309(3)]
(1)	I.27	260203		(932)	10.III.17	[170310]
				(934)	13.III.17	[170313(1)]
						[170313(2)]

NOVYI MIR(NY)

				(935)	14.III.17	[170314]
(564)	6.I.16	[160106]		(936)	15.III.17	[170315(1)]
(565)	7.I.16	[160106]				[170315(2)]
(568)	11.I.16	[160106]		(937)	16.III.17	[170316(1)]
(569)	12.I.16	[160106]				[170316(2)]
(851)	6.XII.16	161114(3)		(938)	17.III.17	[170317(1)]
(886)	16.I.17	[170116(2)]				[170317(2)] ++++

NOVYI MIR(NY)   ++++

(940)	19.III.17	[170319]		(2)	III.31	270600(1)
(941)	20.III.17	[170320(1)]				300900(1)
		[170320(2)]				[301000(2)]
(942)	21.III.17	[170321]				310311
(943)	22.III.17	[170322(1)]		(3)	IV.31	270600(2)
		[170322(2)]				290925(2)
		[170322(3)]				310325
(948)	27.III.17	[170327]				310415
(1143)	9.XI.17	171106(2)/		(4)	IX.31	270801
		171106(3)/				310715(1)
				(5)	10.XII.31	271023
						280628
						311017

NOVYI PUT(Riga)

(--)	29.IX.21	[210929]		(I.1)	1.IV.32	311126
				(I.2)	8.IV.32	311126
						320301

ODESSKI NOVOSTI

(7510)	6.V.08	[080506]		(I.3)	15.IV.32	300000(1)
						320329
(8852)	19.X.12	[121019(1)]		(I.4)	22.IV.32	300000(1)
(8902)	19.XII.12	[121219]				300825
						320412
				(I.5)	1.V.32	300000(1)
				(I.6)	6.V.32	311208
				(I.7)	13.V.32	281000(1)
						320504

OMSKII VESTNIK

(7)	11.I.18	180102(1)/		(I.8)	20.V.32	281000(1)
(8)	12.I.18	180102(2)/		(I.12)	17.VI.32	300000(1)
						320524(2)
				(I.13)	24.VI.32	320613(3)
				(I.14)	1.VII.32	320625
				(I.15)	8.VII.32	310708(2)

OSVOBOZHDENIE

(1)	I.31	240122(1)		(I.16)	15.VII.32	320512
		280628				320522(2)
		301126		(I.17)	22.VII.32	310825
		301129(1)				[311200]
		[301200(1)]				320613(1)
		[301200(3)]		(I.18)	29.VII.32	310825 ++++

OSVOBOZHDENIE   ++++

(I.19)	5.VIII.32	310825
		320423
(I.20)	12.VIII.32	310825
		320628
(I.21)	19.VIII.32	320215(2)
		320423
		320628
(I.22)	26.VIII.32	310404
		320628
(I.23)	2.IX.32	300207(1)
		310404
		320809
(I.24)	9.IX.32	300207(1)
		310404
		320809
(I.25)	16.IX.32	320817
(I.26)	23.IX.32	⌊320500⌋
		320818(2)
(I.27)	30.IX.32	320804(2)
		320922(2)
(I.29)	14.X.32	⌊300800(1)⌋
		320802
		320806
(I.30)	21.X.32	⌊300800(1)⌋
		320831
(I.31)	28.X.32	⌊300800(1)⌋
		320910
		321006
		321013(1)
		321013(2)
(I.35)	6.I.33	320917
		321219
(I.36)	13.I.33	320917
		321127
(I.37)	20.I.33	⌊321200(2)⌋
		321200(3)
(I.38)	27.I.33	321200(3)
		321228(2)

(I.39)	23.III.33	⌊321200(2)⌋
(I.40)	18.X.33	330512(1)
(I.41)	6.XI.33	330321
(II.39-40)	16.XI.33	330715(2)
(II.43)	14.XII.33	330330
(II.41-42)	18.XII.33	331100

===============================

PETROGRADSKAYA PRAVDA

(122)	13.VI.18	180613(5)
(125)	16.VI.18	180613(3)
(127)	19.VI.18	180614(2)
(17)	25.I.20	⌊200122(1)⌋
(21)	30.I.20	200128
(65)	24.III.20	⌊200324⌋
(71)	31.III.20	200330
(76)	6.IV.20	200404(1)
(79)	14.IV.20	200409(2)
(94)	1.V.20	200420
		200429(2)
(95)	4.V.20	200430(2)
		200501(2)
(97)	6.V.20	200505(1)
(101)	11.V.20	200510(3)
		200510(5)
(106)	16.V.20	200509(2)
(115)	28.V.20	⌊200525⌋
(117)	30.V.20	⌊200530⌋
(119)	3.VI.20	200602
(122)	6.VI.20	200605
(130)	16.VI.20	200616(2)
(131)	17.VI.20	200615
		200616(1)
(159)	21.VII.20	200711(2)
(160)	22.VII.20	200717
(170)	3.VIII.20	200731(1)
(183)	18.VIII.20	200817(1) ++++

PETROGRADSKAYA PRAVDA   ++++

(192)	31.VIII.20	200830(2)	(5)	6.I.22	⌊220104(1)⌋
(195)	3.IX.20	200826	(25)	2.II.22	⌊220131(1)⌋
(196)	4.IX.20	200828	(35)	14.II.22	220211
(214)	25.IX.20	⌊200823⌋	(43)	23.II.22	220223(1)
(218)	30.IX.20	200928	(49)	2.III.22	220225
(222)	5.X.20	201002	(57)	11.III.22	220308
(251)	7.XI.20	201027(3)	(60)	15.III.22	220312
(252)	10.XI.20	201106(1)	(65)	22.III.22	220314
(264)	24.XI.20	201117	(73)	31.III.22	220329(1)
		201122	(83)	13.IV.22	220411(1)
(274)	5.XII.20	201202(1)	(194)	31.VIII.22	220826
(278)	10.XII.20	201208(2)	(210)	19.IX.22	220916(2)
		201209(1)	(230)	12.X.22	⌊221012⌋
(279)	11.XII.20	201208(2)	(231)	13.X.22	221011
(283)	16.XII.20	201215	(232)	14.X.22	221011
(287)	21.XII.20	⌊201219⌋	(243)	27.X.22	221024(2)
(290)	24.XII.20	[201220⌋	(258)	16.XI.22	221114(2)
(293)	28.XII.20	201225(2)	(273)	3.XII.22	221201(2)
		201227	(274)	5.XII.22	221201(2)
(296)	31.XII.20	201229(1)	(8)	12.I.23	221221
		201229(2)	(27)	6.II.23	230205(1)
(11)	18.I.21	⌊210115(1)⌋	(35)	15.II.23	230210
(12)	19.I.21	210116	(39)	20.II.23	230218
(23)	3.II.21	⌊210201(1)⌋	(42)	23.II.23	230205(2)
(47)	3.III.21	210302	(50)	4.III.23	230227
(58)	15.III.21	⌊210315⌋	(51)	6.III.23	230304
(60)	17.III.21	210314(2)	(65)	23.III.23	230321
(126)	15.VI.21	210613(1)	(66)	24.III.23	230321
(134)	28.VI.21	210624	(95)	1.V.23	230430(2)
(140)	6.VII.21	210418	(96)	3.V.23	230430(2)
(148)	16.VII.21	210623	(97)	4.V.23	230430(2)
(154)	23.VII.21	210717(1)	(105)	13.V.23	230512(1)
(205)	4.X.21	⌊211001⌋	(107)	16.V.23	230515
(235)	11.XI.21	211110(1)	(145)	1.VII.23	230629(1)
(246)	24.XI.21	211118	(152)	10.VII.23	⌊230710⌋
(263)	14.XII.21	211211	(153)	11.VII.23	⌊230711⌋
(276)	29.XII.21	211226	(154)	12.VII.23	⌊230712⌋ ++++

919

PETROGRADSKAYA PRAVDA		++++
(156)	14.VII.23	⌊230714⌋
(159)	18.VII.23	230717
(181)	14.VIII.23	230806
(182)	15.VIII.23	230806
(184)	18.VIII.23	230808
(186)	21.VIII.23	230808
(207)	14.IX.23	230908(1)
(208)	15.IX.23	230908(1)
(209)	16.IX.23	230908(1)
(215)	23.IX.23	⌊230523(2)⌋
(216)	25.IX.23	230916
(218)	27.IX.23	230916
(220)	29.IX.23	230916
(221)	30.IX.23	230916
(235)	17.X.23	⌊231017⌋
(236)	18.X.23	231016
(239)	21.X.23	231019(1)
(241)	24.X.23	231023(3)
(246)	30.X.23	231029(1)
(247)	31.X.23	231030
(253)	7.XI.23	231105
(267)	24.XI.23	231123(2)
(277)	6.XII.23	⌊231206(2)⌋
(282)	12.XII.23	231208(1)
(294)	29.XII.23	231222
(295)	30.XII.23	231223

PETROGRADSKII GOLOS

(21)	23.XII.17	⌊171221/⌋

PLANOVOE KHOZYAISTVO

(6)	VI.25	250525
(1)	I.26	260118

POD ZNAMENEM MARKSIZMA

(1-2)	I-II.22	220227
(5-6)	1922	220425

PRAVDA

(69)	31.V.17	170527/
(75)	7.VI.17	170604/
(80)	13.VI.17	170612/
(97)	2.VII.17	⌊170702/⌋
(170)	27.X.17	171025(5)/
(172)	29.X.17	171026(1)/
(173)	30.X.17	171028(1)/
(174)	31.X.17	171029(3)/
(175)	1.XI.17	171031/
(181)	5.XI.17	171104(4)/
(182)	7.XI.17	171104(4)/
(184)	9.XI.17	171108(1)/
		171108(2)/
		171108(3)/
(185)	10.XI.17	171106(1)/
(186)	11.XI.17	⌊171111(1)/⌋
(187)	12.XI.17	171109/
		⌊171112/⌋
(188)	13.XI.17	⌊171113(1)/⌋
(190)	15.XI.17	171115(2)/
(193)	18.XI.17	171116(3)/
(194)	19.XI.17	171117(1)/
(195)	21.XI.17	171120/
(199)	25.XI.17	⌊171125(1)/⌋
		⌊171125(2)/⌋
(200)	26.XI.17	171124(1)/
(201)	27.XI.17	171126(2)/
(202)	30.XI.17	171126(3)/
(203)	1.XII.17	⌊171201(1)/⌋
(207)	6.XII.17	⌊171206(1)/⌋
		⌊171206(2)/⌋
		⌊171206(3)/⌋ ++++

PRAVDA   ++++

(208)	7.XII.17	⌊171207(2)/⌋	(80)	25.IV.18	180422(1)
(210)	9.XII.17	⌊171209(2)/⌋			180422(2)
(213)	13.XII.17	171201(2)/	(81)	26.IV.18	180422(1)
		⌊171213/⌋			180422(2)
(215)	15.XII.17	171214(2)/	(107)	31.V.18	180530(2)
(217)	17.XII.17	171214(1)/			⌊180531(6)⌋
		⌊171217(1)/⌋	(108)	1.VI.18	180530(1)
(218)	18.XII.17	171214(1)/	(129)	27.VI.18	180626(2)
		⌊171218(1)/⌋	(142)	11.VII.18	180710(2)
		⌊171218(2)/⌋	(152)	23.VII.18	180723(13)
(220)	21.XII.17	171219(1)/	(158)	30.VII.18	180729(2)
(221)	22.XII.17	⌊171209(1)/⌋	(188)	4.IX.18	180902(1)
		⌊171222(4)/⌋	(192)	8.IX.18	180903(2)
		⌊171222(5)/⌋	(197)	14.IX.18	180910
(222)	23.XII.17	171222(1)/	(214)	5.X.18	181003
		171222(2)/	(244)	12.XI.18	181109
(1)	3.I.18	171231(1)/	(247)	15.XI.18	181113
(2)	4.I.18	171231(2)/	(283)	27.XII.18	⌊181226(1)⌋
(5)	7.I.18	180105(1)/	(4)	5.I.19	⌊190105(1)⌋
(8)	12.I.18	180110/	(8)	14.I.19	190109(1)
(11)	16.I.18	180113(1)/	(16)	24.I.19	190124
		180116/	(17)	25.I.19	190109(2)
(12)	17.I.18	180113(1)/	(26)	5.II.19	190113
(20)	26.I.18	180117(2)/	(30)	9.II.19	190110(2)
(21)	27.I.18	180118(1)/	(42)	23.II.19	⌊190223(2)⌋
(23)	30.I.18/	180310(2)	(43)	25.II.19	190220
(25)	1.II.18	⌊180201⌋	(51)	6.III.19	⌊190306(2)⌋
(26)	15.II.18	180214	(52)	7.III.19	190306(1)
(27)	16.II.18	180214			190306(3)
(30)	20.II.18	180219(1)	(54)	11.III.19	190309(2)
(32)	22.II.18	⌊180222(1)⌋	(64)	25.III.19	190318(1)
(33)	23.II.18	180222(2)			190318(3)
(39)	2.III.18	180216(2)			190318(4)
(46)	10.III.18	180301(1)	(70)	1.IV.19	190324(1)
(48)	14.III.18	⌊180314⌋	(83)	17.IV.19	190407(1)
(49)	15.III.18	⌊180314⌋	(84)	18.IV.19	190409
(51)	21.III.18	180319(1)	(85)	23.IV.19	190417
(58)	26.III.18	⌊180324(1)⌋	(86)	24.IV.19	190327 ++++

PRAVDA   ++++

(87)	25.IV.19	190413		(283)	17.XII.19	191216
(88)	26.IV.19	190414		(284)	18.XII.19	191217(2)
(111)	24.V.19	190511		(288)	23.XII.19	[191222(1)]
(127)	14.VI.19	190610		(289)	24.XII.19	191222(2)
(128)	15.VI.19	190602		(293)	28.XII.19	191227(1)
(137)	26.VI.18	190617				191227(2)
(170)	3.VIII.18	[190719(2)]				
(185)	22.VIII.18	[190819]		(2)	3.I.20	[200103]
(189)	27.VIII.19	190826(2)		(4)	6.I.20	191220
(194)	3.IX.19	[190901(1)]		(10)	16.I.20	200115(2)
(209)	20.IX.19	190911(1)				200115(5)
(210)	21.IX.19	190916(1)		(14)	22.I.20	[200122(1)]
(217)	30.IX.19	[190929]		(18)	28.I.20	200124(1)
(219)	2.X.19	190930		(19)	29.I.20	200124(1)
(223)	7.X.19	191004		(20)	30.I.20	200128
(233)	18.X.19	191016(2)		(24)	4.II.20	200203(1)
(234)	19.X.19	191018(2)		(63)	23.III.20	[200323(1)]
(236)	22.X.19	191020(1)		(65)	25.III.20	[200323(1)]
		191021(1)		(70)	31.III.20	200330
(239)	25.X.19	191024(1)		(75)	6.IV.20	200404(1)
		191024(2)		(84)	21.IV.20	200419(1)
(249)	6.XI.19	191104(4)		(86)	23.IV.20	200423
(250)	7.XI.19	191030(2)		(92)	30.IV.20	200429(4)
(251)	9.XI.19	191107(2)		(93)	1.V.20	200429(1)
(254)	13.XI.19	[191113]		(94)	4.V.20	200430(2)
(257)	16.XI.19	[191116]				200501(1)
(260)	20.XI.19	191120				200501(2)
(270)	2.XII.19	191130		(95)	5.V.20	200502(2)
(271)	3.XII.19	191203		(96)	6.V.20	200505(5)
(274)	6.XII.19	191205(1)		(97)	7.V.20	200504
		191205(2)		(100)	11.V.20	200508(1)
(276)	9.XII.19	191206				200510(5)
(277)	10.XII.19	191200		(101)	12.V.20	200509(1)
		191207				200510(3)
		191208		(104)	15.V.20	200509(2)
(278)	11.XII.19	191206		(106)	18.V.20	200508(3)
(279)	12.XII.19	191206		(107)	19.V.20	200518
(280)	13.XII.19	191212(1)		(113)	27.V.20	[200527]
				(114)	28.V.20	[200525] ++++

PRAVDA ++++

(115)	29.V.20	200522
		200528
(121)	6.VI.20	200605
(128)	15.VI.20	200614
(130)	17.VI.20	200616(1)
(131)	18.VI.20	⌊200618(1)⌋
(142)	1.VII.20	200630
(143)	2.VII.20	⌊200702⌋
(150)	10.VII.20	200707
(157)	18.VII.20	200717
(159)	21.VII.20	200711(2)
(160)	22.VII.20	⌊200722⌋
(169)	2.VIII.20	200731(1)
(171)	5.VIII.20	200723
(177)	12.VIII.20	⌊200812⌋
(180)	15.VIII.20	200814
(182)	18.VIII.20	200817(1)
(191)	31.VIII.20	200830(4)
(196)	5.IX.20	200903
(198)	8.IX.20	⌊200908(3)⌋
(199)	9.IX.20	⌊200908(3)⌋
(202)	12.IX.20	⌊200912⌋
(203)	14.IX.20	200910
(204)	15.IX.20	200911
(206)	17.IX.20	[200917]
(213)	25.IX.20	200924(1)
(216)	29.IX.20	200928
(231)	16.X.20	⌊201016⌋
(233)	19.X.20	201017
(237)	23.X.20	⌊201023⌋
(250)	7.XI.20	201106(1)
(260)	19.XI.20	201116
(263)	23.XI.20	201117
(269)	30.XI.20	201126(1)
(273)	4.XII.20	201202(1)
(274)	5.XII.20	201202(1)
(275)	7.XII.20	201202(1)
(276)	8.XII.20	201208(2)
(277)	9.XII.20	201208(2)
(278)	10.XII.20	201208(2)
		201209(1)
(279)	11.XII.20	201209(2)
(286)	19.XII.20	⌊201219⌋
(293)	28.XII.20	201227
(294)	29.XII.20	201227
(296)	31.XII.20	201229(1)
		201229(2)
(5)	11.I.21	⌊210111⌋
(8)	14.I.21	⌊210114⌋
(9)	15.I.21	⌊210115(1)⌋
(12)	19.I.21	⌊210119⌋
(19)	29.I.21	⌊210129⌋
(21)	1.II.21	⌊210201(1)⌋
		⌊210201(2)⌋
(47)	3.III.21	210302
(51)	8.III.21	210305
(56)	15.III.21	⌊210315⌋
(57)	16.III.21	⌊210313⌋
(58)	17.III.21	210314(1)
		210314(2)
(62)	23.III.21	210323(2)
(63)	24.III.21	210323(1)
(86)	21.IV.21	⌊210421⌋
(128)	14.VI.21	210613(1)
(136)	25.VI.21	210623
(137)	26.VI.21	210624
(146)	7.VII.21	210702
(149)	10.VII.21	210705
(150)	12.VII.21	⌊210712⌋
(154)	16.VII.21	210714(2)
(159)	22.VII.21	210717(1)
(201)	10.IX.21	210907(1)
(203)	13.IX.21	210911
(206)	16.IX.21	⌊210916⌋
(209)	20.IX.21	210913(2)
(215)	27.IX.21	210926
(219)	1.X.21	⌊211001⌋
(229)	12.X.21	211011 ++++

PRAVDA   ++++

(240)	25.X.21	211020		(109)	18.V.22	⌊220518⌋
(241)	26.X.21	211020		(117)	28.V.22	220526
(242)	27.X.21	211020		(127)	10.VI.22	220608
(243)	28.X.21	211020		(128)	11.VI.22	220610
(254)	11.XI.21	211107		(134)	18.VI.22	⌊220618⌋
		211110(1)		(138)	24.VI.22	220623
(256)	13.XI.21	211113		(144)	1.VII.22	220628
(263)	22.XI.21	211118		(145)	2.VII.22	220628
(264)	23.XI.21	211120		(149)	7.VII.22	⌊220707⌋
(279)	10.XII.21	⌊211210(2)⌋		(150)	8.VII.22	220708(2)
(281)	13.XII.21	211211		(168)	29.VII.22	⌊220727⌋
(286)	18.XII.21	211212		(209)	17.IX.22	220916(2)
(287)	20.XII.21	211212		(210)	19.IX.22	220916(2)
(292)	25.XII.21	211221		(221)	1.X.22	220916(2)
(294)	28.XII.21	211226		(222)	3.X.22	220916(2)
(295)	29.XII.21	211227		(224)	5.X.22	220916(2)
		[211229]		(230)	12.X.22	221010
						[221012]
(3)	4.I.22	⌊220104(1)⌋		(231)	13.X.22	221011
(5)	6.I.22	220104(2)		(234)	17.X.22	⌊221017⌋
(12)	17.I.22	220116		(238)	21.X.22	221020
(13)	18.I.22	220116		(243)	27.X.22	221024(1)
(16)	22.I.22	220121		(253)	9.XI.22	221031
(43)	23.II.22	220223(1)				221105
(45)	25.II.22	220000(5)				221107
(48)	1.III.22	220228(2)		(259)	16.XI.22	221114(1)
(49)	2.III.22	220302(1)		(275)	5.XII.22	221202(3)
(50)	3.III.22	220302(1)		(276)	6.XII.22	221201(1)
(59)	14.III.22	220312		(286)	17.XII.22	[221218]
(64)	21.III.22	220314		(287)	20.XII.22	[221218]
(71)	29.III.22	220328		(292)	24.XII.22	221222
(73)	31.III.22	220329(1)		(1)	3.I.23	⌊230101⌋
		220329(3)		(34)	15.II.23	230210
(92)	27.IV.22	220426				[230215]
(95)	30.IV.22	220429		(38)	20.II.23	230218
(100)	7.V.22	⌊220504⌋		(41)	23.II.23	230205(2)
		⌊220507⌋		(48)	3.III.23	230227
(102)	10.V.22	220508(5)		(50)	6.III.23	230304 ++++
(107)	16.V.22	220513				
		⌊220516⌋				

PRAVDA ++++

(56)	14.III.23	230313	(207)	14.IX.23	230908(1)
(61)	20.III.23	230319(2)	(208)	15.IX.23	230908(1)
(64)	23.III.23	230321	(209)	16.IX.23	230908(2)
(67)	27.III.23	230325	(215)	23.IX.23	⌊230923(2)⌋
(74)	4.IV.23	230403	(216)	25.IX.23	230916
(78)	11.IV.23	230306(1)	(217)	26.IX.23	230916
		230405(3)	(220)	29.IX.23	230929
(79)	12.IV.23	230405(3)	(221)	30.IX.23	230929
(88)	22.IV.23	230420(1)			⌊230930⌋
(89)	24.IV.23	230421	(222)	2.X.23	230923(1)
		230422(2)	(236)	18.X.23	231016
(90)	25.IV.23	⌊230425(2)⌋	(239)	21.X.23	231019(1)
(95)	1.V.23	230430(2)	(240)	23.X.23	231023(1)
(96)	3.V.23	230501	(246)	30.X.23	231029(1)
(99)	6.V.23	230504(1)			231029(2)
(103)	11.V.23	230508	(247)	31.X.23	231030
(105)	13.V.23	230512(1)	(253)	7.XI.23	231105
(107)	16.V.23	230515	(264)	21.XI.23	⌊231121⌋
(114)	25.V.23	230518	(267)	24.XI.23	231123(2)
(116)	27.V.23	230526	(270)	28.XI.23	⌊231128⌋
(118)	31.V.23	230529	(275)	4.XII.23	231203
(121)	3.VI.23	230530	(277)	6.XII.23	⌊231206(2)⌋
(123)	6.VI.23	230601	(279)	8.XII.23	⌊231208(2)⌋
(136)	21.VI.23	230616(3)	(280)	9.XII.23	231207
(139)	24.VI.23	230618	(281)	11.XII.23	231208(1)
(140)	26.VI.23	230618	(287)	18.XII.23	231217
		230625	(294)	28.XII.23	231222
(143)	29.VI.23	230628	(295)	29.XII.23	231223
(144)	30.VI.23	230630	(19)	24.I.24	240122(1)
(145)	1.VII.23	230629(1)	(44)	23.II.24	240223
(152)	10.VII.23	⌊230710⌋	(71)	28.III.24	240319
(153)	11.VII.23	⌊230711⌋	(86)	15.IV.24	240412(1)
(154)	12.VII.23	⌊230712⌋			240412(3)
(155)	13.VII.23	⌊230713⌋			240413
(156)	14.VII.23	⌊230714⌋			240414
(166)	26.VII.23	230719	(87)	16.IV.24	⌊240416⌋
(181)	14.VIII.23	230806	(88)	17.IV.24	240415(1)
(183)	17.VIII.23	230808			240415(2) ++++

PRAVDA ++++

(89)	18.IV.24	240406		(16)	20.I.25	250115
(90)	19.IV.24	240411		(73)	31.III.25	250327
(91)	20.IV.24	240406		(104)	9.V.25	250403
(92)	22.IV.24	240419(2)		(120)	28.V.25	250000(5)
(93)	23.IV.24	240406		(123)	2.VI.25	250531
(95)	25.IV.24	240423		(125)	4.VI.25	250000(5)
(97)	30.IV.24	240429(1)		(127)	6.VI.25	⌊250606⌋
		240429(3)		(130)	11.VI.25	250000(5)
(98)	1.V.24	240421(2)		(135)	17.VI.25	250000(5)
(103)	9.V.24	240507		(161)	17.VII.25	250706
(104)	10.V.24	⌊240510(2)⌋		(163)	19.VII.25	250712
(106)	13.V.24	⌊240513(1)⌋		(166)	23.VII.25	250612(1)
(107)	14.V.24	⌊240514(2)⌋		(172)	30.VII.25	⌊250730(1)⌋
(108)	15.V.24	240512		(194)	27.VIII.25	250817
(112)	20.V.24	240519(1)		(195)	28.VIII.25	250817
		240519(2)		(196)	29.VIII.25	250828(1)
(118)	27.V.24	240523		(198)	1.IX.25	250828(2)
		240525		(199)	2.IX.25	250828(2)
		240526		(204)	8.IX.25	250903
(126)	5.VI.24	⌊240605⌋		(211)	16.IX.25	250915(1)
(128)	8.VI.24	240607		(212)	17.IX.25	250915(1)
(133)	14.VI.24	240610(1)		(215)	20.IX.25	250915(1)
(135)	18.VI.24	⌊240618(2)⌋		(216)	22.IX.25	250910
(151)	6.VII.24	240705				250915(1)
(154)	10.VII.24	240703		(217)	23.IX.25	250911
(157)	13.VII.24	240621		(223)	30.IX.25	250923
(165)	23.VII.24	240717		(251)	1.XI.25	251031
(176)	5.VIII.24	240728		(253)	5.XI.25	251025
(183)	14.VIII.24	240723		(255)	7.XI.25	251107(2)
(190)	23.VIII.24	240818		(259)	13.XI.25	251102
(193)	27.VIII.24	240827		(261)	15.XI.25	251107(1)
(197)	31.VIII.24	⌊240831⌋		(272)	28.XI.25	251108
(202)	6.IX.24	240729(1)		(278)	5.XII.25	251205
(228)	7.X.24	240928		(288)	17.XII.25	251207(1)
(229)	8.X.24	240930		(6)	8.I.26	251226
(237)	17.X.24	240922		(14)	17.I.26	⌊260117⌋
(239)	19.X.24	241018		(15)	19.I.26	260119
(250)	1.XI.24	241015(1)		(16)	20.I.26	260113(2)
(255)	7.XI.24	⌊241107⌋		(25)	31.I.26	260129 ++++

PRAVDA	++++		PRAVDA(Vienna)		
(26)	2.II.26	260129	(1)	3.X.08	⌊081003⌋
(33)	10.II.26	260209	(2)	17.XII.08	⌊081217(1)⌋
(34)	11.II.26	260211			⌊081217(2)⌋
(50)	2.III.26	260215			⌊081217(3)⌋
(51)	3.III.26	260215	(3)	27.III.09	⌊090327(1)⌋
(52)	4.III.26	260215			⌊090327(2)⌋
(53)	5.III.26	260215			⌊090327(3)⌋
(60)	14.III.26	260310			⌊090327(4)⌋
(118)	25.V.26	251222(2)	(4)	2.VI.09	⌊090602⌋
		251228	(5)	20.IX.09	⌊090920(1)⌋
(119)	26.V.26	251225			⌊090920(2)⌋
		260106			⌊090920(3)⌋
		260107	(6)	5.XI.09	⌊091105(1)⌋
		260113(1)			⌊091105(2)⌋
		260305			⌊091105(3)⌋
		260513	(7)	21.XI.09	⌊091121(1)⌋
		260519			⌊091121(2)⌋
(125)	2.VI.26	260528(1)			⌊091121(3)⌋
(168)	24.VII.26	260721	(8)	8.XII.09	⌊091208(1)⌋
(240)	17.X.26	261016			⌊091208(2)⌋
(257)	6.XI.26	261101			⌊091208(3)⌋
(274)	26.XI.26	261125			⌊091208(4)⌋
(289)	14.XII.26	261208			⌊091208(5)⌋
(68)	25.V.27	270325	(9)	1.I.10	⌊100101(1)⌋
(161)	19.VII.27	⌊270719⌋			⌊100101(2)⌋
(180)	10.VIII.27	270808			⌊100101(3)⌋
(181)	11.VIII.27	270808			⌊100101(4)⌋
(191)	24.VIII.27	270819	(10)	12.II.10	⌊100212(1)⌋
(251)	2.XI.27	271023			⌊100212(2)⌋
(254)[x]	5.XI.27	271100(2)	(11)	18.III.10	⌊100318(1)⌋
(263)[x]	17.XI.27	271100(2)			⌊100318(2)⌋
(13)	15.I.28	280114(1)	(12)	3.IV.10	⌊100403(1)⌋
		280114(2)			⌊100403(2)⌋
					⌊100403(3)⌋

[x] Diskussionyi listok, Nos. 3,5.

⌊100403(4)⌋
⌊100403(5)⌋   ++++

PRAVDA(Vienna)   ++++

(13)	15.V.10	⌊100403(2)⌋
		⌊100515⌋
(14)	24.VI.10	⌊100403(2)⌋
		⌊100624(1)⌋
		⌊100624(2)⌋
(15)	1.VIII.10	⌊100801(1)⌋
		⌊100801(2)⌋
		⌊100801(3)⌋
(16)	24.IX.10	⌊100924(1)⌋
		⌊100924(2)⌋
(17)	20.XI.10	⌊101120(1)⌋
		⌊101120(2)⌋
		⌊101120(3)⌋
(18-19)	29.I.11	⌊110129(1)⌋
		⌊110129(2)⌋
		⌊110129(3)⌋
(20)	16.IV.11	⌊110416⌋
(21)	25.VI.11	⌊110625⌋
(22)	16.XI.11	⌊111116(1)⌋
		⌊111116(2)⌋
		⌊111116(3)⌋
(23)	10.XII.11	⌊111210⌋
(24)	14.III.12	⌊120314(1)⌋
		⌊120314(2)⌋
(25)	23.IV.12	⌊120423(1)⌋
		⌊120423(2)⌋
		⌊120423(3)⌋
		⌊120423(4)⌋

=====================

PROLETARII(1908)

| (32) | 2.VII.08/ | 080705 |
| (38) | 1.XI.08 | 081014 |

=====================

PROLETARII(1917)

(1)	13.VIII.17	⌊170813/⌋
(2)	15.VIII.17	⌊170815(1)/⌋
		⌊170815(2)/⌋
(4)	17.VIII.17	⌊170817/⌋
(5)	18.VIII.17	⌊170818/⌋
(7)	20.VIII.17	⌊170820(1)/⌋
		⌊170820(2)/⌋
		⌊170820(3)/⌋
(8)	22.VIII.17	⌊170822/⌋
(10)	24.VIII.17	⌊170823/⌋

=====================

PROLETARSKAYA REVOLYUTSIYA

(--)	1921	⌊180000(55)⌋
(9)	1922	000700
(10)	1922	201107
(6)	1925	190508

=====================

RABOCHAYA GAZETA

| (234) | 17.X.23 | ⌊231017⌋ |

=====================

RABOCHAYA MOSKVA

(140)	27.VII.22	220725
(34)	15.II.23	230210
(39)	21.II.23	⌊230221(2)⌋
(41)	23.II.23	⌊230223(2)⌋
		⌊230223(3)⌋
		⌊230223(4)⌋
(50)	6.III.23	230304
(78)	12.IV.23	230306(1)
(79)	13.IV.23	230306(1)
(86)	21.IV.23	230420(1)
(87)	22.IV.23	230421 ++++

RABOCHAYA MOSKVA   ++++

(94)	3.V.23	⌊230503(3)⌋
(102)	12.V.23	⌊230512(2)⌋
(103)	13.V.23	230512(1)
(104)	15.V.23	230512(1)
(114)	27.V.23	230526
(142)	30.VI.23	230629(2)
(157)	18.VII.23	230717
(219)	30.IX.23	⌊230930⌋

=================================

RABOCHII

(1)	25.VIII.17	[170825/]
(10)	1.IX.17	⌊170901(2)/⌋
(12)	2.IX.17	⌊170901(2)/⌋

=================================

RABOCHII I SOLDAT

(1)	17.X.17	⌊171017(2)/⌋
		⌊171017(3)/⌋
(2)	18.X.17	170725(1)/
		⌊171018(1)/⌋
(3)	19.X.17	⌊171019/⌋

=================================

RABOCHII PUT

(1)	23.VIII.17	⌊170823/⌋
(2)	5.IX.17	170901(1)/
(4)	7.IX.17	170903/
(5)	8.IX.17	⌊170908/⌋
(7)	10.IX.17	⌊170910(1)/⌋
(8)	12.IX.17	170909(2)/
		170909(3)/
		170910(2)/
(15)	20.IX.17	170918(1)/
		170918(2)/
(18)	23.IX.17	170922(1)/

(19)	24.IX.17	170921(2)/
		170922(2)/
(21)	27.IX.17	170925(1)/
		170925(3)/
(23)	29.IX.17	170925(2)/
(31)	8.X.17	171007(1)/
(32)	10.X.17	171009(3)/
		171009(4)/
(33)	11.X.17	171009(1)/
		171009(2)/
(34)	12.X.17	171010(1)/
(35)	13.X.17	171011(1)/
		171011(2)/
		171012(3)/
(36)	14.X.17	171012(2)/
(38)	17.X.17	171012(1)/
(39)	18.X.17	171016(1)/
(41)	20.X.17	171013/
		171018(4)/
		171018(5)/
(42)	21.X.17	171018(2)/
(43)	22.X.17	171018(3)/
		171021(2)/
(44)	24.X.17	171022(3)/
		171024(1)/
(45)	25.X.17	171023(2)/
		171024(2)/
		⌊171025(1)/⌋
(46)	26.X.17	171024(4)/
		171025(2)/
		171025(3)/
		171025(4)/

=================================

RANNEE UTRO

| (121) | 2.VII.18 | 180701(1) |
| | | 180701(3) |

=================================

ROBITNICHI VISTI

(I.3)	15.XII.33	330720(1)
(II.4)	1.I.34	331107
		331110
(II.5)	1.III.34	330805
		331001
(II.6)	15.III.34	331001
(II.7)	1.IV.34	331001
		⌊340304⌋
(II.8)	15.IV.34	340223
(II.9)	1.V.34	⌊340300⌋
(II.10)	15.V.34	340118
(II.11)	1.VI.34	340118
(II.12)	15.VI.34	300108
(II.13)	1.VII.34	300108
(II.14)	15.VII.34	300108
(II.15)	1.VIII.34	300108
(II.16)	15.VIII.34	300108
(II.17)	1.IX.34	300108
(II.18)	15.IX.34	320917
		340715
		340800(3)
(II.19)	1.X.34	321231
(II.20)	15.X.34	321231
(II.21)	1.XI.34	321231
(II.22)	18.XI.34	321231
(II.23)	1.XII.34	340610
		341020
(II.24)	15.XII.34	340610
(III.1)	1.I.35	340610
(III.2)	15.I.35	340610
(III.3)	1.II.35	340610
		341230(1)
(III.4)	15.II.35	341228
(III.5)	1.III.35	341228
		350210
(III.6)	15.III.35	350112
(III.7)	1.IV.35	350126
(III.8)	15.IV.35	350130

(III.10)	15.V.35	350331(1)
		⌊350400⌋
(III.11)	1.VI.35	350201
(III.12-3)	1.VII.35	350201
		350525(2)
(III.1ns)	1.VIII.35	350610(1)
(III.2)	1.VIII.35	350607(2)
		350700(1)
(III.3)	1.IX.35	350722(1)
(III.6)	15.X.35	350926
(III.7)	1.XI.35	350607(1)
(III.8)	1.XII.35	351022
(III.9)	15.XII.35	230405(3)
		351126(4)
(IV.1)	1.I.36	351112
(IV.2)	15.I.36	351031
(IV.5)	1.III.36	360110
		360115(1)
		360128(1)
(IV.6)	15.III.36	360110
		360111
(IV.10)	1.VI.36	360416
(IV.11)	15.VI.36	360325
		360416

RUSSKAYA GAZETA

(383)	9.XI.05	⌊051109⌋
(388)	15.XI.05	⌊051115(1)⌋
(389)	16.XI.05	⌊051116(4)⌋
		⌊051116(5)⌋
(399)	27.XI.05	⌊051127(1)⌋
(404)	2.XII.05	⌊051202⌋

RUSSKAYA VOLYA

(252)   24.X.17   171023(1)/

=====================================

SEVERNAYA KOMMUNA

(31)   9.II.19   ⌊190206⌋
(33)   12.II.19   190110(2)
(34)   13.II.19   190211(1)
                          190211(2)
(36)   15.II.19   190214(1)
                          190214(2)
(--)   1919   190219
(74)   3.IV.19   190401

=====================================

SEVERNAYA RABOCHAYA GAZETA

(11)   21.II.14   ⌊140221⌋

=====================================

SOTSIALDEMOKRAT

(2)   1904   ⌊041100⌋
(3)   1904   ⌊041200⌋

(9)   7.VII.05   ⌊050707⌋

(2)   10.II.09   ⌊090210⌋
(3)   22.III.09   ⌊090322⌋
(7-8)   21.VIII.09   ⌊090821⌋

=====================================

SOTSIAL-DEMOKRAT

(210)   16.XI.17   171115(2)/
(215)   21.XI.17   171114(3)/

=====================================

SOTSIALISTICHESKII VESTNIK

(23-24)   17.XII.23   230306(2)
(11)   28.V.24   231008
                          231023(2)

=====================================

SPUTNIK KOMMUNISTA

(24)   1923   ⌊230923(2)⌋

=====================================

SVOBODA ROSSIYA

(44)   11.VI.18   180610(2)

=====================================

TOVARISHCH

(106)   5.XI.05   051104

=====================================

TRUD

(11)   3.III.21   210302
(20)   15.III.21   ⌊210315⌋
(91)   17.VI.21   210615

(57)   14.III.22   220312
(71)   31.III.22   220329(2)
(94)   3.V.22   220501(1)
(107)   18.V.22   ⌊220518⌋
(167)   28.VI.22   ⌊220727⌋
(191)   27.VIII.22   220826
(192)   30.VIII.22   220826
(228)   11.X.22   221010
(229)   12.X.22   221011
(248)   3.XI.22   ⌊221103(2)⌋
(252)   9.XI.22   221031
                          221107
(258)   16.XI.22   221114(1)
(272)   2.XII.22   221201(2)   +++

TRUD	++++	
(273)	3.XII.22	221202(1)
(295)	29.XII.22	221228
(104)	13.V.23	230512(1)
(132)	17.VI.23	230616(3)
(158)	18.VII.23	230717
(238)	21.X.23	231019(1)
(19)	24.I.24	240122(1)
(67)	23.III.24	⌊240323⌋
(92)	22.IV.24	240419(2)
(95)	25.IV.24	240423
(96)	26.IV.24	⌊240426⌋
(105)	11.V.24	240511
(106)	13.V.24	⌊240513(1)⌋
		⌊240513(2)⌋
(118)	27.V.24	240526
(176)	5.VIII.24	240728
(228)	7.X.24	240928
(229)	8.X.24	240930
(16)	20.I.25	250115
(124)	3.VI.25	250531
(171)	29.VII.25	⌊250729⌋
(221)	27.IX.25	250925
(14)	17.I.26	260113(2)
(24)	30.I.26	260129
(290)	20.XII.27	271203(1)
		271213

TRUDOVAYA NEDELYA

(—)	19.IV.20	200208

URALSKII RABOCHII

(39)	19.II.20	200217

VECHERNAYA POCHTA

(3)	**3.XI**.17	⌊171102(1)/⌋

VESTNIK KOMISSARIATA VNUTRENNIKH DEL

(10)	15.IV.18	180401(1)
		180405(3)
		180408(2)
(11)	24.IV.18	180411(2)
(12-13)	16.V.18	⌊180425(1)⌋
		⌊180516(3)⌋
(15-16)	14.VI.18	⌊180614(9)⌋
		⌊180614(10)⌋
		⌊180614(11)⌋
		⌊180614(12)⌋
		⌊180614(13)⌋
		⌊180614(14)⌋

VESTNIK PUTEI SOOBSHCHENIE

(2)	1918	180422(3)
		⌊180515(1)⌋
(3)	1918	180516(2)
		180529(1)
		180529(7)
		180530(4)
		⌊180530(5)⌋
		180531(5)
		180601(2)
		180601(3)
		⌊180604(6)⌋
(4)	1918	180610(4)
(5)	1918	180614(8)
		180626(2)

VESTNIK SOTSIALISTICHESKOI AKADEMII

(4-5)	IV-VI.23	230621

VESTNIK ZHIZNI

(6)	1907	[070700]
(7)	1907	[070700]

VOENNAYA NAUKA I REVOLYUTSIYA

(2)	1921	211205
(1)	1922	220218

VOENNOE DELO

(2)	1919	190109(1)
(5-6)	23.II.19	190110(2)
		[190223]
(23-24)	1919	190710
(25)	1919	190724
		190805(4)
(26)	IX.19	[190900]

VOSTOCHNOE OBOZRENIE

(230)	15.X.00	[001015]
(284)	22.XII.00	[001222]
(285)	23.XII.00	[001223]
(286)	24.XII.00	[001222]
(287)	25.XII.00	[001222]
(289)	30.XII.00	[001222]
(10)	14.I.01	[010114]
(19)	25.I.01	[010125]
(33)	14.II.01	[010214]
(34)	15.II.01	[010214]
(36)	17.II.01	[010217]

(56)	13.III.01	[010313]
(57)	14.III.01	[010313]
(61)	18.III.01	[010318]
(70)	29.III.01	[010329]
(88)	22.IV.01	[010422]
(91)	26.IV.01	[010422]
(99)	5.V.01	[010505]
(102)	9.V.01	[010505]
(117)	30.V.01	[010530]
(121)	3.VI.01	[010603]
(122)	4.VI.01	[010603]
(126)	9.VI.01	[010603]
(135)	20.VI.01	[010620]
(136)	21.VI.01	[010620]
(154)	13.VII.01	[010713]
(162)	22.VII.01	[010722]
(164)	25.VII.01	[010722]
(165)	26.VII.01	[010722]
(173)	4.VIII.01	[010804]
(176)	9.VIII.01	[010809]
(189)	20.VIII.01	[010820]
(194)	2.IX.01	[010902]
(197)	8.IX.01	[010908]
(212)	26.IX.01	[010926]
(225)	13.X.01	[011013]
(251)	14.XI.01	[011114]
(253)	17.XI.01	[011117]
(89)	19.IV.02	[020419]
(114)	18.V.02	[020518]
(115)	19.V.02	[020518]
(129)	5.VI.02	[020605]
(192)	17.VIII.02	[020817]

VPERED

(1)	2.VI.17	[170600(1)/]
		[170602(1)/]
		[170602(2)/] ++++

VPERED ++++

(2)	7.VI.17	⌊170607/⌋
(3)	15.VI.17	170605(1)/
		⌊170615/⌋
(4)	17.VI.17	170609(2)/
		⌊170617/⌋
(5)	28.VI.17	⌊170628(1)/⌋
		⌊170628(2)/⌋
		⌊170628(3)/⌋
(6)	9.VII.17	⌊170709/⌋
(7)	25.VII.17	⌊170725(2)/⌋

===============================

V PUTI

(20)	1919	190107(1)
(21)	11.I.19	190109(2)
(22)	11.II.19	190211(1)
(--)	17.III.19	⌊190317(1)⌋
(27)	6.IV.19	190324(1)
		190327
(29)	11.IV.19	190409
(30)	1919	190410(1)
(31)	15.IV.19	190412(2)
		190413
(32)	18.IV.19	190414
		⌊190418(1)⌋
(34)	20.IV.19	⌊190420(2)⌋
(35)	24.IV.19	190423(1)
		190424(2)
(36)	1919	190424(1)
(37)	27.IV.19	190427
(38)	28.IV.19	⌊190428⌋
(39)	1919	190430
(40)	1919	190503(1)
		190503(2)
(41)	1919	190504
(43)	1919	190507(1)
(44)	1919	190512(1)
(45)	1919	190511

(46)	1919	190516(1)
(47)	1919	190516(2)
(49)	1919	190526(1)
(50)	2.VI.19	190601(1)
(51)	1919	190602
(52)	5.VI.19	190604(1)
(53)	1919	190610
(54)	1919	190617
(55)	28.VI.19	190627(2)
		⌊190628(1)⌋
(56)	1919	⌊190628(2)⌋
(59)	1919	190711(1)
(61)	1919	190715
		190716
(64)	1919	190718(1)
(65)	1919	190719(1)
(66)	19.VII.19	190719(2)
		⌊190719(3)⌋
(73)	1919	190802(2)
(74)	1919	190803
(75)	1919	190804
(80)	12.VIII.19	⌊190812⌋
(83)	1919	190818(1)
(84)	19.VIII.19	190818(2)
		⌊190819⌋
(86)	1919	190904(3)
(88)	1919	190906(1)
(90)	1919	190908
(93)	12.IX.19	190911(1)
		190911(2)
(94)	1919	190913
(95)	17.IX.19	190916(1)
(96)	6.X.19	191006
(97)	16.X.19	191005
		⌊191016(1)⌋
(98)	18.X.19	191016(2)
(99)	22.X.19	191021(1)
(100)	24.X.19	191023 ++++

V PUTI	++++	
(101)	1919	191025(1)
(102)	26.X.19	191025(2)
		[191026]
(103)	1919	191103(2)
(104)	22.XII.19	[191222(1)]
(--)	1920	200200(1)
(106)	8.II.20	[200208]
(107)	10.II.20	200209(2)
(110)	8.V.20	[200508(2)]
(112)	10.V.20	200509(2)
(114)	12.V.20	200511(1)
(115)	14.V.20	200513
(116)	16.V.20	200515(1)
(117)	23.VIII.20	[200823]
(119)	25.VIII.20	200825
(120)	29.VIII.20	200828
(121)	30.VIII.20	200830(2)
(122)	8.IX.20	[200908(2)]
(124)	11.IX.20	200910
(125)	12.IX.20	200911
(132)	11.X.20	201010(1)
(134)	1920	201013(1)
(135)	1920	201027(1)
(136)	27.X.20	201027(2)
(142)	1921	210902
(145)	1921	210907(1)

ZA NOVYI BYT

	XII.25	251200

ZHIVOE DELO

(7)	2.III.12	120222
(16)	28.IV.12	[120428]

ZHIZN NATSIONAL'NOSTEI

(4:61)	1.II.20	200128
(13:70)	29.IV.20	200429(4)

ZNAMYA TRUDOVOI KOMMUNY

(22)	15.IX.18	[180914(1)]

ZNAMYA TRUDA

(84)	30.XI.17	[171130/]
(90)	9.XII.17	[171208(3)/]

ZVEZDA

(106)	1.V.19	190414

PERIODICALS LIST

Other scripts

	*ACCION OBRERA		*BORBA
ActSoc	ACTION SOCIALISTE	Bote	BOTE DER RUSSISCHEN
	(LocIISG)		REVOLUTION (∉ LocIISG)
ActSocRév	ACTION SOCIALISTE	BulCom	BULLETIN COMMUNISTE
	RÉVOLUTIONNAIRE		(LocIISG)
	(LocIISG)		
	*ADELANTE	CahiersCom	*Les CAHIERS COMMUNISTES
	AFTENPOSTEN (LocAAO)	Cahiers duBol	CAHIERS DU BOLCHEVISME
	*AKSHAM(Turkey)		(LocIISG)
	Die AKTION (LocIISG)		The CALL(Ln) (LocBM)
	AMERICAN MERCURY		*The CALL(NY)
	(LocNYPL)		CE QU'IL FAUT DIRE
	La ANTORCHA (∉ LocIISG)		(LocBDIC)
	La ANTORCHA		CHALLENGE OF YOUTH
	(Madrid) (∉ LocIISG)		(LocPer)
	*ARAB STUDIES		*CHICAGO DAILY NEWS
	ARBEIDERBLADET (LocULO)		*CLARIDAD
Arbeiter-Lit	*ARBEITER-LITERATUR		CLARTÉ (LocIISG)
	ARBEITERPOLITIK(∉ LocIISG)		*CLARTÉ
	ARBEITER-STIMME(∉ LocIISG)		(Denmark)
	ARBEITERZEITUNG(LocIISG)		CLASS STRUGGLE (LocNYPL)
	ARIZONA DAILY STAR		CLASS STRUGGLE(Ln)
	(LocPer)		(LocPer)
	ART AND ARTISTS(LocPer)		CLASS STRUGGLE(NY)
	ATLANTIC MONTHLY		(LocBM)
	(LocNYPL)		CLAVE (LocNYPL)
	*AUSSIGER TAGEBLATT		CLÉ (LocHIS)
	*L'AVANT-GARDE		*COMBAT(Shanghai)
	*AVANTI		La COMMUNE (LocIISG)
		TheCom	THE COMMUNIST (LocO)
			THE COMMUNIST(B)
Baan	De BAANBREKER (LocIISG)		(LocPer)
	BABEL (∉ LocPer)	Le Com	Le COMMUNISTE (LocPer)
	*BAMIFNE	CI	The COMMUNIST
	BANNER (∉ LocPer)		INTERNATIONAL
	La BATALLA (∉ LocIISG)		(LocBM)
	*BERLINER TAGEBLATT	CI(Ln)	The COMMUNIST
	BLACK DWARF (LocPer)		INTERNATIONAL(Ln)
	Der BOLSCHEWIK (∉ LocIISG)		(LocO)
	*BOLSHEVIK-LENINIST	ComReview	The COMMUNIST
	(India)		REVIEW (LocBM)

	COMUNISMO	(LocIISG)	Fahne desKom	FAHNE DES KOMMUNISMUS	
El Com	El COMUNISTA	(LocIISG)			(∅ LocIISG)
Contre leC	CONTRE LE COURANT			De FAKKEL	(LocIISG)
		(LocIISG)		FIGHT	(LocPer)
	CONTRE LE		FI(S)	FJÄRDE INTERNATIONALEN	
	COURANT(B)	(LocABC)		(Sweden)	(LocPer)
	CONTROVERSY	(LocBM)	4I(D)	4 INTERNATIONALE	
CorInt	CORRESPONDANCE			(Denmark)	(LocABC)
	INTERNATIONALE			FOREIGN AFFAIRS	(LocBM)
		(LocBDIC)		FORUM	(LocNYPL)
	*CORRIERE DELLA SERA			FORWARD	(LocNLS)
	*CRITICA		FI	FOURTH INTERNATIONAL	
	CRITIQUE SOCIALE				(LocPPA)
		(LocIISG)	FI(Ln)	FOURTH INTERNATIONAL	
IV Int	IV INTERNACIONAL			(London)	(LocPer)
		(LocIISG)	FI(P)	FOURTH INTERNATIONAL	
	CURRENT HISTORY	(LocNYPL)		(Paris)	(LocPer)
				*FRANKFURTER ZEITUNG	
	*DAGBLADETT			FREE EXPRESSION	(LocPPA)
	DAILY EXPRESS	(LocBM)		FRONT(Minsk)	(∅ LocIISG)
	DAILY HERALD	(LocBM)			
	DAILY NEWS	(LocBM)		Der GEGNER	(∅ LocABC)
	*DAILY NEWS(NY)			GLASGOW HERALD	(LocBM)
	*DAVAR			GLASGOW WORKER	(LocBM)
	DEMAIN	(LocPer)			
	*DEUTSCHE ALLGEMEINE			*HAAREZ	
	ZEITUNG			*HAPOEL HATZAIR	
	DIETHNISTES	(LocPer)		HARPERS MAGAZINE	
DrapR	Le DRAPEAU ROUGE				(LocNYPL)
		(LocPer)		*HASHOMER HATZAIR	
				*HASHOMER HATZAIR(Warsaw)	
EWeg	Der EINZIGE WEG	(LocIISG)		L'HERNE	
	*Der EMES		Huma	L'HUMANITÉ	
EnigeW	De ENIGE WEG	(LocIISG)		Les HUMBLES	
EM	ETUDES MARXISTES				
		(∅ LocPer)		INDEPENDENT	(LocBM)
	*EUROPE NOUVELLE			INITIATIVE	
	*El EXCELSIOR			SOCIALISTE	(∅ LocPer)

IP   INTERCONTINENTAL   *KETUVIM
            PRESS   (LocPPA)   KLASSE KAMP   (LocABC)
Int   Die INTERNATIONALE   Klassen   KLASSENSTRIJD   (LocIISG)
            (1925)   (∉ LocIISG)   Klassen(A) KLASSENSTRIJD
Int   Die INTERNATIONALE   (Amsterdam) (LocIISG)
            (1948)   (LocIISG)   Klassen(G) KLASSENSTRIJD
Int(M)   Die INTERNATIONALE   (Gent)   (LocIISG)
            (1970)   (LocPer)   KLORKEIT   (LocPPA)
Int   De INTERNATIONALE   *KOLNISCHE ZEITUNG
            (LocIISG)   KOMMUNISMUS   (LocABC)
De Int   De INTERNATIONALE   Der Kom   Der KOMMUNIST   (LocIISG)
            (LocIISG)   Der KOMMUNIST
IC   L'INTERNATIONALE   (Bremen)   (∉ LocIISG)
            COMMUNISTE (LocBDIC)   KOMMUNISTISCHE
Inprekor   INTERNATIONALE   ARBEITERZEITUNG
            PRESSE-KORRESPONDENZ   (∉ LocIISG)
            (LocIISG)   KomInt   Der KOMMUNISTISCHE
IntNews   INTERNATIONAL NEWS   INTERNATIONALE
            (∉ LocPer)   (LocABC)
Inprecor   INTERNATIONAL PRESS   KaI   Den KOMMUNISTISKA
            CORRESPONDENCE   INTERNATIONALEN
            (LocPPA)   (LocAAS)
IntReview   INTERNATIONAL REVIEW   KeI   Den KOMMUNISTISKE
            (LocNYPL)   INTERNATIONALE
IntSoc   INTERNATIONAL   (LocABC)
            SOCIALISM   (LocPer)   *KOMUNARAS
ISR   INTERNATIONAL SOCIALIST KomFon   *KOMUNISTISHE FON
            REVIEW   (LocPPA)   *KUNTRAS

            JELGAWAS KOMUNISTS   LABOR ACTION
            (∉ LocKBS)   (San Francisco)
            JISKRA   (∉ LocIISG)   (LocPPA)
            JOHN O'LONDON (LocBM)   LabChal   LABOR CHALLENGE(LocIISG)
Jug-Int   JUGEND-INTERNATIONALE   LABOUR MONTHLY (LocBM)
            (LocABC)   LabReview   LABOUR REVIEW   (LocPer)
            *JUMRURIET (Turkey)   The LACE CURTAIN
                                                        (LocPer)
            Der KAMPF   (LocIISG)   LEFT REVIEW   (∉ LocPer)
            KEEP LEFT   (LocPer)   *LEIPZIGER VOLKSZEITUNG
                                                 Les LETTRES
                                                     NOUVELLES   (LocBN)

	LIBERATOR (∉ LocIISG)	Mil(A)	MILITANT (Australia) (LocIISG)
	LIBERTY (LocNYPL)		
	LIDOVE NOVINY (∉ LocIISG)	MIR	MILITANT INTERNATIONAL REVIEW (LocPer)
	LIFE (LocNYPL)		
	Die LINKE FRONT (∉ LocIISG)		*MILLIET (Turkey)
LitWelt	*Die LITERARISCHE WELT		MISCAREA SOCIALA (∉ LocIISG)
	LIVING AGE (LocNYPL)		MODERN MONTHLY (LocNYPL)
	LOGOTECHNES (LocPer)		The MODERN THINKER (LocPer)
	A LUTA DE CLASSE (∉ LocIISG)		*Le MONDE
	La LUTTE (Saigon) (∉ LocIISG)		MONDE (VERDEN) (Denmark) (LocABC)
	LUTTE DE CLASSE (Belgium) (LocPer)		*MONTAG MORGEN
Lutte deC	La LUTTE DE CLASSES (LocHIS)		MORNING POST (LocBM)
LdesC	La LUTTE DES CLASSES (LocHIS)		MOSKAU (∉ LocABC)
LO(B)	La LUTTE OUVRIÈRE (Belgium) (LocHIS)		MOT DAG (LocAAO)
LO(C)	La LUTTE OUVRIÈRE (Canada) (∉ LocPer)		NATION (LocNYPL)
			*Die NEUE BÜCHERSCHAU
LO(Fr)	La LUTTE OUVRIÈRE (France) (LocHIS)		NEUE FREIE PRESSE (LocBM)
			Der NEUE MAHNRUF (LocIISG)
			*Die NEUE RUNDSCHAU
			*Das NEUE RUSSLAND
ManGuard	MANCHESTER GUARDIAN (LocBM)		*Die NEUE WIENER JOURNAL
	MARXISTIKO DELTIO (∅ LocPer)		*Die NEUE ZEIT
			NEW EUROPE (LocBM)
		NI	NEW INTERNATIONAL (LocPPA)
MarxOut	MARXIST OUTLOOK (India) (∉ LocPer)	NI(WP)	NEW INTERNATIONAL (WP) (LocPPA)
	MARXIST REVIEW (LocPer)		NEW LEADER (LocBM)
			NEW MASSES (LocPer)
MYJ	MARXIST YOUTH JOURNAL (LocPer)	NMil	NEW MILITANT (LocPPA)
	*MEXICO AL DIA	NRep	NEW REPUBLIC (LocNYPL)
Mil	MILITANT (LocPPA)		NEW RUSSIA (LocBM)
			NEW RUSSIA (Shanghai) (∉ LocIISG)

NEWS CHRONICLE (LocBM)

NEWSLETTER (LocPer)   PermRev

*NEW YORK EVENING POST

*NEW YORK GLOBE

*NEW YORK HERALD-

    TRIBUNE

NEW YORK TIMES (LocBM)

*NEW YORK VOLKSZEITUNG

*NEW YORK WORLD-

    TELEGRAM

*NICHIRO SOOFUKAI

NFak   De NIEUE FAKKEL(LocIISG)

De NIEUWE TIJD (∉ LocIISG)

De NIEUWE WEG (LocIISG)   Pol(D)

NOUVELLES ETUDES

    MARXISTES (∉ LocPer)   Pol(S)

NRF   NOUVELLESREVUE

    FRANÇAISE (LocBN)

NOWE PISMO (∉ LocIISG)

NOWE PRZEGLAD (∉ LocIISG)

La NUEVA ERA (LocPer)

NUEVO ORDEN (∉ LocIISG)

NY TID (∉ LocAAO)

El OBRERO MILITANTE

    (∉ LocPer)

OBSERVER (LocBM)

OCTOBER YOUTH (LocPer)

OCTUBRE (∉ LocIISG)

OCTUBRE

    (Buenos Aires)   QI(It)

    (∉ LocPer)

OKTOBER (LocAAO)   QI

L'ORDINE NUOVO (LocIISG)

*OSAKA MAINICHI   QI(OSPE)

Pali   E PALI TON TAKSION

    (∉ LocIISG)

PARIS-MIDI (LocBN)

PARIS-SOIR (LocBN)

PARTISAN REVIEW(LocNYPL)

PERMANENTE

    REVOLUTION (LocIISG)

PERMANENT

    REVOLUTION

    (India) (∉ LocPer)

PERSPECTIVA

    MUNDIAL (∉ LocPer)

PERSPECTIVES (∉ LocPer)

*PESTER LLOYD

POCHODNIA (∉ LocIISG)

POLITICAL

    QUARTERLY (LocBM)

POLITIKEN

    (Denmark) (LocABC)

POLITIKEN

    (Sweden) (LocABS)

*POPOLO D'ITALIA

POUM (∉ LocIISG)

*PRAGER PRESSE

*PRAGER TAGEBLATT

PRAWDA (∉ LocAAS)

*PRESENTE

*Le PROLÉTAIRE

PROLETARJAT (LocIISG)

PROMETEO (LocIISG)

PRZEGLAD SOCYAL-

    DEMOKRATYCZNY

    (LocIISG)

QUARTA INTERNAZIONALE

    (LocPer)

QUATRIÈME INTERNATIONALE

    (LocPer)

QUATRIÈME INTERNATIONALE

    (OSPE) (LocBN)

QUE FAIRE (LocPer)

*RADNICHKE NOVINE

*RADNIK

	RED DAWN	(LocBM)
	RED FLAG	(LocPer)
	RED MOLE	(LocPer)
RepAm	REPERTORIO	
	AMERICANA	(∉ LocIISG)
	RÉVOLUTION	(LocIISG)
	RÉVOLUTION	
	Gilly)	(∉ LocIISG)
RevSoc	De REVOLUTIONAIR	
	SOCIALIST	(LocIISG)
RevProl	La RÉVOLUTION	
	PROLÉTARIENNE	
		(LocMS)
RevCom	The REVOLUTIONARY	
	COMMUNIST	(LocPer)
RevueCom	La REVUE COMMUNISTE	
		(LocIISG)
	*La REVUE MONDIALE	
	*RHENISCHE-WESTFÄLISCHE	
	ZEITUNG	
RodOkt	De RODE OKTOBER(∉ LocIISG)	
	Det RÖDE RYSSLAND	
		(LocABC)
	De ROOD GARDISTE	
		(LocIISG)
	*ROTE FAHNE	
	ROUGE	(LocPer)
	RUDE PRAVO	(LocIISG)
	RUSSIAN INFORMATION	
	REVIEW	(LocGDS)
RusKor	RUSSISCHE KORRESPONDENZ	
		(LocIISG)
	RUSSISCHE RUNDSCHAU	
		(∉ LocIISG)
	*SÄCHSISCHE STAATS	
	ZEITUNG	
	*ST LOUIS POST-DISPATCH	
	SAMTIDEN	(LocULO)
	SAN FRANCISCO NEWS	
		(LocPer)

	SATURDAY EVENING	
	POST	(LocNYPL)
	SATURDAY REVIEW OF	
	LITERATURE	(LocNYPL)
	*SCHLESSISCHE ZEITUNG	
	*SEVEN DAYS	
SocDemok	SOCIAL DEMOKRATEN	
		(∉ LocABC)
Soc(G)	The SOCIALIST	
	(Glasgow)	(LocBM)
SocAp	SOCIALIST APPEAL	
		(LocPPA)
SocAp(C)	SOCIALIST APPEAL	
	(Chicago)	(LocPPA)
SocAp(Ln)	SOCIALIST APPEAL	
	(London)	(∉ LocPer)
SocInf	SOCIALISTIK	
	INFORMATION	(LocPer)
	SOCIALIST VANGUARD	
	(Bombay)	(LocPer)
	SOCIALIST WORKER	
		(LocPer)
	SOCIÁLNÍ DEMOKRAT	
		(∉ LocIISG)
	SOCIJALNA MISAO(∉ LocIISG)	
	An SOLAS	(LocPer)
SDS	SOUS LE DRAPEAU DE	
	SOCIALISME	(LocPer)
	*El SOVIET	
	SOVIET RUSSIA	(LocIISG)
	*SOZIALISTISCHE	
	ARBEITERZEITUNG	
	The SPARK	(∉ LocPer)
	SPARTACIST	(LocPer)
	SPARTACUS	(LocIISG)
	SPARTACUS(1969)(∉ LocPer)	
	SPOKESMAN	(LocPer)
	SUNDAY EXPRESS (LocBM)	
	SUNDAY SUN	
	(Australia) (LocPer)	

	SUNDAY WORKER	(LocBM)
	SWIT	(LocBM)
	SYMPOSIUM	(LocPer)
	*Das TAGEBUCH	
ThurAllgemZtg	*THURINGEN ALLGEMEIN ZEITUNG	
	TIDENS TEGN	(LocAAO)
	TIMES	(LocBM)
	TRIBUNA SOCIALISTA	(¢ LocPer)
	De TRIBUNE	(LocIISG) WIN
	TROTZ ALLEDEM!	(LocPer)
	TRUTH	(LocPer) WIReview
	TWENTIETH CENTURY (Cambridge)	(LocCU)
	UMILLO MOLLO	(¢ LocIISG)
	*El UNIVERSAL	
	UNSER KAMPF	(LocNYPL)
UWort	UNSER WORT	(LocIISG)
	*VADERLAND	
	VANGUARD (Canada)	(¢ LocPer)
	La VERITÁ	(LocIISG)
V	La VÉRITÉ	(LocIISG)
V(M)	La VÉRITÉ(1918)	(LocIISG)
V(OCE)	La VÉRITÉ(OCE)	(LocBN)
VieOuv	La VIE OUVRIÈRE	(LocMS)
IVe Int	De IVe INTERNATIONALE	(LocIISG)
IVe Int(p)	De IVE INTERNATIONALE (processed)	(LocIISG)
	La VOIE DE LÉNINE	(¢ LocPer)
VoixCom	LA VOIX COMMUNISTE	(LocIISG)
Volks	VOLKSWILLE	(¢ LocIISG)
	*VORWAERTS	

*VOSSISCHE ZEITUNG	
WAS TUN?	(¢ LocPer)
*Der WEG	
WELTBÜHNE	(LocIISG)
*WORKER(USA)	
The WORKERS DREADNOUGHT	(LocIISG)
WORKERS FIGHT	(LocPer)
WORKERS' FIGHT (Manchester)	(LocPer)
WORKERS INTERNATIONAL NEWS	(¢ LocNLS)
WORKERS INTERNATIONAL REVIEW	(¢ LocPer)
WORKERS PRESS	(LocPer)
WORKERS REPUBLIC (Manchester)	(LocPer)
*WORKERS VOICE (So. Africa)	
WORKERS WEEKLY	(LocBM)
*WORLD (Sweden)	
WORLD OUTLOOK	(LocPer)
WORLD POLITICS (Ln)	(LocPer)
YALE REVIEW	(LocBM)
YOUNG MARXIST	(LocPer)
YOUNG SOCIALIST(NY)	(LocPPA)
YOUNG SOCIALIST(Ceylon)	(LocPer)
YOUNG SPARTACUS	(LocPer)
Die ZUKUNFT	(LocPer)

CONCORDANCE TO PERIODICALS
Other scripts

ACCION OBRERA

(--)	1941	380923

=================================

ACTION SOCIALISTE

(II.3)	20.I.34	331107
(II.7)	17.II.34	330610
(II.8)	24.II.34	330610
(II.9)	3.III.34	330610

=================================

ACTION SOCIALISTE RÉVOLUTIONNAIRE

(III.35)	31.VIII.35	350729
(III.51)	22.XII.35	350914
(IV.14)	4.IV.36	360318
(IV.22)	30.V.36	360328
(IV.23)	6.VI.36	360328
(IV.25)	20.VI.36	360416
		360605
(IV.26)	27.VI.36	360416
		360609
(IV.30)	25.VII.36	360709(2)
(IV.31)	2.VIII.36	360522
(IV.33)	15.VIII.36	360730(1)
(IV.34)	22.VIII.36	360700(1)

=================================

ADELANTE

(--)	1933	331003(2)

=================================

AFTENPOSTEN

(--)	24.IX.36	360923
(42)	23.I.37	⌊370112(2)⌋

=================================

AKSHAM

(--)	⌊20.III.29⌋	290312

=================================

Die AKTION

(--)	*1920	200000(37)
(XV.2-3)	15.II.25	240915
(XVI.11-12)	XII.26	261016
(XVIII.1)	II.28	261101
(XVIII.2-3)	III-IV.28	280114(1)
(XVIII.10-12)	XII.28	280628
		280712
		280723
		280909(1)
(XIX.1-2)	III.29	271021
		280103
(XIX.3-4)	V.29	240122(1)
		281216(2)
		290225
		290329
(XIX.5-8)	IX.29	290422
		290522(1)
		290600(1)
		290612
		290615
		290701
		290727(1)
		290804
		291004
(XX.1-2)	VIII.30	⌊300500(1)⌋
		⌊300500(2)⌋
		300528
(XXI.1-2)	IV.31	⌊301200(1)⌋
		310308 ++++

AKTION   ++++

(XXI.3-4)	VII.31	310404
		310528(1)
(XXII.1-4)	VIII.32	⌊320415⌋
		320613(2)

==================

AMERICAN MERCURY

	I.34	330622

==================

La ANTORCHA

(III.59)	12.I.23	221114(1)
(III.61)	26.I.23	221114(1)
(III.62)	2.II.23	221114(1)
(III.63)	9.II.23	221114(1)
(III.85)	13.VII.23	⌊230215⌋
(III.95)	21.IX.23	⌊230711⌋
(IV.114)	1.II.24	240122(1)
(IV.115)	8.II.24	230313
(IV.118)	29.II.24	230313
(IV.128)	16.V.24	231200(3)
(VI.250)	17.IX.26	260000(7)
(VI.251)	30.IX.26	260000(7)
(VI.252)	8.X.26	260000(7)
(VI.253)	15.X.26	260000(7)
(VI.254)	22.X.26	260000(7)
(VI.257)	12.XI.26	260000(7)
(VI.258)	19.XI.26	260000(7)
(VI.259)	26.XI.26	260000(7)
(VI.260)	3.XII.26	260000(7)
(VI.261)	10.XII.26	260000(7)
(VI.262)	17.XII.26	260000(7)
(VI.263)	24.XII.26	260000(7)
(VI.264)	31.XII.26	260000(7)
(VI.265)	7.I.27	260000(7)

==================

La ANTORCHA(Madrid)

(I.1)	1.V.34	340331
(I.2)	30.VI.34	310124

==================

ARAB STUDIES

(11)	IX.69	⌊101100⌋

==================

ARBEIDERBLADET

(--)	27.VII.29	290422
(--)	3.VIII.29	290225
(--)	21.VIII.29	290225
(--)	3.IX.29	290225
(--)	4.IX.29	290225
(180)	26.VII.35	350726(1)
(194)	21.VIII.36	360821
(196)	24.VIII.36	360824
(197)	25.VIII.36	360823(1)
		360825

==================

ARBEITER-LITERATUR

(1: 106-18)	1924	210204
: 199-213)		240319
: 303-24)		240000(24)

==================

ARBEITERPOLITIK (Bremen)

(II.4)	27.I.17	151100(2)
(II.33)	18.VIII.17	⌊170617/⌋
(II.34)	25.VIII.17	⌊170617/⌋
(II.41)	13.X.17	100000(2)

==================

ARBEITER-STIMME

(19)	3.XII.27	070212
(37)	XI.28	271021
		280712
(39)	I.29	281021
(45)	VII.29	⌊290626⌋
(59)	IX.30	⌊300900(2)⌋
(91)	XII.31	311126
(102)	V.32	⌊300800(1)⌋
		⌊320127⌋
(103)	VI.32	⌊300800(1)⌋
		⌊320127⌋
(108)	VIII.32	320725
		330400(2)
(109)	IX.32	330400(2)
(111)	X.32	330400(2)

================

ARBEITERZEITUNG

(62)	3.III.29	290225

================

ARIZONA DAILY STAR

	13.XII.38	⌊381213⌋
	13.XII.42	⌊381213⌋

================

ART AND ARTISTS

(IV.5)	VIII.69	380725(2)

================

ATLANTIC MONTHLY

	X.35	330510

================

AUSSIGER TAGEBLATT

	13.VII.31	310000(1)

================

L'AVANT-GARDE

(I.2)	⌊--⌋	⌊400820(4)⌋
		⌊400820(6)⌋

================

AVANTI

	3.III.23	180000(55)

================

De BAANBREKER

(I.29)	9.XI.29	291004
(I.30)	16.XI.29	291004
(I.31)	23.XI.29	291004
(I.34)	14.XII.29	291109
		291113
(II.32)	29.XI.30	⌊280900⌋
(II.33)	6.XII.30	⌊280900⌋
(II.34)	13.XII.30	⌊280900⌋
(II.35)	20.XII.30	⌊280900⌋
(II.36)	27.XII.30	⌊280900⌋
(II.37)	3.I.31	⌊280900⌋
(II.40)	24.I.31	240122(1)
(III.4)	23.V.31	310415
(III.17)	22.VIII.31	310624
(III.40)	30.I.32	320102
(IV.3)	21.V.32	320215(1)
(IV.29)	19.XI.32	321013(2)
(IV.31)	3.XII.32	321022(1)
(IV.32)	10.XII.32	321022(1)
(IV.33)	17.XII.32	321022(1)
(IV.34)	24.XII.32	321022(1)
(IV.35)	31.XII.32	321022(1)

++++

BAANBREKER	++++		BABEL		
(IV.36)	7.I.33	321022(1)	(2)	1939	390304(3)
(IV.37)	14.I.33	321022(1)	(5)	1939	381010
(IV.38)	21.I.33	321022(1)	(11)	1940	391215(2)
		330111(2)	(15-16)	I-IV.41	250917
(IV.39)	28.I.33	321022(1)			330401
(IV.40)	4.II.33	330111(1)			380212
(IV.41)	11.II.33	330111(1)			390121
(IV.42)	18.II.33	330111(1)			390807
(V.7)	16.VI.33	330525			
(V.9)	1.VII.33	330523			
(V.11)	15.VII.33	330613(1)	================		
(V.18)	2.IX.33	330720(1)	BAMIFNE		
(V.19)	9.IX.33	330720(1)		1932	320423
(V.20)	16.IX.33	330720(1)			
		330817(3)	================		
		330826			
(V.23)	7.X.33	330828	BANNER		
(V.24)	14.X.33	330828		X.37	370828
(V.25)	21.X.33	330920			
		331001	================		
(V.29)	18.XI.33	331110	La BATALLA		
(V.31)	2.XII.33	331107	(I.10)	1.III.23	⌊180000(55)⌋
(V.41)	10.II.34	340118	(I.11)	8.III.23	221114(1)
(V.42)	17.II.34	340118	(I.17)	4.V.23	230000(9)
(V.43)	24.II.34	340118	(I.20)	17.VIII.23	230630
(V.44)	3.III.34	340222	(I.25)	28.IX.23	⌊230711⌋
(V.48)	31.III.34	340316			
(V.49)	7.IV.34	⌊340300⌋			
		340323			
(VI.4)	26.V.34	⌊340427⌋	(II.22)	27.VIII.36	360730(1)
(VI.11)	14.VII.34	340610	(II.69)	21.X.36	300000(1)
(VI.37)	12.I.35	341230(2)			
(VI.41)	9.II.35	350126	(XXI.149)	III.65	330714
(VI.43)	23.II.35	350210	(XXIV.163)	II.68	330401
(VI.44)	2.III.35	350130	(XXIV.164)	III.68	330401

BERLINER TAGEBLATT

1928	280115	(I.36)	14.X.20	200723
1930	⌊300215⌋	(I.46)	2.XII.20	200731(2)
		(I.47-48)	9.XII.20	201010(2)
		(I.50-51)	23.XII.20	191005
				200000(37)

==============================

BLACK DWARF

(XIV.27)	30.I.70	380725(2)	(II.2)	13.I.21	201208(2)
			(II.3)	20.I.21	200000(37)
			(II.4)	27.I.21	201202(1)
			(II.5)	3.II.21	⌊201219⌋

==============================

Der BOLSCHEWIK

(20)	30.XI.22	⌊221130(2)⌋	(II.26)	23.VI.21	210613(2)
					210623
			(II.29)	14.VII.21	210623
					210704
			(II.30)	21.VII.21	210613(2)
					210623

==============================

BOLSHEVIK-LENINIST

VIII.42	381230	(II.34)	18.VIII.21	201124
		(II.51)	17.XI.21	211127
		(III.13)	30.III.22	220226(1)

==============================

BORBA

(II.17)	1910	⌊101101⌋	(III.14)	6.IV.22	220226(1)
			(III.15)	13.IV.22	⌊220413(2)⌋
(IV.21)	1911	⌊111101⌋	(III.20)	11.V.22	220226(2)
			(III.21)	25.V.22	220000(5)
(VII.208)	1914	*⌊140000(4)⌋	(III.22)	1.VI.22	210000(7)
			(III.26)	22.VI.22	220523

==============================

(III.28)	6.VII.22	220519(1)
(III.30)	20.VII.22	220526

BOTE DER RUSSISCHEN REVOLUTION

(7)	27.X.17	171010(1)/	(III.33)	10.VIII.22	220508(4)
			(III.34)	17.VIII.22	220519(2)
			(III.35)	24.VIII.22	220519(2)
			(III.36)	31.VIII.22	220608

==============================

(III.37)	7.IX.22	220512(1)
		220610

BULLETIN COMMUNISTE

(I.3)	1.IV.20	190914	(III.45)	9.XI.22	221020
(I.10)	20.V.20	190118	(III.48)	30.XI.22	221103(1)
(I.11)	27.V.20	191030(2)			
(I.12)	3.VI.20	191218	(IV.2-3)	18.I.23	221201(2)
(I.23-24)	12.VIII.20	200000(37)	(IV.4)	25.I.23	221201(1)
(I.30-31)	16.IX.20	200722	(IV.7)	15.II.23	221205

++++

BULLETIN COMMUNISTE   ++++

(IV.9)	1.III.23	230127(1)		(VIII.24-25)	XII.27	270507
(IV.11)	15.III.23	230210				270517(1)
		⌊230215⌋		(IX.26)	I-III.28	270507
(IV.12)	22.III.23	220112				270517(1)
(IV.15)	12.IV.23	230321		(IX.29-30)	VIII-XII.28	271021
(IV.16)	19.IV.23	221114(1)				
(IV.18)	3.V.23	230306(1)				

========================

(IV.19)	10.V.23	230420(1)
(IV.30)	26.VII.23	230630

CAHIERS COMMUNISTES

(IV.36)	6.IX.23	⌊230710⌋
(IV.40)	4.X.23	230325

(3)	1924	170000(1)

========================

(IV.47)	22.XI.23	170000(1)
(IV.49)	6.XII.23	⌊231123(2)⌋

CAHIERS DU BOLCHEVISME

(IV.50)	13.XII.23	230313
		230319(2)

(I.3)	5.XII.24	240728
(I.4)	12.XII.24	240728

(IV.51)	20.XII.23	220425
(IV.52)	27.XII.23	151222

(I.5)	19.XII.24	240915
(I.6)	26.XII.24	240915

(V.3)	18.I.24	231222
(V.4)	25.I.24	231223

(II.45)	25.III.26	⌊260000(33)⌋
(II.51)	15.VI.26	260215

(V.6)	8.II.24	⌊231200(1)⌋
(V.11)	14.III.24	231200(4)
(V.21)	23.V.24	200000(37)

(II.53)	15.VII.26	260503
(--)	20.XII.26	261016
		261101

(V.27)	4.VII.24	240607
(V.29)	18.VII.24	161011

(III.79)	1.IX.27	270808

(VI.3)	6.XI.25	201107
(VI.5)	20.XI.25	240305

========================

(VIII.16-17)	I-III.27	⌊270300(1)⌋
(VIII.18-19)	IV-VI.27	261016
		261214(2)
		⌊270400⌋

The CALL(London)

	10.I.18	⌊171217(2)/⌋
	17.IV.19	190304
	31.VII.19	161211
(VIII.20-21)	VII-IX.27	270526(2)
		270527(1)
		270528(1)
		270528(2)
		270808

	11.IX.19	⌊190306(2)⌋
	4.XII.19	190901(3)
	23.XII.19	190716
	15.I.20	180422(4)

(VIII.22-23)	X-XI.27	260412
		271100(2)

	15.IV.20	200228(2)
	29.IV.20	200404(2)

========================

The CALL(New York)

| | 1917 | 170115 |
| | | 170116(1) |

(VI.14)	15.X.27	250828(2)
(VI.15)	XI.27	250828(2)
(VI.16)	XII.27-I.28	250828(2)

==

CE QU'IL FAUT DIRE

| 26.VIII.16 | ⌊160826⌋ |
| 22.XII.17 | ⌊170617/⌋ |

CLARTÉ(Denmark)

| (V) | 1940 | 390925 |

==

The CHALLENGE OF YOUTH

X.37	370522
III.38	380204
20.IX.40	371117

CLASS STRUGGLE

(--)	XI-XII.17	⌊170617/⌋
(II.2)	III-IV.18	⌊170602(2)/
(III.4)	XI.19	180328(1)

==

CHICAGO DAILY NEWS

| 7.XI.19 | 191031 |
| 18.V.32 | 320423 |

CLASS STRUGGLE(London)

| (1) | ⌊1939⌋ | 390925 |

==

CLASS STRUGGLE(New York)

(I.1)	V.31	301126
(I.2)	VI.31	310415
(I.5)	XII.31	311010
(II.7)	VIII.32	320519(1)
		320522(1)
		320524(1)

CLARIDAD

| (328) | VIII.38 | 371217 |

(III.1)	I.33	321205
(III.3-4)	III-IV.33	321228(2)
		330128(2)
(III.6)	VI.33	321003
(III.9)	IX-X.33	330622
(III.10)	XI.33	330622
		330800(1)

CLARTÉ

	1922	220512(2)
(22)	1.X.22	220515
(II.30)	1.II.23	220710(1)
(II.41)	15.VIII.23	⌊230710⌋
(II.46)	1.XI.23	230000(9)
(III.58)	1.V.24	231200(3)
(V.1)	15.VI.26	260119
		260215

++++

CLASS STRUGGLE(NY)   ++++

(IV.1)	I.34	330610	(I.8)	1.V.39	390318
(IV.2)	II.34	⌊340200(1)⌋			390501
(IV.4-5)	IV-V.34	330602	(I.9)	1.VI.39	381222(1)
(IV.6-7)	VI-VII.34	320917			390214
(IV.8)	VIII.34	340222			390310
		340323	(II.1)	1.IX.39	390307(2)
(IV.9-10)	X.34	331130			390422(1)
(VI.3-4)	VIII.36	360124(1)			390725
		360124(2)	(II.2)	X.39	390925
			(II.3-4)	XI-XII.39	390729
					391018

====================

CLAVE			(II.5)	I.40	391204(2)
					391211
(I.1)	1.X.38	371217	(II.6)	II.40	391215(2)
		380725(2)	(II.10-13)	VI-IX.40	400526
		380919(1)			400630
		380919(2)			
(I.2)	XI.38	380903			

====================

		380926	CLÉ		
		381010			
		381022(3)	(2)	II.39	381222(3)
(I.3)	XII.38	380500(1)			

====================

(I.4)	I.39	380500(1)			
		381108	COMBAT		
		381214			
(I.5)	II.39	380619	(1)	15.I.36	350610(1)
		390130(1)			

====================

		⌊390217⌋			
(I.6)	1.III.39	390130(2)	La COMMUNE		
		⌊390200(2)⌋	(25)	22.V.36	360328
		390304(1)	(36)	18.XII.36	360827
		390304(2)	(50)	2.IV.37	370209
		390304(3)	(66)	3.IX.37	370706
		⌊390321⌋	(74)	19.XI.37	370921
(I.7)	1.IV.39	390311	(82)	14.I.38	371104 ++++
		390324(1)			

La COMMUNE ++++

(83)	21.I.38	371104
(84)	28.I.38	371104
(92)	24.II.38	191024(2)
(96)	9.III.38	380309
(118)	30.IV.38	380312
(120)	3.V.38	⌊380400(1)⌋
(126)	19.V.38	380307
(128)	24.V.38	300528
(129)	28.V.38	300528
(131)	3.VI.38	380309
(132)	10.VI.38	380308(1)
(142)	26.VIII.38	380719(2)
		380801
(147)	7.X.38	380127(1)
(148)	21.X.38	330818(1)
(--)	XII.38	380824

The COMMUNIST

	13.I.21	201208(2)
	16.VII.21	210623
		210705
	6.VIII.21	210706
		⌊210712⌋
(88-94)	8.IV-20.V.22	220000(5)
(112)	23.IX.22	⌊220507⌋
(124)	16.XII.22	221114(1)
(125)	23.XII.22	221114(2)

The COMMUNIST(B)

(1)	V.32	311126
(2)	IX.32	311107
		311208
(3)	I.33	321006
(4)	IV.33	330223

(5)	V.33	321006
		321013(2)
		330223
(6)	VI.33	330303(2)
(7)	⌊XII.33⌋	331110
(9)	⌊1934⌋	340105

Le COMMUNISTE

(33)	4.XI.28	280909(1)
(34)	11.XI.28	280712
(35)	18.XI.28	280712
(36)	25.XI.28	280712
(37)	2.XII.28	280712
(38)	9.XII.28	280712
(II.2)	31.III.29	271121
		⌊280103⌋
		280712
(II.7)	5.V.29	290331(1)
(II.10)	26.V.29	290225
(II.13)	16.VI.29	290526
(II.14)	23.VI.29	280900
(II.17)	14.VII.29	⌊290626⌋
(II.19)	28.VII.29	290614
(II.23)	25.VIII.29	231200(3)
(II.24)	1.IX.29	290804
(II.27)	19.X.29	290930
(II.30)	17.XI.29	291004
		291017
(II.31)	1.XII.29	291110
(II.32)	22.XII.29	291113
(III.1)	5.I.30	291113
(III.3)	2.II.30	⌊291225⌋
		300108
(III.4)	16.II.30	300108
(III.5)	2.III.30	300108 ++++

Le COMMUNISTE   ++++

(III.13)	22.VI.30	300525(1)
(III.15)	20.VII.30	⌊300800(3)⌋
(III.21)	19.X.30	300926(1)
(III.22)	16.XI.30	301012
(IV.1)	8.I.31	⌊301200(1)⌋

==============================

The COMMUNIST INTERNATIONAL

(I.1)	1.V.19	190304
		190306(1)
		190306(2)
		190420(3)
(I.5)	IX.19	190901(3)
(I.6)	X.19	190914
(11-12)	VI-VII.20	⌊200600⌋
		⌊200722⌋
(13)	1920	200731(2)
		200807(1)
(III.14-15)	1921	210000(50)
(III.16-17)	1921	201124
		210000(50)
(19)	⌊1922⌋	211205
(25)	1923	230405(1)
(V.1)	1924	190124
(V.5)	IX.24	⌊170617/⌋
(V.30)	1924	240122(1)
(22)	1926	260513

==============================

The COMMUNIST INTERNATIONAL(London)

(5)	21.VII.24	⌊170617/⌋
(III.4)	30.XI.26	261101
(IV.14)	30.IX.27	270808
(IV.15)	15.X.27	270711

(IV.16)	15.XI.27	231008
(--)	5.II.28	280114(1)
		280114(2)

==============================

The COMMUNIST REVIEW

(4)	VIII.21	210706
(--)	VI.22	220223(2)
		220508(5)
(--)	XII.22	221103(1)
(--)	X.23	230630
(--)	XI.23	230618
(--)	XII.24	240928
(--)	III.25	250115

==============================

COMUNISMO

(I.1)	15.V.31	301126
		310412
(I.2)	15.VI.31	310415
(I.3)	1.VIII.31	310528(1)
		310612
(I.4)	1.IX.31	310708(1)
		310715(2)
(I.5)	X.31	300821
		310531
		310618
		310624
(I.6)	XI.31	310629
		310820(1)
(II.8)	I.32	311208
(II.9)	II.32	⌊311200⌋
		320102
(II.11)	IV.32	320127
(II.12)	V.32	320127 ++++

COMUNISMO	++++		El COMUNISTA		
(II.13)	VI.32	320127	(I.26)	20.XI.20	201020
(II.14)	VII.32	320127	(II.31)	26.III.21	200000(37)
(II.15)	VIII.32	320802			210000(50)
(II.16)	IX.32	320628	(II.32)	2.IV.21	200731(2)
		320804(2)	(II.33)	9.IV.21	200722
(II.17)	X.32	320725	(II.35)	20.IV.21	210403
		320809	(II.36)	23.IV.21	210116
(II.18)	XI.32	321013(1)			⌊210313⌋
		321013(2)	(II.37)	27.IV.21	210323(1)
(II.19)	XII.32	320920	(II.61)	23.VII.21	210704
(III.20)	I.33	321127	(II.63)	30.VII.21	210704
		321200(3)	(II.64)	3.VIII.21	210704
		321205	(II.66)	13.VIII.21	210704
(III.21)	II.33	330111(1)			⌊210712⌋
		330111(2)			
(III.22)	III.33	⌊321200(6)⌋			
		330105	CONTRE LE COURANT		
		330205			
(III.23)	IV.33	⌊321200(6)⌋	(I.1)	20.XI.27	271023
		330314	(I.2)	2.XII.27	271023
		330321			⌊271100(2)⌋
(III.24)	V.33	⌊330300(3)⌋	(I.4)	19.XII.27	⌊271030⌋
(III.25)	VI.33	330429	(I.5-6)	30.XII.27	271001
		330512(1)			271021
		330523	(II.7)	22.I.28	070212
		330525			280114(1)
(III.27)	VIII.33	330616			280114(2)
(III.28)	IX.33	330622	(II.13)	5.VIII.28	280310
		330714	(II.15-16)	25.X.28	280712
		330719(1)			280723
(III.29)	X.33	330805			280909(1)
		330920	(II.18-19)	26.XI.28	200000(37)
(IV.31)	I.34	331110	(II.20-21)	15.XII.28	280628
(IV.32)	II.34	331212	(III.22)	28.I.29	281021
(IV.33)	III.34	340118	(III.23)	25.II.29	290304
		340120(1)	(III.24)	9.III.29	281216(1)
(IV.34)	IV.34	340222			290227
			(III.25-26)	1929	280103

++++

CONTRE LE COURANT	++++		CORRESPONDANCE INTERNATIONALE		
(III.25-26)	1929	281100	(I.9)	9.XI.21	211107
		⌊290415(2)⌋	(I.11)	17.XI.21	211024
(III.27-28)	12.IV.29	281004	(—)	I.22	220104(2)
		281200(2)	(II.5)	18.I.22	⌊211225⌋
		290110	(II.20)	15.III.22	220302(1)
		290327	(II.21)	18.III.22	220302(1)
		290331(1)	(II.22)	22.III.22	220000(5)
(III.29-30)	6.V.29	280929	(II.25)	1.IV.22	220303(1)
		281110	(II.38)	17.V.22	220508(5)
		⌊290300(1)⌋	(II.40)	24.V.22	220000(5)
		290300(2)	(II.42)	31.V.22	220000(5)
		290422	(II.45)	10.VI.22	220523
		290424	(II.46)	14.VI.22	220526
(III.31-32)	10.VI.29	280717(1)	(—)	9.XII.22	221125
		⌊280900⌋	(III.1)	15.I.23	221201(1)
		290523	(III.6)	16.II.23	180000(55)
		290526			230127(1)
		290601			
(III.33-34)	19.VII.29	290424	(III.8)	2.III.23	230210
		290612	(III.9)	9.III.23	⌊230215⌋
		290615	(III.13)	7.IV.23	230321
		290707	(III.14)	13.IV.23	230321
		⌊290800(1)⌋			230325
(III.36-37)	21.IX.29	290804	(III.15)	20.IV.23	230325
					230403
	============				230405(3)
			(III.16)	27.IV.23	230405(3)
CONTRE LE COURANT(B)			(III.17)	5.V.23	230420(1)
(1)	X.38	380725(2)	(III.20)	29.V.23	230508
			(III.26)	7.VII.23	230630
	============		(III.29)	28.VII.23	⌊230712⌋
			(III.30)	4.VIII.23	⌊230710⌋
CONTROVERSY			(III.35)	8.IX.23	⌊230711⌋
			(III.36)	15.IX.23	⌊230713⌋
	XII.35	350918	(III.38)	29.IX.23	230908(1)
	VII.36	360522			230908(2)
	VII.38	380308(1)	(III.40)	13.X.23	⌊230923(2)⌋
					++++
	============				

CORRESPONDANCE INTERNATIONALE   ++++

(IV.8)	31.I.24	231208(1)	(VII.105)	16.XI.27	220104(2)	
(IV.13)	19.II.24	231222	(VII.124)	11.XII.27	271100(2)	
		231223				
		240100(1)				
(IV.17)	12.III.24	240223	CORRIERE DELLA SERA			
(IV.26)	14.V.24	240406				
(IV.28)	28.V.24	240406		1927	⌊270727⌋	
(IV.29)	4.VI.24	⌊240514(1)⌋				
(IV.33)	19.VI.24	240523				
(IV.36)	24.VI.24	240607	CRITICA			
(IV.39)	2.VII.24	⌊240618(2)⌋				
(IV.44)	15.VII.24	⌊170617/⌋		21.II.40	⌊400221(2)⌋	
(IV.45)	17.VII.24	240705				
(IV.74)	4.XI.24	240928				
		241023	CRITIQUE SOCIALE			
(IV.77)	19.XI.24	241025	(3)	X.31	⌊260000(31)⌋	
(V.7)	30.I.25	250115				
(V.24)	1925:936	240100(2)				
(V.54)	23.V.25	250403	IV INTERNACIONAL			
(V.62)	17.VI.25	⌊250606⌋				
(V.72)	22.VII.25	250522	(I.1)	3.IX.36	350907(2)	
(V.82)	22.VIII.25	250403			360522	
		250522	(I.2)	15.IX.36	351112	
		250701			360815	
(V.87)	5.IX.25	250828(1)	(I.3)	15.X.36	360730	
		250911	(I.5)	I.37	340610	
(V.111)	11.XI.25	250930	(I.6)	II.37	370000(10)	
		251107(2)			370204	
(VI.22)	26.II.26	⌊260216⌋	(I.7)	III.37	361013	
(VI.32)	2.III.26	260211			370219(1)	
(VI.34)	13.III.26	260211	(I.8)	IV.37	340610	
(VI.67)	29.V.26	260503	(I.9)	V.37	340610	
(VI.69)	2.VI.26	260503	(I.10)	V.37	340610	
(VI.137)	18.XII.26	261209	(I.11)	VI.37	340610	
					370423	
(VII.6)	14.I.27	261209			370600	
(VII.93)	7.IX.27	270819	(I.12)	VII.37	340610	
(VII.104)	15.X.27	170921(2)/	(I.13)	VIII.37	340610	

IV INTERNACIONAL	++++	
(II.17)	XII.37	371213(1)
		371213(2)
(II.19)	VIII.38	380127(1)
		380710
		380719(1)
(II.24)	VIII.39	380903(1)
(II.25-26)	VIII-IX.39	390904
		390906
(II.29)	I.40	391204(2)

=========================

CURRENT HISTORY		
	IV.18	180210(2)
	XI.19	190323(1)
	XII.19	180000(5)
	I.20	180000(5)
	III.24	200423
	V.24	240223
	II.26	[250730(1)]

=========================

DAGBLADETT		
	21.VIII.36	360820(2)
	25.VIII.36	360825

=========================

DAILY EXPRESS		
	27.II.29	290120
		290225
	28.II.29	290225
	1.III.29	290225
	18.III.29	290316
	19.VI.29	[290611]
	18.IX.29	390902

=========================

DAILY HERALD		
	17.III.21	[210313]
	19.I.22	220116
	28.III-	
	3.IV.22	220000(5)
	22.VII.29	290715
	1939	390318
	1939	391023

=========================

DAILY NEWS(London)		
	30.I.18	180116
	25.III.18	180320(2)
	25.II.20	200223

=========================

DAILY NEWS(NY)		
	1938	381228

=========================

DAVAR		
(1152)	1929	290225
(1154)	1929	290225
(1156)	1929	290225

=========================

DEMAIN		
(I.16)	VIII.17	161011
(II.1)	18.X.17	[170617/]

=========================

DEUTSCHE ALLGEMEINE ZEITUNG		
	7.IX.30	310000(1)

=========================

DIETHNISTES

(1)	I.[65]	⌊140000(3)⌋
(10)	X.65	400423(2)
(11-12)	XI-XII.65	310000(1)
		380500(1)
(13)	I.66	390725
		400526
(15)	III.66	351126(1)

═══════════════════════

Le DRAPEAU ROUGE

	30.XII.22	221125
(I.22)	26.I.24	240122(1)
(I.273)	14.XI.24	240928
(I.281)	23-4.XI.24	241025
(II.126)	29.V.25	250403
(II.140)	16.VI.25	[250606]
(III.31)	31.I.26	260129
(III.32)	1.II.26	260129
(IV.334)	1.XII.27	271023
(IV.335)	2.XII.27	271023

═══════════════════════

Der EINZIGE WEG

(1)	XII.37	370828
		370921
		370923
		371102
(2)	I.38	371030
		371125(2)
(3)	III.38	370928
		371213(1)
		371217
(6)	VII.39	390307(1)

═══════════════════════

Der EMES

(87)	16.IV.24	240406
(94)	24.IV.24	240406
(95)	25.IV.24	240406

═══════════════════════

De ENIGE WEG

(I.1)	18.II.38	371217
		380121(1)
(I.3)	10.III.38	380115
(I.4)	30.III.38	380115
		380127(1)
(I.5)	13.IV.38	370828
(I.6)	27.IV.38	370828
(I.7)	11.V.38	370828
(I.8)	25.V.38	380113
(I.9)	8.VI.38	380308(1)
(I.10)	22.VI.38	370809
(I.11)	6.VII.38	370809
(I.13)	3.VIII.38	380522
(I.15)	31.VIII.38	371104
(I.16)	14.IX.38	371125(2)
(I.17)	28.IX.38	380830
(I.18)	12.X.38	380605
(I.20)	9.XI.38	381014
(I.21)	23.XI.38	380919(1)
		380922
		380923
(I.24)	4.I.39	381010
(I.25)	18.I.39	381010
(I.26)	1.II.39	381214
(II.3)	15.III.39	⌊390200(1)⌋
		⌊390200(2)⌋
(II.4)	29.III.39	381222(3)
(II.5)	13.IV.39	380703(2)
		390306
(II.6)	26.IV.39	380216
		⌊390217⌋ ++++

De ENIGE WEG   ++++

(II.7)	10.V.39	380216
		390311
		390324(2)
(II.8)	25.V.39	380216
(II.9)	8.VI.39	380216
		390501
(II.11)	6.VII.39	381220
		390307(1)
(II.13)	7.IX.39	380903(1)
		390609
(II.16)	16.XI.39	390925

========================

ETUDES MARXISTES

(1)	I.69	380115
(2)	II.69	[210712]
		[340600(1)]
		380607

========================

EUROPE NOUVELLE

	7.II.25	250115

========================

El EXCELSIOR

	10.VIII.37	370730

========================

Die FAHNE DES KOMMUNISMUS

(I.36)	18.XI.27	[240700]
(II.3)	20.I.28	[270912]
(II.38)	21.IX.28	280310
(II.40)	5.X.28	280909(1)
(II.43)	26.X.28	280712
(II.44)	2.XI.28	280723

(II.51)	21.XII.28	271215
(II.52)	28.XII.28	271215
(III.1)	4.I.29	281021
(III.2)	11.I.29	280103
(III.3)	18.I.29	240122(1)
(III.4)	25.I.29	[281111]
(III.11)	15.III.29	281100
(III.12)	22.III.29	281100
(III.13)	5.IV.29	281100
(III.14)	12.IV.29	281100
(III.15)	19.IV.29	281100
(III.16)	26.IV.29	281100
		290331(1)
(III.18)	17.V.29	[280900]
(III.19)	24.V.29	[280900]
		290227
(III.21)	14.VI.29	[280900]
(III.22)	21.VI.29	280717(1)
		[280900]
(III.23)	28.VI.29	[280900]
		290425
(III.24)	5.VII.29	290600(1)
		290612
(III.25)	12.VII.29	[290626]
(III.26)	19.VII.29	290701
(III.27)	26.VII.29	[290726]
(III.29)	9.VIII.29	[290800(1)]
(III.30)	16.VIII.29	290727(1)
		[290800(1)]
(III.31)	23.VIII.29	290727(1)
		290804
(III.32)	30.VIII.29	290727(1)
		[290800(1)]
(III.37)	11.X.29	290925(1)
(III.39)	25.X.29	291004
(III.40)	8.XI.29	291017
(III.41)	22.XI.29	290925(2)
(III.42)	6.XII.29	291109
		291113 ++++

FAHNE DES KOMMUNISMUS	++++	
(III.43)	20.XII.29	291113
(IV.1)	10.I.30	291222(1)
(IV.11)	9.V.30	300314
(IV.13)	23.V.30	300213
(IV.14)	30.V.30	300213
(IV.15)	6.VI.30	300213

===============

De FAKKEL

(II.45)	15.IV.33	330310
(II.53)	6.V.33	330303(2)
(II.54)	13.V.33	330303(2)
(II.61)	27.V.33	330303(2)
(II.65)	9.VI.33	330303(2)
(II.67)	16.VI.33	330303(2)
(II.69)	23.VI.33	330528
(II.70)	27.VI.33	330528
(II.74)	11.VII.33	330303(2)
(II.76)	18.VII.33	330303(2)
(II.93)	15.IX.33	330901(1)
(II.97)	29.IX.33	330714
(II.112)	21.XI.33	331110
(II.117)	8.XII.33	331107
(III.14)	20.II.34	340118
(III.16)	27.II.34	340118

===============

FIGHT

(1)	10.X.36	360605
		360704
(—)	12.XII.36	360708
(10)	IX.37	370706
(I.3)	VI.38	370423

===============

FJÄRDE INTERNATIONALEN

(1)	1969	200000(37)
		380500(1)

===============

FJERDE INTERNATIONALE

(I.1)	II.37	280628
(I.2)	III.37	321209
		370219(1)
(I.4)	IX.37	370617(1)
(I.5)	X.37	370730
(III.1)	I.39	380830
(III.2)	III-IV.39	[390200(1)]

===============

FOREIGN AFFAIRS

	IV.34	331130

===============

FORUM

	IV.32	⌊320415⌋

===============

FORWARD

	26.IX.36	360826(1)
	10.IV.37	370316
	6.XI.37	370127(1)
	11.XII.37	371102
	15.I.38	371213(1)
		371213(2)
	12.II.38	380113
	19.II.38	380113
	5.III.38	380218
	26.III.38	380303(1)
	16.IV.38	380310(1)
	7.V.38	380422 ++++

FORWARD ++++

25.VI.38	380605		400818
20.VIII.38	380724		400820(1)
3.IX.38	380811		400820(2)
			[400820(6)]
27.V.39	390318		400820(7)
31.VIII.40	371214	XI.40	400817(1)
	390422(2)	XII.40	[400820(3)]

===================================

FOURTH INTERNATIONAL			
		I.41	390400(2)
			390807
V.40	390729	II.41	[400820(4)]
	400107	III.41	220302(1)
VI.40	290331(1)		400700(1)
	400425	V.41	230621
X.40	381018		390400(2)
	400423(2)	VI.41	320104
	400501		361228
	400514(1)		361230
	400528(2)		370109(1)
	400601		400500
	400617	VII.41	280602
	400618(2)	VIII.41	361231
	400618(3)		400608
	400630	X.41	260108
	400709		260304
	400727		261126
	400729	XI.41	270927
	400802(1)	XII.41	351107(2)
	400802(2)		400700(2)
	400803(1)	I.42	381230
	400803(2)		[400820(8)]
	400807	III.42	061004
	400809	V.42	170512/
	400812	VII.42	230630
	400813		371223
	400816(1)	VIII.42	400214
	400816(2)	IX.42	400214
	400817(2)	X.42	[340600(1)]

++++

FOURTH INTERNATIONAL   ++++

XI.42	390800	IV.45	371217
XII.42	240421(2)	V.45	291004
I.43	180902(2)	VI.45	240728
II.43	330610	VII.45	240728
	390419	VIII.45	190309(2)
III.43	220425		210613(1)
IV.43	260215		221113
V.43	260215		[230711]
VII.43	330715(2)		240728
VIII.43	221228		320613(1)
IX.43	221228		350700(1)
X.43	310618		381010
	310624	IX.45	331130
	310701	X.45	380105
	310802	XI.45	350420
	310901	XII.45	370118
	311115		370222
XII.43	220508(1)		381222(2)
	220508(2)		400700(2)
I.44	211101(2)	II.46	380607
	211101(3)	V.46	290300(2)
II.44	211205		290331(1)
	330712		290425
III.44	211205	VIII.46	290612
IV.44	211205		290806
V.44	220401(1)		380600
VI.44	220401(1)	IX.46	290811
	220401(2)	X.46	290907
VII.44	220401(2)	XI.46	250313
VIII.44	230618	XII.46	290907
	240520	II.47	290907
	[321200(6)]	III.47	290907
IX.44	170512/	IV.47	300206
	220000(33)	VI.47	290925(1)
X.44	[140000(3)]		300422
XI.44	381220	VII-VIII.47	[230923(2)]
III.45	380113		321127
			370417(2)

++++

FOURTH INTERNATIONAL   ++++

	IX-X.47	300619
	I.48	371030
	II.48	371030
	V.48	390404
	VIII.48	[170822/]
	IX.48	390405
		390409
	II.49	390409
	XI.49	390422(1)
	XII.49	390730
	I-II.50	320922(1)
		320926
	III-IV.50	380120
		380618(1)
	VII-VIII.50	360000(10)
	I-II.51	200423
		240122(1)
	III-IV.51	350323(1)
	V-VI.51	[080915]
	VII-VIII.51	371104
		371125(2)
	I-II.52	240406
	Winter '54	380704
	Fall '54	321104
	Winter '55	300329
	Winter '56	331130

=============================

FOURTH INTERNATIONAL(London)

	Summer '64	240621
	Aut-Winter '64	
		[101100]
(II.2)	VIII.65	400615
(III.1)	I.66	240429(2)
		240717
		260225(2)

(IV.2)	VII.67	240509

=============================

FOURTH INTERNATIONAL(Paris)

	Autumn '58	260119
		320613(1)
(7)	Autumn '59	400227(1)
		400207(2)
		400303
(11)	Autumn '60	370417(2)

=============================

FRANKFURTER ZEITUNG

	29.IV.30	300213
	11.VI.31	300000(1)

=============================

FREE EXPRESSION

	XI.42	220425
	III.44	170512/
	IV.44	170512/
	VI.44	170512/
	I.45	240729(1)

=============================

FRONT(Minsk)

(74)	13.X.17	171009(1)/

=============================

Der GEGNER		
(45)	1932	320000(1)

GLASGOW HERALD		
	18.I.28	280115

GLASGOW WORKER		
	6.XII.19	190901(3)
	23.VI.23	230512(1)

HAARETZ		
(4043)	1933	321019
(4044)	1933	321019

HAPOEL HATZAIR		
(XIX.14)	1926	260412

HARPERS MAGAZINE		
	IX.33	330602

HASHOMER HATZAIR		
(1)	X-XI.33	330610

HASHOMER HATZAIR(Warsaw)		
(III.9)	1929	260203

L'HERNE		
(5)	1965	330510

L'HUMANITÉ		
	24.VII.21	210704
	4.VIII.21	210717(1)
	10.VIII.21	⌊210712⌋
	24.VIII.21	210600
	22.I.22	151100(1)
	17.IV.22	220414
	7.V.22	220303(1)
	13.V.22	220512(2)
	22.V.22	220429
	12.VI.22	220508(5)
	7.X.22	220801
	23.XI.22	221114(1)
	24.XII.22	221125
	14.III.23	170313(1)
	1.IV.23	230000(9)
	25.I.24	240122(1)
	1.X.25	250908

Les HUMBLES		
(XVII.7-8)	VII-VIII.32	⌊320400⌋
(XIX.5-6)	V-VI.34	151100(1)
		161011
		340220
(XX.6)	VI.35	350610(1)
(XX.12)	XII.35	351031

INDEPENDENT		
	9.III.18	171200(2)

INITIATIVE SOCIALISTE

(17)	VI.68	240729(1)

===========================

INTERCONTINENTAL PRESS

(VI.21)	3.VI.68	351126(1)
(VII.16)	28.IV.69	240411
(VII.17)	5.V.69	240411
(VII.28)	8.IX.69	390723
(VII.30)	22.IX.69	380601(2)
(VII.33)	13.X.69	381220
(VII.40)	1.XII.69	370923(2)
(VIII.9)	9.III.70	370617(2)
		380306
(VIII.12)	30.III.70	[231128]
(VIII.16)	27.IV.70	330715(1)

===========================

Die INTERNATIONALE

(VIII.2)	II.25	250115

===========================

Die INTERNATIONALE

(2)	XII.48	390800
(3)	II-III.49	390800
(--)	XI.56	361013
(II.1)	I-III.57	361013
(IV.3-4)	XII.59	400227(1)
		400227(2)
		400303

===========================

Die INTERNATIONALE(Mannheim)

(III.2)	1970	370429

===========================

De INTERNATIONALE

(I.2)	V.35	[350328]
(I.5)	VIII.35	350729
(I.7)	X.35	350420
(I.8)	XI.35	350918
(I.9)	XII.35	351104(1)
		351126(1)

===========================

De INTERNATIONALE

(I.2-5)	1.IV-1.X.57	321231
(II.9)	1.V.58	370209
(III.12)	15.II.59	260301
(VIII)	V.65	350201
(XI.12)	1968	350201
(XII.6-7)	1969	230618

===========================

L'INTERNATIONALE COMMUNISTE

(1)	1919	190306(1)
		[190306(2)]
		190420(3)
(3)	VII.19	190302(1)
(5)	1919	190901(3)
(6)	1919	190914
(7-8)	XI-XII.19	191218
(9)	1920	191005
(II.11)	VI.20	200000(37)
		[200600]
(II.12)	30.VII.20	[200722]

===========================

INTERNATIONALE PRESSE-KORRESPONDENZ

[Combining 2 series and Special
Issues in date sequence]

(I.18)	3.XI.21	190914
(I.25)	19.XI.21	211025
(II.4)	10.I.22	211227
(II.6)	14.I.22	220104(2)
(II.4)	16.I.22	[211225]
(II.29)	11.III.22	220000(5)
		220226(1)
(II.33)	21.III.22	220000(5)
(II.34)	23.III.22	220000(5)
(II.44)	8.IV.22	220303(1)
(II.61)	6.V.22	220426
(II.66)	13.V.22	200000(37)
(II.69)	18.V.22	220429
(II.80)	30.V.22	220513
(II.84)	8.VI.22	220526
(II.92)	13.VI.22	220523
(II.94)	14.VI.22	220608
(II.100)	17.VI.22	220609
(II.112)	24.VI.22	[220618]
(II.175)	2.IX.22	220826
(II.201)	17.X.22	[221012]
(II.202)	19.X.22	221010
(II.204)	24.X.22	221011
(II.206)	26.X.22	221011
(II.220)	18.XI.22	221103(1)
(II.223)	23.XI.22	221105
(II.230)	7.XII.22	221121
(II.237)	16.XII.22	221201(1)
(II.241)	21.XII.22	221200(2)
		221201(1)
(III.30)	16.II.23	230127(1)
(III.33)	21.II.23	230205(2)
(III.38)	28.II.23	[230215]
(III.66)	20.IV.23	230321
(III.67)	23.IV.23	230321
(III.69)	23.IV.23	230405(3)
	21.V.23	230512(1)
(III.87)	25.V.23	230512(1)
	26.V.23	230512(1)
(III.107)	27.VI.23	230605(1)
(III.114)	6.VII.23	230630
(III.123)	25.VII.23	[230712]
(III.145)	12.IX.23	230504(1)
(III.150)	24.IX.23	[230711]
(III.152)	26.IX.23	[230923(2)]
(III.184)	27.XII.23	231200(4)
(IV.4)	10.I.24	211227
(IV.8)	21.I.24	231208(1)
		231210
(IV.13)	28.I.24	231222
		231223
(IV.14)	28.I.24	240122(1)
(IV.5)	2.II.24	240122(1)
(IV.30)	4.III.24	240223
(IV.10)	8.III.24	240223
(IV.53)	9.V.24	240411
(IV.19)	10.V.24	240406
		240411
(IV.59)	27.V.24	240421(2)
(IV.22)	31.V.24	240421(2)
(IV.62)	4.VI.24	240526
(IV.65)	10.VI.24	240523
(IV.69)	17.VI.24	240607
(IV.25)	21.VI.24	240607
(IV.83)	8.VII.24	[170617/]
(IV.92)	9.VII.24	240705
(IV.40)	4.X.24	240818
(IV.52)	23.XII.24	211206
(V.15)	I.25	240915
(V.18)	29.I.25	240915
		250115
(V.93)	12.VI.25	[250606]
(V.24)	13.VI.25	[250606]

+++

INTERNATIONALE PRESSE-KORRESPONDENZ   ++++

(V.111)	21.VII.25	250522	(—)	13.III.23	[230215]
(V.123)	21.VIII.25	250403	(III.33)	19.IV.23	230325
		250701	(III.35)	3.V.23	230323
(V.34)	22.VIII.25	250403	(III.36)	9.V.23	220112
		250522	(III.41)	7.VI.23	230512(1)
		250701	(III.43)	14.VI.23	230508
(V.41)	10.X.25	250908	(III.48)	5.VII.23	230605(1)
(V.45)	7.XI.25	250930	(III.50)	12.VII.23	230630
(VI.19)	26.I.26	[260117]	(III.56)	16.VIII.23	230618
(VI.4)	30.I.26	[260117]	(III.64)	4.X.23	230504(1)
(VI.26)	16.II.26	[260216]	(III.66)	11.X.23	[230923(2)]
(VI.7)	20.II.26	[260216]	(III.67)	18.X.23	[230711]
(VI.34)	2.III.26	260211	(IV.1)	4.I.24	231200(4)
(VI.9)	6.III.26	260211	(IV.8)	31.I.24	240122(1)
(VI.77)	26.V.26	260503	(IV.12)	15.II.24	231208(1)
(VI.78)	28.V.26	260506	(IV.16)	29.II.24	231222
(VII.87)	30.VIII.27	270819	(IV.19)	13.III.24	240223
			(IV.30)	22.V.24	240406
			(IV.31)	29.V.24	240421(2)
			(IV.33)	10.VI.24	240523
			(IV.35)	19.VI.24	240411
					240607

INTERNATIONAL NEWS

(I.2)	X.35	350610(2)	(IV.36)	26.VI.24	240607
(I.3)	[X.35]	341101	(IV.45)	21.VII.24	[170617/]
		[341200]	(IV.48)	12.VIII.24	240629
			(IV.72)	9.X.24	240818
				23.I.25	211206
				7.II.25	250115

INTERNATIONAL PRESS CORRESPONDENCE

(II.44)	1922	220429	(V.16)	26.II.25	240915
(II.76)	1922	[220827]	(V.51)	18.VI.25	[250606]
(II.91)	1922	221010	(V.60)	30.VII.25	250522
(II.92)	1922	[221012]	(V.68)	3.IX.25	250701
(II.95)	1922	221020	(V.81)	19.XI.25	251107(2)
(II.101)	21.XI.22	221103(1)	(VI.13)	18.II.26	[260216]
(II.110)	1922	221020	(VI.19)	11.III.26	260211
(II.115)	19.XII.22	221125	(VI.45)	3.VI.26	260503
(III.3)	9.I.23	221201(1)	(VI.46)	10.VI.26	260506
(III.20)	27.II.23	230205(2)	(VI.79)	25.XI.26	261101 ++++
		230210			

INTERNATIONAL PRESS CORRESPONDENCE ++++

(VII.49)	18.VIII.27	270808
(VII.53)	8.IX.27	270819
(VII.54)	22.IX.27	170922(3)/
(VII.55)	29.IX.27	170918(1)/
(VII.56)	6.X.27	170921(2)/
(VII.63)	10.XI.27	171024(4)/
(VII.70)	12.XII.27	271100(2)
(VIII.3)	19.I.28	280114(1)
		280114(2)
(VIII.7)	9.II.28	270830
	1928	271203

Winter '57	300715
Summer '58	230430(2)
Winter '64	380000(14)
Fall '66	350420
I-II.70	[300500(1)]
III-IV.70	240729(1)
V.70	321200(4)

INTERNATIONAL REVIEW

	IX-X.36	360709(1)

INTERNATIONAL SOCIALISM

(38-39)	VIII-IX.69	300926(1)
		311126
		320000(1)
		320802
		320804(2)
		320809
		320910
		320912
		320913
		320914
		330610
(43)	V-VI.70	330228
		390404

INTERNATIONAL SOCIALIST REVIEW

	Summer '56	350201
	Fall '56	300715

JELGAWAS KOMUNISTS

(34)	14.III.19	190306(1)
(35)	15.III.19	190306(1)
(36)	16.III.19	190306(1)

JISKRA

(III.2:11)	V.36	360318
(III.4:13)	IX.36	350201
		360700(1)
		360727
		360820(2)
		360827
(III.5:14)	X.36	290701
		360820(1)

JOHN O'LONDON

	20.IV.29	290323

JUGEND—INTERNATIONALE

(10)	X.17	[170617/]
(11)	V.18	[140000(3)]
(I.22)	VII-VIII.20	[200305]
(II.7)	III.21	200000(37)
(III.3)	XI.21	210921
(III.11)	VII.22	070000(3)
(III.12)	VIII.22	070000(3)
(IV.1)	IX.22	070000(3)
		220227
(IV.2)	X.22	070000(3)
(IV.3)	XI.22	070000(3)
(IV.4-5)	I.23	070000(3)
(IV.6)	II.23	221020
(IV.12)	VIII.23	230618

===============

JUMRURIET

	20.III.29	290312

===============

Der KAMPF

(II.1)	1.X.08	[081001]
(IV.2)	1.XI.10	[101101]
(IV.9)	1.VI.11	[110601]
(V.2)	1.XI.11	[111101]
(VII)	1913-4:519	[140619]

===============

KEEP LEFT

(XIX.2)	II.70	190113
(XIX.3)	III.70	[110129(1)]
		[130208(1)]
		[130713]

(XIX.5)	V.70	[150717(2)]
(XIX.6)	VI.70	[150717(2)]
(XIX.7)	VII-VIII.70	220425

===============

KETUVIM

	1929	230618

===============

KLASSE KAMP

(3)	1939	390925
(4)	[1939]	391023

===============

KLASSENSTRIJD

(II.9)	IX.27	270500
(II.12)	XII.27	270526(1)
		270526(2)
(III.2)	II.28	270903
(III.4)	IV.28	270903
(III.7)	VII.28	270903

===============

KLASSENSTRIJD(Antwerp)

(1)	[1932]	311208
(2)	[1932]	311208
(3)	[1932]	311208
(I.3)	19.XII.36	341000
(I.6)	6.III.37	331001
(I.7)	10.IV.37	331001
(I.8)	1.V.37	331001
		370219(1)

===============

KLASSENSTRIJD(Ghent)

(2)	26.IX.37	370808
		370828
(3)	5.XII.37	371102

==========================

KLORKEIT

(1)	IV.30	300108
(2)	V.30	300108
(3)	VI.30	300108
		300413(1)
		300510
(4)	VII.30	300108
		300207(1)
(5)	VIII.30	300108
(6)	IX.30	300108
		300900(1)

==========================

KOLNISCHE ZEITUNG

	11.V.27	[270411]

==========================

KOMMUNISMUS

(I.41-42)	26.X.20	200615
(II.27-28)	1.VIII.21	210706

==========================

Der KOMMUNIST

(I.1)	IV.30	300108
		300206
(I.2)	V.30	200423
		300314
(I.3)	V.30	300213
(I.4)	VI.30	300213
(I.6)	VII.30	300213
(I.7)	VIII.30	300413(1)
(I.8)	VIII.30	300413(1)
(I.9)	IX.30	300413(1)
		[300700(1)]
(I.10)	IX.30	[300900(2)]

==========================

Der KOMMUNIST(Bremen)

(II.27)	1.II.19	180000(5)
(III.1)	3.I.20	190901(3)
(III.2)	15.I.20	190118

==========================

KOMMUNISTISCHE ARBEITERZEITUNG

(I.40)	18.VI.19	180328(1)
(I.132)	3.X.19	[190429]
(II.15)	15.I.20	190118

==========================

Der KOMMUNISTISCHE INTERNATIONALE(Berlin)

(1)	VIII.19	190124
		190304
		190306(1)
(3)	1919	190302(1)
(5)	IX.19	190901(3)
(6)	X.19	190914
(7-8)	XI-XII.19	191218
(II.9)	1920	191005
(II.10)	1920	200000(37)
		200429(1)
(II.11)	1920	200000(37)
(II.12)	1920	200722
(II.13)	1920	200731(2)
		200807(1)

++++

KOMMUNISTISCHE INTERNATIONALE(Berlin)   ++++

(II.16)	VI.21	210115(2)	(5)		VII.21	210115(2)
		210116	(6)		IX.21	201124
		210215				210813(3)
(II.17)	1921	201124				
		210429				

KOMUNARAS

(6)	VI.22	200000(37)
		220508(5)

(II.19)	1922	211205
(III.20)	1922	220220
(III.21)	1922	220608
		220610

KOMUNISTISHE FON

(19)	24.I.24	240406
(20)	25.I.24	240122(1)
(22)	27.I.24	200423
(75)	22.IV.24	240406

(5-6)	V-VI.26	251222(1)
		251225
		251228
		260105
		260106
		260107
		260112
		260113
		260305
		260506
		260513
		260519

KUNTRAS

(—)	1924	200423
(146)	1924	230630

Der KOMMUNISTISCHE INTERNATIONALE
   (Petrograd)

(I)	1919: 73-4	[190306(2)]

LABOR ACTION(San Francisco)

(II.4)	III.46	380220
(II.11)	VII.46	370118
		381222(2)
(II.12)	VII.46	[400820(4)]
(II.13)	VIII.46	[400820(4)]
(II.18)	X.46	381018
(III.1)	I.47	240122(1)
(V.8)	VIII.49	391215(2)

Den KOMMUNISTISKA INTERNATIONALEN

(1)	1920	200000(37)

Den KOMMUNISTISKE INTERNATIONALE

(1)	1920	200000(37)
(2)	XII.20	200731(2)

LABOUR MONTHLY

VIII.21	210704
VIII.22	220515
VII.23	230306(1)
VIII.23	230306(1)
XI.23	⌊230710⌋
I.24	⌊230923(2)⌋
VII.24	240406
XI.25	250828(2)
XII.25	250828(2)

===============================

LABOUR REVIEW

(II.6)	XII.57	260301
(IV.2)	VII-VIII.59	190110(2)
(VII.3)	Autumn '62	260203
		380725(2)

===============================

The LACE CURTAIN

(1)	⌊1970⌋	⌊160704(1)⌋

===============================

LEFT REVIEW

IV.38	371030
V.38	371030

===============================

LEIPZIGER VOLKSZEITUNG

18.X.18	180000(5)
3.III.32	320000(1)

===============================

LIBERATOR

III.18	171017(1)/

===============================

LIBERTY

27.II.32	⌊320227⌋
14.I.33	320917
18.XI.33	330712
23.III.35	350323(1)
13.XI.37	370809
26.XI.38	⌊381126⌋
27.I.40	391204(2)
10.VIII.40	⌊400810⌋

===============================

LIDOVE NOVINY

(XLI.631)	17.XII.33	⌊331214⌋

===============================

LIFE

2.X.39	390922

===============================

Die LINKE FRONT

(II.1-2)	1.XII.32	320825
		321024(2)

===============================

Die LITERARISCHE WELT

(VI.39)	1930	230908(2)

===============================

LIVING AGE

5.IV.19	190219	
15.V.20	200124(1)	
26.VI.20	200124(1)	
18.III.22	211226	
25.XI.22	⌊161227⌋	
9.XII.22	⌊161227⌋	
28.IV.23	⌊180000(55)⌋	
1.VI.27	⌊270411⌋	
VII.29	⌊290400(3)⌋	
15.II.30	⌊300215⌋	
V.31	310100	
VI.34	330829	

===============

LOGOTECHNES

(I.4)	XI.56	⌊080915⌋
(I.5)	XII.56	⌊080915⌋

===============

A LUTA DE CLASSE

(III.9)	I.33	321013(1)

===============

La LUTTE(Saigon)

(VI.161)	1.XI.37	370209
(VI.162)	4.XI.37	370209
(VI.163)	8.XI.37	370209
(164)	11.XI.37	370209
(178)	28.XI.37	370923
(182)	9.I.38	371107
(183)	16.I.38	371107
(191)	27.III.38	371217
(192)	7.IV.38	370612
		371217

(193)	14.IV.38	370612
		371217
(205)	14.VIII.38	380605
(206)	28.VIII.38	370416(1)

===============

LUTTE DE CLASSE(Belgium)

(6)	IV.64	221125

===============

La LUTTE DE CLASSES

(III.1)	II-III.28	250828(2)
(III.6)	VIII-IX.28	280310
(III.8)	II.29	281021
(III.9)	III.29	290225
(12)	10.IX.29	290811
(15)	XI.29	⌊291000(1)⌋
(17)	I.30	291021
(18)	II.30	291130(2)
(19)	III.30	301100(1)
(20)	IV.30	300300(2)
		300323
(21-22)	V-VI.30	300425
		⌊300500(1)
		301100(1)
(23)	VII.30	300413(1)
		300422
		300425
		300514
		300619
(24)	VIII.30	⌊300600(1)⌋
		⌊300600(3)⌋
(25-26)	IX-XII.30	300715
		300900(1)
		301022
(28-29)	II-III.31	301126

++++

La LUTTE DE CLASSES   ++++

(30)	IV.31	310412
		310415
(31)	VI.31	310612
(32-33)	VI-VII.31	⌊310600(3)⌋
		310613
		⌊310700(2)⌋
(36)	VIII-IX.31	320000(1)
(37)	15.III.32	320127
(38)	15.IV.32	320301
(39)	15.VI.32	⌊320400⌋
		320613(2)
(40-41)	VII-VIII.32	320628
(42)	IX.32	⌊320415⌋
(43)	X.32	320519(1)
		320922(1)
		320926
(44)	XI.32	321022(1)
(45)	XII.32	310325
		321019
(46-47)	I-II.33	290703
		⌊300800(1)⌋
		321003
		321104
		330103
(51-52)	IV-VI.35	350210

===============================

La LUTTE DES CLASSES

(14)	30.XI.22	221103(1)

===============================

La LUTTE OUVRIÈRE(Belgium)

(II.43)	23.X.37	370923
(II.45)	6.XI.37	171031/
(II.48)	27.XI.37	371102
(II.52)	25.XII.37	371129(2)

(III.1)	1.I.38	370905
(III.2)	8.I.38	371213(1)
(III.3)	15.I.38	371217
(III.4)	22.I.38	371217
(III.5)	29.I.38	371217
(III.8)	19.II.38	370816
		380115
(III.9)	26.II.38	380115
(III.20)	14.V.38	380312
		380331
(III.21)	21.V.38	370809

===============================

LUTTE OUVRIÈRE(Canada)

(V.1)	I-II.69	371030

===============================

La LUTTE OUVRIÈRE(France)

(1)	12.VI.36	360605
(4)	18.VII.36	360609
(7)	8.VIII.36	360700(1)
		360730(1)
(8)	15.VIII.36	360727
(9)	22.VIII.36	351112
		360815
(10)	5.IX.36	351112
		360819(1)
		360820(1)
		360820(2)
		360823(1)
(11)	12.IX.36	360826(1)
(15)	10.X.36	360923
(31)	12.II.37	361218(1)
(32)	19.II.37	361218(1)
(33)	26.II.37	361218(1)
		370219(1)

++++

La LUTTE OUVRIÈRE(France)   ++++

(37)	26.III.37	370305
		370313(1)
(39)	9.IV.37	370308
	[1937]	370323
(44)	14.V.37	370423
(45)	21.V.37	370423
(48)	10.VI.37	370512
(50)	24.VI.37	370601
(53)	6.VIII.37	370617(1)
(54)	27.VIII.37	370429
		370730
		370808
		370809
(55)	10.IX.37	370706
		370816
(59)	4.XI.37	370923
(61)	25.XI.37	370921
		371102
(62)	9.XII.37	370905
(63)	23.XII.37	371129(2)
(III.65)	20.I.38	371217
(III.66)	3.II.38	371217
(III.67)	17.II.38	380115
(III.70)	17.III.38	380220
		380301(1)
(III.71)	24.III.38	380220
(III.72)	31.III.38	380220
(III.77)	5.V.38	380331
(III.86)	22.VII.38	380610
		380618(1)
(III.88)	2.IX.38	380803
(III.89)	16.IX.38	380811
(III.92)	30.IX.38	380920
(III.95)	21.X.38	380717
		380919
(III.97)	4.XI.38	381014
(III.100)	25.XI.38	381010
(III.101)	2.XII.38	381010
		381022(1)

(III.102)	16.XII.38	381108
		381114
(IV.103)	6.I.39	381214
(IV.107)	3.II.39	381228
(IV.3)	3.III.39	[390200(1)]
		[390200(2)]
(IV.115)	7.IV.39	390306
(IV.117)	21.IV.39	390311
		390318
		390324(1)

========================

MANCHESTER GUARDIAN

24.XI.17	171108(1)/
4.I.18	[171217(1)/]
	171219(1)/
8.I.18	171209(3)/
30.XII.19	191031
16.VIII.20	200814
27.IX.20	200924(2)
23.X.22	221021
1.III.23	221031
16.XI.27	271023
27.III.31	310100
28.III.31	310100
16.VIII.31	[310716]
22.III.33	330310
21.VI.33	330602
22.VI.33	330602
10.III.34	[340304]
1.I.35	341230(2)
17.IX.36	360826(2)

++++

MANCHESTER GUARDIAN   ++++

25.I.37	370123(3)
26.I.37	370124(1)
2.II.37	370201
16.III.37	370316

========================

MARXISTIKO DELTIO

(VII.43)	IX.66	380600

========================

MARXIST OUTLOOK

(I.2)	III.66	240729(2)
(I.10)	XI.66	291130(2)

========================

MARXIST REVIEW

⌊1949⌋	311110

========================

MARXIST YOUTH JOURNAL

(I.2)	⌊XII.69⌋	220226(1)

========================

MEXICO AL DIA

1937	370816

========================

MILITANT

15.XI.28	280628
1.XII.28	280628
15.XII.28	280628
	280723
1.I.29	280628
15.I.29	280628

1.II.29	281021
1.III.29	280103
	280628
15.III.29	280628
	280909(1)
1.IV.29	280628
	281216(1)
15.IV.29	280628
	⌊290415(2)⌋
1.V.29	290327
15.V.29	280628
	290327
1.VI.29	280628
	290300(1)
1.VII.29	280628
	290522(1)
1.VIII.29	280628
	280717(1)
	290526
	⌊290626⌋
15.VIII.29	⌊280900⌋
	290425
15.IX.29	⌊280900⌋
	290804
1.X.29	⌊280900⌋
	290612
15.X.29	⌊280900⌋
1.XI.29	⌊280900⌋
30.XI.29	⌊280900⌋
	291017
	291019
	291110
7.XII.29	291004
14.XII.29	291014
21.XII.29	290907
28.XII.29	290907
	⌊291000(1)⌋

++++

MILITANT ++++

4.I.30	290907	14.VI.30	300323
	[291000(1)]		300402
	291113		300422
11.I.30	290907	21.VI.30	300413(1)
	291113	28.VI.30	300413(1)
18.I.30	290907	12.VII.30	300530
	291221	26.VII.30	300416
25.I.30	290907		300600(2)
	291218		300610
1.II.30	291222(1)		[300700(2)]
	291227	7.VIII.30	300514
8.II.30	300103(1)	15.VIII.30	300600(2)
	300103(2)		[300700(1)]
15.II.30	291021	1.IX.30	[300800(3)]
	300105(2)	15.IX.30	300715
22.II.30	[291225]		[300800(2)]
	300108	1.X.30	300715
1.III.30	291130(2)		300900(1)
	300105(1)		[300900(2)]
	300122	15.XI.30	300715
8.III.30	271021		[301000(2)]
15.III.30	300213		[301000(4)]
22.III.30	271021	1.XII.30	300715
	290925(1)	1.I.31	[301100(2)]
29.III.30	300122		[301100(3)]
	300206		301121(1)
	300208	15.I.31	300926(2)
	300301		301022
5.IV.30	280628		301126
	300212	1.II.31	300917
12.IV.30	[290300(1)]		[301200(2)]
	300314	15.II.31	310107
19.IV.30	280628	15.III.31	[301200(1)]
	[300300(2)]	1.IV.31	[301200(1)]
26.IV.30	[300400(1)]	15.IV.31	[301200(1)]
10.V.30	300329		[310300(3)]
17.V.30	300329		310311
24.V.30	300323		++++
7.VI.30	300323		

MILITANT ++++

1.V.31	310308	12.XII.31	311107
15.V.31	310325	19.XII.31	310901
1.VI.31	310415		311117
15.VI.31	310209	26.XII.31	300826
4.VII.31	310424	2.I.32	300826
	310501	9.I.32	311208
11.VII.31	261208	16.I.32	311115
	310414(2)	30.I.32	⌊320130⌋
18.VII.31	310618	6.II.32	320102
25.VII.31	310624	13.II.32	311222
	310701	12.III.32	320215(1)
1.VIII.31	291100(2)	19.III.32	311126
	310600(3)	26.III.32	320127
	310612	2.IV.32	320127
	⌊310700(2)⌋		320301
	310708(1)	9.IV.32	320127
8.VIII.31	310600(3)		320301
	310708(2)	16.IV.32	320127
15.VIII.31	310715(1)	23.IV.32	320127
	310719	30.IV.32	320127
22.VIII.31	310715(1)	7.V.32	320127
	310715(2)	14.V.32	320127
5.IX.31	310629	28.V.32	320127
15.IX.31	310713	4.VI.32	320127
	310825		320423
26.IX.31	310730	11.VI.32	320127
	310825		320509
10.X.31	310825		320519(1)
17.X.31	310820(1)	18.VI.32	320127
24.X.31	310820(1)		320512
31.X.31	310929	25.VI.32	⌊300800(1)⌋
14.XI.31	⌊310900(1)⌋	2.VII.32	⌊300800(1)⌋
	310927		320613(1)
21.XI.31	310912	9.VII.32	320616
	311114	16.VII.32	⌊320415⌋
28.XI.31	281004		320613(2)
	311010	30.VII.32	⌊320500⌋
5.XII.31	311110	6.VIII.32	320628 ++++

MILITANT   ++++

13.VIII.32	320628	7.I.33	321022(1)
20.VIII.32	320625		[321200(2)]
	320802		321205
27.VIII.32	320725	14.I.33	[321208(2)]
	320806	21.I.33	321127
3.IX.32	320804(2)	28.I.33	330104(1)
10.IX.32	320524(1)	4.II.33	330111(1)
	320809	11.II.33	330111(2)
17.IX.32	270418		330114
	320818(2)	20.II.33	311208
24.IX.32	320817	24.II.33	330205
		3.III.33	330126
15.X.32	320910	6.III.33	[321200(6)]
	320922(1)	18.III.33	330303(2)
22.X.32	320902	25.III.33	330303(2)
	320926	1.IV.33	330223
29.X.32	320902	8.IV.33	330314
5.XI.32	211206		330321
	321013(2)		330323(2)
12.XI.32	[290800(1)]	15.IV.33	330223
	320912		330306
	321013(1)		330323(1)
	321019		[330415]
	[321020(2)]	29.IV.33	330310
	321022(1)		330323(1)
19.XI.32	321019	6.V.33	330409
	321022(1)	13.V.33	330409
26.XI.32	321019	20.V.33	330300(3)
	321101		[330400(3)]
3.XII.32	321022(1)	27.V.33	330429
	321123(1)	3.VI.33	330429
17.XII.32	321022(1)		330503
24.XII.32	321030(1)		330507
31.XII.32	321013(3)	10.VI.33	330512(1)
	321022(2)		330523
	321022(3)		330525
	321104	17.VI.33	330522
			[330609(1)]
			330613(2)

++++

MILITANT   ++++

1.VII.33	330421	30.XII.33	331123
8.VII.33	330410	6.I.34	331001
	330604		331123
	330613(1)	20.I.34	331001
15.VII.33	330401		331212
	330406	27.I.34	331212
	330528		340105
22.VII.33	330519	29.I.34	330712
	330616	10.II.34	340120(1)
29.VII.33	330706		340124
5.VIII.33	330615	17.II.34	330323(1)
12.VIII.33	320818(1)	10.III.34	340118
	330715(4)		⌊340304⌋
26.VIII.33	330714	17.III.34	340222
	330719(1)	31.III.34	⌊340300⌋
	330719(3)	14.IV.34	340316
2.IX.33	330602	21.IV.34	330827
	330813		340323
9.IX.33	330602	28.IV.34	340331
16.IX.33	330805	19.V.34	340419
23.IX.33	330817(3)	16.VI.34	⌊340616⌋
	330826	30.VI.34	⌊340600(1)⌋
	330827		⌊340608(1)⌋
	330828	8.IX.34	⌊340817(1)⌋
	330901(1)		
	⌊330901(2)⌋		
	⌊330903(1)⌋	10.V.41	400820(5)
30.IX.33	330715(1)	4.X.41	370617(1)
	330904		
	330910	7.VIII.43	300514
7.X.33	330913	13.VII.46	381028
	330920	27.XI.50	371129(1)
14.X.33	330715(2)		
21.X.33	330720(1)	23.VII.56	400423(2)
	331002(1)		
4.XI.33	⌊331000(2)⌋	18.IV.60	381228
25.XI.33	331110	20.II.70	⌊200305⌋
9.XII.33	331107		
16.XII.33	331102		

MILITANT(Australia)

(IV.1)	19.IV.37	361218(1)
(IV.3)	31.V.37	370118
		370313(1)
		370313(3)
(IV.5)	7.VII.37	370127(1)
(V.1)	10.I.38	371116(1)
		371125(1)
		371127(1)
(V.2)	24.I.38	371102
(V.3)	7.II.38	371102
		371213(1)
(V.6)	11.IV.38	380218
(V.7)	1.VII.38	370214
(I.2)	1.X.38	380725(1)
(II.5)	VII.39	390311
		390324(1)

========

MILITANT INTERNATIONAL REVIEW

(2)	Spr-Sum '70	320000(1)

========

MILLIET

	29.II.29	[290229]

========

MISCAREA SOCIALA

(IV.1)	I.33	321205

========

MODERN MONTHLY

	III.33	321104
	III.34	330715(3)
	[1937]	371015

========

The MODERN THINKER

	VI.32	320415
(III.6)	X.33	330610

========

Le MONDE

	1.IX.28	[080915]

========

MONDE(VERDEN)

(I.3)	XII.28	[080915]
(I.9)	VI.29	[290600(7)]

========

MONTAG MORGEN

	1932	320512

========

MORNING POST

	17.XII.17	[171201(1)/]
	11.II.22	220202
	12.V.25	250506

========

MOSKAU

(48)	22.VII.21	210717(1)

========

MOT DAG

(XII.1)	26.I.34	340101

========

NATION

9.X.21	210907(1)	(IV.14)	VII.32	320613(2)
				320616
14.IX.27	270808			
5.X.27	270819	(IV.20)	X.32	290727(1)
29.V.29	290327			

4.VII.36   360609
8.VIII.36   360709(2)

======================

Die NEUE RUNDSCHAU

(II)	1930: 301-34	310000(1)
	1930: 590-605	310000(1)
(I)	1931: 215-35	310000(1)

4.VII.36   360609
8.VIII.36   360709(2)
10.X.36   360826(1)

27.III.37   370308

======================

Die NEUE BÜCHERSCHAU

(V)	1927: 147-8	⌊270000(15)⌋
(VII)	1929: 293-9	290225

Das NEUE RUSSLAND

(III.3-4)	1926	251200
(IV.3-4)	1927	260203
(IV.5-6)	1927	250203

======================

NEUE FREIE PRESSE(Vienna)

11.X.25	⌊250730(1)⌋
19.IV.29	290225
12.IV.31	300000(1)

======================

Die NEUES WIENER JOURNAL

20.XII.27	⌊271200⌋

======================

Der NEUE MAHNRUF

(III.6)	III-IV.31	310124
(III.7)	IV.31	310124
(III.16)	VIII.31	310715(1)
(III.18)	IX.31	310100
(III.22)	IX-X.31	310715(1)
(III.23)	XI.31	310715(1)
(III.25)	XII.31	311126
(IV.2)	I.32	311208
(IV.3)	II.32	311110
(IV.6)	III.32	320000(1)
(IV.7)	III-IV.32	320000(1)
(IV.8)	IV.32	320301

Die NEUE ZEIT

(XXV.ii)	VI.07	⌊061200(1)⌋
(XXV.ii)	1906-7	⌊070600⌋
(XXVI.i)	1907-8	⌊070100⌋
(XXVI.ii)	1907-8	080214
(--)	IV.08	⌊080400(1)⌋
(XXVI.ii)	1907-8	⌊080400(3)⌋
(XXVI.ii)	1907-8	080500(2)
(XXVI.ii)	15.IX.08	⌊080915⌋
(XXVII.i)	1908-9	⌊081200⌋
(XXVII.i)	III.09	⌊090322⌋
(XXVII.ii)	V.09	⌊090500⌋
(XXVIII.ii)	1910	⌊100000(3)⌋

++++

Die NEUE ZEIT   ++++

(XXVIII.ii)	9.IX.10	[100909]
(XXIX.ii)	1910-11	[110200(1)]
(XXXII.i)	XI.13	[131100]

========================

NEW EUROPE

	20.XII.17	171109/

========================

NEW INTERNATIONAL

VII.34	270924	II.36	351100(1)
	321231		360110
	[340700(4)]	IV.36	280302
VIII.34	321231	VI.36	351015
	340715		360321
IX-X.34	270925		360422
	340710	I.38	201107
	340800(3)		371030
XI.34	271001	II.38	310913(1)
	271004		320614
	280911		371030
XII.34	330719(1)	III.38	270403
I.35	231200(2)	IV.38	270403
III.35	210204		380115
	350130	V.38	260700(2)
V.35	[350328]	VI.38	380216
VII.35	350201	VII.38	220226(1)
	350424		380522
VIII.35	350610(1)	VIII.38	220226(1)
	350624(1)		380706
X.35	270516	X.38	380830
	350729	XI.38	380917
	350900(4)		381014
	350914	XII.38	381010
XII.35	350918	II.39	381108
	351031	III.39	380108
			390130(1)
		IV.39	360412
			390304(3)
		V.39	381222(1)
			390214
			390307(1)
			390307(3)
		VI.39	390501
		VII.39	390307(2)

++++

NEW INTERNATIONAL   ++++

VIII.39	390607		IV.45	370000(25)
	390609		XI.45	390800
	390610(2)		IX.46	350819
IX.39	390725		X.46	⌊230923(2)⌋
X.39	390715			
XI.39	390925		VIII.48	390422(1)
II.40	250917		V-VI.51	310820(1)
	380418(1)			
	391018			
III.40	391215(2)	NEW LEADER		
	400124		25.VIII.33	⌊330800(1)⌋
			13.X.33	330829
			21.VIII.36	360815
			3.IX.37	370306

NEW INTERNATIONAL(WP)

IX.40	⌊290300(1)⌋	NEW MASSES		
IV.41	231200(3)			
V.41	370222	(I.2)	VI.26	260119
X.41	300715			
XI.41	300715	NEW MILITANT		
XII.41	281100			
II.42	281100		19.I.35	341230(1)
VIII.42	261101		9.II.35	350112
IX.42	290323(1)		30.III.35	350210
X.42	390701		4.V.35	350331(1)
XI.42	220000(12)		18.V.35	⌊350426⌋
	261101		8.VI.35	350525(2)
XII.42	261101		15.VI.35	⌊350400⌋
IV.43	281111		29.VI.35	350607(2)
VI.43	190306(1)		27.VII.35	350607(1)
VII.43	330714		3.VIII.35	350700(1)
	331107		7.IX.35	350807
I.44	300514		28.IX.35	350907(2)
V.44	240319		5.X.35	350829
VII.44	300514		12.X.35	⌊350900(1)⌋
I.45	350610(1)		26.X.35	280628
III.45	340109			

++++

NEW MILITANT   ++++

2.XI.35	350926
30.XI.35	351104(1)
	351107(1)
14.XII.35	351126(1)
4.I.36	351022
1.II.36	360115(1)
	360128(2)
15.II.36	360111
	360123
	360128(1)
22.II.36	360130
21.III.36	[170317(1)]
4.IV.36	360318
11.IV.36	[360400(3)]
25.IV.36	360328
2.V.36	360328
	[360400(2)]
	360412
9.V.36	360328
	360416
16.V.36	360325
	[360500(3)]
6.VI.36	360101

=================

NEW REPUBLIC

22.V.29	290225
5.VII.33	330528
1.XI.33	[331101]
3.I.34	[331214]

=================

NEW RUSSIA

(I.6)	2.III.20	200124(1)
(I.12)	22.IV.20	200212(1)
(II.17)	27.V.20	200429(4)
(II.19)	10.VI.20	200509(2)
(II.23)	8.VII.20	200616(1)
(II.24)	15.VII.20	200522
(III.38)	21.X.20	[200823]

=================

NEW RUSSIA(Shanghai)

(II.35)	29.XI.23	[230711]
		[230713]

=================

NEWS CHRONICLE

27.VIII.36	360826(2)
16.III.40	390922
19.III.40	400214
20.III.40	400214
21.III.40	400214
23.III.40	400214
25.III.40	400214
26.III.40	400214

=================

NEWSLETTER

(II.41)	22.II.58	220223(2)
(IV.153)	28.V.60	240818
(V.208)	15.VII.61	260113(2)
(V.215)	16.IX.61	231123(2)
		240419(1)

=================

NEW YORK EVENING POST

1937	370219(1)

=================

NEW YORK GLOBE

[1917]   171106(3)/

==

NEW YORK HERALD-TRIBUNE

24.XI.17   171111(3)/

1940   400727

==

NEW YORK TIMES

19.I.22	⌊220117⌋
26.II.22	220223(3)
5.V.22	⌊220504⌋
31.V.22	⌊220518⌋
27.VIII.22	220826
	⌊220827⌋
15.X.22	⌊221015⌋
21.I.23	⌊230121⌋
18.VI.23	230616(2)
3.X.23	⌊230930⌋
13.IV.24	240412(2)
1.V.24	240429(1)
19.V.24	240419(1)
7.V.25	250506
2.VI.25	250531
7.VI.25	⌊250606⌋
30.XII.25	251218
6.II.26	260113(2)
1.III.27	270228(2)
20.XI.27	271119(1)
26.II.29	290225
27.II.29	290225
28.II.29	290225
1.III.29	290225
19.VII.31	310714

24.I.32	320123
27.II.32	320215(2)
	[320226(1)]
5.III.32	320215(1)
8.V.32	⌊320508⌋
12.XII.32	321211
18.III.33	330317(2)
13.I.35	341230(2)
27.VII.35	350726(1)
28.II.36	360227
19.VII.36	360522
20.VIII.36	360819(2)
	360819(3)
25.VIII.36	360824
26.VIII.36	360825
30.VIII.36	360815
2.IX.36	360820(2)
7.IX.36	360823(2)
10.I.37	370109(2)
13.I.37	370112(1)
21.I.37	370120
24.I.37	370123(1)
	370123(2)
25.I.37	370124(3)
28.I.37	370127(2)
30.I.37	370129(3)
31.I.37	370130
16.II.37	370215
24.V.37	370523
26.V.37	370518
13.VI.37	370612
18.VI.37	370617(2)
1.VIII.37	370730
1.X.37	370930(1)
7.XII.37	371203
14.XII.37	371213(3)

++++

NEW YORK TIMES	++++		De NIEUWE FAKKEL		
	3.III.38	380302	(I.14)	26.IV.35	350300(1)
	4.III.38	380303(1)	(I.16)	3.V.35	[350400]
	5.III.38	380304(2)	(I.31)	28.VI.35	350610(1)
	6.III.38	380305	(I.37)	19.VII.35	350700(1)
	7.III.38	380306(1)	(I.57)	27.IX.35	350607(1)
	8.III.38	380307			350914
	9.III.38	380308(1)	(I.60)	8.X.35	350914
	21.III.38	380317(2)	(I.74)	26.XI.35	351031
	29.XI.38	381128	(II.97)	10.IV.36	360318
	13.XII.38	[381213]	(II.107)	19.VI.36	360605
	4.X.39	391003	(II.108)	26.VI.36	360522
	23.XI.39	391117	(II.113)	31.VII.36	360709(2)
	18.XII.39	391207	(II.115)	14.VIII.36	360704
	27.XII.39	391226(1)	(II.116)	21.VIII.36	360730(1)
			(II.117)	28.VIII.36	360823(1)
	1.VII.56	230417	(II.118)	4.IX.36	360815
			(II.120)	18.IX.36	360819(1)
			(II.121)	25.IX.36	360819(1)
					360820(2)

=================================

NEW YORK VOLKSZEITUNG					
	1917	170200	(III.5)	28.I.37	370122
	1930	300610	(III.14)	9.IV.37	370313(1)
			(III.39)	24.IX.37	370730
					370808

=================================

NEW YORK WORLD-TELEGRAM			(III.40)	1.X.37	360113
			(III.41)	8.X.37	370930(1)
	1920	200223	(III.44)	29.X.37	370923
	4.VII.33	330613(2)	(III.52)	24.XII.37	371213(1)
			(IV.7)	19.II.38	371030
			(IV.8)	25.II.38	371030

=================================

NICHIRO SOOFUKAI			(IV.33)	19.VIII.38	380803
			(IV.34)	26.VIII.38	380801
	1924	[240618(2)]	(IV.36)	9.IX.38	380719(2)
			(IV.43)	28.X.38	381007

=================================

			(V.3)	20.I.39	381114
			(V.32)	11.VIII.39	390501
			(V.33)	18.VIII.39	390501 ++++

De NIEUWE FAKKEL   ++++

(V.38)	22.IX.39	390911
(V.40)	6.X.39	390904
(V.42)	20.X.39	390311

=====================

De NIEUWE TIJD

(XXI.2)	II.16	⌊150712(2)⌋

=====================

De NIEUWE WEG

(IV.5)	V.29	290327
(IV.11)	XI.29	291014
(V.3)	III.30	291113
(V.6)	VI.30	300314
(V.7)	VII.30	300314
(V.8)	VIII.30	300530
(V.9)	IX.30	300425
(V.10)	X.30	300425
(V.11)	XI.30	300926(1)
(V.12)	XII.30	300926(1)
(VI.1)	I.31	300213
(VI.2)	II.31	300213
(VI.5)	V.31	310124
(VI.7)	VII.31	310308
(VI.10)	X.31	310715(1)
(VI.12)	XII.31	310225
(VII.1)	I.32	311208
(VII.7)	VII.32	320301
(VII.8)	VIII.32	320628
(VII.9)	IX.32	320802
		320804(2)
(VII.10)	X.32	320809
		320817
		320818(2)
(VII.11)	XI.32	320902
(VII.12)	XII.32	320910
		320912
		320914

(VIII.1)	I.33	260000(31)
		⌊290800(1)⌋
(VIII.4)	IV.33	321104
		330314
(VIII.5)	V.33	321003
		330223
(VIII.6)	VI.33	330223
(VIII.7)	VII.33	330429
(VIII.8)	VIII.33	330429
(VIII.9)	IX.33	330607(1)
		330817(3)
		330826
		330901(1)
(IX.1)	I-II.34	340101
		⌊340200(1)⌋
(IX.4)	IV.34	340316
(IX.5)	V.34	331130
(IX.10)	X.34	340700(2)
		340800(3)
		340922

=====================

NOUVELLE REVUE FRANÇAISE

	IV.31	310209
	III.34	330610
		331102

=====================

NOUVELLES ETUDES MARXISTES

(2)	⌊1970⌋	370828

=====================

NOWE PISMO

(III.15:110)	11.III.34	340120(1)

=====================

NOWY PRZEGLAD

| (I.3-4) | VIII-IX.22 | 220513 |
| (I.5) | X.22 | [220518] |

==

La NUEVA ERA

| (I.6) | VII.36 | 360522 |

==

NUEVO ORDEN

| (I.1) | 3.IX.21 | 210623 |

==

NY TID

24.XI.17	171108(1)/
30.XI.17	171115(2)/
18.XII.17	171203(3)/
5.I.18	[171218(2)/]
16.I.18	171229(1)/
23.II.18	180222(2)
4.III.18	[180222(1)]
1.IV.19	190306(1)
2.IV.19	190306(1)
29.XII.19	191031
14.V.20	200429(4)
20.IX.20	[200912]
8.III.21	210305
16.III.21	[210313]
5.VII.21	210623
8.VII.21 ++	210706
4.VIII.21	210730
29.X.21	211025
19.V.22	220414
7.IX.22	220826

	14.IV.23	[180000(55)]
	28.IV.23	[180000(55)]
	27.X.24	240728

==

El OBRERO MILITANTE

| | VIII-IX.62 | 380500(1) |

==

OBSERVER

| | 5.XI.22 | 221101 |

==

OCTOBER YOUTH

| (5) | X-XI.33 | 331003(1) |

==

OCTUBRE

(I.1)	1.X.35	341000(1)
		350610(1)
		350700(1)
(I.2)	XI.35	341000
		350729
		350914

==

OCTUBRE(Buenos Aires)

| (II.4) | III-V.47 | 370923 |

==

OKTOBER

(1)	IV.37	361218(1)
		370219(1)
(4-5)	VIII-IX.37	370617(1)

++++

OKTOBER ++++

(4-5)	VIII-IX.37	370730
		370808
(7)	XI.37	310000(1)
		370828
(II.1)	I.38	371102
		371213(3)
		371219
(II.2)	II.38	371116(2)
		371217
(II.3)	III.38	371217
(II.5)	X.38	371217
(II.6-7)	XI-XII.38	380500(1)
		380830
(III.1)	III.39	381214
		381222(3)
(III.2)	V.39	380703(2)
		390304(3)
		390318
(III.3)	IX.39	390422(1)

===========

L'ORDINE NUOVO

(I.13)	13.I.21	200109(2)
(I.77)	18.III.21	200000(37)
(I.120)	1.V.21	190710
(I.145)	26.V.21	210000(50)
(I.169)	16.VI.21	201208(2)
(I.190)	10.VII.21	210623
(I.204)	24.VII.21	210704
(I.206)	26.VII.21	210704
(I.225)	14.VIII.21	[210717(3)]
(I.226)	15.VIII.21	[210712]
(I.236)	25.VIII.21	200000(37)
(I.309)	6.XI.21	[211001]
(II.4)	4.I.22	211227
(II.15)	15.I.22	190118
(II.27)	27.I.22	[211225]

(II.44)	13.II.22	151100(1)
(II.92)	2.IV.22	220302(1)
		220328
(II.98)	8.IV.22	220303(1)
(II.142)	23.V.22	[220518]
(II.158)	8.VI.22	220513
(II.165)	15.VI.22	220526
(II.184)	4.VII.22	[220618]

===========

OSAKA MAINICHI

	1924	[240424]

===========

E PALI TON TAKSION

(302)	18.VII.33	330409

===========

PARIS-MIDI

	16.II.37	370211

===========

PARIS-SOIR

	15.VI.33	330607(1)
	16.VI.33	330607(1)

===========

PARTISAN REVIEW

	VIII.38	380618(1)
	Fall '38	380725(2)
	Winter '39	381222(3)
	Fall '68	[120304]

===========

PERMANENTE REVOLUTION

(I.1)	VII.31	310501	(II.24)	X.32	321013(2)
(I.2)	VII.31	310708(2)			[321020(2)]
		310715(1)	(II.25)	X.32	320922(1)
(I.3)	IX.31	[300800(1)]	(II.26)	XI.32	321006
		310820(1)			321013(1)
		310825	(II.27)	XI.32	321030(1)
(I.5)	XII.31	[300800(1)]	(II.28)	XI.32	320920
		[311200]	(II.29)	XI.32	321003
(II.1)	I.32	[300800(1)]	(II.31)	XII.32	[321200(2)]
		311208	(II.33)	XII.32	320917
(II.2)	I.32	311110			321200(3)
		311222	(II.34)	XII.32	321127
		320102	(III.1)	I.33	321104
		320130			321205
(II.4)	II.32	320127			321228(2)
(II.6)	III.32	320301	(III.2)	I.33	320229
(II.7)	IV.32	310708(4)	(III.3)	I.33	330111(1)
		320315			330111(2)
(II.9)	V.32	320215(1)			330114
(II.10)	V.32	320423	(III.5)	II.33	312108
(II.11)	VI.32	320512			330128(2)
(II.13)	VII.32	300821	(III.7)	II.33	330105
		320613(1)			330126
		320613(2)			330205
		320616	(III.8)	II.33	180319(1)
(II.14)	VII.32	300821			
		320625			

=================================

PERMANENT REVOLUTION(India)

(--)	I.43	381230
(I.3)	IX.43	391124

=================================

PERSPECTIVA MUNDIAL

(I.11-12)	2.XII.66	310000(1)
(24-25)	I.68	230621

(II.15)	23.VII.32	320628
(II.17)	VIII.32	[320415]
(II.18)	VIII.32	[320415]
(II.19)	VIII.32	320804(2)
		320806
(II.20)	VIII.32	270418
		320809
		320817
(II.21)	IX.32	320818(2)
(II.22)	IX.32	[320500]

=================================

PERSPECTIVES

(52)   V-VI.69   230621

==================================

PESTER LLOYD

        26.IV.31   310000(1)

        1932   320423

==================================

POCHODNIA

        ⌊1920⌋   200618(1)

==================================

POLITICAL QUARTERLY

        VII-IX.32   ⌊320508⌋

==================================

POLITIKEN(Denmark)

        26.II.29   281216(2)
        27.II.29   290225
        28.II.29   290225
        1.III.29   290225
        22.V.29   ⌊290522(2)⌋
        9.VII.29   300000(1)
        16.VII.29   300000(1)
        17.VII.29   300000(1)
        23.VII.29   300000(1)
        24.VII.29   300000(1)
        30.VII.29   300000(1)
        31.VII.29   300000(1)
        6.VIII.29   300000(1)
        7.VIII.29   300000(1)
        13.VIII.29   300000(1)
        14.VIII.29   300000(1)
        20.VIII.29   300000(1)
        21.VIII.29   300000(1)
        27.VIII.29   300000(1)

        28.VIII.29   300000(1)
        3.IX.29   300000(1)
        10.IX.29   300000(1)
        17.IX.29   300000(1)
        18.IX.29   300000(1)
        25.IX.29   300000(1)
        26.IX.29   300000(1)
        1.X.29   300000(1)
        8.X.29   300000(1)
        9.X.29   300000(1)
        15.X.29   300000(1)
        24.XI.32   ⌊321123(3)⌋
        28.XI.32   321127
        11.II.37   370209

==================================

POLITIKEN(Sweden)

(III.1)   2.I.18   171202(5)/
(III.3)   4.I.18   171214(1)/
(III.30)   6.II.18   180202(1)
(III.44)   21.II.18   180219(2)
(III.45)   22.II.18   180219(3)
(III.186)   13.VIII.18   180801(1)

==================================

POPOLO D'ITALIA

        1924   ⌊240510(2)⌋

==================================

POUM

(I.3)   9.IX.36   351112
                          360730(1)
(I.4)   16.IX.36   360819(1)
                          360821
(I.7)   7.X.36   300000(1)

==================================

PRAGER PRESSE

4.XI.28	271021	

==

PRAGER TAGBLATT

1929	[290400(3)]

==

PRAWDA

(15)

5.VIII.17	170723/

==

PRESENTE

XI.38	380500(1)
XI.61	380605

==

Le PROLÉTAIRE

1.VII.30	290600(1)

==

PROLETARJAT

(1)

V.32	290701
	311126
	311208
	320000(1)
	320301

==

PROMETEO

(I.9)	15.XI.28	240915
(II.13)	15.II.29	240122(1)
(II.14)	15.III.29	281216(1)
(II.15)	15.IV.29	280103
(II.16)	1.V.29	290327
(II.18)	15.VI.29	290523
(II.21)	15.IX.29	270801
(II.22)	1.X.29	270801
(II.24)	15.XI.29	291004
(II.25)	1.XII.29	290925(1)
		291109
(III.27)	1.II.30	291113
(III.28)	1.III.30	291113
(III.30)	1.V.30	300213
(III.31)	1.VI.30	300422
(III.33)	15.VII.30	300619
(III.34)	1.VIII.30	300514
(III.37)	15.IX.30	300900(1)
(III.40)	1.XI.30	240915
(III.41)	15.XI.30	300926(1)
(III.42)	1.XII.30	300926(1)
		[301100(3)]
(III.43)	15.XII.30	300926(1)
		301126
(IV.44)	1.I.31	[301200(1)]
(IV.46)	15.II.31	310107
(IV.47)	1.III.31	310124
(IV.48)	15.III.31	310124
(IV.49)	1.IV.31	310124
(IV.50)	15.IV.31	310124
(IV.51)	1.V.31	301126
(IV.52)	15.V.31	291130(2)
(IV.53)	7.VI.31	310405
(IV.55)	5.VII.31	291130(2)
(IV.56)	19.VII.31	291130(2)
(IV.57)	2.VIII.31	291130(2)
(IV.58)	23.VIII.31	310404
(IV.59)	13.IX.31	310404
(IV.60)	27.IX.31	310404
		310414(3)
		310528(1)
		310528(2)

++++

PROMETEO   ++++

(IV.61)	11.X.31	310404
(IV.62)	25.X.31	310404
(IV.63)	8.XI.31	310404
(IV.64)	29.XI.31	310404
(IV.66)	27.XII.31	311126
(V.67)	17.I.32	311126
(V.68)	31.I.32	311126
(V.75)	22.V.32	320301
(V.76)	19.VI.32	320301
(VI.83)	1.I.33	321200(3)
		⌊330101⌋

=====================================

PRZEGLAD SOCYAL-DEMOKRATYCZNY

(IV.1)	III.08	⌊080300⌋
(IV.2)	IV.08	⌊080400(2)⌋
(IV.3)	V.08	⌊080500⌋
(IV.4)	VI.08	⌊080600(1)⌋
		⌊080600(2)⌋
(IV.5)	VII.08	⌊080700⌋
(IV.6)	VIII.08	⌊080800⌋
(IV.8-9)	X-XI.08	081014
(IV.10)	XII.08	081216
(V.11)	V.09	⌊090327(4)⌋
(V.12)	VI.09	⌊090600⌋
(V.14-15)	VIII-IX.09	⌊090821⌋

=====================================

QUARTA INTERNAZIONALE

(I.1)	XII.67	390409

=====================================

QUATRIÈME INTERNATIONALE

(1)	X.36	360700(1)
		360708
(2)	II.37	330401
		350300(1)
		370118
(3)	III-IV.37	361218(1)
		370209
		370211
(4)	I.38	370816
		370817
		370828
		370913
		370920(2)
		370922
		370925
		370928
		370929
(5)	II.38	370809
		371217
		380115
(6-7)	III-IV.38	370809
		371030
		380121(1)
(8)	V.38	380500(1)
(9)	VI.38	371125(2)
(--)	VI.38	371104
(10)	VII.38	380319
		380522
(11)	VIII.38	380618(1)
		380706
(12-13)	IX-X.38	380500(1)
		380830
(14-15)	XI-XII.38	380703(2)
		380719(2)
		380824
		380923

++++

QUATRIÈME INTERNATIONALE   ++++

(16)	IV.39	221125		VII-VIII.47	230618
		⌊390217]		IX-X.47	170512/
		390304(3)		XI-XII.47	170512/
(2)	XII.43	390725	(VII.1-2)	I-II.49	280302
(3)	I.44	240728	(VIII.8-10)	VIII-X.50	391018
(8-10)	1944	350300(1)			391215
(14-15)	I-II.45	191024(2)			400124
		390800	(XI.5-7)	VII.53	230000(9)
(16-19)	III-VI.45	390800	(XI.8-10)	XI.53	230000(9)
(20-21)	VII-VIII.45	390725	(XII.6-8)	VI-VIII.54	[230711]
(22-24)	IX-XI.45	301100(1)			
		320613(1)		VI.55	300329
(25-26)	XII.45-I.46	390422(1)	(XIV.1-3)	III.56	371116(2)
	II.46	390925		VII.56	321231
	VI-VII.46	[340600(1)]	(XIV.10-12)	XII.56	220425
		380519			230927
	VIII-IX.46	400501			260203
		400514(1)	(XV.7-10)	X-XI.57	321127
		400528(2)	(2)	IV.58	260301
		400709	(3)	VII.58	240319
		400729		X-XI.58	370828
		400802(2)			
		400803(1)	(XVII.6)	V.59	320613(1)
		400803(2)	(XVII.7)	IX-X.59	400227(1)
		400806			400227(2)
		400807			400303
		400809	(30)	VI.68	351126(1)
		400812		II.69	360000(6)
		400816(1)			
		400817(2)			
		400818			

QUATRIÈME INTERNATIONALE(OSPE)

	400820(1)	(2)	XII.43	390725
	400820(2)	(3)	I.44	240421(2)
	400820(3)			260215
	400820(6)	(8-10)	VI-VIII.44	350201
X-XI.46	380600			
	380605			

QUE FAIRE

(3-4)	V.70	240319

===================

RADNICHKE NOVINE

(21)	1910	[100000(5)]
(271)	1911	[100101(2)]
(272)	1911	[100101(2)]
(43)	1913	[130315]
(44)	1914	[130314]

===================

RADNIK

| (15) | 1909 | [090300] |

===================

RED DAWN

| (II.6) | VIII.20 | 180422(4) |

===================

RED FLAG

(1)	V.33	330314
(2)	VI.33	330323(1)
		330323(2)
(3)	VII.33	330429
(4)	VIII.33	330427
		330523
(5)	IX.33	330714
(6)	X-XI.33	330720(1)
		330826
		330828
(7)	I.34	330104(1)
		331102
		331107
(8)	II-IV.34	340222

(9)	V-VI.34	250000(5)
(11)	X.34	340817(1)
(II.1)	XI.34	311110
		340710
(1)	V.36	360318
(2)	VI-VII.36	360328
(3)	IX.36	360730(1)
		360815
(4)	X.36	360820(2)
(5)	I.37	231206(2)
(6)	II.37	361013
(7)	III-IV.37	361218(1)
		370219(1)

===================

RED MOLE

| (I.2) | 1.IV.70 | 231200(3) |

===================

REPERTORIO AMERICANA

(XXVII.12)	23.IX.33	321127
		321205
(XXVII.16)	28.X.33	321127
(XXVII.18)	11.XI.33	330401

===================

RÉVOLUTION

(II.16)	XII.35	351104(1)
(II.17)	7.XII.35	351104(1)
(III.25)	28.II.36	360111
(III.27)	27.III.36	360318
(III.30)	15.V.36	200000(37)
		360321
(III.31)	22.V.36	360101
(IV.40)	15.IV.37	351107(1)
(IV.42)	15.VII.37	370522 ++++

RÉVOLUTION   ++++

(V.49)	VI.38	370809
(V.51)	VII.38	370809
(VI.55)	I.39	360000(10)

==================

RÉVOLUTION(Gilly)

(9)	IX.37	370730
(II.5)	V.38	380220

==================

De REVOLUTIONAIR SOCIALIST

(II)	1936	360325
(II.5)	V.36	360412
(II.6)	VI.36	360412
(II.7-8)	VII-VIII.36	360708
(III.2-3)	VI.37	370423

==================

The REVOLUTIONARY COMMUNIST(India)

	VIII.45	240421(2)

==================

La RÉVOLUTION PROLÉTARIENNE

(I.1)	I.25	240728
(I.2)	II.25	250115
(I.10)	X.25	250908
(V.79)	1.V.29	281216(1)
		290212
		290225
(V.84)	15.VII.29	290601
(VII.114)	5.II.31	301205
(230)	30.IX.36	360820(2)

==================

La REVUE COMMUNISTE

(I.1)	III.20	190118
(I.2)	IV.20	180328(1)
(I.3)	V.20	180328(1)
(I.6)	VIII.20	200429(4)
		200807(2)
(I.7)	IX.20	200429(4)
(I.9)	XI.20	190914

==================

La REVUE MONDIALE

(150)	15.X.22	[161227]
(151)	1.XI.22	[161227]

==================

RHENISCH-WESTFÄLISCHE ZEITUNG

	21.III.29	290312

==================

De RODE OKTOBER

(I.1)	I.36	360111
(I.2)	II.36	360111
(I.5)	V.36	360416
(I.6)	VI.36	360328
(I.7)	VII.36	360609
(I.8)	VIII.36	360700(1)
(I.9)	IX.36	360709(1)
		360820(1)
(I.10)	X.36	351112
		⌊360400(2)⌋
(II)	1937: 75-91	370209
	:127-41	371116(2)
	:227-37	371116(2)
	:249-62	371116(2)
(III.6)	VI.38	380312 ++++

De RODE OKTOBER   ++++

(IV)	1939:33-40	381214	(II.146)	24.VI.21	210613(2)
	:69-72	380725(2)	(II.150)	29.VI.21	210623
	:117-20	390318	(II.167)	19.VII.21	180000(5)
	:164-8	390422(1)	(II.169)	21.VII.21	180000(5)
	:239-42	390902			[210712]
(LocPer)			(II.171)	23.VII.21	180000(5)
			(II.173)	26.VII.21	180000(5)
(1)	VIII.46	370118			210623
		370222	(II.174)	27.VII.21	210623
		381222(2)	(II.175)	28.VII.21	180000(5)
		400700(2)	(II.176)	29.VII.21	210702
(2)	X.46	[400820(4)]	(II.177)	30.VII.21	180000(5)
(3)	XII.46	320628	(II.179)	2.VIII.21	180000(5)
			(II.181)	4.VIII.21	180000(5)
			(II.183)	6.VIII.21	[210800(3)]
Det RÖDE RYSSLAND			(II.185)	9.VIII.21	210714(2)
(44)	7.XI.20	200000(37)	(II.186)	10.VIII.21	180000(5)
	4.XI.22	[221012]	(II.188)	12.VIII.21	180000(5)
			(II.189)	13.VIII.21	180000(5)
			(II.192)	18.VIII.21	180000(5)
De ROOD GARDISTE			(II.193)	19.VIII.21	210624
(1)	X-XI.35	351016	(II.194)	20.VIII.21	210706
			(II.195)	21.VIII.21	210706
			(II.197)	24.VIII.21	180000(5)
					210706
ROTE FAHNE			(II.198)	25.VIII.21	210706
	[1923]	[231017]	(II.199)	26.VIII.21	180000(5)
					210706
			(II.202)	30.VIII.21	180000(5)
					210706
ROUGE			(II.203)	31.VIII.21	210706
(26)	2.VII.69	[400820(4)]	(II.204)	1.IX.21	210706
					210714(3)
			(II.205)	2.IX.21	180000(5)
			(II.209)	7.IX.21	180000(5)
RUDE PRAVO [including RUDE PRAVO VEČERNIK]			(II.216)	15.IX.21	180000(5)
(40)	7.XI.20	190914	(II.220)	20.IX.21	180000(5)
(48)	17.XI.20	200807(1)	(II.221)	21.IX.21	180000(5)
(65)	7.XII.20	[140000(3)]	(II.228)	29.IX.21	180000(5)

++++

RUDE PRAVO   ++++

(II.229)	30.IX.21	210830
(II.230)	1.X.21	180000(5)
		210921
(II.233)	5.X.21	180000(5)
(II.235)	7.X.21	180000(5)
(II.236)	8.X.21	180000(5)
(II.237)	9.X.21	⌊210916⌋
(II.239)	12.X.21	180000(5)
(II.240)	13.X.21	180000(5)
(II.274)	23.XI.21	211020
(III.3)	4.I.22	211025
(III.5)	6.I.22	⌊211229⌋
(III.22)	26.I.22	211221
(III.24)	28.I.22	211221
(III.40)	16.II.22	211011
(III.49)	26.II.22	151100(1)
(III.53)	3.III.22	220223(3)
(III.56)	7.III.22	220228(2)
(III.61)	12.III.22	220308
(III.64)	16.III.22	220226(1)
(III.67)	19.III.22	220116
(III.79)	4.IV.22	220329(1)
(III.93)	21.IV.22	220414
(III.114)	17.V.22	220508(5)
(III.142)	21.VI.22	220519(1)
(III.144)	23.VI.22	220519(1)
(III.210)	8.IX.22	⌊220827⌋
(III.247)	21.X.22	⌊221012⌋
(242)	24.X.22	221010
(III.256)	2.XI.22	221020
(III.257)	3.XI.22	221020
(III.290)	12.XII.22	221121
		221201(2)
(IV.43)	22.II.23	230210
(IV.44)	23.II.23	230210
(IV.88)	17.IV.23	221201(1)
(IV.106)	9.V.23	230405(1)
(124)	2.VI.23	230512(1)

(IV.161)	13.VII.23	230630
(IV.266)	13.XI.23	231019(1)
(V.21)	24.I.24	200423

=================================

RUSSIAN INFORMATION REVIEW

	8.VI.22	220501(1)
	20.X.23	⌊230930⌋
	10.XI.23	231021

=================================

RUSSISCHE KORRESPONDENZ

(I.i.3)	II.20	200128
(I.i.4)	II.20	⌊200122(1)⌋
(I.i.6–7)	IV–V.20	200219(1)
		200228(2)
(I.i.8–9)	VI.20	200124(1)
		200423
		200429(1)
		200429(4)
		⌊200501(3)⌋
(I.i.10)	VII.20	200330
		200404(1)
(I.ii.11)	VIII.20	200510(4)
		200731(1)
		200800
(I.ii.12–13)	IX.20	200000(37)
(I.ii.14–16)	X.20	180000(5)
		190914
(I.ii.17–18)	XI.20	200418
(II.i.1–2)	I–II.21	201202(1)
		⌊201219⌋
		201222(2)
(II.i.3–4)	III–IV.21	201225(2)
		210000(13)
(II.i.5)	V.21	210314(2)

++++

RUSSISCHE KORRESPONDENZ	++++	
(II.ii.10-11)	X-XI.21	210830
		[210916]
(II.ii.12)	XII.21	211024
(III.i.4-5)	IV-V.22	220000(5)
		[220223(1)]
		220303(1)
(III.i.6)	VI.22	220526
		[220618]
(III.ii.7-10)	VII-X.22	221010
		221103(1)
		221114(1)
(III.ii.11-12)	XI-XII.22	221103(1)
		221201(1)

=================================

RUSSISCHE RUNDSCHAU		
(13)	8.XII.20	201108
(14)	15.XII.20	201108
		201202(1)
		201208(2)
(15)	22.XII.20	201208(2)
(16)	29.XII.20	[201219]
		201224(3)
(18)	14.I.21	201202(2)
		201229(1)
(19)	21.I.21	210000(13)
(22)	8.II.21	210115(2)
		210125
(27)	15.III.21	210305
(35)	10.V.21	210000(50)

=================================

SÄCHSISCHE STAATS ZEITUNG

	23.III.29	[290323(2)]

=================================

St LOUIS POST-DISPATCH		
	17.I.37	370116
	1940	400214

=================================

SAMTIDEN		
(XLIV.7)	VII.33	330602

=================================

SAN FRANCISCO NEWS		
	1.II.37	370129(4)

=================================

SATURDAY EVENING POST		
	25.IV-	
	30-V.32	310000(1)
	27.VIII.32	310000(1)
	3.IX.32	310000(1)
	26.V.34	340313

=================================

SATURDAY REVIEW OF LITERATURE		
(XV.18)	27.II.37	361013

=================================

SCHLESSISCHE ZEITUNG		
	23.III.29	[290323(2)]

=================================

SEVEN DAYS		
	30.XII.34	341230(2)

=================================

SOCIAL DEMOKRATEN

	24.XI.32	⌊321123(4)⌋
	28.XI.32	321127

====================

The SOCIALIST(Glasgow)

(XVIII.222)	17.VII.19	190306(1)
(XVIII.223)	24.VII.19	190600
(XVIII.224)	31.VII.19	190600
(XVIII.225)	7.VIII.19	190600
(XVIII.227)	21.VIII.19	190600
(XVIII.238)	6.XI.19	180328(1)
(XVIII.239)	13.XI.19	180328(1)
(XVIII.240)	20.XI.19	180328(1)
(XVIII.245)	24.XII.19	190716
(XIX.24)	1.VII.20	190901(1)
(XIX.43)	25.XI.20	201020
(XXI.4)	26.I.22	211226

====================

SOCIALIST APPEAL

	21.VIII.37	370706
	28.VIII.37	370429
	18.IX.37	370905
	25.IX.37	370829
	2.X.37	370829
	9.X.37	370920(2)
		370930(1)
	16.X.37	370612
		370925
	23.X.37	371006
	30.X.37	370600
		371019
	6.XI.37	370600
		370921
	20.XI.37	371102
	27.XI.37	371116(1)
		371127(1)

4.XII.37	371125(1)
11.XII.37	371015
	371129(2)
18.XII.37	371213(3)
25.XII.37	371213(2)
1.I.38	371129(1)
8.I.38	371217
15.I.38	371217
12.II.38	380127(1)
26.II.38	380218
5.III.38	380224
12.III.38	380228
	380301(1)
19.III.38	380303(2)
26.III.38	380310(2)
	380312
	380313
2.IV.38	⌊170617/⌋
16.IV.38	380319
23.IV.38	380331
14.V.38	380422
25.VI.38	380605
2.VII.38	380618(2)
30.VII.38	380718
	380719(1)
13.VIII.38	380719(2)
	380801
20.VIII.38	380803
	380804
27.VIII.38	380811
10.IX.38	380824
1.X.38	380919(1)
8.X.38	380921
	381007
22.X.38	380500(1)
29.X.38	380929
5.XI.38	380923
	381018

++++

SOCIALIST APPEAL   ++++

19.XI.38	381110		22.VI.40	400617
24.XII.38	381214		29.VI.40	400526
				400625(2)
14.I.39	381228		6.VII.40	400618(2)
10.II.39	⌊390200(1)⌉			400618(3)
14.II.39	⌈390200(2)⌉			400625(1)
17.II.39	⌊390217⌋			400630
21.III.39	⌈390321⌋		10.VIII.40	400727
28.III.39	390306			400802(3)
31.III.39	390324(2)		17.VIII.40	400809
4.IV.39	390318		24.VIII.40	240122(1)
7.IV.39	390311		31.VIII.40	400423(2)
	390324(1)			400806
21.IV.39	390304(1)			400821
	390419			
9.V.39	390422(1)		25.I.41	240416
9.IX.39	390904			
11.IX.39	390902		================	
	390905		SOCIALIST APPEAL(Chicago)	
15.IX.39	390730			
	390911		IX.36	360730(1)
18.IX.39	390730			360815
20.IX.39	⌊230215⌋		1.X.36	360820(2)
	390914			
10.X.39	390925		================	
24.X.39	390906		SOCIALIST APPEAL(London)	
27.X.39	⌊390921⌋	(V.12)	VI.43	381018
31.X.39	390805	(V.20)	X.43	300514
3.XI.39	391023			
14.XI.39	391018		================	
16.XII.39	391207			
23.XII.39	391204(1)		SOCIALISTIK INFORMATION	
	391212			
30.XII.39	391211		III-IV.70	200000(37)
	391217			
			================	
27.IV.40	190113		SOCIALIST VANGUARD(India)	
4.V.40	400423(1)	(I.2)	IV.52	371125(2)
11.V.40	400423(2)			
15.VI.40	400601		================	
	400605			

SOCIALIST WORKER

(183)   22.VIII.70   400227(1)

===============

SOCIÁLNÍ DEMOKRAT

(II.36)   5.XI.20   200000(37)
(II.37)   12.XI.20   200000(37)
(II.38)   18.XI.20   200000(37)
(II.39)   26.XI.20   200000(37)
(II.40)   3.XII.20   200000(37)
(II.41)   10.XII.20   180328(1)

===============

SOCIJALNA MISAO

(VI)   IX.33   310000(38)
                             330314

===============

An SOLAS

(15-16)   Aut-Winter'66
                             340222

===============

SOUS LE DRAPEAU DU SOCIALISME

(41)   IX-X.67   390922
(42)   XI-XII.67   390715

===============

El SOVIET

               [1931]   310929

===============

SOVIET RUSSIA

               31.I.20   191130
               14.II.20   190718(2)
               6.III.20   191029

5.VI.20   ⌊200501(3)⌋
12.VI.20   200208
4.IX.20   200615
27.XI.20   200000(37)
25.XII.20   190309(2)

15.I.21   200000(37)
22.I.21   201107
29.I.21   200000(37)
5.II.21   200000(37)
               201126(1)
12.II.21   200000(37)
5.III.21   201108
12.III.21   201108
26.III.21   200000(37)
2.IV.21   200000(37)
23.IV.21   210306
14.V.21   210323(1)
XI.21   ⌊210916⌋
XII.21   ⌊210929⌋

1.II.22   211110(1)
15.II.22   210819
1.III.22   210000(7)
15.III.22   210000(7)
1.IV.22   210000(7)
15.IV.22   210000(7)
15.V.22   220303(1)
15.VII.22   220513

===============

SOZIALISTISCHE ARBEITERZEITUNG

               [1933]   330126

===============

The SPARK

               VIII.35   350610(1)
               IX.35   350700(1)
               X.35   350722(1)

++++

The SPARK   ++++

(IV	IV.36	360115(1)
	IX.36	360609
	X.36	360730(1)
	II.37	360416
		360708
		360823(2)
		360823(4)
		360827
		361218(1)
	IV.37	370219(1)
	V.37	370313(1)
	VII.37	370423
	VIII.37	370601
	X.37	370808
	XII.37	370612
	III.38	371217
	IV.38	371217
(IV.5)	V.38	371030
(IV.6)	VI.38	380113
(IV.8)	VIII.38	370809
(IV.9)	IX.38	370809
(V.2)	II.39	381010
(V.3)	III.39	381010

=============================

SPARTACIST

| (9) | I-II.67 | 340822 |

=============================

SPARTACUS
(V.21)	29.VI.35	350610(1)
(V.24)	17.VIII.35	350607(1)
		350607(2)
		350700(1)
(V.26)	7.IX.35	350807
(V.30)	19.X.35	350722(1)
		350906
(V.34)	14.XII.35	351031

(VI.11)	30.V.36	360115(1)
		360416
(VI.15)	18.VII.36	360522

=============================

SPARTACUS(Germany)

| (12-13) | IV-V.70 | ⌊400820(4)⌋ |

=============================

SPOKESMAN

| (4) | VI.70 | ⌊160200⌋ |

=============================

SUNDAY EXPRESS

| | 6.III.38 | ⌊380306(2)⌋ |
| | 17.III.40 | 400313 |

=============================

SUNDAY SUN(Australia)

| | 21.XI.37 | 370817 |

=============================

SUNDAY WORKER

| | 10.V.25 | 250403 |
| | 19.VII.25 | 250701 |

=============================

SWIT

| | 13.XII.19 | 191130 |

=============================

SYMPOSIUM

| (III.4) | X.32 | ⌊321000⌋ |

=============================

Das TAGEBUCH

(IX)	1928: 1882	271021
(X)	2.III.29	290225
(X)	9.III.29	290225
(X.46)	16.XI.29	300000(1)

==================

THURINGEN ALLGEMEIN ZEITUNG

| | 26.III.29 | [290323(2)] |

==================

TIDENS TEGN

(19)	24.I.38	371102
		371219
(55)	7.III.38	[380306(2)]
(67)	21.III.38	[380301(2)]
(73)	28.III.38	380303(1)

==================

TIMES

	7.XII.17	171119/
	24.XII.17	171208(2)/
	26.XII.17	[171209(1)/]
	30.XII.17	[171130/]
	3.I.18	171219(3)/
	14.I.18	171228(1)/
	1.II.18	180115/
	6.II.18	180202(1)
	13.II.18	180210(3)
	18.II.18	180217(2)
	25.II.18	[180222(1)]
	27.II.18	180219(3)
	25.VIII.36	360824
	26.VIII.36	360825

==================

TRIBUNA SOCIALISTA

| (4) | IV.63 | 351112 |

==================

De TRIBUNE

(180)	6.V.20	[200425]
(296)	18.IX.20	200128
(74)	27.XII.20	200807(1)
(182)	7.V.21	210429
(227)	30.VI.21	210623
(236)	11.VII.21	210624
(243)	19.VII.21	[210712]
(263-9)	14-18.VIII.21	
		210623
(2)	3.X.21	210907(1)
(11)	13.X.21	210704
(18)	21.X.21	210830
(68)	19.XII.22	221205
(139)	15.III.23	221021
(234)	10.VII.23	230630
(253)	1.VIII.23	[230712]
(254)	2.VIII.23	230618
(86)	11.I.24	[231206(2)]
(90)	26.I.24	240122(1)
(108)	6.II.24	230515
(137)	11.III.24	240223

==================

TROTZ ALLEDEM!

| (II.3) | II.37 | [370200(3)] |

==================

TRUTH

IV.37	370122	
	370127(1)	
	370200(2)	
	370215	
	370313(2)	
	370316	

===========================

TWENTIETH CENTURY(Cambridge)

IV.32	311126
V.32	311126

===========================

UMLILO MOLLO

(I.2)	X.36	360730

===========================

El UNIVERSAL

1937	371129(2)
23.IV.38	380422
7.VI.38	380606

===========================

UNSER KAMPF

(I.1)	1.II.32	271021
		311208
(I.2)	15.II.32	271021
		310325
(I.3)	1.III.32	271021
		311222
		[320130]
(I.4)	15.III.32	271021
		290327
(I.5)	1.IV.32	320301

(I.6)	15.IV.32	271021
		310715(1)
(I.7)	1.V.32	271021
		320000(1)
(I.8)	15.V.32	271021
		320000(1)
(I.9)	1.VI.32	271021
		320509
(I.10)	1.VII.32	271021
		320519(1)
(I.11)	1.VIII.32	271021
		320613(2)
		320616
(I.12)	15.VIII.32	[320500]
		320625
(I.13)	1.IX.32	320802
		320806
(I.14)	15.IX.32	270417
		271021
		320804(2)
(I.15)	15.X.32	320831
(I.16)	15.XI.32	271021
		320000(1)
		321013(1)
		321013(2)
(II.1)	15.I.33	190118
		[321200(2)]
		321200(3)
		321205
(II.2)	II.33	321127
(II.3)	IV.33	330105
(II.4)	1.VI.33	330409
(II.5)	15.VI.33	330330
		330512(1)
		330523
		330525
(II.6)	1.VII.33	330503 ++++

UNSER KAMPF ++++

(II.7)	15.VII.33	330613(1)	(II.1)	I.34	331212
(II.8)	XI.33	330715(1)	(II.2)	I.34	340105
		330817(3)	(II.3)	II.34	340118
					340123
==================			(II.7)	III.34	340222
			(II.8)	III.34	[340300]
UNSER WORT			(II.10)	III.34	340316
(I.2)	IV.33	330223	(II.11)	IV.34	340323
		330310	(II.12)	IV.34	340331
		330314	(II.27)	VII.34	340715
		330323(1)	(II.31)	VIII.34	340710
(I.3)	IV.33	330303(2)	(II.33)	IX.34	340800(3)
		330323(1)			340817(1)
(I.4)	V.33	330303(2)	(II.34)	IX.34	340800(3)
		[330400(3)]	(II.35)	XI.34	310423
		330409	(II.36)	XII.34	330904
(I.5)	V.33	330303(2)			
		330503	(III.1)	II.35	341230(1)
		330507			341230(2)
(I.6)	VI.33	330429			[350200(3)]
		330512(1)	(III.2)	III.35	350130
		330522			350210
		330525	(III.3)	IV.35	350331(1)
		[330609(1)]	(III.4)	V.35	350201
(I.7)	VI.33	330604			[350400]
		330613(1)	(III.5)	V.35	350424
(I.10)	VIII.33	330714	(III.6)	VI.35	350201
		330715(4)			350525(2)
		330719(3)	(III.7)	VII.35	350201
(I.11)	VIII.33	330715(2)			350610(1)
		330813	(III.8)	VIII.35	350607(2)
(I.12)	IX.33	330817(3)			350624(1)
		330828			350700(1)
(I.13)	X.33	330720(1)	(III.9)	IX.35	350607(1)
		330920			350729
		[331000(2)]			350811(1)
(I.14)	XI.33	331001	(III.10)	X.35	[350900(1)]
(I.15)	XI.33	331107			350907(2)
		331110			++++

UNSER WORT ++++

(III.11)	XI.35	350926	(VI.4-5)	X.38	380216
(III.12)	XII.35	351031			380605
(IV.1)	I.36	351126(1)	(VI.6-7)	XII.38	380717
(IV.3)	II.36	350918			380830
		360110			380919(1)
(IV.4)	II.36	350918	(VII.1)	II.39	381108
		360115(1)			381214
		360123		1939	381220
(IV.5)	III.36	360111			
(IV.8)	IV.36	360318			
		360321			
		⌊360400(3)⌋	VADERLAND		
(IV.9)	V.36	⌊360400(2)⌋		1922	⌊220518⌋
		360403			
		360412			
(IV.10)	V.36	360325	VANGUARD(Canada)		
		360416			
		360422		7.I.36	351126(1)
		⌊360500(2)⌋			
(IV.11)	VI.36	360110			
(IV.12)	VI.36	360605	La VERITÀ		
		360609	(1)	III.34	340325
(—)	VIII.36	360815			
		360820(1)			
(IV.14)	IX.36	⌊360500(3)⌋	La VÉRITÉ		
		360700(1)	⌊Note: There are 2 issues numbered (1).		
		360730(1)	The first is dated 15.VIII.29.⌋		
(IV.15)	X.36	360823(1)			
(V.2)	V.37	370219(1)	(1)	13.IX.29	290800(2)
		370316			290804
(V.3)	VIII.37	370617(1)			⌊290900(4)⌋
(V.4)	XI.37	370429	(3)	27.IX.29	290806
(VI.1)	I.38	371129(2)	(5)	11.X.29	290925(2)
(VI.2)	III.38	⌊380308(3)⌋	(7)	25.X.29	291004
(VI.3)	V.38	380308(1)	(8)	1.XI.29	291014
		380309	(9)	8.XI.29	291017
		380331	(11)	22.XI.29	291110
			(14)	13.XII.29	291113 ++++

La VÉRITÉ   ++++

(15)	20.XII.29	291113	(59)	24.X.30	300926(1)
(17)	3.I.30	291221	(60)	31.X.30	300926(1)
(18)	10.I.30	291222(1)	(61)	7.XI.30	301022
(19)	17.I.30	300103(1)	(62)	14.XI.30	300000(1)
(20)	24.I.30	291218	(63)	21.XI.30	220226(1)
(21)	31.I.30	291222(2)	(64)	28.XI.30	291021
		291225	(65)	5.XII.30	⌊301100(3)⌋
		⌊300109⌋	(66)	12.XII.30	⌊301200(1)⌋
		300120	(67)	19.XII.30	⌊301200(1)⌋
					301205
(22)	7.II.30	291227			
(23)	14.II.30	300108	(68)	26.XII.30	⌊301200(1)⌋
(24)	21.II.30	300108	(69)	2.I.31	⌊301200(1)⌋
(25)	28.II.30	300108	(71)	16.I.31	310104
(26)	7.III.30	300213			310107
(27)	14.III.30	300213	(74)	6.II.31	310124
		300301			310126
(29)	28.III.30	300314	(75)	13.II.31	310124
(33)	25.IV.30	300400(1)	(76)	20.II.31	310124
(35)	9.V.30	⌊300500(1)⌋	(78)	6.III.31	300821
(36)	16.V.30	⌊291205⌋	(79)	13.III.31	⌊310300(3)⌋
		⌊300500(2)⌋	(80)	20.III.31	310308
(40)	13.VI.30	300525(1)	(81)	27.III.31	310209
(42)	27.VI.30	300528			310311
(44)	11.VII.30	300514	(84)	17.IV.31	310325
(45)	18.VII.30	300228	(87)	8.V.31	310405
(46)	25.VII.30	300600(2)	(88)	15.V.31	310404
		300610	(89)	22.V.31	310404
		⌊300700(1)⌋	(90)	5.VI.31	310404
		⌊300800(3)⌋	(91)	12.VI.31	310424
(47)	1.VIII.30	⌊300800(3)⌋			310501
(48)	8.VIII.30				
(53)	12.IX.30	300825	(92)	19.VI.31	300525(2)
		300900(1)			301121(2)
(55)	26.IX.30	300600(2)			301212
		300926(2)			310131(1)
(56)	3.X.30	300600(2)			310205
		300926(2)			310213
(57)	10.X.30	280712			310215
		300926(1)			310313 ++++

La VÉRITÉ ++++

(92)	19.VI.31	310414(1)	(131)	10.XI.32	320920
		310420			321030(1)
		310423	(132)	17.XI.32	321006
		310517	(133)	8.XII.32	321122
		310520			321127
		310528(1)			321200(3)
(93)	26.VI.31	310404			⌊321208(2)⌋
(95)	17.VII.31	310708(2)	(134)	15.XII.32	321205
(96)	1.VIII.31	310708(4)	(138)	19.I.33	⌊321200(2)⌋
		310715(1)			330111(2)
		310715(2)	(139)	26.I.33	330111(1)
(98)	1.IX.31	310713			330114
		310714	(142)	16.II.33	⌊321200(6)⌋
(99)	15.IX.31	310825			330205
(106)	28.XI.31	⌊310900(1)⌋	(143)	23.II.33	320613(3)
(107)	12.XII.31	311126			330126
(108)	26.XII.31	311110	(144)	2.III.33	220521
		311208	(145)	9.III.33	220521
(110)	23.I.32	320102			330223
(112)	1.III.32	320127	(146)	16.III.33	330223
(113)	15.III.32	320215(2)			330303(2)
(114)	8.IV.32	320215(1)	(147)	24.III.33	330314
		320301	(148)	31.III.33	330310
(116)	18.V.32	320423			330321
(117)	1.VI.32	320512	(149)	7.IV.33	330323(1)
(120)	i.VII.32	320615			330323(2)
(121)	15.VII.32	320625	(150)	14.IV.33	⌊330300(3)⌋
(122)	1.VIII.32	320613(1)			330323(1)
(123)	15.VIII.32	320802			⌊330400(3)⌋
		320806	(151)	21.IV.33	⌊330300(3)⌋
(124)	5.IX.32	320809			330409
(125)	22.IX.32	320817			330410
(126)	29.IX.32	320818(2)	(152)	28.IV.33	⌊330428⌋
(127)	6.X.32	320913	(153)	5.V.33	⌊330428⌋
(129)	20.X.32	⌊321020(2)⌋	(154)	12.V.33	330429
(130)	3.XI.32	171025(1)/			330503
		321013(1)			⌊330512(2)⌋
		321013(2)	(155)	19.V.33	330507 ++++

La VÉRITÉ   ++++

(156)	26.V.33	330406	(187)	26.I.34	340120(1)
(157)	2.VI.33	330523	(188)	2.II.34	340118
		330525			340123
(158)	9.VI.33	330421	(193)	16.II.34	340118
		330522	(195)	2.III.34	340222
		⌊330609(1)⌋	(196)	9.III.34	⌊340300⌋
		⌊330609(2)⌋	(198)	23.III.34	340316
(159)	16.VI.33	330604	(200)	6.IV.34	340331
(160)	23.VI.33	330613(1)	(202)	20.IV.34	340323
		330618	(203)	27.IV.34	340419
(163)	14.VII.33	330615			⌊340427⌋
		330715(4)	(208)	1.VI.34	⌊340601⌋
(165)	28.VII.33	⌊330728⌋	(209)	8.VI.34	⌊340608(1)⌋
(166)	4.VIII.33	330726			⌊340608(2)⌋
(167)	11.VIII.33	330714	(211)	VI.34	⌊340600(1)⌋
		330719(1)	(216)	3.VIII.34	340715
		330719(3)	(218)	17.VIII.34	340710
		330805			⌊340817(1)⌋
(168)	18.VIII.33	330622	(220)	IX.34	340800(3)
		330813	(225)	2.XI.34	⌊341102⌋
		⌊330818(3)⌋	(226)	9.XI.34	341000(1)
(169)	25.VIII.33	330622	(227)	1.XII.34	⌊341201⌋
(170)	1.IX.33	330817(3)	(228)	15.XII.34	340610
		330826	(229)	5.I.35	341230(1)
		⌊330901(2)⌋	(230)	20.I.35	350112
(171)	8.IX.33	330720(1)	(231)	10.II.35	350126
(172)	15.IX.33	330828	(232)	28.III.35	⌊350328⌋
		330910	(233)	5.IV.35	⌊350405(2)⌋
(174)	6.X.33	330904	(234)	12.IV.35	350130
		330920			350331(1)
(175)	13.X.33	331001	(235)	19.IV.35	350130
(180)	17.XI.33	331107	(236)	26.IV.35	⌊350426⌋
		331110	(237)	3.V.35	⌊350400⌋
(183)	8.XII.33	331123	(238)	10.V.35	350201
(184)	22.XII.33	331212	(240)	25.V.35	350525(2)
			(243)	21.VI.35	350610(1)
			(245)	21.VII.35	350624(1)

++++

La VÉRITÉ ++++

(247)	23.VIII.35	350700(1)
		350722(1)
		350807
(249)	11.X.35	350906
(251)	8.XI.35	350914
(252)	20.XI.35	350918
		351031
(253)	26.XI.35	351126(1)

[New series]

(2)	VI.38	370417(2)
		371030
		380200
		380301(1)
		380310(1)
(3)	15.III.39	191016(2)
(4)	5.V.39	240728
		290711
		380310(3)
		380410
		380418(2)
		380900
		390115
		390116
(6)	VIII.39	390422(1)

[New series]

| (519) | V-VI.60 | 350610(1) |

===

⌐a VÉRITÉ(OCC)

| (20) | 15.IX.41 | 400820(6) |

===

La VÉRITÉ(M)

(II.26)	5.I.18	171209(3)/
(II.27)	6.I.18	161011
(II.67)	15.II.18	[150214]
(II.71)	19.II.18	180217(2)

===

La VIE OUVRIÈRE

(3)	1916	161011
	21.XI.19	190901(3)
	26.XI.20	200731(2)
	15.VII.21++	210704
	2.VI.22	210000(7)
	24.XII.22	221103(1)
	11.V.23	221114(1)
	10.X.23	[230923(2)]
	8.II.24	231208(1)
	21.III.24	210204
	19.III.25	250000(5)
	4.VI.25	250000(5)
	10.VII.25	[250606]
	6.XI.25	240000(24)
	18.XII.25	250828(2)

===

De IVe INTERNATIONALE

(I.1)	XII.38	370828
		380919(1)
		380922
(I.2)	[I.39]	380830
(I.3)	[II.39]	381010
		[390200(1)]
(I.5)	VIII.39	380113
		381007
		381220

De IVe INTERNATIONALE

[New series]

(1)	1938	370824
(2)	1938	371217

========================

La VOIE DE LÉNINE

(1)	IV.39	380216
(11)	15.I.42	[400820(6)]
(IV.5)	11.IX.44	310000(1)
(V.14)	21,28.I.45	380500(1)

========================

La VOIX COMMUNISTE

(I.2)	25.I.31	300213
(I.3)	8.II.31	300213
(I.4)	22.II.31	300213
(I.5)	8.III.31	310124
(I.6)	22.III.31	310124
(I.7)	5.IV.31	300213
		310124
(I.8)	19.IV.31	300213
		310124
(I.9)	3.V.31	310124
(I.10)	17.V.31	310124
		310405
(I.11)	31.V.31	310404
(I.12)	14.VI.31	310404
(I.13)	28.VI.31	310424
(I.16)	9.VIII.31	310715(1)
		310715(2)
(I.17)	23.VIII.31	310715(1)
(I.18)	6.IX.31	310404
(I.20)	4.X.31	310825
(I.25)	13.XII.31	[310900(1)]
(I.26)	27.XII.31	311126

(II.1)	10.I.32	311208
(II.2)	24.I.32	311110
(II.8)	17.IV.32	320301
(II.12)	12.VI.32	320512
(II.14)	10.VII.32	320616
(II.15)	24.VII.32	320625
(II.18)	14.VIII.32	320802
(II.23)	18.IV.32	320804(2)
(II.24)	25.IX.32	320809
(II.25)	2.X.32	320817
(II.26)	9.X.32	320817
(II.28)	23.X.32	320818(2)
(II.29)	30.X.32	321013(2)
		[321020(2)]
(II.30)	6.XI.32	321013(1)
(II.34)	4.XII.32	321123(1)
(II.36)	18.XII.32	321022(1)
		321205
(III.1)	1.I.33	321127
		321220(1)
(III.5)	29.I.33	330111(1)
		[330111(2)]
(III.12)	19.III.33	330223
(III.13)	26.III.33	330223
(III.14)	2.IV.33	330314
(III.15)	9.IV.33	330321
(III.16)	16.IV.33	[330323(1)]
		330323(2)
(III.17)	23.IV.33	[330323(1)]
(III.19)	7.V.33	330409
(III.21)	21.V.33	330429
		330503
(III.22)	28.V.33	330421
		330507
		330512
(III.23)	4.VI.33	[330300(3)]

++++

La **VOIX COMMUNISTE** ++++

(III.24)	11.VI.33	330406	(V.1)	6.I.35	341230(1)
		330523			341230(2)
		330525	(V.2)	13.I.35	341228
(III.25)	18.VI.33	330522	(V.3)	20.I.35	341228
		330525	(V.8)	24.II.35	240729(1)
(III.26)	25.VI.33	330604	(V.9)	3.III.35	240729(1)
		330613(1)	(V.10)	10.III.35	240729(1)
(III.30)	23.VII.33	330715(4)	(V.12)	24.III.35	240729(1)
(III.34)	20.VIII.33	330805	(V.13)	31.III.35	240729(1)
		⌊330818(3)⌋	(V.14)	7.IV.35	350201
(III.35)	27.VIII.33	330719(1)	(V.16)	21.IV.35	350130
(III.36)	3.IX.33	⌊330901(2)⌋			⌊350328⌋
(III.37)	10.IX.33	330622	(V.17)	28.IV.35	350130
(III.38)	17.IX.33	330622			⌊350328⌋
(III.40)	8.X.33	330715(2)			
		330904			

========================

(III.49)	3.XII.33	331107	VOLKSWILLE		
		331110			
(III.52)	24.XII.33	331123	(159)	7.IX.28	271021
			(162)	14.IX.28	271021
(IV.4)	28.I.34	340109	(165)	21.IX.28	271021
		340120(1)	(170)	1.X.28	271021
(IV.6)	11.II.34	340108	(171)	3.X.28	271021
(IV.9)	4.III.34	⌊340304⌋	(172)	6.X.28	271021
(IV.10)	11.III.34	340222	(173)	6.X.28	271021
(IV.15)	15.IV.34	340316	(174)	8.X.28	271021
		340331	(175)	10.X.28	271021
(IV.17)	13.V.34	⌊340513⌋	(176)	13.X.28	271021
(IV.25)	24.VI.34	⌊340608(1)⌋	(178)	15.X.28	271021
(IV.32)	12.VIII.34	340715	(179)	17.X.28	271021
(IV.34)	26.VIII.34	340710	(180)	20.X.28	271021
		⌊340817(1)⌋	(181)	20.X.28	271021
(IV.35)	2.IX.34	340700(3)	(182)	22.X.28	271021
(IV.38)	23.IX.34	240806	(186)	29.X.28	271021
(IV.42)	21.X.34	331107	(209)	8.XII.28	280628
(IV.46)	18.XI.34	341000	(211)	12.XII.28	280628
(IV.47)	25.XI.34	341000	(215)	19.XII.28	280628
(IV.48)	2.XII.34	341000	(216)	22.XII.28	280628 ++++

VOLKSWILLE	++++		
(217)	22.XII.28	280628	
(218)	24.XII.28	280628	
(219)	29.XII.28	280628	
(221)	31.XII.28	280628	
(II.5)	9.I.29	280628	
(II.6)	11.I.29	280628	
(II.7)	12.I.29	280628	
(II.8)	14.I.29	280628	
(II.9)	16.I.29	280628	
(II.14)	26.I.29	280628	
(II.36)	6.III.29	280628	
(II.41)	15.III.29	290212	
(II.54)	10.IV.29	290327	
(II.85)	7.VI.29	290526	
(IV.17)	1.V.31	310100	
(IV.18)	8.V.31	310100	
(IV.19)	15.V.31	310100	
		310415	
(IV.20)	22.V.31	310100	
(IV.21)	30.V.31	310100	
(IV.22)	5.VI.31	310100	
(IV.38)	25.IX.31	⌊310820(1)⌋	
(IV.43)	30.X.31	310912	
(IV.45)	13.XI.31	310825	
(IV.46)	20.XI.31	310825	
(V.17)	27.V.32	320512	
(VI.3)	1.II.33	311208	

===================

VORWAERTS

(201)	28.VIII.10	⌊100828⌋
(72)	26.III.12	⌊120326⌋
	18.XI.17	171111(3)/

===================

VOSSISCHE ZEITUNG

	14.IX.18	180000(5)
	12.VII.31	310708(3)

===================

WAS TUN

(III.12)	⌊VI.⌋70	⌊400820(4)⌋

===================

Der WEG

	1937	370118

===================

WELTBÜHNE

(12)	23.III.26	260215
(9)	1.III.32	320000(1)

NEUE WELTBÜHNE

(4-5)	8.XI.32	320800
(23)	8.VI.33	330528
(25)	22.VI.33	330602
(26)	29.VI.33	330602
(28)	13.VII.33	330610
(30)	27.VII.33	330622
(31)	3.VIII.33	330622
(48)	30.XI.33	331123
(49)	7.XII.33	⌊331101⌋
(50)	14.XII.33	⌊331214⌋
(52)	28.XII.33	331130
(2)	11.I.34	340101
(7)	15.II.34	340120(1)

===================

WORKER(USA)

	1.XII.23	231021

===================

The WORKERS DREADNOUGHT

(V.43)	18.I.19	180930(1)
(VI.33)	11.VIII.19	190306(1)
(VI.38)	13.XII.19	190710
(VI.41)	3.I.20	191031

=========================

WORKERS FIGHT

(I.5)	X.38	370809
(II.2)	I.39	381214
(II.3)	V.39	390311
		390324(1)
(II.4)	IX.39	381220

=========================

WORKERS' FIGHT(Manchester)

(1)	X.67	321127
(7)	VI.68	061004/
		350918

=========================

WORKERS INTERNATIONAL NEWS

(I.1)	18.XII.37	371102
		371116(1)
	II.38	370612
	IV.38	380224
		380301(1)
	V.38	380319
		380331
	VI.38	380309(1)
	VII.38	380113
	VIII.38	380522
	IX.38	380719(2)
		380804
	X.38	370809

I.39	381010
II.39	381010
	381214
III.39	⌊390200(1)⌋
	⌊390200(2)⌋
IV.39	380500(1)
	380618(1)
	390306
VI.39	390311
	390422(1)
X.39	390904
IV.40	391018
VI.40	190113
VII.40	400425
IX.40	371102
	400617
XII.40	400709
	400813
	400817(2)
II.41	⌊400820(6)⌋
III.41	400807
V.41	⌊400820(4)⌋
IX.41	270516
XI.41	⌊400820(3)⌋
XII.41	350918
X-XII.42	260108
	260304
	261126
I.43	380522
	400709
IV.43	330610
	390800
VI.43	390607
VIII.43	⌊400820(4)⌋
I.44	330715(2)
X.44	300514 ++++

WORKERS INTERNATIONAL NEWS		++++
	VII–VIII.45	340710
		340800(3)
	XI.45	321127
	XII.45	250524
	II–III.46	[170317(1)]
	VI–VII.46	[230711]
		370118
		370222
		381222(2)
		400700(2)
	IX–X.46	371125(2)
	I–II.47	320900(1)
	VIII.48	380600
	I–II.49	250000(5)

=======================

WORKERS INTERNATIONAL REVIEW		
(II.2)	IV–V.57	340120(1)
(II.3)	VI–VII.57	280628

=======================

WORKERS PRESS		
(151)	29.IV.70	240728
(152)	30.IV.70	240728
(154)	2.V.70	260215
(155)	5.V.70	260215
(188)	16.VI.70	[160704(1)]

=======================

WORKERS REPUBLIC		
(17)	Spring '67	200423
(18)	V–VI.67	[400820(4)]
(20)	Winter'67-8	230621
(25)	Autumn '69	[400820(4)]

=======================

WORKERS VOICE(So.Africa)		
	XI.44	350420
(V.1)	III.46	[340200(1)]

=======================

The WORKERS WEEKLY		
	23.VI.23	230512(1)
(40)	9.XI.23	231019(1)
(52)	1.II.24	240122(1)

=======================

WORLD(Sweden)		
	1917	171023(3)/

=======================

WORLD OUTLOOK		
(IV.31)	14.X.66	380725(2)
(VI.4)	2.II.68	310820(1)
(VI.11)	22.III.68	350900(4)

=======================

WORLD POLITICS		
	II.67	220302(1)

=======================

YALE REVIEW		
	XII.33	330610
	VI.38	370809

=======================

YOUNG MARXIST		
	Fall '48	350722(1)

=======================

YOUNG SOCIALIST(NY)

| (XII.9) | IX.69 | 220227 |

———————————————————

YOUNG SOCIALIST(Ceylon)

(III.1)	[XI.64]	220226(1)
(III.2)	[1965]	370000(25)
(III.3)	VI.65	390725

———————————————————

YOUNG SPARTACUS

| | III.33 | 320613(3) |
| | XI-XII.35 | 350722(1) |

———————————————————

Die ZUKUNFT(NY)

	II.17	161011
		170121
	III.17	[170300]
	IV.17	[170400(1)]

———————————————————

LIST OF INTERNAL BULLETINS, etc.

of Sections of the Fourth International

and related Organizations

ACD	News Bulletin: American Committee for the Defense of Leon Trotsky.	(LocIISG)
BAO	Boletin de Informacion. Publicado por el Buro Americano-Oriental de la 4 Internacional.	(∉ LocPer)
BCD	Information Bulletin. Issued by the British Committee for the Defence of Leon Trotsky.	(LocIISG)
BI	Bulletin d'Information ⌊de la⌋ 4° Internationale.	(∉ LocABC)
BII	Bulletin intérieur international.	(∉ LocABC)
BIJ	Bulletin intérieur. Edité par le SI des Jeunes pour la QI.	(∉ LocABC)
BIM	Boletino interno. (Seccion mexicana de la LCI.)	(∉ LocPer)
BInt	Bulletin international.	(∉ LocABC)
BIP	Bulletin d'Information et de Presse sur l'URSS.	(∉ LocHIS)
BISI	Bulletin International, édité par le SI (Paris).	(∉ LocABC)
BMIP	Bulletin mensuel d'Information et de Presse du Comité pour l'Enquête sur le Procès de Moscou.	(∉ LocIISG)
BMS	Bulletin of Marxist Studies (New York).	(LocPer)
BMS(E)	Bulletin of Marxist Studies (England).	(LocPer)
BOC	Bolletino dell'Opposizione Comunista Italiana.	(∉ LocIISG)
BQI	Bulletin de la Quatrième Internationale.	(LocHIS)
CES	Bulletin publié par la Comité européenne du Secrétariat International ⌊de la 4° Internationale⌋.	(∉ LocIISG)
CIste	Correspondance Internationaliste.	(∉ LocPer)
CLA	Internal Bulletin: Communist League of America.	(LocPPA)
ClarProl	Claridad Proletaria. Boletin en español de la Liga Comunista e America (Oposicion de Izquierda).	(∉ LocIISG)
CLB	Internal Bulletin: Communist League (British Section), International Left Opposition (Bolshevik-Leninist).	(LocPer)
CLO	International Bulletin: Communist Left Opposition (Internal Bulletin).	(∉ LocPer)
DCL	Internal Document: Communist League of America.	(∉ LocPer)
Doc	Document. Source unspecified.	(LocPer)
DocSI	Document: Secrétariat International.	(LocPer)
EB	Educational Bulletin: Socialist Workers Party (USA).	(LocHIS)
EB(A)	Eerste Bundel: Comite van Revolutionnaire Marxisten, Amsterdam.	(LocPer)

GBL	Bulletin Intérieur: Groupe Bolchevik-Léniniste.	(∉ LocPPA)
IBF	Information Bulletin, issued by the International Bureau, Fourth International.	(LocHIS)
ICE	Boletin Hispano-Americano, publicado por la Izquerda Comunista Española (Seccion española de la Op. Com. Int.)	(∉ LocPer)
ICL	International Bulletin: International Communist League.	(∉ LocPer)
IDB	Informatie en Discussie Bulletin (IS FI).	(∉ LocPer)
IenP	Informatie en Persdienst van het Comité voor Recht und Waarheid.	(LocPer)
IIB	International Information Bulletin: IS FI.	(∉ LocPPA)
IIB(G)	Internes Internationales Bulletin.	(∉ LocABC)
III	International Internal Bulletin: IS FI.	(∉ LocPPA)
IIM	Internal Bulletin: CLA. International Information Material.	(∉ LocPer)
IJI	Internationale Jugend-Information.	(∉ LocABC)
IKD	Informationsdienst: Internationale Kommunisten Deutschland (früher Linke Opposition).	(∉ LocABC)
Het Kompas	Het Kompas	(LocIISG)
KLO	Internationales Bulletin der Kommunistischen Links-Opposition. (cf OCG.)	(LocHIS + IISG)
LCA	Bulletin de la Ligue des Communistes Internationalistes (Amsterdam)	(LocHIS + IISG)
LCB	Bulletin Interieur de la Ligue Communiste Internationaliste (Belgium).	(LocHIS + IISG)
LCI	Bulletin de la LCI: publié par le SI.	(∉ LocABC)
LKI	Bulletin der Liga der Kommunisten-Internationalisten (Bolschewiki-Leninisten).	(LocABC + IISG)
NIB	New International Bulletin: League for Revolutionary Workers Party. [Note: This organization is not a section of the Fourth International.]	(LocIISG)
OCG	Bulletin International de l'Opposition de Gauche. (cf. BInt and KLO)	(LocHIS + IISG)
OCI	Bulletin de l'Opposition Communiste Italienne (Paris). (cf. BOC)	(LocIISG)

PDB	Pre-Plenum Discussion Bulletin, SWP(USA).	(LocHIS)
POI	Bulletin Intérieur: Parti Ouvrière Internationaliste.	(∅ LocPer)
PSR	Bulletin Interieur: Parti Socialiste Révolutionnaire.	(∅ LocABC)

RSL	Internal Discussion Bulletin, Revolutionary Socialist League (Britain).	(LocPer)
RSP	Bulletijn der RSP (Trotskysten).	(LocPer)

SIP	Service d'Information et de Presse.	(LocABC + HIS+ IISG)
SPC	Internal Bulletin of the Organizing Committee for the Socialist Party Convention, USA.	(LocPPA)
SWP	Internal Bulletin: Socialist Workers Party, USA.	(LocPPA)

Voz	La Voz Leninista. (Boletin del Gruppo Bolchevique-Leninista de España).	(∅ LocPer)

WP	International Information Bulletin: National Committee, Workers Party, USA.	(LocPPA)

CONCORDANCE TO BULLETINS

ACD				BIM		
(3)	3.II.37	370127(1)		(3)	VII.38	380422
		370203				380606

==================

==================

BAO				BInt		
(3)	I.38	380607		(5)	III.31	300516
		380830				310108
				(6)	IV.31	310217
				(8)	VI.31	310609

==================

			(9-10)	VII-VIII.31	310531
BCD					310618
(2)	VII.37	370306			310624
		370518			310629
					310702
			(13)	XI.31	311107
			(14)	III.32	311228

==================

==================

BI				BIP		
(2)	IV.38	380102		(1)	VI.39	381222(1)
		380126				390214
(3)	V.38	360711				390310
		371202				390422(1)
		380121(1)				390501
		380121(2)		(2)	VIII.39	390307(2)
(--)	XI.39	390730				390607
						390609

==================

==================

BII				BISI		
(1)	IV.37	370323		(2-3)	IV.33	330307
						330312

==================

					330317(1)
BIJ				(4)	V.33	330421
	10.XI.[36]	360101				330427

==================

==================

BMIP

(2-3)	II-III.37	370127(1)
		370215

====================

BMS		BMS
(1)	VIII.57	240421(2)
		270403
		280302
		320922(1)
		320926
		380105
(4)	VII.62	330228
		390409

====================

BMS(E)

(I.2)	Autumn '68	230923(2)

====================

BOC

(2)	15.VI.31	310415
(3)	15.VIII.31	310609
(4)	20.XI.31	310715(1)
(5)	15.XII.31	311126
(6)	15.I.32	311208
(7)	15.II.32	⌊311200⌋
		320000(1)
(8)	15.IV.32	320301
(11)	15.IX.32	320802
(12)	15.XII.32	321127
(13)	1.II.33	330111(1)
(16)	15.VI.33	330604
		[330609(1)]

====================

BQI

(1)	VI.39	381222(1)
		390214
		390310 ++++

(1)	++++	VI.39	390422(1)
			390501
(2)		VIII.39	390307(2)
			390607
			390609

====================

CES

(4)	30.X.39	381007
		390306
		390311
		390904

====================

CIste

(9)	5.XI.39	390730
(10)	12.XI.39	391003
(11)	20.XI.39	390925
(12-13)	8.XII.39	390925
(2)	25.IV.40	400214

====================

CLA

	1931	310728
(2)	VII.32	310523(2)
		311125(1)
		311125(2)
		320105
		320115
		320210
		320519(1)
		320519(2)
(4)	1932	320818(1)
		321020(1)
		321113
(6)	15.I.33	321013(4)
(8)	28.I.33	321228(1)
		321228(2)
		330104(2) ++++

CLA   ++++

(9)	1933	321216
(11)	31.III.33	330317(1)
(12)	19.IV.33	330329(1)
(13)	29.IV.33	330307
		330417
		330715(2)
		330720(1)
		330727
(15)	VI.34	331008
		340405
(16)	IX.34	340700(2)
(17)	X.34	340700(3)
		340806

=============================

ClarProl

(5)	I.34	330720(1)

=============================

CLB

(8)	[VI.33]	330615
(11)	12.VIII.33	330715(1)
		330715(2)
(12)	28.VIII.33	330727
(13-14)	27.IX.33	330831(1)
		330901
		330910
(15-16)	24.X.33	330903(2)
		330916
		330925
		331002(2)

=============================

CLO

(2)	1.III.31	301004
		301012
		[301100(6)]
		301126
(3)	1931	301129(1)
(4)	1931	310124

(5)	VIII.31	300516
		310108
		310131(2)
(6)	1931	310217
(8)	1931	310609
(17)	I.33	310115
(II.1)	II.33	330400(1)
(II.2-3)	III.33	330400(1)

=============================

DCL

	1932	311222

=============================

Doc

A		290331(1)
B		391018
C		351118
E		341101
F		341216
G		350302
H		[350200(3)]
		390925

=============================

DocSI

	1932	320520(2)

=============================

EB

	V.48	320519(1)
		380400(2)
		380531(1)
		380720

=============================

EB(A)

	14.IV.45	370809
		370828
		371217
		380113
		380115
		380308(1)

=================

GBL

(4)	[VIII.31]	310820(2)
		310820(3)
(—)	10.IV.32	311222
(5)	22.IX.33	330918
(9)	XII.35	350703
		350711
		350722(2)
		350730(1)
		350801
		350811(2)
		350907(1)
		351118
		351121
		351125
		351129(1)
(10)	13.XII.35	351203(1)
		351204
		351205
		351206
		351209
(15)	10.V.36	360327
		360422

=================

IBF

	VII.37	370320
		370323
		370512

=================

ICE

(I.2)	1.VIII.33	330413

=================

ICL

(2)	IX.34	331204(2)
		[340900(2)]
		[340900(3)]

=================

IDB

(1)	1.VII.37	360715
		370323
(3)	XI.37	370921
		370928
(4)	I.38	370306
		371102

=================

IenP

(3)	VII.37	370518
(4-5)	VIII-IX.37	370417(2)

=================

IIB

	XI.35	350223
(2)	IV.38	370824
		380102
		380126

=================

IIB(G)				Het KOMPAS		
(1)	IV.38	370824			III.46	400630
		370914			IX.46	⌊400820(4)⌋
		380102			XI.47	291014
		380126			III.48	291014
	V.38	380500(1)			I.52	360427

===========

III		
(3)	1938	370914
		371001
		380102
		380126
		380531(2)
		380602

KLO		
(2)	XI.30	301004
		301012
		301126
(3)	I.31	301129(1)
(4)	II.31	310124
(6)	IV.31	310217
(12)	XI.31	310929
(15)	III.32	320307(2)
(17)	VI.32	310115
		320509

===========

IIM		
	1932	310925(1)
		320307(1)
		320522(2)

===========

IJI		
(II.2)	III.36	351107(1)

===========

IKD		
(I.9)	20.XII.33	331116

===========

LCA		
(1)	1.V.35	350305
(2)	1.VI.35	350424
(3)	VII.35	350700(1)
(4)	1.IX.35	350729
		350811(1)
		350823(2)
(5)	X.35	350420
		⌊350900(3)⌋
		350914
		350926
(6)	XII.35	350918
		351016
		351020
		351022 ++++

LCA	++++		
(7-8)	V.36	360123	
		360403	
		360412	
		360422	

=================

LCB			
	IV.35	350302	
(3)	IX.35	350718	
		350728	
		350811(4)	
		350812	
	1935	350900(2)	
(4)	XI.35-I.36	351016	
		351104(2)	
		351113	
		351126(3)	
		351230	

=================

LCI			
(2)	XI.33	331116	
(4)	VI.34	340405	
(5)	VII.34	⌊340300⌋	
(7-8)	V.36	360123	
		360403	
		360412	
		360422	

=================

LKI			
(1)	I.34	330818(2)	
		331204(2)	
		340111	
(2)	VI.35	350305	
		350415	
(4)	VIII.35	350420	
(5)	X.35	350823(2)	

=================

NIB			
(II.1)	III.37	370118	

=================

OCG			
(2)	XI.30	301004	
		301126	
(3)	I.31	301129(1)	
(5)	III.31	300516	
		310108	
		310131(2)	
(6)	IV.31	310217	
(8)	VI.31	310609	
(10)	X.31	310900(2)	
(12)	X.31	310929	
(13)	I.32	311107	
		311117	
(14)	III.32	311228	
(15)	III.32	320315	
(17)	VI.32	310115	
		320509	
		320522(1)	
		320524(1)	
(19)	XII.32	321216	++++

OCG   ++++

(2)	II.33	[321200(2)]
(4)	IV.33	310927
		330221
		330312
		330329(1)
		330400(1)
		330417
(5)	V.33	[330400(5)]
(6)	VI.33	330206
(7)	VIII.33	330715(2)
		330720(1)
(9)	IX.33	330901(1)
(10)	XII.33	331116
		331130

==============

OCI

(2)	VI.31	310415
(3)	[VIII.31]	310609
(5)	1931	311126
(8)	1932	320501
(11)	1932	320802

==============

PDB

| (III.1) | VIII.40 | 400612 |
| (III.2) | IX.40 | 400615 |

==============

POI

(1)	15.XI.37	371022
(4)	20.II.38	370914
		380102
		380127(2)

==============

PSR

(7)	VIII.37	360718
		360719
(9)	XI.37	370824
(10)	XII.37	370811
		370903
		371027
(11)	I.38	371104
(12)	II.38	370118
(13)	IV.38	371125(2)
		380126
(14)	V.38	371202
		380121(1)
		380121(2)

==============

RSL

| (1) | X.38 | 380602 |

==============

RSP

| | I.40 | 390925 |

==============

SIP

	20.VI–4.VII.36	
		360522
(8)	13.IX.36	360820(2)
		360826(1)
(11)	2.X.36	360923
(14)	1.XII.36	360823(2)
		360823(4)
		360827
(18)	16.III.37	370118
(19–20)	VI.37	370323 ++++

SIP   ++++

(21-22)	VIII.37	370518
		370706

=================

SPC

(1)	X.37	370824
		370914
		370923
		370928
		370929
(2)	XI.37	371104
(3)	XII.37	370811
		370903
		371027
		371127(2)
(5)	XII.37	371208

=================

SWP

(I.2)	1938	380519
		380531(1)
(I.3)	VIII.38	371001
		380102
		380126
		380531(2)
		380602
(I.5)	VIII.38	360718
		360719
		371022
		371202
		380121(1)
		380121(2)
(I.6)	VIII.38	380607
		380704
(I.7)	VIII.38	380720
		380729

(I.9)	VI.39	390404
		390405
		390411
(II.1)	10.X.39	390925
(II.2)	6.XI.39	391018
		391021
		391022
(II.4)	20.XII.39	391106
(II.5)	XII.39	391124
(II.6)	I.40	391219
		391220
		400103
		400104
		400105
(II.7)	I.40	390400(2)
		391215(2)
(II.9)	I.40	400107
(II.11)	II.40	400124
(III.2)	1940	400807
(VII.2)	IV.45	371208
(XV.10)	IV.53	400615

=================

SYL

	XI.35	350323(1)

=================

VOZ

(2)	VII.39	390501

=================

WP

(1)	1935	[350200(2)]
		350226
		350228 ++++

<u>WP</u>   ++++

(2)   7.IX.35   350610(2)
                      350613
                      350730(3)
                      350811(2)
                      350811(4)

(3)   12.II.36   351118
                      350811(3)
                      351130

====================

CONCORDANCE TO HARVARD ARCHIVES

T

3	180126/	792	*230328	1019	271001
7	180118(3)/	794	230416	1021	271004
9	180202(2)	795	230417	1023	271006
34	180815(2)	796	230418	1030	*⌊271000(2)⌋
67	181101			1032	271024
		818	240702	1039	271100(2)
108	190101	868	260304	1048	*271109
118	190110(1)	870	260325	1053	271115
119	190111(2)		260400(2)	1061	271218
139	190322(1)	873	*260402		
152	190410(2)	875	260414	1108	280200
194	190512(3)	881	260723	1161	280228
		894	260919	1179	280310
204	190517(1)	896	261016	1189	280302
254	190601(2)	908a	261214(1)		280400(1)
		908b	261214(2)	1197	280305
321	190727(1)	913	270106		
342	190811	918	270120	1401	⌊280000(11)⌋
355	190906(3)	928	270221		
369	191017(2)	934	270304	1509	280523
		937	270318	1516	280524
422	200122(2)	938	270329	1530	280525
431	200211(2)	941	270526(2)	1541	280526(1)
		946	270418	1578	⌊280000(11)⌋
516	200511(3)	950	270517(2)	1588	*⌊280600⌋
533	200604	951	270517(2)		
544	200713(1)	955	*270505	1613	280602
545	200713(2)	958	270604		
565	200817(3)	959	270609(1)	1738	280526(2)
		965	*270628(1)	1770	280624
623	201119	966	270628(2)		
661	210321	979	270713	1943	280714
671	210503	993	*270804	1968	280717(2)
		994	270808		
714	211206			2148	280800
746	220418	1001	*⌊270900(3)⌋		
747	*220419	1007	270903	2418	280830(2)
764	221212	1009	270900(2) ?		
773	230115	1010	270906	2538	280911
774	210807	1015	270912		
	220803	1018	270930	2642	280922
	230120				
775	230125			2712	281002(1) ?
778	230213			2713	281002(2)
				2766	281013
				2768	281014

T

2819	281020	3028	*270219	3106	271119(1)
2820	281020	3033	270322(2)	3107	271118
2868	281107	3036	270331	3108	[271119(2)]
2874	281110	3038	270403	3112	280509
2899	281124	3039	270405	3115	280628
2912	281216(1)	3040	270405	3116	280628
2945	290120	3041	270412	3117	280628
2950	290212	3042	270414	3118	280712
2952	180912(2) ?	3047	270416	3119	280712
2953	181201(1)	3053	270507	3120	280712
2954	190300(2)	3055	270609(2)	3121	280712
2956	190805(1)	3057	270516	3122	280103
2962	230213	3058	270516		300207(1)
2963	230223	3061	270524	3124	280715
2964	230306	3062	270528(2)	3125	280717(1)
2969	241130	3064	270527(2)	3126	280723
2975	251222(1)	3065	270528(1)	3127	280820
2976	260108	3066	270528(1)	3128	[280900]
2978	260119	3071	270600(1)	3129	[280900]
2979	260213(1)		270600(2)	3130	280909(1)
2980	260213(2)	3072	270623	3131	280912
2983	260412	3073	270625	3132	280912
2985	260519	3074	270627	3136	280929
2986	260606	3075	270628	3140	281000(2) ?
2987	260609	3080	270801	3141	281004
2989	*[260700(1)]	3081	270802	3142	281004
2990	*[260700(3)]	3085	*270806	3143	281100
2993	260711	3089	270900(1)	3144	281100
	320804(1)	3092	270924	3145	281021
2995	260727	3093	270925	3146	281021
2996	260723 ?	3094	270927	3150	281111
2997	*260813(1)	3098	271108(1)	3151	281111
2998	*260813(2)	3099	271021	3154	281200
3003	260700	3100	271022	3155	281200
3006	260919	3101	271102(1)	3160	290600(3)
3007	260923	3102	271023	3161	290600(3)
3008	260927	3103	271108(2)	3162	[310000(34)]
3016	261209	3104	271113	3168	290600(2)
3017	[261212]	3105	271113	3169	290600(2)
3024	320804(1)				

T

3173	290225	3229	⌊290900(3)⌋	3300	300213
3174	290415(2)	3231	⌊290900(4)⌋	3301	300208
3176	290304(1)	3232	⌊290900(5)⌋	3302	300301
3177	290305		290930	3303	300329
3178	290308	3233	290804 ?	3304	300400(1)
3179	290320	3234	290907	3305	⌊300400(3)⌋
3183	290323(1)	3239	290925(2)	3306	300402
3185	⌊290323(2)⌋	3240	290925(1)	3307	300413(1)
3186	290329	3242	⌊291000(1)⌋	3308	300422
3188	290331(1)	3243	291004	3309	300425
3192	301100(1)	3244	291014	3310	⌊300500(3)⌋
3193	290422	3245	291017	3311	⌊300500(1)⌋
3195	290424	3247	291021	3312	300514
3197	290425	3249	⌊291100(1)⌋	3315	300525(1)
3198	290522(1)	3250	291100(2)	3316	300528
3200	290526	3253	291107	3317	300530
	290707	3254	291109	3318	⌊300800(2)⌋
3202	290600(1)	3255	⌊291126⌋	3319	300600(2)
3204	290601	3256	291130(2)	3320	300600(2)
3205	⌊290611⌋	3258	291220	3321	300600(2)
3206	290612	3259	291221	3324	300715
3207	290614	3260	291221	3326	⌊300700(2)⌋
3209	⌊290626⌋	3261	291222(1)	3327	⌊300800(1)⌋
3210	⌊290300(1)⌋	3262	291228	3328	⌊300800(3)⌋
3211	⌊290726⌋	3279	*300000(35)	3330	⌊300700(1)⌋
3212	⌊290726⌋	3280	⌊300109⌋		300801
3213	⌊290700⌋	3282	300103(1)	3331	⌊300800(2)⌋
3214	⌊290700⌋	3285	300108	3332	300801
3215	290701	3288	300120	3333	300821
3216	290715	3289	300120	3334	300825
3217	290727(2)	3290	300122	3335	300826
3218	290727(1)	3292	⌊300300(2)⌋	3337	⌊300900(2)⌋
3219	290806	3293	300206	3338	300900(1)
3220	290811	3294	300207(2)	3339	⌊301000(2)⌋
3223	290824	3295	300207(1)	3340	⌊301000(3)⌋
3224	290824	3296	300207(1)	3341	⌊300900(2)⌋
3227	⌊290900(1)⌋	3297	300207(1)		⌊301000(4)⌋
3228	⌊290900(2)⌋	3298	300209	3343	⌊300900(2)⌋
		3299	300209	3345	301004

T

3346	300917	3403	310802	3457	321007
3349	301121(1)	3405	[310900(3)]	3462	321123(1)
3350	⌊301100(3)⌋	3406	310902	3463	321104
3352	301205	3409	310913(1)	3466	321122
3356	310104	3410	310925(1)	3469	321127
3357	310107	3412	311107	3470	321127
3358	310124	3413	311117	3471	321127
3364	310217	3414	311126	3472	321127
3366	[310300(3)]	3416	311208	3475	321200(3)
3367	[310300(3)]	3417	311222	3476	321205
3368	[310300(4)]	3421	[311200]	3479	321208(1)
3369	[310200(3)]	3422	320102	3480	321211
3370	⌊310300(5)⌋	3423	320104	3481	321216
3371	⌊310300(3)⌋	3426	320229	3484	321220(1)
3373	310308	3427	320423	3486	321228(2)
3375	310311	3428	⌊320508⌋	3487	321231
3377	310325	3429	320519(1)	3490	240618(1)
3378	310100	3431	[320700(2)]	3497	320512
3379	310404	3432	320613(1)	3498	330111(1)
3380	310412	3433	320613(2)	3500	330111(2)
3381	310415	3434	320613(3)	3501	330114
3383	310528(1)	3436	320725	3502	330126
3384	310501	3437	320804(1)	3503	330128(1)
3385	310523(1)	3438	320806	3505	⌊321200(6)⌋
3387	310609	3439	320917	3509	330223
3388	310612	3441	320818(1)	3511	330228
3389	310613	3443	321030(1)	3512	⌊330400(3)⌋
3391	310618	3444	320831	3514	330303(2)
3392	310624	3445	320902	3516	[330300(1)]
3393	310701	3446	320902	3517	330306
3394	310708(1)	3447	320902	3518	330307
3395	310708(2)	3448	320902	3519	330310
3397	310713	3449	320902	3520	330312
3398	310715(2)	3450	[320900(2)]	3522	330513
3399	310715(1)	3452	320920	3523	330317(1)
3400	310714	3453	320922(1)	3526	330321
3401	310728		320926	3527	330323(1)
3402	310730	3456	321003	3530	330329(1)

T

3531	330330	3576	330805	3657	340316
3532	⌊330400(3)⌋	3579	⌊330800(1)⌋	3660	340325
3533	330401	3583	330813	3662	340323
3534	330409	3584	330817(3)	3664	⌊341200⌋
3536	330410	3587	330903(1)	3665	340817(2)
3538	330421	3589	330826	3666	341000
3540	⌊330400(5)⌋ ?	3590	330828	3669	350110
3541	330427	3591	330831(1)	3670	350300(1)
3542	330429	3592	330901	3671	⌊350328⌋
3543	330507	3593	330904	3672	350420
3546	330510	3595	330910	3673	350700(1)
3547	330512(1)	3597	330916	3674	350607(2)
3548	330519	3599	330918 ?	3675	350610(2)
3550	330522	3603	330925		350613
3551	330523	3607	331001	3677	350624(1)
3552	330525	3608	331002(1)	3682	350722(1)
3553	330528	3613	331107	3683	350722(1)
3554	330602	3614	331110	3685	350729
3555	330604	3618	⌊340200(1)⌋ ?	3686	350729
3556	330607(1)	3622	331204(1)	3687	350811(2)
3557	330610	3625	331123	3688	351118
	331102	3627	331130	3689	350823(1)
3558	330613(1)	3630	331212	3690	350823(1)
3559	330615	3632	340610 ?	3691	350829
3560	330616	3634	331130	3692	350829
3561	330617	3635	340101	3693	⌊350900(3)⌋
3563	330622	3637	340105	3694	⌊350900(3)⌋
3564	330609(1)	3638	340109	3695	⌊350900(1)⌋
3565	330613(2)	3641	340111	3696	⌊350900(1)⌋
3566	330706	3642	340118	3697	350926
3567	330712	3643	340120(1)	3698	350926
3568	330714	3645	340120(2)	3699	350907
3569	330715(3)	3647	340124	3700	350914
3570	330715(4)	3649	340222	3701	350907(2)
3571	330719(2)	3651	340313	3702	350907(2)
3572	330719(1)	3652	340313	3703	350918
3573	330719(3)	3653	340313	3704	350918
3574	330720(1)	3654	331110	3706	351001
3575	330726	3656	340316	3707	351001

T

3709	351015	3909	360328	3954	360815
3710	351015	3910	360328	3955	360820(2)
3711	351020	3911	360328	3956	360821
3712	351022	3912	360403	3958	360823(1)
3713	351022	3913	360412	3960	360826(2)
3714	351016	3914	⌊360500(3)⌋	3962	360825
3715	351031	3915	⌊360500(3)⌋	3965	⌊360700(3)⌋
3716	351031	3916	360416	3966	361000(1)
3717	351100(2)	3917	360416	3967	361218(1)
3718	351100(2)	3920	360422	3968	370109(1)
3719	351104(1)	3921	360422	3970	370112
3720	351104(1)	3922	360522	3971	370116
3721	351107(1)	3923	360603	3973	370118
3722	351107(1)	3924	360605	3975	370120
3723	351107(2)	3925	360605	3976	370120
3724	351107(2)	3926	360609	3978	370122
3725	351112	3927	360609	3979	370122
3726	351112	3928	360610	3980	370122
3728	351126(1)	3929	360610	3981	370122
3729	351126(1)	3934	360704	3987	370123(1)
3740	351100(1)	3935	360708	3988	370123(1)
		3936	360708	3989	370123(2)
3892	360110	3937	360709(1)	3990	370123(2)
3893	360110	3938	360709(1)	3992	370123(3)
3894	360111	3939	360709(2)	3993	370124(1)
3895	360111	3940	360709(2)	3994	370124(2)
3896	360115(1)	3942	360727	3995	370124(2)
3897	360115(1)	3943	360727		
3898	360123	3944	360730	4008	370126(1)
3899	360123	3945	360730	4009	370126(1)
3900	360128(1)	3946	361013	4010	370126(1)
	360128(2)	3947	361013	4011	370126(2)
3903	360318	3948	361013	4012	370126(2)
3904	⌊360400(3)⌋	3949	361013	4013	370126(2)
3905	⌊360400(3)⌋	3950	361013	4014	370126(3)
3906	360321	3951	361013	4015	370126(3)
3907	360325	3952	361013	4016	370126(3)
3908	360325	3953	361013	4019	370127(1)
				4020	370127(1)

T

4021	370127(2)	4084	370209	4147	370512
4022	370127(2)	4085	370209	4148	370518
4023	370127(2)	4086	370209	4149	370518
4029	370128	4087	370209	4151	370522
4030	370128	4088	370209	4152	370522
4031	370128	4089	370209	4157	370617(1)
4034	370200(2)	4090	370209	4158	370617(1)
4035	370200(2)	4093	370214	4159	370617(2)
4036	370200(2)	4094	370214	4162	370629
4037	370129(2)	4095	370214	4163	370629
4038	370129(2)	4096	370214	4164	371116(2)
4039	370129(1)	4097	370211	4165	371116(2)
4040	370129(1)	4098	370211	4166	371116(2)
4041	370129(1)	4099	370211	4167	371116(2)
4042	370129(3)	4100	370215	4168	371116(2)
4043	370129(3)	4101	370215	4169	371116(2)
4044	370129(3)	4102	370215	4170	371116(2)
4048	370130	4103	370219(1)	4171	371116(2)
4049	370130	4104	370219(1)	4172	371116(2)
4050	370130	4105	370222	4173	371116(2)
4055	370131(3)	4106	370222	4174	371116(2)
4056	370131(3)	4117	370303(1)	4175	371116(2)
4057	370131(3)	4118	370303(1)	4176	370706
4058	370131(4)	4119	370305	4177	370706
4059	370131(4)	4120	370305	4179	370730
4060	370131(4)	4121	370306	4180	370730
4061	370131(1)	4122	370306	4181	370900
4062	370131(1)	4123	370308	4183	370808
4063	370131(1)	4124	370308	4184	370808
4064	370131(2)	4125	370313(1)	4185	370809
4065	370131(2)	4126	370313(1)	4186	370809
4066	370131(5)	4127	370313(2)	4187	370809
4067	370131(5)	4128	370316	4188	370809
4068	370131(5)	4129	370316	4189	370809
4069	370131(6)	4131	370323	4190	370809
4070	370131(6)	4141	370423	4192	370816
4074	370201	4142	370423	4193	370816
4075	370201	4145	370429	4194	370816
4076	370201	4146	370429	4195	370817

T

4196	370817	4245	371208	4297	380303(2)
4199	370824	4250	371213(1)	4301	380304(1)
4200	370824	4251	371213(1)	4302	380305
4201	370828	4252	371213(1)	4303	380306(1)
4202	370828	4253	371213(2)	4305	⌊380306(2)⌋
4203	370903	4254	371213(2)	4308	380307
4204	370905	4255	371213(3)	4309	380307
4205	370905	4257	371217	4311	380308(2)
4206	370905	4258	371217	4312	380308(1)
4207	370913	4260	380102	4313	380308(1)
4208	370914	4261	380105	4315	380309
4209	370921	4262	380105	4316	380309
4210	370921	4263	380108	4317	380310(1)
4211	370922	4264	380108	4318	380310(1)
4212	370923	4265	380108	4319	380310(2)
4213	370925	4266	380113	4320	380310(2)
4214	370928	4267	380113	4321	380311
4215	371001	4268	380115	4322	380311
4216	371006	4269	380115	4323	380312
4221	371022	4270	380121(1)	4324	380312
4222	371027	4271	380121(1)	4325	380313
4223	371030	4272	380126	4326	⌊380300(2)⌋
4224	371030	4273	380127(1)	4327	⌊380300(2)⌋
4225	371030	4274	380127(1)	4328	⌊380400(1)⌋
4226	371102	4275	380216	4329	⌊380400(1)⌋
4227	371102	4276	380216	4330	380317(1)
4229	371104	4277	380216	4331	380317(1)
4230	371104	4278	380218	4332	380317(2)
4231	371116(1)	4279	380218	4333	380319
4233	371125(1)	4280	380220	4334	380319
4234	371125(1)	4281	380220	4337	380331
4235	371125(2)	4282	380204	4338	380331
4236	371125(2)	4284	380224	4339	380400(2)
4237	371129(1)	4285	380224	4340	380500(1)
4238	371129(1)	4286	380224	4341	380500(1)
4239	371129(2)	4291	380302	4342	380500(1)
4240	371203	4292	380302	4343	380418(1)
4241	371203	4293	380303(1)	4344	380418(1)
4244	371208	4294	380303(1)	4345	380422

T

4346	380519	4394	380725(2)	4451	380105
4348	380522	4395	380729	4452	380105
4349	380522	4400	380801	4456	381108
4352	380531(1)	4401	380801	4457	381108
4353	380531(1)	4402	380803	4465	381114
4354	380531(2)	4403	380804	4473	381128
4355	380531(2)	4406	380811	4474	381201
4356	380601(2)	4407	380811	4475	381201
4357	380607	4412	380824	4478	381202
4358	380605	4413	380824	4479	381202
4359	380605	4415	380830	4484	381214
4360	380610	4416	380830	4485	381214
4365	380618(1)	4421	380917	4486	381220
4366	380618(1)	4422	380917	4487	381220
4367	380618(2)	4423	380919(1)	4488	381222(1)
4368	380618(2)	4424	380922	4489	381222(1)
4370	380703(1)	4425	380919(2)	4490	381222(2)
4371	380703(1)	4426	380919(2)	4491	381222(2)
4372	380703(2)	4426.9	380920	4492	381222(3)
4373	380703(2)	4427	380921	4493	381222(3)
4374	380705	4428	380921	4494	381228
	[cf. 4362-4]	4429	380923	4495	381228
4376	380706	4430	380923	4496	381230
4377	380706	4431	380929	4504	390111
4379	380710	4432	380929	4505	[390217]
4380	380717	4433	381009	4506	[390217]
4381	380717	4434	381009	4507	[390200(1)]
4384	380718	4435	381010	4508	[390200(1)]
4385	380718	4436	381010	4509	390130(1)
4386	380719(1)	4440	381018	4510	390130(1)
4387	380719(1)	4441	381018	4511	390130(2)
4388	380719(2)	4442	381018	4513	[390200(2)]
4389	380719(2)	4443	381022(1)	4514	[390200(2)]
4390	380723	4444	381022(1)	4517	390214
4390.9	380720	4447	381022(2)	4518	390214
4391	380723	4448	381022(2)	4519	390418
4392	380724	4449	381022(3)	4523	390418
4393	380724	4450	381022(3)	4524	390418

T

4525	390418	4572	390609	4615	390905
4526	390418	4573	390609	4616	390905
4527	390418	4574	390610(2)	4617	390906
4528	390418	4575	390610(2)	4618	390906
4529	390418	4576	390610(3)	4620	390907
4530	390418	4577	390610(3)	4621	390907
4532	⌊390321⌋	4578	390610(4)	4622	390911
4533	[390321]	4579	390610(4) ?	4623	390911
4534	390304(1)	4580	390610(5)	4624	390914
4535	390304(1)	4581	390610(5)	4625	390914
4536	390304(2)	4582	390610(6)	4626	390918
4537	390304(2)	4583	390610(6)	4627	390918
4540	390304(3)	4584	390610(1)	4629	390922
4541	390304(3)	4585	390610(1)	4630	390922
4542	390306	4586	390621	4631	390922
4543	390306	4587	390621	4632	390925
4544	390307(1)	4588	390621	4633	390925
4545	390307(1)	4589	390701	4634	391001
4546	390307(2)	4594	390715	4635	391001
4547	390307(2)	4595	390715	4641	391018
4548	390307(3)	4596	390715	4642	391018
4549	390307(3)	4597.1	390723(1)	4643	391021
4550	390310	4598	390725	4644	391021
4551	390310	4599	390725	4647	391117
4552	390311	4600	390725	4648	391117
4553	390311	4601	390729	4649	391117
4555	390318	4602	390729	4650	391117
4557	390324(2)	4603	390730	4651	391204(1)
4559	390400(2)	4604	390730	4652	391204(1)
4560	390400(2)	4605	390730	4653	391204(2)
4561	390409	4606	390805	4654	391204(2)
4562	390409	4607	390805	4655	391204(2)
4563	390411	4608	390807	4656	391207
4564	390422(1)	4609	390807	4657	391211
4565	390422(1)	4610	390807	4658	391211
4567	390501	4611	390902	4659	391212
4568	390501	4612	390902	4660	391212
4570	390607	4613	390904	4661	391215(1)
4571	390607	4614	390904	4662	391215(2)

T

4663	391215(2)
4664	391215(2)
4665	391211
4666	391226(1)
4667	391226(2)
	391227
4668-	
4814	410000(1)
4782	390800
4815	400500
4816	400820(3)
4819	400107
4820	400107
4821	400107
4822	400124
4823	400124
4824	400214
4825	400214
4826	400214
4827	400221
4828a	400227(1)
4828b	400227(2)
4828c	400303
4829	400229
4830	400304
4833	400313
4834	400313
4835	400313
4837	400423(1)
4838	400423(1)
4839	400423(2)
4840	400423(2)
4841	400425
4842	400425
4845	400514(2)
4846	400514(2)
4847-	
4876	400526

4876.1	400527	
4876.4	400531	
4880	400601	?
4881	400601	?
4882	400602	
4884	400608	
4885	400608	
4886	400608	
4887	400608	
4888	400608	
4889	400608	
4891	400615	
4894	400617	
4895	400617	
4896	400618(2)	
4897	400618(2)	
4898	400618(2)	
4899	400625(1)	
4900	400625(2)	
4901	400625(2)	
4902	400625(2)	
4903	400630	
4904	400630	
4905	400528(3)	
4906	400528(3)	
4908	400705	
4909	400705	
4910	400705	
4911	400703(2)	
4912	400703(2)	
4913	400711	
4914	400711	
4917	400726	
4918	400726	
4919	400727	
4920	400727	
4923	400802(1)	
4924	400807	
4925	400807	

4926	400817(1)
4927	400817(1)
4928	400817(1)

————————

V	
46	330727
104	[340300]
105	[340300]
106	[340300]
111	340700(2)
112	340700(3)
113	[340800(3)]
114	340715
120	340806
121	[341200]
124	350130
125	350201
126	350210
127	350210
128	350228
130	350331(1)
131	[350400]
133	350424
140	350807
141	350807

D	
10	300427
100	370529
116	330430
119	361012
167	330531
168	330607(2)
173	330707
175	330707
209	330730(1)
210	330730(2)
211	330731(1)
212	330731(2)
213	330731(3)
324	361126
350	340610
411	331003(2)

PART III

From PERVAYA RUSSKAYA REVOLYUTSIYA. Ukazatel literatury. Izdatel´stvo
     Kommunisticheskoi Akademii, 1930. (LocO)

An On; Antid Oto; Kruks; L´vov; Neofit; O,A; Pero; Petr Petrovich; SS;
T; Takhotskii, L; Tanas, P; T—ii; T—kii, N; Trotskii, N; Vladimirov, L;
Yanovskii, L.

From Krozmin(B.P.), PISATELEI SOVREMENNOI EPOKHI. Tom I. (LocCU)

Yanov, L.

From Deutscher(I), THE PROPHET ARMED

Antid Oto; Arbuzov; Lvov; Pero; Petr Petrovich; Samokovlieff; Takhotsky, N;
Tanas, P; Vikentiev; Vivos Voco; Yanovsky.

Other signatures in Part I

Cyrillic
A; Al´fa; D; Én; G.G.; Gurov,G; K; Kh; Lyud; N,L; N,M; N,N; Neunvyvayushchii;
Postoronii; T,L; T, N; T—ii, L; Trotskii, Lev N; T—skii;

Other scripts
Alpha; [Breton, A &] Rivera, D; Clave; Cornell; Crux; D,L; G.G.; G—off; Gourov;
Gourov, G; Hansen, Joseph; Heny; Lee; Leo; Lund; Lund,L; O,V.T.; O'Brien, V.T.;
Onken; Opmerker; Parabellum; R,W; Rork, W; Sympathizer; Vidal; Wolfe; Your
Old Man.

PROSPECTUS OF SOCHINENIYA, 1925

[See end-paper in SOCH. XII]

SERIYA I   ISTORICHESKOE PODGOTOVLENIE OKTYABRYA

      Tom I   O KHARAKTERE RUSSKOI REVOLYUTSII

        II   1905

        III   1917

  II   PERED ISTORICHESKIM RUBEZHOM

      Tom IV   POLITICHESKAYA KHRONIKA

        V   VNUTRIPARTIINYE VOPROSY

        VI   BALKANY I BALKANSKAYA VOINA

        VII   NA MEZHDUNARODNYE TEMY

        VIII   POLITICHESKIE SILUÉTY

  III   VOINA

      Tom IX   VOINA V POLITIKE

        X   FRANTSIYA V VOINE

        XI   RABOCHEE DVIZHENIE V EPOKHU VOINY

  IV   PROBLEMY MEZHDUNARODNOI PROLETARSKOI REVOLYUTSII

      Tom XII   OSNOVNYE VOPROSY PROLETARSKOI REVOLYUTSII

        XIII   KOMMUNISTICHESKII INTERNATSIONAL (Ot kruzhkov k

                      partiyam: 1917-1921 g.g.)

        XIV   KOMMUNISTICHESKII INTERNATSIONAL (Novyi etap: 1921-1924 g.g.)

  V   NA PUTI K SOTSIALIZMU

      Tom XV   KHOZYAISTVENNOE STROITEL'STVO SOVETSKOI RESPUBLIKI

        XVI-XVII   SOVETSKAYA RESPUBLIKA I KAPITALISTICHESKII MIR

                   (Vnutrennee i mezhdunarodnoe polozhenie respubliki)

        XVIII   NA PARTIINYE TEMY

  VI   PROBLEMY KUL'TURY

      Tom XIX-XX   KUL'TURA STAROGO MIRA

        XXI   KUL'TURA PEREKHODNOGO PERIODA

        XXII   LITERATURA I REVOLYUTSIYA

  VII   LENIN I LENINIZM

      Tom XXIII   Kniga o Lenine

MATERIAL PUBLISHED IN SOCHINENIYA

FROM ARCHIVES

060212   060614   [061100]

070000(5)

121112   [121200]

[130320]

150116

160000(2)

[170600(1)]

180117(1)/   [180319(3)]   180614(1)   180912(2)   181030

190118   190300(1)   190329   190401   190809(1)   190829   190906(2)   190916(2)

[191000]   191019   191107(1)   191230

[200000(87)]   [200000(88)]   [200000(89)]   200101(2)   200106   200109(1)   200112

200113   [200114]   200115(1)   200115(3)   200115(4)   200123   200200(2)   200209(1)

200211(1)   200211(2)   200212(2)   200219   200222   200224(2)   200226(2)   200302

200308   200312   200323(2)   200409(2)   200415   200418   200420   200500   200507(1)

200621   200629   [200700(1)]   200721   200800(1)   200810(2)   200817(1)   200817(2)

200831   200901   [201100(1)]   [201100(2)]   201106(1)   201106(2)   201112

201115   201118   201119   201128

210104   210217(1)   210905(5)   211020   211025   211101(3)   211102   211210(1)

[211223]

220000(32)   [220117]   220316   [220321]   220324   220401(3)   221025(1)

230512   230605(1)   230605(2)   230625   230927   231019(1)

240906

260000(30)   260225(2)

TRANSLATIONS: BY LANGUAGES

AFRIKAANS   371030

ARABIC   [101100]   [640000(8)]   650000(4)

BENGAL   690000(6)   [690000(12)]   [700000(3)]

BULGARIA   100000(1)   *180000(1)   190000(5)   *210000(17)   *210000(18)
                   *210000(19)   220000(10)   *220000(11)   *220000(37)   *240000(38)
                   240122(1)   270600(1)   270600(2)   270801   271023   280628
281000(1)   290925(2)   300207(1)   [300800(1)]   300825   300900(1)   [301000(2)]
301126   301129(1)   [201200(1)]   [301200(3)]   *310000(2)   *[310000(4)]   310311
310325   310404   310415   310708(2)   310715(1)   310825   311017   311126   [311200]
311208   320215(2)   320301   320329   320412   320423   [320500]   320504   320512
320524(2)   320613(1)   320613(3)   320625   320628   320802   320804(2)   320806
320809   320817   320818(2)   320831   320910   320922(2)   321013(1)   321013(2)
321127   [321200(2)]   321200(3)   321203(2)   321219   321228(2)   330000(1)
*[330000(3)]   *[330000(4)]   *[330000(5)]   *[330000(6)]   330321   330330   330512(1)
330715(2)   331110   *360000(13)

CHINA   *[200000(96)]   *300000(5)   *300000(12)   *300000(23)
                   *[300000(31)]   *310000(36)   *310000(37)   *[320000(36)]
                   *[320000(37)]   340000(21)   *380000(16)   *[380000(17)]
*380000(18)   380000(19)   *[390200(3)]   *400000(2)   *460000(15)   *470000(1)
*470000(3)   470427   [700000(13)]

CZECHO-SLOVAKIA   [140000(3)]   151100(1)   180000(5)   180328(1)   *[190000(62)]
                   *200000(65)   200423   200807(1)   201107   *210000(38)   *210000(40)
                   210000(62)   210613(2)   210623   210624   210702   210706
[210712]   210714(2)   210714(3)   210830   [210916]   210921   211011   211020
211025   [211129]   211121   220116   220223(3)   220226(1)   220228(2)   220308
220329(1)   220414   220508(5)   220519(1)   [220827]   221010   [221012]   221022
221121   221201(1)   221201(2)   230210   230405(1)   230512(1)   230630   231019(1)
*240000(47)   *250000(28)   *250000(35)   *260000(23)   270507   270516   270517(1)
270526(1)   270526(2)   *300000(18)   *300000(30)   [310000(32)]   *[310000(33)]
320000(12)   *[320000(25)]   *[320000(27)]   330000(21)   *[330000(33)]   *330000(37)
*330000(38)   340000(2)   *340000(3)   *[340000(14)]   *[340000(16)]   *[340000(17)]
*[360000(13)]   *[360000(22)]   *[360000(23)]

DENMARK   [180000(49)]   190000(61)   190306(1)   200000(37)   250000(31)
                   280628   281216(2)   290225   [290522(2)]   291130(2)   300000(1)
                   310000(25)   [320223]   [321123(3)]   [321123(4)]   321127

++++

DENMARK   ++++   321209   ⌊350000(15)⌋   ⌊370000(22)⌋   370209   370219   370617(1)
370730   380830   ⌊390200(1)⌋   390925   391023   600000(30)
⌊680000(5)⌋

ESPERANTO   290424

ESTHONIA   *190000(52)

FINLAND   180000(39)   180000(61)   ⌊190000(72)⌋   190124   190306(1)
⌊190306(2)⌋   210000(60)   210000(61)   700000(15)

GREECE   ⌊080915⌋   330409   351126(1)   380500(1)   380600   390725
400423(2)   400526   450000(6)   450000(7)   460000(6)   *470000(6)
590000(1)   610000(19)   620000(18)   630000(10)   630000(11)
630000(12)   650000(2)   650000(9)   660000(6)   660000(7)   660000(8)   660000(9)
660000(10)   670000(15)

HEBREW   200423   220000(32)   230618   230630   260203   260412   290225
300000(6)   310000(24)   *320000(11)   320423   321019   330610
*370000(5)   410000(4)

HOLLAND   150000(1)   ⌊150717(2)⌋   ⌊200000(8)⌋   200000(70)   ⌊200000(83)⌋
210000(33)   ⌊210000(47)⌋   ⌊220518⌋   230618   240122(1)
⌊260000(31)⌋   260301   270000(7)   270500   270516   270526(2)
270800   270903   ⌊280900⌋   290329   290331(1)   ⌊290800(1)⌋   291004   291014
291109   291113   300000(17)   300213   300314   300425   300525(1)   300530
300926(1)   310000(21)   ⌊310000(28)⌋   ⌊310000(29)⌋   *⌊310000(30)⌋   310124
310225   310308   310415   310624   310715(1)   311208   320102   320215(1)   320301
320628   320802   320804(2)   320809   320817   320818(2)   320902   320910   320912
320914   321003   321013(2)   321022(1)   321104   321231   ⌊330000(31)⌋   ⌊330000(32)⌋
330111(1)   330111(2)   330223   330303(2)   330310   330314   330319   330429
330523   330525   330528   330607(1)   330613(1)   330714   330720(1)   ⌊330800(2)⌋
330817(3)   330826   330828   330901   330920   331001   331107   331110   331130
340000(15)   340101   340118   ⌊340200(1)⌋   340222   ⌊340300⌋   340316   340323
⌊340427⌋   340610   340700(2)   340922   341000   341230(2)   350000(13)   ⌊350000(14)⌋
350126   350130   350201   350210   350300   ⌊350328⌋   ⌊350400⌋   350420   350607(1)
350610(1)   350700(1)   350729   350914   350918   351016   351031   351104(1)
351112   351126(1)   360000(2)   ⌊360000(18)⌋   360111   360113   360318   360325
360328   ⌊360400(2)⌋   360412   360416   360522   360605   360609   360700(1)
360704   360708   360709(1)   360709(2)   360718   360719   360730   360815(1)

++++

HOLLAND   ++++   360819(1)   360820(1)   360820(2)   360823(1)   370118   370122
370209   370219   370222   370306   370313(1)   370323   370417(2)
370423   370730   370808   370809   370824   370828   370921
370923   370928   370930   371102   371104   371117   371125(2)   371213(1)   371217
380113   380115   380121(1)   380127(1)   380216   380304(2)   380308   380522
380605   380703(2)   380719(2)   380801   380803   380830   380903(1)   380919(1)
380922   380923   381007   381010   381014   381114   381214   381220   381222(2)
381222(3)   390000(3)   *⌊390000(6)⌋   ⌊390200(1)⌋   ⌊390200(2)⌋   ⌊390217⌋   390306
390307(1)   390311   390318   390324(1)   390324(2)   390422(1)   390501   390609
390902   390904   390911   390925   391018   ⌊400000(6)⌋   400000(9)   400700(2)
⌊400820(4)⌋   ⌊450000(5)⌋   460000(2)   ⌊470000(4)⌋   490000(1)   510000(2)   600000(6)
⌊630000(3)⌋   670000(14)   690000(16)

HUNGARY   *190000(73)   *190000(75)   *190000(76)   *⌊190000(77)⌋
*⌊190000(78)⌋   300700(3)   *320000(3)   *⌊320000(26)⌋   321022(1)
321205   330303(2)   330714   330715(2)   ⌊360000(19)⌋   ⌊380000(9)⌋

ICELAND   360000(20)

ITALY   090000   130401   151100(1)   *⌊180000(51)⌋   ⌊180000(55)⌋
190000(43)   190000(50)   190118   190710   200000(37)   200000(54)
200000(55)   200109(2)   201208(2)   210000(28)   *210000(29)
*210000(41)   210000(50)   210623   210704   ⌊210712⌋   ⌊210717(3)⌋   ⌊211101⌋
211206   ⌊211225⌋   211227   220302(1)   220303(1)   220328   220513   ⌊220518⌋
220526   ⌊220618⌋   ⌊220727⌋   240122(1)   ⌊240510(2)⌋   ⌊240519⌋   *250000(15)
260302   270801   280103   ⌊281000(1)   281216(1)   *⌊290000(13)⌋   290229   290523
290525(1)   291004   291109   291113   291130(2)   *300000(16)   300213   300300(1)
300412   300514   300619   300900(1)   300926(1)   ⌊301100(3)⌋   301126   ⌊301200(1)⌋
310107   310124   310404   310405   310414   310415   310528(2)   310609   310700(1)
310715(1)   311126   ⌊311200⌋   311208   ⌊320000(1)⌋   320301   320802   321127
321200(3)   *330000(14)   ⌊330101⌋   330111(1)   330604   330609(1)   340325
*360000(8)   *390000(9)   390409   *400000(10)   ⌊430000(3)⌋   *⌊450000(1)⌋
*460000(9)   480000(1)   *480000(3)   *490000(3)   560900(2)   570400   581000
*600000(31)   600100   610400   620000(20)   620404   640100   640110   *640600
641200   ⌊660000(2)⌋   *661200   670121   670310   670315   670831   671100(4)
680000(6)   680200(2)   681000   690224   690500(1)   690500(2)   690610   700000(16)
700000(17)   700000(18)

JAPAN [240424] [240618(2)] *250710 250720 251016 *251028
260807 260915 260930 *270000(18) 270901 *290621 *300000(8)
*300723 *310601 *310614 370726 *370814 *460000(12)
*490000(4) *500000(3) *520000(4) *540215 561123 *590000(6) *600000(18)
*610000(16) *610000(17) *610325 *610515 *611005 *620000(19) *620000(20)
*620120 *620915 *621130 *630430 631030 631130 640330(1) 640330(2)
640330(3) 640330(4) 641225 650430 660228 660730 661031 661130 670115
670131 680320 680430 680610 *680920 681010 681125 690831 700130

JUGO-SLAVIA See SERBIA, etc.

KARANTSCHAISCH 250000(29)

LATVIA 190306(1) *240000(42)

LITHUANIA 180203(1) 220000(37) 220508(5)

MALAYALAM 570411 580225 621031

NORWAY [080915] 171108(1)/ 171115(2)/ 171203(3)/ [171218(2)/]
171229(1)/ [180000(55)] [180222(1)] 180222(2) 190000(56)
190306(1) 191031 200000(105) 200429(4) [200912] 210305
[210313] 210623 210706 210717(1) 210730 211025 220414 220826 240728
250000(31) 290225 290422 [290600(7)] 310000(1) [320508] 330602 340101
350000(9) 350607(3) 350611 350612 350726(1) 351001 360820(2) 360821
360823(1) 360824 360825 360923 361218(1) 370000(4) 370000(16) *370112(2)]
370617(1) 370730 370808 370828 371102 371116(2) 371213(3) 371217
371219 380301 380303(1) [380306(2)] 380500(1) 380703(2) 381214 381222(3)
390304(3) 390318 390422(1) [690000(10)]

POLAND [080300] [080400(2)] [080500] [080600(1)] [080600(2)]
[080700] [080800] 081014 081216 090000 [090327(4)]
[090600] [090821] 171009(1)/ [191026] *200000(66)
*200000(97) *200000(98) *200000(99) *200000(103) 200618(1) 211206 220513
[220518] *290000(15) 290701 *300000(32) 311126 311208 320000(1)
*320000(29) *320000(30) *320000(31) 320301 321006 *330000(41) *330000(42)
*330000(43) [331214] 340120(1) *370000(28)

PORTUGAL [200000(91)] 200000(106) 310000(9) 321013 330000(11)
*[330000(18)] 340000(6) *[340000(12)] *430000(1) *440000(1)

RUMANIA   180000(35)   *⌊180000(55)⌋   *180000(56)   190000(39)
                   *⌊270000(13)⌋   330000(7)

SCANDINAVIA   200000(37)   200731(2)   201124   210115(2)   210717(4)

SERBIA, etc.   040000   *⌊090300⌋   *⌊100000(5)⌋   ⌊100101(2)⌋   ⌊101101⌋
                   ⌊111101⌋   ⌊130314⌋   ⌊130315⌋   *⌊140000(4)⌋   *190000(80)
                   200000(37)   310000(38)   330314   361013

SINHALA   471001   510000   510400   570200   631200   640000(5)   650500

SPAIN   ⌊010217⌋   041220   050120   061004/   061200(1)   ⌊080915⌋
                  150915   170505/   190000(41)   *190000(42)   190000(45)
                  *190000(66)   190000(69)   190118   ⌊190429⌋   *200000(77)
200000(80)   ⌊200000(85)⌋   *⌊200000(86)⌋   200423   ⌊200722⌋   200731(2)   201020
*210000(49)   *210000(55)   210116   ⌊210313⌋   210323(1)   210403   210613(1)
210704   ⌊210712⌋   220000(38)   221114(1)   ⌊230215⌋   230313   230515   ⌊230711⌋
⌊240000(45)⌋   240122(1)   240411(1)   240421(2)   ⌊240711⌋   250828(2)   250917
*260000(35)   260203   260301   270000(6)   270000(9)   270418   271021   *280000(3)
*280000(5)   *280000(12)   290000(5)   *⌊290000(12)⌋   290329   290600(2)   *300000(7)
*300000(10)   *300000(15)   300821   301126   310000(5)   *310000(8)   310000(10)
*310000(13)   *310000(14)   310000(15)   310000(16)   *310000(17)   *310000(19)
*⌊310000(31)⌋   310325   310412   310415   310531   310612   310618   310624   310708(1)
310715(1)   310715(2)   310820(1)   310929   ⌊311200⌋   311208   311222   320000(1)
⌊320000(22)⌋   ⌊320000(24)⌋   *⌊320000(28)⌋   320102   320127   ⌊320130⌋   320301
⌊320500⌋   320509   320519   320616   320625   320628   320725   320802   320804(2)
320806   320809   320831   320920   321013(1)   321013(2)   321022(1)   321127
⌊321200(2)⌋   321200(3)   321205   *330000(9)   ⌊330000(28)⌋   *⌊330000(34)⌋
330000(36)   330105   330111(1)   330111(2)   330200(2)   330205   ⌊330300(3)⌋
*330300(4)   330303   330314   330321   330330   330400(3)   330400(5)   330401
330409   330413   330429   330512(1)   330523   330525   330610   330613(1)   330622
330714   330715(1)   330720(1)   330805   330817(3)   330920   331003(2)   331110
331212   *⌊340000(13)⌋   340118   340120(1)   340222   ⌊340600⌋   340610   341000
350000(3)   *⌊350000(22)⌋   *⌊350000(23)⌋   350610(1)   350700(1)   350729   350907(2)
350914   351112   360000(5)   360000(27)   360328   360522   360730(1)   360815
370000(8)   370000(10)   ⌊370000(23)⌋   370000(26)   370000(30)   370204   370219
370423   370600   370700   370730   370816   370900   370923   371102   371129(2)
371213(1)   380000(7)   *⌊380000(10)⌋   *380000(15)   380127(1)   380422   380423
380500(1)   380606   380710   380719(1)   380830   380903(1)   ⌊380903(4)⌋   380919(2)
380923   381009   381010   *381100   390000(1)   390000(3)   *390000(8)   390301

++++

SPAIN   ++++   390304(3)   390418   390501   390725   390904   390906   400000(1)
                 *400000(11)   *⌊400000(13)⌋   *400000(16)   400526   400618(1)
                 ⌈400820(4)⌉   *460000(11)   *470000(8)   *470000(9)   *480000(4)
*480000(5)   *490000(2)   *530000(4)   *540123   *560000(8)   580130   600000(32)
600730   610501   610622   611025   620000(10)   620000(16)   620000(17)   *⌊620700(2)⌋
620719   630000(4)   630501   631126   *640000(6)   640617   640900(1)   *640900(2)
650000(1)   ⌈650000(11)⌉   *650000(12)   *⌊650000(13)⌋   *651000(2)   670000(5)
670900   671100   680000(9)   690000(8)   690500(3)   690700(2)

SWEDEN   130000   171023(3)/   171117(4)/   171128(3)/   171214(1)/
                  180000(38)   180000(41)   180202(1)   180219(2)   180801
                  190306(1)   210000(35)   ⌊221012⌋   230000(25)   *240000(46)
250000(30)   270000(8)   270000(14)   270000(19)   280000(4)   290000(10)   370000(9)
690600(1)   691100(2)   691100(3)

TATAR   180000(10)   230000(41)   *240000(11)

TURCOMAN   240000(56)

TURKEY   290000(9)   *⌊290229(2)⌋   *290312

UKRAINE   210000(7)   *⌊230000(24)⌋   230405(3)   250000(36)   300108
                  321203(2)   330720(1)   330805   331107   331110   340000(24)
                  340000(26)   340118   340222   ⌊340300⌋   340310   340610   340715
340922   341020   341228   350000(24)   350000(25)   350130   350210   350331(1)
⌊350400⌋   350525(2)   350607(1)   350607(2)   350610(1)   350700(1)   350722(1)
350926   351022   351126(4)   360110   360111   360115(1)   360128(1)   360325
360416   370000(29)

VIETNAM   *480000(11)

YIDDISH   161011   170121   *⌊170300⌋   ⌊170400(1)⌋   *180000(30)
                  *190000(54)   190000(68)   190118   190510   200423   *210000(34)
                  *210000(37)   210000(51)   *220000(35)   *⌊220000(36)⌋   240122(1)
240406   270418   270903   271021   *290000(3)   290329   *300000(14)   300108
300207(1)   300413(1)   300510   300900(1)   *310000(35)   310325   310715(1)
311222   320000(1)   *320000(33)   *320000(34)   *320000(35)   ⌊320130⌋   320301
⌊320500⌋   320509   320519(1)   320613(2)   320616   320625   320802   320804(2)
320806   320831   321013(1)   321013(2)   321022(1)   321127   ⌊321200(2)⌋   321200(3)
321205   330000(22)   330000(23)   *330000(44)   330105   330303   330330   330409
330512(1)   330523   330525   330613(1)   330715(1)   330817(3)   340000(20)   370118

SUBJECT-INDEX

POLITICAL PARTIES

POLITICAL PORTRAITS

POLITICAL THEORY

Prefaces. See

      LITERATURE: Prefaces

Pre-Parliament. See

      RUSSIA (1917): Pre-Parliament

PROGNOSES

Programme. See

      INTERNATIONAL: Fourth:

      Programme

PROLETARIAN INTERNATIONALISM

PROLETARIAN MARTYRS

PROLETARIAN REVOLUTION

RAKOVSKY

RED AIR FORCE

RED ARMY

RED NAVY

Reiss. See

      GPU: Reiss

Rumania. See

      BALKANS: Rumania

RUSSIA (Tsarist)

RUSSIA (1905)

RUSSIA (1917)

RUSSIAN DUMA

RUSSIAN REVOLUTION

RUSSIAN SOCIAL-DEMOCRATIC PARTY

Ryazanov. See

      TRIALS: Ryazanov

Second International. See

      INTERNATIONAL: Second

SEDOV

Serbia. See

      BALKANS: Serbia

Siberia. See

      AUTOBIOGRAPHY: Siberia

SOCIAL DEMOCRACY

SOCIAL PATRIOTISM

SOCIALIST WORKERS PARTY

SOCIOLOGY

South Africa. See

      INTERNATIONAL LEFT OPPOSITION:

      South Africa

Soviet. See

      RUSSIA (1905)

SOVIET RUSSIA

SOVIET UNION

SPAIN

Specialists. See

      RED ARMY: Specialists

SR Trials. See

      TRIALS: SR

STALIN

STALINISM

SYNDICALISM

TERRORISM

Third International. See

      INTERNATIONAL: Third

TRADE UNIONS

TRIALS

TROTSKYISM

Tsar Trial. See

      TRIALS: Tsar

TURKEY

Two-and-a-half International. See

      INTERNATIONAL: Two-and-a-half

UKRAINE

UNITED FRONT

United States of Europe. See

      EUROPE: United States of

USA

WORKERS CONTROL

WORLD AFFAIRS

WORLD WAR I

WORLD WAR II

YOUTH

Zimmerwald. See
        CONFERENCE: Zimmerwald

AGRARIAN QUESTION

  Russia ⌊180427(1)⌋ 190322(1) 190322(2) 230000(7) 240000(22)
       250923 251205 260000(16) *260000(32) 260612
       *⌊270000(14)⌋

  Bolivia 370424

ANARCHISM   230000(12) 260000(18) 380127(1)

  Kronstadt 230000(7) 260000(18) 380115 380706

ART   230000(9) 260000(12) *⌊270000(15)⌋ 380725(2)
     381222(3)

AUSTRIA   See also: INTERNATIONAL LEFT OPPOSITION: Austria
     220000(3) 260000(17) 310000(12) 330000(15) 330323(1)
     330503 330507 330613(1) 551115

AUTOBIOGRAPHY See also: GPU; SEDOV; TRIALS: Moscow
     970000 980000(1) 980000(2) 980000(3) 070000(3)
     100000(4) ⌊110200(2)⌋ 170115 170116(1) ⌊180000(55)⌋
181200 190000(2) ⌊220321⌋ ⌊231123(3)⌋ 231217 270414 *⌊271200⌋
⌊280000(11)⌋ 280200 280401 290200 290316 ⌊290415(2)⌋ 300000(1) 310000(38)
310000(39) 310414(3) 310708(2) 310708(3) 310715(2) ⌊310716⌋ ⌊211200⌋
320000(2) 320123 320215(2) ⌊320226(1)⌋ 320301 320413 320625 321122
321123(2) 321200(3) 321205 321208(1) ⌊321208(2)⌋ 321211 330715(3)
330719(2) 330719(3) 330726 ⌊330728⌋ 340220 ⌊340427⌋ 360128(1) 360128(2)
370308 370310 370313(1) 371116(2) 380212 380303(2) 380305 381027
381028 381128 ⌊390114⌋ 390419 390422(2) 391226(1) 400000(1) 400531
400601 400618(2) 400618(3) 400625(2) 400803(1) 400803(2) 400816(1)
400818 400820(1) 400820(2) 400821

  Britain ⌊290600(4)⌋ ⌊290600(5)⌋ ⌊290600(6)⌋ 290611 290715
  Denmark ⌊320223⌋ ⌊321123(3)⌋ ⌊321123(4)⌋ 321209
  Diaries 180000(33) 220000(3) 220000(4) 330700 580000(4)
  Dies Committee 391207 391211 391212 391217
  Family ⌊280300(1)⌋ ⌊280300(2)⌋ 330111(2) 361218(2) 370127(2)
     380310(3) 380410 380418(2) 380900 380919(3) 390116
  France ⌊160800(2)⌋ 220000(3) 240000(32) 260000(17)
  Mexico 370109(2) 380710 380719(1) 381110
  Norway 371116(2)
  Siberia 070000(3) 220916(1) 270000(3)
  Spain ⌊161105⌋ 190600 220000(3) 260000(5) 270000(1)
  Turkey *⌊290229(2)⌋ *290312 320104 330715(3)

BALKANS   [101101]   [120926]   [121016]   140000(1)   260000(1)
                                   270000(1)

        Armenia   260000(1)

        Bulgaria   See also: INTERNATIONAL LEFT OPPOSITION: Bulgaria
                                   230000(19)   260000(1)

        Macedonia   230000(19)   260000(1)

        Montenegro   260000(1)

        Rumania   180115/   230000(20)   260000(1)   260000(18)

        Serbia   *[090300]   190000(1)   260000(1)

BALKAN WAR   230000(19)   260000(1)

BELGIUM   See also: INTERNATIONAL LEFT OPPOSITION: Belgium
                                   190000(1)   340109   580000(4)

BOLSHEVISM   370828   390607

BREST-LITOVSK   171204(2)/   171228(5)/   171231(2)/   180100(1)
                                 [180100(2)]   180110/   180111/   180115/   [180201]
                                 [180206(1)]   180206(2)   180210(3)   180210(4)   180219(2)
180219(3)   [180314]   260000(18)   300000(1)   410000(1)   640000(1)

BRITAIN   See also: AUTOBIOGRAPHY; INDEPENDENT LABOUR PARTY;
                                 INTERNATIONAL LEFT OPPOSITION: Britain
                                 200604   221114(2)   230000(7)   240419(2)   [240711]
                                 241015(2)   250000(5)   260000(11)   270000(2)   [270300(2)]
310300(1)   580000(4)
        Anglo-Russian Committee   260129   [270000(12)]   270516   270925

CHINA   See also: INTERNATIONAL: Fourth; INTERNATIONAL LEFT
                                 OPPOSITION: China; JAPAN: China
                                 240818   [250606]   260400(2)   260927   [270000(12)]
270228(2)   270322(1)   270331   270405   270412   270418   270623   281200(2)
[301000(3)]   301100(1)   320600(2)   [330100(2)]   370913   370925   371001   371203
380105   400700(1)   470427   551115   570000(2)

CIVIL WAR   240729(1)

CIVIL WAR (Russia)   180224   [180525(5)]   [180526]   180607(2)   180610(2)
                                 180723(13)   180724(1)   180727(1)   180903(1)   181018
                                 181028   181201(1)   [181226(1)]   250000(8)   410000(1)
                                 640000(1)   ++++

CIVIL WAR (Russia)   ++++

      Czecho-Slovaks 180525(6)   180613(3)   181113   230000(7)   260000(18)

      Insurrection   310000(1)

COMMUNIST PARTY (Russia) 230000(5)   230223   230427   240000(28)   240412(3)

                    250701   251218   251222(1)   410000(1)

COMMUNIST PARTY (Soviet Union)   280723   281100   300413(1)   ⌊300800(2)⌋

                    ⌊301100(2)⌋   301121(1)   330330   330706   340120(1)

                    551115

CONFERENCE

      Zimmerwald   151100(2)   160113(2)   ⌊160200⌋   ⌊160511(2)⌋   190304

              220000(3)

CONGRESS

      Anti-Fascist   330000(7)   330000(8)   330300(3)   ⌊330400(3)⌋

      Anti-War   320613(2)   320725

      Copenhagen   ⌊091208(4)⌋   ⌊100403(2)⌋   ⌊100801(3)⌋   ⌊100924(2)⌋

CZECHO-SLOVAKIA   See also: CIVIL WAR (Russia): Czecho-Slovakia; INTERNATIONAL

                        LEFT OPPOSITION: Czecho-Slovakia

                        210717(2)

      World War II   380602   380917

DENMARK   See AUTOBIOGRAPHY: Denmark

DEWEY COMMISSION   370518   370529   370630   371014   371213(1)   371213(2)

                        371213(3)

ECONOMIC PLANNING   331130   340109   380000(4)

      NEP   211028   211029   221114(1)   221114(2)   230127(1)

      Soviet Russia   210807   *220419   220802   220823   230000(41)   230115

                    230120   230125   230129   300425

ECONOMY

      Soviet Russia   171200(2)   171201(4)/   180216(2)   180226   ⌊180228(1)⌋

              ⌊180228(2)⌋   ⌊180306(2)⌋   180416(1)   ⌊180604(6)⌋

              ⌊180611(2)⌋   ⌊180614(10)⌋   ⌊180614(12)⌋   ⌊180614(14)⌋

    180615(1)   ⌊200103⌋   ⌊200324⌋   ⌊200414⌋   ⌊200416⌋   ⌊200419(2)⌋

      ⌊200425⌋   201215   ⌊201219⌋   201227   210000(23)   ⌊221015⌋   230000(7)

    230213   231200(6)   240000(22)   240000(32)   240610(2)   240702   250531

                                              ++++

ECONOMY   ++++

    Soviet Russia   ++++   250612(1)   ⌊250630⌋   250729   250828(2)
                250901   250925   251119   260000(18)   ⌈260117⌋   270000(4)

    Soviet Union   300821   ⌈301200(1)⌋   ⌈310300(5)⌋   ⌊310327⌋   310715(1)
                321022(1)   321022(2)   330126   330303(2)   361013

ENTRISM   340700(2)   340700(3)   340710   340800(3)   ⌊340803⌋
                340806   340922   341101   341216   350415   351230

EUROPE   220000(3)   260000(12)   260000(17)   270000(1)   291004
                330607(1)   551115

    United States of   230630

FASCISM   311115   320512   320804(1)   ⌈330512(2)⌋   330714   340715
                350819   ⌊390200(2)⌋   ⌊400820(6)⌋   590600

FINLAND   See also: SOVIET RUSSIA: Finland; SOVIET UNION: Finland
                180301(1)   230000(7)   260000(16)   260000(18)

FOREIGN AFFAIRS   See also: RUSSIAN REVOLUTION: Foreign Affairs
    Soviet Russia   220312   ⌊220504⌋   230000(7)

FRANCE   See also: AUTOBIOGRAPHY: France; INTERNATIONAL: Fourth:
                France; INTERNATIONAL: Third: France; INTERNATIONAL LEFT
                OPPOSITION: France; JEWRY: France; PROLETARIAN REVOLUTION:
                France; SOCIAL PATRIOTISM: France;
151100(1)   ⌊151105⌋   190000(10)   220000(3)   240000(32)   250908   260000(18)
331100   ⌊340600(1)⌋   ⌊340601⌋   ⌈340608⌋   341000(1)   360000(6)   381222(1)
390214   580900

GERMANY   See also: INTERNATIONAL: Fourth: Germany; INTERNATIONAL:
                Third: Germany; INTERNATIONAL LEFT OPPOSITION: Germany;
                PROLETARIAN REVOLUTION: Germany; SOVIET UNION: Germany
050700(2)   *080000(1)   220000(3)   230000(7)   230000(11)   ⌊230723⌋   231029(2)
240000(29)   260000(10)   260000(12)   260302   270000(1)   310414(2)   320512
330310   330417   ⌊330512(2)⌋   330528   330602   330604   330622   ⌊331104⌋   331123
⌊331214⌋   580000(4)   590600

    SAP   320825   321024(2)
    Soviet Russia   *180106/   ⌊240513(1)⌋   311121   320301   330317(1)
                330321   350729   381007

GPU   280117   280125   290305   290308   ⌊300700(1)⌋   ⌊300800(2)⌋   371102   400000(1)   400802(2)   400806   400817(1)

     Klement   380718   380723   380801   380803   380804   381201

     Reiss   370921   370930   371019   371127(1)   380717   ⌊390921⌋

IMPERIALISM   220000(3)   270000(1)   390000(2)   390304(2)   410000(1)

     Lenin   381230

INDEPENDENT LABOUR PARTY   ⌊330800(1)⌋   330828   330829   330903(2)   330904   330916   330925   330930   331002(1)   351100(1)   360403

     Fourth International   340105   350918

INDIA   300530   390725   391124

INDUSTRY

     Soviet Russia   200201   200507(2)   200509(1)   ⌊200530⌋   ⌊210111⌋   ⌊210114⌋   ⌊210119⌋   211227   ⌊211229⌋   220418   230000(7)   230000(12)   230306(1)   230422(3)   230503(1)   230503(2)   240000(28)   250000(3)   250706   250716   ⌊250730(2)⌋   250804   250903   ⌊250913⌋   ⌊250915(2)⌋   250930   251002   251207(2)   260000(18)   260400(1)   270000(4)   270325

INTERNATIONAL

     Amsterdam   240000(6)

     Fourth   See also: INDEPENDENT LABOUR PARTY: Fourth International; POLITICAL THEORY: Centrism

        320825   330715(1)   330715(2)   330720(1)   330727   330817(3)   330826   330827   330901   330913   331230   340120(2)   ⌊340300⌋   340610   350700(1)   350722(1)   360700(1)   360704   370305   370601   370706   380000(13)   380127(2)   380531(2)   380830   381018   381022(1)   381202   381220   390907

         Australia   371223

         China   ⌊380903(4)⌋

         France   390310

         Germany   340111

         Holland   380102   380121(1)   380121(2)

         Manifesto   380903(1)

         Mexico   370204   380612   390111   390130(1)

         Programme   380500(1)   380519   380522   380607   421200

         Soviet Union   331001   360111   360325   ⌊360400(2)⌋   360708   390307(3)   ++++

INTERNATIONAL   ++++

    Second   140000(1) [151009] 220000(3) 240000(29) 260000(17)
                      390729

    Third   See also: INTERNATIONAL LEFT OPPOSITION: Third International
                      190304   190306(3)   190313   190420(3)   [200600]
                      200807(2)   210000(50)   210717(1)   [210717(4)]   220225
220226(2)   221121   230000(7)   240000(6)   240000(29)   [240700]   240705
260000(10)   260000(17)   280909   300108   [300109]   [301000(2)]   301100(1)
321012(2)   340118   350525(2)   350607(1)   350823(1)   350914   590600

             France   200726   201224(3)   210127   220508(4)
                           220512(2)   [221100(3)]   221202(1)
                           230000(8)   240000(29)   250908

             Germany   [210717(4)]   210813(1)   210813(3)
                           330613(1)

             Italy   200109(2)   [210717(3)]   [221100(2)]
                           221200(2)

             Jugo-Slavia   201010(2)   [210813(2)]
             Poland   260702
    Two-and-a-half   210115(2)   580000(4)

INTERNATIONAL LEFT OPPOSITION   230306   [270000(12)]   270221   270414
                                 [280000(9)]   280114(1)   280114(2)   280115
                                 280228   280305   280310   280317   [280500]
280509   280525   280526(1)   280526(2)   280602   280624   280715   280717(1)
280717(2)   280800   280820   280830(1)   280830(2)   280911   280922   280929
281000(2)   281002(1)   281013   281014   281020   281107   281110   281111   281124
281200(1)   290000(1)   290000(14)   290110   290227   290304   290523   290600(3)
290727(2)   290824   [290900(1)]   [290900(2)]   [290900(3)]   [290900(4)]   [290900(5)]
[291000(2)]   291012   [291100(2)]   291208   291220   [291225]   300000(1)   300105(1)
300120   300122   300208   [300300(2)]   300301   300323   300427   [300500(2)]
[300600(1)]   300600(2)   [300600(3)]   [300900(2)]   301022   310714   310728
[310900(3)]   311222   320315   320520(2)   320522(2)   320613(1)   [320700(2)]
320900(2)   321007   321200(4)   [321200(6)]   321203(1)   321216   330104(2)
[330300(1)]   330306   [330415]   330430   330531   330607(2)   330615   330617
330618   330820(2)   330826   330831(1)   330831(2)   330901(1)   331008   331107
331212   350302   [350900(3)]   350907(2)   351112   351212(1)   360422   360606
360711   551115

    Austria   310000(12)   330319
    Belgium   301013   321220(1)   331116   [340900(2)]   [340900(3)]
                    341101   [350300(2)]   350811(3)   350823(2)   350900(2)

                                                ++++

INTERNATIONAL LEFT OPPOSITION   ++++

Belgium   ++++ 360923

Britain   311107   311110   330903(2)   340105   ⌊360700(3)⌋

Bulgaria   301004   301129(1)   311017   320329   320412   320504
                320524(2)   320922(2)   321219

Canada   331003(1)

Chile   330413

China   290600(1)   291222(1)   300900(1)   320600(2)   320922(1)
                320926   321003   350305   350809   350813   370811   370903
                371027   470427

Czecho-Slovakia   290701

Danzig   370429

France   See also: ENTRISM
                290425   ⌊290600(8)⌋   290703   290711   290800(2)   290811
                300413(2)   300510   300626   300825   301009   301205
⌊310617⌋   310820(2)   310922   310925(1)   310925(2)   311118   320115
320520(2)   330707   330730(1)   330730(2)   330731(1)   330731(2)   330731(3)
330817(1)   330818(1)   ⌊330820(1)⌋   330821   330825   350415   350610(1)
350610(2)   350613   350703   350711   350722(2)   350726(2)   350730(1)
350730(3)   350730(4)   350801   350807   350810   350907(1)   350913
350916   351024   351026   351104(2)   351113   351117   351121   351125
351126(2)   351126(3)   351128(1)   351128(2)   351128(3)   351129(1)
351129(2)   351130   351203(1)   351203(2)   351203(3)   351204   351205
351206   351209   351213(1)   351213(2)   351216   351220   351226   360104
360107   360114   360131   360304   360316   360607   360716   360727
370323   670306

Germany   290612   290712   291104   300206   300516   300707   300918
                310000(12)   310131(2)   310217   310708(4)   311117
                320130   320509   321007   321013(4)   ⌊321020(2)⌋   321105
321228(1)   321228(2)   330104(2)   330128(2)   330312   330329(1)   330409
330421   330427   330522   ⌊330609(2)⌋   330818(2)   331204(2)   340111
340124   ⌊350200(3)⌋   551115   590600

Greece   310900(2)   340405

Holland   350226   350811(1)   351016   351118   360718   360719

Hungary   300821

Italy   260302   290925(1)   300422   300514   300619   310115
                310414(3)   310528(2)   ⌊330101⌋   340325

Norway   371219

Poland   320831   350718   350728   370429

South Africa   320613(1)   350420

++++

INTERNATIONAL LEFT OPPOSITION   ++++

Soviet Union   281021   ⌊290600(7)⌋   ⌊291000(1)⌋   ⌊291100(1)⌋   ⌊291126⌋
                300104   300213   300323   ⌊300400(2)⌋   ⌊310300(4)⌋
                310501   ⌊310900(1)⌋   320616   321017   321024   321030(2)
330330   ⌊340817(1)⌋
Spain   See also: NIN
                *300212   310424   310523(2)   310618   310700(1)   310802
                310927   320307(1)   320307(2)   320613(3)   331200   360727
370320   370323   370824   370920(1)   370928   590600
Third International   ⌊290626⌋   ⌊290726⌋   300108   ⌊300109⌋
USA   ⌊290300(1)⌋   291019   300416   300610   310719   311010
                311225(1)   311225(2)   320105   320210   320522(1)
                320524(1)   321013(3)   321020(1)   321022(3)   321101
321113   330307   ⌊340700(4)⌋   ⌊350200(2)⌋   350811(4)   350812   360124(1)
360124(2)   360309   370309   370525   370615   370625   270826   370918
Youth   330410   ⌊341200⌋   350323(3)   350811(2)   360427   370522
War   320613(2)

INTERVENTION (Russia)   180301(2)   180305(1)   180320(1)   180321(2)   ⌊180329⌋
                         180607(2)   180625(6)   180702   180801   230000(7)
                         240000(40)   260000(18)   300000(1)   410000(1)
Japan   180320(2)

ITALY   See also: INTERNATIONAL: Third: Italy   INTERNATIONAL LEFT
                OPPOSITION: Italy
                190000(10)

JAPAN   See also: INTERVENTION (Russia): Japan
                230000(7)   ⌊230101⌋   270000(1)   330712   370920(2)
                371001   400500   400501
China   370730   370923   371027
Soviet Russia   ⌊240424⌋   ⌊240618(2)⌋
Soviet Union   ⌊320227⌋   380811

JEWRY   230000(20)   260000(16)   ⌊340200(1)⌋   341000(2)   370118
                370222   381222(2)   400700(2)   700700
France   300510

LABOUR ARMY   230000(7)   260000(18)   270000(4)

LEFT OPPOSITION   230306(2)   *230328   231008   231023(2)   231217
                   240000(22)   240523   240526   [240530]   240629   241130
                   250115   250403   250506   250522   250701   260108
260304   *260402   [260700(3)]   260723   *260813(1)   *260813(2)   261016   261101
261102   261209   261214(2)   [270000(12)]   270200   *270219   270500   *270505
270517(2)   *270628(1)   270711   270802   *270804   *270806   270808   *[270900(3)]
270903   270912   270924   *[271000(2)]   271001   271004   271022   [271030]
271100(2)   *271109   *271117   271119(1)   271203   271215   271218   [280000(9)]
*[280600]   290000(1)   290320   *300000(33)   320000(2)   320102   330128(1)
390400(2)

        International: Third   270927
        Soviet Union: Economy   260412

LENIN   See also: IMPERIALISM
                   040000   130401   190000(2)   211206   240000(24)   240423
                   240812   260000(31)   [280000(9)]   290323(1)   300000(1)
*[310411]   321231   360000(10)   390610(4)   410000(1)   580000(4)

LIEBKNECHT   190000(10)   220000(3)   260000(17)

LITERATURE   220000(34)   230000(9)   230923(1)   240000(8)   260000(12)
                   [320400]   330510   330616   370000(25)   380601(2)
                   380610   380618(1)   380725(2)   381222(3)   580000(4)
        Prefaces   050700(2)   051200   190906(4)   190906(5)   [200000(91)]
                   210204   230000(7)   230000(8)   230127(1)   231102
                   240000(32)   240000(54)   *240000(55)   240319   240522
        241102   270000(4)   321006   330406   331107   350811(1)   351107(1)
        360607   371030   380105   390418
LUXEMBURG   260000(17)   320628   350624(1)

MARX, MARXISM   051200   [070100]   260000(16)   270000(2)   330104(1)
                   371030   380418(1)   [390217]   390307(1)   390418   390609

MEXICO   See also: AUTOBIOGRAPHY: Mexico; INTERNATIONAL: Fourth:
                   Mexico
                   380423   380605   381228

MILITARY SCIENCE   190000(2)   220403   230000(2)   230000(7)   240319   270000(1)

NATIONAL QUESTION [180616(2)]   240922   241102   300000(1)   331130   410000(1)
        Esthonia   640000(1)
        Soviet Russia   220000(3)   230000(41)   260000(16)   270000(1)

NIN   310901   330400(1)   360123   370808

OBITUARIES   060000(3)   *⌊100000(5)⌋   170000(1)   220000(3)   230000(7)

                       240511   250000(6)   250320   250910   260000(17)   260119

                       260721   261125   ⌈300500(1)⌉   310300(4)   ⌊320700(1)⌋

330715(4)   340101   360709(1)   370921   381108   390304(3)

ORDERS OF THE DAY   171124(4)/   ⌊171128(6)/⌋   180320(3)   180330(2)   180401(1)

                         180401(2)   180401(3)   180403(1)   180403(2)   180404

                         180405(1)   180405(2)   180405(3)   180408(1)   180408(2)

180408(3)   180409   180410   180411(1)   180411(2)   180411(3)   180413   180415(1)

180415(2)   180416(2)   180416(3)   180417(1)   180417(2)   180417(3)   180418

180420(1)   180420(3)   180420(4)   180420(5)   180420(6)   180420(7)   180420(8)

180420(9)   180420(10)   180422(5)   180422(6)   180422(7)   180423(2)   180423(3)

180423(4)   180423(5)   180423(6)   180424(1)   180424(2)   ⌊180424(5)⌋   180425(2)

180425(3)   180425(4)   180426   180427(2)   180429(1)   180429(2)   180429(3)

180430   180503(2)   180503(3)   180503(4)   180503(5)   180507(1)   180507(2)

180507(3)   180507(4)   180507(5)   180507(6)   180508(1)   ⌊180508(2)⌋   180508(3)

180508(4)   ⌊180508(5)⌋   ⌊180508(6)⌋   ⌊180508(7)⌋   ⌊180508(8)⌋   ⌊180508(9)⌋

180508(10)   180508(11)   180508(12)   180508(13)   180508(14)   ⌊180509(2)⌋

180509(3)   180509(4)   180509(5)   180509(6)   180509(7)   180509(8)   180509(9)

180509(11)   180509(12)   180509(13)   180509(14)   180510(2)   ⌈180511⌉   180512(1)

180512(2)   180512(3)   180512(5)   180513(1)   180513(2)   180513(3)   180513(4)

180514   180515(2)   180515(3)   180516(1)   180516(2)   ⌊180516(3)⌋   180516(4)

180516(5)   180516(6)   180517   180520(1)   180520(2)   180520(3)   180520(4)

18052L(1)   180521(2)   180521(3)   180521(4)   180523(2)   180523(3)   180523(4)

180523(5)   180524(1)   180524(2)   180524(3)   180524(4)   180524(5)   180524(6)

180524(7)   180525(1)   180525(2)   180525(3)   180525(4)   180527(2)   180527(3)

180528(1)   180528(2)   180529(3)   180529(4)   180529(5)   180529(6)   180530(7)

180531(3)   180531(4)   180531(5)   180531(7)   180531(8)   180601(2)   180601(3)

180601(4)   180602   180603(1)   180603(2)   180603(3)   180604(5)   180604(7)

180605(1)   180605(2)   180606(1)   180606(2)   180606(3)   180606(4)   180606(5)

180606(6)   180606(7)   180607(3)   180607(4)   180607(5)   180610(1)   180611(3)

180611(4)   180613(4)   180614(2)   180614(3)   180614(4)   180614(5)   180614(6)

180614(7)   180614(15)   180615(1)   180615(2)   180615(3)   180615(4)   180615(5)

180615(6)   180615(7)   180615(8)   180615(9)   180615(10)   180615(11)   180615(12)

180615(13)   180615(15)   180617(2)   180617(3)   180618(2)   180618(3)   180618(4)

180618(5)   180618(6)   180618(7)   180618(8)   180618(9)   180618(10)   180618(11)

180618(12)   180620(2)   180621   180622(2)   180622(3)   180622(4)   180623(1)

180623(2)   180624(1)   180624(2)   180624(3)   180624(4)   180624(5)   180625(1)

++++

ORDERS OF THE DAY ++++ 180625(2) 180625(3) 180625(4) 180625(5) 180625(7)
180626(1) ⌊180626(3)⌋ 180627(1) 180627(2) 180627(3)
180627(4) 180627(5) 180627(6) 180627(7) 180627(8)
180627(9) 180627(10) 180627(11) 180627(12) 180627(13) 180627(14)
180627(15) 180627(16) 180627(17) 180627(18) 180627(19) 180627(20)
180627(21) 180627(22) 180627(23) 180627(24) 180627(25) 180627(26)
180629(6) ⌊180629(7)⌋ 180630(1) 180630(2) 180630(3) 180630(4) 180630(5)
180630(6) 180701(2) 180703(1) 180703(2) 180704(4)180706(1) 180706(2)
180706(3) 180706(4) 180708(3) 180710(3) 180710(4) 180711(1) 180711(2)
180712(3) 180712(4) 180712(5) 180712(6) 180715(1) 180715(2) 180716(2)
180716(3) 180716(4) 180716(6) ⌊180717(2)⌋ 180717(4) 180717(5) 180717(6)
180717(7) 180717(8) 180717(9) 180717(10) 180717(11) 180717(12) 180717(13)
180717(14) 180717(15) 180718(1) 180718(2) 180718(3) [180718(4)]
[180718(5)] 180718(6) 180718(7) 180719(1) 180719(2) 180719(3) 180719(4)
180720(1) 180720(2) [180721] 180722(1) 180722(2) 180722(4) 180723(4)
180723(5) 180723(6) 180723(7) 180723(8) 180723(9) 180723(10) 180723(11)
180723(11) 180723(12) 180723(14) 180723(15) 180724(2) 180724(3) 180724(4)
180725 180726(1) ⌊180726(2)⌋ ⌊180726(3)⌋ ⌊180726(4)⌋ ⌊180726(5)⌋
⌊180727(2)⌋ 180727(3) 180727(4) 180727(5) 180727(6) 180727(7) 180729(3)
180729(4) 180729(5) 180729(6) 180729(7) ⌊180730(1)⌋ ⌊180730(2)⌋ ⌊180730(5)⌋
⌊180730(6)⌋ ⌊180730(7)⌋ ⌊180730(8)⌋ ⌊180730(9)⌋ ⌊180730(10)⌋ ⌊180731⌋
180802(2) 180802(3) 180803(3) 180803(4) 180803(5) 180803(6) 180803(7)
180803(8) 180804(1) ⌊180804(3)⌋ ⌊180804(4)⌋ ⌊180804(6)⌋ ⌊180804(7)⌋
⌊180804(8)⌋ ⌊180804(9)⌋ 180805(1) 180805(2) 180805(3) 180805(4) 180805(6)
180805(7) 180805(9) 180806(1) 180806(2) 180806(3) 180806(6) 180806(9)
180806(10) 180806(11) 180806(12) 180806(13) 180806(14) 180806(15)
180807(2) 180807(3) 180807(4) 180807(5) 180807(6) 180807(7) 180807(8)
180807(9) 180807(10) ⌊180808(1)⌋ ⌊180808(2)⌋ 180808(3) 180808(4) 180808(5)
180808(6) 180808(7) 180808(8) 180808(9) 180809(2) 180810(1) 180810(2)
180811(1) 180811(2) 180812(1) ⌊180817(1)⌋ ⌊180817(2)⌋ ⌊180817(3)⌋
⌊180817(4)⌋ ⌊180817(5)⌋ ⌊180817(6)⌋ ⌊180817(7)⌋ ⌊180817(8)⌋ ⌊180817(9)⌋
⌊180817(10)⌋ 180825(1) 180829(1) 180829(2) ⌊180917(1)⌋ ⌊180917(2)⌋
181004(3) 181007(2) 181007(3) 181009(1) 181009(2) 181009(3) 181009(4)
181009(5) 181009(6) 181011(2) 181011(3) 181011(4) 181011(5) 181011(6)
181011(7) 181011(8) 181012 181014 181021(1) 181021(2) 181021(3)
181022(1) 181022(2) 181022(3) 181022(4) 181123 181203 190102(1) 190128
191211(2) 191212(2) 200115(5) 200331(2) 200331(3) 200331(4) 200404(3)
200404(4) 200408 200501(4) 200502(2) 200503 ⌊200505(2)⌋ 200505(3)
⌊200505(4)⌋ 200506 200507(3) 200531 200614 200616(2) 200922 200926
201116 201209(2) 220113(2) 230000(7) 240429(3) ⌊240531(1)⌋ 640000(1)

PARIS COMMUNE   051200   200000(37)   210204   220000(3)

PEACE PROGRAMME   ⌊160129⌋   ⌊171115(2)/⌋   171119/   171208(4)/   190000(2)
                  220000(3)   240000(32)   260000(18)

PERMANENT REVOLUTION   070000(2)   080000(3)   080705   220000(12)   ⌈310700⌉
                       ⌊320500⌋   331204(2)   551115

PERSIA   ⌊180116(2)⌋   240000(32)

POLAND   See also: INTERNATIONAL: Third: Poland; INTERNATIONAL LEFT
          OPPOSITION: Poland; SOVIET UNION: Poland
          200128   201008(1)   230000(7)   260000(18)   320000(2)
          410000(1)

POLITICAL PARTIES   240000(32)   250000(6)   260000(16)
        Left SR   220526   230000(7)   260000(18)

POLITICAL PORTRAITS   180000(36)   ⌈201023⌉   220000(3)   230000(20)   260000(1)
                      260000(17)   330104(1)   330510   351031   331107(2)

POLITICAL THEORY   See also: WORKERS CONTROL
                   050700(2)   ⌊081200⌋   ⌊140223(3)⌋   ⌊191116⌋   220000(19)
                   230000(8)   240000(29)   250000(8)   260000(12)   301126
330223   330920   ⌈341201⌉   350610(1)   351015   360321   370824   371022   371202
380919(1)   380921   380923   390501   400630   400813   400816(2)   421200
590600
        Centrism   300528   340222   340316   340323   350228   350424
                     351022   390310
        Revisionism 421200
        War   340610   ⌊370200(1)⌋   380126   400526   400709   400817(2)

PROGNOSES   390610(5)   390610(6)

PROLETARIAN INTERNATIONALISM   ⌊150115(2)⌋   ⌊150223⌋   ⌊150723⌋   190000(2)
                                190000(10)   220000(3)   270000(1)

PROLETARIAN MARTYRS   ⌊190929⌋   230000(7)   260000(17)

PROLETARIAN REVOLUTION   ⌈080800⌉   171124(2)/   180000(37)   180801   210000(7)
                         *210613(2)   230000(7)   230000(18)   240000(6)   240000(29)
                         240000(32)   241029(1)   250000(8)   260000(7)   260000(10)
261126   311117   360700(1)

++++

PROLETARIAN REVOLUTION   ++++

    France   340710   340922 ⌊341102⌋ ⌊350405(2)⌋ 351107(1)
                 360000(6)   381214

    Germany   171205/   200928   231023(3)   240412(1)   240915
                 310414(2)   310708(4)   310913(1)   320614 ⌊321108⌋
                 ⌊400820(5)⌋   590600

RAKOVSKY   190000(10)   220000(3)   260000(17)   300400(2)   320315
                 330323(2)   330525   340310   340331   340419   580000(4)

RED AIR FORCE   230000(7)   230629(2)   240601

RED ARMY   See also: ORDERS OF THE DAY
                 ⌊171128(4)/⌋   171203(6)/   180321(3) ⌊180324(1)⌋   180324(2)
                 ⌊180330(1)⌋ ⌊180425(1)⌋   180504   180509(2) ⌊180530(6)⌋
⌊180531(2)⌋   180601(5)   180601(6)   180607(6)   180613(5) ⌊180614(9)⌋ ⌊180614(11)⌋
180629(2)   180629(3)   180629(4)   180629(5)   180716(1)   180722(5)   180727(4)
180727(5) ⌊180730(3)⌋ ⌊180730(4)⌋   180803(2) ⌊180804(2)⌋   180805(11)
⌊180807(1)⌋   180807(12)   180810(3)   180814(3) ⌊180830(4)⌋ ⌊180917(2)⌋
181004(1) ⌊181005(3)⌋   181019 ⌊181225(1)⌋   190204   190220 ⌊190226⌋ ⌊190730(2)⌋
190906(4)   190906(5)   191104(4) ⌊191228⌋   200000(2)   200504   200505(5)
200511(3) ⌊200525⌋   200602   200605 ⌊200702⌋   200830(4)   201229(2) ⌊210201(1)⌋
⌊210404⌋   210600 ⌊210800(4)⌋211025   220113(3)   220117   220308 ⌊220313⌋
⌊220618⌋   220708(2) ⌊220710(2)⌋ ⌊221103(2)⌋ ⌊221225⌋   230000(7) *⌊230000(23)⌋
⌊230121⌋   230205(1)   231019(2)   231207 *240000(7)   240000(28)   240000(29)
240000(32) ⌊240103⌋   240223 ⌊240513(2)⌋ ⌊240514(1)⌋ ⌊240514(2)⌋   240531(2)
⌊240605⌋   240610(3)   240731(1)   260000(18) *⌊260700(1)⌋   300000(1)   320000(2)
340313 ⌊350400⌋   361013   370617(1)   371116(2)   410000(1)   640000(1)
        Specialists   230000(7)   240000(24)   260000(18)

RED NAVY   ⌊180501(2)⌋ ⌊180515(1)⌋ ⌊180917(1)⌋ ⌊221017⌋
                 230000(7)   230000(39) ⌊231121⌋

RUSSIA (Tsarist)   000000 ⌊030415⌋ ⌊041100⌋ ⌊051109⌋ ⌊051112(2)⌋
                 ⌊051116(4)⌋   060711   070000(1) ⌊070100⌋ ⌊070221⌋
                 ⌊070225⌋ ⌊070227⌋ ⌊080300⌋ ⌊080400(2)⌋ ⌊080500⌋
⌊080600(2)⌋ ⌊080700⌋ ⌊090821⌋ ⌊091105(2)⌋ ⌊091105(3)⌋   100000(2) ⌊100000(3)⌋
⌊100212(2)⌋ ⌊100403(4)⌋ ⌊101120(3)⌋ ⌊110129(3)⌋ ⌊110200⌋ ⌊110601⌋ ⌊111100⌋
⌊111116(3)⌋ ⌊120314(2)⌋ ⌊120428⌋ ⌊130313(2)⌋   220000(8)   220000(12)   230000(9)
230000(19)   240000(32)   250000(6)   250000(7)   250000(11)   260000(1)   260000(12)

                                        ++++

RUSSIA (Tsarist)　++++　260000(16)　260000(17)　270000(1)　300000(1)　310000(1)

RUSSIA (1905)　060000(6)　100000(2)　220000(12)　220628　⌊220707⌋
250000(6)　250000(7)　260000(17)

　　　　Soviet　060000(3)　220000(12)　250000(6)

RUSSIA (1917)　170116(1)　170608/　170825/　170903/　171007(2)/
220000(3)　240000(24)　240000(32)　410000(1)

　　Democratic Conference　240000(32)　310000(1)
　　July Days　240000(32)　⌊270719⌋　310000(1)
　　Pre-Parliament　240000(32)　310000(1)

RUSSIAN DUMA

　　　Second　070000(1)　⌊070221⌋　260000(16)
　　　Third　220000(12)　250000(6)　260000(16)
　　　Fourth　⌊140222(3)⌋　⌊160331⌋　220000(3)　260000(12)　260000(16)
270000(1)

RUSSIAN REVOLUTION　171022(2)/　171023(3)/　171029(4)/　171101(1)/
171101(3)/　⌊171102(1)/⌋　171102(2)/　171103(2)/
171106(2)/　171106(3)/　171110(2)/　171111(3)/　171111(4)/
171116(2)/　171124(3)/　⌊171124(6)/⌋　⌊171124(7)/⌋　⌊171125(5)/⌋　171125(6)/
⌊171128(5)/⌋　⌊171208(3)/⌋　⌊171216/⌋　⌊171222(5)/⌋　⌊171224/⌋　180000(5)
180000(53)　180926(1)　190211(2)　211107　231105　240000(24)　240000(32)
⌊241107⌋　251108　260000(18)　⌊270719⌋　300000(1)　310000(1)　320000(2)
321013(1)　321127　330401　331204(2)　351104(1)　381114　410000(1)　551115
　　　Foreign Affairs　171116(1)/　171118(4)/　171118(5)/　171124(5)/
171202(5)/　171219(3)/　⌊171222(3)/⌋　240000(32)
　　　Germany　171205/　⌊180000(50)⌋

RUSSIAN SOCIAL-DEMOCRATIC LABOUR PARTY　030700　030900　030920　031126
040000　⌊040315⌋　⌊040625⌋　070000(1)　⌊070225⌋
⌊070227⌋　070501　070502　070508　070516(1)　⌊070700⌋
⌊080600(2)⌋　⌊081001⌋　⌊090210⌋　100000(2)　⌊100403(5)⌋　⌊100828⌋　⌊100909⌋
120225　⌊120314(1)⌋　⌊120326⌋　⌊120423(3)⌋　⌊120423(4)⌋　⌊120500⌋　121003(2)
⌊130202(1)⌋　⌊130202(2)⌋　130205　130207　⌊130306⌋　⌊130331⌋　130401
⌊140222(2)⌋　⌊140409⌋　⌊160331⌋　170510/　220000(13)　240000(32)　250000(6)
270600(1)　300000(1)

SEDOV　380218　380220　380719(2)　380824　390115

SOCIAL DEMOCRACY　220000(3)　260000(1)

SOCIAL PATRIOTISM [150718(1)] [151113] [160116] [160201] [160216]
[160419] [160423] [160506(2)] 220000(3) 230000(19)
260000(1) 381014 390307(2) 391023 400514(1)

    France [151005] 161011 310126

SOCIALIST WORKERS PARTY (USA) 340700(4) 371129(1) 371208 391028
400615 400729 400807 400820(7) 421200

SOCIOLOGY 230000(3) 230000(9) [230412] 230717 [231101]
240000(4) 240000(5) 240000(37) 240518 260000(12)
270000(2) 380216 390609

SOVIET RUSSIA See also: ECONOMIC PLANNING: Soviet Russia; FOREIGN AFFAIRS: Soviet Russia; GERMANY: Soviet Russia; INDUSTRY: Soviet Russia; JAPAN: Soviet Russia; NATIONAL QUESTION: Soviet Russia; TRADE UNIONS: Soviet Russia

180305(2) [180305(3)] 180306(1) 180315 180316 180319(2) 180520(1)
180522 180523(1) 180530(3) [180530(4)] [180531(6)] [180601(1)] [180614(3)]
180617(1) 180628 191031 [191113] 191205(1) 191206 [191209] 200000(90)
200219(2) 200223 200331 [200501] 200502(3) 200510(5) [200527] [210201(2)]
210314(1) [210315] 210730 310907(2) [210929] [220413(2)] 220623
[221103(2)] 221105 230000(7) 230000(37) [240711] 240727 240731(2)
[240831] [250730(1)] 260000(10) 260000(18) 260209 [260216] 270000(2)
320000(2) 410000(1) 640000(1)

    Finland 180301(1)
    Poland 200128 260000(8).II
    Ukraine 180508(2) [180509(1)] 201122 640000(1)

SOVIET UNION See also: ECONOMY: Soviet Union; INTERNATIONAL: Fourth: Soviet Union; INTERNATIONAL LEFT OPPOSITION: Soviet Union; Japan: Soviet Union; USA: Soviet Union

281021 281100 281111 290400(3) 300314 [300400(3)] 300413(1) 300425
[300500(2)] [300700(2)] [300800(2)] [300900(2)] [301000(4)] [301100(2)]
301121(1) [301200(2)] [310300(3)] 310404 [310600(3)] 310715(2) 310902
320226(2) [320508] 321203(2) 321228(2) 330111(1) 330114 [330300(2)]
330429 330512(1) [331101] [340200(2)] [340616] 350201 350210 350300(1)
351100(2) 360101 360110 360227 360318 [360400(3)] 360416 [360500(2)]
[360500(3)] 360522 360603 361013 370617(2) 370900 371104 371125(2)
371129(2) 380108 380113 380306(1) 380317(1) 380703(1) 380703(2) [381126]
390610(1) 390621 390701 391117 391204(1) 400423(2) 421200 590600

SPAIN   See also: AUTOBIOGRAPHY: Spain; INTERNATIONAL LEFT OPPOSITION:
Spain
310618   310624   310701   310708(1)   310730   310802   310901
331003(2)   360412   360707   360730(1)   370116(1)   370219(1)   370512   370816
370824   370914   371006   371217   [390200(1)]   [390321]   390324(2)   [400820(3)]
590600

STALIN   200511(3)   291221   300000(1)   300209   [300400(1)]   [300400(3)]
[300700(1)]   300715   300800(1)   [301200(3)]   320000(2)
[321200(1)]   [321200(2)]   321228(2)   330114   350610(1)
[350900(1)]   360115(1)   360318   360823(2)   [380306(2)]   380309   380331
[380400]   380705   390922   400313   410000(1)   640000(1)

STALINISM   300610   320000(2)   330406   [330609(1)]   331110   350130
[350426]   350829   [350900(1)]   350926   370612   370828   380108
381022(2)   381220   390501

SYNDICALISM   230000(8)   310300(1)

TERRORISM   200000(37)   260000(16)   360820(1)   [390200(2)]

TRADE UNIONS   310300(1)   310325   380929   [400820(4)]
    Soviet Russia   201225(2)   201230(1)   201230(2)   210000(2)
    210000(13)   [210129]   [210213]   [210217(2)]   210314(2)
    210314(3)   220329(1)   251005

TRIALS
    Menshevik   [301100(3)]   310311
    Moscow   341230(1)   341230(2)   350000(1)   350331(1)   360130
    360815   360819(1)   360819(2)   360819(3)   360820(1)
    360820(2)   360821   360823(1)   360823(2)   360823(4)
360824   360825   360826(1)   [360826(2)]   360827   [360900(2)]   360915(1)
360915(2)   361012   361030   361202   361218(1)   370000(10)   370111
370120   370123(1)   370123(2)   370123(3)   370124(1)   370124(3)   370129(3)
370130   [370200(3)]   370201   [370203]   370211   370214   370215   370306
370313(2)   370316   370410(1)   370410(2)   370412(1)   370412(2)   370413(1)
370413(2)   370414(1)   370414(2)   370415   370416(1)   370416(2)   370417(1)
370417(2)   370529   370629   370905   370922   370930(1)   370930(2)
371116(1)   371116(2)   371125(1)   380204   280228   [380300(2)]   380301(1)
[380301(2)]   380302   380303(1)   380303(3)   380304(1)   380304(2)
[380306(2)]   380307   380308(1)   380308(2)

++++

TRIALS   ++++

        Moscow   ++++   ⌊380308(3)⌋   380309   380310(1)   380310(2)   380311

                             380312   380313   380317(2)   ⌊380400⌋   ⌊380618(2)⌋

                             380724   390610(3)

        Ryazanov   310308   310501

        SR   220513

        Tsar   300000(1)   580000(4)

TROTSKYISM   320000(2)   330813   381009   390715

TURKEY   See also: AUTOBIOGRAPHY: Turkey

                               260000(1)

UKRAINE   See also: SOVIET RUSSIA: Ukraine

                               240000(32)   260000(18)   390422(1)   390730   390805

                               390906   410000(1)   640000(1)

UNITED FRONT   230000(8)   240000(32)

USA   See also: INTERNATIONAL LEFT OPPOSITION: USA; SOVIET UNION:

                               USA

                               220000(3)   230616(2)   250524   ⌊310328⌋   321104   321123(1)

                               330317(2)   360701   371015   380319   380929

                               480000(2)   ⌊620000(15)⌋

      Negro Question   ⌊230215⌋   670600

      Soviet Union   270819   ⌊321200(2)⌋   321228(2)   330114

      World War II   391003

WORKERS CONTROL   310820(1)   310912   320000(1)   380600

WORLD AFFAIRS   201020   ⌊220504⌋   ⌊220507⌋   ⌊220518⌋   ⌊220727⌋   ⌊220827⌋

                               221021   221101   221113   230000(7)   ⌊240323⌋   240412(2)

                               240413   240414   240415(2)   ⌊240420⌋   ⌊240510(2)⌋

250525   260000(18)   260129   291004   300314   300821   320215(1)   320229

320804(1)   320818(1)   330607(1)   331130   340715   350900(4)   370817   371001

400214

WORLD WAR I   ⌊140000(3)⌋   ⌊141125⌋   ⌊141127⌋   ⌊150115(2)⌋   ⌊150213⌋

                               ⌊150223⌋   ⌊150409⌋   ⌊150416⌋   ⌊150604⌋   ⌊150711(2)⌋

                               151100(1)   151100(2)   ⌊151124⌋   ⌊151127⌋   ⌊151128⌋

                               ⌊151130⌋   ⌊151229(2)⌋   ⌊170203⌋   ⌊171115(2)/⌋   190000(1)

                               190000(2)   190000(10)   220000(3)   240000(32)   260000(17)

                               270000(1)   300000(1)

WORLD WAR II

See also: CZECHO—SLOVAKIA: World WarII; SOVIET UNION: World War II; USA: World War II

320423   370809   380919(1)   381010   381213   390318
390729   390905   ⌊400820(5)⌋   ⌊400820(6)⌋   590600
700126

YOUTH

See also: INTERNATIONAL LEFT OPPOSITION: Youth

⌊200305⌋   240522

Komsomol

230000(7)   231019(2)   240000(28)   240000(29)   240522
270000(2)

SECONDARY SOURCES

SECONDARY SOURCES: Russian

*Belotski (M.L.), (Red.), VOENNAYA AKADEMIYA ZA PYAT LET (1918-1923 g.g.).
*BOR'BA ZA BOL'SHEVIKOV.
Byulleten tretego kongressa K.I. (LocIISG)
*Byulleten 2-go Vserossiiskogo s"ezda Gornorabochikh.

IV VSEMIRNYI KONGRESS KOMMUNISTICHESKOGO INTERNATSIONALA. (LocBM)
*CHTO NUZHNO ZNAT O GERMANSKOI REVOLYUTSII. Sbornik.

DEKRETY, POLOZHENIYA I PRIKAZY PO KRASNOI ARMII. (LocBDIC)
*DELO KIEVSK. GUB. ZHAND. ZA 1905 g. [Nos. 127, 146, 193]
DOKUMENTY VNESHNEI POLITIKI SSSR. (LocCU)
*DUBROKHIM. Sbornik.
*Dunaevskii i Kuznetsov, PRAVA O OBYAZANNOSTI KRASNOARMEITSA.

EZHEGODNIK KOMINTERNA. (LocLSE)

*GEROI I MUCHENIKI PROLETARSKOI REVOLYUTSII. Sbornik.
*GOD PROLETARSKOI DIKTATURY.
Gorbachev (G.), SOVREMENNAYA RUSSKAYA LITERATURA. (LocBM)

Ioffe (A.A.), (Red.), MIRNYE PEREGOVORY V BREST-LITOVSKE. (LocO)
ISKRA ZA DVA GODA. (LocO)
*IZ MATERIALOV PARTIINOI DISKUSSII.

*Kedrov (M.S.), BEZ BOL'SHEVISTSKOGO RUKOVODSTVA.
KOMENTARII K PROTOKOLAM VTOROGO S"EZDA RSDRP. (LocBM)
KRASNYI PETROGRAD. (LocABC)
KRASNYI VOENNYI FLOT. (LocBDIC)
*Krupskaya (N.K.), (Red.), NA MOGILU IL'ICHA
K 7-mu VSEROS. S"EZDU SOVETOV. (LocLSE)
*K VOPROSU O NOVYKH ZADACHAKH PARTII.
*K VOPROSU O NOVYKH ZADACHAKH PARTII. [Trans. Georgian]

*Lebedev (N), KINO.
Lenin (V.I.), POLNOE SOBRANIE SOCHINENIYA. [All editions]
        *SBORNIK
LENINGRADSKIE RABOCHIE V BOR'BE ZA VLAST SOVETOV, 1917 g. (LocBDIC)
LENIN O TROTSKOM. (LocBDIC) [Also under Safarov(G), (Red.)]
LETUCHII LISTOK, (1), V.17. (LocABC)
Levin (M) i Yurgens (O), KHOZYAISTVO SSSR: Khrestomatiya. (LocGDS)
LITERATURNYI RASPAD. (LocBM)

Maksakov i Turunov, KHRONIKA GRAZHDANSKOI VOINY V SIBIRI (1917–1918 g.g.). (LocCU)

*MATERIALY K ISTORII RUSSKOI KONTR–REVOLYUTSII. Tom I.

*Melnikov (D.), (Red.) PARIZHSKAYA KOMMUNA.

*MIROVAYA BOINYA I MIROVAYA REVOLYUTSIYA. (LocBDIC)

*NA DISKUSSIONYE TEMYE. Sbornik.

*NAVSTRECHU. Sbornik.

Nevskii (A.), SOVETSKAYA PECHAT I LITERATURA O SOVETAKH. (LocGDS)

OB UROKAKH OKTYABRYA. (LocIISG)

OTCHET S"EZD SOVETOV.

OTSTAVKA TROTSKOGO. (LocHIS)

PETLYA VMESTO KHLEBA. (LocHIS)

*Piontkovskii (S.), KHRESTOMATIA.

PIS´MA P.B.AKSELRODA i Yu. MARTOVA. (LocCU)

PRODOVOL´STVENNAYA POLITIKA. (LocBDIC)

PROTSESS ÉSEROV. (LocBDIC)

*PYAT LET. Sbornik.

RKP ... PROTOKOLY. (LocSEES) [Reprints LocCU)

RSDRP ... PROTOKOLY. (LocSEES)

Safarov (G.), (Red.), LENIN O TROTSKOM. (LocBDIC)

*SBORNIK ISTPART.

*S"EZD SOVETOV.

SHIROKAYA KONFERENTSIYA FABRICHNO–ZAVODSKIKH KOMITETOV. (LocBM)

SOEDINENNOE ZASEDANIE. (LocO)

*SOVESHCHANIE VOENNYKH DELEGATOV IX S"EZDA SOVETOV.

*SOVREMENNYI MIR.

Stalin (J.), OB OPPOZITSII. (LocCU)

Sukhanov (N), ZAPISKI O REVOLYUTSII. (LocCU)

*TOVARISHCH IL´ICH. Sbornik.

*TOVARISHCH LENIN. Sbornik.

TROTSKII PERED SUDOM KOMMUNISTICHESKOI PARTII. (LocNYPL)

U VELIKOI MOGILY. (LocPer)

*VESTNIK KVD.

*VLADIMIR IL´ICH LENIN. Sbornik.

*VOENNAYA MYSLI I REVOLYUTSIYA.

*VOENNYI VESTNIK

VOPROSY ELEKTROPROMYSHLENNOSTI I ELEKTROFIKATSII. (LocNYPL)

VOPROSY KUL´TURY PRI DIKTATURE PROLETARIATA. (LocIISG)

*VOPROSY STENOGRAFII.

*VOPROSY ZHIZNI I BOR´BY.

*VOZHD ZHELENSKOI KOGORTY.

*ZA GRAMOTU.

*ZNAMYA PIONEROV LENIN.

SECONDARY SOURCES: Other languages

A LA MÉMOIRE DE RAYMOND LEFEBVRE, LEPETIT, MARCEL VERGEAT. (LocPer)

ALMANACH DES VERLAGES DER KOMMUNISTISCHEN INTERNATIONALE. 1921. (LocABC)

AN DEN PRANGER! (LocABC)

*ANNUAIRE DU TRAVAIL.

EN ANTOLOGI OM DEN PERMANENTE REVOLUTION. (LocAAC)

Antonelli (E.), BOLSHEVIST RUSSIA. (LocBM)

ANUALI FELTRINELLI: 1966. (LocIISG)

Armstrong (H.F.), FOREIGN AFFAIRS READER. (LocLSE)

L'ASSASSINAT DE LÉON TROTSKY. (LocBDIC)

Bailey (H.C.F.), MISSION TO TASHKENT. (LocBM)

Barbusse (H), (Ed.), THE SOVIET UNION AND PEACE. (LocBM)

Bauer (E.), ÖSTERREICH EINE LEHRE FÜR ALLE. (LocIISG)

Baume (E.), I LIVED THOSE YEARS. (LocBM)

Bergmann (H.), L'ESERCITO ROSSA. (LocSEES)
          DIE RUSSISCHE SOZIALISTISCHE ROTE ARMEE. (LocLSE)

Bernstein (H.), CELEBRITIES OF OUR TIME. (LocBM)

Bjedny (D.), DIE HAUPSTRASSE. (LocNYPL)

BOJ. See Pollak (A.).

Brandt (C.), STALIN'S FAILURE IN CHINA. (LocBM)

Braun (N.), L'ORGANE DE MASSE. (LocPer)

Breton (A.), LA CLÉ DES CHAMPS. (LocBN)

Broué (P), (Ed.), LA QUESTION CHINOISE DANS L'INTERNATIONALE COMMUNISTE. (LocPer)

Browder (E.) & Kerensky (A.), THE RUSSIAN PROVISIONAL GOVERNMENT. (LocCU)

*Bukharin (N.), NIEDER MIT DER FRAKTSIONSMACHEREI.

Bulletin des III. Kongresses der Kommunistischen Internationale. (LocIISG)

Bulletin des Exekutiv-Komitees der Kommunistischen Internationale. (LocIISG)

Bulletin des Petrograder Büros. (LocIISG)

Bulletin des IV. Kongresses der Kommunistischen Internationale. (LocIISG)

Bulletin du Bureau d'Information de la IIIe Internationale Communiste. (LocIISG)

Bulletin du IIIème Congrès de l'Internationale Communiste. (LocIISG)

Bulletin of the 4th Congress of the Communist International. (LocIISG)

Bunyan (J.), INTERVENTION, CIVIL WAR AND COMMUNISM IN RUSSIA. (LocHIS)

Bunyan (J.) & Fisher (H.N.), THE BOLSHEVIK REVOLUTION. (LocHIS)

*BYROKRACIE NE, -- REVOLUCE ANO.

Campbell (J.R.), SOVIET POLICY AND ITS CRITICS. (LocBM)

Cannon (J.P.), THE STRUGGLE FOR A PROLETARIAN PARTY. (LocPHA)

Carr (E.H.), THE BOLSHEVIK REVOLUTION (LocBM)

  THE INTERREGNUM (LocBM)

  SOCIALISM IN ONE COUNTRY. (LocBM)

THE CASE OF LEON TROTSKY. (LocBM)

Chamberlin (W.H.), THE RUSSIAN REVOLUTION. (LocBM)

DIE CHINESISCHE FRAGE. [Feltrinelli Reprint]. (LocPer)

*Christman (H.M.), ONE HUNDRED YEARS OF THE "NATION".

Coates (W.P.) & (Z.K.), ARMED INTERVENTION IN RUSSIA, 1918-1922. (LocBM)

Copeland (L.), (Ed.), WORLD FAMOUS SPEECHES. (LocNYPL)

LA CRISE DES BOLCHEVIKS-LÉNINISTES. I (LocHIS)

  II (LocBM)

Cumming (C.K.) & Pettit (W.W.), RUSSIAN-AMERICAN RELATIONS. (LocBM)

Daniels (R.V.), THE CONSCIENCE OF THE REVOLUTION. (LocBM)

Davis (J.), (Ed.), LABOR SPEAKS FOR ITSELF: ON RELIGION. (LocNYPL)

DECREES, ORDERS AND PROCLAMATIONS OF THE PROVISIONAL WORKMEN'S AND PEASANTS'

  GOVERNMENT OF THE RUSSIAN REPUBLIC. (LocO)

Degras (J.), DOCUMENTS OF THE COMMUNIST INTERNATIONAL. (LocBM)

  SOVIET DOCUMENTS OF FOREIGN POLICY. (LocBM)

DEMOKRATIKUS JELSZAVANRÓL VESZEDELEMBEN A SZOVJETGAZDÁL KODÁS. (LocBN)

Dennis (A.L.P.), FOREIGN POLICIES OF SOVIET RUSSIA. (LocBM)

Deutscher (I.), THE PROPHET ARMED. (LocBM)

  THE PROPHET UNARMED.(LocBM)

  THE PROPHET OUTCAST.(LocBM)

  STALIN. (LocBM)

DOCUMENTS OF NEGRO STRUGGLE. (LocPPA)

Dosch-Fleurot (A.), THROUGH WORLD REVOLUTION. (LocBM)

Drahn (E.), BREST-LITOVSK. (LocNYPL)

Draper (Th.), THE ROOTS OF AMERICAN COMMUNISM. (LocBM)

Duker (A.), JEWISH SURVIVAL IN THE WORLD TODAY. (LocPer)

Eastman (M.), PORTRAIT OF A YOUTH: LEON TROTSKY. (LocBM)

  SINCE LENIN DIED. (LocBM)

EENHEIDSFRONTTAKTIEK. (LocIISG)

Eliacheff (B), in: Démocratie, (190), 13.VI.63. (LocBN)

ENCYCLOPEDIA BRITANNICA. 14th ed. (LocBM)

THE ERRORS OF TROTSKYISM. (LocBM)

Etiemble, "The Tibetan Dog" in: Yale French Studies, (31), May 1964: 127-34.

Eudin (X.J.) & Fisher (H.H.), SOVIET RUSSIA AND THE WEST. (LocHIS)

Farbman (M.S.), RUSSIA IN RETREAT. (LocBM)

Fischer (O.), LENINISMUS GEGEN STALINISMUS. (LocPer)

Fischer (R.), STALIN AND GERMAN COMMUNISM. (LocBM)

Flugschriften der Kommunistischen Internationale. ⌊Nos. 1, 6⌋ (LocABC)

Footman (D.), CIVIL WAR IN RUSSIA. (LocBM)

*Fossa (M.), in <u>Accion Obrera</u>, 1941.

THE FOUNDING CONFERENCE OF THE FOURTH INTERNATIONAL. (LocHIS)

Freund (G.), THE HOLY ALLIANCE. (LocBM)

Freymont (J.), (Ed.), CONTRIBUTIONS A L'HISTOIRE DU COMINTERN. (LocPer)

5. JAHRSTAG DER RUSSISCHEN REVOLUTION. (LocPer)

FÜR RECHT UND WARHEIT. (LocIISG)

Gankin (O.) & Fisher (H.H.), THE BOLSHEVIKS AND THE WORLD WAR. (LocHIS)

Georgevic (J.), (Ed.), BIROKRATIJA I TEKHNOKRATIJA. (LocPer)

Godden (G.M.), RUSSIA UNDER THE RED FLAG. (LocBM)

Golder (F.A.), DOCUMENTS OF RUSSIAN HISTORY. (LocBM)

Guérin (D.), LA DÉCOLONISATION DU NOIR AMÉRICAIN. (LocBDIC)

    FRONT POPULAIRE. ⌊1970 ed.⌋ (LocPer)

HAIMSON (L.H.), THE RUSSIAN MARXISTS AND THE ORIGINS OF BOLSHEVISM. (LocCU)

DIE HELDEN DER WIENER KONFERENZ. (LocIISG)

*Hillman (G.), SELBSKRITIK DES KOMMUNISMUS.

Humbert-Droz, (J.), "L'OEIL DE MOSCOU" A PARIS. (LocBN)

    L'ORIGINE DE L'INTERNATIONALE COMMUNISTE. (LocPer)

L'INTERNATIONALE COMMUNISTE ET SA SECTION FRANÇAISE. (LocBN)

Isaacs (H.), THE TRAGEDY OF THE CHINESE REVOLUTION. ⌊1st ed. only.⌋ (LocPer)

JAHRBUCH FÜR POLITIK-WIRTSCHAFT ARBEITERBEWEGUNG 1922-23. (LocIISG)

KAPITALISTINEN MAAILMA JA KOMMUNISTINEN INTERNATIONALE. (LocULH)

Kapsukas (V.), RAŠTAI (t.7). (LocPer)

Kaun (A.), MAXIM GORKY AND HIS TIMES. (LocBM)

Kendall (G.W.), THE REVOLUTIONARY MOVEMENT IN BRITAIN: 1900-21. (LocBM)

Kennan (G.F.), THE DECISION TO INTERVENE. (LocBM)

Kriegel (A.), in: Cahiers du monde russe et soviétique, (IV.3), VII-IX.63. (LocBN)

    LE CONGRÈS DE TOURS. (LocBN)

    AUX ORIGINES DU COMMUNISME FRANÇAIS. (LocBN)

LABOUR CONDITIONS IN SOVIET RUSSIA. (LocSHL)

Lademacher, DIE ZIMMERWALDER BEWEGUNG. (LocIISG)

Lenin (V.I.), COLLECTED WORKS. (LocBM)

SELECTED WORKS. (LocBM)

Lenin, Trotsky, Liebknecht, GEGEN DER BÜRGERLICHEN MILITARISMUS! (LocABC)

*LENIN. [Kiev. Trans. Yiddish.]

LENIN, LEBEN UND WERK. (LocIISG)

*Lenin (W.I.), [DETSKOI BOLEZNI LEVIZNY V KOMMUNIZME]. (CatZK)

Léon (A.), LA CONCEPTION MATÉRIALISTE DE LA QUESTION JUIVE. (LocPer)

LEO TROTSKI: EEN LEVEN VAN STRIJD. (LocIISG) [With book list.]

Lerski (G.J.), ORIGINS OF TROTSKYISM IN CEYLON. (LocHIS)

*UNE LETTRE AU PARTI SOCIALISTE FRANÇAIS.

LETTRE AUX ABONNÉS DE La Vie Ouvrière. (LocHIS)

Levine (I.D.), THE MIND OF AN ASSASSIN. (LocBM)

Lévy (R.), TROTSKY. (LocBM)

Lewin (M.), LENIN'S LAST STRUGGLE. (LocBM)

Lie (T.), OSLO -- MOSKVA -- LONDON. (LocAAO)

LIVRE ROUGE. Recueil des documents diplomatiques relatifs aux relations entre la
Russie et la Pologne. (LocABC)

Lloyd George (D.), WAR MEMOIRS. (LocBM)

Lockhart (R.Bruce), MEMOIRS OF A BRITISH AGENT. (LocBM)

*Luce (R.B.), (Ed.), THE FACES OF FIVE DECADES: "The New Republic".

Lukacs (G.), in: Survey, (47), IV.63. (LocBM)

Lutz (R.H.), THE FALL OF THE GERMAN EMPIRE. (LocHIS)

McCullagh (F.), in: Fortnightly Review, (DCXLVI), 1.X.20.

McNeal (R.), STALIN: A Bibliography. (LocHIS)

Magnes (J.L.), RUSSIA AND GERMANY AT BREST-LITOVSK. (LocNYPL)

Maitan (L.), DAI PROCESSO DI MOSCA ALLA CADUTA DI KRUSCIOV. (LocPer)

Maitron (J.) & Chambelland (C.), SYNDICALISME RÉVOLUTIONNAIRE ET COMMUNISME. (LocBN)

Majstrenko (I.), BOROT'BISM. (LocCU)

MARXISMO E SINDACATO. (LocPer)

MATERIAL OF THE 3rd CONGRESS OF THE COMMUNIST INTERNATIONAL. (LocPer)

Melgounov (S.P.), THE RED TERROR. (LocBM)

MOSCOW TRIALS. (LocPer)

Morizet (A.), CHEZ LÉNINE ET TROTSKI. (LocBN)

Naville (P.), TROTSKI VIVANT. (LocBN)

Nettl (J.F.), ROSA LUXEMBURG. [2-vol. ed.] (LocBM)

Niessel (H.A.), LE TRIOMPHE DES BOLCHEVIKS. (LocBM)

Neumann (M.), ICH KANN NICHT MEHR... (LocPer)

NOT GUILTY. (LocBM)

OKTOBERREVOLUTION. (LocPer)

Oldenbourg (S.), LE COUP D'ETAT BOLCHEVISTE. (LocCU)

ONE YEAR OF REVOLUTION. (LocPer)

PÅBUD OCH FÖRORDNINGAR UTFÄRDADE AV DE REVOLUTIONÄRA FOLKENS STYRELSE. (LocABC)

LE PARTI BOLCHEVIK RESTERA BOLCHEVIK. [Feltrinelli Reprint] (LocPer)

PARTIJA PROLETARIJATA. (LocPer)

*Pereyra (C.), LA TERCA INTERNACIONAL.

Pollak (A.), BOJ O KOMINTERNU. (LocIISG)

Poretski (E.), LES NÔTRES. (LocPer)

POUR L'ACTION. (LocIISG)

Procacci (G.), LA "RIVOLUZIONE PERMANENTE" E IL SOCIALISMO IN UN PAESE SOLO. (LocPer)
STALINE CONTRE TROTSKY: 1924-1926: LA RÉVOLUTION PERMANENTE ET LE
SOCIALISME EN UN SEUL PAYS. (LocPer)

Reed (J.), TEN DAYS THAT SHOOK THE WORLD. (LocBM)

LA RÉVOLUTION ALLEMANDE DE 1918-1919. (LocBDIC)

LA RÉVOLUTION ESPAGNOLE (1936-9). (LocPer)

Rosenberg (A.), THE HISTORY OF BOLSHEVISM. (LocBM)

Rosmer (A.), LE MOUVEMENT OUVRIER PENDANT LA GUERRE. (LocIISG)

Ross (E.A.), THE HISTORY OF THE RUSSIAN BOLSHEVIK REVOLUTION. (LocNYPL)
*RUSSIA IN UPHEAVAL.

Rossum (L. van), in: International Review of Social History, (XIV.2), 1969. (LocIISG)

RÜSTZEUG (8). 7 NOVEMBER. DIE RUSSISCHE REVOLUTION. (LocABC)

S.(M.), LENIN-TROTZKI. DE BLODIGE DAGE I RUSSLAND. (LocAAO)

Sack (H.), THE BIRTH OF THE RUSSIAN DEMOCRACY. (LocBM)

Sadoul, (J.), NOTES SUR LA RÉVOLUTION BOLCHEVIQUE. (LocBN)

Scheffer (P.), SEVEN YEARS IN SOVIET RUSSIA. (LocBM)

Schuster (M.L.), A TREASURY OF THE WORLD'S GREAT LETTERS. (LocBM)

Sedov (L.), LE LIVRE ROUGE. (LocIISG)

Seibert (T.), RED RUSSIA. (LocBM)

Serge (V.), VIE ET MORT DE TROTSKI. (LocBN)

Seydewitz (M.), STALIN ODER TROTZKI. (LocCU)

Shachtman (M.), BEHIND THE MOSCOW TRIALS. (LocNYPL)
THE STRUGGLE FOR THE NEW COURSE. [in Am. ed. of T., THE NEW COURSE.]

Slavik (J.), RUSKÁ REVOLUCE LISTOPADOVÁ. (LocCU)

Slonim (M.), MODERN RUSSIAN LITERATURE. (LocCU)

SOVIETUNIONEN OG SOCIALISMEN. (LocAAO)

SOWJET-RUSSLAND UND POLEN. (LocBDIC)

Sternberg (F.), in: Survey, (47), IV.63. (LocBM)

Strakhovsky (L.I.), THE ORIGINS OF AMERICAN INTERVENTION IN NORTH RUSSIA, 1918.

(LocCU)

Strong (A.L.), THE FIRST TIME IN HISTORY. (LocBM)

SURREALISM AND REVOLUTION. [Processed] (LocPer)

DIE TAKTIK DER KI GEGEN DIE OFFENSIVE DES KAPITALS. (LocABC)

*Tasin (N.), LA DICTATURA DEL PROLETARIADO SEGUN MARX, ENGELS, KAUTSKY, BERNSTEIN,
     LENIN, TROTSKI, AXELROD Y BAUER.

Tcherikower (E.), DI UKRAYINER POGROMEN IN YOR 1919. (LocCU)

THESEN UND RESOLUTION DES III. WELTKONGRESSES. (LocABC)

THÈSES, MANIFESTES ET RÉSOLUTIONS adoptés par les Ier, IIe, IIIe et IVe Congrès de
     l'Internationale Communiste (1919-1927). (LocIISG)

DET 3die INTERNASJONALE. (LocABC)

DEN TREDJE INTERNATIONALE. (LocABC)

DEN TREDJE INTERNATIONALEN. (LocABC)

TROTSKI ED IL TROTSKISMO. (LocBDIC)

TROTSKI ET LE TROTSKISME. (LocBM)

UM DEN OKTOBER. (LocBM)

Unruh (F. von), MEINE BEGEGNUNG MIT TROTZKI. (LocPer)

Venkataramani (M.S.), in: International Review of Social History, (IX.1), 1964.

VOM BÜRGER KRIEG. (LocIISG)

Vulliamy (C.E.), THE RED ARCHIVES. (LocBM)

Warde (Wm.F.), in: International Socialist Review, Winter 1964. (LocPPA)

*Weber (H.), DIE KOMMUNISTISCHE INTERNATIONALE.

Wheeler-Bennet (J.W.), THE FORGOTTEN TREATY. (LocBM)

Wolfe (B.D.), in: American Slavic & East European Review, (IX.3), X.50. (LocO)

*Yuditzki (A.), OKTYABER TEG.

Zeller (F.), THE REVOLUTIONARY ROAD FOR SOCIALISTS. (LocPPA)

DATE DUE